SERIOUS STATS

SERIOUS STATS

A GUIDE TO ADVANCED STATISTICS FOR THE BEHAVIORAL SCIENCES

THOM BAGULEY
Professor of Experimental Psychology, Nottingham Trent University, UK

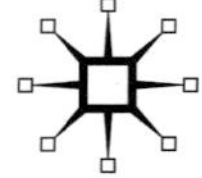

First published 2012 by
PALGRAVE MACMILLAN

Palgrave Macmillan in the UK is an imprint of Macmillan Publishers Limited, registered in England, company number 785998, of Houndmills, Basingstoke, Hampshire RG21 6XS.

Palgrave Macmillan in the US is a division of St Martin's Press LLC, 175 Fifth Avenue, New York, NY 10010.

Palgrave Macmillan is the global academic imprint of the above companies and has companies and representatives throughout the world.

Palgrave® and Macmillan® are registered trademarks in the United States, the United Kingdom, Europe and other countries.

ISBN 978-0-230-57717-6 hardback
ISBN 978-0-230-57718-3 paperback

This book is printed on paper suitable for recycling and made from fully managed and sustained forest sources. Logging, pulping and manufacturing processes are expected to conform to the environmental regulations of the country of origin.

A catalogue record for this book is available from the British Library.

A catalog record for this book is available from the Library of Congress.

10 9 8 7 6 5 4 3 2 1
21 20 19 18 17 16 15 14 13 12

Printed in China

Contents overview

Contents

List of tables

List of figures

List of boxes

List of key concepts

Preface

About this book

This book is a bridging text for students and researchers in the human and behavioral sciences. The ideal reader will have some familiarity with inferential statistics – perhaps as part of an undergraduate degree in a discipline such as psychology, cognitive science or ergonomics – and be interested in deepening their understanding or learning new material. This book aims to bridge the gap between a reader's existing understanding of statistics and that required to apply and interpret more advanced statistical procedures.

I have also tried to make the book a helpful resource for experienced researchers who wish to refresh their statistical knowledge or who have good understanding of a 'narrow' but fairly advanced topic such as analysis of variance. I hope it will allow these readers to expand from islands of existing expertise to new territory.

The book starts with a review of basic inferential statistics, beginning with descriptive statistics, probability distributions and statistical inference (in the form of confidence intervals and significance tests). If you are already familiar with these topics I would encourage you to look through these chapters to refresh your understanding. In addition, this material may be presented in a slightly different way (e.g., from a different perspective or in greater depth).

Later chapters introduce core topics such as, regression, correlation and covariance, effect size, and statistical power. Unless you have advanced training in statistics it is likely that you will benefit from looking closely at this material – it is fundamental to an appreciation of later content. Two further chapters consider the messiness inherent in working with real data (particularly data from human participants). The approach I adopt is to give a taster of some methods for exploring and dealing with messy data, rather than provide a comprehensive recipe for checking and solving every possible problem. This is both for practical reasons (as each of these chapters could be a book in its own right) and because the best approach in any particular situation depends on what you are trying to do and the context from which the data are drawn.

Later chapters cover what I consider to be advanced material: multiple regression, analysis of variance, analysis of covariance, and the general linear model. Before covering these topics I review alternatives to classical, frequentist inference (and significance tests in particular). In order to get the most out of the more advanced material in the book, you will need to understand the problems inherent in relying (solely) on a p value from a significance test for inference. I also think it important to go beyond criticism of the p value approach and present viable alternatives. Three are presented here: Bayesian, likelihood, and information theoretic approaches to inference. There are important connections (and distinctions) between these three approaches. In this chapter, I sacrifice depth for breadth (though there is sufficient material to run a range of analyses using each approach).

The final chapters explore the most challenging topics. Also included are chapters on interaction effects and contrasts. These topics are extremely important for researchers in the human and behavioral sciences, but are often covered only briefly (if at all) in introductory classes. My goal here is to remedy this deficit. The final two chapters introduce generalized linear models (for discrete outcomes) and multilevel models (with emphasis on repeated measures models). I have tried to emphasize the links between these advanced topics and the general linear model and to demonstrate what they offer over and above simpler models.

If you want to learn and understand what is covered, it is essential that you have a go at applying it. Each chapter contains worked examples. Many of these use real data sets. These are necessarily a bit messy and don't always lead to clear answers (and several data sets are chosen because they have interesting or unusual quirks). My aim is to illustrate some of the challenges of working with real data sets (and the importance of data exploration and model checking). In other cases I have resorted to creating artificial data sets to illustrate a particular point, or to make it easier to conduct calculations by hand. These data sets are carefully constructed to meet the requirements of the example – though you will sometimes encounter real data sets with similar properties. In general, the early examples use hand calculation while later examples require you to use a computer.

Hand calculation can sometimes help you to understand how an equation works or demystify a (supposedly) complex technique. This will depend on your confidence and ability with basic mathematical operations. This doesn't work with every procedure, and in many examples I explain how to use a computer package to provide intermediate values that, when put together in the right way, illustrate what is going on. From time to time the mathematics is sufficiently challenging that I merely describe the gist of what is happening (and rely on the computer to provide a complete solution). Where necessary, I refer interested readers to a more detailed mathematical account of what is taking place.

The contents of the book differ from the coverage of a typical introductory or intermediate statistics course in the behavioral or human sciences. One difference is the breadth of coverage, which runs from descriptive statistics to generalized linear and multilevel models. Another is the reduced emphasis on null hypothesis significance tests and increased emphasis on confidence intervals or other inferential tools. Several topics have more prominence than you might expect: graphical methods; effect size; contrasts and interactions. Other topics have less emphasis or are presented differently: psychometrics, multivariate analysis of variance, non-parametric statistics; and pairwise comparisons. I have chosen to focus on univariate methods – methods for the analysis of a single outcome measure (though there may be many predictor variables). Covering multivariate statistics (in the sense of modeling multiple outcomes) and psychometrics would probably have doubled the page count. Nonparametric statistics are covered, but in an atypical way. Several methods, often considered to be 'nonparametric' (e.g., bootstrapping, kernel density estimation, the rank transformation and robust regression), are integrated into the text at appropriate points. I have, in particular, avoided describing a large number of rank transformation tests in detail. My preference is to emphasize the link between parametric and so-called non-parametric approaches and to encourage consideration of robust methods as alternatives to the usual (e.g., least squares) models.

If there is a single message to take away from this book, it is that statistical modeling is not a set of recipes or instructions. It is the search for a model or set of models that capture the regularities and uncertainties in data, and help us to understand what is going on.

Software

Many of the statistical tools described in the book require specialist software to run them. Nearly all the examples were implemented in the free, open source statistical programming environment R (R Core Development Team, 2011). This will run on PC, Mac and Linux operating systems. Installation on a Mac or PC is generally very easy. For details on downloading and installing R see: http://cran.r-project.org/

R works slightly differently on PC, Mac and Linux machines and for this reason I have, for the most part, avoided referring to platform-specific features of R (e.g., resizing windows, printing, opening or saving files). There are many online guides and books that run through the basics of installing and running R (in addition to the information available when you download R for the first time).

At the end of each chapter, I provide a detailed description of the R code used to reproduce the examples in that chapter. Data sets and R scripts for each chapter are available with the online resources for this book. I assume no previous knowledge of R (and only limited familiarity with statistical computing). Although I am not trying to teach R *per se*, I have tried to include enough explanation of how R works for readers, if they wish, to learn it as they go along. To this end, the complexity of the R code being used increases gradually from Chapter 1 through to Chapter 18. In some cases I have glossed over fine grain technical details about how R works (e.g., the difference between 'modes' of vector) and used generic terms such as 'string' alongside R-specific terms such as 'data frame'.

As well as R code, I provide very brief notes on relevant SPSS syntax at the end of each chapter (where relevant). SPSS is the most widely used statistics package in the human and behavioral sciences (in the UK at least). These notes are included for two reasons: (1) to reveal some of the hidden features and capabilities of SPSS, and (2) to highlight the advantages of using R alongside or in place of SPSS.

Mathematics

To get the most from this book you will need to have basic mathematical competence. I assume readers will have mastered basic arithmetic (e.g., addition, subtraction, division and multiplication) and be familiar with concepts such as, fractions, decimals, rounding, negative numbers, squares and square roots, and cubes and cubed roots. Knowing the order in which to apply arithmetic operations (e.g., PEMDAS or BODMAS) is also necessary. You should also have some understanding of percentages, probabilities and ratios (and perhaps reciprocals, exponents, logarithms and factorials) and simple algebra. If you are rusty on any of these topics don't worry too much – as there will be some 'refresher' material in each chapter.

I would expect readers to be able to answer the following arithmetic problems without much difficulty:

$$
\begin{array}{ccc}
4+3\times 5=? & 6(3-1)=? & \sqrt{9}=? \\
10^2=? & \dfrac{9}{2}=? & 0.5\times 0.5=?
\end{array}
$$

I would also expect readers to understand what the following equations mean, and (perhaps with a little help) be able to solve them:

$$
\begin{array}{ccc}
3x+1=10 \Rightarrow x=? & 4!=? & \sqrt{2}\times\sqrt{2}=? \\
P(A)+P(\sim A)=? & \sqrt[3]{27}=? & -2\times -3=?
\end{array}
$$

In addition to mathematical competence, I anticipate some familiarity with data collection, exploration and analysis. This may include experimental design, descriptive statistics and simple graphical methods such as line graphs or scatter plots (and technical terms such as x-axis and y-axis). Again, the text contains refresher material on most of these topics.

Many of the examples refer to 'hand calculation'. This is a fuzzy concept, but I take it to mean reproducing the calculations step-by-step as if doing them by hand. It therefore includes using paper and pencil, mental arithmetic, pocket calculators or spreadsheets (if used in the correct way). In fact, a spreadsheet is one of the best ways to organize hand calculations to understand what they are doing (provided you know how to use one and are careful to set out all the intermediate steps).

Boxed sections and online supplements

As well as learning features (such as examples, sections on R code, and SPSS notes), there are two types of boxed section used throughout the book. One type covers key concepts or important ideas that are referred to in several different chapters. These are referred to as 'key concepts' and numbered by chapter and serial position within chapter (e.g., Key Concept 2.1 is the first key concept box in Chapter 2). The other is a more traditional boxed section that is used to improve the flow of the text and contains material that is relatively self-contained (and that is generally referred to again only within that chapter). These are referred to as 'boxes' and numbered by chapter and serial position within chapter (e.g., Box 1.2 is the second boxed section in Chapter 1).

In addition to the boxed sections there are five online supplements. Supplements 1, 2 and 5 cover advanced topics that are not central to the text, but will be very useful for some readers (meta-analysis, dealing with missing data and loglinear models). Supplements 3 and 4 provide more detail on peripheral topics that are mentioned in the main text (replication probabilities and pseudo-R^2 measures).

Acknowledgments

I would like to thank the following people who have contributed suggestions for the book, read chapters or provided encouragement: Jaime Marshall; Andrew Dunn; Danny Kaye; Mark Andrews; Stanislav Kolenikov; Dave Atkins; Tim Wells; Tom Dunn; Mark Torrance; James Houston and Zoltan Dienes.

THOM BAGULEY

1

Data, samples and statistics

Contents

1.1 Chapter overview

The aim of this chapter is to review some basic statistical ideas, with particular emphasis on the use of descriptive statistics to explore data. The main focus is on statistics for summarizing the central tendency and dispersion of a sample. Key ideas introduced here include the distinction between sample statistics and population parameters, and between inferential or descriptive statistics.

1.2 What are data?

To understand what data are, it helps to consider the distinction between *numbers* and *data*. Numbers are abstract tokens or symbols used for counting or measuring. Data are numbers that represent 'real world' entities.[1] The crucial feature that distinguishes data from numbers is that they are connected to a particular context and acquire meaning from that connection.

Example 1.1 Take a look at this set of numbers (labeled D_1 for later reference):

12 14 9 11 15 11 D_1

Their interpretation would be very different if they described the ages (in years) of six children than if they described the number of words remembered by a participant from a series of six 20-word lists. Not only is the context vital in understanding what the numbers describe, it also has profound implications for what you might want to do with them (and on the subsequent findings of a statistical analysis). Knowing that 11 is an age (in years) makes it reasonable to represent it as $11 \times 12 = 132$ months. Alternatively, knowing that the six numbers represent repeated memory measures from the same individual makes it likely that the numbers can be considered as some combination of the participant's learning ability, improvement with practice and chance factors (influences that are potential components of what, in statistics, is usually termed *error*).

The context, in turn, depends on the process that generated the data. This process can for many sciences be characterized as collecting a subset (a *sample*) of observations from a larger set (the *population*) of observations that are of interest. The idea of taking a sample from a population is central to understanding statistics, and at the heart of most statistical procedures.

Working with samples is attractive to researchers because the populations themselves are usually considered to be infinitely large (and so beyond reach). Even where a population might reasonably be considered finite it is rarely possible, in practice, to sample the whole population. This presents a fundamental difficulty for researchers. A sample, being a subset of the whole population, won't necessarily resemble it. Therefore, the information the sample provides about the population is inherently uncertain. Statistics involves finding ways to deal with this uncertainty. For example, the uncertainty can be quantified and expressed in terms of *probability* (see Box 1.1).

Box 1.1 Probability

There are many ways to represent the uncertainty of an event numerically, but probability is the most common. A probability is a number between zero and one, where one indicates that the event is certain to occur and zero that it is certain not to occur. The probability of an event x can be written as $P(x)$ or $Pr(x)$.

A probability can be interpreted in several ways, but a reasonable place to start is to consider the probability as the relative frequency with which an event such as x occurs in the long run. For instance, if the event H was the occurrence of heads on tossing a fair coin then, in the long run, equal numbers of heads and tails would be observed, and $Pr(H)$ would be 0.5. For example, if a fair coin were tossed 1 million times you'd expect to see 500,000 heads out of 1 million coin tosses and so $Pr(H) = 500,000/1,000,000 = 0.5$.

The problem of dealing with the uncertainty inherent in taking a sample from a population is fundamental to understanding even the simplest statistical tools – the descriptive statistics that are the focus of this chapter. The next section considers these issues in a little more detail, before turning to consider a range of tools for describing and summarizing data.

1.3 Samples and populations

An important point to understand about the concept of a population in statistics is that it is an abstraction. Rarely, if ever, does it refer to a particular set of things (e.g., objects or people). The customary assumption is that samples are drawn from an infinitely large, hypothetical population defined by the *sampling procedure*. A well-designed study will use (or attempt) a sampling procedure that draws from a population that is relevant to the aims of the research. For most (and perhaps all) research, the sampling procedure is imperfect and introduces potential bias into the sample (e.g., because not every member of the population has an equal chance of being chosen). Therefore, the sample will almost never match the intended population exactly. A good study is one that minimizes these problems and thus limits their impact on the statistical model and on the research findings.

Treating a sample as drawn from an infinite population may at first seem unreasonable. However, it represents a fairly cautious position for a researcher to take in practice. Before we examine why, we need to introduce a few technical terms. The first term is the *sample size* – the number of observations (data points) in a sample – usually abbreviated to n. The sample size can, in theory, vary from one to ∞ (infinity). The larger the population, the less information (proportionately) a sample of size n provides about the population of size N.[2] The *sampling fraction* is the ratio of sample to population size: n/N. In theory, the larger the sampling fraction the more closely the sample matches the population and the more likely that characteristics of the sample are also true of the population. Therefore, treating the population as infinitely large is a very cautious option, one that regards the sampling fraction as negligible. The consequence of this cautious position is that conclusions drawn from looking at the sample are assessed more carefully before deciding that they are likely to generalize to the population. The practical limits on generalization from a statistical model depend on the adequacy of the sampling procedure in relation to the objective of the research.

For example, if a researcher collects data from an opportunity sample of 100 healthy people from the city of Nottingham this limits the generalizability of any findings (e.g., to people broadly similar to those making up the sample). For some research questions, this restriction would be severely limiting, but for others it would not. Assessing the adequacy of the sample depends on extra-statistical factors – notably an understanding of the research domain. This is why it helps greatly if researchers have routinely obtained information about the context of the data (e.g., demographic data about human participants). An opportunity sample from Nottingham might be adequate to assess the impact of caffeine on simple reaction time, but not to determine the relative popularity of different UK soccer teams. For the caffeine example it is probably reasonable to assume a certain degree of similarity in physiological response to caffeine among healthy adults. For the football example the sample is likely to be biased (e.g., by support for local teams).

1.3.1 Exploring data

There are many good reasons to explore data, but a very important one is to understand the relationship between a sample and the population from which it is drawn. In order to extrapolate from information in any sample it is necessary to have at least some knowledge of that population. This process of extrapolation from sampled data is known as statistical generalization. The methods used are termed *statistical inference* or *statistical modeling* depending on whether the primary interest is in testing a specific hypothesis or in understanding the process that generated the observed data (e.g., by predicting new observations). This book looks broadly at statistical modeling – building a statistical model of the process that generated the observed data. Statistical inference is a special case of statistical modeling where the primary purpose of the model (perhaps the only purpose) is to test a specific hypothesis.

In combination with graphical techniques, descriptive statistics form the core methods of *exploratory data analysis* (Tukey, 1977). Exploratory analyses are used to become familiar with a data set and will often throw up specific hypotheses (e.g., potential explanations of what is happening). In contrast, *confirmatory data analysis* is employed to test hypotheses. Sometimes these are derived from scientific theory, but they also often emerge from exploratory analyses. Although this distinction is useful, it is not always clear-cut. In particular, thoughtful use of descriptive statistics and graphical techniques can be a very powerful method for testing hypotheses, while confirmatory analyses sometimes lead to reinterpretation of data (e.g., when checking the quality inferences or predictions).

Descriptive statistics, also called *summary statistics*, are an excellent starting point for most statistical analyses and are a good way to summarize and communicate information about a data set. In some situations, descriptive statistics are sufficient to settle a research question (e.g., on the rare occasions when the sample comprises most or all of the whole population of interest). For example, if you want to know what proportion of babies are male and what proportion female it is probably sufficient to look at descriptive statistics for hospital births (the proportion of males is between 0.48 to 0.49). It can also happen that patterns in the data are strong or clear enough to support inferences using descriptive statistics (e.g., that men tend to be taller than women). However, in my view, the main role for descriptive statistics is to get a feel for a data set. A lot of time and effort can be saved and many mistakes avoided by even a quick exploratory analysis of data. Using appropriate descriptive statistics and graphical methods will often catch basic problems before they cause any serious trouble and will help guide you toward an appropriate statistical model. Take three of the most elementary descriptive statistics: the sample size (*n*), the minimum (*min*) and the maximum (*max*). These will often reveal problems in coding, transcribing or data entry errors.

Example 1.2 Imagine that we have collected data from 100 students in an introductory statistics class. These students all rate their understanding of statistics after completing the class on a scale from one ('no understanding') to seven ('excellent understanding').

The sample size, minimum and maximum for the ratings appear as follows in computer output:

n	101
min	1
max	77

This sort of output is fairly common for manual entry of data onto a computer. Although there were 100 students the apparent sample size is 101. This is most likely because one of the ratings was entered into the computer twice by accident. The *min* of one is plausible (though disappointing), but the *max* of 77 is a clear error – probably arising from hitting a key twice in computer entry. While it is always good practice to check data entry (even if the data are plausible) these descriptive statistics alert us to serious mistakes.

This may seem like mere common sense – hardly worth mentioning – but trivial errors such as these are often missed (even by experienced researchers). They are also more likely to be missed in a complex analysis – where an unusual outcome may be attributed to all sorts of other causes. There is much more to exploratory analysis than this, but embarking on a statistical analysis without getting the basics right is extremely dangerous.

1.3.2 Types of data

Different contexts provide us with different kinds of data. One of the simplest and most important distinctions is between *discrete* and *continuous* data. Discrete data are restricted in the values that can legitimately occur. For example, binary discrete data can take on only two possible values (usually represented as zero or one). Another common type of discrete data used in research is *frequency* data – often known as *count* data (because it involves counting things). Continuous data can take on intermediate values within a given range, for example, physical measures, such as, time and distance can (in principle) take on any value from zero to infinity. The difference between two such measures can therefore range between minus infinity and infinity.

A widely taught, but controversial, distinction was proposed by Stevens (1946; 1951). He proposed *scales of measurement* that classify data as *nominal* (also known as *categorical*), *ordinal*, *interval* or *ratio*. He argued that these measurement scales are derived from the underlying relationships between the numbers used to represent a data set. Furthermore, he argued that they limit the mathematical operations that are permitted on data of a given type. Nominal data can be represented by numbers, but the relationship between the numbers is arbitrary (e.g., assigning one to represent blue eye colour and two to represent brown eye colour). If data are ordinal, the numbers preserve information about the relative magnitude of what is measured, but not the absolute magnitude (e.g., data about ages are often collected in the form of age groups or bands with one representing 21–30-year olds, two representing 31–40-year olds and so forth). Interval data preserve continuous, linear relationships between what is measured (e.g., temperature in degrees Centigrade). This means that a given interval between two numbers on the scale (e.g., $5 - 3 = 2$) is equivalent to any other interval of the same magnitude (e.g., $10 - 8$). Ratio scales are interval measurements that have a 'true' zero point (e.g., weight in kilograms or temperature in degrees Kelvin). This means that the number zero represents the point at which the quantity being measured is absent (i.e., nothing is left).

According to this scheme, nominal data is limited to operations, such as counting and ordinal data, to operations, such as placing numbers in rank order, whereas interval data also permits addition and subtraction. Ratio scales permit the full range of arithmetic operations and, as the name suggests, allow meaningful ratios between numbers on the scale to be constructed (e.g., $10/5 = 2$ implies ten is twice as large as five). Ratio scales are probably quite rare for simple measurements, but an interesting observation is that the difference between two numbers on an interval scale is a ratio (because zero represents a 'true' absence of the difference).

There are many critiques (and some defenses) of Stevens' measurement scales (e.g., see Velleman and Wilkinson, 1993, for an overview). Among the more cogent criticisms is the observation that a measurement scale is not a fixed property of data – it also depends on the use to which the data are put. Lord (1953) used the example of football shirt numbers. For many purposes they would be considered nominal data, but it is easy to imagine situations where the numbers convey additional information (perhaps because players derive status from lower or higher numbers, or because they indicate the order in which players joined a team). A major drawback is that the system may also lead people to neglect rather important characteristics of their measurements. Many measurements are bounded in some way (e.g., at zero). Such limits are often much more important for both theoretical and practical purposes when selecting a statistical model or procedure. For example, a statistical model that predicts impossibly low or high values for a measure is problematic (though it may be adequate for some purposes).

Understanding the context of the data that have been sampled and being sensitive to the constraints that context places on a statistical model is important. Classification of data in types (such as those proposed by Stevens) is probably not the best way to go about this. Classification schemes inevitably lose information about the context, so using them in a rigid way to determine what to do is dangerous. Velleman and Wilkinson (1993) go as far as to say, "the single unifying argument against proscribing statistics based on scale type is that it does not work".

An alternative approach – that advocated here – is to consider a range of factors of data that impact on the statistical model you are considering. These factors include whether data are discrete or continuous, but other factors, such as the probability distribution being assumed, the size of the sample and what the model is being used for, are also important. Later chapters will consider several of these factors in greater detail.

1.4 Central tendency

One way to describe data is to reduce it to a single number; a number that is in some way typical or representative of the data as a whole. This corresponds to the everyday notion of an *average*; a notion that encompasses a range of meanings from 'typical', 'most common' to 'mediocre'.

No single way to communicate central tendency will work for all data sets, so it is useful to distinguish between different measures of central tendency. Some common measures, such as the *mode*, *median* and *mean* (and a few less widely known ones) are reviewed below.

As well as being used to describe or summarize samples, many of these measures are also vital in relation to making inferences about the population from which a sample was taken. The mode, median and mean of a sample will nearly always differ from those of the population being sampled. This is an example of the uncertainty that arises through sampling from a population. Even in the ideal situation that every observation in the population has an equal chance of being sampled (e.g., because observations are sampled at random) any sample that does not exhaust all members of the population will almost always differ from it in some way. This leads to the important distinction between a *statistic* and a *parameter* (see Key Concept 1.1).

KEY CONCEPT 1.1

Parameters, statistics and the law of large numbers

A *parameter* can be defined as a property of a population, in contrast to a statistic (which is a property of a sample). Taking a subset of the population makes it unreasonable to conclude that a characteristic of the sample, such as its mean, is the same as that of the population. Instead, the statistic provides a way to estimate a population parameter. It is customary to distinguish statistics from the parameters they estimate by using different (but usually related) symbols. One convention is to use a Greek letter for the population parameter and a Latin letter for the sample statistic. Another convention is to use the same symbol, but differentiate a sample estimate by the 'hat' symbol (^). Thus the population mean is often designated μ (the Greek letter 'mu', pronounced 'myoo') and the sample statistic could be represented by M or $\hat{\mu}$ ('mu-hat'). This is only a convention (and both Latin and Greek letters can have other roles). The mean can also be denoted by a placing a horizontal bar over another symbol. Thus $\bar{x}$ ('x-bar') represents the mean of x.

It is easy to show that statistics are likely to resemble the population parameters they estimate by invoking the notion of the sampling fraction n/N introduced earlier. As sample n approaches N (i.e., the sampling fraction increases) sample statistics tend to resemble population parameters ever more closely. When the sampling fraction is 1 (i.e., $n = N$) a statistic such as the mean is necessarily equal to the parameter being estimated.

It is possible to go further by appealing to the *law of large numbers*. According to this law, a sample average converges on its *expected value* as the sample size n increases.* One way to understand this is to consider sampling without replacement from a finite population of size N. Sampling without replacement means that no data point can be sampled more than once. When sampling with replacement, it is possible to resample the same value at a later stage. As a sample of size n increases, the sample mean, $\hat{\mu}$, computed from n data points is likely to be closer to the population mean μ (computed from N data points). Even though the effective N is infinite $\hat{\mu}$ will be indistinguishable from μ for all practical purposes when n is sufficiently large. A further implication of this law is that parameters that are also averages can be interpreted as the expected value of a statistic in the long run (i.e., repeatedly taking a large number of observations).

* If the statistic is unbiased its expected value is the population parameter.

A parameter is a property of a population whereas a statistic is a property of a sample. The connection between them is that descriptive statistics, for instance a mean, provide estimates of parameters, such as the population mean. The quality of the estimate depends on a range of factors, including (among others) the nature of the process that generated the sample, the amount of uncertainty in the population and – as already mentioned – the size of the sample.

1.4.1 Mode

The mode is the most common value in a sample. The sample labeled D_1 (from Example 1.1) comprised the following numbers:

12 14 9 11 15 11 D_1

The mode of D_1 is, therefore, 11 (and $n=6$). One of important features of the mode is that a set of numbers may have a single mode (being *unimodal*) or more than one mode (being *multimodal*). For example, a set of numbers with two modes would be *bimodal*. The mode is often chosen to summarize frequency or count data (particularly for small numbers of unordered categories).

For continuous data the mode can be useful, but it is also common to find samples where the mode is not very informative. For the following nine numbers, the mode is 14:

14 14 18 35 43 51 62 88 91

Although this enables you to predict the most common value in the set, it is atypical of the set as a whole. The mode ignores information about the quantitative relationship between the numbers in the set. This makes it more suitable for categorical data – a situation where the numbers may have no inherent relationship with each other.

The mode – in common with other measures of central tendency – can be used to predict future outcomes. The mode would be the best value to guess if you wanted to predict the *exact* value of a number taken at random from the sample. This tends to work better for discrete outcomes than continuous ones. For instance, if you wanted to know what ice cream flavor people prefer, a random sample of 100 people might reveal that chocolate was the modal choice. Chocolate would be, therefore, the best guess for the favorite flavor in the sample (the guess with the best chance of being correct) and a good estimate of the best guess for the population. For continuous data the situation is slightly different. The mode is still the best guess for the sample, but might be wildly wrong. For instance, if you asked a random sample of 100 people how much they weighed (to the nearest kilogram) the mode might be 105 kg. This would be the best guess for the exact weight of someone in the sample, but might be very far from typical. In addition, it is unlikely to be a good estimate for the population.

Example 1.3 Consider the responses made by a group of ten people to the question: *What colour eyes do you have?* If two people respond 'blue', five respond 'brown' and three respond 'green' the modal eye colour would be brown. Figure 1.1 shows these responses in the form of a bar plot of the frequencies (a standard way of plotting count data).[3] The modal eye colour (brown) is indicated by the tallest bar in Figure 1.1. One advantage of plotting the data in this way is being able to spot the mode or modes immediately (which can be hard to detect in even a short list of numbers). The plot also shows that the sample is unimodal (as the plot has a single peak). Here the mode could be used to predict the most likely eye colour of a random member of the group. If the group were a random sample from a set of people (e.g., university students), and in the absence of any other information, brown would also be the best guess for eye colour for members of that set (being correct with probability $5/10 = 0.5$). Treating the mode as a best guess at the exact value in the population being sampled can work quite well for discrete data.

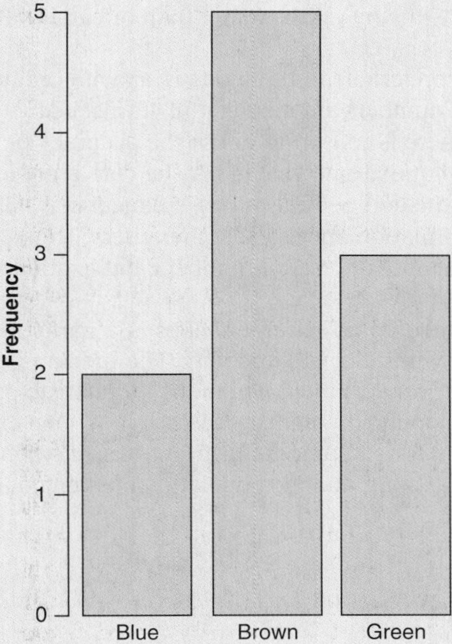

Figure 1.1 Frequency of eye colour for a sample of ten people

1.4.2 Median

The median is one of the most intuitively appealing measures of central tendency. It is the central or middle value in a set of n numbers. If n is odd the median requires little effort to determine. If the numbers are placed in rank order (e.g., lowest to highest) the median is the middle value. So, for the numbers,

23 42 65 108 111

the median is 65. If n is even, then the median is – in a strict sense – undefined (except in the unlikely case that the two central numbers take the same value). When n is even the convention is to take the mid-point between the two central values as the median. If the numbers, 64, 11, 7, 10, 4, 22, are placed in rank order, the resulting set is:

4 7 10 11 22 64

The two middle values are ten and 11. The median can therefore be computed as $(10+11)/2=10.5$.

The median has some potentially very valuable properties. Any set of numbers can be described by a single *median* value and the median divides the set roughly in half (exactly so, if n is even and there are no ties). Because the median only uses the central one or two values in its calculation it is not sensitive to extreme scores. For example, the value 64 in the previous example could be replaced with any value greater than or equal to 11 and the median wouldn't change.

The median is generally preferable to the mode if, as with ordinal and continuous data, the relationships within a set of numbers are meaningful. Its insensitivity to non-central values also makes it a good choice if there is reason to doubt the accuracy or authenticity of some of the numbers (e.g., if you think that extreme values may be data entry errors). On the other hand, if someone is interested in all the non-central values, the median is not a good choice. The median ignores potentially vital information about a set of numbers. The median is usually preferred as a description of a typical member of a set of numbers, but is not adequate as a summary of all the numbers in the set.

The insensitivity of the median to extreme values is a particularly attractive feature when sampling from populations with a lot of variability. The median generally provides good estimates of a typical population value in these situations – tending to produce values that are close in absolute distance to the population median (see Box 1.5). One exception, where the median can be rather misleading, is for multimodal distributions (distributions with several modes), where the modes could be far apart and the population median might not be close to any of the modal values.

1.4.3 Arithmetic mean

The arithmetic mean is probably the most widely used measure of central tendency: so widely employed that it is often referred to (without qualification) as the *average* or *mean*. The adjective 'arithmetic' distinguishes it from other forms of mean (some of which will be considered later). An arithmetic mean is calculated by adding up a set of numbers (i.e., taking their sum) and dividing by n. The set of numbers D_1

12 14 9 11 15 11 D_1

has a sum of 72 and because $n=6$, the arithmetic mean is $72/6=12$. It is common to report the arithmetic mean as M (e.g., $M=12$) when reporting results, but to refer to it as $\hat{\mu}$ or $\bar{x}$ in formulas.[4] The symbol $\hat{\mu}$ emphasizes its role as an estimate of the population mean μ.

One way to present the calculation procedure for the arithmetic mean (and other statistics) is in the form of the equation:

$$\hat{\mu} = \frac{\sum_{i=1}^{n} x_i}{n} \qquad \text{Equation 1.1}$$

This type of formula is ubiquitous in statistics and can be intimidating at first. A brief explanation of how they work is given in Box 1.2.

Box 1.2 Equations involving Σ

Perhaps the simplest way to understand a formula such as that reproduced below is to view it as a set of instructions:

$$\hat{\mu} = \frac{\sum_{i=1}^{n} x_i}{n}$$

The Σ symbol (the Greek capital letter sigma) stands for 'sum' and can be interpreted as an instruction to add up the quantities immediately to its right. Underneath sigma is the element of the instruction that indicates where to start adding the numbers (when $i = 1$) and above the sigma it indicates where to stop (when $i = n$, the sample size). The x in the formula refers to the set of numbers in the sample, whereas i is an 'index' value for each data point. So, the first number in the sample D_1, 12, is x_1 and the last number, 11, is x_6. The final element of the instruction involves dividing the resulting sum by n. Putting all this together, the formula is an instruction to add up the set of numbers x_1 to x_n and then to divide the resulting total by n.

Although this type of equation can be off-putting, they are necessary for communicating the exact procedure used in a calculation. In this case the calculation could easily be communicated in words, but for a more complex formula (such as Equation 1.10 below) precise notation of some kind is indispensable.

An important property of the arithmetic mean is that the sum of the distances of each point from the mean (the deviations from the mean) is zero. Thus, a different way of thinking about the mean is that it is the value that balances out these deviations (at least when considering simple arithmetic operations such as addition and subtraction). An important observation is that, unlike the mode or median, the arithmetic mean uses all n numbers in its calculation. Changing any number would therefore always have some impact on the mean (though this impact diminishes as n increases). This has, historically at least, been considered an attractive property for a descriptive statistic because it implies that all the information in the original set of numbers has contributed to the final result.

Example 1.4 The 2009 UK *Annual Survey of Hours and Earnings* reports the median and mean income for a sample of 18,835 employees as £21,320 and £26,470 respectively. For continuous data such as earnings, the mode isn't particularly helpful (perhaps just reflecting the legal minimum wage for a full-time employee). The mean is a bit higher than the median because the data are not evenly distributed either side of the median – the high earners are more spread out than the low earners. This phenomenon is known as *skew* (specifically positive skew – see Key Concept 2.2). So a small number of very high earners pull up the mean relative to the median; someone in the sample might earn £100,000 more than the median, but no one can earn less than zero (£21,320 below median).

Which is the better measure of central tendency here? It depends on what you are trying to measure. The median tells you what a typical member of the sample earns. More people earn close to £21,320 than earn close to £26,470. On the other hand if you want to know how much money the sample as a whole have to spend, the mean is probably a better figure – it better reflects the total earnings in that period.

Faced with data such as these it is tempting to think the median is the most informative measure of central tendency. However, the median can sometimes be very misleading. In 1985 the biologist Stephen Jay Gould wrote the article 'The median isn't the message', in which he described being diagnosed with a rare form of cancer three years earlier. He quickly learned that median mortality for this form of cancer was eight months. Gould (1985) describes his initial 'stunned' reaction, before realizing that while the median might be a reasonable description of a typical patient, he was probably atypical (e.g., being younger and with an early diagnosis). If half of all patients live between zero and eight months after diagnosis, the other half includes patients who survived from eight months upwards. Gould doesn't report the mean survival, but this would have added further information (because it would incorporate those patients still alive many years after diagnosis).

Measures of central tendency can provide reasonable predictions of observations from the same population, but there may well be other information that can be taken into account. The quality of prediction will also depend on the dispersion of observations around the mean. Both incomes and survival times are very variable and so neither the median nor the mean would lead to a particularly accurate prediction on its own. Gould himself lived for another 20 years after diagnosis.

1.4.4 Geometric mean

An important alternative to the arithmetic mean for certain situations is the *geometric* mean. Where the arithmetic mean involves taking the sum of n numbers and dividing by n, the geometric mean involves first calculating the product of n numbers and then taking their n^{th} root.[5] Writing the procedure in equation form gives:

$$\hat{\mu}_{geometric} = \sqrt[n]{X_1 \times X_2 \times \ldots \times X_n} \qquad \text{Equation 1.2}$$

To see how it works, plug the numbers five and 20 into the equation. Their product is 100 and the square root of this product (because $n=2$) gives a geometric mean of ten:

$$\hat{\mu}_{geometric} = \sqrt[n]{X_1 \times X_2 \times \ldots \times X_n} = \sqrt[2]{5 \times 20} = \sqrt[2]{100} = 10$$

Because Equation 1.2 involves multiplication rather than addition, using Σ would be inappropriate. The equivalent symbol for multiplication is Π (the capital Greek letter *pi*). The geometric mean can therefore be expressed more compactly as:

$$\hat{\mu}_{geometric} = \left(\prod_{i=1}^{n} x_i\right)^{1/n} \qquad \text{Equation 1.3}$$

In what sense is this mean similar to an arithmetic mean? The connection between the arithmetic mean and the geometric mean becomes obvious if you switch to working with logarithms (see Box 1.3). In the examples that follow we will assume that the natural logarithm (*ln*) is used.

Box 1.3 Arithmetic with logarithms

Logarithms are very convenient mathematical functions that provide a link between addition and multiplication (and hence also between subtraction and division). Each logarithm has a *base* that is needed to scale the link between numbers and the logarithms (but is not that important otherwise). In statistics, two popular choices of base are 10 or e (where e is a mathematical constant approximately equal to 2.718282). The logarithm of a number x is defined such that if $base^y = x$, then $\log_{base}(x) = y$. For instance, if you are working with *base* 10, then the logarithm 2 is $10^2 = 100$. Conversely, the logarithm of 100 in base 10 is 2 (i.e., $\log_{10}(100) = 2$).

A major reason for working with logarithms is to simplify mathematical operations using multiplication. This works because addition of logarithms is equivalent to multiplication of the original numbers. Consider the following:

$$\log_{10}(100) = 2$$
$$\log_{10}(1000) = 3$$
$$\log_{10}(100) + \log_{10}(1000) = 5$$

Given that $\log_{10}(100) = 2$ and $\log_{10}(1,000) = 3$, the answer 5 represents $100 \times 1000 = 100,000$ (or 10^5) on the original scale. Adding logarithms of the original numbers gives $2 + 3 = 5$. Although the answer 5 was arrived at by addition using the logarithms, multiplication of the numbers on the original scale gives the same answer. The base 10 logarithm of 5 represents 100,000 (a 1 followed by five zeroes). This is also the answer obtained by multiplying 100 by 1000. This property is true of all addition involving logarithms, hence

$$\log_{base}(a) + \log_{base}(b) = \log_{base}(a + b)$$

is equivalent to

$$base^a \times base^b = base^{(a+b)}$$

Going back to the previous example: $10^2 \times 10^3 = 10^5$.

Subtraction of logarithms is equivalent to division. Thus $\log_{10}(1,000) - \log_{10}(100) = \log_{10}(100/10) = \log_{10}(10) = 1$ on a logarithmic scale (or 10 on the original scale). Less obvious is that logarithms reduce *exponentiation* (raising a base to the power of another number) to multiplication. For example

$$\log_{10}(100,000) = \log_{10}(10^5) = 5 \times \log_{10}(10) = 5$$

The link between exponentiation and multiplication also provides the inverse of the logarithmic function; if $\log_{base}(x) = y$ then $base^y = x$. It follows that the function 10^x is the inverse for $\log_{10}(x)$.

Logarithms to base e are known as *natural logarithms* and usually denoted by the function $\ln(x)$ rather than the clumsier $\log_e(x)$. The inverse is usually denoted by e^x. Most statistical procedures use natural logarithms, but because the choice of base is purely an issue of scaling this is largely a matter of preference (provided the same base is used throughout a set of calculations). This scale shift involves multiplication by a constant (e.g., by $\ln(10) \approx 2.3026$ to convert from base 10 to natural logarithms). Natural logarithms are usually just as easy to work with as those for any other base when you have real data (because it is unusual to have real data that are neat multiples of 10). For instance:

$$\ln(2) + \ln(3) = \ln(6) = 1.791759 \text{ and}$$
$$e^{1.791759} = 6$$

There are restrictions on the values a base can take (for routine uses of logarithms at least) and bases other than e, 10 or 2 are uncommon. In general, bases are positive numbers greater than one and logarithms can only be computed for real numbers greater than zero. Needing to take the logarithm of zero sometimes makes using logarithms awkward (though there are ways to cope with this problem).

The arithmetic mean of the logarithms of n numbers is given by the equation

$$\frac{\sum_{i=1}^{n} \ln(x_i)}{n} \qquad \text{Equation 1.4}$$

(In this case natural logarithms have been used, but remember that the choice of base is not critical – it just represents a shift of scale.) The statistic expressed by Equation 1.4 is on a logarithmic scale and not easy to interpret in relation to the scale of the original sample. This can be resolved by the transformation e^x (the inverse function for the natural logarithm). The geometric mean is therefore:

$$\hat{\mu}_{geometric} = e^{\left(\frac{1}{n}\sum_{i=1}^{n} \ln(x_i)\right)} \qquad \text{Equation 1.5}$$

Example 1.5 To see how this works in practice, we'll apply the calculation to D_1:

12	14	9	11	15	11	D_1

For these values $M = 12$, and the natural logarithms are:

2.48491	2.63906	2.19722	2.39790	2.70805	2.39790

The arithmetic mean of these values is 2.47084 and $M_{geometric} = e^{2.47084} = 11.83$. Quite a few statistical procedures work with numbers on a logarithmic scale rather than the original scale. In most cases the geometric mean will be much easier to interpret than the arithmetic mean of the numbers on the logarithmic scale. For example, if the original data were earnings per hour in dollars, the value 11.83 is easy to interpret (as $11.83). The value 2.47084 is not (although it represents the same quantity on a logarithmic scale where e is the base).

1.4.5 Harmonic mean

Where the geometric mean is a generalization of the arithmetic mean using logarithms, the harmonic mean is a generalization using reciprocals (see Box 1.4).

Box 1.4 Reciprocals

A reciprocal is a mathematical function that involves dividing a number into one. The reciprocal of x is therefore $1 \div x$ (usually written as $1/x$). One consequence of this is that when x is a fraction (e.g., 1/2) or a ratio (e.g., 0.25 meters/second) calculating the reciprocal of x just involves 'inverting' the fraction or ratio. For example, 1/2 becomes $2/1 = 2$ and 0.25 meters/second becomes four seconds/meter.

Like logarithms, reciprocals are often used in mathematics to make arithmetic easier. For example, multiplication of the reciprocal of x is equivalent to division by x:

$$5 \times 1/x = 5/x$$

Taking the reciprocal of x is the same as raising x to the power of -1. Hence $1/x = x^{-1}$. The reciprocal function is also its own inverse. So taking the reciprocal of a reciprocal reverses the operation:

$$(1/x)^{-1} = x$$

One drawback of working with reciprocals is that taking the reciprocal of zero is not possible (for standard arithmetic, at least) and, as with logarithms, using the reciprocal function when a set of numbers contains zero can cause problems.

The arithmetic mean of the reciprocals of a set of numbers is

$$\frac{\sum_{i=1}^{n}\left(\frac{1}{x_i}\right)}{n} \qquad \text{Equation 1.6}$$

Taking the reciprocal gives the harmonic mean:

$$\hat{\mu}_{harmonic} = \frac{n}{\sum_{i=1}^{n}\left(\frac{1}{x_i}\right)} \qquad \text{Equation 1.7}$$

Note that Equation 1.7 simply 'flips' the right side of Equation 1.6 – itself a ratio – upside down. As with the geometric mean, symbols for the harmonic mean vary, with both H and $\tilde{x}$ (pronounced 'x-tilda' by analogy to $\bar{x}$ and x-bar) being fairly common.

Example 1.6 Again, let's apply this formula to the sample D_1:

12	14	9	11	15	11	D_1

The reciprocals of the numbers are:

0.083333	0.071429	0.111111	0.090909	0.066667	0.090909

The sum of the reciprocals is .514. The arithmetic mean of these numbers is 12 and $M_{harmonic}$ is 11.67 (because $n = 6$, the harmonic mean equals six divided by .514).

When the numerator is fixed at some total and the denominator of a ratio varies, the harmonic mean is often a sensible choice.[6] If the denominator is fixed, the arithmetic mean is probably more appropriate. Consider the rate at which errors occur on two tests. Test A has an error rate of ten per minute and Test B an error rate of five per minute. If both tests take one minute to complete then the appropriate average is 7.5 (the arithmetic mean). If the tests were of different durations and stopped when a participant made ten errors (i.e., the numerator is fixed), the appropriate average is 6.67 (the harmonic mean).

Why does the appropriate mean change? In the different duration scenario, B takes two minutes relative to one minute for A. The harmonic mean 'weights' the result for the additional length of time that B took. Doing this produces a number that correctly reflects the fact that a total of 20 errors were produced in three minutes ($20/3 = 6.67$).

The harmonic mean is not widely used as a descriptive measure (e.g., perhaps when working with reciprocals rather than data on their original scale). However, it arises from time to time when working with ratios and fractions, such as when averaging rates or ratios within other procedures.

1.4.6 Trimmed mean

A trimmed mean is a measure of central tendency designed to reduce the influence of extreme scores. Consider the following samples:

12	14	9	11	15	11	D_1
12	14	8	11	34	11	D_2

The respective arithmetic means are 12, for D_1, and 15, for D_2. A trimmed mean can be calculated for these samples by discarding the smallest and largest k numbers in each sample. This procedure can be described by the equation

$$\hat{\mu}_{trimmed} = \frac{\sum_{i=k+1}^{n-k} x_{(i)}}{n-2k} \qquad \text{Equation 1.8}$$

The new element to the notation here is $x_{(i)}$. This indicates that the data have been ordered from highest to lowest.

Trimmed means vary according to the extent of trimming. The usual convention is to indicate this by the percentage of data trimmed. It is usual to set k so that between 5% and 20% of each end or 'tail' of the sample is trimmed (where this percentage is $100 \times k/n$). For the above samples, if $k = 1$, the percentage trimmed from each end of the distribution is 1/6 or roughly 16.7%.[7] The 16.7% trimmed mean, $M_{16.7\%}$, is therefore 12 for both D_1 and D_2. It so happens that the remaining observations of the two samples (11, 11, 12, 14) are identical (though identical trimmed means merely require the untrimmed observations to have the same arithmetic mean).

The trimmed mean forms a natural link between the arithmetic mean and the median. The former is a special case of the trimmed mean when $k=0$, while the latter is a special case when $n-2k=1$ (if n is odd) or $n-2k=2$ (if n is even). This makes the trimmed mean a compromise between the mean (that weights all observations equally) and the median (that ignores all non-central values). Trimming can be applied to other statistics (e.g., the geometric or harmonic mean), though this is uncommon in practice. Calculating trimmed means for large data sets can be awkward by hand, but is implemented in most statistics software. As the percentage of trimming approaches 50% in each tail (i.e., 100% in total) the trimmed mean will converge on the sample median.

1.5 Dispersion within a sample

Measures of central tendency such as the median, trimmed mean or arithmetic mean reduce data to a single number. While this can be a very convenient way to summarize a set of numbers, it will fail to capture some essential characteristics of the data. Compare one of the earlier examples in this chapter with a new sample:

12	14	9	11	15	11	D_1
11	22	7	12	15	5	D_3

D_1 and D_3 have identical arithmetic means and medians (12 and 11.5 respectively), but are very different. Both the sample mean and median are a better description of numbers in the sample D_1 than in D_3. The numbers in D_1 fall no more than three units from the mean, whereas D_3 includes one observation that is ten units away from the mean. The numbers in D_3 have greater *dispersion* (i.e., are more spread out) than those in D_1.

Just as a single number can be used to characterize the central tendency of a sample, various options exist to describe the dispersion in a sample. As with measures of central tendency, no single measure is entirely satisfactory for all situations. This section will consider several of the most important measures in relation to a sample of n numbers.

1.5.1 Range

A very simple and intuitive measure of sample dispersion is the *range*: the difference between the *minimum* and *maximum* values of the sample. The range is simple to compute and easy to understand, but it is extremely limited as a measure of dispersion.

From the range alone, it is hard to assess how far a typical data point might be from the mean or median (though halving the range gives an idea of how far the extremes are from the center, provided the sample is fairly symmetrical about the median). A further problem is that the range is determined only by the most extreme values in a sample. Ignoring the dispersion of less extreme numbers implies that the range is particularly vulnerable to aberrant or extreme values – values that researchers will probably not want to dominate the outcome of a statistical procedure.

Example 1.7 Finding the range is easy enough if the numbers are arranged in order. Ordering D_1 and D_2 from highest to lowest gives:

9	11	11	12	14	15	D_1
5	7	11	12	15	22	D_3

The minimum of D_1 is five and its maximum is 15 giving a range of $15 - 9 = 6$.

For D_3 the range is $22 - 5 = 17$. In this case the range does a rather fine job of describing the differences in spread of the two samples. To see why the range is sometimes problematic, compare these results with those for D_4.

5	10	11	12	12	22	D_4

This has the same range as D_3 but most of the numbers are very close to the mean and median. The range is completely insensitive to this clustering of data in the center. This insensitivity to central values is a particular problem in large samples where there are proportionately more central values.

1.5.2 Quartiles, quantiles and the interquartile range (*IQR*)

An alternative to computing the range on the full sample is to compute the range on a trimmed sample. By discarding a proportion of extreme values it is possible to obtain a measure of dispersion that better describes the spread of less extreme, more central values. In principle, this could be carried out for any level of trimming, but it is rare to see anything other than the *interquartile range* (*IQR*) chosen. The *IQR* is defined as the difference between the upper and lower quartile of a set of numbers.

Quartiles are the points on the number line that separate a set of n ordered numbers into subsets of $n/4$ (or as close to $n/4$ as possible). The first (lower) quartile separates the smallest 25% of the numbers from larger numbers. The second (middle) quartile is the median, while the third (upper) quartile separates 25% largest numbers from the smallest. If you are wondering why there are only three quartiles, think about how many cuts you need to make along a length of pipe to divide it into four equal pieces. It should take three cuts. One cut in the middle creates two halves, and then two further cuts are required to divide each of those pieces in half. These cuts are equivalent to the three quartiles. The quartiles are the boundaries used to divide up a set of numbers, they are not the subsets created by the boundaries.

Quartiles are a special case of *quantiles*. Quantiles are the points on the number line used to divide up a set of numbers into q subsets of equal (or as near to equal as possible) size. So for quartiles $q = 4$ and for 'quintiles' $q = 5$. It takes $q - 1$ quantiles to split a set of numbers up in this way (e.g., for quintiles there are $5 - 1 = 4$ boundaries). This makes the size of each subset n/q (or as close to this as you can get). Quartiles are very popular as descriptive statistics. Another common choice is the centile (also called a percentile) where $q = 100$. Centiles therefore describe the percentage of values in the lower portion of a set of numbers (e.g., the 12th centile defines the smallest 12% of the set). It is often convenient to express quartiles as centiles and you will often see the first, second and third quartile referred to as the 25th, 50th and 75th centile. Thus the *IQR* can also be defined as the difference or distance between the 75th and 25th centile.

Example 1.8 As noted above, the samples D_3 and D_4 have identical means, medians and ranges:

5	7	11	12	15	22	D_3
5	10	11	12	12	22	D_4

The *IQR* for D_3 is 6.25 and for D_4 it is 1.75. The *IQR* therefore does a good job of capturing the clustering of the non-extreme values in each sample (relative to the median or mean). Halving the *IQR* also gives a very rough sense of how far the more central values are from the mean or median (provided the sample is fairly symmetrical).

Deriving an *IQR* for small samples such as these (and more generally when n is not neatly divisible by four) is awkward and different methods exist to resolve the problems for such situations (e.g., the figures reported here can be replicated in R or via the QUARTILE() function in Excel, but differ from those provided by SPSS). Software will also sometimes depart from standard conventions when data are very sparse (e.g., for a sample such as D_3). These departures are usually designed to produce plots that are easier to interpret – but it is worth checking exactly what is plotted when n is small. A more detailed discussion of calculation methods can be found in Hyndman and Fan (1996).

While the *IQR* is widely used, it is not common as a stand-alone measure of dispersion. It is usually encountered alongside other descriptive statistics – in particular in graphical summaries of data such as a *box plot*. A box plot is a handy summary of a number of descriptive statistics and can be useful as a quick exploratory tool. Figure 1.2 shows the anatomy of a typical box plot for a sample of simulated data. The dark central line shows the sample median. The *hinges* (the top and bottom of the box) show the upper and lower quartiles respectively. The *whiskers* (the dashed lines extending vertically from the box) show the minimum and maximum values of the sample.

The software that produced the plot extends the whiskers as a multiple of the *IQR* (typically 1.5) from the hinges, provided they do not extend beyond the most extreme values in the data (as would happen in this case). Extreme values that fall beyond the whiskers are often also displayed. One such value occurs in Figure 1.2 and it is labeled here as a 'potential' outlier. Such values can cause problem for a statistical analysis, but are not necessarily unusual or particularly extreme. Working out whether a potential outlier is unusual or extreme is a difficult problem (and dealt with in more detail in Chapter 9). The box plot also indicates the range (this is the distance along the y-axis between the two most extreme features – whether whiskers or individual data points). While box plots can be constructed in many different ways, nearly all will display the median, *IQR* and range. Regardless of how they are defined, the whiskers tend to give an indication of where the 'bulk' of the data fall, while the *IQR* gives an indication of the clustering around the median.

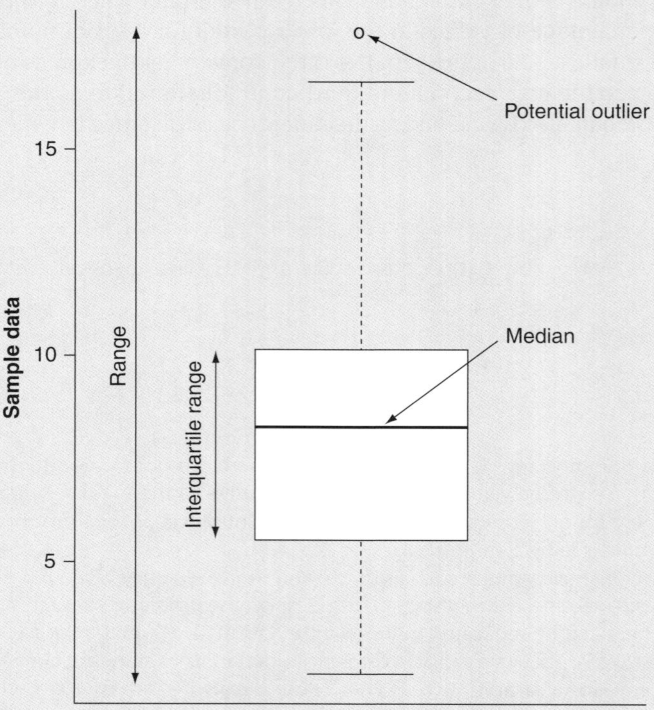

Figure 1.2 The main features of a box plot

1.5.3 Sums of squares

Measures of dispersion such as the range and *IQR* are often reported alongside measures of central tendency that do not use all sample data in their calculation (e.g., measures such as the median, trimmed mean or mode). If you are working with the mean it is natural to report a measure of dispersion that also uses the whole sample.

It might be tempting to start by using the average deviation of each point from the arithmetic mean but, as noted earlier, the sum of these deviations is always zero. The arithmetic mean is the point that balances these deviations (and so they will cancel out when summed). A plausible alternative is to use *absolute deviations* from the mean (i.e., discarding the sign of the deviations). Using absolute deviations is unfortunately not as simple as might first appear (see Box 1.5). Instead, the most widely employed measures of dispersion are based on *squared deviations* from the mean. If the mean is ten and an observation is six, its corresponding deviation would be $6 - 10 = -4$. Its squared deviation would therefore be $(-4)^2 = 16$.

Box 1.5 Advantages and disadvantages of using absolute deviations

Calculating the absolute deviations from the arithmetic mean merely involves subtracting the mean from every number in the sample and discarding the sign of the difference. For D_2 the raw deviations (*residuals*) are:

−3 −1 −7 −4 19 −4

The corresponding absolute deviations are therefore:

3 1 7 4 19 4

The arithmetic mean of these absolute deviations – the *mean absolute deviation* (*MAD*) is $38/6 = 6.33$. Using the absolute distance from the mean isn't necessarily the best way to go.

One consideration is that the measure of central tendency that minimizes the absolute deviations is the median (not the mean). For example, the corresponding raw and absolute deviations from the median are

0.5 2.5 −3.5 −0.5 22.5 −0.5

and

0.5 2.5 3.5 0.5 22.5 0.5

Here the total absolute distance from the median is 30 (not 38) and the *MAD* for the median is 5.

This suggests a link between using the arithmetic mean in conjunction with squared deviations (and statistics such as *SS*, variance or *SD*) and using the median with absolute deviations. One reason for preferring squared deviations is therefore the prevailing preference for the mean over the median in statistics. This default use of the mean is not always reasonable. The median is generally a more robust measure (e.g., it is less sensitive to extreme values).

A second consideration is that squared deviations tend to be easier to work with than absolute deviations. This is true both in the sense of deriving the mathematical proofs upon which statistical procedures are based, and in terms of the complexity of the calculations required to implement statistical analyses. Most statistical work still relies on squared deviations from the mean, but owing to advances in computing power and the increasing availability of suitable software other approaches are becoming more popular.

The basic building block for any measure of dispersion using squared deviations from the mean is a *sum of squares* (*SS*). Sums of squares are calculated by squaring each of the deviations from the mean and adding these squared values together. The can be represented as the equation

$$SS = \sum_{i=1}^{n} (x_i - \hat{\mu})^2 \qquad \text{Equation 1.9}$$

where $\hat{\mu}$ is the arithmetic mean of the sample.

Summing squared deviations from the mean is a very convenient way to capture variability within a sample (and many other statistical procedures have this basic calculation at their core). Even so, there are several difficulties inherent in using sums of squares as a descriptive measure. First, summing deviations from the mean ensures that if n increases, SS increases too (assuming some variability in the sample). This makes comparison between samples with different n awkward. Second, sums of squares are scaled in terms of the squared deviations from the mean. Interpreting these squared values in terms of the original (unsquared) units can be tricky.

Note also that any measure using the squared deviations has disadvantages (as well as advantages) relative to using alternatives such as absolute deviations (see Box 1.5). Measuring dispersion in terms of the squared deviations from the mean produces statistics that may be oversensitive to extreme values (although this is not inevitable). This can cause serious problems (e.g., a single very extreme value can sometimes distort the outcome of a study).

Example 1.9 This example will again use the sample D_1:

12	14	9	11	15	11	D_1

For D_1 the deviations from the mean (often termed *residuals* in this context) are obtained by subtracting the mean of 12 from each observation to get:

0	2	−3	−1	3	−1

The corresponding squared deviations are therefore:

0	4	9	1	9	1

The sum of squares is thus $0+4+9+1+9+1=24$.

Now compare this to D_3, a sample with the same mean, but more widely dispersed values. For D_3 the $SS=184$. While for D_4, a sample with the same mean, median and range, $SS=154$. This is consistent with the observation that central values in D_4 tend to be closer to the mean than for D_3. Because sums of squares use the whole data set they are sensitive to the dispersion of both extreme and central values.

1.5.4 Variance

The variance is closely related to sums of squares, but incorporates an adjustment to the SS to account for different sample sizes. This is achieved by dividing the sums of the squared deviations by n. The equation for the variance can therefore be denoted as:

$$Var = \frac{\sum_{i=1}^{n} (x_i - \hat{\mu})^2}{n} \qquad \text{Equation 1.10}$$

This equation can be interpreted as the arithmetic mean of the sums of the squared deviations from the arithmetic mean. This is an important point: the variance of a sample is itself a form of arithmetic mean. Thus both the variance and the arithmetic mean are averages and findings such as the law of large numbers apply to both (see Key Concept 1.1).

The variance is a fundamental concept in statistics that, like *SS*, has many further applications. Here the focus is on the variance as a descriptive statistic. Although it deals with the problem of differences in sample size it shares all the other limitations of *SS*. Its main limitation as a descriptive statistic is a consequence of using squared deviations from the mean. Knowing that the mean is ten and that the variance is 16 doesn't make it easy to tell how the data are dispersed around the mean because the number ten (in unsquared units) and the number 16 (in squared units) are on different scales.

Example 1.10 In the previous example, the *SS* of the samples D_1, D_3, and D_4 were reported as 24, 184 and 154 respectively. In each case $n = 6$, so the corresponding variances of the samples can be calculated as $24/6 = 4$, $184/6 = 30.67$, and $154/6 = 25.67$. Because the samples have identical *n*, the variance is only marginally more informative than the *SS*.

To understand the advantages of the variance requires a comparison of samples of different sizes. Let's combine D_3 and D_4 into a single sample with $n = 12$. The variance of the combined sample is *SS*/12 and because the two samples have the same mean there is a shortcut to calculate its overall *SS*. This shortcut is simply to add the *SS* of D_3 and D_4 together. (This won't work if the means differ, because the residuals of the combined and individual samples would no longer be calculated relative to a common value). The new *SS* is $184 + 154 = 338$, and the variance of the combined sample would be $338/12 = 28.17$.

Doubling the sample has little impact on the variance (which necessarily takes a value somewhere between the variances of the two original samples). In contrast, the *SS* of the combined sample is around twice the size of the original *SS* for D_3 and D_4 separately (338 versus 154 or 184). The combined sample and the two subsamples all have similar dispersion and this produces similar variances (25.67, 28.17 or 30.67). The variance is a better statistic than *SS* (or even the range or *IQR*) for comparing otherwise similar samples with different *n* (e.g., different classes in a school).

1.5.5 Standard deviation

The *standard deviation* (*SD*) is a measure of dispersion related to the variance, but scaled to use the same units as the original data. It is the square root of the arithmetic mean of the sum of the squared residuals (where the residuals are deviations of observations from the arithmetic mean). Because the arithmetic mean of the sum of the squared residuals is the variance, the standard deviation is the square root of the variance. This is illustrated by the equation:

$$SD = \sqrt{Var} = \sqrt{\frac{\sum_{i=1}^{n} (x_i - \hat{\mu})^2}{n}} \qquad \text{Equation 1.11}$$

As a description of sample dispersion the *SD* has all the advantages of the variance, being a far more sensitive measure of dispersion than measures such as the range or the *IQR*, because it uses all the data (not just extreme or intermediate values) in its calculation. As with the *SS* or variance, it can sometimes be unduly influenced by extreme values (in which case a trimmed measure such as the *IQR* might be preferred). Taken together, the advantages of using the *SD* often outweigh the disadvantages. For this reason, the *SD* is a popular statistic for summarizing the dispersion of a sample (and it is the standard choice for reporting dispersion alongside the arithmetic mean). Its most important property is that, unlike the variance or *SS*, the *SD* can be directly interpreted as a measure of the degree of clustering of a sample around the mean in a sample. It is therefore an excellent statistic for comparing the dispersion of samples of different sizes on a common scale.

A convenient guideline is to treat the *SD* as an estimate of the distance a typical data point lies from the mean. In a sample with a mean of ten and a variance of 16 the *SD* is four. It is usually reasonable to interpret this as indicating that a typical observation falls roughly four units from the mean.[8]

Example 1.11 In the preceding example the variances of D_1 and D_4 were calculated to be four and 25.67. The *SD*s are $\sqrt{4} = 2$ and $\sqrt{25.67} = 5.07$ respectively. Because the samples are fairly symmetrical and evenly spread around the mean, the *SD* gives a good indication of the distance a typical sample member is from the mean. A typical observation is around two units from the mean of D_1 and around five units from the mean of D_4. If samples are less evenly distributed around the mean the *SD* will still give a rough idea of the average spread of points around the mean (though it might not be the case that any single observation falls around this point). Getting a feel for the distribution of a small sample is easy. In larger samples it is a good idea to plot the data to reveal the overall shape of the distribution. A box plot is one way to do this, but there are many other methods (only one of which will be considered at this point).

A drawback of the box plot (and alternatives such as histograms) is that individual observations are not shown. A simple alternative that does show individual data points is the *stem and leaf plot.* In a stem and leaf plot the numbers are ordered low to high and the first two significant digits (i.e., both digits for numbers in the range −99 to 99) are plotted. Of these digits the first digit is the 'stem' and placed on the left (followed by a vertical line). The second digit is the 'leaf' and placed to the right of the vertical line. Numbers sharing the same stem have their second digit added to the right. Numbers with a larger stem value are added below. So a basic stem and leaf plot of D_3 looks like this:

0 | 5 7

1 | 1 2 5

2 | 2

Here the stem digits are 'tens' and the plot indicates a fairly even and symmetrical spread with no obvious gaps. The *SD* of 5.5 is therefore broadly consistent with typical distance of points from the mean. Contrast this with a stem and leaf plot for D_4:

0 | 5

1 | 0 1 2 2

2 | 2

The *SD* here is 5.1, but most points are much closer to the mean than this (with two points a little further out).

Stem and leaf plots are easy to generate (not requiring sophisticated software) but are not common in published work. Their inclusion here is to show the value of even a simple plot that includes all observations (albeit in an abbreviated form). Such plots can be helpful in deciding what measure of dispersion to report.

1.5.6 Other measures of dispersion

The measures of dispersion described here are among the most popular. Alternative measures of dispersion using absolute deviations from the median or arithmetic mean such as the *MAD* can be constructed (see Box 1.5). It is also possible to calculate measures of dispersion appropriate for the geometric mean, harmonic mean and trimmed mean. For example, the *SD* of the natural logarithms of a sample is very simple to calculate. Taking the exponent of this value (to base *e*) would rescale the *SD* in terms of the original units and give the *geometric SD*. Likewise a trimmed or harmonic *SD* or variance could be calculated for a sample.

1.6 Description, inference and bias

There are a number of properties that are desirable in estimates of a parameter such as the mean or median. A statistic should, for example, be an *unbiased* and *efficient* estimator of the relevant population parameter.

An efficient estimate has less error (i.e., tends to be close to the population parameter). The degree of error can be assessed in different ways, but the most common criterion is to use the sum of the squared residuals. An efficient estimator assessed using this criterion is therefore one that tends to have a small *SD*. If the estimator is also unbiased, it has zero bias, where bias is defined as the difference between the expected value of the statistic and the true value of the parameter. In the long run (e.g., given sufficient sample size) an unbiased statistic will converge exactly on the parameter it estimates.

The accuracy of an estimate is a combination of its error and bias. Imagine a large number of darts thrown at a target. If the throws are unbiased they will be scattered more-or-less evenly around the center of the target. If they fall consistently slightly right or left (or above or below) the center of the target, this indicates bias. The overall accuracy depends on the sum of the error and bias. An efficient estimator could be very inaccurate if the bias is large (just as a set of throws could be tightly clustered but all land a long way from the target). In the same way, being unbiased doesn't imply accuracy (your throws could fall evenly around the center of the target and yet still fall a long way away from it on average). On the other hand, a known bias can sometimes be corrected, whereas error tends to be quite hard to eliminate. For this reason it is sometimes better to adopt a biased estimator with small error rather than an unbiased but inefficient estimator.

Descriptive statistics such as means, medians and trimmed means are unbiased estimators of central tendency. The expected value of the statistic is the true population parameter (e.g., $\hat{\mu}$ estimates the population mean μ with zero bias). This is not the case, however, for sample statistics used to estimate population dispersion. The expected value of a descriptive measure of dispersion in a sample (e.g., the range or variance) is an underestimate of the true population value. Where the *law of large numbers* applies, this underestimate declines, as n approaches N. However, for infinitely large populations (i.e., when $N = \infty$) any finite sample will have some bias (though with sufficiently large n this bias will become too small to detect).

Why is the sample dispersion an underestimate of the population dispersion? To understand how this bias arises, consider the case of a finite sample taken without replacement from some population. For example, imagine we have obtained a random sample of the ages (in years) of n people from the population of Nottingham ($N \approx 300,000$). When n is small the sample is unlikely to capture the extremes of the population and will underestimate its dispersion. The lowest age in the population will be zero years and we'll assume that the population maximum is 100 years. A random sample of size, say, $n = 10$ will hardly ever include both a newborn baby and a 100-year-old adult. For this reason the sample *range* will tend to underestimate the population range. As n increases, the probability of sampling the extremes increases (e.g., assuming there is only one 100-year-old in the population the probability of him or her being in the sample increases from $P \approx 1/30,000$ to $P \approx 1/3,000$ as n increases from ten to 100). As n approaches N the sample range is likely to get closer and closer to 100 years (the population range). This argument applies equally to infinite populations (and a mathematical proof is possible).

Other measures of dispersion in a sample will also underestimate the population dispersion (for exactly the same reasons). Measures such as the variance or *SD* require the full range of values in the sample or population for calculation; omitting the extreme values will necessarily reduce the final result. A moment's reflection should suffice to show that it also applies, albeit to a lesser extent, to measures such as the *IQR* or trimmed variance, even though they exclude the minimum and maximum. Excluding the most extreme values just shifts the problem to the next most extreme values (e.g., the first and third quartiles for the *IQR*).

1.6.1 Unbiased estimation of the population variance or *SD*

The aim of collecting data is often to use sample statistics to estimate population parameters. It is therefore undesirable if the descriptive formula for calculating the variance (or other measures of dispersion) provides an underestimate of the population variance.

Fortunately because the degree of bias is known, it can be eliminated. For this reason, a different formula is adopted for estimating the population variance from a sample than for description of the sample itself. Confusingly, both formulas are often labeled as the 'sample variance'. A more sensible designation is to label one formula the *descriptive* formula (which treats the sample as if it were a population) and one as the *inferential* formula (which regards the sample as an estimate of the population): Equation 1.9, Equation 1.10 and Equation 1.11 are all descriptive formulas.

The formulas differ by what is termed a correction factor (which can be derived from the mathematical proof that a sample variance underestimates the population variance) applied to the inferential formula. To go from the uncorrected descriptive formula to the corrected inferential formula requires multiplying the variance by this correction factor. Dividing by the correction factor (or multiplying by its reciprocal) allows you convert the (inferential) population variance estimate back to the (descriptive) sample variance. The correction factor is $n/(n-1)$. As you might expect, it is relatively large only for small n and becomes negligible when n is very large. In practice, the largest possible value of the correction factor is two (when $n = 2$) and approaches one for large samples (e.g., it would be ≈ 1.01 for $n = 100$ and ≈ 1.001 for $n = 1000$).

The population variance is usually represented by the symbol σ^2 (pronounced 'sigma squared' because σ is a lower-case form of the Greek letter sigma). So the descriptive sample *SD* is a biased estimator of σ^2. Knowing the correction factor is $n/(n-1)$, it is possible to construct an unbiased estimate of σ^2. The unbiased estimator of σ^2 can be labeled $\hat{\sigma}^2$ ('sigma-hat squared'). Incorporating the correction factor, the unbiased, inferential formula is:

$$\hat{\sigma}^2 = \frac{\left(\frac{n}{n-1}\right) \times \sum_{i=1}^{n} (x_i - \hat{\mu})^2}{n} = \frac{\sum_{i=1}^{n} (x_i - \hat{\mu})^2}{n-1} \qquad \text{Equation 1.12}$$

Apart from the correction factor, this is identical to Equation 1.10. Many inferential statistical procedures include a similar correction to form estimators of population parameters. However, some measures (e.g., the range or *IQR*) tend to be encountered almost exclusively as descriptive measures (although they remain biased estimates of dispersion in the population). Sums of squares are also used purely as descriptive measures. The *SS* tends to infinity as n increases (and is therefore not a sensible estimate of any population parameter). Using *SS* as a descriptive statistic is not necessarily inappropriate, but there is a tendency for people to interpret measures based on *SS* as if they were inferential statistics. So understanding the difference between *SS* and variance – particularly inferential measures of variance – is important.

Given the relationship between the variance and *SD* it is also possible to derive an inferential formula for the population standard deviation σ. The usual sample estimate of σ can be labeled $\hat{\sigma}$ ('sigma-hat'), and is the square root of the unbiased variance estimate:

$$\hat{\sigma} = \sqrt{\hat{\sigma}^2} = \sqrt{\frac{\sum_{i=1}^{n} (x_i - \hat{\mu})^2}{n-1}} \qquad \text{Equation 1.13}$$

A curious property of the estimator $\hat{\sigma}$ is that, although derived from an unbiased estimator, it is not itself an unbiased estimate of σ. Equation 1.13 underestimates the magnitude of σ (the underestimate arising, in this case, because the square root function is nonlinear). The underestimate is relatively small and can be safely ignored for most applications.

From this point on, the inferential formulas for the variance and standard deviation will be used by default. However, for the sum of squares (and some closely related statistics) descriptive formulas based on Equation 1.9 will be used.

1.7 R code for Chapter 1

1.7.1 Getting started

Once R is installed (a fairly easy procedure on most desktop computer systems) you will be presented with the *R console* window. Most interaction with R involves typing input into this window and hitting the return key. When R is ready to accept input you will see the following prompt:

```
>
```

Most of the work in R involves assigning things to entities called 'objects' and using functions (themselves types of objects) to manipulate other objects. The most basic object type in R is called a vector and it is a one-dimensional container of information. Vectors can contain all sorts of information, but for the moment we'll just consider vectors as containers of numbers. To assign a number to a vector is very simple. For instance, to assign the number 36 to a vector named `num.vect`[9] just enter (followed by the return key):

```
num.vect <- 36
```

To confirm that the assignment has indeed occurred, just type the name of the vector and hit return. This should bring up the following output:

```
[1] 36
```

The `[1]` in square brackets indicates that the object has a single dimension (and can be ignored for the moment). The `<-` arrow is an example of an assignment operator (there are others) and works – as you have probably realized – by taking the object on the right and assigning it to the object on the left. An alternative that would have worked just as well is:

```
36 -> num.vect
```

If you are new to R you will be tempted to assign objects left to right (as when writing) but in many cases you'll find it helpful to work right to left. One reason for this is that naming the object tends to be very easy, and it helps to get the easy part out of the way before typing out a complex instruction or formula.

In this way, R allows you to type in data and assign it to an object. It is also possible to read in data from external files (e.g., Excel or SPSS files). To keep things very basic, the examples in this chapter won't require reading in any external data files. On the other hand, the examples do require samples containing more than one data point. How do you get several numbers into an R object? One way is to use the combine function: `c()`. This is one of the most important and useful functions in R. To combine several numbers just use the combine function with the numbers separated by commas:

```
num.vect <- c(36, 49, 64)
```

Now, by entering `num.vect` (typing the object name and hitting return) the R console will generate:

```
[1] 36 49 64
```

The original contents of the vector have now been over-written (and are lost). You now know enough to enter data sets into R. Note that the vector is returned with `[1]` preceding it, indicating that the line starts with the first element of the vector. For large data sets this allows you to find the row with, for example, the 379th observation more easily.

Once you start entering data into R, your workspace (the bit of R that keeps track of objects such as vectors) may start to get untidy. When you quit R you will have the opportunity to save your default workspace (the one that R opens in). You could keep things tidy by not saving your work, saving workspaces under a different name or by saving work in a text editor.[10] It helps to keep track of your workspace and tidy it up as you go along. To see what objects are in R, you can list them with:

```
ls()
```

The above call requires no arguments. You can remove (i.e., delete) objects with `rm()`, but be sure to use the name of the correct object. To remove `num.vect` enter:

```
rm(num.vect)
```

1.7.2 Arithmetic

All basic arithmetic operators are also built into R, so it is possible to perform a range of calculations either with numbers, objects or both. Standard operators such as + and − behave as expected. For multiplication, R uses the asterisk character *; for division, R uses the forward slash character /. Try out the following examples:

```
2 + 6
9 - 2
3 * 7
100/4
```

Using R as a calculator pays off when you start integrating calculations with assignment to objects. This makes it possible to store the output from a calculation. One application for this is to update objects:

```
num.vect <- c(36, 49, 64)
num.vect <- num.vect + 4
num.vect

[1] 40 53 68
```

As well as basic arithmetic operators, R has functions for square roots, logarithms and exponentiation (raising to different powers or orders). These follow the standard order of operations (e.g., associated with acronyms such PEMDAS in the US and BODMAS in the UK). These place operations in parentheses (brackets) first, followed by exponentiation and then division and multiplication. Addition and subtraction bring up the rear. To raise a number (or object) to a power, place the ^ operator after the number, followed by the required power. To square a number you raise it to the power of two (e.g., to square 15 you would enter `15^2` into R). This procedure is quite flexible and allows square, cube and other roots to be found. (To get the nth root of a number you need to raise it to the power of $1/n$.)

One more feature of R is worth introducing here. If a vector contains several numbers you can apply the same operation to every number in the vector simultaneously (if you wish). This is extremely valuable in statistics, because you will often want to do exactly this. We'll illustrate this by taking the square root of several numbers within a vector.

```
num.vect^0.5
```

```
[1] 6 7 8
```

Sometimes there are several ways to do the same thing in R (or more generally in mathematics). R has a built-in square root function called `sqrt()`. We could express the preceding operation as `num.vect^.5` or `num.vect^(1/2)` with the same outcome. The preceding example displayed the outcome of the calculation, but was not assigned to an object, so would be lost. To store the results we'd need to use assignment, as below.

```
sqrt.vect <- sqrt(num.vect)
```

1.7.3 Simple functions and measures of central tendency

R has functions for most common descriptive statistics, the exception being the mode. This is usually easy to determine in small samples. For large samples the sample mode is rarely used for continuous data (and different approaches are appropriate).

If the data are discrete (e.g., frequency or count data) then the modal response is the largest count (and obtained as the maximum of the counts). For such data a bar plot or histogram is usually a good idea. The bar plot in Figure 1.1 is produced by the R code below. This creates a vector of the counts for each eye colour and a separate vector of labels for the eye colors. The vector of labels uses text strings enclosed by single or double quotes (the choice is irrelevant – although consistency is important). Strings such as 'Blue' or 'two' can be stored and retrieved by R and are required to label output (e.g., to put titles or legends on figures).[11]

```
eyes <- c(2, 5, 3)
labels <- c('Blue', 'Brown', 'Green')
```

The plot itself uses the `barplot()` function. A basic plot just requires one argument to be defined when the function is 'called'. The arguments are the information supplied to the function. The most basic bar plot just requires a vector of data points to define the heights of the bars.

```
barplot(eyes)
```

This resulting plot has no labels on the *x* or *y*-axis and additional arguments have to be supplied to get a satisfactory plot. Commas must separate all arguments. Depending on the function, the arguments can be defined by order of entry or (if some arguments can be omitted) may need to be named. To tell R that the labels represent the names of the bars the `names.arg` argument is used. To specify the label on the *y*-axis the `ylab` argument is used.

```
barplot(eyes, names.arg = labels, ylab = 'Frequency')
```

This reproduces Figure 1.1 almost exactly. The main difference is the size and shape of the plot. This can also be manipulated via R code, but it is usually easiest just to resize the plot window manually. Manual resizing might sometimes distort the plot, but if so, re-running the command should clean it up. To return to a previous command just use the up arrow key in the R console window. Repeated use of the up arrow cycles back through previously executed commands. In the preceding call, the text string defining the *y*-axis label is specified within the function (but it could be defined as a separate object such as a vector). Once you are happy with the plot you can save it in one or more common different formats (depending on the platform R is running on).

The flexibility to change the output of a function by specifying different arguments is a considerable benefit, but it can also be frustrating to keep track of the names of all the arguments a function can take. It is worth making your own reference sheet of common functions (or downloading one of the dozens available on the internet). To remember what arguments are available and how to specify them when calling a function, try out the `help()` function. You can get help for any function in the base installation packages (the packages of R functions that are installed by default) with the call `help(function.name)` or the shortcut `?function.name`. The help output may at first appear confusing, but it follows a fairly strict structure across all the main packages and will make more sense as you learn more about R. Try it out with the call `?c` to get help for the combine function. Some functions also have examples that can be accessed via the `example()` function:

```
example(c)
```

To compute the median or mean of a sample the functions `median()` and `mean()` are used. To illustrate this, let's do the calculations for the sample D_1. (Note that R is case sensitive and so the object D1 is different from d1.)

```
D1 <- c(12, 14, 9, 11, 15, 11)
median(D1)
mean(D1)
```

The `mean()` is very versatile and will also calculate a trimmed mean. As a second argument it expects the trimmed proportion in each tail. If you look at the help for this function using `?mean` you will see that the function has a trim argument with a default value of zero. This is designated by the `trim = 0` argument under 'Usage'. Many functions have default values, allowing the function to show quite sophisticated behavior. So a 16.7% trimmed mean for D1 is obtained with the command:

```
mean(D1, .167)
```

Increasing the trim proportion would eventually produce the median (and is guaranteed for `trim = .5`). In this case the trimmed mean doesn't differ from the mean, but for a sample such as D_2 it does matter:

```
D2 <- c(12, 14, 8, 11, 34, 11)
mean(D2, .167)
```

What about the geometric and harmonic mean? Functions to calculate them can be found in user-contributed packages for R, but it is also very easy to calculate them yourself. For the geometric mean, one method is to calculate the logarithms of the sample data (using whatever base you wish). We'll use natural logarithms. The natural logarithm is the default for the R `log()` function. This can be changed by using the `base` argument: the default being `base = exp(1)`. There is also a separate `log10()` function for logarithms to base ten. The inverse of the natural logarithm is e^x and is provided by the `exp()` function. Thus `exp(1)` is one way to obtain the constant e.

To compute the geometric mean of D_1, first calculate the natural logarithms of the sample. The geometric mean is then obtained by using the inverse of the mean of the natural logarithms:

```
D1.ln <- log(D1)
D1.ln.mean <- mean(D1.ln)
exp(D1.ln.mean)
```

Doing it in three steps is not necessary, and R can roll all the steps into a single command:

```
exp(mean(log(D1)))
```

This instantiates the formula in Equation 1.5. To instantiate the formula in Equation 1.3 it helps to use the `prod()` command for taking the product of a set of numbers.

```
prod(D1)^(1/6)
```

The sample size can also be obtained from the `length()` function – which will count the number of things (in this case numbers) in a vector.

```
prod(D1)^(1/length(D1))
```

The harmonic mean can be obtained by instantiating Equation 1.7. Either of these commands will give the harmonic mean of D_1:

```
1/mean(1/D1)
mean(D1^-1)^-1
```

One final function is worth introducing here. This is the `summary()` function. Summary is a very general function that produces different outputs depending on the type of object in the call. For a vector of numbers it will return the minimum, maximum, mean and the three quartiles (including the median, which is the middle or second quartile).

```
summary(D1)

Min.  1st Qu.  Median  Mean  3rd Qu.  Max.
9.0   11.0     11.5    12.0  13.5     15.0
```

1.7.4 Measures of dispersion

Although the `range()` function in R returns the minimum and maximum of a sample (often even more informative than the range itself), getting the range is easy using the functions `min()` and `max()` directly:

```
D1.range <- max(D1) - min(D1)
D1.range

[1] 6
```

The `summary()` function also returns the minimum and maximum for a numeric vector along with the quartiles. Unlike the range, the *IQR* has a dedicated function called `IQR()`. To calculate *IQR* for samples D_3 and D_4:

```
D3 <- c(11, 22, 7, 12, 15, 5)
D4 <- c(10, 22, 11, 12, 12, 5)
IQR(D3)
IQR(D4)
```

R also has a general quantile function that defaults to reporting the minimum, maximum and quartiles (labeled as the 0%, 25%, 50%, 75% and 100% centiles). Note that different computer software may calculate the quartiles in slightly different ways (and may produce different *IQR* values when n is small). Hyndman and Fan (1996) describe nine different methods for calculating quantiles – all of which are implemented by `quantile()`. Details are given in the help documentation (e.g., via `?quantile`).

There is no sum of squares function, but R is designed to carry out similar calculations on objects. Calculating the sum of squares for D_1 is therefore not at all hard. The new function required here is the `sum()` function.

```
resids <- D1 - mean(D1)
sq.resids <- resids^2
sum(resids^2)
```

Again it can be combined into a single expression:

```
sum((D1 - mean(D1))^2)
```

To calculate sums of squares for any other numeric vector replace D_1 with the relevant vector name. You can make the procedure more generic by separating the object name from the expression using another vector:

```
vect <- D1
sum((vect-mean(vect))^2)
```

This means we just have to change the line `vect <- D1` to read `vect <- D2` to get the *SS* for D_2. (We could write a function to do this, but for the present it is useful to work through the details of each calculation.)

For the descriptive formulas in Chapter 1, calculating the variance of a sample involves dividing sums of squares by n. For a vector this works out as:

```
vect <- D1
sum((vect - mean(vect))^2)/length(vect)
```

Taking the square root of this gives the descriptive *SD* of the sample:

```
(sum((vect - mean(vect))^2)/length(vect))^.5
```

R also has built-in functions for the inferential variance and inferential *SD* of a vector. These are `var()` and `sd()`.

```
var(D1)
sd(D1)
```

1.7.5 Plotting dispersion

This chapter introduced two very basic ways to plot the dispersion of a sample in R (in addition to the bar plot used for frequency data in Figure 1.1). The first of these was the box plot. A box plot can be plotted in a number of different ways. The plot in Figure 1.2 uses the R defaults.

The box is defined by the quartiles (with the median, the second quartile, a line across the middle). The length of the whiskers is defined as either as 1.5 times the *IQR* or as the distance up to the values of the largest or smallest data points (whichever is least extreme). Any points outside the whiskers (potential outliers) would be marked as open circles. A basic box plot using the `boxplot()` function requires only a vector of data points:

```
boxplot(D3)
```

This illustrates the power of R for quick plotting and exploration of data – especially if combined with descriptive data functions such as `summary()`. To make it prettier you can add labels such as the *y*-axis label in Figure 1.2.

```
boxplot(D3, ylab = 'Sample Data')
```

A second plot type considered here is the stem and leaf plot. Again the basic command for this is very easy to run:

```
stem(D3)
stem(D4)
```

One complication is that R default scales the stem of the plot in units of five (rather than units of ten used in Example 1.11). For larger samples the R defaults will usually be very helpful, but to reproduce the plots in this chapter exactly it is possible to tweak the scale argument of the `stem()` function:

```
stem(D3, scale = .5)
stem(D4, scale = .5)
```

1.8 Notes on SPSS syntax for Chapter 1

The examples in this chapter were either worked out by hand or using R (rather than SPSS). The notes below give some pointers for getting broadly equivalent output using SPSS syntax.

1.8.1 Basic descriptive statistics and plots

To obtain common descriptive statistics such as *n*, min, max, mean, *SD* and range use the DESCRIPTIVES command with a /STATISTICS subcommand. It is good practice to separate out the command and subcommand onto different lines like this:

SPSS data file: D1toD4.sav

```
DESCRIPTIVES VARIABLES=D1
 /STATISTICS=MEAN STDDEV MIN MAX.
```

This example assumes you have opened the data file (D1toD4.sav) with each sample specified as a separate variable (and that this is the active data file). To use the syntax you can open a new syntax window and type or paste it in. Highlight the syntax you need from the syntax window, and then go to the <Run> menu and choose <Selection>. You can also access these commands directly from the <Analyze> menu. Choose <Descriptive Statistics> and <Descriptives . . . > to open a dialog box that allows you to generate the syntax you require and either run it by clicking on the 'OK' button or pasting it into the syntax window by clicking on 'Paste'. The latter is an excellent way to explore how SPSS syntax works (and gives your more flexibility than a pure menu-driven approach).

The output from the function includes a box with the requested descriptive statistics for sample D_1. To get the same for D_2, edit the syntax so that the variables statement reads VARIABLES=D1 D2. The DESCRIPTIVES command is rather limited. For a broader set of descriptive statistics including 5% trimmed mean, median and *IQR* use the EXAMINE command.

```
EXAMINE
 VARIABLES=D1
 /PLOT NONE
 /STATISTICS DESCRIPTIVES
```

The EXAMINE command will include plots by default (and the syntax above suppresses that with the /PLOT NONE subcommand. SPSS can produce a wide range of plots, but it is not as versatile as R. A plot similar to the bar plot in Figure 1.1 can be produced with the following syntax:

SPSS data file: eyes.sav

```
GRAPH
 /BAR(SIMPLE)=COUNT BY eye_colour
 /TITLE= 'Frequency of eye colour for a sample of 10 people'.
```

Box plots and stem and leaf plots are also available. A box plot similar to that in Figure 1.2 can be plotted with the following syntax:

SPSS data file: D1toD4.sav

```
EXAMINE VARIABLES=D3
 /PLOT=BOXPLOT
 /STATISTICS=NONE.
```

For a stem and leaf plot (such as that in Example 1.11) try:

```
EXAMINE VARIABLES=D3
 /PLOT STEMLEAF
 /STATISTICS NONE.
```

1.8.2 Other descriptive statistics

SPSS provides a wide range of descriptive statistics and exploratory plots – notably from the EXAMINE and EXPLORE commands. Arithmetic can be performed on variables via the COMPUTE command. For simple arithmetic, however, you may find it easier to do calculations by hand (or to use spreadsheet software such as EXCEL).

The following syntax uses the compute command to calculate the natural logarithms of a variable and DESCRIPTIVES to calculate the mean of the transformed variable. The simplest way to obtain the geometric mean is then to take the exponent e^X of the result (2.478) using a calculator or spreadsheet.

SPSS data file: *C1 sample data.sav*

```
COMPUTE ln_D1 = LN(D1).
EXECUTE.

DESCRIPTIVES
 VARIABLES=ln_D1
 /STATISTICS=MEAN.
```

1.9 Bibliography and further reading

Gould, S. J. (1985) The Median isn't the Message, *Discover*, 6, 40–2.
Tukey, J. W. (1977) *Exploratory Data Analysis*. Reading, MA: Addison-Wesley.
Velleman, P. F. and Wilkinson, L. (1993) Nominal, Ordinal, Interval, and Ratio Typologies are Misleading, *The American Statistician*, 47, 65–72.

2
Probability distributions

Contents

2.1 Chapter overview

This chapter introduces common probability distributions for discrete and continuous data. The main focus is on distribution functions for determining probability or probability density, cumulative probability and quantiles of a distribution. Key characteristics of probability distributions (e.g., skew and kurtosis) and key ideas such as the central limit theorem are reviewed. A central theme is the role of selecting an appropriate probability distribution in building a statistical model.

2.2 Why are probability distributions important in statistics?

The presence of uncertainty is fundamental to statistical inference. If there were no uncertainty when sampling from a population then there would be no need for inferential statistics. In the absence of uncertainty, there will be zero variability and the sample will match the population perfectly.

Example 2.1 Consider the set of numbers {1, 1} as a finite population (of size $N = 2$). As there is no uncertainty in the population there is no role for statistical inference. A sample of size $n = 1$ or $n = 2$ taken from the set {1, 1} will always estimate the population mean (or any other parameter) with perfect accuracy. Because the population does not vary, this would not change even if the population were infinitely large. This could be confirmed by sampling the finite population with replacement (replacing observations after they are sampled and, in effect, sampling from an infinite population). Nor does the probability with which an observation is sampled matter when the population does not vary – the lack of uncertainty makes the relative probability of sampling any particular population value (e.g., the first observation) irrelevant.

Contrast the above situation with the numbers {0, 1} also considered as a population. The probability of sampling a particular value (0 or 1) is now of the utmost importance in estimating a population parameter. For example, if the probability of sampling zero is .25 when sampling with replacement (i.e., $Pr(0) = .25$), then this is effectively sampling from an infinite population where 25% of the population take the value 0 and 75% take the value 1. The distribution of values in this population determines how accurately a sample of size n will estimate the population mean. So even this rather simplistic situation requires us to consider the *probability distribution* defined by the population.

Example 2.1 suggests that without knowing the distribution of the population being sampled it will be difficult to make accurate inferences about a population. An immediate difficulty is how to determine the distribution of values in the population. This may seem like an impossible obstacle to overcome. But it is important to realize that the sample itself contains some information about the population from which it was sampled (and this information increases with n). In addition, at least some further information about the distribution is available in any real study (e.g., about its upper or lower bound). Last, but far from least, you will nearly always be able to get by without knowing the precise population probability distribution. What is required is sufficient information about the distribution to meet the goals of the research (e.g., estimating one or more parameters with a certain degree of accuracy).

For many purposes it is possible to rely on a relatively small set of probability distributions that can capture many of the key characteristics of population. These distributions act as useful building blocks for a statistical model. The distributions focused on here are just a few of those most commonly used in statistical modeling in the human and behavioral sciences. Methods also exist for dealing with situations when data are not easily modeled by assuming one of these distributions (e.g., robust methods). Whatever assumptions are required for a model, however, some understanding of the most important characteristics of the probability distribution being sampled is required (see Box 2.1).

Box 2.1 Characteristics of discrete and continuous probability distributions

One of the most fundamental characteristics of a probability distribution is whether the distribution is *discrete* or *continuous*. A discrete distribution is one where the population (and hence sample) only contains specific values, usually integers, such as {0, 1} or $\{-3, -2, -1, 0, 1, 2, 3\}$. A probability distribution for discrete data involves a mutually exclusive pairing of a probability with each population value that could be sampled. This can be done, in the simplest case, by listing each value with its corresponding probability. If the range of possible population values is large, then this can be done more conveniently by specifying a functional relationship* between the population values and their probability:

$$f(x) = p(X = x) = \text{probability of } X \text{ taking the value } x$$

For discrete data the functional relationship $f(x)$ gives the probably of X taking a particular value and is called a *probability mass function* (*pmf*).

It is common to represent the *pmf* as a plot of probability (from 0 to 1) on the y-axis and the values (x) that the distribution can assume on the x-axis. A *pmf* for the number of heads obtained when tossing a fair coin ten times is shown in Figure 2.1. In a *pmf* the probabilities of different values (denoted by the height of the lines in Figure 2.1) must sum to 1.

It is possible to obtain the arithmetic mean or expected value of the distribution by multiplying each probability on the y-axis by the value on the x-axis and summing the results. In this case the expected value is:

$$\begin{aligned} E(x) = 0.0009765625 \times 0 + 0.0097656250 \times 1 + 0.0439453125 \times 2 + \\ 0.1171875000 \times 3 + 0.2050781250 \times 4 + 0.2460937500 \times 5 + \\ 0.2050781250 \times 6 + 0.1171875000 \times 7 + 0.0439453125 \times 8 + \\ 0.0097656250 \times 9 + 0.0009765625 \times 10 = 5 \end{aligned}$$

For a discrete distribution the mode is simply the value (or values, if more than one) with the highest probability and therefore the tallest line (e.g., 5 in Figure 2.1). The median is the value that is halfway through (or at the 50th centile) of the probability distribution. This is easiest to show by plotting a *cumulative distribution function* (*cdf*) for the distribution.

A *cdf* is very similar to a *pmf* except that rather than the probability of a value being plotted, the probability of obtaining that value or lower – the cumulative probability of x – is plotted on the y-axis. Figure 2.2 shows the *cdf* for the number of heads from ten tosses of a fair coin. In this figure the lengths of the lines indicate the probability of observing x or fewer successes (and hence each line is taller than its height in the *pmf* by an amount equal to the height of the preceding *cdf*

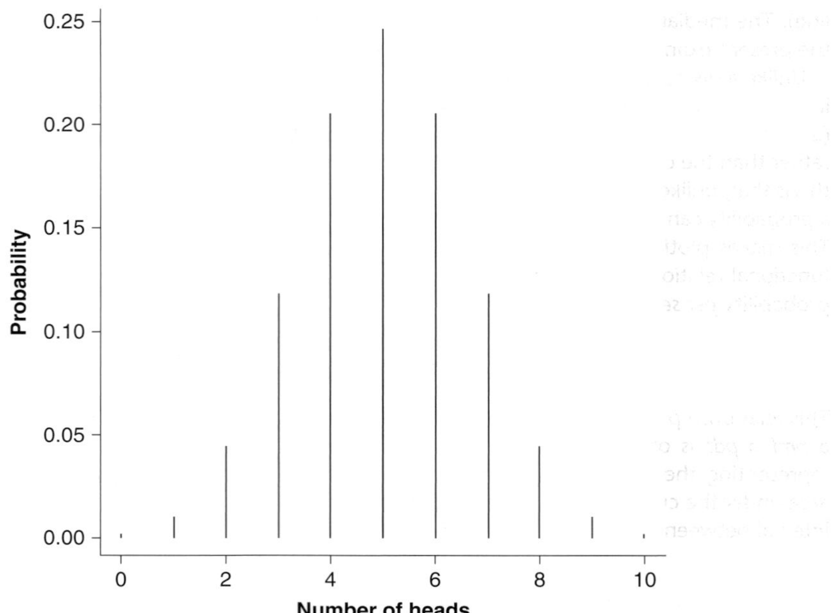

Figure 2.1 Probability mass function for the number of heads observed from 10 tosses of a fair coin

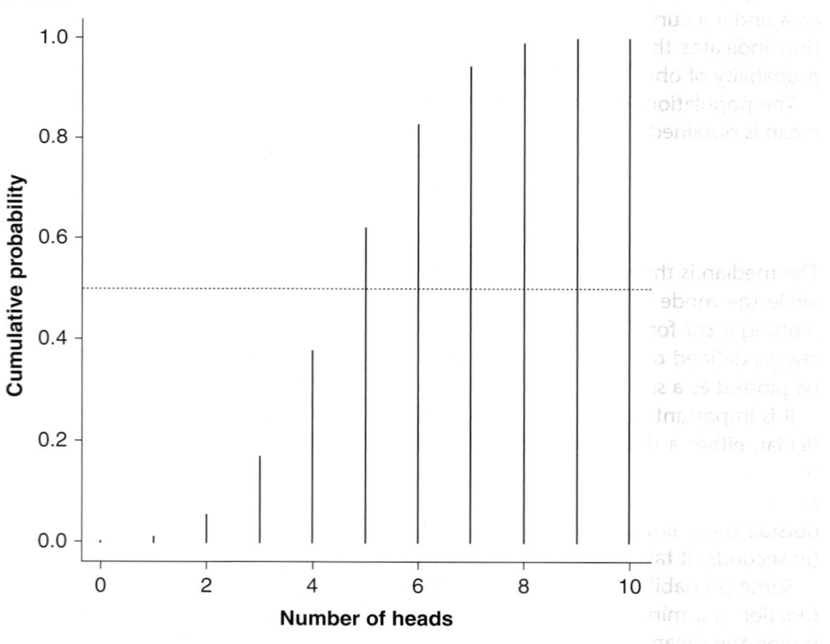

Figure 2.2 Cumulative distribution function for the number of heads observed from 10 tosses of a fair coin

line). The median is the first value for which the probability (or height of the line) includes .5. For the present example this is again 5 (as can be seen by following the dotted line at $P = .5$).

Unlike a discrete distribution, continuous distributions are not restricted to specific values such as integers and can, as a rule, take any value in between the lower and upper bound of the population (assuming it is bounded). A continuous probability distribution therefore has a smooth function rather than the characteristic 'spiky' function of a discrete probability distribution. An implication of this is that, unlike the discrete case, the probability of any particular value is zero. As a consequence, a probability can only be obtained for an interval (a range of values) within a continuous distribution. This makes plotting the probability directly as a *pmf* problematic. The solution is to specify the functional relationship between the population values and their *probability density* rather than the probability *per se*:

$$f(x) = p(X = x) = \text{probability density of } X \text{ at the value } x$$

This relationship for a continuous distribution is known as the *probability density function* (*pdf*). Like a *pmf* a *pdf* is often represented in graphical form, but in this case the *pdf* is a smooth curve representing the density at a given population value, while the probability is represented by the area under the curve (with the total area summing to 1). The probability of observing a value in the interval between the values a and b is

$$Pr(a \leq X \leq b) = \int_a^b f(x)dx \qquad \text{Equation 2.1}$$

This equation appears more complex than it is. The right-hand side of the equation is the *integral* for the *pdf* between the values a and b. (Integration is a mathematical procedure for calculating the area under a curve and an *integral* is the calculated area under a section of the curve.) Equation 2.1 thus indicates that calculating the area under the curve of a *pdf* between two values gives the probability of obtaining values in that range.

The population mean, median and mode can also be derived from continuous distribution. The mean is obtained via integration of the product of each value and its probability density:

$$\mu = \int_{-\infty}^{\infty} x\, f(x)\, dx \qquad \text{Equation 2.2}$$

The median is the value that divides the area under the probability density function exactly in half, while the mode is the value with highest peak (or peaks if more than one) in the *pdf*. Note that plotting a *cdf* for a continuous distribution is not a problem (because cumulative probabilities are always defined over intervals from zero to *P*). A *cdf* for a continuous function can also legitimately be plotted as a smooth curve.

It is important to realize that probability distributions also differ in other important ways. In particular, either a discrete or continuous distribution could be *bounded* or *unbounded*. For example the *pmf* in Figure 2.1 is for a distribution bounded at 0 and at 10. Many continuous distributions are also bounded (e.g., heights or weights are bounded at 0). Placing such limits means that values outside these limits are logically impossible. Therefore a continuous distribution such as the time (in seconds) it takes to drink a cup of coffee is bounded at 0 but has no logical upper limit.

Some probability distributions (e.g., that in Figure 2.1) are *symmetrical*, such that the probability function is a mirror image (i.e., identical but reversed) about the median. In a symmetrical distribution the mean and median take the same value. If the distribution is also unimodal (has a single peak and hence mode) then the population median, mean and mode are usually also all equal.** (More generally, in a multimodal *symmetrical* distribution, one of the modes will coincide with the mean only if there are an odd number of modes.) These relationships also hold between sample distributions and sample statistics (e.g., if the sample is symmetrical around the sample median, this value is also the sample mean).

A vital step in statistical modeling is to match characteristics of the data – more accurately characteristics of the process that generated the data – to a suitable probability distribution (or at least to narrow the choice down to a family or set of related distributions). Particularly important characteristics for this purpose are whether a distribution is discrete or continuous, symmetrical or asymmetrical and whether it is bounded in some way.

*The term $f(x)$ is just a general way to express the output of a function f when the input is the observation x.

**The exception is for discrete distributions with even number population values (see Key Concept 2.2).

2.3 Discrete distributions

2.3.1 The binomial distribution

In introducing probability distributions, the notion of sampling with replacement from a very simple population – a population containing only the values 0 and 1 – was invoked (see Example 2.1). If the probability of sampling the value 1 is fixed at, say, $Pr(1) = .75$ then a single sample of $n = 1$ from such a population is known as a *Bernoulli trial* and its distribution is termed a *Bernoulli distribution*. A Bernoulli trial can be used to model the outcomes of a process that has two mutually exclusive outcomes (e.g., the sex of a newborn baby – in which case the values represent 'male' and 'female').[1] A convenient shorthand is to label 1 as 'success' and 0 as 'failure'. The expected value or mean of a Bernoulli trial is equal to P (defined as the probability of a 'success'). The variance is equal to $P(1 - P)$, where $1 - P$ is the probability of a 'failure'.

What happens if n independent observations are sampled from such a population? The resulting probability distribution is known as the *binomial distribution*. As it happens, just such a situation is shown Figure 2.1 (which shows the probability mass function for a fair coin tossed ten times). Figure 2.1 shows the *pmf* for a binomial distribution with $P = .5$ and $n = 10$ (where 1 represents 'heads').

The binomial distribution is a theoretical distribution that is fundamental to many statistical models. For example, consider a recognition memory experiment in which 20 participants are presented with an item and then offered five options (the correct item and four foils) at test. In this situation, random guessing can be modeled as a binomial distribution with $n = 20$ and $P = .2$.

The *pmf* of a binomial distribution for a variable X is:

$$f(x; n, P) = \binom{n}{x} P^x (1 - P)^{n-x} \qquad \text{Equation 2.3}$$

Again, this formula may appear complex, but if you understand the notation (and some basic probability theory) it is reasonably simple (see Box 2.2). The symbols n and P refer to the number of independent binomial trials and the probability of success respectively, while x is the observed number of 'successes'. Thus $1 - P$ is the probability of a failure and $n - x$ is the observed number of 'failures'. Overall, the equation indicates that the probability of observing x successes is obtained by multiplying the number of possible combinations of trials with x successes by the probability of a sequence with x successes: $P^x(1-P)^{n-x}$. The number of possible combinations is given by the binomial coefficient described in Box 2.2.

Box 2.2 Probability, combinations and the binomial coefficient

A full introduction to even the basics of probability theory is outside the scope of this chapter, but it is worth introducing (or reviewing) some important points. First, if a and b are independent events (that is, the outcome of one has no influence on the other) then the probability of a occurring followed by b is $Pr(a) \times Pr(b)$. For example, if you toss a fair coin twice the probability of it coming up heads followed by heads again (HH) is

$$Pr(H) \times Pr(H) = Pr(HH) = .5 \times .5 = .5^2 = .25$$

Similarly, the probability of tails followed by tails (TT), or the probability of heads followed by tails (HT) is also .25. Together, these probabilities sum to .75 (not to 1). Why is that? Because a fourth option, tails followed by heads (TH) – also with probability .25 – has been missed out.

To find out how likely any set of outcomes (two heads, two tails or one head and one tail) is, you need to know not just the probability of each particular outcome, but also the number of ways in which it can occur. The number of ways an unordered outcome can occur is known as the number of *combinations* (and is distinct from the four ordered permutations HH, HT, TH and TT). In the above example, two heads can only occur in one way (HH), whereas one head and one tail can occur two ways (HT or TH). While it often helps to think of combinations in terms of sequences, the same principles apply to any set of independent events (e.g., tossing two coins labeled A and B simultaneously; thus HT could indicate that A is heads and B tails, and TH that A is tails and B is heads).

Thus in the *pmf* for the binomial distribution the $P^x(1-P)^{n-x}$ term represents the probability of obtaining a particular combination of x successes in n trials. For two fair coins $n = 2$ and $P = .5$ so the probability of two heads is $.5^2(1-.5)^{(2-2)} = .25(1-.5)^0 = .25(1) = .25$. To get the number of possible combinations there are two main methods. The first method is to list all the possible outcomes and count the relevant ones. Although time-consuming, it is a good way to understand what is going on when n is small. The second method is to use the following formula to find $\binom{n}{x}$:

$$\binom{n}{x} = \frac{n!}{x!(n-x)!} \qquad \text{Equation 2.4}$$

The exclamation mark denotes the factorial function. The factorial of a non-zero integer x (e.g., 4) is obtained by multiplying all integers from 1 up to x together (e.g., $1 \times 2 \times 3 \times 4 = 24$). The factorial of zero is a special case and defined as $0! = 1$. When tossing two coins, there is only one combination of two heads (or two tails):

$$\binom{2}{2} = \frac{2!}{2!(2-2)!} = \frac{2}{2} = 1$$

The term $\binom{n}{x}$ is known as the *binomial coefficient* and is a general way to refer to the number of ways of selecting x combinations from a total of n things.

The mean (expected value) of a binomial distribution can be obtained by summing the probability of x successes over all possible outcomes:

$$\mu = \sum_{x=0}^{n} f(x; n, P) = nP \qquad \text{Equation 2.5}$$

Equivalently, given that there are n independent trials, each has P chance of being a success and hence the mean of a binomial distribution is nP. The corresponding variance is $nP(1-P)$.

Although the binomial distribution is unimodal, it is symmetrical only if $P = .5$. In this case, nP is also the median. The median itself always falls between $nP - 1$ and $nP + 1$, while the mode is the largest integer smaller than $(n+1)P$. This carries the implication that the mean, median and mode are also identical if the mean is an integer. When the median and mode differ the mean lies between them (Kaas and Buhrman, 2008). This is necessarily true if the mean is not an integer: it will lie in between the median and the mode (one of which must be $nP + 1$ and the other $nP - 1$).

If a variable X has a binomial distribution this can be written as:

$$X \sim B(n, P)$$

B is shorthand for binomial while n and P refer to the parameters of the distribution (the tilde symbol can be read as 'is distributed as'). Here a particular sense of the term *parameter* is invoked. If you know both n and P, and that the distribution of X is binomial then no other information is needed – between them these parameters completely specify a binomially distributed variable. The estimators of such a set of parameters are sometimes termed *sufficient statistics* (see Box 2.3). Any other parameter of the binomial distribution (e.g., median, mode, range or variance) can be deduced once n and P are known.

Box 2.3 Sufficient statistics

Sufficient statistics are summaries of data that preserve all the information a sample provides about a population parameter. For example, $\hat{P}$ is a sufficient statistic for a Bernoulli distribution, whereas n and $\hat{P}$ are (in combination) sufficient statistics for a binomial distribution. A better-known example is that $\hat{\mu}$ and $\hat{\sigma}$ are sufficient statistics for the normal distribution.

When data are assumed to have been sampled from a particular distribution, sufficient statistics play a particularly crucial role as descriptive statistics. If the assumption is correct then the sufficient statistics offer a complete description of the population distribution. In practice it is unreasonable to assume data are sampled from a perfect binomial or other distribution. Even so, if the distribution is closely approximated by some ideal distribution, sufficient statistics for that distribution are undoubtedly a very powerful way to summarize and communicate what is going on (e.g., potentially allowing readers to check, re-analyze or conduct alternative tests of published data). Strong distributional assumptions are not always adopted, but sufficient statistics (usually in conjunction with other descriptive statistics and checks on a statistical model) are the starting point for most summaries of research. For example, they are the standard for reporting many statistical procedures in psychology (e.g., APA, 2010).

Applications of the binomial distribution often involve not the number of successes x but the proportion of successes x/n. For example, a researcher might be interested in the proportion of successes from n trials in a memory experiment (e.g., because this might be comparable between experiments with similar stimuli but different n). This follows the same distribution, except that dividing by n produces a mean of P and a variance $P(1-P)$. A sample estimate of the probability of successes is therefore also an estimate of the proportion of successes in the population. I will refer to this sample estimate as $\hat{P}$ ('P-hat') to distinguish it from the population parameter P.

Example 2.2 Consider a rudimentary extra-sensory perception experiment in which a supposed psychic (the 'sender') concentrates on one of three shapes (a circle, square or triangle). On each trial a participant (the 'receiver') is presented with pictures of the three shapes and asked to pick out the one that the sender is concentrating on. This procedure is repeated until $n=6$ trials are completed. If the receiver is guessing at random then all options are equally probable and the probability of success $P=1/3$. The assumed population mean is $nP=6(1/3)=2$ (as is the median and mean). The variance of this distribution is $nP(1-P)=2(2/3)=4/3$ or approximately 1.33. This could easily be re-expressed in terms of proportions of successes rather than number of successes. Dividing by n gives a mean of 1/3 and a variance of $4/18=2/9$ or about .22. The corresponding standard deviation (*SD*) could be estimated as .47 (the square root of .22). If four successes are observed then $\hat{P}=4/6=.67$. Although the observed proportion is fairly high it is not inconsistent with the assumed distribution of random guesses. Its *SD* of .47 gives a rough idea of how far a typical sample proportion might fall from the true mean.

Given these assumptions about the population it is possible to work out the probability of any particular outcome using Equation 2.3 and Equation 2.4. The probability of four successes turns out to be:

$$\left(\frac{6!}{4!(2)!}\right)\times\left(\frac{1}{3}\right)^4\times\left(\frac{2}{3}\right)^2=\frac{720}{48}\times\frac{1}{81}\times\frac{4}{9}=15\times\frac{4}{729}\approx.0823$$

Cumulative probabilities can also be calculated using these equations. The probability of four or more successes $Pr(x\geq 4)$ would be approximately 0.0823 plus the probability of five successes (0.0165) and six successes (0.0014) for a total of around 0.10. Although these calculations might seem precise, it is important to remember that they are limited in several ways. First, as noted earlier, the variance is probably quite large. Second, the probability model required an assumption (albeit a fairly reasonable one) about the value of the parameter P. Third, the binomial distribution assumes that the six trials are independent (which is almost certainly not true in this case – as all six responses are made in sequence by the same person). This would be violated if both receiver and sender have a preference for selecting a particular shape or sequence of shapes. Such a problem could be dealt with by generating the targets at random. Thus the design of the study can have an impact on the suitability of the probability model.

2.3.2 The Poisson distribution

The *Poisson distribution* is often selected to model frequency or count data – data that arise from counting the number of occurrences of an outcome within a particular area or time period. A *Poisson process* (something that generates a Poisson distribution) is one in which independent, discrete events occur over time or space at a continuous rate. This means that the number of events observed depends only on the length of the time period or the size of the area sampled.

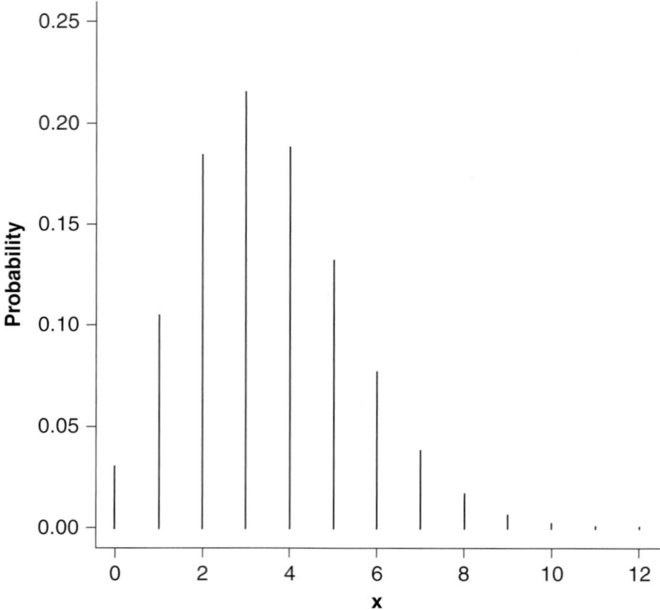

Figure 2.3 Probability mass function for a Poisson distribution with $\lambda = 3.5$

It is important to realize that, although each event is discrete, the time period or area sampled is continuous and could be divided into smaller segments (or pooled into a larger segment). The Poisson distribution is a natural starting point for modeling, say, the number of hits on a website or accidents reported in a one-week period in a particular workplace. The Poisson distribution has a single rate parameter λ (lambda) that determines the number of outcomes observed in a given sample. Figure 2.3 shows a Poisson probability mass function for $\lambda = 3.5$. A Poisson distributed variable, X, can be denoted as:

$$X \sim Pois(\lambda)$$

The probability mass function for the Poisson is:

$$f(x;\lambda) = \frac{\lambda^x e^{-\lambda}}{x!} \quad \text{Equation 2.6}$$

A fundamental characteristic of the Poisson distribution is that the single rate parameter is both the mean and the variance of the distribution. Also, as one would expect from a discrete distribution used to model count data, it is bounded at zero (but has no upper bound). A consequence of this is that the distribution is notably asymmetric when λ is small (the distribution tends to be squashed together toward zero and stretched out toward the upper bound, indicating *positive skew* – see Key Concept 2.2), but becomes more symmetrical as λ increases. Figure 2.4 illustrates this using the *pmf* for the Poisson distribution for $\lambda = 2$ and $\lambda = 5$. Also apparent is how the distribution spreads out as the mean (and hence its variance) also rises.

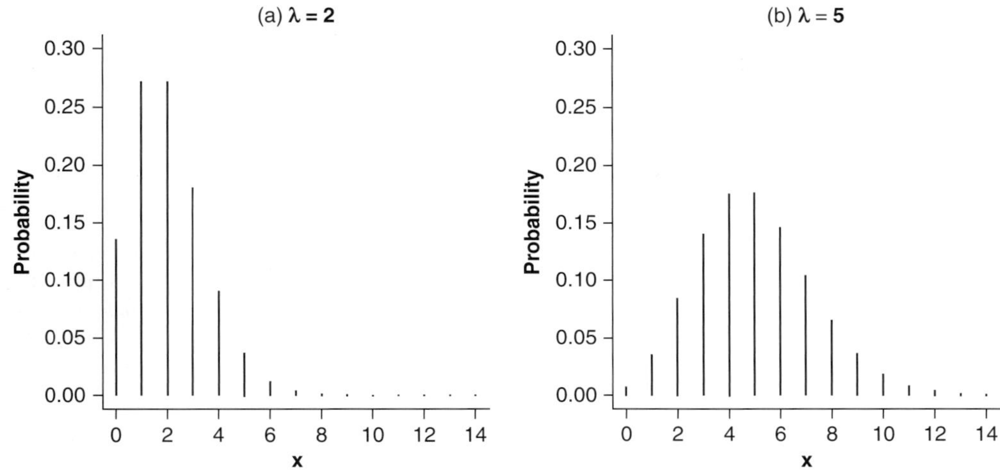

Figure 2.4 Probability mass functions for Poisson distribution with different rates

This relationship between mean and variance in the Poisson distribution offers one indication of its appropriateness in a statistical model. If the mean and variance of a sample differ markedly then a Poisson distribution may not be appropriate (at least not without considering additional factors that may be influencing the variability of the observed counts). Although generally asymmetrical, the Poisson distribution is unimodal. Its mode is the largest integer less than λ, unless λ is an integer (in which case both λ and $\lambda - 1$ are modes[2]). The median is less easy to pin down because of the asymmetry of the distribution. The median will often be close to λ, but there is no simple rule to describe its location (see von Hippel, 2005).

In the preceding section the binomial distribution was introduced as the sum of n independent Bernoulli trials with a fixed probability. What happens if two or more independent Poisson distributions are summed? It turns out that the sum of independent Poisson distributions is also a Poisson distribution with λ equal to the sum of the rates of the constituent distributions. For example, if the frequency of arguments between two couples undergoing therapy is rates of two per week and three per week respectively, the total rate of arguments is five per week. This is useful, because any number of couples (or other measurement units) with different rate parameters might, in principle, be modeled (provided the observations on each unit are independent).

So far, the discussion has focused on the Poisson distribution as the number of independent, discrete events occurring at a given rate. It is also possible to consider the Poisson distribution as an approximation of the binomial distribution appropriate when events are rare (i.e., P is very small). Under these circumstances the binomial distribution approaches the Poisson distribution with $\lambda = nP$ for a fixed value of λ as n becomes very large. Hence you can think of the Poisson distribution as a distribution for rare events if there are very many independent opportunities for the event to occur. At any point in time, a large number of people might potentially carry out some act (e.g., make a fraudulent insurance claim) but each does so with only a small probability. Thus a binomial distribution with $n = 5000$, $P = .001$ is approximated by a Poisson distribution with $\lambda = 5$. The binomial probability of observing exactly two such rare events is 0.08416534, while the Poisson approximation is 0.08422434.

Example 2.3 Consider the case of the number of arguments reported by a couple undergoing therapy. If a couple reported seven arguments in two weeks then $\lambda = 3.5$ per week and the probability of a couple reporting exactly two arguments in a week would be:

$$\frac{3.5^2 e^{-3.5}}{2!} = \frac{12.25 \times .030197}{2} = \frac{.36992}{2} = .18496$$

You'd expect such a couple to report two arguments in a week around 18% of the time. As just noted, this can also be thought of as an approximation to a binomial distribution where arguments occur with fixed probability $\hat{P}$ and an unknown number of trials. Working with a binomial distribution directly would be problematic – partly because it would not be practical to estimate the number of opportunities for arguments in any week.

2.3.3 Other discrete distributions

There are many other common (and many less common) discrete distributions of interest to researchers. Two, in particular, are worth a brief mention for their links to the binomial and Poisson distribution.

The first is the *negative binomial distribution* (sometimes known as the *Pascal distribution*). This is the distribution of the number of independent trials required to achieve a certain number of successes or failures, where P – the probability of a success – is fixed. Thus the negative binomial distribution is a kind of reverse form of the binomial (where the number of outcomes is fixed but n varies). The negative binomial model is also widely employed in a different context, where it acts as a substitute for the Poisson. This application arises because the negative binomial can be set up to mimic the behavior of the Poisson. Because it has an additional parameter it can model count data where the mean is not equal to the variance (see Chapter 17).

The second distribution is the *multinomial distribution*. This can be thought of as a generalization of the binomial distribution to situations with k discrete outcomes each with a fixed, independent probability (P_k) and where $P_1 + P_2 \ldots P_k = 1$. Furthermore, k independent Poisson distributed variables will have a joint distribution that is multinomial (and with parameters determined by the number of Poisson trials and their respective λ). The multinomial distribution is a natural choice when modeling categorical outcomes with more than two options.

2.4 Continuous distributions

2.4.1 The normal distribution

The *normal distribution* (also known as the *Gaussian distribution*) is a symmetrical, unimodal, continuous distribution that plays a key role in many areas of statistics. One way to derive the normal distribution is as the sum of an infinite number of independent, random variables. Thus the normal distribution seems appropriate for situations in which data arise from a process that involves adding together contributions from a large number of independent, random events. For example, the distribution of male heights might reasonably be considered the outcome of many independent, random genetic or environmental influences and hence (at least approximately) normal. The importance of the distribution in statistics derives primarily from its role in the *central limit theorem* (see Key Concept 2.1).[3] The central limit theorem suggests that under certain, fairly reasonable conditions, many statistics will follow an approximate normal distribution when *n* is large.

KEY CONCEPT 2.1

Sampling distributions and the central limit theorem

The central limit theorem (CLT) is the justification for many statistical procedures that assume a normal distribution (or at least approximate normality). It is a theorem about the *sampling distribution* of a statistic (a statistic being the sample estimate of a population parameter). The sampling distribution of a statistic is the distribution that is obtained by calculating the same statistic from an infinite number of independent samples of fixed *n*. It is therefore the hypothetical population distribution of sample statistics for a given sample size. Such a distribution is known as the sampling distribution of the statistic (e.g., in the case of the mean you would refer to it as the *sampling distribution of the mean*). The mean of a sampling distribution is the expected value (i.e., mean) of the original population the samples were drawn from. The *SD* of a sampling distribution is known as its *standard error* (the importance of which will become apparent when statistical inference is introduced). So the *SD* of the sampling distribution of the mean is termed the *standard error of the mean*.

There are a number of reasons why sampling distributions are interesting. First, these distributions determine the probability of observing a particular value of a statistic in any given sample (information essential for statistical inference). Second, the sampling distribution of a statistic can – and often does – differ from the population distribution of the data used to calculate the statistic. Don't assume that a sampling distribution has the same distribution as the population the original data are sampled from.

The central limit theorem states that the sampling distribution of a statistic approaches the normal distribution as *n* approaches infinity (its *asymptote*). This asymptote is the limit referred to in the theorem. (It is 'central' in the sense that it is fundamental to probability theory and statistics.)

There are restrictions on the generality of this result. The central limit theorem applies to any statistic that is computed by summing or averaging quantities. Thus it holds for variances or means, but not for all descriptive statistics (e.g., the *SD* is the square root of an average and the CLT does not hold for it). It also holds only for distributions with finite mean and finite variance. This might appear to include all possible distributions, but there are distributions (and not necessarily esoteric ones) that do not have finite means or variances. Nevertheless, for many practical applications a finite mean or variance is a reasonable assumption.

What is the practical impact of this? In essence it means that, provided certain fairly plausible assumptions are met and *n* is sufficiently large, the sampling distribution of a statistic will be approximately normal. In addition, the larger *n* gets, the better the approximation gets. Armed with the mean and *SD* of the sampling distribution it is therefore possible to use the normal distribution to estimate the probability of observing a particular statistic value or range of values. It should be immediately obvious that this makes the normal distribution incredibly versatile (even if the population that data are sampled from is decidedly non-normal).

Consider data sampled from a binomial distribution. It has finite mean and variance. The number of successes in a sample from a binomial distribution is the sum of *n* independent Bernoulli trials. It follows that the distribution of successes from a binomial distribution approaches the normal distribution asymptotically. Figure 2.5 shows histograms (frequency bar graphs) of the sampling distribution of successes from a binomial distribution when $n = 10$, 30 or 100 for $P = .35$ and $P = .15$. Each plot is based on only 100,000 samples (but this is enough to show the sampling distribution reasonably clearly). When $n = 100$

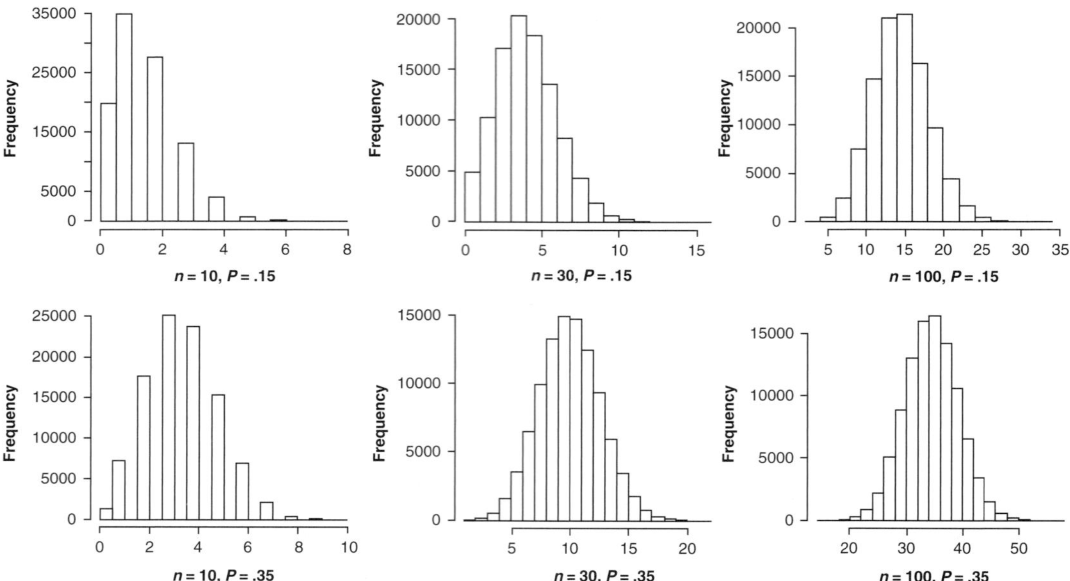

Figure 2.5 Histograms for 100,000 simulated samples from binomial distributions, with $P = .15$ (top row) or $P = .35$ (bottom row) and sample sizes of $n = 10$, $n = 30$ or $n = 100$

the distributions for both $P = .15$ and $P = .35$ look approximately normal, while both distributions look rather asymmetrical when $n = 10$. The main insight to be derived from Figure 2.5, however, is that the rate of convergence of the binomial distribution on the normal depends on P. Remember that the binomial distribution is symmetrical only when $P = .5$ and becomes increasingly asymmetrical as P approaches 0 or 1. Thus, when $P = .35$ the binomial distribution is more symmetrical than when $P = .15$. The similarity to the normal is evident for $P = .35$ even when $n = 30$ (and some skew is evident for $P = .15$ even when $n = 100$).

In general, the closer the original distribution is to the normal in shape, the more swiftly its sampling distribution converges on the normal.

As Figure 2.5 shows, different sampling distributions may well have very different rates of convergence. This poses a problem because it means it is not possible to state with any certainty that a given sample size (e.g., $n = 30$, $n = 100$ or even $n = 1,000,000$) allows the CLT to be invoked. In other words, no matter what n is selected there is no guarantee that the sampling distribution of a statistic will be even approximately normal (without additional conditions being imposed). That said, given some idea of the original distribution of the data (e.g., that it is approximately binomial with $P = .4$ or Poisson with $\lambda = 6$), it is easy to estimate what value of n will provide a reasonable approximation. Figure 2.5 suggests that for $n = 30$ the normal distribution provides a very satisfactory approximation to the binomial if $P = .35$, but might not be adequate for more extreme values of P such as .15 or .85.

Joliffe (1995) provides a neat example of the problem of convergence using the Poisson distribution. Recall that the sum of independent Poisson distributions itself has a Poisson distribution. Let's start by assuming that a distribution has $\lambda = 2$. If this distribution is, let's say, the sum of 100 independent Poisson distributions with $\lambda = 0.02$ it follows that the sum of means from a Poisson distribution is not guaranteed to be approximately normal when $n = 100$ (see Figure 2.4a). Thus Joliffe shows that while it tempting to use the Poisson to illustrate the CLT in action, the scenario works both ways. When λ is large the Poisson distribution is very well approximated by a normal distribution (e.g., Figure 2.4b suggests that the approximation may be acceptable even for $\lambda = 5$). However, we could pick any finite value of n and show that summing n distributions would not be approximately normal (provided λ for the summed distribution was itself small). This state of affairs is not confined to the Poisson. A similar argument can be made for the binomial distribution as a sum of n Bernoulli trials for rare events (i.e., when P is small).

Although the central limit theorem is a remarkably powerful tool, it is worth reflecting on three common misunderstandings of it. The first misunderstanding is that it applies without restriction. This is not the case – and although widely applicable – there are some statistics and some distributions that are excluded. Second, it is often assumed that a given value of n (e.g., $n = 30$ is common) ensures that the theorem can be invoked. Again, this is untrue. Required n depends on the distribution of the original data (its shape and the precise parameters involved) and on how close an approximation is desired. The third misconception is the most troubling. The CLT is sometimes interpreted as a statement about the distribution of the original data rather than a statement about the sampling distribution of a statistic. It is possible that this arises because some distributions (e.g., the binomial or Poisson) can themselves be thought of as sampling distributions of statistics. Nevertheless, a moment's reflection should be sufficient to counteract this misunderstanding. If you were to sample a completely flat, uniform distribution (e.g., a process that generates random real numbers between 0 and 1) and calculate the mean, repeating this process a few thousand or million times will produce a reasonable approximation to the sampling distribution (an approximate normal distribution). However, the shape of this sampling distribution will in no way have had any influence on the process that generated those numbers. How could it? Its distribution remains uniform. A related argument could be made for any discrete distribution such as the occurrence of heads or tails when a coin is tossed. Even if the sampling distribution of the number of heads is close to normal (which it will be with large n) and well-described by a continuous function, the outcome remains discrete. So someone might predict, but never observe, 4.5 heads from nine tosses of a coin.

The parameters of a normal distribution are its mean μ and its variance σ^2. A normally distributed variable X can therefore be denoted as:

$$X \sim N(\mu, \sigma^2)$$

The probability density function for a normal distribution with $\mu = 100$ and $\sigma = 15$ is shown in Figure 2.6. For convenience, the variability of a normal distribution is often described in terms of σ (sigma) the population *SD* – for the same reasons that the sample *SD* is preferred to the variance as a descriptive statistic. Many psychological scales are deliberately constructed to be approximately normal and Figure 2.6 happens to show the hypothetical population distribution for many common IQ tests. All normal distributions have this characteristic 'bell' shape (though note that a number of other common distributions can also be described as 'bell-shaped'). As the normal distribution is both symmetrical and unimodal, its mean, median and mode are identical in the population.

The probability density function for a normally distributed variable, X is:

$$f(x; \mu, \sigma^2) = \frac{1}{\sqrt{2\pi\sigma^2}} e^{-\frac{(x-\mu)^2}{2\sigma^2}} \qquad \text{Equation 2.7}$$

This function looks rather more difficult to understand than it really is – bear in mind that both e and π are constants (and π, the ratio of the diameter of a circle to its circumference, is found in many functions that describe curves). Hays (1973) explains that the 'working' part of the function is $-(x-\mu)^2/2\sigma^2$ (where x appears). For any particular normal distribution $x - \mu$ (the

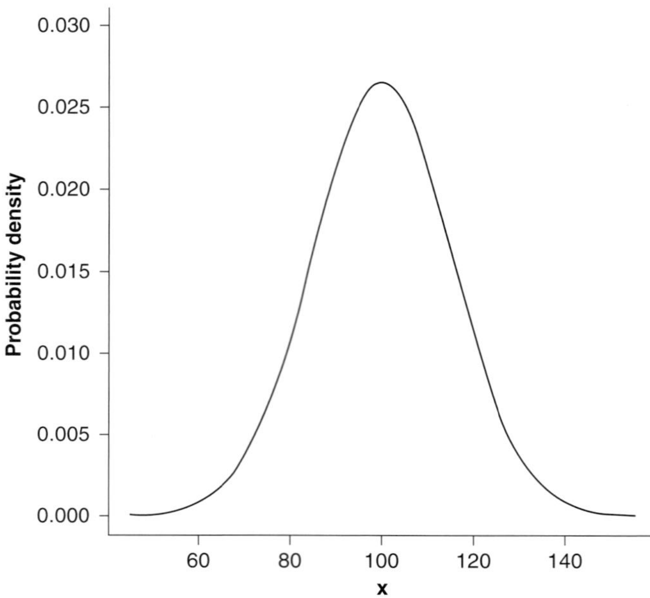

Figure 2.6 Probability density function for a normal distribution, with $\mu = 100$ and $\sigma = 15$

distance from the mean) determines its density. As this quantity is squared in Equation 2.7, the density is symmetrical around the mean. This part of the function appears as an exponent with a negative sign. Larger distances from the mean produce a more negative exponent, so the density is smallest when x is very far from μ and largest when $x = \mu$. Thus the distribution has a single mode. No matter what value x takes, the exponent of a positive number (such as the constant e) always produces an outcome greater than 0, therefore the probability density can never fall below zero (and hence the distribution is unbounded). All this holds provided σ is larger than zero (i.e., provided that there is any variability in X whatsoever). As with any continuous distribution, probabilities are defined by the area under the curve for a given interval (obtained by the integral of the curve between those points). Thus the total area under the curve equals the total probability:

$$Pr(-\infty \leq X \leq \infty) = \int_{-\infty}^{\infty} f(x)dx = 1$$

The spread of points around μ is determined entirely by σ (or equivalently by σ^2). Figure 2.7 shows normal distributions where μ and σ vary. It should be evident that changing the mean merely shifts the distribution right or left along the x-axis, while changing the standard deviation increases or decreases its spread (in the same way that constricting the x-axis would). This constriction is, in effect, just a rescaling of the x-axis: the same visual result is achieved by multiplying all the value labels on the x-axis by two or by halving σ.

An important feature of the normal distribution that is not particularly evident when it is plotted is that the probability density never reaches zero (and one convention is to terminate the left and right ends of the plotted curve in 'mid air' to suggest this). This is because the distribution

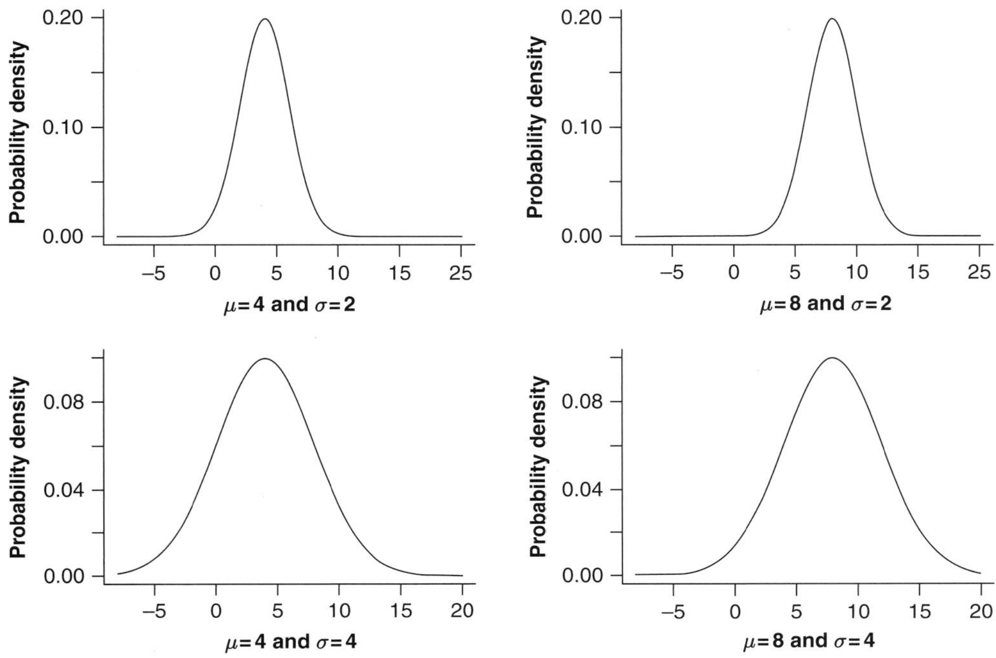

Figure 2.7 Normal distributions with differing parameters

is unbounded; ranging from $-\infty$ to ∞. In principle a value any distance from the mean might be observed (though the probability becomes extremely small as the distance exceeds several multiples of σ). This property may make the normal distribution unsuitable for some purposes (e.g., because the true population values are bounded or because the probability of very extreme values being observed is poorly represented).

If a variable has the distribution

$$z \sim N(0, 1),$$

then it is said to follow the *standard normal distribution*. The *pdf* and *cdf* of the standard normal are depicted in Figure 2.8.

The standard normal distribution (often abbreviated to *z*) is frequently used to simplify working with normal distributions. For the reasons considered above, any normal distribution can be shifted right or left, so that $\mu = 0$ (by subtracting its mean from all values). Likewise you can squash or stretch the distribution, so that $\sigma = 1$, by dividing all values by its *SD*. Aside from simplifying calculation (arithmetic using 0 and 1 being generally quite easy) it also simplifies some mathematical proofs involving the normal distribution. Particularly useful (historically at least) is the fact that the quantiles (and particularly centiles) of the standard normal distribution can be so easily mapped onto any other normal distribution and vice versa. A single set of tables of *z* quantiles, combined with a little arithmetic, can substitute for any normal distribution (and is particularly convenient when working without a computer). For example, the 50th centile (the median) lies at zero and approximately two-thirds of the distribution lie between -1 and 1.

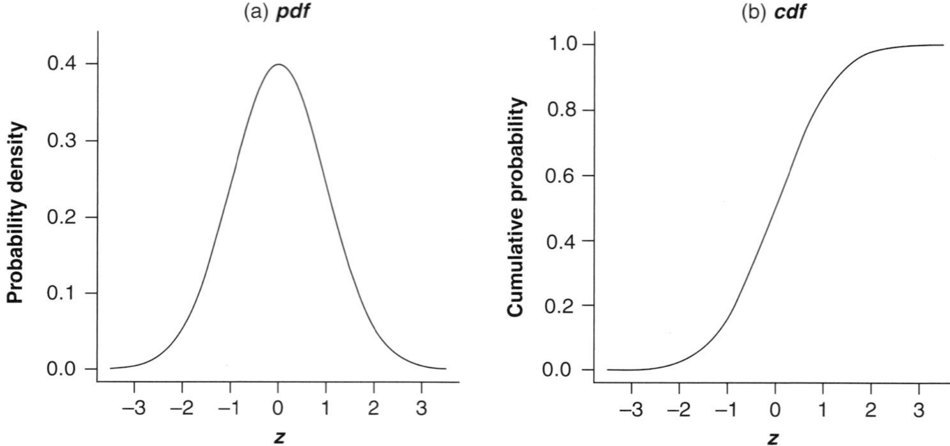

Figure 2.8 Probability density and cumulative distribution functions for the standard normal (z) distribution

For any normal distribution, around 67% of the population lie within $\mu \pm \sigma$, and around 95% of the population lie within $\mu \pm 2\sigma$. As the distribution is symmetrical it follows that about 2.5% lie above $\mu + 2\sigma$ and about 2.5% below $\mu - 2\sigma$. While these integer approximations are handy, more precise values can determined by computer or from tabulated values of z. These values could also be calculated by integrating the area under the standard normal curve bounded by particular values of z. The usual trick here is to use the *cdf* to obtain the cumulative probability for a particular tail value. When using the z distribution, this function is often labeled Φ (the Greek capital letter 'phi') and its inverse as Φ^{-1}. Hence $\Phi(-1.96) = .025$. This gives the cumulative probability of the left tail of z up to and including -1.96. You should be able to check this visually using Figure 2.8b. Because the *pdf* is symmetrical (see Figure 2.8a) you only need to look up values for the lower tail and double it to get the proportion of values falling $+/-1.96\sigma$ from the mean. (Using the left tail is easiest because the convention is to cumulate left-to-right.) Likewise, $\Phi(1.96)$ gives the cumulative probability up to and including $z = 1.96$. This is .975 and implies $1 - .975 = .025$ is the probability for values of z exceeding 1.96. To include 66.67%, 90%, 95% and 99% of the distribution, the correct values of z (to three decimal places) are ± 0.968, ± 1.645, ± 1.960 and ± 2.576.[4]

This property of the normal distribution makes the sample *SD* an especially useful descriptive statistic. Even if a distribution is known not to be normal, there is a theorem (*Tchebycheff's inequality*) that provides limits on the proportion of a distribution that can fall in each tail (see Hays, 1973). For any distribution with finite mean and variance, the probability of obtaining a value $\pm j\sigma$ from the mean of a distribution is always less than or equal to $1/j^2$. For example, the probability of obtaining a value $\pm 2\sigma$ from the mean is no more than .25. This can also be applied to the distribution as a whole. At least 75% of values from any distribution are no further than $\pm 2\sigma$ and at least 93.75% are no further than $\pm 4\sigma$ from the mean. If the distribution is both unimodal and symmetrical, it is possible to narrow the limits a little further using the *Vysochanskij-Petunin inequality*. Here the relevant quantity is $4/9\,(1/j^2)$. This more than halves the tail probability, so that around 89% of observations are no further than $\pm 2\sigma$ from the mean. Thus, even if a variable is not normal, $\hat{\sigma}$ provides at least a rough indication of how unusual an observation is.

Example 2.4 Researchers in the UK have recently argued that differences in teaching ability can have a substantial impact on public examination grades (Slater *et al.*, 2009). One estimate is that the difference between having a teacher in the top 5% or bottom 5% of teaching ability, relative to an average teacher, is around one letter grade (the difference between A and B or B and C) at GCSE (the main public exam for 16-year-olds in England and Wales). If teaching ability is assumed to follow a normal distribution (probably quite a strong assumption), the effect of teaching ability on GCSE grades could be modeled as a normal distribution with $\mu = 0$ and $\sigma \approx 0.3$.

On this basis, what is the expected impact of a teacher on the 25th centile of teaching ability? This can be from $\Phi^{-1}(.25) \approx -0.67$. A teacher at the 25th centile might be expected to reduce grades by about $.67\sigma$ or $0.67 \times 0.3 = 0.2$. This amounts to a fifth of a letter grade lower than they would otherwise obtain. It follows that a teacher on the 75th centile would be expected to increase performance by about a fifth of a grade.

The calculations also work the other way. What proportion of teachers would be expected to increase grades by a whole letter grade? This is approximately $1/0.30 = 3.33\sigma$. As $\Phi(3.33) \approx .9996$ it follows that this proportion is about $1 - .9996 = .0004$. This equates to .04% (or around one teacher in 2500). Note that by requesting the lower (left) tail cumulative probability I would have got directly to $\Phi(-3.33) \approx .0004$.

Although these estimates seem reasonable, they required quite strong assumptions about the distribution. If the distribution is not normal the estimated probabilities – particularly the extreme tail probabilities – could be very inaccurate.

2.4.2 The lognormal distribution

The lognormal distribution is an asymmetric, continuous probability distribution that, as the name implies, is normal under a logarithmic transformation. If a variable X has a normal distribution then e^X has a lognormal distribution. Correspondingly, if Y has a lognormal distribution then $\ln(Y)$ is normal. (Note that the base of the logarithm is irrelevant to this relationship – it merely acts as a scaling factor.) While the normal distribution is *additive* – arising as the sum of an infinite number of independent, random variables, the lognormal distribution is *multiplicative*. The lognormal thus applies when many independent, random variables are multiplied together (i.e., as the distribution of their product rather than their sum). This is reasonable when the effect of many independent and random influences is to induce a proportionate change in something (rather than merely adding or subtracting from it). Just as the sum of independent normal variables is normal, so the product of independent lognormal distributions is lognormal.

It is natural to exploit the link between the lognormal and the normal. For example, the parameters of the lognormal are usually defined as μ and σ^2 where μ and σ^2 are the mean and variance of the logarithms of the population sampled (rather than of the original population). A lognormal variable X can be written as

$$X \sim LogN(\mu, \sigma^2)$$

with the probability density function:

$$f\left(x;\mu,\sigma^2\right) = \frac{1}{x\sqrt{2\pi\sigma^2}} e^{-\frac{(\ln(x)-\mu)^2}{2\sigma^2}} \qquad \text{Equation 2.8}$$

Representing the lognormal in this way (using natural logarithms) means that exponentiation to base e of μ and σ gives e^{μ}, the geometric mean, and e^{σ}, the geometric standard deviation. The variance of X is given by $\left(e^{\sigma^2} - 1\right) e^{2\mu+\sigma^2}$, while the arithmetic mean of the original values is given by $e^{\mu+\frac{\sigma^2}{2}}$. The geometric mean of a lognormal distribution, e^{μ}, is also its median, whereas the mode is $e^{\mu-\sigma^2}$. These values are consistent with the asymmetry of the lognormal distribution – the median, geometric mean and mode are smaller than the arithmetic mean (which is weighted toward the long right tail of the distribution). This is shown clearly in Figure 2.9, which depicts the standard lognormal distribution (i.e., with $\mu = 0$ and $\sigma = 1$).

Data from a lognormal distribution are constrained to be greater than zero, but have no upper bound. The distribution is therefore a popular choice of continuous distribution for real world data bounded in this way (e.g., response times). The lognormal distribution is a common example of a positively skewed distribution (see Key Concept 2.2). The degree of skew depends on σ. When σ is small the skew is negligible (approaching symmetry as σ approaches zero). One implication of this is that, as skew decreases, the mean $e^{\mu+\frac{\sigma^2}{2}}$ and geometric mean e^{μ} become more similar.

It is therefore difficult to distinguish samples from normal and lognormal distributions if μ is large relative to σ. Limpert *et al.* (2001) make exactly this argument for much real world data; the normal distribution is often assumed when the lognormal is at least as plausible.

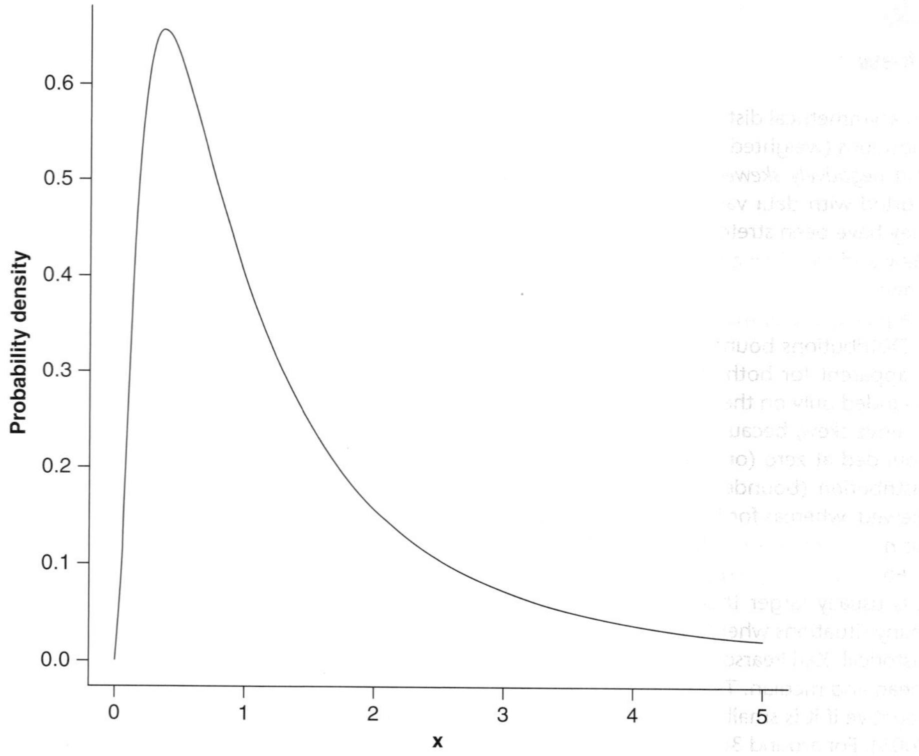

Figure 2.9 Probability density function for the standard lognormal

Example 2.5 Limpert *et al.* (2001, Table 2) report numerous examples of data sets with an approximate lognormal distribution. One, based on historic data from Boag (1949), is for survival after a diagnosis of mouth and throat cancer. Subsequent examples refer to these as the cancer survival data.

Survival data are notable for their positive skew (see Gould, 1985), and it seems reasonable that the lognormal distribution could be used to describe it. The geometric mean (also the median) is approximately 9.6 months with a geometric *SD* of 2.50. This distribution could be modeled as a normal distribution of the natural logarithm of the survival time (in months) or as a lognormal distribution with $\mu = \ln(9.6)$ and $\sigma = \ln(2.50)$. The advantage of using a lognormal distribution is that it retains the original units (survival in months).

Using this information one can predict the survival for patients in the left and right tails of the distribution, or the probability or surviving a certain length of time after diagnosis for a patient picked at random. The probability of surviving two years or more after diagnosis $Pr(x \geq 24)$ is about .16. A patient in the bottom 10% has an estimated survival time of about 3.0 months (6.6 worse than median). The skew of the distribution is obvious when you consider that estimated survival for a patient in the top 10% is about 31.1 months (21.5 months better than median). These summary data are now over 60 years old and survival after diagnosis will probably be much improved (though it may well still be adequately modeled by a lognormal distribution).

KEY CONCEPT 2.2

Skew

An asymmetrical distribution is said to be *skewed*. It is sensible to distinguish between *positively skewed* distributions (weighted to the right of the number line where the larger, more positive numbers are located) and *negatively skewed* distributions (weight toward smaller, more negative numbers on the left). When plotted with data values on the *x*-axis (e.g., for a *pmf* or *pdf*), positively skewed distributions look as if they have been stretched out to the right and negatively skewed stretched out to the left. The terms *right skew* and *left skew* are therefore often used interchangeably with positive and negative skew respectively. However, positive and negative skew are more general terms; if the data values are plotted vertically (on the *y*-axis) the terms right and left skew will be misleading.

Distributions bounded only at their left-most tail (e.g., at or near 0) tend to be positively skewed. This is apparent for both Poisson and lognormal distributions (see Figure 2.3 and Figure 2.9). Distributions bounded only on the right tend to have negative skew. Negative skew is less frequently encountered than positive skew, because many real world processes (e.g., response times, income, number of children) are bounded at zero (or close to zero). However, negatively skewed distributions are not rare. The binomial distribution (bounded on both the left and the right) is a good example. When $P < .5$ it is positively skewed, whereas for $P > .5$ it is negatively skewed. Figure 2.10 shows the *pmf* for the binomial distribution for $n = 20$ when $P = .08$ and $P = .92$.

For a positively skewed distribution the median is typically smaller than the mean. For negative skew it is usually larger than the mean. A common misconception is that this is always true, but there are many situations where this pattern does not hold (von Hippel, 2005). One reason for this misconception is historical. Karl Pearson proposed two simple measures of skew (*skewness*) based on the difference between mean and median. These measures define skewness as positive if the mean is larger than the median (and negative if it is smaller). The Poisson distribution is a particularly useful counter-example (see von Hippel, 2005). For around 30% of all values of λ the median is larger than the mean (even though the Poisson can never have negative skew). For example, if $\lambda = 1.9$ the median is 2. When $\lambda = 2$ the median is also 2, but the distribution is far from symmetrical. If you look back at Figure 2.4a it should be possible to see why.

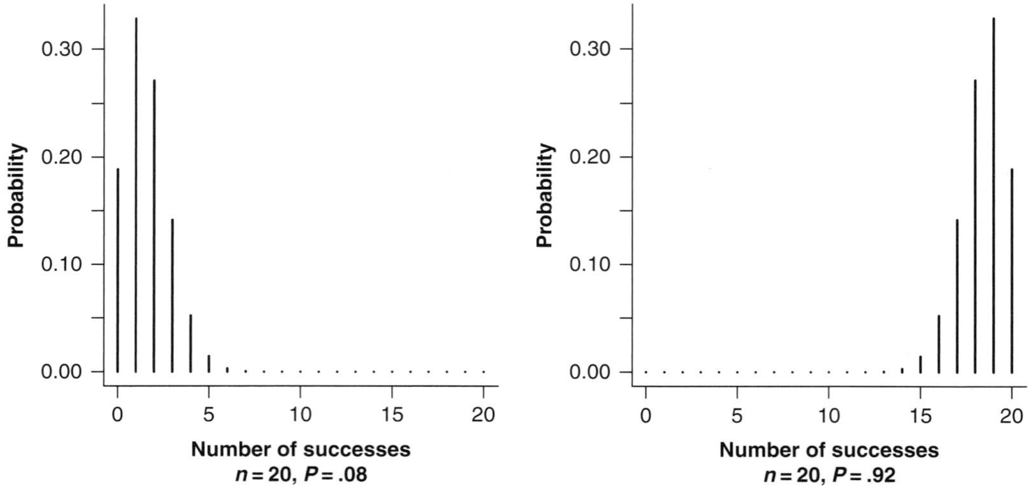

Figure 2.10 An illustration of the asymmetry of the binomial distribution, when $P \neq .5$

First, note that the mode is spread across 1 and 2. When λ falls just below 2, the peak shifts slightly so that the mode equals 1. The median is harder to shift and remains at 2.

Skew is more correctly defined in terms of the 3rd 'moment' (μ_3) of a probability distribution (where the mean is defined as the 1st moment and the variance the 2nd). This indicates that the skew depends on the cubed deviations of values from the mean (while the variance depends on the squared values and the mean on the unsquared, uncubed values). When comparing distributions, skewness is often 'standardized' (i.e., scaled in terms of σ). For example, skewness is typically represented as μ_3/σ^3 (and will be zero if a distribution is symmetrical).

In general, violations of the supposed 'rule' that the median is shifted away from direction of skew (relative to the mean) occur most often for discrete and bimodal (or multimodal) distributions. For continuous distributions such a pattern is never found if a distribution is unimodal, but can sometimes occur when a distribution is not unimodal. In addition, it is important to understand that a sample distribution can (and typically does) differ in shape from the distribution it is drawn from – so a negatively skewed sample could be drawn from a positively skewed population. Furthermore, if measurements are discrete (e.g., because of rounding error or the nature of the measurement tool being used), samples from a continuous distribution might behave somewhat erratically (relative to the continuous distribution they are supposedly sampled from).

2.4.3 The chi-square (χ^2) distribution

A good starting point for understanding the *chi-square* distribution[5] is to consider a squared observation, z^2, drawn at random from the z (i.e., standard normal) distribution. The sampling distribution of z^2 is a chi-square distribution – specifically it is a chi-square with 1 *degree of freedom* (*df*). Figure 2.11 shows the *pdf* for the chi-square distribution with 1 *df*.[6]

If k independent observations were sampled from a z distribution and each observation squared and summed (added together), the distribution would be chi-square with ν degrees

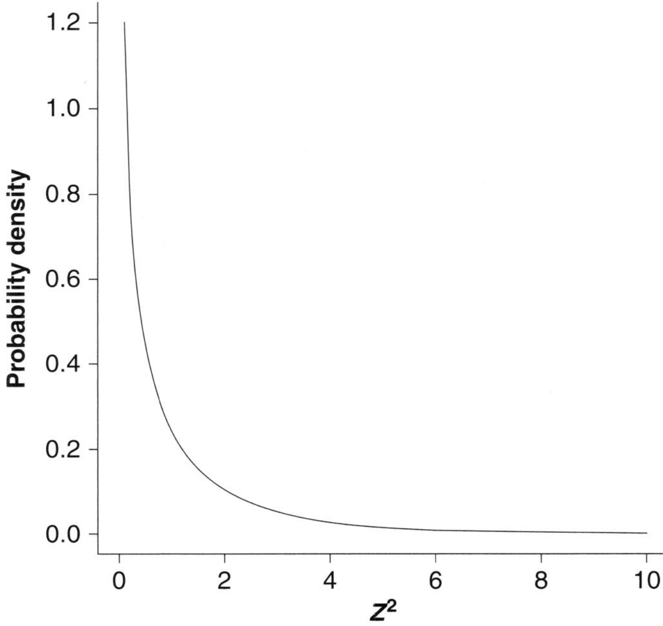

Figure 2.11 Probability density function for a chi-square distribution with 1 *df*

of freedom (where ν is the Greek lower-case letter 'nu'). The distribution has a single parameter ν, and this is always greater than zero. Why might we be interested in this distribution? The fundamental insight here is that z^2 is a special case of *sums of squares* where the data have a variance of 1. Given the intimate link between the calculation of sums of squares and the variance it turns out that the chi-square distribution is useful for modeling variances of samples from normal (or approximately normal) distributions.

If a variable X has a chi-square distribution with ν *df* it can be denoted as:

$$X \sim \chi^2_\nu$$

The mean or expected value of χ^2 is equal to its degrees of freedom ν and its variance is 2ν. Knowledge of the expected value of a chi-square statistic is particularly useful for large ν; it provides a quick way to gauge the fit of a statistical model (which tends to be good if the statistic is similar in value to its *df* and poor when markedly different from its *df*). The mode is $\nu - 2$ if $\nu > 2$ (and zero otherwise). In contrast, the median tends to be in the region of $\nu - 2/3$. Figure 2.12 shows the *pdf* for chi-square when for $\nu = 3$ and $\nu = 10$.

The chi-square distribution is positively skewed and bounded at zero – as should be expected for a distribution derived from sums of squares. Figure 2.12 hints that as the *df* rise, the distribution will become more symmetrical (and, in accordance with the CLT, it will ultimately converge on the normal distribution). This is indeed the case – and follows from the fact that chi-square is itself a form of sampling distribution (for the sums of squares of independent z).

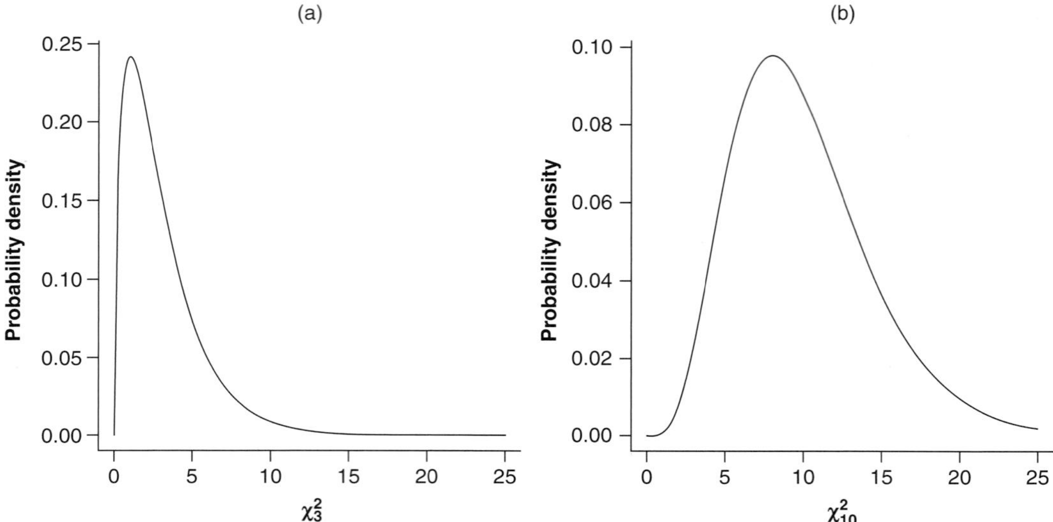

Figure 2.12 Probability density functions for chi-square distributions, with (a) $\nu = 3$, and (b) $\nu = 10$ *df*

The link between sums of squares and χ^2 is not restricted to the standard normal. The sums of squares of independent, random normal variables with variance σ^2 have a chi-square distribution scaled by σ^2:

$$\sum_{i=1}^{n} (x_i - \mu)^2 \sim \sigma^2 \chi^2_{n-1} \qquad \text{Equation 2.9}$$

An oddity of the chi-square distribution is that, although it can be derived as the distribution of sums of squares of discrete observations, the *df* are not restricted to integer values (though $\nu \geq 1$). Some statistical procedures make use of fractional *df* and it is helpful to realize that this is not necessarily an error.

Strictly speaking, the preceding discussion applies to the *central chi-square distribution*, and for some situations a *non-central chi-square distribution* is appropriate. This point is also relevant for the final two continuous distributions discussed in this chapter – the central *t* and central *F*. The distinction between central and non-central distributions is dealt with later, in relation to statistical power (see Chapter 8).

2.4.4 The *t* distribution

The *t distribution* (also called *Student's t*) is a sampling distribution for means from a normal distribution. As has already been established, the sampling distribution of means from a normal population is itself normal. However, estimating this distribution when the population standard deviation σ is unknown presents a practical difficulty. William Gossett (publishing under the pseudonym 'Student') addressed this problem by showing that if σ is estimated from the unbiased variance estimate $\hat{\sigma}^2$, the resulting 'standardized' sample mean has what is now known as a t distribution with *df* equal to $\nu = n - 1$ (Student, 1908). A variable, X, with a t distribution can be denoted as:

$$X \sim t(\nu)$$

The t distribution is closely linked to both z and the χ^2 and it is the probability distribution of the ratio:

$$\frac{Z}{\sqrt{V/\nu}} \qquad \text{Equation 2.10}$$

The numerator Z is a variable with a standard normal distribution. The denominator is a chi-squared variable V with ν *df*. In addition, Z and V are assumed to be independent.

A common misconception is that the t distribution applies to the sampling distribution itself (whereas it applies only to this standardized form). This is, however, the form that is most likely to arise in practice, because σ^2 is rarely known for real data sets. Figure 2.13 shows the t distribution relative to the standard normal when $\nu = 1$ and $\nu = 29$ (corresponding to a single sample with $n = 2$ and $n = 30$).

Like the normal distribution t, is always symmetrical, but it tends to have a relatively narrower peak and 'fatter' or 'heavier' tails than z (at least when n is small). This characteristic is known as *leptokurtosis* (see Key Concept 2.3). Notably, the t distribution converges rapidly on z and is only barely distinguishable from z in Figure 2.13b when $n = 30$. Even so, the difference between z and t can be substantial for very small samples.

Being related to z (and hence unimodal and symmetrical), the median and mode of t are both equal to zero (and the mean is also zero if $\nu > 1$). If t has at least 2 *df* it has a variance of $\frac{\nu}{\nu - 2}$. When t has only 1 *df* its mean and variance are undefined and it coincides with the standard

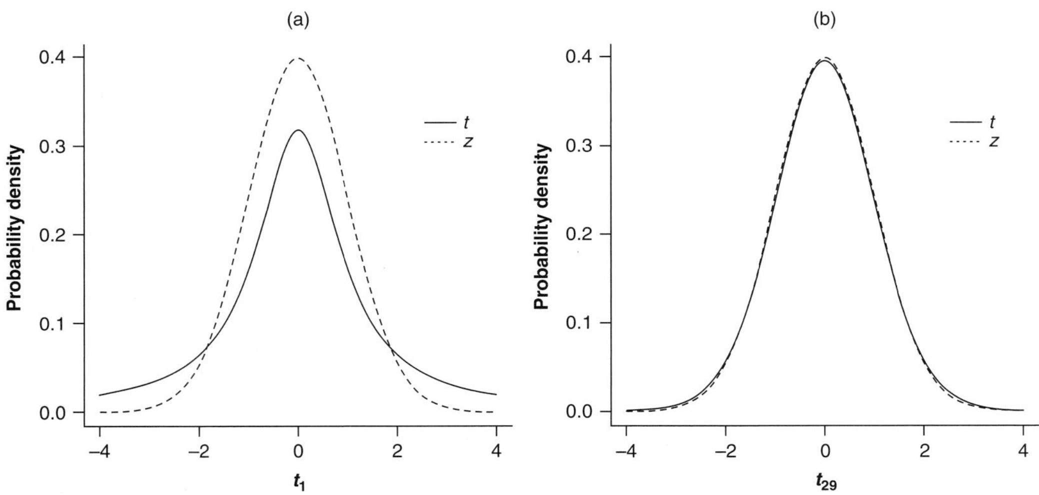

Figure 2.13 Probability density of t_1 and t_{29} relative to z

Cauchy distribution (a distribution which is the ratio of two standard normal distributions). This is an important reminder that the distribution of something as 'basic' as a *t* distribution with 1 *df* can fall outside the scope of the CLT. The CLT requires that the mean and variance are finite (see Key Concept 2.1).[7]

KEY CONCEPT 2.3

Kurtosis

Kurtosis is a term describing the relative proportions or 'weight' of a probability distribution in its middle versus its tails. For unimodal, symmetrical distributions (such as the normal or *t* distributions) it therefore refers to the relative weight of the distribution in its peak or its tails. A distribution with flat peak and relatively 'thin' or 'light' tails indicates *platykurtosis* (i.e., it is *platykurtotic*). A distribution with 'pointy' peak and relatively 'fat' or 'heavy' tails indicates *leptokurtosis* (i.e., it is *leptokurtotic*).

Kurtosis is widely misunderstood and is often incorrectly described solely in terms of how 'pointy' or 'peaked' a distribution is (see DeCarlo, 1997). Think about the normal distribution – it has the same degree of kurtosis regardless what values μ and σ take, yet it can be made arbitrarily more or less 'pointy' simply by decreasing or increasing σ. So adjusting the 'pointiness', either by altering σ or by adjusting the aspect ratio (the ratio of the scales of the *x*-axis and *y*-axis) of a plot, has no impact on kurtosis. Kurtosis must involve a *relative* shift of probability density (or mass) to or from the middle to the tails such that the variance is unchanged. For this reason the weight of density falling on the 'shoulders' of a unimodal distribution (the bits either side of the peak) tends to be particularly important.

Kurtosis is defined formally in terms of the 4th moment around the mean (μ_4). Although a normal distribution has positive standardized kurtosis (with $\mu_4/\sigma^4 = 3$), it is common to represent kurtosis as *excess kurtosis* relative to the normal distribution (which is defined as having zero excess kurtosis). For example, the *t* distribution with 5 *df* has excess kurtosis of 6 (relative to 0 excess kurtosis for the normal). The kurtosis of a distribution is a somewhat neglected topic in statistics (relative to skew), but the relative weight of data in the middle and tails of a distribution can be vital for statistical inference. Distributions with heavy tails (i.e., leptokurtosis) are particularly awkward to work with.

2.4.5 The *F* distribution

The *F distribution* (sometimes termed the Fisher or Fisher-Snedecor distribution) is a probability distribution for the ratio of variances of independent, random samples from populations with a normal distribution. The distribution is appropriate if the sample variances are unbiased estimates and provided the population variances (but not necessarily the means) are equal. If they are not equal, the *non-central F distribution* is appropriate. If a variable, *X*, has an *F* distribution it can be written as:

$$X \sim F(\nu_1, \nu_2)$$

The parameters ν_1 and ν_2 are the number of observations in each sample minus 1 (i.e., the denominator used in calculating an unbiased variance estimate $\hat{\sigma}^2$). Thus ν_1 and ν_2 are the *df* of two independent χ^2 variables. This is because *F* can also be defined as the ratio of two chi-square distributions divided by their respective *df*. Equation 2.9 indicates that (assuming a normal distribution) independent sums of squares have the distribution: $\sigma^2\chi^2_{n-1}$. This implies that an unbiased sample variance has the distribution:

$$\hat{\sigma}^2 \sim \frac{\sigma^2\chi^2_{n-1}}{n-1} \qquad \text{Equation 2.11}$$

If it is assumed that the populations the two samples are drawn from have equal variance (as is the case for the *central F* distribution) then the unknown σ^2 will cancel out and the ratio of the two sample variances has the distribution

$$F = \frac{\chi^2_{\nu_1}/\nu_1}{\chi^2_{\nu_2}/\nu_2} \qquad \text{Equation 2.12}$$

where ν_1 and ν_2 are $(n_1 - 1)$ and $(n_2 - 2)$ respectively.

The shape of *F* distribution (being a ratio of two other distributions) is difficult to characterize. Figure 2.14 shows the *F* distribution with values of ν_1 ranging from 1 to 10 and with ν_2 set at

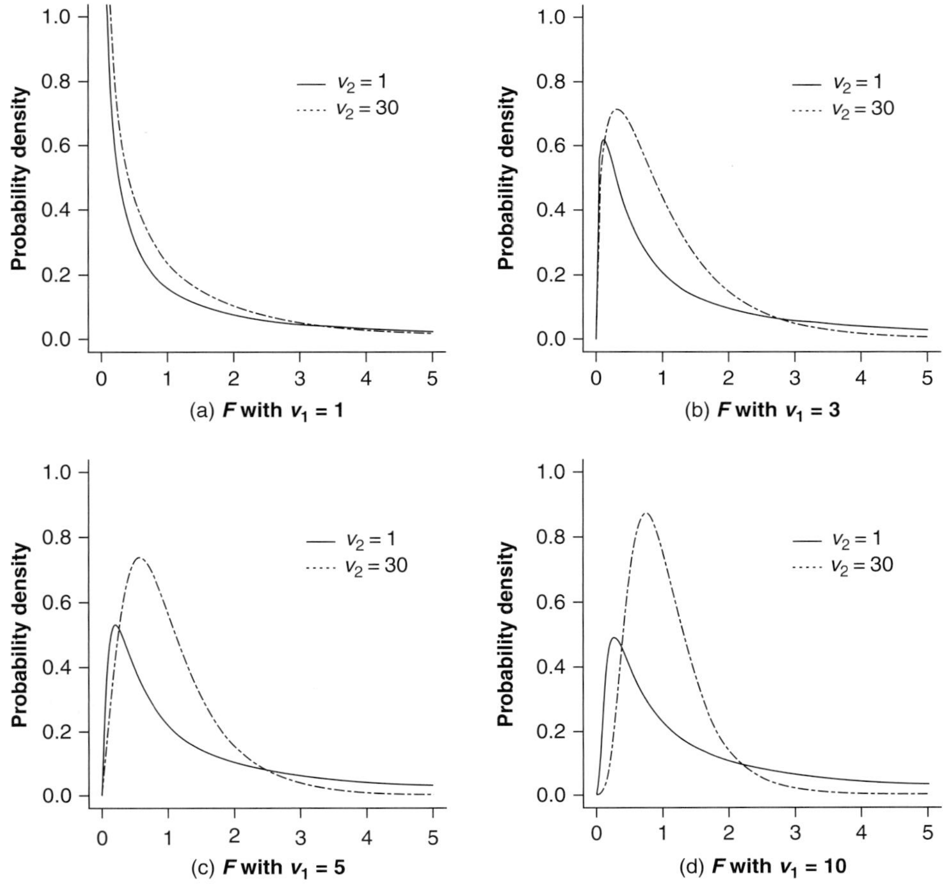

Figure 2.14 Probability density of *F*, with denominator *df* of $\nu_2 = 1$ or $\nu_2 = 30$ with numerator *df* equal to (a) $\nu_1 = 1$, (b) $\nu_1 = 3$, (c) $\nu_1 = 5$, or (d) $\nu_1 = 10$

either 1 or 30. This gives a rough idea of how the shape of the distribution can vary. As a ratio of two quantities that must be greater than zero, F is also bounded at zero (but can take any positive value greater than zero). Provided both that ν_1 is smaller than ν_2 and that ν_2 is larger than 2 (which is commonly the case for real applications) the distribution is positively skewed and unimodal. For these values of ν_2 the mean of the F distribution is $\nu_2/(\nu_2 - 2)$. This, you may recall, is also the variance of a t distribution when $\nu > 1$. As ν_2 approaches infinity the value of F tends toward 1.

F and t are intimately related (through the chi-square distribution). Using Equation 2.10 it is easy to show that

$$t^2 = \left(\frac{Z}{\sqrt{V/\nu}}\right)^2 = \frac{Z^2}{V/\nu}$$

The square of a standard normal variable such as Z has, by definition, a chi-square distribution with 1 *df* (i.e., $Z^2 \sim \chi_1^2$). V is chi-square with ν *df*. Given Equation 2.12 it follows that

$$t_\nu^2 = \frac{\chi_1^2/1}{\chi_\nu^2/\nu} = F_{1,\nu} \qquad \text{Equation 2.13}$$

In other words t^2 is distributed as F with numerator *df* (ν_1) equal to 1 and denominator *df* (ν_2) equal to ν. It is therefore not surprising that the shape of F be similar to a χ_1^2 distribution when $\nu_1 = 1$ (as can be seen by comparing Figure 2.11 and Figure 2.14a). It is necessarily also true that $\sqrt{F_{1,\nu}} = t_\nu$.

Example 2.6 Distribution functions for the χ^2, t and F distribution can be employed in the same way as for the normal or standard normal. As they are continuous distributions the *pdf* tends to be preferred for plotting, but the *cdf* and its inverse are used more heavily in calculations. As with the Φ function and z, the *cdf* gives cumulative probabilities from the lower, left tail of the distribution up to a desired value, while its inverse produces quantiles of the distribution for a given cumulative probability (and the inverse of a *cdf* is therefore a quantile function).

Of the three distributions, t (being symmetrical) is the easiest to work with. Just as for z, either tail can be interrogated to get a particular tail probability. If ν (the *df*) is very large the *cdf* for t will return values identical to z for all practical purposes. Thus $Pr(t_{999} \leq 1.96)$, the cumulative probability of t up to and including 1.96 is .975 (rounding these and subsequent values to 3 decimal places). Likewise, $t_{999,\,.025}$ (the quantile of t with cumulative probability .025 and 999 *df*) is approximately −1.96. Discrepancies between the z and t distribution are apparent for low *df*. For a single sample with $n = 10$, $Pr(t_9 \leq 1.96) = .960$ and $t_{9,\,.025} \approx -2.26$.

The *cdf* and its inverse (the quantile function) can be applied to obtain the tail probability for any quantile, or the quantile (often expressed as a percentage) for any tail probability. For instance, you might need to find the tail probability for an observed t of 2.14 with 29 *df*. Using the symmetry of the distribution this can be obtained directly by looking for the cumulative probability for $t_{29} = -2.14$ which is .020. (The cumulative probability for $t_{29} = 2.14$ is $1 - .020 = .98$.) Alternatively, you may want to find the upper limit of t that covers 90% of the distribution when $df = 29$. To do this you'd want to know the value of t that excludes the most extreme 5% at either end. These values are $t_{29,.05} \approx -1.70$ and $t_{29,\,.95} \approx 1.70$ respectively. So with $df = 29$, 90% of the distribution falls in the range $-1.70 \leq t \leq 1.70$.

Working with χ^2 or F is different. For these distributions interest will almost always focus on one tail of the distribution. Because the distributions are related to the square of z or t, extreme values of the data correspond to cumulative probabilities or quantiles for the right or upper tail only. An observed chi-square value of 6.63 with 1 *df*, has the right tail probability $Pr(\chi^2_1 \geq 6.63) = .01$. The quantile of the same distribution that has a cumulative probability of .95 is $\chi^2_{1,.95} = 3.84$. This quantile leaves $1 - .95 = .05$ or 5% of the distribution in the right tail. As $\chi^2_1 = z^2$, the value 3.84 should be the square of the corresponding tail value for z. To check this, compute $\sqrt{3.84}$. The answer is either +1.96 or −1.96 (matching the values obtained for z or for t when ν is large).*

Cumulative probability or quantile calculations for the F distribution are similar to chi-square except that both numerator and denominator *df* must be specified. When $\nu_1 = 1$ and $\nu_2 = 29$ the cumulative probability of the observed F ratio 4.58 is $Pr(F_{1,29} \leq 4.58) = .96$. Thus the right tail probability $Pr(F_{1,29} \geq 4.58)$ is $1 - .96 = .04$. This is exactly twice the value for $t_{29} = -2.14$ or $t_{29} = 2.14$. This follows because $-2.14^2 = 2.14^2 = 4.58$ and $(t_{29})^2 = F_{1,29}$. The right tail of the F distribution here is equivalent to the most extreme t statistics in either direction. Hence the probability obtained from F is equivalent to the sum of the two tail probabilities for t. Switching to the quantile function, the value of $F_{1,999}$ that excludes 95% of the distribution is 3.85. This is very close to the same value for χ^2_1 (because when $\nu_1 = 1$ and ν_2 is large the two distributions converge – exactly as t approaches z in large samples).

* A square root may take either a positive or negative value. The usual convention is to return the positive root by default. Here both roots are of potential interest.

2.5 R code for Chapter 2

2.5.1 Functions for discrete distributions

R distribution functions combine *d* (for density or mass), *p* (for the cumulative probability or *cdf*), *q* (for quantile, the inverse of the *cdf*) and *r* (for random number generation) with a distribution 'nickname'. The nickname for the binomial is *binom* and the nickname for Poisson is *pois*. This system is extremely versatile and makes it easy to work with probability distributions.

For the moment the focus is on the *pmf* and *cdf* functions. To obtain the probability of four heads from ten tosses of a fair coin (i.e., assuming $P = .5$) use the following call to `dbinom()`:

```
dbinom(x=4, size = 10, prob = .5)
```

There is no need to name the arguments for this function (as long as the order is preserved), so it can be simplified to:

```
dbinom(4, 10, .5)
```

Both functions return the probability .2050781. The argument `x` (the observed number of successes from n trials) could be a number (as above) or a vector. For discrete distributions it is handy to be able to specify `x` as an integer sequence. This is easily done in R by expressing the sequence in the form `a:b`, which R interprets as an instruction to count up from a to b in steps of one.[8] So typing `0:4` and hitting return will produce the output:

```
[1] 0 1 2 3 4
```

Example 2.2 involves working out the four, five or six successes from a binomial distribution with $n = 6$ and $P = 1/3$. This can be obtained from the call:

```
dbinom(4:6, 6, 1/3)
```

The results from this call match those reported in Example 2.2. Summing these gives the cumulative probability of four or more successes:

```
sum(dbinom(4:6, 6, 1/3))
```

However, as there is also a *cdf* function `pbinom()`, the following will also work:

```
1 - pbinom(3, 6, 1/3)
```

The `pbinom(3, 6, 1/3)` bit gives the cumulative probability of up to three successes. Subtracting this from one gives the cumulative probability of more than three successes. The default of cumulating the probability from low values to high (in the lower or left-hand tail) can be over-ridden by including the argument `lower.tail = FALSE`.

```
pbinom(3, 6, 1/3, lower.tail = FALSE)
```

All three calls return the output 0.1001372. For further information call the help function using `?dbinom`.

The *pmf* for the Poisson distribution is even easier to work with. Just specify a value or range of values for `x` and λ. To get the probability of observing `x` = 2 from a Poisson distribution with $\lambda = 3.5$ type:

```
dpois(2, 3.5)
```

Like many R functions the distribution functions can also take numeric vectors as input. So to get the probability of zero through to ten events from a Poisson distribution with $\lambda = 5$ you could use either of the following approaches:

```
dpois(0:10, 5)
```

```
counts <- 0:10
dpois(counts, 5)
```

To get cumulative probabilities use `ppois()`. So the probability of up to three events when $\lambda = 2$ is:

```
ppois(3, 2)
```

Likewise, the probability of four or more events can be obtained in either of these ways:

```
1 - ppois(3, 2)
ppois(3, 2, lower.tail=FALSE)
```

The Poisson distribution can be considered an approximation to the binomial for rare events when n is large. To calculate an exact binomial probability for exactly two successes from 5000 trials with probability of success $P = .001$ you could enter:

```
dbinom(2, 5000, .001)
```

This would be approximated by two successes from a Poisson distribution with $\lambda = 5000 \times .001 = 5$ using the call `dpois(2, 5)`. The resulting approximation of .0842 is accurate to four decimal places.

2.5.2 Plotting *pmf* and *cdf* functions

Probability mass functions can be plotted many different ways. A basic scatter plot is very easy. In this example, the probability mass function for zero to 12 events from a Poisson distribution with $\lambda = 3.5$ is obtained and assigned to a vector named `x`. This is the default plot for this type of object using the generic `plot()` function:

```
x <- dpois(0:12,3.5)
plot(x)
```

You could also create a bar graph, and in this case I have added x- and y-axis labels and a main title:

```
barplot(x, names.arg = 0:12, xlab = 'Count', ylab =
   'Probability', main = 'Poisson pmf with lambda = 3.5')
```

The *pmf* plots in this chapter are line plots created by drawing an empty plot and then using the `segments()` function to draw lines between specified pairs of x and y coordinates. Because the function can take input from a vector, and because functions such as `dpois()` default to returning outputs as vectors, it is possible to draw multiple lines with a single call to `segments()`. The plot in Figure 2.1 was drawn using these commands:

```
heads <- 0:10
prob.mass <- dbinom(heads, 10, .5)
plot(heads, prob.mass, pch = NA, xlab = 'Number of heads',
  ylab = 'Probability')
segments(x0 = heads, y0 = 0, x1 = heads, y1 = prob.mass)
```

The first command draws an empty plot by defining the point character for the dots of the scatter plot as 'not applicable' (`pch=NA`) in place of the default of open circles. Although the points are not visible, by using the x-coordinates from a `heads` vector (containing the numbers 0 to 10) and the y-coordinates defined by the probability mass to be plotted, the plot sets up the correct limits for the x- and y-axis. The second command use `segments()` to draws lines for integer values for the number of heads (zero through to ten). These lines start at $y = 0$ in each case and end in the probabilities defined by `prob.mass`. Note that the value 0 for the starting y-coordinate (`y0`) is 'recycled' 11 times to match the length of the other arguments in the function (all vectors with 11 elements).

Although this illustrates some useful plotting functions, there is an even simpler way to set up this kind of line plot:

```
plot(heads, prob.mass, type = 'h')
```

This over-rides the default R dot plot and replaces it with vertical lines via the argument `type = 'h'` (and `xlab` or `ylab` arguments can be added if required – see `?plot`). A binomial *cdf* can be created in more-or-less the same way as any of the above methods using `pbinom()`. Here is the basic R code for drawing a *cdf* similar to that in Figure 2.2:

```
plot(heads, cprob.mass, type = 'h', xlab = 'Number of heads',
  ylab = 'Probability')
```

2.5.3 Functions for continuous distributions

Distribution functions for discrete and continuous variables follow the same format of pre-fix *d*, *p*, *q* or *r* to a nickname. The nickname for the normal distribution is *norm* while for lognormal, chi-square, *t* and *F* they are *lnorm*, *chisq*, *t*, and *f* respectively.

The functions for the normal distribution have built-in defaults for parameters $\mu = 0$ and $\sigma = 1$. Thus they all default to the standard normal (*z*) distribution. The following three calls are therefore equivalent:

```
dnorm(x = 1, mean = 0, sd = 1)
dnorm(1, 0, 1)
dnorm(1)
```

It is trivial to change μ and σ to take on other values. The call `dnorm(100, 100, 15)` would return the density for an observed value of 100 from a normal distribution with $\mu = 100$ and $\sigma = 15$.

For continuous functions the density is preferred for plotting, and the *cdf* and quantile functions are employed for calculation of critical values. The `pnorm()` function gives the cumulative probability function (Φ) for *z* by default, while `qnorm()` gives Φ^{-1} (the quantile function for *z*). To get the cumulative probability for $z = 1.645$ enter:

```
pnorm(1.645)
```

For the tail probability of a value (a value of *z* as extreme as this or more extreme) many people will enter values of *z* in the left tail (i.e., negative values) to take advantage of the symmetry of *z*, such as:

```
pnorm(-1.645)
```

An alternative approach is to request a probability from the right (upper) tail:

```
pnorm(1.645, lower.tail = FALSE)
```

The `quantile()` function is similarly easy to apply. The following R code produces values of the standard normal that exclude the most extreme 33.3%, 10%, 5% and 1% respectively.

```
quants <- c(.333, .10, .05, .01)
qnorm(quants/2)
```

There is no need to use a vector, but it often keeps the code neater. Dividing the desired probabilities by two means that the function returns the quantile that excludes the correct proportion in the left, lower tail (and hence the desired total probability in both tails). The output can be tidied up by requesting the right tail probabilities and by rounding to three decimal places using the `round()` function.

```
round(qnorm(quants/2, lower.tail=FALSE), 3)
```

Example 2.4 shows how you might model the effect of teaching ability on student grades using the z distribution. The effect is assumed to have the distribution: $N(0, 0.3)$. The z value for a teacher at the bottom 25% of ability is given by:

```
qnorm(.25)
```

To estimate the impact on a student's exam grade, multiply this value by 0.3 (the assumed value of σ). An alternative method is to work directly with the $N(0, 0.3)$ distribution. The following commands therefore produce identical results:

```
qnorm(.25) * 0.3
qnorm(.25, 0, 0.3)
```

To estimate the proportion of teachers that could lift exam outcomes by a whole grade, either work out the required multiple of σ for this outcome using z or work directly with the $N(0, 0.3)$ distribution:

```
msig <- 1/0.3
pnorm(msig, lower.tail=FALSE)

pnorm(1, 0, 0.3, lower.tail=FALSE)
```

Either the normal functions or the lognormal function can be employed if you are working with the lognormal distribution. The lognormal functions follow the convention of scaling μ and σ in terms of the natural logarithm of the geometric standard deviation and mean. Example 2.5 explores a lognormal distribution for historic cancer survival data with a median of 9.6 months and a geometric standard deviation of 2.50 months. To determine the probability of surviving at least 24 months after diagnosis the following R code could be used:

```
plnorm(24, log(9.6), log(2.5), lower.tail=FALSE)
```

Being able to use the logarithm function (which has natural logarithm as its default base) within another function is an advantage. Note also that the distribution is asymmetric, so interrogating the right tail probability is essential. The asymmetry is apparent when comparing the top and bottom of the distribution. The bottom 10% and the top 10% have survival times obtained with the following commands:

```
qlnorm(0.1, log(9.6), log(2.5))
qlnorm(0.9, log(9.6), log(2.5))
```

These are 2.966816 and 31.06361 respectively.

2.5.4 Plotting *pdf* and *cdf* functions

The `curve()` function facilitates drawing continuous functions and it is particularly handy for *pdf* and *cdf* plots. It takes as its principal argument a function of `x` such as `x^2` (for $y = x^2$) and plots it as a line graph (opening a new window by default). For this purpose R accepts both density and cumulative probability functions. To plot a z distribution all that is required is:

```
curve(dnorm(x))
```

However, as the default limits of x are 0 to 1, these need to be adjusted to see the characteristic 'bell shape' of the normal curve:

```
curve(dnorm(x), xlim=c(-4,4))
```

Figure 2.6 was obtained with the following R code (which also adds labels):

```
curve(dnorm(x,100,15), xlim=c(45,155), ylab='Probability density')
```

The *cdf* is also easy to plot using this method. Figure 2.8 combines the *pdf* and *cdf* for the z distribution in a plot with two panels. The two panels are set up using the graphical parameters function `par()`. This allows all sorts of properties of a plot to be specified. In this case, the *mfrow* argument specifies a vector indicating the number of rows and columns for the panel – thus `mfrow=c(1,2)` sets up a plot containing two panels arranged in a one row by two column 'matrix'. The `mar` argument sets the margin width of each plot (in terms of number of lines for bottom, left, top and right margins in order), while `pty='s'` constrains the plot to a ('pretty') square shape. The final parameter (which can also be called within a plot command) sets the character expansion factor – and hence relative size – of the main title:

```
par(mfrow=c(1,2), mar=c(4,4,2,1), pty='s', cex.main = 1.1)

curve(dnorm(x), xlim=c(-3.5,3.5), ylab = 'Probability
  density', xlab=expression(italic(z)),
  main=expression(paste('(a)', italic(pdf))))

curve(pnorm(x), xlim=c(-3.5,3.5), ylab = 'Cumulative
  probability', xlab=expression(italic(z)),
  main=expression(paste('(b)', italic(cdf))))
```

Each panel is plotted separately (and you may want to manually resize the plot window to the shape of the plot for best results). To get the labels, the `expression()` function is used to special characters (such as statistical notation or particular text styles) to `xlab`. The `paste()` function concatenates text strings and other characters together. This allows plain text to be joined with italics in this example. The `italic()` function just changes the style of the text in parentheses to italic.

Other *pdf* or *cdf* plots can be constructed in the same way. Figure 2.12 combines two χ^2 distributions in the same panel using the `dchisq()` density function. The x-axis label here incorporates `chi[3]^2` or `chi[10]^2` within the pasted expression. R evaluates this as a text expression 'χ^2' (with the subscript 3 or 10).

```
par(mfrow=c(1,2), mar = c(4,4,0.5,0.5), pty='s', cex.main = 1)

curve(dchisq(x,3), xlim=c(0,25), ylab='Probability density',
  xlab=expression(paste('(a)', chi[3]^2)))

curve(dchisq(x,10), xlim=c(0,25), ylab='Probability density',
  xlab = expression(paste('(b)', chi[10]^2)))
```

In some plots you will want to overlay two or more curves on the same panel. This is done by getting `curve()` to add a new line (via `add=TRUE`). This prevents the existing plot being replaced by a new one in the plot window. Figure 2.13 overlays lines for the t and z distribution in another two-panel plot.

```
par(mfrow=c(1,2), mar=c(4,4,0.5,0.5), pty='s')

curve(dnorm(x), xlim=c(-4,4), ylab='Probability density', xlab
  =expression(paste('(a)', italic(t)[1])), lty=2)
curve(dt(x,1), xlim=c(-4,4), add=TRUE)

curve(dnorm(x), xlim=c(-4,4), ylab='Probability density', xlab
  =expression(paste('(b)', italic(t)[29])), lty=2)
curve(dt(x,29), xlim=c(-4,4), add=TRUE)
```

The second curve is differentiated in each plot by changing the line type to dashed by the argument `lty=2`. A legend could be added after each panel by the command:

```
legend(2.25, .35, legend=c(expression(italic(t)),
  expression(italic(z))), lty=c(1,2), bty='n')
```

The first two arguments set the x- and y-coordinates for the legend, while the legend argument takes a vector of labels for each line. Within the legend function the `lty` argument also requires a vector containing the numeric identifier of the line type (e.g., 1 for solid, 2 for dashed and 3 for dotted) – one for each label. The `bty='n'` argument tells R not to place a box round the legend. Further details are given by the help call: `?legend`.

2.5.5 Simulating data using distribution functions

The random number generation functions enable you to simulate real data drawn from a variety of different functions. Figure 2.5 uses the `rbinom()` function to simulate 100,000 random draws of ten, 30 or 100 trials from a binomial distribution (with two different *p* values). These are assigned to a vector, *x*, and a histogram (frequency bar graph) plotted. In this case the parameter `par(mfrow=c(2,3)` is used to create a 2 by 3 grid of panels. Each panel can then be created using `rbinom()`. Here is the code for the first panel:

```
x <- rbinom(100000, 10, .15)
hist(x,xlab=expression(paste(italic(n), ' = 10, ', italic(P),
  ' = .15')), main=NULL)
```

The `hist()` function is very widely used to generate histograms of real or simulated data. The argument `main=NULL` suppresses the default title in the histogram.

Random numbers from a normal distribution (or indeed any other of the distribution functions in this chapter) could be simulated in the same way. For instance, a simulated standard normal sample of size $n = 100$ could be generated with the command `rnorm(100)`.

2.6 Notes on SPSS syntax for Chapter 2

2.6.1 Distribution functions

SPSS has density and cumulative distribution functions for all discrete and continuous functions covered in this chapter. These are drawn on by other SPSS commands, but also available via syntax and – in particular – via the `COMPUTE` command (though it is less flexible in handling output from them than R). Use of the `COMPUTE` commands with the binomial *pmf* and *cdf* functions for the binomial and standard normal is illustrated below.

Open a new data window and (after selecting 'Variable View') enter a new variable called *x*. Then (after re-selecting 'Data View') enter the number 4 as the value of the case (row) 1 for variable *x*. Open a new syntax window and run the following syntax (e.g., typing it in, selecting it and then running your selection):

```
COMPUTE prob=PDF.BINOM(x,10,.5).
EXECUTE.
```

The spreadsheet should now contain a new variable called *prob* with the value .21. The function expects the observed value, followed by *n* and then *P*. The *cdf* function for the binomial works in a similar fashion:

```
COMPUTE cumprob=CDF.BINOM(x,10,.5).
EXECUTE.
```

These values are rounded to two decimal places, but changing the SPSS preferences (or 'Variable View') can alter how many digits are displayed; `pdf.Poisson` and `cdf.Poisson` work in a corresponding fashion. Selecting one via the menus: <Transform> then <Compute . . . > allows you to browse the functions and displays some help text when you select it.

For the standard normal distribution create a new variable (here called *quant*) and enter the values 1.645 and 1.96 as cases. The following syntax should generate cumulative probabilities for these quantiles:

```
COMPUTE cprob=CDF.NORMAL(quant,0,1).
EXECUTE.
```

The quantile functions are labeled 'Inverse DF' (inverse distribution functions) and use the suffix IDF. To calculate the quantiles of *cprob* you could use the following syntax:

```
COMPUTE newquant=IDF.NORMAL(cprob,0,1).
EXECUTE.
```

The resulting quantiles are slightly different from *quant* (because of cumulative rounding error).

2.6.2 Random number generation

SPSS also has random number generation facilities. Accessing it via the COMPUTE command will create one random number for each active case. A simple way to generate ten random numbers is therefore to open a new data file, create a new variable (e.g., called *id*) and type or paste in the numbers 1 to 10. Then run the following syntax:

```
COMPUTE rn_1=RV.NORMAL(100,15).
EXECUTE.
```

More detail on all these commands can be found in the SPSS help files.

2.7 Bibliography and further reading

DeCarlo, L. T. (1997) On the Meaning and Use of Kurtosis. *Psychological Methods*, 2, 292–307.

Hays, W. (1973) *Statistics for the Social Sciences* (2nd edn). New York: Holt.

von Hippel, P. T. (2005). Mean, Median, and Skew: Correcting a Textbook Rule. *Journal of Statistics Education*, 13, 2.

3
Confidence intervals

Contents

3.1 Chapter overview

This chapter introduces interval estimation in the form of frequentist confidence intervals. Confidence intervals for means and differences between means from normal samples, for a binomial proportion and for a Poisson count, are considered. Key ideas include the relationship between standard errors for a single sample and difference between samples, the use of Monte Carlo methods (such as the bootstrap) for obtaining interval estimates, and the interpretation of a confidence interval as a plausible range of values for a population parameter.

3.2 From point estimates to interval estimates

Inference – going beyond the data at hand – is at the heart of scientific research. It is possible to classify statistical inference into four broad (but intimately related) types: *point estimation*, *interval estimation*, *hypothesis testing* and *prediction*. All of these techniques, and in particular prediction, can be subsumed under the term *statistical modeling* (a general attempt to model data or processes that incorporate uncertainty).

This chapter focuses on interval estimation, emphasizing classical (frequentist) statistical methods that are widely taught and applied in many areas of science, medicine and engineering. These are important because of they will be encountered by any professional dealing with quantitative data, but also because they introduce many issues and problems central to statistical inference. Later chapters will cover prediction and statistical modeling before turning to challenges arising from the application of classical methods and consider alternative methods such as *likelihood* and *Bayesian inference* (see Dienes, 2008).

The distinction between a point and interval estimate is both of theoretical and practical importance. One of the easiest ways to understand a point estimate is to think of it as a 'best guess' of the true population parameter. Descriptive statistics such as the sample mean and median are thus excellent examples of point estimates, as are statistics such as the sample standard deviation (*SD*) or variance. A point estimate summarizes information about a parameter with a single number. It therefore communicates no information about the uncertainty or quality of the estimate it provides.

This is the fundamental drawback of a point estimate: it conceals the uncertainty in the estimate. Imagine that two studies have different point estimates of the same parameter; one suggests that the mean is 25 and the other suggests the mean is 18. The uncertainty of each estimate depends on a number of factors (e.g., the size of the sample, the variability of the sample and the distribution it is drawn from). All this information could be reported alongside each point estimate, but integrating and weighting the information appropriately requires considerable effort and expertise. Instead, it is convenient to wrap all this information up in a separate calculation that integrates and weights the different factors correctly. An interval estimate is a way of achieving this. Interval estimates are also 'best guesses', not of the exact value of a parameter, but of a range of values that the parameter might plausibly take. There are several ways to calculate an interval estimate, but the most common method involves constructing a *confidence interval* (CI).

3.3 Confidence intervals

Confidence intervals specify a range of values that have a high probability of containing the true population parameter. The probability of a CI containing the true population parameter is its *confidence level* (usually expressed as a percentage). CIs constructed to have a .99 probability of containing the parameter are labeled 99% CIs. The distinction between confidence and probability is an important one. Classical frequentist statistics views a probability as a statement about the frequency with which events occur in the long run. According to this perspective, it is meaningful to make a statement such as: 'If a great many confidence intervals are constructed then a 99% CI will, on average, contain the true population parameter 99 times out of 100.' In contrast, a statement such as 'This 99% CI has a probability of containing the true population parameter equal to .99' is not meaningful to a strict frequentist. Put crudely, the CI either contains the true value (with probability 1) or it does not (with probability 0).

A formal interpretation of a CI with *C*% confidence is therefore that, of the many CIs that might be constructed, *C*% are expected to contain the true population parameter. Despite this formal definition, it is often reasonable to treat a CI as an expression of confidence or belief that a CI does contain the true parameter value (see Loftus, 2001). It may even be reasonable to express this as a probability (as long as you appreciate that this is not the formal, frequentist definition of probability). For example, in everyday language most people (including frequentist statisticians) are happy to make statements such as: 'It will probably rain tomorrow.' The formal interpretation of a CI can be contrasted with an informal interpretation of it as a range of plausible values that the true parameter might take. Values inside the interval are plausible values of the parameter, whereas values outside the interval are relatively implausible parameter values (Cumming and Finch, 2005). This informal interpretation of a CI is typically more useful than its formal interpretation.

The range of values encompassed by a CI – its width – will vary with its confidence level. As the confidence level increases, the CI gets wider. At one extreme, a 100% interval encompasses the whole range of possible values of a parameter (and is thus too wide to be useful). At the other extreme (for a continuous distribution, at least) a 0% confidence interval reduces to a point estimate. In general, high confidence is preferred, with a 95% CI being the most common choice. For reasons that will become apparent (when significance testing is introduced in Chapter 4), it is common to express the confidence level as a probability using the criterion α (the lower-case Greek letter 'alpha'). According to this convention, α is the total tail probability (i.e., the proportion of the distribution in both tails) and $C = 100(1 - \alpha)$. Thus $\alpha = .01$ is equivalent to 99% confidence and $\alpha = .05$ is equivalent to 95% confidence.

3.3.1 Standard errors and confidence intervals

A confidence interval can be defined in terms of two points. These form the limits (or lower and upper bounds) of the interval. In simplest case of a symmetrical interval the point estimate lies in the center of the CI. If so, the interval can be described in terms of the point estimate plus or minus half the width of the interval. This half width is widely known as a *margin of error* (*MOE*).

The width (and therefore margin of error) of the interval depends on the desired level of confidence and on the *sampling distribution* of the statistic. The sampling distribution of the statistic determines the probability of observing values at a particular distance from the point estimate (e.g., from the mean). A sampling distribution is therefore the probability distribution of a statistic (see Key Concept 2.1).

The width of the CI depends on the parameters of this probability distribution – most notably the standard deviation (*SD*). The *SD* of a sampling distribution is different from the *SD* of the population the data are drawn from. For this reason the *SD* of a sampling distribution is termed its *standard error* (*SE*). Because different statistics give rise to different standard errors it is also common to distinguish them by explicitly referring to the statistic that generated the sampling distribution (e.g., standard error of the mean, standard error of the median or standard error of the difference).

A simple formula underlies any symmetrical CI. The interval is equal to $\hat{\theta}$ ('theta-hat') the point estimate of θ (theta[1]), plus or minus the margin of error (half the width of the interval):

$$CI = \hat{\theta} \pm MOE \qquad \text{Equation 3.1}$$

The margin of error of a symmetrical CI usually takes the form

$$MOE = \Phi^{-1}_{1-\alpha/2} \times \hat{\sigma}_{\hat{\theta}} \qquad \text{Equation 3.2}$$

where $\hat{\sigma}_{\hat{\theta}}$ is an estimate of the *SE* of $\hat{\theta}$ and Φ^{-1} is the inverse (quantile function) of a probability distribution. Thus $\pm\Phi^{-1}_{1-\alpha/2}$ are the quantiles that include *C*% of the distribution. This assumes, as is common, that you are working with a standardized, symmetrical probability distribution such as *z* or *t*. Quantiles are commonly scaled in terms of probabilities (and hence proportions of the distribution) rather than percentages. An equivalent way to express this is by stating that a $100(1-\alpha)\%$ interval includes $(1-\alpha)$ proportion of the distribution. It therefore excludes $\alpha/2$ probability in each tail. Putting the two equations together gives a generic form for the CI as:

$$CI = \hat{\theta} \pm \Phi^{-1}_{1-\alpha/2} \times \hat{\sigma}_{\hat{\theta}} \qquad \text{Equation 3.3}$$

The *MOE* therefore depends on the shape of the distribution and the level of confidence required. If the sampling distribution and its *SD* (i.e., the standard error or *SE*) are known, an exact CI can be constructed. In practice, both are usually unknown, but reasonable assumptions about the approximate form of the distribution can often be made, and the *SE* can usually be estimated. The central limit theorem (CLT) provides a justification for using a normal approximation (see Key Concept 2.1). In many cases these approximations will be fairly accurate even with only moderately large sample sizes (but this is not always true; and recall that there are exceptions to the CLT). On the other hand, even an approximate CI is almost always more informative than a point estimate alone.

KEY CONCEPT 3.1

The standard error of the mean

The standard error of the mean is fundamental to statistical inference. For a sampling distribution derived from the means of samples of size *n*, the *SD* of the distribution is the standard error of the mean ($\sigma_{\hat{\mu}}$). The magnitude of $\sigma_{\hat{\mu}}$ depends on both n and the standard deviation (σ) of the population being sampled:

$$\sigma_{\hat{\mu}} = \frac{\sigma}{\sqrt{n}} \qquad \text{Equation 3.4}$$

The more variable the population, the larger $\sigma_{\hat{\mu}}$ becomes and the more variable the sampling distribution. More interesting is the relation between $\sigma_{\hat{\mu}}$ and n. As n increases, $\sigma_{\hat{\mu}}$ decreases. Why is this? The sampling distribution is the distribution of statistics calculated from samples of a fixed size. It reflects the precision with which the statistic has been measured (i.e., how good an estimate you have). The law of large numbers ensures that the larger the sample the closer its expected value (the mean) will be, on average, to the true population mean (see Key Concept 1.1). This ensures that large samples tend to have means closer to the population mean. Their sampling distribution is thus less spread out, and hence their *SD* decreases when n is large. Large samples are therefore doubly useful. Not only is $\hat{\sigma}_{\hat{\mu}}$ smaller, but the sampling distribution is also more likely to be approximately normal (and hence approximately symmetrical and unimodal).

In practice, σ is usually unknown and $\hat{\sigma}$ (the square root of the unbiased sample estimate of the variance) is used in its place. This allows $\sigma_{\hat{\mu}}$ to be estimated as:

$$\hat{\sigma}_{\hat{\mu}} = \frac{\sqrt{\frac{\sum_{i=1}^{n} (x_i - \hat{\mu})^2}{n-1}}}{\sqrt{n}} = \frac{\hat{\sigma}}{\sqrt{n}} \qquad \text{Equation 3.5}$$

Regardless of which formula is used, a crucial observation is that the precision of the estimate, as defined by the size of $\sigma_{\hat{\mu}}$, is inversely proportional to $\sqrt{n}$.* You'd need to quadruple n to halve the size of $\sigma_{\hat{\mu}}$. Increasing sample size by a fixed amount (e.g., increasing n by 10) will bring relatively rapid gains in precision or efficiency at first, but the gains soon diminish.

* Precision can also be defined in terms of the sampling variance (the variance of the sampling distribution which is the square of the standard error). For this reason some statisticians define 'precision' as the reciprocal of a variance (particularly a sampling variance).

Given that the standard deviation of z is 1, $z_{1-\alpha/2}$ specifies a multiple of standard deviations from the mean that includes C% and excludes 100-C% of the population. For a symmetrical distribution, such as z, the excluded percentage is split evenly to exclude (100-C)/2 % in each tail.[2] This is illustrated for $\alpha = .05$ in Figure 3.1. This shows the standard normal probability density function (*pdf*) with the shaded area representing the 5% most extreme values of z (2.5% in each tail). This shaded area starts $\pm 1.96\ \sigma$ from the mean of zero. Thus 1.96 is the appropriate multiple of σ for the margin of error of a 95% CI of a normally distributed statistic.

3.3.2 Confidence intervals for a mean from a normal distribution

For a mean μ from a normal distribution, the CI will be symmetrical and follows the standardized form given in Equation 3.3. Thus any CI for a normal distribution can be represented as:

$$\hat{\mu} \pm z_{1-\alpha/2} \times \hat{\sigma}_{\hat{\mu}} \qquad \text{Equation 3.6}$$

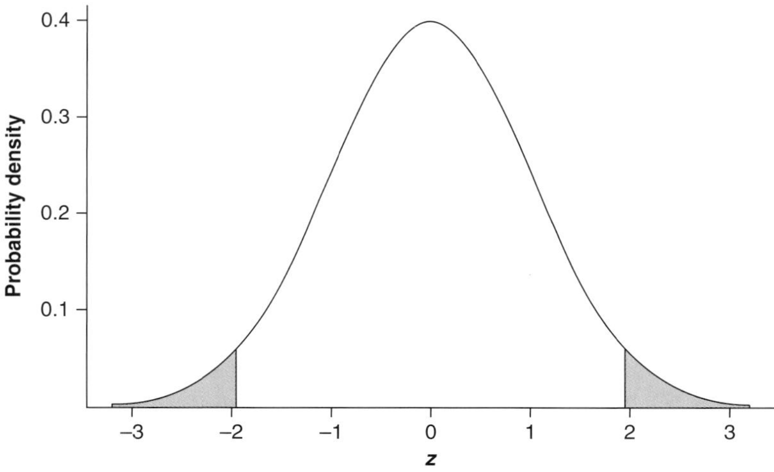

Figure 3.1 The 5% most extreme values (tail probabilities) of the standard normal (z) distribution

In this equation $\hat{\mu}$ is the usual sample estimate of the arithmetic mean, $z_{1-\alpha/2}$ is the required quantile of the standard normal distribution and $\hat{\sigma}_{\hat{\mu}}$ is the sample estimate of the standard error of the mean (see Key Concept 3.1).

Example 3.1 Imagine that a researcher takes a random sample of 50 people and keeps them awake for 24 hours prior to taking an IQ test. She finds that their mean IQ after sleep disruption is 94.6. Subsequent examples will refer to this as the sleep loss data. If the IQ scale is constructed, as is common, to have the distribution $N(100, 15)$, a 95% CI for the sample mean will be:

$$94.6 \pm z_{.975} \times \hat{\sigma}_{\hat{\mu}} = 94.6 \pm 1.96\hat{\sigma}_{\hat{\mu}}$$

As σ is known and equal to 15, $\hat{\sigma}_{\hat{\mu}} = 15/\sqrt{50} = 2.121$ and the CI is 94.6 ± 4.16. The CI could also be reported as the statistic (here the mean) together with its lower and upper bounds. This is the preferred format in publication (and it is suitable for both symmetrical and asymmetrical intervals). The American Psychological Association publication manual (APA, 2010) – used by many journals – suggests reporting the outcome as $M = 94.6$, 95% CI [90.4, 98.8]. Best practice is to report the statistic and its limits to the same level of precision (here one decimal place). Reporting too many digits in your results may give a misleading impression of precision (though as many digits as possible should be retained during the calculation process to prevent rounding errors from accumulating).

This CI excludes the expected population mean of 100 (suggesting that sleep disruption lowers IQ). If IQ in the population sampled follows a normal distribution with $\sigma = 15$, then this CI is exact (see Box 3.1). However, no matter how well the test is constructed, the distribution of test scores will not be perfectly normal and the CI is best considered an approximation (albeit a fairly accurate one). Furthermore, there must be some doubt that $\hat{\sigma} = 15$ in the population being sampled (e.g., because of differences between the sample and the population the test was constructed for, or because sleep loss itself influences the variability of the test scores).

Box 3.1 Exact versus approximate inferences

A common objective in statistical inference is to provide 'exact' solutions. This may seem odd – given that estimation involves uncertainty – but an exact solution in this context is one that gives an exact statement about the uncertainty in an estimate. Exact solutions are highly attractive in theory, but can be difficult to find. One exception is for statistics based on the normal distribution (for which exact solutions to many common problems have been found). For distributions, such as the binomial or Poisson, exact, analytic solutions (derived from analysis of the mathematical form of the problem) exist, but may be awkward to work with. Furthermore exact solutions sometimes have practical limitations. Researchers may therefore rely on approximate solutions (e.g., provided they are convenient and deemed sufficiently accurate).

Agresti and Coull (1998) make this point very neatly when considering exact versus approximate solutions for the CI of a binomial proportion. The best-known exact solution is the *Clopper-Pearson* CI. The *Wald* CI (the usual normal approximation) is simple, but typically performs worse than the Clopper-Pearson CI. However, despite the label 'exact', some approximate solutions may outperform it. This happens because the Clopper-Pearson CI is constructed to always have at least *C*% confidence and thus tends to be conservative (i.e., the interval is too wide).

An important concept here is the *coverage* of the CI (its capture rate). Under this definition the 95% CI is exact because it has a capture rate that never falls below 95%. In the long run, no fewer than 95 out of 100 intervals calculated using this method will contain the true population parameter. Approximate solutions may outperform exact ones if they have average coverage closer to 95% (even though the coverage sometimes falls below the nominal level).

It may not always be possible to employ an exact method (perhaps because the solution is unknown). In these situations *Monte Carlo methods* (see Box 3.3) are often employed. Whatever the methods being used, only rarely can you be sure that data are sampled from a known probability distribution; for most problems even supposedly exact solutions give only approximate answers.

3.3.3 Confidence intervals using the *t* distribution

If σ^2 (the population variance of a normal distribution) is unknown it is possible to estimate it using the sample variance. Under these circumstances the standardized sampling distribution of the mean follows a *t* distribution. A more accurate CI for the mean can be formed using quantiles of the *t* distribution with appropriate degrees of freedom (*df*) in place of *z*:

$$\hat{\mu} \pm t_{\nu,1-\alpha/2} \times \hat{\sigma}_{\hat{\mu}} \qquad \text{Equation 3.7}$$

Here $t_{\nu,1-\alpha/2}$ is the $(1-\alpha)/2$ quantile of the *t* distribution with ν *df* (see Box 3.2) and $\hat{\sigma}_{\hat{\mu}}$ is the standard error of the mean estimated from the sample.

Box 3.2 Degrees of freedom

The *degrees of freedom* (*df*) of a statistic are determined by the number of independent data points or observations that contribute to it, and hence the number of independent data points that are used to estimate the corresponding population parameter. For the mean $\hat{\mu}$ of a single sample of *n* independent observations the *df* are equal to $n-1$. This is because only $n-1$ of the observations are free to vary. This may seem counterintuitive, but happens because the *df* are determined only after calculation of $\hat{\mu}$. Before $\hat{\mu}$ is known, all n observations are free to vary.

A common way to explain this is to consider how many observations you need to know before you have all the information in the sample. Start with a sample of size $n=4$ and no other information (e.g., no knowledge of the sample mean). In this case you need all four observations. What happens if you also know $\hat{\mu}=5$? In this case any three observations will suffice. This is because if $n=4$ and $\hat{\mu}=5$ their sum will be 20. Knowing three of the four observations will allow you to deduce the value of the fourth (e.g., if three of the values sum to 12, the remaining value must be $20-12=8$).

More mathematical accounts of *df* are possible, but the preceding explanation helps to introduce the role of *df* in a statistical model. Even a basic statistical procedure such as calculating a sample mean involves constructing a statistical model. In this case the model is for the point estimator of the population mean, where n observations are used to estimate the parameter μ, the total *df* for the model is n. However, each parameter that you estimate 'uses up' 1 *df*. If the number of parameters is designated q then $df=n-q$. This quantity is often known as *residual* or *error df* and represents the upper limit on the number of parameters that could, in theory, be estimated. This way of thinking about *df* extends to more complex models. Thus the model for a difference between two sample means has $n_1+n_2=N$ total *df*, but the difference in means requires $q=2$ parameters to be estimated (one for each sample mean) and the residual *df* for this model are $N-2$.

Example 3.2 It is probably unwise to assume that σ is known for the sleep loss data in Example 3.1. A more appropriate CI can be constructed with t in place of z. Assume that the researcher uses the raw data to estimate σ and that $\hat{\sigma}=19.6$. The estimate standard error $\hat{\sigma}_{\hat{\mu}}$ is therefore

$$\hat{\sigma}_{\hat{\mu}}=\frac{\hat{\sigma}}{\sqrt{n}}=\frac{19.6}{\sqrt{50}}=2.77$$

with *MOE* for the 95% CI equal to

$$t_{49,.975}\times 2.77=2.01\times 2.77\approx 5.6$$

Putting this together produces a 95% CI of 94.6 ± 5.6, or (in APA style): $M=94.6$, 95% CI [89.0, 100.2].

This interval includes 100. Thus a range of plausible values for the population mean includes the expected population mean for people without disrupted sleep (suggesting, contra Example 3.1, that lack of sleep might not reduce IQ test scores). The CI is wider than when σ^2 is known, but will not necessarily be true. The main reason for the difference in widths is simply that $\hat{\sigma}$ is larger than the value of σ assumed in Example 3.1. As $\hat{\sigma}$ is estimated with error it will sometimes be larger and sometimes smaller than σ. The use of t in place of z also has an impact – but it is usually very minor. A quantile of the t distribution always leads to a larger multiplier than the equivalent quantile of z, yet the difference will be negligible in large samples (and substantial only when n is tiny).

On the other hand, given an identical estimate of σ, an interval using t is never narrower than the corresponding interval using z. For this reason – and because σ^2 is rarely known – t is typically preferred to z.

Although the normal and t distributions are symmetrical, they can readily be adapted to deal with some asymmetrical distributions. For instance, it is not uncommon for positively skewed distributions to be approximately lognormal in shape. If so, a CI can be constructed around the geometric mean using t or z by taking logarithms of the raw data. This CI will be symmetrical on the log scale, but exponentiation of the upper and lower bounds produces an asymmetrical interval on the original scale. This interval is exact if the population is lognormal (and will often provide a decent approximation if not).

Example 3.3 The cancer survival data in Example 2.5 come from a sample of $n = 338$ (Boag, 1949; Limpert *et al.*, 2001). The geometric mean is approximately 9.6 months and the geometric *SD* 2.50 months. The survival data are positively skewed and an asymmetric CI is desirable. Given that data are well described by lognormal distribution (see Boag, 1949), the initial step is to use the natural logarithm of the geometric mean and *SD* to construct a symmetric CI using the *t* distribution:

$$\ln(9.6) \pm t_{337,.975} \times \ln(2.5)/\sqrt{338}$$
$$= 2.261763 \pm 1.967028 \times 0.04983965$$

The resulting 95% CI is 2.261763 ± 0.098036 or [2.163727, 2.359799]. This CI is symmetrical, but on the wrong scale. To get an interval on the original scale (months of survival post diagnosis) the function e^x is applied. This gives the lower limit as $e^{2.163727} = 8.703516$ months and the upper limit as $e^{2.359799} = 10.58882$ months:

$$M = 9.6, 95\% \text{ CI } [8.7, 10.6]$$

The large sample size here ensures a relatively narrow CI. This reveals a fairly precise estimate of the median (geometric mean) survival post diagnosis (but note that these data are historic and more recent data would not necessarily be similar). The CI is also only slightly asymmetric – partly because the sample size is large – with the geometric mean close to the center of the interval.

3.3.4 Confidence intervals for a binomial proportion

A number of methods exist to construct a CI for the proportion of successes from a binomial distribution. One surprisingly effective method is to use a normal approximation. This exploits the fact that the proportion of successes is the mean of a binomial distribution. It is the first approach introduced here, both because it is so simple and because it is a good general illustration of how to construct a CI based on a normal distribution.

For a normal approximation only two parameters, μ and σ^2, are estimated. The mean of a binomial proportion is P (the probability of a success) and its variance is $P(1-P)$. The population mean P can be estimated from the sample mean. This is the ratio of the number of successes x and the number of Bernoulli trials n:

$$\hat{\mu} = \hat{P} = \frac{x}{n} \qquad \text{Equation 3.8}$$

The estimator $\hat{P}$ ('P-hat') also provides an estimate of the variance of the proportion, which is a simple function of the mean:

$$\hat{\sigma}^2 = \hat{P}\left(1-\hat{P}\right) \qquad \text{Equation 3.9}$$

Plugging these estimates into Equation 3.5 gives an estimate of the standard error of a binomial proportion:

$$\hat{\sigma}_{\hat{P}} = \frac{\hat{\sigma}}{\sqrt{n}} = \frac{\sqrt{\hat{P}(1-\hat{P})}}{\sqrt{n}} = \sqrt{\frac{\hat{P}(1-\hat{P})}{n}} \qquad \text{Equation 3.10}$$

The estimate $\hat{\sigma}_{\hat{P}}$ can be used to construct a CI for the mean $\hat{P}$ using Equation 3.6. The resulting interval estimates, and several similar normal approximations, are often termed Wald CIs (see Box 3.1). The justification for the procedure is that, provided the requirements of the CLT are met (see Key Concept 2.1), the sampling distribution of the statistic in question will be asymptotically normal. The sampling distribution of a binomial proportion conforms to the CLT and so with sufficiently large samples it will be approximately normal. The Wald CI for a binomial proportion is therefore:

$$\hat{P} \pm z_{1-\alpha/2} \times \hat{\sigma}_{\hat{P}} \qquad \text{Equation 3.11}$$

Although this approximation is sometimes very good, serious problems can arise. The binomial distribution is asymmetrical (except when $P = .5$). As the normal distribution is symmetrical, a CI calculated using Equation 3.11 is inevitably also symmetrical. This won't matter much when P is close to .5 or if n is large, but it can lead to serious inaccuracy. The closer that P is to 0 or 1 the more likely that a Wald CI will be unsuitable (see Agresti and Coull, 1998). A large n helps ensure approximate symmetry of the sampling distribution of the proportion, but the practical performance of the method depends on both P and n (being worst when n is small and P far from .5). The more asymmetric the distribution, the larger the sample size required to obtain an approximation adequate for inference.

Some improved CIs are considered below. However, a simple correction to the Wald CI – the *adjusted Wald* CI – performs reasonably well and is extremely easy to compute (Agresti and Coull, 1998). This is implemented by adding two successes and two failures (thus incrementing x by 2 and n by 4) to the observed data.

Example 3.4 A participant in a memory experiment correctly recognizes 19 out of 25 words on a list. A 99% Wald CI for the proportion of words correctly recalled has the form:

$$\hat{P} \pm z_{.995} \times \hat{\sigma}_{\hat{P}}$$

The quantile of z for a 99% CI that excludes the most extreme 0.5% of the distribution in each tail is 2.576. From Equation 3.8, the sample mean $\hat{P}$ is the proportion $x/n = 19/25 = .76$, thus

$$\hat{\sigma}_{\hat{P}} = \sqrt{\frac{\hat{P}(1-\hat{P})}{n}} = \sqrt{\frac{.76(1-.76)}{25}} = \approx .0854^*$$

The 99% Wald CI is $.76 \pm 2.576 \times .0854 = .76 \pm .22$ or:

$$\hat{P} = .76, 99\% \text{ CI } [.54, .98]$$

This interval estimate is probably not too inaccurate, as n is not very small and because P is likely to be close to .5 (or at least far from 0 or 1). Adding two successes and two fails treats the interval as if 21 successes were obtained from 29 trials. This gives:

$$\tilde{P} = .72, 99\% \text{ CI } [.51, .94]$$

This estimate of P (labeled $\tilde{P}$ to distinguish it from $\hat{P}$) is slightly closer to .5 and exhibits a property known as shrinkage. Shrinkage makes point estimates less extreme and, in theory, makes them better estimates for some purposes. Although the use of shrunken estimators is not to everyone's taste, there is little doubt that the adjusted interval is superior to the usual Wald CI (Agresti and Coull, 1998).

The problems with the Wald CI can be highlighted by looking at what happens for $x = 24$. For this number of successes $\hat{P} = .96$ and the 99% CI is:

$$\hat{P} = .96, 99\% \text{ CI } [.86, 1.06]$$

This interval is unsatisfactory both because it includes impossible values for the proportion (which can not exceed 1) and because – if interpreted as [0.859, 1.00] – it will be too narrow (Agresti and Coull, 1998). The situation can be rescued a little by switching to the adjusted Wald CI.

$$\tilde{P} = .90, 99\% \text{ CI } [.75, 1.04]$$

This interval is more realistic than the Wald CI, but still problematic (because the upper bound exceeds one).

*It would be trivial to transform this into a CI for the number of successes x by multiplying $\hat{\sigma}_{\hat{P}}$ by n.

3.3.5 Improved intervals for a binomial proportion

One approach to finding an improved CI for a binomial proportion (or indeed any discrete distribution) is to work directly with its distribution function (i.e., its *pmf* or *cdf*). An obstacle to this approach is that it is unlikely that discrete distributions will return probability values that match the required confidence levels exactly. The traditional solution is to pick limits that have at least the required tail probability. For the binomial distribution the best-known interval of this kind is the Clopper-Pearson interval and is exact (being based on the binomial *cdf*). At the same time it is conservative because its coverage (the expected capture rate of P) is always at least C%, and sometimes quite a bit larger than 95% (see Box 3.1). Agresti and Coull (1998) recommend an approximate solution known as the *Wilson CI*. Newcombe (1998a) reaches a similar conclusion, but recommends using the *Wilson CI* with a continuity correction. Recent work has also provided an improved exact interval estimate in the form of the *Blaker CI* (Blaker, 2000; Fay, 2010). Table 3.1 summarizes the results of the Wald, adjusted Wald, Wilson, Wilson continuity-corrected (*Wilson-cc*), Clopper-Pearson and Blaker CIs for the data in Example 3.4 (with $n = 25$ and either $x = 19$ or $x = 24$).

Table 3.1 Approximate and exact 99% confidence intervals for binomial proportions, with $n=25$ and either $x=19$ or $x=24$

	$x=19, n=25, \hat{P}=.76$		$x=24, n=25, \hat{P}=.96$	
	Lower bound	**Upper bound**	**Lower bound**	**Upper bound**
Wald	.5400	.9800	.8590	1.0610
Adjusted Wald	.5104	.9379	.7509	1.0422
Wilson	.5024	.9085	.7318	.9953
Wilson-cc	.4826	.9199	.7051	.9986
Clopper-Pearson	.4864	.9337	.7382	.9998
Blaker	.5000	.9235	.7388	.9996

Table 3.1 shows several patterns that reflect the conclusions in the literature (Newcombe, 1998a; Fay, 2010). The Wald and adjusted Wald CIs have unacceptable behavior when P is extreme. The Clopper-Pearson interval tends to be wider than the others. The Wilson CI has average coverage that is probably closest to the nominal confidence level (i.e., closest to 99% for a 99% CI) and is thus more liberal than the other tests. This is consistent with the narrow intervals reported in Table 3.1. On the basis of average coverage the Wilson CI is the best choice. However, Newcombe (1998a) notes that its minimum coverage is poor (83.2% for a nominal 95% CI or 88.7% for a nominal 99% CI). This implies that you would not be certain that the coverage is close to $C\%$ for any particular sample. Minimum coverage improves dramatically for the continuity-corrected Wilson CI and will be precisely $C\%$ for either exact CI.

For this reason I would recommend the exact Blaker CI under most circumstances, with the continuity-corrected Wilson CI a reasonable alternative in large samples (or for hand calculation). The adjusted Wald or the uncorrected Wilson CI are probably only justified in large samples if P is in the region of .5 (e.g., $.2 \leq P \leq .8$). The Wilson CI can also be justified if average coverage close to $C\%$ is deemed paramount.

3.3.6 Confidence intervals for a Poisson rate parameter

The Poisson distribution can be considered an approximation to the binomial distribution for large numbers (high n) and rare events (low P). Thus it is perhaps unsurprising that the construction of an interval estimate for a Poisson rate could be approached in the same way (via a normal approximation). These intervals are harder to construct than usual because n is usually unknown.[3] Ulm (1990) provides relatively simple exact method using the χ^2 distribution if n is unknown. Using this method, the upper and lower bounds ($\hat{\lambda}_L$ and $\hat{\lambda}_U$) are:

$$\hat{\lambda}_L = \frac{\chi^2_{2\hat{\lambda},\alpha/2}}{2}$$

$$\hat{\lambda}_U = \frac{\chi^2_{2(\hat{\lambda}+1),1-\alpha/2}}{2} \qquad \text{Equation 3.12}$$

The equation is simple to compute from the estimated rate $\hat{\lambda}$, provided appropriate quantiles of the χ^2 distribution can be obtained. Like the Clopper-Pearson and many other exact tests, it tends to be conservative. It is also possible to compute a form of the Wilson CI or a Blaker CI for a Poisson rate. Again, I would therefore recommend using the Blaker CI (Blaker, 2000; Fay, 2010). Subsequent chapters will consider other methods for modeling count and rate data and alternative methods for obtaining interval estimates using the Poisson distribution.

Example 3.5 In Example 2.3 a couple were observed to have had seven arguments over a period of two weeks. This is an estimated rate of $\hat{\lambda} = 3.5$ arguments per week. Assuming a Poisson distribution, the 95% CI for the number of arguments per two-week period could be calculated using Ulm's method as:

$$\hat{\lambda}_L = \frac{\chi^2_{2\times\hat{\lambda},.025}}{2} = \frac{\chi^2_{14,.025}}{2} = \frac{5.628726}{2} \approx 2.81$$

$$\hat{\lambda}_U = \frac{\chi^2_{2\times(\hat{\lambda}+1),.975}}{2} = \frac{\chi^2_{16,.975}}{2} = \frac{28.84535}{2} \approx 14.42$$

This gives an interval of [2.81, 14.42] for that period. To express this as a rate per week requires the interval to be rescaled (dividing all values by two). The resulting interval could be reported as $\hat{\lambda} = 3.5$, 95% CI [1.41, 7.21].

The corresponding Blaker CI, calculated using the `exactci` package in R (Fay, 2010), is $\hat{\lambda} = 3.5$, 95% CI [1.58, 7.04]. This interval is somewhat narrower and illustrates the superior average coverage of this exact method (see Blaker, 2000).

3.4 Confidence intervals for a difference

Often the focus of inference is not on a single parameter but the difference between two parameters. An obvious way to approach this problem is to calculate a CI for each of the two sample statistics. This turns out to be problematic – because the combined length of the two intervals is too large if the sample statistics are independent (which is generally the case if the statistics are from different samples). What width should the CI for a difference be? The correct width is largely determined by the *standard error of the difference*.

Consider the specific case of a difference in means sampled from a normal distribution. The difference between two normal distributions is itself normal, so a CI can be constructed for the difference using either z or t (depending on whether σ for the difference is known or estimated from the samples). Assuming that σ is estimated from the samples, a CI will take the form

$$\hat{\mu}_1 - \hat{\mu}_2 \pm t_{\nu,1-\alpha/2} \times \hat{\sigma}_{\hat{\mu}_1-\hat{\mu}_2} \qquad \text{Equation 3.13}$$

where $\hat{\mu}_1 - \hat{\mu}_2$ is the estimated difference in means and $\hat{\sigma}_{\hat{\mu}_1-\hat{\mu}_2}$ is the estimate of the standard error of the difference. The degrees of freedom ν are equal to $(n_1 - 1) + (n_2 - 1)$ or $n_1 + n_2 - 2 = N - 2$ (see Box 3.2). The subscripts 1 and 2 serve to keep track of the two samples (e.g., $\hat{\mu}_1$, $\hat{\sigma}_1$ and n_1 refer to the mean, *SD* and size of the first sample). The larger effective sample size for the difference ensures that the quantile $t_{\nu,1-\alpha/2}$ will be slightly smaller than for a CI computed for a single mean. The impact of this is rarely substantial and negligible for larger sample sizes (because the *t* distribution converges on *z* quite rapidly). The crucial consideration is that $\hat{\sigma}_{\hat{\mu}_1-\hat{\mu}_2}$ depends both on sample size and on the variance of the differences between the samples.

For two independent (and therefore uncorrelated) distributions, the variance of the difference between them is $\sigma_1^2+\sigma_2^2$ (i.e., the sum of their separate variances). This is a special case of the *variance sum law* (see Key Concept 3.2).

KEY CONCEPT 3.2

The variance sum law

The *variance sum law* states that the variance of a sum or difference of two variables, X_1 and X_2, is equal to the sum of their variances plus or minus twice their covariance. This is usually represented as

$$\sigma^2_{X_1 \pm X_2} = \sigma_1^2 + \sigma_2^2 \pm 2\sigma_{X_1,X_2} \qquad \text{Equation 3.14}$$

where $\sigma^2_{X_1 \pm X_2}$ is the variance of the sum or differences and σ_{X_1,X_2} is the *covariance* between X_1 and X_2. A covariance is measure of shared variance between two variables (see Chapter 6). For present purposes it is sufficient to note that a positive covariance indicates that X_1 tends to be high when X_2 is high (and implies the two variables are correlated). Similarly, a negative covariance indicates that X_2 tends to be low when X_1 is high and *vice versa*. If two variables are independent they are uncorrelated and $\sigma_{X_1,X_2}=0$. The variance sum law then reduces to:

$$\sigma^2_{X_1 \pm X_2} = \sigma_1^2 + \sigma_2^2 \qquad \text{Equation 3.15}$$

Some further thought is required to interpret the variance sum law when the covariance is not zero. For the sum of two variables a negative covariance reduces $\sigma^2_{X_1+X_2}$ (because the deviations from the mean of X_1 will tend to cancel out deviations from the mean of X_2). In contrast, a positive covariance tends to make the deviations in the summed variable more extreme. For variables that co-vary, the equation then becomes:

$$\sigma^2_{X_1 + X_2} = \sigma_1^2 + \sigma_2^2 + 2\sigma_{X_1,X_2} \qquad \text{Equation 3.16}$$

One analogy is with pushing a child on a swing. If each push coincides with the swing moving away from you, the pushes will tend to increase the speed of the child, whereas pushes coinciding with movement toward you will slow the child down. Positive and negative covariance will increase or decrease variation in the summed variable in a similar way.

For the difference between two variables the opposite pattern holds and the corresponding equation is:

$$\sigma^2_{X_1 - X_2} = \sigma_1^2 + \sigma_2^2 - 2\sigma_{X_1,X_2} \qquad \text{Equation 3.17}$$

This is relevant, because the standard error of a difference is itself the square root of a variance (the variance of a sampling distribution). This variance is, in turn, a function of the variance of the differences in the population: $\sigma^2_{X_1-X_2}$. If two independent samples are drawn from populations with the same variance (σ^2), Equation 3.15 indicates that $\sigma^2_{X_1-X_2}$ would then be $\sigma^2+\sigma^2=2\sigma^2$. Under these conditions $\sigma_{X_1-X_2}$, the standard deviation of the differences in

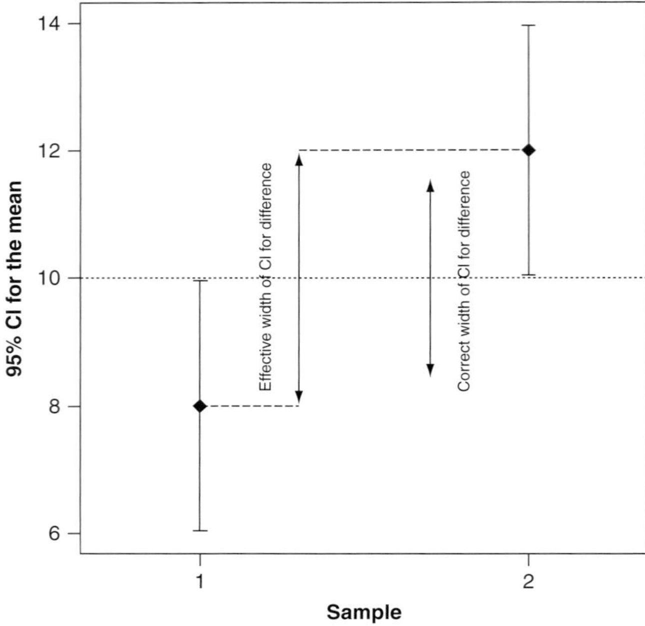

Figure 3.2 The effective width of a 95% CI for a difference, inferred from the intervals plotted around separate sample means relative to the correct width of the 95% CI for a difference

the population becomes $\sqrt{2\sigma^2} = \sqrt{2}\sigma \approx 1.4\sigma$. As a consequence, $\hat{\sigma}_{\hat{\mu}_1-\hat{\mu}_2}$ (the standard error of the difference) will be $\sqrt{2} \approx 1.4$ times larger than $\hat{\sigma}_{\hat{\mu}}$. Unequal population variances, unequal n and correlated samples all alter this relationship, but for independent samples with $n_1 \approx n_2$ and $\hat{\sigma}_1 \approx \hat{\sigma}_2$, the standard error of the difference in means will be larger than the standard errors of the original samples by a factor of approximately $\sqrt{2}$.

An important insight that follows from this is that the CI of a difference is narrower than the combined width of the CIs around the means.

Figure 3.2 shows 95% CIs for two independent, equal n samples where $\hat{\mu}_1 = 8$ and $\hat{\mu}_1 = 12$ and $\hat{\sigma}_{\hat{\mu}_1} = \hat{\sigma}_{\hat{\mu}_2} = 1$. The 95% CI for each mean is assumed to be $\hat{\mu} \pm 1.96$. If the means are separated so that they just fail to overlap, the total width separating them is $2 \times 1.96 = 3.92$. In contrast, the CI for the difference has width $\pm\sqrt{2} \times 1.96 \approx 2.77$. The effective width inferred from the separate sample CIs is too large by a factor of:

$$\frac{2 \times 1.96}{\sqrt{2} \times 1.96} = \frac{2}{\sqrt{2}} = \sqrt{2}$$

The precise difference between the effective and correct width of the interval depends on several factors, but the effective width of the separate sample intervals is almost always considerably larger than is required (see Schenker and Gentleman, 2001).

3.4.1 Differences in means from normal samples

If σ^2 is estimated from the samples, the CI for a difference in the means of samples from normal populations takes the form:

$$\hat{\mu}_1 - \hat{\mu}_2 \pm t_{(n_1+n_2-2),1-\alpha/2} \times \hat{\sigma}_{\hat{\mu}_1-\hat{\mu}_2} \qquad \text{Equation 3.18}$$

The standard error of the difference $\hat{\sigma}_{\hat{\mu}_1-\hat{\mu}_2}$ depends on the size of the two samples and on the population variance of the difference in means. Equation 3.18 produces accurate interval estimates under certain fairly restrictive conditions. The first condition is that the samples are taken from populations with a normal distribution. The second is that the observations in each sample are independent (and therefore the covariance in Equation 3.14 is zero). The third is that the populations the samples are taken from have the same variance (often termed *homogeneity of variance*). These assumptions – particularly the latter two – simplify the calculations considerably.

The CI for a difference in means therefore requires that $\hat{\sigma}_{\hat{\mu}_1-\hat{\mu}_2}$ can be accurately estimated. Adapting Equation 3.4 and Equation 3.15, it is possible to represent it as:

$$\sigma_{\hat{\mu}_1-\hat{\mu}_2} = \sqrt{\frac{\sigma_1^2}{n_1} + \frac{\sigma_2^2}{n_2}} \qquad \text{Equation 3.19}$$

If $\sigma_1^2 = \sigma_2^2$ this equation can be simplified and either σ_1 or σ_2 used to define the standard error. The simplified equation could be written as:

$$\sigma_{\hat{\mu}_1-\hat{\mu}_2} = \sigma_1\sqrt{\frac{1}{n_1} + \frac{1}{n_2}} = \sigma_2\sqrt{\frac{1}{n_1} + \frac{1}{n_2}} \qquad \text{Equation 3.20}$$

In practice it would be sensible to estimate $\sigma_{\hat{\mu}_1-\hat{\mu}_2}$ using all the available data, not just one of the two samples. This can be achieved by pooling data from both samples. The resulting estimator, $\hat{\sigma}_{pooled}$, should provide a more accurate estimate of σ than either sample on its own.

KEY CONCEPT 3.3

Pooled estimates of variances and standard deviations

All other things being equal, an estimate that uses all available data will be more accurate than one that uses only a fraction of the available data. This general principle leads naturally to the idea of combining different sample estimates to increase accuracy. In many cases the combination is trivial: you just combine the data into one large 'super-sample', but in other cases the approach will fail. Obtaining a pooled variance or *SD* is good illustration of the problem. The samples are assumed to be drawn from populations with the same variance or *SD* (e.g., $\sigma_1 = \sigma_2$), but are not necessarily similar in other respects: they probably have different means (i.e., $\mu_1 \neq \mu_2$). Combining all the data into a single super-sample would lead to an inflated estimate of variability by confounding variability in each sample with variability due to the difference in sample means.

If the populations have different means, but equal *n*, the mean of the combined samples, the *grand mean,* will be an unbiased estimator of the mean of the combined population mean $(\mu_1 + \mu_2)/2$. The problem is that the residuals (deviations from the mean) calculated for the super-sample would on average be too large (by half the differences in population means). The solution to this problem is to strip out the effects of differences between μ_1 and μ_2 by combining the residuals ($x - \hat{\mu}_1$ and $x - \hat{\mu}_2$) rather than the raw data from each sample. The relationship between the residuals of a sample and its variance estimate are given by Equation 1.12. Rearranging this equation produces a convenient expression of the residuals in terms of the sample variance:

$$(n-1)\hat{\sigma}^2 = \sum_{i=1}^{n}(x_i - \hat{\mu})^2 \qquad \text{Equation 3.21}$$

Using this relationship in conjunction with Equation 3.15 gives a pooled variance estimate for two independent samples:

$$\hat{\sigma}^2_{pooled} = \frac{(n_1-1)\hat{\sigma}_1^2 + (n_2-1)\hat{\sigma}_2^2}{n_1+n_2-2} \qquad \text{Equation 3.22}$$

This is an unbiased estimate of the population variance of either sample (assuming homogeneity of variance). Taking the square root of $\hat{\sigma}^2_{pooled}$ provides an estimate of the pooled standard deviation: $\hat{\sigma}_{pooled}$. As the square root of an unbiased estimator, it has a small – generally negligible – bias associated with it. The calculations can be simplified somewhat if the two samples have equal n, in which case

$$\hat{\sigma}^2_{pooled} = \frac{\hat{\sigma}_1^2 + \hat{\sigma}_2^2}{2} \qquad \text{Equation 3.23}$$

and

$$\hat{\sigma}_{pooled} = \sqrt{\frac{\hat{\sigma}_1^2 + \hat{\sigma}_2^2}{2}} \qquad \text{Equation 3.24}$$

Pooling estimates in this manner has a wide range of applications in statistics and is not limited to just two samples. Thus, a general formula for the pooled *SD* (extending the approach from two to J samples) is:

$$\hat{\sigma}_{pooled} = \sqrt{\frac{(n_1-1)\hat{\sigma}_1^2 + \cdots + (n_J-1)\hat{\sigma}_J^2}{(n_1-1)+\cdots+(n_J-1)}} = \sqrt{\frac{\sum_{j=1}^{J}(n_j-1)\hat{\sigma}_j^2}{\sum_{j=1}^{J}(n_j-1)}} \qquad \text{Equation 3.25}$$

Combining the residuals of each sample to obtain the pooled estimate provides an estimate of the standard error of the difference as:

$$\hat{\sigma}_{\hat{\mu}_1-\hat{\mu}_2} = \hat{\sigma}_{pooled}\sqrt{\frac{1}{n_1}+\frac{1}{n_2}} \qquad \text{Equation 3.26}$$

The pooled *SD* in Equation 3.26 is:

$$\hat{\sigma}_{pooled} = \sqrt{\frac{(n_1-1)\hat{\sigma}_1^2 + (n_2-1)\hat{\sigma}_2^2}{n_1+n_2-2}} \qquad \text{Equation 3.27}$$

This is the standard approach to calculating the CI for a difference between independent, normal means. It makes the strong assumption that $\sigma_1 = \sigma_2$. If this is not true the sampling distribution will not follow a t distribution and alternative approaches should be considered.

Example 3.6 Calculating the CI for a difference is only marginally more difficult than calculating the CI for an individual mean. Baguley and Payne (2000a; Experiment 1) report data from 56 participants who read spatial descriptions and then performed a comprehension task. This required them to select which of two diagrams matched a written description. Participants were randomly assigned to either a high study condition ($n_1 = 28$) or a low study condition ($n_2 = 28$). In the high study condition they read the descriptions and performed the task three times, while in the low study condition they completed the task only once. Those in the high study condition correctly matched a greater proportion of descriptions ($M = 87.2\%$, $SD = 24.0\%$) than in the low study condition ($M = 74.1\%$, $SD = 8.5\%$). Subsequent examples refer to this data set as the comprehension data.

Assuming equal population variances, the 95% CI for the difference in means is

$$\hat{\mu}_1 - \hat{\mu}_2 \pm t_{(n_1+n_2-2),1-\alpha/2} \times \hat{\sigma}_{pooled}\sqrt{\frac{1}{n_1}+\frac{1}{n_2}}$$

Where

$$\hat{\sigma}_{pooled} = \sqrt{\frac{(28-1)\,8.5^2+(28-1)\,24.0^2}{28+28-2}}$$

This simplifies to

$$\hat{\sigma}_{pooled} = \sqrt{\frac{8.5^2+24.0^2}{2}} = \sqrt{\frac{72.25+576}{2}} = \sqrt{324.125} \approx 18.0$$

It is convenient, but not essential, to subtract the smaller from the larger mean to get a positive difference. This difference in means is $87.2 - 74.1 = 13.1$. The 95% CI is:

$$13.1 \pm t_{54,.975} \times 18.0\sqrt{\frac{1}{28}+\frac{1}{28}} = 13.1 \pm 2.005 \times 4.811$$

This produces a 95% CI for the difference in accuracy between the low and high study conditions of $13.1\% \pm 9.6\%$ or:

$$M_1 - M_2 = 13.1, 95\%\ \text{CI}\ [3.5, 22.8]$$

This suggests that there is greater accuracy for the high study condition than for the low study condition. Because the interval estimate is fairly wide, the CI is consistent with quite a small difference (4%) or one that is fairly large (23%).

It would be wise to treat this CI with some caution. Different participants were assigned to conditions of the experiment at random and so the observations in the two samples should be independent, but neither normality nor homogeneity of variance seems plausible. As the accuracy scores are bounded at 100%, the distribution is likely to be skewed – particularly for the higher scoring group (where the mean is close to 90%). Such a large difference in *SD*s (24 versus 8.5) is also unlikely if the population variances are equal.

3.4.2 Unequal sample variances: the Behrens-Fisher problem

Gossett's original work on the t distribution dealt only with the case of samples from normal distributions with different means, but identical variance. If the distributions do not have the same variance the sampling distribution of the standardized mean is no longer a t distribution. It follows some other distribution (usually designated t'). Both Behrens and Fisher attempted to solve this problem and proposed approximate solutions. Subsequent work has provided exact solutions, but it is an approximate solution derived from work by Welch and Satterthwaite that is usually employed to deal with unequal variances. The popularity of the *Welch-Satterthwaite* approximation is that as well as being fairly accurate it does not require abandoning the t distribution entirely (e.g., allowing existing tables for t to be employed).

The Welch-Satterthwaite correction works by adjusting the degrees of freedom, treating t' as if it were a genuine member of the t family (but with non-standard *df*). In addition, the usual pooled standard deviation estimate is inappropriate. It was derived on the assumption that there is a single population variance common to both samples and so pooling the samples will estimate this quantity more accurately. Instead, using Equation 3.19, $\sigma_{\hat{\mu}_1-\hat{\mu}_2}$ can be estimated from the separate sample variances:

$$\hat{\sigma}_{\hat{\mu}_1-\hat{\mu}_2} = \sqrt{\frac{\hat{\sigma}_1^2}{n_1} + \frac{\hat{\sigma}_2^2}{n_2}} \qquad \text{Equation 3.28}$$

If the sample sizes are equal this quantity is identical to the pooled *SE*, but it can differ dramatically if sample sizes are unequal (with large variances in small samples having the biggest impact). The Welch-Satterthwaite correction requires the following adjustment to the *df*:

$$\nu' = \frac{\left(\frac{\hat{\sigma}_1^2}{n_1} + \frac{\hat{\sigma}_2^2}{n_2}\right)^2}{\frac{\hat{\sigma}_1^4}{n_1^2(n_1-1)} + \frac{\hat{\sigma}_2^4}{n_2^2(n_2-1)}} \qquad \text{Equation 3.29}$$

The interval estimate is then formed using a t distribution with ν' *df*:

$$\hat{\mu}_1 - \hat{\mu}_2 \pm t_{\nu',1-\alpha/2} \times \hat{\sigma}_{\hat{\mu}_1-\hat{\mu}_2} \qquad \text{Equation 3.30}$$

Experts recommend adopting this correction by default (and certainly if the homogeneity of variance assumption is in doubt). The loss of accuracy when applying the Welch-Satterthwaite solution if homogeneity of variance is true is considered negligible (see Zimmerman, 2004). The approach is also robust (see Hayes and Cai, 2007), performing well unless both the variances and sample sizes are very unequal (and even then only performing very badly with samples from populations that are decidedly non-normal).

Example 3.7 It was unreasonable to assume equal variances for the comprehension accuracy data from Example 3.6. One group had more time to study the descriptions than the other. The low study group might be more inclined to guess on some trials and therefore their overall performance may be more variable, while variability in the high study group is restricted by performance close to 100% (a ceiling effect). Constructing a CI using the Welch-Satterthwaite correction is therefore appropriate. The standard error of the difference calculated using the separate variance estimate is

$$\hat{\sigma}_{\hat{\mu}_1-\hat{\mu}_2} = \sqrt{\frac{24^2}{28} + \frac{8.5^2}{28}} = \sqrt{20.57 + 2.58} = \sqrt{23.15} \approx 4.81$$

and identical to the value from the pooled variance estimate. This will always occur with equal sample sizes (but not if they are unequal). Calculating the *df* is harder:

$$\nu' = \frac{\left(\frac{\hat{\sigma}_1^2}{n_1} + \frac{\hat{\sigma}_2^2}{n_2}\right)^2}{\frac{\hat{\sigma}_1^4}{n_1^2(n_1-1)} + \frac{\hat{\sigma}_2^4}{n_2^2(n_2-1)}} = \frac{\left(\frac{24^2}{28} + \frac{8.5^2}{28}\right)^2}{\frac{24^4}{28^2(27)} + \frac{8.5^4}{28^2(27)}}$$

Note that the top half of the fraction is the square (rather than square root) of the value of 23.15 already used to calculate the *SE*) and so:

$$\nu' == \frac{23.15^2}{\frac{331776}{21168} + \frac{5220.0625}{21168}} = \frac{535.9225}{15.6735 + 0.2466} \approx 33.7$$

The 95% CI is therefore:

$$\hat{\mu}_1 - \hat{\mu}_2 \pm t_{33.7,.975} \times 4.81$$

Because the *SE* is identical, the crucial change is that the *t* quantile was determined using 33.7 *df*. The quantile $t_{33.7,.975}$ is 2.033 and the CI is:

$$13.1 \pm 2.033 \times 4.81 = 13.1\% \pm 9.8 \text{ or}$$

$$M_1 - M_2 = 13.1, 95\% \text{ CI } [3.3, 22.9]$$

Despite the large difference in the sample variances this interval is only slightly wider than had equal variances been assumed. With unequal *n* the width of the CI could have been much narrower or much wider (the latter occurring if the smaller sample also has less variance). For example, if $n_1 = 20$ and $n_2 = 36$ $\hat{\sigma}_{\hat{\mu}_1-\hat{\mu}_2}$ would be 4.43, $\nu' \approx 48.1$ and the margin of error ± 8.9. Reversing this pattern (so that $n_1 = 36$) gives an $\hat{\sigma}_{\hat{\mu}_1-\hat{\mu}_2} = 5.55$, $\nu' \approx 21.7$ and a margin of error of ± 11.5. Fairly large discrepancies in sample size and variance are required to have a big influence on the width of the CI. The Welch-Satterthwaite approach is also fairly robust to moderate degrees of non-normality (except in very small samples).

3.5 Using Monte Carlo methods to estimate confidence intervals

If there are good reasons to doubt the assumption of normality holds for a given situation, or if an analytic solution is unknown or unavailable, it may be convenient to switch to Monte

Carlo methods (see Box 3.3). Finding the lower and upper bounds for a confidence interval is a good illustration of the utility of this approach. Modern computer software makes it increasingly attractive to use such methods. In this section the approach will first be illustrated using *simulation* for the CI of binomial proportion and then a percentile *bootstrap* CI for a sample median. More sophisticated (and accurate) analytic or Monte Carlo methods are available, and the aim here is to outline the principles behind these methods.

Box 3.3 The bootstrap, jackknife, resampling and other Monte Carlo methods

'Monte Carlo methods' (named after the renowned casino district of Monaco) is a general term for a way of solving mathematical or statistical problems through repeated generation of random or pseudo-random numbers. Many of these methods involve simulation of a particular model using random numbers with particular properties. For example, Monte Carlo simulations are often used to explore what happens when samples are drawn from populations where the assumptions of a statistical procedure are violated. This has advantages over using real data – the main one being that the presence or absence of particular violations can be controlled in a simulation (but is usually uncontrolled and unknown for real data). Thus, Monte Carlo simulations could be used to assess the performance of a statistical procedure under a wide range of circumstances.

Many Monte Carlo methods in statistics involve *resampling*. Resampling methods work by drawing data points at random from observed data. These methods are further divided into *permutation* methods (also known as *randomization* tests), the *jackknife* and the *bootstrap*.

Resampling methods differ in terms of their sampling plans (how they sample from observed data). Rodgers (1999) provided a taxonomy of these based on: i) the size of sample and ii) whether sampling is with or without replacement (see Figure 3.3).

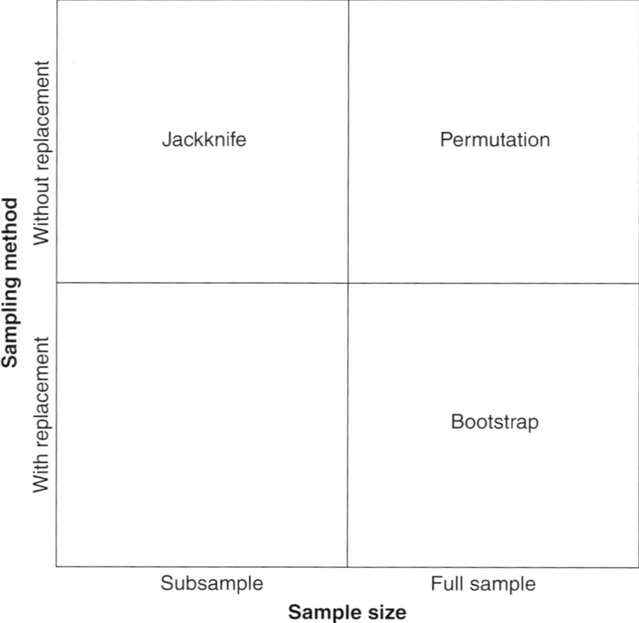

Figure 3.3 A taxonomy of sampling plans for resampling statistics

Randomization tests, the earliest permutation statistics, were devised by R. A. Fisher (Yates and Mather, 1963). For permutation statistics, values are drawn at random from the original data set (without replacement) and assigned randomly to categories, groups or other structures. A statistic (e.g., a median, mean or difference) can then be computed for each resampled data set. This procedure is then repeated until all possible permutations of the data are exhausted. The resampled data sets can then be used for inference. For instance, the standard error for the statistic being calculated is obtained as the arithmetic mean of the standard errors of all the resampled data sets. Such inference is exact (see Box 3.1) if all permutations of the data were sampled. For large data sets, searching through all the possible permutations may not be possible and a random or systematic sample of the full set of permutations (e.g., 10,000 or 50,000) might be taken. Such statistics are not exact (but approach the exact solution as the number of permutations increases).

In contrast to permutation tests (which resample all n observed data points) the jackknife takes fewer than n values without replacement (e.g., taking $n-1$ per sample). It is most often used to assess the stability and bias of parameter estimates. The jackknife can be contrasted with the bootstrap where it is usual to sample n observations from the original sample. However, the most important distinction between the bootstrap and the previous methods is that sampling is done with replacement.

The bootstrap is particularly useful for data sampled from unknown distributions. The advantage of resampling with replacement is that a finite sample can, in principle, behave like an infinite population. Thus very large numbers of bootstrap samples can be generated (and these samples will not necessarily resemble the original data closely).

In a simulation, the true population distribution is assumed known (e.g., with parameters equal to those of the observed sample estimates) and a large number of random samples with the properties of this ideal distribution are generated. Table 3.1 summarized several exact and approximate procedures for generating a 99% CI for a binomial proportion with $n=25$ and either 19 or 24 successes. This serves as a useful benchmark for a simulation approach. We will start by simulating the number of successes from a single sample of $n=25$ from a population in which $P=.76$ (equivalent to expecting 19 successes out of 25). Dividing the number of successes in the simulated sample by 25 gives the simulated observed proportion. Repeating this process 10,000 times gives 10,000 simulated proportions. The mean of these simulated proportions gives the parameter estimate (and the difference between the simulated mean and the observed proportion is a measure of bias in the simulation).

In this case the simulated mean is 0.75978 (indicating little bias) and the .005 and .995 quantiles of the 10,000 simulated proportions provide a simulated CI of [.52, .96]. The width of this interval is similar to that of the Wald CI, though the interval is asymmetrical and therefore somewhat more realistic. For an observed P of .96 the simulated CI gives a mean of 0.959936 (again indicating little bias in the simulation). The corresponding CI is [.84, 1.00] which is probably a little too narrow (but again similar to the Wald CI). Repeating the exercise with another 10,000 simulated samples should produce broadly similar results. Even very basic simulation methods like these can sometimes produce adequate results (although either the Wilson or Blaker CI would be a better option in this case). Furthermore, it is possible to develop simulations that produce more accurate answers (something that is particularly important for situations in which an analytic solution is not feasible).

3.5.1 Bootstrap confidence intervals

Bootstrapping differs from simulation in that few prior assumptions are required about the population. Instead, the observed data are used to estimate the sampling distribution.

A bootstrap sample of size n is taken by randomly sampling n values with replacement from the observed data. If the original sample consisted of the observations {2, 3, 8, 8} a bootstrap sample might start by drawing an 8. This would then be put back. The next observation might be the 3. It too would then be put back. The process could then be repeated until $n = 4$ observations had been drawn and then replaced. This would leave the original sample of {2, 3, 8, 8} intact but have created a bootstrap sample such as {8, 3, 2, 3} or {8, 3, 8, 8}. Each observation (including duplicated observations) has an equal chance of being included in the bootstrap sample. Because all sampling is done with replacement, any observation can be sampled more than once (in theory up to n times). In a real application, the process is repeated until a large number (e.g., hundreds or thousands) of bootstrap samples are obtained. The bootstrapped samples are then used to estimate one or more parameters of the population originally sampled.

By sampling with replacement, bootstrapping treats the observed data as if it were an infinite population of to-be-sampled values. Provided the sample is representative of the population it is drawn from, the bootstrap population should have similar characteristics to the true population (though any idiosyncrasies in the sample will be replicated over and over in the bootstrap population – see Rodgers, 1999).

Figure 3.4 shows a histogram of percentage accuracy for the comprehension task data (the data used in Examples 3.6 and 3.7). The y-axis shows the frequency with which accuracy scores fall into certain ranges ('bins'). The graph shows marked negative skew (consistent with a ceiling effect where high performance meets the upper bound of 100%). Although the true distribution is unknown, bootstrapping may provide a more accurate CI for these data because it is sensitive to these properties of the sample (that are assumed to reflect those of the true population).[4]

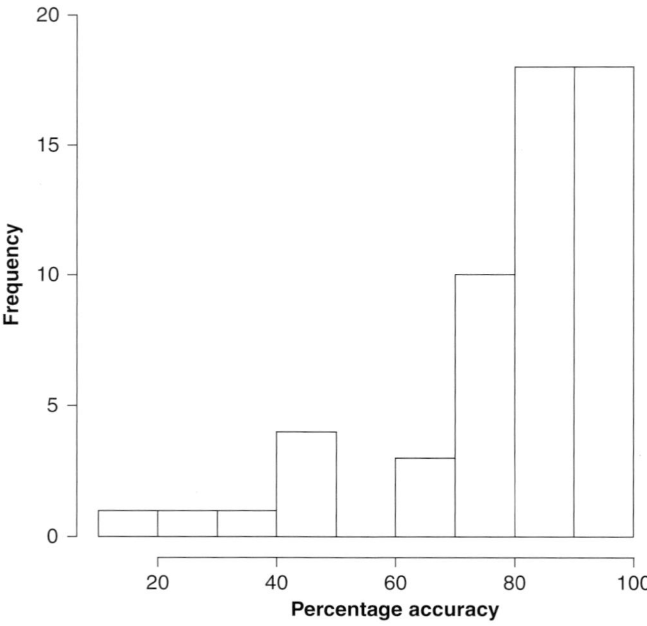

Figure 3.4 Frequency of observed percentage accuracy scores for the comprehension data

To obtain a bootstrap sample of differences it is perhaps simplest to start with a bootstrap sample for each of the two conditions. A bootstrap sample from the low study condition is obtained by sampling with replacement 28 new values from the original 28 observed values. The same process gives a single bootstrap sample from the high study condition. Figure 3.5 shows histograms of the observed data and a bootstrap sample separately for each condition. As you might expect, the bootstrap samples are similar to the original data – but there are also obvious differences. These differences represent sampling variability within the population of possible bootstrap samples. Having created two bootstrap samples, the next step is to calculate the difference between the mean of each sample. The means of the bootstrap samples in Figure 3.5, panels (c) and (d), are 76.3 and 88.4 respectively (with a difference of 12.1). To derive a bootstrap CI it is necessary to resample the original data many times in order to simulate a sampling distribution for the bootstrapped statistic (in this case the difference between the sample means). The CI is obtained from the relevant quantiles of the distribution of differences in the bootstrap samples (e.g., .025 and .975 for a 95% CI). This procedure is termed a *percentile bootstrap*. Other statistics can also be computed from the bootstrap distribution. For instance, the *SD* of a bootstrap distribution is an estimate of the

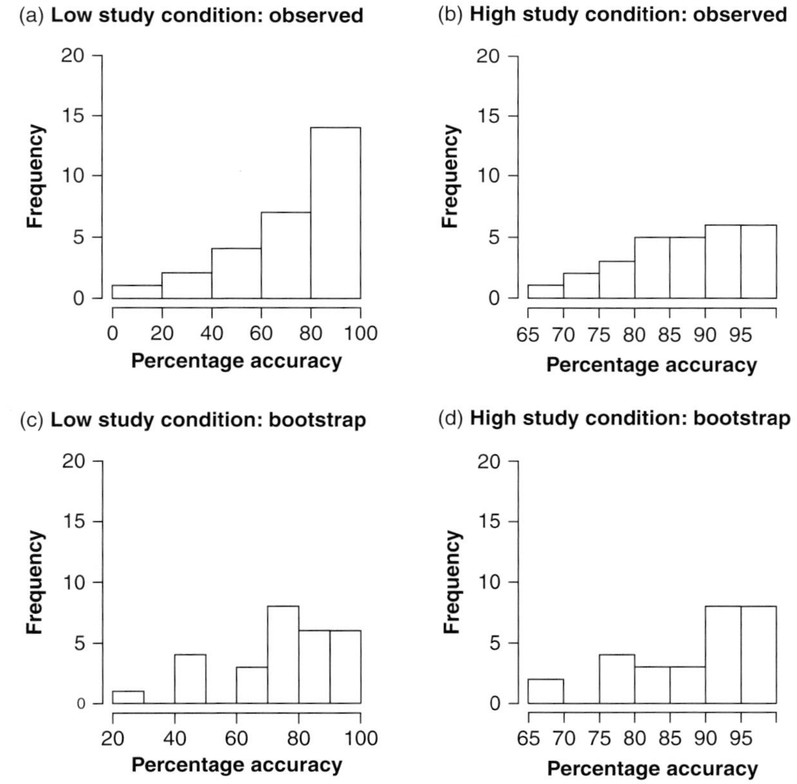

Figure 3.5 Comparison of observed and a single bootstrap sample by condition for the comprehension data

standard error of the bootstrapped statistic (because a standard error is the *SD* of a sampling distribution).

The percentile bootstrap is among the simpler bootstrap approaches that can be employed. It produces good results if the bootstrap distribution is fairly symmetrical and unbiased (i.e., centered on the parameter of interest). This makes it a reasonable choice for statistics such as means and medians, but a poor choice for statistics such as variances that tend to have highly skewed sampling distributions. In addition, because small samples tend to underestimate variability in the population, the coverage of the CI will often be too narrow when the original sample size is small. In common with other Monte Carlo methods, the accuracy of the method also depends on the number of bootstrap samples B that are taken. As B is an integer, the bootstrap distribution will be discrete even if the original data are continuous (Hall, 1986). Nevertheless, Hall (1986) shows that, for the percentile bootstrap, the bootstrap distributions behave like random variables from a continuous distribution (under some fairly general conditions) – provided B is chosen so that $\alpha/2(B+1)$ is a positive integer. For a 95% CI the smallest value of B that satisfies this constraint is 39, because $.025 \times (39+1) = 1$. Even with B at its smallest value a percentile bootstrap CI can be surprisingly accurate, and as $B \to \infty$ the interval becomes indistinguishable from an exact permutation test.

Example 3.8 Figure 3.5 illustrates a bootstrap sample for each of the groups using the comprehension data from Examples 3.6 and 3.7. To compute a 95% percentile bootstrap CI for the mean group difference, a large number of bootstrap replications must be generated. Let's start with $B=9,999$ replications for each group and compute the difference between each pair of replications. This produces a set of 9,999 differences. It is a good idea to check the distribution of the bootstrap statistics at this stage.

Figure 3.6 shows a histogram of the distribution of 9,999 bootstrap replications. This distribution looks fairly symmetrical and its mean is 13.11 (very close to the observed mean difference of 13.1, indicating negligible bias). Indeed the simulated sampling distribution is not far from normal even though the original data are highly skewed (as expected for a sampling distribution that meets the assumptions of the CLT). These properties suggest that the percentile bootstrap method is suitable. The .025 and .975 quantiles of the bootstrap sampling distribution are 4.16667 and 22.767857 and so the interval estimate for the difference in percentage accuracy is 13.1, 95% CI [4.2, 22.8]. This interval is similar, but slightly narrower than the Welch-Satterthwaite CI of [3.3, 22.9]. Despite the superiority of the bootstrap CI for these data (which are not remotely normal in shape) the normal approximations in Example 3.6 and 3.7 are not wildly different (and adequate for most purposes). The *SD* of the bootstrap distribution can also be used to estimate the standard error for the difference. This is 4.74 (slightly lower than the estimate of 4.81 obtained from either the separate or pooled variance estimates).

In theory the accuracy of the bootstrap CI can be improved by increasing the number of replications B. For $B=99,999$ the interval estimate is [4.2, 22.6]. Further increases to B have little impact on the outcome, though for other data sets a larger number of replications might be required. There are procedures available to check whether sufficient simulated or bootstrapped samples have been obtained. In practice two rules of thumb can be applied. First, decide upon a desired level of accuracy and repeat the process several times. If the answers don't change at the desired level of accuracy, the number of samples is sufficient. Second, stop when the calculations begin to tax the processing capacity of your computer. At this point it is usually better to repeat the process and average over several 'runs' to achieve the desired level of accuracy – a practice termed *bagging*.

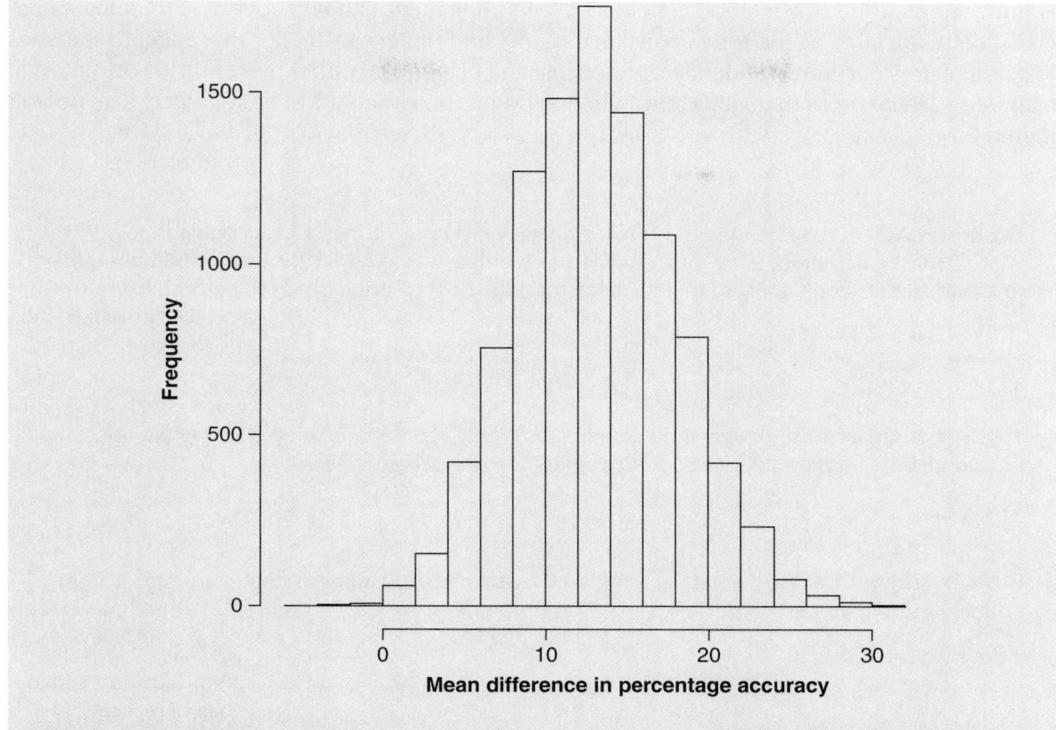

Figure 3.6 Distribution of mean between-group differences for 9,999 bootstrap samples from the comprehension data

The example here focused on the difference between two means for non-normal distribution. It would be trivial to alter the computations to calculate other statistics such as the trimmed mean or median (or their differences).

3.5.2 Bias-corrected and accelerated (BC_a) confidence intervals

Bootstrapping is an extremely versatile statistical tool for dealing with awkward problems in statistical inference. Although the percentile bootstrap requires a large number of computations to be performed, each operation is trivial provided you have a way to generate random numbers with suitable properties (and sufficient computing power). For problems that are not amenable to the percentile bootstrap, a number of alternatives exist.

DiCiccio and Efron (1996) review different bootstrap methods and favor the *bias-corrected accelerated* (BC_a) bootstrap. As the name suggested, this incorporates a bias correction (first estimating the degree of bias and then adjusting the bootstrap samples accordingly). Acceleration refers to a similar adjustment to counter the skew of the bootstrap sampling distribution. A BC_a bootstrap therefore corrects for estimates that are not centered on the true parameter (bias) and for distributions that are not symmetrical (acceleration). These are the main deficiencies of the percentile bootstrap and so it makes sense to switch to the BC_a bootstrap if the simpler method is not accurate. The BC_a method is not as easy to implement and it is advisable to employ specialist software such as the R `boot` package (Canty and Ripley, 2010). For most simple statistics (e.g., measures of central tendency, differences, and dispersion) either percentile or BC_a interval estimates will be more than sufficient. When in doubt, BC_a intervals are a relatively safe default method.

Example 3.9 It may be interesting to compare the output of the `boot` package in R with the 95% CI for the comprehension data obtained in Example 3.8. With $B = 99,999$ replications (albeit that Hall's results don't apply to the BC_a bootstrap) the boot package gives the percentile bootstrap CI as:

$$13.1, 95\% \text{ CI } [4.3, 22.5]$$

This is very similar to the interval obtained with 99,999 replications using a percentile bootstrap procedure built from scratch. The corresponding BC_a interval estimate is:

$$13.1, 95\% \text{ CI } [4.6, 22.9]$$

Either bootstrap CI offers a potential advantage over one that assumes samples are drawn from a normal distribution.

3.6 Graphing confidence intervals

A particularly effective way to report and convey patterns among data, including interval estimates, is to plot them (Cleveland, 1985; Cumming and Finch, 2005). A number of factors – not least personal preference – determine the best way to plot any given CI. A common method is to employ a bar plot of the statistic (e.g., mean) with 'whiskers' (error bars) representing the distance of the upper and lower bound from the mean. Figure 3.7 shows a basic bar plot with a 95% CI (based on the t distribution) for the separate sample means of the low and high study conditions of the comprehension data. In panel (a) the bar plot is drawn so that the y-axis runs from 0 to 100 (sometimes called zero referencing), while in panel (b) the scale runs from 50 to 100.[5]

Zero referencing is often recommended for comparing quantities with a meaningful zero point. Starting the plot from a point above zero would enhance any differences between the groups (potentially exaggerating small differences to make them appear large). This does not imply that zero referencing is always correct. The data here are from a two-alternative forced choice recognition task. While it is possible that participants could score as low as 0%, it is unlikely. A more sensible minimum would be 50% (the score expected if participants had no memory and were guessing at random). Panel (b) is arguably a superior graphic, because the means are scaled relative to a meaningful reference point (expected chance performance).

Plotting the means and interval estimates together, as in Figure 3.7, has several advantages. One is that the difference in precision of each group is immediately visible. For unequal sample sizes it would help to add n below each bar (to indicate that some of the difference in precision

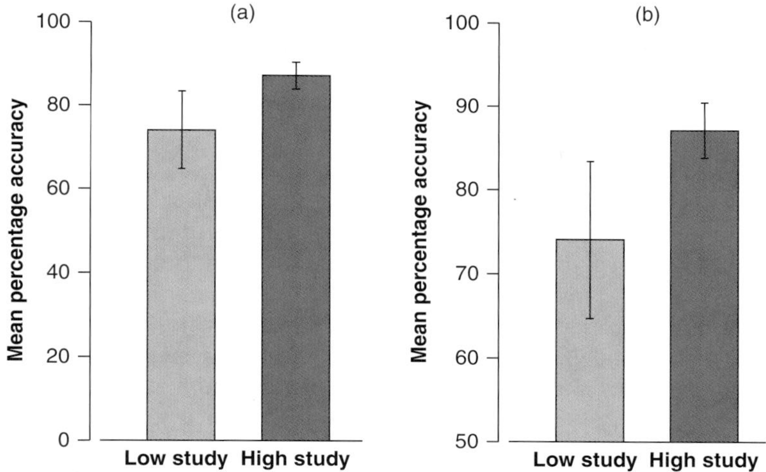

Figure 3.7 Mean percentage accuracy and 95% confidence intervals by group for the comprehension data

stems from differences in sample size). Plotting the CI also supports inferences about the individual means. For these data it shows clearly that performance in each group is above chance (with both intervals comfortably excluding 50% accuracy). The plot also has disadvantages. It can be hard to gauge the exact location of the whiskers in relation to other features of the plot (though this only matters if a high level of precision is required). A more serious concern arises if the objective is to illustrate differences between independent groups. If so, it may be better to plot the CI for the differences between groups directly.

As noted earlier, Cumming and Finch (2005) point out that when 95% CIs for two separately plotted means overlap, it is still possible that the CI for the difference would not include zero (see Figure 3.2). However, is possible to adjust a plot to reflect the correct width of the CI for a difference. One very relatively simple solution is to adjust each interval so that they overlap only when the total distance between the means is equal to the width of a CI for their difference. Overlap or lack of overlap of this kind of *difference-adjusted CI* around the individual means can then be interpreted as if it were a CI for their difference. Difference-adjusted CIs can be obtained in several ways, but a very general approach is to use a normal approximation. Goldstein and Healy (1995) show that, for independent means with equal standard errors, the required width of a difference-adjusted 95% CI is $\pm 1.39\hat{\sigma}_{\hat{\mu}}$.[6] If the standard errors are unequal, it is possible to adjust the multiplier accordingly. For small samples, a more accurate approach is to use the t distribution to obtain a multiplier (Goldstein and Healy, 1995; Afshartous and Preston, 2010). Afshartous and Preston (2010) provide an R code to obtain a multiplier, and extend the approach to work with correlated (non-independent) samples. The Goldstein and Healy approach is convenient for plotting large numbers of means or other statistics, and assumes a common multiplier for all the statistics being plotted (but distinct standard errors).

A related approach is to plot a CI in the usual way, but adjust the width so that absence of overlap corresponds to the required CI for the difference. For independent samples with equal variances and equal n, the total width of the CI for a difference is – as already discussed – larger than that for an individual mean by a factor of $\sqrt{2}$. The following equation produces intervals around a set of J sample means so that the total width between each pair corresponds to the width of a CI for their difference:

$$\hat{\mu}_j \pm t_{n-1,1-\alpha/2} \frac{\sqrt{2}}{2} \times \hat{\sigma}_{\hat{\mu}_j} \qquad \text{Equation 3.31}$$

Except for the $\sqrt{2}/2$ adjustment factor, this is identical to the usual CI. The adjusted factor ensures that the total width of error bars between two means is around $\sqrt{2}/2 + \sqrt{2}/2 = \sqrt{2}$ times wider than the interval for an individual mean (and exactly so if the variances are equal). Thus the $\sqrt{2}$ factor in Equation 3.31 is halved to allow for the fact there are two error bars rather than one. This approximation works well for independent samples with similar n and roughly equal variances (see Schenker and Gentleman, 2001). Equation 3.31 assumes that separate standard errors are computed for each of the independent means. The width of these intervals will therefore be sensitive to differences in the variances and sizes of each sample. In situations where it is reasonable to assume homogeneity of variance it may be more accurate to replace $\hat{\sigma}_{\hat{\mu}_j}$ with a pooled standard error. The separate standard error approach is, however, safer. It can also be more informative. For equal n samples, separate error terms may reveal patterns in the variances among the means: intervals will be larger for more variable samples (Loftus, 2001).

Graphed in this way, overlap indicates that it is plausible that there is no difference between the means (because the CI for the difference would include zero), while lack of overlap suggests there are systematic differences between the means. A more radical solution is to indicate both the 95% difference-adjusted and the 95% CI for each sample mean on the same plot. This could be done in several ways, but a neat solution is to use two-tiered error bars such as those described by Cleveland (1985). With two-tiered error bars, the ends of each bar could be drawn at $\pm t_{n-1,1-\alpha/2}\hat{\sigma}_{\hat{\mu}_j}$ (the required distance for a 95% CI of the sample mean) to create the outer tier. The inner tier could be created by drawing a line (at right angles to the error bar) at $\pm t_{n-1,1-\alpha/2}\sqrt{2}/2\hat{\sigma}_{\hat{\mu}_j}$.

In a dot plot, the sample mean is displayed as a single point with error bars for the CI. Dot plots are often preferred to bar plots because they reduce visual 'clutter'. This will usually make it is easier to focus on the details that are important. A downside is that it is perhaps easier to get away with picking reference points on the y-axis that distort the size of the differences between the means than it is for bar charts. Figure 3.8a shows a conventional dot plot of means with error bars depicting a 95% CI. This plot is roughly the equivalent of the bar plot in Figure 3.7b. Figure 3.8b depicts two-tiered error bars. The outer tier corresponds to a 95% CI around the sample mean, while the inner tier corresponds to a difference-adjusted 95% CI. As the inner tiers do not overlap, it suggests that the two means are likely to be different. Figure 3.8 also shows a simple alternative to zero referencing: adding a line at an important value (in this case expected chance performance of 50%). The outer tier error bars are far from this line – indicating that it is highly implausible that either group is simply guessing.

An important final consideration is whether to plot standard error bars ($\pm 1\hat{\sigma}_{\hat{\mu}}$) or CIs. Plotting one standard error is broadly equivalent to plotting a 68% CI (not a particularly common choice of confidence level). Cleveland (1985) suggests that the practice of plotting a single standard error arises from a tradition of numerical reporting (in which the numeric value of the *SE* can then be plugged into other calculations). For visual display of data, the goal is not to provide exact numbers for additional analysis, but to illustrate or summarize particular patterns among the data. It therefore makes sense to pick the confidence level more carefully. Adopting a 95% confidence level provides a reasonably strict level of confidence and has the convenience of

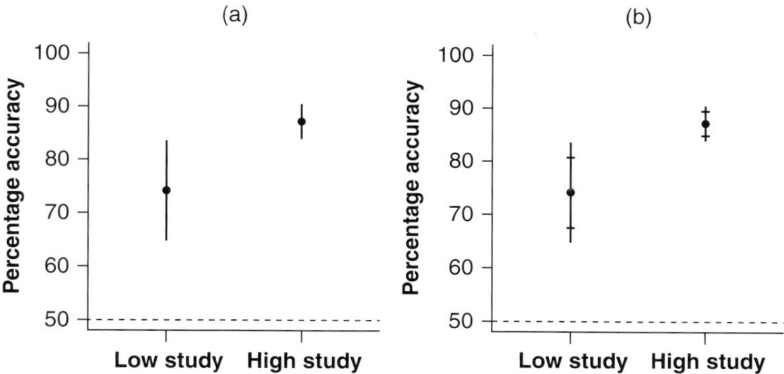

Figure 3.8 Mean percentage accuracy for the comprehension data, with (a) conventional 95% CI error bars, and (b) two-tiered error bars depicting 95% CI for the individual means (outer error bars) and a difference-adjusted 95% CI (inner error bars)

consistency across different publications (as this is almost certainly the most popular choice). Whatever you choose to plot, it is vital to label the plot clearly (e.g., axes, figure title and legend, if required). Being unable to tell whether standard errors, confidence intervals or some other quantity has been plotted is extremely frustrating.

Plotting data in an informative and visually appealing way is part art and part science. Appropriate choices depend on the background and expertise of your audience, the message you want to convey and – at least partly – on aesthetics. A good starting point for understanding how best to plot your data is Cleveland (1985).

3.7 R code for Chapter 3

3.7.1 Normal CI with known variance (Example 3.1)

Many statistical procedures in R calculate CIs from raw data. Calculating a CI from summary statistics is also possible using arithmetic and distribution functions. Example 3.1 is for a normal CI assuming known variance. The following code assigns the known *SD*, sample mean, sample n and required confidence to vectors and then computes α, the estimated *SE*, margin of error, lower and upper bound.

```
m.hat <- 94.6
sigma <- 15
n <- 50
conf <- 95

alpha <- (100-conf)/100
se.hat <- sigma/n^0.5
moe <- se.hat * qnorm(1-alpha/2)
lower <- m.hat - moe
upper <- m.hat + moe
```

To print the interval just type `lower` and `upper` separately or enter:

```
c(lower, upper)
```

It is not necessary to set everything out in this laborious way (although the step-by-step approach is clearer if you are unfamiliar with R). In addition, because the input is by assignment to vectors, the calculation can be updated by changing the assigned values.

This basic structure can be adapted for most CIs that use a normal approximation. Only minor changes are required to adapt it for CIs using a *t* distribution.

3.7.2 CI for the mean of a single sample using *t* (Examples 3.2 and 3.3)

When the variance is unknown, the CI for a mean from a normal distribution uses the *t* distribution in place of *z* and the population *SD* (σ) is estimated from the sample. Adapting the previous example for the new estimate and the *t* distribution gives:

```
m.hat <- 94.6
sigma.hat <- 19.6
n <- 50
conf <- 95

alpha <- (100-conf)/100
se.hat <- sigma.hat/n^0.5
moe <- se.hat * qt(1-alpha/2,n-1)
lower <- m.hat - moe
upper <- m.hat + moe

c(lower, upper)
```

The interval is wider (mainly owing to `sigma.hat` being larger than `sigma`) and not the small difference between `qnorm(1-alpha/2)` and `qt(1-alpha/2,n-1)`.

The equivalent code without vector input (and merging the steps) is harder to read and edit, but more compact:

```
lower <- 94.6 - qt(.975, 49) * 19.6/50^0.5
upper <- 94.6 + qt(.975, 49) * 19.6/50^0.5
c(lower, upper)
```

Using vectors and separating steps out is recommended until you become more comfortable with R (and for code that you want to share or re-use).

The same procedure that works for a sample from an approximately normal distribution can be adapted for a non-normal distribution – as long as a suitable transformation is available. For the mouth and throat cancer survival data in Example 3.3 the data are positively skewed and the data approximately lognormal. Here the interval is constructed for the logarithm of the mean survival. The transformation e^X used to obtain lower and upper bounds in months. This time, α (the total excluded tail probability) is set directly rather than calculating it from the confidence.

```
mu.hat <- log(9.6)
sig.hat <- log(2.5)
n <- 338
alpha <- .05
se.hat <- sig.hat/n^0.5
moe <- qt(1 - alpha/2, n-1) * se.hat
ll <- mu.hat - moe
ul <- mu.hat + moe

exp(ll)
exp(ul)
```

3.7.3 Confidence intervals for discrete data (Examples 3.4 and 3.5)

The Wald CI – a normal approximation for a binomial CI – uses an estimate of the *SE* of a proportion and the mean (the sample proportion itself) to calculate a CI using the known variance approach. For 19 successes out of 25 trials the interval would be:

```
s <- 19
n <- 25
alpha <- .01

p.hat <- s/n
se.p <- ((p.hat*(1 - p.hat))/n)^0.5
moe <- qnorm(1 - alpha/2) * se.p
c(p.hat - moe, p.hat + moe)
```

The same code produces the interval for 24 successes out of 25 by changing the first line to:

```
s <- 24
```

The adjusted Wald CI simply edits the number of successes and n:

```
s <- 24 + 2
n <- 25 + 4
```

In practice there is no reason to use either of these approaches in R. The Wilson CI (with or without continuity correction) is available from the `prop.test()` function. The call

```
prop.test(19, 25)$conf.int
```

gives a 95% CI for 19 successes from 25 trials. To adjust the confidence level to 99% simply alter the `conf.level` argument from its default value (but note that it takes input as a probability not a percentage).

```
prop.test(19, 25, conf.level = .99)$conf.int
```

The default version includes a continuity correction, which can be over-ridden if necessary:

```
prop.test(19, 25, conf.level = .99, correct = FALSE)$conf.int
```

Exact CIs are also available. The Clopper-Pearson CI is given by `binom.test()`. The following code generates a 99% CI for 24 successes from 25 trials:

```
binom.test(24, 25, conf.level = .99)$conf.int
```

The Clopper-Pearson is a poor choice in practice and a far better exact alternative (and a good general choice) is a Blaker CI. This is available from the `exactci` package (Fay, 2010). If you have an active internet connection the following will install and load the package before computing the interval:

```
install.packages('exactci')
library(exactci)

binom.exact(19, 25, tsmethod='blaker', conf.level=.99)
```

The default CI for the `binom.exact()` function is the Clopper-Pearson interval, so it is important to specify the required method.

For count data a CI could be obtained using the Poisson distribution. Ulm's method produces a conservative 'exact' CI analogous to the Clopper-Pearson (using a link between the Poisson and χ^2 distribution). This code mimics the hand calculations in Example 3.5 (for the 95% CI of an observed count of seven events in a two-week period):

```
l.hat <- 7
alpha <- .05

ll <- qchisq(alpha/2, 2*l.hat)/2
ul <- qchisq(1-alpha/2, 2*(l.hat+1))/2

c(ll, ul)
```

To get the rate in a one-week period the interval can be rescaled by dividing the observed count and its upper and lower bounds by two:

```
c(ll, ul)/2
```

Alternatively `poisson.test()` – a function very similar to `binom.test()` – gives an exact CI equivalent to Ulm's method (though it uses the Poisson distribution directly). A useful feature is that the time period to rescale the interval can be set directly. To express the interval as events per week simply set the argument `T` to the number of weeks observed:

```
poisson.test(7, T = 2, conf.level = .95)$conf.int
```

The exactci package also provides Blaker intervals for the Poisson distribution. Once the package is installed and loaded, the Blaker CI for the weekly rate of events (if seven are observed in two weeks) is returned as part of the output from the call:

```
poisson.exact(7, T = 2, tsmethod='blaker')
```

The confidence level defaults to 95% unless explicitly altered (see the help file for this function by calling ?poisson.exact).

3.7.4 CI for a difference in independent means (Examples 3.6 and 3.7)

The following code loads the foreign package and uses it to read the comprehension task data into R from the SPSS file baguley_payne_2000.sav. It is then assigned to a list object named bp2000. foreign is part of the core R installation and contains functions for working with files from other software packages (e.g., SPSS). Lists are complex R objects that can contain other R objects (and the default is to import SPSS data files as lists). SPSS data files can also be imported as a data frame (an R object that is a bit like a bundle of vectors joined together as 'named' columns). For convenience the next two lines take the fourth object (the percentage accuracy data) and assign it to a new vector. The file needs to be in R working directory or you need to change the working directory to the one containing the file for this to work. If not, you will need to specify the full path in place of the file name.

```
library(foreign)
bp2000 <- read.spss('baguley_payne_2000.sav')
pc.acc <- bp2000[[4]]
```

Using a single set of square brackets unpacks an item from a list (e.g., [1] for the first item or [4] for the fourth item). Unfortunately, on this occasion the fourth item is itself a list (albeit with only one object within it). To get at the vector inside this list you need to use a second set of square brackets (e.g., [[4]] as above). List elements can also be identified by name. For the moment we will work with each sample separately and so we will extract the first 28 values and the last 28 values into separate vectors for the low and high study conditions respectively.

```
lsc <- pc.acc[1:28]
hsc <- pc.acc[29:56]
```

As raw data are now available it is possible to use the t.test() function in R to calculate a CI for each sample from raw data (rather than the summary statistics).

```
t.test(lsc, conf.level=.95)$conf.int
t.test(hsc, conf.level=.95)$conf.int
```

Again the default is conf.level= .95 and t.test(hsc)$conf.int also gives a 95% CI for the high study condition using the t distribution. The t.test() function can be called in many different ways. In fact, there is no need to assign the data to a vector – it can be used from within another object. Here are two equivalent examples:

```
t.test(bp2000$percent_accuracy[1:28])$conf.int
t.test(pc.acc[1:28])$conf.int
```

A CI for the difference between two independent means can also be calculated in R. The following code mimics the hand calculation for the difference between low and high study group means in Example 3.6. Code separated by a semi-colon is treated as if entered on separate lines:

```
m1 <- 87.2 ; m2 <- 74.1
sd1 <- 8.5 ; sd2 <- 24.0
n1 <- n2 <- 28
alpha <- .05

var.p <- ((n1-1)*sd1^2+(n2-1)*sd2^2)/(n1+n2-2)
sd.p <- var.p^.5
se.p <- sd.p*(1/n1+1/n2)^.5
moe <- qt(1-alpha/2,n1+n2-2) * se.p
ll <- m1-m2 - moe
ul <- m1-m2 + moe

c(ll, ul)
```

This calculation and that in Example 3.7 is rather tedious. A more reliable solution is to use the `t.test()` function. This assumes that a call including two vector names for two independent means is required:

```
t.test(hsc, lsc)$conf.int
```

This should return the Welch-Satterthwaite corrected version of the 95% CI. In general this interval is preferred to the uncorrected CI. An equal variances assumed version could also be obtained:

```
t.test(hsc, lsc, var.equal=TRUE)$conf.int
```

Using raw data produces almost identical results to the hand calculations (but without the rounding errors that occur when calculating by hand).

Working with data sets can sometimes be made easier by 'attaching' an R object (e.g., one imported from external file formats such as for Excel or SPSS). This is done with the `attach()` command. Provided the data set is imported as a list or a data frame, this instructs R to search within that object first when looking for named objects. For an unattached list or data frame, objects inside it need to be addressed using both the name of the container and the object inside (e.g., `bp2000$group` or `bp2000$percent_accuracy`). The following commands attach the list and then produce a CI using the original SPSS variable names:

```
attach(bp2000)
t.test(percent_accuracy[29:58], percent_accuracy[1:28])$conf.int
detach(bp2000)
```

Working with data frames is often easier than with lists. The following command imports the SPSS as a data frame and displays the contents on screen. The `attach()` and other functions work just as before:

```
bp2000 <- read.spss('baguley_payne_2000.sav', to.data.frame = TRUE)
attach(bp2000)
t.test(percent_accuracy[29:58], percent_accuracy[1:28])$conf.int
detach(bp2000)
```

A data frame structure is, in essence, a set of vectors or similar objects bundled together as named columns. To the see this structure enter:

```
bp2000
```

For a large data frame you may want to use `summary()` to get some descriptive statistics for each column or to use `head()` to see the first few rows of the data frame:

```
summary(bp2000)
head(bp2000)
```

Some people prefer not to attach lists or data frames because it can make the R workspace very 'untidy'. It may also have unintended consequences (e.g., if R matches an object name to something in an object you had forgotten was attached). If you do attach objects, try to detach them as soon as you have finished (and avoid having multiple data objects attached). Alternatives to using `attach()` are the `with()` or `within()` commands. These allow you to specify data or a 'place' to look for the data (e.g., a data frame or list):

```
with(bp2000, t.test(percent_accuracy[29:58],
  percent_accuracy[1:28])$conf.int)
```

3.7.5 CI for a difference in proportions

One of the many applications of a normal approximation is for the difference between two statistics (using the variance sum law to adjust the standard error). CIs for a difference in proportions constructed this way tend to be worse approximations than the usual Wald CI for a single proportion. A better option is to use bootstrap methods such as the BC_a approach or a continuity corrected version of the Wilson CI (see Newcombe, 1998b). The `prop.test()` function will produce a pretty accurate Wilson CI for the difference between two binomial proportions. It takes input as two vectors (one for successes and one for the number of trials). Thus the 95% CI for the difference between 19 and 24 successes out of 25 trials is:

```
s <- c(24, 19)
n <- c(25, 25)

prop.test(s, n)$conf.int
```

The uncorrected version is also available:

```
prop.test(s, n, correct = FALSE)$conf.int
```

3.7.6 Monte Carlo methods

Monte Carlo methods are relatively straightforward to set up in R because the distribution functions can simulate draws from a population with specified parameter values. R also has other functions to support sampling with or without replacement.

The following code implements the simulation of a 99% CI for a binomial proportion for 19 successes out of 25 trials using $B = 999$ simulated samples. The crucial step here is the use of `rbinom()` to create B samples from a distribution with n successes where $P = s/n$. As this function returns the number of successes it has to be turned into a proportion by dividing by the n trials. This is assigned to a vector x and the `quantile()` function used to obtain the values that exclude the required percentage in each tail.

```
s <- 19
n <- 25
alpha <- .01
B <- 999
P <- s/n
x <- rbinom(B, n, P)/(n)
mean(x)
quantile(x, c(alpha/2,1-alpha/2))
```

Changing s to 24 would give the simulated CI for $P = .96$ with 25 trials. The mean of the simulated proportions is useful because the difference `P - mean(x)` is a measure of bias. Here the bias should be negligible.

3.7.7 Setting up a percentile bootstrap (Example 3.8)

The `sample()` function allows you to take a random sample from a vector with or without replacement (the default is without replacement). This procedure is at the heart of any bootstrap calculation. A good place to start is to simulate a single bootstrap sample from the observed sample data. In Example 3.8 bootstrap samples are taken separately from vectors (`lsc` and `hsc`) containing the 28 data points (percentage accuracy) from the low and high study conditions of the comprehension task data set.

```
bl1 <- sample(lsc, 28, replace=TRUE)
bh1 <- sample(hsc, 28, replace=TRUE)
```

The second argument determines the size of the bootstrap samples (set equal to the size of the observed samples). Figure 3.5 compares histograms of the observed data and the bootstrap samples. This R code uses the `ylim` argument to fix the y-axis limits to facilitate comparisons.

```
par(mfrow=c(2,2), mar = c(4,4,3.5,2), pty='s')
hist(lsc, ylim = c(0,20), xlab = 'Percentage accuracy',
  main='(a) Low study condition: observed')
hist(hsc, ylim = c(0,20), xlab = 'Percentage accuracy',
  main='(b) High study condition: observed')
hist(bl1, ylim = c(0,20), xlab='Percentage accuracy', main='
  (c) Low study condition: bootstrap')
hist(bh1, ylim = c(0,20), xlab = 'Percentage accuracy',
  main='(d) High study condition: bootstrap')
```

The bootstrap samples generated earlier will differ somewhat from those plotted in Figure 3.5 (to be expected given a single random sample has been taken). Repeating the plot commands would give an idea of the variability present in the data.

Although taking the samples without replacement is crucial, the ability to work with thousands of bootstrap samples is essential for most applications. This can be done in R using the `replicate()` function. This is a way to repeatedly evaluate output from another function. Here the objective is to calculate the mean of a bootstrap sample (of $n = 28$) for `lsc` or `hsc`, repeat the process 9,999 times and then assign the output to a new vector.

```
set.seed(1234)
B <- 9999

mbl <- replicate(B, mean(sample(lsc,28,replace=TRUE)))
mbh <- replicate(B, mean(sample(hsc,28,replace=TRUE)))
```

To bootstrap a median or other statistic simply replace the `mean()` with the function you require. The `set.seed()` function serves no purpose except to allow you to replicate the bootstrap output in Example 3.8 (by fixing the value of the 'seed' used as input to the random number generator). The mean, *SD* and quantiles of the bootstrap distribution (containing 9,999 means in this case) are obtained in the usual way. The mean is the bootstrap point estimate of the statistic, the *SD* is its bootstrap standard error and the quantiles give the bounds of a percentile bootstrap CI for the individual samples. To obtain the bootstrap CI for the difference between independent samples, simply subtract the 9,999 bootstrap means for the one sample from those for the other.

```
mdiffs <- mbh - mbl
```

The *SD* of the vector of differences samples gives a bootstrap estimate of its standard error. The quantiles provide an estimate of the 95% CI.

```
sd(mdiffs)
quantile(mdiffs, c(.025,.975))
bias <- mean(mdiffs) - (mean(hsc)-mean(lsc))
bias
```

Here the mean is very close to the observed mean difference of 13.1 and so bias is negligible. To increase the number of bootstrap replications, replace *B* with a larger value. Depending on the available computing resource it would be wise to start with small values of B (e.g., 999). Larger values of B may take a while to run (or overload the processing power of your machine).

An important check is to plot the bootstrap samples (as done in Figure 3.6). A basic form of this plot (using default titles and labels) is obtained via the call:

```
hist(mdiffs)
```

3.7.8 Percentile and BC_a bootstrap methods in R (Example 3.9)

A more sophisticated approach is to use the R `boot` package. This supports four methods (including the percentile and the BC_a bootstrap). It operates by creating a bootstrap object via the `boot()` function. This object can then be used by the `boot.ci()` function (which generates intervals for the four different bootstrap methods).

The `boot` package is not particularly user-friendly (because it involves defining a function for the bootstrapped statistic). For a gentle introduction see Wright and Field (2009). To bootstrap a statistic for a single sample, the function you need to define is that for the statistic in question. Hence, to bootstrap a 95% CI of the median of the low study condition (`lsc`) you might do the following:

```
library(boot)
medboot <- boot(lsc, function(x,i) median(x[i]), R = 9999)
boot.ci(medboot, conf=.95)
```

As the default confidence level is 95%, the argument `conf=.95` can be omitted. The argument `R` sets the number of bootstrap replications. The function definition `function(x,i) median(x[i])` won't make much sense until you become familiar with creating your own functions, but `x` is the object the function applies to and `i` is an index of values within that object. For a more complex bootstrap calculation (such a difference in means) it might help to have data in a matrix or data frame format. Wright and Field (2009) give a data frame example, so we will use a matrix format (which is sometimes easier to work with). The first step is to rearrange the two samples into a matrix of two columns and 28 rows (i.e., dimension 28 by 2) by creating an empty matrix of this size and putting each sample into one of the two columns.

```
pm <- matrix(nrow=28, ncol=2)
pm[,1] <-lsc
pm[,2] <-hsc
```

In R the columns of a matrix or similar object are indexed second, so `pm[,1]` is the first column and `pm[1,]` would be the first row. The next step is to bootstrap a BC_a interval for the differences between the means of the low and high study conditions using the `pm` matrix:

```
bootdiffs <- boot(pm, function(x,i) mean(x[i,2])-mean(x[i,1]), R=9999)
boot.ci(bootdiffs, type='bca')
```

To obtain a percentile bootstrap use `type='percentile'`. To get a histogram of the bootstrap distribution, the simulated statistics need to be extracted from the bootstrap object (which is a form of list). They are contained in the second list object (which is named `t`). Thus, either of these calls will plot the bootstrap distribution:

```
hist(bootdiffs[[2]])
hist(bootdiffs$t)
```

3.7.9 Plotting CIs

A number of R packages provide functions to plot CIs. However, it is also possible to build up plots using functions in the base package. An advantage of this approach is that the same functions and parameters are useful in customizing plots from other packages (or creating novel plots).

First, consider a bar plot with error bars for a confidence interval like those in Figure 3.7. Prior to plotting it helps to set up vectors with the statistics and labels to be plotted. Assigning names to the means allows the `barplot()` function to adopt the names as bar labels automatically.

```
cmeans <- c(mean(lsc), mean(hsc))
names(cmeans) <-c('Low Study','High Study')
n <- c(28,28)
csd <- c(sd(lsc), sd(hsc))
se <- csd/sqrt(n)
cl <- cmeans + qt(.025, n[2]-1) * se
cu <- cmeans + qt(.975, n[1]-1) * se
```

The plot in panel (a) of Figure 3.7 can now be reproduced, using `segments()` to draw line segments between *x*-*y* coordinate pairs for the error bars and the little tick marks that usually accompany them. Bar heights are defined by the vector of means and various parameters of the plot (e.g., spacing, color and density of bar shading) can be controlled.

```
cbars <- barplot(height=cmeans, beside=TRUE, ylab='Mean
  percentage accuracy', ylim = c(0,100), xlim = c(0,4),
  space=0.7, density=c(50,90), col=c('light gray', 'dark
  gray'), cex.main=.925)

segments(x0 = cbars, x1 = cbars, y0=cl, y1=cu)
segments(x0 = cbars-.05, x1 = cbars +.05, y0=cl, y1=cl)
segments(x0 = cbars-.05, x1 = cbars +.05, y0=cu, y1=cu)
segments(x0 = 0, x1=max(cbars)+1, y0=0, y1=0, lty=1, lwd = 2)
```

The last line segment draws the *x*-axis. To generate panel (b) the limits are changed, the default *x*-axis dropped and a customized *x*-axis drawn at $y = 50$.

```
cbars <- barplot(height = cmeans, beside = T, ylab='Mean
  percentage accuracy', ylim = c(50,100), xlim = c(0,4),
  space=0.7, density=c(50,90), col=c('light gray', 'dark
  gray'), cex.main=.925, xaxt='n', xpd=FALSE)
```

```
segments(x0 = cbars, x1 = cbars, y0=cl, y1=cu)
segments(x0 = cbars-.05, x1 = cbars +.05, y0=cl, y1=cl)
segments(x0 = cbars-.05, x1 = cbars +.05, y0=cu, y1=cu)
segments(x0 = 00, x1 = max(cbars)+1, y0=50, y1=50, lty = 1, lwd = 2)
axis(1, at = cbars, labels=names(cmeans), tick = FALSE)
```

Bar plots are widely used to display CIs, but dot plots are increasingly the preferred choice (having less visual clutter). A dot plot version of the previous figure is shown in Figure 3.8a and produced using the default `plot()` function in R. A useful trick is to specify a blank plot and customize it by using the `points()` function to add the data points. The vector `index` contains the x coordinates of the points to be plotted (i.e., the numbers 1 and 2).

```
index <- 1:2
plot(0,0, ylim=c(50,100), xaxt='n', xlim = c(0.5,2.5),
  ylab='Percentage accuracy', xlab=NA)
points(cmeans, pch = 19)
segments(index, cl, index, cu, lwd=1.5)
axis(1, at=1:2, labels=names(cmeans))
abline(h=50, lty=2, lwd=0.5)
```

Once the basic plot is complete, it is easy to customize. You may want to add horizontal lines at the end of the error bars (though they are customary, they are unnecessary and dropping them reduces visual clutter). Figure 3.8b uses two-tiered error bars to depict a 95% CI for the individual means and an approximate 95% CI for the difference in the means. The outer and inner limits of the two-tiered error bars are:

```
ol <- cl
ou <- cu

il <- cmeans + qt(.025, n[2]-1) * se * sqrt(2)/2
iu <- cmeans + qt(.975, n[2]-1) * se * sqrt(2)/2
```

Note that the calculation for the inner limits uses equation 3.31 and is thus difference-adjusted. Plotting is now just a matter of tweaking the locations of the line segments:

```
plot(0,0, ylim=c(50,100), xaxt = 'n', xlim = c(0.5,2.5),
  xlab='(b)', ylab='Percentage accuracy')
points(cmeans, pch = 19)
segments(index, ol, index, ou, lwd=1.5)
segments(index-.02, il, index+.02, il, lwd=1.5)
segments(index-.02, iu, index+.02, iu, lwd=1.5)
axis(1, at=1:2, labels=names(cmeans))
abline(h=50, lty=2, lwd=.5)
```

The final shape of the plot can be altered by resizing the graphics window before printing, saving or exporting it.

There are many other ways to get a similar plot. One of the easiest is to use the `gplots` package. This produces an acceptable plot with very little prompting (and uses a formula approach common to R packages). This requires the quantity plotted and the group or sample identifier to be separated out. The first step here just creates group identifiers for the 56 points:

```
group <- c(rep('1: low study', 28), rep('2: high study', 28))
```

Then instal and load the package (if you haven't already):

```
install.packages('gplots')
library(gplots)
```

The plot (with adjusted limits for *Y*) is obtained from:

```
plotmeans(pc.acc ~ group, connect=FALSE, ylim=c(50,100))
```

Remember that `pc.acc` is the original vector of data containing the percentage accuracy scores from all 56 participants. The argument `connect=FALSE` tells the function not to connect the points with lines. This function makes producing a plot very straightforward (though it only works if raw data are available).

3.7.10 R packages

Canty, A., and Ripley, B. D. (2010) *boot*: Bootstrap R (S-Plus) Functions. R package version 1.2–42.
Fay, M. P. (2010) Two-sided Exact Tests and Matching Confidence Intervals for Discrete Data. *The R Journal*, 2, 53–8.
R-core members, DebRoy, S., Bivand, R., *et al.* (2011) *foreign*: Read Data Stored by Minitab, S, SAS, SPSS, Stata, Systat, dBase. R package version 0.8–42.
Warnes, G. R. *et al.* (2010) *gplots*: Various R Programming Tools for Plotting Data. R package version 2.8.0.

3.8 Notes on SPSS syntax for Chapter 3

3.8.1 Confidence intervals

Many commands in SPSS provide CIs automatically or as options for output. For instance the Welch-Satterthwaite CI is provided automatically for any *t* test with independent samples. Descriptive statistics and graphing commands also have options to report or plot CIs. The default intervals are for the arithmetic mean and based on the *t* distribution. If only the interval (and no plot) is required the `EXAMINE` command can be used. For a simple CI of percentage accuracy for the comprehension data this syntax is appropriate:

SPSS data file: `baguley_and_payne.sav`

```
EXAMINE VARIABLES=percent_accuracy
  /PLOT NONE
  /STATISTICS DESCRIPTIVES
  /CINTERVAL 95.
```

This returns the CI as part of the usual table of descriptive statistics. The plot option would return a stem-and-leaf plot or histogram. The default confidence for pasted syntax is a 95% CI, but this can be altered by editing the /CINTERVAL subcommand.

The preceding syntax gives a CI for the mean of the percentage accuracy scores, but in this case separate CIs for the two groups are desirable. This can also be achieved using EXAMINE.

```
EXAMINE VARIABLES=percent_accuracy BY group
  /PLOT NONE
  /STATISTICS DESCRIPTIVES
  /CINTERVAL 95.
```

SPSS also produces dot plots with error bars. For a single sample mean the syntax is:

```
GRAPH
  /ERRORBAR(CI 95)=percent_accuracy.
```

For separate 95% CIs by group the syntax follows the same pattern as above:

```
GRAPH
  /ERRORBAR(CI 95)=percent_accuracy BY group.
```

A more flexible approach is to use the SPSS chart builder. This has a 'drag and drop' interface and, provided variables are appropriately coded (in variable view) as nominal, ordinal or scale (corresponding to categorical, ordinal and interval variables), will readily produce an acceptable plot. Using chart builder to select an error bar plot, dragging the percentage accuracy variable to the y-axis and the group to the x-axis produces the following syntax:

```
* Chart Builder.
GGRAPH
  /GRAPHDATASET NAME='graphdataset' VARIABLES=group
MEANCI(percent_accuracy,
    95)[name='percent_accuracy' LOW='percent_accuracy_LOW'
HIGH='percent_accuracy_HIGH']
    MISSING=LISTWISE REPORTMISSING=NO
  /GRAPHSPEC SOURCE=INLINE.
BEGIN GPL
  SOURCE: s=userSource(id('graphdataset'))
  DATA: group=col(source(s), name('group'), unit.category())
  DATA: MEAN_percent_accuracy=col(source(s),
name('percent_accuracy'))
  DATA: LOW=col(source(s), name('percent_accuracy_LOW'))
  DATA: HIGH=col(source(s), name('percent_accuracy_HIGH'))
  GUIDE: axis(dim(1), label('group'))
  GUIDE: axis(dim(2), label('Mean percent_accuracy'))
  GUIDE: text.footnote(label('Error Bars: 95% CI'))
  SCALE: cat(dim(1), include('0.00', '1.00'))
```

```
  SCALE: linear(dim(2), include(0))
  ELEMENT: point(position(group*MEAN_percent_accuracy))
  ELEMENT:
interval(position(region.spread.range(group*(LOW+HIGH))),
shape.interior(shape.ibeam))
END GPL.
```

This uses the SPSS graphical programming language (GPL). Many SPSS users – even experienced ones – don't program the GPL directly. Most users elect to paste the GPL syntax from an appropriate menu. The pasted syntax can then be edited within SPSS (or in an external text editor).

As of version 18 it appears that CIs for a binomial proportion or Poisson count are not implemented in SPSS (see Newcombe, 1998a), though there are ways to obtain normal approximations from some of the regression commands. SPSS users have, however, written macros for some common interval estimates – notably the Wilson CI for a binomial proportion (and these are available free online). In addition, the SPSS bootstrapping add-on can be used to bootstrap CIs where other methods are unavailable (e.g., the documentation gives examples of how to bootstrap a CI for a proportion or for a median).

3.9 Bibliography and further reading

Cumming, G., and Finch, S. (2005) Inference by Eye: Confidence Intervals, and How to Read Pictures of Data. *American Psychologist*, 60, 170–80.

DiCiccio, T. J. and Efron, B. (1996) Bootstrap Confidence Intervals. *Statistical Science*, 11, 189–228.

Loftus, G. R. (2001) Analysis, Interpretation, and Visual Presentation of Experimental Data. In J. Wixted and H. Pashler (eds), *Stevens' Handbook of Experimental Psychology* (3rd edn), Vol. 4: Methodology in Experimental Psychology (pp. 339–90). New York: Wiley.

4
Significance tests

Contents

4.1 Chapter overview

This chapter introduces null hypothesis significance tests. The link between confidence intervals and null hypothesis significance tests is explained, and the standard rationale for significance testing is reviewed. Concepts central to significance testing: the interpretation of a significance probability (p), the role of the significance threshold (α), and distinction between one-sided and two-sided tests are explored. t tests (for hypotheses about means of normal samples with unknown variance) as well as exact and approximate tests for discrete data (e.g., binomial test and Pearson χ^2 tests) are introduced.

4.2 From confidence intervals to significance tests

A confidence interval (CI) provides an interval estimate of a parameter. This interval estimate supplements the point estimate provided by a statistic (e.g., a sample mean or median). An informal interpretation of a CI is that it provides a range of plausible values that a population parameter might take (Loftus, 2001; Cumming and Finch, 2005). Confidence intervals can also be used for formal inference about a parameter. Formal inference with a CI is a form of significance testing.

A formal *significance test* involves explicitly or implicitly setting up a hypothesis about the value of a population parameter (e.g., $\mu = 10$). If the CI for the estimate of that parameter (e.g., the CI for a sample mean) excludes the hypothesized population value then the hypothesis is rejected with C% confidence. Although this procedure is easy to accomplish with a CI, it is common to construct and perform significance tests without calculating a CI. Significance tests of this kind are the most common form of statistical inference in scientific work (though their widespread application is controversial). Interval estimation (e.g., via a CI) is widely regarded as superior to the application of significance tests alone (see Rozeboom, 1960; Gardner and Altman, 1986; Loftus, 2001; Cumming and Finch, 2005; Dienes, 2008).

Example 4.1 In Example 3.2 a CI was constructed for sleep loss data using the t distribution. The researcher was interested in whether lack of sleep did or did not decrease IQ. As IQ tests are constructed to have a mean of 100 in the population, a reasonable hypothesis is that $\mu = 100$. The estimate was reported as $M = 94.6$, 95% CI [89.0, 100.2]. This interval includes 100, so the hypothesis that $\mu = 100$ cannot be rejected at the 95% confidence level. Formal interpretation of a CI that fails to exclude a hypothesized parameter value is awkward. While the hypothesis that $\mu = 100$ has not been rejected by the test, it would be incorrect to infer that μ equals 100. This is one reason to prefer an informal interpretation. The value 100 is one of a range of plausible values for the mean IQ of people with disrupted sleep (based only on the information in this sample). Other values are also plausible, with values close to the mean of 94.6 being more likely than values near the limits.

This application of a CI based on the t distribution is equivalent to a formal significance test known as the *one sample t* test. As a rule, any CI will have a corresponding significance test associated with it (but not *vice versa*).

4.3 Null hypothesis significance tests

Point and interval estimates of parameters are useful tools for understanding data, but often play a limited role in scientific research. At the heart of empirical research is the idea of testing theories. A good theory will make predictions that can be tested and the *null hypothesis significance test* (NHST) is the most prevalent statistical tool for testing such predictions.[1] NHSTs are controversial – not least because standard application of NHSTs is a hybrid of two different (and not necessarily compatible) theoretical positions. These positions stem from the fundamental work of R. A. Fisher on the one hand, and Jerzy Neyman and Egon Pearson on the other (see Yates and Mather, 1963; Dienes, 2008). The focus in this chapter is on understanding NHSTs as widely practiced, leaving aside for the moment the debate surrounding them.

The first step in significance testing is to set up a hypothesis. This statistical hypothesis is derived from, but is different to, a *substantive hypothesis* that might follow from a particular theory. For example, an evolutionary psychologist might predict that adult males will lower the pitch of their voice in the presence of a potential mate (on the basis that lower voice pitch is a cue to fertility). This is a substantive hypothesis that follows from a particular theory, but is not a statistical hypothesis. The substantive hypothesis leads to the researcher collecting data (e.g., in the form of an experiment). Perhaps a researcher decides to record the pitch of a sample of males when viewing either a neutral image or an image of a potential mate. In this case, a statistical hypothesis might be that the mean voice pitch of participants is lower for the potential mate than for the neutral image. Assume that the mean difference in pitch between the samples is 5 hertz (and ignore the practical difficulty in measuring something as complex as voice pitch). The researcher wants to know whether this sample statistic corresponds to a true effect in the populations being sampled. The uncertainty inherent in sampling from a population makes it impossible to know this with certainty. A more modest goal is to determine the probability that the corresponding population parameter takes a particular value. This too turns out to be extremely difficult.

The approach adopted by NHSTs is to calculate the probability of an effect of a certain size or larger being observed if there were no true effect. This is done by testing a *null hypothesis* rather than the hypothesis of interest (the latter being termed the *alternative hypothesis*).[2] The null hypothesis is typically denoted as H_0 and the alternative hypothesis as H_1.

What is the advantage of setting up a null hypothesis: a hypothesis in which the size of an effect (e.g., a difference between means) is zero? In order to calculate the precise probability of a statistic being observed if the true parameter takes a particular value, you need to know the distribution it is sampled from. This distribution and its parameters are, by definition, unknown for almost any real research question. Settling on a particular value of the population parameter enables a probability to be calculated (even if it is not the probability you are really interested in). A further complication is that it is not that meaningful to calculate the probability of a particular value of a statistic. Indeed, if the data are continuous – rather than discrete – this probability is zero (see Chapter 2). An NHST therefore calculates the probability that an observed statistic *or one more extreme than it* would arise if the true population parameter took a particular value. The value of the population parameter chosen for the null hypothesis (H_0) is often, but not always, zero.

Returning to the earlier example, an NHST would calculate the probability of obtaining a difference in pitch of 5 or more hertz if the true population difference was zero hertz (i.e., H_0 is true). This probability is termed the *significance probability*, but is nearly always abbreviated to

p. Keep in mind that p is not the quantity that the researcher is really interested in. It is just a necessary step in the decision procedure defined by a significance test. According to the logic of significance testing, however, p is sufficient to support inferences about the true population parameter. If p is very small, the logic goes, it is reasonable to *reject the null hypothesis*. This is justified on the basis that the observed difference (or one larger) is unlikely to have arisen if H_0 is true. In contrast, if p is large the observed statistic (or one more extreme) could easily have arisen by chance, even if H_0 were true. The test now indicates a *failure to reject the null hypothesis*. These two potential outcomes – rejecting or failing to reject H_0 – form the basis of null hypothesis significance tests as a tool for making decisions about a hypothesis.

This logic is quite subtle, and it is worth reviewing the main points:

i) A null hypothesis (H_0) is set up
ii) The probability (p) of obtaining the observed statistic (or one more extreme) if H_0 is true is calculated
iii) If p is small, the outcome is to reject H_0, and if p is large the outcome is a failure to reject H_0

What do these outcomes mean in practice? Rejecting H_0 implies that the hypothesis that a parameter θ takes a particular value (e.g., $\theta = 0$) is considered false. By implication H_1, the alternative hypothesis that the parameter differs from this value (e.g., $\theta \neq 0$), is accepted and considered true. In contrast, a failure to reject H_0 does not allow the null hypothesis to be rejected.[3] The conventional interpretation of a failure to reject H_0 is that the test is inconclusive. It is not possible, on the basis of the data at hand, either to accept or to reject H_0. Both $\theta = 0$ and $\theta \neq 0$ remain plausible.

This treatment of H_0 and H_1 may seem unbalanced. It occurs because it is usually unreasonable to decide that the true population parameter takes some exact value every time the observed p value is large. Obtaining a difference of 5 hertz with low significance probability (e.g., $p = .01$) allows you to reject the hypothesis that the population difference is 0 hertz. Had the same experiment produced a large significance probability (e.g., $p = .80$) you would not be able to conclude that the true difference was exactly zero. For instance, the observed data suggest that a true mean difference of 0.5 or 1 hertz are more plausible than zero (being closer to the 'best guess' of 5 hertz).

Despite its popularity, null hypothesis significance testing incorporates a number of very demanding features. One is the nature of the p value. The p value is calculated not in relation to the hypothesis of interest (the alternative or experimental hypothesis H_1), but for the null hypothesis H_0. Second, p is a *conditional probability*, a probability that only applies given some precondition (e.g., that H_0 is true). Conditional probabilities are known to be difficult for people to interpret (even more so than simple probabilities). This increases the difficulty of interpreting a significance test.

As well as being difficult to interpret, employing a p value presents an additional challenge. An essential feature of a significance test is determining whether p is sufficiently small to reject H_0. How small does p have to be to do this?

4.3.1 Statistical significance, confidence and α

One solution to the problem of determining whether p is sufficiently small to reject H_0 is to allow each researcher to set their own decision criterion or threshold. The principal objection to selecting the criterion in this way is that is difficult to set thresholds in an unbiased, objective way. A p value of .12 might be taken as support for the alternative hypothesis in one study (e.g., support for the researcher's own theory), but be insufficient to reject H_0 in another (e.g., if it goes against the researcher's theory).

For this reason formal inference with NHSTs requires that you fix the criterion prior to collecting data. Deciding on the criterion for significance is equivalent to setting a confidence level for a confidence interval. The criterion is denoted as α and is related to a C% confidence interval by the formula $C = 100(1 - \alpha)$. This relationship is sufficiently well known that the terms 'confidence level' and 'significance level' are often used interchangeably in statistics.

In an ideal world a researcher would select an appropriate α level for each test, but in practice this rarely happens. One of the main reasons is that there is no realistic way to know that any researcher has fixed α at a particular value prior to collecting data. Even discounting deliberate deception (which, thankfully, is probably rare) it would be easy for researchers to 'misremember' the criterion that had been set or unconsciously shift to a more favorable criterion at a later time. Particular fields or subfields of research therefore tend to adopt either a common criterion or a range of alternative α levels for different situations.

Across many disparate areas of research the criterion of $\alpha = .05$ has emerged as standard (with both $\alpha = .01$ or $\alpha = .10$ also common). The origins of $\alpha = .05$ as a threshold for statistical significance can be traced to remarks by Fisher (1925) in the early history of significance testing (though these were probably not intended to be so widely and rigidly applied).

In a typical application of significance testing, if the observed p value is less than $\alpha = .05$ statistical significance is declared. The use here of 'statistical' should be noted; significance is being used in a narrow, technical sense and should not be taken to imply any other kind of significance (e.g., in terms of the importance, meaningfulness or size of the observed outcome). A common interpretation of a statistically significant test is that it provides evidence of some effect (e.g., a difference or association). This interpretation is controversial and difficult to justify. A safer way to interpret the outcome involves acknowledging the role of an NHST as a tool for deciding between two hypotheses. In this spirit, Wright (2003; see also Dienes, 2008) has suggested that statistical significance implies that an effect has been 'detected'. This term seems to evade some of the difficulties of interpreting p as a conditional probability, without implying either importance or evidential strength. Likewise, if an effect is declared statistically non-significant, terms such as insignificant (that implies unimportance) are best avoided. A more neutral phrase such as 'failed to detect an effect' seems preferable.

The selection of α as a decision criterion has an important implication. If H_0 is true and an accurate p value calculated, then the proportion of tests that reach statistical significance should, in the long run, equal α. This property of α – the expected long-term rate of statistical significance under H_0 – is known as the *Type I error* rate. A second kind of error – a *Type II error* – occurs when the null hypothesis is false but statistical significance is not obtained. The two error rates are linked: the Type II error rate decreases as α increases (but the rate of Type II errors also depends on other factors).

4.3.2 Calculating *p* for one-sided and two-sided tests

In order to construct a significance test, at least three components are required. The first is the null hypothesis (and by implication a corresponding alternative hypothesis). The second is the criterion for determining statistical significance: α. The third is a way of calculating p. Numerous ways of calculating or estimating p exist. When data are sampled from a well-known probability distribution an exact p value can be calculated. If the probability distribution is not known, it may be possible to estimate p.

The p value is defined as the probability of obtaining a statistic as extreme or more extreme than the one observed. It is therefore defined by the tail probability of a cumulative distribution function (*cdf*). Using the *cdf* ensures that the tail probability represents the proportion of statistics as extreme or more extreme than that observed. For a symmetrical distribution, such as the normal distribution, an observation can be extreme in either tail. For such distributions p is most often determined by summing probability of extreme values in the left and right tail of the distribution. This p value is termed a two-tailed or two-sided probability. The resulting procedure is a non-directional, two-sided test.

Under certain circumstances it may be reasonable to restrict the test to one tail (treating the probability of observing a statistic in the other tail as zero). This leads to a directional, one-sided test. For a two-sided test with a symmetrical test statistic, it is as if α is divided evenly between the tails of the distribution, whereas a one-sided test behaves as if the full value of α is assigned to one of the two tails.[4] For other distributions – such as χ^2 or F – extreme values are confined to a single tail. Although such a test is, by one definition, 'one-tailed', inference is inherently non-directional (because extreme observations in any direction lead to large values of a statistic such as χ^2 or F). Thus p values from distributions such as χ^2 or F correspond to inferences from two-sided non-directional tests with symmetrical distributions such as z or t (for those situations where both are applicable).

Even if the distribution is not known, many test statistics are constructed so that they follow a familiar distribution such as z, t, χ^2 or F to some degree of approximation. The central limit theorem (CLT) provides a justification for many of these approximations (see Key Concept 2.1). Monte Carlo methods such as the bootstrap can be also be used to obtain p values (either as a method of last resort or because the method is convenient).

Example 4.2 Armed only with the information that a statistic is approximately normal in distribution it is possible to estimate a p value. Vasquez *et al.* (2007, Table 3) report data from a large study (pooling data from many other researchers) about risk factors for diabetes. One such risk factor is body mass index (BMI). They report BMI measurements for European adults as: $M = 26.3\,kg/m^2$, $SD = 3.4\,kg/m^2$. Even this limited information is sufficient to construct a test statistic using a normal approximation.

A researcher samples 64 European adults who use a particular brand of game console. She wants to know whether their average BMI ($M = 27.0$) differs from that of the general population. An obvious null hypothesis is that the sample is from the general population with a mean BMI of around 26.3. This can be set out formally as:

$$H_0 : \mu = 26.3 \text{ and } H_1 : \mu \neq 26.3$$

On the assumption that $\sigma = 3.4$, the standard error of the mean $\sigma_{\hat{\mu}}$ is $\sigma/\sqrt{n} = 0.425$. A test statistic can now be formed for the difference between the population mean under the null hypothesis (μ_0) and the sample mean of 27.0. Provided the distribution of BMI is normal, the difference will also be normal and the ratio of the difference to the standard deviation of its sampling distribution ($\sigma_{\hat{\mu}}$) has a z distribution:

$$\frac{\hat{\mu} - \mu_0}{\sigma_{\hat{\mu}}} = z \qquad z \sim N(0,1)$$

A significance test constructed in this way is known as a *one sample z test.* This approximation is reasonable if σ is known (or is estimated with sufficient accuracy) and the distribution is at least approximately normal.

As the observed mean BMI is 27.0 kg/m^2, the observed test statistic is:

$$z = \frac{\hat{\mu} - \mu_0}{\sigma_{\hat{\mu}}} = \frac{27.0 - 26.3}{0.425} = 1.65$$

The p value for this test is the probability of getting a z statistic more extreme than 1.65. For a two-sided test this is the probability that z is less than −1.65 or greater than 1.65.

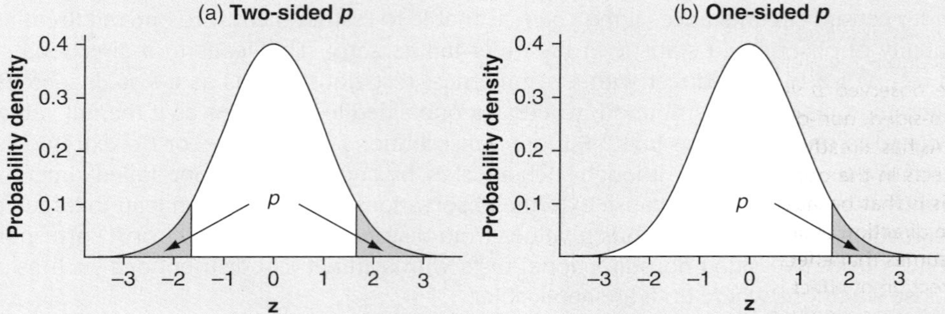

Figure 4.1 Areas representing (a) two-sided and (b) one-sided p values for a z test, with an observed test statistic of $z = 1.65$

The p value is the sum of the tail probabilities for absolute values of $z \geq 1.65$. Figure 4.1 plots the tail probabilities for an observed test statistic of $z = 1.65$ with panel (a) plotting the relevant tail probabilities for a two-sided test and panel (b) for a one-sided test. For a two-sided test statistic the left tail probability can be found from the standard normal *cdf* and is $\Phi(-1.65)$ or .049 (to 3 d.p.). The right tail probability is $1 - \Phi(1.65) = 1 - .951$, which, because the distribution is symmetrical is also .049. So the two-sided p value is approximately .098. Adopting the conventional criterion of $\alpha = .05$ this is not statistically significant (because $p > .05$). The test could be reported formally as $z = 1.65$, $n = 64$, $p > .05$.

The one-sided p value depends on the direction of the hypothesized difference. For the one-sided test the null hypothesis and alternative hypothesis are either:

$$H_0 : \mu \geq 26.3 \text{ and } H_1 : \mu < 26.3$$

Or

$$H_0 : \mu \leq 26.3 \text{ and } H_1 : \mu > 26.3$$

Figure 4.1b assumes the latter is correct and therefore that the sample is from a population with a mean BMI larger than 26.3. In this case the probability of observing $z \geq 1.65$ is the right tail probability of .049. As one-sided $p < .05$ this is statistically significant. The one-sided test, unlike the two-sided test, detects a difference between the mean of the sample and the general population. According to this test, the sample of game console owners appears to have a larger than average BMI.

Employing a one-sided, directional test is only rarely a good idea. Had the observed mean been 25.0, the observed statistic would be $z = -3.06$. This would be statistically significant with a two-sided test. However, with a one-sided test and the null hypothesis H_0: $\mu \geq 26.3$, the left tail probability is zero (see Figure 4.1b). The smaller p value of a one-tailed test comes at the cost of only looking for effects in one direction (and ignoring any effects observed in the other for which, in effect, $p = 1$). For this reason directional tests should be used with great caution (see Box 4.1).

Box 4.1 One-sided (directional) versus two-sided (non-directional) tests

The advantage of a directional test is that it tends to produce smaller p values than a non-directional test and is therefore more likely to detect an effect. For test statistics with a symmetrical distribution the observed p value for a one-sided, directional test will always be half that of the equivalent two-sided, non-directional test.* This superficially desirable property brings disadvantages.

As has already been noted, one disadvantage of looking for an effect in only one direction is that effects in the opposite direction are ignored (and can be considered to have $p = 1$). A corollary of this is that because the hypothesis is directional, the test itself does not support inferences about the direction of an effect. This may appear paradoxical, but follows from the calculation of p (which assumes that effects other than those in the hypothesized direction cannot or will not occur). If the direction of effect is in question, a two-sided, non-directional test is required.

Another disadvantage is that, like α, a one-sided test needs to be chosen in advance of looking at the outcome. This stipulation is difficult to enforce. It is very tempting to report a one-sided p value if the two-sided p value falls just beyond statistical significance (e.g., $p = .07$ when $\alpha = .05$). Routinely switching to one-sided tests in this way would mean that real α would be larger than the nominal, stated α level.

A final issue is that it is almost always preferable to report a CI in addition to or in place of a significance test. For a two-sided test this is generally straightforward (as this is the standard method for constructing any CI). While it is possible to construct a one-sided CI, the result is unsatisfactory, because it runs counter to the rationale for interval estimation (e.g., to provide a plausible range of values for the population parameter and to indicate the precision with which a parameter has been estimated). A possible compromise is to plot a $100(1-2\alpha)\%$ CI. This is a two-sided interval estimate equivalent to a one-sided significance test with criterion α in each direction.

A common misunderstanding of directional testing is to believe that it should be employed whenever a researcher predicts an effect in a particular direction. This is almost always bad practice. A one-sided test should be employed only if the direction of an effect is already known or if any outcome in the non-predicted direction would be ignored. The crucial question is not whether you think an effect lies in a particular direction, but whether you are willing to declare an effect in the wrong direction non-significant (no matter how interesting or how important it is). The answer to such a question is usually 'no' and for this reason one-sided tests should typically be avoided.

* One-sided p is always less than or equal to two-sided p for the same test statistic.

4.4 *t* tests

To construct a test statistic for a sample mean or a difference between sample means from a normal distribution the main options are to work with the z or t distribution. The z distribution assumes known variance, whereas the t distribution relaxes this assumption, producing more accurate results when n is small. As the z and t distribution are almost indistinguishable when n is large, there is no benefit in switching from t to z as the sample size increases and so t tests are often preferred. Several of the most common t tests are considered here.[5]

4.4.1 One sample *t*

The *one sample t test* is a null hypothesis significance test for a single sample constructed using $\hat{\sigma}$ (the sample estimate of σ). If H_0 is true the test statistic has the form:

$$t = \frac{\hat{\mu} - \mu_0}{\hat{\sigma}_{\hat{\mu}}} = \frac{\hat{\mu} - \mu_0}{\hat{\sigma}/\sqrt{n}} \quad \sim t(\nu) \qquad \text{Equation 4.1}$$

μ_0 is the population mean specified by H_0, while $\hat{\sigma}_{\hat{\mu}}$ is the standard error of the mean computed from $\hat{\sigma}$ (see Key Concept 3.1). The null and alternative hypotheses for a two-sided test are therefore H_0: $\mu = \mu_0$ and H_1: $\mu \neq \mu_0$. This test statistic is evaluated against a t distribution with $\nu = n - 1$ degrees of freedom (*df*). The one sample test is equivalent to formal inference with a CI around a mean calculated using the t distribution $C = 100(1\text{-}\alpha)\%$ confidence (see Example 4.1).

Example 4.3 For the sleep loss data the observed sample statistics ($M = 94.6$, $SD = 19.6$, $n = 50$) give a 95% CI of [89.0, 100.2]. Example 4.1 indicated that a test of the null hypothesis H_0: $\mu = 100$ is not statistically significant. As $C = 95\%$ this interval is equivalent to a one sample t test with $\alpha = (1 - C/100) = .05$ and two-tailed $p < .05$.

From Example 3.2, $\hat{\sigma}_{\hat{\mu}} = 19.6/\sqrt{50} \approx 2.77$ and therefore the observed test statistic is:

$$t = \frac{\hat{\mu} - \mu_0}{\hat{\sigma}_{\hat{\mu}}} = \frac{94.6 - 100}{2.77} \approx -1.95$$

This statistic has $n - 1 = 49$ *df*. One-sided p is therefore $Pr(t_{49} \leq -1.95) = 0.03$ and two-sided $p = .06$. A formal report of the test (in APA style) would go something like this:

> No significant difference was detected between the sample mean ($M = 94.6$, $SD = 19.6$) and average population IQ, $t(49) = 1.95$, $SE = 2.77$, $p = .06$.

It is quite common to drop the sign of the t statistic when it is reported. If you want to emphasize the direction of the effect (e.g., for similar tests with outcomes in different directions) you may want to retain the sign.

Although the two-sided test is the default choice, a one-sided test might be defensible. The justification here is that the researcher would be uninterested in (and probably willing to discount) an observed effect that suggested sleep disruption raised IQ. In any case, a better-designed study would incorporate a control condition (with no sleep disruption).

4.4.2 Independent *t*

The *independent t test* is the NHST of a difference between the means of two independent, normal samples with unknown, but equal σ. As with the equivalent CI, the equal variance assumption leads to the construction of a test statistic for the difference in means that uses a pooled variance estimate (see Key Concept 3.3). If the null hypothesis is true, the test statistic is:

$$\frac{\hat{\mu}_1 - \hat{\mu}_2 - \delta_0}{\hat{\sigma}_{\hat{\mu}_1 - \hat{\mu}_2}} = \frac{\hat{\mu}_1 - \hat{\mu}_2 - \delta_0}{\hat{\sigma}_{pooled}\sqrt{\frac{1}{n_1} + \frac{1}{n_2}}} \sim t(\nu) \qquad \text{Equation 4.2}$$

In this equation δ_0 is the hypothesized difference under H_0 and $\hat{\sigma}_{\hat{\mu}_1 - \hat{\mu}_2}$ is the pooled estimate of the standard error of the difference from Equation 3.26. This statistic has a t distribution with $\nu = n_1 + n_2 - 2$ df (or $N - 2$ df where N is the total sample size $n_1 + n_2$).

A two-sided independent t test of the hypothesis that the difference between population means is zero has the null hypothesis H_0: $\mu_1 = \mu_2$ and the alternative hypothesis H_1: $\mu_1 \neq \mu_2$ The hypotheses can also be expressed in terms of a difference between population means H_0: $\mu_1 - \mu_2 = 0$ and H_1: $\mu_1 - \mu_2 \neq 0$. For this null hypothesis $\delta_0 = 0$ and will drop out of the equation, which becomes:

$$\frac{\hat{\mu}_1 - \hat{\mu}_2}{\hat{\sigma}_{\hat{\mu}_1 - \hat{\mu}_2}} = \frac{\hat{\mu}_1 - \hat{\mu}_2}{\hat{\sigma}_{pooled}\sqrt{\frac{1}{n_1} + \frac{1}{n_2}}} \sim t(\nu) \qquad \text{Equation 4.3}$$

This is equivalent to a CI for the difference in independent samples using the same pooled estimate of $\hat{\sigma}_{\hat{\mu}_1 - \hat{\mu}_2}$. It therefore has similar limitations if the assumptions of independent, normal samples and equality of variance are not met. If the equal variances assumption is implausible, the Welch-Satterthwaite correction can be employed. The resulting test statistic is:

$$t' = \frac{\hat{\mu}_1 - \hat{\mu}_2}{\hat{\sigma}_{\hat{\mu}_1 - \hat{\mu}_2}} = \frac{\hat{\mu}_1 - \hat{\mu}_2}{\sqrt{\frac{\hat{\sigma}_1^2}{n_1} + \frac{\hat{\sigma}_2^2}{n_2}}} \sim t(\nu') \qquad \text{Equation 4.4}$$

This has an approximate t distribution with ν' df, where ν' is computed using Equation 3.29.

Example 4.4 Examples 3.6 and 3.7 produced 95% CIs for the comprehension data as [3.5, 22.8] if equal variances are assumed and [3.3, 22.9] using the Welch-Satterthwaite correction. The difference in sample means is 13.1% and $\hat{\sigma}_{\hat{\mu}_1 - \hat{\mu}_2} = 4.81$ for both tests. Thus both t and t' are equal to:

$$\frac{\hat{\mu}_1 - \hat{\mu}_2}{\hat{\sigma}_{\hat{\mu}_1 - \hat{\mu}_2}} = \frac{13.1}{4.81} \approx 2.72$$

The tests differ only in the *df* which are $56 - 2 = 54$ for the equal variance t test and $\nu' = 33.7$ for the corrected test. Using the *cdf* of the t distribution to calculate p values, the independent t test could be summarized as $t(54) = 2.72$, $SE = 4.81$, $p = .0088$, and the Welch-Satterthwaite t test could be reported as $t(33.7) = 2.72$, $SE = 4.81$, $p = .0100$.

With $\alpha = .05$ both tests comfortably reject the null hypothesis of zero difference (which they must, because both 95% CIs comfortably excluded zero as plausible value for the difference). Accordingly, a difference between high study ($M = 74.1\%$) and low study ($M = 87.2\%$) conditions has been detected. Increasing the amount of study seems to increase performance on the comprehension task.

Although a superior CI was obtained using a bootstrap method in Example 3.8 and Example 3.9, there is no reason to use bootstrap methods on this occasion (as both the percentile and BC_a 95% intervals also exclude zero). However, some non-normal distributions (e.g., those with very heavy tails) can cause problems for the Welch-Satterthwaite *t* test, and might make alternative tests such as the BC_a bootstrap more attractive.

4.4.3 Paired *t*

Thus far only tests for a single mean or for the difference between two independent means have been considered. Independence can be violated in various ways, but the most common is when two or more measurements are correlated. Dealing with such data is difficult, but for paired data it is possible to evade these difficulties by working with the differences between paired observations (see Box 4.2). These differences are treated as a single sample of size n for which the mean and standard deviation of differences $\hat{\mu}_D$ and $\hat{\sigma}_D$ can be computed. These in turn are used to create a test statistic by adapting Equation 4.1. The paired *t* test is therefore just a special case of the one sample *t* test.

Box 4.2 Correlated measures, repeated measures and paired data

In a study with an *independent measures* design, data are collected such that having information about one observation provides no additional information about any of the other data points (e.g., one data point per person, with people randomly assigned to different groups). One consequence of this is that the observations are not correlated with each other. Many statistical procedures treat observations as independent in this way (though it is unlikely to be strictly true except in a controlled experiment).

It is also possible to design an experiment with *repeated measures*. In a repeated measures design each unit (e.g., each person in a study with human participants) is sampled more than once. The samples therefore contain measurements that are correlated – by virtue of being taken from the same unit. Correlations among observations can occur in other ways, perhaps because the data are naturally correlated, perhaps by accident or by deliberate matching of units (thus ensuring that they are correlated). The latter is known as a *matched design* and is useful in controlling for a confounding variable if experimental control is not feasible (e.g., the socioeconomic status or age of children in educational research).

Working with correlated data is more difficult than working with independent samples because the standard errors used to construct significance tests and CIs depend not just on population variances but also on covariances (and hence correlations) between measurements. For independent samples the covariance between samples is exactly zero and can be ignored – a good example is the variance sum law which reduces to a simple form when samples are uncorrelated (see Key Concept 3.2).

How to deal with correlated data in general – such as from a matched or repeated measures design – will be considered in more detail in Chapters 16 and 18. This section focuses on the special case of paired data. With paired measurements, the data are structured so that a correlation exists between corresponding observations from two different samples. This could happen if each sampling unit is measured twice or through matching (e.g., each person in a treatment group is matched with a similar person in a control group).

One way to deal with correlated data is to treat the correlation as a 'nuisance parameter' and get rid of it in some way. For paired data there is a very simple way to do this. This involves setting aside the raw data and working with the differences between pairs. This works because the correlation between paired observations has the same influence on both members of a pair (e.g., tending to make them larger or smaller by the same amount). Subtracting one observation from the other will – on average – remove the within-unit correlation between observations and hence do away with the nuisance parameter.

Working with the differences between pairs has other advantages. First it greatly simplifies the calculations (because where there were two samples there is now just a single sample). Second, because paired samples are usually positively correlated, the standard error of the difference is usually smaller than it would be for two uncorrelated samples. This is not always the case. Where samples are negatively correlated, the variance and hence standard error of the differences will be larger than for uncorrelated samples (see Key Concept 3.2).

A number of statistical tests use paired data in this way. The best known of these are probably the paired *t* test and the sign test. Other methods (e.g., bootstrapping) can also be implemented with paired data in the same way.

A typical null hypothesis for the paired *t* test is that the mean of the differences is equal to zero (and hence the means of the original samples are equal). Thus for a two-sided test H_0 is that $\mu_D = 0$ and H_1 is that $\mu_D \neq 0$ (where $\mu_D = (\mu_1 - \mu_2)$). As $t = (\hat{\mu} - \mu_{D_0})/\hat{\sigma}_{\mu_D}$ and it is usually the case that the expected mean under the null hypothesis (μ_{D_0}) is zero, the test statistic under H_0 can be expressed as

$$t = \frac{\hat{\mu}_D}{\hat{\sigma}_{\hat{\mu}_D}} = \frac{\hat{\mu}_D}{\hat{\sigma}_D/\sqrt{n}} \sim t(\nu) \qquad \text{Equation 4.5}$$

where n is the number of pairs and $\nu = n - 1$. The corresponding CI for the paired differences is:

$$\hat{\mu}_D \pm t_{\nu,1-\alpha/2} \times \hat{\sigma}_{\hat{\mu}_D} \qquad \text{Equation 4.6}$$

If the original pairs are positively correlated, the standard error of the paired differences will tend to be smaller than for independent, uncorrelated samples. It is not necessary to assume equality of variance or normality of the original samples. The differences are, however, assumed to be sampled from a normal distribution. This assumption should be checked (e.g., using graphical methods).

Example 4.5 Brennen *et al.* (1990, Experiment 1) compared the effectiveness of two difference cues in resolving tip-of-the-tongue (TOT) states. Subsequent examples will refer to this data set as the TOT data. Fifteen participants were asked a series of questions containing information about the identity of a famous person. If the participant entered a TOT state (in which someone knows a word but is unable to bring it to mind) either a picture of the famous person (a face cue) or a repetition of the question (a question cue) was provided. The hypothesis of interest was whether the face cue produced a larger number of correct answers than the question cue.

Table 4.1 shows data consistent with the summary statistics reported by Brennen *et al.* (the raw data being unavailable). The face cue mean is 0.6 and the question cue mean is 0.8, thus the observed difference in means is 0.6 − 0.8 = −0.2. The *SD* of the differences is 1.32 and so the paired *t* statistic is:

$$t = \frac{\hat{\mu}_D}{\hat{\sigma}_D/\sqrt{n}} = \frac{-0.2}{1.32/\sqrt{15}} = \frac{-0.2}{0.3408} \approx -0.59$$

Table 4.1 Correct responses by cue and the difference between cues for the TOT data

Participant	Face cue	Question cue	Difference
P1	2	0	2
P2	2	1	1
P3	1	0	1
P4	1	0	1
P5	1	0	1
P6	0	3	−3
P7	0	2	−2
P8	1	2	−1
P9	0	1	−1
P10	0	1	−1
P11	0	1	−1
P12	1	1	0
P13	0	0	0
P14	0	0	0
P15	0	0	0

This statistic has 15 − 1 = 14 *df* and two-sided *p* is .57. The test could therefore be reported as $t(14) = .59$, $SE = 0.34$, $p = .57$. This is not statistically significant at $\alpha = .05$ and indicates that no difference between the cues has been detected. The corresponding confidence interval is:

$$\hat{\mu}_D \pm t_{14,.975} \times \hat{\sigma}_{\hat{\mu}_D} = -0.2 \pm 2.145 \times 0.3408$$
$$\approx -0.2 \pm 0.73$$

The CI could therefore be reported as $M = -0.2$, 95% CI [−0.93, 0.53]. This CI includes zero (as it must, because the paired *t* test is non-significant), but is also quite wide. There is little indication that cues differ in effectiveness, but a range of differences (in either direction) remains plausible.

Another issue is that as these data are discrete, the differences themselves may not be well approximated by a normal distribution. Does this matter? In this case (because there is so little sign of an effect) probably not, but the sample is quite small and a test designed for discrete data might be safer.

4.5 Tests for discrete data

There are a number of approaches to constructing significance tests for discrete data. Tests typical of the two main approaches are introduced here. The first approach, one that typically works well for parameter estimates from a single sample, is to calculate a p value directly from the *pmf* or *cdf* of a discrete distribution. The second approach, one that tends to be used for more complex statistical problems, is to use a normal approximation to construct a test statistic that follows a continuous distribution. In this case the statistic is often asymptotically distributed as χ^2 (a distribution created by summing squared observations from the z distribution). The *binomial test* is a good example of the former, while the χ^2 goodness-of-fit test is a good example of the latter.

4.5.1 Binomial test

The binomial test uses the binomial distribution to determine the statistical significance of x or more successes from n trials, given a fixed probability of success specified by the null hypothesis. The test assumes that observations are independent and that the probability of success P is the same for all trials. The significance probability p can be calculated directly from the *pmf* or (more likely) the *cdf* of the binomial distribution. The binomial test is thus an example of an exact test – a test that depends on calculating an exact probability using a known probability distribution. The relationship between the number of successes (x) for a binomial distribution and a binomial proportion ensures that the binomial test is also a test of the binomial proportion x/n. In either case the null hypothesis specifies that the parameter P lies between 0 and 1, with H_0: $P = .5$ being typical (indicating that success and failure are equally likely or *equiprobable*).

The binomial *pmf* gives the probability of obtaining x successes from n trials with probability of success P. The p value is computed by adding the probability of x successes to the probability of all outcomes as extreme or more extreme. This allows a one-sided p value to be calculated directly from the *cdf* of the distribution. This distribution, obtained by summing over values of the binomial *pmf* is given by the equation:

$$F(x;n,P) = \sum_{i=0}^{\lfloor x \rfloor} \left[\binom{n}{i} P^i (1-P)^{n-i} \right] \qquad \text{Equation 4.7}$$

By convention, the *cdf* cumulates from the lower, left tail up to $\lfloor x \rfloor$ (which is the largest integer less than or equal to the observed value). As the total probability is 1, the right (upper) tail probability is given by $1 - F(x;n,P)$. Getting a probability directly from the distribution function avoids the need to derive a test statistic and provides an exact test for n independent binomial trials where P is fixed.

While this procedure is sufficient to define one-sided p, there is more than one way to define two-sided p for an exact test for discrete distributions. Only two of these will be considered here. The definition preferred for a significance test is to add the probability of the smaller observed tail to the smallest probability of the other tail that does not exceed it. Fay (2010) labels this the Blaker method (because it is the same definition used to construct a Blaker CI). One alternative – widely used for confidence intervals such as the Clopper-Pearson CI – is to double the probability of the smaller tail. This is known as the central method.

The choice of definition for two-sided p is important. If the methods used to calculate p and to construct a CI do not match, there will be frequent inconsistencies between the outcomes of the test and the outcomes of the CI. The Clopper-Pearson CI illustrates this. It frequently includes a parameter value that is rejected by a two-sided binomial test (using the usual Blaker method to define p). Using the same method for tests and CIs eliminates inconsistencies for the central method, and they become 'very rare' for the Blaker method (*ibid*.). As standard practice is to define two-sided p for an NHST using the Blaker method, this is an additional argument in favor of preferring the Blaker CI to the Clopper-Pearson CI.

The principles behind the binomial test can easily be generalized to compute exact p values for other discrete distributions. A case in point is the Poisson distribution, where matching tests and CIs can also be constructed using this approach (see *ibid*.).

Example 4.6 Assume that the prevalence of left-handedness in the population is 15% (this is at the upper extreme of actual estimates). A researcher is interested in whether left-handed people are more likely to enter some occupations than others. In a sample of ten engineers, four are left-handed, and she wishes to test the hypothesis that engineers are more likely to be left-handed than the general population. This can be done using a binomial test with H_0: $P = .15$. A two-sided test is appropriate because observing no left-handed engineers in a sample might also be regarded as interesting.

The probability of observing four or more left-handed engineers in a sample of $n = 10$ is a right tail cumulative probability (summing the probability of four through to ten engineers). The corresponding left-tail probability is three or fewer engineers and this is given by:

$$\sum_{i=0}^{|3|}\left[\left(\frac{10!}{i\,(10-i)\,!}\right).15^{i}\,(1-.15)^{10-i}\right] = .9500302$$

Subtracting this from one gives the probability of four or more engineers and the one-sided p value for the binomial test is $1 - .9500302 = .04997$.

The two-sided Blaker p value combines this with the smallest value from the opposite tail that does not exceed it. In this case the probability of zero or fewer left-handed engineers is .1968744. Thus all the left tail probabilities will exceed it and so the two-sided Blaker p value remains .04997. In effect, there are no outcomes in the opposite tail that are more extreme than the observed outcome and the probability of extreme outcomes in the other direction can be ignored.

The 95% Blaker CI for the proportion is [.150, .717] which just excludes .15 (though this is not obvious because of rounding). Thus a higher rate of left-handedness has been detected among these engineers than might be expected in the general population (even after adopting a conservative estimate of the prevalence of left-handedness).

4.5.2 Pearson χ^2 goodness-of-fit test

The *Pearson* χ^2 *goodness-of-fit test* aims to compare an observed frequency distribution against its expected probability of occurrence. Its full name derives from the use of a Pearson χ^2 statistic (a normal approximation for independent frequency or count data attributed to Karl Pearson).[6] For this statistic to apply, the observations must fall naturally into two or more categories and be independently sampled. For small samples an exact test based on a multinomial distribution could be used (or the binomial test when there are only two categories), but in large samples the χ^2 approximation is often excellent.

It is customary to set out the observed frequencies or counts in a table with r cells (one for each category that could be observed). The goodness-of-fit test proceeds by comparing the observed counts O_i to the expected counts E_i (where i is a subscript indicating which of the r

cells that the observations fall into). In its purest form the test applies to natural categories, but it is not unusual to create artificial categories for ordinal or continuous data (a process known as 'binning' that is often employed to create histograms). The expected values for each cell are determined by the null hypothesis of the test. The cell probabilities may be derived from theory, previous research or a known probability distribution (such as the normal). A typical hypothesis is one of equiprobability; that the observed frequencies or counts fall into categories at random. If there are r cells with a total observed count of n the expected cell counts under equiprobability are:

$$E_i = \frac{n}{r} \qquad \text{Equation 4.8}$$

The Pearson χ^2 statistic for the test is based on the residual (the observed minus expected count) for each cell:

$$\sum_{i=1}^{r} \frac{(O_i - E_i)^2}{E_i} \sim \chi^2_{r-1} \qquad \text{Equation 4.9}$$

Equation 4.9 divides the squared residuals for each cell by its expected value and sums the results for all r cells. Each of the r cells is made up of O_i independent binomial counts with $P_i = 1/r$ (assuming equiprobability). If n is large, the central limit theorem implies that the distribution of the residuals is approximately normal and the squared residuals divided by the expected value follow a z^2 distribution. Summing these values gives a χ^2_{r-1} rather than a χ^2_r distribution because the observed count in the last cell is not free to vary (being n minus the sum of observed values in the other cells).

The normal approximation to the binomial distribution is excellent for moderate to large sample sizes where P is close to .5. The goodness-of-fit test is therefore suspect for sparse tables where low n and P combine to give small expected values. A reasonable recommendation is that $E_i \geq 5$ for at least 80% of cells and that no cells have expected values of 0. One way of viewing this problem is in relation to the continuity of the test statistic for discrete data. The χ^2 and z distributions are continuous. They therefore sometimes approximate discrete distributions such as the binomial or multinomial very poorly.

A goodness-of-fit test differs slightly from a standard NHST in that the emphasis is on finding a satisfactory or good fit rather than on detecting an effect. A statistically significant outcome for the test indicates that a departure from the expected values (under H_0) – and hence a poor fit – has been detected. A non-significant test outcome indicates a failure to detect a poor fit. Thus the observed data are not inconsistent with the expected probability distribution. Both outcomes need to be interpreted with caution. Not detecting a poor fit is not strong evidence of a good fit. In addition, detecting a poor fit (particularly if n is large) does not imply that the departure from the expected values is of theoretical or practical importance. Although more sophisticated methods are available, a quick way to index the degree of departure from the expected values is to use the ratio χ^2_ν/ν. The mean (expected value) of a χ^2 distribution is ν (its *df*) and therefore the expected value of χ^2_ν/ν (sometimes called the *reduced* χ^2 statistic) equals 1 if the fit is perfect. Thus $\chi^2_\nu/\nu \approx 1$ suggests a good fit and values that exceed this suggest a progressively worse fit.[7]

Where there are departures from the expected frequencies, the residuals of the cells can be used to explore the contribution of each cell to the overall lack of fit. The raw residual $(O_i - E_i)$

gives some indication of what is going on. However, because cells with large expected values tend to have large residuals it is better to use the contribution of each cell to the χ^2 statistic itself: $(O_i - E_i)^2/E_i$. As each cell has an approximate χ^2_1 distribution, its square root has an approximate z distribution. This is the *standardized Pearson residual* of the cell:

$$\sqrt{\frac{\left(O_{ij} - E_{ij}\right)^2}{E_{ij}}} = \frac{O_{ij} - E_{ij}}{\sqrt{E_{ij}}} \sim z \qquad \text{Equation 4.10}$$

This provides a convenient scale for deviations from the expected frequencies (and could be used as an approximate test statistic for extreme cells).[8] A cell's contribution is strongly influenced by small expected values – partly explaining why sparse data are so problematic.

Example 4.7 With only $r = 2$ cells the goodness-of-fit test is a normal approximation to the binomial test. With $r > 2$ it is an approximation to a multinomial test. For the test to function properly it is important that the *contingency table* (the table of frequencies or counts for each possible outcome) includes counts for occurrence and non-occurrence of events. Thus observing three heads from ten independent coin tosses should be tabulated as:

H	*T*
3	7

For H_0: $P = .5$, the expected value for each cell is $10/2 = 5$. Observing three successes from ten trials thus produces a χ^2 statistic of

$$\sum_{i=1}^{r} \frac{(O_i - E_i)^2}{E_i} = \frac{(3-5)^2 + (7-5)^2}{5} = 1.6$$

with $r - 1 = 1$ *df*. The corresponding two-sided *p* value is .21, which can be compared to that of $p = .34$ obtained for the binomial test.

Extending the procedure to more than two cells ($r > 2$) is trivial. The main challenge is to determine the expected probability distribution for the cells (assuming equiprobability is inappropriate). This may follow from theory, from a known probability distribution or from prior data. To illustrate the latter, consider a professor interested in whether the proportions of degree classifications awarded to students in his or her department are similar to those awarded nationwide. According to the UK Higher Education Statistics Agency (HESA), the proportion of degree classes awarded in each category in England and Wales for full-time students graduating in 2009 was:

1st	2nd (upper division)	2nd (lower division)	3rd (or other)
.141	.494	.297	.068

The 3rd class category includes all lower classifications (e.g., non-honours degrees). The proportions can be used to generate the expected frequencies for each cell (under the null hypothesis that a sample is drawn randomly from this population). A hypothetical sample for the same year in the professor's department might have the following frequency distribution:

1st	2nd (upper division)	2nd (lower division)	3rd (or other)
12	56	43	8

As $n = (12 + 56 + 43 + 8) = 119$, the expected values for each cell are obtained by multiplying the population proportions by N to get:

1st	2nd (upper division)	2nd (lower division)	3rd (or other)
16.8	58.8	35.3	8.1

The test statistic is therefore:

$$\frac{(12-16.8)^2}{16.8} + \frac{(56-58.8)^2}{58.7} + \frac{(43-35.3)^2}{35.3} + \frac{(8-8.1)^2}{8.1}$$
$$= \frac{(-4.8)^2}{16.8} + \frac{(-2.8)^2}{58.7} + \frac{(7.7)^2}{35.3} + \frac{(-.01)^2}{8.1} \approx 3.2$$

This has $r - 1 = 3$ *df* and two-sided $p = .36$. This could be reported (in APA style) as: $\chi^2(3, N = 119) = 3.2$, $p = .36$. The test is not statistically significant and therefore a poor fit has not been detected – the data are not inconsistent with the national profile. The reduced χ^2 statistic is 1.05 and suggests a good fit to the random sample from the 2009 cohort of graduates. The largest standardized Pearson residual is 1.3 (for 2nd class (lower division)). This indicates that relatively more 'poor' classifications were awarded in the sample than nationally, but the observation is far from extreme (with around 80% of standardized residuals expected to be within ± 1.3 *z*).

4.5.3 Pearson χ^2 test of independence

The χ^2 *test of independence* is the single most widely used test involving the χ^2 distribution. It is a special case of the goodness-of-fit test applicable when dealing with independent counts arranged in a contingency table with two or more rows (r) and two or more columns (c). If each variable is dichotomous $r = 2$ and $c = 2$ and this produces a 2×2 table with $r \times c = 4$ cells set out as follows:

	A_1	A_2	
B_1	$O_{1,1}$	$O_{1,2}$	R_1
B_2	$O_{2,1}$	$O_{2,2}$	R_2
	C_1	C_2	n

The 2×2 table is the simplest form of χ^2 *test of independence* and by far the most common. In this arrangement, A_1 and A_2 are the possible outcomes of variable A while B_1 and B_2 the outcomes for variable B. Each $O_{r,c}$ cell contains the observed value for one of the four joint outcomes of A and B. The *marginal cells* contain the total observations in each column or row (e.g., $R_1 = O_{1,1} + O_{1,2}$). The sample size n can be calculated either by adding up the cell values, the row marginals or the column marginals:

$$n = \sum_{i=1,j=1}^{r,c} O_{i,j} = \sum_{i=1}^{r} R_i = \sum_{j=1}^{c} C_j \qquad \text{Equation 4.11}$$

If the observed outcomes of A and B are independent of each other, the outcome of A has no association with the outcome of B (or vice versa). If this condition holds, how would the observations be expected to fall into cells? When A_1 is independent of B then the observations in the column should fall into either B_1 or B_2 according to which is more numerous. For example, if B_1 is three times more common than B_2, the observations in A_1 will fall into B_1 three times more often on average than B_2. Calculating the expected values for a contingency table, assuming independence, thus requires each cell to be weighted by the prevalence of those outcomes. The prevalence can be estimated using the marginal totals; if A_1 is more common than A_2 this will be reflected in the relative size of the column totals. Putting this insight into equation form defines the expected values under independence as:

$$E_{i,j} = \frac{R_i}{n} \times \frac{C_j}{n} \times n = \frac{R_i C_j}{n} \qquad \text{Equation 4.12}$$

Equation 4.12 thus determines the probability of an observation falling into each cell under the null hypothesis of independence (the probability of it falling into a given row multiplied by the probability of it falling into a given column) and multiplies the result by n. This is a generic formula for a contingency table, but if the marginals (row and column totals) are equal it reduces to the familiar equiprobability model.[9] Thus in the trivial case that $R_1 = R_2 = C_1 = C_2$, the expected value in all cells is $n/4$.

The Pearson χ^2 statistic for the test is:

$$\sum_{i=1,j=1}^{r,c} \frac{\left(O_{ij} - E_{ij}\right)^2}{E_{ij}} \sim \chi^2_{(r-1)(c-1)} \qquad \text{Equation 4.13}$$

This is identical to Equation 4.9 except that: i) summation is over cells defined by both rows and columns of the table and ii) the *df* are computed differently. A 2×2 table has four cells but only $(2-1)(2-1) = 1$ *df* (whereas a goodness-of-fit test with four cells has three *df*). The reason for the change is that the test of independence uses information from the row and column totals to calculate the expected values (in addition to n). If the column and row totals are known then any single cell count can be use to determine the other three cell counts – so only one cell is free to vary (see Box 3.2).

Yates' continuity correction (Yates, 1934) is sometimes applied to Equation 4.9 in order to improve the approximation when n is small. It involves subtracting half a count from the absolute value of the residuals before squaring:

$$\sum_{i=1,j=1}^{r,c} \frac{\left(\left|O_{ij} - E_{ij}\right| - 1/2\right)^2}{E_{ij}} \qquad \text{Equation 4.14}$$

The correction is conservative. It therefore decreases p for the test (and this is sometimes offered as an argument against it). An argument for the correction is that it brings us into closer agreement with p values from exact tests (Fleiss, 1973). These tests tend, on average, to be conservative. Uncorrected tests are therefore preferred by some experts (e.g., Haviland, 1990). Delucchi (1993) summarizes the situation pithily by writing that 'the debate over the use of the Yates correction for continuity is unresolved'.

The popularity of the test of independence is down to several factors. First, it is relatively easy to calculate. The formulas given above apply for any $r \times c$ table. For a 2×2 table they can be further simplified after some minor relabeling:

	A_1	A_2	
B_1	a	b	$a+b$
B_2	c	d	$c+d$
	$a+c$	$b+d$	n

Using the new labels the test statistic is:

$$\chi_1^2 = \frac{n\,(ad-bc)^2}{(a+b)(c+d)(a+c)(b+d)} \qquad \text{Equation 4.15}$$

without continuity correction. With continuity correction the test is:

$$\chi_1^2 = \frac{n\,(|ad-bc|-1/2n)^2}{(a+b)(c+d)(a+c)(b+d)} \qquad \text{Equation 4.16}$$

As $\chi_1^2 = z^2$, the critical value of z required for $100(1-\alpha)\%$ confidence provides a critical value for a significance test of independence with the criterion α. For 95% confidence $z = 1.96$, so $1.96^2 = 3.84$ is the threshold for a two-sided significance test at $\alpha = .05$. If $p < \alpha$ the null hypothesis of independence can be rejected, implying that an association between the two variables has been detected.

Problems associated with the goodness-of-fit test also apply with the test of independence – notably violations of the assumption of independent observations and sparse data (leading to low expected counts). The two tests are also often misused in similar ways. Lack of independence between observations and failure to include non-occurrence of events are among the most serious and persistent abuses (Delucchi, 1993).

Example 4.8 The data in Example 4.7 are also provided in the form of raw (albeit rounded) counts and reported for subcategories such as gender. Subsequent examples will refer to this data set as the degree class data.

For 2009 the number of full-time students by degree class and gender was:

	1st	2nd (upper)	2nd (lower)	3rd	
Male	17,975	55,710	38,175	10,400	122,260
Female	21,370	81,590	44,485	8,465	155,910
	39,345	137,300	82,660	18,865	278,170

A test of the hypothesis that degree classification is independent of gender is of potential interest as it is a test of whether the proportions of degree classifications differ between male and female students. From Equation 4.12, the expected values for the test are:

	1st	2nd (upper)	2nd (lower)	3rd
Male	17,292.7	60,345.5	36,330.3	8,291.5
Female	22,052.3	76,954.5	46,329.7	10,573.5

The χ^2 contribution $(O_{ij} - E_{ij})^2/E_{ij}$ for each cell is:

	1st	2nd (upper)	2nd (lower)	3rd
Male	26.9	356.1	93.7	536.2
Female	21.1	279.2	73.4	420.5

Summing these contributions gives: $\chi^2(3, N = 278,170) = 1,807.1$, $p < .0001$. Because n is very large, reduced χ^2 is also very large (and almost useless as an indicator of model fit). Even very tiny discrepancies may reach statistical significance with a sample size of around 280,000.

How should these results be interpreted? In large tables deviations from expected values can be hard to interpret (as can the standardized residuals). Plotting the data (e.g., in the form of a bar or line plot) is recommended. Figure 4.2 plots the raw counts for each degree class by gender in panel (a) and the corresponding proportions in panel (b).

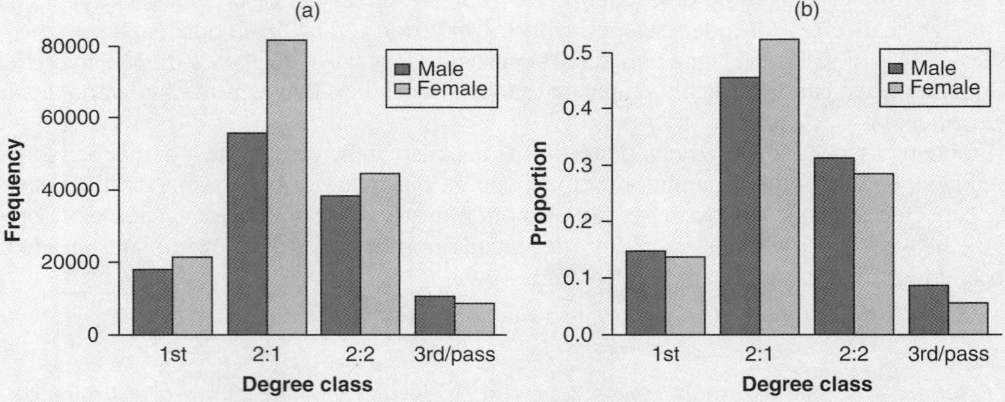

Figure 4.2 Degree class awarded by gender in 2009 to students in England and Wales (a) as a frequency and (b) as a proportion of total classifications

Panel (a) appears to indicate that female students have fewer degrees in the lowest classifications (3rd class and non-honours pass degrees), but more in the other categories. This is plot is misleading because the sample sizes for males and females differ. Plotting the proportion clarifies the pattern. Female students have proportionately more 2:1 (upper second class) degrees but fewer in all other categories.

One finding that stands out is that while more female students gain first class degrees, the proportion is lower than for male students. The question of whether female students gain proportionately fewer first class degrees is of some interest (e.g., Mellanby *et al.*, 2000). Further analysis to compare the proportions of first class degrees is possible. This illustrates a common strategy for exploring contingency table data: 'collapsing' large tables into smaller tables. In this case a focused test of the alternative hypothesis that female students gain fewer firsts than male students can be constructed by collapsing the degree classifications into a 2 × 2 table with first and non-first classifications by gender. An important feature of the construction of the table is that all observations from the original table are included. Just comparing the numbers of firsts without including their rates of non-occurrence would be a violation of the test (because the marginal totals are needed to account for the differences in the numbers of male and female students).

	1st	*Other*	
Male	17,975	104,285	122,260
Female	21,370	134,540	155,910
	39,345	238,825	278,170

The test statistic for this table is:

$$\chi_1^2 = \frac{n(ad-bc)^2}{(a+b)(c+d)(a+c)(b+d)} = \frac{278{,}170\,(17{,}975 \times 134{,}540 - 104{,}285 \times 21{,}370)^2}{122{,}360 \times 155{,}910 \times 39{,}345 \times 238{,}825} \approx 55.9$$

This is well in excess of the critical value of 3.84 (for $\alpha = .05$) and indicates that the null hypothesis of independence (i.e., that the proportion first class degrees does not depend on gender) has been rejected. Males gain 17,975/122,260 = .147 and females 21,370/155,910 = .137 of first class degrees. The difference is statistically significant, $\chi^2(1, N = 278{,}170) = 55.9$, $p < .0001$. At this stage it is sufficient to understand that a difference in the proportions has been detected. The interpretation of effects such as these is considered in more depth when measures of effect size are explored in Chapter 7. Neither of the above tests employed a continuity correction. For these sample sizes the choice is largely irrelevant.

4.5.4 Sign test

The sign test is a very simple test for paired data. The procedure for the sign test involves first calculating the difference between the n paired scores. Tied pairs produce a difference of 0 and are ignored. For the remaining n differences (ignoring the ties) the numbers of positive and negative signs are counted. Disregarding ties and only looking at the sign of the differences reduces the paired data to a simple dichotomous outcome: a positive difference or a negative difference. This can be modeled with the binomial distribution (e.g., treating pluses as successes and minuses as failures).

If there is no difference between the means of the two paired samples the sign of each difference would be determined entirely at random (with $P = .5$). Thus the two-sided null hypothesis for the test is H_0: $P = .5$, and the alternative hypothesis is H_1: $P \neq .5$. The *sign test* is therefore a form of binomial test performed on the signs of the differences between untied pairs and with H_0 set to $P = .5$ for a two-sided test. H_0 for a one-sided test, if warranted, is set to $P \leq .5$ or $P \geq .5$.

The test makes relatively few assumptions: that the differences (but not raw data) are independent and that the probability of a positive or negative sign does not vary across trials. The main drawback of the sign test is that it throws information away (in the form of the magnitude of the differences). This reduces its ability to detect effects (and more powerful tests are available). In addition, if an interval estimate for the difference (rather than the proportion of positive differences) is required, the sign test is inappropriate. Potential alternatives include a paired *t* test or a bootstrap test of differences in means, trimmed means or medians.

The sign test is easy to apply and is often used as a quick test in small samples for 'eyeballing' data (or when raw data are unavailable). For example, many researchers are aware that the one-sided probability of five successes in five trials is less than .05 (the exact value is $.5^5 = .03125$). So if five out five differences are in the predicted direction and $\alpha = .05$, the pattern is statistically significant by a one-sided test. Likewise, for a two-sided test, six successes from six trials implies $p = .03125$.

Example 4.9 The sign test is a possible alternative for the TOT data analyzed by paired *t* test in Example 4.5 (and was the test reported by Brennen *et al.*, 1990). Referring to Table 4.1 reveals that there are four ties and effective *n* is 11 (relative to the original 15 pairs). Of these, six are positive (favoring the question cue) and five are negative (favoring the face cue). A formal test is hardly warranted; no result can be less extreme than six successes or five failures and two-sided $p = 1$.

4.5.5 McNemar test for correlated proportions

The sign test can be calculated for paired observations that differ in terms of either a discrete or continuous measurement that is at least ordinal in scale. The *McNemar test correlated for proportions* (*McNemar test for change*) is a test for paired categorical (or nominal) data. Each of the paired samples (X) and (Y) must be dichotomous, taking one of two possible outcomes (usually coded 0 and 1). The test looks at the direction of differences or 'changes' in outcome for each pair (comparing the number of cases where $X = 0$ and $Y = 1$ with the number where $X = 1$ and $Y = 0$). Pairs that do not change are ignored.

It is usual to set out the data in the form of a 2 × 2 contingency table in which the rows and columns represent the possible outcomes for X and Y respectively and the cells a, b, c and d represent the number of pairs matching each combination of outcomes:

	$Y = 0$	$Y = 1$
$X = 0$	a	b
$X = 1$	c	d

The cells a and d are tied pairs and are ignored. The cells b and c represent outcomes that have changed. Setting out the data in this way produced data that can be analyzed with a sign test in which b can be considered the number of positive signs and c the number of negative signs. The effective number of pairs is then $n = b + c$. The McNemar test can therefore be considered a form of sign test and p can be calculated as for a binomial test with H_0: $P = .5$ (see Conover, 1980).

Although calculating an exact p value using the binomial distribution is an entirely logical approach, it is very common to use a normal approximation that produces a test statistic with an approximate χ^2 distribution:

$$\frac{(b-c)^2}{b+c} \sim \chi_1^2 \qquad \text{Equation 4.17}$$

As $\chi_1^2 = z^2$, this test statistic is inherently non-directional. The chief attraction of the normal approximation is ease of hand calculation when sample sizes are large. However, the binomial test is superior (especially if a one-sided test is required).

Edwards (1948) proposed a continuity correction for the test, which involves subtracting one from the absolute value of the numerator in Equation 4.17:

$$\frac{(|b-c|-1)^2}{b+c} \sim \chi_1^2 \qquad \text{Equation 4.18}$$

As with Yates' correction, the adjusted test statistic is lower and produces p values closer to those of the exact test than the uncorrected form does.

Example 4.10 Bertenthal and Fischer (1978) investigated self-recognition in $n = 48$ infants using the rouge task (a test of self-awareness). In this task a red spot is placed on an infant's nose. At a later stage the infant is placed in front a mirror and observed to see if they touch the mark. As part of the study the researchers carried out a crucial check; comparing behavior in the presence of the mirror with that during a five-minute familiarization phase (with no mirror present). The question of interest is whether presence (coded 1) or absence (coded 0) of nose touching differs between familiarization (F) and the rouge task (R). The table below, adapted from Bertenthal and Fischer (1978, Table 2), summarizes the pattern of data collected.*

	$R=0$	$R=1$
$F=0$	35	10
$F=1$	0	3

Of the $n = 10$ changes from familiarization to rouge task, all ten involve infants touching their nose in the rouge task but not during the familiarization period. For the sign test (a binomial test with $P = .5$), two-sided $p = .00195$. This is statistically significant, suggesting that it is the introduction of the mirror in the rouge task that leads children to touch their nose. The χ^2 approximation is $(10-0)^2/(10-0) = 10$ without continuity correction or $(|10-0|-1)^2/(10-0) = 8.1$ with continuity correction. The χ^2 statistic has 1 *df* and $p = .00157$ and $p = .00443$ respectively. The relatively large discrepancy between p values stems from the small effective n and the relatively extreme outcome. With larger samples the outcome for the continuity corrected test and the binomial test should be more similar.

* Data for the $n = 35$ infants failing the rouge task are not reported (cells a and c). The proportions falling into each cell are estimated from quantities that are reported.

4.6 Inference about other parameters

The majority of significance tests considered so far have been for means and differences between means (of which proportions are a special case). Options for testing hypotheses about other parameters follow the same pattern as for earlier tests. If an exact analytic solution is unavailable (being either unknown or not implemented in available software), a normal approximation is often employed. A normal approximation may be adequate, but it is often sensible to compare the results to that of a more robust approach (e.g., the bootstrap).

This section will illustrate the approach by comparing an analytic solution using the χ^2 distribution with a bootstrap hypothesis test for a variance. The same strategy could be generalized to tests for other parameters (e.g., medians or trimmed means).

4.6.1 Tests and confidence intervals for a variance

Sometimes researchers wish to test a hypothesis about a population variance or *SD*. In principle, this situation lends itself to hypothesis testing almost as readily as for other sample statistics. The two-sided null and alternative hypotheses can be stated as H_0: $\sigma^2 = \sigma_0^2$ and H_1: $\sigma^2 \neq \sigma_0^2$.

Directional hypotheses are also possible and (keeping in mind that a variance cannot fall below zero) it could be argued that hypotheses of the form H_0: $\sigma^2 = 0$ and H_1: $\sigma^2 \geq 0$ are particularly appropriate when testing for the presence of variation in a sample. Given that most samples contain uncertainty, this hypothesis is rarely of genuine interest. Far more likely is that a researcher would wish to construct a CI for a variance or to test a substantive hypothesis about σ^2 (in which case a two-sided interval or test may be appropriate).

Given that independent, normal sums of squares have the distribution $\sigma^2\chi^2_{n-1}$, a test statistic for H_0 can be obtained by dividing the sample sum of squares $(n-1)\hat{\sigma}^2$ by the expected value of the population variance under H_0. The resulting test statistic is:

$$\frac{(n-1)\hat{\sigma}^2}{\sigma_0^2} \sim \chi^2_{n-1} \qquad \text{Equation 4.19}$$

The same approach can be used to construct an asymmetric $100(1-\alpha)\%$ CI with lower and uppers bounds ($\hat{\sigma}_L^2$ and $\hat{\sigma}_U^2$) defined as:

$$\hat{\sigma}_L^2 = \frac{(n-1)\hat{\sigma}^2}{\chi^2_{n-1,1-\alpha/2}}$$

$$\hat{\sigma}_U^2 = \frac{(n-1)\hat{\sigma}^2}{\chi^2_{n-1,\alpha/2}} \qquad \text{Equation 4.20}$$

The NHST can also be considered a test of H_0: $\sigma = \sigma_0$ and the square root of these bounds provides an approximate interval estimate for σ.

Although this procedure is easy to implement there are at least two reasons to be cautious about it. First, the skew of the χ^2 distribution can be severe – particularly in small samples – and makes reliably estimating variances particularly awkward. Second, the procedure is more sensitive to departures from normality than tests and intervals for means (see Hays, 1973). The chi-square distribution can be considered a sampling distribution for the sum of independent squared z scores. While the CLT may be invoked for large samples, convergence toward the normal distribution is not rapid (especially if the populations sampled are not even approximately normal). Alternative methods such as bootstrapping are suitable if n is moderately large, but with small n satisfactory tests and CIs for variances are not feasible (in the absence of additional information).

Example 4.11 For the sleep loss data, $n = 50$ and the sample estimate of σ is 19.6. It may therefore be of interest to test the null hypothesis that $\sigma = 15$ (as expected for an IQ test of this type). The test statistic for H_0: $\sigma_0 = 15$ is therefore:

$$\chi^2_{49} = \frac{(n-1)\hat{\sigma}^2}{\sigma_0^2} = \frac{(50-1) \times 384.16}{15^2} \approx 83.7$$

The one-sided probability of obtaining a χ^2 as large or larger than this is around .0015 (2 d.p.). Owing to the asymmetry of the χ^2 distribution, transforming this statistic into a two-sided p value is not trivial, but a conservative approach is to use a central p value, doubling .0015 to give $p = .003$.

A more convenient approach in this case is to construct the two-sided CI for the variance. The bounds of a 95% CI are:

$$\hat{\sigma}^2_L = \frac{(n-1)\hat{\sigma}^2}{\chi^2_{n-1,1-\alpha/2}} = \frac{49 \times 384.16}{70.22241} \approx 268.1$$

$$\hat{\sigma}^2_U = \frac{(n-1)\hat{\sigma}^2}{\chi^2_{n-1,\alpha/2}} = \frac{49 \times 384.16}{31.55} \approx 596.5$$

Taking the square root of these limits gives an interval estimate that could be reported as $SD = 19.6$, 95% CI [16.4, 24.4]. Both the test and the CI allow H_0 to be rejected and indicate that a difference between the sample *SD* and expected population *SD* has been detected. The sample data appear to be more variable. The sample may therefore differ from the population, or sleep loss may increase the variability of the scores (or perhaps the test is out of date or badly designed).

The sample size of 50 is fairly large and so the interval estimate may be fairly accurate. One check is to use a BC_a bootstrap estimate. This requires raw data. As the example is fictional, a simulated sample of normal data with $n = 50$ and $SD = 19.6$ can be used to illustrate the procedure. Using the `boot` package in R for one simulated sample gives a BC_a 95% CI as [16.8, 23.2]. This interval is slightly narrower, but otherwise similar to the estimate above. This is not surprising. The simulated data are from an independent, normal distribution and the sample size is not too small. Under other conditions a bootstrap CI might produce a very different interval estimate.

4.7 Good practice in the application of significance testing

Significance testing is an ingenious solution to the hard problem of statistical inference. Although it is undoubtedly the most popular method of statistical inference, its use is controversial. One reason for its continued use is the lack of an agreed alternative (an argument considered further in Chapter 11). At this stage it is sufficient to realize that statistical significance is only one, relatively modest, component in the evaluation of quantitative data.

This point has been articulated by a number of experts, notably by Abelson (1995). Abelson's position is that statistics can be viewed as a form of principled argument. Statistical significance, in the form of a conventional NHST, is only one potential element of such an argument. Abelson lists five elements in total: magnitude, articulation, generality, interestingness and credibility (generating the acronym MAGIC). A significance test tells you how probable a particular statistic (or one more extreme) is if the data were generated by a random process, assuming H_0 is true. If this probability is low it may reduce the credibility or generality of a finding, but other factors influence its credibility and generality too.

Aside from not focusing narrowly on statistical significance, are there other things that will improve the practical application of significance testing? The consensus is that there are. Interval estimation is generally more informative than point estimation and therefore CIs should be preferred to NHSTs (which, in essence, focus on point estimates). CIs indicate the precision with which a statistic is measured and suggest a set of plausible values for the true parameter. The main drawback of making the switch to CIs is that it can be difficult to translate some tests into equivalent interval estimates that are both easy to interpret and easy to plot (e.g., tests with multiple degrees of freedom). These situations provide the strongest case for retaining NHSTs.

A final point is that NHSTs cannot, in isolation, indicate how important, large or useful an effect is. The p value has a very narrow interpretation as the conditional probability of a statistic that is as extreme (or more extreme) than that observed if H_0 is true. This conditional probability is not what most researchers are really interested in, yet it is easy to focus on p values and statistical significance at the expense of what really matters. Including appropriate descriptive statistics and graphs will also enhance communication of findings when NHSTs have been used. Descriptive statistics and graphical summaries of data are often sidelined (or perhaps missing entirely) when NHSTs are reported. Any method of statistical inference will be largely useless without also providing a transparent summary of the data. The summary data should also always include one or more measures of effect size (to communicate the magnitude of an effect).

4.8 R code for Chapter 4

4.8.1 Calculating *p* values from a *t* or *z* test statistic

For a test statistic with a symmetrical distribution (e.g., z, t or the binomial distribution when $P = .5$), calculating p involves using the *cdf* of the distribution to obtain one of the tail probabilities from the observed statistic. In Example 4.2 the statistic of $z = 1.65$ is positive and, because the lower tail is the default, the upper (right) tail probability is given by either of the following:

```
1 - pnorm(1.65)
pnorm(1.65, lower.tail=FALSE)
```

The same output is also obtained (under symmetry) from the lower tail probability for $z = -1.65$:

```
pnorm(-1.65)
```

The call returns .04947147, which is a one-sided p value. A two-sided p value is obtained by doubling this value:

```
2 * pnorm(-1.65)
2 * pnorm(1.65, lower.tail=FALSE)
```

This works in exactly the same way for the t distribution (except df are specified). For Example 4.3 the observed one sample t statistic with 49 df is -1.95. Thus one-sided p is given by `pt(-1.95, 49)` and two-sided p by `2 * pt(-1.95, 49)`. In Example 4.2 the observed t statistic is 2.72 with 54 df (or 33.7 if the Welch-Satterthwaite correction is used). Two-sided p values for the equal variance test can be obtained by any of the methods above:

```
2 * pt(-2.72, 54)
2 * pt(2.72, 54, lower.tail = FALSE)
```

The t distribution functions happily accept fractional df and can also be employed for the Welch-Satterthwaite correction:

```
2 * pt(-2.72, 33.7)
```

4.8.2 *t* tests from summary statistics (Examples 4.3 and 4.4)

The test statistic for a t test is a difference (e.g., between a sample mean and population mean or between two sample means) divided by the *SE* of the difference. Calculating a t test from summary statistics just requires the difference and the *SE*. Example 4.3 calculated t for a single sample of $n = 50$ with $\hat{\mu} = 94.6$ and $\hat{\sigma} = 19.6$. Example 3.2 gives the basic procedure for calculating the *SE* for a single normal sample with unknown variance.

```
m.hat <- 94.6
sigma.hat <- 19.6
n <- 50
se.hat <- sigma.hat/n^0.5
```

If the H_0 is that $\mu = 100$, then the t statistic is:

```
m.null <- 100
t.obs <- (m.hat-m.null)/se.hat
t.obs
```

The corresponding two-sided p value is:

```
2 * pt(t.obs, n-1)
```

One trick for getting the correct p value from a t or z statistic assigned to a vector (if you don't know the sign of t in advance) is to take the absolute value of t and reverse its sign:

```
2 * pt(-abs(t.obs), n-1)
```

For an independent *t* test the procedure is very similar. Example 3.6 computed the *SE* for the difference between independent samples as follows:

```
m1 <- 87.2 ; m2 <- 74.1
sd1 <- 24.0 ; sd2 <- 8.5
n1 <- n2 <- 28
var.p <- ((n1-1)*sd1^2+(n2-1)*sd2^2)/(n1+n2-2)
sd.p <- var.p^0.5
se.p <- sd.p*(1/n1+1/n2)^0.5
```

The *t* test statistic and two-sided *p* are therefore:

```
t.ind <- (m1-m2)/se.p
t.ind
2 * pt(-abs(t.ind), n1+n2-2)
```

The Welch-Satterthwaite correction can be computed in the same way by adjusting the *df* (and a function to compute ν' is introduced in Section 15.7.2).

4.8.3 *t* tests from raw data (Examples 4.3, 4.4 and 4.5)

The `t.test()` function has already been used to obtain CIs using the *t* distribution. The function is versatile and, if called by a single vector, will return a one sample *t* test. The 95% CI for the mean and two-sided *p* value are included by default. The following examples use the comprehension data, loaded into R as follows:

```
library(foreign)
bp2000 <- read.spss('baguley_payne_2000.sav')
pc.acc <- bp2000[[4]]
lsc <- pc.acc[1:28]
hsc <- pc.acc[29:56]
```

The one sample *t* tests for the low and high study conditions are given by:

```
t.test(lsc)
t.test(hsc)
```

In this case the *t* tests default to an uninteresting null hypothesis (H_0: $\mu = 0\%$). As the data are percentage accuracy in a two-alternative response task, H_0: $\mu = 50\%$ is a more interesting hypothesis (being the level of accuracy expected by random guessing). This requires an extra argument:

```
t.test(lsc, mu = 50)
t.test(hsc, mu = 50)
```

Calling the function with two vectors defaults to returning the Welch-Satterthwaite t test and a 95% CI for the difference in means:

```
t.test(lsc, hsc)
```

This returns almost exactly what was calculated in Example 4.4 (allowing for rounding error). As here, R will usually select sensible defaults for common analyses (as the Welch-Satterthwaite should usually be preferred to the equal variance test). To obtain the equal variance test again requires just a change in one argument:

```
t.test(lsc, hsc, var.equal=TRUE)
```

The same function works for paired data. A paired t test is returned for two vectors of equal length if the argument `paired=TRUE` is specified. Example 4.5 uses the TOT data. These data can be entered by hand or imported into R from an SPSS file. The `summary()` or `head()` function can be used to get a quick overview of the variables in the data frame (scores for the face and question cue conditions).

```
library(foreign)
bren.dat <- read.spss('brennen_et_al_1990.sav', to.data.frame = TRUE)
summary(bren.dat)
head(bren.dat)
```

Don't forget to change the working directory or move the file to the right place (otherwise you will need to give R the full path as well as the file name).

The paired t test and a 95% CI for the difference in conditions is given by:

```
t.test(bren.dat$face, bren.dat$question, paired=TRUE)
```

An alternative route, arguably much simpler, is to perform a one sample test of the differences (either from summary statistics as above) or using the `t.test()` function:

```
pdiffs <- bren.dat$face - bren.dat$question
t.test(pdiffs)
```

Using summary statistics, the test is simply:

```
n.paired <- length(pdiffs)
t.paired <- mean(pdiffs)/(sd(pdiffs)/sqrt(n.paired))
t.paired
p.obs <- 2 * pt(-abs(t.paired), n.paired-1)
p.obs
```

The `length()` function just counts the number of elements in an object – in this case the number of differences in the vector `pdiffs` (and hence supplies n).

Use the help function (e.g., `?t.test`) to find out more about the function (e.g., to work out how to get a one-sided p value using the `alternative` argument).

4.8.4 The binomial test (Example 4.6)

The binomial test obtains one-sided p values directly from the *pmf* or *cdf* of the binomial distribution. Example 4.6 requires a one-sided p value for four successes from a sample of ten when $P = .15$. Using the binomial *pmf* function this is the sum of the probabilities for four through to ten successes:

```
sum(dbinom(4:10, 10, .15))
```

Using the *cdf*, this is $1 - Pr(x \leq 3)$ and is given by either of these calls:

```
1 - pbinom(3, 10, .15)
pbinom(3, 10, .15, lower.tail = FALSE)
```

The one-tailed p value is also computed directly by the `binomial.test()` function. This gives an exact p value and the 95% Clopper-Pearson CI:

```
binom.test(4, 10, .15, alternative = 'greater')
```

For a two-sided test the procedure is problematic (because the CI and the p value are computed by different methods). Fay (2010) describes options for matching the calculations. The Blaker method from his `exactci` package is recommended.

```
install.packages('exactci')
library(exactci)
binom.exact(4, 10, .15, tsmethod='blaker')
```

It is also possible to calculate both p and CI using the minimum likelihood `'minlike'` or `'central'` methods (though the latter matches the Clopper-Pearson CI and can be very conservative).

The `prop.test()` function also gives p values for the Wilson CI with or without continuity correction. This is part of the R base installation. The main advantage of this function is that it provides one of the recommended options (see Newcombe, 1998b) for testing the difference between two proportions (here comparing the difference between 19 and 24 successes from 25 trials):

```
prop.test(c(24, 19), c(25, 25))
```

An exact alternative to this test using the `exact2x2` package (Fay, 2010) is considered below in relation to contingency tables.

Exact tests for other situations can also be constructed if required, though for the multinomial distribution it is often easier to use a χ^2 approximation. For an exact test using the Poisson distribution use `poisson.test()` or `poisson.exact()` from `exactci`. The following code provides exact Poisson tests for the hypothesis that an observed count of 18 in five time periods has a rate different from two:

```
poisson.test(18, T=5, r=2)
```

The matching Blaker CI and two-sided p value are given by:

```
poisson.exact(18, T=5, r=2, tsmethod='blaker')
```

4.8.5 The Pearson χ^2 goodness-of-fit test (Example 4.7)

A Pearson chi-square goodness-of-fit test is readily computed using the `chisq.test()` function. If the input is a single vector it performs a goodness-of-fit test with the null hypothesis of equiprobability (via the default argument `p=rep(1/length(x))`, equivalent to $P = 1/r$). Example 4.7 first calculates a test statistic for observing three heads from ten independent coin tosses and H_0: $P = 1/r = .5$. Using `chisq.test()` this is:

```
chisq.test(c(3,7))
```

The equivalent binomial test is:

```
binom.test(3,10)
```

This is followed by a substantive example in which degree classifications for a sample of university graduates are compared to the proportions expected from national data. To calculate goodness-of-fit using χ^2, it helps to separate out the hypothesized proportions from the observed counts:

```
observed <- c(12, 56, 43, 8)
expected.prop <- c(.141,.494,.297,.068)
chisq.test(observed, p=expected.prop)
```

The expected proportions must sum to one, but if you enter raw counts or percentages you can use the argument `rescale.p = TRUE` to rescale them:

```
chisq.test(observed, p=expected.prop, rescale.p = TRUE)
```

The expected counts can be extracted if required, as can the standardized Pearson residuals:

```
chisq.test(observed, p=expected.prop)$expected
chisq.test(observed, p=expected.prop)$residuals
```

Summing the squared residuals gives the Pearson χ^2 statistic:

```
sum(chisq.test(observed, p=expected.prop)$residuals^2)
chisq.test(observed, p=expected.prop)$statistic
```

The manual calculation can be replicated using the observed and expected values if required:

```
expected <- expected.prop * sum(observed)
chi.obs <- sum((observed-expected)^2/expected)
chi.obs
```

For the χ^2 statistic only the upper tail probability is of interest (because extreme values are represented by large values of the statistic). Thus the p value is given by either of the following:

```
pchisq(chi.obs, length(observed)-1, lower.tail = FALSE)
1 - pchisq(chi.obs, length(observed)-1)
```

This is an inherently non-directional test. Patterns can be revealed by graphical methods and directional tested by collapsing categories to form a 1 *df* test (perhaps better analyzed as a binomial test).

4.8.6 The Pearson χ^2 test of independence (Example 4.8)

The χ^2 test of independence can also be obtained with the `chisq.test()` function. The best way to use this function is to assign the contingency table data to an r x c matrix. One way is to define an empty matrix and then assign vectors to the rows or columns. Here I have set up the data for male and female degree classifications in Example 4.8 as vectors.

```
males <- c(17975, 55710, 38175, 10400)
females <- c(21370, 81590, 44485, 8465)
```

Labels for the matrix rows and columns are not essential, but make it easier to interpret the output:

```
row.names <- c('male', 'female')
col.names <- c('1st', '2:1', '2:2', '3rd/pass')
```

The empty 2×4 matrix is set up using the code:

```
observed <- matrix(,2,4, dimnames=list(row.names, col.names))
```

As r and c are the dimensions of a matrix, the labels are the dimension names (set with the `dimnames` argument). The final step in setting up the matrix is to fill the rows. Then take a look to check there are no errors.

```
observed[1,] <- males
observed[2,] <- females
observed
```

The function produces a χ^2 test of independence when called with a matrix as input:

```
chisq.test(observed)
```

The standardized residuals and expected counts are given by:

```
chisq.test(observed)$residuals
chisq.test(observed)$expected
```

A plot of the counts similar to that in Figure 4.2a is given by the `barplot()` function. This recognizes the structure of the table if the input is a matrix, but stacks the bars by default. Plotting the categories as juxtaposed bars is a preferable method, setting `beside=TRUE`:

```
barplot(observed, beside = TRUE)
```

A neater plot comes from adjusting the space between bars, adding labels and an *x*-axis line, and manually resizing the plot window:

```
barplot(observed, beside = TRUE, space = c(0,0.4),
  legend=row.names, xlab='Degree class', ylab='Frequency')
abline(h=0)
```

As the raw counts are misleading when the numbers of males and females are unequal, it is better to plot the proportions. Do this by creating a matrix of proportions (dividing each row by its marginal *n*):

```
obs.prop <- matrix(,2,4, dimnames=list(row.names, col.names))
obs.prop[1,] <- males/sum(males)
obs.prop[2,] <- females/sum(females)

barplot(obs.prop, beside = TRUE, space = c(0,.4),
  legend=row.names, xlab='Degree class', ylab='Frequency')
abline(h=0)
```

For a 2×2 contingency table the input is also a matrix. To set this up for the degree classification data requires reworking the original data into new vectors for first class versus non-first class degrees by gender:

```
males.2 <- c(males[1], sum(males[2:4]))
females.2 <- c(females[1], sum(females[2:4]))
```

The 2×2 matrix is now:

```
new.obs <- matrix(,2,2, dimnames=list(row.names, c('1st','not 1st')))
new.obs[1,] <- males.2
new.obs[2,] <- females.2
```

The test, standardized residuals and expected values are given by:

```
chisq.test(new.obs)
chisq.test(new.obs)$residuals
chisq.test(new.obs)$expected
```

This could be compared with an exact test of the differences between independent proportions (Fay, 2009, 2010). This test is analogous to the well-known Fisher's exact test, but computes two-sided *p* using the Blaker, minimum likelihood or central method. Here the central method is used because the sample size is too taxing and the calculations take too long (even on a fairly fast desktop computer) if the Blaker method is selected.

```
install.packages('exactci')
library(exact2x2)
exact2x2(new.obs, tsmethod = 'central')
```

The CI reported here is for the odds ratio rather than the difference in proportions. In addition, these exact tests are conditional on the marginals of the contingency table being fixed. This approach is controversial. Unconditional exact tests exist, but are not (as of writing) implemented in `exact2x2`.

4.8.7 The sign test and the McNemar test (Examples 4.9 and 4.10)

Both the sign test and the McNemar test can be considered variants of the binomial test (though the latter is most often implemented as a χ^2 approximation). In Example 4.9 six of the 11 non-tied differences indicate superior performance for the question cue. The binomial test

```
binom.test(6, 11)
```

returns the significance probability: $p = 1$ (it is not possible to observe a less extreme outcome). As the CI for the sign of the difference is rarely of interest, there is no incentive to use the `binom.exact()` function here.

The McNemar test can be implemented as either an exact binomial test – in which the `binom.exact()` is recommended – or using the `mcnemar.test()` function. The latter takes input from a matrix that expresses the full 2×2 contingency table for the observed data and returns the usual χ^2 test statistic. For the rouge task data in Example 4.10 a matrix for the contingency table is set up as above (though labels have been omitted).

```
rouge.data <- matrix(c(35,0,10,0), 2, 2)
mcnemar.test(rouge.data)
```

The default is for the continuity-corrected test and the call for the uncorrected test is:

```
mcnemar.test(rouge.data, correct=FALSE)
```

The exact binomial test with 95% CI for the proportion using the Blaker method is given by:

```
library(exactci)
binom.exact(0, 10, tsmethod='blaker')
```

4.8.8 NHSTs and CIs for a variance (Example 4.11)

An analytic solution, assuming independent observations sampled from a normal population generated a χ^2 test statistic. The R code below reproduces the analysis in Example 4.11. For convenience, $\hat{\sigma}$ and σ_0 have been selected as input (rather than the variances).

```
n <- 50
sig.hat <- 19.6
sig.null <- 15
var.stat <- ((n-1)*sig.hat^2)/sig.null^2
```

The one-sided p value is given by:

```
pchisq(var.stat, n-1, lower.tail=FALSE)
```

The 95% CI for the *SD* is given by:

```
alpha <- .05
lb <- ((n-1)*sig.hat^2)/qchisq(1-alpha/2, n-1)
ub <- ((n-1)*sig.hat^2)/qchisq(alpha/2, n-1)
c(lb, ub)^0.5
```

To demonstrate a bootstrap CI requires raw data (which do not exist for this example). Using `rnorm()` it is possible to simulate sample data with $\hat{\sigma} = 19.6$.

```
set.seed(147)
sim.sample <- round(rnorm(50,0,19.6),1)
sd(sim.sample)
```

The boot package can then be used to generate a BC_a bootstrap CI:

```
library(boot)
sd.boot <- boot(sim.sample, function(x,i) sd(x[i]), R = 99999)
boot.ci(sd.boot, type='bca')
```

The distribution of bootstrap replications is shown by:

```
hist(sd.boot$t)
```

The plot looks reasonably symmetrical and helps explain the similarity of the two interval estimates.

4.8.9 R packages

Canty, A., and Ripley, B. D. (2010) *boot*: Bootstrap R (S-Plus) Functions. R package version 1.2–42.
Fay, M. P. (2009) Confidence Intervals that Match Fisher's Exact or Blaker's Exact Tests. *Biostatistics*, 11, 373–4.
Fay, M. P. (2010) Two-sided Exact Tests and Matching Confidence Intervals for Discrete Data. *The R Journal*, 2, 53–8.
R-core members, DebRoy, S., Bivand, R., *et al.* (2011) *foreign*: Read Data Stored by Minitab, S, SAS, SPSS, Stata, Systat, dBase. R package version 0.8–42.

4.9 Notes on SPSS syntax for Chapter 4

4.9.1 Significance probability and *p* values

One of the strengths of SPSS is that it implements a wide range of NHSTs (often with options for CIs). SPSS calculates *p* values automatically for most of the relevant commands (though these can in many cases also be calculated using its distribution functions). One unusual feature is that SPSS typically labels *p* values as 'Sig.' – short for significance probability rather than the more common probability abbreviations 'p', 'P' or 'Pr'.

4.9.2 *t* tests

To run a *t* test, use the T-TEST command either via syntax or from the <Analyze> menu, selecting <Compare means> and either <One-Sample T-Test . . . >, <Independent Samples T-Test . . . >, or <Paired-Samples T-Test . . . >. To illustrate the one sample *t* test we will use the TOT data set. The goal is to run a one sample test of the differences in means (equivalent to paired *t* test) for the paired face and question cue conditions. The first step is to obtain the differences using `COMPUTE`.

SPSS data file: `brennen_et_al_1990.sav`

```
COMPUTE pdiffs = face-question.
EXECUTE.

T-TEST
 /TESTVAL = 0
 /VARIABLES = pdiffs
 /CRITERIA = CI(.95).
```

By default a 95% CI is included. The `/TESTVAL` = 0 subcommand sets the null hypothesis (defaulting to $\mu = $ zero).

For the independent *t* test I'll switch to the comprehension data. Both syntax and menu interface for this use the group codes in the SPSS data view spreadsheet (0 and 1 in this case) to specify the groups to be compared. This can be frustrating when non-standard codes have been used in data entry (rather than 1 and 2 or 0 and 1). However, it has the advantage of allowing tests between two groups when the grouping variable codes for three or more groups (e.g., you can select 3 and 5 if there are five groups coded 1 to 5). A Welch-Satterthwaite correction is always reported alongside the uncorrected *t* test (without needing to request it).

SPSS data file: `baguley_and_payne.sav`

```
T-TEST
 GROUPS = group(0 1)
 /VARIABLES = percent_accuracy
/CRITERIA = CI(.95).
```

The default output also includes a 95% CI based on *t*. Also included automatically is a version of the Levene test of equality of variances (see section 9.3.5). The Levene test should not be used to decide which t test output to refer to. If you are unsure which to choose, a simple rule is to select the Welch-Satterthwaite test.

The paired t test can be run as a one sample test of the differences, or by specifying the paired data structure:

SPSS data file: `brennen_et_al_1990.sav`

```
T-TEST
 PAIRS = face WITH question (PAIRED)
 /CRITERIA = CI(.95)
```

4.9.3 Pearson χ^2 tests

There are several ways to obtain χ^2 tests of independence, and in SPSS. We – will consider only the most common here. If the data are in the form of counts it is important to use the `WEIGHT CASES` command prior to the analysis. This ensures that SPSS recognizes the counts as aggregated, discrete cases (rather than continuous quantities). Using the degree class data, suitable syntax is:

SPSS data file: `hesa_2009.sav`

```
WEIGHT
 BY count.

CROSSTABS
 /TABLES=gender BY degree
 /FORMAT= AVALUE TABLES
 /STATISTIC=CHISQ
 /CELLS= COUNT EXPECTED RESID SRESID
 /COUNT ROUND CELL.
```

The same analysis can be run via menus from <Analyze> < Descriptive Statistics> and selecting the `CROSSTABS` command (specifying one variable as a row and one as a column). The menu default for `CROSSTABS` does not, however, include the χ^2 test of independence (which needs to be selected using the 'Statistics . . . ' button). The `/CELLS=` subcommand can be adjusted to include various values (here the raw counts, expected values, residuals and standardized residuals).

To add a bar chart of the frequencies by gender and degree include the `/BARCHART` subcommand (though this can be misleading when n is not equal for all categories). Exact and Monte Carlo methods are also implemented. For the former add `/METHOD=EXACT TIMER(5)` and for the latter add `/METHOD=MC CIN(99) SAMPLES(10000)`. The `CIN` argument sets the confidence level, `SAMPLES` sets the number of simulations and `TIMER` sets a time limit (in minutes) in case exact estimation takes too long. To get a bar chart for percentages rather than raw frequencies use the graphing commands directly:

```
GRAPH
 /BAR(GROUPED)=PCT BY degree BY gender.
```

The same data file also contains the data organized by first or non-first degree class and a revised count. This allows you to run the test of independence using the same commands:

```
WEIGHT BY revised_count.

CROSSTABS
 /TABLES=gender BY first
 /FORMAT= AVALUE TABLES
 /STATISTIC=CHISQ
 /CELLS= COUNT EXPECTED RESID SRESID
 /COUNT ROUND CELL.
```

The goodness-of-fit test is also available, but via the <Chi-Square . . . > option of the <Analyze> <Nonparametric Tests> menu path. The following example assumes you have entered two new variables, each with four cases: one called *observed* (with the values 12, 56, 43 and 8) and one called *degree* with category codes (e.g., 1, 2, 3 and 4). Using syntax the analysis is:

```
WEIGHT BY observed.

NPAR TESTS
 /CHISQUARE=degree
 /EXPECTED= .141 .494 .297 .068.
```

The `/METHOD` subcommand can be added (as above), but plots must be run separately. For a null hypothesis of equiprobability set `/EXPECTED= EQUAL`.

4.9.4 Binomial, sign and McNemar tests

The binomial test, sign test, and McNemar test are all implemented in SPSS. The binomial test (available from <Analyze> <Nonparametric Tests>) requires two variables, each with two cases. One specifies the categories (e.g., coded 0 and 1) and the other the observed count. If these variables were named *cat* and *count* the syntax would be:

```
WEIGHT BY count.

NPAR TESTS
 /BINOMIAL (0.50)=cat.
```

The `/BINOMIAL (0.50)` subcommand can be edited to change the null hypothesis from the default of .5 to any other value between 0 and 1.

The sign or McNemar tests can be run as exact tests using the binomial test function or directly. Both are available from <Analyze> <Nonparametric Tests> <2 Related Samples . . . >. Run this way, the sign test has syntax similar to the paired *t* test:

SPSS data file: `brennen_et_al_1990.sav`

```
NPAR TEST
 /SIGN= face WITH question (PAIRED).
```

The McNemar test could be set up exactly as the χ^2 test of independence for a 2×2 table (including the weight cases command), but with the /STATISTIC=CHISQ subcommand replaced with /STATISTIC=MCNEMAR. Alternatively, it can be run using the NPAR test command rather than CROSSTABS (with data in the same format). If the observed counts are in a variable called *pcounts* and the two categorical variables are designated *cat1* and *cat2* the following syntax will run the analysis:

```
WEIGHT BY pcount.

NPAR TESTS
 /MCNEMAR=cat1 WITH cat2 (PAIRED).
```

4.10 Bibliography and further reading

Abelson, R. P. (1995) *Statistics as Principled Argument*. Hillsdale, NJ: Erlbaum.
Dienes, Z. (2008) Understanding Psychology as a Science: *An Introduction to Scientific and Statistical Inference.* Basingstoke: Palgrave Macmillan.

5
Regression

Contents

5.1 Chapter overview

This chapter introduces regression in the context of a simple linear regression model with a single predictor X and an outcome Y. Central topics include the mathematics of a linear function, least squares estimation and the use of a regression equation to predict future outcomes. Confidence intervals and null hypothesis significance tests of the intercept and slope, based on the t distribution, are described. Issues surrounding the fitting and interpretation of simple linear regression models (including the relationship between regression and the independent t test) are explored.

5.2 Regression models, prediction and explanation

Regression is a statistical technique for modeling relationships between variables. It is a very general technique that encompasses point estimation, interval estimation and hypothesis testing. Although the focus of this chapter is on simple regression models – involving only two variables – it is possible to extend the approach to deal with much richer and more complex data sets.

Even though regression models can be used to derive point and interval estimates or to test hypotheses, the form of inference most firmly associated with regression is *prediction*. Once you understand the relationship between two variables you should be able to predict what happens to one as a function of the other. Prediction is not only important as an application of a statistical model, but as a form of scientific explanation. A good model should both fit the observed data and be able to predict new observations. This is a very powerful way to assess the quality of a statistical model.

To understand regression it is sensible to think about how to model the relationship between two unbounded, continuous variables. By convention the predictor variable is labeled X and the variable being predicted (the outcome) is labeled Y. How can the relationship between X and Y be quantified? This is not as obvious as it might at first seem. It is always possible to find some function of X, $f(x)$, that predicts Y perfectly within a sample. For instance, $f(x)$ could simply map the observed values of X in the sample onto the corresponding observed values of Y. Thus $f(x)$ might simply involve looking up X in a table and reporting the mean Y value associated with that value of X. Such a function would not help you understand the relationship between X and Y outside the sample (e.g., in the population that was sampled). Nor would it allow you make inferences about the population. In fact, it would merely be a re-description of the sample. The aim of a regression model is to use the sample to extract information about the relationship between X and Y in the population. Even a crude relationship (e.g., one tends to increase as the other decreases) is informative, and with enough data more sophisticated relationships can be modeled.

There are a number of obstacles to determining the relationship between X and Y. Perhaps the most serious is that there is an infinite number of ways that the two variables could be related. How can the correct form of the relationship be selected? Two main classes of solution can be adopted. One is to select a mathematical function based on theoretical consideration of the situation being modeled. Although this is a very attractive option, it is difficult to implement, because it requires a good theoretical understanding of the factors that might be at work. It also requires a high degree of skill in representing those factors mathematically. The second solution is to reduce the space of possible models by starting with a very basic one: a linear function.

This approach is so common that, in many contexts, regression is synonymous with this form of linear statistical model.

Although assuming a linear function might seem like a severe limitation, this is far from true. This is partly because a linear function is not quite what many people (excepting mathematicians and statisticians) think it is. However, it is also because simpler models are sometimes 'better' explanations than complex ones. Many phenomena studied by scientists are complex and so the correct models will also be complex. However, finding the correct model is much harder than finding a simple model that works 'well enough'. This is related to the principle of *parsimony* sometimes referred to as *Occam's razor* (because of the frequency with which the eponymous philosopher used the principle). Occam's most common phrasing of the principle (Thorburn, 1918) was 'numquam ponenda est pluralitas sine necessitate' which can be (very) loosely interpreted as 'never propose an unnecessarily complex explanation'. All other things being equal, you should prefer a simple explanation to a complicated one. There is a sound statistical basis for Occam's razor. Simple models tend to produce worse predictions for the sample that generated the model than complex models do, but they often generate better predictions for new data. In statistical terms, a complicated model tends to over-fit the sample data and over-generalize when applied to new data. Simple models are also easier to falsify, and falsification is one of the hallmarks of a scientific theory (Dienes, 2008).

5.3 Mathematics of the linear function

5.3.1 The equation for a straight line

Before introducing regression, it is essential to understand the basic mathematics of a linear function, and what statisticians mean when they use a technical term such as 'linear'. If two variables X and Y are related linearly the relationship can be expressed as an equation of the form:

$$Y = b_0 + b_1 X \qquad \text{Equation 5.1}$$

This equation states that Y is equal to b_0 plus b_1 times the value of X. People often refer to this as the 'equation for a straight line'. Any straight line can be described by this equation by selecting appropriate values of b_0 and b_1.[1] These are the *coefficients* of the equation; constant, multiplicative terms.[2] The coefficient b_0 is referred to as the *intercept* or *constant.* The coefficient b_1 is known as the *slope* or *gradient* of the line.

These labels will make more sense if the equation is represented graphically. Figure 5.1 is a plot of the equation $Y = 2 + 0.5X$ (in which $b_0 = 2$ and $b_1 = 0.5$). The intercept is the point at which the straight line crosses the *y*-axis (conventionally plotted at $X = 0$).[3] This occurs because when $X = 0$ the value of Y is determined solely by the value of b_0. The slope of the line in Figure 5.1 is governed by b_1. If b_1 is positive, the line slopes up (from left to right). If b_1 is negative the line slopes down (from left to right). If $b_1 = 0$ then the line is flat.

A simple way to interpret the slope – one that follows directly from the equation – is that it is the number of units that Y increases for a unit increase in X. Here, the slope indicates that if X increases by 1, Y increases by only 0.5.

Figure 5.2 depicts this relationship, and thereby illustrates a general graphical method for determining the slope of a line. This method involves picking a fixed interval of X and determining the corresponding increase in Y.

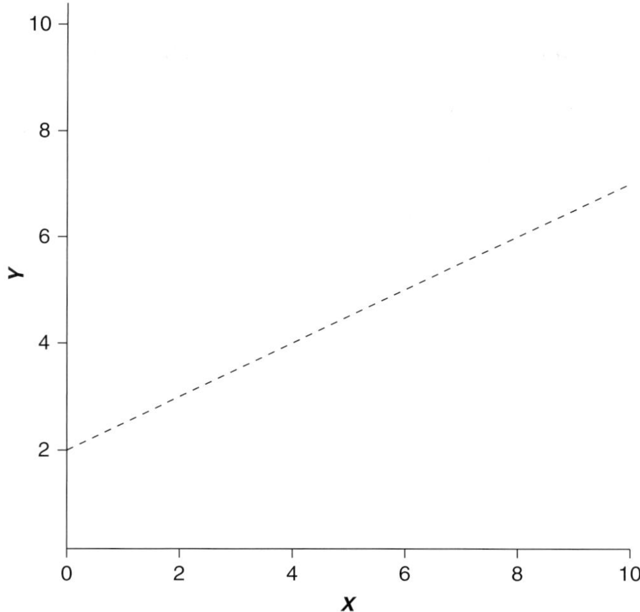

Figure 5.1 The straight line described by the equation $Y = 2 + 0.5X$

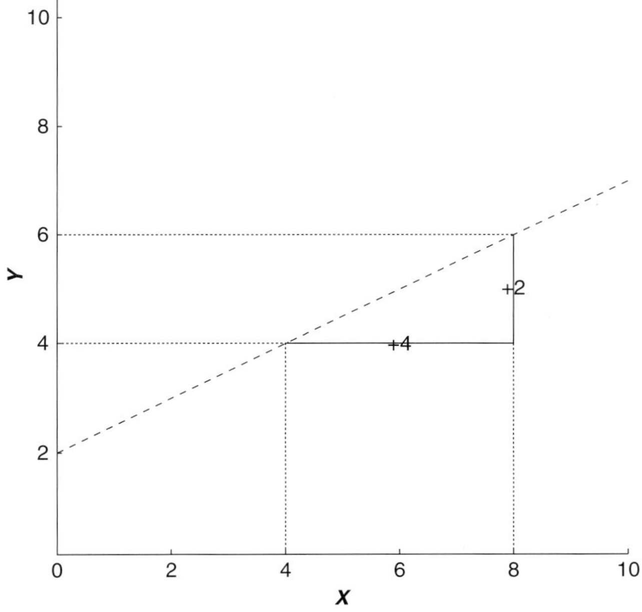

Figure 5.2 A graphical method to calculate the slope of a straight line

The ratio of the increase in Y to the increase in X is, by definition, the slope. Thus the slope in Figure 5.1 is $\Delta Y/\Delta X = +2/+4 = 0.5$.[4] It is a good idea to pick values of X and corresponding values of Y that can be easily read from the graph (e.g., where there are axis tick marks).

For any two points i and j on the line (where x_i and x_j are the corresponding values of X and y_i and y_j are the corresponding values of Y) the relationship can be expressed as:

$$b_1 = \frac{y_i - y_j}{x_i - x_j} \qquad \text{Equation 5.2}$$

This ratio is the same at any point on a straight line, and this is – in essence – what a straight line is. It is a function that produces a fixed, constant change in one variable every time another variable increases by a fixed amount. If the change in Y is negative the slope will be negative (and the line will slope down). If the change in Y is identical to the increase in X the slope will be one and the equation takes the form $Y = b_0 + X$. If it is also true that $b_0 = 0$ then the variables would be identical and the equation reduces to $Y = X$. Changing the intercept (or constant) moves the whole line up or down the y-axis by a fixed amount. Thus the intercept in the equation has an important (but limited) role in describing the line – influencing its 'height' up or down the graph.

The equation for a straight line is, of course, a linear function. It is, in a way, the most fundamental linear function. What may be surprising is that a linear function does not always describe a straight line.

To a understand a linear regression model in statistics you need to start by thinking of a linear function as one that expresses a variable as an *additive* function of one or more other variables (e.g., Y as an additive function of X). In this context, 'additive' means that the variables are added together, but they are also scaled (i.e., multiplied) by some coefficient. According to this definition, the slope of a line is just a way of scaling one variable to match another variable. The slope of a line will, in fact, change in exactly this way if the scale of either variable is changed. Thus, if all values of Y in Figure 5.2 were to be multiplied by ten, the new slope would be $10 \times 0.5 = 5$ (and if the y-axis was relabeled to read 20, 40, 60 and so on, the figure otherwise would look identical).

One consequence of this definition is that linear regression models are not necessarily restricted to explaining or predicting straight-line relationships between variables. Contrary to a common misconception, linear functions can be used to model curvilinear relationships. Many curves can be described by relatively simple linear functions.

5.4 Simple linear regression

In *simple linear regression* the linear relationship between two variables is modeled. One variable is predicted as a linear (i.e., additive) function of another. Linear regression is widely used in many fields and terminology also varies widely (e.g., simple linear regression is also termed *bivariate regression*). We will use the label X for the *predictor* variable (usually plotted on the x-axis of a graph) and the label Y for the *outcome* being predicted (usually plotted on the y-axis of a graph). Common terminology is described in Box 5.1.

Box 5.1 Regression terminology

A range of terms is commonly used to describe variables in regression. Many borrow from the language of experimental design. This is slightly unfortunate because regression is often used for non-experimental designs (where those terms can be misleading). In an experimental design the *independent variable* (*IV*) is manipulated by the experimenter in order to determine its effect on the *dependent variable* (*DV*). Thus the *IV* and *DV* in an experiment correspond to the predictor and outcome in a simple regression. A true experiment (one in which the appropriate method of randomization is in place as an experimental control) entitles a researcher to conclude that the *IV* has caused a change in the *DV*. It is the nature of the experimental control (not the statistical technique or the use of labels such as *IV* and *DV*) that determines a true experiment. While regression can be used for the analysis of an experimental design, this is not a requirement of the technique. Hence it is safer to use more neutral labels to describe variables in regression.

Aside from independent or predictor variable, *X* may also be called an explanatory variable, regressor or covariate. In addition to being called an outcome or dependent variable *Y*, is sometimes termed a response, regressand, criterion, or measurement variable.

Simple linear regression proceeds by attempting to find the intercept and slope of the straight line that fits the observed data best. The data consist of paired observations of X and Y (e.g., heights and weights from the same individuals). Once obtained, the line can be used for prediction and to understand the quantitative relationship between the two. If the relationship is perfectly linear this process is trivial. To appreciate why, look at the data plotted in Figure 5.3. Both panel (a) and panel (b) show the best fitting line for a sample size of $n = 7$ (where n represents the number of observations on Y, and hence also the number of associated predictor values).

The data in panel (a) show a perfect linear relationship. Finding the line of best fit is simply a matter of joining the points. The intercept and slope can be found using graphical methods. For the data in panel (b) the situation is more difficult, because the relationship is not

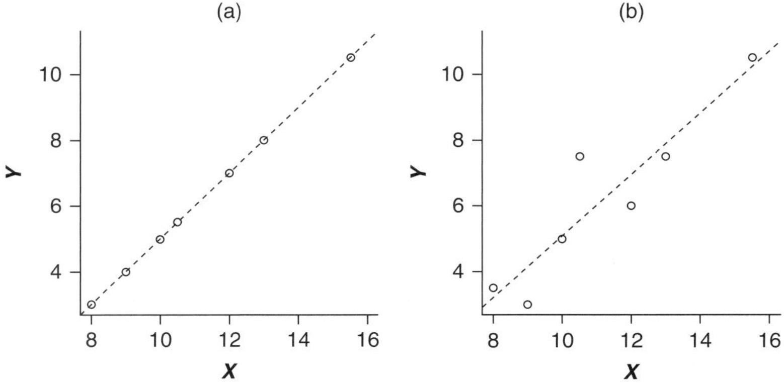

Figure 5.3 Lines of best fit for simple linear regression in (a) a sample without error and (b) a sample with error

perfectly linear. Although both relationships appear linear, the difference (in statistical terms) is that one sample contains error and the other does not. The initial difficulty is therefore how to determine the intercept and slope of the best fitting line when error is present. The resulting line of best fit – known as a regression line – is an estimate of the relationship between X and Y in the population.

5.4.1 Fitting a regression line

To find the best-fitting regression line you first need to decide what it means to have a good fit. In a perfect fit like that of Figure 5.3a the regression line passes through all the points. This implies that for a good fit all the points will be close to the line, while for a poor fit the points will be far from the line. The problem of finding the best fit thus shifts to the problem of deciding what measure of distance to use. The best-fitting straight line is then defined as the line that minimizes this distance measure.

A large number of difference measures have been proposed, but the most common measure is *ordinary least squares* (*least squares*). This method involves minimizing the squared difference between the predicted values of y (those on the line) and the observed values. This corresponds to minimizing the squared vertical distance of each point from the regression line. The least squares criterion has a number of attractive features (see Key Concept 5.1).

KEY CONCEPT 5.1

Least squares

Why use least squares to determine the line of best fit in a regression? The first advantage of this approach is that provides a direct connection between the method of fitting a statistical model and familiar, widely used statistics such as the arithmetic mean, sums of squares, variance and standard deviation. One of many potential alternatives would be to minimize the absolute deviations. This would produce a line of best fit that estimated median Y. These alternatives also tend to be more difficult to work with than least squares (though this is less of an issue with modern computing resources).

Another reason for adopting least squares as an estimation method is the *Gauss-Markov theorem*. This theorem states that a linear regression model in which the errors have a mean of zero, are uncorrelated and have equal variance is a *best linear unbiased estimator.* This collection of attributes – known as *BLUE* for short – is highly desirable for a statistical model. It ensures that the estimator provides optimal and unbiased predictions of a linear function. Furthermore it is not too restrictive – it isn't necessary to assume the errors (the differences between the predicted values and true values in the population) have a particular type or shape of distribution (or that the distribution is identical for all values of X). The only assumptions are that these errors sum to zero, are not correlated and that their variance does not change as a function of X. (This latter assumption is often referred to as *homogeneity of variance.*)

The assumption that the errors are uncorrelated is sometimes phrased in terms of independence of the observations. Independence is a slightly stricter condition (implying that knowing one quantity provides no information about another). Being uncorrelated merely requires that two things have a *covariance* of zero. The errors are always uncorrelated if they are independent, but it is still possible for non-independent errors to have a covariance of zero.

A final advantage of least squares estimation is that it is possible to calculate the estimates directly. Alternative methods often rely on iterative solutions. This would involve selecting estimates for the slope and intercept, calculating the criterion being minimized and then repeating this procedure after adjusting the estimates to produce a better fit. Iterative estimation usually continues until the criterion cannot be minimized further (to some degree of measurement), until it is deemed good enough, or a stopping condition is met.

Using least squares estimation, the slope of the regression line is

$$b_1 = \frac{\sum_{i=1}^{N} (x_i - \hat{\mu}_X)(y_i - \hat{\mu}_Y)}{\sum_{i=1}^{N} (x_i - \hat{\mu}_X)^2} \qquad \text{Equation 5.3}$$

where $\hat{\mu}_X$ and $\hat{\mu}_Y$ are the sample means of X and Y, and x_i and y_i are the ith observations of X and Y. The quantities $(x_i - \hat{\mu}_X)$ and $(y_i - \hat{\mu}_Y)$ are therefore the deviations of the observed values of X and Y from their respective means. The calculation can be streamlined (if you are working it out by hand) by appreciating that the mean is identical for all observations. Subtracting the mean from every observation is therefore equivalent to subtracting $N \times \hat{\mu}$ from summed totals that ignore the mean. A less cumbersome version of Equation 5.3 lumps the subtractions together in one go:

$$b_1 = \frac{\sum_{i}^{n} (x_i y_i) - N\hat{\mu}_X\hat{\mu}_Y}{\sum_{i}^{n} (x_i^2) - N\hat{\mu}_X^2} \qquad \text{Equation 5.4}$$

Why does Equation 5.3 work? Think about what happens to this equation if the deviations for X always match the deviations for Y exactly. The numerator would then effectively be the square of the deviations for X. This is also the denominator of the ratio and so the slope would be exactly 1. If the absolute values of the deviations always matched, but the signs differed, the slope ends up as -1. Similarly, if the deviations from Y are always twice those of X, the slope will end up being 2. What the equation does is to capture the tendency for Y to increase or decrease in relation to X and express it as a ratio. The change in Y won't always be consistent. If it is very inconsistent then the term $\sum_{i=1}^{n} (x_i - \hat{\mu}_X)(y_i - \hat{\mu}_Y)$, and therefore the slope itself, will be close to zero. For example, if the deviations for x_1 and x_2 are +2 and −2, but the deviations for y_1 and y_2 are both 5 then:

$$\sum_{i=1}^{n} (x_i - \hat{\mu}_X)(y_i - \hat{\mu}_Y) = (2)(5) + (-2)(5) = 10 + (-10) = 0$$

With real data the relationship will generally be somewhat inconsistent. The slope reflects the average balance of the relationship. If small increases in X tend, on average, to be associated with large increases in Y, b_1 will be large and positive. On the other hand, if large increases in X are associated with small decreases in Y, b_1 will be small and negative.

Once the slope is known, it is possible to determine the intercept using the equation:

$$b_0 = \hat{\mu}_Y - b_1\hat{\mu}_X \qquad \text{Equation 5.5}$$

This equation works because the intercept is a constant that adds or subtracts from Y, shifting the line of best fit up or down the y-axis (without altering its slope). The term $b_1\hat{\mu}_X$ is the expected (i.e., mean) value of Y if there were no intercept, and $\hat{\mu}_Y$ is the mean of Y in the sample. The difference between the two is the degree to which the best-fitting line needs to be shifted to match the observed data.

A fitted regression line has some interesting properties. First, the line of best fit always passes exactly through the coordinates $(\hat{\mu}_X, \hat{\mu}_Y)$. This may be easier to notice if Equation 5.5 is re-arranged. Adding $b_1\hat{\mu}_X$ to both sides produces $b_0 + b_1\hat{\mu}_X = \hat{\mu}_Y$, indicating that when $X = \hat{\mu}_X$ the corresponding value of Y is $\hat{\mu}_Y$. Second, both b_0 and b_1 are expressed in terms of units of Y. This is perhaps obvious for b_0 (which represents a shift of the line of best fit up and down the y-axis). The slope b_1 is a ratio and therefore expresses the expected number of units Y changes by if X increases by exactly one unit. Looking at the denominator of Equation 5.3 it might appear that the slope is expressed in terms of squared units of X. This is not the case, because $(x_i - \hat{\mu}_X)^2$ is $(x_i - \hat{\mu}_X) \times (x_i - \hat{\mu}_X)$ and the $(x_i - \hat{\mu}_X)$ term in the numerator cancels out one of the $(x_i - \hat{\mu}_X)$ terms in the denominator. Thus the ratio expresses the change in Y in units of X. This is an incredibly useful property for prediction. For instance, it would allow you to predict height from weight, or risk of disease from severity of symptoms.

Example 5.1 Consider a simple experiment. Six participants are given a picture to view for between three and 18 seconds. The next day they are shown an empty picture frame and asked to locate an object from the original picture within the frame. The distance of their response from the correct location of the object is then measured in centimeters (*cm*). Table 5.1 shows how hypothetical data from this experiment might look. Subsequent examples will refer to this data set as the location memory data.

Table 5.1 Hypothetical data from a simple location memory experiment

Participant	***X* (presentation time)**	***Y* (distance)**
P1	3	6.3
P2	6	3.9
P3	9	2.3
P4	12	2.0
P5	15	2.8
P6	18	1.6
$\hat{\mu}$	10.5	3.15
Σ	63.0	18.90

As you might expect, responses tend to be closer to the original location of the target object for longer presentation times.

How well can this relationship be represented by a simple linear regression? A good start is to determine the intercept and slope of the line of best fit.

Figure 5.4a shows a scatter plot of the data. Equation 5.3 and Equation 5.5 can be applied to calculate the line of best fit. For hand calculation it is a good idea to set out intermediate terms in a table (or to use a spreadsheet). These intermediate terms include the deviations from the mean of

X and Y and the product of these quantities. Table 5.2 shows these quantities for the n participants. It also includes some additional terms useful for later examples.

Using the information in Table 5.2, the slope and intercept are:

$$b_1 = \frac{\sum_{i=1}^{N} (x_i - \hat{\mu}_X)(y_i - \hat{\mu}_Y)}{\sum_{i=1}^{N} (x_i - \hat{\mu}_X)^2} = \frac{-40.65}{157.50} = -0.2581$$

$$b_0 = \hat{\mu}_Y - b_1 \hat{\mu}_X = 3.15 - (-0.2581 \times 10.5) = 3.15 + 2.71 = 5.86$$

The equation for the best-fitting straight line for these data is therefore:

$$Y = 5.86 - 0.2581X$$

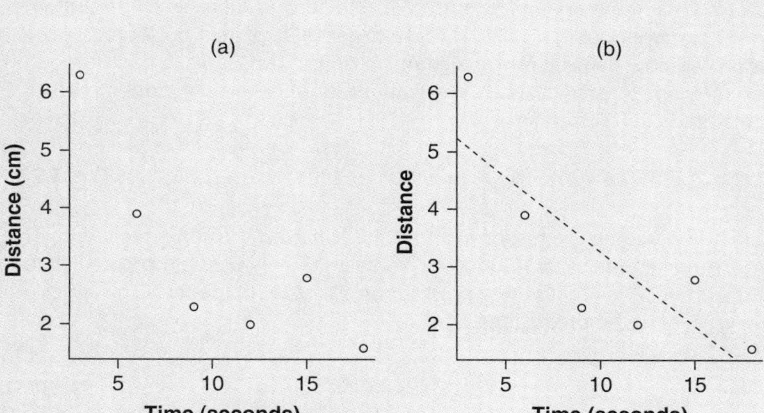

Figure 5.4 Scatter plots of the location memory data (a) without, and (b) with the best-fitting simple linear regression line

Table 5.2 Intermediate quantities for calculating the slope and intercept for a simple linear regression on the location memory data

Participant	$x_i - \hat{\mu}_X$	$y_i - \hat{\mu}_Y$	$(x_i - \hat{\mu}_X)(y_i - \hat{\mu}_Y)$	$(x_i - \hat{\mu}_X)^2$	$x_i y_i$	x_i^2
P1	−7.5	3.15	−23.625	56.25	18.9	9
P2	−4.5	0.75	−3.375	20.25	23.4	36
P3	−1.5	−0.85	1.275	2.25	20.7	81
P4	1.5	−1.15	−1.725	2.25	24.0	144
P5	4.5	−0.35	−1.575	20.25	42.0	225
P6	7.5	−1.55	−11.625	56.25	28.8	324
$\hat{\mu}$	0	0	−6.775	26.25	26.3	135.5
Σ	0	0	−40.650	157.50	157.8	819.0

Using Equation 5.4 with values from Table 5.1 and 5.2, the slope is:

$$b_1 = \frac{\sum_i^n (x_i y_i) - N\hat{\mu}_X \hat{\mu}_Y}{\sum_i^n (x_i^2) - N\hat{\mu}_X^2} = \frac{157.8 - 6 \times 10.5 \times 3.15}{819 - 6 \times 10.5^2} = \frac{-40.65}{157.50} = -0.2581$$

A regression equation is often easier to understand if meaningful variable names are added. Two common formats are:

$$distance = 5.86 - 0.2581 \times time$$

$$Y_{distance} = 5.86 - 0.2581 X_{time}$$

To properly interpret the equation it is essential to know the scales that distance and time are measured on (e.g., centimeters and seconds). A one second increase in presentation time (X) is associated with the target being recalled 0.26*cm* closer to its correct position.

The equation can now be used for prediction. To do this, just replace the X term in the equation by the value you want to predict for. A presentation time of ten seconds (for which there are no data) leads to a prediction of:

$$Y_{distance} = 5.86 - 0.2581 X_{time} = 5.86 - 0.2581 \times 10 = 5.86 - 2.581 \approx 3.27$$

Thus the predicted outcome is a response about 3.27*cm* from the correct location. This is the basis of prediction in regression: by measuring or knowing X it is possible to predict the value of Y. When dealing with uncertain data these predictions will never be perfect. The logical next step is to determine the quality of the predictions.

5.4.2 Residuals, prediction and error

Using a simple regression line for prediction involves 'plugging in' a specific value of X into the equation for the best-fitting line. Prediction has obvious practical applications and can be an important way to demonstrate understanding in science. Prediction is also a useful way to check the quality of a model. If a statistical model predicts implausible or impossible values, this is often an indication of problems with the model (though even a problematic model may have useful applications or scientific merit). More generally, researchers are often interested in assessing the quality of a statistical model. One way to do this is to use a measure of the closeness of the predictions to the observed values of Y (the true value of Y in the population usually being unknown).

Central to the assessment of the quality of prediction are the residuals of the linear regression model: the deviations between the observed and predicted values of Y. The idea of using the residuals of a model to assess its quality is already familiar to you – albeit in a very simple form. The mean of a sample represents a very crude statistical model in which the predicted value is a constant ($\hat{\mu}$) and the residuals from the model are used to measure the quality of this prediction (e.g., in the form of sums of squares, $\hat{\sigma}^2$ or $\hat{\sigma}$).

As the line of best fit is determined using least squares, what is being predicted is the arithmetic mean of Y (the value that minimizes the squared distance of deviations calculated from it). The regression line therefore represents the relationship between the expected (mean) value of Y conditional on a given value of the predictor X. The deviation between this value and an observed value of Y in a sample is its residual. Together the residuals are indication of the observed level of uncertainty or 'error' in the data. Residuals are sometimes also called *errors*, though strictly speaking errors are population values (and the residuals are samples from the population of errors).

The errors in the population are often represented by the symbol ε (the Greek letter epsilon) and the sample residuals by e_i (indicating the residual of the ith observation). A residual, being the difference between the predicted outcome for a given data point $\hat{y}_i$ and the observed outcome y_i, is therefore

$$e_i = y_i - \hat{y}_i \qquad \text{Equation 5.6}$$

This relationship can be plotted using the vertical distances of points from the regression line. Figure 5.5 does this for the location memory data.

The regression line shows the predicted values of Y. The points depict the observed values of Y and the vertical distances of the points from the line are the residuals. Points above the line produce positive residuals and points below produce negative residuals.

The full form of the simple linear regression model is:

$$y_i = b_0 + b_1 x_i + e_i \qquad \text{Equation 5.7}$$

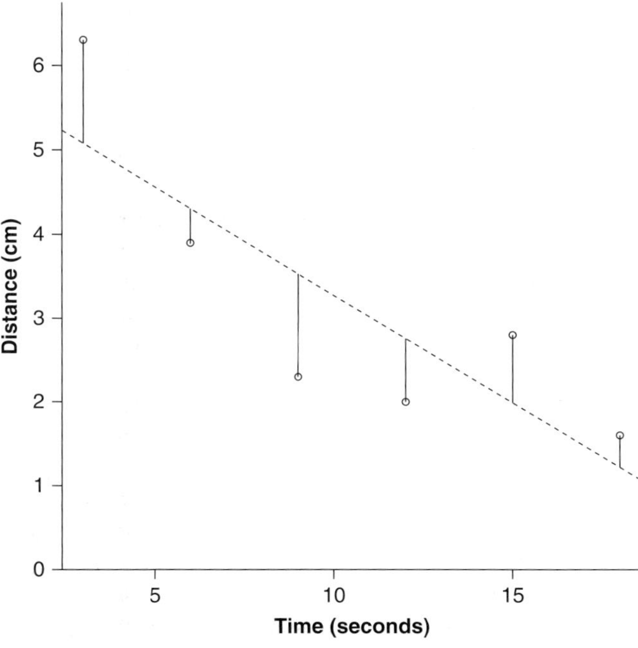

Figure 5.5 Residuals depicted as the vertical distance between observed and predicted Y for a simple linear regression of the location memory data

This differs in two respects from Equation 5.1, first by adding subscripts (indexing the $i = 1$ to n observations) and second by adding the residual term e_i. Remember that the predictions of the regression model ($\hat{y}_i$) are the expected, mean value of Y for a particular value of the predictor. Subtracting the residual term from Equation 5.7 therefore produces a *prediction equation* expressing $\hat{Y}$ in terms of the predictor. A prediction equation therefore has the form:

$$\hat{Y} = b_0 + b_1 X \qquad \text{Equation 5.8}$$

The intercept b_0 and the slope b_1 define the relationship between X and Y, as estimated from the data at hand. The residuals quantify the degree of 'misfit' for this relationship in the sample. If the fit is perfect (e.g., as in Figure 5.3a) the residuals are all zero. If the fit is poor then the observed and predicted values of Y are far apart and the residuals will tend to be large. Exploring the fit of the model to a data set therefore involves looking at the residuals.

The residuals are estimates of the errors of a statistical model in the population sampled, and therefore of the uncertainty inherent in prediction with the model. This uncertainty can be measured in a number of ways. One of the simplest measures of fit is the residual sum of squares:

$$SS_{residual} = \sum_{i=1}^{N} (y_i - \hat{y}_i)^2 = \sum_{i=1}^{N} e_i^2 \qquad \text{Equation 5.9}$$

$SS_{residual}$ (sometimes labeled SS_{error}) is a useful descriptive statistic for quantifying the variation in the sample, but has the usual drawback of sums of squares measures that it increases as n increases. One solution is to scale $SS_{residual}$ by $N - 1$ to turn it into an estimate of the error variance (the variance of ε). For a regression model there is also an option to scale $SS_{residual}$ by the total sum of squares for Y. (In most applications of regression, the predictor X is assumed to be measured without error, and the focus is on variation in the outcome Y.) The total sum of squares for the regression represents all potential variance to be explained in the sample. The sums of squares total is obtained by applying the standard formula for sample sums of squares in Equation 1.9 to the outcome Y. As with Equation 5.4, it is often encountered in this streamlined form to facilitate calculation by hand:

$$SS_{total} = \sum_{i=1}^{N} (y_i - \hat{\mu}_Y)^2 = \sum_{i=1}^{N} \left(y_i^2\right) - N\hat{\mu}_Y^2 \qquad \text{Equation 5.10}$$

The following ratio therefore expresses the uncertainty in the sample as a proportion of the total variance:

$$\frac{SS_{residual}}{SS_{total}} = \frac{\sum_{i=1}^{N} e_i^2}{\sum_{i=1}^{N} (y_i^2) - N\hat{\mu}_Y^2} \qquad \text{Equation 5.11}$$

This ratio is the proportion of the total variance accounted for by the residuals and therefore the proportion of *unexplained variance* in the sample. It is a plausible measure of the lack of fit of the model, because it is zero when the fit is perfect and one when there is no relationship between X and Y in the sample. Working with the unexplained variance can be awkward and people often prefer to express the ratio directly in terms of *explained variance* (the proportion of sample variance explained by X). This is accomplished by subtracting the quantity in Equation 5.11 from 1. The explained variance is assigned the label R^2 ('R-square')[5] and, for simple linear regression, is defined as:

$$R^2 = 1 - \frac{SS_{residual}}{SS_{total}} = 1 - \frac{\sum_{i=1}^{n} e_i^2}{\sum_{i=1}^{N} (y_i^2) - N\hat{\mu}_Y^2} \qquad \text{Equation 5.12}$$

R^2 is probably the most popular way to measure the fit of a linear model. This quantity could also have been arrived at directly by considering the sums of squares of the regression model (termed SS_{model} or $SS_{regression}$). The sums SS_{model} can be obtained by squaring the deviations of the predicted values from their mean $\mu_{\hat{Y}}$ (which is also the mean of Y):

$$SS_{model} = \sum_{i=1}^{N} (\hat{y}_i - \hat{\mu}_Y)^2 = \sum_{i=1}^{N} (\hat{y}_i^2) - N\hat{\mu}_Y^2 \qquad \text{Equation 5.13}$$

Thus R^2 can also be expressed directly in terms of explained variation:

$$R^2 = 1 - \frac{SS_{residual}}{SS_{total}} = \frac{SS_{model}}{SS_{total}} \qquad \text{Equation 5.14}$$

More generally, the statistical model for simple linear regression – or indeed any linear regression – can be framed as:

$$SS_{total} = SS_{model} + SS_{residual} \qquad \text{Equation 5.15}$$

This is a fundamental property of linear regression models, which divide up or 'partition' the total variance in the sample into that which is explained by the model and that which is not. One caveat is that the terms explained and unexplained are used in quite a weak sense; there is no implication that X causes Y to change. The predictor X accounts for a proportion of the total observed variance in Y, but the mechanism that produced this relationship (if one exists) is not addressed by the statistical model.

Example 5.2 Table 5.3 displays the residuals and predicted values for the location memory data. It also includes squared residual, predicted and observed values of Y (for use in later calculations). Referring back to Table 5.1 and to Table 5.3, $\hat{\mu}_Y = 3.15$ and $\sum y_i^2 = 74.59$. SS_{total} is therefore

$$\sum_{i=1}^{N} (y_i^2) - N\hat{\mu}_Y^2 = 74.59 - 6 \times 3.15^2 = 74.59 - 59.535 = 15.055$$

and $SS_{residual}$ is $\sum e_i^2 = 4.5634$. Putting these quantities together gives:

$$R^2 = 1 - \frac{SS_{residual}}{SS_{total}} = 1 - \frac{4.5634}{15.055} = 1 - .303 \approx .697$$

Table 5.3 Predicted, residuals, squared predicted, residual and observed *Y* for the location memory data

Participant	$\hat{y}_i$ **(predicted)**	e_i **(residuals)**	$\hat{y}_i^2$	e_i^2	y_i^2
P1	5.0857	1.2143	25.8645	1.4745	39.69
P2	4.3114	−0.4114	18.5884	0.1693	15.21
P3	3.5371	−1.2371	12.5114	1.5305	5.29
P4	2.7629	−0.7629	7.6334	0.5820	4.00
P5	1.9886	0.8114	3.9544	0.6584	7.84
P6	1.2143	0.3857	1.4745	0.1488	2.56
$\hat{\mu}$	3.1500	0.0000	11.6711	0.7606	12.43
Σ	18.9000	0.0000	70.0266	4.5634	74.59

Working directly from SS_{model} gives the same result. SS_{model} is

$$\sum_{i=1}^{n}(\hat{y}_i) - N\hat{\mu}_Y^2 = 70.0266 - 6 \times 3.15^2 = 10.4916$$

and the explained sample variance is

$$R^2 = \frac{SS_{model}}{SS_{total}} = \frac{10.4916}{15.055} \approx 0.697$$

The presentation time explains about 69.7% of the total sample variance in a simple linear model. In many domains researchers would be very pleased with a model that fitted this well, but interpreting statistics such as R^2 is a tricky business. This is particularly true for researchers used to collecting data from human participants (where there are many potential sources of error). There are reasons to be suspicious of this model (leaving aside the fact that the data are artificial).

First, with small N it is relatively easy to get a good linear fit by chance. If $N = 2$ the regression line necessarily produces a perfect fit; it is always possible to find a straight line that exactly passes through two points. This is the 'degrees of freedom' concept under another guise. Only with three or more points are there sufficient degrees of freedom (*df*) for the line of best fit to miss some of the points. For $N = 6$ the line of best fit is based on only 4 *df*. The remaining two are absorbed by the parameters of the model (the intercept b_0 and the slope b_1). Second, because very good fits are rare with data from human participants, one should always consider whether the sampling strategy is biased or problematic in some way. This experiment uses a single picture, so the quality of prediction may simply reflects characteristics of that item. (Such extra-statistical issues are essential for researchers to consider when interpreting a statistical model.) Third, there may be fundamental problems with the model itself. All statistical models are approximations, so it may be that this approximation relies on assumptions that are untenable. Here, there is no particular reason to doubt that the measurements are independent of each other, but there are insufficient data to assess the assumption that the errors in the population (from which the residuals are sampled) do not meet the homogeneity of variance requirement.

There are also reasons to doubt the 'form' of the model. The linear nature of the predictions implies that at some point the presentation time will reduce the predicted outcome below zero *cm* (this happens when the time is longer than $5.86/0.2581 = 22.7$ seconds). As this result is impossible, the model is far from ideal. Is it therefore a bad model? Not necessarily. Within the ranges of X for which data were collected the model predicts surprisingly well. As long as someone is aware of the limitations of the model it may still be useful. The model is also adequate to establish that the distance tends to decrease as presentation time increases. A more plausible model would involve fitting a curvilinear relationship for these data.

A final issue is that the statistical model employed here has assumed that X is measured without error (in other words the residual variance is associated only with sampling form Y). For experimental research – such as this – this is often a reasonable assumption (e.g., the presentation times may be carefully controlled and have negligible error). For non-experimental studies it may not be reasonable, though some predictors (e.g., age or gender) may be measured with little or no error.

5.5 Statistical inference in regression

Fitting a model using least squares provides a regression model of the form

$$y_i = b_0 + b_1 x_i + e_i$$

where Y is being predicted from X. This is a form of parameter estimation. Specifically, the sample data are being used to estimate two population parameters. These parameters are the population intercept β_0 and the population slope β_1. The relationship between X and Y in the population can therefore be expressed as:

$$y_i = \beta_0 + \beta_1 x_i + \varepsilon_i \qquad \text{Equation 5.16}$$

Getting estimates of the best linear fit (defined in terms of minimizing the squared residuals) does not require strong assumptions about the population. This is not true of statistical inference about the population parameters. Without an understanding of the probability distribution of the population being sampled – specifically the population of errors (ε_i) – it is hard to determine the appropriate margin of error for an interval estimate or p value for a significance test. The standard assumptions for linear regression models are that the errors are independently sampled from a normal population with constant variance. The independence and constant variance assumptions derive from the Gauss-Markov theorem (see Key Concept 5.1). The normality assumption is justified by appeal to the central limit theorem (CLT); the distribution of the sum of a large number of independently sampled residuals from a population with finite mean and variance should be approximately normal. Bear in mind though, that neither obtaining the best-fitting regression line nor R^2 assume a normal distribution of errors. A common misunderstanding of regression is that the linear fit itself requires a normal distribution of X, Y or the errors.

On this basis, the errors of a regression model can be characterized as:

$$\varepsilon_i \sim N\left(0, \sigma_E^2\right) \qquad \text{Equation 5.17}$$

That is, they have a normal distribution with mean of 0 and unknown *error variance* σ_E^2. A sample estimate of the error variance is obtained in a similar fashion to the variance of a sample (using $SS_{residual}$ and the *df* of the model). This estimate is the *mean square error* (MS_{error} or MS_e) because it is the average $SS_{residual}$ per *df* of the model. The model *df* are $N-2$ (the number of data points being predicted minus the two parameters being estimated). Hence the sample estimate of the *error variance* is:

$$\hat{\sigma}_E^2 = MS_{error} = \frac{\sum_{i=1}^{N} e_i^2}{N-2} = \frac{SS_{residual}}{df} \quad \text{Equation 5.18}$$

The square root of this quantity is effectively the standard deviation of the errors and is termed the *standard error of the estimate*:

$$\hat{\sigma}_E = \sqrt{MS_{error}} = \sqrt{\frac{\sum_{i=1}^{N} e_i^2}{N-2}} = \sqrt{\frac{SS_{residual}}{df}} \quad \text{Equation 5.19}$$

The standard error of the estimate provides information about the prediction of Y from values of X in the sample.[6] While this captures the error in predicting Y from X, it is not suitable for inference about the population parameters themselves. Later sections consider how to form confidence intervals (CIs) and null hypothesis significance test statistics (NHSTs) for these parameters. Before considering how these are constructed it is useful to consider how the regression line depends on the spread of observed X values as well as the uncertainty inherent in predicting Y.

5.5.1 Leverage

Not all points have equal impact on the regression line. What happens if an additional point is added to a regression? Its contribution to the slope of the regression line depends on two factors: the value of X and the distance from the original line. The first factor is termed the *leverage* of the point, while the second (the size of the residual) captures the uncertainty in the regression model.

Why is leverage important? If the new point x_{n+1} is sampled at the mean of X, it will have no effect on the slope of the regression line whatsoever. If the new point is far from the mean of X then the slope of the regression line may have to shift up or down substantially to fit the data point. The degree to which the regression line shifts depends on the size of the residual (or more accurately the size of the residual relative to the original regression line) and the original sample size n. To see why the slope of the regression line won't change when $x_{n+1} = \hat{\mu}_X$, recall that the best-fitting line always passes through the coordinates ($\hat{\mu}_X$, $\hat{\mu}_Y$). Adding a point such as ($\hat{\mu}_X$, $\hat{\mu}_Y + 2$) will produce a line that still passes through $\hat{\mu}_X$ (that quantity being unaltered). On the other hand, $\hat{\mu}_Y$ will change, and therefore the whole line (and intercept) will be shifted up by $2/(n+1)$. Figure 5.6 illustrates this with the location memory data by adding a seventh point where $x_7 = 10.5$ and $y_7 = 6$. The slope of the regression in Figure 5.6b is unchanged, but the intercept is $(6 - \hat{\mu}_Y)/7$ higher. Although the slope of the line hasn't changed, the overall fit of the line is worse. The new point has a relatively large residual and therefore inflates $\sum e_i^2$.

If leverage is high then a new point could have a substantial impact on the estimate of the slope parameter. This is not guaranteed, because if the observed outcome of a new point y_{n+1}

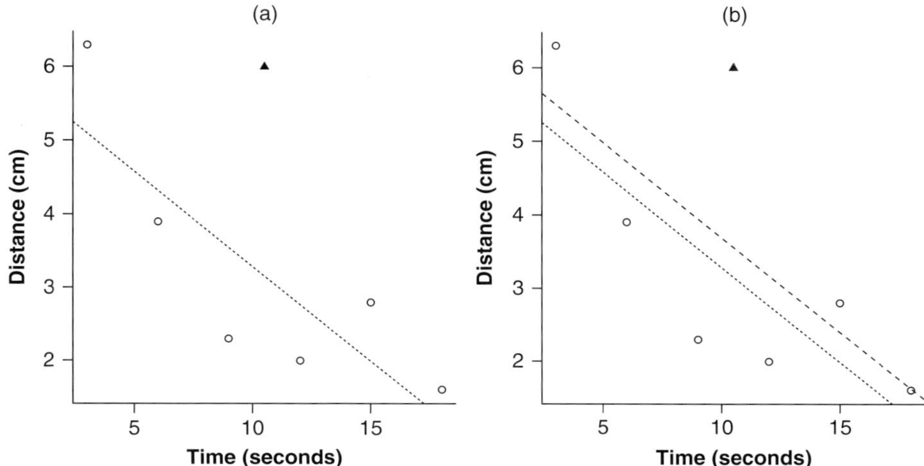

Figure 5.6 How the regression line for the location memory data changes after adding a new observation (the black triangle) at the mean of *X*: (a) depicts the original regression line, while (b) shows the new regression line alongside the original line

falls exactly on the original regression line then the line does not need to shift to accommodate it. In other words, if its residual is zero then the slope is unaltered (regardless of leverage). In contrast, large residuals combined with high leverage have a huge impact on the regression line. What matters is whether the residual is extreme relative to the original model. Figure 5.7 illustrates this by showing what happens when a point with high leverage and a large residual

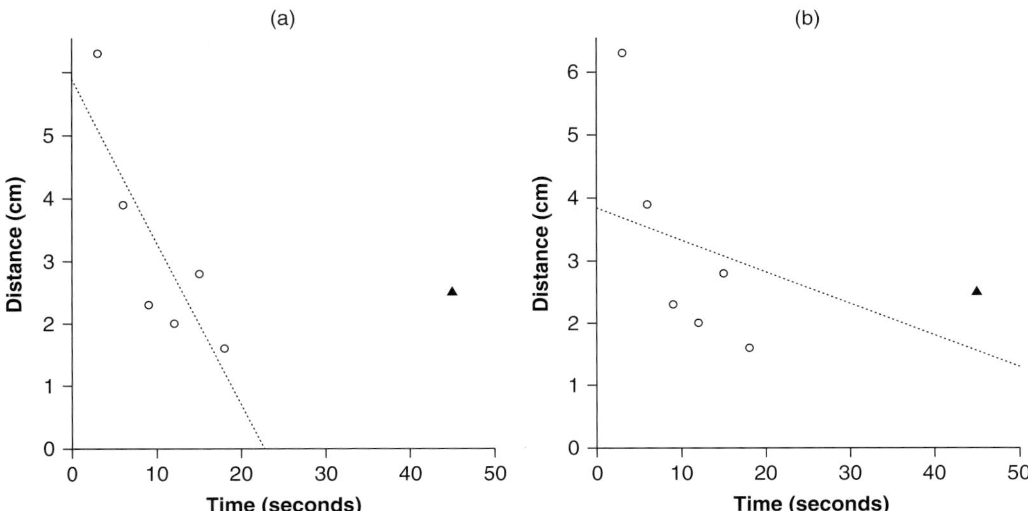

Figure 5.7 How the regression line for the location memory data changes after adding a new observation (the black triangle) with high leverage and a large residual: (a) depicts the original slope and (b) depicts the new slope

($x_7 = 45$ and $y_7 = 2.5$) is added to the location memory data. Again panel (a) shows the original regression line, while panel (b) shows the regression line refitted for the additional data point.

The new slope is still negative, but much shallower than that for the original data. High leverage observations have the potential to dramatically alter both the slope and intercept of a model.

Leverage could be measured in several ways, but a standard measure for simple linear regression is h_i (called a *hat* value). Hat values are given by the equation:

$$h_i = \frac{1}{N} + \frac{(x_i - \hat{\mu}_X)^2}{\sum_{i=1}^{N} (x_i - \hat{\mu}_X)^2} \qquad \text{Equation 5.20}$$

This might seem an *ad hoc* measure (e.g., the minimum is not zero), but expressing leverage in this way turns out to be very helpful. With hat values leverage is always $\geq 1/N$. One feature that helps scale hat values is that they always sum to two. This can be helpful for detecting excessively influential points in a regression model. Even though h_i can exceed one, values at or approaching one in a large data set imply high leverage relative to other points in the regression.

Consider what happens if a sample is taken only for a small region of the possible values of X (assuming X is continuous and unbounded). As the value of X moves further from the mean (the center of the sampled region), prediction moves closer to the unsampled region. At the fringes of the sampled regions (or beyond it) the ability to predict Y with confidence is greatly reduced, because there is little or no data to inform the model. Predicting a new value is rather like adding a data point to the sample. Its impact on the sample variance would be proportional to $1/N$ (indicating equal weight if they all have the same value of X) and the impact on the *SE* is equal to the square root of that. The minimum hat value of $1/N$ is therefore equivalent to the value expected when all data points make the same contribution to prediction and are hence equally informative.

High leverage is not necessarily a bad thing. High leverage points carry more information about the slope than low leverage points. If all observations were sampled at the same value of X it would be impossible to estimate the slope at all. However, having only a few points with high leverage (as is common in small samples) is problematic; the parameter estimates may be unduly influenced by those few observations.

Example 5.3 The new point added to the location memory data set in Figure 5.6 has leverage of:

$$h_i = \frac{1}{N} + \frac{(x_i - \hat{\mu}_X)^2}{\sum_{i=1}^{N} (x_i - \hat{\mu}_X)^2} = \frac{1}{7} + \frac{0}{157.5} = \frac{1}{7}$$

This is the minimum possible. Despite the unchanged slope, the new observation has a relatively large residual (the mean of Y being 3.15 for the original data and the residual being $6 - 3.15 = 2.85$). The reduction in fit using R^2 is from .697 to .477. The new prediction equation differs only in the intercept and is:

$$\hat{Y}_{distance} = 6.267 - 0.2581 X_{time}$$

In contrast, high leverage points can change the slope. For example, if a seventh point was added to the location memory data such that $x_7 = 45$ (i.e., a presentation time of 45 seconds), its leverage would be:

$$h_7 = \frac{1}{7} + \frac{(45 - 15.42857)^2}{1177.714} \approx 0.8853$$

The new point increases both the mean and the squared deviations for X (10.5 and 157.5 in the original sample). The resulting leverage is high relative to the minimum possible leverage of 1/7 (and the next highest leverage is 0.274 for the first point). In Figure 5.7 the observation $x_7 = 45$, $y_7 = 2.5$ is added to the original data. The refitted prediction equation differs both in the intercept and slope:

$$\hat{Y}_{distance} = 3.841 - 0.0508X_{time}$$

The fit is also much poorer ($R^2 = .197$).

5.5.2 Confidence intervals and significance tests for the slope

The standard error of the slope depends not just on the error variance (and therefore $\hat{\sigma}_E$) but also on the range of X used to predict Y. This can be seen in Equation 5.3. The slope is the ratio of the change in Y to a given increase in X. If a large spread of X is used then Y will also show a large spread of values, but the ratio should remain relatively stable between samples. The *standard error of the slope* $\hat{\sigma}_{b_1}$ therefore combines the standard error of the estimate (error in the model) with the spread of X:

$$\hat{\sigma}_{b_1} = \frac{\hat{\sigma}_E}{\sqrt{\sum_{i=1}^{N}(x_i - \hat{\mu}_X)^2}} = \frac{\hat{\sigma}_E}{\sqrt{\sum_{i=1}^{N}(x_i^2) - N\hat{\mu}_X^2}} \qquad \text{Equation 5.21}$$

Calculation of $\hat{\sigma}_{\hat{b}_1}$ assumes an independent, normal distribution of errors with constant, but unknown variance (σ^2_{error}). Inference should therefore refer to the t distribution. This distribution has $\nu = N - 2$ *df* (the *df* associated with the estimate of error variance used in Equation 5.21). A CI for the slope is therefore formed as

$$b_1 \pm t_{N-2,1-\alpha/2}\hat{\sigma}_{b_1} \qquad \text{Equation 5.22}$$

where $t_{N-2,1-\alpha/2}$ is the quantile of the t distribution associated with $N - 2$ *df* and $100(1-\alpha)\%$ confidence. The t distribution can be used to derive a test statistic for the corresponding NHST. A typical H_0 for the slope is that $\beta_1 = 0$, indicating that there is no linear relationship between X and Y in the population. The appropriate test statistic for H_0: $\beta_1 = 0$ is

$$t_{b_1} = \frac{b_1 - 0}{\hat{\sigma}_{b_1}} = \frac{b_1}{\hat{\sigma}_{b_1}} \sim t(\nu) \qquad \text{Equation 5.23}$$

where $\nu = N - 2$. An equivalent test (one often reported by regression software) uses an F distribution with the statistic $F_{1,\nu}$ (for which it is trivial to show that $t^2 = F$).

Example 5.4 The slope of the location memory data is −0.2581 and the relationship between the presentation time (*X*) and distance of responses from the target (*Y*) accounts for about 70% of the variance in the sample ($R^2 = .697$). How confident should you be in this estimate? One way to assess it is to compute a CI for the slope. The *SE* of the slope is:

$$\hat{\sigma}_{b_1} = \frac{\hat{\sigma}_E}{\sqrt{\sum_{i=1}^{N}(x_i^2) - N\hat{\mu}_X^2}} = \frac{\sqrt{SS_{residual}/(N-2)}}{\sqrt{\sum_{i=1}^{N}(x_i^2) - N\hat{\mu}_X^2}} = \frac{\sqrt{4.5634/4}}{\sqrt{819 - 6(10.5^2)}} \approx 0.0851$$

The 95% CI for the slope is therefore:

$$-0.2581 \pm t_{4,.975} \times 0.0851$$

As $t_{4,.975} = 2.776445$ this evaluates as -0.2581 ± 0.2363 and the resulting interval estimate can be reported as:

$$b_1 = -0.26,\ 95\%\ \text{CI}\ [-0.49, -0.02]$$

This interval is very wide: indicating that a plausible range for the effect is a decrease of between a 50th of a *cm* and half a *cm* distance from the target per extra second of presentation time. A significance test of the null hypothesis that there is no effect of presentation time on responses (and hence no relationship between *X* and *Y*) produces the test statistic

$$t_{b_1} = \frac{b_1}{\hat{\sigma}_{b_1}} = \frac{-0.2581}{0.08511} \approx -3.033$$

with two-sided $p = .039$. As the 95% CI excludes zero it necessarily agrees with the NHST (rejecting H_0 because $p < .05$). Both the test and the CI have detected an effect of presentation time on distance from the target (because the null hypothesis of no relationship was rejected). However, the CI is more informative, indicating that the effect could be very small or fairly substantial.

5.5.3 Confidence intervals and significance tests for the intercept

Inference using regression models usually focuses on the relationship between *X* and *Y* and thus the slope rather than the intercept. Inference about the intercept is also possible (and is instructive because it is a special case of prediction). A CI for the intercept is an interval estimate of the predicted value of *Y* at the point when *X* is zero. The *standard error of the intercept* can be obtained from the equation:

$$\hat{\sigma}_{b_0} = \hat{\sigma}_E \sqrt{\frac{\sum_{i=1}^{N} x_i^2}{N\left(\sum_{i=1}^{N}(x_i - \hat{\mu}_X)^2\right)}} \qquad \text{Equation 5.24}$$

Because $x_i = 0$ at the intercept, this equation can be rearranged to yield:

$$\hat{\sigma}_{b_0} = \hat{\sigma}_E \sqrt{\frac{1}{N} + \frac{\hat{\mu}_X^2}{\sum_{i=1}^{N} (x_i - \hat{\mu}_X)^2}} \qquad \text{Equation 5.25}$$

Compare this to Equation 5.20. You will see that the right-hand side is, in effect, a leverage calculation for the predicted value (i.e., when $X = 0$). This value tends to be high when N is small or when, relative to the spread of the data, $\hat{\mu}_X$ is large (i.e., when most data points lie far from zero). This is an important idea – fundamental to prediction. Prediction works best (i.e., has a smaller margin of error) for observations similar to those in the sample. When predictions are made outside the range of observed data, prediction tends to be poor.

CIs and tests for the intercept again use the t distribution with $N - 2$ degrees of freedom. The CI for the intercept is therefore

$$b_0 \pm t_{N-2,1-\alpha/2} \hat{\sigma}_{b_0} \qquad \text{Equation 5.26}$$

and a significance test of H_0: $\beta_0 = 0$ has a test statistic of the form:

$$t_{b_0} = \frac{b_0 - \beta_0}{\hat{\sigma}_{b_0}} = \frac{b_0}{\hat{\sigma}_{b_0}} \qquad \text{Equation 5.27}$$

Although other null hypotheses are possible, this is a typical implementation of the NHST. Because the intercept is the value of Y when $X = 0$, it is a test of the hypothesis that the regression line passes through the origin (0, 0). However, as explained in Section 5.6.1, it is dangerous to fit a model without an intercept even if the context of the study or a test of the intercept suggests that the population regression line does pass through the origin.

Example 5.5 For the location memory data the intercept is 5.86. Referring to Table 5.2 and using the result that $\hat{\sigma}_E = \sqrt{4.5634/4} \approx 1.0681$ the *SE* of the intercept is:

$$\hat{\sigma}_{b_0} = 1.0681 \sqrt{\frac{1}{6} + \frac{10.5^2}{157.5}} \approx 0.9944$$

The 95% CI for the intercept is therefore $5.86 \pm 2.7764 \times 0.9944$, or $b_0 = 5.86$ 95% CI [3.10, 8.62]. The corresponding NHST has a test statistic of

$$t = \frac{b_0}{SE_{b_0}} = \frac{5.86}{0.994} \approx 5.90$$

with two-sided $p = .004$. Although this is statistically significant (if $\alpha = .05$), there are reasons to be suspicious of both the interval estimate and test. It is not clear that the prediction of the distance is meaningful when presentation time is zero. In addition, the intercept is highly dependent on straight-line fit (which seems doubtful).

5.5.4 Confidence and prediction intervals

Thus far the term prediction has been used in a loose sense (more or less synonymous with estimation of the slope of intercept parameters). Prediction in its strictest sense is the application of statistical methods to derive estimates of a new or unknown outcome (Y) from known values of a predictor or set of predictors (see Snedecor and Cochran, 1989). As the population mean is the expected value of an observation, the mean is also the 'best guess' for predicting an unknown Y value. However, the margin of error is greater for prediction of individual observations than for estimation of the mean. Except in the case of no error variance (i.e., perfect prediction), new observations rarely fall exactly on the mean (or even very close to it). Estimation only considers the variability of the true mean relative to the predicted mean. Prediction must take into account an additional source of variability: the scatter of observed values around the population mean.

If the goal is to estimate the value of future observations from the same population, a standard CI is inadequate (as it provides an interval estimate for the population mean). For predicting individual outcomes a different form of confidence interval known as a *prediction interval* is required. The prediction interval is formed in the same way as the regular CI, but uses a standard error that takes account of the additional variability. A general expression for the *SE* for a prediction interval is:

$$\hat{\sigma}_{prediction} = \hat{\sigma}_E \sqrt{\frac{1}{m} + \frac{1}{n} + \frac{(x_{n+m} - \hat{\mu}_X)^2}{\sum_{i=1}^{n} (x_i - \hat{\mu}_X)^2}} = \hat{\sigma}_E \sqrt{\frac{1}{m} + h_{n+m}} \qquad \text{Equation 5.28}$$

Here x_{n+m} is the value of the m unknown observations for which predictions are sought, while h_{n+m} is the leverage or hat value for those m observations (and n is the original sample size). Using leverage reiterates the point that predicting observations depends on where the weight of observed data lie. If you collect data for a narrow range of X, your predictions will be best for new values of X central to that range. As you go beyond the available information the predictions become increasingly uncertain.

This general form of the equation is, in effect, an interval estimate for the mean of a future sample of size m. By comparing Equation 5.28 and Equation 5.25 it is possible to see that a CI could be viewed as special case of a prediction interval. A CI is a prediction interval for a parameter (the mean of an infinitely large population) rather than for the mean of a finite number of observations. When only a single observation is predicted $m = 1$ and the formula reduces to

$$\hat{\sigma}_{prediction} = \hat{\sigma}_E \sqrt{1 + h_{n+1}} \qquad \text{Equation 5.29}$$

where h_{n+1} is the leverage of the unknown observation to be predicted. On the other hand if m is very large, the ratio $1/m$ approaches zero, and when m is infinite the object of prediction becomes the population mean. This is what happens in Equation 5.25 for the intercept (and because $x_{n+1} = 0$, that also disappears from the equation). The intercept is therefore the predicted value of Y if the entire population were sampled (provided $x_{n+1} = 0$). Generalizing this equation to other values of X gives the following expression for the standard error of prediction for a population mean:

$$\hat{\sigma}_{prediction} = \hat{\sigma}_E \sqrt{h_{n+1}} \qquad \text{Equation 5.30}$$

A prediction interval can therefore be constructed as:

$$\hat{Y} \pm t_{n-2,1-\alpha/2} \hat{\sigma}_{prediction} \qquad \text{Equation 5.31}$$

The quality of prediction depends on the appropriateness of the model and the assumptions that underlie the choice of the t distribution.

Example 5.6 For the location memory data, the predicted distance for a presentation time of six seconds is $5.860 - 0.2581 \times 6 = 4.311$ *cm*. The interval estimate for predicting Y from X is:

$$4.311 \pm 2.776 \times \hat{\sigma}_{prediction}$$

If the mean is the object of prediction $\hat{\sigma}_{prediction}$ is:

$$\hat{\sigma}_E \sqrt{h_{n+1}} = 1.068 \sqrt{\frac{1}{6} + \frac{(6-10.5)^2}{157.5}} \approx 0.580$$

However, if prediction is for a single observation $\hat{\sigma}_{prediction}$ becomes:

$$\hat{\sigma}_E \sqrt{\frac{1}{m} + h_{n+m}} = 1.068 \sqrt{1 + \frac{1}{6} + \frac{(6-10.5)^2}{157.5}} \approx 1.216$$

This gives a 95% CI for the mean of Y when $x_{n+m} = 6$ of [2.70, 5.92], and a 95% prediction interval of [0.94, 7.69]. In this case the prediction interval is nearly twice as wide as the CI for the mean. Both intervals are wide because the original sample size is so small.

While prediction intervals for individual observations or for the mean of the outcome are informative, they can be frustrating to work with. You may not be interested in the interval estimate for a single point on the regression line. It is more likely you are interested in the overall relationship between X and Y. It will often be preferable to plot the confidence or prediction intervals for a range of predictor values rather than for a single point. A rather elegant approach is to plot *confidence bands* around the regression line (or, by analogy, prediction bands).

This involves plotting the upper and lower limits of the interval estimate as a function X. Figure 5.8 illustrates this by plotting 95% confidence bands for the location memory data. The curvature of the confidence bands is very marked (partly because of the small sample size). The narrowest gap between these limits and the regression line is at the mean of X. Thus the curvature neatly illustrates the impact of leverage on the interval estimates.

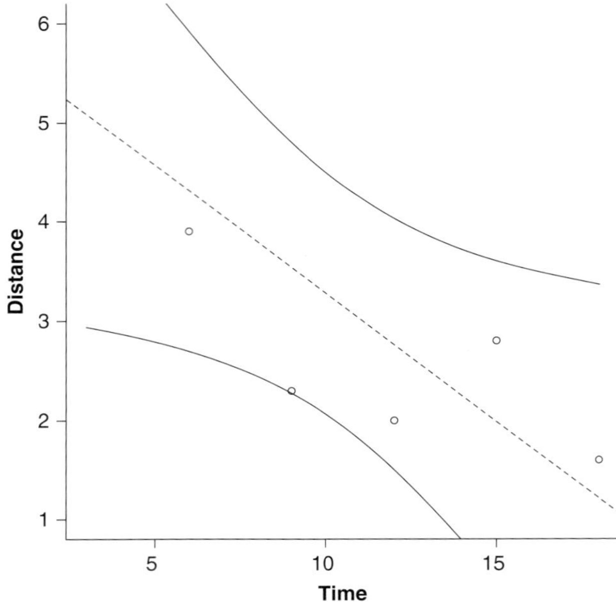

Figure 5.8 Regression line with 95% confidence bands for the location memory data

5.6 Fitting and interpreting regression models

5.6.1 Regression with no intercept

Regression without an intercept is rarely a good idea. A regression with no intercept assumes a model where the regression line goes through the origin (the point where $x = 0$ and $y = 0$). This type of model is, in theory, attractive because it implies that when X is zero Y is zero. For example, in predicting vocabulary size from age you might presume a vocabulary of zero for a newborn child. This form of model is usually discouraged, even if the true relationship were of the correct form. Forcing the regression line through the origin (the implication of not including an intercept) nearly always causes problems. Such a model effectively fixes the intercept to be exactly zero and the regression model becomes:

$$y_i = b_1 x_i + e_i \qquad \text{Equation 5.32}$$

Why is such a model so bad? First and foremost, the regression line will not, as a rule, be the best-fitting straight line (or even close to it). Even if the true intercept in the population is zero, forcing a regression to go through the origin has unpleasant consequences. It is probably unreasonable to assume that Y is measured without any bias whatsoever in a given sample (though its expectation may be unbiased). If the error in measuring Y biases observed values up or down this has the effect of shifting the intercept in the same direction. Including an intercept in the model allows it to soak up this kind of consistent (additive) bias and the estimate of the slope will be unbiased. Not including the intercept will dramatically change the slope. In effect,

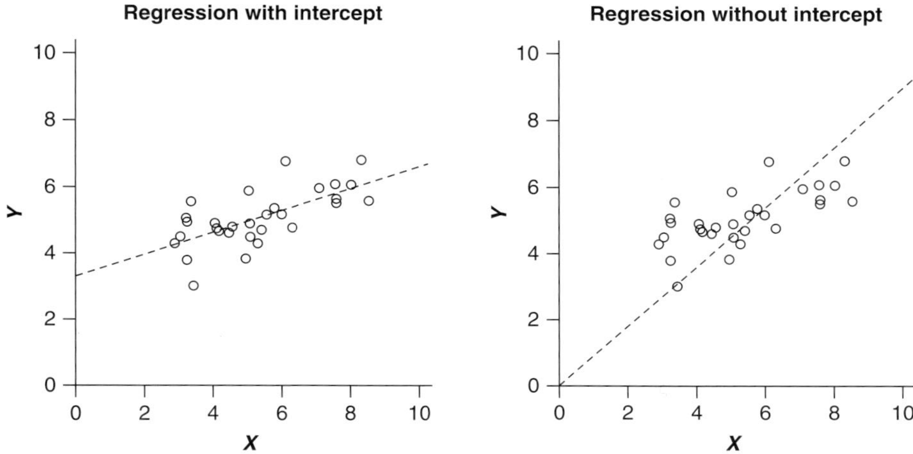

Figure 5.9 The impact of forcing the intercept through the origin on the estimate of the regression slope

b_1 will no longer be a pure estimate of the population slope but a mixture of contributions from both intercept and slope.

Figure 5.9 shows (using artificial data constructed to have a positive slope and intercept) how the slope can change for a model without an intercept relative to one with an intercept.

In addition, the no-intercept model often appears to account for a larger proportion of the sample variance than the standard model including an intercept. For example, for data plotted in Figure 5.9 the no-intercept model R^2 is .9475 compared with .4515 for the R^2 of the with-intercept model. This apparently superior fit is spurious – arising from a switch in the definition of R^2. This is because the proportion of variance explained by each model is assessed relative to a different total (at least with most common software). In the no-intercept model R^2 is calculated from SS_{total} assuming that the mean of Y is zero. (Although not helpful in this situation, there are situations where this characterization of R^2 is warranted.) Formulas for no-intercept regression are provided by Snedecor and Cochran (1989).

Fitting a no-intercept model also places an additional burden on the suitability of a linear model. For a simple linear regression a straight line will often produce a good approximation to a curvilinear relationship (at least for the range of X values that are sampled). One reason it can do this is because the intercept allows it to get a close fit to the observed section of a curve (particularly if the curvature is not marked).

Although a no-intercept regression model should mostly be avoided, there are some unusual situations where it is appropriate. It can also be a useful trick to change the way computer software parameterizes a regression model (see Chapter 13).

5.6.2 Impact of the addition or multiplication of *X* or *Y* on regression

It is not uncommon for X and Y to be rescaled by addition or multiplication prior to analysis. As long as the effect of rescaling is to add or multiply X or Y by a constant (or subtract or divide by a constant) the regression model will largely be unaffected.

Adding a constant c to Y will increase the intercept (and hence all predicted values) by c. Adding a constant c to X will increase the intercept and predicted values by exactly b_1 times c. This sort of shift arises from a change in reference point (e.g., altitude can be measured as height above sea level or height above ground). Multiplying Y by a constant k will increase the values of all coefficients (slope and intercept) by k and hence all predicted values will increase by a factor of k. Similarly, variances and sums of squares will be increased by a factor of k^2, but this has no adverse effect on estimation or prediction (because the standard errors will be increased by k, thus rescaling everything correctly). For quantities that use the sums of squares directly – such as R^2 – the increase in variance by a factor of k^2 also cancels out (as both the numerator and denominator are k^2 times larger). Such multiplication is very common when changing measurement units.

The location memory example used seconds as the unit for time and *cm* as the unit for distance. This could easily be changed to minutes by multiplying X by 60^{-1} and inches by multiplying distance by 2.54^{-1}. The resulting regression equation is:

$$distance_{inches} = 2.3071 - 6.0967 \times time_{minutes} + e_i$$

This is an identical statistical model, provided you are aware of the change in units. Parameters and standard errors remain exactly in line with the rescaled data and the inferences drawn from tests, confidence and prediction intervals will not change.

This property of regression – aside from being essential to keep arbitrary changes of measurement scale from changing important properties of a statistical model – has practical applications. Specialist statistical software (e.g., SPSS or R) uses carefully designed algorithms that can deal with very large and very small data values. Non-specialist software (e.g., generic spreadsheet software such as Excel) is not designed this way. For example, where the mean of a sample is very small (e.g., 0.0000001) statistical operations that calculate quantities such as residuals and square them can lose accuracy (because software may discard digits after perhaps 15 decimal places). Even specialist software may have difficulty with displaying such small values (e.g., because it introduces clutter to the labels on graphs). Multiplying the values by a suitable constant will get round these difficulties. It can also aid interpretation (because most people find it more comfortable working with whole numbers rather than small fractions).

A more important application arises for data with an arbitrary scale. A common case is a Likert-type scale. On such a scale, responses are usually coded as positive integers such as 1 to 5, or by summing such responses over a number of items. If so, the intercept of the model is unlikely to be meaningful. Also, if Y is coded in this way, there is no point testing the hypothesis that the intercept is 0 (because such a value is impossible). To aid interpretation you may prefer to *center* either the codes or Y prior to regression.

Centering a variable involves subtracting its mean from each observation. So if Y is the variable to be centered:

$$y_{C,i} = y_i - \hat{\mu}_Y \qquad \text{Equation 5.33}$$

The new, centered variable will now have a mean of zero, though its distribution and variance (or *SD*) are unchanged. If both X and Y have arbitrary scales and are centered then the intercept becomes zero. This can aid interpretation if the intercept isn't meaningful (e.g., if it is an impossible value). The regression will then take the form:

$$y_{C,i} = (y_i - \hat{\mu}_Y) = 0 + b_1 x_{C,i} + e_i$$

This is not a no-intercept model – the intercept is a parameter in the model (but its estimate is zero). Interpretation of the model is potentially simpler: zero for either variable now represents its mean. If only X is centered, the intercept represents the value of Y when X is at its mean (i.e., the predicted mean for an 'average' X). Centering is sometimes applied in simple linear regression, and is standard practice for some regression models employing variables on arbitrary scales. Centering the codes for a Likert-style scale works in an analogous way – but the intercept is not necessarily zero. The advantage is that codes such as 1 to 5 are replaced by the set of codes $\{-2, -1, 0, +1, +2\}$ and zero represents the midpoint of the scale (usually a neutral point and quite often close to the mean).

5.6.3 Residuals and influence

Not all points have equal impact on the regression line. Think about what happens when an additional point is added to a regression. As noted earlier, its contribution to the slope of the regression line depends on two factors: its leverage and its vertical distance from the regression line (the size of the residual).

Leverage determines the potential impact a point could have on the slope of the regression – being zero at $\hat{\mu}_X$ and increasing with distance from $\hat{\mu}_X$. The degree of impact is scaled by the residual. To measure the impact on the regression model it helps to rescale the residuals. Perhaps the best-known option is to standardize the residual – dividing it by $\hat{\sigma}_{estimate}$ (which is the square root of the error variance and hence its *SD*). As the residuals are assumed normal and have mean zero, dividing by $\hat{\sigma}_{estimate}$ should give the residuals a z distribution:

$$z_{residual} = \frac{e_i}{\hat{\sigma}_E} \sim z \qquad \text{Equation 5.34}$$

Standardized residuals are relatively easy to interpret (e.g., if $n = 100$ one would expect about 5% of observations to have absolute z scores above two and only a few observations above three). Standardized residuals are sometimes weighted by leverage. For convenience these can be denoted as:

$$r_{standard} = \frac{e_i}{\hat{\sigma}_E \sqrt{1 - h_i}} \qquad \text{Equation 5.35}$$

This latter formula will not guarantee that the residuals have an *SD* of one (but has the advantage of weighting influential points more heavily than $z_{residual}$).

While the standardized residuals are convenient, they underestimate the potential impact of a new point on the regression line. This is because – as pointed out when leverage was calculated for a seventh point in the location memory data – the new point will change n (and other statistics may change dramatically too). When the new point has high leverage this inflates the sums of squares for X. Thus its leverage and residual in the new model underestimate its impact relative to the parameter estimates of the original model. The solution is to use *deletion residuals*. These are obtained by deleting each point from the regression in turn. Impact can then be assessed relative to a model that excludes it (i.e., with sample size $N - 1$). Standardized residuals calculated in this way no longer have a z distribution. Instead they should follow a t distribution with $(N - 1) - (q + 1) = N - q - 2$ *df*, where q is the number of predictors and $(q + 1)$

is the total number of parameters being estimated. For simple linear regression there is one predictor and the number of parameters being estimated is $(q+1)=2$ and $df = N-3$. The loss of an extra degree of freedom is a trivial consequence of having one fewer observation after deletion. Residuals obtained in this way are *Studentized residuals* (because of the link to Student's t distribution):

$$t_{residual} = \frac{e_i}{\hat{\sigma}_{deletion}} \sim t(N-q-2) \qquad \text{Equation 5.36}$$

Here $\hat{\sigma}_{deletion}$ is $\hat{\sigma}_{estimate}$ calculated from the deletion residuals (the residuals of the regression model with the ith point deleted). A version incorporating leverage is:

$$r_{student} = \frac{e_i}{\hat{\sigma}_{deletion}\sqrt{1-h_i}} \qquad \text{Equation 5.37}$$

Studentized residuals offer a method to construct a test statistic for the impact of extreme observations on the regression. These tests are a little suspect and should generally be avoided. They depend strongly on the assumptions of the model and can be misused (e.g., to hunt down and remove 'inconvenient' data points from an analysis).

A crucial point arising from this discussion is that it is not whether an observation is extreme, but whether a residual is extreme that matters. When extreme residuals combine with high leverage this changes the parameter estimates. This principle is illustrated in Figure 5.7. The slope of the regression line in panel (b) is estimated using an additional data point with high leverage and a large residual. This dramatically reduces the estimate of the strength of relationship between X and Y. The new point (depicted by a black triangle) therefore has high *influence*. Influence is the degree to which an observation alters the parameter estimates of a model. Leverage alone is not problematic (it being useful to have information from a range of predictor values), and large residuals don't necessarily alter the parameter estimates (though they do increase error variance).

Measures of influence combine leverage and residuals into a single statistic. A number of measures exist, but we will focus on a widely available and relatively simple measure known as Cook's distance (Cook, 1977). A general formula for Cook's distance is

$$D_i = \frac{e_i^2}{qMS_{error}}\left(\frac{h_i}{(1-h_i)^2}\right) \qquad \text{Equation 5.38}$$

where q is the number of parameters in the regression model and MS_{error} is the sample estimate of error variance (i.e., $\hat{\sigma}_E^2$). Given that simple linear regression only involves $q=2$ parameters this reduces to:

$$D_i = \frac{e_i^2}{2MS_{error}}\left(\frac{h_i}{(1-h_i)^2}\right) \qquad \text{Equation 5.39}$$

The absolute value of Cook's distance can be hard to interpret, but a rough guide is that any data point with $D_i \geq 1$ is highly influential. With at least moderate sample sizes, Cook's distances as large as one are rare and worthy of further investigation.[7] Furthermore, somewhat smaller values of D_i also indicate very influential points (e.g., $D_i \approx 0.5$).

Influence statistics should be interpreted with care. Influential points should never automatically be discarded from the model. Observations with high leverage are more informative about the linear relationship between X and Y than those with low leverage. Discarding influential points necessarily involves discarding highly informative observations. A better solution is to design a study to sample many high leverage points and so reduce the influence of a single large residual with high leverage (see McClelland, 1997).

Example 5.7 The six residuals for the location memory data are shown below in relation to increasing presentation time ($x_i = 3, 6, 9, 12, 15$ or 18 seconds).

$$1.214 \quad -0.411 \quad -1.237 \quad -0.763 \quad 0.811 \quad 0.386$$

The residuals themselves are measured in *cm* because they are on the same scale as Y. The second largest residual (in absolute terms) is that for the three-second presentation which has a standardized residual of:

$$z_{residual} = \frac{e_i}{\hat{\sigma}_E} = \frac{1.214}{1.068} \approx 1.14$$

Incorporating leverage of 0.524 for the same point gives:

$$r_{standard} = \frac{e_i}{\hat{\sigma}_E\sqrt{1-h_i}} = \frac{1.21}{1.068\sqrt{1-0.524}} \approx 1.64$$

Neither measure is particularly extreme relative to the full sample.

Studentized residuals require recalculating $\hat{\sigma}_{estimate}$ for a data set. Doing so for the three-second presentation gives $\hat{\sigma}_{deletion} = 0.6993$ and therefore:

$$t_{residual} = \frac{e_i}{\hat{\sigma}_{deletion}} = \frac{1.214}{0.6993} \approx 1.74$$

Incorporating leverage produces:

$$r_{student} = \frac{e_i}{\hat{\sigma}_{deletion}\sqrt{1-h_i}} = \frac{1.214}{0.6993\sqrt{1-0.524}} \approx 2.52$$

This latter measure suggests greater cause for concern than the other measures. The corresponding Cook's distance is:

$$D_i = \frac{e_i^2}{2MS_{error}}\left(\frac{h_i}{(1-h_i)^2}\right) = \frac{1.214^2}{2 \times 1.068^2}\left(\frac{0.524}{(1-0.524)^2}\right) \approx 1.49$$

As values above one indicate highly influential points this confirms the impact of this observation on slope. In a larger data set this would be a genuine worry, but with such a small sample highly influential observations are almost inevitable. With only six observations, each data point necessarily has a big impact on the model. The optimum solution is to design a study to gain more data with high leverage. Influence can also be used to justify exclusion of data from a model, but this should be avoided if possible. If you do exclude data, best practice is to explain the rationale for exclusion and to report the impact of excluding data on the analysis.

5.6.4 Regression with discrete variables

Regression was introduced as a technique for understanding the relationship between two continuous variables. Although this is a good starting point, regression can also be applied when X or Y are discrete. As a rule, this works better for the predictor (X) than the outcome (Y). Regression using least squares does not involve strong assumptions about the continuity of the predictor. The properties of the outcome are much more important. Even so, there are many cases where regression with discrete Y is more than adequate. If necessary, linear regression models can also be generalized to explicitly model discrete outcomes (see Chapter 17).

Major difficulties arise in modeling the relationships between discrete variables, not because they are discrete *per se*, but because they are often bounded. This may pose serious problems if the goal is to make predictions. A fundamental insight is that for bounded variables the true relationship cannot be linear (though it may be approximately linear within the range sampled). Discrete data (e.g., scores on a Likert-type scale) are frequently bounded in this way. Two general principles can guide regression modeling with such data:

i) regression produces sensible output if the assumptions of the statistical model are not severely violated;
ii) prediction outside the sampled range of X should be done only with extreme caution.

The first principle will sometimes be justified by reference to the CLT. Thus regression with a dichotomous response (an extreme case of a discrete, bounded Y variable) will be fairly accurate if the true outcome is binomial, N is moderately large (e.g., approaching 30) and the probability of observing a success is not too low or too high (e.g., between .25 and .75).[8] In such a case the binomial converges rapidly on the normal distribution.

5.6.5 Regression with a dichotomous predictor

A particularly important application of regression occurs when the predictor is dichotomous. For instance, in an experimental study participants may belong to either a control group or an experimental group. Provided the participants are independent observations (e.g., randomly assigned to only one of the two groups) simple linear regression is appropriate. Here group membership could be coded by any two values, though to keep things simple *dummy coding* using the values zero and one are usually selected (e.g., zero representing controls and one representing the experimental group). Regressing Y on X thus produces the model:

$$y_i = \hat{\mu}_0 + (\hat{\mu}_1 - \hat{\mu}_0)x_i + e_i \qquad \text{Equation 5.40}$$

Under dummy coding, this is a standard regression equation with $b_0 = \hat{\mu}_0$ and $b_1 = (\hat{\mu}_1 - \hat{\mu}_0)$ because X is either zero or one. This model can also be set out as separate regression equations for the two groups:

$$y_i = \hat{\mu}_0 + e_i \qquad (X = 0)$$

$$y_i = \hat{\mu}_0 + (\hat{\mu}_1 - \hat{\mu}_0) + e_i \qquad (X = 1)$$

Expressed this way it is perhaps clearer that the intercept is the control group mean, and the slope is the difference between the control group and experimental group means: $\hat{\mu}_1 - \hat{\mu}_0$.

The CI or NHST for the slope is therefore an inference about the difference between the means of two independent groups from a normal distribution with unknown variance. These inferences use a t distribution with $N-2$ *df*. The t test of the slope is therefore equivalent to the independent t test. It follows that the independent t test is a special case of simple linear regression when X is dichotomous. If dummy coding hadn't been used, the test of slope would still have been equivalent to the independent t test, but the parameter estimates would have to be interpreted slightly differently. Changing the group coding *reparameterizes* the regression. Reparameterization doesn't fundamentally change the statistical model, but switching to an alternative parameterization can make a model easier to interpret. Regression can be used as a framework to integrate a large number of superficially disparate statistical techniques. For instance, a one sample t test is equivalent to a regression model with an intercept but no predictor.

Example 5.8 The equivalence between independent t and simple linear regression with dichotomous X can be demonstrated by reanalyzing the comprehension data first introduced in Example 3.6. This analysis requires a dummy coded grouping variable (or regression software that can recognize and automatically code a categorical predictor).

In this case I have coded the low study group zero and the high study group one. This defines the predictor X. Percentage accuracy is then treated as the outcome Y.

Figure 5.10 shows the fitted regression line for these data. The corresponding prediction equation is:

$$\hat{Y} = \hat{\mu}_0 + (\hat{\mu}_1 - \hat{\mu}_0)X = 74.1 + 13.1X$$

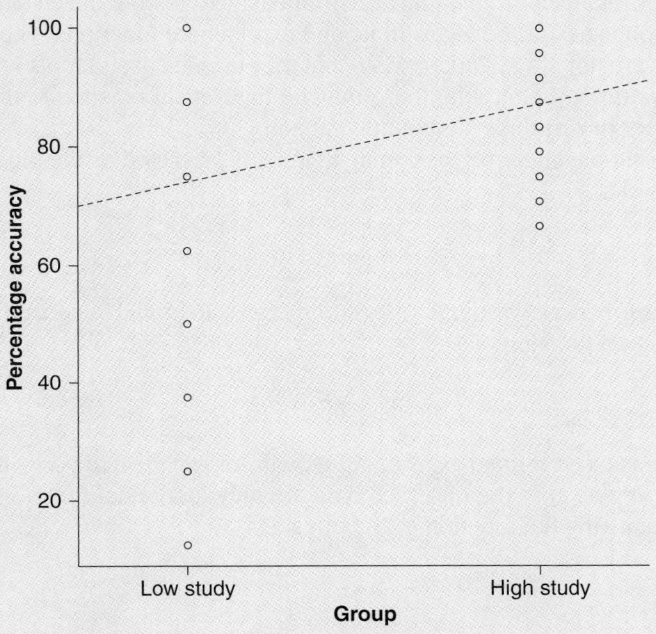

Figure 5.10 Regression line for a simple linear regression of percentage accuracy by group (dummy coded) for the comprehension data

The intercept is the mean of the low study group ($M=74.1\%$) and the slope of 13.1 is the difference in percentage accuracy between the high study group ($M=87.2\%$) and the low study group (i.e., $74.1\%+13.1\%=87.2\%$). As $\hat{\sigma}_E$ is the square root of the error variance, it should match the pooled standard deviation from the *t* test. Also identical are *t*, *df*, *p* and the 95% CI. This identity may not hold if the Welch-Satterthwaite correction is employed; this correction is typically implemented in software for the independent *t* test, but not regression. For this reason, while regression is very flexible, there may be practical reasons not to run all analyses as regressions.

5.7 Fitting curvilinear relationships with simple linear regression

A simple linear regression is linear in the sense that it fits a model that is an additive function of a constant and a single predictor. This results in a straight-line fit to the data (though linear models in general are not limited in this way). It may seem unlikely, but it is even possible to model some curvilinear relationships between X and Y with a simple linear regression (and its 'straight-line' fit).

Where any set of points has only one best-fitting straight line (assuming least squares estimation), infinitely many curves could be generated that fitted the same data. With a sufficiently large number of parameters a curve can always be found that will fit any sample perfectly. This strategy violates the principle of Occam's razor (which suggests researchers should prefer curves produced by relatively simple functions). One way to restrict the choice of curves in simple linear regression is to use the logarithmic and exponential functions. The models produced by these functions are not always appropriate, but they provide useful tools when it is necessary to fit curvilinear patterns. Better still, there may be theoretical reasons to use these functions (e.g., when predictor or response are bounded at zero).

First consider a simple linear regression in which Y is predicted as the logarithm (usually the natural logarithm) of X:

$$Y = b_0 + b_1 \ln(X) \quad \text{Equation 5.41}$$

This is sometimes termed a *logarithmic* or *logarithmic growth* model. A second option is to model the logarithm of Y as a function of X:

$$\ln(Y) = b_0 + b_1 X \quad \text{Equation 5.42}$$

This form of curve is often termed *exponential growth* (or *exponential decay* if the slope is negative). The model implies that the observed data are an exponential function of X. This can be demonstrated by applying the function e^X to both sides:

$$Y = e^{b_0 + b_1 X} \quad \text{Equation 5.43}$$

A third option is to take logarithms of both X and Y:

$$\ln(Y) = b_0 + b_1 \ln(X) \quad \text{Equation 5.44}$$

This produces what is known as a *power law*. All three are still linear functions in the sense that Y is modeled as an appropriately scaled additive function of X. The logarithm of X or Y may also have a theoretical justification if the variables are bounded at zero, particularly if the effect of a variable might be multiplicative rather than additive (see Section 2.4.2).

All these regression models involve assumptions that are not always apparent to researchers. By transforming X and Y so that a nonlinear relationship becomes a straight line (which is what these methods do), the assumptions of least squares regression now apply to the errors of the transformed model (see Snedecor and Cochran, 1989). For the exponential model it is assumed that the errors in predicting $\ln(Y)$ have constant variance. For inference it would be further assumed that the errors are normal. Thus this model assumes a lognormal distribution of errors when Y is predicted. If these assumptions are not tenable then simple linear regression will not be appropriate and either a more sophisticated linear model or a nonlinear model is required.

Example 5.9 The location memory data involves two variables (time and distance) that are bounded at zero. For this reason a curvilinear fit may be particularly suitable (noting also that the pattern of the data also looks somewhat curvilinear). Figure 5.11 shows regression lines for logarithmic, exponential and power law fits to the data.

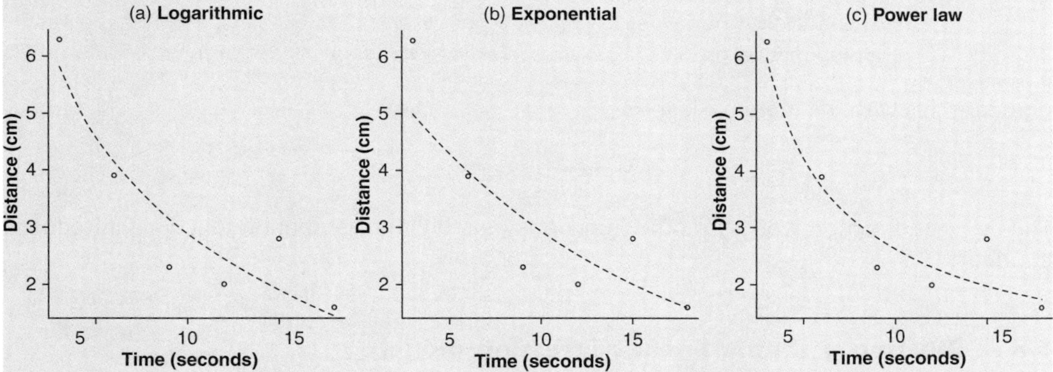

Figure 5.11 Curvilinear fits to the location memory data, using (a) logarithmic, (b) exponential, or (c) power law fits

Of these curves, the logarithmic model is marginally the best fit ($R^2 = .8655$) with the power law a close second ($R^2 = .8427$) and the exponential the poorest ($R^2 = .7396$). However, no model should ever be selected purely on its fit to observed data. Considering only these three options, the power law is the most theoretically plausible. While the power law predicts a distance of 0.93*cm* at for a presentation time of 45 seconds, the exponential model predicts a distance of −0.78*cm*. Neither function may capture the 'true' relationship between X and Y, and (as here) the best-fitting regression model is not necessarily the most convincing. As both X and Y are bounded at zero, a regression of $\ln(Y)$ on $\ln(X)$ is appealing because it prevents prediction of negative responses.

Applying simple linear regression to curve fitting is a reminder that simple models can be surprisingly powerful. Nevertheless, curve fitting is a very difficult business. While it is often easy to fit a particular sample, there are perhaps several (and maybe hundreds of) plausible curves that will fit well, even if choice is restricted to relatively simple mathematical functions. Only very rarely will there be sufficient data to select decisively from the most plausible alternative models.

5.8 R code for Chapter 5

5.8.1 Plotting a mathematical function

The `curve()` function provides a general-purpose method for plotting a range of mathematical functions. This is shown in Figure 5.1 (where a straight line is plotted). The first argument in the function `2+0.5*x` specifies the equation for the curve as a function of `x`. Straight lines can also be fitted with the `abline()` function and sections of straight lines with `segments()`. The `xlab` and `ylab` arguments provide the labels for each axis, while `lty` specifies the line type (1 for solid, 2 for dashed and 3 for dotted). For further details try `?par` or `help(par)`.

```
par(mar=c(4,4,0.5,0.5), pty='s')
curve(2+0.5*x, xlim=c(0,10), ylim=c(.5,10), xaxs='i', lty=2,
  xlab=expression(italic(X)), ylab=expression(italic(Y)))
```

Compare this with the more basic form:

```
curve(2+.5*x)
```

The `curve()` function works for other functions (notably the distribution functions introduced in Chapter 2.)

5.8.2 Plotting a simple linear regression model

In most cases you will want to add a regression line to plot with the observed data – to be able to visually assess the fit. This can be done with the `plot()` function defaults. This produces a scatter plot if called with two vectors containing X and Y. Here, `time` and `distance` are vectors containing the predictor and outcome for the location memory data. The data sets are sufficiently small to be typed in.

```
time <- c(3, 6, 9, 12, 15, 18)
distance <- c(6.3, 3.9, 2.3, 2, 2.8, 1.6)

plot(time, distance, ylab='Distance', xlab='Time')
abline(5.86, - 0.2581, lty=2)
```

Here, the `abline()` function works with the intercept and slope, but it can also take other forms of input.

5.8.3 Fitting a regression model (Examples 5.1, 5.2, 5.4 and 5.5)

The `lm()` function fits a linear model using least squares estimation. At its simplest, it takes a regression formula such as $Y = b_0 + b_1 X$ as input. This is represented in R as `Y ~ X`, where `X` and `Y` are R objects (e.g., vectors or variables defined by columns of a data frame).

```
lm(distance ~ time)
```

This default output from the regression model is:

```
Call:
lm(formula = distance ~ time)

Coefficients:
(Intercept)      time
   5.8600     -0.2581
```

The basic output from the `lm()` linear model function is quite sparse. It reproduces the call to the function (and therefore the regression equation) and duplicates the parameter estimates calculated by hand in Example 5.1 (which could also be repeated step-by-step using R's arithmetic functions).

The output of this fitted regression model can be assigned to a new object (of class `lm`, and usually called a 'model object' – a special form of list):

```
locmem <- lm(distance ~ time)
```

Assigning the output to a model object has many advantages. These will become apparent as you learn more about R. The main advantage is that it can be interrogated in different ways. For instance, the `abline()` function can extract the coefficients of a linear fit directly from a model:

```
abline(locmem)
```

You can extract elements of a fitted model object by name or the element number. These three methods all return the coefficients, though the first one is a one-element list. The other two methods extract the coefficients from the list as a vector:

```
locmem[1]
locmem$coefficients
locmem[[1]]
```

A useful function here is `names()`. This reveals that the element in the list has the name `'coefficients'` and that the elements of the vectors are `'(Intercept)'` and `'time'`.

```
names(locmem[1])
names(locmem$coefficients)
names(locmem[[1]])
```

Knowing the names of parts of an object makes it easier to access its contents.

A model object stores much more than the basic output. To get a fuller idea of what it contains use `str()` to see its internal structure:

```
str(locmem)
```

A more useful report of a model is available from the `summary()` function. This recognizes the object as the output of a regression model and also provides statistics such as R^2. Alternatively, to get the sums of squares and *df* of the model and residuals you can use `aov()`. The results calculated by Example 5.2 could be reproduced by the calls:

```
aov(locmem)
summary(locmem)$r.square
```

The `summary()` function provides more detailed output for linear models and includes NHSTs based on the *t* distribution as well as an overall *F* test of the relationship between *X* and *Y*. Note that $\hat{\sigma}_E$ (the square root of MS_{error}) is labeled the residual standard error rather than standard error of the estimate. The full output for the call `summary(locmem)` is:

```
Call:
lm(formula = distance ~ time)

Residuals:
     1       2       3       4      5      6
1.2143 -0.4114 -1.2371 -0.7629 0.8114 0.3857

Coefficients:
             Estimate Std. Error t value Pr(>|t|)
(Intercept)   5.86000    0.99436   5.893  0.00415 **
time         -0.25810    0.08511  -3.033  0.03868 *
---
Signif. codes: 0 '***' 0.001 '**' 0.01 '*' 0.05 '.' 0.1 ' ' 1

Residual standard error: 1.068 on 4 degrees of freedom
Multiple R-squared: 0.6969, Adjusted R-squared: 0.6211
F-statistic: 9.196 on 1 and 4 DF, p-value: 0.03868
```

This reproduces all the results from Examples 5.4 and 5.5 except that no interval estimates are included. To obtain the corresponding CIs use `confint()`. The call

```
confint(locmem, level=.95)
```

gives the output:

```
                 2.5 %       97.5 %
(Intercept) 3.0992265   8.62077346
time       -0.4943956  -0.02179484
```

This defaults to 95% confidence so the call `confint(locmem)` is equivalent. Coefficients can also be addressed by name or numeric order in the formula. So a 95% CI for the slope is obtained by either of these calls:

```
confint(locmem, 2)
confint(locmem, 'time')
```

Although it easier to work with a stored model, this doesn't prevent you nesting the model call within another call:

```
summary(lm(time ~ distance))
confint(lm(time ~ distance))
```

5.8.4 Residuals, leverage and influence (Examples 5.3, 5.6 and 5.7)

A model object can be interrogated to produce residuals, leverage and influence statistics. The residuals can be obtained via the `residuals()` function:

```
residuals(locmem)
```

The model `locmem` is a type of list containing named elements that are themselves R objects (one of which is a vector of residuals). You can extract the residuals by name using the `$` separator or by its numeric order in the list:

```
locmem$residuals
locmem[[2]]
```

Use `?lm` to see the full list of components. Leverage is available from the `hatvalues()` function. Similar functions exist for standardized and Studentized residuals (which use Equation 5.35 and Equation 5.37 incorporating leverage) and for Cook's distance:

```
hatvalues(locmem)
rstandard(locmem)
rstudent(locmem)
cooks.distance(locmem)
```

The $z_{residual}$ values can be computed if you divide the residuals by $\hat{\sigma}_E$. For example, standardized residuals without incorporating leverage are:

```
se.estimate <- summary(locmem)$sigma
residuals(locmem)/se.estimate
```

5.8.5 Confidence and prediction intervals for fitted values (Example 5.6)

R has a number of functions for exploring fitted regression models. The `predict()` function is a generic one that calls other functions – in this case `predict.lm()` for the linear model. While you rarely need to use the full function name to call it, it is more informative to use `?predict.lm` or `help(predict.lm)` than `?predict` if you need to look up the function. The following commands obtain predicted values from `locmem` and the relevant *SE*s with either confidence or prediction intervals. The R default is to produce interval estimates with 95% confidence for the observed values of X (though this can be altered with the `level` argument). The argument `se.fit` determines whether the *SE*s are also reported:

```
predict(locmem, interval='confidence', se.fit=TRUE)
predict(locmem, interval='prediction', se.fit=TRUE)
```

Note also that the predicted values for observed X (but not the intervals) could be obtained from `locmem` with `locmem$fitted.values` or `locmem[[5]]`.

The `predict()` function can also be used to obtain predictions for new X values. This can be a bit fiddly, because the new X values need to be defined as a data frame. They must also have the same name as the predictor used in the model object for which predictions are required (here `time`). The following code sets up a data frame for two new values, 10.5 seconds and 45 seconds, and generates point and interval estimates for the population mean of Y given these values of X:

```
new.data <- data.frame(time = c(10.5, 45))
predict(locmem, newdata = new.data, interval='confidence')
```

This can be altered to obtain prediction intervals and standard errors.

5.8.6 Confidence bands

Plotting confidence bands – as done in Figure 5.8 – can be done with basic R functions (though more sophisticated methods exist). First obtain predictions for the model. The `matplot()` function is used here. It is able to render a sequence of discrete confidence limits into a smooth line for the final plot. First generate the upper and lower limits as a sequence of points:

```
alpha <- .05
n <- 6
predx <- data.frame(time = seq(3, 18, 1/100))
moe <- predict(locmem, newdata = predx, interval='confidence',
  se.fit=TRUE)[[2]] * qt(alpha/2,n-2)
ub <- predict(locmem, newdata = predx, se.fit=FALSE)+moe
lb <- predict(locmem, newdata = predx, se.fit=FALSE)-moe
```

The mysterious part here is the `seq()` function. It creates a sequence of numbers starting with three, ending with 18 and moving in steps of 1/100. This is used to predict a large number (1501) of X values (presentation times in seconds) to use in prediction. In other respects, the upper and lower CI bounds are created as for a single point.

For the confidence bands use `matplot()` and specify `type='l'` to get a line plot. Set the lines to the color and style you prefer:

```
matplot(predx$time, cbind(lb,ub), type='l', lty=1,
  ylim=c(1,6), xlim=c(3,18), col= 'black', xlab= 'Time',
  ylab='Distance')
```

The first argument `predx$time` specifies X and the second argument specifies a matrix of Y values to be plotted by column. In this case the matrix is created by using `cbind()`. This binds the lower and upper bound vectors together into a matrix with two columns and 1501 rows. The regression line and the points can be added in the usual way:

```
points(time, distance)
abline(locmem, lty=2)
```

An alternative approach is to plot the points first and add the confidence bands using `lines()`.

5.8.7 Regression with no intercept

Regression with no intercept (i.e., forcing the line of best fit through the origin) merely involves a change to the formula used to call `lm()`. This formula forces the intercept through the origin:

```
lm(distance ~ 0 + time)
```

This formula fits an equivalent model by removing the intercept:

```
lm(distance ~ time - 1)
```

The formulas make more sense if you know that + adds a term to the model and - tells R to drop a term from the model. So the former term fits the constant zero to the model plus the predictor `time`, while the latter fits `time` and - 1 instructs R to drop the constant.

The following commands plot a model with and without intercept. First, `rnorm()` is used to generate a random variables from a normal distribution and `set.seed(6)` duplicates the data from Figure 5.9. Adding `x` to `y` ensures that they are correlated. Later commands fit models with and without intercepts for plotting. Note that axis limits are adjusted to make sure that the origin is visible in both plots.

```
set.seed(6)
x <- rnorm(30,5,1.5)
y <- (x + rnorm(30,5,1.5))/2

int.model <- lm(y ~ x)
no.int.model <- lm(y ~ 0 + x)

par(mfrow=c(1,2), pty='s')
```

```
plot(x,y, ylim = c(0.375, 10), xlim = c(0.375, 10),
  sub='Regression with intercept')
abline(int.model)
plot(x,y, ylim = c(0.375, 10), xlim = c(0.375, 10),
  sub='Regression without intercept')
abline(no.int.model)
```

5.8.8 Regression with a dichotomous predictor (Example 5.8)

The following commands demonstrate the equivalence of the test output for a *t* test and the slope of a linear regression if *X* is dichotomous and dummy coded. The first step is to load in the data. This time the comprehension data are loaded as a data frame (but the following commands also work if it is a list)

```
library(foreign)
bp2000 <- read.spss('baguley_payne_2000.sav', to.data.frame=TRUE)
```

If you use `summary(bp2000)` you may notice that the variable group is treated differently from the other variables. R has recognized that it is categorical and coded it as a factor (a technical term for a categorical predictor in certain regression models). In general, R tends to treat text strings as factors by default when loading data. To look at the group variable type:

```
bp2000$group
```

It consists of 56 labels (28 'low study' and 28 'high study'). The default is for R to dummy code this kind of variable, so the regression

```
lm(bp2000$percent_accuracy ~ bp2000$group)
```

will fit a model equivalent to an independent *t* test as in Equation 5.40. The `with()` and `within()` commands allow you to address the contents of a data frame or list directly:

```
with(bp2000, lm(percent_accuracy ~ group))
```

One of the most useful features of these regression functions is that you can specify a data frame or list. This makes it easier to work with large data sets. Setting `data=bp2000` forces R to look for named objects inside `bp2000` before searching elsewhere. This provides a neat way to avoid the use of `with()` or `attach()`.

```
bp2000.mod <- lm(percent_accuracy ~ group, data=bp2000)
```

Compare this model with that of the independent *t* test without Welch-Satterthwaite correction, which can also be called with a formula:

```
t.test(percent_accuracy ~ group, data=bp2000, var.equal = TRUE)
summary(bp2000.mod)
```

If X is a factor the default is not a scatter plot. A simple way to get a scatter plot is to create a new vector with the dummy codes and use that for the regression and the plot. The `rep()` function can be used to create them, or they can be done by direct assignment (the semi-colon here allows you to include two commands on a single line):

```
group.dc <- c(rep(0,28), rep(1,28))

group.dc[1:28] <- 0 ; group.dc[29:56] <- 1
```

A plot similar to Figure 5.10 is obtained as:

```
plot(group.dc, bp2000$percent_accuracy, xlab='Group',
  ylab='Percentage accuracy', xaxt='n', xlim=c(-0.25, 1.25))
abline(bp2000.mod, lty = 2)
axis(1, labels = c('Low study', 'High study'), at = c(0,1))
```

5.8.9 Fitting curves using simple linear regression

It is easy to fit certain curvilinear relationships using simple linear regression and the functions `log()` and `exp()`. The following code generates the fitted power law curve shown in Figure 5.11 with values taken from the simple linear regression output.

```
summary(lm(log(distance) ~ log(time)))
plot(time, distance)
curve(exp(2.5475-.6877*log(x)), add = TRUE)
```

You can fit and plot an exponential relationship by taking the logarithm of Y:

```
summary(lm(log(distance) ~ time))
plot(time, distance)
curve(exp(1.83652-.07606*x), add = TRUE)
```

Likewise, you could fit a logarithmic function by taking the logarithm of X:

```
summary(lm(distance ~ log(time)))
plot(time, distance)
curve(8.4979-2.4362*log(x), add = TRUE)
```

5.8.10 R packages

R-core members, DebRoy, S., Bivand, R., *et al.* (2011) *foreign*: Read Data Stored by Minitab, S, SAS, SPSS, Stata, Systat, dBase. R package version 0.8-42.

5.9 Notes on SPSS syntax for Chapter 5

5.9.1 Obtaining regression output (including the line of best fit)

The following SPSS syntax uses the file `loc_mem.sav`. A range of regression commands can be run from the menu <Analyze> selecting <Regression> and <Linear . . . >. For a simple bivariate linear regression these menus generate SPSS syntax with the basic form:

SPSS data file: `loc_mem.sav`

```
REGRESSION
  /STATISTICS COEFF
  /DEPENDENT distance
  /METHOD=ENTER time.
```

This syntax provides unstandardized ('B') and standardized regression ('Beta') coefficients and the associated *SE* for the coefficients. Also included are *t* and *p* values (the latter labeled 'Sig.'). Additional statistics can be obtained by adding terms to the `/STATISTICS` subcommand. For instance adding `R` gives R^2 and related statistics, while adding `ANOVA` gives the ANOVA table providing the *SS* and *MS* for the regression model (including the MS_{error} and the error *df* used for the test of the slope or intercept). Adding `CI` also includes a 95% CI for the unstandardized slope and intercept.

```
REGRESSION
  /STATISTICS COEFF R ANOVA CI(95)
  /DEPENDENT distance
  /METHOD=ENTER time.
```

5.9.2 Scatter plots for simple linear regression

Plotting a scatter plot for the location memory data is easy via <Graphs> <Interactive> <Dot . . . > or <Graphs> <Legacy Dialogs> <Scatter/Dot . . . >. The latter uses the basic syntax

```
GRAPH
 /SCATTERPLOT(BIVAR)=time WITH distance.
```

Although getting the plot is easy, adding the line of best fit is not. One way is to select the plotted graph in the output window. Double clicking on it allows you edit many properties of the graph. Go to the menu <Elements> and select the submenu <Fit Line at Total>, then click on the 'Close' button and close the Chart Editor window. The fitted regression line should now have been added to the plot.

The above method seems to be the most popular, but there is a simpler one. This is to use the `CURVEFIT` command (available from <Analyze> <Regression> <Curve Estimation . . . >). This relies on the fact that a straight line is a special case of a curve (and is the menu default):

```
CURVEFIT /VARIABLES=distance WITH time
  /CONSTANT
  /MODEL=LINEAR
  /PLOT FIT.
```

You can also get the full regression model output this way (including coefficients and tests) by checking the appropriate box after selecting <Curve Estimation . . . > from the menus or by adding a `/PRINT ANOVA` subcommand.

SPSS Chart Builder also has a graphical programming language that allows you to get a line of best fit using syntax. For the location memory data the following syntax will produce a slightly different plot from that using the earlier syntax:

```
GGRAPH
 /GRAPHDATASET NAME='graphdataset' VARIABLES=time distance
MISSING=LISTWISE REPORTMISSING=NO
 /GRAPHSPEC SOURCE=INLINE.
BEGIN GPL
 SOURCE: s=userSource(id('graphdataset'))
 DATA: time=col(source(s), name('time'))
 DATA: distance=col(source(s), name('distance'))
 GUIDE: axis(dim(1), label('Presentation time (in seconds)'))
 GUIDE: axis(dim(2), label('Distance of response from
correction location in cm)'))
 ELEMENT: point(position(time*distance))
 ELEMENT: line(position(smooth.linear(time*distance)))
END GPL.
```

This syntax is slightly cumbersome, but you can use SPSS help topic *Examples (GGRAPH command)* or use Chart Builder to get a basic scatter plot. If you paste the syntax (rather than clicking on OK to generate the plot) it is then fairly easy to add elements such as:

```
ELEMENT: line(position(smooth.linear(time*distance)))
```

Other useful elements that can be added include confidence bands similar to those in Figure 5.8:

```
ELEMENT:
line(position(region.confi.smooth.linear(time*distance, alpha(.95))))
```

5.9.3 Saving residuals, leverage and influence for fitted models in SPSS

Prediction intervals for the mean or for individual data points can also be obtained for all values of the predictor (*time* in this case) using this syntax, but these are saved to the SPSS Data View spreadsheet.

```
REGRESSION
  /STATISTICS COEFF OUTS R ANOVA
  /DEPENDENT distance
  /METHOD=ENTER time
/SAVE ICIN.
```

For example, the above SPSS syntax calculates the 95% prediction interval for a new observation with presentation time of six seconds as (0.93638, 7.68647). Replacing `ICIN` above with `MCIN` would give the prediction interval for the population mean. Editing the same `/SAVE` subcommand can be used to save predicted values, Cook's distance, leverage and residuals (unstandardized, standardized or studentized) to SPSS Data View:

```
/SAVE PRED COOK LEVER RESID ZRESID SRESID.
```

This may seem inconvenient, but turns out not to be. It is now very easy to use SPSS to obtain descriptive statistics for or plots of these quantities. The regression commands give options for obtaining some of these plots via menus, but there is greater flexibility saving the statistics and plotting them yourself. Many SPSS commands, including regression, give the option of saving additional output when accessed via menus. (Look for a button marked 'Save…' whenever you run an analysis this way.)

5.9.4 Regression with no intercept

Running a regression with no intercept involves just adding the `/ORIGIN` subcommand to the regression syntax:

```
REGRESSION
  /STATISTICS COEFF OUTS R ANOVA
  /ORIGIN
  /DEPENDENT distance
  /METHOD=ENTER time.
```

If you access regression commands via the menus the default syntax used includes a `/NOORIGIN` subcommand. If you prefer to use menus to paste syntax and then edit it, simply change the `/NOORIGIN` subcommand to `/ORIGIN` subcommand to get a no-intercept regression. To obtain the no-intercept model directly from menus, set up the analysis as usual and then click on the button marked 'Options…' in the 'Linear Regression' window, uncheck the box marked 'Include constant in equation', then click 'Continue' followed by 'OK'.

Alternatively, with the `CURVEFIT` command, change `/CONSTANT` to `/NOCONSTANT` and run the following syntax:

```
CURVEFIT /VARIABLES=distance WITH time
  /NOCONSTANT
  /MODEL=LINEAR
  /PLOT FIT.
```

5.9.5 Regression with a dichotomous predictor

Regression with a dichotomous predictor proceeds entirely as with a continuous predictor:

SPSS data file: baguley_payne2000.sav

```
REGRESSION
  /STATISTICS COEFF OUTS R ANOVA
  /DEPENDENT percent_accuracy
  /METHOD=ENTER group.
```

5.9.6 Fitting curves using simple linear regression

The following syntax fits a power curve using simple linear regression. The COMPUTE creates new variables comprising the natural logarithms of the *time* and *distance* variables. These are then used for a simple bivariate regression:

SPSS data file: loc_mem.sav

```
COMPUTE log_distance = ln(distance).
EXECUTE.

COMPUTE log_time = ln(time).
EXECUTE.

REGRESSION
  /STATISTICS COEFF OUTS R ANOVA
  /DEPENDENT log_distance
  /METHOD=ENTER log_time.
```

Plotting the data on log scales is possible via the REGRESSION command (because it is just a straight line). To plot on the original scale use the more user-friendly CURVEFIT command. An additional feature is the ease of adding two or more lines to the same plot. The following syntax fits a power law and a simple linear model on the original scale.

```
CURVEFIT /VARIABLES=distance WITH time
  /CONSTANT
  /MODEL=LINEAR POWER
  /PLOT FIT.
```

Other curves can be fitted by specifying different models (e.g., LOGARITHMIC or EXPONENTIAL) in place of POWER. However, plotting more than two curves at a time greatly increases visual clutter.

5.10 Bibliography and further reading

Cohen, J., Cohen, P., West, S. G., and Aiken, L. S. (2003) *Applied Multiple Regression/Correlation Analysis for the Behavioral Sciences*. Mahwah, NJ: Erlbaum.

Snedecor, G. W., and Cochran, W. G. (1989) *Statistical Methods* (8th edn). Ames, IA: Iowa State University Press.

6
Correlation and covariance

Contents

6.1 Chapter overview

This chapter explores the concepts of correlation and covariance, with particular focus on linear correlation, defined by the Pearson product-moment correlation coefficient r. The link between simple linear regression and linear correlation and the role of the Fisher's z transformation in inference with r are introduced. Properties that influence the magnitude of a sample correlation (such as reliability, range restriction and small sample bias) are reviewed, and some common alternatives to Pearson's r are noted.

6.2 Correlation, regression and association

A correlation is a measure of the closeness of the relationship or *association* between variables. In their simplest form, these associations are bivariate (involving two variables). Correlation is closely related to regression, but differs from it in two main respects. First, it does not distinguish between predictor (X) and outcome (Y); it expresses interdependence between variables (sometimes designated X_1 and X_2 for this reason). Second, a correlation is a *dimensionless* quantity. It expresses the relationship between X_1 and X_2 on a common numeric scale (typically -1 to $+1$) divorced from the original units of measurement.[1] While there are many different forms of correlation coefficient, one of these, the Pearson *product-moment correlation coefficient*, is by far the most popular. As the Pearson *product-moment correlation coefficient* is a bit of a mouthful, it is nearly always referred to either as Pearson's r (or just r).

Pearson's r measures the linear association between two variables. It plays a crucial role in many areas of statistics and can be interpreted in many different ways (see Rodgers and Nicewander, 1988). Linking both correlation and regression is the concept of *covariance*. The following discussion therefore starts by looking at covariance, before turning to Pearson's r and its connection to regression.

6.2.1 Covariance

Covariance is often described as a measure of 'shared variance', but it is a more general concept. Moreover, the concept of shared variance is sometimes misleading. Covariance measures the average tendency of two variables to covary (change together). It is quantified as the mean of the cross product of two variables (e.g., X and Y):

$$cov_{X,Y} = \frac{\sum_{i=1}^{N} (x_i - \hat{\mu}_X)(y_i - \hat{\mu}_Y)}{N} \qquad \text{Equation 6.1}$$

This formula is the descriptive formula for a sample. A typical application of covariance involves estimating the population covariance $\sigma_{X,Y}$. A sample estimate suitable for inference is:

$$\hat{\sigma}_{X,Y} = \frac{\sum_{i=1}^{N} (x_i - \hat{\mu}_X)(y_i - \hat{\mu}_Y)}{N-1} \qquad \text{Equation 6.2}$$

To facilitate hand calculation the formula can be rearranged as:

$$\hat{\sigma}_{X,Y} = \frac{\sum_{i=1}^{N} (x_i y_i) - N\hat{\mu}_X\hat{\mu}_Y}{N-1} \qquad \text{Equation 6.3}$$

Covariance is relevant to several areas of statistics (e.g., see Key Concept 3.2). Its connection to regression may already be obvious: the numerator of the covariance is also the numerator of the equation for the slope in a regression (see Equation 5.3 and Equation 5.4). Zero covariance implies a slope of zero (i.e., $\hat{\sigma}_{X,Y} = 0 \Leftrightarrow b_1 = 0$). Furthermore, because the denominator of each equation is never negative, they share the same sign when the numerator is not zero (e.g., a positive covariance implies a positive regression slope).[2]

It is trivial to show that variance is a special case of covariance. If two variables are identical (i.e., $X = Y$) then Equation 6.2 reduces to Equation 1.12.[3] Covariance is therefore a generalization of variance that encompasses non-identical variables. A drawback of the covariance, one that makes it hard to interpret as a descriptive statistic, is that it is scaled in units of the product of X and Y (or, for a variance, squared units of X). One motivation for using either a regression slope or a correlation coefficient is to scale the covariance in a way that makes it easier to interpret. Whereas the slope of a regression uses units of Y/X (a change in Y per unit increase in X), the correlation coefficient r can be regarded as a standardized covariance, scaled in terms of the standard deviations of X and Y (Rodgers and Nicewander, 1988).

If two variables are independent (i.e., one carries no information about the value of another) their covariance will always be zero. The converse is not true: zero covariance does not imply independence. For example, if X has mean zero and $Y = X^2$, X and Y will be uncorrelated, even though Y is entirely determined by X.[4] If two variables are independent they do not covary, but variables that don't covary may still be related in some other way (and therefore not be independent).

6.2.2 Pearson's product-moment correlation coefficient (r)

Pearson's r can be considered a way to scale X and Y in terms of their standard deviations. For a population product-moment correlation, denoted as ρ (the Greek letter 'rhọ') the formula is:

$$\rho_{XY} = \frac{\sigma_{X,Y}}{\sigma_X \sigma_Y} \qquad \text{Equation 6.4}$$

The usual sample estimate of this parameter is:

$$\hat{\rho}_{XY} = r_{XY} = \frac{\hat{\sigma}_{X,Y}}{\hat{\sigma}_X \hat{\sigma}_Y} \qquad \text{Equation 6.5}$$

Using the standard deviation (*SD*) of the variables to scale the covariance constrains r to take values between -1 and $+1$. When $\hat{\rho}_{XY}$ and the simple linear regression slope b_1 are zero, r must also be zero. If the correlation coefficient is not zero, its sign also matches the sign of $\hat{\rho}_{XY}$ and of b_1. Another link to simple linear regression is that the extremes of $+1$ and -1 represent perfect straight-line prediction of X from Y (and vice versa).

Why does scaling in terms of the *SD* of the variables limit r to this range? This is easiest to understand for the case of the variance (a covariance where $X = Y$). A sample variance $\hat{\sigma}_X^2$ can be expressed as $\hat{\sigma}_X \times \hat{\sigma}_X$. The maximum possible value of the covariance is $\pm\hat{\sigma}_X\hat{\sigma}_Y$. When $X = Y$ then $r_{XY} = \hat{\sigma}_{X,Y}/(\hat{\sigma}_X\hat{\sigma}_Y) = \hat{\sigma}_X^2/(\hat{\sigma}_X \times \hat{\sigma}_X) = 1$, and the two variables will be perfectly correlated.

A crucial consequence of the way r is defined is that it is a dimensionless quantity. The units of the covariance (the numerator in Equation 6.5) are the product of X and Y. The units of the denominator are also the product of X and Y (the *SD* being a way to measure dispersion in the original units). Ratios formed in this way can be thought of as 'pure' numbers – they have no natural units. Because they are dimensionless, all relationships fall on the same -1 to $+1$ scale. This is incredibly useful in statistical theory, and correlation crops up in many different contexts. However, the loss of the original units makes it difficult to interpret a correlation coefficient appropriately when it is used as a measure of some real outcome. This is particularly true in applied research (see Baguley, 2004), but can also be the case in other scientific work. Tukey (1969, p. 89) summed it up with the comment: 'being so disinterested in our variables that we do not care about their units can hardly be desirable'.

Example 6.1 To calculate Pearson's r for the location memory data in Table 5.1, the *SD* of each variable ($\hat{\sigma}_X$ and $\hat{\sigma}_Y$) and their covariance $\hat{\sigma}_{X,Y}$ are required. The sum of squares for X is 157.5 (from Table 5.2) so $\hat{\sigma}_X$ is

$$\hat{\sigma}_X = \sqrt{\frac{\sum_{i=1}^{n}(x_i - \hat{\mu}_X)^2}{n-1}} = \sqrt{\frac{157.5}{5}} \approx 5.6125$$

The sum of squares for Y was not previously derived, but the sum of the squared Y values is 74.59 (from Table 5.3) and $\hat{\mu}_Y = 3.15$. Rearranging Equation 1.13 gives:

$$\hat{\sigma}_Y = \sqrt{\frac{\sum_{i=1}^{n}(x_i - \hat{\mu}_Y)^2}{n-1}} = \sqrt{\frac{\sum_{i=1}^{n}(y_i)^2 - n\hat{\mu}_Y^2}{n-1}} = \sqrt{\frac{74.59 - 6 \times 3.15^2}{5}} \approx 1.7352$$

The sum of the cross product of X and Y is -40.650 (from Table 5.2) so the covariance is

$$\hat{\sigma}_{X,Y} = \frac{\sum_{i=1}^{N}(X_i - \hat{\mu}_X)(Y_i - \hat{\mu}_Y)}{N-1} = \frac{-40.65}{5} = -8.13$$

and the Pearson correlation is

$$r_{XY} = \frac{\hat{\sigma}_{X,Y}}{\hat{\sigma}_X\hat{\sigma}_Y} = \frac{-8.13}{5.6125 \times 1.7352} \approx -.835$$

This correlation indicates a negative relationship between the length of time the picture was presented for and the distance of subsequent responses from the target (consistent with the negative slope of the regression).

Given that the correlation has no natural units, how can the strength of this relationship be assessed? There is an obvious (but not necessarily correct) answer; the relationship would seem strong if the correlation is close to a perfect positive or negative correlation (±1) and weak if it is close to zero. While these extremes provide useful boundaries, dimensionless quantities such as correlations are awkward to interpret. For instance, is a correlation of .2 twice as strong as a correlation of .1? The numeric value of the correlation coefficient has doubled, but this does not mean that the strength of the association X and Y has doubled. Nevertheless, the correlation coefficient is widely thought of a measure of the strength of a relationship between variables. Cohen (1988) suggested that .1 should be considered a 'small' correlation in behavioral research, while .3 would be 'medium' and .5 'large'. Others have proposed different benchmarks for interpreting the size of r. Attaching labels such as 'large' or 'small' to correlation coefficients is dangerous and is usually best avoided (Lenth, 2001; Baguley, 2009).[5]

A further illustration of the difficulty of interpreting a correlation in this way is that correlations can be transformed into another popular measure of strength. The square of the correlation coefficient, r^2, is the proportion of variance in Y accounted for by X (or vice versa). Thus, when $r = 0$ this value is zero and when $r = -1$ or $+1$, $r^2 = 1$. For values in between the relationship between r and r^2 is decidedly nonlinear (e.g., $r^2 = .25$ when $r = .5$). There are a number of ways to measure the strength of a relationship been two variables. It is not the case that one is always superior to another (it will depend both on the context and what you are trying to do).

Working out r^2 for the location memory example produces $.835^2 = .697$. This value is identical to R^2 for the regression of Y on X. This will always be true: R^2 for a simple linear regression is identical to r^2 from the corresponding Pearson product-moment correlation coefficient. The reason for the different symbol is merely that regression is a more general technique. It is not restricted to predicting Y from X, and so R^2 has a wider application than r^2 (e.g., in multiple regression where the identity $R^2 = r^2$ does not hold).

6.2.3 Switching between correlation and regression

Correlation and simple linear regression are intimately connected. This connection can be seen in a number of ways (e.g., $R^2 = r^2$), but arguably the clearest way is to show that the correlation coefficient is itself the slope of a regression model.

Think about two variables: X and Y. It is possible to create two new variables, Z_X and Z_Y, that are standardized versions of the originals. Standardization involves two steps. First, center the variable by subtracting its mean, so that the new variable has a mean of zero.[6] The second step is to divide the variable by its *SD*:

$$Z_{X,i} = \frac{x_i - \hat{\mu}_X}{\hat{\sigma}_X}, \quad Z_{Y,i} = \frac{y_i - \hat{\mu}_Y}{\hat{\sigma}_Y} \qquad \text{Equation 6.6}$$

Performing a simple linear regression to predict Z_Y by Z_X creates a regression model of the form:

$$Z_Y = 0 + \hat{\beta} Z_X = \hat{\beta} Z_X \qquad \text{Equation 6.7}$$

In this model the intercept is always zero, because both X and Y have been centered. In this model $\hat{\beta}$ is a standardized slope. For simple linear regression (and only for simple linear regression) it is also equal to the product-moment correlation coefficient: $\hat{\beta} = r$.

Thus, a very useful interpretation of r is that it is the standardized slope of a simple linear regression. Because the standardized slope of the regression of X on Y and the standardized slope of Y on X have standardized units they are equal. In contrast, the unstandardized slopes typically differ (because their units of measurement differ). Regression therefore provides another way to interpret the strength of a correlation. The slope b_1 is a change in units of Y associated with a single unit increase in X. As the units of a standardized slope are *SD* units, Y changes by r standard deviations for an associated increase of one *SD* in X. The relationship between presentation time and distance from target in the location memory example could be expressed as a 0.258*cm* decrease in the distance of responses from the correct location for each additional second of presentation time. Shifting to standardized units, this becomes a .835 $\hat{\sigma}_Y$ decrease in the distance for each 1 $\hat{\sigma}_X$ increase in presentation time.

Although the connection to correlation invokes the idea of a regression with standardized variables, it is possible to arrive at the standardized slope more directly. The move to correlation represents a switch in units of X and Y to $\hat{\sigma}_X$ and $\hat{\sigma}_Y$. You can rescale a regression with Y measured in seconds to one with Y measured in milliseconds by dividing the coefficients by 1000. It is therefore possible to switch between b_1 and r by using $\hat{\sigma}_X$ and $\hat{\sigma}_Y$ to rescale the coefficients. Expressing the correlation between X and Y in terms of the slope gives the formula:

$$r = b_1 \frac{\hat{\sigma}_X}{\hat{\sigma}_Y} \qquad \text{Equation 6.8}$$

Consequently, the slope of the simple regression is:

$$b_1 = r \frac{\hat{\sigma}_Y}{\hat{\sigma}_X} \qquad \text{Equation 6.9}$$

The connection between regression and correlation has practical uses. For example, what is known about least squares estimation in regression applies equally to correlation (as do concepts such as leverage and inference). There are also dangers. Several stem from the difference between a dimensionless quantity such as r and one with meaningful units such as b_1. It is also important to realize that regression distinguishes between the role of predictor and outcome. This places different demands on these variables. In regression, X (but not Y) is assumed to be measured reliably (i.e., without error). Correlation assumes both X and Y are measured reliably. Centering X and Y removes information about the intercept for a correlation, while this information is retained in regression. For these reasons, regression is usually superior to correlation as a scientific tool (although in many disciplines correlation is more widely used – perhaps because it is, incorrectly, perceived as simpler).

Example 6.2 The link between r and b_1 can be demonstrated by plugging r into Equation 6.9 to get the original slope for the location memory data. As $r = -.835$ it follows that the slope is:

$$b_1 = r \frac{\hat{\sigma}_Y}{\hat{\sigma}_X} = -.835 \frac{1.73522}{5.61249} = -0.258$$

The impact of quantities such as leverage and influence on r and r^2 can be demonstrated by omitting the most influential point in this regression model (the first point in this case). Doing so reduces the correlation to −.731, while r^2 falls from −.697 to .534 (a reduction of nearly 25% in the proportion of explained sample variance).

6.3 Statistical inference with the product-moment correlation coefficient

Statistical inference with r is more difficult than with simple linear regression. Although the two techniques are sometimes equivalent, standardizing the slope changes the distribution. This happens because the slope is forced into the range −1 to +1 (introducing bounds that are not assumed in regression). Just as the sampling distribution of the binomial is only symmetrical when $P = .5$, the distribution of r is only symmetrical if $\rho = 0$ (equidistant from −1 and +1). Values of ρ close to the extremes 'squash' the sampling distribution of r (sometimes termed a *boundary effect*). These distributional issues do not matter for calculating a regression or correlation coefficient – the least squares estimates of the linear relationship don't assume a normal distribution – but they do matter for constructing interval estimates or hypothesis tests.

In the case of a population correlation ρ assumed to be zero (H_0: $\rho = 0$) inference with r is equivalent to inference in simple linear regression. Making only the assumptions required for least squares regression (errors from an independent normal distribution with constant variance), it is possible to construct a test statistic for r using the t distribution:

$$\frac{r\sqrt{N-2}}{\sqrt{1-r^2}} \sim t\,(N-2) \qquad \text{Equation 6.10}$$

This is equivalent to the test of the slope of the simple linear regression $t_{N-2} = b_1/\hat{\sigma}_{b_1}$ for the null hypothesis H_0: $\beta_1 = 0$ (that there is no linear relationship between X and Y). This approach is rather restrictive. It is not possible to use it to test other hypotheses or to construct confidence intervals around an observed correlation (unless the observed correlation is zero).

Inference for correlations under more general conditions introduces additional constraints. The most common approach requires a further assumption: that X and Y follow a *bivariate normal* distribution. The bivariate normal is a joint distribution of both X and Y under which not only each variable is normal, but their conditional distributions are also normal (in the populations sampled). Figure 6.1 plots three random samples of size $N = 7000$ from a bivariate normal distribution, each showing the elliptical shape characteristic of bivariate normal samples.

The distribution of Y conditional on X is the distribution of Y for a specific value of X. Recall that the population regression equation has the form:

$$y_i = \beta_0 + \beta_1 x_i + \epsilon_i$$

In a conditional distribution, both the predictor X and the intercept are constants. Hence the bivariate normal distribution requires that the population errors in predicting both Y from X and

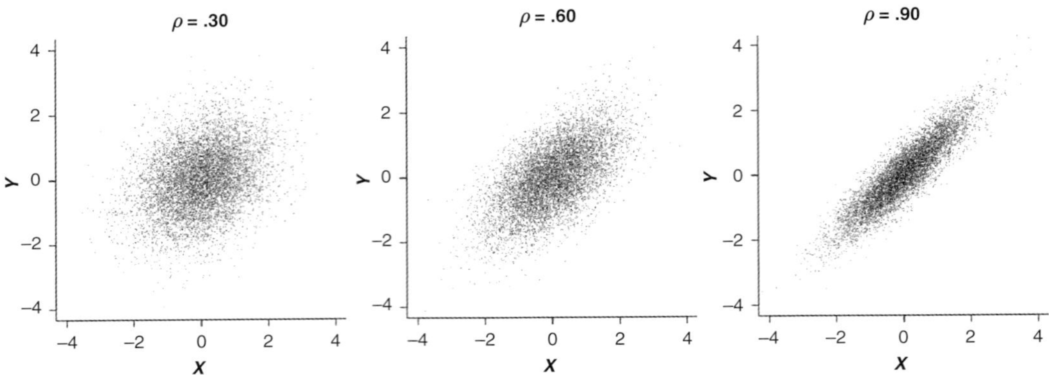

Figure 6.1 Samples of $N = 7000$ from a bivariate normal distribution, with $\rho = .30$, .60 or .90

X from Y are normal. This contrasts with inference in simple linear regression (where only the errors in predicting Y from X are required to be normal). The normal errors on X and Y combine to produce the ellipses depicted in Figure 6.1. As error decreases, the ellipses tend to 'flatten out' and become linear. While the assumption of a bivariate normal distribution is reasonable for some situations, it is unlikely to be met in others (e.g., when the predictor is dichotomous).

With the bivariate normal distribution as a starting point it is possible to use an approximation to transform the bounded and potentially asymmetrical r distribution to an unbounded, symmetrical normal distribution (Fisher, 1915; Bond and Richardson, 2004). The *Fisher z transformation* can be used for a range of inferential procedures when it is not reasonable to assume $\rho = 0$. This is simplest to illustrate by showing how the transformation can be used to derive a CI for a sample correlation. Transforming r to z is achieved with the formula:

$$z_r = 1/2 \ln\left(\frac{1+r}{1-r}\right) \qquad \text{Equation 6.11}$$

Fisher showed that the standard deviation of this sampling distribution, and hence the standard error (*SE*) of the correlation after transformation, is approximately:

$$\hat{\sigma}_{z_r} = \frac{1}{\sqrt{N-3}} \qquad \text{Equation 6.12}$$

This is sufficient information to construct a symmetrical CI for z_r as

$$z_r \pm z_{1-\alpha/2}\hat{\sigma}_{z_r} \qquad \text{Equation 6.13}$$

where $z_{1-\alpha/2}$ is the appropriate quantile of the standard normal distribution.

Reversing the initial transformation provides lower or upper bounds in terms of r. This is accomplished by using the lower and upper bounds of z_r as input to the equation:

$$r = \frac{e^{2z_r} - 1}{e^{2z_r} + 1} \qquad \text{Equation 6.14}$$

This method of obtaining an interval estimate for r can be used to construct one-sided or two-sided significance tests of a null hypothesis that the correlation takes some value within the range −1 to 1. The approximation is known to be very good for the CI around a single correlation coefficient (if the assumptions are not badly violated). It is problematic for other inferences (e.g., concerning r^2 or the differences between two correlations) or if the distributional assumptions are seriously violated (Zou, 2007). BC_a bootstrap methods are generally preferred in the latter case (DiCiccio and Efron, 1996).

Example 6.3 The correlation coefficient of −.835 obtained in Example 6.1 can be represented in terms of z_r as:

$$z_r = 1/2 \ln\left(\frac{1+(-.835)}{1-(-.835)}\right) = 1/2 \ln\left(\frac{0.165}{1.835}\right) \approx -1.2044$$

After transformation the 95% CI is $z_r \pm 1.96\sigma_{z_r}$. Because

$$\hat{\sigma}_{z_r} = \frac{1}{\sqrt{6-3}} = \frac{1}{\sqrt{3}} \approx 0.57735$$

this produces the interval [−2.336, −0.072841]. Hence the lower bound of r is

$$r_{lower} = \frac{e^{2\times(-2.336)}-1}{e^{2\times(-2.336)}+1} = \frac{e^{-4.672}-1}{e^{-4.672}+1} = \frac{-0.99065}{1.0094} \approx -.98$$

and the upper bound is

$$r_{upper} = \frac{e^{2\times(-0.072841)}-1}{e^{2\times(-0.072841)}+1} = \frac{e^{-0.14568}-1}{e^{-0.14568}+1} = \frac{-0.13557}{1.8644} \approx -.07$$

These bounds exclude zero, so $\rho = 0$ is not a plausible value for the population correlation. This CI could be reported in APA style as

$$r(4) = -.835, p < .05, 95\%\ \text{CI}\ [-.98, -0.07]$$

where the number in parenthesis represents the *df* ($N-2$). The t statistic for the NHST is

$$t = \frac{r\sqrt{N-2}}{\sqrt{1-r^2}} = \frac{-.835\sqrt{6-2}}{\sqrt{1-(-.835)^2}} \approx -3.04$$

and two-sided $p = .04$ (and, aside from rounding error, identical to test of the regression slope).

The excessive width of the CI reflects the small sample size. However, even with larger sample sizes the width of a CI for a correlation is often larger than many people expect. For instance with a sample size of 30 a 95% CI for a correlation of $r = .3$ is [−.068, .596], while a 95% CI for $r = .6$ is [.306, .790]. It requires very large samples to obtain precise estimates of standardized statistics such as r.

6.4 Correlation, error and reliability

The correlation coefficient plays a special role in summarizing and reporting the precision of measurements taken by researchers. A precise measurement is one with little error. Determining precision is therefore largely a matter of understanding the proportion of error in a measurement. In *classical measurement theory* (e.g., Lord and Novick, 1968) all observed scores are considered the sum of a true score plus error: $X_{observed} = X_{true} + error$. Under the least squares assumptions of unbiased, uncorrelated errors with a mean of zero, the variance of observed scores can be decomposed in the following way:

$$\sigma^2_{X_{observed}} = \sigma^2_{X_{true}} + \sigma^2_E \qquad \text{Equation 6.15}$$

The *reliability* of a measurement, ρ_{XX}, is the ratio of the true score variance to the variance of the observed scores:

$$\rho_{XX} = \frac{\sigma^2_{X_{true}}}{\sigma^2_{X_{observed}}} \qquad \text{Equation 6.16}$$

The reliability is therefore the fraction (or proportion) of the observed variance that is accounted for by the true variance.

How can the reliability of a measurement be estimated? One method is to obtain two samples of X from units (e.g., people) in the same population. The crucial aspect of this method is that while the same N units (e.g., $x_1, x_2, \ldots x_N$) are sampled, care must be taken to ensure that the two measurements of x_i are independent (and thus the residuals of the two paired measurements are uncorrelated). If the residuals are uncorrelated, the covariance of the paired measurements (X_1 and X_2) is $\sigma^2_{X_{true}}$. If there is no error, the measurements are perfect and the covariance between X_1 and X_2 reduces to the variance of X. Any departure from perfect measurement in this scenario adds to the variability of X (as $\sigma^2_{X_{observed}}$ is always larger than $\sigma^2_{X_{true}}$ by the error variance σ^2_E). The expected variance of both X_1 and X_2 is $\sigma^2_{X_{observed}}$. This means that the population correlation between X_1 and X_2 can be estimated using the formula for Pearson's r:

$$r_{XX} = \hat{\rho}_{XX} = \frac{\hat{\sigma}^2_{X_{true}}}{\hat{\sigma}^2_{X_{observed}}} = \frac{\hat{\sigma}_{X_1X_2}}{\hat{\sigma}_{X_1}\sigma_{X_2}} \qquad \text{Equation 6.17}$$

The correlation between two independently sampled paired measurements of X in a sample (r_{XX}) is therefore an estimate of the reliability of X.

Reliability is a major topic in its own right, and the reliability of measurement can have a major impact on statistical inference. The greater the proportion of error in the estimate of a population parameter, the more difficult inference about it becomes. In the case of correlation itself, both the error in X and Y reduce the ability to detect a relationship. Furthermore, error increases the observed sample variance relative to the true population variance. This means that r will underestimate ρ unless both variables are measured without error (which is unlikely). An advantage of simple linear regression over correlation is that, because regression coefficients are not scaled in terms of the sample *SDs*, b_0 and b_1 are unbiased estimates of population parameters if Y is measured with error (see Baguley, 2009). Measurement error in Y just adds to the noise in estimating these parameters. However, measurement error in X should be avoided where possible as it will influence both the intercept and slope (see Hunter and Schmidt, 2004).

In practice, estimating reliability of measurements is somewhat more complex than has been considered here. Measurement error can be thought of as stemming from a number of different sources – and may vary from sample to sample and study to study as well as between measurement instruments (see Schmidt and Hunter, 1999). Indeed, reliability estimates are themselves subject to random error. Reliability should therefore be reported as an interval rather than a point estimate.

6.4.1 Range restriction

Leverage – the distance of a value of X from the mean of X – is relevant to both correlation and regression. The sampled range of X (or indeed Y) is an important consideration in designing or interpreting a study. The consequence of the range of values sampled is somewhat different for regression and correlation. Compare two situations: one in which the range of X is restricted during sampling and one in which only the extremes of X are selected during sampling. I'll label the former situation as *range restriction* of X and the latter as *extreme groups analysis* (see Preacher *et al.*, 2005), though both are often loosely designated as range restriction.

What happens to regression under range restriction of X? By excluding the extremes and over-sampling central values of X, leverage is reduced. These values are the likely to be the most informative and influential values in the regression. Removing them reduces the efficiency of estimation. However, the parameter estimates of the regression are unbiased. Conversely, preferentially selecting the extremes of X increases efficiency. Indeed, selecting two groups on the basis of extreme values of X is the optimal design (the one having greatest *statistical power*) for detecting a linear effect (Preacher *et al.*, 2005; McClelland, 1997). For curvilinear relationships between X and Y the effect of range restriction will vary and the optimal design will differ (McClelland, 1997).

How does the impact of range restriction differ for correlation? Efficiency is influenced for r in the same way as for simple linear regression; restricting X or Y will decrease efficiency, whereas selecting the extremes increases efficiency. This assumes that the underlying relationship between X and Y is not curvilinear (though any curvilinear relationship that is well approximated by a straight line will tend to show the same pattern). What changes in correlation is that the estimate of the standardized slope in the sample (r or $\hat{\beta}$) is influenced by range restriction (Preacher *et al.*, 2005). Range restriction distorts the standardized slope. In fact, the standardized slope is distorted by any factor – such as reliability – that changes $\hat{\sigma}$ without influencing σ (Baguley, 2009). This is inevitable. The standardized slope (and hence r) is the unstandardized slope of the regression scaled by the ratio $\hat{\sigma}_X/\hat{\sigma}_Y$. Restricting the range of either X or Y tends to decrease r. Selecting the extremes tends to increase r. This follows from Equation 6.8. If a correlation exists (i.e., $\rho \neq 0$), then restricting X will also tend to restrict Y and the *SD* of both variables (being calculated from squared deviations closer to the mean than in the unrestricted situation) will be reduced. Unless the correlation is perfect, restriction of X will also reduce $\hat{\sigma}_X$ more than $\hat{\sigma}_Y$. This in turn ensures that restricting X decreases both $\hat{\sigma}_X/\hat{\sigma}_Y$ and r.

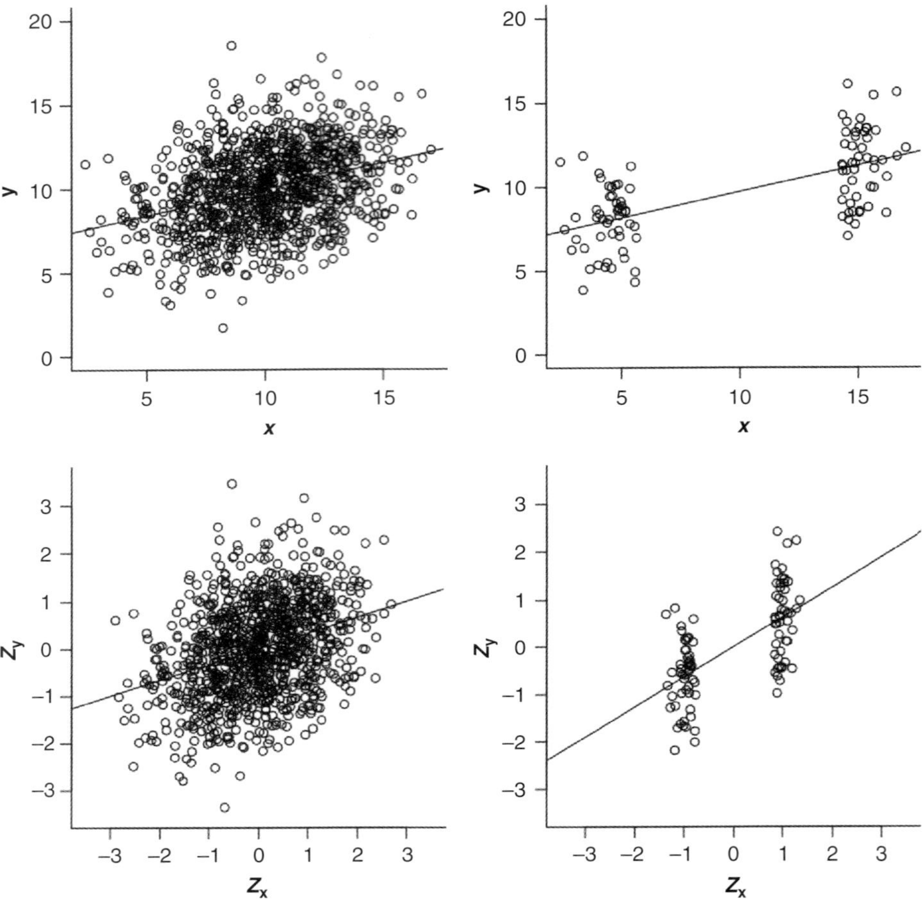

Figure 6.2 The impact of selecting the extremes of X (extreme groups analysis) on the unstandardized slope (upper panels) and the standardized slope (lower panels) of a regression line

Exactly the same happens (in reverse) for an extreme groups analysis. Figure 6.2 shows the impact of selecting the extremes of X on b_1 and on r. The two variables are randomly generated samples from a $N(10, 2.5)$ distribution with $\rho_{XY} = .25$. The upper panels show the simple regression of X and Y for the full sample ($N = 1000$) on the left and for the 5% most extreme X values in each tail ($N = 100$) on the right. The lower panels show the corresponding regressions for the standardized variables (Z_X and Z_Y). The slope of the regression is largely unchanged by selecting the extremes; it shifts from $b_1 = 0.314$ to $b_1 = 0.311$. This difference is a consequence of sampling error. Sampling error could easily lead to a greater discrepancy in slopes when N for the extreme groups analysis is small (but is on average unbiased). The standardized slope is $\hat{\beta} = .633$ for the restricted sample, compared to the full sample estimate of $\hat{\beta} = .333$ (fairly close to the true value of $\rho_{XY} = .25$). Not only does range restriction distort $\hat{\beta}$ or r (relative to ρ_{XY}), the degree of distortion can be substantial.

Range restriction is a somewhat neglected phenomenon that can lead to extremely inaccurate estimates of ρ (a serious issue if that is your aim). More importantly – as estimating ρ is only rarely the primary goal of research – it leads to inefficient research designs. Range restriction is quite common, arising either by directly selecting one or more variables or as an indirect consequence of the sampling strategy (Sackett and Yang, 2000). One common situation that induces range restriction is when group membership is correlated with Y. For example, gender will be correlated with an outcome such as aggression (because males and females tend to differ in levels of aggression). In an all-male or all-female sample the correlation of aggression with a third variable would thus tend to be lower than in a sample of males and females combined.

The preceding discussion focused largely on direct range restriction. Indirect selection is also common, but harder to detect. Many psychological studies use undergraduate students as participants and, if academic ability is related to the variables under investigation, indirect range restriction will be present. Such studies should be particularly cautious about interpreting correlation coefficients or standardized regression coefficients. In addition, the combination of indirect range restriction and unreliability of X may reduce the regression intercept and slope (Hunter and Schmidt, 2004).

6.4.2 Small sample correction and adjusted R^2

Pearson's r tends to overestimate the population correlation ρ in small samples. The bias is sufficiently low to be ignored except for the smallest sample sizes. Even if it is not worth correcting the bias, familiarity with the correction is useful because it has more general applications in correlation and regression. A perfect correlation could, in theory, arise by chance in any sample (even if $\rho \neq 1$ in the population). The probability of this is vanishingly small in large samples, but in tiny samples is not that unlikely. If $N = 2$ the points always lie on a straight line (and estimating ρ is meaningless). For $N = 3$ even randomly scattered points will often lie close to a straight line. So in small samples a near-perfect correlation becomes more likely. This biases r toward 1 or -1. The size of the bias is also related to ρ itself. If $\rho = 1$ Pearson's r will be unbiased, whereas the bias is maximized when $\rho = 0$.

The oldest known correction formula is due to Ezekiel (1929) and although several alternatives have since been proposed, evidence suggests that it is among the best performers (Wang and Thompson, 2007). The correction is widely employed, though not as a correction to r or r^2. It is usually encountered as a correction to R^2 in linear regression models. In this context it is known as *adjusted* R^2 and has the formula:

$$R^2_{adj} = 1 - \frac{(1 - R^2)(N - 1)}{N - q - 1} \qquad \text{Equation 6.18}$$

In the context of Pearson's r (or simple linear regression) where the number of predictors q is 1 this becomes:

$$r_{adj} = \sqrt[\pm]{1 - \frac{(1 - r^2)(N - 1)}{N - 2}} \qquad \text{Equation 6.19}$$

For Equation 6.19 the positive or negative root should be selected so that r_{adj} has the same sign as r.

Example 6.4 The correlation of $-.835$ with $N=6$ produced $r^2=.697$. Adjusted r^2 is

$$r^2_{adj}=1-\frac{(1-r^2)(N-1)}{N-2}=1-\frac{(1-(-.835)^2)(6-1)}{6-2}\approx .622$$

and its negative square root is $r_{adj}=-.788$. The sizable reduction in the estimate of ρ or is a consequence of small N.

In comparison, correlations of .8 or .2 with sample sizes of 100 would produce adjusted correlations of .798 and .174 respectively. Care should be taken when interpreting adjusted r and R^2. First, while their long run average corrects the overestimation of r, they do not eliminate sampling error (so any given sample could still be an underestimate or overestimate of the population value). r_{adj} and r^2_{adj} are attempts to provide a 'best guess' at the true population correlation by correcting the sample values for expected chance relationships. However, it is possible for r^2_{adj} to be negative. For example, if $r=0$ and $N=10$, then $r^2_{adj}=-.125$. This happens because the observed value is lower than the expected chance value for $\rho=0$ and $N=10$.

6.5 Alternative correlation coefficients

Many other correlation coefficients have been proposed. A few are widely used, though none are as popular as Pearson's r. Several of these coefficients are closely related to r, while others have a very different origin. The focus here is on coefficients related to r.

6.5.1 Point-biserial correlation

A point-biserial correlation r_{pb} is the correlation between a true dichotomy and a continuous variable. This situation is problematic for correlation. A true dichotomy, a variable in which only two states are possible (e.g., 'success' or 'fail'), will not follow a normal distribution. The solution to calculation of r_{pb} lies in the realization that this situation is equivalent to simple linear regression when the predictor is dichotomous (e.g., see Figure 5.10). The standardized slope of the simple linear regression between a dichotomous X and a continuous Y variable is r_{pb}. This is useful because it is not necessary to assume normality of X for the regression (and because the familiar tests and interval estimates can be employed).

The point-biserial correlation coefficient can either be calculated as the standardized slope of a regression or from the usual Pearson product-moment formula. In either calculation it is usual for the dichotomous variable to be dummy coded. While any numerical coding could be used (e.g., X could be coded 27 and 132) using zero and one simplifies the calculations. Because of the link between regression and the independent t test, the value of r_{pb} can also be obtained from t (obtained either from the independent t test or the test of the unstandardized slope of the XY regression):

$$r_{pb}=\sqrt{\frac{t^2}{t^2+N-2}}$$ Equation 6.20

A test statistic for r_{pb} is obtained as:

$$\frac{r_{pb}\sqrt{N-2}}{\sqrt{1-r_{pb}}} \sim t(N-2) \qquad \text{Equation 6.21}$$

The statistic r_{pb} can also be calculated directly using the formula

$$r_{pb} = \frac{\hat{\mu}_{X_1} - \hat{\mu}_{X_0}}{SD_Y}\sqrt{\frac{n_1}{N}\frac{n_2}{N}} \qquad \text{Equation 6.22}$$

where SD_Y is the descriptive SD of Y, using Equation 1.11 rather than 1.13, and N is the sum of the sample sizes n_1 and n_2.[7] This formula is only rarely used to calculate r_{pb}, but helps to illustrate an important property of the coefficient. McGrath and Meyer (2006) discuss how the value of the point-biserial coefficient is base rate sensitive. It reaches its maximum only when the group sizes n_1 and n_2 are equal. If dummy coding is used, $\sqrt{(n_1/N)(n_2/N)}$ is also the descriptive SD of X. It is worth reflecting on two implications of this observation. First, r_{pb} will only be an unbiased estimator of ρ if the proportion n_1/n_2 reflects the base rate of X (the relative proportions of the groups defined by X in the population). Second, sampling X so that $n_1 = n_2$ will make it easier to detect an effect (because it maximizes statistical power). This may cause problems if a researcher designs a study to ensure $n_1 = n_2$, but does not realize that this could bias r_{pb} as an estimate of ρ.

Why is point-biserial r considered a special case (rather than a routine application) of r? The main reason is that the coefficient calculated from a dichotomous X and continuous Y is not a point-biserial correlation if the dichotomy is artificial (e.g., created by using the median to split a continuous variable into two groups). For a correlation between two continuous predictors when one of them has been dichotomized, the appropriate statistic is the *biserial correlation* coefficient. If both X and Y are artificial dichotomies, the *tetrachoric correlation* coefficient is appropriate. The biserial correlation is always at least as large as the point-biserial (and usually larger). Likewise the tetrachoric correlation is at least as large as the biserial correlation. They tend to be larger because dichotomizing a continuous variable throws away information about the true relationship between X and Y (MacCallum *et al.*, 2002). The biserial and tetrachoric correlation coefficients adjust the estimate for this loss of information, but are less efficient than estimates computed from the original (continuous) variables. For this reason, dichotomizing a continuous predictor is hardly ever a sensible move.

Also bear in mind that that unless X and Y have the same shape of distribution, a correlation coefficient can't attain its maximum value (Carroll, 1961). If this is not obvious, recall that perfect prediction requires that one variable be a simple linear function of the other. This is not possible unless you can go from one to another purely by multiplying by or adding a constant – in which case the distributions will have the same shape. For instance, if the continuous predictor has a normal distribution, the maximum attainable value of r_{pb} is $\pm.79$.

6.5.2 *Phi*

Phi (ϕ) is a Pearson correlation coefficient calculated between two dichotomous variables. Like r_{pb} it assumes that both dichotomous variables are true dichotomies. Phi can be calculated by numeric coding of each variable (e.g., using dummy coding) and calculating r from Equation 6.5. Simple linear regression between X and Y will also work, if both variables have been dummy coded.

As ϕ involves two dichotomous variables it is frequently encountered in the context of a 2×2 contingency table. It captures the linear relationship between the two variables. This is a natural form of relationship to consider for dichotomous categorical variables. If coded numerically, any relationship will be linear (e.g., see Figure 5.10). However, while simple linear regression can be used to calculate ϕ, the usual test is made using the χ^2 distribution with 1 df and the formula:

$$n\phi^2 \sim \chi_1^2 \quad \text{Equation 6.23}$$

This χ^2 statistic is mathematically equivalent to the Pearson χ^2 for a 2×2 table. Thus ϕ and ϕ^2 can be derived directly from the χ^2 statistic.

The quantity ϕ^2 is the proportion of the maximum sum of squares accounted for by the observed sum of squares:

$$\phi^2 = \frac{\chi^2_{observed}}{\chi^2_{max}} \quad \text{Equation 6.24}$$

For a 2×2 test of independence (but not necessarily for other χ_1^2 statistics – see Rosenberg, 2010) $\chi^2_{max} = N$, and:

$$\phi = \sqrt{\phi^2} = \sqrt{\frac{\chi_1^2}{\chi^2_{max}}} = \sqrt{\frac{\chi_1^2}{N}} \quad \text{Equation 6.25}$$

Using this formula, the calculated value of ϕ is usually reported as positive. The appropriate sign for ϕ (or indeed r_{pb}) depends on which variable is coded one. Sometimes a sign is useful to preserve quantitative information (e.g., if success is coded as one and failure as zero). It is also important to be consistent about reporting the direction of correlations (e.g., if the direction changes between correlations where X or Y is common to both).

Example 6.5 The degree class data in Example 4.8 looked at the proportion of first class university degrees awarded to male and female students in England and Wales. The test of independence for these data was reported as: χ^2 $(1, N = 278{,}170) = 55.9$, $p < .0001$. This summary can be used to calculate the correlation coefficient ϕ:

$$\phi = \sqrt{\frac{\chi_1^2}{N}} = \sqrt{\frac{55.9}{278170}} \approx .014$$

The proportion of variance explained by the correlation is $\phi^2 \approx .0002$ (or 1/50th of a percent). This might seem tiny, but it is still an effect of potential practical significance (e.g., because the outcome is important and applies to a large number of people).

This demonstrates an important, and arguably undesirable, feature of ϕ. Proportion of variance explained is often very small – especially for correlations from 2×2 contingency tables. Such small effects are not necessarily unimpressive. Rosnow and Rosenthal (2003) note that $\phi \approx .011$ for the successful trial of the Salk polio vaccine (explaining around 1/100th of a percent of the total sample variance). A key factor is the rarity of the outcome. Polio was relatively rare among children given the vaccine, and (like all correlation coefficients) the maximum obtainable value of ϕ requires the dichotomous outcomes to have the same distribution. Because around half the children were given the vaccine, the rarity of the disease constrains the absolute value of the correlation to be low (even if the vaccine is highly effective). A surprising number of alternative ways of measuring and communicating the magnitude of effect for a 2 × 2 contingency table exist. Determining the best measure or measures of effect size to use can be difficult. This issue is revisited in Chapter 7.

An extension of ϕ, known as Cramer's V (or ϕ_C) can be used for contingency tables with more than 1 *df*. Cramer's V is calculated as

$$\phi_C = \sqrt{\frac{\chi^2_v}{\chi^2_{max}}} = \sqrt{\frac{\chi^2_v}{\min(r, c) - 1}} \qquad \text{Equation 6.26}$$

where $v = (r-1)(c-1)$ and $\min(r, c)$ is the smaller of r and c (the number of rows and columns of the contingency table). Interpreting a correlation coefficient for such tables is, however, problematic. For instance, direction of effect and linearity are awkward concepts when dealing with more than two unordered categories. It will usually be easier to interpret ϕ^2_C (the proportion of total variance accounted for by the effect). An even better strategy may be to break down associations or comparisons into several 2 × 2 tables. This allows effects to be compared using simpler, less ambiguous metrics.

6.5.3 Correlation coefficients for ordinal data

A number of methods exist for detecting associations where one or both variables are ordinal (and too many to cover in detail here). For instance, Agresti (1996) describes an application of Pearson's r to situations where both X and Y are ordered categories. In this procedure, both X and Y need to be coded numerically for all N observations (e.g., using codes such as 0, 1 and 2 if a variable has three ordered outcomes). Where information about the spacing of the categories is unavailable it is reasonable to select equally spaced categories. If additional information is available this can be used to adjust the spacing (e.g., 0, 1 and 3 to reflect 0, 10 and 30 *mg* doses of a drug). Once coded in this way a correlation coefficient can be computed via the usual formula for r.

The correlation between two categorical variables coded in this way is sometimes referred to as a *linear by linear association* (e.g., in SPSS software). The test statistic for this correlation is

$$M^2 = r^2(N-1) \quad \sim \chi^2_1 \qquad \text{Equation 6.27}$$

which can be evaluated against a χ^2 distribution with 1 *df* (or the equivalent $z = r\sqrt{N-1}$ statistic). It provides a test of the null hypothesis of independence versus the alternative hypothesis of a linear association between the ordered categories.

Agresti (1996) notes that this form of χ^2 is less susceptible to problems with small sample sizes than the standard test of independence. An additional advantage is that the χ^2 statistic can be meaningfully compared to the χ^2_ν statistic of an $r \times c$ table that treats both categories as unordered, where $\nu = (r-1)(c-1)$. When $r^2 = 1$ the linear component accounts for the all of the observed deviations and $M^2 = \chi^2_\nu$. Thus, not only does r^2 represent the proportion of the total χ^2 accounted for by the linear trend, but also the difference $\chi^2_\nu - M^2$ provides a test of the departure from linearity. This difference has an expected $\chi^2_{\nu-1}$ distribution under the null hypothesis of linearity (see Howell, 2002).

Example 6.6 The full 2×4 table for the degree class data can be explored using the correlation approach described here. The χ^2 test of independence was reported as: $\chi^2(3, N = 278{,}170) = 1{,}807.1$, $p < .0001$. If gender is dummy coded (0 = male and 1 = female) and degree class coded as 1, 2, 3 or 4 (from first through to 3rd/other) the Pearson correlation between gender and degree class is $r = -.049$. Other equally spaced codes would give the same result.

This suggests that there is negative correlation between being female (coded 1) and getting a lower degree class (because lower degree classes are coded as high). In general female students tend to obtain better degree classifications than male students. The pattern is consistent with that in Figure 4.2b, which indicates that the proportion of 'good' degrees (first class or 2:1 degrees) is higher for females than for males. The test statistic for the linear correlation is:

$$M^2 = r^2(N-1) = (-.049)^2 \times (278100 - 1) \approx 675.7$$

It exceeds the critical value of $\chi^2_{1,.95}$ of 3.84 and is therefore statistically significant (if $\alpha = .05$). The test of non-linearity is likewise statistically significant: $\chi^2_2 = 1807.1 - 675.7$ (as $\chi^2_{2,.95} = 5.99$). The fact that both linear and non-linear patterns have been detected suggests that, in addition to the general trend for female students toward better degree classes, there is something else going on. Example 4.8 established what that might be: a greater proportion of males get first class degrees (in opposition to the linear correlation). The linear correlation accounts for $r^2 = .0024$ or .24% of the total sample variance. A more relevant quantity is how much of the observed deviation in the samples is accounted for by the linear trend. This is 675.7/1807.1 = .374 (37.4%). The linear component accounts for around a third of the overall effect.

6.5.4 Spearman's rho

Spearman's rho – typically denoted as r_S – is also a way to adapt r to deal with ordinal relationships. Spearman's statistic is identical to Pearson's r except that it makes use of a *rank transformation* (see Section 10.4.4). Prior to calculation of r, the data are replaced by their ranks. The Pearson correlation coefficient computed on the ranks is r_S.

As the assignment of ranks produces a finite set of discrete values, the distribution of the ranks will neither be continuous or normal. Thus, the usual hypothesis test and CI for Pearson's r will be unsatisfactory when N is small (though normal approximations for the distribution of ranks perform very well in moderate to large sample sizes). Because the ranks for a sample of size N are known being, in the absence of ties, some arrangement of the numbers 1 to N it is possible to calculate exact probabilities for different permutations of ranks. If ties are present these permutation tests will only be approximate. When N is large, exact or permutation versions of the tests can be replaced by resampling tests or normal approximations. Alternatively, the t distribution can be used to determine the statistical significance of r_S via Equation 6.10. All of these approaches produce similar outcomes when N is large.

In switching to analysis of the ranks, rather than raw scores, the null hypothesis of the significance test also changes. Rather than being a test of a linear relationship between X and Y, it is a test of a linear relationship between their respective ranks. This is less awkward to interpret than it may appear. A positive or negative linear relationship between ranks implies a monotonically increasing or decreasing relationship between the raw scores. The ranks ignore the information in the differences between successive values of X or Y, treating the differences as equal in magnitude. If the true relationship is that Y increases by some amount (whether large or small) every time X increases, the correlation between ranks will be perfect (i.e., $r_S = 1$). If Y always decreases when X increases, then r_S will be -1. This is the definition of a monotonic increase or decrease. This pattern includes any curve that is always increasing or decreasing (e.g., the exponential). Spearman's rho is therefore a sensitive measure for testing hypotheses about increasing or decreasing functions when a linear relationship is implausible.

Although r_S is convenient for some analyses, a difficulty with the rank transformation is that it destroys the link between the correlation and the original data. This makes constructing a CI for the raw data tricky (though approximate CIs are possible). An alternative to Spearman's rho, not considered here, is Kendall's τ (the Greek letter 'tau'). τ is based on the order of the observed values of X and Y. It is calculated from the degree of disorder in the paired scores (measured by inversions – the number of times adjacent values in one variable have to be swapped so that the ranks of X and Y match). Conover (1980) discusses τ in further detail.

Example 6.7 Table 6.1 reproduces the location memory data (from Table 5.1) in order of increasing presentation time, and adds the ranks of both X and Y.

Table 6.1 Reproduction of location memory data (from Table 5.1) in order of increasing presentation time, adding ranks of X and Y

Participant	***X* (presentation time)**	***X* (ranks)**	***Y* (distance)**	***Y* (ranks)**
P1	3	*1*	6.3	*6*
P2	6	*2*	3.9	*5*
P3	9	*3*	2.3	*3*
P4	12	*4*	2.0	*2*
P5	15	*5*	2.8	*4*
P6	18	*6*	1.6	*1*

The assignment process for these data is very clean (there are no ties). Computing r for the ranks gives $r_s = -.829$. Two-sided $p = .058$ for the exact test. The approximate test (calculated from Pearson's r applied to the ranked data) gives $p = .0416$, and the statistical significance of Pearson's r calculated from the raw data was reported earlier as $p = .0369$. The outcome of the three procedures differs slightly here (though the p values are similar in magnitude). The outcomes would match more closely in larger samples.

6.6 Inferences about differences in slopes

The typical focus of regression or correlation is on point or interval inferences for a single slope parameter. Several methods exist for testing differences in slopes. Methods for comparing regression slopes within a sample (e.g., moderated multiple regression) are considered in later chapters. This section introduces methods for comparing slopes from two independent samples.

6.6.1 Differences in slopes from independent simple linear regressions

Independent simple linear regressions arise when the regression equations for identical X and Y variables are computed for two different samples (e.g., for a replication and the study being replicated). Under these circumstances the slopes and intercepts will rarely be identical. Inference about the difference in the regression slope b_1 between two independent studies is related to the difference in means from two independent samples. Assuming homogeneity of variances, the standard error of the difference in two slopes is simply

$$\hat{\sigma}_{b_1-b_2} = \sqrt{\hat{\sigma}^2_{b_1,1} + \hat{\sigma}^2_{b_1,2}} \qquad \text{Equation 6.28}$$

where $\hat{\sigma}^2_{b_1,1}$ and $\hat{\sigma}^2_{b_1,2}$ are the standard errors of the slopes in the respective samples. This can then be used to construct a CI around the difference $b_1 - b_2$ as

$$b_1 - b_2 \pm t_{(N_1+N_2-4),1-\alpha/2}\hat{\sigma}_{b_1-b_2} \qquad \text{Equation 6.29}$$

where N_1 and N_2 are respective total sample sizes of the studies. The null hypothesis of no difference in the slopes can be tested using a t statistic of the form:

$$\frac{b_1 - b_2}{\hat{\sigma}_{b_1-b_2}} \sim t(N_1 + N_2 - 4) \qquad \text{Equation 6.30}$$

It is important to realize that this is not a test of the difference in correlation between the samples. The correlation coefficients may differ even if the regression slopes are identical and vice versa (e.g., because the standard deviations of X and Y differ between samples). The correlation, being related to R^2, depends on the degree of clustering of residuals around the regression line (something that influences the p value or width of a CI but not the estimate of an unstandardized slope).

6.6.2 Differences between two independent correlations

A first step in evaluating two independent correlations is to consider whether the two correlations are indeed comparable. It is usually obvious that comparing slopes measured in different units is unlikely to be sensible (e.g., weight and temperature). With correlations – which are dimensionless – the units may seem comparable, even when the underlying quantities being correlated are not.

For the comparison to be sensible it is necessary to assume not only that the relationships being compared are sufficiently similar, but also that the *SD*s of the variables in each sample are equally representative of the populations sampled. Thus it must be assumed that factors such as reliability or range restriction that influence the sample *SD*s are not in play (or have a similar impact on each correlation). Even so, there are some applications for the CI of a difference in correlations that are both sensible and useful (e.g., the difference in reliability coefficients from two independent samples).

Confidence intervals for r (and significance tests other than for the null hypothesis that $\rho = 0$) are usually based on the Fisher z transformation because the distribution of r is bounded. This transformation can also be used to derive a significance test of the hypothesis that $\rho_1 - \rho_2 = 0$ (although it is not possible to obtain a CI from this procedure). The most common approach is to rely on simple asymptotic methods to obtain a CI for a difference between correlations or to apply methods such as the BC_a bootstrap (DiCiccio and Efron, 1996; Zou, 2007). Neither of these solutions is wholly satisfactory. Zou (2007) proposed a modified asymptotic method based on the lower and upper bounds of CIs formed around separate correlations (where these are based on z_r). This modified asymptotic method provides superior CI coverage to the simple asymptotic method. For small and moderate sample sizes the modified asymptotic 95% CI contains ρ at between 94% and 96% of the time for samples as small as $N = 15$. In contrast, the coverage of the simple asymptotic method ranged from 90% to 93% (see *ibid.*).

To obtain a CI for the difference between two independent correlations (r_1 and r_2) using the modified asymptotic method, start by calculating CIs for single correlations at the desired confidence level (e.g., 95%). This uses the Fisher z transformation. The lower bounds of the CI for r_1 and r_2 are designated L_1 and L_2, and the upper bounds are designated U_1 and U_2. The CI for their difference is $[L, U]$. Estimates of L and U are given by:

$$\begin{aligned} L &= r_1 - r_2 - \sqrt{(r_1 - L_1)^2 + (U_2 - r_2)^2} \\ U &= r_1 - r_2 + \sqrt{(U_1 - r_1)^2 + (r_2 - L_2)^2} \end{aligned} \qquad \text{Equation 6.31}$$

Zou's modified asymptotic method can be extended to deal with situations where the correlations are themselves correlated (either because they overlap or because of some other dependency) or for differences in R^2 between comparable models (*ibid.*). Note that it is not advisable to use interval estimates of r to derive CIs for r^2 or R^2, because the relationship between r and r^2 is not linear (and thus the sampling distribution of one is not a simple rescaling of the other).

Example 6.8 Two versions of the same psychological scale often report different point estimates for reliability. Merely detecting or failing to detect a difference between these point estimates might not be very useful. An interval estimate of the difference in reliabilities is more informative. Assume version 1 and version 2 of a scale have different reliabilities so that $r_{XX,1} = .5$ and $r_{XX,2} = .6$ (and $N_1 = N_2 = 400$).

The usual 95% CI is [.4227, .5701] for $r_{XX,1}$ and [.5333, .6593] for $r_{XX,2}$. With these lower and upper bounds for the individual correlations as input, the lower bound for the difference is

$$\begin{aligned} L &= -.1 - \sqrt{(.5 - .4227)^2 + (.6593 - .6)^2} \\ &= -.1 - \sqrt{.005975 + .003516} \approx -.1974 \end{aligned}$$

and the corresponding upper bound for the difference is

$$U = -.1 + \sqrt{(.5701 - .5)^2 + (.6 - .5333)^2}$$
$$= -.1 + \sqrt{(.004914 + .004449} \approx -.0033$$

The resulting 95% CI for the difference could be reported as:

$$-.100, 95\% \text{ CI } [-.197, -.003]$$

This is equivalent to a test of H_0: $\rho_1 - \rho_2 = 0$, and thus the procedure has detected a difference in reliability between the scales. It appears that the second version of the scale is likely to be more reliable than the first, although the interval is quite wide. Thus, it is plausible that the second version is as reliable, and perhaps more reliable, than the first version. The interval estimate also suggests that it unlikely to be much worse than the first version.

6.7 R code for Chapter 6

6.7.1 Covariance and correlation (Examples 6.1 and 6.3)

The functions `cov()` and `cor()` provide the covariance and Pearson correlation between two variables (and can also be applied to a matrix to obtain covariance or correlation matrices). As `cov()` uses the inferential formula, it can also be used with `sd()` to compute r. For instance, for the location memory data, compare:

```
cov(time, distance)
cor(time, distance)
cov(time, distance) / (sd(time)*sd(distance))
```

With these functions, getting r^2 from r is also trivial:

```
cor(time, distance)^2
```

An r^2 value can also be obtained from the linear model summary:

```
summary(lm(distance ~ time))$r.square
```

The unstandardized regression slope b_1 is:

```
b1 <- lm(distance ~ time)$coefficient[[2]]
```

This can be converted into a correlation coefficient using the ratio of the *SD* of Y and X:

```
b1 * sd(time)/sd(distance)
```

6.7.2 Centering and standardizing (Example 6.2)

Centering involves creating a new variable with a mean of zero by subtracting the original mean:

```
dist.cent <- distance - mean(distance)
```

Standardizing involves also dividing by its *SD*:

```
dist.z <- dist.cent / sd(distance)
```

This can be done in one step as

```
dist.z <- (distance - mean(distance)) / sd(distance)
```

As standardizing is a common procedure, there is a built-in function called `scale()` that defaults to standardizing a variable (usually a vector):

```
dist.z <- scale(distance)
```

This function has arguments `center` and `scale` that by default are set to `TRUE`, but can be set to `FALSE`. This will center the `distance` vector:

```
dist.z <- scale(distance, scale = FALSE)
```

The main advantage of the `scale()` function is that it can be called within another function (e.g., to standardize or center variables in a regression model formula). This is helpful because model formulas assume arithmetic operators are part of the formula (rather than operators applying to predictor or outcome variables). The following linear model therefore generates the standardized slope between *X* and *Y* (using the location memory data):

```
lm(scale(distance) ~ scale(time))
```

6.7.3 Tests and CIs for Pearson's *r* (Examples 6.3 and 6.4)

The function `cor.test()` gives detailed output for Pearson's *r* (including the usual NHST and a CI obtained from z_r). The default is a 95% CI:

```
cor.test(time, distance, conf.level = .95)
cor.test(time, distance)
```

It is also possible to get an NHST for *r* from the summary method for the linear model of the standardized variables:

```
summary(lm(scale(distance) ~ scale(time)))
```

It is important to note that this linear model cannot be used to obtain accurate CIs for the standardized slope. However, it can be exploited to get the adjusted r^2 (Ezekiel small sample correction) for a correlation:

```
summary(lm(distance ~ time))$adj.r.square
```

This adjusted R^2 value matches the small sample correction calculated in Example 6.4 (disregarding rounding error).

If you wish to obtain a CI for a correlation coefficient in the absence of raw data, several methods could be employed. One is to use the Fisher z transformation and its inverse. Fisher z transformation functions exist in several packages, but there is also a built-in function. This uses the mathematics of hyperbolic functions, as the Fisher z transformation is a hyperbolic function of r (see Bond and Richardson, 2004). The hyperbolic arc-tangent `atanh()` function transforms r into z_r, while its inverse is the hyperbolic tangent `tanh()`. To get a 95% CI for a correlation you can therefore run these commands:

```
r <- cor(distance, time)
zr <- atanh(r)
n <- 6
alpha <- .05

zr.se <- 1/(n-3)^0.5
moe <- qnorm(1-alpha/2) * zr.se
zu <- zr + moe
zl <- zr - moe

tanh(c(zl, zu))
```

Alternatively, you can use the `CIr()` function from the `psychometric` package:

```
install.packages('psychometric')
library(psychometric)

CIr(r, n)
```

6.7.4 Other correlation coefficients (Examples 6.5, 6.6 and 6.7)

It is possible to use `cor()` to compute ϕ from dummy coded X and Y variables. To demonstrate this using the number of firsts and non-firsts for the degree class data requires creating new vectors for the gender (1 = male, 0 = female) and degree class (1 = first, 0 = non-first) from the matrix `new.obs` (from Section 4.8.6):

```
first.1 <- rep(c(1,1,0,0), new.obs[1:4])
gender.1 <- rep(c(1,0,1,0), new.obs[1:4])

cor(gender.1, first.1)
```

This matches the result in Example 6.5. The calculation in that example used the χ^2 test statistic. This can be replicated by:

```
phi.sq <- chisq.test(new.obs)$statistic / sum(new.obs)
phi <- phi.sq^0.5
phi
```

Example 6.6 uses r to estimate the linear correlation between two categorical variables when one or both variables are ordinal. The example uses the full 2×4 table for the degree class data. This time it is simplest to recode the data as vectors (using codes 1 to 4 for degree class).

```
males <- c(17975, 55710, 38175, 10400)
females <- c(21370, 81590, 44485, 8465)
gender <- rep(0:1, c(sum(males), sum(females)))
degree <- c(rep(1:4, males), rep(1:4, females))

cor(gender, degree)
cor(gender, degree)^2
```

The r^2 value here gives the proportion of the maximum possible χ^2 statistic of the independence test that is accounted for the linear correlation. Thus, the test statistic for the linear correlation is:

```
chisq.lin <- cor(gender, degree)^2 * (sum(observed)-1)
chisq.lin
```

As the p value for this test is very, very small, it is convenient to compare the observed χ^2 statistic to the critical value for 2 df for $\alpha = .05$. This is:

```
qchisq(.95, 2)
```

Expressing the proportion as a function of the observed variance for the table is also straightforward:

```
chisq.lin / chisq.test(observed)$statistic[[1]]
```

The `cor()` and `cor.test()` functions are quite versatile and can compute Spearman's r_S and Kendall's τ.

```
cor(time, distance, method='spearman')
cor.test(time, distance, method='spearman')

cor(time, distance, method='kendall')
cor.test(time, distance, method='kendall')
```

You can also get r_S using the `rank()` function on the two original vectors followed by calculating Pearson's r for the ranks:

```
t.rank <- rank(time)
d.rank <- rank(distance)
cor(t.rank, d.rank, method='pearson')
```

With $N < 10$ an exact test for Spearman's rho is computed, so for inference `method='spearman'` is preferred. The exact test can be requested (though it is the default for this sample size):

```
cor.test(time, distance, method='spearman', exact=TRUE)
```

User-contributed packages can be installed that calculate other correlation coefficients (Carroll, 1961). For example, the `polycor` package will calculate a tetrachoric correlation using the `polychor()` function for two dichotomously coded continuous variables.

6.7.5 Writing an R function

One of the big attractions of R is the ease with which you can write your own functions. This and subsequent chapters contain examples of functions written by the author – either to help illustrate a procedure or to allow you to reproduce an analysis. These functions can be pasted into R and called as needed (or saved to your R workspace if you prefer).

Writing functions is useful if you need to repeat or automate complex statistical calculations. A function is a type of named object created via the function `function()`. Here is a simple example:

```
ssc.R <- function(R, N, q = 1) {
    # Ezekiel (1929) small sample correction for r
    R.out <- (1 - (((1 - R^2) * (N - 1))/(N - q - 1)))^0.5
    if (R < 0)
        R.out <- R.out * -1
    R.out
}
```

If you paste the function into R, hit the return key and call the function with

```
ssc.R(-.835, 6)
```

it returns the value −0.7883725 from the vector `R.out`. This is Ezekiel's small sample correction for r. The function has a built-in default of $q = 1$ predictors and so expects a simple correlation as input. This can be over-ridden by changing the call. The objects `R`, `N`, `q` and `R.out` are internal or 'local' to the function (a useful feature that prevents you over-writing other objects). The `if` statement changes the sign of the output to match the input if `R` is negative. When writing a function, curly brackets { } must enclose all the code that forms part of the function. Lines or phrases beginning # are ignored by R and are used to annotate or add comments to the code. A function will normally return the result of the last evaluated expression as output (e.g., here `R.out`), though this can be altered using `return()`.

A full guide to writing functions in R is not possible here. You can see how some functions are written by typing the function name (though this will not work for many built-in or primitive functions). R is open source, and you may use, adapt and share these or other functions (provided you acknowledge the original author).

The next example creates a function that calculates the CI for a single correlation using the Fisher *z* transformation. This duplicates the `CIr()` function described earlier (though the function is written in a different way).

```
rz.ci <- function(r, N, conf.level = 0.95) {
    zr.se <- 1/(N - 3)^0.5
    moe <- qnorm(1 - (1 - conf.level)/2) * zr.se
    zu <- atanh(r) + moe
    zl <- atanh(r) - moe
    tanh(c(zl, zu))
}
```

You can check it by comparing calls such as `rz.ci(.5, 10)` with `CIr(.5, 10)`.

6.7.6 Differences between correlation coefficients (Example 6.8)

It is possible to set up a function for the CI of a difference in two independent correlations using Zou's modified asymptotic method. This example uses the `rz.ci()` function from the previous section:

```
r.ind.ci <- function(r1, r2, n1, n2=n1, conf.level = 0.95) {
    L1 <- rz.ci(r1, n1, conf.level)[1]
    U1 <- rz.ci(r1, n1, conf.level)[2]
    L2 <- rz.ci(r2, n2, conf.level)[1]
    U2 <- rz.ci(r2, n2, conf.level)[2]
    lower <- r1 - r2 - ((r1 - L1)^2 + (U2 - r2)^2)^0.5
    upper <- r1 - r2 + ((U1 - r1)^2 + (r2 - L2)^2)^0.5
    c(lower, upper)
}
```

The function may look complicated, but most of the code is taken up by assigning the output from `rz.ci()` to vectors called `L1`, `U1`, `L2`, and `U2`. The real work is done by the last few lines. Although the function could be written more efficiently, it is usually sensible (at least to start with) to use multiple steps within a function to make it easier to see what is going on. To check the function against Example 6.8 use this call:

```
r.ind.ci(.5, .6, 400, 400)
```

6.7.7 R packages

Fletcher, T. D. (2008) *psychometric*: Applied Psychometric Theory. R package version 2.1.
Fox, J. (2010) *polycor*: Polychoric and Polyserial Correlations. R package version 0.7-8.

6.8 Notes on SPSS syntax for Chapter 6

6.8.1 Covariance and correlation

Correlations can be obtained either with the CORRELATIONS or NONPAR CORR command. For the location memory data the basic syntax for Pearson's r including a two-sided p value – labeled 'Sig. (2-tailed)' – is:

SPSS data file: loc_mem.sav

```
CORRELATIONS
  /VARIABLES=time distance.
```

Spearman and Kendall correlations can be obtained from the syntax:

```
NONPAR CORR
  /VARIABLES=time distance
  /PRINT=BOTH TWOTAIL.
```

The /PRINT subcommand can be edited to provide either correlation on its own (by replacing BOTH with KENDALL or SPEARMAN). Likewise a /PRINT subcommand can be added to the CORRELATIONS command and edited to provide one-sided p values (replacing TWOTAIL with ONETAIL). These functions can also be accessed via the <Analyze> menu by selecting <Correlate> <Bivariate . . . >.

Although obtaining CIs for a correlation in SPSS is not easy using standard commands (requiring macros or step-by-step computation), one interesting feature of the correlation commands is that they produce a correlation matrix by default. This allows a matrix of all possible bivariate correlations between a set of variables to be produced. For example, the syntax below would produce a matrix with correlations between x1 and x2, x1 and x3, and x2 and x3:

```
CORRELATIONS
  /VARIABLES=x1 x2 x3.
```

SPSS will also compute ϕ and related statistics. To get ϕ for the degree class data (as in Example 6.5) use the following syntax:

SPSS data file: hesa_2009.sav

```
WEIGHT BY revised_count.

CROSSTABS
  /TABLES=gender BY first
  /STATISTIC=PHI.
```

The output also includes ϕ_C, though this is identical to ϕ in a 2×2 table. SPSS also provides what it calls a linear by linear association by default if you request /STATISTIC=CHI. This is identical to the usual statistic for a 2×2 table, but different for larger two-way tables. This example uses the full 2 × 4 gender by degree class table (first changing the frequency variable back to *count* from *revised_count*):

```
WEIGHT BY count.

CROSSTABS
  /TABLES=gender BY degree
  /FORMAT= AVALUE TABLES
  /STATISTIC=CHISQ PHI.
```

To standardize or center variables you can use the COMPUTE command, though standardization is usually applied via <Analyze> <Descriptives . . . > where the analysis window has a check box for 'Save standardized variables'. The following syntax will also work:

SPSS data file: `loc_mem.sav`

```
DESCRIPTIVES VARIABLES=time distance
 /SAVE.
```

This provides default descriptive statistics output and also saves the standardized variables to the SPSS Data View spreadsheet as `Ztime` and `Zdistance`.

6.9 Bibliography and further reading

Agresti, A. (1996) *An Introduction to Categorical Data Analysis*. New York: Wiley.

Carroll, J. B. (1961) The Nature of Data, or How to Choose a Correlation Coefficient. *Psychometrika*, 26, 347–72.

Rodgers, J. L., and Nicewander, W. L. (1988) Thirteen Ways to Look at the Correlation Coefficient. *The American Statistician*, 42, 59–66.

7
Effect size

Contents

7.1 Chapter overview

This chapter reviews the concept of effect size, starting with a definition of effect size and the role of effect size in research. A central theme is the challenge of selecting an appropriate effect size metric. Important distinctions are made between simple and standardized effect size, metrics for continuous outcomes (including *d* and *r* family standardized measures), and metrics for discrete outcomes (with emphasis on those for 2×2 contingency tables).

7.2 The role of effect size in research

7.2.1 What is effect size?

All effects can be reduced either to a difference between two things (e.g., $\hat{\mu}_1 - \hat{\mu}_2$) or an association between two things (e.g., r_{XY}). The distinction between a difference or association is largely one of convenience. For instance, a difference in means between two independent groups for outcome (Y) is equivalent to the slope of the regression of Y on X (where X is a dummy coded predictor identifying group membership). For any effect, whether a difference or an association, the question of how big or small the effect is – its magnitude – is almost always vital. Determining the magnitude of an effect involves selecting a metric (or measure). The term *effect size* is used to distinguish a particular measure from the general concept of magnitude of an effect. A number of definitions of effect size have been proposed, though some are quite narrow in scope (and potentially too restrictive). Preacher and Kelley (2011) propose a broad definition that encompasses the range of effect size metrics discussed here. The definition they propose is 'any measure that reflects a quantity of interest, either in an absolute sense or as compared to some specified value' (*ibid.*, p.95). In most cases the quantity of interest is a population parameter, and an estimate of that quantity is an effect size statistic.

Having adopted a definition of effect size, two further questions need to be considered. First, why do researchers need to know the magnitude of an effect? To answer this question it is necessary to consider what applications effect size is used for. Second, how should you decide which effect size metric to select? This is one of the hardest questions to answer in statistics. The answer depends on what you are trying to do, what kind of data you have and the audience you are trying to communicate your findings to.

7.2.2 What is effect size used for?

Effect size has a range of potential uses. Steinberg and Thissen (2006) suggest there are three broad uses for effects sizes: i) statistical power, ii) research synthesis and iii) reporting findings. Baguley (2009) discusses how to report findings in published work and summarizes the uses of effect size as: i) understanding the importance of an effect, ii) comparison of effect sizes and iii) secondary analysis. A single effect size metric is very unlikely to be suitable for every purpose. This is unfortunate, because guidelines often advocate reporting effect size without considering what the effect size will be used for (e.g., APA, 2010), though good advice exists if you know where to look (see Wilkinson and APA Task Force on Statistical Inference, 1999).

Applications of effect size can be classified along three broad dimensions: *style* (formal or informal), the *source* of the data (primary or secondary) and *application* (interpretation or inference). An informal method might involve a verbal description of an effect (e.g., labeling it as 'small' or 'large'), whereas a formal method involves the application of some principled method (e.g., cost-benefit analysis or interval estimation). A primary analysis has access to the raw data and is usually carried out by people intimately familiar with the research. In contrast, secondary analysis relies on published reports or archived data, and is likely to be carried out by researchers who did not collect the original data. Interpreting an effect – particularly the practical impact of an effect – is a major motivation for reporting effect size. This is especially true in applied research (Baguley, 2004). Inference with effect size can take several forms, but involves using an effect size to estimate some quantity of interest (e.g., the sample size required for a new study). Inference also includes inferences about the effect itself (e.g., comparing effects within or between studies). A good example of the latter is *meta-analysis*, a form of *research synthesis* that is concerned with combining effect size estimates.[1]

Using this typology it is possible to characterize some common uses of effect size. Verbal comments about the size of effect are informal applications for interpreting a finding. Evidence suggests that these can mislead people – in particular when a verbal label is attached to a point estimate (Robinson *et al.*, 2003). Verbal comparison of the sizes of effects between studies is likewise an informal form of inference. This is less likely to be misleading. Baguley (2009) characterizes this distinction as being between absolute and relative judgments of the magnitude of an effect. Merely commenting that an effect is 'large' tends to be misleading because there is insufficient context to clarify what the label means (and because the uncertainty in the estimate is ignored). For these and other reasons, this practice has been heavily criticized (e.g., Baguley, 2004, 2009; Lenth, 2001; Steinberg and Thissen, 2006). Lenth (2009) memorably christened verbal labels such as 'small', 'medium' and 'large' as 'T-shirt' effect sizes.

Formal methods of inference include significance tests and confidence intervals (CIs) as well as tools to aid interpretation such as cost- or risk-benefit analysis. These tools can be applied for both primary and secondary data. Research synthesis is a catch-all term for methods that aggregate findings from different studies. These methods range from informal, narrative reviews to formal, systematic reviews (e.g., meta-analysis).

Among formal methods, statistical power and sample size estimation are particularly interesting. These are employed by primary researchers to help assess the impact of a finding, or to estimate sample size required to detect an effect. Secondary researchers use them to assess the impact of previous findings (e.g., by assessing whether research had sufficient power to detect an effect) or to make inferences about future studies based on published research (e.g., to estimate the required sample size to replicate an effect).

While these dimensions can be used to classify typical uses of effect size statistics, the boundaries between them can be fuzzy. For instance, systematic reviews try to eliminate the deficiencies of informal reviews of previous studies (e.g., by minimizing bias in the way previous research is sampled), but may stop short of formal meta-analytic methods. Secondary research that assesses the importance of an effect tends to draw on a mixture of formal and informal methods. Thus, a published meta-analysis will often involve a systematic review of the literature with a narrative interpretation, as well as a statistical model of effect size (constituting meta-analysis in the strictest sense).

What does looking at the uses of effect size in this way reveal? First, it will be difficult to anticipate all the uses to which published reports of effect size might be put. Some researchers will want to assess its practical or clinical importance, whereas others will use the information to plan new studies. Second, formal methods, if properly applied, can be used to reduce biases or deficiencies in informal methods.

The typology also ignores the identity of readers or consumers of published work. These consumers range from other researchers (interested in replicating or extending the work) to practitioners, policy-makers or members of the general public. The audience for the work will vary considerably in their scientific and mathematical experience and have different preferences (e.g., for familiar, easy to display effect sizes). What works for communicating to other researchers might not work for a client, patient or journalist.

The principal motivation for estimating the size of an effect (the one to which nearly all uses of effect size feed in to) is to gauge its importance. Small effects can be important – particularly for testing or distinguishing between theories – but larger effects tend to be of greater importance and be more impressive than small effects.[2] Thus Kirk (1996) proposed that researchers in education, psychology and other disciplines focus on *practical significance* rather than on statistical significance. Reporting and interpreting effect size as a measure of practical significance is at the heart of his proposal. Similarly, in medical and health research, there is increasing emphasis on the *clinical significance* of an effect, in contrast to the 'statistical' significance that a null hypothesis test (NHST) provides (Kraemer and Kupfer, 2006).

7.2.3 Small effects can be impressive too

Factors other than its magnitude will influence the interpretation of any effect. Small effects (or effects that appear small) can be impressive too. For scientists engaged in theory testing, very tiny effects may be critical (e.g., if theory A predicts the presence and direction of an effect, but theory B does not).

In relation to practical significance, large effects are more likely to be important than small effects. Even so, determining what constitutes a large effect is a tricky business. Supposedly 'small' effects can have substantial practical significance. This can occur for two broad reasons.

First, people may misunderstand the effect size metric that they are using. Some of the most profound misunderstandings occur with proportion of variance explained metrics (e.g., R^2). Rosenthal and Rubin (1979) give the example of an old and new treatment, each applied to 50 people. Under the new treatment, 70% of patients are alive after one year, whereas only 30% survive this long under the old treatment. This constitutes a very impressive effect, yet the proportion of variance explained is only .16. Rosnow and Rosenthal (2003) provide further striking examples from real studies (e.g., the Salk vaccine trial mentioned in Example 6.5). Part of the problem is that people judge effects expressed in terms of small numbers as less impressive than equivalent effects expressed as large numbers. People may also assume that standardized effect sizes are 'pure' measures of effect sizes (e.g., unaware that problems such as unreliability that may distort them). Furthermore, correlation coefficients and proportion of variance explained can also only rarely attain their theoretical maximum. This could be because the distributions of the predictor and response are not the same (Carroll, 1961), or because predictors not included in the model explain the remaining variance (O'Grady, 1982). Indeed, for any complex outcome, a single predictor would only rarely be expected to predict more than a small fraction of the total variance. Thus, a predictor that explained 10% of the variance might be of huge importance.

The second reason is that the importance (practical, clinical or otherwise) of an effect cannot be properly determined without some context. The relevant contextual information includes issues such as how hard the outcome is to influence, the seriousness of an outcome and the costs associated with it (Prentice and Miller, 1992; Baguley, 2004). A striking example of how 'small' effects can have impressive consequences comes from Abelson (1985). Abelson showed that, for most major league baseball players, skill explains only about 0.33 of a percentage point of the variance of a single batting performance (and not much above 1% for even the greatest players). In this case the answer isn't simply that the effect size measure gives an incorrect impression of what is going on: skill really doesn't have that much impact on a single batting performance at this level. Abelson's main argument is that – in this context – skill has impact not through a single performance, but through cumulative performances over a season. In a situation where effects are cumulative, even a tiny effect may have enormous impact on the outcome. Consider a brief intervention that increases a child's reading age by a fraction of 1 percent. Such an intervention might be dismissed as negligible, but if it was easy to implement repeatedly, and its effects were cumulative, it could produce a substantial improvement in literacy after several years of schooling.

While important and substantial effects sometimes appear small, it is also true that relatively unimpressive effects can seem large. In small samples, the true size of an effect won't be measured with precision (though an interval estimate of the effect should reveal this). Moreover, small samples tend to underestimate the population variance and therefore overestimate standardized effect size (because the sample distribution of variances from independent samples are highly skewed). More generally, because all studies have some bias and sampling error, any surprisingly large effect is likely to have overestimated the true effect size (i.e., it is more likely to be a product of random noise or bias – a 'fluke' – than a small effect). Publication bias is particularly relevant here. While unexpectedly small effects do occur, they are much less likely to be published. So, in the absence of additional data (e.g., from a replication), it is wise to be cautious about large effect size estimates – particularly those that are surprisingly large or from small studies (Ioannidis, 2005a, 2005b).

7.3 Selecting an effect size metric

7.3.1 Criteria for selecting a metric

Selecting an effect size metric involves understanding what effect size metrics are available and matching the features you require from a metric to what is available. It is not necessarily the case that an ideal metric exists for a given situation, and – as already discussed – a single effect may need to be reported in a way that facilitates a range of applications. Selecting an effect size metric to report requires compromising between different criteria. Nevertheless, there are some properties that are likely to be desirable for all effect size measures. Preacher and Kelley (2011) propose three main 'desiderata': i) an appropriate scale, ii) the ability to calculate an interval estimate and iii) a point estimate that is independent of sample size. They also note that, as with any statistic, it should ideally be unbiased, efficient and consistent. This does not exhaust the requirements of the metric, but other requirements will depend on the context in which it is applied (e.g., on the particular audience you have in mind).

There are dozens of effect size metrics in common use and perhaps hundreds of measures proposed in published work (e.g., see Rosenthal, 1994; Fleiss, 1994; Kirk, 1996). Rather than survey the full range of options it is more productive to consider the main characteristics used to select an appropriate metric. A good starting point is whether the effect in question involves a continuous or categorical outcome – as different options exist for each type. Following Preacher and Kelley's desiderata, the next step is probably to decide what constitutes an appropriate scale. The main choice here is between a *simple* or *standardized effect size* metric (Frick, 1999; Baguley, 2009). Once the appropriate scale is decided, it is usually possible to meet the remaining desiderata – having a point estimate independent of n and being able to construct an accurate interval estimate – without difficulty (at least for the effect size statistics considered in this chapter). Properties such as lack of bias, efficiency and consistency should also be considered. The choice must also take into account the purpose of reporting the effect and how best to communicate the findings to the intended audience. It is also best practice to provide sufficient information (in the form of summary statistics) for alternative metrics to be computed.

One final property of an effect size statistic needs to be considered. Any substantive hypothesis (and the appropriate effect size statistic associated with it) can be focused or unfocused. A focused effect size statistic provides information about the direction or precise pattern of the effect in addition to its magnitude. Good examples are a difference between two means or a correlation between two variables. An unfocused effect is one that merely summarizes the magnitude of the effect without information about the direction or pattern of effect. A technical way to define this distinction is that of single degree of freedom (1 *df*) effects versus multiple degree of freedom (multiple *df*) effects. For most purposes it makes little sense to use multiple *df* effect size metrics (see Baguley, 2009). Single *df* effects are more informative than multiple *df* effects. If different studies are being compared (e.g., in a meta-analysis) it is relatively rare that multiple *df* effects will be similar enough to be compared. A multiple *df* effect aggregates information about several effects (e.g., a set of differences or associations) using the same numeric outcome (e.g., $R^2 = .60$), but might correspond to any number of different patterns among the effects. The individual effects might also differ between studies. For this reason it is usually better to break down multiple *df* effects into 1 *df* effects when reporting and interpreting effect size (Baguley, 2009; APA, 2010). The emphasis here is therefore almost exclusively on 1 *df* effects, though some widely reported multiple *df* effect size metrics (such as R^2) are addressed in passing.

7.3.2 Simple versus standardized effect size

A straightforward way to report the magnitude of an effect is to use the original units of measurement. Thus a study investigating memory accuracy might report a difference between conditions in terms of the number of items recalled from a list, while a study looking at the effect of age on speed of processing might predict reaction times in milliseconds as a function of age. Such effect sizes are frequently labeled as raw or unstandardized effect sizes – terms that might suggest these metrics are inferior in some way. To avoid this suggestion I adopt the more neutral term *simple effect size* (see Frick, 1999). Simple effect size crops up in many situations, but the canonical example is the slope of a simple linear regression in the original units of measurement (b_1). Thus any unstandardized regression coefficient (including the intercept) can also be considered a simple effect size statistic.

Regression coefficients are good exemplars of simple effect size and there is a long history of preferring simple to standardized effect size metrics in regression (e.g., Fisher, 1925; Tukey, 1954). One feature that makes simple effect size metrics particularly attractive is that the slope of a linear regression is also a measure of *causal efficacy* (Abelson, 1995). That is to say, it is the ratio of the size of an effect to the size of its cause. Even when causal efficacy has been obscured (e.g., because of the way groups are implicitly coded in an independent t test or a regression with categorical predictors), it is usually quite easy to extract this information from simple effect size metrics. A simple difference between two group means is one of the most common ways to report the magnitude of an effect (and itself a form of regression slope). If the groups are defined by the dose of a drug (e.g., a 0*mg* placebo group and a 30*mg* experimental group) the effect of the drug on an outcome such as reaction time can be reported as the simple difference between conditions or as the mean change in reaction time per *mg* of the drug. For this reason, while dummy coding is useful for incorporating categorical variables into regression, it is sometimes better to replace group codes with meaningful values (e.g., 0 and 30 in the preceding example).[3]

In contrast, *standardized effect size* does not use the original units of measurement. The magnitude of effect is instead scaled either in terms of the standard deviation ($\hat{\sigma}$) or variance ($\hat{\sigma}^2$). This shift from the original scale to a standardized scale has an intuitive appeal, particularly when comparing effects across two or more different scales (e.g., accuracy and time) or two or more different versions of a measure (e.g., long and short forms of a psychometric instrument). However, it rests on a fundamental assumption that the units of 'standardization' (the *standardizer*) are identical for each effect. Thus, if standardization is achieved using the standardizer $\hat{\sigma}$, the assumption is that $\hat{\sigma}$ is equivalent across all the effects being compared (Morris and DeShon, 2002; Kirk, 2007). This assumption is likely to be unreasonable in many cases (Baguley, 2009). The canonical form of a standardized effect size is the standardized slope of a simple linear regression ($\hat{\beta}$) or the equivalent Pearson product-moment correlation coefficient (r). Any standardized regression or correlation coefficient is therefore a form of standardized effect size metric (as are related statistics, such as z_r or R^2).

The appeal of standardized effect size metrics is twofold. First, many researchers appear to believe that standardized metrics such as correlation offer a universally agreed standard by which to measure the magnitude of an effect. This is problematic because, while there are many attempts to codify magnitude of effect in this way (e.g., T-shirt effect sizes), there is no general agreement on this. An implicit (and sometimes explicit) aspect of this belief is that measures such as r or r^2 provide a mathematical ideal for determining the magnitude of an effect (e.g., strength of a relationship). This is not the case (except in very limited circumstances). Imagine two studies looking at the association between hours of exercise per week and scores on a positive mood scale. The first study reports a regression slope of $b_1 = 0.6$ scale points per hour of exercise. Even if the two studies have identical correlations (e.g., $r = .25$) it would be unlikely that the second study would also have a slope of $b_1 = 0.6$. This is only guaranteed if the ratio of the variances of the exercise and mood scale measures were identical in each sample – see Equation 6.8 and Equation 6.9. The more the two studies differ (in terms of sample characteristics, measurement instruments or design) the less likely the sample *SD*s, and hence regression slope, are to be similar. This is well understood by most experts in statistics: r depends on the degree to which residuals cluster around the slope of the regression (something arguably irrelevant to the magnitude of the relationship between X and Y). That said, there are situations – such as the assessment of reliability – where measures such as r fit the bill exactly (*ibid.*). A reliable measurement is expected to approach zero measurement error and hence perfect correlation. Likewise, if the only substantive hypothesis of interest is that the true effect is zero then standardized and simple effect metrics are equivalent.

The second main appeal of standardized effect size is to side-step practical difficulties in comparing effects that are scaled in different ways. A researcher measuring problem-solving performance might have diverse measures such as solution rate, solution times, number of correct moves and number of incorrect moves. All these measures capture some aspect of the broader, abstract notion of problem-solving ability. Standardization seems to offer a neat solution for making these measures equivalent. This issue arises frequently in meta-analysis of standardized effect size metrics, where considerable effort is required to ensure that the process of standardization does not introduce error and bias (see Hunter and Schmidt, 2004). However, the hidden assumptions of standardization (in terms of the equivalence of the standardizer) are largely ignored outside the context of meta-analysis (and sometimes within it). Careful use of standardization can make it easier to compare effects on different scales, but standardization is not a magical procedure for making these difficulties disappear. It may even conceal these difficulties by making the measures appear to be on a common scale when they are not (Tukey, 1969; Baguley, 2009).

On balance, simple effect size metrics have three advantages over standardized effect size metrics and should be preferred for most applications (Baguley, 2009). Simple effect size is:

1) scaled independently of $\hat{\sigma}$ or $\hat{\sigma}^2$
2) scaled in its original units, and
3) easy to compute.

Why are these advantages? Scaling effect size in terms of $\hat{\sigma}$ or $\hat{\sigma}^2$ confounds the magnitude of an effect with its variability. This is a serious problem because $\hat{\sigma}$ is influenced by many factors that don't necessarily influence the magnitude of the effect in the population. These include reliability, range restriction, distributional assumptions, small sample bias and differences in study design (e.g., choice of independent or repeated measures). In addition, $\hat{\sigma}$ is itself an estimate (and hence measured with error). Standardized effect size is thus influenced by two different sources of error. This makes the statistic more imprecise than would be the case if only the magnitude of the effect were estimated.[4] This is not to argue that the uncertainty in the sample should be ignored. A neater solution is to present the estimate of a parameter in addition to an estimate of its precision. One way to do this is in the form of a CI for a simple effect size metric (*ibid.*).

Using the original units has obvious advantages in terms of the interpretation of an effect – especially in applied research (Baguley, 2004). Knowing that a new device decreases the time taken to complete a routine task by an average of two minutes will usually make it easier to assess its practical significance than knowing that $r = .37$. Some of the most influential guidance on statistical practice – widely interpreted as advocating the reporting of standardized effect size – explicitly notes that simple effect size metrics should be preferred when measurement units are meaningful (Wilkinson and APA Task Force on Statistical Inference, 1999). Even with arbitrary measures such as rating scales, there is a case that simple effect size is easier to interpret (see Baguley, 2009). This is particularly true when the arbitrary measures are well known to researchers and consumers of research (Tukey, 1969; Abelson, 1995; Preacher and Kelley, 2011).

The final advantage – ease of computation – carries the least weight, yet should not be dismissed entirely. The more steps there are in the computation of a statistic the easier it is to make errors (and errors in reporting statistical findings are not uncommon). If two statistics have an identical interpretation, it seems more sensible to report the one that is easier to compute. Although many common standardized effect sizes are not hard to compute, correcting them for reliability, range restriction, small sample bias or study design adds considerably to the complexity. For routine applications the extra computation seems unnecessary and simple effect size suffices (Baguley, 2009). Furthermore, obtaining interval estimates for simple effect size metrics is much easier than for standardized metrics.

Standardized effect size only rarely provides advantages over simple effect size. Exceptions are for situations where the objective is to estimate a standardized population parameter such as ρ or where it aids the interpretation of some substantive hypothesis. For instance, if one expects that (under ideal circumstances) ρ should approach 1 (or -1) then r may be a more suitable measure than b_1. Psychometric measures such as reliability and validity fall into this category. Likewise, a theory that predicted that an increase in X always produces an increase in Y would, in effect, be claiming a monotonically increasing relationship. This is equivalent to a perfect correlation for Spearman's rho (r_S) in the population (i.e., $\rho_S = 1$).

There are also some data for which standardization may help make effects more comparable. Standardization is most attractive if the standardizer is σ rather than $\hat{\sigma}$ (the latter only rarely being an accurate estimate). There are two broad ways that this can be achieved. One is to obtain an accurate estimate of σ (e.g., from a meta-analysis that includes many high-quality studies or from population norms). The other is to correct the sample estimates for sources of bias (Hunter and Schmidt, 2004). Where this is not feasible, perhaps because necessary information to make the corrections is unavailable or of poor quality, other options should be considered. Kim and Feree (1981) note that not all variables in an analysis need to be standardized (preferring not to standardize those variables measured in meaningful units). Cohen *et al.* (1999) argue that for variables on arbitrary scales *percentage of maximum possible* (POMP) scores may be more informative than standardized regression coefficients.

POMP scores also illustrate that very simple transformations of the original units can sometimes greatly aid interpretation. For instance, in memory research the number of items remembered is often reported in terms of percentage accuracy (to account for different numbers of items between conditions or between experiments).

A point of caution arising from this discussion is that while the original units of measurement are often a good choice for reporting effects that are meaningful and easy to interpret, this does not imply that they are necessarily the best units of measurement. Even a basic memory experiment might offer several plausible alternative measures of accuracy for the same raw data (e.g., percentage correct, percentage corrected for guessing, or a signal detection measure such as d' or a'). Each measure implies a different theoretical account of memory. Neither simple effect size nor standardized effect size guarantees that the original measure selected by the researcher will be the best one. Finding the best measure for testing a theory is among the most fundamental and difficult challenges in science (of which the statistical properties of the measure are just one facet).

7.4 Effect size metrics for continuous outcomes

For continuous outcomes many effect size metrics are available. With simple effect size the choice reduces to two basic options: a simple difference in means (e.g., $\hat{\mu}_1 - \hat{\mu}_2$) or the (unstandardized) slope of a regression (e.g., b_1). In essence, almost any 1 *df* effect can be represented in one of these forms. For standardized effect size there are too many options to list even a tiny fraction of the possible choices. Rosenthal (1994) classifies these into two main families: the *d* family and the *r* family.

7.4.1 Standardized mean differences: the *d* family

The *d* family of standardized effect sizes are effect sizes based on differences in means scaled by a standard deviation (termed the standardizer). Statistics that make up the *d* family are therefore also known as standardized mean differences. For many researchers, *d* family statistics are synonymous with Cohen's *d*, a measure identified by the equation:

$$\delta = \frac{\mu_1 - \mu_2}{\sigma_j} \qquad \text{Equation 7.1}$$

Cohen (1969, 1988) defined his measure of effect size in terms of population parameters: μ_1 and μ_2 are the population means of two independent groups and σ_j is the population *SD* of one of the two groups. Subsequent researchers have estimated the population standardized mean difference (δ) in different ways, all of which can more or less legitimately be referred to as Cohen's *d*. Authors have employed different symbols for this parameter and for its various estimates. McGrath and Meyer (2006) proposed a common standard, and their recommendations are adopted here.

Members of the *d* family of effect size statistics (if some of the more distant cousins, only loosely based on a standardized mean difference, are excluded) have an expected value of zero if there is no true effect, but can range from negative to positive infinity. Standardizing provides an interpretation of the difference in means in terms of the standard deviation of the outcome *Y*. Thus $\delta = 0.5$ represents a difference of half a standard deviation of *Y* between the groups. For normally distributed scores this corresponds to an overlap of 67% between the two samples. Cohen (1988) originally motivated his choice of labels for effect sizes by considering the degree of separation (or overlap) of the sampled distributions. The benchmarks relate to whether someone could readily detect the effect without statistical analysis (e.g., 0.5 is a 'medium' effect in this scheme and represents the degree of separation just visible to a typical observer). Although widely, and usually incorrectly, interpreted as a measure of the magnitude of an effect, the origin of Cohen's *d* is therefore as a measure of the discriminability or detectability of an effect. This may explain why Cohen's *d* is sometimes calculated as a descriptive measure rather than an inferential one.

Most *d* family statistics are for focused (1 *df*) effects appropriate for a variety of two independent group designs. It is also possible to adapt the most common *d* family statistics to one sample or non-independent designs (e.g., for paired or pre-post designs). The sign of the statistic preserves information about the direction of the observed effect, in common with the simple mean difference, unstandardized slope or the correlation coefficient. For unfocused (multiple *df*) effects *d* family statistics are less useful and harder to interpret. It is therefore not surprising that they are relatively uncommon. A popular multiple *df* generalization of *d* is Cohen's f^2. This statistic, convenient for statistical power or sample size estimation, is reviewed briefly in Chapter 12.

7.4.2 Standardized mean differences: independent samples

Although Equation 7.1 implies that an estimator of either σ_1 or σ_2 should be used to estimate δ, in practice a pooled variance estimate is more likely to be employed (see Key Concept 3.3).

Pooling variances should produce a more accurate estimate, though it also implicitly assumes homogeneity of the population variances (i.e., that $\sigma_1^2 = \sigma_2^2$).

One variant of Cohen's d is to obtain the standardized mean difference in the sample:

$$d = \frac{\hat{\mu}_1 - \hat{\mu}_2}{\sqrt{\frac{\sum_{i=1}^{n_1}(x_i - \hat{\mu}_1)^2 + \sum_{i=1}^{n_2}(x_i - \hat{\mu}_2)^2}{n_1 + n_2}}} = \frac{\hat{\mu}_1 - \hat{\mu}_2}{\sqrt{\frac{(n_1 - 1)\hat{\sigma}_1^2 + (n_2 - 1)\hat{\sigma}_2^2}{n_1 + n_2}}} = \frac{\hat{\mu}_1 - \hat{\mu}_2}{SD_{pooled}} \quad \text{Equation 7.2}$$

This is a descriptive measure because the standardizer is the pooled SD with $n_1 + n_2 = N$ rather than $N-2$ as a divisor (i.e., Equation 1.11 is used to calculate the SD for each sample). This descriptive measure is analogous to R^2 (the proportion of sample variance explained by a regression). Both R^2 and d are potentially useful descriptions of a sample, but are problematic as inferences about the population (over-estimating the population effect size in small samples). If N is large, d may nevertheless provide a reasonable estimate of δ.

Another variant, perhaps the most widely used, employs the usual inferential sample estimate $\hat{\sigma}_{pooled}$ from Equation 3.27 as a standardizer. This estimate is attributed to Hedges (1981) and often known as Hedges' g:

$$g = \frac{\hat{\mu}_1 - \hat{\mu}_2}{\sqrt{\frac{(n_1 - 1)\hat{\sigma}_1^2 + (n_2 - 1)\hat{\sigma}_2^2}{n_1 + n_2 - 2}}} = \frac{\hat{\mu}_1 - \hat{\mu}_2}{\hat{\sigma}_{pooled}} \quad \text{Equation 7.3}$$

Being smaller than d by a factor of $\sqrt{(N-2)/N}$, g is less biased than d as an estimate of δ. However, it still slightly overestimates δ in small samples. Hedges (1981) also describes a small sample correction (similar to Ezekiel's correction for r). The small sample correction for g exists in several forms, but one convenient expression is:

$$\hat{\delta} = \frac{(N-3)}{N-2.25}g \quad \text{Equation 7.4}$$

Unless N is very small, the correction only has a marginal impact on the estimate and (like r_{adj}) it is rarely reported in published work outside meta-analysis. Nevertheless, $\hat{\delta}$ is an unbiased estimator and is only marginally more troublesome to compute than g.

A convenient short-cut formula for g uses the test statistic t from an independent t test. Using the relationship between $\hat{\sigma}_{pooled}$ and $\hat{\sigma}_{\mu_1 - \mu_2}$ Hedges' g can be expressed as:

$$g = t\sqrt{\frac{1}{n_1} + \frac{1}{n_2}} \quad \text{Equation 7.5}$$

If $n_1 = n_2$ this reduces to:

$$g = \frac{2t}{\sqrt{N}} \quad \text{Equation 7.6}$$

To convert to $\hat{\delta}$ from t combine Equation 7.5 and Equation 7.4. To obtain d from t, multiply the right-hand side of Equation 7.5 by $\sqrt{N/(N-2)}$.

If the homogeneity of variance assumption is not justified, it is sensible to use a standardizer that does not pool variances. This statistic is referred to as Glass' Δ (Glass, 1976). It standardizes the difference using $\hat{\sigma}$ calculated from a baseline or control group:

$$\Delta = \frac{\hat{\mu}_e - \hat{\mu}_C}{\hat{\sigma}_C} \qquad \text{Equation 7.7}$$

This is a sensible strategy as it allows effects sharing a common control group (or some other reference group) to be compared on a similar scale. However, if there is no logical reference group, unequal variances present a problem for standardized mean differences (because the effect size depends either on an arbitrary decision or on a pooled estimate that reflects neither group). Violations of normality can also distort d family statistics (Grissom and Kim, 2001). Switching to an alternative estimator of the difference (e.g., a difference in trimmed means) or a different standardizer can produce effect size metrics that are more robust to violations of assumptions.

Example 7.1 Let's take a look at how these effect sizes are computed in practice. Table 7.1 shows summary data adapted from Buchner and Mayr (2004, Experiment 1), reporting the size of the observed negative priming effect (measured in milliseconds) for young and old participants.

Table 7.1 Buchner and Mayr (2004) negative priming data

Group	***n***	$\hat{\mu}$	$\hat{\sigma}$
Young	52	53 *ms*	63 *ms*
Old	52	79 *ms*	135 *ms*

The simple mean difference is $79 - 53 = 26\,ms$ in favor of older participants.

Calculating the standardized mean difference for the negative priming effect between the two groups can be done in several ways. A descriptive measure of the standardized difference is:

$$d = \frac{\hat{\mu}_1 - \hat{\mu}_2}{\sqrt{\frac{(n_1-1)\hat{\sigma}_1^2+(n_2-1)\hat{\sigma}_2^2}{n_1+n_2}}} = \frac{26}{\sqrt{\frac{(52-1)63^2+(52-1)135^2}{104}}} \approx 0.249$$

This measure indexes the discriminability of the negative priming effect in the sample, but overestimates δ. Less biased estimates are given by

$$g = \frac{\hat{\mu}_1 - \hat{\mu}_2}{\hat{\sigma}_{pooled}} = \frac{26}{\sqrt{(63^2+135^2)/2}} \approx 0.247$$

and

$$\hat{\delta} = \frac{(N-3)}{N-2.25} g = \left(\frac{(N-3)}{N-2.25}\right)\left(\frac{26}{\sqrt{(63^2+135^2)/2}}\right) \approx 0.245$$

The estimate of δ is therefore in the region of 0.25 for all three metrics.

As these estimates were inferred from the summary statistics reported in Table 7.1 it is useful to check the results via an alternative route. Buchner and Mayr (2004) also report a test statistic for this difference: $F_{1,102} = 1.47$, $MS_{error} = 11,364$, $p > .05$. The square root of MS_{error} should be identical to $\hat{\sigma}_{pooled}$ from above. The two agree as closely as can be expected in the presence of rounding error: $\sqrt{11364} \approx 106.6$ and $\sqrt{(63^2 + 135^2)/2} \approx 105.3$. Using $\hat{\sigma}_{pooled}$ calculated from MS_{error} would therefore slightly decrease the standardized effect size estimate.

An F statistic with 1 df in its numerator is the square of a t statistic with the same error df. Using the relationship $\sqrt{F} = t$, Equation 7.5 can be used to calculate Hedges'g as:

$$g = t\sqrt{\frac{1}{n_1} + \frac{1}{n_2}} = \sqrt{1.47\left(\frac{1}{52} + \frac{1}{52}\right)} \approx .238$$

Multiplying by $\sqrt{N/(N-2)} = \sqrt{104/102}$ gives $d = .240$ and using Equation 7.4 gives $\hat{\delta} = .236$. The sample sizes here are reasonable and d, g and $\hat{\delta}$ are therefore in close agreement. Either g (for ease of computation) or $\hat{\delta}$ (for accuracy) are reasonable choices. In very small samples $\hat{\delta}$ should always be preferred.

Calculating d using two or more different methods from summary data isn't entirely pointless. Published summary data often have minor errors (and sometimes major ones). Calculating a statistic using different inputs confirms that the value of $\hat{\delta}$ calculated from the raw data would be around 0.24. The statistic derived from F (on the assumption that F was calculated by computer from the raw data) is marginally preferable. One lesson here is that even basic descriptive statistics are extremely useful for secondary analysis. Having the raw data would be best (but tracking down raw data from older studies is a major challenge). This sort of analytic detective work is the bread and butter of formal methods of research synthesis such as meta-analysis. If raw data are not available, researchers will typically use several methods to estimate (and therefore check) the effect size statistic they are interested in.

Glass' Δ is a potential option here, given the disparity in the sample variances (and ample evidence from other studies that older participants have more variable responses). In particular, one could make a case that the young participants are an appropriate baseline or comparison group: different studies are likely to use similar young samples (18–21 year old students), whereas the ages of older participants probably vary considerable between studies. Glass' Δ can therefore be estimated as $26/63 \approx 0.413$. Δ is infrequently used in published research, but there are good reasons to employ it if the choice of standardizer is unambiguous. While it can be better than d for comparing effects, it isn't as useful as d or g for power or sample size estimation (because the pooled SD takes the uncertainty of both samples into account).

A final peculiarity is that although the older group show greater negative priming in terms of simple effect size they have a smaller standardized effect size. This is a rather striking example of how (on occasion) standardized and simple effect size metrics might lead to very different conclusions. The much larger variance for the old group means that their larger priming effect (79 *ms* versus 53 *ms*) produces a smaller standardized difference (0.58 versus 0.83). Not only can changing metric from simple to standardized difference alter the apparent size of an effect – it may sometimes reverse the direction. Buchner and Mayr (2004) make exactly this point, and note that use of the wrong effect size metric could cause researchers to miss important findings (or see effects where none are present). This could happen when comparing data within or between studies whenever d family statistics are calculated using different standardizers (and is almost inevitable in some situations). This kind of difficulty adds to the arguments favoring simple effect size metrics over standardized ones (Baguley, 2009). With a standardized metric it is essential to ensure that any comparisons between effects use an equivalent standardizer.

7.4.3 Standardized mean differences: paired or correlated samples

How can d family statistics be generalized to non-independent differences? Studies with paired or correlated samples are common, but the problem of how to generalize d family measures does not have an unambiguous solution.

Standardized effect size statistics such as d are very sensitive to the design of the study – because this impacts on the calculation of, among other things, test statistics. Analysis of paired data has to take the covariance between samples into account. This can be done by modifying how $\hat{\sigma}_{\hat{\mu}_1-\hat{\mu}_2}$ (the standard error of the difference) is calculated to take account of the correlation between samples. For paired data the differences between correlated samples are also often analyzed by a one sample CI or t test of the differences. Using the standard error of the differences $\hat{\sigma}_{\hat{\mu}_D}$ is equivalent to adjusting $\hat{\sigma}_{\hat{\mu}_1-\hat{\mu}_2}$ to account for the correlation. In a paired design, $\hat{\sigma}_{\hat{\mu}_D}$ decreases as the correlation between samples becomes more positive (and increases if the correlation becomes more negative). Because paired measurements are typically positively correlated, paired designs tend to be better at detecting effects (producing larger t statistics and narrower CIs by virtue of a smaller standard error).

This raises a major dilemma when computing a standardized effect size statistic. If the standardized mean difference is calculated from the means and standard deviations of the samples, it will produce different estimates than if calculated from a t statistic (e.g., Equation 7.3 and Equation 7.5 would disagree). Which approach is correct? The answer is that it depends on what the statistic will be used for. Some applications – those that can safely assume a common design (e.g., for determining the statistical power of an identical or near-identical replication) – need to take into account the correlation betweens samples. Other applications such as those involving comparison of effects between studies with different designs, or those looking at the practical significance of an effect, will probably want to ignore the correlation (Dunlap *et al.*, 1996; Morris and DeShon, 2002).

Reports of standardized effect size from paired designs (or other designs with correlated measures) do not always mention which approach was used or why it was selected. For primary interpretation and analysis it is mostly likely that a researcher will want to report an effect size estimate that corresponds to the equivalent independent groups design (i.e., one where N participants are allocated two groups of size n_1 and n_2 at random). The appropriate default option is therefore to calculate d, g or $\hat{\delta}$ as you would for independent samples (treating the raw data as if they were from a two independent groups design). Following Morris and DeShon (2002), it seems reasonable to label these statistics as d_{IG}, g_{IG} or $\hat{\delta}_{IG}$ to indicate the attempt to create equivalence with an independent groups design (i.e., as estimates of δ_{IG}).[5] Corresponding measures that do not ignore the correlation can be labeled d_{RM}, g_{RM} or $\hat{\delta}_{RM}$.

This approach presupposes that the choice of design does not bias the estimates of any of the parameters. This is a strong assumption, but not unreasonable if the paired design has appropriate controls in place (e.g., order of testing is counterbalanced). In some designs this equivalence is extremely unlikely. A case in point is the pre-post design. The post measure, as well as being correlated with the pre measure, will also typically have a different variance. The recommended approach in this case is to calculate g_{IG} or $\hat{\delta}_{IG}$ using $\hat{\sigma}_{pre}$ as a standardizer (Morris and DeShon, 2002). The reasoning here is similar to that for Glass' Δ; $\hat{\sigma}_{pre}$ provides a sensible benchmark for comparing between designs.

One route for calculating d family statistics that take account of the correlation between paired observations is to define the effect in terms of the paired t statistic and the number of pairs (n). An alternative route is to use $\hat{\sigma}_D$ (the standard deviation of the paired differences) as a standardizer. These routes should produce identical results. Thus g_{RM} can be defined as:

$$g_{RM} = \frac{\hat{\mu}_1 - \hat{\mu}_2}{\hat{\sigma}_D} = \frac{t}{\sqrt{n}} \qquad \text{Equation 7.8}$$

For positively correlated pairs, g_{RM} is often substantially larger than g_{IG}. This 'increase' in effect size is illusory. The magnitude of the effect (e.g., the effectiveness of a drug) has not increased, because it is not a property of the experimental design used to measure it. On the other hand – the ability to discriminate between the groups (the original rationale behind d family measures) has improved. Converting to statistics other than g_{RM} is achieved through multiplication by the appropriate factor. Thus d_{RM} is $\sqrt{n/(n-1)} \times g_{RM}$ and $\hat{\delta}_{RM}$ is $\sqrt{(n-3)/(n-2.25)} \times g_{RM}$.

A more in-depth treatment of how to calculate d family statistics – particularly in pre-post designs – is provided by Morris and DeShon (2002). Olejnik and Algina (2000) consider d family statistics for more complex designs.

Example 7.2 Alter and Oppenheimer (2008, Experiment 2a) looked at the effect of priming a city name on judgments of how close the city was. Table 7.2 shows summary data adapted from their paper.

Table 7.2 Effect of priming a city name on judged closeness of city

Condition	**n**	$\hat{\mu}$	$\hat{\sigma}$
Unprimed	32	1416.5 miles	230.4
Primed	32	1273.0 miles	284.0

Source: Adapted from Alter and Oppenheimer, 2008.

The paired t test can be reported as $t_{31} = 2.32$, $SE = 61.9$, $p < .05$, and g_{IG} is calculated as follows:

$$g_{IG} = \frac{\hat{\mu}_P - \hat{\mu}_U}{\sqrt{\frac{(n-1)\hat{\sigma}_P^2 + (n-1)\hat{\sigma}_U^2}{2n-2}}} = \frac{1416.5 - 1273}{\sqrt{\frac{(32-1)230.4^2 + (32-1)284^2}{2 \times 32 - 2}}} \approx .555$$

Multiplying by $\sqrt{(2n-3)/(2n-2.25)}$ gives $\hat{\delta}_{IG} = .552$

Using the paired t test statistic gives:

$$g_{RM} = \frac{t}{\sqrt{n}} = \frac{2.32}{\sqrt{32}} \approx 0.410$$

Multiplying by $\sqrt{(32-3)/(32-2.25)}$ would give $\hat{\delta}_{RM}$. The difference in these statistics reflects the correlation between samples. $\hat{\delta}_{RM}$ is a useful estimate for sample size or statistical power calculations (assuming a replication with a near identical design). $\hat{\delta}_{IG}$ is a reasonable estimate of δ from an independent samples design.

Although (as expected) the values of $\hat{\delta}_{IG}$ and $\hat{\delta}_{RM}$ or g_{IG} and g_{RM} are different, there is something slightly unexpected going on. The usual pattern, reflecting a positive correlation between the paired samples, is that $g_{IG} < g_{RM}$, but for these data $g_{IG} > g_{RM}$. It appears that the paired observations are negatively correlated. Someone who reports shorter distances in one condition tends to report longer distances in the other. This sort of pattern is found mainly in observations that compete for some shared resource (e.g., rats in a litter will compete for their mother's milk, so one rat getting more milk reduces the growth of its siblings) or where there is some compensatory or other mechanism at work (e.g., perhaps the priming effect decreases or reverses for the closest cities).

7.4.4 Standardized effect size metrics: the *r* family

The *r* family is larger and more varied than the *d* family. Members of the family fall into two main classes (Rosenthal, 1994). In the first class are correlation coefficients such as r, r_{pb} and ϕ. At root all these coefficients can be interpreted as the standardized slope of a regression. The second class comprises statistics based on squared correlation coefficients such as r^2, R^2 and adjusted R^2. These statistics are commonly interpreted as the proportion of variance explained (and need not be calculated from a correlation coefficient). There are also a number of hard-to-classify metrics such as z_r (a Fisher *z* transformed correlation). The z_r statistic is usually grouped within the *r* family, but could almost as easily be placed among the *d* family (because it has a symmetrical distribution, running from minus infinity to infinity).

One advantage of the *r* family over the *d* family is that the key members of the family (r and R^2) are in widespread use and thus methods for calculating them are well known. A consequence of this is that there is perhaps not the same confusion between these core statistics as there is between members of the *d* family. Hence there is no need to consider the calculation of *r* and related statistics here. Instead the focus is on the relative merits of r and R^2.

As a rule, there are good reasons to prefer correlation-based metrics such as *r* to proportion of variance explained metrics such as R^2. Two main reasons are cited in favor of correlation (e.g., Rosnow and Rosenthal, 2003; Rosenthal, 1994). First, they preserve information about the direction of effect.[6] This is essential for meta-analysis, and generally a good idea. If two studies reported $r^2 = .16$, it would be tempting to conclude that there was consistent effect. However, r^2 of .16 could arise from values of $r = .4$ and $r = -.4$, in which case, the average correlation would be zero. Meta-analysis exists precisely to account for these sorts of issues, and would usually use a measure such as *r* (or *d*) that preserves the direction of the effect. The second reason to prefer *r* has already been mentioned (in connection to the idea that apparently small effects can be impressive). Correlations of small absolute size (e.g., .1 or .01) can represent effects of huge practical or clinical significance (Rosenthal and Rubin, 1979; Kraemer and Kupfer, 2006). Squaring the correlation measure makes the absolute value of the statistic even smaller. In extreme cases small values of r^2 may be rounded down and reported as zero. Rosnow and Rosenthal (2003, Table 3) list several real cases where rounding important effects to two decimal places suggests $r^2 = .00$.

Even so, proportion of variance explained measures are widely used, particularly as measures of 'goodness-of-fit' for linear regression models. R^2 is a descriptive measure of the proportion of variance explained in a sample: SS_{model}/SS_{total}. This statistic is often misinterpreted as an inferential (population) estimate. A number of measures have been proposed as estimates of the proportion of variance explained in the population (Hays, 1973; Olejnik and Algina, 2003). The connection to regression makes R^2 and related measures convenient descriptive statistics. Furthermore, if an effect has multiple *df*, the direction of effect argument for selecting *r* does not hold (because direction of effect cannot be inferred unambiguously from a multiple *df* effect size statistic). Proportion of variance explained measures such as R^2 are therefore natural choices for unfocused, multiple *df* effects (though alternatives such as R^2_{adj} should also be considered). However, it is wise to be cautious about using proportion of variance explained as an effect size statistic. It is most useful as a descriptive statistic comparing similar models using the same data. R^2 based statistics can also be convenient for statistical power calculations. In this context there is a straightforward link between R^2 and the *d* family statistic Cohen's f^2 (see Section 12.3.4).

7.4.5 The relationship between *d* and *r* family statistics

The two families will only be directly comparable for data where both *d* and *r* family statistics can legitimately be computed. The links between the two are therefore best illustrated with the point-biserial correlation coefficient r_{pb}. The Pearson correlation between a dichotomous X and a continuous Y variable denoted by r_{pb} is mathematically equivalent to an independent *t* test. This equivalence is tricky to arrive at intuitively because ρ runs from -1 to 1 and δ from $-\infty$ to ∞ (with only the point $\rho = \delta = 0$ in common). It may be worth thinking about what happens when $\rho = -1$ or 1. Such perfect correlations can only happen if the shape of the distribution of X and Y is the same. This only occurs if Y is also dichotomous – specifically when a given value of X is always associated with the same Y value (e.g., $X = 0 \Rightarrow Y = 1$ and $X = 1 \Rightarrow Y = 2$). Under these circumstances both groups defined by X (X_0 and X_1) have zero variance and therefore the pooled standard deviation is also zero. Provided the difference between the mean of X_0 and X_1 is not zero, the resulting value of δ can be treated as infinitely large (with the sign depending on which has the larger mean).[7] It follows that even tiny differences in means can produce very large δ values (and near perfect correlations). In very small samples, perfect or near perfect correlations arise by chance rather too often (and hence the requirement to correct for small sample bias).

One formula for r_{pb}, reproduced here from Equation 6.22, is:

$$r_{pb} = \frac{\hat{\mu}_{X_1} - \hat{\mu}_{X_0}}{SD_Y}\sqrt{\frac{n_1}{N}\frac{n_2}{N}}$$

McGrath and Meyer (2006) show how this formula can be developed to reveal the connection between r_{pb} and *d* (and by implication *g* or $\hat{\delta}$). The term $\sqrt{(n_1/N)(n_2/N)}$ is the descriptive of *SD* of X if X has been dummy coded (because X is, in effect, a binomial proportion). The base rates (i.e., the relative proportion of observations in the groups defined by the dummy codes) matter because they influence the *SD* of X. This implies that r_{pb} is base rate sensitive, whereas *d* family statistics such as *d*, *g* or $\hat{\delta}$ are not. A correlation is standardized using both the *SD* of X and the *SD* of Y. In contrast, *d* family statistics are standardized using only the variability of Y (specifically the variability within each group). This is at the heart of the difference between the two families.

This relationship means that getting r_{pb} from *g* requires incorporating a standardizer for X as well as Y. The following formula (Aaron *et al.*, 1998; McGrath and Meyer, 1996) combines these adjustments to give:

$$r_{pb} = \frac{g}{\sqrt{g^2 + (N-2)\left(\frac{1}{n_1} + \frac{1}{n_2}\right)}} = \frac{g}{\sqrt{g^2 + \frac{N^2 - 2N}{n_1 n_2}}} \qquad \text{Equation 7.9}$$

If $n_1 = n_2$, this can be simplified to:

$$r_{pb} == \frac{g}{\sqrt{g^2 + 4\left(\frac{N-2}{N}\right)}} \qquad \text{Equation 7.10}$$

Rearranging Equation 7.9 in terms of g for the unequal n case gives

$$g = \frac{r_{pb}}{\sqrt{\left(1 - r_{pb}^2\right) \frac{n_1 n_2}{N^2 - 2N}}} \qquad \text{Equation 7.11}$$

and simplifying this for equal n produces:

$$g = \frac{r_{pb}}{\sqrt{\frac{\left(1 - r_{pb}^2\right)}{4 - 8/N}}} \qquad \text{Equation 7.12}$$

A number of variants of these formulas exist (notably in terms of d) including some approximations that drop terms that are negligible when N is large.

Example 7.3 To appreciate the implications of the link between r_{pb} and d family statistics such as g, consider three hypothetical studies: A, B and C. Each collects data using a two independent group design with $N = 200$ (as set out in Table 7.3). One group is coded 0 and the other 1. The difference in means is $\hat{\mu}_1 - \hat{\mu}_2 = 12$ for each study.

Table 7.3 Sample size per group and summary statistics for three hypothetical studies with two independent group designs

Study	n_0	n_1	$\hat{\mu}_1 - \hat{\mu}_2$	$\hat{\sigma}_{pooled}$
A	10	190	12	16
B	25	175	12	16
C	100	100	12	16

As Table 7.3 shows, the only difference between the studies is in terms of n per group. In each case $g = 12/16 = 0.75$ (as are d and $\hat{\delta}$ to two decimal places). The point-biserial correlation is different for A, B and C. Equation 7.9 indicates that the correlation is:

$$r_{pb} = \frac{g}{\sqrt{g^2 + \frac{N^2 - 2N}{n_1 n_2}}} = \frac{0.75}{\sqrt{0.75^2 + \frac{200^2 - 2 \times 200}{n_1 n_2}}}$$

For study A this evaluates as

$$r_{pb} = \frac{0.75}{\sqrt{0.75^2 + \frac{200^2 - 2 \times 200}{10 \times 190}}} \approx .162$$

for study B it is .242 and for study C it is .353. Varying n per group more than doubles the correlation in study C relative to study A (even though g is unchanged). This reflects the fact that r_{pb}

standardizes on the total variability in Y and X while d family statistics standardize using only those within group variability of Y. This generates the base rate sensitivity of r_{pb}. Because the base rate sensitivity arises from changes in the standard deviations of X, it can also be viewed as a special case of range restriction (in which the variability of X is suppressed relative to its maximum variance when $n_1 = n_2$).

If n per group is known, it is trivial to go from r_{pb} back to g. You can check this by using the correlation of .162 for study A. This calculation returns:

$$g = \frac{r_{pb}}{\sqrt{\left(1 - r_{pb}^2\right)\frac{n_1 n_2}{N^2 - 2N}}} = \frac{.162}{\sqrt{(1 - .162^2)\frac{10 \times 190}{200^2 - 2 \times 200}}} \approx 0.75$$

Which statistic is better? The invariance of g suggests that it should be preferred, because it accurately reflects the group mean differences. However, it isn't quite that simple. If the goal is to estimate the population correlation ρ then r_{pb} computed from a study with appropriate base rates is the ideal choice. If the data at hand do not have appropriate base rates, Equation 7.9 can be adapted to estimate ρ provided the true base rates are known. Even so, g or $\hat{\delta}$ will be best for most practical applications. Only rarely is the primary aim of research to estimate ρ.

What happens if you use r_{pb} to compute the proportion of variance explained for each study? The correlations of .162, .242 and .353 become r^2 values of .026 (2.6%), .059 (5.9%) and .124 (12.4%) respectively. Such base rate effects are a common side effect of differences in study design (e.g., observational versus experimental or quasi-experimental research).

7.4.6 Confidence intervals for standardized effect size statistics

Confidence intervals for standardized effect size metrics are much more difficult to derive than for simple effect size. The principal problem is that the distribution of the statistic depends on the true population value. These distributional problems will be considered in more detail in relation to statistical power and sample size calculations in Chapter 8 (when the problem of obtaining accurate interval estimates will be revisited).

Rather than attempt to construct exact interval estimates, it is possible to employ an approximation. Good approximations exist for both r and g. The former uses the familiar Fisher z transformation (see Example 6.3). For the latter, Rosenthal (1994) reports that the standard deviation of Hedges' g is approximately:

$$\hat{\sigma}_g = \sqrt{\frac{n_1 + n_2}{n_1 n_2} + \left(\frac{g^2}{2(n_1 + n_2 - 2)}\right)} \qquad \text{Equation 7.13}$$

As this is an estimate of the *SD* of the sampling distribution of g it is therefore an estimate of the standard error of $\hat{\delta}$ or g. The distribution of these statistics is approximately normal and so a CI can be formed using quantiles of the z distribution. For $\hat{\delta}$ this interval estimate is:

$$\hat{\delta} \pm z_{1-\alpha/2}\hat{\sigma}_g \qquad \text{Equation 7.14}$$

Cumming and Fidler (2009) have shown that symmetrical CIs constructed using this approximation generally perform very well. Rosenthal (1994) also reports an expression for the *SD* of Glass' Δ:

$$\hat{\sigma}_{\Delta} = \sqrt{\frac{n_e + n_c}{n_e n_c} + \left(\frac{\Delta^2}{2n_c - 2}\right)} \qquad \text{Equation 7.15}$$

This can be used to construct a CI for Δ in the same way as for g or $\hat{\delta}$.

Example 7.4 In Example 7.1 the size of a difference in negative priming between the 52 young and 52 old participants was estimated as $g = 0.247$ and $\hat{\delta} = 0.245$. Using Rosenthal's equation, $\hat{\sigma}_g$ is approximately:

$$\hat{\sigma}_g = \sqrt{\frac{n_1 + n_2}{n_1 n_2} + \left(\frac{g^2}{2(n_1 + n_2 - 2)}\right)} = \sqrt{\frac{52 + 52}{52 \times 52} + \left(\frac{0.245^2}{2(52 + 52 - 2)}\right)} \approx 0.197$$

Assuming a normal distribution the 95% CI is then:

$$\hat{\delta} \pm z_{1-\alpha/2}\hat{\sigma}_g = 0.245 \pm 1.96 \times 0.197$$

This gives an interval estimate of:

$$\hat{\delta} = 0.245, 95\% \text{ CI } [-0.14, 0.63]$$

One thing that may puzzle you at this point is why this CI includes zero (given that the original NHST was statistically significant). A partial answer is that the CI for the true population effect is an attempt to estimate a plausible range of values for the true population effect (not a test of the difference in means). The two goals are distinct (see Maxwell *et al.*, 2008). Although this CI is an approximation, the observation that it is much wider than that implied by the CI for the simple difference in means suggests that it incorporates an additional source of uncertainty (that related to estimating the population *SD* necessary for estimating the standardized effect).

7.4.7 Correcting for reliability

Range restriction and reliability are potentially very serious problems in research with human participants. Devising ways of sampling people so they are representative of a population is a major challenge (even presuming that a target population can be identified). The typical proportion of measurement error in psychological research has been estimated at around .5 (Schmidt and Hunter, 1999). Corrections for both these factors have a long history in the context of correlation, but are less well known for standardized mean differences (and are rarely used outside meta-analysis). Correction formulas for the simplest cases are instructive and are discussed here (though for most applications more sophisticated approaches are required).

The best-known correction for reliability was proposed by Spearman (1904) and is still widely used today. This equation is often first encountered as the attenuation formula of classical test theory. It shows that the observed correlation r_{XY} is a function $r_{X_tY_t}$ (the correlation of the 'true' scores measured without error) and the reliabilities of X and Y (r_{XX} and r_{YY}):

$$r_{XY} = r_{X_tY_t}\sqrt{(r_{XX}r_{YY})} \qquad \text{Equation 7.16}$$

Rearranging this formula gives Spearman's (*ibid.*) correction for reliability, sometimes called the disattenuation formula:

$$r_{X_tY_t} = \frac{r_{XY}}{\sqrt{(r_{XX}r_{YY})}} \qquad \text{Equation 7.17}$$

In principle, the connection between ρ_{pb} and δ means that you could convert any given g value to r and disattenuate the estimate that way. This would be legitimate if both X and Y were measured unreliably. However, in a two independent group design the dichotomous X variable that defines the groups is often measured without error. This is likely to be true for experimental designs, but can also hold for quasi-experiments and observational studies. For instance if X is gender (male or female), its measurement can be considered perfect for most purposes. On the other hand, if X represented young and old groups of participants (as in Example 7.1) this assumption would be questionable (as not all participants within each group have the same age). This needs to be considered on a case-by-case basis; it can't be assumed that any independent variable – even in a true experiment – is measured with perfect reliability. Assuming X is measured reliably, Bobko *et al.* (2001) present a version of the disattenuation formula for g:

$$g_t = \frac{g}{\sqrt{r_{YY}}} \qquad \text{Equation 7.18}$$

This can be derived from Spearman's disattenuation formula by substituting g for r_{XY} and assuming $r_{XX} = 1$.

Some caution needs to be exercised before applying these formulas. The quality of the correction depends crucially on obtaining accurate estimates of reliability (see Box 7.1). The estimate of reliability itself is subject to error, so reliability coefficients from small samples are problematic. Deciding on what form of reliability coefficient to use is more difficult than it may first appear (Hunter and Schmidt, 1999; DeShon, 2003). More subtly, these formulas – as is common in classical test theory – assume that the errors of X and Y are independent. If the errors are correlated, then the corrections will overestimate the true correlation (Zimmerman, 2007). It is also a bad idea to correct using a reliability statistic that is estimated from the same sample the correction is applied to. The estimate needs to be external to the sample. Even so, the correction can be informative about the plausible range for the population value of g or r (especially when combined with a CI for the statistic). Interval estimates can be obtained by disattenuating the lower and upper bounds of the usual CI (rather than forming a CI for a disattenuated point estimate, as this produces intervals that are too narrow).

Example 7.5 Dedousis-Wallace and Shute (2009) looked at the perceived seriousness of direct and indirect bullying for a sample of teachers ($N = 55$). The initial correlation between their seriousness of indirect bullying scale and a likelihood of intervening scale is reported as: $r = .74$, 95% CI [.59, .84].

The reported internal reliabilities for these measures range from .75 to .89 for the seriousness scale and .79 to .89 for the intervention scale. The measure of internal consistency reliability they report (Cronbach's alpha) is taken from a smallish sample (the same sample used to calculate the correlation to be corrected). For a conservative correction (i.e., one less likely to overcorrect r) it makes sense to use the highest of the reported reliability coefficients ($r = .89$).

Entering Spearman's disattenuation formula for the point estimate of the correlation gives:

$$r = \frac{.74}{\sqrt{(.89 \times .89)}} \approx .83$$

The same formula applied to the lower and upper bounds of the CI gives

$$r_{lower} = \frac{.59}{\sqrt{(.89 \times .89)}} \approx .66$$

and

$$r_{upper} = \frac{.84}{\sqrt{(.89 \times .89)}} \approx .94$$

This gives an estimate for the corrected correlation of .83, 95% CI [.66, .94].

Even with what are normally thought of as very high reliabilities (around .90) the correction has a fairly substantial impact. This shouldn't really be a surprise. Reliability of .90 is not that good: if both r_{XX} *and* $r_{YY} = .90$ then the total measurement error is approaching 20% (as $1 - .90^2 = .19$). In addition, the interval is wider than the original uncorrected interval. Even if you believe the correction has increased the accuracy of the point estimate, it has done so at the expense of its precision. Worse still, this CI has not explicitly taken into account any concerns about the quality of the reliability estimates. These include the uncertainty in estimating r_{XX} *and* r_{YY} with such a small sample (and using the same sample to estimate internal reliability and the correlation). There are also specific concerns about using Cronbach's alpha, because it tends to underestimate consistency between items (Cortina, 1993). Relying on internal consistency also neglects the transient error that arises between measurement points in time (see Box 7.1).

Given these problems, how useful is the corrected CI? As there are good reasons for thinking that the true correlation is higher than the observed one, the correction does give a slightly better idea of the real relationship between the predictors. However, it is essential to remember that the corrected point estimate and the associated CI are not particularly accurate. As a consequence it would be risky to use the corrected values for formal inference.

Box 7.1 What reliability estimate to use?

From time to time researchers are interested in reporting or using reliability coefficients, but do not necessarily have much interest in how they are estimated. The correct reliability estimate to use depends on the kind of data you have. Different estimates are appropriate for data recorded directly from participants, for ratings of directly observed behavior and coded responses for data not directly observed (Schmidt and Hunter, 1999; Hunter and Schmidt, 2004). Response data (recorded directly from participants) are the most common and are the focus here.

You can distinguish between three main components of measurement error that a reliability estimate needs to account for in response data: random response error, specific error and transient error (Schmidt and Hunter, 1999; Hunter and Schmidt, 2004). Random response error is variability among observations that has no discernable cause or pattern and that can be thought of as truly random. Specific error arises from idiosyncratic responses by people for specific items. For example, if asked to remember a list of 50 proper names, each participant might find a few names particularly easy to recall (e.g., because they are the names of close friends or family). While this source of error isn't random for any given person it is random from the perspective of the researcher (as the specific errors are not readily predictable and vary from person to person). Transient error is error related to measurements taken at different time points. Many factors that influence performance, such as arousal or health, vary over time but are not systematically related to the variables being studied; these give rise to transient error.

Different reliability estimates capture different components of error. Cronbach (1947) distinguished between the coefficient of equivalence (CE), the coefficient of stability (CS) and the coefficient of equivalence and stability (CES). A measure of internal consistency addresses equivalence. It does this by correlating different 'parallel' forms of the same measure. Split-half reliability is one way to do this: a set of items is split into two halves (at random) and the scores for the first half are correlated with the scores for the second half. Cronbach's alpha is an estimate of the average reliability of all possible random splits of the items – though it tends to be biased and is best treated as a lower bound on this value (Cortina, 1993). An estimate of test-retest reliability assesses the stability of the measure in relation to transient error.

What about random response error? Because this is pervasive, both test-retest and parallel form estimates will be influenced by it. What is required is the CES; an estimate of reliability that combines random response, specific error and transient error. This is achieved using delayed parallel forms of the measure. This involves correlating data from two forms of the measure sampled at different time points. It is more difficult to collect data for a delayed parallel forms estimate (and researchers typically rely on either test-retest reliability or internal consistency). Hunter and Schmidt argue that this implies that most reliability corrections are underestimates. However, given the likelihood that Cronbach's alpha (the most widely used CE estimate) underestimates internal consistency, this is not necessarily the case. There may also be situations in which some components of error – such as transient error – should not be corrected for, because they are part of the phenomenon of interest (DeShon, 2003).

As well as requiring the appropriate estimate, the accuracy of the corrections depends on the precision with which reliability is estimated. This can be assessed by calculating a CI for the reliability coefficient, but necessitates large samples to be of sufficient accuracy. The assumption of zero correlation between the errors of X and Y also needs to be taken into account. This assumption is incredibly hard to check. One of the few situations when it seems reasonable is if X is measured with perfect or near-perfect reliability. In large samples the degree of correction can be used to assess the impact of the uncorrelated errors assumption (Zimmerman, 2007). A small correction implies both high reliability and negligible violation of the assumption. A large correction implies either reliability is low, the errors are correlated, or both. The effect of correlated errors is to overcorrect. Low reliability makes the problem of correlated errors worse. So large corrections are a cause for suspicion. On the other hand, reliability estimated from small samples will rarely produce accurate corrections (though the disattenuation formula may still be informative if used to explore the effect of reliability on the effect).

The preceding discussion focused on corrections for a single effect. Some of these problems may be mitigated in meta-analysis. Reliability coefficients in meta-analysis are more likely to be obtained from large samples or themselves estimated from a meta-analysis of smaller studies (Hunter and Schmidt, 2004). Even in meta-analysis, however, some authors have argued strongly against routine use of such corrections, preferring to model the effect of reliability in other ways (Hox, 2010).

7.4.8 Correcting for range restriction

Corrections for direct range restriction (in which the sampled range of X or Y is restricted) also have a long history in the context of correlation (Pearson, 1903). Corrections for indirect range restriction (in which a variable correlated with X or Y is restricted) are less widely used, and adequate methods for dealing with indirect range restriction are more difficult to implement (Hunter and Schmidt, 2004). Although indirect range restriction is probably a more serious problem (at least where perfect measurement of predictors can't be assumed), this section focuses on the simpler case of direct range restriction. Direct range restriction illustrates the nature of the problem and helps explain why indirect range restriction is more difficult to deal with.

With direct range restriction of X, the predictor is deliberately (or at least knowingly) selected so that σ_X is restricted (or, in an extreme groups analysis, enhanced), but Y is unrestricted (except as a consequence of ρ_{XY}). A formula for range restriction in this situation is

$$r_{X_tY_t} = \frac{kr_{XY}}{\sqrt{k^2r_{XY}^2 - r_{XY}^2 + 1}} \qquad \text{Equation 7.19}$$

where k is $\sigma_{X_u}/\sigma_{X_r}$ (the ratio of unrestricted to restricted *SD* of X). Although $\sigma_{X_u}^2$ is usually unknown, it is possible to estimate k provided the degree of restriction and the approximate distribution of X are known. Hunter and Schmidt (2004) show how to do this for a normal distribution, and it would be relatively easy to infer for other distributions (e.g., by simulation).

The basic formula for direct range restriction on Y works in an analogous fashion. Extending this to indirect range restriction can be done in several ways, and one of the simplest is to adapt the direct range restriction formula. The indirect case differs from the direct case because the restriction is not on the variances of the measured scores, but on the variances of the true scores (Hunter and Schmidt, 2004; Hunter *et al.*, 2006). This happens because indirect selection influences the variability of X in general, but has no way to influence any specific measurement made on X. For example, if selection is made on academic ability (e.g., for university entrance) this will reduce the variability of undergraduate student IQ relative to the general population (assuming academic ability and IQ are correlated). However, the academic selection process (e.g., based on public examination grades) can't influence measurement error on a particular IQ test. In contrast, direct selection of X – such as selecting the best 50% of performers on the task – involves selecting on combination of true IQ scores and measurement error. Only in the special case of X being measured with perfect reliability (zero error) are the direct and indirect range restriction formulas equivalent.

Only by estimating k_t (the ratio of the variances of the unrestricted true scores to the restricted true scores) with reasonable accuracy is a correction feasible.

The solution to the problem of estimating k_t depends on understanding that the true score variances can be obtained by stripping out measurement error (i.e., using the disattenuation formula). Thus indirect range restriction corrections can't be considered separately from reliability corrections. In particular, the precise order of reliability and range restriction corrections is essential (Hunter and Schmidt, 2004). Hunter *et al.* (2006) set out these calculations in a detailed step-by-step fashion for both direct and indirect range restriction.

Reliability and range restriction are very important whenever the focus is on standardized effect size statistics. Simple effect size metrics are less likely to be distorted by these factors, particularly when predictor (X) variables are measured with little or no error (see Ree and Carretta, 2006). Uncorrected standardized effect sizes statistics should therefore be interpreted with caution (Baguley, 2009). The corrections are often useful for exploring the impact of reliability and range restriction for a single effect, but require accurate information (e.g., about reliability or the unrestricted variances) and large sample sizes for accuracy. Even then, the potential for assumptions of the corrections to be violated suggests that researchers need to be cautious whenever there are big differences between the uncorrected and corrected statistics (Zimmerman, 2007).

Example 7.6 Rozencwajg and Bertoux (2008) looked at taxonomic categorization – the ability to group items such as words within some high-level category based on their common features. For abstract words they report a negative correlation among older participants ($n = 20$) between age (in years) and taxonomic categorization: $r = -.48$, 95% CI [−.76, −.05]. The age range of these participants was reported as 62 to 79 years ($n = 20$, $SD = 4.66$). Age in years can be considered to be measured with near perfect reliability.* Thus Equation 7.19 should suffice to correct the correlation for either indirect or direct range restriction.

In studies such as this, it is quite likely that older participants are indirectly selected on age (e.g., selecting older adults who are well educated and score in the normal range for healthy adults on various screening measures). Age may be restricted relative to the population of older adults a researcher may be interested in. If older adults were selected from a uniform distribution ranging from 60 to 90 years the *SD* of age would be 8.6. This gives us a rough idea that the restriction ratio for the *SD*s might be as large as $8.6/4.66 \approx 1.85$. Putting this into the formula gives:

$$r_{X_t Y_t} = \frac{1.85 \times -.48}{\sqrt{1.85^2 \times -.48^2 - .48^2 + 1}} \approx -.71$$

Repeating this procedure for the lower and upper confidence bounds gives an approximate estimate of −.71, 95% CI [−.91, −.09]. Hunter and Schmidt (2004) show how to calculate more a precise CI, though they note that this simple method is a good approximation.

The sample size here does not seem sufficient to estimate *r* with any precision. This raises the question of what the corrected correlation is for. Is it sensible to estimate the true correlation for a wider range of older people? Hunter *et al.* (2006, p. 607) propose that 'this [indirect] correction should be applied whenever the independent variable *SD*s are different in one's sample and the population of interest'. Here the population of interest is ambiguous: is it the restricted population of healthy older people or is it a hypothetical unrestricted population? There is a potential dilemma in deciding when indirect selection has merely refined a sample to contain members of the population of interest and when it has restricted that sample. In this case, screening is employed to ensure that the older participants are comparable to younger participants (e.g., not impaired by ill health). It may be nonsense to imagine what the correlation would be for a wider range of healthy older people – because the distribution of ages in the sample may already accurately reflect those of healthy older people in the population.

Moreover, the effect of age on taxonomic categorization may not be linear. An implicit assumption of these corrections is that the effect is linear and the variance of the errors constant (i.e., that the true correlation is the same for all values of *X*).

*A back-of-the-envelope calculation based on the likely error in measuring age in years rather than days for this range of ages suggests r_{XX} is around .99.

7.5 Effect size metrics for discrete variables

Discrete variables pose a particular problem for interpretation because there are several popular, plausible effect size metrics. The discussion can be simplified by focusing on single *df* effects and on effect sizes for 2×2 contingency tables. Although this is a fairly narrow focus, it encompasses the common case of a dichotomous predictor and a dichotomous outcome. This happens in a two independent group design when participants are assigned to one of two experimental conditions (e.g., treatment and placebo) and the outcome can take only two values (e.g., disease present and disease absent). The discussion here considers three broad types of effect size metric: simple difference in proportions, standardized effect size metrics and ratio measures. Both the simple differences in proportions and standardized metrics can be misleading when interpreting effects for discrete variables. Ratio measures are superior for many purposes. A number of ratio measures have been proposed, though they have very different characteristics and are suited for different applications.

7.5.1 Simple difference in proportions: absolute risk reduction

The simple difference in proportions or percentages of outcomes is one of the most basic effect size metrics for a 2×2 contingency table. This is identical to a simple difference in means for a dichotomous outcome (coded one or zero). Suppose that there is a clear outcome measure that is either a 'success' (+) or 'failure' (−) and that there are two groups: a treatment group (G_1) and a control group (G_0). These labels can be added to a contingency table with a, b, c and d representing the observed counts (see Section 4.5.3):

	$A_1(+)$	$A_2(-)$	
$(G_0)\ B_1$	a	b	$a+b=n_0$
$(G_1)\ B_2$	c	d	$c+d=n_1$
	$a+c=n_+$	$b+d=n_-$	n

The proportions of successes $\hat{P}_0$ and $\hat{P}_1$ for the control group and the treatment group respectively are given by:

$$\hat{P}_0 = \frac{a}{a+b} = \frac{a}{n_0}, \quad \hat{P}_1 = \frac{c}{c+d} = \frac{c}{n_1} \qquad \text{Equation 7.20}$$

The difference $\hat{P}_1 - \hat{P}_0$ is a measure of the magnitude of the treatment effect. This is a difference between independent proportions, and is often termed the *absolute risk reduction* (*ARR*) if the outcome is an adverse event (such as presence of a disease).[8] I will either stick with the label *ARR* or use the more general term difference in proportions. The *ARR* can therefore be defined as:

$$ARR = \hat{P}_1 - \hat{P}_0 = \frac{a}{n_1} - \frac{c}{n_0} \qquad \text{Equation 7.21}$$

This is an estimate of the population difference in proportions $\Delta_{\Pi} = P_1 - P_0$.[9] It is also a simple difference between group means (because $\hat{P}_0$ and $\hat{P}_1$ are also the mean number of successes of the two groups).

The difference in proportions for a 2 × 2 table has a number of characteristics that make it useful as an effect size metric. An obvious advantage is that it is easy to calculate. A key characteristic is that it is sensitive to the base rates of the outcome measure, but insensitive to the base rates of the non-outcome variable.[10] This is usually a desirable property in contexts where there is a clear, unambiguous outcome variable. In these situations the group base rate is arguably a 'nuisance' variable to be ignored (e.g., the sample sizes of the treatment and control group). In contrast, the base rate for the outcome may be essential for interpreting the practical importance of the effect (with the proviso that the sampled base rates reflect the population of interest). The *ARR* is therefore an important measure to report in many clinical studies (Kraemer and Kupfer, 2006), or in non-clinical studies with a similar set-up. A final advantage is that good methods exist for producing CIs for a binomial proportion or for a difference between proportions (see Chapter 3).

There are also serious drawbacks to using the difference in proportions as an effect size metric. Although simple to calculate, it has undesirable statistical properties. One potential issue is that the magnitude of a difference in proportions will not be comparable between outcomes with different base rates. A difference of, say, .03 (or 3%) needs to be interpreted differently if the base rate is low (when it probably represents a large effect) than when base rates are high (when it represents a small effect). This is not necessarily a problem for a randomized clinical trial (RCT) where patients are assigned to a treatment or control condition at random and baselines are expected to be similar to those in the population. However, it may be a problem if the aim is to generalize findings to a different type of patient.

What about situations where outcome base rates are known to vary? Consider a problem-solving experiment where two problems, one easy and one hard, are presented to participants. In one condition participants are rewarded for solving the problem and in the other they are not. The reward increases solution rates for the hard problem from .05 to .25 and for the easy problem from .20 to .40. Is it reasonable to conclude that reward had the same effect $(.25 - .05) = (.40 - .20) = .15$ for both problems? In one case, the solution rate increased fivefold and in the other it only doubled. Deciding the correct interpretation is not trivial (Walter, 2000).

Serious problems arise if there is no obvious or natural choice of outcome measure. In such situations the difference in proportions depends on the variable designated as the outcome. Only if base rates are identical for both variables is the choice of outcome immaterial. A study of personality type and its association with heart disease might find that 20 out of 500 people with Type A personality have heart disease compared to only 10 out of 500 with Type B personality. In this kind of observational study, it is just as valid to look at the difference of .17 in proportions of Type A personality (between heart disease and those without), as it is to look at the difference in heart disease rates of .02 (between Type A and Type B personality types).

This sort of problem leads some authors (e.g., Fleiss, 1994) to discount the difference in proportions as a viable effect size metric for comparing effects. Fleiss points out that variability in Δ_{Π} is limited by the values of P_1 and P_0. Only rarely will the theoretical range of Δ_{Π} (−1 to 1) be a plausible range for a sample statistic. This can make it appear that there are substantive changes in Δ_{Π} between studies, when the changes merely reflect 'mathematical constraints imposed on [the] probabilities' (*ibid.*, p. 247). A related problem is that using the difference in proportions to predict outcomes for individuals or subgroups with difference base rates can result in predictions greater than one or less than zero (Walter, 2000).

Although a difference in proportions is easy to calculate, it is not always obvious how to interpret it (even in applications with an unambiguous outcome measure). One proposal is to use the *ARR* to derive a statistic known as *number needed to treat* (*NNT*).[11] This is the reciprocal of *ARR*:

$$NNT = \frac{1}{ARR} = \frac{1}{\hat{P}_2 - \hat{P}_1} \quad \text{Equation 7.22}$$

NNT was formulated for communicating clinical information about the effectiveness of a treatment and it is not well suited for inference (Cook and Sackett, 1995; Walter, 2000, 2001). It can be interpreted as a measure of the amount of clinical effort required to obtain a positive outcome or to avoid an adverse outcome (Walter, 2001). If $ARR = .01$, then 100 patients have to be treated to obtain a positive outcome, whereas if $ARR = .25$ the *NNT* is only four. This is useful when comparing treatments with similar base rates and can lead to more realistic evaluation of findings than other metrics. However, like *ARR*, it is dangerous to compare effects calculated with different baselines or to generalize findings to make predictions about individuals or subgroups with different base rates. A final consideration is that *NNT* can be badly biased (overestimating or underestimating *NNT*) when reliability is low – though it is possible to correct this (Marschner *et al.*, 2004).

The simple difference in proportions (*ARR*) and its reciprocal (*NNT*) can aid the interpretation of studies with both an unambiguous outcome and equal group sizes. If the observed base rates are similar to those in the population of interest they can be used to compare two or more studies or to generalize findings (Haddock *et al.*, 1998).

Example 7.7 Haynes *et al.* (2009) report the results of the introduction of a surgery safety checklist on the outcomes of surgery in eight hospitals. Subsequent examples will refer to this data set as the surgical checklist data.

Table 7.4 shows the mortality data (estimated from the original percentages) in terms of the number of patients alive or dead 30 days after surgery, both before and after the introduction of the checklist.

Table 7.4 Mortality before and after surgical checklist intervention is introduced

	Alive	**Dead**	
Before	3677	56	3733
After	3924	31	3955
	7601	87	7688

The test of independence without continuity correction for this table, $\chi^2(1, N = 7688) = 8.81$, $p < .05$, is statistically significant, as is the continuity corrected test, $\chi^2(1, N = 7688) = 8.18$, $p < .05$.* The *ARR* expressing the difference in the proportion of people not surviving 30 days after surgery is:

$$ARR = \frac{56}{3733} - \frac{31}{3955} \approx .0150 - .0078 \approx .0072$$

This is reported here as a positive number (though it is not uncommon to express risk reductions as a negative number). A value of .0072 or 0.72% may appear small, but is potentially impressive. An approximate 95% CI for the difference in proportions obtained is [.002, .012] suggesting a plausible range for the true population difference of 0.2% to 1.2%.

Taking the reciprocal of the *ARR* gives *NNT*. The resulting *NNT* statistic is 140, 95% CI [82, 469]. This interval is obtained by taking the reciprocal of the upper and lower bounds of the CI for the difference in proportions. If the NHST for the difference is non-significant at the reported confidence level, the upper bound for *NNT* will be infinity. This can make reporting and plotting CIs for *NNT* tricky (Kraemer and Kupfer, 2006; but see Altman, 1998). *NNT* is therefore not ideal for inference.

How should the difference in the proportion of post-surgery deaths be interpreted? Although 0.72% seems like a small quantity, the context also matters. Mortality is as serious an outcome as there is, so even small reductions in mortality rates are valued. Furthermore, the safety checklist is (in comparison to many medical interventions) probably both inexpensive and easy to implement. The *NNT* is also useful here. The estimate suggests one death is prevented for every 140 operations performed with the checklist. In the context of the many thousands of operations being performed in these hospitals (let alone worldwide) this is a substantial effect, and would remain so even if the *NNT* were closer to the upper bound of 469). Context is very important. If an intervention is expensive or has other risks or harms associated with it, this *NNT* would be less impressive (Kraemer and Kupfer, 2006).

* This table collapses over all eight hospitals in the study and many different types of operation. This violates the assumption of independence. Subsequent examples consider other approaches. The original paper reports additional analyses and shows similar patterns for several different outcomes in each hospital.

7.5.2 Standardized effect size metrics for 2 × 2 contingency tables

Several standardized effect size statistics can be calculated for 2 × 2 tables. For the r family, the most commonly calculated statistic is ϕ (phi). This correlation coefficient is appropriate when the variables represent true dichotomies.[12] Working directly from a 2 × 2 table, a convenient expression for ϕ is:

$$\phi = \frac{ad - bc}{\sqrt{(a+b)(c+d)(a+c)(b+d)}} = \frac{ad - bc}{\sqrt{n_0 n_1 n_+ n_-}} \qquad \text{Equation 7.23}$$

Several d family variants can also be calculated from a 2 × 2 table. The choice depends on whether the variables are true dichotomies or not. As already mentioned, differences in proportions are also differences in the mean number of successes ($\hat{P}_1 - \hat{P}_0 = \hat{\mu}_1 - \hat{\mu}_0$). A standardized mean difference can therefore be calculated from $\hat{P}_1 - \hat{P}$ with $\hat{\sigma}_{pooled}$ as the standardizer (calculated for the two groups when the outcome is dummy coded). Another option is to estimate g from ϕ using Equation 7.11. These measures, labeled g_P and g_ϕ respectively, are problematic as effect size statistics for dichotomized continuous variables (Sánchez-Meca *et al.*, 2003), though their properties as effect size measures for true dichotomies are less well understood.

Even though d family statistics can be calculated, ϕ is more likely to be encountered in the context of a 2 × 2 table. Like r_{pb}, the value of ϕ depends on the base rates of the categories (i.e., marginals) and is at its maximum when they are equal. This causes problems when comparing ϕ between effects or studies with different base rates (Fleiss, 1994; Haddock *et al.*, 1998). As with all correlation coefficients, a perfect correlation is only possible if the distributions have the same shape. This limits the maximum correlation observed. These problems have led to the view that ϕ is unsuitable for comparing effects between 2 × 2 tables – especially for meta-analysis (Fleiss, 1994; Haddock *et al.*, 1998). To this can be added cautions about interpreting the magnitude of ϕ or ϕ^2 calculated from dichotomous variables (Rosenthal and Rubin, 1979; Rosenthal, 1994; Rosnow and Rosenthal, 2003).

Standardized measures of effect size are therefore discouraged as measures of the magnitude of effects with a dichotomous outcome. They are generally not as simple to calculate and interpret as differences in proportions and have several undesirable mathematical properties. One point in their favor (relative to differences in proportions) is that correlations do not require an unambiguous outcome measure.

Example 7.8 For the surgical checklist data, the correlation between survival and introduction of the safety checklist is:

$$\phi = \frac{3677 \times 31 - 56 \times 3924}{\sqrt{7601 \times 87 \times 3733 \times 3955}} = \frac{-105757}{3124620} \approx -.0338$$

The same value could be obtained from the uncorrected χ^2 statistic (though the sign is lost by taking the positive square root):

$$\phi = \sqrt{\frac{8.81}{7688}} \approx .0338$$

This corresponds to a seemingly tiny $\phi^2 = .0011$, illustrating the difficulty of interpreting the practical significance of an effect with a correlation. The maximum possible value of ϕ for a contingency table with these observed marginals can also be determined. This is accomplished by putting all 87 deaths into the smaller group (the 'before' category) as shown in Table 7.5. As the table has 1 *df*, all other values can be derived by subtraction.

Table 7.5 The largest possible effect for the observed marginal totals of the surgical checklist data

	Alive	**Dead**	
Before	3646	87	3733
After	3955	0	3955
	7601	87	7688

An estimate of the maximum possible absolute value for ϕ is therefore:

$$\hat{\phi}_{\text{max}} = \frac{87 - 0 \times 3955}{3124620} \approx .11$$

Because the group sizes aren't equal, putting all the adverse outcomes in the other group gives a smaller value ($\phi = .10$). The estimate $\phi = +/- .0338$ needs to be interpreted in terms of the maximum possible for that table (and is thereby more impressive).

A final concern is producing an accurate CI for ϕ. Fleiss (1994) gives a large sample approximation, but recommends using the Monte Carlo methods such the Jackknife.

7.5.3 Relative risk and relative risk reduction

The *relative risk* (*RR*) and *relative risk reduction* (*RRR*) are widely used ratio measures for reporting the magnitude of effects for 2 × 2 tables.[13] Where *ARR* is the difference in the proportions of an outcome (usually the reduction in negative outcomes for clinical studies), *RR* is the ratio of the two proportions. This can be computed directly from the 2 × 2 table or from the proportions themselves:

$$RR = \frac{\hat{P}_1}{\hat{P}_0} = \frac{b/n_1}{d/n_0} \qquad \text{Equation 7.24}$$

RR runs from zero to infinity, with $RR = 1$ representing no difference in the proportions. Relative risks less than one indicate a decrease in risk for the treatment group, while relative risks greater than one indicate that risk has increased.

The relative risk reduction (*RRR*) is meaningful when $RR < 1$ and is:

$$RRR = 1 - RR = 1 - \frac{\hat{P}_1}{\hat{P}_0} \qquad \text{Equation 7.25}$$

When risk increases, the term *relative risk increase* (*RRI*) is sometimes used. The reduction or increase in relative risk can also be expressed in terms of *ARR*:

$$-\frac{ARR}{\hat{P}_0} \qquad \text{Equation 7.26}$$

If this value is negative its *absolute* value represents *RRR* (the reduction in risk). If positive its value is *RRI* (the increase in risk).

RRR is widely reported as a measure of clinical significance in medicine. Many health professionals are familiar with it, and, expressed as a percentage, it is popular with journalists reporting medical studies. One reason for its popularity may be that it makes both treatment benefits (for *RRR*) and negative outcomes (for *RRI*) appear more striking when base rate risks are low. A difference in positive outcomes of .0002 and .0001 represents an *ARR* of .0001 (0.01%). The corresponding *RRR* depends on the rate of adverse outcomes in the reference group ($\hat{P}_0$). If this is very low (e.g., .0002) then *RRR* will be high (e.g., $.0001/.0002 = .5$ or 50%). If $\hat{P}_0$ is higher (e.g., .1) then the *RRR* will be less impressive (e.g., $.0001/.1 = .001$ or 0.1%).

The effect of low base rates is even more striking with *RRI*. When $ARR = .0001$ and $\hat{P}_0 = .00005$, the *RRI* is $.0001/.00005 = 2$ (200%). When base rates are low, the risks and benefits of treatment are exaggerated. The mathematical deficiencies of *RR* and *RRR* are outlined by Fleiss (1994). The values depend crucially on the proportion of the relevant outcomes in the reference group. When this value is high then the values that *RR* or *RRR* can take are restricted (e.g., when $\hat{P}_0 = .4$ the *RRR* ranges between 0 and 2.5). Furthermore, like *ARR*, relative risk measures require an unambiguous outcome variable. For *ARR* this was illustrated by considering an observational study looking at heart disease and personality type. The proportions of heart disease outcomes were .04 for Type A personality and .02 for Type B personality. Thus, using Equation 7.26 relative risk increase (*RRI*) of heart disease for Type A personality relative to Type B is $(.04-.02)/.02 = 1$ (a 100% increase). The proportions of Type A personality were .04 for those with heart disease and .02 for those without. The *RRI* of Type A personality for those with heart disease relative to those without is $(.667-.495)/.495 \approx .35$ (a 35% increase). Neither absolute nor relative risk type measures can be used as general measures of association. They are unsuitable when there is no clear distinction between predictor and outcome.

The problems with respect to base rates are well known in the clinical literature, but are more often presented in terms of study design (e.g., Fleiss, 1994; Walter, 2000). It may be reasonable to calculate *RR* for a prospective study or cross-sectional study because the base rates are likely to be representative of the population of interest in this type of design (though this can't be guaranteed if sampling is biased or there is differential drop-out between groups). In contrast, a retrospective study (e.g., a case-control study) is likely to sample cases in a way guaranteed to introduce bias (by looking at cases with a known outcome and matching them with an equal number of controls). Indeed, one of the reasons for conducting such studies is to increase statistical power by over-sampling rare outcomes. They also tend to be less expensive than prospective or cross-sectional studies. Both Fleiss (1994) and Agresti (1996) describe relatively simple procedures for obtaining CIs for the *RR*.

Example 7.9 For the surgical checklist data the relative risk is:

$$RR = \frac{\hat{P}_1}{\hat{P}_0} = \frac{b/n_1}{d/n_0} = \frac{31/3955}{56/3733} \approx \frac{.00784}{.01500} \approx .52$$

The relative risk of death 30 days after surgery is .52 (52%) after the introduction of the checklist. The change in relative risk is therefore:

$$-\frac{ARR}{\hat{P}_0} \approx -\frac{.0072}{.0150} \approx -.48$$

This corresponds to a reduction in relative risk (*RRR*) of .48 (48%). This was the headline figure in a BBC news story about the study: 'Using a simple surgical checklist during major operations can cut deaths by more than 40%'.*

Reporting the mortality data as a 0.72% reduction in deaths might have been less newsworthy. For this particular effect it seems that both *RR* and *RRR* provide a useful measure of the clinical or practical significance of the finding. However, they do so almost by accident. The importance of the finding has more to do with the seriousness of the outcome and the total number of operations performed annually in a single hospital (let alone nationally or internationally). The relative simplicity, lack of expense and low risk of harm of the intervention also make the intervention more impressive. The *NNT* estimate of 140 would be a sensible compromise here. Members of the general public would perhaps be more sensitive to factors such as the number of operations being performed if told that one life was saved for every 140 operations performed after the introduction of the checklist.

* Retrieved from http://news.bbc.co.uk/1/hi/health/7825780.stm on 22 May 2009.

7.5.4 Odds and odds ratios

Many common effect size metrics for dichotomous variables are based on proportions. Among the advantages of these measures is a natural link between binomial proportions and probabilities. The sample proportion $\hat{P}$ is an estimate of the probability of the outcome. An alternative way of representing probabilistic information is in terms of odds rather than probabilities. The odds of an outcome are defined as the ratio of the probability of its occurrence (P) to its non-occurrence ($1-P$):

$$o = \frac{P}{1-P} \qquad \text{Equation 7.27}$$

Odds are therefore relative probabilities.

If $o = 4$, then an outcome or event is four times more likely to happen than not to happen. The choice of event to define as P is often arbitrary, though many people prefer to form the ratio based on the more probable of two events (which ensures that $o > 1$). Being a ratio, it is easy to flip the odds around by taking its reciprocal. Thus odds of occurrence of four imply odds of non-occurrence of $1/4$. Odds range from zero to infinity with negative odds being impossible (because the $P \geq 0$). If the two probabilities are equal (i.e., $P = .5$) the odds are one. Odds above one arise because the probability of occurrence of an event is higher than its non-occurrence (i.e., $P > .5$). Likewise, odds below one indicate that the event is more likely not to occur than to occur (i.e., $P < 1$).[14] It is also trivial to switch back from odds to probability:

$$P = \frac{o}{1+o} \qquad \text{Equation 7.28}$$

Why might you want to switch from probabilities to odds? Not only do odds make some statistical calculations easier, they have attractive mathematical properties that probabilities do not. Reporting an effect size metric for a 2×2 table is a case in point. In a two independent group design with a dichotomous outcome, the proportion of positive or negative outcomes within a group is an estimate of the probability of that outcome. Odds for the positive outcome ('successes') in the treatment group are therefore:

$$\hat{o}_{1+} = \frac{\hat{P}}{1-\hat{P}} = \frac{c/n_1}{d/n_1} = \frac{c}{d}$$

and odds of the negative outcome ('failures') are:

$$\hat{o}_{1-} = \frac{\hat{P}}{1-\hat{P}} = \frac{d/n_1}{c/n_1} = \frac{d}{c}$$

Switching between outcomes is therefore simply a matter of inverting the ratio (i.e., the odds of success are the reciprocal of the odds of failure and vice versa). The population odds for each group or category are estimated directly from the ratio of occurrence to non-occurrence of an outcome within that category. The relative odds of an outcome for each of the two groups can be expressed as an *odds ratio* (*OR*). An estimate of the population odds ratio for the treatment effect for the negative outcome (i.e., odds of the selected outcome for treatment relative to the odds for control) is:

$$OR = \frac{\hat{o}_{1+}}{\hat{o}_{0+}} = \frac{\hat{P}_1/\left(1-\hat{P}_1\right)}{\hat{P}_0/\left(1-\hat{P}_0\right)} = \frac{a/b}{c/d} \qquad \text{Equation 7.29}$$

Inverting the ratio would give the *OR* in terms of positive outcome for the treatment group. The *OR* can also be calculated as the ratio of the cross product of the observed values in the 2×2 table:

$$OR = \frac{ad}{bc} \qquad \text{Equation 7.30}$$

The *OR* is widely employed for statistical inference with 2×2 tables, its mathematical properties making it an attractive alternative to statistics based on probabilities (Fleiss, 1994; Agresti, 1996; Haddock *et al.*, 1998). Like odds, odds ratios range from zero to infinity (with one representing even, equal or unchanged odds). An *OR* above one indicates that the odds have increased by a factor equal to the *OR*. An *OR* below one indicates that the odds have decreased by a factor equal to the *OR*.

What properties make it attractive? First, it is insensitive to changes in the base rates (i.e., marginals). In this respect the distinction between *RR* and *OR* is broadly similar to that between *r* and *d* (McGrath and Meyer, 2006). Furthermore, the *OR* isn't influenced by the choice of the outcome measure. The *OR* is meaningful even when there is no natural or unambiguous outcome measure (and in this respect is similar to a correlation coefficient such as ϕ). In combination, these characteristics make it incredibly versatile. It can be calculated legitimately for a wide variety of experimental and observational designs including both prospective and retrospective (e.g., cross-sectional) studies.

7.5.5 Odds ratios for the McNemar test

The equations introduced here apply to a 2×2 table of independent counts, but odds ratios can also be derived for other situations. A good example is the McNemar test for correlated proportions, where the odds ratio can be computed as:

$$\hat{o} = \frac{b}{c} \qquad \text{Equation 7.31}$$

This follows from the link between McNemar's test and the binomial test (as *b* is the number of 'positive' changes and *c* is the number 'negative' changes). This link can be exploited to obtain an exact CI for this odds ratio from the lower and upper bounds of the CI for a binomial proportion (Fay, 2010). The bounds are estimates of *P* and can therefore be transformed into limits of a CI for the *OR* using Equation 7.27.

7.5.6 Odds ratios and the logistic transformation

Inference with odds ratios usually involves a *logistic transformation*. This transformation uses the *logit*, the natural logarithm of the odds, as its basic unit:

$$logit = \ln(\hat{o}) = \ln\left(\frac{\hat{P}}{1 - \hat{P}}\right) \qquad \text{Equation 7.32}$$

For a binomial proportion with probability *P* the logit has a symmetrical, approximately normal distribution, running from $-\infty$ to ∞ (see Key Concept 17.1). As $\ln(1) = 0$, a logit of zero represents equal odds ($OR = 1$). A good example of the logistic transformation in action is to derive an interval estimate for the *OR* of a 2 × 2 contingency table (Fleiss, 1994; Agresti, 1996). This interval takes the form:

$$\ln\left(\frac{\hat{o}_1}{\hat{o}_0}\right) \pm z_{1-\alpha/2}\hat{\sigma}_{\ln(\hat{o}_1/\hat{o}_0)} \qquad \text{Equation 7.33}$$

The standard error for the log odds ratio is given by:

$$\hat{\sigma}_{\ln(\hat{o}_1/\hat{o}_0)} = \sqrt{\frac{1}{a}+\frac{1}{b}+\frac{1}{c}+\frac{1}{d}} \qquad \text{Equation 7.34}$$

Reversing the logistic transformation by applying the function e^x to the lower and upper limits of the interval gives an asymmetrical CI in terms of the odds ratio (rather than the log odds).

The approximate normality of the log odds has other applications. The variance of the standard logistic distribution is $\pi^2/3$. Dividing the log odds for a 2 × 2 table by $\pi/\sqrt{3} \approx 1.81$ gives a *d* family estimate of the standardized mean difference appropriate for dichotomized continuous variables (Haddock *et al.*, 1998). A related approximation that divides by 1.65 rather than 1.81 appears to perform slightly better in practice (Sánchez-Meca *et al.*, 2003).

A practical problem with the *OR* is that, in common with all ratio measures, it is undefined when the denominator is zero. As a consequence, the usual *OR* estimate is not available if any of the cells in the 2 × 2 table contains zero. Several solutions have been proposed for this problem, but a relatively unbiased and reasonably efficient one is to add 0.5 to all the observed values (not just the empty cells) prior to calculating the *OR* and its CI (Fleiss, 1973). This solution is sometimes known as the *Haldane estimator* after the noted biologist J. B. S. Haldane (Walter, 1985).

Example 7.10 For the surgical checklist data, the odds of the negative outcome (death of the patient) after the introduction of the checklist relative to the odds before can be expressed as:

$$OR_{dead} = \frac{\hat{o}_1}{\hat{o}_0} = \frac{a/b}{c/d} = \frac{3677/56}{3924/31} \approx 0.519$$

Thus, the odds of dying 30 days after surgery are almost halved after the surgical checklist is introduced. You get exactly the same *OR* comparing the odds for time of surgery (after versus before checklist) between patients who died and those who survived:

$$OR_{after} = \frac{31/56}{3924/3677} \approx 0.519$$

A 95% CI for this ratio is

$$0.519 \pm 1.96\hat{\sigma}_{\ln(\hat{o}_1/\hat{o}_0)}$$

where

$$\hat{\sigma}_{\ln(\hat{o}_1/\hat{o}_0)} = \sqrt{\frac{1}{3677}+\frac{1}{56}+\frac{1}{3924}+\frac{1}{31}} \approx 0.225$$

As $\ln(0.519) = -0.656$ the interval estimate on the log odds scale is $-0.656 \pm .441$, or $[-1.097, -0.215]$. Reversing the transformation gives:

$$OR = 0.519, 95\% \text{ CI } [0.33, 0.81]$$

This CI excludes zero and thus the null hypothesis that $OR = 1$ is rejected with $p < .05$ (and an effect of the surgical checklist on mortality is detected).

Strikingly, the *OR* is very similar in value to the *RR*. This is not inevitable (but will happen for whenever the outcome is rare). Contrast these findings with the *OR* and *RR* obtained for the hypothetical treatment comparison described by Rosenthal and Rubin (1979). In their example, 15 out 50 people recovered under the first treatment and 35 out 50 under the second. This gives an *OR* of 5.44 in favor of the second treatment whereas *RR* is only 2.33.

7.5.7 Odds ratios versus relative risk

Although odds ratios have their proponents, there is also a strong sentiment against their use as effect size metrics, particularly in medical research (see Sackett *et al.*, 1996). The main argument against odds ratios is that they are sometimes misinterpreted as relative risks. It is not unreasonable to treat the *RR* and the *OR* as equivalent when the outcome is rare. Agresti (1996) demonstrates this using the following equation:

$$OR = \frac{\hat{P}_1/\left(1-\hat{P}_1\right)}{\hat{P}_0/\left(1-\hat{P}_0\right)} = RR \times \frac{1-\hat{P}_0}{1-\hat{P}_1} \qquad \text{Equation 7.35}$$

When the outcome is rare, both $\hat{P}_0$ and $\hat{P}_1$ are close to zero. The right-hand fraction will therefore be close to one and $OR \approx RR$.

For more frequent outcomes *OR* and *RR* may diverge substantially. Thus opponents of the *OR* are quite right to criticize those who misinterpret odds ratios (interpreting them as if they were relative risks even when the outcome is common). A stronger argument is sometimes asserted or implied: that because its value does not always match the *RR*, odds ratios are bad or improper estimates of effect size for 2×2 tables. This criticism assumes that the *RR* is the 'correct' metric. Walter (2000) emphasizes that *OR* and *RR* are estimates of different parameters and should not be expected to agree under all conditions. Neither is the 'correct' metric.

RR or RRR have advantages in communicating the practical significance of an effect if there is an unambiguous outcome variable. However, they require that the base rates are accurate estimates of the base rates in the population of interest. Even in these cases, other effect size metrics, such as *ARR* or *NNT*, may be more appropriate (e.g., leading to more cautious or balanced assessments). Odds ratios are superior to *RR* if there is no clear outcome variable or if the study design does not allow the base rates to be estimated accurately. The mathematical properties of the *OR* make it a good choice for statistical and scientific inference – particularly for comparing studies with different characteristics (Fleiss, 1994; Walter, 2000). For reporting results and explaining them (e.g., to practitioners or the general public) the *OR* needs to be combined with metrics that are easier for people to interpret. For example, a base rate sensitive measure such as *ARR*, *RR* or *NNT* (particularly the latter) will often be better for communicating the practical importance of an effect, provided a good estimate of the correct base rates is available. Measures such as *ARR* and *NNT* can also be recalculated for a range of different base rates – if the goal is to present benefits or harms for people with different risk profiles.

7.6 R code for Chapter 7

7.6.1 Computing standardized mean differences (Example 7.1)

Several packages provide functions for calculating d, g and Δ from raw data or summary statistics. This example employs the `MBESS` package. The `smd()` function computes Hedges' g and $\hat{\delta}$ while `smd.c()` will compute Glass' Δ. For example, `smd(a,b)` will compute g from raw data in the vectors `a` and `b`, while `smd(a,b, Unbiased=TRUE)` will do the same for $\hat{\delta}$. When using summary statistics, the functions require additional input. The following commands calculate d and g and Δ for the data in Example 7.1:

```
install.packages('MBESS')
library(MBESS)

smd(Mean.1=79, Mean.2=53, s.1=135, s.2=63, n.1=52, n.2=52)
smd(Mean.1=79, Mean.2=53, s.1=135, s.2=63, n.1=52, n.2=52,
  Unbiased=TRUE)
smd.c(Mean.T=79, Mean.C=53, s.C=63, n.C=52, Unbiased=FALSE)
```

To calculate g or $\hat{\delta}$ from summary data you could also define your own functions. The following calculate d, g or $\hat{\delta}$ (and assume $n_2 = n_1$ by default):

```
smd.d <- function(m1, m2, s1, s2, n1, n2 = n1) {
    num <- m2 - m1

    denom <- (((n1-1) * s1^2 + (n2-1) * s2^2)/(n1+n2))^0.5
    num/denom

}

smd.g <- function(m1, m2, s1, s2, n1, n2 = n1) {
    num <- m2 - m1
    denom <- (((n1-1) * s1^2 + (n2-1) * s2^2)/(n1+n2-2))^0.5
    num/denom

}

smd.unb <- function(m1, m2, s1, s2, n1, n2 = n1) {
    num <- m2 - m1
    denom <- (((n1-1) * s1^2 + (n2-1) * s2^2)/(n1+n2-2))^0.5
    num/denom * (n1+n2-3)/(n1+n2 - 2.25)

}
```

The following commands, therefore, almost exactly match the output of the MBESS functions (which are really designed for raw data):

```
smd.g(53, 79, 63, 135, 52)
smd.unb(53, 79, 63, 135, 52)
```

while

```
smd.d(53, 79, 63, 135, 52)
```

generates d and matches:

```
(104/102)^0.5 * smd(Mean.1=79, Mean.2=53, s.1=135, s.2=63,
  n.1=52, n.2=52)
```

Similarly you can define a function to obtain d, g or $\hat{\delta}$ from an independent t statistic:

```
t.to.d <- function(t, n1, n2 = n1) {
    t * (1/n1 + 1/n2)^0.5 * ((n1 + n2)/(n1 + n2 - 2))^0.5
}

t.to.g <- function(t, n1, n2 = n1) {
    t * (1/n1 + 1/n2)^0.5
}

t.to.g.unb <- function(t, n1, n2 = n1) {
    g <- t.to.g(t, n1, n2)
    g * (n1 + n2 - 3)/(n1 + n2 - 2.25)
}
```

To get g from an F ratio of 1.47 and equal samples of $n = 52$ use the call:

```
t.to.g(1.47^0.5, 52)
```

7.6.2 Standardized mean difference for paired designs (Example 7.2)

Estimates of d_{IG}, g_{IG}, and $\hat{\delta}_{IG}$ can be obtained from MBESS or the functions `smd.d()` , `smd.g()` and `smd.unb()` defined above. Estimates of d_{RM}, g_{RM}, and $\hat{\delta}_{RM}$ can be obtained be rewriting the functions based on t:

```
t.to.d.rm <- function(t, n) {
    t * (1/n)^0.5 * (n/(n - 1))^0.5
}

t.to.g.rm <- function(t, n) {
    t * (1/n)^0.5
}
```

```
t.to.g.unb.rm <- function(t, n) {
    g <- t.to.g.rm(t, n)
    g * (n - 3)/(n - 2.25)
}
```

So g_{IG} can be obtained from these commands

```
smd(Mean.1=1416.5, Mean.2=1273, s.1=230.4, s.2=284, n.1=32,
  n.2=32)

smd.g(1416.5, 1273, 230.4, 284, 52)
```

while g_{RM} is computed from:

```
t.to.g.rm(2.32, 32)
```

These results should match those in Example 7.2.

7.6.3 Converting between *g* and r_{pb} (Example 7.3)

The following functions convert between *g* for an independent samples design and r_{pb} (and back again):

```
g.to.r <- function(g, n1, n2 = n1) {
    N <- n1 + n2
    g/(g^2 + (N^2 - 2 * N)/(n1 * n2))^0.5
}

r.to.g <- function(r, n1, n2 = n1) {
    N <- n1 + n2
    r/((1 - r^2) * ((n1 * n2)/(N^2 - 2 * N)))^0.5
}
```

Using input from Example 7.3, the following commands convert the *g* of .75 for study A to a correlation coefficient and back again:

```
g.to.r(.75, 10, 190)
r.to.g(.162, 10, 190)
```

To confirm the calculation is an exact reversal of the transformation, call `r.to.g()` with the output from the other function:

```
r.pb <- g.to.r(.75, 10, 190)
r.to.g(r.pb, 10, 190)
```

7.6.4 An approximate CI for g and Δ (Example 7.4)

An approximate 95% CI, using the approximation provided by Rosenthal (1994), for g or $\hat{\delta} = .245$ is:

```
g <- 0.245
n1 <- 52
n2 <- 52
se.g <- ((n1 + n2)/(n1 * n2) + g^2/(2 * (n1 + n2 - 2)))^0.5
moe <- se.g * qnorm(0.975)
c(g - moe, g + moe)
```

Rosenthal's approximation for the standard deviation of Glass' Δ allows a 95% CI for Δ to be constructed as:

```
nC <- 52
nE <- 52
smg.D <- smd.c(Mean.T=79, Mean.C=53, s.C=63, n.C=nC,
  Unbiased=TRUE)
se.D <- ((nC + nE)/(nC * nE) + smg.D^2/(2 * nC - 2))^0.5
moe <- se.D * qnorm(0.975)
c(smg.D - moe, smg.D + moe)
```

7.6.5 Disattenuation for reliability (Example 7.5)

Correcting a correlation coefficient using the Spearman disattenuation formula is not difficult. It requires the observed correlation and the reliability estimate:

```
r.obs <- .74
r.xx <- .89
r.yy <-.89
r.t <- r.obs/sqrt(r.xx * r.yy)
r.t
```

This gives a value of `0.8314607` which (given that the original correlations are not known to any degree of accuracy) is best reported as $r = .83$. Putting the calculations into a formula allows you to combine it with the `CIr()` function from the `psychometric` package:

```
r.true <- function(r.obs, rxx) {
    r.obs/sqrt(r.xx * r.yy)
}

r.true(r.obs, r.xx)

library(psychometric)
r.true(CIr(.74, 55), .89)
```

7.6.6 Correction for direct range restriction on *X* (Example 7.6)

The `psychometric` package also includes the function `cRRr()` that corrects for direct range restriction on *X*, as well as for meta-analysis of correlation coefficients using the Hunter and Schmidt (2004) approach. The following R code computes an uncorrected CI for the observed correlation of $r = -.48$ in Example 7.6 and computes a correction via a call to `cRRr()`:

```
CIr(-.48, 20)
cRRr(-.48, 4.66, 8.6)
```

A 95% CI for the corrected correlation is obtained by nesting one call within the other:

```
cRRr(CIr(-.48, 20), 4.66, 8.6)
```

7.6.7 Effect sizes for 2 × 2 contingency tables

As an *ARR* is a difference in independent proportions, a CI for the *ARR* can be obtained using `prop.test()` or the `exact2x2()` function from the `exact2x2` package (Fay, 2009, 2010). The `prop.test()` function also gives the chi-square test of independence.

```
n.dead <- c(56, 31)
n.per.group <- c(3733, 3955)

prop.test(n.dead, n.per.group)

ARR <- 56/3733 - 31/3955
ARR
```

Using `exact2x2()` provides an estimate of the odds ratio and a Blaker CI for the odds ratio. The first part sets up the table as a matrix (with labels).

```
checklist <- matrix(c(3677,56,3924,31), 2, 2, byrow=TRUE,
  dimnames = list(c('Before', 'After'),c('Alive', 'Dead')))

library(exact2x2)
exact2x2(checklist, tsmethod = 'blaker')
```

As *NNT* is simply the reciprocal of *ARR*, obtaining *NNT* is also straightforward. A useful trick is taking the reciprocal of a vector containing the confidence limits. The limits are in the list element `conf.int` (which can be addressed by `$conf.int`).

```
NNT <- 1/ARR
NNT
1/prop.test(n.dead, n.per.group)$conf.int[2:1]
```

Calculating ϕ is easy from the χ^2 statistic, but can also be done from the cells:

```
phi <- (56*3924 - 3677 * 31) / (7601*87*3733*3955)^.5
phi
```

The calculations for all the effect size statistics are simple enough to do by hand, but the `epitools` package includes functions for calculating several statistics and their CIs. The `epitab()` function comes with methods for calculating the *RR* and *OR*. To get the *RR* the specify `method='riskratio'`. The main output is a matrix, so computing *RRR* (1−*RR*) involves specifying the appropriate cell of the matrix (or some further arithmetic):

```
install.packages('epitools')
library(epitools)

epitab(checklist, method='riskratio')
RRR = 1 - epitab(checklist, method='riskratio')$tab[2,5]
RRR
```

Getting the *OR* and its CI just involves changing the method:

```
epitab(checklist, method='oddsratio')
```

For the McNemar test, a CI for the binomial proportion can be obtained using familiar methods. The *OR* and a CI for the *OR* is obtained from the `mcnemar.exact()` function in the `exact2x2` package (but detach the `epitools` package first, because some `exact2x2` functions are masked by it). The input is 2×2 matrix of paired counts:

```
detach(package:epitools)
library(exact2x2)

sample.data <- matrix(c(10,3,12,2),2,2)
mcnemar.exact(sample.data)
```

7.6.8 R packages

Aragón, T. (2010) *epitools*: Epidemiology Tools. R package version 0.5.6.

Fay, M. P. (2009) Confidence Intervals that Match Fisher's Exact or Blaker's Exact Tests. *Biostatistics*, 11, 373–4.

Fay, M. P. (2010) Two-sided Exact Tests and Matching Confidence Intervals for Discrete Data. *The R Journal*, 2, 53–8.

Fletcher, T. D. (2010) *psychometric*: Applied Psychometric Theory. R package version 2.2.

Kelley, K., and Lai, K. (2010) *MBESS*: MBESS. R package version 3.2.0.

7.7 Notes on SPSS syntax for Chapter 7

7.7.1 Standardized effect size

Calculating *d* family effect sizes will be easier by hand or using common spreadsheet software such as Excel than using SPSS syntax (point estimates for many *r* family metrics are easily obtained). SPSS syntax for obtaining CIs for standardized effect sizes including for δ is described by Smithson (2001) and Fidler and Thompson (2001).

7.7.2 Effect sizes for 2 × 2 contingency tables

Using the CROSSTABS command it is possible to obtain several common effect size measures for 2 × 2 contingency tables as well as the more usual χ^2 statistic. The following example uses the data file checklist.sav. Remember to use the WEIGHT cases command in SPSS for the count or frequency variable before running CROSSTABS.

SPSS data file: checklist.sav

```
WEIGHT
BY count.

CROSSTABS
/TABLES=mortality BY checklist
/FORMAT= AVALUE TABLES
/STATISTIC=CHISQ PHI RISK
/CELLS= COUNT.
```

Here specifying PHI ensures that ϕ is reported, while specifying RISK ensures that the odds ratio and its 95% CI is reported. Note that the *ARR*, *RR* and *RRR* are not reported when adding RISK to the /STATISTIC subcommand, but can be calculated by hand from the cell counts and marginal totals.

7.8 Bibliography and further reading

Baguley, T. (2009) Standardized or Simple Effect Size: What should be Reported? *British Journal of Psychology*, 100, 603–17.

Fleiss, J. L. (1994) Measures of Effect Size for Categorical Data. In H. Cooper and L. V. Hedges (eds), *The Handbook of Research Synthesis*. New York: Sage, pp. 245–60.

Rosenthal, R. (1994) Parametric Measures of Effect Size. In H. Cooper and L. V. Hedges (eds), *The Handbook of Research Synthesis*. New York: Sage, pp. 231–44.

7.9 Online supplement 1: Meta-analysis

For an introduction to meta-analysis – with particular emphasis on meta-analysis of simple (rather than standardized) differences in means, go to the online supplement at www.palgrave.com/psychology/baguley.

8
Statistical power

Contents

8.1 Chapter overview

This chapter explores statistical power to detect an effect with a null hypothesis significance test or to obtain the desired width for a confidence interval. Key ideas include the relationship between effect size, statistical power and statistical significance, and the role of noncentral distributions in statistical power. Statistical power analysis is illustrated for sample size and *a priori* power estimation, and the dangers of retrospective or *post hoc* power estimates are reviewed. The chapter ends with an introduction to accuracy in the parameter estimation approach to determining the expected width of a confidence interval.

8.2 Significance tests, effect size and statistical power

Anyone using a significance test needs to understand the relationship between effect size, statistical significance and statistical power. Although statistical power can be interpreted more broadly than implied by its role in significance testing, its origins are tied to the Neyman-Pearson philosophy of significance testing as a method of controlling long-term error rates (Dienes, 2008).

There are two principal types of errors that can arise from a statistical decision. For a null hypothesis significance test (NHST), these are termed Type I and Type II errors. A Type I error is the error of obtaining statistical significance when H_0 is true; the false positive error of deciding there is an effect when none exists. A Type II error is failing to obtain statistical significance when H_0 is false; the false negative error of deciding there is no effect when one does exist. Type I errors occur with probability α, while Type II errors occur with probability β.[1] Statistical power is $1 - \beta$ (the probability of avoiding a Type II error). This is the probability of detecting a difference or association if one is present in the population.

In the Neyman-Pearson philosophy of significance testing, statistical power is an essential consideration. Only when statistical power is high is it at all reasonable to use a significance test as a decision procedure. Only high statistical power makes it possible to keep α and β, the long run rate of both types of error, low. However, keeping the rate of errors low does not guarantee that effects that are detected will be important or interesting. The effect might be so small that it is entirely uninteresting (e.g., a drug that prolonged the life of people who took it by only a few hours or days might have little or no clinical benefit). The distinction between practical and statistical significance is a particular concern when statistical significance is obtained in large samples.

Rosenthal illustrates the link between statistical significance, effect size and sample size with a 'conceptual equation' (Rosenthal, 1994):

$$\textit{significance test} = \textit{size of effect} \times \textit{size of study}$$

This conceptual equation indicates that statistical significance (e.g., a large value for a test statistic such as t or z) depends on both effect size and sample size. Statistical significance can be achieved from a large effect in a small sample or a small effect in a large sample. In the absence of other information, statistical significance says almost nothing about the size of an effect. It is foolish to assume that a small p value implies a large or important effect.

Rosenthal (1994) illustrates how the equation works for a number of common standardized effect size metrics. It is worth looking at one of these metrics in detail. A good place to start is the independent *t* test. Here statistical significance depends on *t* (because as *t* increases the observed *p* value will fall). Fleshing out the conceptual equation gives:

$$t = g \times \sqrt{\frac{n_1 + n_2}{n_1 n_2}} \qquad \text{Equation 8.1}$$

Statistical significance in Equation 8.1 is a function of standardized effect size (Hedges' *g* in this case) and the sample size (n_1 and n_2). The size of the study has its impact through the reduction in sampling error as *N* increases. The standardized difference in means captures the remaining influence on *t*. Standardized measures of effect such as *g* are therefore good at summing up the efficiency of an NHST. They do so by stripping out the confounding influence of sample size. Also, recall that independence of sample size is one of the desiderata for measures of effect size proposed by Preacher and Kelley (2011). However, even this fleshed out conceptual equation obscures some important details of how NHSTs work.

What happens if the equation is unpacked further? Equation 7.3 defines Hedges' *g* as:

$$\frac{\hat{\mu}_1 - \hat{\mu}_2}{\hat{\sigma}_{pooled}}$$

While it is true that statistical significance can be achieved via large *g* and small *N* or via small *g* and large *N*, this obscures its relationship to variability in the sample. If $\hat{\sigma}_{pooled}$ is large then *t* will tend to be small, and if $\hat{\sigma}_{pooled}$ is small *t* will be large (assuming $\hat{\mu}_1 - \hat{\mu}_2$ and sample size are constant). Standardized effect size metrics are ratios of the magnitude of an effect to its variability (not 'pure' measures of the magnitude of effects). Following this logic, the conceptual equation becomes:

$$\textit{significance test} = (\textit{magnitude of effect} \; / \; \textit{variability of effect}) \times \textit{size of study}$$

For independent *t* this can be fleshed out as:

$$t = \frac{\hat{\mu}_1 - \hat{\mu}_2}{\hat{\sigma}_{pooled}} \times \sqrt{\frac{n_1 + n_2}{n_1 n_2}} \qquad \text{Equation 8.2}$$

Simple effect size is a measure of the magnitude of the effect while standardized effect size is the ratio of this magnitude to its variability. Comparing standardized effect sizes between samples or studies is therefore only legitimate if the variability of the effects being compared is constant (Morris and DeShon, 2002; Baguley, 2009).

Under this conceptualization, standardized effect size is a 'signal to noise' ratio that indexes the 'detectability' of an effect. The conceptual equation can be presented explicitly in those terms.[2] Presenting the equation in this way – as well clarifying that the standardized effect size is not a pure measure of magnitude – also makes it clear that statistical power is influenced by at least three separate factors: the sample size, the magnitude of an effect and the variability of an effect.

Standardized effect size metrics, while not usually interpretable as the magnitude (or indeed size) of an effect, do separate out the detectability of an effect from the sample size of a study that attempts to detect it. This explains the central role of standardized effect size statistics in statistical power analysis. If you want to estimate the sample size to detect an effect, or the statistical power to detect an effect for a given sample size, measures such as g or r package together crucial information about the magnitude and variability of the effect in a convenient form.

8.3 Statistical power and sample size

As well as being $1 - \beta$ (the probability of avoiding a Type II error), statistical power is an illustration of a much broader concept – that of measurement precision. Obtaining high statistical power in a significance test requires that one or more parameters are estimated with sufficient precision to detect the effect of interest.

Why is statistical power central to the logic of the Neyman-Pearson decision theory? The first reason is that unless the power of a significance test is high, significance tests are not much use. A non-significant finding is uninformative if power is low, because it could easily be a Type II error. Worse, it is downright misleading if you conclude that failing to detect an effect implies no effect exists. A test with statistical power of $1 - \beta = .35$ has a .65 (65%) chance of not detecting a genuine effect (should one exist). Even if an effect is detected, an NHST may not be very informative if the Type I error is very high (e.g., $\alpha = .40$). Such high levels of α may seem implausible, but are easily achieved through data dredging (performing lots of tests not motivated by theory) or simultaneous testing of multiple hypotheses (Maxwell, 2004).[3] The second reason is a practical one. Researchers have limited resources. Statistical power – employed correctly – can help maximize resources by providing more efficient parameter estimates and tests. Maximization of resources is often presented as an issue of cost or efficiency, but it also has an ethical dimension (Baguley, 2004). Research that is underpowered is wasteful of resources that might be used more productively and may expose people or animals to unnecessary risk or harm (given that the study has little prospect of finding anything useful). Conversely, overpowered studies may have a very high probability of detecting important or interesting effects, but at the cost of exposing more people or animals than necessary to adverse consequences. Bodies responsible for research governance often require statistical power to be explicitly considered in applications for ethical approval. The practical application of statistical power is largely about balancing risks, harms and costs against potential benefits.

For NHSTs these risks, harms and costs are usually related to the Type I and Type II error rates. For a single test, correctly applied, the long-run probability of a Type I error is equal to α (and often fixed at .05 or 5%). The long-run probability of a Type II error is β. Neither β nor statistical power $(1 - \beta)$ are easy to control. Even estimating β or $1 - \beta$ is difficult. A further challenge is that all three quantities are conditional probabilities. Relaxing your decision threshold by increasing α will tend to decrease β and increase statistical power for a large set of tests, but for any single effect only one of α or β is a meaningful probability. As you won't know for certain whether H_0 is true or false you'll need to consider both potential outcomes when you plan a study.[4]

The same concerns arise for other inferential tools – notably confidence intervals (CIs) – but the framework for considering them is less well developed. A recent approach, *accuracy in parameter estimation* (AIPE), is concerned with the broader issue of precision in estimation (Kelley *et al.*, 2003). Although the following sections start by explaining statistical power from a classical NHST perspective, the goal is to build up a picture of statistical power in a broader sense (one that necessarily includes measurement precision).

8.3.1 Statistical power and the efficiency of a statistical procedure

The term 'statistical power' is used in at least two (slightly) different ways. These differ with regard to whether the term is applied to a class of statistical procedure or to a specific instantiation of the procedure. The former application involves determining which statistical procedure will be most efficient for a certain class of situations (e.g., is the paired t test more powerful than the sign test?). The latter involves estimating the statistical power or sample size of a particular study (ideally one which is being planned rather than one that has already been completed).

Determining the statistical power of a class of statistical procedures is incredibly hard because it depends on factors such as sample size and the precise distributions being sampled. The usual solution is to consider relative efficiency for samples from populations with well-understood distributions (e.g., the normal). Relative efficiency is ratio of sample sizes (N_1/N_2) required to achieve the same power for two procedures. As this value itself varies with sample size, *asymptotic relative efficiency* (*ARE*) is the usual standard of comparison. Procedures that use more information from the sample have greater statistical power than those that use less information. For instance, the *ARE* of the sign test relative to paired t is $2/\pi \approx .637$ for paired differences sampled from a normal distribution (Conover, 1980). To achieve the same power to detect an effect, you'd expect the sign test to require a sample size $1/.637 \approx 1.6$ times larger. The sign test uses only the direction of the differences between pairs and not the size of the differences. This explains part of the efficiency advantage of paired t. The t test, because it assumes normality, also incorporates additional information about the probability of a difference of a particular size being observed. In general, stronger assumptions (e.g., about distributions) allow the procedure to incorporate more information and increase the efficiency of the test.

This approach has several drawbacks. While the asymptotic efficiency is a useful standard of comparison, it isn't ideal for comparison involving realistic sample sizes. Moreover, the precise distribution of the populations being sampled is rarely known. There is now sufficient evidence that procedures once widely regarded as being powerful and reasonably robust to violations of assumptions (e.g., t tests) can perform very poorly when the assumptions are violated (Wilcox, 2005a). Much of the evidence for these conclusions comes from Monte Carlo simulations. As well as being useful for comparing the power of different classes of procedure, such simulations are excellent tools for estimating power when standard methods fail. Simulation methods researchers make it possible to explore the effects of assumptions and parameter values on the ability to detect an effect or obtain a CI with accurate coverage.

8.3.2 Factors that influence statistical power

Several factors influence the power of a statistical procedure (see Baguley, 2004; Hayes, 1973). The principal ones are:

i) α
ii) magnitude of the effect
iii) variability of the effect
iv) sample size.

How the significance threshold impacts on the ability to detect an effect is reasonably straightforward: α is the lower limit that statistical power can take. As α is the long-run Type I error rate,

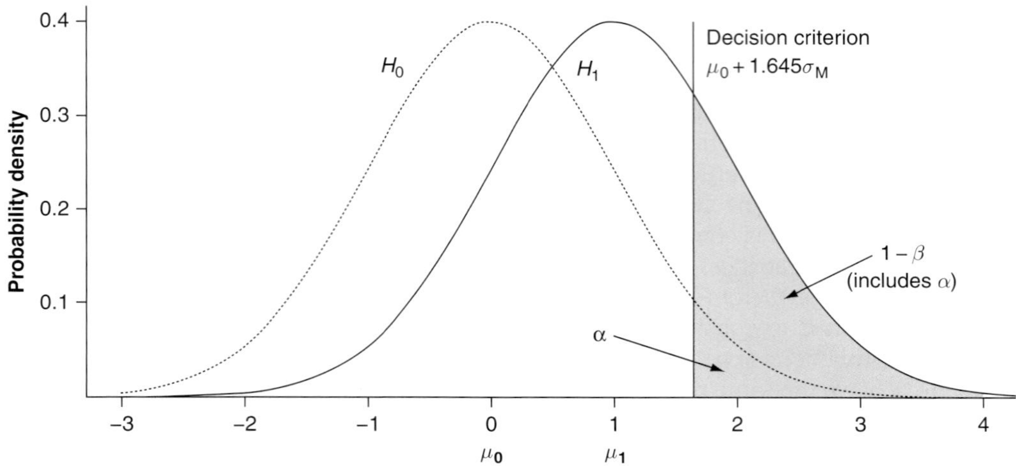

Figure 8.1 The relationship between statistical power and one-sided α

it is the probability of statistical significance when the effect size equals zero. Even for very tiny effects (those virtually indistinguishable from zero), power must equal or exceed α. Figure 8.1 shows α and statistical power $(1-\beta)$ for an alternative hypothesis (assumed to be true for this illustration) when $\alpha = .05$. The curve labeled H_1 is the sampling distribution of the test statistic z for the true alternative hypothesis. The curve labeled H_0 is the distribution of z under the null hypothesis. The shaded area α under the curve H_0 is the familiar rejection region of a z distributed test statistic for a one-sided test.[5]

The decision criterion for the test statistic depends on α. For a one-sided test with $\alpha = .05$ the value of z at the cut-off is approximately 1.645. Thus every sample mean that is 1.645 or more standard errors larger than μ_0 (the mean expected under H_0) is statistically significant at $\alpha = .05$. The area of the H_1 curve (to the left of the decision criterion) represents non-significant test outcomes. As the alternative hypothesis is true, these are Type II errors. Thus the unshaded area of curve H_1 has an area equal to β. The shaded area to the right of the criterion is the statistical power of the test $(1-\beta)$. The area $1-\beta$ always includes α, because the same criterion is applied to each curve. In Figure 8.2 the curves defined by H_0 and H_1 have been placed closer together (relative to Figure 8.1). As the two curves converge, the area $1-\beta$ will shrink and eventually coincide exactly (in this case almost exactly) with α. Relaxing the decision criterion (by increasing α) increases statistical power. This is sometimes helpful, but quite risky. Unless Type I errors are low in cost (e.g., if the research involves negligible risk or is exploratory in character) then messing about with α is a poor strategy. It just shifts errors from one category to another (decreasing Type II by increasing Type I errors).

An exception is for research where all of the factors that influence statistical power are fixed and cannot be altered. In this situation, a sensible strategy is to decide on the ratio of Type I and Type II errors and select α so that this ratio will be met (given the information at hand). This option is implemented in software such as G*Power (e.g., Faul *et al.*, 2007).

A striking feature of Figure 8.1 and Figure 8.2 is that statistical power (the shaded area in each graph) depends heavily on the separation of the two curves. The overlap of the curves depends

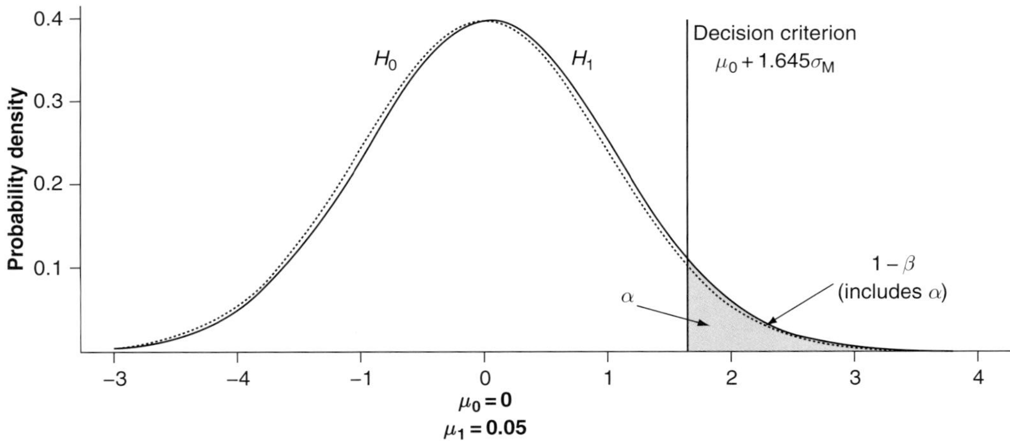

Figure 8.2 The relationship between statistical power and α when the separation of H_0 and H_1 is small

on the gap between μ_0 and μ_1 and on the standard deviation (*SD*) of their sampling distribution (the standard error of mean $\sigma_{\hat{\mu}}$). As the separation gets larger, power $(1-\beta)$ increases. The separation between curves is defined by:

$$z = \frac{\mu_1 - \mu_0}{\sigma_{\hat{\mu}}} = \frac{\mu_1 - \mu_0}{\sigma / \sqrt{n}} \qquad \text{Equation 8.3}$$

Anything that increases z will increase statistical power, while anything that reduces the separation will decrease statistical power.

Consider each of the terms $\mu_1 - \mu_0$, σ and n in turn. $\mu_1 - \mu_0$ is the population effect size (the simple difference between the true population parameter and that assumed under H_0). The larger the difference between μ_1 and μ_0, the greater the separation (and the better the chance of detecting an effect). This should not be surprising: bigger effects are easier to find (with or without statistical tests). The bottom half of the ratio is the standard error of the mean $\sigma_{\hat{\mu}}$, comprising σ (the population *SD*) divided by the square root of the sample size n. As this ratio goes up (because σ increases or n decreases) statistical power goes down. Power increases when the ratio decreases. It becomes harder to detect an effect when data are more variable, because any 'signal' gets swamped by the 'noise' in the sample. Large samples counteract this because the sampling distribution of a statistic converges on the true population parameter as n approaches infinity. This happens because, as n increases to encompass the whole population, the sample and population become identical. At that point even the tiniest effects can be detected.

It is crucial to understand that the separation of the distributions under the null and alternative hypotheses depends not just on the distance between the means but on their variability. Figures 8.1 and 8.2 obscure this by presenting the distributions in terms of a standard normal (z) test statistic where $\sigma_z = 1$. Figure 8.3 shows the statistical power for samples from a normal distribution with $\mu = 15$ and with H_0: $\mu = 10$. Panel (a) shows the statistical power for $\sigma_{\hat{\mu}} = 2.5$, while panel (b) shows the power for $\sigma_{\hat{\mu}} = 1.5$.

Statistical power increases because the null and alternative distributions become more tightly clustered around their means. A consequence of this is that the decision threshold shifts

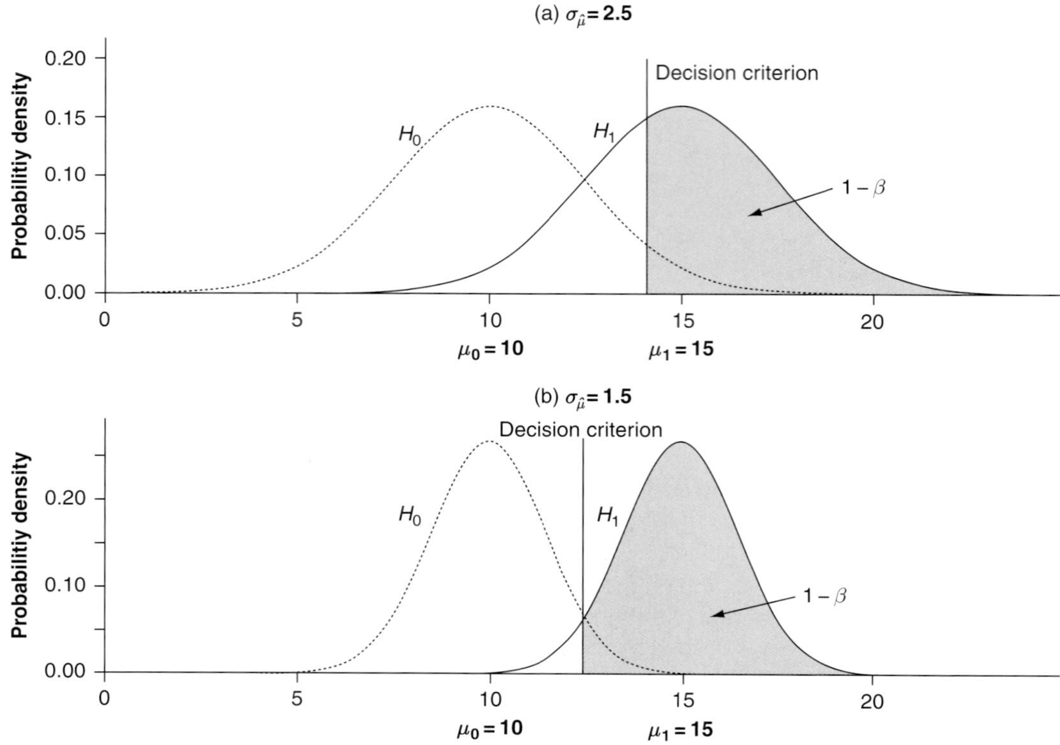

Figure 8.3 The influence of (a) larger and (b) smaller standard errors of the mean on statistical power $(1 - \beta)$

closer to the mean of the null distribution. The threshold for this one-sided test is entirely determined by the 5% most extreme values in the null distribution, and this region gets closer to $\mu_0 = 10$ as $\sigma_{\hat{\mu}}$ decreases. For the purposes of statistical power it does not matter whether $\sigma_{\hat{\mu}}$ varies because of σ or because of n. A value of $\sigma_{\mu} = 2.5$ could arise because $\sigma = 25$ and $n = 100$ or because $\sigma = 250$ and $n = 10{,}000$.

When thinking about statistical power it can make sense to sift out sample size from the other factors that influence the separation of the sampling distributions. For a z test, this gives an equation of the form:

$$z = \frac{\mu_1 - \mu_0}{\sigma} \times \sqrt{n} \qquad \text{Equation 8.4}$$

The first term in the equation is a form of standardized effect size (a standardized difference in means). Standardized effect size estimates can be employed to simplify power calculations. One of the most widely used frameworks for statistical power analysis does precisely this (Cohen, 1988, 1992). This application of standardized effect size metrics requires some qualification. For a statistical power calculation the important quantity is not σ_T (the true population σ), but σ_U (the σ of the population of measurements being sampled). The difference is that σ_U is uncorrected with respect to phenomena such as range restriction or reliability. It needs to include all sources of variability that influence the sample (and which may not all influence σ_T). This implies that an estimate of standardized effect size that is most informative about the practical or clinical benefit of an effect, or for comparing between studies with different designs (one that it is corrected for reliability, range restriction or study design), will typically be inappropriate for statistical power estimation.

Statistical power analysis has several applications, three of which are addressed below. The first, and possibly most important, is to inform researchers about the things they can manipulate to increase the statistical power of a study. The second is to estimate the sample size required to achieve a desired level of statistical power (once all the other characteristics of a test are fixed). The third is to estimate the statistical power of a test when all other characteristics (including sample size) are fixed. These applications overlap in practice, because most statistical power estimates (e.g., for sample size planning) look at a range of factors that influence sample size.

8.3.3 Noncentral distributions

The previous explanation of factors that influence power focused on the normal distribution. Many statistical tests (and power calculations) involve a test statistic with a t, F or χ^2 distribution. These statistics are easy to work with when H_0 is true (as assumed in a classical significance test) because computing a test statistic invokes the central form of the distribution (e.g., central t). If H_0 is false, the distribution of test statistics depends on the size of the effect, and noncentral distributions are required. These are families of distributions that differ in terms of a *noncentrality parameter* (*ncp*). A central distribution is a special case of a noncentral distribution where the *ncp* equals zero.

The bigger the true effect, the less the shape of a noncentral distribution resembles the corresponding central distribution. Depending on the distribution in question, noncentral and central distributions can differ in several ways. For instance, with the t distribution, the larger the true effect, the larger the *ncp* and the less symmetrical the distribution becomes. This asymmetry is more pronounced for small sample sizes (when *df* are low). Noncentral t converges on the normal distribution asymptotically – but this convergence is much slower than for central t. Figure 8.4 shows a comparison of central and noncentral t for $df = 6$ and $df = 29$ when $ncp_t = 3$.[6] The difference in symmetry of the two distributions is clear when $df = 6$ (even though the degree of noncentrality implied by $ncp_t = 3$ is modest). For the larger of the two sample sizes ($df = 29$) the distribution looks fairly symmetrical, but the shift of density away from the center of the distribution is shown by the reduced height of the central peak. As the noncentrality parameter depends on sample size (increasing for large n) this contributes to its slow convergence toward the normal in large samples.

Noncentral t can be likened to the binomial – which is also a kind of noncentral distribution (Smithson, 2001). The difficulties that arise with the asymmetry of the binomial distribution also apply to noncentral t (e.g., constructing an interval estimate for asymmetric distributions is harder than for symmetrical ones). It poses a particular problem for statistical power calculations because the goal is to estimate the probability of obtaining a given value of test statistic if there really is an effect. This implies H_0 is false and that the test statistic has a noncentral distribution.

Consider a one sample t test. The noncentrality parameter for this test statistic is:

$$ncp_t = \frac{\mu_1 - \mu_0}{\sigma_{\hat{\mu}}} \qquad \text{Equation 8.5}$$

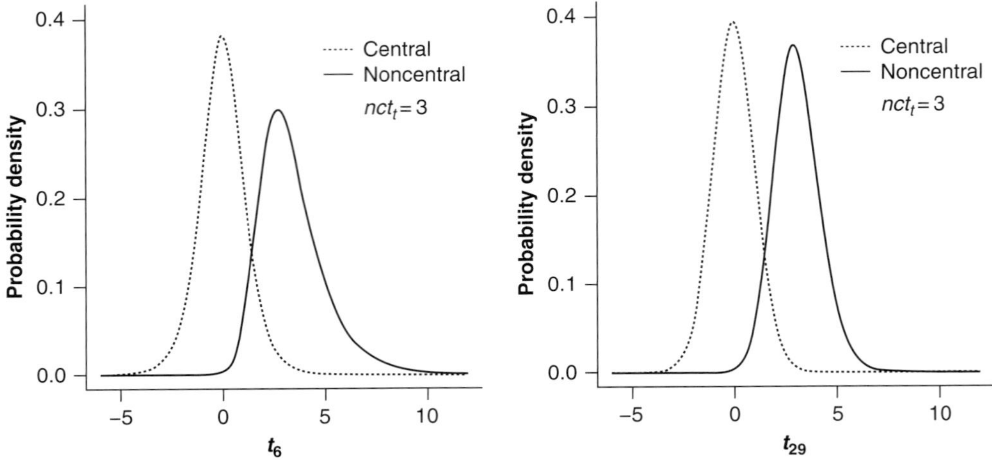

Figure 8.4 Comparing central and noncentral *t* distributions with 6 and 29 degrees of freedom

This is the separation between two normal sampling distributions. Cumming and Finch (2001) show this could also be represented in terms of the population standardized mean difference:

$$ncp_t = \delta\sqrt{n} \qquad \text{Equation 8.6}$$

Provided $\delta = (\mu_1 - \mu_0)/\sigma_U$(the standardized mean difference for a one sample *t* test using σ uncorrected for factors such as reliability), a sample estimate of the noncentrality parameter is given by:

$$n\hat{c}p_t = \frac{\hat{\mu}_1 - \mu_0}{\hat{\sigma}_{\hat{\mu}}} \qquad \text{Equation 8.7}$$

This should look familiar because it is the test statistic for one sample *t*. In contrast, Equation 8.5 and Equation 8.6 are expressions for the *ncp* in the population.

Accurate interval estimates for standardized effect size also involve noncentral distributions. Cumming and Finch (*ibid*.) point out that a CI for the ncp_t can be used to obtain a CI for δ. However, there is no exact analytic solution to the problem, and either an approximation or an iterative method needs to be employed (*ibid*.; Smithson, 2001).[7] In principle, a CI for a noncentrality parameter could also be used to estimate power or sample size when planning a study. More often a researcher decides on a single estimate of the standardized effect size (and by implication the noncentrality parameter).

Example 8.1 Example 7.4 looked at the CI for a standardized mean difference. The difference in negative priming between a young and old sample was estimated (using approximate methods) as: $\hat{\delta} = 0.245$, 95% CI [−0.14, 0.63]. How does this CI compare with the more accurate method proposed by Cumming and Finch (2001)? Kelley (2007a) describes how to use the MBESS package in R to calculate exact CIs for g using noncentral distributions. This iterative solution is:

$$\hat{\delta} = 0.245, 95\% \text{ CI } [-0.14, 0.63]$$

The approximation is therefore very impressive (being identical to two decimal places). This will generally be true for small *ncp* values and moderate to large *n*. Both methods assume normality, and so other methods (e.g., bootstrapping) might be required when approximate normality is not tenable (Kelley, 2005).

8.3.4 Increasing the power of a study

Discussion of how to increase the power of a study usually revolves around a single factor – sample size – to the neglect of other factors. In particular, it is common to neglect the design of the study and its influence on measurement precision or statistical power (but see Baguley, 2004; Sackett, 2001). Sometimes there is a tacit assumption that factors such as the magnitude of the effect or its variability are immutable (or at least difficult to change). This is only occasionally true. This section reviews some of the main ways that factors other than sample size can be manipulated.

Recall that α determines the lower bound for power. Any procedure that increases effective α also increases power. Researchers are generally reluctant to alter α because there is a perception that this will make results less credible. This doesn't really fit with the philosophy of significance testing. Type I and Type II errors are equally important (unless the relative costs of the two errors differ). If missing a real effect is the more costly of the two errors (e.g., in exploratory research that will be followed up later) then a modest increase in α is sensible. If the two errors are equally undesirable, a good strategy is to balance the two errors (e.g., by targeting statistical power of $1 - \alpha$). This is rarely done – perhaps because achieving high levels of power and low Type I error rates is difficult with sample sizes typical of research with human participants. Furthermore, the nominal α level of a test is rarely accurate: the effective α level is often much lower or much higher. The main culprits here are violations of statistical assumptions (e.g., normality), adopting conservative statistical procedures (where true α differs from nominal) or not operating with a stopping rule (see Chapter 11).

The magnitude of an effect (e.g., $\mu_1 - \mu_2$) can also be manipulated. For this purpose it helps to think in terms of the 'dose' of the treatment used in a study. This can be helpful even if the treatment isn't a true independent variable (*IV*) manipulated by the researcher. Thus, in a memory experiment, a researcher can manipulate all sorts of variables that may influence how much or what is remembered. If the hypothesis of interest concerns the effect of delay on recall of words, the researcher could manipulate the dose of this variable by increasing or decreasing the delay or by decreasing the time participants have to learn the words. What if the outcome is something – such as state anxiety – that can't be manipulated in an experiment? The dose can still be adjusted by disproportionately sampling people with low or high scores on the variable. This is what an extreme groups analysis does. Sampling in this way increases statistical power, but makes it harder to estimate standardized population parameters such as ρ or δ (Preacher *et al.*, 2005). This may or may not matter. Researchers typically care more about detecting an effect than estimating population standardized effect size. Also, if the study is designed this way, range restriction will be direct (and the information required to correct the sample estimates of ρ or δ relatively easy to determine).

If the effect is linear then sampling two extreme groups with equal n is the optimal design. For nonlinear effects there are different optimal sampling strategies (McClelland, 1997). One misunderstanding of these optimal approaches needs to be avoided. It is never sensible to throw data away. Sampling a range of low to high values and excluding the middle values is always a bad idea (because it ignores potential information about the effect and reduces overall N). A strategy for sampling the extremes needs to be found that deploys the available resources efficiently and does not discard data. One strategy might be to pre-screen participants (e.g., for one of the predictors) using an easy-to-administer measure, or to target groups that are expected to be low or high on the predictors of interest. This isn't always practical (or theoretically justified), but it is surprising how few researchers target large effects (even when the effect of interest is known to be hard to detect).

The variability of the effect is likewise open to manipulation. Many of the measures routinely used by researchers have poor reliability. Schmidt and Hunter (1999) assert that a typical measurement error in a field such as psychology is 50% (i.e., reliability $\approx .7$). Selecting or developing more reliable measures will increase power. Measurement errors from other sources can be reduced by careful experimental control (Sackett, 2001). Something as basic as making instructions clear and easy to follow, or providing practice items, can reduce aberrant responses by participants. Likewise, piloting materials and removing items that elicit unusually variable or bizarre responses can reduce measurement error (though it is worth looking closely at unusual responses before eliminating an item). Using samples with more homogeneous responses can also increase statistical power by reducing measurement error (though whether this is sensible depends on the research question).

Other characteristics of a design can increase statistical power. One feature – already considered at length for 2×2 tables and for r_{pb} – is ensuring equal n per group in two group designs. In multiple group designs the best option varies depending on the research question (McClelland, 1997). Repeated measures designs – including paired designs – usually increase power. They do so by excluding individual differences from the error term used to compute a test statistic. Increasing the number of items given to each participant is also sometimes an option. This increases power by making the measurement more reliable if the analysis involves an outcome averaged over all items. This type of analysis is not always appropriate and an alternative solution is to model individual responses within participants (e.g., using a multilevel model). The latter also typically increases power (because the increase in effective sample size by including more items often exceeds that lost by other features of the design; see Chapter 18). Increasing the sensitivity of measures by increasing the precision with which people can make a response (e.g., moving from a five- to seven-point scale) may also increase power. These factors can apply in reverse. For instance, dichotomizing or categorizing continuous variables reduces power (MacCallum *et al.*, 2002).

This by no means exhausts ways to improve the power of a study. Thinking through all the possible factors might seem daunting, but for a given study the options are limited. A good way to approach it is to go through a series of simple questions. Can you increase the magnitude of the effect in some way? Can you reduce the variability of the measurements? What other features of the design can you manipulate? Are there alternative methods of analysis that use more information and increase statistical power?

8.4 Statistical power analysis

8.4.1 Estimating the sample size required to detect an effect

Statistical power analyses can be used to estimate a suitable sample size when planning a study. There are a number of stages to a power analysis, starting with determination of α. This can be set directly or indirectly (e.g., by deciding on the ratio α/β). A researcher also needs to think about the level of statistical power that is required. This should involve a decision about the relative costs of Type I and Type II errors. A common, but problematic, practice is to decide on statistical power without thinking about the context (e.g., always selecting .80; a level suggested – but not mandated – by Cohen, 1988). Once armed with the desired level of power and α, you need two further pieces of information: the magnitude of the effect and its variability.

The main obstacle to getting reasonable sample size estimates is not the difficulty of the calculation. Although the involvement of noncentral distributions makes hand calculation difficult, this obstacle can be eliminated by using a computer. The real obstacle is getting hold of sensible estimates for the magnitude and the variability of the effect. Almost any other source of uncertainty or inaccuracy in the calculation is likely to be overwhelmed by the uncertainty in these estimates. This is inevitable. If precise, accurate estimates of these quantities were available there would be no point doing the study. Why collect data to see if a treatment works if you already know whether there is an effect and how big it is?

The magnitude and variability can be considered separately or jointly (in the form of a standardized effect size metric). In either case the fundamental problem is the same: how do you get a good estimate? One option is to derive the estimates from data (e.g., from a prior study or pilot study). A second option is not to estimate the magnitude and variability at all, but to calculate the statistical power to detect an effect of theoretical or practical significance. This is possible if a theory makes quantitative predictions about the size of an effect. Similarly, practitioners often have an understanding about the size of an effect that would make a practical difference (possibly taking into account costs or harms associated with the effect). An advantage of this strategy is that – provided power is set at a suitable level – a non-significant effect can be interpreted as evidence for an effect of little practical or theoretical significance. A third option, proposed as a last resort method by Cohen (1988), is to use T-shirt-style benchmarks for 'small', 'medium' and 'large' effects (Lenth, 2009). This is almost always a bad idea. It implies that a researcher is clueless about the size of effect they are interested in (or has not bothered to come up with a better estimate). You can also mix and match the first two options. If you have an idea of the magnitude of effect that is clinically important, it is easy to combine this with an estimate of variability from another study (using a similar measure in a similar sample).

Things are easier if you want to replicate an effect that somebody else has reported. Summary statistics in published research usually contain sufficient data to estimate the magnitude and variability of the effect. Standardized effect size (e.g., g or r) can also make things even easier. Even so, it is wise to cross-check the calculations against summary data, test statistics or p values (if available).[8] If using someone else's study to obtain information for a sample size calculation, try to avoid two common errors. The first error is simply to replicate the same sample size as the original study. This will result in low power whenever the original study was only barely statistically significant (i.e., when $p \approx \alpha$). Under these circumstances the original study could easily have tipped either way ($p > \alpha$ or $p < \alpha$). An identical replication would therefore expect $p \approx \alpha$. If the test statistic has a symmetrical distribution (e.g., z or t), this implies that power will be around .5 (and usually not far off for other test statistics). The second error is more subtle. No two studies are identical replications, and it is important to consider factors that differ between the studies. Switching between repeated measures and independent measures, changing measurement instruments, changing the dose of the treatment and many other factors will have an impact on statistical power.

Example 8.2 The Beck Depression Inventory (BDI) is a measure of the severity of depressive symptoms (Beck *et al.*, 1961). Seggar *et al.* (2002) reported BDI scores for clinical samples ($M = 25.45$, $SD = 9.99$, $n = 3,339$) and community samples ($M = 7.22$, $SD = 6.33$, $n = 28,905$) of depressed individuals, as well as a small asymptomatic sample ($M = 2.88$, $SD = 2.88$, $n = 81$). Reliability for BDI tends to be high (typically > .90). This information can be used to plan sample size for a new study. As long as measurements in the planned studies have similar reliability to those in the Seggar *et al.* study, this aspect of the study can be ignored (as the reliability of the measure is built in to the observed *SD* of each group).

The difference between the community and clinical samples is 18.33 points. As a rough guide to clinical significance, scores on the BDI below 11 are generally considered in the healthy range, scores around 11–20 suggest mild depression, while 21–30 is associated with moderate depression and 31–63 with severe depression. What size of effect might be of clinical value? This is a difficult judgment for a non-clinician to make, but a sample size able to detect a reduction of ten points with high probability (e.g., .95) may be a good starting point. This is more than half the difference between the clinical and community sample and is also sufficient to move someone from moderate to mild depression (or out of the mild depression category altogether). Given the variability of the clinical sample, this corresponds to $\delta = 10/9.99 \approx 1.0$. The goal here is to design a study that is very unlikely to miss an effect that could make a practical difference to a patient.

Although this is probably a reasonable estimate of the desired effect size, there are additional concerns. The BDI scores are positively skewed. This is suggested by the way that the *SD* rises in line with the mean (and tends to occur for measures with scores close to a lower bound). For participants with severe symptoms you'd expect variability to increase and this estimate of δ will be too large. The standard power calculations also assume normality and equal variances (which may not hold in this case). An alternative option is to simulate power for a suitably skewed distribution (e.g., the lognormal distribution). You might also explore the impact of more than one type of analysis on power (e.g., considering robust alternatives to the t test such as bootstrapping). Although these steps are worth considering, the quality of the effect size estimate is likely to be the single most important factor in the accuracy of a sample size calculation.

Going for a power of .95 with $\alpha = .05$ implies a target of $\beta = .05$ (consistent with equal cost of Type I and Type II errors). For an untested treatment, it is sensible to use a two-sided test (as it is not unknown for new treatments to harm people). If there is prior evidence of efficacy it may be reasonable to use a one-sided test. For a one-sided test with $\alpha = .05$, the sample size for a 95% chance to detect an effect of $\delta = 1$ is 46 (or 23 per group) when estimated with G*Power. An equivalent analysis in R using the `pwr` package returns an estimate of 22.35635 per group. Standard practice is to round n per group up to the nearest whole number. This gives 23 per group and matches the G*Power output.

This is the number of participants needed at the end of the study. A study such as this would take weeks or months to complete. It is therefore essential to plan for loss of data (e.g., due to participants withdrawing from the study, moving to another clinic or not complying with treatment). Looking at similar published studies should give an idea of the likely level of 'dropout'. The study should include additional participants to allow for this. It is also wise to put in place mechanisms to support participants and reduce dropout (Sackett, 2001). This is often highly cost effective (because dropout rates of 50% or more are not unheard of).

8.4.2 Estimating statistical power ($1-\beta$)

The usual focus of statistical power analysis is on sample size estimation. In some situations it is desirable to estimate the probability $1 - \beta$ for a given sample size before any data are collected. This is an *a priori* power calculation, and is handy if the maximum sample size is restricted (e.g., by cost). The same calculations can be performed after the study has been run. The use of statistical power calculations in the latter case – sometimes known as retrospective or *post hoc* power – is dangerous and should generally be avoided (or at least approached with great care).

For *a priori* power, information about the magnitude of the effect, its variability and the sample size defines the separation of the distribution for test statistics under H_0 and H_1 (see Figure 8.1). Provided you also know where the decision threshold lies – as determined by α – and provided you know the shape of the two distributions it is possible to calculate $1-\beta$. This is the shaded area in Figures 8.1 or 8.2. For an independent t test the underlying distributions of the means are presumed normal and therefore the test statistic has a noncentral t distribution. The equations used to arrive at a sample size estimate therefore also work for statistical power. The difference is that, for the former, $1-\beta$ is considered known and n unknown, while n is known and $1-\beta$ unknown for the latter. Once again, the major difficulty is to find sensible estimates of the magnitude and variability of the effect. Best practice is to establish these in a pilot study (which may be impractical if n is restricted) or to use values of theoretical or practical importance.

Example 8.3 A tacit assumption in Example 8.2 was that there was no restriction on n. What if this was not true? This could happen if recruitment was limited to a single hospital or outpatient clinic. Imagine the case of a clinic treating patients with relatively severe depression as measured by BDI ($M=30$, $SD=15$). In this clinic, a maximum of 50 patients are available to take part in the study. For the same difference of ten points on the BDI scale, a conservative estimate of δ is now $10/15 \approx 0.667$. It is conservative because if the new treatment works, the variance of the treated group should decrease (given that BDI is positively skewed). In fact, both groups may improve over time, as the usual control for this kind of study is 'treatment as usual' rather than no treatment at all.

Again the aim is to have a high probability of detecting a relative reduction of ten points in BDI. The statistical power, assuming normality and equal variances (with one-sided $\alpha=.05$ and $N=50$) depends on the split of participants between groups. The best allocation is $n=25$ per group and the estimate of statistical power to detect an effect of $\delta=.667$ is .751715. It would be foolhardy to think that these estimates – with many so many sources of uncertainty 'built-in' – are worth reporting to more than two decimal places of accuracy. The chance of detecting a ten-point reduction in BDI – should such an effect exist – is about 75%. Because sample size is limited it would probably be worth investing in other procedures to maximize statistical power (e.g., working hard to prevent dropout).

Software such as G*Power is also able to plot power curves with minimal effort (and similar plots can be constructed in R). A power curve plots the power of a test as a function of other factors (e.g., total sample size). Figure 8.5 shows power curves for statistical power versus sample size for the effect sizes of $\delta = 1$ and $\delta = .667$.

These curves show the characteristic nonlinearity of statistical power as a function of sample size; rising sharply at the start and flattening out as statistical power approaches one. The approach is steeper for large standardized effect sizes (and the flattening out more pronounced). With smaller standardized effect sizes (e.g., $\delta < .5$), very large sample sizes may be required to obtain adequate statistical power.

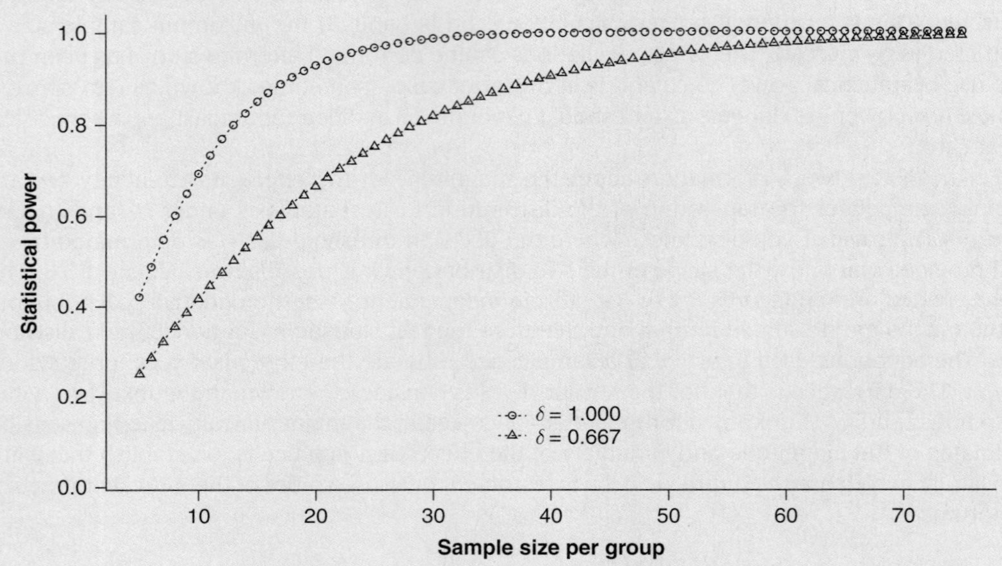

Figure 8.5 Statistical power as a function of *n* per group for effect sizes of $\delta = 1$ and $\delta = .667$

8.4.3 The dangers of *post hoc* power estimates

The main application of *a priori* power estimates is to identify when a study is likely to be overpowered or underpowered if *n* is limited. This can allow researchers to allocate resources to increasing statistical power by other means or (if a study is overpowered) to reallocate resources to other projects. Contrast this with retrospective or *post hoc* power calculations – particularly in the form of retrospective power calculations. These are argued to be dangerous (Baguley, 2004; Hoenig and Heisey, 2001; Lenth, 2001; Zumbo and Hubley, 1998). Understanding why they are dangerous has two facets.

First, the idea of estimating the statistical power of a test that has already been conducted is pure nonsense. Assuming the effect exists, the test is either statistically significant – in which case statistical power is one – or the test is non-significant and statistical power is zero. It is possible to rescue the concept of *post hoc* statistical power only by considering it as an estimate of an entirely different probability. For example, you might want to find out the probability of a future study detecting a specified effect (in which case it would be preferable to obtain *a priori* estimates of the sample size required to replicate). Alternatively, you might want to find out the statistical power of a study exactly like yours, had a different (but independent) sample been taken. This is an estimate of a counterfactual probability – the probability of an outcome had circumstances been other than they actually were. Most people find probabilistic reasoning rather hard, and counterfactual probabilistic reasoning even harder, so it is no surprise that counterfactual probabilities such as *post hoc* power are often misinterpreted.

Second, *post hoc* power calculations are at best useless and at worst highly misleading if inappropriate estimates of the magnitude and variability of the effect are used. A number of authors have highlighted the dangers of using observed sample statistics as estimates of population parameters in *post hoc* or retrospective power calculations (Baguley, 2004; Hoenig and Heisey, 2001; Lenth, 2001; Zumbo and Hubley, 1998). Although the observed sample statistics could be used to inform a power calculation for a future replication, they do not add value to the analysis of the observed data. The information they provide already contributes to formal inferences (including tests and CIs) that have been made.

Even though such calculations add no value to an analysis whatsoever, some computer software calculates statistical power in this (entirely wrong) way. SPSS provides such values, as an option for some analyses, under the misleading label 'observed power'. It has two possible uses: 1) as an estimate of *a priori* statistical power in the unlikely event of an identical replication with identical sample size; 2) as a warning not to report blindly any apparently useful statistic that your software provides. The observed power that SPSS provides is simply the statistical power obtained from entering the observed sample statistics (including n) into an *a priori* power calculation. To demonstrate its lack of value, think about what would happen if the original p value of an independent t test were exactly .05 (with $\alpha = .05$). Retrospective power (SPSS observed power) would be .50. For $p < .05$ retrospective power would be greater than .50. If $p > .05$, retrospective power would be less than .50. In fact, 'observed power' in this simple case is a monotonic function of the observed p value – rising as p falls and falling as p rises (Hoenig and Heisey, 2001). This might not seem too bad, but it can lead to serious errors in the interpretation of findings.

If you thought that the 'observed power' value was informative you might interpret any small p value as also being from a test with moderate or high statistical power. Statistically significant results are therefore treated as receiving more support than they warrant; not only would the finding be deemed statistically significant, but the test also has high statistical power. To make matters worse, any non-significant p value will tend to have low retrospective power. If you believed that the 'observed power' statistic is informative, you would tend to discount non-significant studies (on the basis that they never had a good chance of detecting the effect of interest). This is nonsense. Think about the relationship between retrospective power and observed effect size. As the observed effect size approaches zero the retrospective power decreases, but the evidence for H_0 increases. It would be absurd to argue that an observation that increases your confidence that there is no effect also simultaneously makes you less confident in that finding (Baguley, 2004).

This is why it is essential to carry out any *post hoc* power analysis with extreme care. In order to add information, *post hoc* estimates must use estimates of the magnitude and variability of an effect that are independent of the observed sample estimates. Only then is it reasonable to estimate the counterfactual probability of detecting an effect had a different sample been taken. How might this work? Well, one way is if the experiment was designed to replicate an earlier study that had found a particular effect (e.g., $r = .46$). It might then be reasonable to ask whether your study (the study that failed to find the effect) had sufficient power to detect that correlation. Even this approach has drawbacks. Leaving aside the inherent difficulty of counterfactual reasoning, it is quite easy to convince yourself (after the fact) that your study had sufficient power to detect an effect of apparent importance. You will find potential examples of this in any paper that claims to have had sufficient power to detect a 'medium' or 'large' effect (on Lenth's T-shirt scale), particularly if there is no attempt to justify this choice.

Example 8.4 Data investigated in Example OS1.1 (see Online Supplement 1) explored whether an experimental manipulation improved memory for the location of a target. Under a range of conditions Baguley *et al.* (2006) failed to find a statistically significant effect. One possible explanation is that each of the separate conditions that were tested was underpowered. The researchers estimated *post hoc* statistical power for a number of these tests. Crucially, they did not use the observed sample statistics to derive a power estimate (i.e., they did not calculate 'observed power'). Instead they looked at the statistical power to detect the size of effect predicted by a particular theoretical model of the task (an independence model).

For the best performing (intentional learning) conditions $\hat{\delta}$ was around 0.10, whereas the independence model predicted δ of around 0.87. The smallest sample size in Experiment 1 was 30 per group. Statistical power to detect an effect of $\delta = 0.87$ with one-sided α of .05 and n per group of 30 is .95. Therefore those conditions had a 95% chance of detecting the size of effect predicted by this model. For intentional learning conditions the experiments do not seem to be underpowered.

8.5 Accuracy in parameter estimation (AIPE)

For most research questions it is preferable to report and interpret an interval estimate – usually a CI – as opposed to a point estimate or significance test. One potential drawback of this strategy is that standard methods for sample size planning are not necessarily suitable. An alternative approach is to focus on accuracy in parameter estimation (AIPE). Advocates of AIPE propose planning for an accurate interval estimate, rather than merely to detect a non-zero effect (Kelley *et al.*, 2003; Maxwell *et al.*, 2008).

The accuracy of an interval estimate depends on two factors: the narrowness of the CI and whether it contains the true population value (Maxwell *et al.*, 2008). It is therefore important, where possible, to select methods for constructing CIs that are unbiased and precise. For instance, it is wise to avoid a symmetrical CI if the sampling distribution of the statistic is asymmetrical.

In AIPE the goal n is required to estimate a population parameter with a CI width of W. To accomplish this you first need to decide on a confidence level for the interval (e.g., $C = 95\%$), the desired width W and an estimate of the variability of the effect. This estimate of variability, like that for other forms of sample size planning, should not be corrected for factors such as measurement error. It should include all the sources of variability likely to be present in the new sample.

AIPE can be applied to simple differences, regression slopes and standardized effect sizes such as g, r or R^2 (Kelley, 2007a; Kelley *et al.*, 2003). The following sections illustrate the approach for the CI for a simple difference in means. An important advantage of AIPE for a simple difference in means is that an estimate of the magnitude of the effect is not required (Kelley *et al.*, 2003). This is convenient, because getting a sensible estimate of the magnitude of an effect is probably the main source of inaccuracy in sample size estimation. It also helps explain why the CI for a standardized mean difference need not be equivalent to the CI for the mean (and hence the usual NHST). The width of the interval for a standardized effect depends on an additional parameter (see Kelley and Rausch, 2006).

8.5.1 AIPE for the expected width of a CI for a simple mean difference

Kelley *et al.* (2003) present a simple method for determining the sample size to achieve an expected margin of error of $W/2$ for an unstandardized difference between independent means. The calculations assume a CI formed using the t distribution (and make the usual assumptions of normality and equality of variances). For the equal n case, the required sample size can be expressed in terms of n per group required to obtain a CI of width W:

$$n = 2\hat{\sigma}_U^2 \left(\frac{t_{2n-2,1-\alpha/2}}{W/2} \right)^2 \qquad \text{Equation 8.8}$$

The quantile $t_{2n-2,1-\alpha/2}$ is obtained from the central t distribution (an advantage of AIPE for the CI of a simple mean difference) rather than a noncentral distribution. Noncentral distributions are still required for AIPE with standardized effect sizes.

A serious obstacle to applying Equation 8.8 in practice is that n appears on both sides of the equation: both in the solution and in the degrees of freedom of the t statistic. This obstacle can be overcome through an iterative solution. This solution involves first selecting a starting value for the problematic term on the right-hand side of the equation (in this case a $t_{1-\alpha/2}$ statistic with df of $2n$-2). The initial estimate of n can then be then plugged back into the $t_{2n-2,1-\alpha/2}$ term to produce a more accurate estimate of n. This process is repeated (i.e., iterated) until the solution is identical to the previous estimate (to within some tolerable limit). Iteration for a sample size calculation can be stopped when the n per group (rounded up to the nearest integer) is identical for two successive iterations. Iteration using Equation 8.8 is nearly always very rapid (Kelley *et al.*, 2003).

Example 8.5 How large does n need to be to achieve a 95% CI for a difference with an expected width of ten? In Example 8.2 the sample size required to detect a difference in BDI of ten with 95% confidence was $n = 23$ per group (46 in total). That example used a one sample test. A two-sided test would require $n = 27$ per group (54 in total). The earlier estimates assumed $\sigma = 9.99$, and it makes sense to use the same estimate here.

The iterative calculation requires a starting value for t. Kelley *et al.* (2003) use the equivalent standard normal quantile of $z_{1-\alpha/2}$ (which does not require n to determine). For $\alpha = .05$ this value is

1.96. As the choice of starting value only influences the efficiency of the iterative procedure, other plausible (e.g., $t = 2$) values could also be used. With $t = 1.96$ as a starting value, the first step of the iterative solution is:

$$n_{step=1} = 2 \times (9.99)^2 \left(\frac{1.96}{10/2}\right)^2 \approx 30.67$$

Using the initial outcome of $n = 31$ suggests a t value of $t_{60,.975} = 2.0003$ (to four decimal places). This can be plugged into the equation for the second step:

$$n_{step=2} = 2 \times (9.99)^2 \left(\frac{2.0003}{10/2}\right)^2 \approx 31.95$$

Using $n = 32$ produces $t_{62,.975} = 1.9990$. As this is very similar to the old t value, iteration is nearly complete. The third iteration is:

$$n_{step=3} = 2 \times (9.99)^2 \left(\frac{1.9990}{10/2}\right)^2 \approx 31.90$$

Iteration now stops, as the last two steps both generated values of $n = 32$ per group (after rounding up). The final estimate is a total sample size of $N = 64$ to obtain a 95% CI with expected width of ten.

8.5.2 Degree of certainty in the width of a CI

For Equation 8.8 good approximations exist and an iterative solution could be avoided altogether. The method illustrated above plans for an expected with of W (or margin of error $W/2$). The observed width in a sample (w) could be narrower or wider than this. Depending on the parameter being estimated, you'd expect w to be wider than W in perhaps 50% of all samples (assuming that the estimate of σ_U was accurate). This degree of uncertainty is probably unsatisfactory for sample size planning.

To increase the probability that $w \leq W$ it is possible to modify Equation 8.8 to express the *degree of certainty* (*assurance*) that $w \leq W$ (Kelley *et al.*, 2003). The degree of certainty is denoted by the probability $1 - \gamma$.[9] Incorporating degree of certainty into the equation gives:

$$n = 2\hat{\sigma}_U^2 \left(\frac{t_{2n-2,1-\alpha/2}}{W/2}\right)^2 \left(\frac{\chi^2_{2n-2,1-\gamma}}{2n-2}\right) \qquad \text{Equation 8.9}$$

The χ^2 term enters the equation as the distribution of the variance of w. This too is an iterative solution, and it is roughly equivalent to Equation 8.8 when $\gamma = .5$ (because $\chi^2_{2n-2,.5} \approx 2n - 2$). Although iteration is tedious to perform by hand, the equation is easy to automate and tends to converge rapidly. The R package MBESS incorporates degree of certainty into its AIPE sample size functions.

Example 8.6 The previous example suggests that n per group to obtain a 95% CI of width $W = 10$ is around 32 if $\sigma = 9.99$. The degree of certainty that $w \leq 10$ is somewhere around 50%. This corresponds to $1 - \gamma = .5$. To be reasonably sure that $w \leq 10$, it seems better to set certainty to $\gamma = .10$ (corresponding to a 90% chance of getting a CI as narrow as, or narrower than, ten).

For the first iteration we will arbitrarily set the starting value of the χ^2 term to one and the t term to two. The outcome is:

$$n_{step=1} = 2 \times (9.99)^2 \left(\frac{2}{10/2}\right)(1) \approx 31.93$$

Using $n = 32$ it is possible to generate quantiles from the t and χ^2 distributions for the next iteration. These inputs are $t_{62,.975} = 1.9990$ and $\chi^2_{62,.90} = 76.6302$ (to four decimal places) and the second iteration is:

$$n_{step=2} = 2 \times (9.99)^2 \left(\frac{1.9990}{10/2}\right)^2 \left(\frac{76.6302}{62}\right) \approx 39.43$$

The third iteration therefore uses $n = 40$. As $t_{78,.975} \approx 1.9908$ and $\chi^2_{78,.90} \approx 94.3735$ this gives n per group of:

$$n_{step=3} = 2 \times (9.99)^2 \left(\frac{1.9908}{10/2}\right)^2 \left(\frac{94.3735}{78}\right) \approx 38.29$$

Taking $n = 39$ generates $t_{76,.975} \approx 1.9917$ and $\chi^2_{76,.90} \approx 92.1662$. The fourth iteration is therefore:

$$n_{step=4} = 2 \times (9.99)^2 \left(\frac{1.9917}{10/2}\right)^2 \left(\frac{92.1662}{76}\right) \approx 38.41$$

Steps 3 and 4 both suggest $n = 39$ and therefore iteration can stop. To be 90% certain that a 95% CI of the difference in BDI scores has $w \leq 10$ you would need about 78 people in total.

Requiring this level of certainty only results in a relatively modest increase in N (from 64 to 78). The sensitivity of different parameters on w or γ can be explored using `MBESS` (e.g., $N = 88$ would provide 99% certainty of $w \leq 10$).

8.6 Estimating σ

The biggest challenge to finding accurate sample size or power estimates is typically that the true magnitude of the effect is unknown. If a researcher already had a good estimate he or she probably wouldn't be doing the research in the first place. Even so, estimating the variability of the effect (e.g., in the form of σ_U) is important too. In addition, while you don't always need the magnitude of the effect (e.g., in AIPE for simple mean differences), an estimate of σ_U is always required.

Locating a potential estimate of σ_U is less challenging than locating an estimate of the magnitude of the effect. Previous studies may have looked at different predictors, but often use similar participants, measures and study designs. It is possible to use appropriate estimates from other studies to estimate σ_U for a new study. An obvious starting point is to find $\hat{\sigma}$ for comparable conditions of previous studies as estimates of σ_U. If the predictors (or independent variables) in prior studies don't seem to influence variability, then $\hat{\sigma}_{pooled}$ or $\sqrt{MS_{error}}$ over two or more conditions or studies can be used. Pooling can be done via an unweighted average of the variances (see Key Concept 3.3) or a weighted average similar that used in meta-analysis. Pooled or weighted averages allow a researcher to estimate σ_U more precisely (by increasing the aggregate sample size). Weighting allows estimates from large studies to be more influential in estimating σ_U.

If the estimate of σ_U comes from a single sample with small n, an additional problem arises. The sampling distribution of a variance has a scaled χ^2 distribution. The sampling distribution of σ_U is therefore highly positively skewed when n is small. The degree of skew reduces as n increases (e.g., see Figure 2.12), but is a serious concern because many researchers use pilot studies with very small n to estimate σ_U. Vickers (2003) looked at published research that reported sample size estimates based on pilot data (or other small n samples). Many people's intuition is that overestimates of statistical power should be as common as underestimates. This is not what Vickers found. The published studies were, in effect, drawing from the left tail of a positively skewed distribution and so most samples underestimated σ_U (and hence overestimated statistical power).

It is possible to remove the bias from estimates of σ_U prior to a power analysis. For a sample of $n = 30$ from a standard normal distribution the lower bound of a two-sided 90% CI is approximately .78.[10] Only $(100 - 90)/2 = 5\%$ of samples should σ_U be smaller than .78 (Browne, 1995). Only the lower bound matters here because the goal is to correct for the degree of the likely underestimate of σ_U (and in a 90% CI half of the 10% tail probability is at the lower end). This implies that the ratio $1/0.78 \approx 1.28$ is a potential correction factor (because $\sigma = 1$ for the z distribution). If a pilot study has $n = 30$ you'd expect σ_U to be less than $1.28\hat{\sigma}$ about 95% of the time. Vickers (2003) provides correction factors for different percentages and different sample sizes. Table 8.1 provides correction factors for n in the range of ten to 20, and for percentage certainty ranging from 70% to 95% (for a wider range of values see Vickers, 2003, Table 3).

While small sample sizes tend to underestimate σ_U (and hence overestimate standardized effect size), using a correction factor to avoid underestimates can lead to overpowered studies.

Table 8.1 Approximate correction factors for σ as a function of n and required degree of certainty

	Percentage certainty that $\hat{\sigma} \leq \sigma_U$					
n	**70%**	**75%**	**80%**	**85%**	**90%**	**95%**
10	1.187	1.235	1.293	1.367	1.469	1.643
11	1.173	1.219	1.272	1.340	1.433	1.593
12	1.163	1.205	1.256	1.318	1.406	1.552
13	1.152	1.192	1.240	1.299	1.380	1.517
14	1.145	1.183	1.228	1.285	1.360	1.487
15	1.137	1.173	1.215	1.268	1.340	1.458
16	1.131	1.165	1.206	1.257	1.324	1.436
17	1.126	1.159	1.198	1.246	1.312	1.419
18	1.121	1.153	1.190	1.237	1.299	1.400
19	1.116	1.147	1.183	1.227	1.287	1.384
20	1.113	1.142	1.177	1.220	1.278	1.370

Evidence suggests that research is more likely to be underpowered than overpowered (see Maxwell, 2004). However, under certain circumstances, overpowered studies may be undesirable (e.g., if Type I errors are more costly than Type II errors or if exposing people to an intervention or treatment is very risky). Therefore, try to obtain estimates of σ from large samples (e.g., by pooling estimates from similar studies) and perhaps use a correction factor if underpowered studies are considered more risky or harmful than overpowered ones.

Example 8.7 A pilot study with $n = 14$ has $\hat{\sigma} = 22$. To be 85% certain that the sample size uses an estimate that is at least as large as σ_U, the appropriate correction factor is approximately 1.285. Sample size calculations should therefore use an estimate of $\sigma_U = 22 \times 1.285 = 28.27$.

What if $n = 23$ in a pilot study, but you require 99% certainty of not underestimating σ_U? In this case you could work out a 98% CI for $\hat{\sigma}$ in the pilot and use the ratio of the lower bound to the point estimate as the correction factor (e.g., using the method in Example 4.11). An alternative approach is to simulate thousands of random samples of size $n = 23$ from a standard normal distribution and find the 2nd percentile (the quantile for which 2% of the distribution are lower and 98% higher). This was the method used to generate the values in Table 8.1 (and should be reasonably accurate when a large number of simulated samples are used). The correction factor for $n = 23$ and 98% certainty is found to be approximately 1.52 via such a simulation.

8.7 R code for Chapter 8

8.7.1 CIs for δ using noncentral distributions (Example 8.1)

The `MBESS` package has a number of functions for calculating CIs for standardized effect size using noncentral distributions. The `ci.smd()` function provides estimates for the population standardized mean difference (δ). The following code shows how to obtain a 95% CI for the difference in negative priming between the 52 young and 52 old participants from Example 8.1.

```
install.packages('MBESS')

library(MBESS)

ci.smd(smd=0.245, n.1=52, n.2=52)
```

The functions `ci.R()` and `ci.R2()` provide noncentral CIs for R and R^2 from a regression model (see `?ci.R` and `?ci.R2` for details of how they work).

8.7.2 Statistical power analysis (Examples 8.2, 8.3 and 8.4)

Statistical power analysis using Cohen's approach is implemented in the `pwr` package. Sample size for the t test uses the `pwr.t.test()` function. These commands replicate the results obtained in Examples 8.2 and 8.3.

```
install.packages('pwr')
library(pwr)

pwr.t.test(d=1, power=.95, type='two.sample',
  alternative='greater')

pwr.t.test(d=.667, power=.95, type='two.sample',
alternative='greater')

pwr.t.test(d=.87, n=30, type='two.sample',
alternative='greater')
```

The default is a two-sided test and $\alpha = .05$; thus all the following give power for a two-sided test when $\delta = .667$.

```
pwr.t.test(d=.667, power=.95, type='two.sample')

pwr.t.test(d=.667, power=.95, sig.level=.025,
type='two.sample', alternative='greater')

pwr.t.test(d=.667, power=.95, sig.level=.05,
type='two.sample', alternative='two.sided')
```

The same command is used to obtain n per group as is used to obtain power. As long as two out of the three parameters `d` (the standardized mean difference), `power` and `n` are entered, the third parameter is estimated. So, as in Example 8.3, statistical power when total $N = 50$ is given by:

```
pwr.t.test(d=.667, n=25, type='two.sample',
  alternative='greater')
```

A basic power curve is possible using plot and power functions. Figure 8.5 plots one-sided power for independent t for samples five through to 75 per group (i.e., $N = 10$ to 150) when $\delta = .667$ or $\delta = 1$:

```
sample.size <- 5:75
power.1 <- pwr.t.test(d=1, n=sample.size, type='two.sample',
  alternative='greater')$power
power.2 <- pwr.t.test(d=0.667, n=sample.size,
  type='two.sample', alternative='greater')$power

plot(sample.size, power.1, pch=NA, ylim=c(0, 1),
  ylab='Statistical power', xlab='Sample size per group', cex
  = 0.8)

grid()
points(sample.size, power.1, pch=1, cex=0.8)
points(sample.size, power.2, pch=2, cex=0.8)
lines(sample.size, power.1, lty=3, cex=0.8)
lines(sample.size, power.2, lty=3, cex=0.8)
```

```
legend(35, 0.2, legend = c(expression(paste(delta, '=
  1.000')), expression(paste(delta, '= 0.667'))), lty = 3,
  pch = c(1, 2), bty = 'n', cex = 0.9)
```

The `grid()` function is used here to draw grid lines to an empty plot, but before adding the points and lines (so that the grid lines are backgrounded). `grid()` has reasonable defaults if called with no arguments. Color, spacing and type of grid lines can be altered by adding appropriate arguments (see `?grid`).

8.7.3 Accuracy in parameter estimation (Example 8.5 and 8.6)

Kelley *et al.* (2003) describe R code for an iterative approximation to obtain an expected margin of error ($W/2$) for the CI of a simple mean difference with the *AIPE* approach. The following example adapts the code to work with the full width W rather than $W/2$ as input (with values corresponding to those in Example 8.5):

```
sigma <- 9.99
W <- 10
alpha <- 0.05
n <- 2 * ((qnorm(1 - alpha/2) * sigma)/(W/2))^2
tol <- 1e-07
dif <- tol + 1
while (dif > tol) {
    previous.n <- n
    n <- 2 * ((qt(1 - alpha/2, 2 * n - 2) * sigma)/(W/2))^2
    dif <- abs(n - previous.n)
}
Per.Group.n <- ceiling(n)
Per.Group.n
```

If you require more than 50% certainty that the width of the CI will be smaller than the target value you can again adapt the Kelley *et al.* code. The following provides the solution to Example 8.6 for 90% certainty expressed as $\gamma = .10$ (and corrects a typographical error in the original R code). Other input is picked up from the earlier example:

```
gamm <- 0.1
n <- 2 * ((qnorm(1 - alpha/2) * sigma)/(W/2))^2
tol <- 1e-07
dif <- tol + 1
while (dif > tol) {
    previous.n <- n
    n <- 2 * ((qt(1 - alpha/2, 2 * n - 2) * sigma)/(W/2))^2 *
        (qchisq(1 - gamm, 2 * n - 2)/(2 * n - 2))
    dif <- abs(n - previous.n)
}
```

```
Per.Group.Modified.n <- ceiling(n)
Per.Group.Modified.n
```

In both cases, iteration is governed by the `while` loop and stops when the difference between successive estimates is less than one plus tolerance. The AIPE approach for many other types of CI is implemented in the MBESS package (Kelley, 2007b). Although there is no AIPE function for simple mean differences, `ss.aipe.c()` will calculate n per group for any contrast (of which a difference in means is a special case). The previous examples can therefore be replicated using the following calls:

```
ss.aipe.c(error.variance=sigma^2, c.weights=c(1, -1), width=W)

ss.aipe.c(error.variance=sigma^2, c.weights=c(1, -1), width=W,
  assurance=.90)
```

This function takes error variance (the square of the *SD* estimate) and the required width of the interval as input. The contrast weights argument must also be entered, but will always be `c.weights=c(1, -1)` for a simple difference in means. Degree of certainty (assurance) and confidence level can be adjusted if required. The advantage of the contrast approach is that it is more versatile (see Chapter 15).

8.7.4 Correction factors for σ in small samples (Example 8.7)

One method for obtaining a correction factor is to use the tabulated values from Table 8.1 or from Vickers (2003). A crude, but versatile, way to obtain the correction factor for σ from small samples is to use a simulation. The example here uses 10,000 simulated samples and is sufficiently accurate for most purposes:

```
certainty <- .99
replication.n <- 10000
sample.n <- 23
sd.estimates <- replicate(replication.n, sd(rnorm(sample.n)))

mean(sd.estimates)
q.sd <- quantile(sd.estimates, probs = 1 - certainty)
q.sd
1/(q.sd)
```

Although an analytic solution exists, it is possible to get a good enough result from this 'brute force' simulation.

8.7.5 R packages

Champely, S. (2009). *pwr*: Basic Functions for Power Analysis. R package version 1.1.1.
Kelley, K., and Lai, K. (2011). *MBESS*: MBESS. R package version 3.2.1.

8.8 Notes on SPSS syntax for Chapter 8

8.8.1 Statistical power in SPSS

SPSS provides noncentral distribution functions and it is possible to set up macros to run power and AIPE calculations within SPSS. However, for most users it will be easier to use G*Power or R to obtain statistical power and sample size estimates.

8.9 Bibliography and further reading

Baguley, T. (2004) Understanding Statistical Power in the Context of Applied Research. *Applied Ergonomics*, 35, 73–80.

Faul, F., Erdfelder, E., Lang, A.-G., and Buchner, A. (2007) G*Power 3: A Flexible Statistical Power Analysis for the Social, Behavioral, and Biomedical Sciences. *Behavior Research Methods*, 39, 175–91.

Maxwell, S. E., Kelley, K., and Rausch, J. R. (2008) Sample Size Planning for Statistical Power and Accuracy in Parameter Estimation. *Annual Review of Psychology*, 59, 537–63.

9
Exploring messy data

Contents

9.1 Chapter overview

This chapter reviews methods for exploring messy data. Emphasis is on the use of descriptive statistics and graphical methods to assess departures from the assumptions of a statistical model. These methods provide a versatile set of tools for exploring data, assessing departures from statistical assumptions and checking the assumptions of a fitted model.

9.2 Statistical assumptions

A common feature of a statistical model is that it makes assumptions about the world being modeled. These assumptions take many forms, but are rarely met perfectly. This may not matter too much. The defining feature of a statistical model is that it tries to capture the uncertainty in our knowledge of the world. It would be unrealistic to suppose that this uncertainty is perfectly captured by these models. Nevertheless, there are times when the assumptions are so badly awry that a model will be wildly inaccurate. For this reason it is essential to think carefully about what the model assumes when planning research and when building or checking a statistical model.

Real world data are often pretty messy. They rarely fit neatly into the patterns you would like or expect to see. There are ways to limit the impact of this messiness, provided you can spot potential problems early enough. It is also possible to adapt many routine statistical procedures to cope with these problems. This includes the option of switching to less restrictive, more robust methods. Even so, a certain degree of pragmatism is in order: 'far better an approximate answer to the right question, which is often vague, than the exact answer to the wrong question, which can always be made precise' (Tukey, 1962, p.13). The usual goal is to get a statistical model good enough to answer a particular question rather than strive for an 'exact' answer that provides false certainty.

9.2.1 A pragmatic framework for thinking about statistical assumptions

Statistical assumptions vary from procedure to procedure. It is easy to get overwhelmed by the range of assumptions that need to be thought through when selecting a test or constructing a statistical model. This is exacerbated by the variety of ways in which statistical assumptions are presented. Rather than try and set out a single approach to dealing with assumptions, I'll take a more pragmatic approach. This involves adopting a heuristic distinction between *general assumptions* and *specific assumptions.* The main focus here will be on the specific assumptions required for least squares regression. Regression models are a convenient focus because they encompass a number of other statistical models, including procedures that many researchers don't think of as statistical models at all (e.g., *t* tests). Many of the methods that are useful in assessing violations of regression assumptions generalize to other statistical models.

To understand the distinction between general and specific assumptions, it helps to think about how research is planned and conducted. In an ideal world, a researcher plans a study with a more or less clear idea of the type of statistical procedure he or she wants to use. Once data are collected the analyst will decide on a small set of potential procedures that could be employed to model the data. This set could consist of procedures explicitly considered by a researcher, or it could be implicit (e.g., representing the set of statistical procedures common or well known in a field). General assumptions are those that are common to all (or nearly all) of the potential procedures under consideration. These include the assumption that samples are drawn at random from a population, that the predictors in regression models are measured without error (i.e., are reliable), and that the measures are valid. In every case a central, but typically implicit, assumption is that the statistical model is appropriate (see Section 10.2). Once the data have been collected, general assumptions are likely to be hard (perhaps impossible) to deal with. This does not mean they should be ignored, but it does mean that they tend to be most important when planning research or interpreting findings. They may have a peripheral role in the analysis itself.

Specific assumptions are those that are not common to a set of potential procedures under consideration. These are assumptions that are central to the choice of statistical procedure and need – where possible – to be checked during the analysis. The process of checking these assumptions is not primarily about determining whether they are violated, but about assessing the degree of violation.

For most analyses it is wise to assume the assumptions are, to some small degree, violated. What matters, is not whether assumptions are violated, but if the departure from the assumptions is sufficient to have a material impact on inference. Severe violations can partially or completely undermine the conclusions of an analysis (see Box 9.1). On the plus side, once a departure from a specific assumption (e.g., sampling residuals from a normal population of errors) has been identified, it may be possible to assess its impact and deal with it. The main methods for dealing with violations of specific assumptions are either to correct the analysis in some way or to switch to an alternate approach – one that avoids the assumption or lessens its impact.

In proposing a distinction between general and specific assumptions I am not attempting to place all assumptions firmly into one category or the other. That approach would be doomed to fail – not least because some assumptions straddle both categories. For instance, some violations of the independence assumption are readily assessed and dealt with, whereas others are not. In the former camp are situations where data are correlated because of the design of the study (e.g., paired or matched data). Many methods exist for dealing with correlated data, provided the correlated structure of the data is understood. If this information is unknown – because the dependency is hidden or because the structural factors that cause the lack of independence were not measured – then any analysis will be affected by the problem. The rationale for making the distinction is to help separate out what to focus on during the process of constructing and checking a statistical model. A corollary is that thinking about specific assumptions may make the repertoire of statistical procedures being considered more explicit. You can then identify gaps that require statistical methods outside your standard repertoire. Alternative models or approaches may make it possible to construct an adequate model where standard approaches fail. Switching to other models has costs – so it is important to try and assess the impact of any problems when thinking about switching to an alternative procedure. Does the benefit of switching pay off relative to the costs? Answering this question requires being able to assess the degree to which specific assumptions are violated and their likely consequences.

Box 9.1 What happens when statistical assumptions are violated?

If a statistical assumption is violated there are two main consequences. Departures from the assumption may introduce systematic bias into the procedure, or they may make the model of uncertainty unreliable.

Non-random sampling is a good example of how violating an assumption can introduce bias. Many statistical procedures assume that observations are sampled at random from the population of interest. If the sampling is non-random then, in effect, a population other than the one you are interested in has been sampled. The observed parameter estimates and inferences will be biased. Whether this matters depends on the degree of bias and the goals of the research. If the non-random sample is similar to the population of interest it may be that the degree of bias will be acceptable. In addition, a non-random sampling procedure doesn't mean that bias is inevitable.

The key to dealing with bias is, in principle, very simple. If bias can be measured, it can be corrected. The problem is that direct measurement of bias isn't always possible. A common solution is to use known differences between the sample and the population to correct the results (e.g., by weighting the estimates in some way). For instance, if the ratio of males to females is 50:50 in the population but 20:80 in a sample, this could be taken into account in your analysis. This can be done as part of the formal modeling process or informally (e.g., by adjusting your interpretation of the findings).

If a probability distribution assumed by a statistical model is incorrect, this will make the model of the uncertainty in the data unreliable (and may also bias results). This is true for regression, where sampling of residuals from a population of normal, independent errors with constant variance is typically assumed. The distribution of the test statistic depends on these properties. For a null hypothesis significance test (NHST) the impact of such violations is to make the p values approximate rather than exact. Some violations are sufficiently minor that the approximation will be acceptable. Other violations are so severe that the approximate p values will be worthless. The equivalent problem for confidence intervals (CIs) is that the coverage probability will be incorrect (e.g., a 95% CI might capture the true parameter at a much lower or higher rate). The nominal α (Type I) and β (Type II) error rates will therefore differ from the true α and β rates. This may have an adverse impact on the statistical power of any tests and the precision of interval estimates.

If the central limit theorem (CLT) applies, sufficiently large samples will ease concerns over the distribution of a test statistic and the accuracy of any inferences. The required sample sizes might, however, be very large indeed. Furthermore, the CLT will not always apply (and has no impact on bias).

9.2.2 Designing to avoid or manage messy data

Statistical assumptions are sometimes an afterthought in the research process – something to be checked and dealt with during an analysis (but not before). This is not good practice. General assumptions are rarely met perfectly. A good design will minimize or control for known sampling biases at the design stage.

A good starting point is to select measures with known – and where possible – high validity and reliability. It is also good to retain information about potential sources of biases (e.g., individual differences) and structural characteristics of the design. This may have cost or ethical implications, but it is worth building into data collection for most studies. Without this information many violations of assumptions cannot be detected, let alone remedied. Violations of independence are a prime example – one of the most basic forms of violation is *autocorrelation* – where successive measurements are correlated with each other. This is likely when measuring the same unit (e.g., person) several times in succession, but can also occur measuring different units using the same procedures or equipment (e.g., through measurement drift or calibration error). For example, one case involved a software bug that meant that the timing on successive trials within an experiment was not reset properly (causing response times to increment steadily over trials). This was spotted when piloting the experiment, but could easily have been missed if the order and identity of trials had not been retained.

For experimental and quasi-experimental research, randomization is probably the single most important tool for reducing bias. It also plays an important role in dealing with some violations of the independence assumption. Random selection from a population (on the rare occasions that it is possible to identify one) won't ensure a representative sample, but will eliminate systematic sampling bias. This point needs clarification: in any given sample the parameter estimates will not necessarily be accurate, but random selection ensures that the expected long-run value of an unbiased sample statistic is the population parameter. Random sampling is rarely possible in practice. It does not eliminate bias introduced by the structural characteristics of a study. If you sample people at random, and then ask a leading question (such as 'How strongly do you oppose gun control?') the hard work in obtaining an unbiased sample would be undone.

Randomization can also be used to eliminate structural biases in the design of an experiment or quasi-experiment. In an independent groups design it is used first and foremost to allocate people to groups. The beauty of randomization in this situation is that if there are any hidden dependences or correlations between participants on the variables of interest, randomization should neutralize them. How does this work? Think about a study investigating reading ability in a small school. The sample will include a number of siblings (and most likely several pairs of twins). The reading ability of siblings will be correlated. A child who is a skilled reader will tend, on average, to have siblings that are skilled readers. If you randomly assign each child to one of the two groups in the study, then the correlation between them is neutralized (for the purposes of the statistical analysis). For a given pair of children with correlated scores, half the time the correlation will lead to increased differences and half the time it will lead to decreased differences. These increases and decreases will, in the long run, cancel out.

If a study involves repeated measurements over time, random allocation to conditions isn't possible. The ideal approach here is to randomize the order of measurements. This will, for the purposes of the analysis, reduce or eliminate problems such as autocorrelation. A typical memory experiment involves presenting many different stimuli to participants (e.g., faces or words). Autocorrelation may arise through the predictability of stimuli, practice effects, fatigue effects and so forth. Randomly ordering stimuli will therefore reduce or eliminate these effects and prevent them biasing the results. Randomization of the order of presentation or testing is sometimes problematic. This tends to happen with small numbers of trials and small numbers of participants. Randomization works well over long sequences, but not for short bursts. In a paired (repeated measures) design with two conditions (A and B), randomly determining whether a participants receives the sequence A-B or B-A will probably work out well for 100 participants, but poorly for only ten.[1] The solution in the latter case is to counterbalance the order of testing. This is easy if there are only two conditions: half the participants are randomly assigned the order A-B and the remaining participants are assigned B-A. A *Latin square* can be used if there are more than two conditions (see Box 9.2).

A somewhat neglected consideration is the impact of violated assumptions on statistical power. Statistical power is influenced by violations of distributional assumptions. A common consequence is low statistical power, but statistical power can sometimes end up being spuriously high (i.e., nominal α is lower than true α).

Box 9.2 Counterbalancing and Latin squares

The aim of counterbalancing is to eliminate the influence of order on subsequent measurement. This is accomplished by distributing order effects evenly over sampling units (e.g., across participants). The canonical example is where participants experience two or more conditions in a repeated measures design, but it can also arise for other aspects of a design (e.g., to counterbalance the order in which stimuli are presented).

For convenience, assume that the order ($1^{st}, 2^{nd}, 3^{rd}, \ldots J^{th}$) of J experimental conditions ($C_1, C_2, C_3, \ldots C_J$) is being counterbalanced across n participants ($P_1, P_2, P_3 \ldots P_n$). A Latin square is a tool to plan the order of presentation of the J conditions in this situation. The simplest Latin square, for $J = 2$ and $n = 2$ is:

	1st	2nd
P_1	C_1	C_2
P_2	C_2	C_1

This illustrates the basic structure of a Latin square. Participant 1 receives condition C_1 followed by condition C_2, while Participant 2 receives C_2 followed by C_1. If the experiment had two conditions, but $n > 2$, the procedure is to re-use the Latin square for the additional pairs of participants (or equivalently add rows until there are n in total). Bear in mind that if n is not divisible by the number of rows in the square, order effects will not be fully counterbalanced; there will be unequal numbers of A-B and B-A orders. This is a general feature of any Latin square.

If $J > 2$ then the construction of a Latin square depends on whether J is odd or even. If $J = 4$ it is even, and then the obvious (but generally incorrect) Latin square to construct is:

	1st	2nd	3rd	4th
P_1	C_1	C_2	C_3	C_4
P_2	C_2	C_3	C_4	C_1
P_3	C_3	C_4	C_1	C_2
P_4	C_4	C_1	C_2	C_3

Although this appears fully counterbalanced, it is not. Every condition appears equally often in each position (1st to 4th), but the Latin square is unbalanced because pairs of conditions do not co-occur equally often forward and backwards (e.g., $C_1 - C_2$ occurs three times and $C_2 - C_1$ never occurs). If there are any dependencies between adjacent conditions – perhaps because some sequences are harder than others – then those order effects will not be eliminated by counterbalancing. The simplest solution, evident in the $J = 2$ case, is to make sure that every forward sequence is elsewhere balanced by the same sequence in reverse. This can be done by hand or by computer (and the computer option also makes it easy to randomly select different balanced Latin squares for each participant if desired).

Creating a balanced Latin square by hand can be done using a simple algorithm when J (the number of conditions) is even. Step (1) is to enter the first row according to the sequence:

$$C_1, C_2, C_J, C_3, C_{J-1}, C_4, C_{J-2}, C_5, C_{J-3}, C_6 \ldots$$

Only the first J values of the sequence are used (thus ensuring no values are duplicated). Step (2) is to complete the remaining rows of the square by incrementing condition numbers. Thus, if the row above has C_2 in the first position, the row below should have C_3 in the first position. If the condition index exceeds J, start again with C_1 (e.g., if $J = 6$ and the cell above contains C_6 then the cell below, if there is one, will contain C_1).

For $J = 4$ the first row in a Latin square constructed using this algorithm is:

	1st	2nd	3rd	4th
P_1	C_1	C_2	C_4	C_3

Filling down the remaining $J - 1$ rows gives:

P_2	C_2	C_3	C_1	C_4
P_3	C_3	C_4	C_2	C_1
P_4	C_4	C_1	C_3	C_2

An easy way to check that the sequences are balanced is to check whether forward sequences are balanced by reversed sequences elsewhere (e.g., row P_3 is P_1 in reverse).

What if J is odd? The problem with an odd number of rows is that no Latin square can ever fully control sequence effects (one or more rows will not be balanced by another row). The solution is to construct a second Latin square (or equivalently add J rows to the first square). In this second square, each of the J new rows reverses the sequence of one of the original J rows. For instance if $J = 5$ an unbalanced square is given by:

	1st	2nd	3rd	4th	5th
P_1	C_1	C_2	C_5	C_3	C_4
P_2	C_2	C_3	C_1	C_4	C_5
P_3	C_3	C_4	C_2	C_5	C_1
P_4	C_4	C_5	C_3	C_1	C_2
P_5	C_5	C_1	C_4	C_2	C_3

Adding five rows that reverse the earlier sequences gives:

	1st	2nd	3rd	4th	5th
P_6	C_4	C_3	C_5	C_2	C_1
P_7	C_5	C_4	C_1	C_3	C_2
P_8	C_1	C_5	C_2	C_4	C_3
P_9	C_2	C_1	C_3	C_5	C_4
P_{10}	C_3	C_2	C_4	C_1	C_5

The second square could also have been completed by reversing the initial row of the first square and incrementing the rows below.

Employing a Latin square involves following the specified sequence for each participant. Ideally participants would also be randomly allocated to the rows and the conditions randomly allocated to the condition labels. Fully counterbalancing also requires that *n* is a multiple of the number of unique rows (*J* for even or 2*J* for odd numbers of conditions).

Even a balanced Latin square does not necessarily control all potential order effects. It merely controls for the most obvious ones (the ones most likely to have large effects). Counterbalancing will also not allow all possible sequences to be sampled. Randomizing the order should therefore be preferred if the number of participants and conditions is large enough to avoid highly unbalanced outcomes.

9.3 Tools for detecting and assessing problems

For any given data set there are many possible tools for detecting and assessing problems. These tools fall into three main categories: descriptive statistics, graphical methods and significance tests. The first two categories are exploratory tools that can be employed prior to a formal analysis, as part of modeling checking, or to help interpret the results. Graphical methods, including many tools used for exploring data and checking a model, are also excellent ways to communicate findings. The third approach – significance testing – is generally best avoided, though it is important to understand why.

Two guiding principles for detecting and assessing violations of statistical assumptions are to avoid relying on a single method, and to be cautious about automatic or default methods (e.g., those provided by many statistics packages). All methods have blind spots, being better at detecting some violations of assumptions than others (or perhaps missing certain problematic patterns entirely). Automatic or default methods reported by computer software are problematic, not least because these methods are perceived as being the best or most appropriate methods available. Rather, they tend to be the most popular methods or the methods with the longest history of use. Even where the methods are among the best available (which is rare), they are not necessarily the correct method for every analysis. Using automatic methods also removes the collateral benefits of exploring data and model checking. Exploratory methods allow you to get to know your data, and help you to understand and communicate what is going on.

Of the many descriptive statistics and graphical methods employed for exploratory analysis of data, only a few are reviewed here. For descriptive statistics, the focus is on the measures widely reported in summaries of data. While descriptive statistics are valuable, graphical methods are typically better for examining both broad patterns and subtle features of a data set. Several common graphical methods also incorporate familiar summary statistics such as the mean or median. Two of the most popular types, box plots and histograms, are considered in detail. Both are useful for exploring or comparing samples, but have important limitations (though these can be overcome). A third type – the scatter or dot plot – is reviewed later in the chapter (in relation to correlation and regression).

9.3.1 Descriptive statistics

Descriptive statistics should be the starting point for most analyses. One of the advantages of many graphical methods is that they offer a way to display common descriptive statistics (as well as showing more subtle patterns in large data sets). Notwithstanding the advantages of graphical methods, numerical reports of descriptive statistics – particularly the minimum, maximum, sample size, arithmetic mean, median and standard deviation (*SD*) – are extremely useful. These need to be obtained separately for each sample or sub-sample used in later analyses (particularly in a large data set). For example, in both paired and independent groups designs it is important to look at some descriptive statistics separately for each sample (as well as for the whole data set).

The simplest descriptive statistics are particularly useful in checking the integrity of the data. Depending on the method of data entry, errors can arise through simple mistakes (e.g., coding, transcription or typing errors) or more serious problems (e.g., bugs in software). Errors can also occur when correct observations are accidentally added, deleted or overwritten. Checking that sample sizes in the data set match the data collected and subsequently analyzed requires overall N as well as n per sample. The minimum and maximum can help identify potential outliers and extreme values (see Box 9.3), and alert you to values that are impossibly small or large (e.g., coding or data entry errors). At this preliminary stage of analysis, minimum and maximum values are generally more useful than their difference (the range).

Box 9.3 Outliers, potential outliers and extreme values

There is no generally accepted definition of an outlier (Hayden, 2005). It may be helpful to group the definitions into three classes. The first class treats outliers as being values that are relatively extreme (e.g., low or high) given the context of the sample. The second class is for algorithmic definitions. These invoke a strict rule for determining whether an observation is an outlier. For instance, SPSS labels data points outside the whiskers of a box plot either as outliers (circles) or extreme values (asterisks). The cut-offs for these depend on the inter-quartile range (*IQR*). SPSS outliers are observations more than 1.5 times the *IQR*, while extreme values are three times the *IQR*. Another algorithmic method is to use absolute z scores of three or four as a cut-off (see Schiffler, 1988). The last class defines outliers as unusual or aberrant values. For example, some people consider an outlier to be an observation that is not from the population of interest, or that is generated by a process not relevant to the aims of the research. This third class is the most interesting, because it implies that an outlier need not be extreme or particularly rare (see Hayden, 2005).

Algorithmic methods for outlier detection are known to be problematic. As an exercise I generated box plots for 25 random samples ($n = 100$) from a normal distribution. Out the 25 plots, 15 had one or more points outside the whiskers. Thus, by any reasonable definition, the 1.5 *IQR* criterion labels points to outliers that are not extreme, aberrant or even particularly uncommon. Using z scores is also problematic. For large samples from a normal distribution, z scores of three or more are fairly common. They are not unexpected in moderately sized samples. The chance of a residual with a z score more extreme than $z = \pm 3$ is about 7.8% in a normal sample of size 30 and about 23.7% for a sample of size 100. It increases to about 93.3% for $n = 1000$. A z score more extreme than $z = \pm 4$ occurs at a rate of about 0.2% for $n = 30$, 0.6% for $n = 100$ and 6.1% for $n = 1000$. A z score can't be interpreted independently of the sample size. The distribution is also relevant. The value of $z = -2$ might be extreme for a positively skewed distribution, whereas $z = 4$ might not.

Using z scores is particularly problematic for small samples. Schiffler (1988) has shown that the absolute value of the largest residual in a sample can't exceed $(n - 1)/\sqrt{n}$. For a sample size of 15 this value is about 3.6 and for a sample size of ten it is about 2.8. No sample with $n < 18$ can have a standardized residual as extreme as -4 or $+4$, while no sample of $n < 11$ can have a standardized residual as extreme as -3 or $+3$. As these are maximums, real samples only rarely get close to these extremes. Adjusting standardized residuals for leverage (as is done by default in some software such as R) makes a little difference. Studentized residuals are better still.

All told, automatic algorithmic methods are best avoided (certainly if used as the sole method). It is suggested that observations detected by such methods be treated as *potential outliers*. Potential outliers may deserve further scrutiny, but could be perfectly reasonable members of the sample (and should not automatically be deleted or trimmed).

For simple two sample designs, comparing the numeric values of a pair of means or medians is sufficient to establish the direction of a difference. Graphical methods are therefore unable to reveal further information about the pattern of the effect, but can add information about the variability of an effect (e.g., in the form of a CI). However, CIs are limited as tools for exploratory analyses unless all comparisons involve similar sample sizes (because the width of the CI depends on both n and $\hat{\sigma}$).

Common descriptive statistics are of limited value in detecting and assessing violations of statistical assumptions. There is at least one important exception. For experimental designs comparing the means of two or more independent groups a typical assumption is *homogeneity of variance*. This is the assumption that the variances are equal in the populations from which the groups are sampled ($\sigma_1^2 = \sigma_2^2 = \ldots = \sigma_J^2$). This is a special case of the constant variance assumption in regression (which can be assessed via graphical methods). For a categorical predictor defining group membership, it is simple to summarize the variance in each group with a single number. This value could be the sample variance $\hat{\sigma}^2$, though it is more convenient to use $\hat{\sigma}$. If the homogeneity of variance assumption is met, the variances or *SD*s of the samples should be similar. Exactly how similar you'd expect them to be depends on sample size. Figure 9.1 is a histogram showing $\hat{\sigma}$ computed from 10,000 random, normal samples (with $\mu = 10$ and $\sigma = 2$). The left-hand panel plots the results for $n = 10$ and the right-hand panel plots results for $n = 100$.

Figure 9.1 illustrates the variability of $\hat{\sigma}$ in samples of different sizes. A useful rule of thumb is to consider the ratio of the smallest and largest sample $\hat{\sigma}$. If $\hat{\sigma}$ for one of the samples is

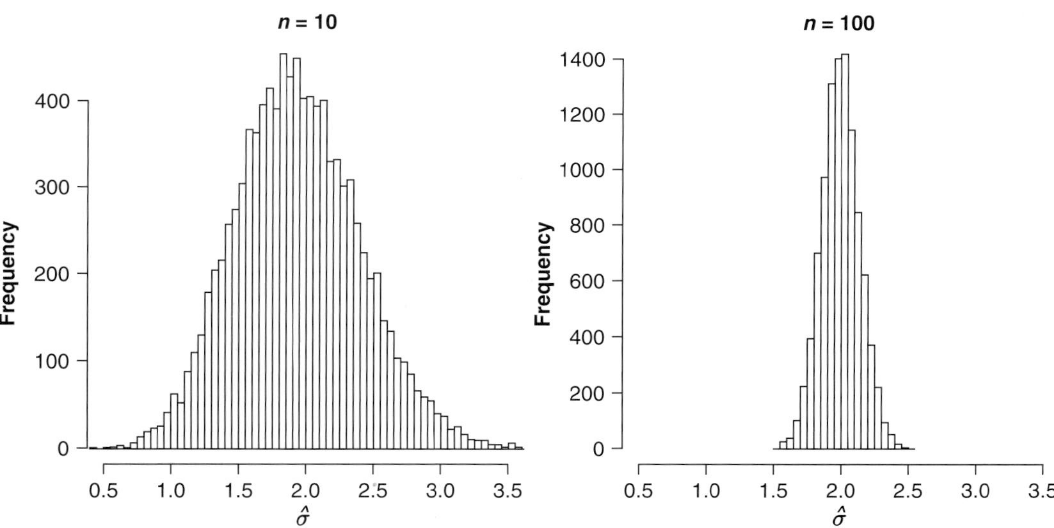

Figure 9.1 The influence of sample size ($n = 10$ or $n = 100$) on the sample standard deviation ($\hat{\sigma}$) for 10,000 simulated samples from a normal distribution (with $\mu = 10$ and $\sigma = 2$)

two or more times larger than for another, this is a strong hint that there are problems with the homogeneity of variance assumption (unless a very large number of groups are being compared or some of the samples are very small).

The 2:1 ratio for $\hat{\sigma}$ is easy to remember and, because $(2\hat{\sigma})^2 = 4\hat{\sigma}^2$, translates into a 4:1 rule for the variance. The rule works well in practice for the sample sizes common in independent group designs. Ratios close to 1:1 indicate that heterogeneity of variance is unlikely to have much impact on the analysis. As the ratio increases, the seriousness of any violation – and its likely impact on inference – increases.

Basic descriptive statistics are not very useful for assessing departures from a normal distribution (though see Section 2.4.1). However, under certain circumstances the relationship between $\hat{\mu}$ and $\hat{\sigma}$ can be revealing. If a variable is bounded at zero, then the absolute value of $\hat{\sigma}$ should be comfortably smaller than the absolute value of $\hat{\mu}$ for a normal or approximately normal distribution.[2] This is a useful property for any moderate or larger-sized sample (even allowing for sampling error). Under these circumstances $\hat{\sigma}$ close to or larger than $\hat{\mu}$ (e.g., $\hat{\mu} = 5$, $\hat{\sigma} = 4$) indicates a substantial departure from normality. The usual culprit is asymmetry (skew) in the sample distribution, although it could also be due to a small number of extreme values.[3]

Other descriptive statistics can be used to detect skew, but have limitations. The mean and median of a perfect normal distribution are identical in value, but samples from a normal distribution will almost always have a mean and median that are not identical. On the other hand, a big difference between the mean and median (relative to $\hat{\sigma}$) is usually a sign of skew (but see Key Concept 2.2). Skewness can also be estimated for a sample. For symmetrical distributions the expected sample skewness is zero, but the sample statistic is difficult to interpret on its own (because of sampling error). The same is true for kurtosis (see Key Concept 2.3). Although most specialist software calculates and reports excess kurtosis (relative to zero for a normal distribution), it can be difficult to detect and appreciate the impact of platykurtosis or leptokurtosis from this sample statistic alone.

Example 9.1 The BDI scale (see Example 8.2) has minimum zero and maximum 63. A sample with $\hat{\mu} = 10$ and $\hat{\sigma} = 6.88$ therefore suggests a substantial departure from a normal distribution. A likely cause is one or two extremely high scores. For instance, the following observations have $\hat{\mu} = 10$ and $\hat{\sigma} = 6.88$:

9 8 10 12 7 3 7 5 11 28

Without the extreme score of 28 the mean is not that different ($\hat{\mu} = 8$), but the $\hat{\sigma}$ statistic of 2.9 is more reasonable (because the impact of the extreme score on the variance depends on the square of the distance from the mean).

Having scores bounded at zero makes this pattern easy to spot, but it works with other limits. A clinical sample of BDI scores with $\hat{\mu} = 48$ and $\hat{\sigma} = 15.2$ might (at first glance) appear fine, but the mean of 48 is less than one standard deviation from the maximum of 63. Now the most likely culprits are one or two particularly low scores. Although the relationship between $\hat{\mu}$ and $\hat{\sigma}$ suggests the presence of skew or extreme scores, there is a better approach: plotting the raw data. Knowing how to detect skew from descriptive statistics is nevertheless useful. Plotting the raw data isn't an option if you don't have access to raw data (e.g., if you are trying to make sense of summary statistics in published work or in a newspaper report).

9.3.2 Histograms and density estimators

Histograms are bar plots of the frequencies of variable values. To facilitate plotting of continuous data, the frequencies are counted for fixed intervals of the variable (termed *bins*). Figure 9.1 is a good example and demonstrates some of the advantages and disadvantages of the technique. With large numbers of observations it is easy to get a good sense of the underlying distribution (e.g., Figure 9.1 plots 10,000 observations in each panel). However, the appearance of the histogram is nearly always quite lumpy – the degree of lumpiness depending on the width of the vertical bars. This is the *bin size* of the histogram. Most statistical software chooses the bin size automatically (based on sample characteristics). Although the default bin size is typically sensible, software sometimes makes poor choices. Too large a bin size will miss important features of the distribution, while too small a bin size will tend to leave gaps and make the plot look spiky. This may make a sample appear bimodal or multimodal when it is not. More generally, it may give a misleading idea of shape of the population distribution. Figure 9.2 shows an extreme example by plotting ten random observations sampled from a normal distribution with $\mu = 20$ and $\sigma = 4$. Panel (a) shows the histogram when the bin size is too large, panel (b) applies the R default bin size and (c) shows the plot when the bin size is too small.

While not perfect, histograms are excellent exploratory tools and there are several ways to enhance them. A common enhancement is to add a line showing an ideal distribution (e.g., the normal distribution) with μ and σ estimated from the sample. This is easiest to do if the histogram is scaled to have a total area of one (with the y-axis plotting probability density rather than frequency). A histogram plotted in this way is sometimes termed *a true histogram* and (apart from scale) is identical to one based on frequencies.

Figure 9.3 plots true histograms for nine random samples of size $n = 30$ (from a normal population with $\mu = 20$ and $\sigma = 4$). For each histogram, a normal curve with parameters estimated from the sample is added.

Overall, the histogram does a good job, but sampling error means that several of the samples look neither particularly normal nor symmetrical. This is characteristic of small and moderate sample sizes – even if the population is normal, they often appear non-normal. The normal curve in each panel is estimated from the sample. The departures would look even

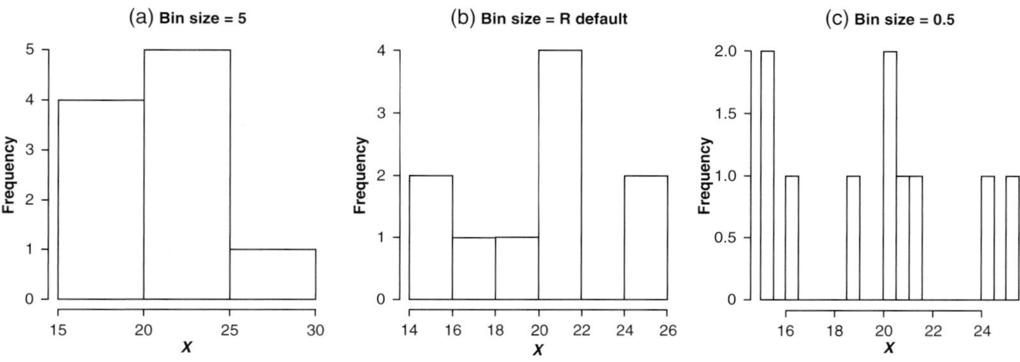

Figure 9.2 The influence of bin size on a histogram

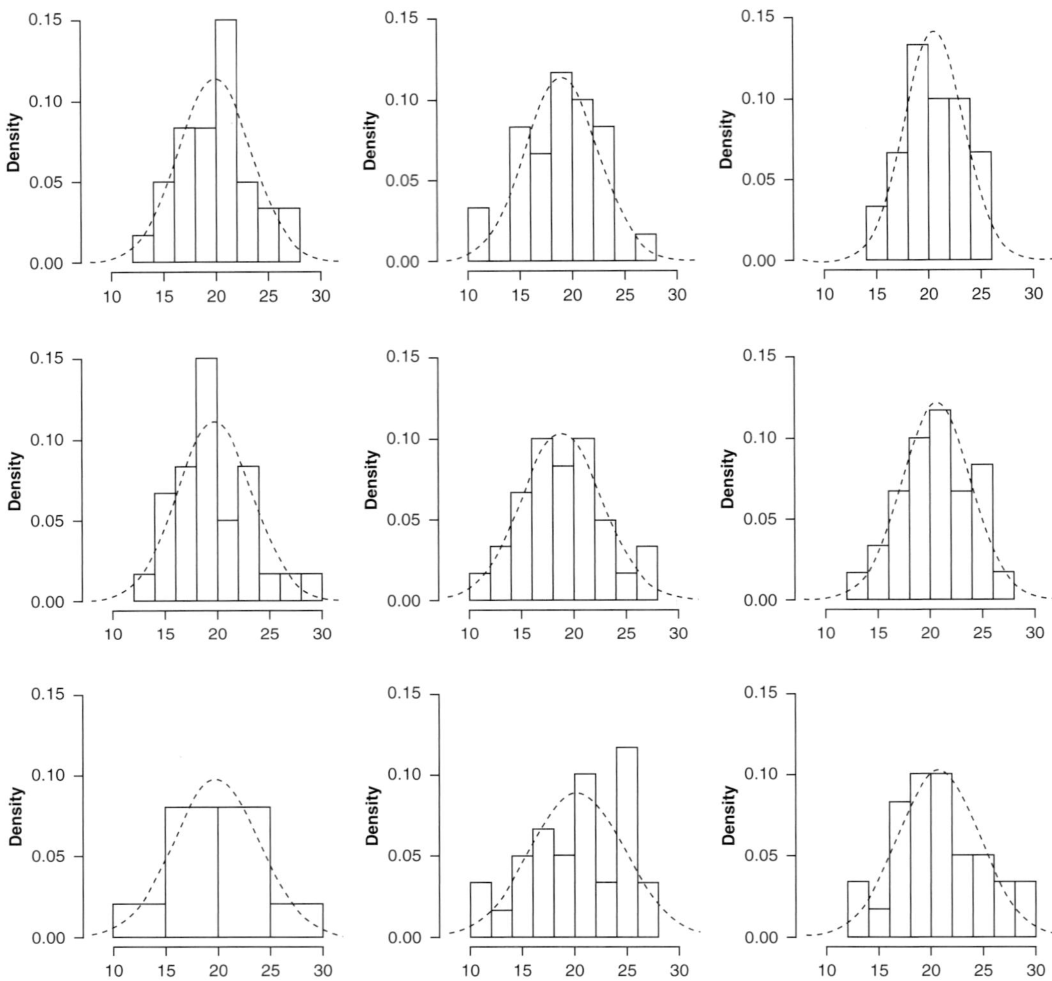

Figure 9.3 True histograms for nine random samples ($n = 30$) from the same normal population ($\mu = 20$ and $\sigma = 4$)

more striking if the true population distribution was added (though this distribution is usually unknown).

An alternative to a histogram that attempts to overcome the spikiness and lumpiness is a *kernel density estimator* (KDE).[4] A KDE estimates a smooth distribution by adding up several different probability distributions (kernels). Each data point is, in effect, replaced by a probability distribution. Summing these provides a continuous density function (see Wilcox, 2004). The choice of kernel varies, but a common selection is a normal distribution with a mean centered on the observation being replaced and σ determined (at least partly) by the dispersion in the sample.

In KDE the problem of bin size manifests itself as an issue of 'bandwidth'. Each kernel can have its probability distribution clustered tightly round the mean or 'smeared' widely over a wider range. Wilcox (*ibid.*) discusses alternative KDE methods for selecting kernels and bandwidth, but it is sufficient for present purposes to know that a KDE can provide a smooth estimate of a population distribution that complements simpler methods such as histograms. R has a built-in KDE function and alternatives are found in several other R packages. KDE works best for continuous data (where probability density as a concept makes most sense) but can be extended to deal with discrete data (where it is more usual to think of probability mass rather than density). Figure 9.4 displays histograms of random samples of $n = 30$ from either a normal distribution (upper panels) or a χ^2_5 distribution (lower panels).

Each of the left-hand panels includes a line showing a kernel density estimate of the population distribution, whereas the right-hand panels superimpose the true population distribution.

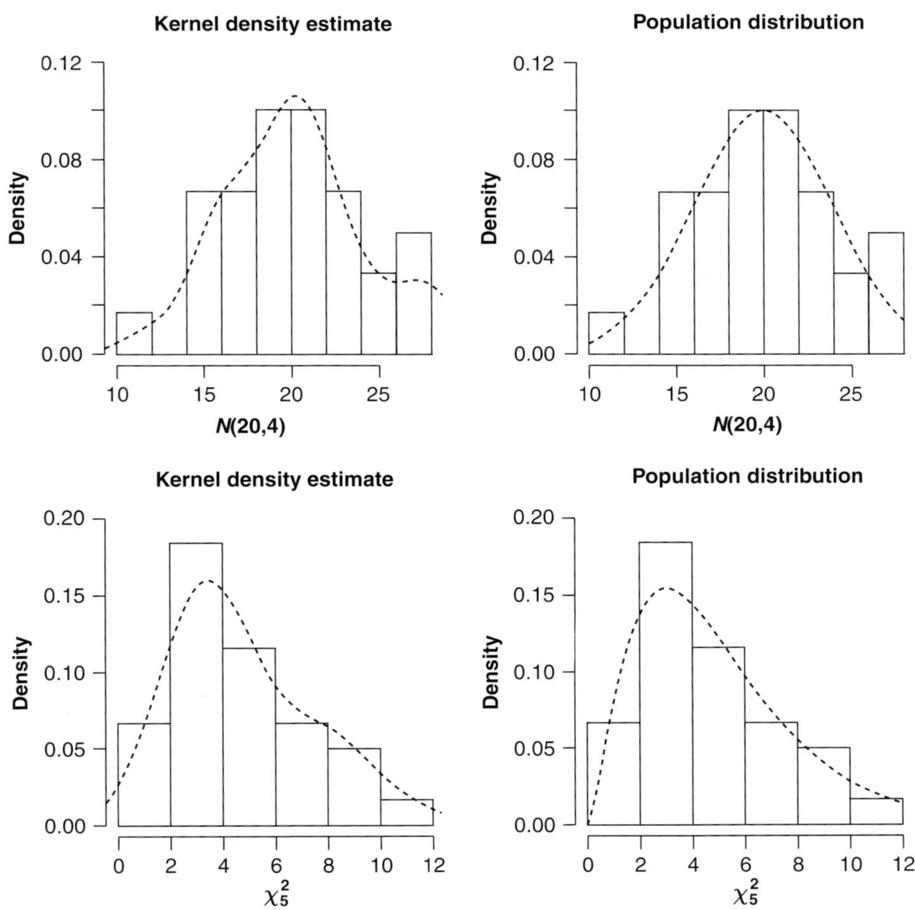

Figure 9.4 True histograms with lines plotting kernel density estimates or the population distribution for either a normal distribution (upper panels) or χ^2 distribution (lower panels)

These examples help explain the appeal of KDE. For samples from many common distributions – particularly continuous ones – the default software settings tend to produce estimates that capture some of the quirks of the sample while also hinting at characteristics of the true population.

9.3.3 Box plots

With histograms and kernel density estimates, the focus is on using the sample to understand the population distribution. Box plots can also be used to examine distributional assumptions, though their main application is as a quick way to check several features of a sample at once. Because most box plots include the median, *IQR* and range and extreme values (see Figure 1.2) they work best for detecting asymmetry and may help identify potential outliers or extreme scores.

The symmetry of a sample can be assessed by comparing the distance from the median to key features above and below it. In a symmetrical distribution, the median should split the *IQR* and the range in half; the tops and bottoms of the box and the whiskers should be equidistant from the median. If there is no skew, other features (such as potential outliers and extreme observations) are as likely to appear above the box or below the box. A quick check is to gauge the distance from the median to the furthest features above and below it. These distances indicate where the top and bottom half of the sample lie, and should be roughly equal in samples from a symmetrical distribution.

Skewed, asymmetric samples thus have characteristic features that are, with practice, easy to detect in a box plot. Figure 9.5 shows nine samples of $n = 30$ from a lognormal distribution with parameters $\mu = 2$ and $\sigma^2 = 0.75$ (and hence a mean of $e^{\mu+\sigma^2/2} \approx 10.75$). A lognormal distribution with these parameters is positively skewed, but how easy is it to detect this? In nearly every panel of Figure 9.5 there are features characteristic of skewed distributions, but also features characteristic of symmetrical distribution such as the normal distribution (e.g., whiskers of roughly equal length).

In every case, the smallest 50% of the observations are squashed into less than half the height of the plot. The largest 50% of the data points (from the median to largest value – indicated by either the upper whisker or the largest value beyond the whisker) are spread out much more widely than smallest values.

Contrast this with samples from a normal distribution. Box plots of three $N(10.75, 3)$ samples of size $n = 30$ are displayed in Figure 9.6. Of these, the sample in panel (c) produces a near perfect box plot in terms of symmetry, while panel (a) looks negatively skewed and (b) looks positively skewed. Points outside the whiskers are fairly common – even in samples from a perfect normal distribution. It is reasonable to treat them as potential outliers, but this does not necessarily imply that they are particularly extreme or unusual (or that they will distort the results of an analysis).

A tendency for points to be labeled as outliers just because they fall beyond the whiskers is one of the weaknesses of a box plot. Another weakness is that the plot only captures relatively crude features of a distribution. It can easily miss some striking patterns. For instance, box plots are rather poor at detecting bimodal and multimodal distributions. They also work rather poorly for small samples (e.g., n less than ten or 15).

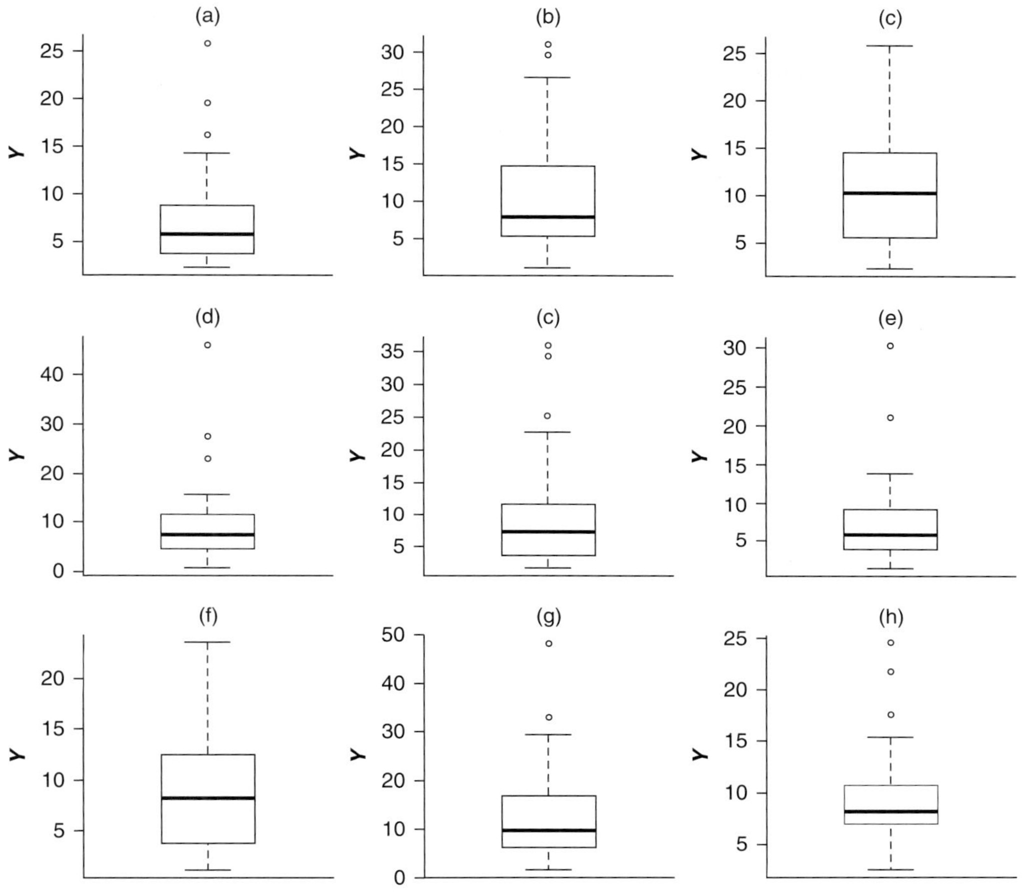

Figure 9.5 Box plots of samples from a (positively skewed) lognormal distribution

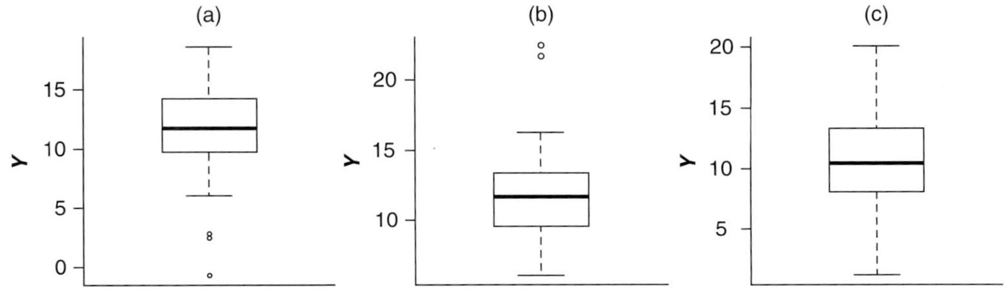

Figure 9.6 Box plots of random samples from a (symmetrical) normal distribution

Example 9.2 Hayden (2005) reports a rather unusual data set that provides an interesting test of exploratory methods. Subsequent examples will refer to this data set as the Hayden (2005) data. The sample consists of 43 observations measured in days ($M = 1865.7$, $SD = 915.5$).* For reasons that will become clear (and following Hayden's example), I will not mention the source of the data at this stage. A box plot of the observations is shown in Figure 9.7.

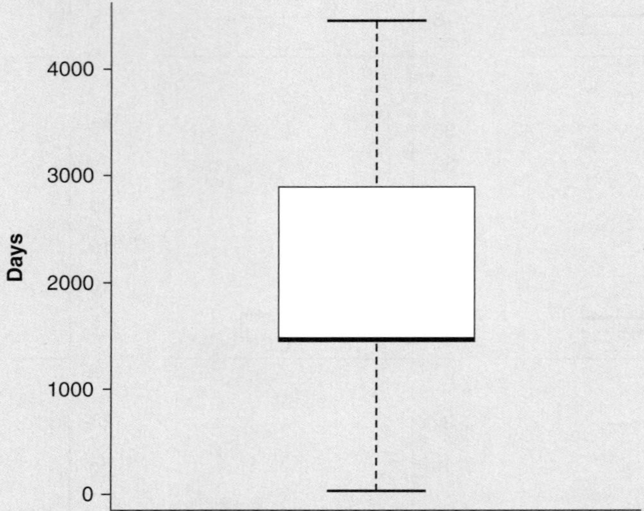

Figure 9.7 A basic box plot of the Hayden (2005) data

The only indication (from the box plot) that the sample distribution is not symmetrical and not even approximately normal is that the sample median is close to the bottom hinge of the box (the 25th centile). This distribution is bimodal – as can be shown by either the histogram or the kernel density estimate in Figure 9.8. The two modes lie roughly at 1500 and 3000 days. Hayden asserts that 44% of his original data set can be considered outliers by some definitions. This should bring home part of his message; the definition of outlier is somewhat slippery (see Box 9.3). None of the data points falling away from the modal peaks of 1460 to 1461 or 2921 to 2922 are flagged as potential outliers by the usual rules.

The central values – those in between the modes – are also, in a sense, outliers. They are the 'correct' or 'expected' outputs from the process that generated the data and any departures are aberrations of some kind.**

What is the process that could produce such an unusual distribution? The data are the days in office of the first 43 US presidents. This period is limited by convention (and later by constitutional amendment) to two terms. The two modes therefore represent presidents who completed one or two full terms. Further details are given in Hayden (2005), but the 'outliers' represent presidents who died or left office prematurely (and the one president who was elected to a fourth term). Thus Hayden seems justified in his position that periods of 1886 and 2027 days (although closer to the mean than any other values in the data set) are atypical – perhaps 'extreme' – observations.*** These data confirm that real world data can be rather messy. Neither ignoring the 'mess', nor throwing away data would be appropriate. Indeed, the 'outliers' here may be more interesting than the rest of the data. On the other hand, if you wanted to do something as mundane as predict the period

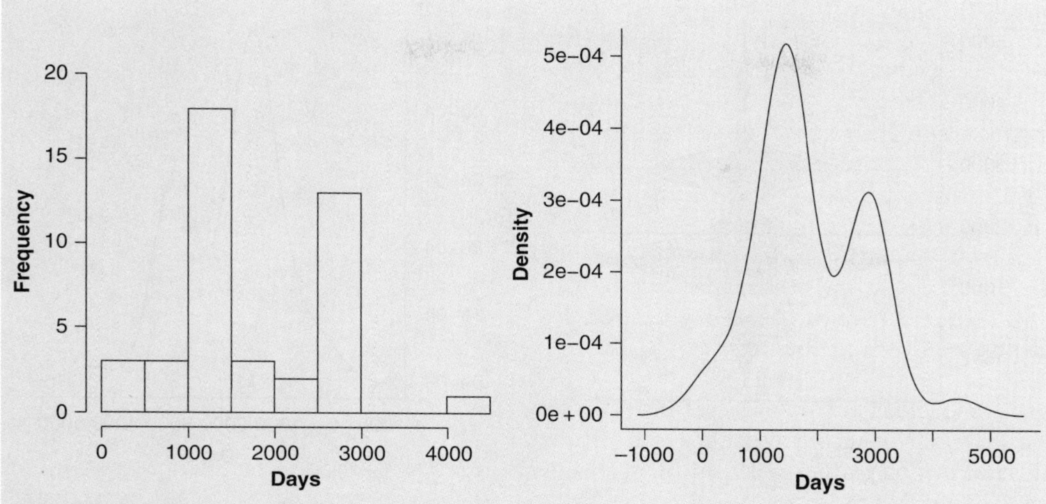

Figure 9.8 Histogram and kernel density estimate for the Hayden (2005) data

in office of the 44th president you might want to ignore the outliers and select the values 1461 or 2922 with a fair degree of confidence. The proper treatment of unusual or atypical values depends on the context of the data and what you are aiming to achieve.

* I have taken the liberty of updating the 43rd observation from 1110 to 2922.
** Hayden (2005) calls the aberrant central values *inliers*. It is preferable to avoid the term as it is sometimes applied to any non-extreme observation (i.e., any non-outlier).
*** The value of 2027 refers to Nixon (who resigned following the Watergate scandal) and 1886 to Johnson (who became president after Kennedy's assassination).

9.3.4 Enhanced box plots and density plots

Unusual data sets such as those presented by Hayden (2005) provide challenges for many exploratory methods. Example 9.2 shows how a box plot can be misleading – partly because the sample is bimodal and partly because the plot conceals interesting detail among the data. A histogram is better, but still lacks detail. The kernel density estimate picks up more detail than the histogram, but Figure 9.8 also shows one of the weaknesses of KDE. Depending somewhat on the choice of kernel, the estimated distribution will often spread out to include impossible values (in this case negative numbers).

Is it possible to design an exploratory tool that overcomes some of these weaknesses? A number of alternatives to box plots have been proposed, including several that combine a box plot with density estimation. A well-known example of this form of plot is a *violin plot* (Hintze and Nelson, 1998), though we will illustrate the approach with the *bean plot* (Kampstra, 2008). The bean plot combines a KDE with a one-dimensional scatter plot (sometimes known as a strip chart). This works by showing individual observations as lines within a 'bean' created by mirroring a KDE curve. Longer lines are used for multiple observations – making it easy to spot duplicate values. The resulting plot combines a density estimate and individual observations in

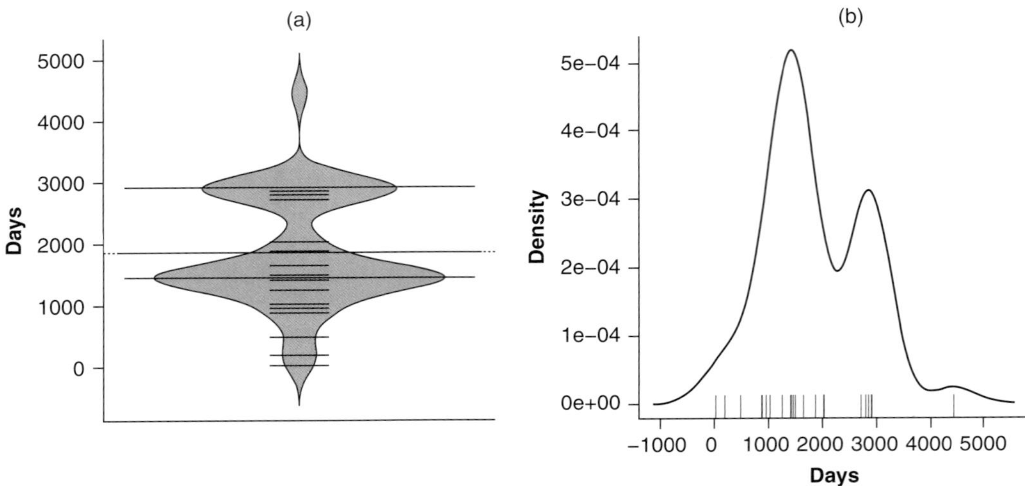

Figure 9.9 The Hayden (2005) data displayed (a) as a bean plot, and (b) as a density estimate with a rug

a format similar to that of a box plot. Unlike a box plot, the mean rather than median is depicted by default (as a thick black line). Figure 9.9a shows a bean plot of the Hayden (2005) data.

With the bean plot the bimodality is immediately obvious. The outline of the bean is a mirrored version of the kernel density estimate in Figure 9.8. The bean still extends into impossible territory – but this is less of a problem, because the individual observations (all greater than zero) can also be seen. The plot has some drawbacks. Its visually complex, densely packed lines can blend to together for some samples. Alternatives with less visual clutter include one-dimensional scatter plots (strip charts) or even a stem and leaf plot (see Example 1.11). A useful compromise between the visual complexity of a bean or violin plot and a simple box plot or density plot is to add a one-dimensional plot to the display as a 'rug'. Figure 9.9b shows a density plot of the Hayden (2005) with a rug added as vertical lines along the *x*-axis. Although not as detailed as the bean plot, it is less cluttered and gives a clear sense of the shape of the distribution. Displaying the raw data reveals the gaps in the distribution and the observed range (from near zero to around 4500).

For exploratory analyses it is wise to look at the data in several ways. Simple plots such as the histogram and box plot are useful starting points, though enhanced plots such as violin plots or bean plots are more powerful. A compromise is to add a rug to a basic plot such as a box plot or, better still, to a density estimate.

9.3.5 The dangers of using significance tests to check statistical assumptions

A popular way to check whether an assumption is violated is to use a significance test. There are serious problems with this approach. Before describing these problems it necessary to understand a little about how such significance tests work. Consider a test for heterogeneity of variance. The homogeneity of variance assumption is that the variances of two or more samples are identical in the population being sampled. Many statistical procedures that compare two or more independent groups make this assumption. In a two group design, a significance test of the homogeneity of variance assumption has the null hypothesis H_0: $\sigma_1^2 = \sigma_2^2$ and the alternative hypothesis H_1: $\sigma_1^2 \neq \sigma_2^2$. Rejecting H_0 corresponds to a decision to accept H_1 (and indicates that a violation of the assumption is detected). This is perhaps the first indication that all is not well with such tests. NHSTs are least effective in situations where a researcher is interested in the strength of evidence for H_0.

The most obvious way to test the equality of two population variances involves constructing a variance ratio. Each variance has a scaled χ^2 distribution and, on the assumption that $\sigma_1^2 = \sigma_2^2$, the scaling factor cancels out (see Section 2.4.5). For samples from independent, normal populations the variance ratio will have an F distribution. This raises the second problem with such tests. In order to test one assumption you first have to assess a different one – the assumption of normality. This is both a practical issue and a conceptual one. Of the two, the conceptual issue is probably the most troublesome. If it is appropriate to check the assumption of test 1 by applying test 2, should you not start by testing the assumptions of the test 2 test with a third test? This suggests the absurd possibility of testing the assumptions of the test 3, 4, 5 and so on *ad infinitum*.

In many cases (e.g., independent t), the properties of the initial test are well known. In contrast, tests of assumptions tend to be less well understood. Several widely used tests of statistical assumptions perform poorly when their assumptions are violated. For instance, the F test of equality of variances is very sensitive to departures from normality (Hays, 1973; Nordstokke and Zumbo, 2007). Many tests of distributional properties involve calculating sample statistics (e.g., skewness or kurtosis) and their standard errors. The standard formulation of these tests assumes that the ratio of the statistic to its standard error (*SE*) follows a z or t distribution. Thus a normal distribution is assumed, although it is unlikely to be met (except asymptotically). The problem of testing assumptions of relatively robust tests with tests of poor or unknown robustness was aptly summed up by Box (1953).[5] His pithy summary of the problem was made in the context of testing equality of variances, but is relevant to other scenarios: 'To make the preliminary test on variances is rather like putting to sea in a rowing boat to find out whether conditions are sufficiently calm for an ocean liner to leave port!' (*ibid*., p. 333).

Finding a robust test does not necessarily solve the problem. The usual alternative for the F test is a form of *Levene's test for equality of variances*. Nordstokke and Zumbo (2007) point out that Levene's test is really a strategy for comparing the dispersion of two or more samples, rather than a specific procedure. It can take several forms. The simplest versions involve only two groups. Levene's proposal was to obtain the absolute deviations of each sample from an average value and to compare the difference in absolute deviations between groups. This could be done with an independent t test (or more commonly with an F test that generalizes to multiple groups). This test is implemented by default in many statistics packages (e.g., SPSS) in the form of a test of differences in absolute deviations from the sample means. It is fairly robust when the distributions are symmetrical, but far from robust when they are not (*ibid*.). Replacing absolute deviations from the mean with the absolute deviations from the median makes the test robust against asymmetry. Robust tests of distributional properties such as skewness or kurtosis can be obtained via bootstrapping (DiCiccio and Efron, 1996).

A further consideration is statistical power. Even if the test of assumptions is itself robust, it will be next to useless whenever the statistical power of the test is too low or too high. Low power means you will often fail to detect serious problems that are present. Low power is the norm for many studies because power to detect distributional problems will almost always be lower than for differences in central tendency (e.g., means). If statistical power is too high, you will reject H_0 even for trivial violations (ones too small to have a material impact on inference).

This leads to the final problem with using NHSTs to test statistical assumptions. The NHST is asking completely the wrong question. Only in a few special cases is it reasonable to believe that a statistical assumption is true. It is not the presence of a violation, but the degree of departure from the assumption (i.e., effect size) that matters. There is presumably an ideal sample size for each test that provides exactly the right statistical power to detect a serious problem. But a study optimized to detect an effect of a particular size (or with a certain degree of precision) is unlikely to be optimal for testing homogeneity of variance or normality. Statistical power is also problematic for another reason. If the choice of test procedure is conditional on a test of assumptions, this can inflate Type I and Type II error rates on the subsequent test (Zimmerman, 2004; Hayes and Cai, 2007; Schucany and Ng, 2006; Rochon and Kieser, 2011).

If you wish to employ an inferential method, it is better to obtain a CI for a relevant descriptive statistic than rely on a significance test. This should give an idea of the degree of violation. If severe violations of assumptions look likely you can use simulation methods to determine the impact on the intended analysis, or switch to an alternative procedure that makes less restrictive assumptions.

Example 9.3 Example 4.4 compared differences in accuracy between groups for the comprehension data using independent t. The *SD*s of the two groups are 24.0 and 8.5. As $\hat{\sigma}$ for the low study group is 2.8 times as large as for the high study group, this violates the rule of thumb that the ratio of largest to smallest $\hat{\sigma}$ should not exceed 2:1.

SPSS automatically provides Levene's test for equality of variances (based on absolute deviations from the sample means) if an independent t test is run. The F ratio and p value for the Levene test are reported, but it is not immediately clear what form of test is applied. In particular, it is not clear whether the appropriate error df for the test is that for the Satterthwaite-Welch correction or equal variances assumed test. Some digging suggests SPSS uses $N - 2 = 54$ (from the uncorrected test). Thus the SPSS version of Levene's could be reported as:

$$F(1,54) = 19.11, p < .005$$

This test is statistically significant (for $\sigma = .05$) and therefore the null hypothesis of equal variance (H_0: $\sigma_1^2 = \sigma_2^2$) is rejected.

It is very easy to calculate the equivalent Levene test based on the medians (e.g., using R) and this provides the output:

$$F(1,54) = 14.19, p < .005$$

This is also a clear rejection of H_0. Both tests have detected a difference in the dispersion of the two groups. The distribution of the comprehension data is far from symmetrical (being negatively skewed) so it is not surprising that, although the median and mean versions are both statistically significant, the test statistics are somewhat different. Neither test provides direct information about the degree to which the assumption is violated. Large samples or a very consistent pattern of differences in dispersion could both produce statistically significant Levene tests (even if the samples had similar but non-identical variances). The relevant information, sufficient to suggest heterogeneity of variance on its own, is the 2.8:1 ratio for the sample standard deviations.

9.4 Model checking in regression

9.4.1 Normal probability plots

Discussion so far has concentrated on graphical methods for general exploration of a data set. If the aim is to compare the sample distribution to a theoretical distribution then a *quantile-quantile* (Q-Q) plot can be employed. If the theoretical distribution in question is the normal distribution, the Q-Q plot is termed a *normal probability plot*.

In a Q-Q plot the observations are plotted in order (e.g., lowest to highest) and the quantiles of the sample distribution are compared to their expected value from a theoretical distribution. In a normal probability plot the sample quantiles are on one axis and the expected values from a normal distribution are on the other.

What makes these plots excellent for comparing two distributions is the pattern you'd expect to see when the sample distribution is a perfect match to the theoretical distribution. Under these circumstances, the observed quantile and expected quantile would be the same for each x-y pair being plotted. Thus the observations should form a straight line (described by the function $Y = X$). This line is commonly included in many normal probability plots. A major advantage of this kind of plot is that any departure from the theoretical distribution is easy to spot as a deviation from linearity. In fact, you don't need to use the observed quantiles to see this departure from linearity at all – you could plot data or residuals on the original scale against the expected quantiles (though a perfect fit will then be characterized by a different straight line).

For ease of interpretation it is common to plot the standardized residuals against the expected values from a standard normal distribution. A more accurate approach for least squares regression models is to plot studentized residuals versus a t distribution. As both the observed data and the expected values in this form of plot are z or t statistics, extreme points can be identified in terms of their observed score relative to its theoretical expectation. Normal probability plots are thus able to detect potential outliers and extreme values. Regression models usually assume that residuals (not raw data) are sampled from a normal distribution. This means it is always safest to plot the residuals (standardized, studentized or unstandardized) rather than raw data in the form of the outcome Y. Only for very simple regression models are the distributions of residuals $(y_i - \hat{y}_i)$ identical to that of the outcome (y_i).[6]

Figure 9.10 shows normal probability plots for simulated random samples from three different populations: one normal, one leptokurtotic (a t distribution with 5 df), and one positively skewed (a lognormal distribution). Recall that a leptokurtotic distribution has less weight in the 'shoulders' and more weight in the tails. Such distributions are particularly troublesome to work with. The samples are arranged in order of increasing size ($n = 30$, $n = 100$, or $n = 1000$) from left to right. Departures from a normal distribution tend to show up as marked curvature on the plots. The patterns are very easy to detect with large sample sizes, and can also be spotted in smaller samples – depending on the degree of the departure from linearity (i.e., from normal).

Skew is usually the easiest pattern to detect. It shows up as a curve away from the 'perfect normal' diagonal line. In positively skewed samples the quantiles are larger than expected from the theoretical distribution. This shows up as upward curvature for large values (i.e., in the top right of the plot) when – as here – the theoretical values are plotted on the x-axis. Plotted like this, negative skew shows up as downward curvature for the smaller quantiles (i.e., in the bottom left of the plot). Kurtosis also shows up as curvature, but produces a sigmoidal

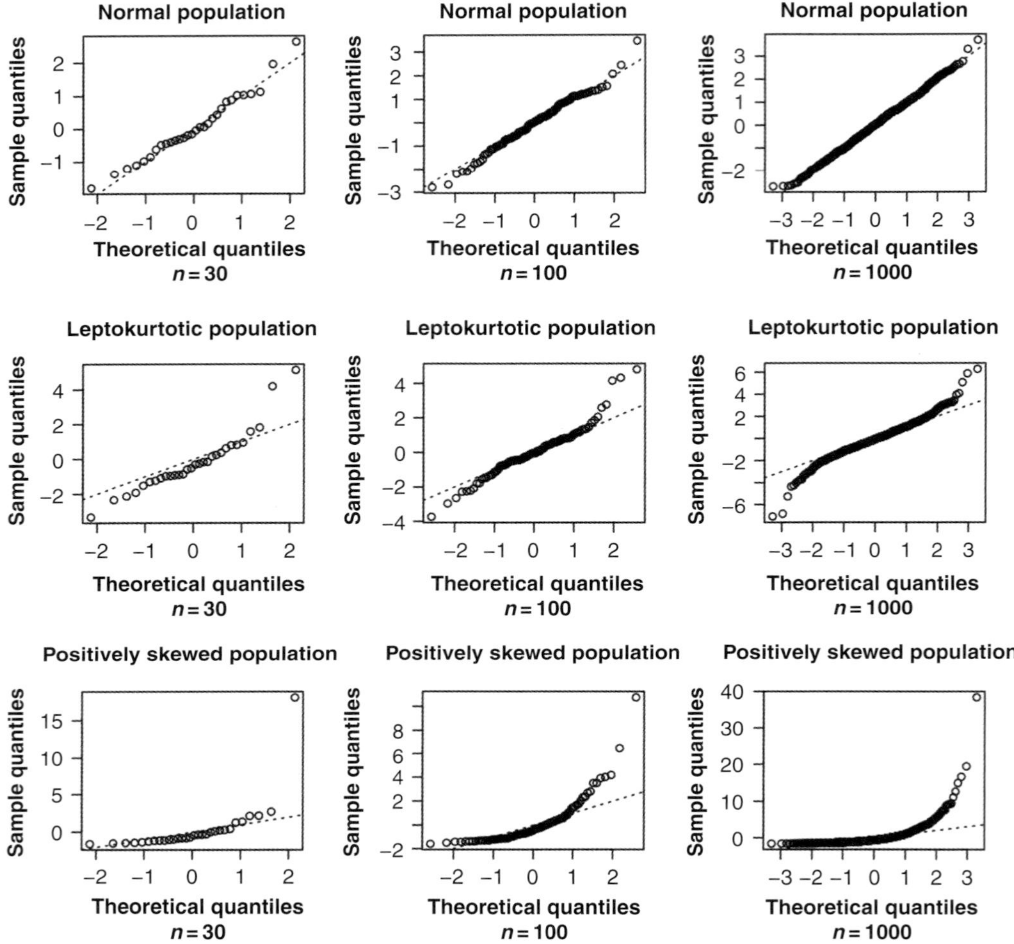

Figure 9.10 Normal probability plots of samples from normal, leptokurtotic or positively skewed distributions, with sample sizes of $n = 30$, $n = 100$ or $n = 1000$

(S-shaped) pattern. In leptokurtotic samples the quantiles in both tails are more extreme than the theoretically expected values. Because the theoretical quantiles in Figure 9.10 are plotted on the x-axis the leptokurtotic distribution tends to curve down on the left of the plot and up on the right. For platykurtosis the pattern would be reversed, with sample quantiles in both tails being less extreme than the expected normal quantiles. This would give the same sigmoidal shape but with the tails curving in the opposite direction.

These patterns come across clearly when $n = 1000$, but are progressively harder to spot in the smaller samples. In the smallest samples, departures from normal show up as potential outliers or extreme values (rather than as part of a clear overall pattern). One tip, when using standardized or studentized residuals, is to look closely at the sample distribution to see what range of residuals – effectively z or t statistics – has been plotted. For normal samples, the ranges of the observed and theoretical quantiles should be similar. For leptokurtotic and skewed samples the range should be consistently wider than for the normal distribution (and a platykurtotic sample would tend to have a narrower range). This is visible in Figure 9.10 where, even for the smallest samples, the ranges of the theoretical quantiles of the non-normal distributions are quite different from those of the normal samples.

For very small samples a normal probability plot may be too sparse to detect any marked curvature. In these situations you could use a *halfnormal probability plot*. This plots the absolute value of the residual against its absolute expected value. Curvature with halfnormal plots also suggests a departure from normal – but interpreting the pattern is harder than for the full plots. As noted earlier, working with studentized residuals is also possible, but requires quantiles to be plotted against a theoretical t distribution with $n - q - 2$ *df*. You may also prefer to work with density estimates (e.g., a histogram or KDE) rather than a Q-Q plot (Fox, 2002a).

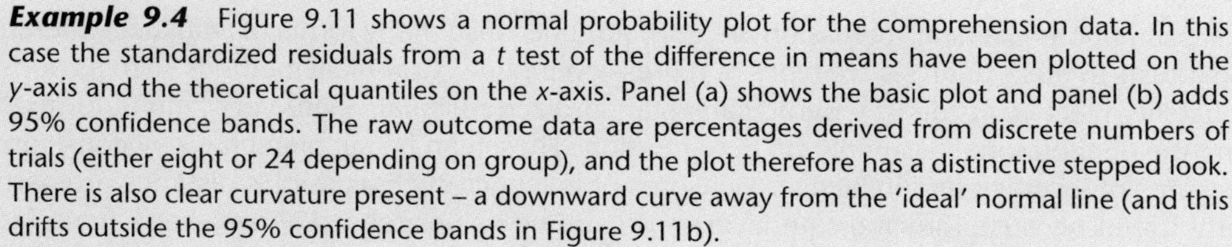

Example 9.4 Figure 9.11 shows a normal probability plot for the comprehension data. In this case the standardized residuals from a t test of the difference in means have been plotted on the y-axis and the theoretical quantiles on the x-axis. Panel (a) shows the basic plot and panel (b) adds 95% confidence bands. The raw outcome data are percentages derived from discrete numbers of trials (either eight or 24 depending on group), and the plot therefore has a distinctive stepped look. There is also clear curvature present – a downward curve away from the 'ideal' normal line (and this drifts outside the 95% confidence bands in Figure 9.11b).

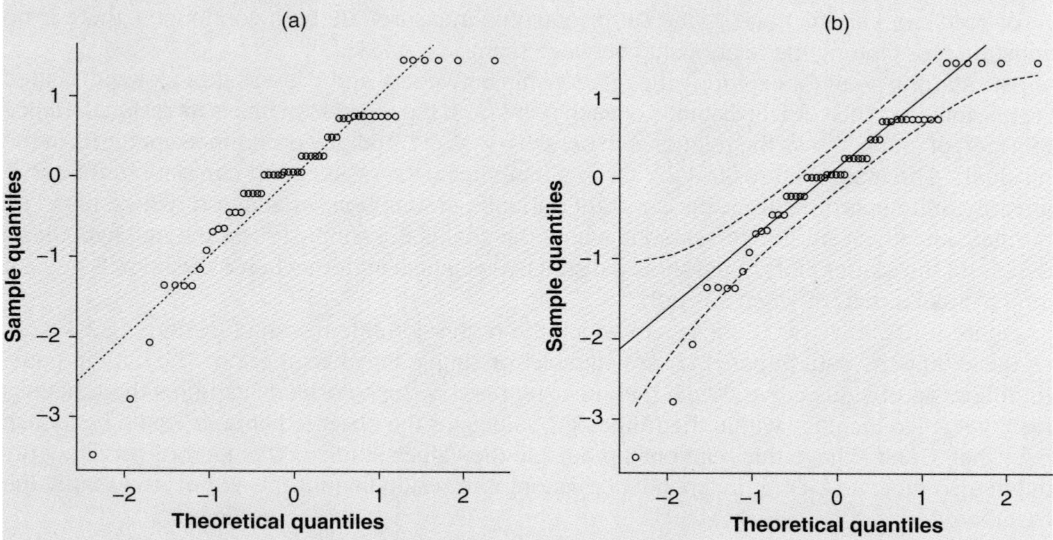

Figure 9.11 Normal probability plot of standardized residuals from a t test of the comprehension data versus the expected quantiles from a normal distribution (a) without, and (b) with 95% confidence bands

The sample quantiles are spread more widely at the lower end of the distribution. They are more extreme than expected from a normal distribution when the outcome is low. This is characteristic of negative skew. To confirm this, the sample skewness is -1.08 (negative numbers indicating negative skew).

What about kurtosis? This is harder to spot than skew – particularly if skew is also present. The sample kurtosis (excess kurtosis relative to the normal distribution) is 1.69. As it is positive, this indicates that the residuals are leptokurtotic. It is the kurtosis, rather than the moderate skew, that probably explains the discrepancy between the bootstrap and normal CI obtained for these data in Example 3.8. Together the skew and kurtosis also suggest that the relatively extreme observations (more than two $\hat{\sigma}$ from the group mean) should not be classed as outliers. They are extreme relative to a normal distribution, but are a natural part of a skewed, leptokurtotic distribution.

9.4.2 Assessing assumptions in correlation and regression

The assumptions of linear regression are important because many forms of statistical inference from *t* tests to meta-analysis are types of regression model.[7] Graphical methods such as normal probability plots of residuals – particularly standardized residuals – are very helpful for examining the distributional assumptions in regression. These can be supplemented by considering measures of leverage and influence. Measures of influence such as Cook's distance are particularly useful because they indicate leveraged extreme values: observations that have a large impact on parameter estimates. All these methods are valuable. Nevertheless, where X (the *IV* or predictor variable) and Y (the *DV* or outcome measure) are both continuous, there is no substitute for plotting the relationship between them.

The starting point for exploring the relationship between X and Y is a scatter plot with a fitted regression line. The vertical distance of each point from the regression line is its residual. Hence this kind of graph shows the relationship between X and Y and any pronounced patterns in the residuals. The main features to look for in simple linear regression and correlation are curvilinearity and departures from the constant variance assumption. In addition, where bivariate normality is important (for correlations where the goal is not simply to test the null hypothesis that $\rho = 0$) the scatter plot should show a distinctive elliptical pattern when correlation is present (and a circular pattern when it is not).

Figure 9.12 shows two data sets in which the regression line has the function $Y = 3 + 0.5X$. Of these only the data in panel (a) are suitable for simple linear regression. The data in panel (b) follow an obvious curve. While the linear regression slope correctly captures the tendency for Y values to increase within the range of X values for the observed data, it would be foolish infer that X and Y have this relationship outside the values studied. This kind of curvilinearity might also indicate lack of independence among the residuals (but this is not necessarily the case).

Both data sets plotted in Figure 9.12 use data created by Anscombe (1973). His examples represent perhaps the most influential published argument in favor of graphical exploration.[8] Without plotting the data there is no obvious clue in the parameter estimates or tests that simple linear regression may be inappropriate.

Figure 9.13 shows a scatter plot of the relationship between two new variables. Here, the relationship between X and Y is linear. Despite the linear relationship, it is clear that the

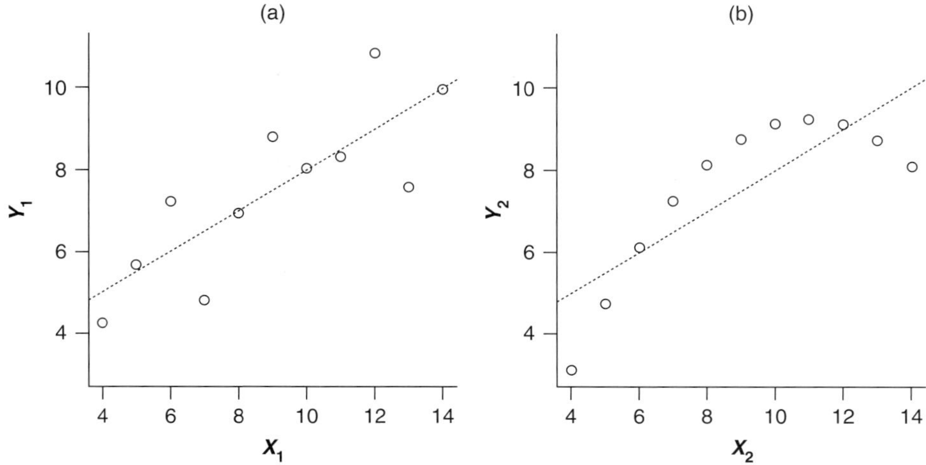

Figure 9.12 Two data sets with identical simple linear regression fits

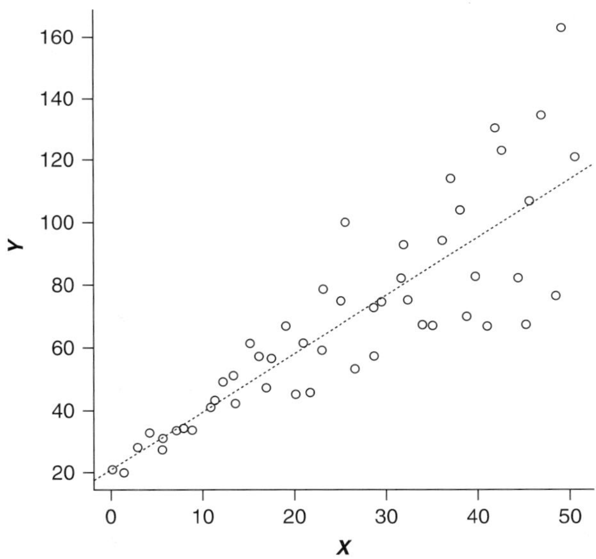

Figure 9.13 Detecting a violation of the homogeneity of variance assumption in simple linear regression

variances of the residuals of the regression in Figure 9.13 are not constant for all values of X. They increase in size as X increases (a pattern that is fairly common in real data sets). Other patterns (such as decreasing variability as X increases, or tight clustering in the center and wider dispersion at the extremes) can also be revealed this way.

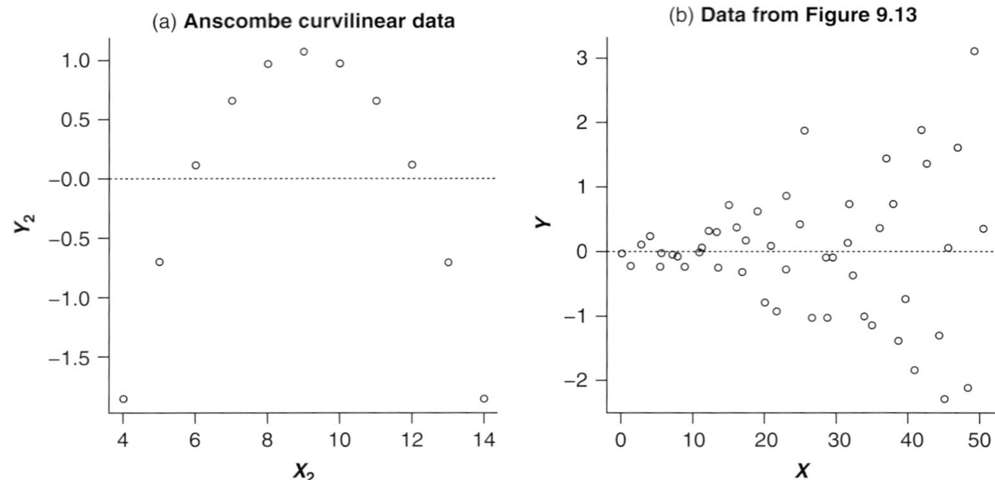

Figure 9.14 Standardized residuals versus X for two data sets

An alternative approach is to plot the residuals or standardized residuals against X. This removes the relationship between X and Y from the equation (literally as well as metaphorically) and produces a slightly cleaner plot. Figure 9.14 shows the standardized residuals as a function of X for the Anscombe curvilinear data (from Figure 9.12b) and for data violating the homogeneity of variance assumption (from Figure 9.13). In both cases, the patterns among the residuals visible in the original plots are easy to detect. Although the previous plots are more informative – because they include the relationship between X and Y, plotting the residuals versus a predictor such as X can make it easier to detect patterns in complex data sets.

A bivariate normal distribution can also be detected in a scatter plot, though the characteristic ellipse is easiest to detect in large samples. Figure 9.15 shows samples with a jointly bivariate normal distribution where $\rho = -.80$, 0 or .40. The circular pattern when $\rho = 0$ and the ellipses of $\rho = -.80$ or $\rho = .40$ are clear in the upper panels (where $n = 500$), but harder to spot in the lower panels (where $n = 50$).

One of the features of these plots is the apparent tighter clustering of residuals around the regression line for large and small values of X in the upper panels. This is a function of the lower frequency of observations in the tails of a normal distribution. It can make assessing the homogeneity of variance assumption difficult for bivariate normal distributions – because there may be too few observations to assess the variances of the residuals at the extremes, and it can appear as though data are more variable in the middle of the distribution. Plotting residuals versus their index (if that is uncorrelated with X) can help avoid this problem. Index numbers often record the order of data collection and so plotting residuals against the index number may help detect some violations of independence.

These basic procedures, illustrated for bivariate regression and correlation, can also be extended to more complex regression models. A full treatment of this topic is beyond the scope of this chapter, but an excellent introduction is found in Fox (2002a).

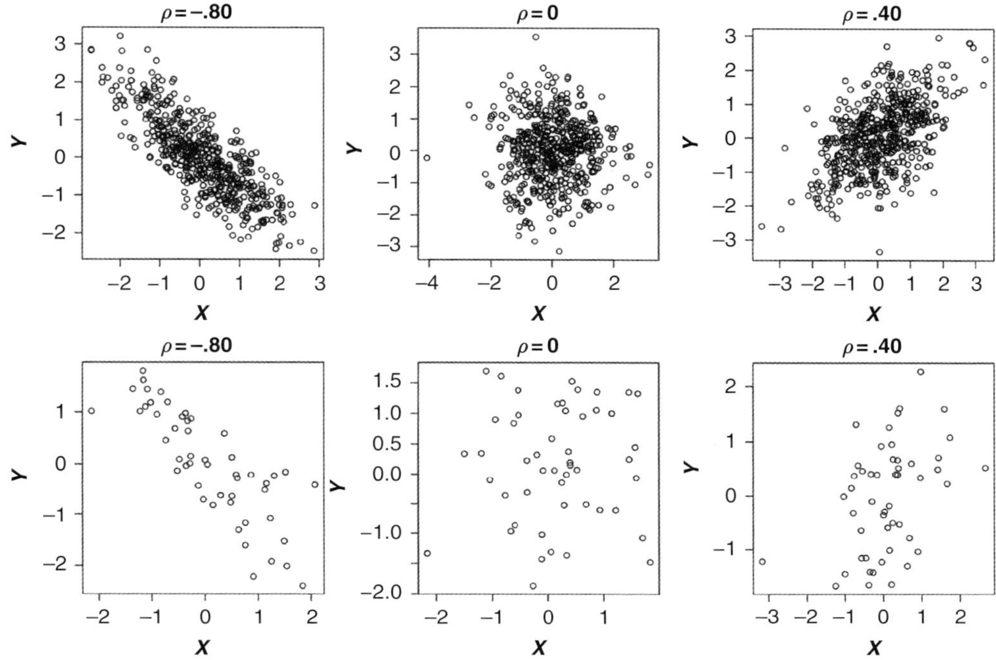

Figure 9.15 Scatter plots of samples from bivariate normal distributions, when $\rho = -.80$, $\rho = 0$ or $\rho = .40$ and for sample sizes of $n = 500$ (upper panels) or $n = 50$ (lower panels)

9.5 R code for Chapter 9

9.5.1 Histograms and true histograms

Histograms plotted with the `hist()` function in R use defaults that generally work well for samples with moderate to large *n*. The default for determining bin sizes is Sturges' method (though other methods are available). As R is open source and because it is not primitive (internal to R), you can inspect the function that calculates the number of bins for this method. Entering `nclass.Sturges` (the name of the function) returns:

```
function (x)
ceiling(log2(length(x)) + 1)
<environment: namespace:grDevices>
```

This function takes a single parameter (`x`) and applies the calculation `ceiling(log2(length(x)) + 1)`. Sturges' method uses `length(x)` to calculate the sample size *n*, computes the logarithm of *n* to base two, adds one and rounds the result up with the `ceiling()` function. This is how much of R works; via functions that call other functions in turn. This modular style is powerful, but makes it hard to keep track of everything R can and can't do. The number of `breaks`, rather than the bin size (n divided by the number of breaks) is used as input to the `hist()` function. If n is ten and there are two breaks, the bin size is five. This can be seen in the functions that plot the three histograms in Figure 9.2. The first line draws a random, normal sample of size ten and subsequent commands draw the plots. The `hist()` argument `main=NA` suppresses the default title for each histogram.

```
set.seed(3)
bad.hist <- rnorm(10,20,4)
par(mfrow=c(1,3), pty='s', mar=c(4,4,3,2), cex.main=1.4)
hist(bad.hist, 2, xlab=expression(italic(X)),
  main='(a) bin size = 5')
hist(bad.hist, xlab=expression(italic(X)), main='(b) bin size
  = R default')
hist(bad.hist, breaks=20, xlab=expression(italic(X)),
  main='(c) bin size = 0.5')
```

Adding a curve to a histogram is easiest for a true histogram (i.e., placing probability density rather than frequency on the y-axis). This is done by setting the `hist()` parameter `freq=FALSE`. A normal (or other) curve can then be overlaid with `curve()` and `dnorm()`. This is done in Figure 9.3, where each panel is constructed from:

```
nh <- rnorm(30,20,4)
dev.off()
hist(nh, xlab=NULL, main=NA, freq=FALSE, xlim=c(8,32),
  ylim=c(0,.15))
curve(dnorm(x,mean(nh),sd(nh)), add = TRUE, lty=3,
  xlim=c(8,32))
```

The call `dev.off()` closes the graphics device (and is a quick way to reset the graphics parameters to their original settings).

9.5.2 Kernel density estimation

A number of kernel density estimators are available in R. The main one is `density()` from the base package. The kernel parameter supports a choice of kernel with the default of Gaussian (i.e., normal). The `density()` function calculates the density estimates, but does not plot them. This allows the output to be passed to other plot functions. The following R code mimics the left-hand panels from Figure 9.4 (in which a kernel density estimate is first added to a histogram of 30 random, normal observations and then to 30 random observations from a χ^2 distribution).

```
par(mfrow=c(1,2), pty='s')
nh <- rnorm(30,20,4)

hist(nh, freq=FALSE, ylim = c(0,.125), xlab='N~(20,4)',
  main = NA)
```

```
lines(density(nh), lty=3)
ch <- rchisq(30,5)

hist(ch, freq=FALSE, ylim = c(0,.2),
  xlab=expression(chi[5]^2), main = NA)
lines(density(ch), lty=3)
```

9.5.3 Plots for the Hayden (2005) data (Example 9.2)

The original Hayden (2005) data set is available from the *Journal of Statistics Education*. A slightly more up-to-date version is available in the SPSS data file `hayden_2005.sav`. The commands below import the data from the SPSS file.

```
library(foreign)
hayden2005 <- read.spss('hayden_2005.sav', to.data.frame=TRUE)
```

Subsequent commands produce the box plot for Figure 9.7, and the combined histogram and kernel density plot for Figure 9.8. Note that `with()` is used to get the `plot()` function to look inside the `hayden2005` data frame for the object `days` (to avoid attaching the data frame).

```
with(hayden2005, boxplot(days, ylab='Days'))

par(mfrow=c(1,2), pty='s')
with(hayden2005, hist(days, main=NA, ylim=c(0,22)))
with(hayden2005, plot(density(days), main=NA, xlab='Days'))
```

Two enhanced plots are shown in Figure 9.9. The left-hand panel is a bean plot and the right-hand panel is a kernel density plot with a rug. The package `beanplot` must be installed first (violin plots are obtained from the package `vioplot`).

```
install.packages('beanplot')
library(beanplot)

with(hayden2005, beanplot(days, col = 'gray', ylab='Days'))
with(hayden2005, plot(density(days), main=NA, xlab='Days'))
with(hayden2005, rug(days, ticksize = .06))
```

The `rug()` function is a part of the basic installation and is very versatile. For some data sets (those with many ties) it may help to add a small amount of random noise or 'jitter' to the data before adding a rug. This is done with the `jitter()` function, though it isn't really needed here. The following examples add the rug to different sides of a kernel density plot and to a box plot. The color and length of the lines can also be edited:

```
with(hayden2005, boxplot(days, ylab='Days'))
with(hayden2005, plot(density(days), main=NA, xlab='Days'))
with(hayden2005, rug(jitter(days), side = 3, col='blue'))
```

Any of these plot functions can be called with a vector for a quick exploratory plot such as:

```
beanplot(hayden2005$days)
with(hayden2005, beanplot(days))
```

9.5.4 Tests of equality of variances (Example 9.3)

A Levene test of equality of variances based on absolute deviations from the median is available in the `car` package. The following commands import the data from the SPSS file `baguley_payne_2000.sav` and run this test for the comprehension data.

```
library(foreign)
bp2000 <- read.spss('baguley_payne_2000.sav', to.data.frame =
  TRUE)
library(car)

bp.mod <- lm(percent_accuracy ~ group, data=bp2000)
leveneTest(bp.mod)
```

The following command produces the version based on the mean absolute deviations (though of course this version is not recommended).

```
leveneTest(bp.mod, center=mean)
```

This could also be reproduced using basic regression commands, as the test is a form of one-way ANOVA on the absolute deviations, or when there are two conditions (as here), a *t* test on the absolute deviations:

```
attach(bp2000)
m.1 <- median(percent_accuracy[1:28])
m.2 <- median(percent_accuracy[29:56])
ad.g1 <- abs(percent_accuracy[1:28] - m.1)
ad.g2 <- abs(percent_accuracy[29:56] - m.2)

t.test(ad.g1, ad.g2, var.equal=TRUE)
t.test(ad.g1, ad.g2, var.equal=TRUE)$statistic]^2

detach(bp2000)
```

In this case, use of `attach()` to get functions to search inside the `bp2000` data frame for named objects is more convenient, but riskier than using `with()`. The final `detach()` command is not necessary, but prevents attached objects 'masking' access to other R objects with the same name (something that often happens if you have many objects attached).

9.5.5 Normal probability plots, skewness and kurtosis (Example 9.4)

The `qqnorm()` function produces a normal probability plot. There is also a more general Q-Q plot function called `qqplot()`. To plot the residuals required involves extracting them from a fitted model. For Figure 9.11, `rstandard()` was used. The `abline()` function adds the dotted line $Y = X$ (where data sampled from a perfect normal distribution are expected to fall). Rather than attach the data frame, the data frame is named within the `lm()` function.

```
lm.out <- lm(percent_accuracy ~ group, data=bp2000)
qqnorm(rstandard(lm.out))
abline(0,1, lty=3)
```

Confidence bands can be added using the `qqPlot()` function in the `car` package. The color here is switched from red to black and gray.

```
library(car)
qqPlot(rstandard(lm.out), col='black', col.lines='gray')
```

If called with a model object, the function plots studentized residuals against a t distribution. This is a more sensitive test of departures from the theoretical distribution – especially for the tails. The function also bootstraps the confidence bands, but this can be suppressed via the `simulate` argument:

```
qqPlot(lm.out)
qqPlot(lm.out, simulate=FALSE)
```

Skewness and excess kurtosis statistics are available from several packages. Here `fBasics` is used, but the more general `describe()` function from the `psych` package works too.

```
install.packages('fBasics')
library(fBasics)

kurtosis(rstandard(lm.out))
skewness(rstandard(lm.out))
```

9.5.6 Regression assumptions and the Anscombe data sets

The Anscombe data sets are included in the `datasets` package (part of the standard R installation). The `data()` function loads the data set you require. To see what data sets are available from the packages you have installed (including the defaults) use the call `data()`. The following commands reproduce Figure 9.12. The `plot()` function has no data argument, so it makes sense to use `with()` if you want to avoid `attach()`.

```
data(anscombe)

par(mfrow=c(1,2), mar = c(5,4,3,1), pty='s')
with(anscombe, plot(x1, y1, ylim=c(3,11),
  ylab=expression(italic(Y[1])),
  xlab=expression(italic(X[1]))))
abline(3, .5, lty=3)
with(anscombe, plot(x2, y2, ylim=c(3,11),
  ylab=expression(italic(Y[2])),
  xlab=expression(italic(X[2]))))
abline(3, .5, lty=3)
```

To just plot the residuals against X involves extracting the residuals from a fitted model. The left-hand panel of Figure 9.14 is reproduced here. This time the dotted line fitted is a constant zero (the mean of the residuals).

```
par(mfrow=c(1,1))
with(anscombe, plot(x2, rstandard(lm(y2~x2)),
  xlab=expression(italic(X[2])), ylab=expression(italic(Y))))
abline(0,0, lty=3)
```

The remaining regression diagnostics use regular scatter plots. Packages such as `car` also contain other useful diagnostic plots. Once you are familiar with the basics, these are well worth exploring.

9.5.7 R packages

Adler, D. (2005) *vioplot*: Violin plot. R package version 0.2.
Fox, J., and Weisberg, S. (2010) *An R Companion to Applied Regression*, (2nd edn). Thousand Oaks CA: Sage.
Kampstra, K. (2008) *Beanplot*: A Boxplot Alternative for Visual Comparison of Distributions. *Journal of Statistical Software*, Code Snippets, 28, 1–9.
R-core members, DebRoy, S. *et al.* (2011) *foreign*: Read Data Stored by Minitab, S, SAS, SPSS, Stata, Systat, dBase. R package version 0.8-42.
Revelle, W. (2011) *psych*: Procedures for Psychological, Psychometric, and Personality Research. R package version 1.0-95.
Wuertz, D. *et al.* (2010) *fBasics*: Rmetrics – Markets and Basic Statistics. R package version 2110.79.

9.6 Notes on SPSS syntax for Chapter 9

9.6.1 Exploratory graphics

SPSS has a variety of options available for exploring data with descriptive statistics and plots, but is not as flexible as R. Neither KDE, bean plots nor true (i.e., density) histograms are directly available in SPSS. The following syntax produce a basic box plot followed by histogram with a normal curve superimposed for the Hayden (2005) data. Changing features of the plot, including bin size, is probably best done by editing the plot in the output window (rather than via syntax).

SPSS data file: `hayden_2005.sav`

```
GRAPH
  /HISTOGRAM(NORMAL)=days.
EXAMINE
  VARIABLES=days
    /COMPARE VARIABLE
    /PLOT=BOXPLOT
    /STATISTICS=NONE.
```

The best way to get a normal probability plot in SPSS is to use the PPLOT command from the <Analyze> <Descriptive Statistics> <Q-Q Plots . . . > using residuals saved from an earlier analysis. The default plot can also be invoked directly from syntax.

```
PPLOT
  /VARIABLES=ZRE_1
  /TYPE=Q-Q
  /DIST=NORMAL.
```

Here `ZRE_1` is the default name for standardized residuals saved to the SPSS data view spreadsheet (but should be substituted with the appropriate variable name as required).

9.6.2 Tests of equality of variances (Example 9.3)

Levene's test of equality of variances using absolute deviations from the means is produced automatically as part of the independent *t* test output. For the `baguley_payne_2000.sav` data set in Example 9.3 the *t* test syntax would be:

SPSS data file: `baguley_payne_2000.sav`

```
T-TEST
   GROUPS = group(0 1)
   /VARIABLES = percent_accuracy.
```

This procedure is limited to two groups, but the Levene test can also be run via the `EXAMINE` command (allowing a grouping variable with more than two groups to be included). Interestingly, this route to the Levene test includes a version based on absolute deviations from the mean, median, median with adjusted *df* and (presumably 5%) trimmed mean. It also includes a spread level plot. This plots the natural logarithm of the median of the groups versus the natural logarithm of the *IQR*. If this reveals an approximately linear pattern, it suggests that a power transformation (also shown in the plot) will make the variances roughly homogeneous. Spread level plots are also available in the R package `car`, but care should be taken before applying arbitrary power transformations routinely or (as here) when there are only two groups.

9.7 Bibliography and further reading

Fox, J. (2002a) *An R and S-Plus Companion to Applied Regression*. Thousand Oaks, CA: Sage.
Tukey, J. W. (1977) *Exploratory Data Analysis*. Reading, MA: Addison-Wesley.

10
Dealing with messy data

Contents

10.1 Chapter overview

This chapter explores different approaches to dealing with messy data. The chapter starts by considering the robustness of models that rely on least squares estimation, illustrated with the case of a two independent group design. Two main approaches to dealing with violations of assumptions are considered: robust methods and transformations.

10.2 Dealing with violations of statistical assumptions

Exploratory analyses can reveal problems with messy data and assess the degree to which statistical assumptions are violated. Once a problem has been identified there are several options. For minor violations, a valid option is to retain the assumption and accept that a certain degree of inaccuracy has entered the analysis. Whether this is the right option depends on the level of accuracy you require. If accuracy in parameter estimation or prediction is paramount, it is worth exploring alternative approaches. Furthermore, unless you have experience dealing with messy data, it can be hard to judge how much danger an apparently minor violation poses. Some violations of assumptions look innocuous yet have a big impact on the analysis.

Another option is to change the analysis. This could involve modifying the initial analysis in some way, or adopting a more conservative approach (one that makes fewer assumptions). Modifying the analysis usually takes one of two forms: 'correcting' the data or correcting the statistical procedure itself (or perhaps both).[1] Adopting a more conservative method of analysis may involve switching to a closely related technique (e.g., using a paired t test to account for correlations between pairs of measurements) or something radically different (e.g., a bootstrap CI). These distinctions are not hard and fast. In samples with many extreme scores, one solution is to analyze differences between trimmed means (rather than the usual t test of differences between untrimmed means). This can be viewed either as a correction to the data or as a switch to an alternative model.

In discussing these points, a fundamental question needs to be addressed: whether the statistical model or models under consideration are fit for purpose (see Box 10.1). If the model selected is completely wrong, then dealing with violations of specific assumptions (e.g., heterogeneity of variance or non-normal residuals) is unlikely to rescue the situation.

Box 10.1 Messy data or bad models?

When you set out to collect data you usually have an idea of what it will look like and how you will analyze it. Once collected, the data are typically messier than you would like. It is tempting to 'shoehorn' the data into your preferred analysis (e.g., using transformations or corrections). Quite often this will work.

The alternative is to go back to basics and check the generic assumptions that you have made: assumptions that are fundamental to your general approach. Make a list of the assumptions you have made that might be unreasonable (now that you have explored the data). Have you treated continuous data as categorical (losing information in the process)? Have you done the opposite and treated discrete responses as normal and continuous? Have you made distributional assumptions that are unwarranted? Have you assumed a linear model when the outcome is bounded?

Consider the example of count data that have an approximate Poisson distribution. These are routinely analyzed with least squares regression models (e.g., t tests or linear regression). When the mean is large this approach works well. If the mean of a Poisson variable is small these approaches are less satisfactory: a model designed for discrete outcomes may be more suitable (see Chapter 17).

One of the most important issues is whether a statistical model assumes independence when the samples are correlated. Are there sources of non-independence that have been ignored? This kind of non-independence is common to paired or repeated measures, matched samples or where clustering is present (e.g., for children clustered in classes or schools). Once these dependencies are accounted for in the model, the data may appear a lot less messy.

Other factors that may distort a model include unreliable measures, bias or inappropriate selection of a fixed effect rather than a random effects model.* Bias crops up in several ways (e.g., through lack of independence or by ignoring confounding variables). One of most frequent and most ignored sources of bias is missing data. Bias can be reduced and statistical power increased by employing an appropriate method for dealing with missing data (e.g., multiple imputation).**

Once you have selected a method of statistical analysis it is good practice to check the assumptions of the analysis as well as the fit and predictions of the model. Those checks will, from time to time, throw up problems you hadn't anticipated or haven't encountered before. Going back to first principles and rethinking the fundamentals of the analysis will sometimes resolve those problems. Sometimes messy data are merely symptoms of a bad model.***

* This topic is dealt with in more detail in Chapter 18 and in *Online Supplement 1: Meta-analysis.*
** This topic is dealt with in more detail in *Online Supplement 2: Dealing with missing data.*
*** Some people would argue that messy data are always the expression of a bad model, but this is not entirely convincing. In many research contexts, the phenomena being investigated are complex and the effects relatively small. Under these circumstances some messiness seems inevitable.

10.2.1 Model comparisons as model checks

Running more than one analysis and comparing results from different models is a popular strategy for checking and guiding the selection of a statistical model.[2] Discrepancies between results are indications that something is wrong – possibly wildly wrong – with one or both models. On identifying the discrepancy, the immediate objective should be to identify the factor or factors underlying the difference in results. Sometimes this is obvious (e.g., a clear violation of a distributional assumption). On other occasions it requires further exploratory work.

This strategy can be adapted as a form of model checking. This is accomplished by rerunning an initial analysis using a more conservative procedure to see if the results change. While there are good reasons to do this, the practice also has its dangers. The most obvious danger is 'cherry picking': running two analyses and picking the analysis that gives the results you want. This inflates the Type I error rates. In some cases, the Type I error rates will rise only slightly (because both the outcomes are likely to be correlated), but the Type I error can rise dramatically in extreme cases (Zimmerman and Zumbo, 2009).

If in doubt, a cautious approach is to apply the rule of selecting the more robust procedure – the procedure that makes fewest or least stringent assumptions (see Zimmerman, 2011). For example, a bootstrap comparison of differences in trimmed means is more robust to non-normality of residuals than a conventional t test (Wilcox, 2005b, 2005c). A discrepancy between the outcomes of the two procedures indicates the more conservative bootstrap results should be preferred. If genuine doubt remains, it is reasonable to report both analyses. Similarly, it is not uncommon for the outcome of a regression analysis to alter substantially on the inclusion or exclusion of a single influential data point. In the absence of further information about the status of that observation (e.g., that the sampling unit is unusual in some way, or that the observation was recorded incorrectly), the most honest approach is probably to describe findings from both models. In the absence of additional data, it may not be possible to decide which model is superior.

10.2.2 Parametric versus nonparametric statistical procedures

Many statistical methods for dealing with messy data are classified as *nonparametric* methods. Although popular, the term is not always helpful. *Parametric* and nonparametric are broad labels that are used in several different ways. A widely accepted definition is that parametric methods assume data or residuals are sampled from a particular probability distribution or distributions, and hence model the parameters of those distributions. In contrast, nonparametric methods (sometimes termed *distribution-free* methods) do not assume a particular probability model. Parametric methods typically make stronger assumptions than nonparametric methods and, if the assumptions are met, have greater statistical power and precision. Nonparametric methods, by virtue of their weaker assumptions, tend to be more robust. These are sweeping generalizations (and it is possible to find examples of methods that don't fit neatly into these categories, or that defy this pattern).

Several common misconceptions have arisen in relation to the parametric–nonparametric distinction. One is that parametric methods are identified with the normal probability distribution and least squares estimation. This need not be the case. Many statistical models assume a probability model based on other distributions (e.g., the binomial or Poisson). In addition, some normal approximations (e.g., the χ^2 test of independence) are frequently misclassified as nonparametric. A particularly problematic misconception is that there exist parametric and nonparametric data. All data are sampled from some probability distribution or combination of probability distributions. Thus all data are, in a casual sense, parametric. The true distribution may, however, be unknown (and this motivates nonparametric methods). Worrying about whether a method is parametric or nonparametric (or somewhere in between) is largely a dead end. It is better to think about whether the statistical model makes theoretical sense, gives reasonable predictions, supports accurate inference and is robust.

10.2.3 Non-normal distributions

The assumption of sampling from a normal distribution most often arises in connection with the residuals of an analysis. In a simple regression model where each observation is the sum of a constant (its mean) and a residual, the residuals and raw scores have an identical distribution. In other analyses, the distribution of the residuals depends on the model. In some cases, just improving the model will reduce or eliminate distributional problems. For instance, the distribution of residuals will change if a predictor is added to the model.

It is possible to classify departures from a normal distribution under three main categories: i) asymmetry (positive or negative skew), ii) problems with kurtosis (leptokurtosis or platykurtosis), or iii) extreme observations. Problems with extreme values can be hard to distinguish from leptokurtosis (where distributions typically have heavy or fat tails) or skew (where extreme values in the direction of skew are likely). However, extreme values also arise where samples are a mixture of two distributions (e.g., one normal and one containing extreme values).

One solution for distributional problems – and for skewed distributions in particular – is to transform the data. A transformation can be chosen for principled reasons or purely pragmatic ones (e.g., because it produces an approximate normal distribution of residuals). Transformations also often have an impact on kurtosis – sometimes shifting excess kurtosis close to the normal value (and sometimes making it worse). It is also fairly common for transformations primarily aimed at dealing with skew to reduce, and perhaps eliminate, distortions due to outliers. An obvious instance is where a distribution is approximately lognormal. A logarithmic transformation should reduce the impact of extreme scores and eliminate problems with skew or kurtosis.

A central concern is the robustness of least-squared estimation, and hence of statistical inference using the t or F distributions. A widely held belief is that inference using t or F is robust to non-normality, and therefore that Type I errors for significance tests are generally close to the nominal α level. This appears to be true for differences between means from distributions with identical shapes, provided homogeneity of variance is present. However, it is now understood that this robustness breaks down if the shape of the distribution differs between the samples being compared (Wilcox and Keselman, 2003; Wilcox, 2005b). Furthermore, whenever there are extreme scores, inference based on the t or F distribution may have very poor statistical power.[3] Leptokurtotic distributions present a particular difficulty here. Not only do heavy tails produce many apparent extreme scores, but symmetrical distributions with excess kurtosis often appear normal at first glance – particularly in small samples (see Figure 9.10).

Wilcox and Keselman (2003) argue the main solutions are either to use a rank transformation (considered in a later section) or robust estimators of central tendency. These robust estimators include familiar measures such as the median or trimmed mean and less familiar ones such as MM-estimators (Anderson and Schumacker, 2003; Wright and London, 2009). Switching to robust methods involves estimating a parameter other than the arithmetic mean. In many cases this will not matter – because the substantive research hypothesis is of a difference in central tendency (e.g., an expectation that typical members of a group differ). However, if the parameter of interest really is the arithmetic mean, then these methods may be inappropriate.

A final point is that if data are very messy (e.g., if you are comparing samples with differently shaped distributions), you may want to think twice about standard inferential statistics. Showing that two samples have different means may not be that important if the populations they are sampled from have very different characteristics. Graphical comparison using nonparametric methods such as kernel density estimation (KDE) may provide a good starting point for comparing the distributions of such samples (Wilcox, 2004).

10.2.4 Heterogeneity of variances: the two group case

Homogeneity of variance in the two independent group case is a special case of the broader regression assumption that the residuals are sampled at random from a population of independent normal errors with constant variance. The problems with inference about the arithmetic mean in two group designs also apply when the variance of the residuals is not constant in regression.

The simplest case where the problem could arise is that of the independent t test, for which a range of options is available. If n per group is equal (or near equal) and the normal distribution assumption is met, the t test is reasonably robust whenever the sample variances are similar (e.g., the ratio of the larger to smaller $\hat{\sigma}$ is less than 2:1). If the sample variances are dissimilar, the Welch-Satterthwaite correction should be employed. When $n_1 = n_2$, this correction is conservative relative to the uncorrected test; it never produces a narrower CI or smaller p value than the uncorrected test. It therefore avoids inflating Type I error rates due to cherry picking (because the Type I error rate of the Welch test can't exceed that of the uncorrected test). As its performance is close to that of the independent t when homogeneity of variance is met (Zimmerman and Zumbo, 2009), it would also be reasonable to adopt the Welch-Satterthwaite correction routinely for all independent group comparisons.

The true danger signal is not differences in sample variances, but unequal n per group. If $n_1 \neq n_2$, the Welch-Satterthwaite correction should always be preferred to the uncorrected test (Zimmerman, 2004; Zimmerman and Zumbo, 2009). There are two reasons for this. Unlike the equal n case, the correction can be less conservative than the uncorrected test (i.e., it can produce a smaller p value and narrower CI). The second reason is subtler. Because of sampling error, it is possible for the sample variances to look similar even if the population variances differ substantially (and vice versa). This risk is diminished by large sample sizes, but samples are rarely large enough to estimate the population variances with anything approaching certainty. When sample sizes are unequal the corrected test should always be applied, regardless of apparent differences (or lack of them) in the sample variances.

The major limitation of this approach is that the robustness of the Welch-Satterthwaite correction does not extend to samples with non-normal distributions. The impact of non-normality is reduced in large samples (Bonett and Price, 2002). Bonett and Price (*ibid.*) recommend sample sizes of 30 per group as sufficient to cope with the degree of non-normality most likely to be encountered in research. For smaller samples or extreme non-normality (particularly heavy tailed distributions) the robust methods are required.

10.3 Robust methods

Robust methods are statistical procedures that are likely to cope well when problems with common assumptions such as normality and homogeneity of variance are violated. A good robust method has high statistical power (ideally equal to or better than standard methods), has close to nominal Type I error rates when these assumptions are met, and maintains these properties if the assumptions are not met. Although such a method might seem too good to be true, some progress has been made toward finding methods that come close to meeting these criteria.

The main difficulty with robust methods is that there is no principled route to determining the correct method to apply in every situation. Robust methods are defined by a motivation to improve on the performance of least squares estimators. Some general-purpose methods that usually work well – but are probably not optimal – are known. Wilcox and Keselman (2004, pp. 361–2) assert bluntly that 'the only known way of determining whether the choice between modern and conventional methods makes a difference is to try both'.[4] This can lead to cherry picking of results. For this reason it is sensible to pick a robust method on principled grounds (e.g., based on exploratory analysis) rather than try many methods and pick the one that gives the result you prefer. As always, discrepancies in the results of two tests call for further investigation. Once you know why the results differ it should be easier to determine which is most trustworthy.

The following sections consider robust methods for two common applications – comparison of two independent samples and linear regression. A third robust approach (the use of a rank transformation) is considered later in the chapter. These give a flavor of robust alternatives to conventional approaches.

10.3.1 Robust alternatives to the *t* test

Bootstrapping is one of the most popular tools for robust inference. For instance, the BC_a bootstrap is a reasonable all-round solution for inference (DiCiccio and Efron, 1996). Wilcox and others have argued strongly that bootstrapping trimmed means overcomes many of the problems with conventional methods (Wilcox, 2005a; Wilcox and Keselman, 2003). Determining the ideal level of trimming for any given analysis is, however, difficult. There will be some occasions when the median (approaching 100% trimming) is the best choice, and others where 5% or 10% trimming may be optimal. There is also evidence that the percentile bootstrap is superior to BC_a for trimmed means, whereas the latter is better for untrimmed means (Wilcox and Keselman, 2003). By combining trimming with a percentile bootstrap it is possible to derive a more robust alternative to the usual t test. This kind of test will generally have good statistical power when assumptions are met – at least when there is no skew. It also provides a better way of dealing with extreme values and heavy-tailed distributions than *ad hoc* practices such as outlier deletion.

Keselman *et al.* (2004) draw on earlier work by Yuen (1974). This work combines trimmed means with the Welch-Satterthwaite t test to produce a robust alternative to the conventional t test, and is robust to unequal variances. By adding a transformation to reduce skew, first proposed by Hall (1992), it also addresses asymmetry in the sample distributions. We will refer to the resulting test as the *Yuen-Hall (YH)* bootstrap t test. Simulation results with 10% to 20% trimming suggest that this 'new and improved' t test performs well in terms of Type I and Type II errors (even for quite small sample sizes). It provides a robust general alternative to the conventional t or Welch t test. The major drawback is that this method is not widely implemented in software (though it is available for R).

Working with trimmed means has its critics (Bonett and Price, 2002). It can be hard to explain trimmed means to a non-technical audience, and it can be tricky to select the level of trimming in a principled way. Comparison of medians using the bootstrap provides an attractive alternative to conventional least squares statistics if you prefer to avoid trimmed means (Bonett and Price, 2002; Wilcox, 2005c).

Example 10.1 This example compares the performance of some robust methods using the comprehension data first introduced in Example 3.6. These data have negative skew and, owing to the ceiling effect in one of the conditions, it is likely that both skew and kurtosis differ between groups. Table 10.1 shows 95% CIs for the difference in percentage accuracy between the groups for a conventional t test, a Welch-Satterthwaite t test, percentile and BC_a bootstrap CIs and the

YH bootstrap *t* test. Each method is demonstrated for the trimmed mean and, where appropriate, the mean and median (with all bootstrap methods using 9999 bootstrap replications). From Table 10.1 a number of patterns are clear. The median performs relatively poorly compared to methods based on means and trimmed means. Whether the mean or trimmed mean is better depends on the precise method used and the method of trimming employed (Wilcox and Keselman, 2003).

Table 10.1 Comparison of 95% CIs of a difference in means, trimmed mean or medians for the comprehension data using independent *t* and a range of robust methods

Method	Parameter	Lower bound	Upper bound	CI width
Independent *t*	mean	−22.75	−3.44	19.31
Welch-Satterthwaite *t*	mean	−22.89	−3.30	19.59
BC_a bootstrap	mean	−22.62	−4.46	18.16
	10% trimmed mean	−21.35	−1.74	19.61
	median	−16.67	4.17	20.83
Percentile bootstrap	mean	−22.77	−4.32	18.45
	10% trimmed mean	−22.70	−2.08	20.62
	median	−18.75	4.17	22.92
YH bootstrap *t*	mean	−21.62	−4.85	16.77
	10% trimmed mean	−19.32	−2.09	17.23
	20% trimmed mean	−21.57	−0.42	21.15

Given that there are discrepancies, which method is likely to be best? The data are negatively skewed so this suggests that the *YH* bootstrap *t* test of Keselman *et al.* (2004) is probably the best bet, as it is the only one of these methods designed specifically to address skew as well as heterogeneity of variance and heavy tails. However, this method appears to be very sensitive to the degree of trimming. It looks as though 10% trimming is appropriate here, and Wilcox (2009, p. 11) suggests that the *YH* bootstrap *t* test is 'a good choice when trimming is less than .2, say .1 or .15'.

For a paired or one sample *t* test (if homogeneity of variance or differences in skew between groups is not an issue), the percentile bootstrap of a trimmed mean (or a BC_a bootstrap of the mean) should be considered as robust alternatives to *t*. Whatever method is selected, some thought should be given to the parameter being estimated. In some situations a transformation will be sufficient to deal with any distributional problems, and a standard *t* test may suffice.

10.3.2 Robust linear regression

As with differences in sample means, there are many robust methods for regression, of which M-estimators and MM-estimators are good examples (Anderson and Schumacker, 2003; Wright and London, 2009). The mathematical basis for these estimators is beyond the scope of this brief presentation, and only a very broad conceptual overview of these methods will be given.

The basic principle is very simple. Least squares regression estimates are found by minimizing its *loss function*: the squared distance of each observation from the regression line (i.e., minimizing the squares of the residuals). There are good reasons for using the squares of the residuals for samples from an independent, normal population of errors with constant variance (see Key Concept 5.1). If these conditions aren't met, there are loss functions other than least squares (such as the mean absolute deviation) that could be minimized. These loss functions may be more efficient and less biased than least squares when the usual regression assumptions are violated.

M-estimators are a broad class of loss functions, of which least squares estimation is a special case (though one which is not very robust). Robust regression involves employing estimators that work well when the least squares regression assumptions are met, but which have low bias and high efficiency when they are not. Anderson and Schumacker (2003) focus on three properties of robust estimators: efficiency, *breakdown point* and *bounded influence*. An efficient robust estimator has a loss function comparable to least squares regression when the usual regression assumptions are met. The breakdown point is a new idea, but a rather elegant one: it is the proportion (or percentage) of observations needed to completely overwhelm parameter estimation. The worst possible breakdown point is zero, indicating that a single observation could completely overwhelm all $N - 1$ remaining observations. The highest possible breakdown point is 0.5. This can occur only for a procedure where no observation (in isolation) can be more influential than any other – thus it takes an equal number of 'bad' observations to overwhelm the 'good' ones. Least squares estimation of means has a breakdown point of zero (as a single sufficiently extreme value could overwhelm all other data). Estimation using trimmed means has a breakdown point that increases with the proportion of trimming. Thus the median (a 50% trimmed mean) achieves the maximum breakdown point of 0.5. *Bounded influence* is the ability of an estimator to limit the impact of high leverage residuals (those with extreme X values) on the regression.

MM-estimation (Yohai, 1987) is a development of M-estimation to improve the breakdown point and bounded influence of the estimator. Although these methods have good robustness (compared to least squares), better methods exist for dealing with particular patterns of violations (see Wilcox and Keselman, 2004).

Example 10.2 A simple linear regression of the data in Figure 9.13 produces the line of best fit:

$$Y = 21.04 + 1.86X$$

A corresponding robust regression (using the defaults for MM-estimation in R) has the equation:

$$Y = 22.47 + 1.75X$$

The two equations are similar and both provide satisfactory fits to the data. The fits are compared in Figure 10.1. The robust regression (the dashed lines with the shallower slope) is hard to distinguish from the least squares regression for these data. There are slightly more high influence points above than below the line on the right-hand side of the plot, and this probably explains the difference in slope. If a single extreme observation with high leverage (and hence influence) were present, the robust regression would differ more markedly. However, focusing solely on the regression slope misses a crucial advantage of robust regression. Robust regression may have a more efficient loss function and hence smaller standard errors (*SE*s) if the assumptions of least squares regression are violated. The least squares *SE*s are 4.88 for the intercept and 0.17 for the slope. The corresponding robust standard errors are 4.26 and 0.15 for the robust regression.

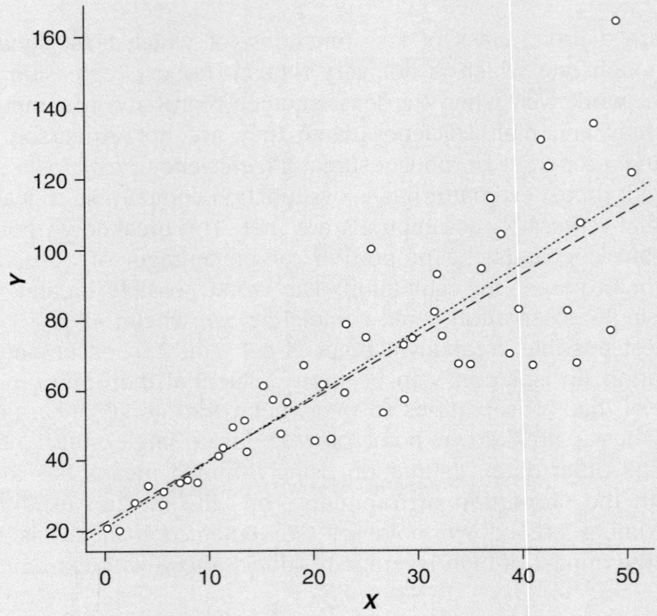

Figure 10.1 Comparing least squares and robust regression fits for the data in Figure 9.13

This gives us an idea of the cost of violating the homogeneity assumption in regression (the least squares *SE* being some 15% larger). The robust regression is more efficient as well as being resistant to extreme observations.

Robust regression methods provide a useful set of tools (of which MM-estimators are only one example). An immediate practical difficulty is obtaining *p* values or interval estimates. As the sampling distributions of the parameters are generally unknown, methods such as the bootstrap are required (Fox, 2002b). A bootstrap interval estimate of the slope is:

$$b_1 = 1.75, 95\% \text{ CI } [1.16, 2.34]$$

This can be compared to the estimate from the simple linear regression:

$$b_1 = 1.86, 95\% \text{ CI } [1.53, 2.19]$$

The bootstrap interval estimates are somewhat wider than the standard regression CIs in this case, but are probably more accurate.

Robust regression won't always work. In particular, if the model that is fitted is fundamentally flawed (see Box 10.1), robust regression isn't likely to rescue the situation. Wright and London (2009) point out that fitting a simple linear or simple robust regression to the curvilinear Anscombe data isn't going to help (see Figure 9.12b). Instead you need come up with a more appropriate model, one that captures the curvilinear relationship between *X* and *Y*.

10.4 Transformations

Transformations usually have one of two main goals: to aid interpretation or to address the assumptions of a statistical model (Tukey, 1957). When first encountered, the idea of transforming data is often treated with suspicion. This is a shame, because when applied sensibly, not only do transformations help deal with messy data, but they may lead to a better model in other ways. Transformed data sometimes provide a clearer interpretation of the findings or a more plausible theoretical account. On the other hand – like many other methods for dealing with messy data – transformations can also be misused. The obvious danger is that people will be tempted to pick the transformation that produces the 'best' result rather than the most appropriate statistical model. Selecting transformations in a principled way reduces this danger.

If you still have some concerns about the use of transformations, reflect on what a transformation is. It is a mathematical function applied to a variable (often the outcome *Y*) that has been measured in some way. It is tempting to think of these measurements as arriving for analysis in their 'natural' state and the transformation as artificial. However, the mere act of measuring or sampling may transform what is being measured. This is most obvious for subjective measures such as psychometric scales, but can also apply to physical quantities. The measurement of sound is a well-known example. This is usually done in decibels (dB) – a logarithmic scale in which a 3 dB increase is equivalent to a doubling of sound intensity. The same logic could easily be applied to other measures such as time or money. Measuring money on an untransformed scale involves the assumption that the difference between, for example, 100 dollars and 200 dollars is the same as 1100 and 1200 dollars. This may be true for some research questions and not others.

Of the many transformations in widespread use, only a fraction is reviewed here.[5] Of these, many are *power transformations* (see Box 10.2). These are particularly important for their role as normalizing transformations (transformations selected to meet the assumption of normality of errors in least squares regression). Three common transformations – each of which is a power transformation – also deserve special mention: the *logarithmic transformation*, the *square root transformation* and the *reciprocal transformation*. The *rank transformation* is also widely used, and constitutes perhaps the oldest and easiest-to-apply robust method.

A general issue that arises in the analysis of transformed data is the question of what summary statistics to report. It is arguably most correct to report the means, standard deviations (*SD*s) and relevant descriptive statistics for the transformed data. This is a good choice if those values are readily interpretable. If not, then it is preferable to report summary statistics after the transformation has been reversed. For a logarithmic transformation this would involve reporting the geometric mean (also its median) and geometric *SD* (in preference to the arithmetic mean and *SD*). If the transformation is not reversible (e.g., the rank transformation) then the choice

Box 10.2 Power transformations and the *ladder of powers*

Tukey (1957, p. 609) noted that: 'the analysis of data usually proceeds more easily if (1) effects are additive; (2) the error variability is constant; (3) the error distribution is symmetrical and possibly nearly normal'. Transforming data can address all three properties. Tukey (1957, 1977) pioneered a principled approach to selecting among the transformations commonly used for this purpose. He argued that it was useful to arrange these transformations in terms of their 'strength'.

Tukey (1957) defined a simple family of transformations based on powers and related functions. If you denote the transformation strength as s then this simple family has the general form:

$$Y_{transformed} = \begin{cases} Y^s, & s \neq 0 \\ \ln(Y), & s = 0 \end{cases} \qquad \text{Equation 10.1}$$

This family can be used to generate a sequence of transformations differing in strength by some multiple of s. This sequence, later termed *a ladder of powers* (Tukey, 1977), makes it easy to pick a transformation of roughly the right strength (e.g., by graphical inspection of the symmetry of adjacent transformations). If s changes by a half on each rung of the ladder, the sequence looks like this:

$$\ldots Y^{-2}, Y^{-3/2}, Y^{-1}, Y^{-1/2}, \ln(Y), Y^{1/2}, Y, Y^{3/2}, Y^2 \ldots$$

Notice that when $s = 1$ there is no transformation (i.e., it is the *identity* transformation Y^1). Values of $s < 1$ are usually selected to reduce positively skewed distributions, while values of $s > 1$ tend to reduce negative skew. Once you have determined that a distribution is positively skewed, a good starting point is a logarithmic transformation such as $\ln(Y)$. If the data are negatively skewed a good starting point is the transformation Y^2. Once transformed, it is easy to plot and compare the outcomes visually – though more formal methods for selecting a transformation exist (see Fox, 2002a).

Transformations to reduce skew work by using a function that tends to decrease big numbers more than small numbers. For instance, a logarithmic transformation (using base 10) reduces 10,000 to 4 and 100 to 2 and hence by 9996 and 98 respectively. On the other hand, the square root function ($Y^{1/2}$) reduces 10,000 to 100 and to 10 (i.e., by 9900 and 90). For stronger transformations the relative impact on big numbers is more marked. Negative skew requires functions such as Y^2 or Y^3. These increase big numbers more than small numbers (e.g., both 1^2 and $1^3 = 1$ whereas $10^2 = 100$ and $10^3 = 1000$). Problems with power transformations may occur for data that ranges close to zero, includes zero or straddles zero. Zero is not defined for the logarithmic or reciprocal transformations. The reciprocal (Y^{-1}) behaves differently for values below 1 (increasing small numbers more than big ones). Squaring a number strips negative observations of their sign, though this can also be useful. Sometimes it is possible to work round these problems (e.g., by adding a constant to all values prior to transformation).

Since Tukey's early work, other families of transformations have been proposed. Only seldom will they satisfy the three criteria of additivity, homogeneity of variance and normality (Sakia, 1992). Even so, they will often reduce problems encountered in a statistical analysis to the level where a satisfactory statistical model can be constructed. Although transformations of the outcome variable in a regression are most common, the same techniques also work for predictors (and can aid interpretation or produce a better-fitting model in much the same way).

of summary statistic is awkward. A compromise is to report more than one summary statistic, but if pressed for a single measure of central tendency then a robust descriptive statistic such as the median or mean absolute deviation (*MAD*) may be satisfactory.

Interval estimates can also be problematic for transformed data. Bland and Altman (1996) note that the CI for a difference in means for transformed data cannot be readily transformed into the CI for a difference on the original scale. Under many common (e.g., power) transformations – with the exception of the logarithmic transformation – the location of the means on the number line can't be ignored when considering the untransformed differences.

10.4.1 Logarithmic transformations

The logarithmic transformation is usually the first choice when dealing with positively skewed distributions. It can also be selected as part of a principled approach to constructing an appropriate model. This might be because of the connection between the normal and lognormal distributions or because of the ability to capture some curvilinear relationships between variables (e.g., in the form of a power law). A fundamental property of the logarithmic transformation is its ability to turn an additive model into a multiplicative one.

Logarithms are used in mathematics to switch from multiplication into addition. A one-unit increase in the natural logarithm of X or Y is equivalent to multiplication by 2.72 in the original units (given that $e \approx 2.72$). This is an increase of 172%. A convenient result is that, for small values, the exponentiation of Y to base e is approximately equivalent to the proportion of change in Y (or percentages if multiplied by 100). If Y is transformed by taking its natural logarithm, a simple linear regression equation can be represented as either $\ln(y_i) = b_0 + b_1 x_i + e_i$ or $y_i = e^{b_0 + b_1 x_i + e_i}$. Thus a coefficient such as $b_1 = 0.05$ is roughly equivalent to a 5% increase in Y (see Gelman and Hill, 2007). A more precise result would be an increase of $(e^{0.05} - 1) = 0.0513$ (5.13%).

A multiplicative model is often more plausible than an additive one when dealing with positive quantities that are bounded at zero. This is partly because the transformation incorporates the limiting value of zero and partly because these distributions are likely be positively skewed. A multiplicative model may also produce more plausible interpretations of the coefficients. Time data are often best interpreted in this way. Assuming Y is transformed, the shift is from a model in which a one-unit change in X is associated with a fixed change in Y (e.g., +0.73) to a model in which a one-unit change in X produces a proportional change in Y (e.g., ×1.12 or +12%). If X rather than Y is transformed, the interpretation is that a proportional increase in X produces a fixed increase in Y. Why might this be more plausible? It depends on context. If X represents the pay of an employee and Y represents the motivation of the employee, it would be odd to think that increasing pay by $1000 always increased motivation by the same amount. More plausible is a model in which increasing pay by a certain percentage increases motivation by a fixed amount. The prospect of a $1000 increase in pay is likely to have less impact on a millionaire than on a pauper.

Some practical difficulties with the logarithmic transformation should be borne in mind. The logarithm of zero is undefined and it is common to add a constant c to the transformed variable if the data contain zeroes:

$$Y_{transformed} = \ln(Y + c) \qquad \text{Equation 10.2}$$

The same practice could be extended to deal with negative values. This will only make sense if the zero point on the scale is arbitrary. If there is a true zero point and the variable can take on negative values, a logarithmic transformation is almost certainly inappropriate. Moreover, the choice of constant may exert influence on the model. A common choice is 0.5 (particularly for discrete data such as counts), but the value should be less than the smallest non-zero observation and almost always ≤ 1.[6] One rule of thumb is to select a constant halfway between zero and the smallest non-zero observation. Why is the choice of constant important? It determines the relative distance between the 'zero' observations and other values (and hence their impact on the analysis). Choosing a small constant makes the transformed zeroes more extreme relative to other values. So the constant will, to some extent, determine the influence of zeroes on the analysis.

An additional advantage of the logarithmic transformation is that the CI for a difference on a logarithmic scale has a direct interpretation for the geometric means when represented on the untransformed scale. Reversing the transformation (e.g., using e^x for the natural logarithm) gives a CI for the ratio of the two geometric means (Bland and Altman, 1996). This ratio will be one if there is no difference between the means, and if the CI includes one it will include zero on the logarithmic scale.

Example 10.3 In the simple regression equation for the location memory data, distance from the target (in *cm*) as a function of presentation time (in seconds) was:

$$Y_{distance} = 5.86 - 0.2581 X_{time}$$

If X is longer than 22.7 seconds, this model makes the absurd prediction that the target is recalled a negative distance from its true location. In Example 5.9 it was suggested that a power law model in which both X and Y are subject to a logarithmic transformation would be more plausible. The best-fitting regression line in this case is:

$$\ln(Y_{distance}) = 2.5475 - 0.6877 \times \ln(X_{time})$$

A presentation time of 120 seconds now makes the prediction of:

$$\ln(Y_{distance}) = 2.5475 - 0.6877 \times \ln(120) \approx -0.745$$

This prediction is on a logarithmic scale, but it is easier to interpret the outcome on the original scale:

$$Y = e^{-0.745} \approx 0.47$$

The model therefore predicts an average error of around half a centimetre for a presentation of two minutes. This is a more plausible model than that for the untransformed data (and fits the curvilinear pattern of the data fairly well). This does not imply that the power law model is the correct one. Other plausible models might perform just as well.

10.4.2 Square root transformations

The square root transformation works in a similar manner to the logarithmic transformation when dealing with positively skewed data and curvilinearity. One application of particular theoretical interest is for data thought to arise from a Poisson distribution. The Poisson distribution is often the first choice for modeling independent counts (i.e., frequency data). Although regression methods for Poisson distributions exist, it is often convenient to apply methods that assume a normal distribution of errors. With large sample sizes these methods often produce fairly accurate inferences. This is likely to be true if the mean of the Poisson distribution (its rate parameter λ) is large and therefore its sampling distribution is approximately normal. Another option is to apply a variance-stabilizing transformation to reduce positive skew and to rescale the variance in relation to the mean. As the mean of the Poisson distribution is also its variance, the obvious choice turns out to be the square root transformation. Thus a common strategy is to model the square root of the counts using least squares regression (or related techniques such as *t* tests).

The justification for the square root transformation is based on its asymptotic behavior for large values of λ. For large λ the variance will be approximately 1/4 and σ approximately 1/2. For small values of λ a number of alternative transformations have been suggested. One of the better known is the Freeman-Tukey transformation (Freeman and Tukey, 1950):

$$Y_{transformed} = \sqrt{Y} + \sqrt{Y+1} \qquad \text{Equation 10.3}$$

This tends to stabilize σ^2 (and hence also σ) at around one, and performs somewhat better (in terms of stabilization) than the simple square root transformation. Figure 10.2 shows histograms from random samples of 10,000 observations from a Poisson distribution with $\lambda = 3$. Panel (a) shows the untransformed data, panel (b) the square root transformation and panel (c) the Freeman-Tukey transformation.

Figure 10.2 provides a clear visual demonstration of the 'normalizing' properties of the square root transformation and close relatives such as Freeman-Tukey. The data in panels (b) and (c) display greater symmetry than the untransformed sample in panel (a). Yet each of the resulting distributions shows some departures from normality – notably the gaps in the lower tails of the transformed distributions. These occur because the Poisson distribution is discrete (and all observations are separated by at least one count). In the transformed distribution, the minimum gap between observations is proportionately larger for small values of Y, leading to

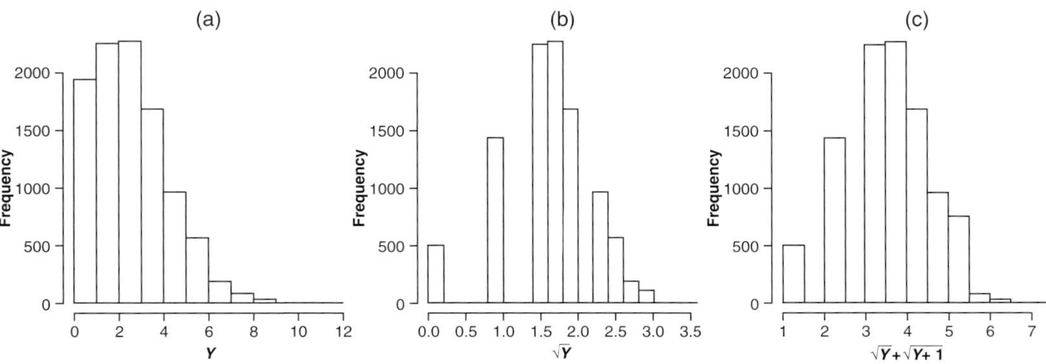

Figure 10.2 Large ($n = 10{,}000$) samples from a Poisson distribution with (a) no transformation, (b) a square root transformation, (c) a Freeman-Tukey transformation

the gaps in the plot. The Freeman-Tukey transformation works better: it has fewer gaps and is generally more symmetrical.

10.4.3 Reciprocal transformations

The reciprocal transformation is a logical choice for a rate or ratio measure. In many cases the designation of denominator and numerator for a ratio is arbitrary. Thus any measure of time per event can be re-expressed as a measure of speed (number of events per unit of time). This is an example of the reciprocal transformation (which swaps the roles of numerator and denominator in a ratio). Many of these re-expressions are at least as easy to interpret as the original ratio format. If so, the choice of transformation can be decided on the basis of the distributional properties of the data.

Example 10.4 For values greater than one the reciprocal transformation reduces big numbers more than small numbers. It is therefore a candidate for positively skewed data under these circumstances (e.g., $10^{-1} = 0.1$ and $100^{-1} = 0.01$). In contrast, for values constrained to be between zero and one the reciprocal transformation has the opposite effect and will reduce negative skew.

For example, a negatively skewed sample such as

.11 .14 .14 .17 .2 .2 .25 .33 1 [D_{5a}]

becomes less skewed after a reciprocal transformation:

9.1 7.1 7.1 5.9 5.0 5.0 4.0 3.0 1.0 [D_{5b}]

If the sample D_{5a} were the number of errors participants made per minute on a task, the transformed data D_{5b} would be the average number of minutes to produce one error for each participant. Both measures have a simple interpretation in the context of the study, but the latter has a more symmetrical distribution and is less likely to cause problems for least squares estimation.

10.4.4 Rank transformation

The rank transformation is often the first, and perhaps only, transformation taught to students learning statistics (though its role is sometimes disguised). Analyses using the rank transformation tend to be robust, and this makes them attractive where the assumptions of least squares regression are not likely to be met or (as with small samples) might be in doubt. Furthermore, replacing raw data with ranks simplifies many calculations. This happens because ranks are relatively easy to work with, and because statisticians can develop test procedures based around the distribution of ranks (common to many data sets) rather than the distributions of the raw data (which vary greatly between data sets). Its chief drawback is that the transformation is irreversible; it is not possible to use the ranks alone to reconstruct the original data.

The transformation works by replacing the observations with their ranks (the procedure first introduced for the Spearman correlation coefficient r_S (see Section 6.5.4). There are several different variants of the rank transformation, each appropriate to a different data structure. For independent group designs the numbers one to n are assigned to all n observations in order (from lowest to highest). Assuming no tied observations, the numbers are allocated across the groups without repetition. Analysis then proceeds on the ranks rather than the raw scores. For instance, an independent t test might compare the mean rank of each group.

In a paired design, the rank transformation is usually applied to the absolute differences between pairs. Positive or negative signs are attached to each rank according to the direction of the unranked difference. The signed ranks could then be analyzed using a one sample t test. For more than two repeated measures it is common to apply the rank transformation to scores within a sampling unit (e.g., within all the scores from a particular person). Zimmerman and Zumbo (1993a) point out that this procedure, the Friedman test, is a version of the sign test adapted to deal with more than two samples. As it ignores information about the size of differences between samples altogether, it produces relatively inefficient tests. Greater statistical power is achieved by ranking all N observations in a single sample prior to repeated measures ANOVA.

A good introduction to the mathematics of the rank transformation can be found in Conover (1980). Its robustness derives from the absence of extreme values. Heavy tails are therefore not a problem for rank transformed data, and the impact of extreme scores is reduced (and perhaps eliminated). In the absence of ties, any data set with the same sample size and design produces an identical set of numbers after rank transformation. The only difference between these rank transformed data sets is arrangement of numbers within each data set. This explains why the transformation is not reversible: an infinite number of untransformed data sets map onto any single set of ranked data.

This simplicity makes it relatively easy to construct exact tests (e.g., permutation tests) for rank transformed data. These tests calculate the exact probability of different combinations of ranks arising in different parts of the data set. For example, two independent groups might be compared by summing the ranks in the more extreme group and looking to see how probable it is that a sum of ranks that extreme (or more extreme) could occur purely by chance. The exact test accomplishes this by generating all possible permutations of ranks for N observations falling into distinct groups of size n_1 and n_2. Calculation of an exact significance probability is trivial using this information (e.g., if only 37 permutations out of 4096 produce a sum of ranks as extreme or more extreme than that observed, one-sided $p = 37/4096 \approx .009$). The history of the rank transformation in statistics is linked to the development of permutation tests for ranked data (*ibid.*). For instance, the test just described is known as the Mann-Whitney-Wilcoxon or Mann-Whitney U test (similar procedures being described by different authors). There are two immediate problems with the exact approach (and some subtler ones to be considered later). One is the complication of computing ranks and permutations in the presence of ties (and the tests are applied in situations where ties are not uncommon). The second problem is that a researcher needs to learn a different (albeit related) procedure for almost every type of analysis they carry out.

A straightforward resolution to both problems is available. Conover and Iman (1981) argue that there is little practical advantage to exact tests of ranks over use of a rank transformation prior to conventional, least squares methods. For example, Conover and Iman show that independent t computed on the ranks of two independent groups takes the value

$$t_R = \frac{T}{\sqrt{\frac{N-1}{N-2} - \frac{1}{N-2}T^2}} \qquad \text{Equation 10.4}$$

where T is the standardized test statistic from the Mann-Whitney-Wilcoxon test and N is the total sample size (*ibid.*). This standardized statistic is used in large samples to perform the test (when exact solutions are difficult to compute). Unless N is very small, the denominator is very close to one in value and the two statistics are virtually identical. Thus only in small samples will there be a noticeable difference between t_R and T (and rarely will there be any practical difference in samples of a reasonable size). A similar case can be made for paired t and other familiar statistics (*ibid.*). It also provides a solution to dealing with ties (which the derivation of T incorporates). Although there are several methods for ranking tied values, the standard solution (assumed here) is to assign the tied values the mean of the ranks they would have obtained had the values not been tied.

Rather than learn a new test for each procedure, it makes sense (except perhaps with very small sample sizes such as $N \leq 10$) to apply conventional least squares tests to the rank transformed data. This strategy is also consistent with the relationship between the Spearman and Pearson correlation (r_S being r computed after a rank transformation).

Rank transformation methods, whether of the exact form or the near-equivalents proposed by Conover and Iman (*ibid.*), are among the easiest robust methods to implement. They are particularly useful for very small data sets where bootstrapping and more computationally intensive robust methods sometimes fail. Siegel and Castellan (1988) provide a gentle introduction to these and related methods (focusing on exact tests that can be readily calculated by hand). However, many statisticians have reservations about using rank transformation methods more widely. A number of reasons for this have been articulated, but they nearly all boil down to the same fundamental concern: rank transformations don't just transform data, they do so in a way that makes it impossible to recover the original scores (unless additional information is recruited).

This has several consequences. It is hard to interpret the statistical model implied by the analysis of ranks in terms of the original data. This won't matter if the sole aim is to construct a significance test, but if you want to make predictions or obtain CIs, use of ranks introduces a potentially unnecessary obstacle. Adequate CIs and predictions are sometimes possible by interpolation (i.e., using known values to make educated guesses about where the inferences fall on the original scale). Nevertheless, given the availability of many other robust methods and alternative transformations, many researchers prefer to avoid the rank transformation except in special cases (e.g., very small samples). A corollary is that when the research question involves trying to understand the quantitative relationships between variables on their original scales (e.g., in regression rather than correlation), rank transformations are particularly unsuitable. This unsuitability increases for statistical models involving more than two variables.

Last of all, it is sometimes asserted that rank transformation methods make no assumptions (or perhaps only weak assumptions) about the distributions the original data are drawn from. This is clearly not the case. Any rank transformation procedure will make generic assumptions about the nature of the sample and the appropriateness of the model. In addition, independent groups procedures assume independence (arguably the most stringent and limiting assumption of least squares regression). Rank transformation tests also assume samples are drawn from distributions with the same shape. Problems such as varying degrees of skew between samples, or large differences in variances are known to influence their performance.[7] Exact tests of ranks also cease to be exact in the presence of ties (and can suffer badly if many ties are present).

For this reason rank transformation tests are not always appropriate. They have two main strengths. One is as robust hypothesis tests for very small samples. The other is for situations where the researcher is primarily interested in the ranks rather than the raw data. Even then, it may sometimes be preferable to use the untransformed data to fit a model and to extract information about the order of different outcomes afterwards (e.g., when trying to predict the winner of a race it may be better to predict the race times and determine the winner from the order of the predictions, rather than trying to predict the order directly).

Example 10.5 The rank transformation was illustrated for the calculation of r_s in Example 6.7. This example will illustrate some of the differences in the computation of ranks for common data structures.

The first illustration considers a single sample. The D_{5a} data (from Example 10.4) represent the rate of errors per minute for a task. The reciprocal transformed data set D_{5b} represents minutes per error. When ranked the observations in data set D_{5a} become (in order):

1 2.5 2.5 4 5.5 5.5 7 8 9

Those in D_{5b} become:

9 7.5 7.5 6 4.5 4.5 3 2 1

This illustrates the standard method of resolving ties (assigning the mean of the ranks they would have received had no ties been present). If, as in D_{5a}, the 2nd and 3rd lowest observations are tied, the mean of ranks 2 and 3 (2.5) is assigned to each observation and 4 is assigned to the next lowest (2 and 3 being 'used up'). The values have the same relative position in the sequence and are perfectly negatively correlated (and ignoring order would be numerically identical if no ties were present). Power family transformations such as the reciprocal are monotonic: they don't change the relative order within a data set (though they can – as in this case – completely reverse it).

For an independent groups design consider the situation of two groups with one extreme value present and $n = 5$. Group 1 consists of the following data (with ranks in brackets):

2 (*1*) 3 (*2*) 6 (*3.5*) 6 (*3.5*) 12 (*6*)

While group 2 contains the data:

8 (*5*) 14 (*7*) 15 (*8*) 21 (*9*) 62 (*10*)

A t test of the untransformed data gives the result $t(8) = 1.84$, $p = .103$. The t test on the ranks gives $t_R(8) = 3.81$, $p = .005$. The exact test on the ranks gives $U\ (N = 10) = 1$, $p = .016$ (where the U statistic is the difference between the observed and minimum possible total of the ranks of the group with the lowest mean rank). Both t_R and the exact test reject the null hypothesis that the mean ranks are equal. The clear superiority of the exact test over the t_R test here stems from the very small sample sizes.

For paired differences the most common method of applying the rank transformation is to rank the differences after excluding ties and assign them a positive or negative sign according to the direction of the differences. This procedure is usually termed the *Wilcoxon signed ranks* or *Wilcoxon T* test. The raw differences for the TOT data from Example 4.5 are

+2 +1 +1 +1 +1 −3 −2 −1 −1 −1 −1 0 0 0 0

The paired data method ranks the absolute differences of the untied scores and produces the ranks:

11 8.5 8.5 8.5 8.5 1 2 4.5 4.5 4.5 4.5

The next step is to assign positive or negative signs to each of these values according to the original direction of the difference. The result is:

$$+9.5 \quad +4.5 \quad +4.5 \quad +4.5 \quad +4.5 \quad -11 \quad -9.5 \quad -4.5 \quad -4.5 \quad -4.5 \quad -4.5$$

If differences between pairs occur at random, you'd expect them to be just as likely to be positive as negative. The null hypothesis that the population difference mean is zero also implies that the population difference in paired ranks is zero. This could be checked with a one sample t test on the signed ranks. This gives the result $t(10) = 0.49$, $p = .633$. The exact Wilcoxon signed-ranks test gives $T\ (N = 11) = 27.5$, $p = .609$. Here the two procedures give fairly similar p values (even though n is small).

For more than two groups, the procedure recommended here is to extend the approach used to rank data in the two independent groups case. The ranks one to N should be assigned as if all observations are from a single sample. The ranked data are then analyzed using independent or repeated measures ANOVA (as appropriate to the design). This produces a test more or less equivalent to the Kruskal-Wallis test for independent measures designs. For repeated measures designs the resulting test has greater statistical power than the usual Friedman test (Zimmerman and Zumbo, 1993a).

10.5 R code for Chapter 10

10.5.1 Robust independent *t* tests (Example 10.1)

Running the YH bootstrap t test in R requires loading the `yhbt()` function from Rand Wilcox's website.[8] This version implemented here is the 10% trimmed test (i.e., trimming 10% from each tail of the sample). The `nboot` parameter specifies the number of bootstrap samples to take (generally it is best to start low or with the default of 600 and increment upwards). The default also fixes the random seed so that the bootstrap samples are identical each time. This is useful for checking and reproducing results, but not ideal for real applications and is set to `FALSE` here). The comprehension data in the data frame `bp2000` are used in this example.

```
bootreps <- 999
trim <- .1

with(bp2000, yhbt(percent_accuracy[1:28],
  percent_accuracy[29:56], tr=trim, nboot=bootreps, SEED =
  FALSE)
```

The bootstrap tests were obtained using the `boot` package used for the earlier bootstrapping examples. For a bootstrapped trimmed mean you could use:

```
library(boot)
pm <-matrix(nrow=28,ncol=2)
pm[,1] <- bp2000$percent_accuracy[1:28]
pm[,2] <- bp2000$percent_accuracy[29:56]
```

```
boot.mdiffs <- boot(pm,function(xmat,ind)
  mean(xmat[ind,2],trim)-mean(xmat[ind,1],trim), R=bootreps)
boot.ci(boot.mdiffs)
```

Replacing mean with median (or increasing the proportion of trimming in each tail to .5) gives a bootstrap test of the differences in medians.

10.5.2 Robust regression (Example 10.2)

There is extensive support for robust regression methods in R. A quick sketch of how to run a robust regression is provided here. The commands below first import data from the .csv file containing the data used in Example 10.2. The robust linear model `rlm()` function is then loaded from the `MASS` package and a robust regression using MM-estimation is calculated.

```
library(foreign)
hov.dat <- read.csv('hov.csv')

library(MASS)

hov.rmod <- rlm(y ~ x, method='MM', data=hov.dat)
summary(hov.rmod)
```

Obtaining an accurate 95% CI for the slope is more difficult for robust regression than least squares regression. An approximation based on the t distribution is unlikely to be particularly accurate. A crude (approximate) 95% CI for the slope is given by:

```
moe <- qt(.975,11.3373) * 0.1545
hov.rmod$coef[2] + c(-1,1)*moe
```

A better option is to bootstrap the regression. Fox (2002b) describes how to do this using the `boot` package. The main requirement is that you specify a function for the coefficient or coefficients you want to bootstrap. Adapting an example from Fox gives this function for the slope of the robust regression:

```
boot.rlm <- function(data, indices, maxit=20) {
  data <- data[indices,]
  rlm(y ~ x, method='MM', data=data, maxit=maxit)$coef[[2]]
}
```

The `maxit` argument is used to increase the maximum number of iterations for the robust linear regression when used within `boot`. The default of 20 may not be enough (and 150 is used below). The boot function produces warnings if the regressions don't converge.

```
bootreps <- 999
boot.slope<- boot(data = hov.dat, statistic = boot.rlm,
  R=bootreps, maxit=150)
boot.ci(boot.slope)
```

Increasing the number of replications (e.g., to 9999) produces more consistent results (but may take some time on a standard desktop computer).

10.5.3 Transformations (Examples 10.3 and 10.4)

Most common transformations are simple to apply in R using `log()`, `sqrt()` or powers (^). The following function refits a power law to the location memory data set (in which both predictor and outcome variable are transformed by taking the natural logarithm).

```
locmem.pl <- lm(log(distance) ~ log(time))
```

The prediction for accuracy (in *cm*) of location memory after 120 seconds presentation time is obtained as set out below. It involves creating a data frame that contains the new predictor value or values (here the time of 120 seconds). Reversing the natural transformation using `exp()` gives the prediction on the untransformed scale:

```
time.new <- data.frame(time = 120)
predict(locmem.pl, time.new)
exp(predict(locmem.pl, time.new))
```

Because the model builds the `log()` function into the formula, the prediction is in the untransformed units. Had the variables `time` and `distance` been transformed and assigned to new variables before calling `lm()`, the prediction would have needed to use `log(120)` to be on the correct scale.

The reciprocal transformation is illustrated by the errors per minute versus minutes per error data in Example 10.4:

```
epm <- c(.11, .14, .14, .17, .2, .2, .25, .33, 1)
mpe <- 1/epm
```

The same data are used for the rank transformation in Example 10.5. The R `rank()` function is extremely handy. Its default tie resolution method is the standard one (but see `?rank` for others).

```
rank(epm)
rank(mpe)
```

For independent group designs, applying the rank transformation is a matter of ranking the raw data (ignoring group) and running the *t* test on the ranks. As the output of this rank transformation is a single variable, it is convenient to use a formula to call the `t.test()` function. Here the categorical grouping variable is first created as using the generate levels `gl()` function:

```
dv <- c(2, 3, 6, 6, 12, 8, 14, 15, 21, 62)
group <- gl(2,5)
t.test(rank(dv) ~ group, var.equal=TRUE)
```

Compare this output to versions of the Mann-Whitney-Wilcoxon test for independent samples using the `wilcox.test()` function and to the *t* test on the unranked data:

```
wilcox.test(dv ~ group, correct=FALSE)
wilcox.test(dv ~ group, correct=TRUE)

t.test(dv ~ group, var.equal=TRUE)
```

The latter includes a continuity correction (because the ranks are not continuous; this can influence the outcome when an exact test of the ranks is not possible owing to ties). If no ties are present an exact version of the test is possible. This is the R default for small samples (unless ties are present). It can be called for larger samples by adding `EXACT=TRUE`. A robust CI (not based on the ranks) can be obtained by adding `conf.int=TRUE`.

For paired samples, getting the signed ranks of the differences is probably easiest to do by hand unless the sample size is large. The following code assigns the signed ranks of the TOT data to a variable and runs a one sample *t* test. This is followed with the `wilcox.test()` function to run the Wilcoxon signed-ranks test with and without continuity correction on the raw differences (contained in the vector `pdiffs` from Example 4.5).

```
signed.diffs <- c(9.5, 4.5, 4.5, 4.5, 4.5, -11, -9.5, -4.5, -4.5,
  -4.5, -4.5)
t.test(signed.diffs)
wilcox.test(pdiffs, correct = FALSE)
wilcox.test(pdiffs, correct = TRUE)
```

The exact Kruskal-Wallis test can be applied for more than two independent samples via `kruskal.test()`. For repeated measures designs with three or more groups the outcome should be ranked as for an independent group design and the analysis run as a repeated measures ANOVA (see Chapter 16). This is superior to the popular, but much less efficient, Friedman test (Zimmerman and Zumbo, 1993a).

10.5.4 R packages

Canty, A., and Ripley, B. D. (2010) *boot*: Bootstrap R (S-Plus) Functions. R package version 1.2-42.

R-core members, DebRoy, S. *et al.* (2011) *foreign*: Read Data Stored by MINITAB, S, SAS, SPSS, Stata, Systat, dBase. R package version 0.8-42.

Venables, W. N., and Ripley, B. D. (2002) *MASS*: Modern Applied Statistics with S. (4th edn) Springer: New York.

10.6 Notes on SPSS syntax for Chapter 10

10.6.1 Transformations and robust methods

Power transformations are easy to obtain in SPSS using the `COMPUTE` command. SPSS has very versatile data manipulation procedures (e.g., from the <TRANSFORM> menu) and these include the rank transformation. The following syntax ranks the percentage accuracy performance from the baguley_payne_2000.sav data set. The method for dealing with ties can be varied – but mean substitution is the default.

SPSS data file: baguley_payne_2000.sav

```
RANK
  VARIABLES=percent_accuracy (A)
  /RANK
  /PRINT=YES
  /TIES=MEAN.
```

As of writing, options for robust regression in SPSS are limited.

10.7 Bibliography and further reading

Wilcox, R. R., and Keselman, H. J. (2003) Modern Robust Data Analysis Methods: Measures of Central Tendency. *Psychological Methods*, 8, 254–74.

Wright, D. B. and London, K. (2009) *Modern Regression Techniques using R*. London: Sage.

10.8 Online supplement 2: Dealing with missing data

For a review of methods for dealing with missing data – with particular emphasis on multiple imputation, providing examples in R and SPSS, go to online supplement 2 at www.palgrave.com/psychology/baguley.

11
Alternatives to classical statistical inference

Contents

11.1 Chapter overview

This chapter introduces alternatives to classical frequentist inference. The chapter begins by reviewing the null hypothesis significance testing controversy. Frequentist responses to this controversy, including potential improvements to or reforms of significance testing, are considered. Subsequent sections introduce two major alternatives to frequentist methods: likelihood and Bayesian inference. The chapter ends by considering information criteria such as AIC and BIC as model comparison tools and briefly explains the connection between information theoretic, likelihood and Bayesian methods.

11.2 The null hypothesis significance testing controversy

In many scientific disciplines statistical inference is synonymous with frequentist methods, and null hypothesis significance tests (NHSTs) in particular. The use of NHSTs in the face of criticism sustained over many years (e.g., Boring, 1919; Rozeboom, 1960; Cohen, 1994; Loftus, 2001; Sedlmeier, 2009) has puzzled many people. In some disciplines – notably psychology, education and economics – there have been calls for the use of NHSTs to be banned or abandoned (see Shrout, 1997; Nix and Barnette, 1998; Ziliak and McCloskey, 2004). The debate surrounding the use of NHSTs, when acknowledged, has become known as the *null hypothesis significance testing controversy*. There is little point trying to summarize the whole debate here; there is at least one excellent review of both the controversy and of attempts to resolve it (Nickerson, 2000).

The main criticisms can be distilled into three main strands. The first is that null hypothesis significance testing is widely misunderstood. The second is that NHSTs can lead to serious problems when applied. Although this may seem a natural consequence of the first point – it is not necessarily inevitable (e.g., the misunderstandings might be inconsequential relative to problems arising from sampling error or violations of statistical assumptions). The third, and potentially most damning, criticism is that NHSTs are the wrong tool for the job: the inferences that they support are not those that researchers require. This latter point is also probably the most interesting. Even if NHSTs are neither misunderstood nor misapplied, they work by making probability calculations that are conditional on the null hypothesis (H_0) being true. Yet H_0 is usually only of secondary or indirect interest to a researcher. Expert opinion is even divided as to whether the H_0 can ever be true.[1] If this final strand of criticism is correct, it suggests that all frequentist methods, including confidence intervals (CIs) should be abandoned in favor of non-frequentist alternatives such as likelihood or Bayesian inference (Dienes, 2008).

The misconceptions surrounding NHSTs are legion. Nickerson (2000) devotes nearly 20 pages of a 60-page review to discussing different misconceptions and their implications. Most of the misconceptions (and certainly the more prevalent ones) involve difficulties understanding or reasoning with conditional probabilities. A p value is the probability of a result (e.g., test statistic) as extreme or more extreme than the one observed if H_0 is true. Many misconceptions simply treat p, or related quantities such as the Type I and Type II error rates (α and β), as unconditional probabilities. It is very tempting to fall into the trap of thinking that p is the probability of H_0 being true or of the alternative hypothesis (H_1) being false.

One way to illustrate that this interpretation of a p value is false is through *Lindley's paradox*.[2] Lindley (1957) set out this apparent paradox with a simple example where $p < .05$ (leading to rejection of H_0 by a conventional NHST) even though the probability of H_0 is .95 or more.

Example 11.1 Lindley's example is expressed mathematically, but demonstrating the phenomenon he describes does not require complex calculations. I'll use a slightly different example from the one considered by Lindley. Imagine a court case in which a mother is accused of a horrific crime: that of killing two infant children born several years apart. There is no known cause of death for either child and the deaths are initially attributed to SIDS (*sudden infant death syndrome*). SIDS is a label attached to unexpected and unexplained deaths in infants when the cause is unknown (Hill, 2004). A prosecutor argues that the probability of a SIDS death in this case is one in 8543 and that the probability of two such deaths is $(1/8543)^2$ or about one in 73 million.* The prosecution argues that this probability is so tiny that the 'null hypothesis' that these were genuine SIDS deaths can be rejected. By implication, the 'alternative hypothesis' (that the children were murdered by their mother) must be true. These causes can be set out as formal hypotheses:

$$H_0 : \text{cause of death} = \text{SIDS}$$

$$H_1 : \text{cause of death} = \text{murder}$$

At this point I'm going to remind you of Lindley's paradox. This, in effect, asserts that no matter how tiny a p value is, H_0 can still be highly probable. To realize that Lindley's paradox is relevant you need to bear in mind that the probability of one in 73 million is a conditional probability. It is the probability of the observed data on the assumption that both deaths were due to SIDS (i.e., that H_0 is true). In fact, the probability that both deaths were due to SIDS is larger (most likely very much larger) than one in 73 million. Given that two tragic deaths have occurred, and given that all natural but explained causes have been ruled out, only two possibilities remain: SIDS and murder. Both these causes of infant death are very rare (relative to natural, explained deaths).

The probability of either cause can't be evaluated without also considering the other. The mathematics of this comparison is rather simple. As there are only two mutually exclusive outcomes, it follows that the probability of either hypothesis depends on the relative rarity of SIDS and murder. If they are equally rare, the ratio of the two conditional probabilities is one (and the probability of either cause being correct is .5). The probability of the either hypothesis being true cannot be evaluated by looking at a p value alone.

In case this example seems far-fetched, it is worth pointing out that it is based on the events that led to the tragic and wrongful conviction of Sally Clark (though both the evidence and statistical arguments have been simplified). In his analysis of the evidence, Hill (2004) estimated that the probability of SIDS as an explanation for two sudden and unexplained infant deaths was around five to nine times more likely than murder. This would put the probability of SIDS being 'true' at about .80 or .90 (very different from the probability of one in 73 million implied by the prosecution).** Confusing a p value for the probability that H_0 is false or the probability that H_1 is true can have serious consequences.***

*This calculation makes the implausible and, as it turns out, false assumption that the events are independent. This error is not central to the flow of the example and will be set to one side.
** For more detail on the legal, scientific and statistical issues arising from this case see Hill (2004).
*** A formal analysis of this problem is trivial using Bayes' theorem (introduced in Box 11.3). If you are already familiar with Bayes' theorem, this example may seem obvious or trivial.

This does not necessarily mean that NHSTs are fatally flawed. It is possible to avoid misinterpreting p values and conditional probabilities such as α and β. One way to avoid these misconceptions is not to get too worked up about the p value itself, but to consider it as a tiny component in a statistical decision procedure, and an even smaller element in a statistical argument (Abelson, 1995). The prevalence of these misconceptions and the ease with which some experts are drawn to them suggests that this may not be easy. Moreover, not all the misconceptions with significance testing are directly related to misunderstandings of conditional probability. People are sometimes misled – particularly if they have little statistical training – into thinking that a statistically significant effect is somehow evidence of the practical or theoretical importance of an effect. This misunderstanding was considered at length in Chapter 7 and Chapter 8 (in relation to effect size and statistical significance). Statistical significance is as a tool for detecting an effect (i.e., discriminating signals from statistical noise). It is not a tool for assessing evidence or determining the importance of an effect.

11.2.1 Some practical problems with significance tests

What of the difficulties of applying significance testing in practice? Some problems (e.g., those related to statistical power) are now widely recognized. NHSTs don't function properly if statistical power is set too low or too high. What makes matters worse is that it isn't immediately clear when a significance test is reported that a study has low statistical power. A CI is superior in this respect (as the width of the CI can give a sense of the precision with which an effect has been measured).

Two related problems are multiple testing and stopping rules. Multiple testing arises for several reasons. One reason is that the research questions rarely reduce to a single hypothesis test. There are usually several hypotheses of interest to a researcher and several tests are conducted. As each test has its own Type I error rate, the overall rate for multiple tests (the chance of at least one Type I error) rises rapidly with the number of uncorrected tests. This problem is well known and many potential solutions have been proposed. A more subtle variation is that studies will often collect data about several different variables. Even if the hypothesis of interest is not supported, it is likely that another interesting pattern will emerge as statistically significant. Maxwell (2004) has argued that this phenomenon accounts for the persistence of low-powered studies in many fields of research; even if a study has low power to detect the effect you are most interested in, one of the other tests will probably achieve statistical significance. One solution – sometimes employed in medical research – is to declare both the hypothesis and the primary outcome measure in advance. However, this is not ideal. It seems wasteful to ignore or discount potentially interesting findings, just because they are unexpected. This is a recurring dilemma with NHSTs (Nickerson, 2000; Dienes, 2008).

Stopping rules are also a problem (and could be considered a variant of the multiple testing problem). A conventional NHST assumes that the sample size is set in advance of data collection. This could be done by specifying n (perhaps as the result of a statistical power calculation) or by setting conditions for terminating data collection (e.g., stopping at a particular time). The former is known as a fixed-sample rule (Botella *et al.*, 2006). The issue is important because the p value calculated for a significance test is only accurate if an appropriate stopping rule is in place. This condition is not always met. A common strategy is to collect an initial quantity of data and, based on a preliminary NHST, stop data collection if $p < \alpha$, but resume if $p > \alpha$. Under this strategy, known as *optional stopping*, data collection then continues until $p < \alpha$ or you run out of time, money or patience.

Optional stopping biases p values downwards. With sufficient resources and persistence this strategy guarantees that p will eventually fall below α, even if H_0 is true (Frick, 1998; Wagenmakers, 2007; Dienes, 2008). Optional stopping is widespread, both in this relatively blatant form and in more subtle forms (e.g., because researchers monitor data as they are collected). It is also not uncommon for journal editors or reviewers to request researchers to collect more data. Optional stopping is almost certainly a more serious threat to evaluating a *p* value than multiple testing. Whereas multiplicity of testing increases the chance of one or more Type I errors occurring among a set of tests, optional stopping biases the *p* value for the outcome of primary interest. Many researchers who use NHSTs seem unaware of the dangers of optional stopping, though there are ways to design stopping rules to reduce or avoid this problem (see Box 11.1).

These three issues – neglect of statistical power, multiple testing and optional stopping – give a flavor of the practical difficulties that arise with NHSTs. These difficulties are widely recognized among frequentist statisticians who use NHSTs. They are not considered controversial and there are active attempts to resolve them within the frequentist approach.

Box 11.1 Simple stopping rules for NHSTs and CIs

Is it possible to apply NHSTs or CIs and correct for the effects of optional stopping? This is a real concern in medical research where it would be unethical to keep going with a clinical trial if a) it is very likely that the treatment is harmful to patients, or b) patients in a control condition are missing out on an effective treatment. Rules for stopping early are often built into a clinical trial, but may need to be individually tailored to the design.

Are there simpler alternatives? Frick (1995) proposed a very simple stopping rule. His rule – called COAST (composite open adaptive sequential test) – works by fixing an arbitrary initial minimum sample size (e.g., $N_1 = 20$) and then performing a significance test. The test operates using two α thresholds (here labeled as α_{lower} and α_{upper}). If observed $p < \alpha_{\text{lower}}$ the test is declared statistically significant, and if $p > \alpha_{\text{upper}}$ it is declared statistically non-significant. If *p* lies between these thresholds (i.e., $\alpha_{\text{lower}} \leq p \leq \alpha_{\text{upper}}$) then data collection resumes. Frick proposed that researchers add to N_1 in small batches and rerun the test at each point until $p < \alpha_{\text{lower}}$ or $p > \alpha_{\text{upper}}$. His simulations show that for a two-sided *t* test, setting $\alpha_{\text{lower}} = .01$ and $\alpha_{\text{upper}} = .36$ maintains true α close to .05. Frick also showed that COAST was fairly robust to changes in N_1 or the size of the incremental increase in *N*, and tends to have greater statistical power than a fixed-sample rule.

Botella *et al.* (2006) proposed a more efficient version of COAST. Their stopping rule, CLAST (composite limited adaptive sequential test), gains efficiency by incorporating a maximum sample size N_{max}. This is a sensible move because there is nearly always some practical limit on the sample size. CLAST works by first determining sample size according to the fixed-sample rule (N_{FSR}). Ideally N_{FSR} should be estimated using a conventional statistical power calculation. The minimum sample size N_1 is set at $\frac{1}{2}N_{FSR}$ and the maximum N_{max} is set at $\frac{3}{2}N_{FSR}$. CLAST is otherwise very similar to the COAST rule. Until N_{max} is reached, statistical significance is achieved if $p < \alpha_{\text{lower}}$ and the test is non-significant if $p > \alpha_{\text{upper}}$. Otherwise data are added in increments of size N_2 (with $N_2 = 1$ being the most efficient increment size) and an additional NHST carried out. Once $N = N_{max}$ the experiment stops. If $p < \alpha$ the test is declared statistically significant and if $p > \alpha$ it is declared non-significant.

For $\alpha_{lower} = .01$, simulations confirm that α_{upper} needs to be set at .36 to maintain true $\alpha = .05$ for a two-sided *t* test (*ibid.*). For a one-sided *t* test the threshold is $\alpha_{upper} = .25$. This will not necessarily generalize to other tests. However, a threshold of $\alpha_{upper} = .35$ will maintain overall α at .05 for the χ^2 test of independence for a 2×2 contingency table. Ximénez and Revuelta (2007) extend the CLAST rule to one-way ANOVA.

An even simpler stopping rule is possible for CIs (Armitage *et al.*, 2002; Dienes, 2008). This rule keeps collecting data until the observed width is narrower than the desired width *W*. Using this approach it is important to select a value of *W* that will always exclude either the effect size expected under H_0 or the effect size you wish to detect. Dienes (2008) gives the example of testing for a difference in means. If the minimally interesting difference in means is five then $W = 4$ would be a sensible choice. This way, the resulting CI can't contain both zero and five.

This method could be combined with AIPE to determine sample size for a CI. This is achieved by setting a minimum sample size (analogous to N_1) that has a reasonable chance (e.g., 20–40%) of the desired W. If the observed width w is greater than W, increment N until the desired width is reached. This works as a stopping rule because it doesn't rely on p. A non-significant effect may be measured precisely, and a significant effect may have a wide interval estimate.

11.2.2 Can the null hypothesis ever be true?

A recurring objection to the use of NHSTs is that a point null hypothesis is rarely – perhaps never – true. This objection is an influential one. If taken literally, it would undermine most (possibly all) experimental science. The argument has been widely deployed (see Nickerson, 2000). For instance, Schmidt (1996, p. 1176) states that 'Type I errors... probably cannot occur in most studies', while Cohen (1994, p.1000) states that 'work in power analysis led me to believe that the nil hypothesis is always false'. The details of the argument rest on the identification of H_0 as a single point on the infinitely long number line.[3] As this point occupies an infinitely small portion of the entire line, the probability of it being true must be zero. Following this line of reasoning, if you manipulate or measure one variable and look to see whether it has an effect on another, there will always be some effect (though it may be exceedingly small). This implies that a large enough sample will always reject H_0.[4]

Not everyone is convinced by this argument. A great deal of science is based on the view that it is possible to identify 'invariances' such as the speed of light (Rouder *et al.*, 2009, p. 225). Even if these invariances are thought to hold approximately and not exactly, a point null hypothesis may serve as a useful proxy unless the sample size is huge (Nickerson, 2000). Moreover, for true experiments (in which allocation to conditions is entirely random) the null hypothesis is sometimes extremely plausible (Frick, 1995). A good illustration of this is for research on paranormal phenomena. Some experimental manipulations may also fall into this category. In an experiment looking at presentations of a masked prime on a response, it is entirely plausible that there might be no effect for very brief presentations. For instance, there may be an effect of a 50 millisecond (*ms*) presentation, but for some shorter presentation (e.g., 5 or 10 *ms*) the presentation might be too quick for the human visual system to respond to.

Thus there appear to be situations in which a point null hypothesis is plausible. Even when it is not, there are two arguments as to why setting up a point null hypothesis might be reasonable. The first is that while some non-zero effect is almost certainly true, you may not know the direction of the effect. Frick (1996) has defended NHSTs on the grounds that rejecting H_0 with a two-sided test is an appropriate decision procedure for determining the direction of an effect. The second argument is that H_0 is a reasonable proxy for a negligible effect (Frick, 1995; Rouder *et al.*, 2009). This line of argument doesn't always hold, but has merit for the sample sizes typical of research with human participants. A lot depends on precisely how large the sample size is. If huge samples are available, it is almost certainly better to focus on obtaining precise parameter estimates (e.g., using CIs) rather than statistical significance. Very large samples will usually give a pretty good sense of the size of an effect (which is probably more interesting than whether it exists).

Example 11.2 Wiseman and Greening (2002) report the results of a large extra-sensory perception (ESP) experiment. The experiment is illuminating for a number of reasons. Unlike many studies that rely on NHSTs, the authors explicitly consider the problem of optional stopping (and had a stopping rule in place). They also report a statistical power calculation based on the average effect obtained in previous reports of ESP. They collected data on a total of 110,959 forced-choice trials from 27,856 participants and report several tests (e.g., for the total number of trials and various sub-samples). None of the tests were corrected for multiple testing (thus true α is larger than the nominal level of $\alpha = .05$). This increases statistical power and inflates the overall Type I error rate, yet none of the tests detected an effect of ESP.

Each trial involved guessing the outcome of a simulated coin toss presented on a computer screen (with the outcome determined by a random number generator). It is convenient to treat these trials as independent (even though some are from the same participants). Non-independent responses would only impact on the analysis if H_0 (no effect of ESP) were false. Out of a total of 110,959 trials, 49.91% (55,375) of the responses were correct. This is a small difference from that expected by random guessing, but in the wrong direction (given that ESP should lead to better than chance performance). The binomial test gives two-sided $p = .532$ and the 95% Blaker CI for the proportion of correct responses is [.496, .502]. Despite an enormous sample size, the effect is resolutely non-significant. H_0 is (to say the least) highly plausible in this case. Even had the researchers collected data from a million trials, then the chance of obtaining a statistically significant result for the overall test would most likely still be around α.

Wiseman and Greening's study is a useful counter-example to the assertion that obtaining very large sample sizes guarantees statistical significance. Even if a study is not a carefully controlled experiment and the point null hypothesis is not plausible, there is no guarantee that a large sample will detect a tiny effect. Consider the statistical power to detect a correlation of $\rho = .01$.* To have a 50% chance of detecting a correlation of this size with a two-sided test requires over 38,000 participants. A 10% chance to detect a correlation this small requires over 4000 participants.

*Although $\rho = .01$ is not necessarily a small or negligible effect, many small effects will equate to correlations of this size small or smaller.

11.3 Frequentist responses to the NHST controversy

11.3.1 Strict Neyman-Pearson inference

One response to the shortcomings of significance tests as generally practiced is to argue for strict adherence to the Neyman-Pearson approach. Many problems associated with the application of NHSTs arise from the confusion inherent in mixing Fisherian with Neyman-Pearson inference (see Hubbard, 2004). Where Fisher appears to have tried to develop a way of assessing the evidence for or against a hypothesis, Neyman and Pearson worked toward a logically coherent decision procedure. Neyman and Pearson were largely successful, provided the aim of the decision procedure is to control the long-run Type I and Type II error rates for a set of tests (Dienes, 2008).

Applying Neyman-Pearson inference correctly is straightforward, provided certain basic steps are taken. The desired levels of α and β (the Type I and Type II error rates) should be determined carefully in relation to the costs of the errors. For instance, if the costs are approximately equal it would be reasonable to set $\alpha = \beta$ and estimate the required sample for a suitably low overall error rate. This may seem self-evident, but recall that most research adopts $\alpha = .05$, and for statistical power, an arbitrary target of $\beta = .20$ is common (i.e., power of $1 - \beta = .80$).[5] In addition, practices that distort the calculated p value (such as multiple testing or optional stopping) must be avoided or dealt with (e.g., by adjusting α or adopting a stopping rule).

Also important is the interpretation of the test. The outcome is a decision to accept or reject H_0 (which is reasonable if the Type I and Type II error rates have been set in accordance with a researcher's goals). According to this view, it doesn't make sense to interpret a p value other than as falling above or below the threshold for statistical significance. Hence the tradition – inconsistently applied – of reporting p values relative to α (e.g., $p > .05$) rather than to some degree of precision (e.g., $p = .08$).[6]

Why doesn't this often happen in practice? One reason is that – following Fisher – we are not primarily concerned about the control of the long-run error rate. A typical researcher cares more about the probability that a particular hypothesis is true or false. This is may be one reason why even experts (e.g., professional statisticians) fall prey to common misconceptions about p values (Lecoutre *et al.*, 2003).

A point in favor of the strict Neyman-Pearson inference is that it includes the use of CIs as a formal tool of inference. CIs were first developed as part of this approach and have some advantages over the simple accept–reject decision of an NHST (e.g., in terms of depicting precision of measurement). The catch is that strict adherence to Neyman-Pearson inference leads to a very restrictive, formal interpretation of a CI. Many proponents of CIs prefer an informal interpretation of them. The informal interpretation of a CI as a range of plausible values for the true effect, although strictly incorrect, is usually reasonable (Gardner and Altman, 1986; Loftus, 2001).

11.3.2 Supplementing frequentist inference

Adhering to a strict Neyman-Pearson approach to the use of NHSTs, although straightforward in principle, is difficult in practice. As the modern application of significance testing is a hybrid of the Fisherian and Neyman-Pearson approach (Hubbard, 2004), this suggests that researchers find its strict tenets difficult to follow. Many potential 'fixes' to classical frequentist inference have been proposed (see Harlow *et al.*, 1997). The most widely advocated ways to augment NHSTs are increased emphasis on confidence intervals, effect size, meta-analysis, replication or statistical power analysis. Of these, increased emphasis on statistical power and the formal use of CIs fall reasonably squarely within the Neyman-Pearson approach. Increased use of CIs as an informal method provides a way to augment or replace NHSTs and p values. It fits with a philosophy in which formal inference is secondary to understanding data. This is exemplified by the work of Tukey (1969, 1977) and Cleveland (1985) on graphical exploration of data.

Increased emphasis on effect size is sometimes advocated as a way to supplement or correct the deficiencies of significance tests (e.g., Thompson, 1999). Reporting effect size is useful for interpreting a genuine effect in a way that a p value, on its own, is not. On the other hand, reporting effect size isn't a simple matter. First, there are many criteria to consider when selecting an effect size metric (Baguley, 2009; Kirk, 1996; Preacher and Kelley, 2011). In addition, a point estimate of an effect size can be just as misleading as a significance test.

Reporting a point estimate of effect size alongside the test can confuse or mislead researchers and consumers of published research (Robinson *et al.*, 2003).

The NHST plus effect size approach offers two potentially conflicting decision rules: an effect is detected if it is statistically significant and it is considered important if it is reasonably large. In underpowered studies it is therefore quite tempting to claim that a non-significant effect is important because its point estimate is large. Large effects – particularly large standardized effects – are not unusual in small, underpowered studies. However, a small, underpowered study provides little evidence about the magnitude, direction or existence of the effect.

It is not suggested here that reporting effect size estimates is wrong, but using effect size as a parallel decision rule is a bad idea. A better approach is to incorporate effect size within your decision rule (or other inferential procedure). A simple way to do this is to use a CI for the effect. A formal frequentist approach is to use an *equivalence test* (see Box 11.2). An equivalence test replaces the point null hypothesis with a range of values that define a negligible effect. Within this range the quantities being compared are treated as equivalent.

Box 11.2 Equivalence tests

The fundamental difference between a traditional NHST and an equivalence test is the switch from a point to a range null hypothesis. This is accomplished by specifying an *equivalence region* (a range of values in which the effect is considered negligible). Equivalent tests arise from a need to determine whether different treatments have similar effects for a particular application. It is common to express the hypothesis in terms of two groups or conditions being 'equivalent' on some outcome measure. A test of differences between means provides a basic introduction to equivalence testing (although the concept of equivalence testing is more general than this).

The most common method in these situations, attributed to Westlake (1981) and Schuirmann (1981), is the *two one-sided tests* (TOST) approach. The equivalence region is a range of differences defined by a lower limit D_{lower} and an upper limit D_{upper}. H_0 is therefore a hypothesis of non-equivalence in which the true difference $\mu_1 - \mu_2$ falls outside this region:

$$H_0\colon \mu_1 - \mu_2 \leq D_{lower} \text{ or } \mu_1 - \mu_2 \geq D_{upper}$$

The corresponding alternative hypothesis is that the true difference falls within the equivalence region:

$$H_1\colon D_{lower} \leq \mu_1 - \mu_2 \leq D_{upper}$$

An equivalence test requires that you set sensible limits for the equivalence region. Symmetrical limits about zero are common (e.g., -5 and $+5$) but symmetry is not necessary. Deciding on the limits is, in essence, about working out the magnitude of an effect that can be safely or reasonable ignored in a particular context. Determining these values is sometimes trivial, but usually involves educated guesswork similar to that required for statistical power and sample size estimation.

Once the equivalence region is defined, the TOST approach is remarkably easy to apply. It involves performing two separate one-sided NHSTs at the desired α level. The first test has the null hypothesis

$\mu_1 - \mu_2 \leq D_{lower}$, while the second test has the null hypothesis $\mu_1 - \mu_2 \geq D_{upper}$. If normality is assumed, *t* tests of the difference between two means are usually applied (with the independent, Welch-Satterthwaite or paired *t* tests chosen as appropriate).

The interpretation of the TOST procedure may not be immediately obvious. If the first test is statistically significant, the hypothesis that the difference is smaller than D_{lower} is rejected. If the second test is statistically significant, the hypothesis that the difference is larger than D_{upper} is rejected. If both tests are statistically significant, you may conclude that the true difference lies within the equivalence region (i.e., between D_{lower} and D_{upper}). This explains why α for an equivalence test is equal to α for the individual tests (and does not require adjustment for multiple testing). Both tests must be statistically significant for a Type I error to occur; performing the second test won't increase the error rate.

One of the beauties of the TOST approach is that it is readily adapted to other situations. Rogers *et al.* (1993) describe the TOST approach with extensions to meta-analysis and differences in proportions. Dixon (1998) describes extensions to rank transformation tests and situations in which the lower and upper limits are expressed as ratios. Goertzen and Cribbie (2010) consider equivalence tests for correlation coefficients.

The TOST approach can be elegantly implemented using a single CI. This involves constructing a $100(1-2\alpha)\%$ CI for the difference in means. If this CI falls entirely within the equivalence region, then the two means are declared equivalent. This is formally identical to a TOST procedure using separate tests at the desired α level. Westlake (1981) explains the rationale for using a CI based on 2α rather than α. If D_{lower} is below the lower bound, or D_{upper} above the upper bound of the CI, each outcome is equivalent to rejecting the null hypothesis of a two-sided test with $100(1 - \alpha)\%$ confidence. Using 2α therefore adjusts the margin of error of the CI so that it is equivalent to a one-sided test in each direction. Thus a 90% CI mimics a TOST procedure with $\alpha = .05$.

If the TOST procedure is combined with a conventional NHST, the joint outcomes fall into several distinct patterns. If it detects an effect within the equivalence region, the NHST may be either statistically significant or non-significant. A non-significant NHST is what most people expect, but with sufficient statistical power even a tiny difference could be detected. Under these circumstances it seems reasonable to conclude that although a difference between the means has been detected, this difference is negligible in magnitude (Rogers *et al.*, 1993). The reasonableness of this conclusion depends critically on whether the limits of the equivalence region were set correctly. If non-equivalence can't be rejected (i.e., the CI does not completely contain the equivalence region) the NHST may be more useful. A significant NHST indicates that a difference has been detected, but that it falls outside the equivalence region. This suggests a potentially important or interesting effect has been detected. If both the equivalence test and the NHST are non-significant – very likely if statistical power is low – there is insufficient information to reach a decision one way or another.

The TOST procedure can be adapted relatively easily to many different situations. Applying it to a rank transformation test is marginally more difficult because it is not usually meaningful to express an equivalence region in terms of ranks. Dixon (1998) explains how to do this by adding or subtracting a constant to one of the samples before computing the ranks for each one-sided test. Thus for a difference in means ($\mu_1 - \mu_2$), and the equivalence region (-2, $+3$), you would reduce the difference in means by two for the first test (e.g., subtracting two from the group with the larger mean) and increase the difference by three for the second test (e.g., adding three to the group with the larger mean).

Although simple to apply, the TOST method is not necessarily the approach with the greatest statistical power. For instance, Goertzen and Cribbie (2010) found that, unless the equivalence region is very large, extremely large samples are required to detect correlations of equivalent magnitude.

Example 11.3 How might a TOST equivalence test be applied to a randomized clinical trial (RCT) comparing a new depression treatment with an old treatment? Assume that old treatment group has a mean reduction in BDI of 8.2 ($SD = 7.8$), the new treatment reduces BDI by 10.5 ($SD = 9.2$), and that the sample sizes are $n_1 = n_2 = 100$. The simplest way to conduct a TOST equivalence test with $\alpha = .05$ is to construct a 90% CI. The difficult bit is deciding the equivalence region. Example 8.2 speculated that a difference in BDI scores of ten could be considered clinically significant. In declaring two treatments clinically equivalent it might be sensible to be more cautious. For this reason I'll use a region of −5 to +5. This effectively declares the two treatments equivalent if you can be confident that the reduction in BDI for the new treatment is within five points of the existing treatment. The 90% CI for the observed difference of 2.3 is [0.32, 4.28]. As this interval is entirely within the region (−5, +5), the two treatments are judged equivalent.

Although this example illustrates the utility of equivalence tests, they have some limitations. First, they often lack statistical power to detect equivalence. Second, determining an appropriate equivalence region is difficult. Perhaps for this reason, equivalence tests are more common in fields such as pharmacology, where there are agreed standards for defining equivalence.

Meta-analysis and replication have also been proposed as ways to supplement significance testing. Meta-analysis is a natural extension to reporting effect size and at least one author has argued in favor of meta-analysis as a replacement for NHSTs (Schmidt, 1992, 1996). Schmidt's arguments rest on several key points. These include the proposition that control of Type I errors is unimportant because the point null hypothesis is almost never true, and that the primary goal of research is (or should be) synthesis across many studies. Both points are debatable. In particular, in many areas – particularly in experimental research – there is a role for a well-constructed individual study (Abelson, 1997). Furthermore, meta-analysis typically involves either significance testing or constructing CIs.

This leaves replication. The suggestion that replication can replace NHSTs seems odd. This is not because supplementing NHSTs with replication is a bad idea, but because replication is central to all science. It is desirable regardless of what inferential tools are adopted. Replication is important for both statistical and non-statistical reasons. An effect that is replicated is more likely to be true than one that is not. Replication by independent researchers using different methods or stimuli is essential for discovering robust and reliable effects, and as a check against rogue (e.g., fabricated) results.

11.3.3 The statistics of replication

A number of attempts have been made to understand or estimate the stability of effects over multiple replication attempts. One approach is to use meta-analysis to combine results from multiple studies. A more radical option is to try and predict the probability of a replication. The best-known attempt at estimating replication probability is the p_{rep} statistic proposed by Killeen (2005). This statistic attempts to determine the probability of an identical replication obtaining an effect in the same direction as that observed in a sample. For example, if a study shows that a drug reduces risk of a disease, p_{rep} attempts to estimate the probability that an identical replication would also show a reduction in disease risk. Killeen's proposal that p_{rep} could replace p values (and therefore NHSTs) attracted initial support in some areas of psychology, but also attracted considerable criticism (e.g., Macdonald, 2005; Iverson *et al.*, 2009).[7] Two criticisms are of particular relevance here. First, the p_{rep} statistic assumes that all values of the true effect size are equally likely, whereas the range of plausible effect sizes in most fields is rather narrow (Iverson *et al.*, 2009). Second, p_{rep} statistics are rather volatile. Even if it correctly estimated the long-run probability of a replication obtaining an effect in the same direction, the observed value of p_{rep} in a particular study would not be particularly informative.

If estimates of replication probability are not particularly stable, do other frequentist statistics fare any better? Researchers who use inferential statistical tools such as CIs and NHST tend to overestimate the stability of these procedures in replications. Even for identical replications, p values are not particularly stable. Cumming and Fidler (2009) illustrate this by comparing CIs, one-sided p and p_{rep} in a Monte Carlo simulation of identical replications (each involving the difference between two independent means). Simulations are ideal for this purpose. Unlike real data, the population parameters used to generate simulated data can be controlled (and therefore the correct outcomes are known). Figure 11.1 (based on Cumming and Fidler, 2009, Figure 1) shows a 95% CI, p and p_{rep} from a one sample t test for 20 simulated samples of $n = 25$ from a normal population ($\mu = 10$, $\sigma = 30$). The column labeled p shows the two-sided significance probability for a one sample t test with H_0: $\mu = 0$. Note that whenever two-sided $p < .05$ the 95% CI necessarily excludes zero. This happens for samples 4, 5, 6, 8, 11, 16, 18 and 19. For a large set of tests, 19 out of 20 CIs should contain the true population mean of ten. As luck would have it, all but one of the 20 intervals in Figure 11.1 do contain the population mean (but it might not have turned out this way). Only the CI for sample 11 (indicated by the filled circle) excludes the population mean.

How does the variability of p or p_{rep} compare to the coverage of the CI? First consider the p values. These are notoriously unstable (and range in this case from .0002 to .8284). The p_{rep} statistics also lack stability. They encompass a range from close to chance levels of replicating the direction of effect (.5609) to near certainty (.9957). The instability of p_{rep} is particularly troublesome. For simulated samples where $\hat{\mu}$ exceeds zero p_{rep} is an estimate of the same outcome: that a future replication with the same study characteristics will have the same sign. Even worse, p_{rep} can still be quite high for samples with effects in the 'wrong' direction (e.g., .56 for sample 2).

What about CIs? The simulation reported here (somewhat luckily) exactly matches the long-run capture rate for the population mean (19 out of 20). The capture rate for the mean of an identical replication is lower than the capture rate for the population mean. Cumming *et al.* (2004) and Cumming and Maillardet (2006) have shown that the capture rate for identical replications tends to be around 83% for a 95% CI in samples from normal populations (provided N is not too small).[8] The rate is lower than 95% because of the sampling error from both the original study and the replication and will influence the outcome. Doubling the sampling variance leads to the capture efficiency being reduced by a factor of around $\sqrt{2}$. For a normal distribution, the 95% CI corresponds to a z score of 1.96. A z score of $1.96/\sqrt{2} \approx 1.39$ corresponds to an 83% CI.

In Figure 11.1 the capture rate for the mean of a future replication can be estimated by looking at the number of intervals that contain the mean of the sample immediately below them. Only three out of 19 (those for samples 10, 11 and 13) don't contain the mean of the sample below them: a capture rate of 84%. This is similar to the expected mean capture rate. Because the distribution of capture percentages is negatively skewed, the observed capture rate is often higher. Cumming and Maillardet (2006) show that the median capture rate is around 90%.[9]

If you are interested in the replicability of findings, it seems that a 95% CI is probably the safest of the three inferential tools considered here. A typical 95% CI should contain the mean of an identical replication about 90% of the time, though an occasional CI will have a

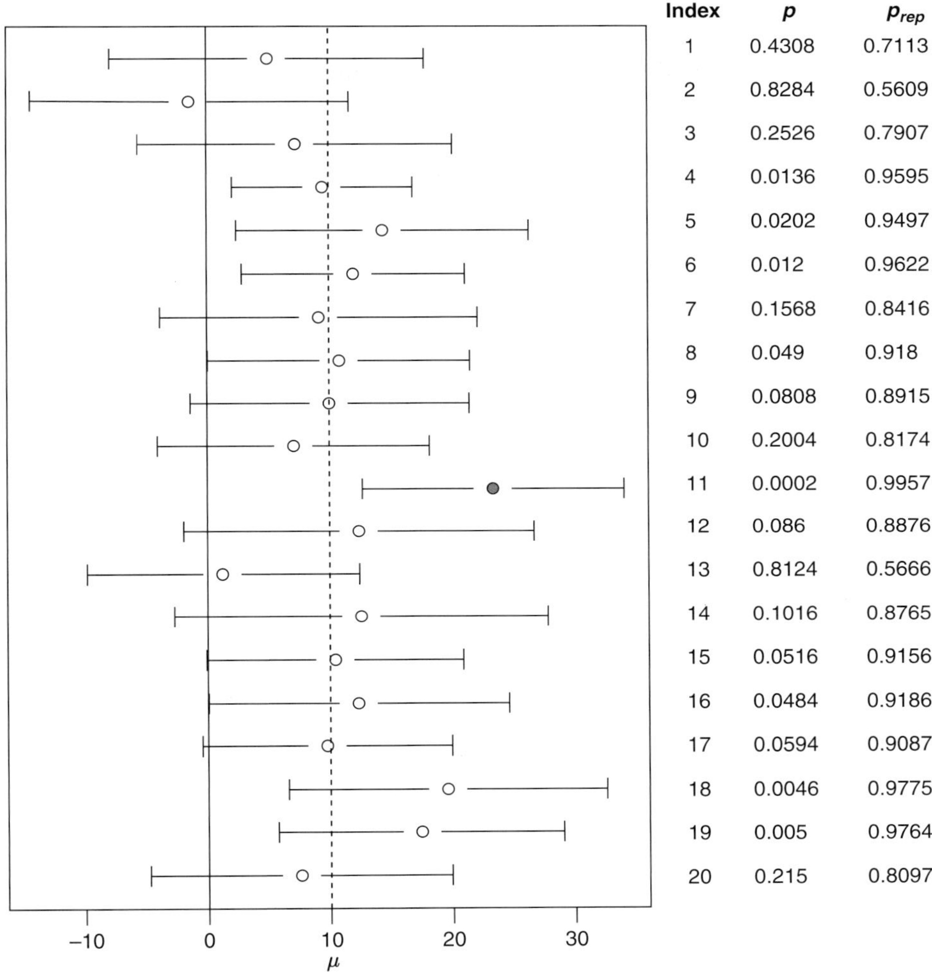

Index	p	p_{rep}
1	0.4308	0.7113
2	0.8284	0.5609
3	0.2526	0.7907
4	0.0136	0.9595
5	0.0202	0.9497
6	0.012	0.9622
7	0.1568	0.8416
8	0.049	0.918
9	0.0808	0.8915
10	0.2004	0.8174
11	0.0002	0.9957
12	0.086	0.8876
13	0.8124	0.5666
14	0.1016	0.8765
15	0.0516	0.9156
16	0.0484	0.9186
17	0.0594	0.9087
18	0.0046	0.9775
19	0.005	0.9764
20	0.215	0.8097

Figure 11.1 The variability of 95% CIs, p and p_{rep} for 20 simulated samples of $n = 25$ from a normal population (with $\mu = 10$ and $\sigma = 30$)

much lower capture percentage (reflected in lower than expected mean capture rate). These rogue CIs provide another argument in favor of genuine replication (rather than replication probabilities).

11.4 Likelihood

The likelihood approach to statistical inference is concerned with measuring the evidence that the data provide (Edwards, 1972; Royall, 1997). Classical frequentist methods are routinely interpreted as if they indicate the evidence for or against a hypothesis, but this is not what they were designed for.[10] They can also fail miserably when applied in this way (e.g., Example 11.1).

The problem of how to measure evidence in frequentist inference is revealed by exploring how sample size influences the interpretation of a significance test. Evidence provided by studies with identical p values is not in general equal. Given two tests of the same hypothesis with different n, but identical p values, which study provides stronger evidence against H_0? A number of factors (e.g., sample size or stopping rules) will influence the calculation of p and alter its evidential status. It is also possible to define 'evidence' in such a way that it leads to almost any answer (Royall, 1986). However, by most reasonable definitions of evidence (e.g., whether there is evidence of a practically important effect, or in terms of the probability of a hypothesis being true) the answer is unequivocal. The study with smaller n provides stronger evidence against H_0 and in favor of H_1 if the p values are equal (*ibid.*). This is easiest to see in terms of the size of effect: in order to achieve an identical p value, the smaller of the two studies must have a larger effect and thus – all other things equal – provide stronger evidence of practical importance. However, Royall's conclusion does not rest solely on the intuition that a larger effect provides stronger evidence. It rests on the belief that the evidence for one hypothesis and against another is determined by their relative likelihood.

Two fundamental and powerful ideas underlie the use of likelihood to quantify evidence. These are the *likelihood principle* and the *law of likelihood*. The likelihood principle states that evidence provided by a sample is fully characterized by the *likelihood function* (e.g., Birnbaum, 1962; Edwards, 1972).[11] This idea can be traced back to Fisher, but its formulation as a fundamental principle of inference is more recent (Edwards, 1974). The law of likelihood (Hacking, 1965) indicates how to apply likelihood functions to quantify evidence. Royall (2004, p. 123) paraphrases the law of likelihood as follows:

> if an event is more probable under hypothesis *A* than hypothesis *B*, then the occurrence of that event is evidence supporting *A* over *B* – the hypothesis that did the better job of predicting the event is better supported by its occurrence. [The law of likelihood] further states that the degree to which occurrence of the event supports *A* over *B* (the strength of evidence) is quantified by the ratio of the two probabilities.

This is the law of likelihood because the likelihood, in its basic form, is the probability of observed data (D), conditional on some hypothesis (e.g., H_1), being true. This can be represented as $Pr(D|H_1)$. A feature that distinguishes a likelihood from a 'regular' conditional probability is that any quantity proportional to $Pr(D|H_1)$ is also a likelihood. One practical advantage of defining likelihood as proportional to probabilities is that, for continuous distributions (where it is not possible to obtain the probability that a parameter takes a particular value), the likelihood function can be obtained directly from the probability density function. A second advantage arises when quantifying the evidence provided by the ratio of two conditional probabilities.

For the same data (D), the strength of evidence in favor of hypothesis H_1 over hypothesis H_2 is quantified by the ratio:

$$\frac{Pr(D|H_1)}{Pr(D|H_2)} \qquad \text{Equation 11.1}$$

The strength of evidence can also be obtained from the ratio of the likelihoods of H_1 and H_2 given the observed data. The likelihood of H_1 given the data is $\ell(H_1|D)$. This quantity is proportional to $Pr(D|H_1)$, being equal to $Pr(D|H_1)$ multiplied by an arbitrary constant c. A formal expression of this relationship is

$$\ell(H_1|D) = cPr(D|H_1) \propto Pr(D|H_1) \qquad \text{Equation 11.2}$$

where $\propto$ means 'proportional to'. Because the observed data are common to both $\ell(H_1|D)$ and $\ell(H_2|D)$, the constant term is identical in each case. It therefore cancels out when the ratio of the two likelihoods is formed:

$$\frac{\ell(H_1|D)}{\ell(H_2|D)} = \frac{cPr(D|H_1)}{cPr(D|H_2)} = \frac{Pr(D|H_1)}{Pr(D|H_2)} \qquad \text{Equation 11.3}$$

Thus the strength of evidence supporting H_1 relative to H_2 is quantified by the *likelihood ratio* (*LR*):

$$LR_{H_1/H_2} = \frac{\ell(H_1|D)}{\ell(H_2|D)} \qquad \text{Equation 11.4}$$

A likelihood theorist believes that likelihood ratios are the fundamental tool of inference. They quantify the evidence in favor of one hypothesis relative to another. Moreover, this belief implies that it is meaningless to assess evidence except by comparing the evidence favoring one hypothesis relative to another.[12] In frequentist inference, the low probability of the null hypothesis for the data at hand is taken as support for the alternative hypothesis. This interpretation is incorrect and may lead to serious errors (as demonstrated in Example 11.1).

A likelihood ratio is the ratio of two positive quantities and has a potential range between zero and infinity, with $LR = 1$ representing equal support for the two hypotheses. Thus $LR = 10$ indicates that H_1 is ten times more probable than H_2 according to the evidence provided by the data at hand. Inverting the ratio provides support for H_2 relative to H_1 ($LR = 0.1$). The striking similarity between the *LR* and the odds ratio (*OR*) is not coincidental. Odds ratios are ratios of the likelihood of the occurrence of an event relative to its non-occurrence.

11.4.1 Likelihood functions and likelihood ratios

Likelihood functions are related to familiar probability distributions such as the binomial and normal, but differ in several respects. As already noted, they are proportional to probabilities conditional on the observed data. In a probability mass or density function, the observed data are a function of the parameters. For likelihood, the parameters are a function of the data.

This is best understood using a specific distribution such as the binomial. The probability mass function (*pmf*) of the binomial distribution is given by Equation 2.3:

$$f(x; n, P) = \binom{n}{x} P^x (1 - P)^{n-x}$$

In classical statistics this function is used to determine the probability of observing x successes from n independent Bernoulli trials. The probability of success on any trial is defined by the population parameter Pr. A likelihood function for the binomial distribution treats both the number of successes and the number of trials as fixed. If a fair coin was tossed ten times and five heads were observed, the likelihood function could be defined as

$$\ell(\theta) \propto f(5; 10, Pr) = \frac{10!}{5!5!} Pr^5 (1 - Pr)^5$$

where $\ell(\theta)$ denotes the likelihood of the parameter P for the observed data (in this case $x = 5$ successes from $n = 10$ trials). Figure 11.2 plots this likelihood function alongside the more familiar *pmf* for observing five heads from ten fair coin tosses. Both functions are plotted with a probability or scaled probability on the y-axis. For the likelihood it is the parameter P that varies and is plotted on the x-axis, whereas for the *pmf* it is the data that vary and are plotted on the x-axis.[13]

The *pmf* shows the characteristic spikiness of a discrete distribution, while the likelihood is a smooth, continuous function. The discrete outcome produces a continuous likelihood function because the observed pattern of five heads and five tails could occur for any value of P in the range: $0 < P < 1$.

The definition of likelihood as proportional to a conditional probability also allows the likelihood function to be simplified. Because the binomial coefficient $\binom{n}{x}$ is a constant for any observed set of data, that term can be dropped. For this reason, the likelihood function $\ell(\theta)$ for a binomial distribution is often represented as

$$\ell(\theta) \propto Pr^x (1 - Pr)^{n-x} \qquad \text{Equation 11.5}$$

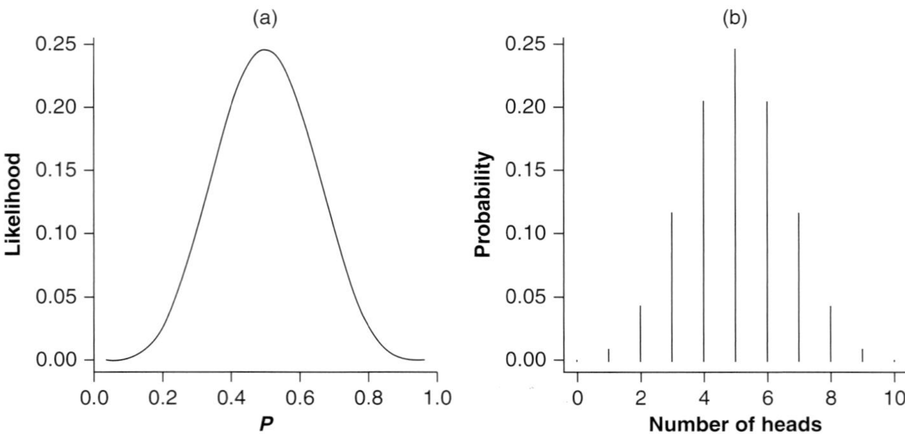

Figure 11.2 Functions for (a) the likelihood and (b) the probability of observing five heads from ten tosses of a fair coin

where $0 \leq P \leq 1$. It is sometimes convenient to rescale likelihood functions to fit the range zero to one. This is accomplished by dividing the likelihood function by its maximum:

$$\frac{\ell(\theta)}{\max[\ell(\theta)]} = \frac{\ell(\theta)}{\ell(\hat{\theta})} \qquad \text{Equation 11.6}$$

The value of θ at the maximum of the likelihood function is its *maximum likelihood estimator* (*MLE*) $\hat{\theta}$. $\hat{\theta}$ is the most plausible or likely value of θ given the data.[14] For binomial data this is $x/n = \hat{P}$ (the mean or proportion of successes in the sample). Figure 11.3 plots the likelihood function $P^x(1-P)^{n-x}$ alongside the standardized likelihood function for 19 successes from 25 trials. The two likelihood functions in Figure 11.3 are identical except for the scale of the y-axis, but (because they are proportional up to an arbitrary constant) they are equivalent. Likelihood functions on any scale can be used for inference (provided the scales match). In a simple (one parameter) statistical model, calculating a likelihood ratio just involves determining the value of the likelihood function for each the two hypotheses of interest (e.g., H_1 and H_2) and taking their ratio.

Likelihood ratios are argued to have many practical and theoretical advantages over classical methods. As they depend only on the probability model and the observed data, factors such as stopping rules or multiple testing don't influence them (Cornfield, 1966; Royall, 1997; Dienes, 2008). In contrast, a frequentist p value or CI is calculated differently depending on how the data arise. The five heads from ten trials in Figure 11.2 could arise because the number of trials was fixed in advance or because the experimenter kept tossing coins until five heads were obtained. If a researcher decided to keep collecting data until $p < .05$ (and failed to correct for optional stopping) he or she could guarantee significance. The same procedure does not guarantee that the *LR* will rise above or fall below a desired threshold. For this reason likelihood methods are suited to studies with sequential designs (see Cornfield, 1966; Van der Tweel, 2005). Another useful property is that evidence can easily be combined in this way. The *LR* for two similar, but

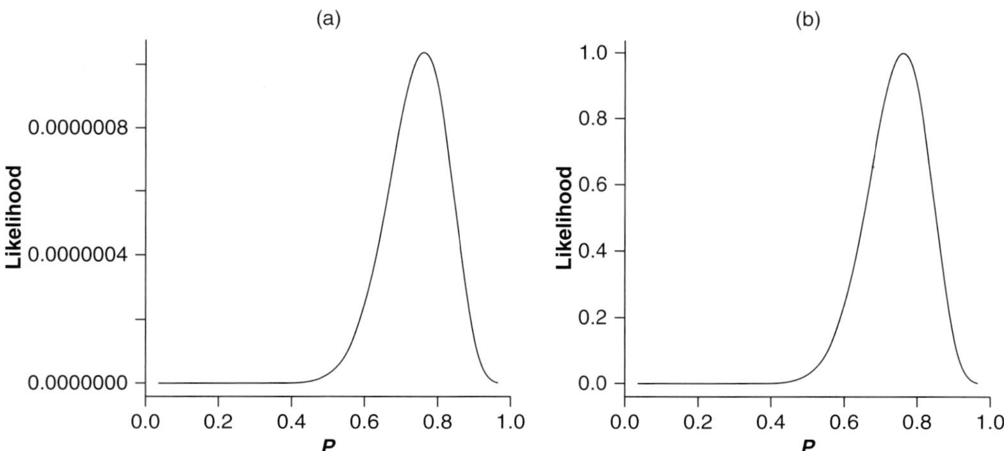

Figure 11.3 Two ways of scaling a likelihood function for 19 successes from a binomial distribution with 25 trials

independent, studies can be obtained by multiplying their individual ratios together (Edwards, 1972).

Example 11.4 In a two-alternative forced-choice recognition memory experiment a participant recognizes 19 words from a list of 25 words; a proportion of .76. If each word is treated as an independent trial (which is slightly unreasonable), it is possible to use the binomial distribution to determine the likelihood function for these data. A researcher might be interested in the hypothesis that the participant's performance is better than that expected by guessing at random. The likelihood function for these data (assuming independent trials) is equivalent to that for 19 successes from 25 trials depicted in Figure 11.3. To assess the evidence that the participants' memory is better than chance you need to compare two hypotheses. One of these is the null hypothesis (H_0) that she is guessing randomly with $P = .5$. Determining the appropriate value of P for the alternative hypothesis (H_1) is not so obvious. Several plausible alternatives could be selected. Let's start with the observed value of $P = .76$. Because .76 is the most likely value of P, this maximizes the evidence against H_0. It would be better to pick a more meaningful value (e.g., one suggested by theory) if one were available. The strength of evidence for H_1 over H_0 is given by:

$$LR_{H_1/H_0} = \frac{\ell(P = .76 \,|\, D)}{\ell(P = .5 \,|\, D)}$$

The likelihood of getting 19 successes from 25 trials if $P = .76$ is:

$$\ell(P = .76 \,|\, D) \propto .76^{19} \times (1 - .76)^{25-19} = .76^{19} \times .24^{6}$$

The likelihood of the same result if $P = .5$ is:

$$\ell(P = .5 \,|\, D) \propto .5^{19} \times (1 - .5)^{25-19} = .5^{19} \times .5^{6}$$

As these numbers are very small, accurate calculation of the LR is best done by computer. Doing so gives:

$$LR_{H_1/H_0} = \frac{\ell(P = .76 \,|\, D)}{\ell(P = .5 \,|\, D)} = \frac{.76^{19} \times .24^{6}}{.5^{19} \times .5^{6}} \approx 34.9$$

The observed data are nearly 35 times more likely under H_1 than H_0. The evidence strongly supports the conclusion that the participant was not guessing.

This ratio strongly favors the hypothesis that $P = .76$ rather than $P = .5$. A binomial test would have rejected H_0 with $p = .01463$ (assuming $\alpha = .05$). What are the advantages of the LR over the NHST? Under the likelihood approach there is no need to worry about factors such as stopping rules, but the main advantage is that the LR provides a meaningful way to quantify the evidence for one hypothesis over another. Unlike the p value, it has a direct interpretation as strength of evidence and can be compared between similar experiments with different n (if the same hypotheses are used).

As this measure is continuous, it is a bad idea to use a strict threshold to determine support for or against a hypothesis (but some guidelines will be reviewed). What if the evidence wasn't as convincing? If the LR were only 2 the support for H_1 would be relatively unimpressive. As the LR is not influenced by collecting more data (i.e., optional stopping is not a problem) an immediate solution to inconclusive or unimpressive evidence is to collect more data. If $P = .5$, adding more data will gradually shift the *LR* toward (and eventually below) one. If $P = .76$, adding more data will gradually shift the *LR* upwards. If $P = (.76 + .5)/2 = .63$ then the *LR* would eventually settle around one (indicating equal support for the two hypotheses).

11.4.2 Comparing likelihood ratios and *p* values

The likelihood can be used to show how a *p* value overstates the strength of evidence against the null hypothesis. Calculating the *LR* for H_0 versus $\hat{\theta}$ (the *MLE* of the observed data) pits it against the strongest possible hypothesis supported by the data and represents a 'worse case scenario' for H_0 (Goodman, 1993). This statistic is sometimes called a standardized *LR* or minimum *LR* (Edwards *et al.*, 1963; Goodman, 1993, 1999) and can be defined as:

$$LR_{\text{min}} = \frac{\ell(H_0|D)}{\ell(\hat{\theta})} = \frac{\ell(\theta_0)}{\ell(\hat{\theta})} \qquad \text{Equation 11.7}$$

For a difference in means from a normal distribution with known variance this statistic is $e^{-z^2/2}$ (Edwards *et al.*, 1963; Goodman, 1993, 1999). When $\alpha = .05$ and $p = .05$ a conventional NHST just reaches statistical significance. Assuming a normally distributed test statistic, this implies $z = 1.96$. The strongest possible evidence for H_0 given by this 'just significant' test is therefore $e^{-1.96^2/2} \approx 0.147$. This is the *LR* in favor of H_0. The maximum *LR* in favor of the alternative hypothesis is then $1/0.147 \approx 6.83$. Assuming the two hypotheses are equally likely *a priori* (and that one of them is true), the probability of H_0 being true is $1/(1 + 6.83) \approx .128$. This is much higher than the level assumed by many researchers or implied by a naive interpretation of the threshold $\alpha = .05$.

This pattern is quite general. The *p* value routinely overestimates the evidence against the null hypothesis. This kind of calculation isn't always sensible for real data, but it does show how a *p* value (where it can be related to a likelihood ratio) is badly biased as an estimate of the evidence for or against H_0. The minimum *LR* is a convenient 'quick and dirty' way to assess the evidence against the H_0, but best avoided for serious work. Edwards *et al.* (1963, p. 224) note that 'it is mathematically possible but realistically preposterous for [the minimum *LR*] to be the actual likelihood ratio'.

11.4.3 Likelihood intervals

A point estimate of a parameter is given by the *MLE* of the likelihood function. This will, depending on the probability model, often coincide with the point estimate from frequentist inference. The *LR* provides an elegant alternative to a significance test, but for many applications an interval estimate is desirable. *Likelihood intervals* (sometimes termed *support intervals*) provide a tool for interval estimation using likelihood.

A likelihood interval for a parameter θ contains all values of θ consistent with the data. This is defined by a likelihood ratio in favor of θ of at most $1/k$ relative to any other possible value of θ. Inverting this limit indicates that, for any value of θ within the interval, no alternative hypothesis is supported by a likelihood ratio of k or more. Blume (2002) explains how the boundaries of the interval are defined to include any value of θ where:

$$\left\{ \frac{\ell(\theta)}{\ell(\hat{\theta})} \geq \frac{1}{k} \right\} = \left\{ \frac{\ell(\hat{\theta})}{\ell(\theta)} \geq k \right\} \qquad \text{Equation 11.8}$$

This condition works because, by definition, the *MLE* $\hat{\theta}$ is the best-supported value. Any value of k can be selected, but the values $k = 8$ and $k = 32$ proposed by Royall (1997) are reasonable. As a rough guide, $LR \geq 32$ provides 'strong' evidence for one hypothesis over another and $LR \geq 8$ 'moderate' or 'fairly strong' evidence (Dienes, 2008; Royall, 2000). Ratios below eight are considered to provide only 'weak' evidence. Despite adopting these labels, it is worth emphasizing that evidence is a continuous function of the *LR*. Any *LR* greater than one provides some evidential support for a hypothesis, and similar ratios (e.g., 7.8 and 8.3) provide broadly similar levels of support.

A plot of the likelihood function for the observed data can be used as a quick graphical method to obtain the interval estimate or as a method of presenting research findings. When plotting the likelihood interval, it is helpful to rescale the function so that its maximum is one. Once scaled in this way, the likelihood interval is shown by a horizontal line at $Y = 1/k$. Figure 11.4 shows 1/8 and 1/32 likelihood intervals for the data in Figure 11.3 (observing 19 successes from 25 binomial trials). Panel (a) shows the likelihood with dotted lines for $Y = 1/8$ and $Y = 1/32$. Where these lines cross the likelihood function they reveal the lower and upper boundaries of the 1/8 and 1/32 likelihood interval respectively. You could read these values from the plot without further calculation. Alternatively, it is possible to obtain precise boundaries by computer and plot each interval as a horizontal line spanning the likelihood curve, as in panel (b) of Figure 11.4. The 1/8 interval estimate is [.5643, .9010] and the corresponding 1/32 interval is [.5033, .9286]. The 1/8 interval indicates that hypothesized parameters in the range $P = .56$

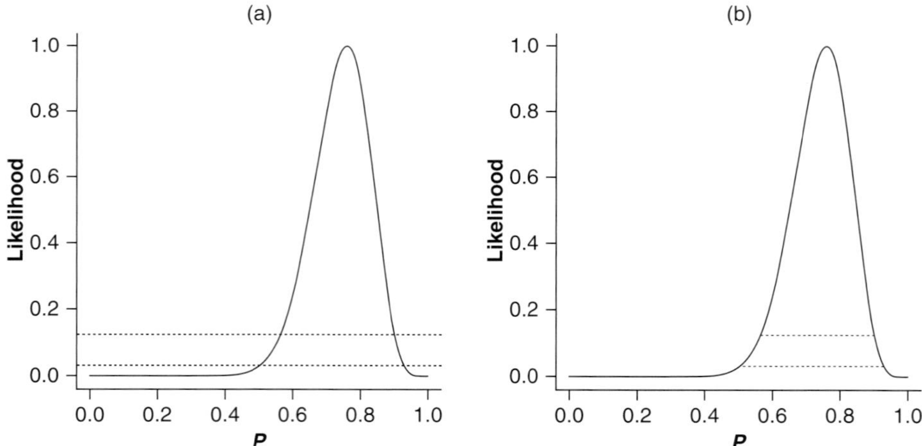

Figure 11.4 The 1/8 and 1/32 likelihood intervals for 19 successes from a binomial distribution with 25 trials

to $P = .90$ have similar levels of evidential support. No parameter in the interval has more than weak support relative to the others (where weak support is defined as $LR < 8$). For a 1/32 interval no hypothesized value of P has more than moderate support relative to any other (where moderate support is defined as $LR < 32$).

As likelihood intervals contain the *MLE,* they can be interpreted as a plausible range of values for the true parameter (taking into account only the data at hand). This is similar to the common, informal interpretation of a CI. One justification for a classical 95% CI is that it is often a close approximation to a 1/8 likelihood interval (and the 99% CI to a 1/32 interval). This link sometimes breaks down (e.g., if α is adjusted for multiple testing).

Example 11.5 It is relatively easy to plot the likelihood interval for a single parameter, provided the *pmf* or *pdf* of a distribution is known. As earlier examples used the binomial distribution, this example will employ the Poisson distribution. Equation 2.6 gives the *pmf* for the Poisson distribution as

$$f(x;\lambda) = \frac{\lambda^x e^{-\lambda}}{x!}$$

As x is the observed count, the denominator (x factorial) will be a constant for any sample. The likelihood function can thus be simplified to

$$\ell(\theta) \alpha \lambda^x e^{-\lambda} \qquad \text{Equation 11.9}$$

where x is the observed rate $\hat{\lambda}$ (the mean, variance and *MLE*).

Figure 11.5 plots a likelihood function as well as the 1/8 and 1/32 likelihood intervals for Poisson distributions with observed counts of three or zero. Again, note that the likelihood function is

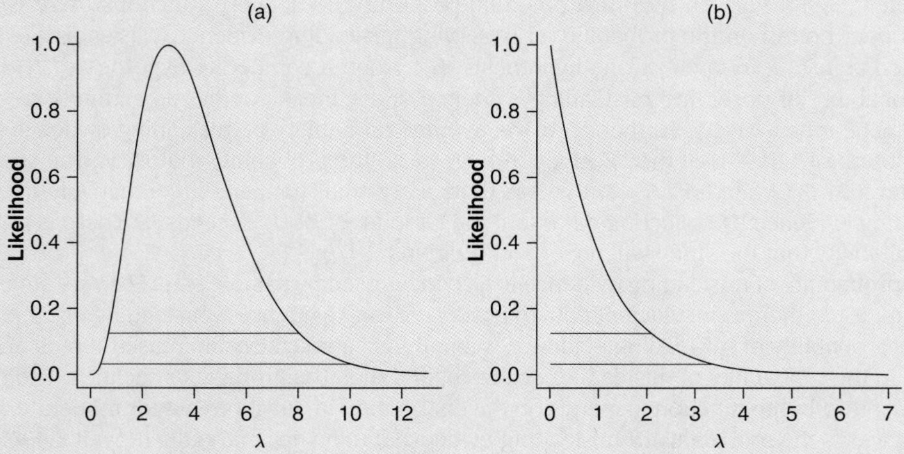

Figure 11.5 Poisson likelihood intervals for (a) $\hat{\lambda} = 3$, and (b) $\hat{\lambda} = 0$

continuous even though the Poisson distribution is discrete. Interpretation of panel (a) is relatively clear. An observed count of three is consistent with a fairly wide range of λ with the 1/8 interval being [0.70, 8.03]. An observed count of zero is at the lower limit of possible outcomes and plausible only for a fairly narrow range of λ, and even the 1/32 interval of [0, 3.47] is relatively narrow.

Likelihood ratios and intervals can be awkward to interpret at boundary values such as $\theta = 0$. Any hypothesis that has a likelihood of zero will necessarily produce $LR = 0$ or $LR = \infty$. This is as it should be. A likelihood of zero means that the hypothesized parameter value is impossible. If an event is hypothesized to occur with rate zero, observing just one event falsifies that hypothesis. The possibility of an infinite *LR* also illustrates the importance of considering only the evidence in favor of one hypothesis relative to another. An infinite *LR* does not imply one of the hypotheses is true (as there are many other hypotheses equally well supported by the data).

11.4.4 Weak or misleading evidence

An intriguing aspect of likelihood theory is that it is not possible for the evidence to be in error (Royall, 2000). Provided you calculate and interpret the likelihood interval or *LR* correctly (e.g., you don't accidentally invert the two hypotheses) an error is impossible. In contrast, significance testing (even properly applied) can give rise to errors. NHSTs are decision procedures, whereas a likelihood ratio is a tool for quantifying evidential support. The evidence is the evidence; a concept such as 'incorrect evidence' is unhelpful. While the evidence can't be wrong, it can be *misleading* (Royall, 2000, 2004). From time to time, the evidence supports one hypothesis when the competing hypothesis is true. Likelihood theorists therefore do not concern themselves with Type I and Type II errors. What does concern them is minimizing the probability of misleading or weak evidence.

Royall (2000) investigated the probability of obtaining misleading or weak evidence for a class of distributions that includes common likelihood functions for inference about a single parameter (e.g., a Poisson rate or a binomial proportion). For these functions there is a universal upper bound on the probability of observing misleading evidence. Misleading evidence is defined as $LR > k$ in favor of one hypothesis (H_2) when a competing hypothesis (H_1) is true. The probability of observing misleading evidence under these conditions cannot exceed $1/k$ (and may be much lower). Furthermore, the average probability of misleading evidence has an upper bound of $1/(k+1)$. If the *LR* in favor of H_2 is 32, the probability that H_1 is true should be less than .03125, while for $LR = 8$ it is less than .125. What happens if you actively try to find misleading evidence by collecting data until the *LR* in favor of H_2 exceeds k? There is at least a $1/k$ probability that the study will never end (Robbins, 1970).

The probability of misleading evidence is also influenced by sample size. For very small samples (e.g., $n < 5$) there is insufficient data to produce strong evidence – misleading or otherwise – and the probability of misleading evidence is small. As sample sizes increase there is an initial 'bump' in the probability of misleading evidence, and then the probability declines. The precise pattern of this 'bump function' depends on the distribution in question, but for moderate sample sizes upwards the probability of misleading evidence diminishes markedly (Royall, 2000).

The probability of observing weak evidence behaves slightly differently. It starts very high with small samples, and declines rapidly as n increases. Also relevant is the difference between the hypothesized values of the parameters. If the hypothesized parameters are close together it will be harder to find evidence for one over the other (and both weak and misleading evidence are more likely). This is a direct analogue of the relation between effect size and statistical power for a significance test. It is harder to provide strong evidence in favor of H_1 over H_2 if the hypothesized difference in parameters is 0.01 than if it is 0.1.

These upper bounds can be used to plan sample sizes for a study based on the *LR* you desire and the anticipated size of the effect (see Royall, 2000). However, this kind of sample size planning is a little more relaxed than for frequentist inference. If the evidence is inconclusive, it is perfectly legitimate to top up the data by additional sampling.

The concepts of misleading or weak evidence are very useful in understanding the practical implications of the likelihood approach when planning a study. A major difference, compared to planning sample size for a significance test, is that the probabilities of weak or misleading evidence are relevant only during planning. Once data are collected, the likelihood principle and law of likelihood say that these probabilities are no longer germane. The evidence is contained in the likelihood function for the observed data and is assessed by the ratio of two likelihoods. Referring to the probability of weak or misleading evidence would, in effect, add information from unobserved data (in violation of the likelihood principle).

11.4.5 Nuisance parameters, profile likelihood and the normal distribution

Extending the likelihood approach to the normal distribution is a little more difficult than for distributions with a single unknown parameter. The normal distribution has two parameters: μ and σ^2. If one of the parameters is known, it is fairly easy to use the *pdf* of the normal distribution to obtain the likelihood of the other parameter, conditional on the observed data (Blume, 2002). More often, both μ and σ^2 are unknown and you will be interested in inferences about only one of them (usually the mean). An unknown parameter that isn't of interest is, rather delightfully, termed a *nuisance parameter*. It is not possible to determine the true likelihood function when nuisance parameters are present.

The solution that is most commonly adopted (at least for inference involving the normal distribution) is to use *profile likelihood*. In a profile likelihood function, nuisance parameters are replaced by their most likely values: their maximum likelihood estimates. The maximum likelihood estimate for σ^2 is the usual estimate of the sample variance: $\hat{\sigma}^2$. The profile likelihood is particularly attractive in relation to the normal distribution, because it is proportional to the t distribution used to solve the equivalent problem in frequentist inference (see Blume, 2002). Profile likelihood for a mean from a normal distribution is:

$$\ell\left(\theta, \hat{\sigma}^2(\theta)\right) \propto \left(1 + \frac{t^2}{\nu}\right)^{-\frac{N}{2}} \qquad \text{Equation 11.10}$$

The *df* are denoted by ν, while N depends on the design (with $N = n$ for paired or one sample tests and $N = n_1 + n_2$ for independent tests). An adjustment to Equation 11.10 can be adopted that replaces N with ν. This makes tests and interval estimates more conservative (Kalbfleisch and Sprott, 1970; Royall, 1997; Blume, 2002).[15]

Because profile likelihoods are not true likelihood functions, they don't necessarily have the same desirable properties. Fortunately, profile likelihood for the normal distribution is well behaved. Royall (2000) has shown that the probability of strong misleading evidence for a normal mean with known variance has a maximum value of:

$$\Phi\left(-\sqrt{2\ln(k)}\right) \qquad \text{Equation 11.11}$$

For $k = 8$ this probability is just over .02 (2%) and for $k = 32$ just over .004 (0.4%). Royall (2000) also demonstrates that this applies as a large sample limit for other distributions, and that the large sample limit also applies to the profile likelihood for a normal mean. In large samples the probability of strong misleading evidence for inference about a normal mean will be low. This implies that the chief constraint for researchers is the probability of weak evidence. Samples large enough to provide strong support for a hypothesis will tend to have very low probabilities of obtaining misleading evidence.

Royall and Tsou (2003) further demonstrated that, for a normal probability model, the profile likelihood function is robust when the parameter of interest is μ (but not if the parameter of interest is σ^2). They define robustness by two properties: continuing to estimate the parameter of interest and adhering to the large sample limit for the maximum probability of misleading evidence. This is a very powerful result, because it implies that even if the probability model is incorrect (e.g., the variances are unequal or the distribution not normal) the probability of strong misleading evidence will be low.

Likelihood methods therefore seem less reliant on assumptions than classical frequentist statistics. In particular, they do not assume a random distribution of independent, identically distributed (e.g., normal) observations or errors. Instead they rely on the weaker assumption of exchangeability. This assumption is a natural consequence of treating parameters as random variables and conditioning on the observed data. The data are considered exchangeable in the sense that they could have been encountered in any order. By conditioning the model on these observations it assumed that data like those observed might be encountered in the future. Independent observations are by definition exchangeable, but exchangeable data are not necessarily independent. Sampling without replacement (i.e., exhaustively) from a sample treats each observation as exchangeable, but not independent (e.g., the probability of sampling each data point depends on what has already been selected).

Example 11.6 This example looks again at the sleep loss data ($\hat{\mu} = 94.6$, $\hat{\sigma}_{\hat{\mu}} = 2.77$, $n = 50$). Using the t distribution, the 95% CI for the mean IQ was found to be [89.0, 100.2]. Figure 11.6 plots 1/8 and 1/32 profile likelihood intervals for these data. The 1/8 likelihood interval is [88.9, 100.3] and the 1/32 interval is [87.1, 102.1]. Notice how the 1/8 interval corresponds fairly closely to the 95% CI (as it should do for a single sample with α unadjusted).

As the researcher might be interested in whether the sample seemed to have IQs lower than typical ($\mu = 100$), this could be tested by calculating the relevant LR. One alternative hypothesis might be that $\mu = 85$ (1σ below the expected population mean). This gives:

$$LR_{\theta_1/\theta_0} = \frac{\ell(\theta_1 = 85 \mid D)}{\ell(\theta_0 = 100 \mid D)} = \frac{0.004165622}{0.1545162} \approx 0.027$$

A reduction of 15 IQ points would be quite a large impairment; a reduction of about 1/3 σ (five IQ points) would be more plausible. This gives:

$$LR_{\theta_2/\theta_0} = \frac{\ell(\theta_1 = 95 \mid D)}{\ell(\theta_0 = 100 \mid D)} = \frac{0.9894195}{0.1545162} \approx 6.40$$

H_1 is not well supported by the data. As $1/0.027 \approx 37.0$, there is strong evidence favoring H_0 over H_1 (i.e., favoring no reduction versus a 15 point reduction). For H_2 there is weak evidence ($LR < 8$)

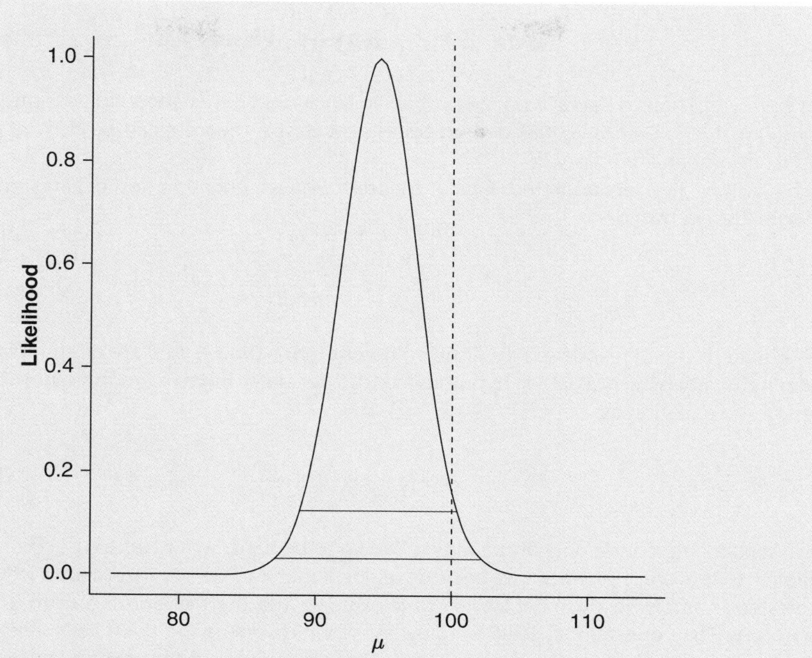

Figure 11.6 The 1/8 and 1/32 likelihood intervals for the sleep loss data

of a modest reduction of five IQ points relative to H_0. Adjusting Equation 11.10 to reduce the probability of misleading evidence gives ratios slightly closer to one in each case (0.029 H_1 versus H_0 and 6.17 for H_2 relative to H_0).

These (fictional) data seem to rule out a large impact of a night's sleep loss on IQ, but there is weak evidence supporting a smaller effect. The likelihood intervals suggest that the study is inconclusive, as the hypothesis that $\mu = 100$ (and that no impairment exists) is consistent with the observed data. A likelihood theorist would probably conclude that there is insufficient data to reach strong conclusions (and probably collect a few more data points).

A key feature of the likelihood approach is that the conclusions depend on both hypotheses. This is an advantage, because having explicit hypotheses with a strong rationale sharpens inference. If precise, quantitative hypotheses are not possible, likelihood intervals provide a simple tool to infer a range of parameter values supported by the data.

11.5 Bayesian inference

The likelihood addresses a fundamental requirement of statistical inference: how to quantify the evidence provided by data. What if you want to do more than this? In Bayesian inference the goal is to go beyond an assessment of the evidence and, as far as possible, obtain an accurate model of the world – one that combines new data with existing knowledge.

Bayesian inference does this by applying *Bayes' theorem* (see Box 11.3), one of the most influential and important results in probability theory (and possibly all of mathematics). Although

Box 11.3 Bayes' theorem

The Reverend Thomas Bayes' work on probability, including Bayes' theorem, was published (posthumously) in 1763. Dienes (2008) demonstrates how Bayes' theorem can be derived from two basic axioms of probability theory.

The author first encountered Bayes' theorem, as an equation for dealing with conditional probabilities, in this form:

$$Pr(A|B) = \frac{Pr(B|A)\,Pr(A)}{Pr(B)} \qquad \text{Equation 11.12}$$

This equation can be expressed in slightly different forms (and A an B are often replaced with more meaningful labels such as H for hypothesis and D for data. In Bayesian inference it is common to present the equation as:

$$Pr(A|B) = Pr(B|A)\,\frac{Pr(A)}{Pr(B)} \qquad \text{Equation 11.13}$$

Understanding conditional probability is known to be hard, so it helps to use a concrete example. Imagine that a brain scanner has been developed that can detect if someone is lying. Police are interested in applying this new device to investigate the theft of an item from a secret research laboratory. They question all 1000 employees, of which one is the thief. Let's label the event A as 'lying' and B as 'failing the lie detector test'. Laboratory tests of the technology establish that if a person is untruthful it will detect their lie 99% of the time and therefore $Pr(B|A) = .99$. Baseline tests show that the false positive rate, the probability of someone failing the test when they are telling the truth, is 2%. This establishes the probability of B given that A is not true as $Pr(B|\sim A) = .02$. This probability is not directly required by the theorem, but is necessary to compute $Pr(B)$ below.

The probability of a random employee being the thief is one in 1000 and so $Pr(A) = .001$. The probability of not being the thief is $Pr(\sim A) = 1 - .001 = .999$. $Pr(B)$ is the probability of failing the test whether A is true or not. Given that there are only two outcomes for A (lying or not lying), the probability of failing the test is simply the probability of B when someone is lying plus its probability when they are not lying:

$$Pr(B) = Pr(B|A)\,Pr(A) + Pr(B|\sim A)\,Pr(\sim A)$$

The overall probability of failing the test is then:

$$Pr(B) = .99 \times .001 + .02 \times .999 = .02097$$

For rare events – such as being the thief here – $Pr(B)$ is dominated by the false positive rate.

Having found the key values to use as input, Bayes' theorem can be applied to determine $Pr(A|B)$. The probability of lying given that someone has failed the test is:

$$Pr(A|B) = .99 \times \frac{.001}{.02097} \approx .0472$$

Even though the test is very sensitive, it is pretty hopeless for this kind of application. Whenever $Pr(B|A)$ is very high, the equation reduces to the ratio of the two base rates: $Pr(A)$ and $Pr(B)$. These base rates provide information about how rare the events are (and their ratio indicates their relative rarity). If guilty people are relatively rare (true for many real applications) the test has to have an extremely low false positive rate, otherwise innocent people (who are more common) make up most of the positive test outcomes. At 2%, the false positive rate is nowhere near good enough to be used for this kind of application. (If this kind of argument is familiar, recall that this calculation provides the underlying rationale for Example 11.1.)

In the context of Bayesian statistical inference, the base rate $Pr(A)$ is the prior. It provides information about how likely the outcome is in the absence of other data. $Pr(B)$ is sometimes termed the *normalizing constant*, because it scales the result into a probability between zero and one. You might also notice that if $Pr(A)/Pr(B)$ is a constant, Bayes' theorem also implies that $Pr(A|B)$ – and hence the likelihood – is proportional to $Pr(B|A)$.

Bayes' theorem is not restricted to two discrete events. It can be extended to deal with more than two events and to continuous outcomes. For a continuous outcome the probability is replaced by the integral of a probability density (see Chapter 2).

the theorem is uncontroversial, some characteristics of Bayesian inference are controversial (though perhaps decreasingly so in recent years). Chief among these is the attempt to quantify existing knowledge using a *prior*. The prior is a probability or probability distribution that reflects the degree of uncertainty of existing knowledge. The outcome of Bayesian inference is also a probability distribution – known as a *posterior*. For some Bayesians these probabilities represent strength or degrees of belief about the state of the world (see Gelman, 2008a, 2008b), or what Edwards *et al.* (1963) term *personal probability*. Determining the appropriate prior for an analysis and how to interpret the posterior probability distribution are stumbling blocks for someone trying to get to grips with Bayesian inference. A further challenge is the computational difficulty of some Bayesian analyses. Except in very simple situations, a Bayesian analysis will involve combining information from two different probability distributions to obtain a third distribution. The advent of Monte Carlo methods and advances in computing now allow Bayesian methods to be applied for a wide class of problems (even if analytic solutions are not available).

11.5.1 Putting a Bayesian model together

Bayesian inference involves modeling the posterior probability distribution of θ as a function of the evidence provided by the data and a prior probability distribution. The quantity θ can be a single parameter or a set of parameters. Adopting the expression of Bayes' theorem in Equation 11.13 and with D representing the observed data, a general equation for this form of statistical model is:

$$p(\theta|D) = p(D|\theta)\frac{p(\theta)}{p(D)} \qquad \text{Equation 11.14}$$

The term $p(D|\theta)$ is the likelihood of the data given the distribution of θ and evidence provided by the data about θ.[16] Thus $p(\theta)$ and $p(\theta|D)$ are the prior and posterior distributions of θ. The probability distribution $p(D)$ takes the role of the normalizing constant (see Box 11.3) and ensures the posterior probability distribution sums to one. The normalizing constant does not need to be evaluated exactly, provided its value is known up to a constant factor that does not change with the parameters. Thus Equation 11.14 can be rewritten as:

$$p(\theta|D) \propto \ell(\theta|D)p(\theta) \qquad \text{Equation 11.15}$$

This states that the posterior probability distribution $p(\theta \mid D)$ is proportional to the likelihood $\ell(\theta \mid D)$ times the prior $p(\theta)$.

It is this equation that summarizes what Bayesian inference does: it combines prior knowledge with evidence from new data in a mathematically coherent and optimal way. It should also be obvious that the role of the prior in the calculation of posterior probabilities is essential. Much of the controversy in Bayesian methods surrounds not the desirability of incorporating prior information, but how to decide on a prior (see Edwards *et al.*, 1963; Dienes, 2008). Both likelihood theorists and frequentists prefer to leave the prior out of formal statistical inference. This may be a sensible way to evaluate a single study in isolation, but has a number of drawbacks. First, it ignores rather than solves the problem of integrating prior information with new evidence. Second, the goal of some research (e.g., applied research) is not to weigh up evidence from a single study but to make a decision about the best or most likely outcome (for which the prior information is essential). Third, merely focusing on the evidence ignores the complexity of the model. An important property of Bayesian inference is that it penalizes complex theories relative to simple ones. To see why, it is necessary to look at how the posterior probabilities are calculated.

Recall that $p(\theta)$ is a probability distribution for a parameter. This probability distribution must sum to one, but the probability can be allocated in different ways. If a researcher thinks that $\theta = 1$ then she could represent her prior expectation as a normal distribution with $\mu = 1$. The standard deviation σ would then represent her confidence or strength of belief that $\theta = 1$. At one extreme she could be absolutely certain about the prior, set $\sigma = 0$, and the entire probability would fall at μ. This would (in effect) be a point null hypothesis. At the other extreme she could set $\sigma = \infty$ and therefore spread the probability more or less evenly over the entire number line. The former is a maximally *informative prior* and the latter an *uninformative* or *diffuse prior*. In practice, neither would usually be a reasonable choice. A realistic prior typically lies somewhere in between these choices. The form of the probability distribution is also up for grabs (though the normal distribution is a common choice).

Bayesian inference uses the prior distribution to calculate a weighted average likelihood $\ell(\theta \mid D)p(\theta)$ for the model. If the probability distribution of the prior is thinly spread over a wide range of parameter values, this means that the weighted likelihood (used to determine the posterior distribution) is also thinly spread. This weakens the evidential support for any particular value. If the prior falls into a narrow range, then the likelihood is focused around those parameter values (increasing support for them). This property is sometimes referred to as a 'fully automatic Occam's razor' (Smith and Spiegelhalter, 1980, p. 216).

All other things equal, a complex theory can explain a wide range of outcomes (having additional flexibility or extra parameters). Figure 11.7 shows this effect in action.

In each panel the likelihood of a normal sample with $\hat{\mu} = 0.25$ and $\hat{\sigma}_{\hat{\mu}} = 0.10$ is depicted. In panel (a) a normal prior ($\mu = 0$ and $\sigma = .10$) is shown alongside the resulting posterior distribution, while panel (b) shows the posterior distribution resulting from a prior with $\mu = 0$ and $\sigma = .20$. Although the prior distributions have the same mean and the data (and hence likelihoods) are identical changing the variance of the prior has a dramatic result. In the upper panel the *SD* of the prior is relatively small and identical to the standard error of the mean $\hat{\sigma}_{\hat{\mu}}$ (which is the *SD* of the likelihood). The posterior distribution lies halfway between the two. In the lower panel the *SD* of the prior is twice as large and the data overwhelm the prior. The more informative and, in a sense, more parsimonious prior has a greater impact on the model than the less informative one.

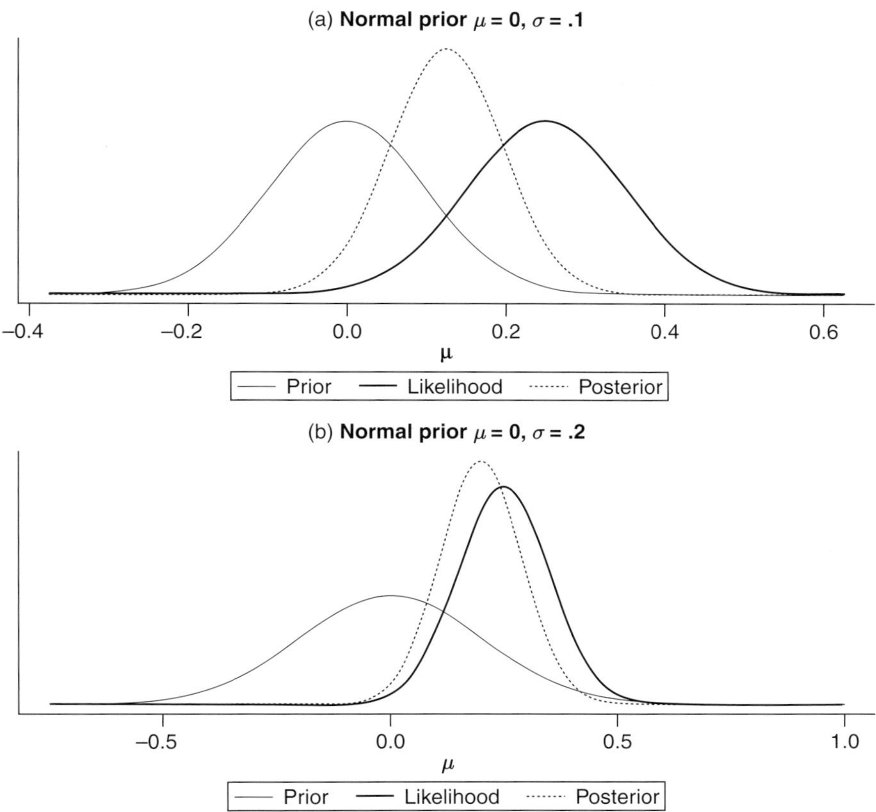

Figure 11.7 How different priors influence the posterior distribution for the same sample data

Wagenmakers *et al.* (2008) explain this with the analogy of gambling on the outcome of a sporting event. The structure of the analogy is as follows. Ricky and Freddie have $100 dollars to bet on the cricket World Cup. Ricky bets $20 each on five teams (Australia, India, England, the West Indies and the Netherlands) while Freddie bets all $100 on England to win. By hedging his bets (spreading his prior belief across five teams) Ricky has a better chance of including the correct outcome, but will gain less from being correct. Freddie, on the other hand, although less likely to win, will get a better return if he does win. In terms of statistical inference, data that are consistent with Freddie's prior provide stronger support for his theory that England will win than they do for Ricky's theory that one of his five teams will win.

11.5.2 Selecting a prior

The choice of prior is central to any Bayesian analysis. If you have no prior knowledge and your prior is diffuse (spread flat over all possible values) the posterior distribution is determined entirely by the likelihood. This in turn implies that frequentist inference (which under certain conditions approximates likelihood inference) approximates a Bayesian analysis with uninformative, diffuse priors. Using a diffuse prior is tempting for some researchers, especially those new to Bayesian methods. It provides a link to more familiar methods and sometimes allows you to duck the difficult decision of how to select a prior. There are several reasons why such an approach is unsatisfactory as a general stance (though there can be principled reasons to select a diffuse prior). One is that selecting a diffuse prior will prevent Bayesian inference acting as an 'automatic Occam's razor'. A second, and more inherently Bayesian, criticism is that there will nearly always be some prior information that a scientist can bring to bear on the problem of selecting a prior. Even if you have complete ignorance about the size of effect you are likely to obtain in a specific study, you will very likely have some idea of the kinds of effects encountered in similar studies. This is precisely the point that Iverson *et al.* (2009) made in their criticism of the p_{rep} statistic. They argued that effect sizes are not free to take any value, but rather tend to be clustered around zero.

How then should you select a prior? There are two main philosophies: *subjective Bayes* and *objective Bayes* (Spiegelhalter and Rice, 2009). Subjective Bayes views the selection of a prior as a matter of personal belief or judgment (e.g., of a suitably expert individual or panel). Objective Bayes involves selecting priors that have some evidential basis. These are often, but not always, weakly informative ones. Objective Bayesian priors can also be characterized as priors that minimize assumptions about the data (Rouder *et al.*, 2009), and thus reflect a degree of consensus about the prior evidence. Although I will concentrate on objective rather than subjective priors, this is not to dismiss the subjective approach, for which Dienes (2008) provides an excellent introduction. In fact, there are distinct advantages to the subjective approach.

A standard criticism of subjective priors is that the interpretation of a study can vary, depending on the subjective prior that is chosen. Furthermore, the philosophy of the subjective Bayes approach promotes these different interpretations of the same data by different individuals as a good thing. My initial reaction to this idea was probably similar to that of most people trained in frequentist inference: a combination of mild shock and confusion. Over time I have come to realize that this initial reaction was probably mistaken. First, all inference from data involves subjective differences in interpretation. Bayesian inference has the distinct advantage that you have to be explicit about this subjectivity (and try to quantify it). Anyone looking at a Bayesian analysis should be able to see what prior was selected and what justification is offered for it. Second, unless you do not have much data, or the data are poor quality, the data tend to dominate the prior. Two people with very different priors will tend to reach similar conclusions as more data is collected (see Howard *et al.*, 2000).

The principal benefits of objective priors are pragmatic. It is usually easier to convince others that your prior is appropriate and probably easier to select a prior on objective grounds. For most research questions, the choice of prior is likely to be a compromise between subjective and objective approaches (Spiegelhalter and Rice, 2009). The most obvious way to elicit an objective prior is to use parameter estimates from a previous study. For instance, if previous studies on a topic have shown a mean difference of 4, 8, −3, 5, 0 and 10 units, the mean is 4 units and the *SD* of the effects is approximately 4.9. This might suggest a normal prior with $\mu = 4$ and $\sigma = 5$. Even selecting this 'objective' prior involves some subjectivity (e.g., have studies been excluded because the designs are too different?). Lack of confidence in the prior can be incorporated by adjusting σ upwards.

The choice of distribution is not limited to the normal distribution. Uniform priors (i.e., a completely flat distribution) are also common, as are priors based on other common probability distributions (e.g., t). On the other hand, when learning Bayesian methods for the first time, a normal prior is likely to be relatively easy to work with.

11.5.3 Normal distributions with known variance

Bayesian inference has many attractive properties for a scientist. Even so, the differences between Bayesian methods and frequentist ones – such as the challenges of selecting a prior – present a stumbling block. With a little preparation and experience it is possible to demonstrate how Bayesian methods are very powerful tools for a researcher. An additional hurdle is that the outcome of a Bayesian analysis can be difficult to compute. The problem is that the posterior distribution is a function of the likelihood times the prior and the normalizing constant. Turning this function into a probability distribution requires computing the integral of this weighted likelihood:

$$p(D) \propto \int \ell(\theta | D) p(\theta) d\theta \qquad \text{Equation 11.16}$$

Depending on the complexity of the model, the distribution of the parameters and the number of parameters, this integral may have a known analytical solution or not.

Some of the potential difficulties are obvious if you consider how to determine the likelihood function. This is relatively easy for simple distributions with one unknown parameter (such as the Poisson or the binomial). If there are nuisance parameters it becomes rather more challenging. In Bayesian analyses these difficulties are compounded because the distribution of the prior (which may differ from the likelihood) also matters. Moreover, it is necessary to integrate the weighted likelihood for a solution. If an analytical solution is not possible or not known, computationally intensive Monte Carlo methods can be applied.

If the prior and likelihood are both normal, the posterior is also normal. Provided the variance of the sample is known there is a very simple analytic solution (see Edwards *et al.*, 1963; Ellison, 1996). If the variance is unknown, an analytical solution exists using the t distribution (though this is not considered here). Berry (1995) also proposes a correction factor for small n that inflates $\hat{\sigma}$ (and hence $\hat{\sigma}_{\hat{\mu}}$) by a factor of $1 + 20/n^2$. This approximate solution is adequate for most purposes.

The likelihood function for a sample from a normal distribution with known variance can be expressed as:

$$\ell(\theta | D) \quad \sim N(\hat{\mu}, \hat{\sigma}_{\hat{\mu}}) \qquad \text{Equation 11.17}$$

If the prior elicited for the analysis is a normal distribution with a mean μ_{prior} and standard deviation σ_{prior}, then the posterior will also be normal. Its mean and *SD* is a function of $\hat{\mu}$, $\hat{\sigma}^2_{\hat{\mu}}$, μ_{prior} and σ^2_{prior}. The variance of the posterior distribution is:

$$\sigma^2_{post} = \left(\frac{1}{\hat{\sigma}^2_{\hat{\mu}}} + \frac{1}{\sigma^2_{prior}} \right)^{-1} \qquad \text{Equation 11.18}$$

The quantity $\hat{\sigma}^2_{\hat{\mu}}$ is the variance of the sampling distribution of the data – and its reciprocal is often termed the precision of the sample. The reciprocal of the prior variance is the precision of the prior. These are combined using standard methods for pooling variances, though sample size is not a factor (as both are estimates for a form of sampling distribution). The final step is to weight the mean of the prior and sample by their respective variances:

$$\mu_{post} = \left(\frac{\sigma^2_{post}}{\hat{\sigma}^2_{\hat{\mu}}}\right)\hat{\mu} + \left(\frac{\sigma^2_{post}}{\sigma^2_{prior}}\right)\mu_{prior} \qquad \text{Equation 11.19}$$

As the posterior distribution is normal it can be used for prediction or to derive an interval estimate for the parameter of interest. These posterior interval estimates are known as *posterior probability intervals* or *credibility intervals*. A posterior probability interval is constructed in a similar way to a $C\%$ frequentist CI (but has a different interpretation). The 95% probability interval for a normal model is therefore:

$$\mu_{post} \pm z_{.975}\sigma_{post} \approxeq \mu_{post} \pm 1.96\sigma_{post} \qquad \text{Equation 11.20}$$

A Bayesian posterior probability interval is an estimate of the range of values likely to contain the true parameter with a fixed probability. This interpretation is at odds with a strict frequentist interpretation of a probability as a long-run average, but is perfectly reasonable from a Bayesian perspective. For a Bayesian inference, probability can be viewed either as an index of the strength of a belief or the degree of certainty with which something is known. If the data are misleading, or if the prior is wrong, this measure may not be very accurate. The goal of Bayesian inference is to use all the information available to produce the best model for the data.

Other combinations of prior and sample distributions have analytic solutions (see Berry, 1995). Wagenmakers (2007), for instance, explains how to use a beta distribution to obtain the posterior distribution from a uniform prior for a binomial sample.

Example 11.7 Howard *et al.* (2000) describe a Bayesian analysis of the effects of a Psychology of Healthy Lifestyles course on student alcohol consumption. They compare the Bayesian analysis to meta-analysis and frequentist inference. The present example reproduces part of their analysis (and only for Study 1). The outcome measure was the self-reported increase in alcoholic drinks per week over the duration of the course. The treatment group received six hours' instruction on the potential adverse effects of alcohol consumption in young people. Data were also collected for a control group (enrolled on different courses). The treatment group ($M = 1.58$, $SD = 2.19$, $n = 13$) increased their alcohol consumption less than the control group ($M = 2.21$, $SD = 2.98$, $n = 36$). This data set is referred to in subsequent examples as the alcohol consumption data.

Howard *et al.* set up priors separately for each group and compared subjective priors for a 'confident optimist' and a 'confident pessimist' with $\sigma_{prior} = 0.5$. The confident optimist anticipates a mean increase of only 1.5 drinks in the treatment group compared to an increase of 5.5 in the control group. The confident pessimist anticipates both groups increase by 5.5 drinks per week. For a normally distributed prior this indicates that both the optimist and pessimist are around 95% certain that the increase will be within $\pm 2\sigma$ (i.e., ± 1 drink per week) of the prior. To calculate the posterior probability distribution requires finding the posterior variance. For the treatment group this is:

$$\sigma^2_{post} = \left(\frac{1}{\hat{\sigma}^2_{\hat{\mu}}} + \frac{1}{\sigma^2_{prior}}\right)^{-1} = \left(\frac{1}{0.6074^2} + \frac{1}{0.5^2}\right)^{-1} = \frac{1}{2.7105 + 4} = \frac{1}{6.7105} \approx 0.1490$$

Taking the square root produces $\sigma_{post} = \sqrt{\sigma^2_{post}} \approx 0.386$. The mean of the posterior distribution is:

$$\mu_{post} = \left(\frac{\sigma^2_{post}}{\hat{\sigma}^2_{\hat{\mu}}}\right)\hat{\mu} + \left(\frac{\sigma^2_{post}}{\sigma^2_{prior}}\right)\mu_{prior} = \left(\frac{0.1490}{0.6074^2}\right)1.58 + \left(\frac{0.1490}{0.5^2}\right)1.5$$
$$= .404 \times 1.58 + .596 \times 1.5 \approx 1.532$$

The multipliers for the observed and prior mean (here .404 and .596) should sum to one. The calculation constructs the posterior mean from 40.4% of the observed mean and 59.6% of the prior mean. The prior is weighted more heavily than the sample mean. This is partly because a confident prior was applied, but mostly because the sample size is so small. The 95% posterior probability interval is:

$$\mu_{post} \pm 1.96 \times \sigma_{post} = 1.53 \pm 0.757$$

With an optimistic prior, you would expect the population increase in drinking for the treatment to be in the range [0.78, 2.29] with a probability of .95 (or 95% certainty).

An alternative way of conceptualizing the prior is to consider it as equivalent to adding a certain number of data points (n_{prior}) to the analysis. Here 40.4% of the information in the analysis is from 13 participants. This means that each participant is about $40.4/13 \approx 3.11\%$ of the information. The remaining 59.6% is therefore equivalent to about $59.6/3.11 \approx 19.2$ participants. A more direct equation is:

$$n_{prior} = \frac{\hat{\sigma}^2}{\sigma^2_{prior}} \qquad \text{Equation 11.21}$$

Greenland (2006) discusses how priors can be added as 'data equivalents' to a frequentist analysis to produce results comparable to a true Bayesian analysis. For instance, in this case you could add n_{prior} data points to the sample such that the data priors have an approximate normal distribution with $\mu = 1.5$ and $\sigma = 0.5$. This kind conceptualization links to the definition of another important prior: the *unit-information prior.* This is a prior that is equivalent to adding one observation to the analysis (i.e., $n_{prior} = 1$). For a normal distribution this means setting σ_{prior} equal to $\hat{\sigma}$.

With a confidently pessimistic prior, the posterior distribution for the treatment group is $\sim N(3.92, 0.386^2)$ giving a 95% posterior probability interval of [3.16, 4.67]. The control group for both optimist and pessimist has the posterior distribution $N(3.84, 0.352^2)$ and 95% posterior probability interval of [3.15, 4.53]. The choice of prior can influence both the mean and variance of the posterior distribution. For this reason a 95% posterior probability interval for an informative prior can be narrower than a 95% CI. The posterior distribution has several applications. An important one is as a prior for a subsequent study, and Howard *et al.* (2000) go on to show that, as more data are added, subsequent analyses converge (regardless of the initial prior).

Berry (1995) suggests applying a small sample correction to $\hat{\sigma}$ when $n < 30$ before calculating $\hat{\sigma}_{\hat{\mu}}$. Recalculating the earlier results for the treatment group ($n = 13$) changes the posterior distribution for the optimistic prior to $N(1.53, 0.403^2)$ and gives a 95% posterior probability interval of [0.74, 2.32]. For the pessimistic prior, the posterior distribution is $N(4.12, 0.403^2)$ and the 95% posterior probability interval is [3.33, 4.91]. The correction has almost no impact on the control group (because $n = 36$).

11.5.4 Bayes factors

A full Bayesian analysis presents an attractive approach to statistical modeling of data that has, albeit at the cost of additional complexity, advantages over frequentist or likelihood methods. These benefits are most obvious when a researcher is interested in parameter estimation and prediction – such as for the applied modeling of complex economic, social or political systems (see Gelman and Hill, 2007). It is also possible to apply the Bayesian philosophy to hypothesis testing. Although it would be ideal to apply a full Bayesian analysis in every case, some situations call for an explicit test of two or more competing hypotheses. A likelihood theorist would accomplish such as a test using likelihood ratios. A Bayesian might use *Bayes factors*. Bayes factors provide a coherent Bayesian method for quantifying the evidential support for one hypothesis over another. A Bayes factor with an informative prior will automatically penalize vague (i.e., complex) theories relative to strong (i.e., parsimonious) ones. A practical benefit is that procedures have been developed to simplify the computation of Bayes factors. A major obstacle is the problem of selecting a prior. Bayes factors are more sensitive to differences in priors than a full Bayesian analysis. One solution is to adopt objective priors that are minimally informative and apply over a wide range of contexts and domains.

Good (1979) credits the development of Bayes factors independently to the scientists and mathematicians Harold Jeffreys and Alan Turing in the 1930s and 40s respectively.[17] To understand what a Bayes factor is, consider Equation 11.15. This expresses the posterior probability distribution in terms of the likelihood of the data and its prior probability:

$$p(\theta|D) \propto \ell(\theta|D)p(\theta)$$

If you want to compare to competing hypotheses H_1 and H_2, this requires the ratio:

$$\frac{p(H_1|D)}{p(H_2|D)} = \frac{p(D|H_1)}{p(D|H_2)} \times \frac{p(H_1)}{p(H_2)} \qquad \text{Equation 11.22}$$

The term on the left-hand side of the equation is the ratio of the two posterior probabilities (the posterior odds). The right-most term is the ratio of the two priors (the prior odds). The central term is the Bayes factor:

$$BF_{H_1/H_2} = \frac{p(D|H_1)}{p(D|H_2)} \qquad \text{Equation 11.23}$$

One way of thinking of the Bayes factor is as a transformation that is applied to the prior probabilities to obtain the posterior probabilities. The form of the Bayes factor is that of an odds ratio; the ratio of the posterior odds to the prior odds. Although Bayes factors are similar to likelihood ratios, they are not the same thing. The key difference is that a Bayes factor is not based on the maximum likelihood but on the marginal likelihood (the weighted average likelihood of Equation 11.16). Only under very restricted conditions, involving nested models with simple hypotheses and no nuisance parameters, does the marginal likelihood equal the maximum likelihood. Under these circumstances the two are equivalent (Kass and Raftery, 1995). Averaging the likelihood rather than maximizing it penalizes complex hypotheses and allows Bayes factors to act as an automatic Occam's razor. This is potentially a major advantage of the Bayesian approach.

The connection with likelihood ratios also extends to interpretation. It is perfectly reasonable, in a Bayesian hypothesis test, to interpret the Bayes factor as the support provided by the data for one hypothesis over another (with the understanding that it penalizes complex models relative to simple ones). Thus a Bayes factor below eight could be interpreted as weak evidence for a hypothesis, one greater than this as moderate evidence and Bayes factors of 32 or greater as strong evidence. Other ways to interpret the magnitude of a Bayes factor exist, but are broadly similar (see Wagenmakers, 2007).

11.5.5 A Bayesian *t* test

For Bayes factors to be an attractive option for hypothesis testing (and therefore a serious competitor to NHSTs or CIs) it is perhaps desirable to automate the process of selecting a prior. In recent years there has been considerable progress toward this end – at least for least squares regression models (including special cases such as *t* tests). Bayes factors can be applied for hypothesis testing in many contexts, but are probably most interesting as Bayesian alternatives to a significance test. For those not looking to replace the convenience of an NHST with an almost equally convenient (but more principled) method, there is much more to the Bayesian approach (see Gelman and Hill, 2007).

To construct a Bayesian test of a null hypothesis involves specifying priors for both H_0 and H_1. For situations where a null hypothesis of zero effect is plausible, the prior for effect size under H_0 is a point mass of probability at μ_0 (e.g., representing zero difference between two means). The alternative hypothesis could also be evaluated for a constant value of μ_1, but this doesn't work very well. Rouder *et al.* (2009) explain how an alternative hypothesis set too far from the observed data will provide 'unbounded' support for the null. It would also be difficult to define a constant value for μ_1 in an objective way.

It is better to consider a distribution for μ_1 that describes a plausible range of effect sizes (and so will be suitable for research in a range of different domains). A common starting point in selecting an objective prior is to use a standardized mean difference (δ). This provides a convenient scale for expressing priors for different contexts. This prior needs to have two main properties: i) it should favor small to moderate effect sizes over large effect sizes, and ii) the variance should not be too large or too small. If the variance is too large it will be uninformative and there would little point in using Bayes factors at all. If the variance is too small, it will be overconfident about the sizes of effects likely to be encountered (e.g., strong evidence for a large effect could be ignored). With a normal prior the first property is easy to obtain if $\mu_1 = 0$ and $\sigma > 0$. With such a prior, small effects close to zero are common (but an effect of exactly $\mu_1 = 0$ will have an infinitely small probability associated with it). This kind of prior is appropriate for a two-sided hypothesis test (because the prior distribution is centered at zero it is not weighted toward an effect in either one direction or the other). Determining the variance of the effect size is a bigger challenge.

One option is to adopt a unit-information prior (Kass and Raftery, 1995; Wagenmakers, 2007). For effects scaled in terms of δ, the relevant distribution is the standard normal: $z \sim N(0, 1)$. Under this prior an effect as extreme as $\delta = 5$ or $\delta = 10$ in either direction would be incredibly rare, but effects between -1 and $+1$ would be relatively frequent.

Rouder *et al.* (2009) argue for a slightly less informative prior known as the Zellner-Siow prior. This prior is less informative because it treats the variance of the prior for the mean as a distribution (rather than a constant such as $\sigma^2 = 1$). In Bayesian terms this amounts to weakening

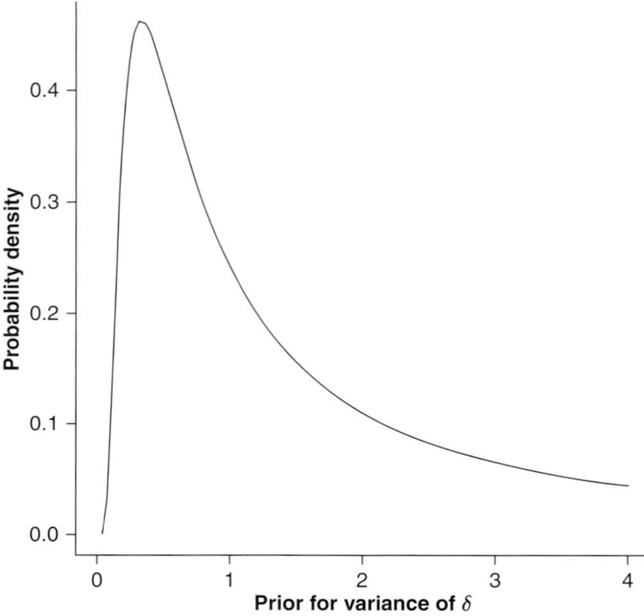

Figure 11.8 Probability density for an inverse χ^2 distribution with 1 *df*

your confidence that the variance of δ is exactly one. In practical terms it ensures that the prior is more conservative than the unit-information prior. The distribution proposed for the variance is an inverse chi-square distribution with 1 *df*. (This is equivalent to the precision of the prior having a χ^2_1 distribution.) Figure 11.8 plots the *pdf* for this prior, and shows that the variance is constrained to be greater than zero. From Figure 11.8 it should be clear that the weight of the density is on small variances (with its mode at $\sigma^2 = 1/3$), but the positive skew ensures that domains with more variable effect sizes are not discounted. This combination of a normal prior with $\mu = 0$ and an inverse χ^2 distribution for σ^2 is mathematically identical to the *standard Cauchy* distribution (Liang *et al.*, 2008). The standard Cauchy is a ratio of two standard normal distributions (and equal to the t distribution with 1 *df*). As a ratio distribution, the Cauchy has some peculiarities (though Figure 11.9 may appear relatively innocuous). It is a good example of the kind of heavy-tailed distribution that causes problems for least squares regression. When selected as an objective prior these properties are an asset. The distribution has an undefined mean and therefore undefined variance. The median and mode do, however, exist (and are zero for the standard Cauchy). Samples from a Cauchy distribution look approximately normal at first glance, but the heavy tails ensure that extreme observations are much more likely. Why is this an asset here? A versatile objective prior needs to be somewhat conservative about the range of effect sizes to be expected. Figure 11.9 shows that, under a Cauchy prior, large effect sizes will be more common than for the unit-information prior. Thus any observed effect favors the null more than for the unit-information prior (it is, therefore, conservative in relation to rejecting the null hypothesis). This might seem counter-intuitive, but is a consequence of the automatic Occam's razor effect of a more diffuse prior versus a less diffuse one. The

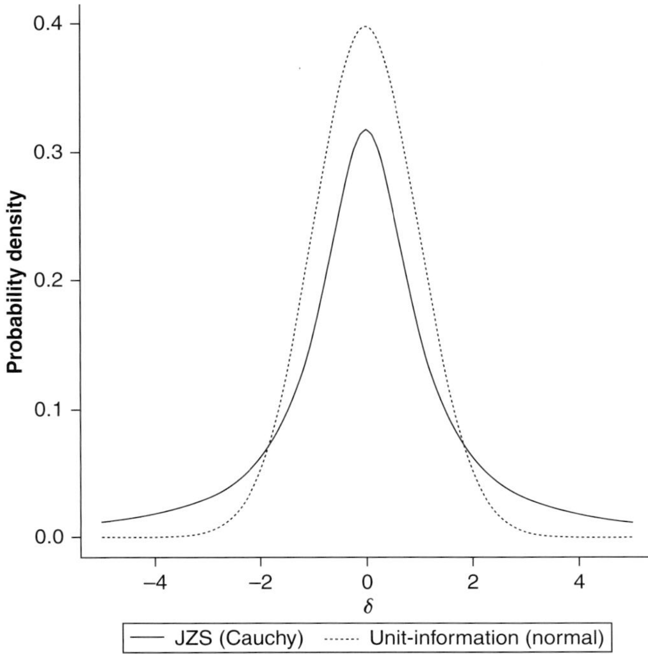

Figure 11.9 The JZS standard Cauchy prior and the unit-information prior for effect size

weight of the alternative hypothesis under the Zellner-Siow prior is spread more thinly than for the unit-information prior. It thus produces a smaller Bayes factor relative to a point null hypothesis.

Having decided on a Zellner-Siow prior for the mean (μ_1), the final ingredient is the prior for the variance (the nuisance parameter σ^2). Rouder *et al.* (2009) propose the common Bayesian default of a Jeffreys prior ($1/\sigma^2$) for the variance. This leads naturally to the label *Jeffreys-Zellner-Siow* (JZS) for the combination of Jeffreys and Zellner-Siow priors. As the variance is a nuisance parameter that applies to both H_0 and H_1, its effect will more or less cancel out (and won't have a substantial impact on the Bayes factor).

Once the priors are determined, the problem of calculating the Bayes factor remains. The input to the calculations could take several different forms, and it turns out to be possible to base the calculations on a t statistic from a standard one or two sample t test. Gönen *et al.* (2005) set out the approach for a unit-information prior. If H_0 is that the difference in means is zero, the formula is simple enough to calculate by hand (but otherwise requires the noncentral t distribution). For a one sample t test with a unit-information prior and H_0: $\mu - \mu_0 = 0$ the Bayes factor is:

$$BF_{H_0/H_1} = \frac{\left(1 + \dfrac{t^2}{n-1}\right)^{-n/2}}{(1+n)^{-1/2}\left(1 + \dfrac{t^2}{(1+n)(n-1)}\right)^{-n/2}} \qquad \text{Equation 11.24}$$

As the *df* of the test are equal to $n-1$, the numerator is the profile likelihood for a normal mean with unknown variance from Equation 11.10. The analytic solution is not always this simple. Rouder *et al.* (2009) provide the corresponding analytic solution for one sample t with a JZS prior:

$$BF_{H_0/H_1} = \frac{\left(1+\frac{t^2}{n-1}\right)^{-n/2}}{\int_0^\infty (1+ng)^{-1/2}\left(1+\frac{t^2}{(1+ng)(n-1)}\right)^{-n/2}(2\pi)^{-1/2}g^{-3/2}e^{-1/(2g)}\,dg}$$

Equation 11.25

The denominator in this equation is an integral. Solving the integral requires using a computer (for any practical application). Rouder *et al.* (2009) show how to extend these solutions to the independent t test and provide a web-based calculator. It is also possible to implement these calculations in appropriate software (e.g., R). These equations deal only with two-sided hypothesis tests and (for the two sample case) equal variances. Wetzels *et al.* (2009) explain how to use MCMC methods to obtain Bayes factors for one-sided hypothesis tests and for the unequal variance case.

While Bayes factors are a (relatively) simple way to implement a form of Bayesian hypothesis test, one of Rouder *et al.*'s central arguments needs to be examined in further detail. A frequentist significance test overestimates the evidence against H_0. This overestimation is more pronounced for large samples (points noted earlier in relation to both stopping rules and likelihood). Rouder *et al.* (2009) propose that a Bayesian t test can be used to assess evidence for a point null hypothesis that is either true or approximately true. Bayes factors (and related statistics) will reduce the bias against the null found with NHSTs in large samples. When H_0 is only approximately true (i.e., the effect is negligible but not exactly zero) the precise performance depends on the prior and the effect size. In addition, there will always be some sample size at which the Bayes factor will switch to favoring the alternative hypothesis (Atkinson, 1978). Weakliem (2004, p. 181) points out that: 'when one obtains a Bayes factor that appears to provide evidence in favor of the null hypothesis, two interpretations are possible: that the null hypothesis is true or that the sample is too small to reveal that it is false'.

Rouder *et al.* (2009) address this concern by looking at the performance of unit-information and JZS prior Bayes factors for an effect size of $\delta = 0.02$. The tipping point turns out to be for sample sizes in the region of 5000 to 50,000. So for $n < 5000$ either test can provide support for a null ($\delta = 0$) or negligible ($\delta \approx 0.02$) effect. For larger samples, or different definitions of a negligible effect, the prior can be adjusted by a 'scale factor' (a multiplier on the prior effect size variance). The default implementation of the Bayesian t test has a scale factor set at one. Increasing it makes the test more conservative (by increasing the expected variance of the effects under H_1).

The availability of software limits the opportunity of researchers to apply even relatively simple Bayesian methods. Dienes (2008) published the Matlab code for examples of Bayesian analyses in his book. Baguley and Kaye (2010) report R functions adapted from Dienes' original Matlab code. Kaye and Baguley (forthcoming) provide R functions that implement the unit-information prior and JZS prior Bayesian t tests described by Gönen *et al.* (2005) and Rouder *et al.* (2009). For more advanced introductions to Bayesian modeling using R, specialist software such as WinBUGS is also available (Gelman and Hill, 2007; Wetzels *et al.*, 2010; Kruschke, 2010).

Bayes factors were developed as hypothesis tests. For the purposes of presentation of results they should generally be supplemented by graphical summaries of data and probably also with interval estimates. Rouder *et al.* (2009) suggest supplementing them with CIs, but likelihood intervals are also an option (because of the link between the likelihood and Bayes factor calculations). Posterior probability or credibility intervals from a Bayesian analysis would be ideal (but may not be practical because Bayes factors are likely to be reported in the absence of a full Bayesian analysis).

Example 11.8 How do the JZS and unit-information prior Bayes factors perform in practice? Example 11.6 looked at sleep loss data using likelihood methods. This suggested weak to moderate evidence for a modest decrease in IQ ($\delta \approx 0.33$) and strong evidence against a large decrease ($\delta = 1$). The likelihood ratios for the effect depend on the alternative hypothesis being considered. The smaller effect seems more plausible, *a priori* and a Bayesian test using the priors described here incorporates this conservative position. The only input required for the analysis is the one sample t statistic $(94.6 - 100)/2.77 = -1.95$ and $n = 50$.

The unit-information prior Bayes factor in favor of H_0 is 1.15 (or 0.87 in favor of H_1). Using the JZS prior the Bayes factor increases to 1.50 in favor of H_0 (or 0.67 in favor of H_1). The JZS prior behaves exactly as expected: it suggests stronger evidence in favor of the null than the unit-information prior. Neither result provides even weak support for the hypothesis that sleep disruption impairs measured IQ.

For the alcohol consumption data (Howard *et al.*, 2000, Study 1), the t statistic for the difference between treatment and control is $t(47) = 0.70$, $SE = .90$, $p > .05$. Calculating a Bayes factor also requires the sample size in each group ($n = 13$ and $n = 36$). The unit-information prior gives a Bayes factor of 2.60 in favor of the null hypothesis of no difference, while the JZS prior gives a Bayes factor of 3.41 in favor of the null.

The Bayes factors in these cases can be compared with the outcome of the corresponding NHST. For the sleep loss example, the one sample t test reports $p = .06$. The Bayes factors provide weak evidence in favor of the null. Interestingly, had the t test been statistically significant (e.g., if $t = 2.01$ rather than 1.95) the Bayes factors (1.03 and 1.34 respectively) would still have favored the H_0.

The Bayes factors provide weak support for the null hypothesis for the alcohol consumption data (rather than the inconclusive interpretation attached to a non-significant p value). It is quite possible, though, for the outcomes to be more starkly at odds. In general, a marginally statistically significant result will not strongly favor H_1 (regardless of whether a JZS or unit-information prior is selected). However, for large samples a marginally significant NHST will increasingly favor H_0. Thus for $n = 1000$ a one sample t statistic of 2.2 will have a JZS Bayes factor of 3.6 in favor of H_0 (even though two-sided $p = .028$).

11.6 Information criteria

Likelihood and Bayesian methods of inference provide clear alternatives to frequentist methods for hypothesis testing: the likelihood ratio and the Bayes factor. Information criteria provide a further option to researchers keen to avoid some of the problems of NHSTs. Information-theoretic approaches view inference as a problem of model selection; selecting the 'best' statistical model from a set of plausible alternatives (Burnham and Anderson, 2004). According to this approach, the best model is the one that is most informative in terms of reducing

Kullback-Leibler information loss (the loss of information in a model relative to the true model).

For finite data and a realistic model it unreasonable to expect to calculate Kullback-Leibler information loss exactly. The true model will be unknown and the sample will be characterized by uncertainty. Information criteria are estimates of this information loss for a specified model and sample. The best-known criterion for estimating information loss in a model is AIC (Akaike, 1974). Akaike modestly named this 'an information criterion', but subsequent work refers to it as *Akaike's information criterion* (AIC). Akaike showed that information loss for a model was closely related to the likelihood of the model and proportional to

$$-\ln(\ell) + k \quad \text{Equation 11.26}$$

where ℓ is the likelihood of the model given the data and k is the number of parameters in the model. His information criterion is defined as:

$$AIC = -2\ln(\ell) + 2k \quad \text{Equation 11.27}$$

As AIC is derived from the likelihood, it is defined only up to an arbitrary constant. Multiplying by two makes no difference to the quality of AIC as an estimate of *Kullback-Leibler* information loss. However, $-2\ln(\ell)$, or 'minus 2 log likelihood', is a widely used quantity in statistics (and, under certain conditions, it has an approximate χ^2 distribution).

Inference using information criteria involves keeping information loss low and therefore selecting a model that minimizes a criterion such as AIC. As with likelihood, the absolute value of AIC is largely meaningless (being determined by the arbitrary constant). As this constant depends on the data, AIC can be used to compare models fitted on identical samples. The best model from the set of plausible models being considered is therefore the one with the smallest AIC value (the least information loss relative to the true model). A common misconception is to think that the goal is to minimize the absolute value of AIC, but the arbitrary constant can (depending on data and model) produce negative values. Negative AIC indicates less information loss than a positive AIC and therefore a better model.

What is the advantage of using AIC rather than the likelihood? If you are comparing models with the same number of parameters, there is no effective difference between AIC and the *LR*. Because k will be identical, the difference in AIC between the models reduces to the difference in $-2\ln(\ell)$. If Δ_{AIC} is the difference in AIC between two models, and provided k is identical for the two models, then the ratio of their likelihoods is:

$$LR = e^{-1/2\Delta_{AIC}} \quad \text{Equation 11.28}$$

This equation indicates that the magnitude of the difference in AIC indexes the evidence supporting one model over another. A modest difference (e.g., $\Delta_{\text{AIC}} = 5$) corresponds to fairly strong evidence ($LR = 12.2$) for one of the models (the one with the lower AIC). This relationship allows researchers to transform AIC into a quantity that is easier to interpret.

AIC is superior to the *LR* if the number of parameters differs between models. Many significance tests compare models with different numbers of parameters. Thus the independent t test compares a model with three parameters (μ_1, μ_2 and σ^2) to a 'null' model with two parameters (μ_{grand} and σ^2). The extra parameter for the model under the alternative hypothesis ensures that it will nearly always fit the data better than the null model (and will never have a worse fit). Extra parameters indicate a more complex model, so information criteria such as AIC can be regarded as different solutions to the problem of parsimony (or different 'brands' of Occam's razor). While the derivation of AIC is all about estimating information loss, it is not uncommon to present AIC and related statistics as being a composite of 'model fit' and a 'penalty for complexity'. According to this view, the $-2\ln(\ell)$ term indicates the fit of a model (e.g., in the form of a χ^2 statistic) and $+2k$ is a penalty for models that are more complex. Not everyone agrees with this way of interpreting AIC, but framing it in this way can help communicate the advantages of the information-theoretic approach.

AIC is not the only possible criterion that could be adopted as an estimate of information loss. The form of the estimate depends on the mathematical assumptions used to derive the criterion. The AIC can be derived as a large sample estimate of the information loss when the true model may not be among the set of models being considered (Burnham and Anderson, 2004). In small samples this approximation may be poor and a corrected statistic AIC_C is preferred (Sugiura, 1978; Hurvich and Tsai, 1989):

$$AIC_C = -2\ln(\ell) + 2k + \frac{2k(k+1)}{N-k-1} \qquad \text{Equation 11.29}$$

As N, the total sample size, increases, the additional right-hand term in AIC_C tends toward zero and AIC_C converges on AIC. For this reason AIC_C should be preferred for most purposes. When k is small the correction has a modest impact for moderate samples sizes (e.g., $N > 30$) and a negligible impact when N is fairly large (e.g., $N > 100$). Nevertheless, unless very precise ranking of models is required or the number of parameters differing between models is large, AIC will be adequate when working with large data sets.

Schwartz (1978) proposed a different estimate of information loss, initially motivated as a Bayesian solution. This criterion is generally known as BIC (*Bayesian information criterion*) or occasionally as the *Schwartz criterion*. Although BIC has a Bayesian motivation, both AIC and BIC can be derived from either a frequentist or Bayesian perspective (Burnham and Anderson, 2004), and it is not necessarily the case that a Bayesian would prefer BIC to AIC (Weakliem, 2004; Gelman and Hill, 2007). The equation for BIC takes the form:

$$BIC = -2\ln(\ell) + k\ln(N) \qquad \text{Equation 11.30}$$

The derivation of BIC assumes (contra AIC) that the true model is within the set of plausible models being considered. This partly explains the difference in the equations. A crude comparison of AIC and BIC focuses on the 'penalty term'. This is $+2k$ for AIC and $+k\ln(N)$ for BIC, and so the estimated information loss will be larger for BIC than AIC whenever $\ln(N)$ is greater than 2. This occurs for all models with $N > 7$ (because $\ln(7) \approx 1.95$ and $\ln(8) \approx 2.08$). BIC therefore selects simpler models relative to AIC except when $N < 8$ (though AIC_C is preferred to AIC when N is this small). For models with the same number of parameters, k and N will be identical and the preference for one model over another depends only on the likelihood.

There is considerable debate – to put it mildly – about the relative merits of AIC and BIC (even leaving aside other criteria). Burnham and Anderson (2004) favor AIC, based on its more plausible derivation (specifically that the set of models under consideration does not contain the true model), and because it selects models with lower prediction error. They also argue that some unfavorable verdicts on AIC stem from simulations that don't apply a small-sample correction. Proponents of BIC (e.g., Raftery, 1995; Wagenmakers, 2007) have tended not to focus on its information-theoretic properties. Instead the difference in BIC for two models is presented as way to approximate a Bayes factor. For many models (e.g., least squares regression models) the BIC is an approximation to a Bayes factor with a unit-information prior (see Kass and Raftery, 1995; Weakliem, 2004). The approximation is quite good in large samples, but it can be poor for smaller sample sizes (e.g., $N \leq 20$). The big advantage is that it is easy to obtain BIC for a wide range of models. Hastie *et al.* (2001) state that AIC tends to choose models that are too complex for large N, and BIC tends to select models that are too simple for finite N. This implies that AIC_C may be a good compromise for small samples, but BIC may be preferable for very large data sets.

BIC and AIC_C are awkward to calculate whenever N is not defined unambiguously. In most cases N is the total number of data points contributing to the statistical model, but in some models (such as those with repeated measures) N has more than one legitimate definition (e.g., total number of participants or total number of observations). Wagenmakers (2007) and Hox (2010) advocate using the number of participants for repeated measures data (although published work often uses the total number of observations).

11.6.1 Transformations of AIC, AIC_C and BIC

The interpretation and reporting of information criteria can be enhanced by transformation. The exact values of each criterion may be useful for replicating an analysis using identical data, though it is probably sufficient to report statistics such as $-2\ln(\ell)$ that can be used to reproduce the exact values. The strength of evidence for one model over another is related to the magnitude of the difference in AIC, AIC_C or BIC between models. Thus the simplest transformation for reporting and interpreting information criteria is to report this difference (e.g., Δ_{AIC} or Δ_{BIC}). When dealing with more than two models it helps to designate the model with fewest parameters as a reference model (e.g., M_0) and report the differences between AIC, AIC_C or BIC relative to this shared reference point. Thus you may calculate

$$\Delta_{IC_i} = IC_{M_i} - IC_{M_0} \qquad \text{Equation 11.31}$$

where IC is the criterion being used (AIC, AIC_C or BIC) and i is a subscript indexing one of the set of models being compared.

The main drawback of reporting the differences is that they are scaled in terms of the logarithm of the likelihood. Researchers familiar with likelihood ratios and Bayes factors may be more comfortable with statistics scaled in the same way. Equation 11.30 indicates that, for models with an identical number of parameters, the LR is $e^{-1/2\Delta_{AIC}}$. The same formula will also transform the AIC, AIC_C or BIC into a form of likelihood ratio. As it is usual for the number of parameters to differ between models, the criterion should be noted when the statistic is reported. This is easy to accomplish by using a subscript such as LR_{AIC}, LR_{AIC_c} or LR_{BIC}. Note that LR_{BIC} (computed as $e^{-1/2\Delta_{BIC}}$) is then an approximation to a Bayes factor with a unit-information prior.

The final transformation is trickier to compute. This involves *Akaike weights* or (for BIC) *Schwartz weights* (see Wagenmakers and Farrell, 2004). Akaike weights represent the relative weight of evidence for a model among a set of J models. As weight of evidence is indicated by the likelihood, this involves dividing the likelihood of each model by the summed likelihood of all the models in the set. The likelihood is proportional to the difference in information criteria between the models, so it makes sense to start with the differences relative to a reference model. To calculate Akaike weights, first obtain these differences using Equation 11.31 and then use them to calculate a weight for each of the J models:

$$w_{IC_i} = \frac{e^{-1/2\Delta_{IC_i}}}{\sum_{j=1}^{J} e^{-1/2\Delta_{IC_j}}} \qquad \text{Equation 11.32}$$

The formulas for AIC, BIC or AIC_C are therefore identical apart from the choice of information criterion plugged into the equations. The weights are relative estimates of how likely each of the models is. As the weights always sum to one, they provide a convenient scale to work with for any set of models (but weights are not comparable between sets).

Akaike and Schwartz weights index the evidential support for one model over another from the set: LR_{IC} for M_1 relative to M_2 is w_1/w_2. Each weight is the probability of a model being the most informative in the set of models being compared (based on the information criterion selected). The weights may also be interpreted as the posterior or predictive probability that a model is true. This assumes that the true model is in the set (something hard to determine with certainty) and that the models were equally plausible *a priori* (except in terms of number of parameters). This can be extended to any subset of models for which weights have been calculated. So an estimate of the posterior probability of M_1 relative to M_2 and M_3 is $w_1/(w_1+w_2+w_3)$.

11.6.2 AIC and BIC for normal models

Information criteria are defined in terms of the likelihood of the model given the data and the number of parameters in the model. For BIC and AIC_C the sample size is also required. If the residuals are sampled from an independent, normal population of errors with equal variance (e.g., for a least squares regression model), alternative formulas can be constructed. These formulas use the relationship between the likelihood of a normal model and the residual sums of squares of the model:

$$-2\ln(\ell) \propto N\ln\left(\frac{SS_{residual}}{N}\right) + N\ln(2\pi) + N \qquad \text{Equation 11.33}$$

Because the two final terms $N\ln(2\pi)$ and N are constants in this context (N being fixed for a given data set) they are often dropped for the purposes of calculating information criteria. This leads to a simplified equation for AIC:

$$AIC = N\ln\left(\frac{SS_{residual}}{N}\right) + 2k \qquad \text{Equation 11.34}$$

The corresponding equation for AIC_C is

$$AIC_C = N\ln\left(\frac{SS_{residual}}{N}\right) + 2k + \frac{2k(k+1)}{N-k-1} \qquad \text{Equation 11.35}$$

while BIC simplifies to

$$BIC = N\ln\left(\frac{SS_{residual}}{N}\right) + k\ln(N) \qquad \text{Equation 11.36}$$

As long as differences in information criteria are compared, and as long as the formulas are applied consistently, choice of the full likelihood formula or the simplified formula will be irrelevant. It is, however, possible to get confused if comparing models fitted using different formulas. This can happen if you switch between software and occasionally within the same software (e.g., R has functions for both full likelihood and the simplified formulas).

A further complication is that formulas may count the total number of parameters k in different ways. The full likelihood formula is usually applied with the total number of free parameters (including nuisance parameters such as σ_E^2 in a regression model). The simplified formulas are often applied with the number of parameters excluding nuisance parameters. For instance, the total number of parameters in a simple linear regression is three, but the number of parameters excluding σ_E^2 is two. When determining Δ_{AIC}, the number of parameters cancels out and will not matter (except for comparing results using different definitions). It is also possible to 'back-transform' the simplified formulas and go directly from LR to LR_{AIC}, $LR_{\text{AIC}c}$ or LR_{BIC} (see Box 11.4).

Box 11.4 Adjusting a likelihood ratio for model complexity

Glover and Dixon (2004) show how to calculate the LR for a variety of least squares regression models using the residual SS:

$$LR_{H_1/H_2} = \left(\frac{SS_{residual_2}}{SS_{residual_1}}\right)^{\frac{N}{2}} \qquad \text{Equation 11.37}$$

This calculation can also be expressed in terms of the proportion of variance explained:

$$LR_{H_1/H_2} = \left(\frac{1-R_2^2}{1-R_1^2}\right)^{\frac{N}{2}} \qquad \text{Equation 11.38}$$

To adjust this likelihood ratio for the different number of parameters in each model requires multiplying the LR by the factor Q_{AIC}, Q_{AICc} or Q_{BIC}. Glover and Dixon (2004) show that the factors are

$$Q_{AIC} = e^{k_1 - k_2} \qquad \text{Equation 11.39}$$

$$Q_{AIC_C} = e^{k_1\left(\frac{N}{N-k_1-1}\right) - k_2\left(\frac{N}{N-k_2-1}\right)} \qquad \text{Equation 11.40}$$

and

$$Q_{BIC} = \left(e^{k_1 - k_2}\right)^{\ln(N)/2} \qquad \text{Equation 11.41}$$

Example 11.9 Information criteria can be calculated with minimal difficulty for least squares models. An independent t test can be used to demonstrate the basic calculations. The null model in this case is a model estimating two parameters (the population grand mean μ_{grand} and the population variance σ_E^2). The alternative model estimates three parameters (μ_1 and μ_2 and σ_E^2).

Obtaining $SS_{residual}$ for a data set (e.g., the comprehension data used here) is not difficult. It is part of the standard output for most regression software. Because $SS_{residual} = \sqrt{MS_{error}/df}$ it is also easily computed from the pooled sample variance:

$$SS_{residual} = (N-2)\,MS_{error} = (N-2)\,\hat{\sigma}^2_{pooled}$$

For the comprehension data $\hat{\sigma}_{pooled} = 18.025$, and $SS_{residual}$ is:

$$(N-2)\,\hat{\sigma}^2_{pooled} = (56-2)\,(18.025)^2 \approx 17544.6$$

The simplified AIC formula for least-squares models with $k = 2$ gives:

$$AIC = 56 \times \ln\left(\frac{17544.6}{56}\right) + 2 \times 2 \approx 325.84$$

In comparison, the full likelihood formula with $k = 3$ gives:

$$AIC = 56 \times \ln\left(\frac{17544.6}{56}\right) + 56 \times \ln(2\pi) + 56 + 2 \times 3$$

$$= 321.84 + 56 \times 1.837877 + 62 \approx 486.76$$

The R functions `extractAIC()` and `AIC()` return 325.8405 and 486.7616 respectively. The `AIC()` function matches the second result (because it works from the full likelihood of the model using the `logLik()` function), and `extractAIC()` matches the first result. For a linear regression model the function works by producing a result equivalent to the simplified formulas (and ignores the nuisance parameter when counting the parameters).

To get the AIC for the null model we could have calculated the residuals directly (by subtracting the grand mean from all 56 observations and then squaring and summing). In fact, I obtained the residuals from the intercept-only model (equivalent to a model with only the grand mean). Either route gives $SS_{residual} = 19945.44$. This is a slightly worse fit, and has one fewer parameters; the residuals are on average further from the grand mean than the two group means. AIC is 333.02 or 491.94, depending on whether the simplified or full likelihood equation is applied. Regardless, the difference in AIC is $(333.02 - 327.84)$ or $(491.94 - 486.76) \approx 5.18$.

This corresponds to $LR_{AIC} = e^{5.18/2} \approx 13.33$, and is fairly strong evidence in favor of the model with lower AIC (which is the alternative model with two means). The small sample corrected AIC_C is a more appropriate choice for these data: $\Delta_{AIC_c} = 4.95$ and $LR_{AIC_c} = 11.86$.

It is possible to calculate Akaike weights or Schwartz weights for these two models (though this is generally only useful if there are three or more models to be compared). This calculation is for Schwartz weights, to illustrate calculation of BIC (using full likelihood):

$$BIC = 56 \times \ln\left(\frac{17544.6}{56}\right) + 56 \times \ln(2\pi) + 56 + 3 \times \ln(56) \approx 492.84$$

The corresponding value for the null model is 495.99. The difference is therefore $(495.99 - 492.84) \approx 3.15$. This corresponds to $LR_{BIC} = e^{3.16/2} = 4.85$ and therefore offers somewhat weaker evidence in favor of the model with the extra parameter. Out of interest, the Bayes factor, using a unit-information prior (of which LR_{BIC} is a large sample approximation), is 6.84.

To obtain the Schwartz weights it is necessary to calculate BIC for each model relative to the reference model (in this case the null model). This is zero for the null model and 4.85 for the alternative model. LR_{BIC} for the alternative model is 4.85 and $e^0 = 1$ for the null model. So

$$\sum_{j=1}^{J} e^{-1/2\Delta_{AIC_j}} \approx 5.85$$

The Schwartz weight for the null model is therefore $1/5.85 \approx .17$ and $4.85/5.85 = .83$ for the alternative model. Switching to AIC_C is preferable for small samples and the corrected Akaike weights (obtained from the R package `bbmle`) are .92 and .08.

11.7 R code for Chapter 11

11.7.1 Equivalence testing using TOST (Example 11.3)

Equivalence testing using TOST can be implemented most easily as a one sample CI. This could be done using the `t.test()` function with a vector of raw data or from the summary statistics (the approach illustrated here). For a 95% confidence equivalence test a 90% CI is required. A quick calculation from summary statistics gives:

```
sd.pooled <- ((7.8^2 * 99 + 9.2^2 * 99)/200)^0.5
diff = 10.5 - 8.2
moe <- sd.pooled * (1/100 + 1/100)^0.5 * qt(0.95, 198)
c(diff - moe, diff + moe)
```

An alternative approach is to use `tost()` from the `equivalence` package. This requires raw data (and works for the one or two sample case). The `tost.stat()` function from the same package uses summary statistics, but only works for the one sample test. The main advantage of these functions is that the decision to reject or not reject the hypothesis of dissimilarity is reported (in Example 11.3 dissimilarity is rejected and equivalence is detected because the 90% interval lies entirely within the equivalence region).

11.7.2 Likelihood function for the binomial (Example 11.4)

There are several ways to calculate likelihoods in R. If you have an equation for the likelihood function, you can use this directly: the likelihood for 19 successes and six fails from a binomial distribution if $P = .76$ is:

```
.76^19 * .24^6
```

The corresponding likelihood for $P = .5$ is:

```
.5^19 * .5^6
```

The likelihood ratio is therefore:

```
(.76^19 * .24^6)/(.5^19 * .5^6)
```

Any quantity proportional to this is also a likelihood function, meaning that *pmf* and *pdf* functions can be used. Here you could use the `dbinom()` function:

```
dbinom(19,25,.76)
dbinom(19,25,.5)
dbinom(19,25,.76)/dbinom(19,25,.5)
```

Although the likelihoods in the preceding equations don't match, the ratios do. A key thing to remember is that a standard call to these functions involves keeping N and P fixed and allowing the number of successes to vary. In a basic likelihood function, the data (the number of trials and successes) are fixed while the parameter (P) varies.

11.7.3 Likelihood intervals

Calculating or plotting likelihood intervals is trickier than likelihood ratios. Functions that calculate the 1/8 and 1/32 intervals for several common distributions are described here. A function for the likelihood interval of a binomial proportion is:

```
binom.lik <- function(successes, trials, accuracy = 1e-05,
  plot = FALSE) {
   P <- seq(0, 1, accuracy)
   like <- P^successes * (1 - P)^(trials - successes)
   max.like <- max(like)
   like <- like/max.like
   P.hat <- P[which(like == max(like))]
   b8.i <- min(which(like >= 1/8))
   e8.i <- max(which(like >= 1/8))
   b8.i <- min(which(like >= 1/8))
   e8.i <- max(which(like >= 1/8))
   b32.i <- min(which(like >= 1/32))
   e32.i <- max(which(like >= 1/32))
   b32.i <- min(which(like >= 1/32))
   e32.i <- max(which(like >= 1/32))
   b8 <- P[b8.i]
   e8 <- P[e8.i]
   b32 <- P[b32.i]
   e32 <- P[e32.i]
```

```
    output <- list('P-hat' = P.hat, '1/8 likelihood interval'
        = c(b8, e8), '1/8 lower' = b8, '1/8 upper' = e8, '1/32
        likelihood interval' = c(b32, e32), '1/32 lower' =
        b32, '1/32 upper' = e32)
    if (plot == TRUE) {
    curve((x^successes * (1 - x)^(trials -
        successes)/max.like), xlim = c(0, 1), xlab =
        expression(italic("P")), ylab = "Likelihood")
    segments(b8, 1/8, e8, 1/8, lwd = 0.2)
    segments(b32, 1/32, e32, 1/32, lwd = 0.2)
   }
   output
}
```

This function is reasonably versatile and called by:

```
binom.lik(19, 25)
```

This returns the *MLE* ($\hat{P}$) and the intervals. If you add `plot=TRUE` it also plots the intervals using `curve()` and `segments()`.

```
binom.lik(19, 25, plot=TRUE)
```

The `accuracy` argument allows you to decrease or increase the accuracy of calculations if desired. The function uses a brute force approach, and tries to adjust the plot axes automatically for the data. It works by slicing the possible range of *P* (zero to one) into thousands of tiny slices and calculating likelihoods at each point. These are then standardized and the values corresponding to 1/8 and 1/32 at either end of the distribution are found using `which()`. See `?which` for further details.

11.7.4 Likelihood inference with Poisson counts (Example 11.5)

Calculating likelihoods for a single unknown parameter distribution with no nuisance parameters is not difficult. Example 11.5 illustrates how to do this for the Poisson distribution. Here the probability mass function for the Poisson is computed directly to obtain the likelihood (assigned to the object `like`), but `dpois()` could be used directly.

The following function also calculates the 1/8 and 1/32 likelihood intervals for the Poisson in a similar fashion to the binomial likelihood function in the previous example.

```
pois.lik <- function(count, plot = FALSE) {
    range <- count * 10 + 10
    lambda <- seq(0, range, range/10000)
    like <- lambda^count * exp(-1 * lambda)
    max.like <- max(like)
    like <- like/max.like
    pois.mle <- count
    b8.i <- min(which(like >= 1/8))
```

```
    e8.i <- max(which(like >= 1/8))
    b8.i <- min(which(like >= 1/8))
    e8.i <- max(which(like >= 1/8))
    b8 <- lambda[b8.i]
    e8 <- lambda[e8.i]
    b32.i <- min(which(like >= 1/32))
    e32.i <- max(which(like >= 1/32))
    b32.i <- min(which(like >= 1/32))
    e32.i <- max(which(like >= 1/32))
    b32 <- lambda[b32.i]
    e32 <- lambda[e32.i]
    output <- list('1/8 likelihood interval' = c(b8, e8), '1/8
        lower' = b8, '1/8 upper' = e8, '1/32 likelihood
        interval' = c(b32, e32), '1/32 lower' = b32, '1/32
        upper' = e32)
    if (plot == TRUE) {
        curve(x^count * exp(-1 * x)/max.like, xlim = c(0,
            count * 2 + 7), xlab = expression(lambda), ylab =
            "Likelihood")
        segments(b8, 1/8, e8, 1/8, lwd = 0.2)
        segments(b32, 1/32, e32, 1/32, lwd = 0.2)
    }
    output
}
```

The function is called with the observed count and plots the likelihood interval if specified:

```
pois.lik(3)
pois.lik(3, plot=TRUE)
```

11.7.5 Profile likelihood and intervals using *t* (Example 11.6)

This example uses profile likelihoods for normal samples with unknown variances to calculate likelihood ratios and intervals. The first function calculates the profile likelihood with or without the adjustment used by Royall (1997). The default is no adjustment. The `independent` argument is required only for the adjustment (because the unadjusted likelihood depends only on t and df).

```
t.lik <- function(t, df, independent = TRUE, adjust = FALSE) {
    if (independent == TRUE)
        N = df + 2
    else N = df + 1
    if (adjust == TRUE)
        N = df
    like <- (1 + t^2/df)^-((N)/2)
    like
}
```

The second function uses `t.lik()` to compute a likelihood ratio from the observed mean (or difference in means), *SE* and *df*. This format is flexible enough to be used for one sample, paired or independent *t* tests (but requires you to enter the *SE* and *df*). In addition, if you are using the adjustment, the `independent` argument needs to be specified). The first two arguments in the call for the function are the population means under the two hypotheses being compared and the third argument is for the observed mean or mean difference.

```
LR.t <- function(mu1, mu2, mu.obs, SE, df, independent = TRUE,
        adjust = FALSE) {
            lik1 <- t.lik((mu1 - mu.obs)/SE, df, independent =
                independent, adjust = adjust)
            lik2 <- t.lik((mu2 - mu.obs)/SE, df, independent =
                independent, adjust = adjust)
            LR.mu1 <- lik1/lik2
            LR.mu2 <- 1/LR.mu1
            return <- list('Likelihood ratios', LR.mu1 = LR.mu1,
                LR.mu2 = LR.mu2)
        return
  }
```

An example of the function in application is:

```
LR.t(85, 100, 94.6, 2.77, 49, independent=FALSE, adjust=FALSE)
```

This call compares the likelihood of the data under the hypothesis that $\mu = 85$ with the likelihood under the hypothesis that $\mu = 100$ (labeled as `LR.mu1`). It also returns the inverse of the ratio (labeled as `LR.mu2`).

A related function returns the 1/8 and 1/32 likelihood intervals and also plots them. As with the binomial version, the `accuracy` argument allows you to decrease or increase the accuracy of calculations if desired. The function takes the mean (or mean difference), *SE* and *df* as input, but also requires the `independent` argument to be specified. The adjustment and plot of the interval are not provided by default.

```
t.lik.int <- function(mean, SE, df, independent = TRUE, adjust
      = FALSE,
        accuracy = 1e-04, plot = FALSE) {
        if (independent == TRUE)
            N = df + 2
        else N = df + 1
        SDest <- SE * N^0.5
        if (adjust == TRUE)
            N <- df
        mu <- seq(mean - SDest, mean + SDest, accuracy)
        like <- (1 + ((mean - mu)/SE)^2/df)^-((N)/2)
        max.like <- max(like)
```

```
            M.hat <- mean
            b8.i <- min(which(like >= 1/8))
            e8.i <- max(which(like >= 1/8))
            b8 <- mu[b8.i]
            e8 <- mu[e8.i]
            b32.i <- min(which(like >= 1/32))
            e32.i <- max(which(like >= 1/32))
            b32 <- mu[b32.i]
            e32 <- mu[e32.i]
            if (plot == TRUE) {
                curve((1 + ((mean - x)/SE)^2/df)^-(N/2), xlim =
                   c(-SDest + mean, SDest + mean), xlab =
                   expression(mu), ylab = "Likelihood")
                segments(b8, 1/8, e8, 1/8, lwd = 0.2)
                segments(b32, 1/32, e32, 1/32, lwd = 0.2)
            }
            output <- list('M-hat' = M.hat, '1/8 likelihood
                   interval' = c(b8, e8), '1/8 lower' = b8, '1/8
                   upper' = e8, '1/32 likelihood interval' =
                   c(b32, e32), '1/32 lower' = b32, '1/32 upper'
                   = e32)
            output
    }
```

The function can therefore be called in several different ways:

```
t.lik.int(94.6, 2.77, 49, independent=FALSE)
t.lik.int(94.6, 2.77, 49, independent=FALSE, plot=TRUE)
t.lik.int(94.6, 2.77, 49, independent=FALSE, adjust=TRUE)
```

11.7.6 Inference with normal prior and known variance (Example 11.7)

The following functions perform inference for a subjective normal prior with known variance (Berry, 1995; Ellison, 1996). The first function provides a posterior mean and *SD* and, by default, a 95% posterior probability interval for the mean.

```
Bayes.norm.1s <- function(M.obs, SD.obs, mu.prior,
     sigma.prior, N, confidence = 0.95, ssc = TRUE, plot =
     FALSE) {
          if (ssc == TRUE) SD.obs <- SD.obs * (1 + 20/N^2)
          SE.adj <- SD.obs/N^0.5
          precision.prior <- 1/sigma.prior^2
          precision.lik <- 1/SE.adj^2
          precision.post <- precision.prior + precision.lik
          mean.post <- (precision.prior/precision.post) *
```

```
          mu.prior + (precision.lik/precision.post) *
          M.obs
     sigma.post <- (1/precision.post)^0.5
     lower <- mean.post + qnorm((1 - confidence)/2) *
          sigma.post
     upper <- mean.post - qnorm((1 - confidence)/2) *
          sigma.post
     post.prob.int <- c(lower, upper)
     min.m <- min(M.obs, mu.prior, mean.post)
     max.m <- max(M.obs, mu.prior, mean.post)
     max.s <- max(SE.adj, sigma.prior, sigma.post)
     y.max <- max(dnorm(mu.prior, mu.prior, sigma.prior),
          dnorm(M.obs, M.obs, SE.adj), dnorm(mean.post,
          mean.post, sigma.post))
     if (plot == TRUE) {
          curve(dnorm(x, mean.post, sigma.post), lty = 3,
               xlim = c(min.m - 3.75 * max.s, max.m + 3.75
               * max.s), yaxt = 'n', ylab = NA, xlab =
               expression(mu))
          curve(dnorm(x, mu.prior, sigma.prior), lwd =
               0.3, add = TRUE)
          curve(dnorm(x, M.obs, SE.adj), add = TRUE)
          legend(max.m + max.s, y.max, legend = c('Prior',
               'Likelihood', 'Posterior'), lty = c(1, 1,
                  3), lwd = c(0.3, 1, 1))
     }
     output <- list('Posterior mean' = mean.post,
          'Posterior SD' = sigma.post, 'Probability
          interval' = post.prob.int, Confidence =
          confidence, lower = lower, upper = upper)
     output
}
```

This assumes a known variance and is called with the observed mean and *SE* as the mean and *SD* for the prior, followed by *n*:

```
Bayes.norm.1s(1.58, 2.19/13^0.5, 1.5, .5, 13, ssc=FALSE)
```

In the above example the *SE* is given by the expression `2.19/13^0.5` using the *SD* and *n* for the treatment group of the alcohol consumption data from Example 11.7. The default is to compute the small sample correction (Berry, 1995) and `ssc=FALSE` overrides this. The function also plots the prior, likelihood and posterior distributions if `plot=TRUE` is added. A similar function does the same for a two sample test, taking the difference in means, *SD* and *n* for each sample (as well as parameters for the prior) as input:

```
Bayes.norm.2s <- function(M.diff, SD.1, SD.2, diff.prior,
     sigma.prior, n1, n2, confidence = 0.95, ssc = TRUE, plot =
     FALSE) {
```

```
        if (ssc == TRUE) {
             SD.1 <- SD.1 * (1 + 20/n1^2)
             SD.2 <- SD.2 * (1 + 20/n2^2)
        }
        SS.pooled <- SD.1^2 * (n1 - 1) + SD.2^2 * (n1 - 1)
        SE.adj <- (SS.pooled/(n1 + n2 - 2) * (1/n1 + 1/n2))^0.5
        precision.prior <- 1/sigma.prior^2
        precision.lik <- 1/SE.adj^2
        precision.post <- precision.prior + precision.lik
        mean.post <- (precision.prior/precision.post) * diff.prior
             + (precision.lik/precision.post) * M.diff
        sigma.post <- (1/precision.post)^0.5
        lower <- mean.post + qnorm((1 - confidence)/2) *
             sigma.post
        upper <- mean.post - qnorm((1 - confidence)/2) *
             sigma.post
        post.prob.int <- c(lower, upper)
        min.m <- min(M.diff, diff.prior, mean.post)
        max.m <- max(M.diff, diff.prior, mean.post)
        max.s <- max(SE.adj, sigma.prior, sigma.post)
        y.max <- max(dnorm(diff.prior, diff.prior, sigma.prior),
             dnorm(M.diff, M.diff, SE.adj), dnorm(mean.post,
             mean.post, sigma.post))
        if (plot == TRUE) {
        curve(dnorm(x, mean.post, sigma.post), lty = 3, xlim =
             c(min.m - 3.75 * max.s, max.m + 3.75 * max.s), yaxt =
             'n', ylab = NA, xlab = expression(mu))
        curve(dnorm(x, diff.prior, sigma.prior), lwd = 0.3, add =
             TRUE)
        curve(dnorm(x, M.diff, SE.adj), add = TRUE)
        legend(max.m + max.s, y.max, legend = c('Prior',
             'Likelihood', 'Posterior'), lty = c(1, 1, 3), lwd =
             c(0.3, 1, 1))
        }
        output <- list('Posterior mean' = mean.post, 'Posterior
             SD' = sigma.post, 'Probability interval' =
             post.prob.int, Confidence = confidence, lower =
             lower, upper = upper)
        output
}
```

The following example illustrates input for the difference in treatment and control, first with the confidently optimistic and then with the confidently pessimistic prior:

```
Bayes.norm.2s(1.58-2.21, 2.19, 2.98, -4, 0.5, 13, 36,
  ssc=FALSE, plot=FALSE)
```

```
Bayes.norm.2s(1.58-2.21, 2.19, 2.98, 0, 0.5, 13, 36,
  ssc=FALSE, plot=FALSE)
```

11.7.7 Bayesian *t* tests (Example 11.8)

Calculations for a Bayesian *t* test using a unit-information prior are relatively simple (see Gönen *et al.*, 2005). Rouder *et al.* (2009) show how to incorporate a scale factor if the effect sizes in your field of research are larger or smaller than that typical in areas such as psychology (where absolute effects in the range $0 \leq \delta \leq 1$ are common). The scaled unit-information prior Bayes factor in R is implemented with the following function for a one sample or paired *t* test.

```
unit.prior.Bf.1s <- function(t, N, scale.factor = 1) {
    df <- N - 1
    numerator <- (1 + t^2/df)^-((df + 1)/2)
    denom.1 <- (1 + N * scale.factor^2)^-0.5
    denom.2 <- (1 + t^2/(df * (1 + N * scale.factor^2)))^-((df
       + 1)/2)
    Bf <- numerator/(denom.1 * denom.2)
    output <- list('Bayes factor for H0' = Bf, 'Bayes factor
       for H1' = 1/Bf)
    output
}
```

The Bayes factor in favor of both H_0 and H_1 are reported. The default `scale.factor` of one assumes the original Gönen *et al.* formula is used. To call this function for the sleep loss data in Example 11.8 you need observed *t* and sample size:

```
unit.prior.Bf.1s(1.95, 50)
```

For a two sample *t* test the following function implements the Rouder *et al.* (2009) scaled unit-information prior Bayes factor. This function needs separate *n* for each sample to be specified (otherwise it assumes equal *n* and that the sample size per group has been entered):

```
unit.prior.Bf.2s <- function(t, n1, n2 = n1, scale.factor = 1)
  {
    df <- n1 + n2 - 2
    N <- (1/n1 + 1/n2)^-1
    numerator <- (1 + t^2/df)^-((df + 1)/2)
    denom.1 <- (1 + N * scale.factor^2)^-0.5
    denom.2 <- (1 + t^2/(df * (1 + N * scale.factor^2)))^-((df
       + 1)/2)
    Bf <- numerator/(denom.1 * denom.2)
    output <- list('Bayes factor for H0' = Bf, 'Bayes factor
       for H1' = 1/Bf)
    output
}
```

To call this function for the alcohol consumption data enter:

```
unit.prior.Bf.2s(.7, 13, 36)
```

Rouder *et al.* (2009) provide a web calculator for the JZS prior Bayesian *t* test and other functions (and this also provides results for the unit-information prior and a Bayes factor estimated from BIC). Kaye and Baguley (forthcoming) provide code to implement both the one sample and two sample JZS Bayes factor in R. This code is adapted below. As the functions are more mathematically challenging to write, they are structured in a modular format (this makes it easy to check they are working and allows several functions to draw on a similar code). The following functions are called by the 'main' `JZS.prior.Bf.1s()` and `JZS.prior.Bf.2s()` functions and won't be called directly to run the Bayesian *t* test.

```
denOneSample <- function(g, N, t) {
  e <- exp(1)
  nu <- N - 1
  ret <- (1+N*g)^(-1/2)*(1+t^2/((1+N*g)*nu))^(-
        (nu+1)/2)*(2*pi)^(-1/2)*g^(-3/2)*e^(-1/(2*g))
  ret
}

denTwoSample <- function(g, N, t, nu) {
  e <- exp(1)
  ret <- (1+N*g)^(-1/2)*(1+t^2/((1+N*g)*nu))^(-
       (nu+1)/2)*(2*pi)^(-1/2)*g^(-3/2)*e^(-1/(2*g))
  ret
}
numTwoSample <- function(N, t, nu) {
  ret <- (1+(t^2)/nu)^(-(nu+1)/2)
  ret
}
numOneSample <- function(N, t) {
  nu <- N-1
  ret <- (1+(t^2)/nu)^(-(nu+1)/2)
  ret
}

crit <- function(N, t, c) {
  ret <- c+1
  while(ret > c)
  {
      t <- t + 0.01
      ret <- BfOneSample(N, t)
  }
  t
}
```

```
JZS.prior.Bf.1s <- function(t, N){
  a <- integrate(denOneSample,0,Inf,N,t)
  Bf <- numOneSample(N, t)/ a$value
  output <- list('Bayes factor for H0'= Bf, 'Bayes factor for
      H1'= 1/Bf)
  output
}

JZS.prior.Bf.2s <- function(t, n1, n2 = n1) {
  N <- n1 * n2 / (n1 + n2)
  nu = n1 + n2 - 2
  a <- integrate(denTwoSample,0,Inf,N,t, nu)
  Bf <- numTwoSample(N, t, nu)/ a$value
  output <- list('Bayes factor for H0'= Bf, 'Bayes factor for
       H1'= 1/Bf)
  output
}
```

These versions are unscaled and are called using t and sample size (as for the unit-prior functions):

```
JZS.prior.Bf.1s(1.95, 50)
JZS.prior.Bf.2s(.7, 13, 36)
```

11.7.8 Information criteria (Example 11.9)

These examples use the comprehension data and assume that the data frame `bp2000` is in the workspace. The residual sums of squares for the independent t test model can be obtained in several ways. One is to run a linear regression of the percentage matching accuracy with group as the predictor. The residuals are given by:

```
lm(percent_accuracy ~ group,data=bp2000)$residuals
```

This means that the expression

```
sum(lm(percent_accuracy ~ group, data=bp2000)$residuals^2)
```

returns the sum of the squared residuals. AIC for the three-parameter independent t test model can be obtained directly from the residuals using the full likelihood formula (here with $k = 3$):

```
56 * log(sum(lm(percent_accuracy ~ group,
  data=bp2000)$residuals^2)/56) + 2*3 + 56*log(pi*2) + 56
```

With the simplified formula that ignores constant terms (here $k=2$) it is:

```
56*log(sum(lm(percent_accuracy ~ group, data =
  bp2000)$residuals^2)/56)+2*2
```

This gives AIC as either 486.7616 or 325.8405. You'd get the same result for the full likelihood calculation using the built-in `AIC()` R function:

```
AIC(lm(percent_accuracy ~ group, data=bp2000))
```

The simplified formula is used by the `extractAIC()` function when applied to a linear model, but it also calculates the number of parameters differently (ignoring the error variance nuisance parameter). The `extractAIC()` function therefore returns 325.8405. This will not matter as long as matching functions are used for model comparison.

For the null model you could calculate the AIC directly from the regression model with no intercept (and therefore just one free parameter for the grand mean) or from the `AIC()` function and get the same result:

```
56*log(sum(lm(percent_accuracy ~ 1,
  data=bp2000)$residuals^2)/56) + 2*2 + 56*log(pi*2) + 56

AIC(lm(percent_accuracy ~ 1, data=bp2000))
```

This gives the value 491.9437 and so the difference in AIC is 5.1821 in favor of the full model. The same difference is obtained with all methods if applied consistently.

To get BIC just apply the usual AIC functions but replace the default $k=2$ multiplier with $k=\log(N)$. This is easiest to demonstrate if the models being compared are stored in R objects like this:

```
m0 <- lm(percent_accuracy ~ 1, bp2000)
m1 <- lm(percent_accuracy ~ group, bp2000)
```

BIC can now be calculated for either model using either of the earlier functions:

```
AIC(m1,k=log(56))
AIC(m0,k=log(56))
AIC(m1,k=log(56)) - AIC(m0,k=log(56))
```

```
extractAIC(m1,k=log(56))
extractAIC(m0,k=log(56))
extractAIC(m1,k=log(56)) - extractAIC(m0,k=log(56))
```

Additional functions are provided in other packages. An extremely useful one is Bolker's `bbmle` package, which has functions for both `BIC()` and `AICc()`. Compare the above output with the following results:

```
install.packages('bbmle')
library(bbmle)

BIC(m0)
BIC(m1)
BIC(m1)-BIC(m0)
AICc(m1)-AICc(m0)
```

Regardless of method, the BIC functions produce a difference of 3.156745 in favor of the more complex 'two mean' model. AIC_C indicates a slighter stronger preference for the more complex model than BIC.

The `bbmle` package has functions for tabulating information criteria and options for Akaike or Schwartz weights (based on AIC, AIC_C or BIC). The most general of these is `ICtab()` function. For full details use R help (e.g., `?ICtab`) once the package is loaded. The following call produces the table of Schwartz weights used to check the calculations in Example 11.9:

```
ICtab(m0, m1, weights=TRUE, base=TRUE, type='BIC', nobs=56)
```

Change `type` to get AIC or AIC_C Akaike weights. All models must use the same data, but more than two models can be compared by adding other models to the list (e.g., `m0`, `m1`, `m2`, `m3` and so forth). The number of observations `nobs` is required for BIC and AIC_C (but not AIC).

```
ICtab(m0, m1, weights=TRUE, base=TRUE, type='AIC')
ICtab(m0, m1, weights=TRUE, base=TRUE, type='AICc', nobs=56)
```

Note that AIC_C can't be accurately calculated using the abbreviated method (because the number of parameters from the full likelihood equation is required).

11.7.9 R packages

Bolker, B., and R Development Core Team (2011). *bbmle*: Tools for General Maximum Likelihood Estimation. R package version 0.9.7

Robinson, A. (2010). *equivalence*: Provides Tests and Graphics for Assessing Tests of Equivalence. R package version 0.5.6.

11.8 Notes on SPSS syntax for Chapter 11

11.8.1 Equivalence testing using TOST (Example 11.3)

Equivalence testing using the TOST approach can be implemented by obtaining a 90% CI for an equivalence test with $\alpha = .05$. This is done by setting the `/CRITERIA` subcommand of the t test to the desired confidence level:

```
/CRITERIA = CI(.90)
```

11.8.2 Using AIC or BIC to compare models (Example 11.9)

AIC and BIC are not available via menus for linear regression or *t* tests. Syntax for linear regression can be persuaded to provide AIC and BIC (but not AIC_C). For a *t* test, it is necessary to run it as a regression with `group` as a predictor. The crucial step is to edit the `/STATISTICS` subcommand to include the `SELECTION` statement. SPSS will now report AIC and BIC (the latter under the label Schwartz Bayesian criterion).

SPSS data file: `baguley_payne_2000.sav`

```
REGRESSION
 /STATISTICS COEFF OUTS R ANOVA SELECTION
 /DEPENDENT percent_accuracy
 /METHOD=ENTER group.
```

This syntax gives information criteria for the model with three parameters (i.e., for the two means and the variance). The AIC is reported as 325.841 and matches the 325.8405 reported by the R `extractAIC()` function. This indicates that SPSS uses the abbreviated equations for calculating AIC or BIC, and that for linear regression it uses a version of the calculation that ignores the nuisance parameter (and not the total number of parameters).

To get the AIC and BIC for the null model with two parameters (i.e., the variance and the grand mean) an intercept-only regression needs to be run. SPSS won't normally allow this, but can be coerced into it. First create a new variable that takes the constant value one. You can do this manually or perhaps via a compute command such as:

```
COMPUTE constant=group*0+1.
EXECUTE.
```

Now run the regression with no intercept, but with *constant* as the only predictor (and request `SELECTION` statistics):

```
REGRESSION
 /STATISTICS COEFF OUTS R ANOVA SELECTION
 /ORIGIN
 /DEPENDENT percent_accuracy
 /METHOD=ENTER constant.
```

This gives the AIC as 331.023 and BIC as 333.048 – again matching output from the R `extractAIC()` function.

The ability to obtain information criteria from SPSS using syntax is one of the best-kept secrets in SPSS. It makes it possible to compare a wide variety of regression models (including ANOVA and *t* tests) using AIC or BIC.

11.9 Bibliography and further reading

Dienes, Z. (2008) *Understanding Psychology as a Science: An Introduction to Scientific and Statistical Inference*. Basingstoke: Palgrave Macmillan.

Kruschke, J. K. (2010) *Doing Bayesian Data Analysis: A Tutorial with R and BUGS*. London: Academic Press/Elsevier.

Royall, R. M. (1997) *Statistical Evidence: A Likelihood Paradigm*. New York: Chapman and Hall.

11.10 Online supplement 3: Replication probabilities and p_{rep}

For a brief review of the problems of estimating replication probability with particular emphasis on the p_{rep} statistic, go to online supplement 3 at www.palgrave.com/psychology/baguley.

12
Multiple regression and the general linear model

Contents

12.1 Chapter overview

This chapter introduces multiple linear regression from the perspective of a general linear model. The problem of fitting a multiple linear regression model when predictors are not orthogonal is considered and illustrated using matrix algebra. Methods for assessing the fit and for comparing regression models are described, as are methods for testing and teasing apart the contribution of individual predictors.

12.2 The multiple linear regression model

Least squares linear regression models with one predictor variable (X) and one outcome variable (Y) are surprisingly flexible. In the familiar simple linear regression model

$$y_i = b_0 + b_1 x_i + e_i \quad e_i \sim N\left(0, \sigma_E^2\right) \qquad \text{Equation 12.1}$$

Y is predicted as an additive function of X, and the errors have an independent, normal distribution with constant variance. In a standard regression model both Y and X are considered to be continuous variables, but need not be. If X is dichotomous the model is equivalent to independent t, while an intercept-only model is equivalent to one sample t. When X and Y are both standardized, the model is equivalent to the Pearson product-moment correlation r. A simple linear regression model is 'simple' in the sense that it is limited to a single predictor.

Extending the model to incorporate multiple predictors is possible. This extended model, with multiple X and a single Y, is known as *multiple linear regression* or *multiple regression*. Multiple linear regression is, in turn, a special case of an even broader model termed the *general linear model*.

If you are interested in the effects of two predictors (X_1 and X_2) on Y, the equation for the regression model becomes:

$$y_i = b_0 + b_1 x_{1,i} + b_2 x_{2,i} + e_i \quad e_i \sim N\left(0, \sigma_E^2\right) \qquad \text{Equation 12.2}$$

Y is now modeled as an additive function of the intercept, the coefficient (b_1) multiplied by X_1, the coefficient (b_2) multiplied by X_2 and error. Although this is an extremely modest change to the equation it has profound implications. It is no longer necessarily the case – for instance – that the equation describes a straight line. The predicted value of Y will be a straight line plotted against X_1 when X_2 is constant (or vice versa), but not in general.

Multiple regression is not restricted to two predictor variables. The equation can be extended to any number of predictors. A general formulation of multiple regression for q predictors can be written as

$$y_i = b_0 + b_1 x_{1,i} + \ldots + b_q x_{q,i} + e_i, \qquad \text{Equation 12.3}$$

or, more compactly, using summation notation:

$$y_i = b_0 + \sum_{p=1}^{q} (b_p x_p) + e_i \qquad \text{Equation 12.4}$$

Being unrestricted in terms of the number of predictors in the model, multiple linear regression is a very powerful way to model data. The model itself is fitted, checked and interpreted in a broadly similar way to simple linear regression – although the additional predictors complicate both estimation and interpretation. As with simple linear regression, it is possible to standardize the predictors and outcome prior to regression, leading to a model of the form:

$$y_i = \hat{\beta}_1 x_{1,i} + \ldots + \hat{\beta}_q x_{q,i} + e_i \qquad \text{Equation 12.5}$$

However, unlike simple linear regression, standardized 'slopes' (sometimes termed *beta weights* such as $\hat{\beta}_1$ or $\hat{\beta}_q$ do not have a simple interpretation as correlation coefficients (see Box 12.1).

The model is fitted by least squares estimation and hence by minimizing the squared residuals. Checking the model involves considering the plausibility of the independence, homogeneity of variance and normality assumptions fundamental to least squares. Robust alternatives to least squares regression (such as MM-estimation) can also be extended to multiple regression. Interpreting the regression model may involve using the regression equation to predict expected Y values from different predictor values or inference with standard tools such as null hypothesis significance tests (NHSTs) and confidence intervals (CIs). Inference is not restricted to frequentist methods. Some alternative approaches – notably information criteria such as AIC or BIC – are particularly valuable for comparing models with multiple predictors.

Example 12.1 Hancock and Rhodes (2008) reported regression models looking at the effect of exposure to other-race faces on the other-race-effect (ORE). The ORE is the advantage people have in recognizing own-race faces relative to other-race faces. Common difficulties in recognizing other-race faces may lie in lack of contact (and hence experience or skill in recognizing them). The researchers recruited Chinese and Caucasian students with differential exposure to other-race faces and used multiple regression to look at the influence of the race of the participant and contact with other races on the ORE (measured as the difference in percentage accuracy between own- and other-race faces). The observed ORE had $M = 6.9\%$ and $SD = 10.0\%$. Contact was measured as an average score on a six-point scale ($M = 3.5$, $SD = 1.2$). Participant race was dummy-coded (zero for Chinese participants and one for Caucasian participants). The prediction equation reported by Hancock and Rhodes (*ibid.*) was:

$$\hat{Y}_{ORE} = 22.25 - 4.29X_{contact} - 0.65X_{Caucasian}$$

$R^2 = .232$, indicating that the predictors jointly account for just over 20% of the sample variance. This multiple regression equation can be interpreted and applied much like a simple linear regression model. It is possible to relate the unstandardized b coefficients to standardized coefficients $\hat{\beta}$ using the standard deviation of X and Y, by adapting Equation 6.8. The standardized coefficient (beta weight) for contact is therefore:

$$\hat{\beta}_{contact} = b_{contact}\frac{\hat{\sigma}_X}{\hat{\sigma}_Y} = -4.29\frac{1.2}{10} \approx -0.51$$

Plugging in values into the prediction equation and looking at how the outcome changes is one of the very best ways to understand a regression model. For example, the minimum possible value on the contact measure is one and the maximum six. So a Caucasian participant having little previous contact with Chinese people might be expected to have an ORE of $22.25 - 4.29 \times 1 - 0.65 = 17.3\%$, whereas a Caucasian student with the highest contact rating has a predicted ORE of $22.25 - 4.29 \times 6 - 0.65 = -4.1\%$.

The contact predictor is more influential than the race predictor by virtue of the range of values it takes (one to six) and the reasonably substantial coefficient. The regression coefficients have a somewhat different interpretation than in simple linear regression. An unstandardized slope in multiple regression is interpreted as the change in Y associated with a one-unit increase in X assuming all other predictors are held constant (i.e., assuming that they don't change in value). The coefficient for contact of $b = -4.29$ is the expected change in the ORE for every one-point increase in the contact scale. However, this is only true if the person is also of the same race.

A similar interpretation applies to standardized regression coefficients. The beta weight of -0.51 implies that a 1σ increase in the contact scale is associated with a 0.51σ decrease in ORE (assuming that race is unchanged). To see that this prediction might be problematic, just consider what happens if you want to predict the ORE from a person's race (leaving aside that this variable isn't a particularly good predictor). It is probably unreasonable to assume that Chinese and Caucasian students have equal contact with people of other races. Ignoring the other predictor (by imagining its value will not change) could be very misleading.

12.2.1 Fitting a multiple regression model with orthogonal predictors

The fit of a least squares regression model can be described by Equation 5.15:

$$SS_{total} = SS_{model} + SS_{residual}$$

In multiple regression, SS_{model} is the sum of the squared deviations from the mean of Y that is jointly explained by all q predictors. $SS_{residual}$ is the sum of the squared residuals of the model. The challenge of fitting a multiple regression model is to find the combination of coefficients $b_0 \ldots b_q$ that minimize the residual term and therefore maximize the joint contribution of the predictors.

Only in the case of *orthogonal predictors* is this relatively trivial. Orthogonal predictors are uncorrelated: r between two orthogonal predictors is equal to zero.[1] Two uncorrelated variables share $r^2 = 0$ proportion of their variance and therefore account for distinct shares of SS_{total}. This simplifies the required calculations; because each orthogonal predictor accounts for a unique portion of the overall variance it is possible to determine b_1 as if X_2 were not present and b_2 as if X_1 were not present. This reduces the difficulty of maximizing the fit to the equivalent problem in simple linear regression. In this very restricted case, you could run separate simple linear regressions to find the best-fitting coefficients. SS_{model} for the multiple regression is then the sum of the SS_{model} terms from each simple regression. The intercept could then be calculated as:

$$b_0 = \hat{\mu}_Y - \left(b_1 \hat{\mu}_{X_1} + \ldots + b_q \hat{\mu}_{X_q}\right) \qquad \text{Equation 12.6}$$

The formula above exploits the property that a regression line passes through the mean of Y at the mean of X (or in this case a weighted combination of X_1 to X_q).

Once b_0 and the individual slopes[2] are estimated, a value of Y can be predicted for each set of observed predictors. The residuals are equal to $y_i - \hat{y}_i$ and $SS_{residual}$, the unexplained portion of the total SS, is the sum of the squared residuals of the model:

$$SS_{residual} = \sum_{i=1}^{n} e_i = SS_{total} - SS_{model} \qquad \text{Equation 12.7}$$

The fit of a simple or multiple linear regression model can be characterized by the proportion of sample variance accounted for by the predictor:

$$R^2 = \frac{SS_{model}}{SS_{total}}$$

Provided the predictors are orthogonal, R^2 will equal the sum of the squared $X - Y$ correlations for each predictor (or equivalently, the summed R^2 values for separate simple linear regressions of X_1 and X_2 with Y). It is also possible to estimate the population variance accounted for by the q predictors in the model using adjusted R^2 using Equation 6.18:

$$R^2_{adj} = \frac{(1 - R^2)(N - 1)}{N - q - 1}$$

These calculations illustrate the connection between simple and multiple linear regression.

Despite these connections, it can be difficult to appreciate what the multiple regression equation represents. With only one predictor it is fairly easy to visualize the relationship as a line in a two-dimensional (2D) space. If there are q predictors, $q + 1$ dimensions are needed to visualize what is happening. For $q = 2$ predictors a multiple regression involves fitting a 2D plane in three dimensions (3D). A plane is a flat surface that slices through a 3D space. This may still be difficult to visualize, though a 3D scatter plot may help. Figure 12.1 shows the best-fitting regression plane for a hypothetical data set with two predictors. Figure 12.1 suggests that the regression plane (defined by the multiple regression equation $Y = -0.2823 + 2.2446X_1 + 1.2277X_2$) is a reasonable fit to the data. No other plane is as good a fit (as defined by minimizing the squared residuals). These residuals are the vertical distances of each observation (the solid black points) from the plane. Plotting a multiple regression in a 3D scatter plot is possible if there are exactly two predictors. For three predictors you'd need a 4D plot, for four predictors a 5D plot and so forth. As multiple regression frequently involves several predictors, and because most people struggle to visualize even a 3D model, it helps to think of alternative ways to represent what is going on.

Another way to think of a multiple regression is by combining all the predictors into a single 'composite' predictor W. This composite variable W is a linear combination of X_1 to X_q, with the slopes b_1 to b_q acting as weights:

$$w_i = b_1 x_{1,i} + \ldots + b_q x_{q,i} \qquad \text{Equation 12.8}$$

Were you to calculate W as set out in Equation 12.8 and run a simple linear regression of Y on W, it would make identical predictions to the full multiple regression model (and have identical R^2). The correlation between W and Y would be $\sqrt{R^2} = R$. This implies that R is itself a kind of correlation coefficient: the *multiple correlation coefficient*. It expresses the correlation between the predictions of a linear regression model and the outcome (i.e., $R = r_{\hat{Y}Y}$).

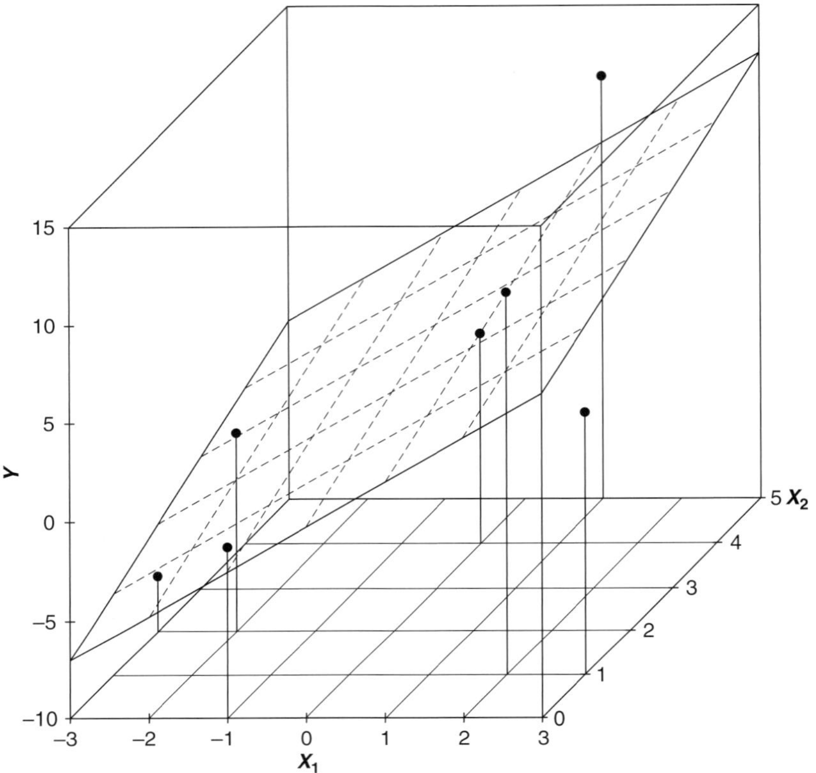

Figure 12.1 The best-fitting regression plane for a data set with two predictors

Composite variables are often used in applications of fitted regression models, because the composite will generate identical predictions, but they are best avoided for inference. There are two reasons for this. One is that inference using the composite treats it as a single predictor. This makes the model seem more parsimonious (less complex) than it really is. Correct inference usually needs to take into account all the predictors that were used to optimize the model. Second, researchers are often interested in understanding the effects of individual predictors or testing hypotheses about them. Using a composite predictor would make this difficult.[3]

Example 12.2 Table 12.1 shows a hypothetical data set with three variables, X_1, X_2 and Y. These data are constructed so that that the correlation between X_1 and X_2 is exactly zero (and hence they are orthogonal).

The multiple regression equation

$$y_i = b_0 + b_1 x_{1,i} + b_2 x_{2,i} + e_i$$

Table 12.1 A small data set with two orthogonal predictors X_1 and X_2 and a continuous outcome Y

Index	X_1	X_2	Y
1	−3	2	−7.15
2	−2	2	0.02
3	−1	0	−1.27
4	0	4	0.68
5	1	5	11.44
6	2	1	9.43
7	3	1	3.29
$\hat{\mu}$	0	2.14	2.35

can therefore be fitted via separate simple linear regressions for each predictor. Fitting the separate regressions with Y produces the prediction equations $\hat{Y} = 2.349 + 2.245\,X_1$ and $\hat{Y} = -0.2823 + 1.2277\,X_2$. Thus $b_1 = 2.245$ and $b_2 = 1.277$. These values can be used to determine the intercept for the multiple regression:

$$b_0 = \hat{\mu}_Y - (b_1\hat{\mu}_{X_1} + b_2\hat{\mu}_{X_2}) \approx 2.35 - (2.245 \times 0 + 1.2277 \times 2.14) \approx -0.28$$

Because the mean of X_1 is zero, the intercept is identical to that of the regression of Y on X_2. The multiple regression equation is therefore:

$$y_i = -0.2823 + 2.245x_{1,i} + 1.2277x_{2,i} + e_i$$

This can be used to predict Y on the basis of known values of the predictors. For instance if $X_1 = 3.5$ and $X_2 = 1$ the expected value of Y is:

$$-0.2823 + 2.245 \times 3.5 + 1.2277 \times 1 \approx 8.80$$

As the predictors are orthogonal, r^2 for the separate correlations or regressions of Y on X_1 and X_2 will sum together to equal R^2 for the multiple regression. The r^2 values are .575 and .116 respectively and so $R^2 = .691$. SS_{model} for the separate regressions are 141.1 and 28.4, making SS_{model} for the multiple regression approximately 169.5.

The equation $Y = -0.2823 + 2.245X_1 + 1.2277X_2$ can be used for prediction in the normal way or by creating a composite predictor. The value of the composite for the first observation is $-3 \times 2.245 + 1.2277 \times 2 \approx -4.28$. To create the composite variable W you'd just repeat this calculation for all seven observed values of Y. A regression of Y on W would predict just as well as a multiple regression of Y on X_1 and X_2. It would account for the same proportion of variance in Y (.691) and have the same SS_{model} and $SS_{residual}$. However, it should not be used for testing the fit of the model (because the model would have only one degree of freedom (*df*) and thus conceal the complexity of the original model with two predictors).

A composite variable used for prediction does not have to use optimized regression weights. An alternative would be to weight the two predictors equally. This kind of 'improper' model can perform surprisingly well (e.g., in this case $R^2 \approx .644$). There are even situations where weighting all predictors equally leads to better prediction than for 'optimized' coefficients (Dawes, 1979; Cohen et al., 2003). This might seem impossible, but happens because the weights are optimized for a particular data set, leading to over-fitting. When optimized weights are used for out-of-sample prediction (i.e., for new data) they tend to perform less well (another application of Occam's razor).

KEY CONCEPT 12.1

Matrix algebra

Matrices simplify many mathematical and statistical calculations, though a bit of effort is required to learn how they work. More detailed introductions can be found in Snedecor and Cochran (1989) and Kirk (1995). Here we will focus on a few key operations that are important for understanding the application of matrix algebra to multiple regression.

A *matrix* is an arrangement of real numbers organized into r rows and c columns. The number of rows and columns is known as the *order* or *dimension* of the matrix. A matrix with only a single row or column is sometimes referred to as a *row vector* or *column vector*. The following matrix has dimension 3×2:

$$\mathbf{A} = \begin{bmatrix} a_{11} & a_{12} \\ a_{21} & a_{22} \\ a_{31} & a_{32} \end{bmatrix} = \begin{bmatrix} 3 & 2 \\ -1 & 0 \\ 5 & -2 \end{bmatrix}$$

Matrices are very often drawn with square brackets and denoted with bold labels (such as the matrix **A** above). It is also typical to use lower-case italics with subscripts to refer to elements of the matrix (e.g., a_{21} is the number in row 2 of column 1 of **A**). Matrix operations are similar, but not necessarily the same as mathematical operations applied to *scalars*. A scalar is an ordinary number such as 4.5 or -7 or a symbol denoting an ordinary number such as μ. Scalars can be distinguished from a matrix or a symbol denoting a matrix such as **X**. Adding and subtracting matrices of the same dimension is similar to scalar addition or subtraction. The corresponding elements are simply added (or subtracted) to produce a new matrix of the same dimension. In the new matrix each element is the sum or difference of the elements of the original matrices:

$$\mathbf{B} + \mathbf{C} = \begin{bmatrix} 1 & -1 \\ 3 & 1 \end{bmatrix} + \begin{bmatrix} 0 & 1 \\ 2 & -1 \end{bmatrix} = \begin{bmatrix} 1 & 0 \\ 5 & 0 \end{bmatrix}$$

Multiplication is not so easy. First you need to appreciate the distinction between *scalar multiplication* and *matrix multiplication*. In scalar multiplication the elements of a matrix are each multiplied by a number to create a new matrix of the same dimension. The scalar multiplication of $3 \times \mathbf{A}$ is:

$$3 \times \mathbf{A} = 3 \begin{bmatrix} 3 & 2 \\ -1 & 0 \\ 5 & -2 \end{bmatrix} = \begin{bmatrix} 9 & 6 \\ -3 & 0 \\ 15 & -6 \end{bmatrix}$$

Matrix multiplication, in contrast, is defined only for an ordered pair of matrices in which the matrix on the left (the *prematrix*) has a number of rows equal to the number of columns of the matrix on the right (the *postmatrix*). Multiplication of matrices with dimensions $r \times m$ and $c \times m$ produces a matrix product of dimension $r \times c$. Because **A** is of dimension 3×2 it can be multiplied with any matrix of dimension $2 \times c$ (or be multiplied by a matrix of dimension $r \times 3$). Matrix multiplication produces an $r \times c$ matrix in which the elements are calculated by multiplying elements in rows of the prematrix with corresponding elements in columns of the postmatrix and taking the sum. For instance, if you multiply **A** by **B**, the first element of the product would be obtained by multiplying elements of the first row of **A** by elements of the first column of **B** and adding the results together:

$$\mathbf{AB} = \begin{bmatrix} 3 & 2 \\ -1 & 0 \\ 5 & -2 \end{bmatrix} \times \begin{bmatrix} 1 & -1 \\ 3 & 1 \end{bmatrix} = \begin{bmatrix} 3 \times 1 + 2 \times 3 & \\ & \\ & \end{bmatrix} = \begin{bmatrix} 9 & \\ & \\ & \end{bmatrix}$$

By repeating this procedure for the subsequent rows of **A** and the remaining column of **B** you get:

$$\mathbf{AB} = \begin{bmatrix} 3 & 2 \\ -1 & 0 \\ 5 & -2 \end{bmatrix} \times \begin{bmatrix} 1 & -1 \\ 3 & 1 \end{bmatrix} = \begin{bmatrix} 3 \times 1 + 2 \times 3 & 3 \times -1 + 2 \times 1 \\ -1 \times 1 + 0 \times 3 & -1 \times -1 + 0 \times 1 \\ 5 \times 1 + -2 \times 3 & 5 \times -1 + -2 \times 1 \end{bmatrix} = \begin{bmatrix} 9 & -1 \\ -1 & 1 \\ -1 & -7 \end{bmatrix}$$

Although matrix multiplication is tedious to do by hand, it is trivial by computer.

The dimension of a matrix is crucial, and some equations require you to switch the number of rows and columns by *transposing* it. The *transpose* of a matrix such as **A** is denoted by **A′** or $\mathbf{A}^t$ and is:

$$\mathbf{A}' = \begin{bmatrix} 3 & 2 \\ -1 & 0 \\ 5 & -2 \end{bmatrix}' = \begin{bmatrix} 3 & -1 & 5 \\ 2 & 0 & -2 \end{bmatrix}$$

Note that here (and in matrix multiplication) the rows are numbered from top to bottom and the columns from left to right. In transposing a matrix, the first row therefore becomes the first column (and vice versa).

A type of matrix that is particularly common in statistics is the *square matrix*. A square matrix is (as you might expect) a matrix where $r = c$ (e.g., like **B** and **C** above). Two very important types of square matrix are a *diagonal* matrix and an *identity matrix*. A diagonal matrix has a main diagonal composed of scalars (that need not be equal) and all other values equal to zero, for example:

$$\begin{bmatrix} 4.4 & 0 \\ 0 & 2.7 \end{bmatrix}$$

An identity matrix is a diagonal matrix in which the main diagonal has elements all equal to one. An identity matrix can be denoted as **I**. An identity matrix with three rows and columns is therefore:

$$\underset{3 \times 3}{\mathbf{I}} = \begin{bmatrix} 1 & 0 & 0 \\ 0 & 1 & 0 \\ 0 & 0 & 1 \end{bmatrix}$$

Sometimes (as above) it is convenient to add the dimension of a matrix as a subscript to its name. The identity matrix has the curious property that, provided matrix multiplication is defined (i.e., the matrices are *conformable*), any matrix multiplied with or by **I** will have a product equal to itself. Hence **AI** = **A**, **BI** = **B** and so forth.

If an identity matrix does not seem very interesting, you may want to consider the problem of dividing a matrix by another matrix. There is no direct analogue of scalar division for matrices, but it is possible to define an operation that has a similar property (for square matrices at least). If you wanted to divide a scalar by six you could multiply it by 1/6 (which is also 6^{-1}). The nearest equivalent matrix operation is to multiply by the *inverse* of a matrix. The inverse of the matrix **M** would be denoted by $\mathbf{M}^{-1}$ and has the property that:

$$\mathbf{MM}^{-1} = \mathbf{M}^{-1}\mathbf{M} = \mathbf{I}$$

The inverse of a matrix can be obtained for a 2×2 matrix as:

$$\mathbf{M}^{-1} = \frac{1}{a_{11}a_{22} - a_{12}a_{21}} \begin{bmatrix} a_{22} & -a_{12} \\ -a_{21} & a_{11} \end{bmatrix} \qquad \text{Equation 12.9}$$

Inverse matrices are very useful for solving equations in mathematics and statistics, though not all matrices have inverses. From the above equation it is easy to see that if the quantity $a_{11}a_{22} - a_{12}a_{21}$ (the *determinant* of a 2×2 matrix) is zero then $\mathbf{M}^{-1}$ can't be calculated. For other square matrices it is still relatively simple to obtain the inverse of a matrix by working out a sequence of transformations that turn a matrix into **I**. The inverse is then obtained by applying these transformations to **I** in reverse order. As this method is time-consuming (particularly for a large matrix) most people will use a computer to find the inverse of a matrix.

12.2.2 Using matrix algebra to fit a regression model

The role of matrix algebra in fitting a regression model is to reduce the difficulty of finding the coefficients that optimize the fit. Solutions can also be obtained using scalar algebra, but are cumbersome even for two predictors, and become increasingly difficult as more predictors are added (see Snedecor and Cochran, 1989). Fitting a multiple regression via matrix algebra has the twin advantages of being relatively easy to explain (provided you understand the basics of matrix algebra – see Key Concept 12.1) and of scaling up gracefully with large data sets or large numbers of predictors.

In multiple regression the same regression equation will be employed to predict every y_i observation. If there were only two data points, y_1 and y_2, and two predictors, X_1 and X_2, the following regression equations would be fitted:

$$y_1 = b_0 + b_1x_{1,1} + b_2x_{2,1} + e_1$$
$$y_2 = b_0 + b_1x_{1,2} + b_2x_{2,2} + e_2$$

The challenge of fitting the model is to find values of b_0 and b_1 common to both equations that minimize the sum of the squared values of e_1 and e_2. Extending this to $q > 2$ and $N > 2$ increases the complexity of the problem. It now involves solving a system of N equations:

$$\begin{aligned} y_1 &= b_0 + b_1x_{1,1} + b_2x_{2,1} + \ldots + b_qx_{q,1} + e_1 \\ y_2 &= b_0 + b_1x_{1,2} + b_2x_{2,2} + \ldots + b_qx_{q,2} + e_2 \\ &\vdots \\ y_N &= b_0 + b_1x_{1,N} + b_2x_{2,N} + \ldots + b_qx_{q,N} + e_N \end{aligned}$$

Matrices simplify this process. To find a solution it is first necessary to structure these equations as a set of four matrices: one for Y, one for the predictors, one for the coefficients and one for the residuals. The equation can then be expressed in terms of the full matrices:

$$\begin{bmatrix} y_1 \\ y_2 \\ \cdot \\ \cdot \\ y_N \end{bmatrix} = \begin{bmatrix} 1 & x_{1,1} & x_{2,1} & \cdot & \cdot & \cdot & x_{q,1} \\ 1 & x_{1,2} & x_{2,2} & \cdot & \cdot & \cdot & x_{q,2} \\ \cdot & \cdot & \cdot & \cdot & \cdot & \cdot & \cdot \\ \cdot & \cdot & \cdot & \cdot & \cdot & \cdot & \cdot \\ 1 & x_{1,N} & x_{2,N} & \cdot & \cdot & \cdot & x_{q,N} \end{bmatrix} \begin{bmatrix} b_0 \\ b_1 \\ \cdot \\ \cdot \\ b_q \end{bmatrix} + \begin{bmatrix} e_1 \\ e_2 \\ \cdot \\ \cdot \\ e_N \end{bmatrix} \qquad \text{Equation 12.10}$$

In this way, any multiple regression (regardless of q and N) can be expressed as an equation for predicting a matrix of responses (**y**) as the product of a predictor matrix (**X**) and a matrix of coefficients (**b**) plus a matrix of residuals (**e**). Lower case is sometimes used to indicate that **y**, **b** and **e** are one-dimensional matrices (i.e., column vectors). Thus a multiple linear regression can be expressed much more compactly via matrix notation as:

$$\mathbf{y} = \mathbf{Xb} + \mathbf{e} \qquad \text{Equation 12.11}$$

An important feature is that, because of the way matrix multiplication works, **X** is always the prematrix and **b** the postmatrix (otherwise the matrices may not be conformable). Also note that by the rules of matrix multiplication the intercept b_0 is premultiplied by a column containing the constant value of one.[4]

None of this explains how the solution is obtained. As the goal is to estimate the regression coefficients (the unknown elements of **b**) it is necessary to express $\hat{\mathbf{b}}$ as a function of matrices with known values. The solution must minimize the squares of the residuals (i.e., the difference between observed and predicted Y). The sum of squares for the predictors is found on the main diagonal of the matrix $\mathbf{X'X}$, while the cross products are in the off-diagonal elements. The former are used to calculate variances and the latter to calculate covariances. Multiplication by its transpose is the matrix equivalent of squaring **X**. The transpose has to be employed because, under the rules of matrix multiplication, **X** cannot, as a rule, be multiplied by itself. It has dimension $N \times (q+1)$ and is only rarely a square matrix. The solution to the equation lies in the fact that $\mathbf{X}\hat{\mathbf{b}}$ is used to predict **y** and prediction error should be minimized when:

$$\mathbf{X'X}\hat{\mathbf{b}} = \mathbf{X'y} \qquad \text{Equation 12.12}$$

In scalar algebra the equation would be solved by dividing both sides by $\mathbf{X'X}$. The matrix algebra equivalent is to premultiply both sides by the inverse of $\mathbf{X'X}$:

$$(\mathbf{X'X})^{-1}\mathbf{X'X}\hat{\mathbf{b}} = (\mathbf{X'X})^{-1}\mathbf{X'y} \qquad \text{Equation 12.13}$$

As any matrix multiplied by its inverse (including $(\mathbf{X'X})^{-1}\mathbf{X'X}$) is the identity matrix, this reduces to:

$$\hat{\mathbf{b}} = (\mathbf{X'X})^{-1}\mathbf{X'y} \qquad \text{Equation 12.14}$$

Using matrix algebra to find the matrix of best-fitting regression coefficients therefore involves some basic matrix multiplication (that could, in principle, be done by hand) and finding the inverse of $\mathbf{X'X}$ (which probably requires a computer).[5] It also follows that if the inverse cannot be obtained, the multiple regression model can't be fitted. This will happen if any X can be perfectly predicted from some combination of the others (termed *perfect collinearity*). Under these circumstances the determinant of the matrix will be zero.

Having found $\hat{\mathbf{b}}$, the residuals are given by the matrix:

$$\hat{\mathbf{e}} = \mathbf{y} - \mathbf{X}\hat{\mathbf{b}}$$ Equation 12.15

What about the variance and covariance estimates associated with $\hat{\mathbf{b}}$? These are contained in the *asymptotic variance-covariance matrix* (see Key Concept 12.2):

$$\hat{\mathbf{V}} = (\mathbf{X}'\mathbf{X})^{-1}\,\hat{\sigma}_E^2$$ Equation 12.16

As $\mathbf{X}'\mathbf{X}$ contains the sums of squares and cross products, multiplying through by $\hat{\sigma}_E^2$ gives a matrix with estimates of the variances of all the parameters on the main diagonal and the covariances between parameters on the off-diagonals. Taking the square root of each variance gives the standard errors of each parameter estimate (because the distribution of a statistic such as a slope or intercept is its sampling distribution).

KEY CONCEPT 12.2

Variance-covariance matrices

A variance-covariance matrix is a square $(q+1) \times (q+1)$ matrix containing variances on the main diagonal and covariances on the off-diagonal. It may also be referred to as a *covariance matrix* (and this is reasonable given that a variance is simply the covariance of a variable with itself). Covariance matrices are encountered in many different contexts, but three types are particularly relevant here. These are the *asymptotic covariance matrix*, the *sample covariance matrix* and the *correlation matrix*.

The asymptotic covariance matrix $\mathbf{V}$ is a matrix of the variances and covariances of the regression coefficients (parameter estimates) in a regression model. Strictly, the matrix contains asymptotic estimates of the sampling variances and covariances and so the matrix $\mathbf{V}$ and the elements it contains should be indicated as such (e.g., as $\hat{\mathbf{V}}$). The general form of the matrix is:

$$\hat{\mathbf{V}} = \begin{bmatrix} \hat{\sigma}_{b_0}^2 & \hat{\sigma}_{b_0,b_1} & \hat{\sigma}_{b_0,b_2} & \cdots & \hat{\sigma}_{b_0,b_q} \\ \hat{\sigma}_{b_1,b_0} & \hat{\sigma}_{b_1}^2 & \hat{\sigma}_{b_1,b_2} & \cdots & \hat{\sigma}_{b_1,b_q} \\ \hat{\sigma}_{b_2,b_0} & \hat{\sigma}_{b_2,b_1} & \hat{\sigma}_{b_2}^2 & \cdots & \hat{\sigma}_{b_2,b_q} \\ \cdots & \cdots & \cdots & \cdots & \cdots \\ \hat{\sigma}_{b_q,b_0} & \hat{\sigma}_{b_q,b_1} & \hat{\sigma}_{b_q,b_1} & \cdots & \hat{\sigma}_{b_q}^2 \end{bmatrix}$$

The main diagonals contain the variance of each of the $q+1$ parameter estimates, starting with the intercept $\hat{\sigma}_{b_0}^2$ and proceeding with the slopes $\hat{\sigma}_{b_1}^2$ to $\hat{\sigma}_{b_q}^2$. The square roots of these values are the standard errors of the regression coefficients. Like all covariance matrices, the off-diagonal cells are mirrored above and below the main diagonal. This happens because the covariance between b_1 and b_2 is by definition the same as that between b_2 and b_1 (as the covariance represents their shared variation). Some software (e.g., SPSS) reports an asymptotic covariance matrix without the intercept. In this format the covariances (off-diagonal elements) are all zero if the design is orthogonal (see Example 12.3).

A sample variance-covariance matrix is a matrix of the variances and covariances of two or more variables. It is usually denoted as $\mathbf{S}$ or Σ, often with a 'hat' symbol indicating that they are estimates of a population covariance matrix (e.g., $\hat{\Sigma}$). For a set of variables A_1 to A_k, the covariance matrix would take the form:

$$\hat{\Sigma} = \begin{bmatrix} \hat{\sigma}_1^2 & \hat{\sigma}_{1,2} & \hat{\sigma}_{1,3} & \cdots & \hat{\sigma}_{1,k} \\ \hat{\sigma}_{2,1} & \hat{\sigma}_2^2 & \hat{\sigma}_{2,3} & \cdots & \hat{\sigma}_{2,k} \\ \hat{\sigma}_{3,1} & \hat{\sigma}_{3,2} & \hat{\sigma}_3^2 & \cdots & \hat{\sigma}_{3,k} \\ \cdots & \cdots & \cdots & \cdots & \cdots \\ \hat{\sigma}_{k,1} & \hat{\sigma}_{k,2} & \hat{\sigma}_{k,3} & \cdots & \hat{\sigma}_k^2 \end{bmatrix}$$

This form of covariance matrix is closely related to the correlation matrix of the variables (**R** or $\hat{\mathbf{R}}$). The Pearson correlation coefficient r is a standardized covariance (created by scaling $\hat{\sigma}_{X,Y}$ by $\hat{\sigma}_X\hat{\sigma}_Y$). Dividing through each element by the product of the *SD* of the variables in the corresponding row and columns (e.g., dividing $\hat{\sigma}_{1,2}$ by $\hat{\sigma}_1\hat{\sigma}_2$) produces a correlation matrix. This takes the value one for the main diagonal elements. Correlation coefficients taking values between −1 and 1 make up the off-diagonals. Because covariances are mirrored above and below the main diagonal it is common to report just the lower or upper half of the correlation matrix (and the main diagonal may also be dropped):

$$\hat{\mathbf{R}} = \begin{bmatrix} 1 & & & & \\ r_{2,1} & 1 & & & \\ r_{3,1} & r_{3,2} & 1 & & \\ \ldots & \ldots & \ldots & 1 & \\ r_{k,1} & r_{k,2} & r_{k,3} & \ldots & 1 \end{bmatrix}$$

Only rarely do people think of a correlation matrix as a covariance matrix, but this is exactly what it is: a matrix of the covariances between a set of standardized variables.

Example 12.3 This example reproduces the output from Example 12.2 using matrix algebra. The matrix form of the regression equation (using the data in Table 12.1) is:

$$\begin{bmatrix} -7.15 \\ .02 \\ -1.27 \\ 0.68 \\ 11.44 \\ 9.43 \\ 3.29 \end{bmatrix} = \begin{bmatrix} 1 & -3 & 2 \\ 1 & -2 & 2 \\ 1 & -1 & 0 \\ 1 & 0 & 4 \\ 1 & 1 & 5 \\ 1 & 2 & 1 \\ 1 & 3 & 1 \end{bmatrix} \begin{bmatrix} b_0 \\ b_1 \\ b_2 \end{bmatrix} + \begin{bmatrix} e_1 \\ e_2 \\ e_3 \\ e_4 \\ e_5 \\ e_6 \\ e_7 \end{bmatrix}$$

To get the matrix of coefficients $\hat{\mathbf{b}}$ involves working out $(\mathbf{X}'\mathbf{X})^{-1}\mathbf{X}'\mathbf{y}$. The transpose of matrix **X** is:

$$\mathbf{X}' = \begin{bmatrix} 1 & 1 & 1 & 1 & 1 & 1 & 1 \\ -3 & -2 & -1 & 0 & 1 & 2 & 3 \\ 2 & 2 & 0 & 4 & 5 & 1 & 1 \end{bmatrix}$$

Using this to premultiply **X** gives:

$$\mathbf{X}'\mathbf{X} = \begin{bmatrix} 1 & 1 & 1 & 1 & 1 & 1 & 1 \\ -3 & -2 & -1 & 0 & 1 & 2 & 3 \\ 2 & 2 & 0 & 4 & 5 & 1 & 1 \end{bmatrix} \begin{bmatrix} 1 & -3 & 2 \\ 1 & -2 & 2 \\ 1 & -1 & 0 \\ 1 & 0 & 4 \\ 1 & 1 & 5 \\ 1 & 2 & 1 \\ 1 & 3 & 1 \end{bmatrix} = \begin{bmatrix} 7 & 0 & 15 \\ 0 & 28 & 0 \\ 15 & 0 & 51 \end{bmatrix}$$

It is also necessary to premultiply **y** by **X′** and this gives:

$$\mathbf{X'y} = \begin{bmatrix} 1 & 1 & 1 & 1 & 1 & 1 & 1 \\ -3 & -2 & -1 & 0 & 1 & 2 & 3 \\ 2 & 2 & 0 & 4 & 5 & 1 & 1 \end{bmatrix} \begin{bmatrix} -7.15 \\ .02 \\ -1.27 \\ 0.68 \\ 11.44 \\ 9.43 \\ 3.29 \end{bmatrix} = \begin{bmatrix} 16.44 \\ 62.85 \\ 58.38 \end{bmatrix}$$

The inverse of **X′X** can be obtained by hand, but for a data set with large numbers of predictors or observations a computer data solution is more practical. Using R, the inverse of **X′X** is:

$$(\mathbf{X'X})^{-1} = \begin{bmatrix} 7 & 0 & 15 \\ 0 & 28 & 0 \\ 15 & 0 & 51 \end{bmatrix}^{-1} = \begin{bmatrix} 0.3863636 & 0 & -0.1136364 \\ 0 & 0.03571429 & 0 \\ -0.1136364 & 0 & 0.0530303 \end{bmatrix}$$

Putting these results into the equation $\hat{\mathbf{b}} = (\mathbf{X'X})^{-1}\mathbf{X'y}$ produces:

$$\hat{\mathbf{b}} = \begin{bmatrix} 0.3863636 & 0 & -0.1136364 \\ 0 & 0.03571429 & 0 \\ -0.1136364 & 0 & 0.0530303 \end{bmatrix} \begin{bmatrix} 16.44 \\ 62.85 \\ 58.38 \end{bmatrix} = \begin{bmatrix} -0.2822727 \\ 2.2446429 \\ 1.2277273 \end{bmatrix}$$

Gratifyingly, these coefficients are identical to the ones from Example 12.2.

Rearranging the equation $\mathbf{y} = \mathbf{X}\hat{\mathbf{b}} + \hat{\mathbf{e}}$ allows us to obtain the residuals:

$$\hat{\mathbf{e}} = \mathbf{y} - \mathbf{X}\hat{\mathbf{b}} = \begin{bmatrix} -7.15 \\ .02 \\ -1.27 \\ 0.68 \\ 11.44 \\ 9.43 \\ 3.29 \end{bmatrix} - \begin{bmatrix} 1 & -3 & 2 \\ 1 & -2 & 2 \\ 1 & -1 & 0 \\ 1 & 0 & 4 \\ 1 & 1 & 5 \\ 1 & 2 & 1 \\ 1 & 3 & 1 \end{bmatrix} \begin{bmatrix} -0.2822727 \\ 2.2446429 \\ 1.2277273 \end{bmatrix}$$

$$= \begin{bmatrix} -7.15 \\ .02 \\ -1.27 \\ 0.68 \\ 11.44 \\ 9.43 \\ 3.29 \end{bmatrix} - \begin{bmatrix} -4.560747 \\ -2.316104 \\ -2.526916 \\ 4.628636 \\ 8.101006 \\ 5.434740 \\ 7.679383 \end{bmatrix} = \begin{bmatrix} -2.589253 \\ 2.336104 \\ 1.256916 \\ -3.948636 \\ 3.338994 \\ 3.995260 \\ -4.389383 \end{bmatrix}$$

Squaring the elements of matrix $\hat{\mathbf{e}}$ and taking the total gives the error sums of squares. Thus $SS_{residual} = 75.71$ and $df_{error} = 7 - q - 1 = 4$. MS_{error} (the estimate of σ_E^2) is 18.92 and the covariance matrix is:

$$\hat{\mathbf{V}} = (\mathbf{X}'\mathbf{X})^{-1}\,\hat{\sigma}_E^2 = \begin{bmatrix} 0.3863636 & 0 & -0.1136364 \\ 0 & 0.03571429 & 0 \\ -0.1136364 & 0 & 0.0530303 \end{bmatrix} \times 18.92$$

$$\approx \begin{bmatrix} 7.313 & 0 & -2.151 \\ 0 & 0.676 & 0 \\ -2.151 & 0 & 1.004 \end{bmatrix}$$

Because X_1 and X_2 are orthogonal, their covariance is exactly zero. The square roots of the variances on the main diagonal provide the standard errors for the intercept and for the slopes of X_1 and X_2. Again these values match the values obtained earlier. The matrix algebra solution would also cope with non-orthogonal predictors.

12.2.3 Testing the fit of a multiple regression model

Sums of squares are descriptive statistics, not inferential statistics: they describe the variance accounted for by a source of variation in the model. Going from sums of squares to an inferential statistic requires dividing the *SS* by its *df*. Doing so for SS_{total} reproduces the standard inferential formula for the variance, but the interest here is in assessing either the fit of the model as a whole or the contribution of individual predictors. For this reason it is necessary to estimate the population variance separately for each source of variance in the model. This requires variance estimates rather than sums of squares. These variance estimates are termed *mean squares* and obtained by dividing *SS* for model and error by their respective *df*. The variance estimate for the model is therefore:

$$MS_{model} = \hat{\sigma}^2_{model} = \frac{SS_{model}}{df_{model}} = \frac{SS_{model}}{q} \qquad \text{Equation 12.17}$$

The corresponding error variance estimate is:

$$MS_{error} = \hat{\sigma}^2_E = \frac{SS_{residual}}{df_{error}} = \frac{SS_{residual}}{N - q - 1} \qquad \text{Equation 12.18}$$

The simple linear regression test statistic is a ratio of the variance estimates for model and variance error. On the assumption of independent, normal errors with constant variance, the sums of squares will have a χ^2 distribution scaled by the population variance. The mean squares are estimates of the population variances for the model and error and thus their ratio has an F distribution (if the distributional assumptions are met). This leads to a test statistic of the form:

$$\frac{SS_{model}/\nu_1}{SS_{residual}/\nu_2} = \frac{MS_{model}}{MS_{residual}} \sim F(\nu_1, \nu_2) \qquad \text{Equation 12.19}$$

This F ratio has df equal to ν_1 and ν_2, where $\nu_1 = q$ for the model (in the numerator) and $\nu_2 = N - q - 1$ for the error term (in the denominator). It is also possible to calculate the test statistic directly from R^2:

$$F_{q,N-k-1} = \frac{(N - q - 1)R^2}{q(1 - R^2)} \qquad \text{Equation 12.20}$$

In simple linear regression $q = 1$, and the F ratio reduces to the square of the t statistic for the slope. The F ratio is therefore a more general test of variances than t (being able to cope with multiple predictors).

In principle there is no upper limit to the number of predictors in the model, provided the sample size is sufficiently large. The sample size N limits the maximum possible number of predictors. To calculate MS_{error}, ν_2 must be at least one and therefore $N - q - 1$ must be greater than zero. This can only happen if q is no larger than $N - 2$. The two remaining df are required to estimate the intercept and the error term. In practice, you will want to keep N much larger than q. Precision of measurement and statistical power depends on keeping MS_{error} small. Equation 12.18 shows that decreasing df_{error} necessarily increases the estimate of the population error variance. As $df_{error} = N - q - 1$, fewer predictors and more observations lead to increased statistical power.

It is customary to set out these calculations in a systematic format known as an *analysis of variance* (*ANOVA*) table.[6] These tables were at first used to organize hand calculations, but are now used as a summary of the regression model. Table 12.2a shows a standard layout for the ANOVA table for a multiple regression.

Several features – common to any ANOVA table – are worth pointing out. The columns on the left include interim results of calculations that feed into the columns on the right. The error term is included below the source of variance that it is an error term for (because it is used to obtain the denominator or lower half of the F ratio). The table also has some redundancy built in. This can help simplify the calculations (because the final df or SS can be obtained by subtraction from the total df or SS) or be used to check the results of hand calculations. Table 12.2b shows the same format including formulas. Filling out the table requires N, q and at least some of SS_{model}, $SS_{residual}$ and SS_{total}.

How does the F statistic work as a test for the fit of the model? Two population variances (σ^2_{model} and σ^2_E) are being estimated. These are the variance in the population accounted for by the predictors in the model and the variance in the population accounted for by the errors (of which the model residuals are assumed to be a random sample). Error variance could be caused by all sorts of things and, depending on how the observations were sampled, might include individual differences between participants, transient error accumulating over time, or

Table 12.2a Analysis of variance (ANOVA) table format for a multiple linear regression model

Source	*df*	*SS*	*MS*	*F*
Model	df_{model}	SS_{model}	MS_{model}	F_{model}
Error	df_{error}	$SS_{residual}$	MS_{error}	
Total	df_{total}	SS_{total}		

Table 12.2b Formulas for computing a multiple regression ANOVA table

Source	***df***	***SS***	***MS***	***F***
Model	q	SS_{model}	$\frac{SS_{regression}}{df_{model}}$	$\frac{MS_{model}}{MS_{error}}$
Error	$N-q-1$	$SS_{residual}$	$\frac{SS_{residual}}{df_{error}}$	
Total	$N-1$	SS_{total}		

measurement error. A fundamental insight is that measurement error influences every outcome that you sample and hence will 'contaminate' all the variance estimates (not just error). This implies that both σ^2_{model} and σ^2_E contribute to MS_{model}. The estimate of the variance accounted for by the predictors will also include some error variance. Conceptually, the F statistic from a regression is therefore an estimate of the ratio:

$$\frac{\sigma^2_{model}+\sigma^2_E}{\sigma^2_E}$$

This makes F appropriate for testing of the null hypothesis H_0: $\sigma^2_{model}=0$. If σ^2_{model} is zero, then the expected value of the F ratio is:

$$E(F|H_0)=\frac{0+\sigma^2_{error}}{\sigma^2_{error}}=\frac{\sigma^2_{error}}{\sigma^2_{error}}=1$$

Because a variance cannot be negative, the true value of σ^2_{model} must be zero or greater. The alternative hypothesis can therefore be expressed as H_1: $\sigma^2_{model}>0$, in which case $E(F|H_1)>1$. If the predictors do influence Y in the population, the expected F ratio is greater than one. An F distribution with df equal to q and $N-q-1$ can be consulted to determine the significance probability p for this null hypothesis. The p value for the test is the probability of obtaining an F test statistic as extreme or more extreme than that observed in the data if H_0 is true.

A major difference between using t and F is that extreme values of the test statistic, corresponding to large positive or negative values of z or t, are found only in the right tail of the F distribution. As with the χ^2 statistic, effects that lead to large absolute values of t or z, produce large F or χ^2 values (because the distributions behave as t^2 or z^2 and are constrained to be positive). This means that the right tail probability of an F distribution is equivalent to a non-directional, two-sided p value for a t distribution. As a rule, only such non-directional tests are of interest for a regression model (and where a directional test is meaningful, such as for tests of individual predictors, t is preferred). The F ratio for the regression model can, in addition, be considered a test of the null hypothesis that R or $R^2=0$. This follows because H_0: $\sigma^2_{model}=0$ implies that the variance accounted for by the predictors in the population is zero. When $R^2=0$ the expected value of F is:

$$E\left(F\middle|R^2=0\right)=\frac{(N-q-1)R^2}{q(1-R^2)}=\frac{(N-q-1)\times 0}{q\times 1}=\frac{0}{1}=0$$

The same information could also be used to obtain other inferential statistics such as information criteria. To calculate AIC for a regression model requires $SS_{residual}$ and the number of parameters, while AIC_C and BIC also require N.

Example 12.4 In Example 12.2 a multiple regression equation was estimated (albeit in a round-about way) for an artificial data set with two orthogonal predictors. Table 12.3a shows the ANOVA table for that multiple regression with SS_{model} added. A good way to understand how ANOVA tables work is to complete the regression table with the information at hand.

Table 12.3a An incomplete ANOVA table for the multiple linear regression of data from Table 12.1

Source	***df***	***SS***	***MS***	***F***
Model	q	169.5	$\frac{SS_{model}}{df_{model}}$	$\frac{MS_{model}}{MS_{error}}$
Error	$N-q-1$	$SS_{residual}$	$\frac{SS_{residual}}{df_{error}}$	
Total	$N-1$	SS_{total}		

As there are seven observations and two parameters being estimated, $N=7$ and $q=2$. $df=2$ for the model and $df=4$ for error (and the total df are $2+4=6$). Filling in the sums of squares column requires a bit more calculation. $SS_{residual}$ is the sum of the squared residuals, while the residuals can be obtained by subtracting predicted Y from observed Y. Another route is via SS_{total}. This is calculated from the deviations of observed Y relative to the mean of Y. $\hat{\mu}_Y = 2.35$. Subtracting this from each Y value, squaring and summing the squares gives $SS_{total} \approx 245.2$. $SS_{residual}$ is therefore $245.2 - 169.5 = 75.7$.

The mean squares are sums of squares divided by their df so $MS_{model} = 169.5/2 \approx 84.8$ and $MS_{error} = 75.7/4 \approx 18.9$. These are the estimates of the population variance attributable to the predictors and to error. Their ratio is $F = 84.8/18.9 \approx 4.5$. Table 12.3b can now be completed.

Table 12.3b A completed ANOVA table for the multiple regression of data in Table 12.1

Source	***df***	***SS***	***MS***	***F***
Model	2	169.5	84.8	4.5
Error	4	75.7	18.9	
Total	6	245.2		

From an ANOVA table you can find the basic ingredients for many common statistics. R^2 is the proportion of sample SS accounted for by the regression model and is equal to $169.5/245.2 \approx .69$. As the NHST based on the F ratio is a test of H_0: $R^2 = 0$, a common format for summarizing the model fit, is to report the significance test and the proportion of sample variance explained together:

$$R^2 = .69, F_{2,4} = 4.5, MS_{error} = 18.9, p = .095$$

Although the predictors account for a fair proportion of the sample variance, their joint contribution is not statistically significant (though this is hardly surprising in such a tiny sample).

AIC for the model can be calculated from the $SS_{residual}$, q and N. Using the simplified likelihood formula (matching the `extractAIC()` function in R) you would need the number of parameters being estimated (excluding the error variance nuisance parameter). This is $q+1$ (one parameter for each predictor plus another for the intercept). AIC is therefore:

$$N \ln\left(\frac{SS_{residual}}{N}\right) + 2(q+1) = 7 \times \ln\left(\frac{75.7}{7}\right) + 2 \times 3 \approx 22.67$$

BIC using the same method would be 22.50.

The full likelihood values would be 44.53 for AIC and 44.32 for BIC. To calculate AIC_C it is essential to set k equal to the total number of parameters (not just the parameters being estimated). This number is $q+2$ for a regression and thus $k = 4$ for this model. The correction factor for AIC_C is $\frac{2k(k+1)}{N-k-1}$. Adding $\frac{2\times4(4+1)}{N-4-1} = \frac{40}{2} = 20$ to the AIC calculated from full likelihood method gives an $AIC_C = 64.53$.

12.3 The impact of individual predictors on the model

12.3.1 Partial and semi-partial correlation

When predictors in a multiple regression or general linear model are orthogonal, this simplifies both the calculation of regression coefficients and their interpretation.[7] When predictors are correlated, the calculations are more challenging. This is part of a broader problem. If you have many inter-correlated variables, how can you tell what is going on? At the heart of this problem is the concept of *partial correlation*.

Partial correlation is a tool for investigating patterns of correlations among a set of three or more predictors. If there are three variables, A, B and C, there are three simple correlations between the possible pairs: ρ_{AB}, ρ_{AC} and ρ_{BC}. A partial correlation is the correlation between two variables considering only individuals who have identical values on a third variable. The partial correlation $\rho_{AB.C}$ is therefore the correlation ρ_{AB} when the third variable is constant. If the correlations are orthogonal then $\rho_{AB} = \rho_{AB.C}$, but (with the exception of experiments designed to have this property) this is unlikely to be true for real data. If a linear model with normal errors is assumed (Hays, 1973) a partial correlation coefficient takes the form:

$$r_{AB.C} = \frac{r_{AB} - r_{AC}r_{BC}}{\sqrt{\left(1 - r_{AC}^2\right)\left(1 - r_{BC}^2\right)}} \qquad \text{Equation 12.21}$$

A crucial feature of this equation is that the partial correlation for A and B depends on the residual variance left over from the correlations of A with C and B with C. Think about why this has to be the case. If C is positively correlated with A, then it accounts for some of the total variation in A. When C is also positively correlated with B then some of the correlation with A will reflect the indirect contribution of C. The partial correlation formula strips out the influence of C on both A and B to estimate the correlation $\rho_{AB.C}$. This is a proportion of the simple correlation not accounted for by the shared variation with C. Hence when $r_{AC} = r_{BC} = 0$, the formula reduces to r_{AB}. If necessary, the same basic formula can be extended to deal with more than three variables (e.g., estimating the partial correlation $r_{AB.CD}$ between A and B when C and D are both constant).

Partial correlation is interesting in its own right. It might be employed when a researcher is interested in the correlation between two variables (e.g., weight and physical fitness) in the presence of a third, confounding variable (e.g., height). For the moment, though, the key idea is that it is possible to strip out the influence of one or more variables from the relationship of two other variables. This is necessary, in a regression model with correlated predictors, to assess the contribution of individual predictors in the model.

Whereas correlation makes no formal distinction between predictor and outcome variable, regression does. As the purpose of regression is to predict Y, there is no need to partial out the effects of Y. What is required is a way to partial out the effects of all of the other predictors apart from one (X_i), to give an estimate of its unique contribution to predicting Y. This is exactly what a regression coefficient does. Because only other predictors are stripped out, b_i is a semi-partial regression coefficient. The regression coefficient b_1 is the effect of X_1 on Y ignoring the effects of any other predictors (i.e., holding their effects on Y constant).

It is also possible to obtain semi-partial correlation coefficients. Notation varies, but the semi-partial correlation of X_1 and Y, partialing out X_2, can be written as $r_{Y1\cdot2}$ or as $r_{Y(X_1\cdot X_2)}$. Remembering the equivalence between the standardized regression coefficient $\hat{\beta}$ in a simple linear regression and the simple Pearson correlation coefficient r, it is tempting to assume that standardized regression coefficients (betas or beta weights) are semi-partial correlation coefficients. This is not true (unless all predictors are orthogonal). The correct interpretation of a beta weight requires more careful consideration (see Box 12.1).

Semi-partial correlations have the useful property that they decompose the total variance of Y into contributions from different predictors or combinations of predictors. Figure 12.2 depicts the contribution of two predictors (X_1 and X_2) to Y in the form of a Venn diagram. This kind of diagram is figurative: it illustrates the decomposition rather than representing it faithfully. The term 'contribution' is used rather than proportion of total variance here, because the areas b, c, d and e represent arithmetic contributions to the total variance without necessarily representing proportions of variance in a strict sense (e.g., the shared contribution c can be negative).[8]

In each panel, the total variance of the predictors and outcomes is shown by circles labeled X_1, X_2 and Y. Assume that the total area of each circle is equal to one. Panel (a) on the left of Figure 12.2 labels regions of interest as a, b, c, d and e. The proportion of the total variance of Y jointly explained by the predictors is the sum of the areas b, c and d. Therefore $R^2 = b + c + d$. It follows that a, the remaining area, is equal to $1 - R^2$ (i.e., the proportion of variance not explained by X_1 and X_2). The area b corresponds to the variance explained by the semi-partial correlation $r_{Y1\cdot2}$ (the correlation of Y and X_1 holding values of X_2 constant). Likewise, area d is the proportion of Y explained by the semi-partial correlation $r_{Y2\cdot1}$. Just as r^2 is the proportion of the variance of Y explained by a simple correlation, squaring a semi-partial correlation gives its contribution to the total explained variance in Y. The squared semi-partial correlations are shown in panel (b).

Figure 12.2 reveals a number of interesting points. First, if you add up the r^2 values for the simple correlation between each predictor and Y you will often overestimate their joint contribution. This is because the squared simple correlations are represented by overlap between X_1 and Y (area $b+c$) and X_2 and Y (area $c+d$). This would end up counting the 'shared' contribution in area c twice. If the simple correlations are high they might also sum to more than one (i.e., 'explain' more than 100% of the variance of Y). The squared semi-partial correlation does not have this problem. If these are summed, the total will always be less than or equal to the joint contribution of X_1 and X_2. This is one of the major difficulties people have in understanding multiple regression with correlated (non-orthogonal) predictors. Many people assume that the total

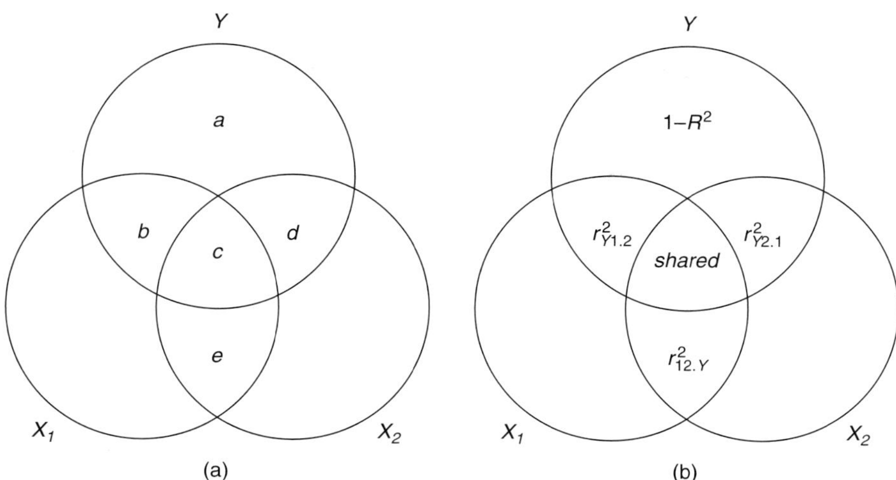

Figure 12.2 Venn diagrams depicting shared and non-shared contribution R^2 in multiple regression

individual contribution of the predictors is equal to R^2. Far from it: total R^2 also includes any shared contribution between predictors (ignored in their individual contributions). Researchers will also want to attribute variance accounted for in Y unambiguously to a particular predictor. This isn't really possible. There is no certain method of attributing the shared portion of R^2 to any one predictor (though it is sometimes possible to make an educated guess).[9]

A final point to take away from this discussion is that the semi-partial correlation between a predictor and Y can be very different from the simple correlation between X and Y. The simple correlation between X and Y could be very high and yet still be entirely explained by one or more other predictors. If so, the semi-partial correlation would be zero. In extreme cases, the simple and semi-partial correlations can have different signs.

Example 12.5 Example 7.5 looked at data on predictors of teacher intervention in relation to indirect bullying (Dedousis-Wallace and Shute, 2009). The correlation between perceived seriousness of indirect bullying and the likelihood of intervening was $r_{SI} = .74$. The correlation of empathy scores with perceived seriousness of bullying was $r_{SE} = .82$. Its correlation with the likelihood of intervening was $r_{IE} = .75$. As these scores are highly intercorrelated it will be hard to tease apart what variables might be influencing the likelihood of intervening. Looking at the partial correlations may help.

The partial correlation between seriousness and intervention (accounting for empathy) is:

$$r_{SI.E} = \frac{r_{SI} - r_{SE}r_{IE}}{\sqrt{(1-r_{SE}^2)(1-r_{IE}^2)}} = \frac{.74 - .82 \times .75}{\sqrt{(1-.82^2)(1-.75^2)}} \approx .33$$

Perceived seriousness correlates with likelihood of intervention at $r_{SI.E} = .33$ when the influence of empathy is stripped out. Empathy has a slightly larger correlation with likelihood of intervention when perceived seriousness is partialed out: $r_{IE.S} = .37$. In statistical terms, these correlations make it difficult to answer questions about which factor is more important or whether the perceived seriousness has a causal effect on the likelihood of intervention. To answer these questions, a different type of study is needed (e.g., one training teachers to be more empathetic).

How do partial correlations fit into Figure 12.2? The squared partial correlation isn't represented directly. If X_1 is perceived seriousness, X_2 is empathy and Y is likelihood of intervention, then the squared partial correlation $r_{SI.E}$ is the area b as a proportion of the area $a+b$ (excluding c and d). So while a squared semi-partial correlation really is a part of the overall R^2, a squared partial correlation is not (and will tend to be much larger than the semi-partial or part correlation). Looking again at the figure you should be able to see that $a+b$ is also $1-(c+d)$. As $c+d$ is the simple r^2 between X_2 and Y ($.75^2$ in this example), it suggests that the squared semi-partial correlation between perceived seriousness and likelihood of intervention should be $.33^2 \times (1-.75^2) = .048$. This makes the semi-partial correlation $\sqrt{.048} = .22$.

A final insight is that the area $a+b$ is the residual variance for the simple regression of Y on X_2 (i.e., $1-r_{Y2}$). This is the area used to scale the partial correlation of X_1 and Y (seriousness and intervention in this example). This means that the partial correlation $r_{Y1.2}$ could also be defined as the correlation between X_1 and the residuals of the regression of Y on X_2.

Box 12.1 What is a standardized regression coefficient?

In a simple linear regression, the slope b is the rate of increase of Y for a unit increase in X. When both variables are z transformed, the resulting standardized slope $\hat{\beta}$ is the Pearson correlation between X and Y (r_{XY}). A natural assumption is that this equivalence holds for the standardized regression coefficients $\hat{\beta}_1$ to $\hat{\beta}_q$ (beta weights) in multiple regression. In fact, the relationship only holds if the predictors are orthogonal (and is necessarily true if there is only one predictor). If the correlations between X_1 to X_q are all zero, the standardized coefficients β_1 to β_q will also be semi-partial correlation coefficients. Furthermore, in this special case, the sum of the squared beta weights will be ≤ 1 and $\hat{\beta}_1$ to $\hat{\beta}_q$ will all fall in the range -1 to $+1$. This special case arises only infrequently (except for experiments designed to have orthogonal predictors). Much more likely is that the predictors will be correlated, in which case the sum of the squared beta weights could exceed one. It is also quite possible for the individual beta weights to exceed -1 or $+1$ in value.

How big could a standardized regression coefficient such as $\hat{\beta}_1$ get in a multiple regression? There is no theoretical upper limit if the predictors are correlated. As collinearity (correlation between predictors) rises, the maximum value that standardized regression coefficients can take also increases. Deegan (1978) explains that for a multiple regression with only two predictors the standardized regression coefficient for X_1 can be represented as:

$$\hat{\beta}_1 = \frac{r_{1Y} - r_{12}r_{2Y}}{1 - r_{12}^2}$$ Equation 12.22

The equation makes it trivial to find correlations between X_1, X_2 and Y that produce values of $\beta_1 > 1$. Consider the following outcomes:

r_{1Y}	r_{2Y}	r_{12}	β_1
0.80	0.00	0.60	1.25
0.60	−0.90	0.50	1.40
0.50	−0.10	0.99	30.10

Large values of $\hat{\beta}_1$ can occur even if collinearity is not in the range usually considered to be high (e.g., .50 or .60). When collinearity is very high a standardized regression coefficient of 20, 30 or 100 should not be surprising.

Despite all this, neither collinearity nor large standardized regression coefficients are necessarily a cause for concern in a statistical model (see Section 12.3.2 below). A more pressing issue is the proper interpretation of a standardized regression coefficient. Deegan (*ibid.*) points out that a regression slope is a rate of change (the ratio of the change in Y to a one-unit change in X). A standardized slope is therefore a standardized rate of change. The coefficient $\hat{\beta}_1$ represents the change in Y associated with one-unit increase in X_1 (with both X_1 and Y scaled in terms of $\hat{\sigma}$). This rate of change interpretation of the standardized semi-partial slope is always correct. Only under very particular circumstances, when all predictors are orthogonal (and this includes simple regression as a special case), will this rate of change also be a simple or semi-partial correlation coefficient.

12.3.2 Interpreting individual predictors

With orthogonal predictors, each effect can be interpreted in isolation. The interpretation of individual predictors then reduces to the problem of interpreting a simple regression coefficient with one crucial difference: reduced *df* for the error term. This, in turn, impacts on the estimate of error variance for the regression and hence on both F and $\hat{\sigma}_{estimate}$ (used to derive standard errors for NHSTs and CIs of the intercepts and slopes). A multiple regression has decreased precision, relative to a simple linear regression, as more parameters are estimated (because df_{error} decreases). This decreased precision may be outweighed by the extra explanatory power of additional predictors. An extra parameter reduces the denominator of MS_{error} by one, but it may decrease the numerator ($SS_{residual}$) by a sufficient margin to maintain or increase overall precision of estimation. In practice, the cost of adding predictors can usually be ignored (except when the number of predictors is high in relation to N or if predictors with low explanatory power are added to a model).

If predictors are orthogonal it is possible to use MS_{error} to obtain a significance test or CI for individual predictors using the t distribution. For correlated predictors, standard errors for the parameter estimates $\hat{\sigma}_{b_0}$ to $\hat{\sigma}_{b_q}$ are obtained from the square root of the diagonal elements of the asymptotic covariance matrix $\hat{\mathbf{V}}$. Test statistics or CIs can then be formed using standard procedures. What do t statistics obtained in this way represent? For orthogonal predictors the t statistics are tests of the total contribution of each predictor to the outcome Y (because the orthogonal predictors share no variance). With reference to Figure 12.2 this would suggest that the circles for X_1 and X_2 do not overlap at all and the shared contribution shrinks to nothing. With correlated predictors b_1 to b_q are semi-partial regression coefficients. Dividing a coefficient b_i by $\hat{\sigma}_{b_i}$ gives a t statistic that tests its unique contribution to the prediction of Y. This unique contribution is expressed as a proportion of total variance by its squared semi-partial correlation coefficient; the variance explained after excluding the unique contribution of any other predictors and any shared contribution with other predictors.

This unique contribution can also be expressed in terms of R^2 (Bring, 1994). If R^2_{full} is the proportion of variance explained by the full model (including the predictor) and $R^2_{reduced}$ is the proportion explained by a reduced model excluding that predictor, then the difference between them is the squared semi-partial correlation:

$$r^2_{semi\text{-}partial} = R^2_{full} - R^2_{reduced}$$ Equation 12.23

Example 12.5 indicated that a squared partial correlation can be derived from the semi-partial correlation expressed as a proportion of the residual variance for a reduced model (including all the other predictors). A formal expression for this is:

$$r^2_{partial} = \frac{R^2_{full} - R^2_{reduced}}{1 - R^2_{reduced}}$$ Equation 12.24

The denominator of this equation is the residual variance of the reduced model. The partial correlation is therefore the extra increment in variance explained by a new predictor as a proportion of previously unexplained variance. In contrast, the semi-partial correlation is the extra variance it explains as a proportion of the total variance.

These equations show that the incremental increase in variance explained by adding a predictor to a model is determined by its unique contribution to the full regression model. Looking at the incremental change is a way of screening out the shared contribution (because that shared contribution with other predictors is already in the reduced model). Bring (*ibid.*) shows how this incremental change is also related to the t statistic used to test the unique contribution of a predictor:

$$t_{predictor} = \sqrt{\frac{(N - q - 1)\left(R^2_{full} - R^2_{reduced}\right)}{1 - R^2_{full}}}$$ Equation 12.25

The standard error can also be obtained from R^2 statistics for the two models (though software that provides R^2 ought also to report $\hat{\sigma}_b$ for each predictor).[10] Confidence intervals for the effect of the predictor can be constructed as $b \pm t_{df_{error},1-\alpha/2}\hat{\sigma}_b$.

In summary, semi-partial regression slopes are the slope of a linear regression when all other predictors are held constant (i.e., do not change in value). The unique contribution of a predictor to the overall R^2 can be tested using a t statistic. It would also be quite reasonable to use an F ratio of the incremental change in R^2 to test this unique contribution relative to the error variance. This F ratio would have 1 *df* in the numerator and therefore equivalent to the usual t test (with $F = t^2$). This interpretation of a regression coefficient is widely taught and entirely correct. Even so, it is widely misunderstood. The difficulty seems to be with the innocuous phrase 'when all other predictors are held constant'. If the predictors are correlated, then the other predictors will tend to vary when X changes in value. As long as predictors are correlated – particularly if they are highly correlated – applications of regression need to consider the joint influence of the predictors in order to generate sensible predictions.

12.3.3 Prediction in multiple regression

Prediction for a new observation is more difficult for multiple regression than simple linear regression because it depends on the leverage (hat value) of the new observation with respect to several predictors. The familiar simple linear regression equations can be adapted with only minor changes when expressed in terms of matrix algebra (see Snedecor and Cochran, 1989). The starting point is to set up a $1 \times (q+1)$ matrix (i.e., a row vector) of predictor values for the mean of the m new observations. This matrix should also include the constant term:

$$\mathbf{X}_{n+m} = \begin{bmatrix} 1 & x_1 & x_2 & . & . & . & x_q \end{bmatrix} \qquad \text{Equation 12.26}$$

The predicted mean of Y can now be expressed very neatly as

$$\hat{y}_{n+m} = \mathbf{X}_{n+m}\hat{\mathbf{b}}, \qquad \text{Equation 12.27}$$

where $\mathbf{b}$ is the $(q+1) \times 1$ matrix (or column vector) of fitted regression coefficients, including the intercept, from a general linear model. This is, in effect, another way of denoting the weighted sum of the regression coefficients and the predictor values.

The difficult part is to obtain the appropriate standard error for the m new observations with these predicted values. Equation 5.28 expressed the standard error of prediction in terms of its hat value h_{n+m}. In multiple regression it is necessary to work with the hat matrix $\mathbf{H}$:

$$\mathbf{H} = \mathbf{X}(\mathbf{X}'\mathbf{X})^{-1}\mathbf{X}' \qquad \text{Equation 12.28}$$

The terms hat matrix and hat value derive from the relationship between $\mathbf{H}$ and the column vector of predicted $\mathbf{y}$ values:

$$\hat{\mathbf{y}} = \mathbf{H}\mathbf{y} \qquad \text{Equation 12.29}$$

Premultiplication by the matrix $\mathbf{H}$ places the 'hat' on $\mathbf{y}$ (transforming it into $\hat{\mathbf{y}}$). Adapting Equation 12.28 for prediction gives an expression for the leverage of a new observation as:

$$h_{n+m} = \mathbf{X}_{n+m}(\mathbf{X}'\mathbf{X})^{-1}\mathbf{X}'_{n+m} \qquad \text{Equation 12.30}$$

It is important to bear in mind the distinction between $\mathbf{X}_{n+m}$ (the predictor values for the m new observations) and $\mathbf{X}$ (the matrix of predictors in the original data). Having obtained the appropriate hat matrix, the standard error of prediction is given by:

$$\hat{\sigma}_{prediction} = \hat{\sigma}_E\sqrt{\frac{1}{m} + h_{n+m}} \qquad \text{Equation 12.31}$$

This is identical to the right-hand expression of Equation 5.28. As with the solutions for simple linear regression this reduces to $\hat{\sigma}_E\sqrt{1+h_{n+m}}$ if $m=1$ and $\hat{\sigma}_E\sqrt{h_{n+m}}$ if the population mean of Y is predicted. In all cases, $\hat{\sigma}_E$ is calculated as $\sqrt{MS_{error}}$.

$\mathbf{H}$ is a diagonal matrix with a main diagonal comprising the hat values (leverage) of the sample data. It can therefore be used to derive leverage adjusted diagnostic statistics (including standardized or studentized residuals and Cook's distance). In simple cases such as Equation 12.30 the solution is scalar (i.e., a 1×1 matrix) and it provides the hat value directly.

Example 12.6 It is possible to use the matrix form of the prediction equation to obtain predictions for the data in Table 12.1. The equation is $\hat{\mathbf{y}} = \mathbf{X}\hat{\mathbf{b}}$ and, drawing on results from Example 12.3, this gives:

$$\hat{\mathbf{y}} = \mathbf{X}\hat{\mathbf{b}} = \begin{bmatrix} 1 & -3 & 2 \\ 1 & -2 & 2 \\ 1 & -1 & 0 \\ 1 & 0 & 4 \\ 1 & 1 & 5 \\ 1 & 2 & 1 \\ 1 & 3 & 1 \end{bmatrix} \begin{bmatrix} -0.2822727 \\ 2.2446429 \\ 1.2277273 \end{bmatrix} = \begin{bmatrix} -4.560747 \\ -2.316104 \\ -2.526916 \\ 4.628636 \\ 8.101006 \\ 5.434740 \\ 7.679383 \end{bmatrix}$$

These are the predictions for observed values of the predictors (those found in the sample). To predict new values is just as easy. If $X_1 = 4$ and $X_2 = -1$, the predicted value of Y is:

$$\hat{y}_{n+m} = \mathbf{X}_{n+m}\hat{\mathbf{b}} = \begin{bmatrix} 1 & 4 & -1 \end{bmatrix} \begin{bmatrix} -0.2822727 \\ 2.2446429 \\ 1.2277273 \end{bmatrix} = 7.468571$$

Assuming that a single new observation is predicted (i.e., $m = 1$), the sampling variance of this prediction is:

$$\hat{\sigma}^2_{prediction} = \hat{\sigma}^2_E (1 + h_{n+m}) = MS_{error} \left[1 + \mathbf{X}_{n+m} (\mathbf{X}'\mathbf{X})^{-1} \mathbf{X}'_{n+m}\right]$$

Using known results for MS_{error} and $(\mathbf{X}'\mathbf{X})^{-1}$ from Example 12.3, h_{n+m} is:

$$\begin{bmatrix} 1 & 4 & -1 \end{bmatrix} \begin{bmatrix} 0.3863636 & 0 & -0.1136364 \\ 0 & 0.03571429 & 0 \\ -0.1136364 & 0 & 0.0530303 \end{bmatrix} \begin{bmatrix} 1 \\ 4 \\ -1 \end{bmatrix} = 1.238095$$

The sampling variance of the prediction is therefore:

$$\hat{\sigma}^2_{prediction} = \hat{\sigma}^2_E (1 + h_{n+m}) = 18.92771\,(1 + 1.238095) = 42.36202$$

Its square root is $\hat{\sigma}_{prediction} \approx 6.51$. The 95% prediction interval for a single new observation is:

$$\hat{y}_{n+m} \pm t_{4,.975}\hat{\sigma}_{prediction} \approx 7.47 \pm 18.07$$

This could be reported as [−10.6, 25.5]. The wide interval reflects the uncertainty of prediction for a single observation and small sample size.

12.3.4 Effect size and statistical power

Effect size considerations for multiple regression are similar to those of simple regression models, except that there is now a clear distinction between effect size for the model versus that for individual predictors. For individual predictors effect size is usually expressed in terms of the unstandardized or standardized slope. The former is preferred for comparing effects between studies with different characteristics and for interpreting practical or clinical significance with meaningful units. For the model both R^2 and adjusted R^2 are popular measures, with the latter being a better population estimate. However, both measures can be misleading when used to compare models with different predictors, samples or measures (including measures with different ranges or reliabilities).

Although proportion of variance explained measures are of limited value in interpreting models, they can simplify sample size and statistical power calculations. The usual effect size estimate for these applications is Cohen's f^2:

$$f^2 = \frac{\hat{\sigma}^2_{explained}}{\hat{\sigma}^2_{error}} = \frac{\Delta R^2}{1 - R^2_{full}} \qquad \text{Equation 12.32}$$

For the overall test of the model $\Delta R^2 = R^2$ (as change is relative to a model with no explanatory power). For a subset of predictors ΔR^2 is the change in R^2 when the predictors are added (or $r^2_{semi\text{-}partial}$ for a single predictor). The calculation can also be expressed in terms of a squared partial correlation:

$$f^2 = \frac{r^2_{partial}}{1 - r^2_{partial}} \qquad \text{Equation 12.33}$$

The square root of this quantity, f, is used as input for sample size and statistical power calculations in G*Power and the R package `pwr` (see Example 13.1).

12.3.5 Collinearity and multicollinearity

Collinearity refers to the linear correlation between two predictors in a multiple regression model. Collinearity refers to the correlation between two predictors (e.g., if only two predictors are present or if all other predictors are orthogonal), whereas *multicollinearity* arises when two or more predictors are correlated (e.g., r_{12}, r_{13} and r_{23} are all different from zero).

Discussion of collinearity and multicollinearity often assumes that the presence of correlated predictors (or at least highly correlated predictors) is inherently problematic. This is not necessarily the case (see Deegan, 1978). Collinearity is a problem under two circumstances: i) when it is so high that it is not possible to fit the model, or ii) when a researcher is interested in teasing apart the effects of individual predictors. In the former situation, specialist computer software is largely robust to the technical difficulties in fitting the model.[11] Only in the extreme situation of two perfectly collinear predictors (i.e., $r_{12} = 1$) should it to be impossible to fit the regression model. With respect to discriminating the effects of different predictors, collinearity is often cited as a problem only when the correlation between two predictors is moderately high (e.g., $r_{12} \pm .8$ or more). This is not true. Much lower correlations will, on occasion, cause problems.

The greater the overlap between two predictors, the harder it will be to tease their effects apart.[12] This will necessarily make interpretation of the individual contribution harder as collinearity increases. Small correlations will only make the interpretation marginally trickier, but can still have negative consequences. As collinearity rises, so must the shared, non-unique contribution of the predictors to R^2 (see Figure 12.2b). In crude terms, this means that each unique contribution is assessed using a smaller and smaller effective sample size as collinearity increases. In the presence of collinearity, standard errors for individual predictors are necessarily larger than for orthogonal predictors. This decreases statistical power and the precision of interval estimates. With low N or high levels of collinearity (or some combination of the two) the parameter estimates begin to behave erratically (e.g., varying dramatically with small changes to the model or between replications). Even though N might be large enough to estimate a single parameter precisely, effective N may not be sufficient to simultaneously estimate two parameters with adequate precision.

This does not contradict the assertion that collinearity needn't be a problem. Collinearity should not impact on the overall fit and test of the model (in the absence of perfect collinearity). The multiple correlation coefficient R is the correlation between an optimal linear combination of all the predictors ($\hat{Y}$) and Y. If your sole interest is in the overall model fit or prediction from the model, collinearity should not be a problem.

Problems occur only for interpreting and testing individual predictors and parameter estimates. Depending on the focus of research, the same degree of collinearity might be a major obstacle or an irrelevance. If the focus of research is on teasing apart contributions of different predictors, serious problems are most likely when the correlations between predictors are .7 or more. With a correlation of .7 roughly half (.49) the variance is shared. Above this level, most of the explanatory power of each predictor is badly compromised. Below this level correlations between predictors account for less than half of the variance of the predictor. This can still cause problems and may reduce statistical power for one or more crucial inferences.

This is only partly a statistical issue. Collinearity depends on the relationships between predictors in the population. Separating their contributions – to the extent that it is possible at all – requires a theoretical understanding of the context. Take a very simple example. If you sample 100 children at random from a school, there will probably be a fairly high correlation between the age of the children and their mathematical ability. You will also find a similarly high correlation between their school year and their mathematical ability. Age and school year will be highly collinear (perhaps $r = .95$). The decision of which predictor is more important (age or years of schooling) isn't primarily a statistical one. Knowledge of the domain suggests that students don't spontaneously acquire understanding of formal mathematics (though it would be pleasant if they did), but are taught it at school. Accordingly, it seems reasonable to interpret these correlations as indicating that schooling rather than mere passage of time is influencing mathematical ability.

Even moderate to low collinearity (e.g., less than $r = .3$) may still have a noticeable impact on statistical power (Graham, 2003). One of the best remedies against problems with collinearity is to increase sample size enough to obtain adequate statistical power. Another remedy is to design your study to avoid correlated predictors. If neither of these solutions is available, it is possible to adjust the statistical model (though this is not the preferred solution). If collinearity is very high, an obvious adjustment is to drop one of the predictors. For example, for most purposes either age or year of schooling (but not both) would be included in a regression model (as one is more or less a surrogate for the other). Another alternative is to add a composite of the two variables or derive a new variable computed from them. If you decide to do this it is essential that any weights or transformations are not optimized for your sample. Any composite or derived variable should be determined from prior experience or theory. Equal weighting or simple transformations (e.g., sums of or differences between predictors) are reasonable options to consider. Many people are skeptical of routinely dropping or combining predictors and emphasize that it may not be necessary, and, if applied, should have a theoretical rationale (O'Brien, 2007).

Multicollinearity is really no different to collinearity in its effects, and presents only one further challenge. Collinearity is very easy to detect. Before running any multiple regression it is sensible to look at the simple correlations between predictors. However, this form of checking can only reliably detect collinearity. The simple correlations may show apparently harmless levels of collinearity (e.g., simple correlations ranging from say −.3 to .3). As this pattern represents at most 10% shared variance between pairs of predictors it would not generally be considered problematic. This misses the point that, while pairs of predictors share only a small proportion of variance, the shared variance will probably not be identical across all predictor pairs. If there are many predictors, the total variance they share could be substantial (and will occasionally conceal perfect collinearity).

Assessing multicollinearity requires a method of determining the degree of overlap between a predictor and the $q - 1$ other predictors in the regression model. Fortunately, such a tool exists: multiple regression. Take each predictor in turn and regress that variable (treating it as the outcome variable) on the remaining $q - 1$ predictors, then calculate the proportion of variance each predictor shares with the other predictors in the full model. To reduce potential confusion with R^2 for the full model, these statistics can be presented as *tolerance* statistics for each predictor. Tolerance is defined as

$$tolerance = 1 - R^2_{X_i} \qquad \text{Equation 12.34}$$

where $R^2_{X_i}$ is the proportion of variance explained in the ith predictor by the remaining predictors. Tolerance will be zero when a predictor is perfectly predicted by some combination of the other predictors and one when it is orthogonal to them.

The tolerance statistic also provides a quick check on the loss of precision implied by the observed level of collinearity or multicollinearity. This is the *variance inflation factor* (*VIF*). The *VIF* is calculated as:

$$VIF_{X_i} = \frac{1}{1 - R^2_{X_i}} = \frac{1}{tolerance} \qquad \text{Equation 12.35}$$

The standard error of a predictor will be inflated by $\sqrt{VIF}$ relative to its theoretical minimum when multicollinearity is not present. O'Brien (2007) points out that this minimum will often be an unrealistic standard of comparison, because orthogonality is typically only found in experiments designed to have orthogonal predictors. The *VIF* also explains why inference in the presence of multicollinearity can still be efficient in large samples. Although an inflation factor of ten is often interpreted as disastrous for an analysis, it merely implies that $\hat{\sigma}_{b_i}$ will be $\sqrt{10} \approx 3.2$ times larger than for an orthogonal predictor. A sample size of 100 and a *VIF* of ten will therefore produce inferences as efficient as a sample size of ten and *VIF* of one, this is a problem that can (at a cost) be overcome. This presumes that multicollinearity matters at all. If the tests of individual predictors are of no real interest (e.g., because they are included as confounding variables) the efficiency of those tests can reasonably be ignored. Including a dozen highly correlated predictors may not be a problem if they are uncorrelated with the predictors you are interested in.

Example 12.7 Calculating tolerance or *VIF* for every predictor in a model is a tedious process, but can be automated. It is also common to precede regression analyses by looking at a correlation matrix of the predictors. This can detect collinearity between pairs of predictors, but may not alert you to multicollinearity (though if correlations between all q predictors are close to zero, serious problems with multicollinearity are unlikely, particularly if q is small).

This example looks at data on voting intentions collected by Healy (2009). Subsequent examples will refer to this as the intention to vote data. It has been argued that one motivation for people to vote is social (see Edlin *et al.*, 2007). A consequence of this hypothesis is that altruistic individuals may be more likely to vote. Healy tested this hypothesis by collecting several measures of altruism and looking at how they predicted intention to vote in a student election (measured by self-report on a seven-point scale from one, 'certain not to vote', to seven, 'certain to vote'). The altruism measures included the Prosocial Motivation Scale *pressure* and *pleasure* subscales, each with scores ranging from one to five (Gebauer *et al.*, 2008).

Healy also asked participants ($N=96$) to report their social network size by estimating the number of other students at their university that were either close friends (*close*) or acquaintances (*acquaint*). Figure 12.3 shows scatter plots for the four potential predictors and the outcome variable (*intention*). The correlations between four of the potential predictors of likelihood of voting are reported below:

	close	*acquaint*	*pleasure*	*pressure*
close	1.00			
acquaint	.62	1.00		
pleasure	.20	.17	1.00	
pressure	.22	.09	.36	1.00

The scatter plots and correlations show fairly weak patterns. This is not too surprising. A complex decision such as whether to vote or not is probably influenced by many factors (and this kind of self-report measure is often unreliable). These exploratory analyses suggest that although the predictors are correlated, they are below typical cut-offs (e.g., $r=.80$) used to detect problems with collinearity.

A multiple linear regression model with all four predictors explains around 15% of the intention to vote variance in the sample: $R^2=.145$, $F_{4,91}=3.86$, $MSE=1.71$, $p=.0061$. The prediction equation is:

$$\hat{Y}_{intention}=2.26+0.0046X_{close}+0.017X_{acquaint}+0.61X_{pleasure}-0.31X_{pressure}$$

Minimum and maximum predictor values (in the sample) and confidence intervals for each regression coefficient are:

	min	*max*	95% CI
close	0	100	[−0.020, 0.030]
acquaint:	1	200	[0.002, 0.031]
pleasure:	2	5	[−0.083, 1.294]
pressure:	2	5	[−1.082, 0.455]

These suggest that the number of acquaintances is predictive of intention to vote, $t_{91}=2.31$, $SE=0.0072$, $p=.023$. The pleasure subscale of the PMS scale also seems positively related to voting intention, though the interval includes zero, $t_{91}=1.75$, $SE=0.35$, $p=.084$. Neither the number of close friends nor the pressure subscale suggests a clear relationship with voting intention (both intervals straddle zero and include reasonably substantial positive and negative effect sizes). As these

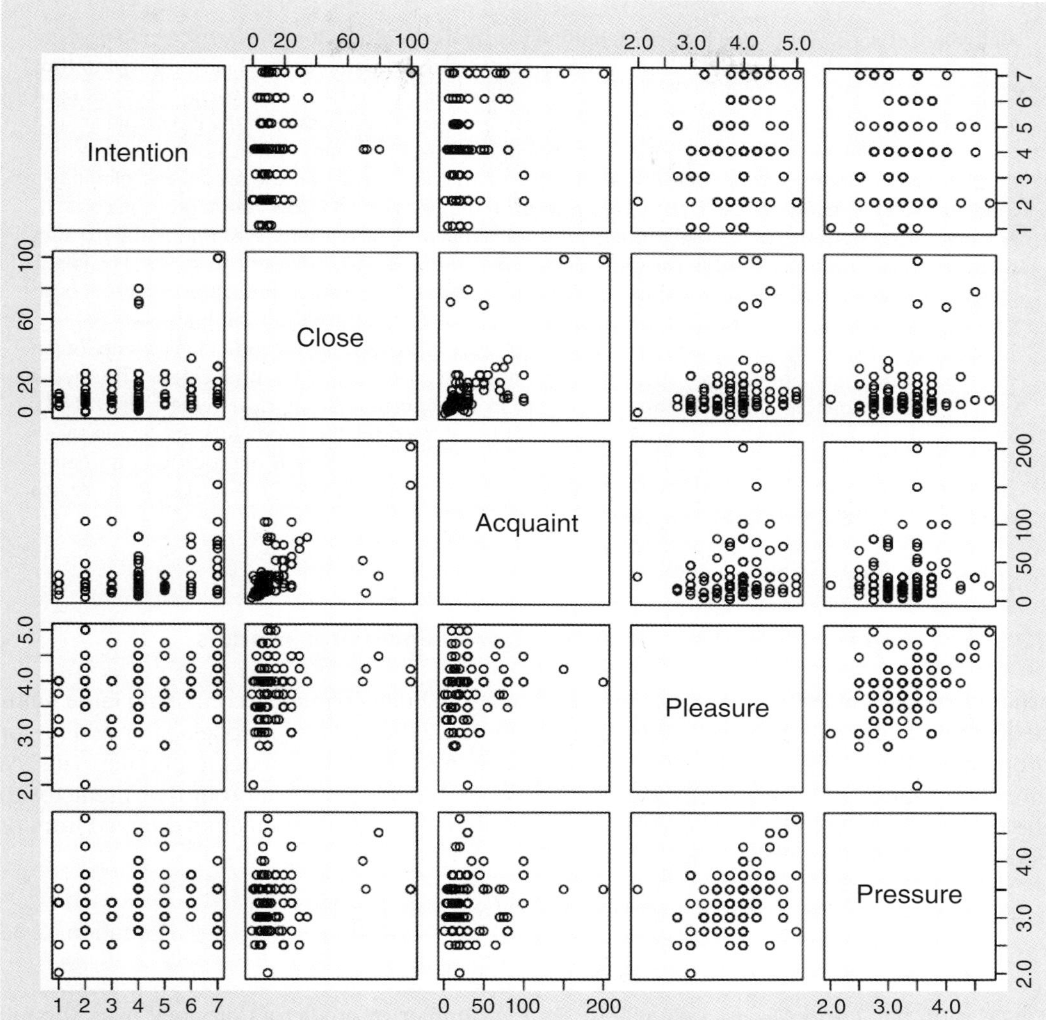

Figure 12.3 Scatter plot matrix of outcome and predictor variables for the intention to vote data

are continuous effects it is vital to take into account the range of possible values in the sample and population (e.g., by looking at the minimum and maximum values). These help explain why the number of acquaintances is a reasonably good predictor even though the coefficient is small: it has a large range. Going from zero to 200 acquaintances indicates an expected $0.017 \times 200 = 3.4$ point change in voting rating (on the basis of this linear model).

The multicollinearity diagnostics are more informative here than the simple pairwise correlations:

close: Tolerance = .59, *VIF* = 1.68
acquaint: Tolerance = .61, *VIF* = 1.63
pleasure: Tolerance = .85, *VIF* = 1.18
pressure: Tolerance = .84, *VIF* = 1.19

All tolerances are closer to one than zero, but the variance inflation factors show that including both *close* and *acquaint* in the model increases the variances of their estimates by at least 60% (and thus their standard errors by around 30%). The sample size required to detect an effect is therefore about 1.6 times larger than if multicollinearity were not present. The two subscales of the PMS scale are not very highly correlated and VIF is modest. Dropping the number of close friends or creating a new predictor by summing acquaintances and friends has a similar impact on the model and eliminates much of the collinearity. Which is the better option? It depends on an understanding of the context, but given that both are unreliable predictors of social network size it might be reasonable to sum them to produce a more reliable measure. For present purposes it is sufficient to report *VIF*, NHST and CI for *acquaint* when *close* is dropped from the model. The p value and standard error both decrease: $t_{92} = 3.19$, $SE = 0.0057$, $p = .0023$, 95% CI [0.007, 0.029], $VIF = 1.03$.

Although collinearity influences the statistical power and precision for individual effects (even when tolerances are quite good), the overall R^2 and test of the model is unaffected. The model with all four predictors explains more variance than the one that drops *close* (where $R^2 = .144$). Including extra predictors is not parsimonious (and highly correlated predictors are less likely to explain additional variance than uncorrelated ones). Models with different numbers of parameters are better assessed in other ways such as adjusted R^2 (or by AIC and BIC). Adjusted R^2 increases from .108 to .116 when *close* is dropped.

12.3.6 Comparing the fit of two or more regression models

Multiple regression makes it possible for a researcher to build up models containing large numbers of predictors with relatively little effort. Comparing the fit of two models after adding (or dropping) a single predictor depends on the change in R^2 from one model to another. This, as already established, is equivalent to the t test of the unique contribution of that predictor to the model. The increment in R^2 can also be compared for a set of J predictors dropped from or added to a model using an F ratio:

$$F_{change} = \frac{(N-q-1)\left(R^2_{full} - R^2_{reduced}\right)}{J\left(1 - R^2_{full}\right)} \qquad \text{Equation 12.36}$$

This F ratio has J and $N-q-1$ *df*, where J is the number of predictors dropped from the full model (or the change in number of predictors) and q is the total number of predictors in the full model. This is similar to Equation 12.25, except that the increment in R^2 is pooled over the number of predictors being added.

The NHST of the change in R^2 is not the only way to compare two regression models. The same information used to obtain the F ratio could also be used to obtain the likelihood ratio (*LR*) comparing the two models. Using Glover and Dixon's (2004) formulas (see Box 11.4), the *LR* for the model comparison is:

$$LR_{full/reduced} = \left(\frac{1 - R^2_{reduced}}{1 - R^2_{full}}\right)^{\frac{N}{2}} \qquad \text{Equation 12.37}$$

This ratio won't take into account the difference in model complexity. It is possible to adjust it in accordance with information criteria such as AIC_C if desired. For AIC_C, the adjusted *LR* is

$$LR_{AIC_C} = \left(\frac{1 - R^2_{reduced}}{1 - R^2_{full}} \right)^{\frac{N}{2}} \times e^{k_{reduced}\left(\frac{N}{N-k_{reduced}-1}\right)-k_{full}\left(\frac{N}{N-k_{full}-1}\right)} \qquad \text{Equation 12.38}$$

where k is the number of parameters (including intercept and nuisance parameters) in the full or reduced model and therefore equal to $q+2$. The corresponding adjustment for BIC is:

$$LR_{BIC} = \left(\frac{1 - R^2_{reduced}}{1 - R^2_{full}} \right)^{\frac{N}{2}} \times \left(e^{q_{reduced}-q_{full}} \right)^{\ln(N)/2} \qquad \text{Equation 12.39}$$

These values can be transformed into differences in AIC$_C$ or BIC via the equation $\Delta_{IC} = -2\ln(LR_{IC})$. This procedure is handy for obtaining Akaike weights or Schwartz weights for a set of models, provided all the models are compared to a single reference model (Wagenmakers and Farrell, 2004). It is also more flexible than the NHST approach. It does not require that the models being compared are nested. This makes it possible to compare models with the same number of parameters, but different predictors. The chief restriction is that the data are identical. Data sets with missing predictor values can cause problems for information criteria – because the data set may change across models. Comparing models with different transformations of the outcome, but not predictors, will also prevent direct comparison of the models (though this can be adjusted for).

For complex regression models, there are strong arguments for going beyond simple hypothesis tests or interval estimates and looking at other characteristics of the models being compared – notably the predictions of the model. This is particularly true for Bayesian data analysis (see Gelman and Hill, 2007).

Example 12.8 In Example 12.7 informal comparisons of different models were made. The two models being compared were a 'full' model of the intention to vote data predicting *intention* from *close, acquaint, pleasure* and *pressure*. This was compared to a 'reduced' model that dropped *close*. R^2 and adjusted R^2 for each model are reproduced in Table 12.4:

Table 12.4 Comparison of full and reduced models for intention to vote data

Model	**Predictors (q)**	**R^2**	**Adjusted R^2**	**df_{error}**
Full	4	.1451	.1076	91
Reduced	3	.1439	.1160	92

The change in R^2 can be tested with the F ratio:

$$F_{change} = \frac{(N-q-1)\left(R^2_{full} - R^2_{reduced}\right)}{J\left(1 - R^2_{full}\right)} = \frac{(96-4-1)(.1451-.1439)}{1\,(1-.1451)} \approx 0.13$$

This test is statistically non-significant: $F_{1,91} = 0.13$, $p > .05$. In this example, the F ratio has 1 *df* and so could also be reported as: $t_{91} = 0.36$, $p > .05$. This t test is equivalent to the test of the *close* effect in the full model. Both procedures are tests of the unique contribution of a single predictor in the model. Change in R^2 is therefore usually reserved for comparing sets of predictors rather than one predictor at a time.

There is no need to use a significance test to compare models, and some alternative methods are arguably superior. The likelihood ratio for the full model relative to the reduced model is:

$$LR_{full/reduced} = \left(\frac{1 - R^2_{reduced}}{1 - R^2_{full}}\right)^{\frac{N}{2}} = \left(\frac{1 - .1438}{1 - .1451}\right)^{\frac{96}{2}} = \left(\frac{.8562}{.8549}\right)^{48} \approx 1.08$$

The full model is therefore only very slightly more informative than the reduced model. This should not be taken as support for the full model. It has an extra parameter and will always be at least as likely as the reduced model. A better approach would be to take account of the extra parameter using AIC_C:

$$LR_{AIC_C} = \left(\frac{.8562}{.8549}\right)^{48} \times e^{5\left(\frac{96}{96-5-1}\right)-6\left(\frac{96}{96-6-1}\right)} \approx 0.34$$

This is the ratio in favor of the full model. When the additional parameter is taken into account, it is clear that the reduced model is more informative than the full model by a ratio approaching 3:1. Adding the number of close friends does not seem to improve the predictions of the model over and above the number of acquaintances.

12.4 Building a statistical model

12.4.1 Model selection

Having small numbers of orthogonal or near-orthogonal predictors and relatively large samples reduces the difficulty of building up a statistical model. All predictors can be entered into the model simultaneously and be interpreted with relative clarity. If predictors are correlated – even if the simple correlations are quite modest – selecting a good model is hard. Building up a statistical model in this context requires expertise and judgment.

Various attempts at 'automatic' selection of the best model have been proposed. These are procedures such as *stepwise regression* or *all subsets regression*. What these procedures do is search through the space of possible models, by adding variables, dropping variables or comparing subsets of predictors systematically. Models can be selected on the basis of R^2, information criteria or other measures (though most often a significance test determines which model is selected). Because the procedures typically search through a very large number of possible models they will inevitably find predictors and combinations of predictors that fit well by chance (unless the number of predictors is small). This leads to biased inference and overestimation of model fit in terms of R^2 and related measures (see Whittingham *et al.*, 2006).

Best practice in selecting a regression model is to keep the number of models small. This is partly to avoid over-fitting and partly because keeping the number of models down requires an explicit strategy for selecting a model or set of models to report. The process of deciding on the strategy obliges you to think about the aims of the research and align those aims with your statistical model. It will also often make reporting the analysis easier. In science, the single most important criterion in selecting predictors to include or exclude from a model should be theory (in its broad sense, rather than the narrow sense of a particular scientific model or hypothesis). If there are strong theoretical grounds to have a predictor in a model, it should be included. If different theories (in the narrow sense) suggest that different predictors should be included in the model, this presents an ideal opportunity to test those competing theories. Recall that evidence in favor of any hypothesis can only be assessed in relation to a competing hypothesis. Inferential tools such as significance testing, likelihood ratios, Bayes factors or information criteria exist precisely to make such comparisons (though they do so in different ways). It is always better, if possible, to compare two plausible hypotheses rather than resort to a 'straw man' hypothesis such as $R^2 = 0$.

Over-fitting when building up a statistical model is a major danger. It is sensible to rely on methods that penalize model complexity where possible (e.g., AIC_C, BIC or Bayes factors rather than NHSTs). A competing tension, however, is that there are often good reasons to keep predictors in a model even if they are not justified in terms of its improved fit – and statistical significance or other strict cut-offs for inclusion or exclusion of predictors can be dangerous. For instance, it is sensible to keep potential confounding variables in a model even if their contribution to fit is modest (or negligible). Confounding variables help in several ways. Where they do predict variance in the outcome, their inclusion will reduce error and make the test of important predictors more sensitive. They can also strengthen the conclusions of an analysis by indicating that alternative explanations are not supported. Such variables usually have a strong pragmatic justification for being in the model. Research with children, for example, will typically include predictors such as the sex of the child because many outcomes (e.g., academic performance) are known, suspected or believed to be associated with this variable. Even if the belief is incorrect, the model is likely to be more credible if the predictor is included.

Although there is unlikely to be a modeling strategy that works well in all situations, it can help to start with general guidelines for building up a model. Gelman and Hill (2007, p. 69) describe a simple set of guidelines that make sense for many domains – particularly when working in the social and human sciences. Other strategies include a hierarchical approach (see Box 14.1) or a theory-driven approach. A hierarchical approach is appropriate for situations where increasingly complex sets of related models are being compared. A theory-driven approach is perhaps the most powerful strategy, but requires that the set of theoretically interesting models can be defined in advance. Even then, if the set is large, over-fitting is possible and approaches such as model averaging could be considered. This can be accomplished by weighting parameter estimates and predictions by the probability of a model within the set (e.g., using Akaike or Schwartz weights).

Building up a statistical model involves combining domain expertise, common sense and statistical understanding. This inevitably brings a degree of subjectivity into the process. This subjectivity can be constrained by checking the model and its predictions. A good model is not overly sensitive to violations of assumptions, has a strong theoretical rationale and makes reasonable predictions.

12.4.2 Expected and unexpected effects of adding a predictor to a model

Adding a predictor to a model often has the effect you expect. Usually this entails the predictor having the same sign and accounting for a similar proportion of variance to that of the simple correlation between predictor and outcome. Sometimes the effect is unexpected (at least to those inexperienced with multiple regression models). The effect could be markedly smaller or larger than for the simple correlation. With a little experience, a researcher should come to realize that the other predictors in the model have an impact on the contribution of any new predictor. If the existing predictors account for a substantial proportion of variance in the model, there is less variance left unexplained. If you add a new predictor that correlates with the outcome Y, there are two main options. Either the predictor will tend to be correlated with existing predictors and contribute little extra to the model, or it will tend to correlate with the residuals, and hence reduce the unexplained variance and increase R^2.

This latter phenomenon is crucial to a proper understanding of regression models of all kinds: the effects of adding a predictor to a statistical model depend not on its ability to explain Y but on its ability to explain residual variance. New predictors that are correlated with the residuals of a model will explain additional variance in Y that other predictors in the model (if there are any) do not. Explaining residual variance has the benefit of reducing the residual variance for the model, making inference more sensitive and prediction more precise. This is true whether NHSTs, CIs or alternatives such as information criteria are used. Statistical inference becomes more efficient when error variance is low.

An extreme form of unexpected effect is found with what is known as a *suppressor* variable. There are several different kinds of suppression discussed in the literature, and the concept dates back at least until the 1940s (see Krus and Wilkinson, 1986). However, focusing on the different ways suppression can occur makes people view it as something abnormal or problematic, when it is neither. Suppression is a readily understandable consequence of fitting a statistical model with multiple predictors (although perhaps not a particularly common one). A suppressor variable is often thought of as a predictor that has a zero (or at least a very small) simple correlation with Y, but nevertheless adds to the overall prediction of the model. Its most obvious characteristic is that it tends to increase the absolute value of regression coefficients for one or more other predictors. In an extreme case, the sign of the suppressor could reverse between simple correlation and regression coefficient.

Suppression is less of a puzzle if you know that a predictor's correlation with Y does not determine its impact on the regression. What matters – as mentioned – is its correlation with the residuals of the reduced model with all predictors other than itself present. Darlington (1968) provides a widely accepted definition of a suppressor (and one of the best discussions of suppression). In his definition, it is first assumed that all predictors are scored so that their population correlation with Y is positive. Suppression occurs when a predictor's population regression slope (its effect after partialing out other predictors) is negative. The slightly convoluted phrasing excludes changes in sign due to sampling error, but includes a population correlation of zero (which can be considered positive) that becomes negative in the regression model. The basic premise is that a zero or positive simple correlation between X and Y changes to a negative correlation when X is included in a regression model with other predictors.

How does suppression come about? It can happen in slightly different ways, but is fairly easy to explain in a regression with only two predictors (X_1 and X_2), where X_2 and Y are uncorrelated (i.e., $r_{Y2} = 0$). X_2 can act as a suppressor variable if it explains error variance in the regression of Y on X_1. You can think of this as improving the reliability of X_1, making it a better predictor of Y. Another way to look at it is in terms of the residuals of the simple linear regression model predicting Y from X_1. Because the predictions are a linear function of X_1 they always incorporate measurement error from X_1 (except in the unlikely situation that Y is perfectly predicted from

X_1). A predictor that explains the errors in X_1 therefore also explains residual variance from that model (and may act as a suppressor in a model with both predictors).

Darlington (*ibid.*, p. 163) provides a frequently cited example of how suppression can arise:

> A typical example in which prediction is improved by assigning a negative weight to a variable might be a situation in which a test of reading speed is used in conjunction with a speeded history achievement test to predict some external criterion of knowledge of history. Since the history test is contaminated by reading speed, assigning a negative weight to the reading-speed test would help to correct for the disadvantage suffered by a student with low reading speed who is competing with faster readers.

In other words, a speeded history test is a bad predictor of historical knowledge because it gives fast readers an advantage. Adding reading ability as a predictor removes this confounding variable and increases the magnitude of the regression coefficient between the speeded test and the measure of historical knowledge.

Suppression is a perfectly reasonable outcome in a regression, but may be relatively rare in published work. This might be because it really is infrequent, but also because scientists may design studies or adjust measures to avoid obvious cases of suppression arising (Cohen, 2007). A researcher who knows in advance that one of the measures is unreliable because of some confound will attempt to correct the measure or control for it in some way.

12.4.3 Causality, mediation and errors in predictors

The overview of multiple regression presented here neglects two major issues: causality and measurement error. The ultimate goal of many researchers is to develop a causal model of the relationship between a set of predictors and one or more outcomes. Establishing a statistical association between a set of predictors and some outcome via regression or correlation does not mean that they are causally related, but it is often the first step in establishing a causal relationship. In some situations a researcher will be able to design an experiment to test this causal relationship directly. For instance, the dose of a drug could be manipulated to see if the outcome is a function of dose (in a randomized controlled trial). In other situations true experiments are not possible and observational studies, quasi-experiments or instrumental variable approaches must be used (see Gelman and Hill, 2007). Where a true experiment is not possible, it is still possible to compare two or more models of the causal processes that relate predictors to outcome. These causal models are not equivalent to direct tests of causality from true experiments. However, if the models of causality being compared are plausible and supported by other evidence, they can be powerful ways to understand what is going on.

Mediation is an example of a relatively simple causal model that can be tested in this way. A basic mediation model involves three variables: a predictor X, a mediator M and an outcome Y. In this situation X could have a direct effect on Y or its effect could be indirect and mediated through M. For instance, X might be workload, M might be workplace support and Y might be stress. Workload could directly increase stress or its effects could be mediated by workplace support. If the effect of workload on stress disappears when workplace support is present, this is *complete mediation*. If the effect of workload is diminished by workload support this is *partial mediation*. In principle, complete and partial mediation models can be tested using simple regression models. In practice, the statistical power of this approach is poor. Preacher and Hayes (2008) provide a good introduction to basic mediation methods for readers familiar with regression.

Regression models work best when all predictors are measured without error. This is unlikely for observational methods, but quite possible for some experimental and quasi-experimental designs. If the predictors are not measured without error, using measures with similarly high levels of reliability is the next best option. If the predictors are measured with error, even unstandardized regression coefficients may be biased. In principle the bias is minimized when the predictors are similarly unreliable (Ree and Carretta, 2006). However, point estimates of reliability are generally imprecise, and error in predictors is likely to be problematic unless the reliability for all predictors is high and is estimated from large samples (Zimmerman, 2007).

Where good estimates of the reliability of the predictors in a model are available it is possible to account for this in the regression model. Culpepper and Aguinis (2011) review several ways of dealing with unreliable predictors in a common form of regression model and describe the R code to implement their favored solution: the *errors-in-variables* approach (Warren *et al.*, 1974). An alternative solution, that may be superior in some situations, is a *structural equation model*. Structural equation modeling is a very general regression approach that permits modeling of measurement error and relationships among large numbers of predictor and outcome variables. It is also widely used for causal modeling, including for both basic and complex mediation models. Kline (2010) provides a gentle introduction to structural equation modeling.

12.5 R code for Chapter 12

12.5.1 Estimating regression coefficients with orthogonal predictors (Example 12.2)

If all predictors in the model are orthogonal, the coefficients for the multiple regression equation (b_0 to b_q) can be obtained by fitting separate regression equations for each predictor with the outcome Y. This example illustrates the approach for the data in Example 12.2. The data are entered as vectors (labeled `X1`, `X2` and `Y`). The correlation (of zero) between the predictors establishes that they are orthogonal:

```
X1 <- c(-3, -2, -1, 0, 1, 2, 3)
X2 <- c(2, 2, 0, 4, 5, 1, 1)
Y <- c(-7.15, 0.02, -1.27, 0.68, 11.44, 9.43, 3.29)
cor(X1,X2)
```

The `lm()` function will fit the separate simple linear regressions for each predictor:

```
lm(Y ~ X1)
lm(Y ~ X2)
```

The output gives the slopes as 2.245 for `X1` and 1.2277 for `X2`. These can be used to compute the intercept.

```
b0 <- mean(Y) -2.2245 * mean(X1) -1.2277 * mean(X2)
b0
```

This returns `-0.2822143`. The R^2 estimate for each of the separate regressions is obtained either from the `summary()` function applied to each model such as `summary(lm(Y~X1))$r.square`, or from the squared correlation coefficient between each predictor and Y. With orthogonal predictors, the proportion of SS_{total} they explain does not overlap and summing them produces R^2 for the regression with both predictors.

```
cor(X1,Y)^2 + cor(X2,Y)^2
```

Putting these numbers together gives the prediction equation: $\hat{Y} = -0.282 + 2.245X_1 + 1.228X_2$. This accounts for roughly .691 (69.1%) of the sample variance. The process of fitting separate regression equations has several drawbacks. It is rather cumbersome, only works for orthogonal regressions and (because each regression only includes one predictor) the interval estimates and tests will be slightly out (having incorrect error df).

Computing a composite predictor involves creating a new vector using the coefficients estimated above. The squared correlation of the composite and Y is also equal to R^2 for the multiple regression.

```
W <- -0.282 + 2.245*X1 + 1.228*X2
cor(W, Y)^2
```

This is always the case because one of the ways to define R^2 is the correlation between observed and predicted Y for the sample data. As the composite is obtained by applying the prediction equation to the observed data, the composite is really just $\hat{Y}$ computed for the values of X_1 and X_2 in the sample. You can check this by comparing the predictions with the composite:

```
Y.hat <- predict(lm(Y~X1+X2))
cor(W, Y.hat)
```

12.5.2 Scatter plot in 3D with fitted regression plane (Figure 12.1)

Plotting in 3D requires specialist functions. Figure 12.1 uses the R `scatterplot3d` package. This requires data in the form of a data frame and a regression equation from a fitted model in R. First, install and load the package and before setting up the data and model in the right way:

```
install.packages('scatterplot3d')
library(scatterplot3d)
ex12.2 <- data.frame(X1, X2, Y)
ex12.2.model <- lm(Y ~ X1 + X2)
```

The following function sets up the basic 3D plot with one of three variables being plotted against each of the three axes (x, y and z). The `pch` parameter allows the plotting character (here a filled circle) to be varied, while `xlab`, `ylab` and `zlab` are the respective axis labels.

```
ex12.2.plot <- scatterplot3d(ex12.2, xlab
  =expression(italic(X[1])), ylab =expression(italic(X[2])),
  zlab =expression(italic(Y)), pch = 16)
```

To add heights for the lines (important to help judge the locations of the points in the 3D space more easily) the `points3d()` function is used, while `plane3d()` adds the regression plane for the model fitted earlier:

```
ex12.2.plot$points3d(ex12.2, type = 'h', lwd=.75)
ex12.2.plot$plane3d(ex12.2.model, lty.box ='solid', lwd=.6)
```

These functions are unusual in that they can only be called in relation to an R object that has already been created by the `scatterplot3d()` function (hence the atypical syntax for these commands).

12.5.3 Some matrix algebra basics (Key Concept 12.1)

R has many built-in functions for working with matrices and a matrix can be set up in several ways. The following commands set up a matrix with seven rows and three columns and then populate it column-by-column:

```
X.mat <- matrix(nrow=7, ncol=3)
X.mat[,1] <- rep(1, 7)
X.mat[,2] <- X1
X.mat[,3] <- X2
```

`X.mat` is a matrix of predictors for the regression in Example 12.3, with the first column being made up of constants (a column of seven ones) used to estimate the intercept. To populate it row-by-row would require addressing the first row by [1,], the second row by [2,] and the third by [3,]. A matrix can also be coerced from a data frame or vector using `as.matrix()`. This example uses the data frame `ex12.2` from the previous example:

```
ex12.2.mat <- as.matrix(ex12.2)
```

The functions `cbind()` and `rbind()` join objects together by adding them as columns or rows. We could have used `cbind()` to create a matrix like `X.mat` from a vector of constants and the first two columns of `ex12.2`:

```
constant <- rep(1,7)
X.mat <- as.matrix(cbind(constant, ex12.2[1:2]))
```

One convenient feature of this route is that the names of the columns of the matrix are inherited from the vector name and the column names of the data frame. To check things have worked as anticipated use `is.matrix()`. This returns `TRUE` for a matrix and `FALSE` for another object type. There are corresponding functions for many R object types (e.g., `as.data.frame()`, `is.data.frame()`, `as.vector` etc.).

Setting up a matrix row-by-row or column-by-column is sensible when getting started with matrix algebra, but you can also set the matrix up much more quickly by including the desired values in the `matrix()` function. The matrices in Key Concept 12.1 were set up like this:

```
C <- matrix(c(0,2,1,-1), 2, 2)
B <- matrix(c(1,3,-1,1), 2, 2)
A <- matrix(c(3,-1,5,2,0,-2), 3, 2)
```

This may seem obvious, but can become confusing for a large matrix (not least because the default is to fill cells column by column, starting in the top left-hand corner). Filling by rows can be accomplished by adding `byrow = TRUE` to the call:

```
C <- matrix(c(0,1,2,-1), 2, 2, byrow = TRUE)
```

It is worth calling the help record via `?matrix` if you are going to be working with matrices frequently. It is not always possible to avoid working with matrices, because many specialist functions are written for them.

Matrix algebra has a number of dedicated functions and operators. Addition, subtraction and scalar multiplication use the standard `+`, `-` and `*` operators. Matrix multiplication uses `%*%` and takes input from both matrices and vectors in R. This means that matrices with only one column or row can be defined as vectors or as matrices. The following command premultiplies `B` by `A`:

```
A %*% B
```

The transpose of a matrix is given by `t()`, the determinant by `det()`:

```
t(A)
det(B)
```

A wonderful timesaver is the `diag()` function. This creates a diagonal matrix with elements defined by its first argument. Thus

```
diag(c(4.4,2.7))
```

creates the matrix:

$$\begin{bmatrix} 4.4 & 0 \\ 0 & 2.7 \end{bmatrix}$$

This can be used to create an identity matrix by specifying one in the first argument and the number of rows or columns in the next. It also assumes that if the first argument is scalar, it is a request for an identity matrix. So a 3×3 identity matrix results from any of these commands:

```
diag(1,3,3)
diag(1,3)
diag(3)
```

If `diag()` is applied to a diagonal matrix, it extracts the elements on the main diagonal. This is useful for working with covariance matrices (see Key Concept 12.2). As they are diagonal matrices, the function will extract the variances (as a vector).

One apparent omission is that R has no matrix inverse function (though these are available in other packages). Calculating the inverse of a matrix is a very inefficient operation. The preferred option is to set up a series of linear equations to be solved simultaneously. This is can be accomplished via the `solve()` function. The first command obtains the inverse of `B` and the second premultiplies `B` by its inverse to obtain an identity matrix:

```
solve(B)
solve(B) %*% B
```

12.5.4 Multiple regression using matrix algebra (Example 12.3)

To obtain the matrix of regression coefficients requires solving $\hat{\mathbf{b}} = (\mathbf{X}'\mathbf{X})^{-1}\mathbf{X}'\mathbf{y}$. The matrix $\mathbf{X}$ for Example 12.3 was previously assigned to `X.mat`. The outcome vector $\mathbf{y}$ already exists as the vector of observed values `Y`. The following command calculates the matrix $\hat{\mathbf{b}}$ in a step-by-step fashion:

```
X.t <- t(X.mat)
XtX <- X.t %*% X.mat
XtX.inv <- solve(XtX)
XtY <- X.t %*% Y
b.mat <- XtX.inv %*% XtY
```

You could also do it all at once (at the risk of making errors):

```
b.mat <- solve(t(X.mat) %*% X.mat) %*% t(X.mat) %*% Y
```

The `t(X.mat) %*% X.mat)` step can also be simplified using the `crossprod()` function:

```
b.mat <- solve(crossprod(X.mat)) %*% t(X.mat) %*% Y
```

To get the residuals you will need to solve $\hat{\mathbf{e}} = \mathbf{y} - \mathbf{X}\hat{\mathbf{b}}$. Start by getting $\mathbf{X}\hat{\mathbf{b}}$, then use it to get the residuals:

```
Y.pred <- X.mat %*% b.mat
e.mat <- Y - Y.pred
```

The residual *SS* and error *MS* are therefore:

```
SS.resid <- sum(e.mat 2)
N <- 7
q <- 2
df.error <- N-q-1
MS.error <- SS.resid / df.error
```

Finding the asymptotic covariance matrix $\hat{\mathbf{V}}$ (the covariance matrix of the regression coefficients) requires the solution to the equation $\hat{\mathbf{V}} = (\mathbf{X}'\mathbf{X})^{-1}\hat{\sigma}^2_{error}$.

```
V.mat <- solve(t(X.mat) %*% X.mat) * MS.error
```

Use `diag()` to extract the sampling variances, and take the square root to get the *SE*s of the regression coefficients:

```
diag(V.mat)^ .5
```

12.5.5 Fitting multiple linear regression models (Example 12.4)

The `lm()` function used previously to fit simple linear regression models is a really a general linear model function. For multiple regression, a formula object with multiple predictors needs to be entered. As a basic multiple regression model involves an additive model of predictors, the formula takes the generic form `Y ~ X1 +···+ Xq` (extending the formula `Y ~ X1` from simple regression). The multiple regression model fitted laboriously earlier is obtained directly from:

```
lm(Y ~ X1 + X2)
```

R echoes this call and returns the regression coefficients as output:

```
Call:
lm(formula = Y ~ X1 + X2)

Coefficients:
(Intercept)          X1          X2
    -0.2823      2.2446      1.2277
```

A more complete view of the model is obtained from `summary()`. This reports significance tests and R^2. As with simpler linear regression, the fitted model can be assigned to an object and the object called by functions such as `AIC()`, or `summary()`. For example, consider:

```
lm.fit <- lm(Y ~ X1 + X2)
AIC(lm.fit)
summary(lm.fit)
predict(lm.fit)
qqnorm(lm.fit$residuals)
```

12.5.6 Partial correlation (Example 12.5)

The partial correlation in Example 12.5 is not difficult to calculate, though to avoid errors it may be easier to define a function to compute it:

```
r.partial <- function(r.ab, r.ac, r.bc) {
    numerator <- r.ab - r.ac * r.bc
    denominator <- ((1 - r.ac^2) * (1 - r.bc^2))^0.5
    output <- numerator/denominator
    output
}
```

The call

```
r.partial(.74, .75, .82)
```

returns 0.3301787. This isn't a particularly efficient function. To partial out multiple correlations (and for hypothesis tests) it is preferable to use matrix algebra. Several functions are available online.

12.5.7 Prediction and the hat matrix (Example 12.6)

The predicted values for the original data are given by $\hat{\mathbf{y}} = \mathbf{X}\hat{\mathbf{b}}$. Thus they can be derived directly from the matrices `X.mat` and `b.mat` or from the fitted model:

```
X.mat %*% b.mat
predict(lm(Y ~ X1 + X2))
lm(Y ~ X1 + X2)$fitted
```

The hat matrix **H** can also be used to obtain the predictions from the data:

```
H.mat <- X.mat %*% solve(crossprod(X.mat)) %*% t(X.mat)
H.mat %*% Y
```

The hat values of the data can be obtained from main diagonal of **H** or from the fitted model:

```
diag(H.mat)
hatvalues(lm(Y ~ X1 + X2))
```

Predictions for new data can be obtained as demonstrated in Example 12.6. First set up a row vector of predictor values (including constant) for the new observations:

```
X.pred <- matrix(c(1,4 ,-1), 1,3)
```

The hat value for the new observation is then calculated as:

```
H.new <- X.pred %*% solve(crossprod(X.mat)) %*% t(X.pred)
```

The predicted outcome value and its standard error are therefore:

```
Y.pred <- X.pred %*% b.mat
se.pred <- ( MS.error * (1 + H.new) )^.5
c(Y.pred, se.pred)
```

A 95% prediction interval is then:

```
moe <- qt(.975, 4) * se.pred
c(Y.pred - moe, Y.pred, Y.pred + moe)
```

A more sensible approach, where possible, is to use the `predict()` function to generate predictions from a fitted model, setting up the predictor values in a data frame (rather than a matrix) first:

```
new <- data.frame(X1 = 4, X2 = -1)
mod.fit <- lm(Y ~ X1 + X2)
predict(mod.fit, newdata = new, interval='prediction')
```

Setting up the new values to predict as a data frame can be time-consuming if you have many predictors. The `expand.grid()` function allows you to set up the data frame very easily. It creates a data frame from all combinations of a specified set of vectors:

```
new.data2 <- expand.grid(X1=seq(1,5,0.5), X2=seq(-5,5,0.5))
```

12.5.8 Collinearity diagnostics (Example 12.7 and Figure 12.3)

Most researchers will assess collinearity by looking at a correlation matrix or scatter plots of the predictors. Although this isn't the best method, it is useful for other reasons (e.g., scatter plots can reveal curvilinear relationships with the outcome). The following commands load the intention to vote data (as a `data.frame`) and produce a correlation matrix.

```
library(foreign)
av.data <- read.spss('altruism_voting.sav', to.data.frame =
  TRUE)
cor(av.data)
```

The default plot for a `data.frame` such as this is a scatter plot matrix. The scatter plot matrix in Figure 12.3 is therefore implemented by the command:

```
plot(av.data)
```

R also offers several methods for collinearity diagnostics, including the `vif()` function in the `car` package. This will work for model objects produced by `lm()` or by the more versatile `glm()` function. The commands here set up a model with all four predictors and calculate *VIF* and tolerance for the model.

```
vote.full <- lm(intention ~ close + acquaint + pressure +
  pleasure, data = av.data)
library(car)
vif(vote.full)
tolerance <- vif(vote.full)^-1
tolerance
```

To see the impact on the CIs it is worth comparing them with and without the *close* predictor. The `confint()` function is very useful here, as is the `drop1()` function. The former provides CIs for each predictor, while the latter provides model information and AIC for the model and compares it to that of models without each predictor in turn.[13] `drop1()` will also report NHSTs if requested:

```
confint(vote.full)
drop1(vote.full)
drop1(vote.full, test = 'F')

confint(lm(intention ~ . - close, data=av.data))
```

In the above example a shortcut was used. In this context, R recognizes the '.' symbol as an instruction to use all predictors from `av.data` not otherwise in the model, while the minus symbol before `close` is recognized as an instruction to drop this term from the model (see `?formula`).

Tolerance and *VIF* could also be obtained by fitting a series of linear models with each predictor taking turns as the outcome. The tolerance for the predictor selected as the outcome is equal to $1 - R^2$. To get tolerance and *VIF* for the predictor `close` therefore requires the following commands:

```
R.sq <- summary(lm(close ~ . - intention,
  data=av.data))$r.square
tol <- 1 - R.sq
VIF <- 1 / tol
VIF
```

This gives a VIF of 1.682500. An identical value was obtained, far more easily, by the earlier call to `vif()`. Note that the output from the `summary()` function is a list containing various R objects. The eighth item in the list is also a list (containing only one item) and has the name `r.squared`. The contents of this object are addressed by either of:

```
summary(lm(close ~ . - intention, data=av.data))$r.sq
summary(lm(close ~ . - intention, data=av.data))[[8]]
```

Had the command above used `[8]` rather than `[[8]]` the named list would have been assigned to the object `R.sq`. Using `[[8]]` extracts the numeric value of R^2 for subsequent calculations. The number is contained within two wrappers, and each set of square brackets 'unwraps' one of these layers. R will also match unique abbreviations of `r.squared` such as `r.sq` to the correct object.

12.5.9 Model comparisons (Example 12.8)

There are many functions to facilitate model building, updating and comparison in R. The `drop1()` function, used in the preceding section, is among the most widely used. There is also an analogous `add1()` function. These functions default to reporting AIC. Here BIC is reported in place of AIC by changing the penalty term:

```
drop1(vote.full, test = 'F', k = log(96))
```

To compare the change in R^2 between two models the `anova()` function can be used. This is useful if more than one term is dropped at a time. If the function is called using a single model it returns a 'pretty' ANOVA table (with *df*, *SS*, *MS*, *F* and *p*) broken down by individual predictors. If called by two models it reports the *df*, *SS*, *MS*, *F* and *p* for the change in R^2. Here the commands display the ANOVA table for the full model and then compare the full model with a reduced model without *close*:

```
anova(vote.full)

vote.red <- lm(intention ~ . - close, data=av.data)
anova(vote.full, vote.red)
```

To make the comparison using AIC_C requires loading the `bbmle` package again.

```
library(bbmle)
AICc(vote.full)
AICc(vote.red)
AICc(vote.red) - AICc(vote.full)
ICtab(vote.full, vote.red, weights=TRUE, base=TRUE, type=
  'AICc', nobs=96)
```

The difference in AIC_C for the models is 2.136509 in favor the reduced model. This can be turned into a form of likelihood ratio in favor the full model by the calculation:

```
exp(-2.136509/2)
```

The output of this calculation is approximately 0.34. Its reciprocal is the penalized *LR* of 2.9 in favor of the reduced model.

```
1 / exp(-2.136509/2)
```

12.5.10 R packages

Bolker, B., and R Development Core Team (2011) *bbmle*: Tools for General Maximum Likelihood Estimation. R package version 0.9.7.
Champely, S. (2009) *pwr*: Basic Functions for Power Analysis. R package version 1.1.1.
Fox, J., and Weisberg, S. (2010) *An R Companion to Applied Regression*, (2nd edn). Thousand Oaks CA: Sage.
Ligges, U., and Mächler, M. (2003) Scatterplot3d – An R Package for Visualizing Multivariate Data. *Journal of Statistical Software 8*, 1–20.
R-core members, DebRoy, S., Bivand, R., *et al.* (2011) *foreign*: Read Data Stored by Minitab, S, SAS, SPSS, Stata, Systat, dBase. R package version 0.8–42.

12.6 Notes on SPSS syntax for Chapter 12

12.6.1 Fitting multiple linear regression models in SPSS

Fitting a multiple linear regression uses the same basic syntax used to fit simple regression. To fit a regression of Y on X1 with these data you could use this syntax:

SPSS data file: table12_1.sav

```
REGRESSION
  /DESCRIPTIVES MEAN STDDEV N
  /STATISTICS COEFF R ANOVA CI(95) SELECTION
  /NOORIGIN
  /DEPENDENT Y
  /METHOD=ENTER X1.
```

A quick alternative is to paste the syntax after setting up the regression menus via: <Analyze> selecting <Regression> and <Linear . . . >. This gives the flexibility to add subcommands such as SELECTION (which reports AIC and BIC). The /DESCRIPTIVES statistics subcommand is a sensible choice here because for any regression it is useful to know the mean and *SD* of each variable when interpreting unstandardized coefficients (the minimum and maximum would also be handy but need to be obtained through other commands).

To run a multiple regression, additional predictors can be added to the /METHOD subcommand. For the moment the goal is to show how the orthogonal predictors account for separate portions of the total sample *SS*. One way to do this is to run the command as a sequential model, entering the two predictors as separate blocks.

```
REGRESSION
  /DESCRIPTIVES MEAN STDDEV CORR SIG N
  /STATISTICS COEFF R ANOVA CHANGE
  /DEPENDENT Y
  /METHOD=ENTER X1
  /METHOD=ENTER X2.
```

Adding the CORR argument to the /DESCRIPTIVES subcommand also confirms the zero correlation between X1 and X2. Repeating the analysis and changing the order of the last two subcommands (entering X2 before X1) would confirm that the coefficients are for orthogonal predictors and unaffected by the order of entry. CIs, prediction intervals and leverage (hat values) are obtained as per simple linear regression. R^2 and adjusted R^2 are part of the general default output.

Using the REGRESSION command allows residuals (e.g., raw or standardized), influence statistics or predictions to be saved. Residual plots are easily obtained from saved residuals using PPLOT. SPSS regression also has good options for collinearity diagnostics. If running multiple regression with two or more predictors added simultaneously it is sensible to request collinearity diagnostics by adding the TOL statement to the /STATISTICS subcommand.

```
REGRESSION
  /DESCRIPTIVES MEAN STDDEV CORR SIG N
  /STATISTICS COEFF R ANOVA TOL
  /DEPENDENT Y
  /METHOD=ENTER X1 X2.
```

In this case the tolerance and *VIF* are necessarily both one because the predictors are orthogonal. Additional collinearity diagnostics can be requested by including `COLLIN`.

SPSS can also provide simple, partial and semi-partial correlations for each predictor with the response (via `/STATISTICS ZPP`). The simple correlation between predictor and response is labeled the 'zero-order' correlation and the semi-partial correlation is labeled a 'part' correlation. A partial correlation command also exists. To get the correlation between `X1` and `Y` partialing out `X2` use the syntax:

```
PARTIAL CORR
  /VARIABLES=X1 Y BY X2.
```

12.7 Bibliography and further reading

Cohen, J., Cohen, P., West, S. G., and Aiken, L. S. (2003) *Applied Multiple Regression/Correlation Analysis for the Behavioral Sciences*. Mahwah, NJ: Erlbaum.

Gelman, A., and Hill, J. (2007) *Data Analysis using Regression and Multilevel/Hierarchical Models*. Cambridge: Cambridge University Press.

Snedecor, G. W., and Cochran, W. G. (1989) *Statistical Methods* (8th edn) Ames, IA: Iowa State University Press.

13
ANOVA and ANCOVA with independent measures

Contents

13.1 Chapter overview

This chapter introduces analysis of variance (ANOVA) and analysis of covariance (ANCOVA) as special cases of regression involving categorical predictors. The chapter starts by considering the impact of dummy and effect coding schemes on a regression model with a single categorical predictor (factor). Emphasis is on the one-way (one factor) ANOVA model with independent measures, including the problem of multiple comparisons and its application to pairwise comparisons following ANOVA. The final section introduces one-way ANCOVA as a method of increasing the power of one-way ANOVA or as a statistical control for confounding variables.

13.2 ANOVA and ANCOVA as special cases of regression

The independent *t* test is a special case of simple linear regression where the predictor is dichotomous. The trick to representing a two independent group design in this way is to find an appropriate coding scheme for the grouping variable (the categorical predictor representing group membership). The default choice is dummy coding, in which group membership is represented by a dichotomous predictor taking the value zero or one. Alternatives to dummy coding are available and allow you to alter the way group differences are represented while preserving the integrity of the overall regression model.

Regression with categorical predictors is not limited to single dichotomous categories. The approach that works for a dichotomous variable – coding the categories via a notionally continuous predictor – will also work for additional variables or categories. Despite this relatively simple way to incorporate categorical predictors in a regression model, it is not as widely employed as might be expected. The reasons for this are largely historical. Researchers working with simple experimental designs (looking at differences between groups) applied, developed and disseminated specialized methods for dealing with categorical predictors. These statistical models have their own terminology. Foremost among these are *analysis of variance* (ANOVA) and *analysis of covariance* (ANCOVA).

From a general linear model perspective, ANOVA is a special case of multiple linear regression with orthogonal, categorical predictors. ANCOVA is an ANOVA-style regression model that adds one or more covariates. A *covariate*, in this context, is simply a continuous predictor (and these need not be orthogonal with respect to the categorical predictors). These labels, ANOVA and ANCOVA, are often deployed more loosely. Software packages may use the terms in different ways, and users may attach those labels to the subsequent analysis (even if the label is not particularly informative). These labels are sometimes misleading or imprecise. Nevertheless, it seems reasonable to label a regression with only categorical predictors as ANOVA, provided the predictors are orthogonal (or nearly orthogonal). The label ANCOVA is reasonable if a covariate is also present, and the label multiple regression is appropriate if all predictors are continuous. While each of these models could be classified as multiple regression (or as a general linear model), the specialist ANOVA and ANCOVA terminology can help communicate the design of a study or the details of a statistical model.

13.2.1 Dummy coding versus effect coding

There are a number of ways to code categorical predictors, but dummy coding and *effect coding* are the most widely employed. In dummy coding the groups or categories are coded zero or one. For a two independent group design with a single predictor this produces a regression model, first introduced in Equation 5.40, in which $\hat{\mu}_0$ is the mean of the group coded zero and $\hat{\mu}_1$ is the mean of the group coded one:

$$y_i = \hat{\mu}_0 + (\hat{\mu}_1 - \hat{\mu}_0)x_i + e_i$$

This model fixes the intercept as the mean of one of the two groups and the slope as the difference between the group means.

Effect coding is a popular alternative to dummy coding in ANOVA and ANCOVA models. For effect coding with a dichotomous predictor, the groups are coded as −1 or 1. This produces a regression model of the form:

$$y_i = \hat{\mu}_{grand} + b_1 x_i + e_i \qquad \text{Equation 13.1}$$

In this parameterization of the model, the intercept is the grand mean (or a weighted grand mean for designs with unequal n per group).[1] The slope in the two group case under effect coding is equal to half the difference in means:

$$y_i = \hat{\mu}_{grand} + 1/2\,(\hat{\mu}_1 - \hat{\mu}_2)x_i + e_i \qquad \text{Equation 13.2}$$

This may seem odd, but it is a trivial consequence of the coding scheme. The difference between −1 and 1 is two, whereas the difference between zero and one is one. A regression slope is expected change in Y for a one-unit increase in X (with any other predictors held constant). The half-group mean difference in slope for a one-unit change under effect coding is equivalent to the slope for dummy coding because the groups are two units apart in the effect coded model and one unit apart in the dummy coded model.

The different interpretation of the slopes can be slightly annoying, and it is common practice with effect coded models (and ANOVA in general) to report and interpret the group means rather than the slopes. This is legitimate because the t or F test of the difference in means is always equivalent to the t or F test of the slope. Although the slope is only half the difference in means, this does not matter. The change in scale imposed by effect coding also changes $\hat{\sigma}_{b_1}$ by the same factor.[2] A potentially neater (but less common) solution is to use the codes −0.5 and 0.5 to identify the groups. This forces the slope to be exactly the difference in groups (because the difference between 0.5 and −0.5 is one unit). If you use specialist software to fit ANOVA models the choice of coding scheme will rarely matter, and may even be hidden from you. ANOVA software typically presents output in terms of the group means (rather than intercepts and slopes). Moreover, if the software uses a general linear model solution it may employ one of several different, but equivalent, parameterizations for ANOVA or ANCOVA models (Green *et al.*, 1999; Kirk, 1995).

One additional property of effect coding is worth stating here. In the two group case, effect coding is equivalent to centering applied to dummy coded predictors (with equal n per group). This is most obvious with the −0.5 versus 0.5 coding version. As the mean of the dummy codes is 0.5 then centering a dummy coded predictor gives values of $(0 - 0.5) = -0.5$ and $(1 - 0.5) = 0.5$.

Effect coding is particularly useful when there are many predictors in the model. To see why, it is instructive to compare coding schemes for a categorical predictor with J categories when $J > 2$. Each coding scheme requires the categories to be represented by $J - 1$ dichotomous indicator variables. Under dummy coding, one category is designated the reference category and always

Table 13.1 Dummy codes for a categorical variable with three categories, representing an independent groups design with groups *G*1, *G*2 and *G*3

Participant	**Group**	**Group 2**	**Group 3**
1	*G*1	0	0
2	*G*2	1	0
3	*G*3	0	1
4	*G*1	0	0
...	...	...	...

receives the code zero.[3] The remaining $J - 1$ categories are represented by one of the $J - 1$ predictors. Apart from the reference category, each predictor is coded one for observations that fall into that category and coded zero when observations fall into another category.

To code three categories therefore requires two predictors. This might be appropriate for an independent groups design with three groups (e.g., two experimental groups and a control). The three groups (*G*1, *G*2 and *G*3) could then be coded as set out in Table 13.1.

It is sensible to label a dummy coded predictor according to the category or group that it codes for. In Table 13.1 *G*1 is the reference group and the dummy variables are labeled *G*2 and *G*3. When $J = 2$, the choice of reference category is largely unimportant (it decides the sign of the slope and determines which category mean is the intercept). For $J > 2$ it can make a difference to tests of individual predictors. This is one motive for switching to effect coding, where the choice is less important.

Effect coding with $J > 2$ categories works in a similar fashion, except that the reference category is coded as -1 for all predictors. This is not as intuitive as dummy coding, but a concrete example may help. Table 13.2 shows the same three-group design as Table 13.1, but with effect coding.

With dummy coding it is reasonably clear that the intercept represents the expected or predicted value of the reference group. If no other predictors are in the model (e.g., when $J = 2$) the intercept will be the reference group mean. If no other predictors are in an effect coded model, the intercept of the regression becomes the grand mean when the categories have equal n (and a weighted mean otherwise). This occurs because the intercept is the value of Y when all predictors are zero. As no category takes the value zero across all predictors, the intercept can't assume the value of any of the category means. All regression lines pass through the mean

Table 13.2 Effect codes for a categorical variable with three categories, representing an independent groups design with groups *G*1, *G*2 and *G*3

Participant	**Group**	**G2 effect code**	**G3 effect code**
1	*G*1	−1	−1
2	*G*2	1	0
3	*G*3	0	1
4	*G*1	−1	−1
...	...	...	...

of X and the mean of Y. Just as centered predictors (predictors with a mean of zero) force the intercept to be equal to the grand mean, effect coded predictors force the intercept to take this value (because it minimizes the squared deviations from the category means).

Effect coding might seem cumbersome, but has several advantages. First, it can sometimes make a model easier to interpret when collinear predictors are entered into a model. Centering a continuous predictor has a similar effect. Second, effect coding is often a natural choice for models where there is no obvious reference group. The slopes for each predictor represent differences not from the reference group, but from the overall grand or weighted mean. This is why, when $J = 2$, the slope is half the difference between means. Assuming equal n, the grand mean lies exactly halfway between the two category means (and in this special case effect coding is a form of centering). These advantages are particularly important for more complex ANOVA and ANCOVA models (and are less obvious for the models with a single categorical predictor).

These differences are solely to do with the interpretation of the model and the specific differences in levels that a researcher is interested in. Dummy coding is often selected when one of the categories is a control or baseline condition. For exploratory work – particularly with complex models – a good strategy is to try more than one coding scheme to determine which works best (as long as the focus is on interpretation rather than hunting for statistical significance). The choice of coding scheme has no impact on the overall model. It only matters when interpreting the coefficients of individual predictors (and their tests), as the coding scheme may not match up neatly with the questions you are interested in.

Several common mistakes occur when incorporating categorical predictors with either form of coding. One mistake is to add J indicator variables as predictors (one for each category). This won't work because it guarantees that the set of J predictors will be perfectly collinear and therefore the regression model can't be fitted.[4] Less common, but probably more dangerous, is that researchers will drop one of a set of $J - 1$ indicators from a model (e.g., because it is statistically non-significant). This is potentially problematic because it leaves one of the categories uncoded. Its effects are then subsumed under the reference category. The reference categories may then no longer have a clear interpretation. It is usually better to add or drop the indicators as a set, and to assess their effect using the overall change in model fit, rather than interpret them as individual predictors. If there are too many categories it is possible to merge some, but categories created this way should be meaningful where possible (e.g., two similar treatments might be merged for comparison with a control).

A drawback of effect coding is that it is occasionally awkward to interpret the parameter estimates in a standard multiple regression. With dummy coding there are parameters representing the differences of all the category means from the reference category (given by the intercept). For effect coding, the intercept represents a different quantity (the mean of Y when all predictors are zero). This means that the reference group mean has to be calculated from the regression equation in a rather round-about way. A quicker solution, depending on your software, is to run a separate regression using a different reference category. The solution adopted in practice is to use specialist software for setting up and running ANOVA and ANCOVA models. Often this involves running a regression or general linear model with some (possibly all) of the messy details hidden from view. Most specialist software also has options for defining a variable as categorical (or for switching dummy or effect coding). It is only rarely necessary to set up dummy or effect codes by hand for an analysis. One further option is the *cell means model* (see Box 13.1). This involves modeling the category means directly and has some advantages over dummy or effect coding.

Example 13.1 Wenzel (2004) carried out a small experiment investigating the effect of different types of diagrams on learning from text. Subsequent examples will refer to this data set as the diagram data. She gave 40 participants a short, four-paragraph text description of how SCUBA diving equipment works. Participants were assigned at random to one of four conditions: *text* (presenting the four paragraphs on separate pages), *picture* (presenting the text alongside a picture of a SCUBA diver), *full diagram* (presenting the text alongside a labeled diagram depicting SCUBA equipment) and *segmented diagram* (presenting a relevant part of the full diagram on each of the four pages). The principal hypotheses were: 1) that diagrams (but not pictures) would facilitate learning and 2) that learning would be better for segmented diagrams than for the full diagram. After a short delay, learning was measured by asking participants to write a brief explanation of how the SCUBA equipment worked. This was scored for description quality (using a method called propositional analysis), and this produced scores ranging from 7 to 38 in the sample.

Table 13.3 shows the mean description quality (*descript*) by condition and the dummy and effect coded indicators for each group. The text condition is adopted as the reference category for both coding schemes. This is an obvious choice because it is a control or baseline condition. Either coding scheme involves adding $J-1=3$ indicator variables as predictors to a regression model with *descript* as the outcome.

Table 13.3 Dummy and effect indicator codes and mean description quality scores by group for the diagram data

Group	M	Dummy codes	Effect codes
Text	17.8	{0, 0, 0}	{−1, −1, −1}
Picture	18.3	{1, 0, 0}	{ 1, 0, 0}
Full diagram	22.4	{0, 1, 0}	{ 0, 1, 0}
Segmented diagram	27.3	{0, 0, 1}	{ 0, 0, 1}

The regression model can be summarized as $R^2 = .193$, $F_{3,36} = 2.87$, $MS_{error} = 67.78$, $p < .05$. Although statistically significant, it does not provide particularly convincing evidence of an effect. The difference in AIC_C between a model with all three indicator variables and an intercept-only model (with the same mean for each group) only weakly favors the more complex model ($\Delta AIC_C = 1.14$, $LR_{AIC_C} = 1.8$).

To appreciate the difference between the coding schemes it is necessary to look at the individual coefficients for the model. The prediction equation for the dummy coded predictors is:

$$\hat{Y}_{descript} = 17.8 + 0.5X_{picture} + 4.6X_{full} + 9.5_{segmented}$$

The text condition is the reference group so the expected description quality for that condition is 17.8 (the intercept). The other regression coefficients represent the difference between each group mean and the text group mean (e.g., the picture group mean of 18.3 − 17.8 produces its coefficient of 0.5). You can therefore reconstruct all four group means using the prediction equation. The *t* tests of individual predictors in this regression model are tests of the differences between each of the group means and the reference group mean.

For the effect coded regression the prediction equation is:

$$\hat{Y}_{descript} = 21.45 - 3.15X_{picture} + 0.95X_{full} + 5.85X_{segmented}$$

In this model, the intercept is the grand mean. In a balanced (equal n) design such as this, it is the sum of the group means divided by the number of groups: $(17.8 + 18.3 + 22.4 + 27.3)/4$. The coefficients therefore represent differences between the means of the groups and the grand mean. However, as there is no coefficient for the reference group (the text group) it is slightly harder to determine its mean than under dummy coding. One option is to rerun the regression with a difference reference category. It can also be worked out by subtraction. The deviations from the grand mean must sum to zero. As the total for the three coded groups is $-3.15 + 0.95 + 5.85 = 3.65$, it implies the reference group mean must be $21.45 - 3.65 = 17.8$. Fitting a cell means model would provide the four means directly (see Box 13.1).

13.3 One-way analysis of variance with independent measures

A one-way analysis of variance can be thought of as a regression model with a single categorical predictor that has least two (and usually three or more) categories. ANOVA has as a separate history as a statistical method and its own specialized terminology. In a traditional application of ANOVA the data are from a designed experiment with appropriate randomization controls and a single independent variable (IV). The IV is a categorical predictor coding for different experimental conditions and the aim of the analysis to determine how these influence a continuous dependent variable (DV).

In such a study, the terms IV and DV are applied in the strict sense of referring to a predictor manipulated by the experimenter and an outcome that can be interpreted as causally dependent on the manipulated variable. For reasons that will become apparent, the IV in ANOVA is usually termed a *factor* and the values it takes are the *levels* of that factor. An experiment with two independent groups is an example of a single factor ANOVA design with two levels (e.g., control and experimental). Hence 'one-way' is short-hand for 'one factor'. Adding factors creates two-way, three-way or higher order ANOVA designs. In an *independent measures* or *between groups* design each sampling unit – assumed to be a person unless stated – provides a single data point. In a true experiment, the sampling units are also randomly allocated to conditions, though independent measures ANOVA is not restricted to true experiments (e.g., it is frequently applied if sampling units are not randomly allocated to conditions or where the factor is not manipulated by an experimenter).

A one-way ANOVA therefore has a single factor with J levels (corresponding to the groups in an independent measures design). Regardless of whether dummy or effect coding is employed, the general form of this regression model for a categorical factor with J levels is:

$$y_i = b_0 + b_1x_{1,i} + \ldots + b_{J-1}x_{J-1,i} + e_i \qquad \text{Equation 13.3}$$

This model is identical to the standard parameterization of a multiple regression model with $J - 1$ predictors; the only difference is that X_1 to X_{J-1} are dichotomous categorical predictors rather than continuous ones. For the reasons discussed earlier, effect coding is often the preferred choice of coding scheme in ANOVA. However, representing the regression model in this way (with the standard regression parameterization) is a little inconvenient.

A more elegant parameterization of the one-way ANOVA model represents the group means as deviations from the grand mean by grouping their coefficients under a single term in the equation:

$$y_{ij} = \mu_{grand} + \tau_j + \varepsilon_{ij} \qquad \text{Equation 13.4}$$

In this equation i is the index of observations within each level of the factor (ranging from one to n) and j is the index of the J levels of the factor (ranging from one to J).

The τ_j term therefore represents the deviation of each of the J levels from μ. In a balanced design, each of the J levels has the same sample size ($n_1 = n_2 \ldots = n_j$) and μ is the grand mean. Figure 13.1 illustrates the deviations represented by the τ_j term for a one-way ANOVA of the diagram data. The grand mean is 21.45 and the level means are 17.8, 18.3, 22.4 and 27.3. Thus $\tau_1 = -3.65$, $\tau_2 = -3.15$, $\tau_3 = 0.95$ and $\tau_4 = 5.8$. This fits together fairly neatly except for one problem. Under this parameterization $J + 1$ parameters (the four τ parameters and μ_{grand}) are estimated for J level means. This kind of model doesn't have a unique solution because the predictors are perfectly collinear. An infinite number of 'correct' solutions to fitting the model are possible; any four numbers could be used as parameter estimates by adjusting the fifth parameter so that

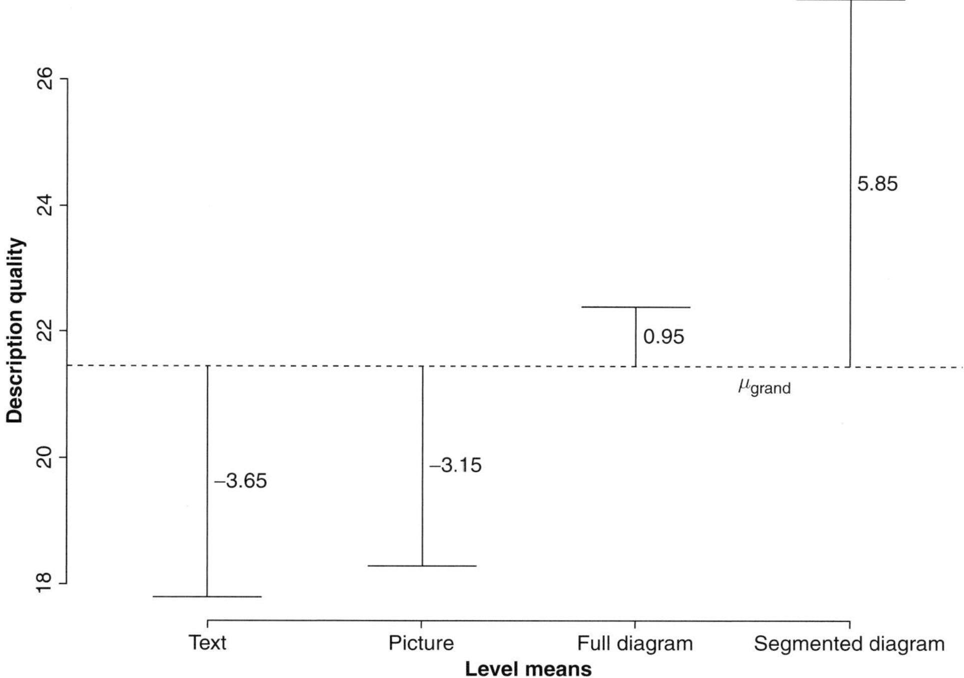

Figure 13.1 Deviations of level means from grand mean for a one-way ANOVA of the diagram data

they sum to zero. This problem is solved in the 'sigma-restricted' parameterization of a general linear model by adding a constraint to the model. This constraint is that the values of τ sum to zero:

$$\sum_{j=1}^{J} \tau_j = 0 \qquad \text{Equation 13.5}$$

This solves the problem because only $J-1$ level means are free to vary. The last level mean is forced to take on the only value that produces a total of zero. A similar trick can be used to fit a general linear model with dummy coded predictors. This leads to the 'overparameterized' general linear model that is implemented in several popular statistics packages (Green *et al.*, 1999).

This grouping of effects in ANOVA is also reflected in the ANOVA table and tests. The ANOVA table for one-way independent measures ANOVA is shown in Table 13.4a. This table follows the standard structure for a regression model, but is likely to be labeled differently. For one-way independent measures ANOVA the sources of variance are often labeled with the terms 'between groups' (for the variance associated with the effects of the factor) and 'within groups' for the error. This is because the sum of squares for the factor is calculated by considering deviations between group means. The residual sum of squares is made up of what is left: deviations within the groups.

Table 13.4b shows how each element of the ANOVA table is calculated. This is not much different from a regular multiple regression. It appears slightly different because the *df* terms are usually defined differently in ANOVA and regression. One-way ANOVA uses the number of levels J, whereas multiple regression employs the number of predictors q. Thus df_{factor} is $J-1$ because the J levels require $q=J-1$ predictors and df_{error} is the difference between df_{total} and df_{factor} which is $(N-1)-(J-1)=N-1-J+1=N-J$. The apparent difference is illusory

Table 13.4a ANOVA table for a one-way ANOVA with independent measures

Source	***df***	***SS***	***MS***	***F***
Factor (between groups)	df_{factor}	SS_{factor}	MS_{factor}	F_{factor}
Error (within groups)	df_{error}	$SS_{residual}$	MS_{error}	
Total	df_{total}	SS_{total}		

Table 13.4b Formulas for a one-way ANOVA with independent measures and J levels

Source	***df***	***SS***	***MS***	***F***
Factor (between groups)	$J-1$	SS_{factor}	$\frac{SS_{factor}}{df_{factor}}$	$\frac{MS_{factor}}{MS_{error}}$
Error (within groups)	$N-J$	$SS_{residual}$	$\frac{SS_{residual}}{df_{error}}$	
Total	$N-1$	SS_{total}		

(because $J-1=q$ and so $N-J=N-q-1$). Given all this, the switch to ANOVA terminology may seem pointless. There are a couple of reasons why it is not. Many experimental researchers use ANOVA almost exclusively, so the terminology is widely used in published work. In addition, ANOVA model and associated terminology becomes more useful in designs with several factors.

As this is a reparameterized multiple regression model, *SS*, *MS* and *F* can be determined using standard regression methods. However, a balanced ANOVA design with equal *n* per level has orthogonal factors. This permits simpler solutions. If *n* is unequal, the factors will no longer be orthogonal and it is usually better to use regression solutions to fit the ANOVA model.

13.3.1 Partitioning variance in orthogonal ANOVA models

If ANOVA predictors are orthogonal it is possible to decompose the total *SS* neatly into non-overlapping components, a process known as *partitioning variance*. Textbook ANOVA formulas are usually optimized for hand calculation. Rearranging the equations in this way can conceal the conceptual basis for them. Cohen (2002) proposes a good compromise: formulas that help reveal the concepts behind the equations, but that use familiar quantities such as $\hat{\sigma}$ in their calculation. The formulas below are adapted from his proposal.[5]

Assuming equal *n* per level, the overall *N* must be $n \times J$ (because in this design each sampling unit (e.g., a participant) contributes only one data point. As *df* are also derived from *n* and *J*, this leaves the sums of squares and mean squares. *SS* for the factor (between groups) is calculated from the squared deviations of the level means from the grand mean. This is the same as calculating *SS* as if the level means were a sample of *J* data points (because their mean will be equal to the grand mean). The *MS* for the factor is simply the *SS* divided by $J-1$. This is equivalent to calculating the variance for a sample consisting of the level means (rather than the raw scores), with *J* acting as the number of 'data points'. A formula for hand calculation of the MS_{factor} is therefore:

$$MS_{factor} = \frac{n\sum_{j=1}^{J}\left(\hat{\mu}_j - \hat{\mu}_{grand}\right)^2}{J-1} = n\hat{\sigma}^2_{means} \qquad \text{Equation 13.6}$$

Thus $\hat{\sigma}^2_{means}$ is the variance of the *J* level means calculated using the usual inferential formula multiplied by *n* (the sample size per group or level). As $\hat{\sigma}_{means}$ is the inferential standard deviation calculated for the group means (rather than raw scores), any statistics package, spreadsheet or calculator that has a function for $\hat{\sigma}$ can be used to obtain this number. The corresponding sum of squares for the factor is:

$$SS_{factor} = n\sum_{j=1}^{J}\left(\hat{\mu}_j - \hat{\mu}_{grand}\right)^2 = n\,(J-1)\,\hat{\sigma}^2_{means} \qquad \text{Equation 13.7}$$

$SS_{residual}$ is the sum of the squared residuals. The residuals of a regression are defined as $y_{ij} - \hat{y}_{ij}$ (the observed minus predicted values of the outcome, and for one-way ANOVA the predictions are the level means ($\hat{\mu}_j$). As the deviations from the level means are also used to compute $\hat{\sigma}_j$ (the standard deviation of the $j=1\ldots J$ levels), it is possible to go directly from the sample variances (squared standard deviations) to MS_{error}. The ANOVA estimate of error variance is the arithmetic mean of the sample variances of the J levels:

$$MS_{error} = \frac{\sum_{j=1}^{J} \hat{\sigma}_j^2}{J} \qquad \text{Equation 13.8}$$

As $\hat{\sigma}_j^2$ represents the error variance within each sample, this is a pooled variance estimate similar to that used to calculate an independent t test, and identical to it when $J = 2$ (see Key Concept 3.3). Because this is an estimate of population error it makes sense to average across the J independent levels to increase accuracy. This pooled estimate is suitable as long as each group is sampled from a population with the same variance. Independent measures ANOVA therefore makes the same homogeneity of variance assumption as independent t (or indeed a least squares regression model, where error variance is assumed constant for all predictor values). The usual regression assumptions of independent, normal residuals also apply.

These terms are sufficient to populate an ANOVA table. For completeness, the sum of squares for the error term is given by:

$$SS_{residual} = (N - J)\frac{\sum_{j=1}^{J} \hat{\sigma}_j^2}{J} = (N - J)\, MS_{error} \qquad \text{Equation 13.9}$$

The total sum of squares can be obtained from $\hat{\sigma}_Y$ (the inferential SD of Y):

$$SS_{total} = (N - 1)\, \hat{\sigma}_Y^2 \qquad \text{Equation 13.10}$$

These quantities provide a check for hand calculation (because $SS_{residual}$ and SS_{factor} must sum to SS_{total}).

13.3.2 Effect size, model fit and inference

The overall R^2 for independent measures ANOVA is $1 - SS_{residual}$ (as it is for any least squares regression). Several specialized standardized effect size measures also exist for ANOVA. The best known are η^2 (eta-squared) and η_p^2 (partial eta-squared). The former is defined as

$$\eta^2 = \frac{SS_{factor}}{SS_{total}} \qquad \text{Equation 13.11}$$

and the latter is

$$\eta_p^2 = \frac{SS_{factor}}{SS_{factor} + SS_{residual}} \qquad \text{Equation 13.12}$$

In a one-way ANOVA with independent measures $SS_{total} = SS_{factor} + SS_{residual}$. Consequently, R^2, η^2 and η_p^2 all take the same value. This equivalence does not hold for other ANOVA designs. Reservations about working with standardized effect size metrics should be borne in mind, but it is worth emphasizing two here. First, ANOVA effects often have multiple *df* and are therefore hard to interpret. Effects with the same observed effect size statistic (e.g., $\eta^2 = .193$) may represent entirely different patterns or direction of effect. Second, R^2, η^2 and η_p^2 are descriptive measures rather than population estimates.

Hays (1973) proposed a population estimate of proportion of variance explained known as ω^2 (omega-squared). This can be estimated either from *SS* and *MS* or from the observed *F* test statistic for the factor:

$$\omega^2 \approx \frac{SS_{factor} - (J-1)\,MS_{error}}{SS_{total} + MS_{error}} = \frac{F-1}{F + \left(\frac{N-(J-1)}{J-1}\right)} \qquad \text{Equation 13.13}$$

This estimate tends to be somewhat smaller than η^2 (which may partly explain why it is less widely reported). The main alternative to standardized effect size metrics is to look at the simple differences between means or relative to a common reference point (e.g., the grand mean or the mean of a control group) in the original units of measurement. Simple effect size metrics are particularly appropriate for designed experiments or quasi-experiments where the categorical predictors may be measured without error. Variance explained measures are nevertheless very useful for sample size calculations (provided the study for which power or sample size is calculated is sufficiently similar in design to that used to estimate the effect size). For instance, η_p^2 is a squared partial correlation coefficient and is related to Cohen's f^2:

$$f^2 = \frac{\eta_p^2}{1 - \eta_p^2} \qquad \text{Equation 13.14}$$

This quantity is convenient for power or sample size estimates in some software (e.g., G*Power – see Faul *et al.*, 2007). For a factor with only two levels f^2 is also related to the descriptive standardized mean difference: $f = d/2$.

The effect of the factor in ANOVA, often termed a *main effect*, is tested using an *F* ratio. In one-way independent measures ANOVA this is equivalent to the *F* ratio for the test of the model in multiple regression (because the effect coded predictors are the only predictors in the model):

$$F_{J-1,N-J} = \frac{MS_{factor}}{MS_{error}} \qquad \text{Equation 13.15}$$

This is an estimate of the ratio of the population variances:

$$\frac{\sigma^2_{factor} + \sigma^2_E}{\sigma^2_E}$$

As σ^2_{factor} depends on the differences between means of the factor levels in the population ($\mu_1 \ldots \mu_j$) this term will be zero if there are no differences between them (in which case the expected *F* ratio is one). For this reason the *F* ratio in one-way ANOVA can be used to test the null hypothesis: H_0: $\mu_1 = \mu_{2=} \ldots = \mu_j$. This is termed an *omnibus* test of the differences among level means (and hence the factor). If H_0 is rejected, it is taken as support for the alternative hypothesis (H_1) that the *J* means are not all equal. The *main effect* of the factor is therefore a sort of pooled or average effect across all levels.

Although ANOVA is usually accompanied by significance tests, other inferential tools such as AIC_C and BIC may be employed. One way to do this is to adjust a likelihood ratio (*LR*) for model complexity. As many ANOVA packages do not report R^2, it is convenient to express the *LR* in terms of sums of squares (which do tend to be reported). The usual comparison of interest in a one-way design is between a model corresponding to the null hypothesis of equal level means and an alternative hypothesis of unequal means. This likelihood ratio, in terms of the *SS* for the one-way model, is:

$$LR_{H_1/H_0} = \left(\frac{SS_{total}}{SS_{error}}\right)^{\frac{N}{2}} \qquad \text{Equation 13.16}$$

Adjusting for model complexity gives the AIC_C adjustment as:

$$LR_{AIC_C} = \left(\frac{SS_{total}}{SS_{error}}\right)^{\frac{N}{2}} \times e^{k_{reduced}\left(\frac{N}{N-k_{reduced}-1}\right)-k_{full}\left(\frac{N}{N-k_{full}-1}\right)} \qquad \text{Equation 13.17}$$

Once more, k is the full number of parameters for each model (and equal to $J+1$ in one-way ANOVA). The corresponding BIC adjustment is:

$$LR_{BIC} = \left(\frac{SS_{total}}{SS_{error}}\right)^{\frac{N}{2}} \times \left(e^{J_{reduced}-J_{full}}\right)^{ln(N)/2} \qquad \text{Equation 13.18}$$

Glover and Dixon (2004) provide examples of how to calculate these statistics from information in an ANOVA table (as well as how to extend these tests to test other plausible hypotheses).

Example 13.2 Table 13.5 shows raw description quality (*descript*) scores for the diagram data. As this is a balanced design, it is possible to use Cohen's formulas to show the relationships between the summary statistics calculated from these data and the ANOVA table.

Table 13.5 Raw description quality score by group for the diagram data

i	Text only	Picture	Full diagram	Segmented diagram
1	35	16	9	20
2	13	15	31	23
3	20	19	28	14
4	15	17	22	35
5	17	10	17	17
6	15	25	38	35
7	28	16	9	37
8	7	32	30	28
9	11	17	15	36
10	17	16	25	28
$\hat{\mu}_j$	17.80	18.30	22.40	27.30
$\hat{\sigma}_j$	8.22	6.07	9.75	8.46
$\hat{\sigma}_j^2$	67.51	36.90	95.16	71.57

The mean square for the group factor is the variance of the sample means multiplied by n.

$$MS_{factor} = \frac{n\sum_{j=1}^{J}(\hat{\mu}_j - \hat{\mu}_{grand})^2}{J-1} = n\hat{\sigma}^2_{means} = 10 \times 19.45667 \approx 194.57$$

SS_{factor} is arrived by multiplying the mean square for the factor by its df. This is $3 \times 194.57 = 583.7$. MS_{error} is the average of the sample variances of the four groups:

$$MS_{errror} = \frac{\sum_{j=1}^{J}\hat{\sigma}_j^2}{J} \approx \frac{67.51 + 36.90 + 95.16 + 71.57}{4} \approx 67.8$$

SS for the error term requires multiplying through by the df which are $(n-1)J = 36$. $SS_{residual}$ is therefore 2440.8 (though some rounding error has crept in; the value from R is 2440.2). The total SS can be calculated from the variance for all 40 raw scores. As $\hat{\sigma} = 8.805$ for the raw description quality scores, the total sum of squares is therefore:

$$SS_{total} = (N-1)\,\sigma_Y^2 = (40-1) \times 8.805^2 = 39 \times 77.528 \approx 3023.6$$

This is close to the exact value of 3023.9 from R. The ratio of MS_{factor} to MS_{error} provides the F test statistic: $194.6/67.8 = 2.87$. The results are summarized in Table 13.6.

Table 13.6 One-way ANOVA table for the diagram data

Source	***df***	***SS***	***MS***	***F***	***p***
Group	3	583.7	194.6	2.87	.050
Error	36	2440.8	67.8		
Total	39	3023.6			

The test could be reported as:

$$F_{3,36} = 2.87, MS_{error} = 67.8, p = .05.$$

This test is statistically significant and overall R^2 for the model is $583.7/3023.6 = .193$. As this is a one-way ANOVA with independent measures, R^2 is identical to η^2 and η^2_p. The adjusted R^2 of .126 provides a population statistic for the whole model. A population estimate of proportion of variance explained is:

$$\omega^2 \approx \frac{F-1}{F + \left(\frac{N-(J-1)}{J-1}\right)} = \frac{2.87-1}{2.87 + \left(\frac{40-(4-1)}{4-1}\right)} = .123$$

This is similar to the adjusted R^2. If there is only one factor, both statistics are forms of population estimate for proportion of variance explained by the model.

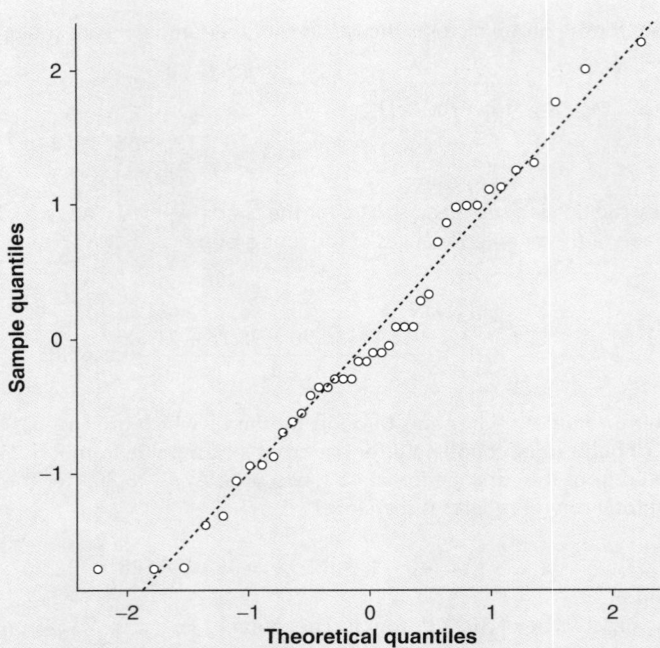

Figure 13.2 Normal probability plot of standardized residuals for one-way ANOVA of the diagram data

Several standard diagnostic checks for regression can be applied in one-way ANOVA. Figure 13.2 shows the normal probability plot for the standardized residuals of the ANOVA model. The plot shows no evidence of extreme observations and, given the small sample size, the residuals are not too far off those expected from a normal distribution. There is some squashing of the distribution at the bottom end (very likely a floor effect for participants with scores close to zero) and some 'cyclic' curvature around the line. The latter may be due to the discrete nature of the description quality measure (which can only be scored as whole numbers). The residuals are not too far off normal, and are probably acceptable. The *SD*s of the groups are similar; homogeneity of variance does not appear to be seriously violated.

No single observation is particularly influential. This is not too surprising. The residuals in Figure 13.2 are not large, and categorical predictors tend to produce modest leverage scores. The greatest influence is for the score of 35, observed in the text condition for participant one. Cook's distance for this point is 0.135 (lower than would trigger serious concern).

Although proportion of variance explained measures are of limited value in interpreting models, they can simplify sample size and statistical power calculations. The usual effect size estimate in these cases is Cohen's *f*, calculated from η_p^2 for a single factor (or from R^2 for the overall model). Thus *f* for both model and factor is:

$$f = \sqrt{\frac{.193}{1 - 1.93}} \approx 0.49$$

This value can be employed to calculate power for a near-identical replication. In this case a replication with $n=20$ per group, $\alpha=.05$ and $f=0.49$ would have statistical power of .96 (e.g., calculated using G*Power). As the sample size is small, the effect may be a slight overestimate. It is good practice to check the sensitivity of power to smaller effect sizes. A more conservative estimate of $f=0.40$ and $n=20$ per group maintains power around .85 and $f=.30$ gives power of .58. This seems an acceptable sample size, provided interest is in the omnibus test (i.e., significance test of the main effect of the group factor).

13.3.3 Unbalanced designs (unequal cell sizes)

Unequal cell sizes occur if n differs between levels of the factor in a one-way ANOVA design. This situation is also referred to as an unbalanced or unequal n design. In a design with more than one factor, combinations of the different factor levels define the 'cells' into which observations fall.

Three main challenges arise with unbalanced designs. The first is the familiar issue of missing data. This can sometimes be rectified by multiple imputation or an equivalent analysis (e.g., fitting an appropriate model using maximum likelihood estimation).[6] Missing data are not the only cause of unequal cell sizes. These also arise as a natural consequence of the sampling strategy in some situations. This leads to the second challenge, that of how to deal with unequal n in the calculations. The third, and most difficult, issue is how to partition SS when there is more than one effect.

For a one-way independent measures ANOVA there are two main solutions. For equal n designs, Equation 13.7 indicates that SS_{factor} is calculated as:

$$SS_{factor} = n\sum_{j=1}^{J}\left(\hat{\mu}_j - \hat{\mu}_{grand}\right)^2$$

This is because n (the sample size per cell) is identical for each of the J levels. One option is to weight each level by its own sample size (n_j) in a *weighted means* solution:

$$SS_{weighted} = \sum_{j=1}^{J} n_j\left(\hat{\mu}_j - \hat{\mu}_{grand}\right)^2 \qquad \text{Equation 13.19}$$

For a one-way ANOVA this matches SS_{model} from a multiple regression with dummy or effect coding (and is the preferred solution). Another alternative, rarely used for one-way designs, is an *unweighted means* approach that replaces n with $\tilde{n}$ (the harmonic mean) of the cell sizes:

$$SS_{unweighted} = \tilde{n}\sum_{j=1}^{J}\left(\hat{\mu}_j - \bar{\mu}_{grand}\right)^2 \qquad \text{Equation 13.20}$$

This equation assumes the cells have the same proportion in the population sampled and therefore weights each mean equally (and hence the unweighted means solution is really an equally weighted means solution).[7] The use of the harmonic mean of the sample size is largely of historic interest (Herr, 1986), but does sometimes crop up in software as an approximate solution when adapting formulas designed for equal cell sizes to unbalanced designs or as an approximate solution in designs with more than one factor.

Having equal cell sizes ensures that the ANOVA design also has orthogonal effects. This guarantees unambiguous allocation of sums of squares to each effect. This property of balanced designs is irrelevant to one-way independent measures ANOVA, because the partitioning of sums of squares involves decomposition into a single effect plus error. Introducing another factor or a covariate to the regression model – as in ANCOVA – complicates matters. Adding a factor violates orthogonality unless the design is completely balanced. Adding a covariate almost always violates orthogonality (except in the unlikely event that the covariate has the same mean for all cells in the design).

The solution adopted by most specialist software is to run an ANOVA or ANCOVA as a general linear model. This deals with the practical problem of estimating the parameters when effects are collinear, but leaves the tricky issue of partitioning sums of squares. In models with orthogonal effects the sums of squares don't overlap and the choice of how to partition sums of squares will not matter. One-way ANOVA with independent measures falls into this category because there is only one effect (the factor or main effect). However, for one-way ANCOVA with independent measures – a design with one factor and one covariate – it matters a great deal.

Two crucial decisions need to be made. The first decision is whether to calculate sums of squares sequentially or non-sequentially. *Sequential sums of squares* (also called Type I *SS*) involves allocating *SS* according to the order in which factors or covariates are entered into the regression model. The second decision, conditional on the first, is which non-sequential method to adopt: *hierarchical sums of squares* or *unique sums of squares* (often labeled Type II and Type III sums of squares).[8] Both non-sequential methods involve determining *SS* for an effect by adjusting the regression model for the presence of other predictors. Hierarchical sums of squares adjusts for the presence of all other effects that do not contain the effect of interest, while unique sums of squares adjusts for all other effects. For some simple models (e.g., one-way ANCOVA) the distinction between the two is immaterial and the more important decision is the first one.[9]

To understand when sequential or non-sequential *SS* are appropriate it is important to know a little bit about how they work. It is also worth repeating that they produce identical results in balanced ANOVA designs. In unbalanced designs (e.g., almost every ANCOVA design), sequential sums of squares produces different results depending on the order of entry of terms into the regression equation. The first term entered will 'grab' all the variance in *Y* that it can. The second entered term will then grab as much as possible of what it left and so on. This means that if a factor and covariate are correlated, the shared variance they explain in *Y* will be assigned to whichever predictor is entered earliest (assuming there are no correlated effects already in the model).[10] A handy feature of sequential *SS* is that sums of squares for the effects will always total to SS_{model} (it will exhaust the sample variance explained by the model). This won't be the case for other *SS* calculations (except in completely orthogonal designs). Sequential SS can also be used to mimic non-sequential *SS* calculations (by varying the sequence of terms). These properties are useful for computational purposes and explain why it is the default choice in some software (notably R).

Non-sequential sums of squares are generally preferred for ANOVA and ANCOVA, because they are unaffected by the order of entry of terms in the regression model (removing an element of subjectivity from the analysis). However, in an unbalanced design the sums of squares for the effects will no longer sum to SS_{model}. Sequential sums of squares are employed by default in several commercial packages. These include SPSS and SAS (where the uninformative labels Type I, Type II and Type III seem to have been coined).

The choice of method for partitioning *SS* for a non-orthogonal design depends on the hypotheses you are interested in. Sequential sums of squares are appropriate if you want to assign the shared variance of two correlated predictors to just one of them. This usually requires some kind of theoretical justification, and is most likely to arise when you want to entirely eliminate the effects of one predictor before estimating the effects of others. A good rule of thumb is that if you can't come up with clear rationale for ordering the predictors, sequential partitioning is probably inappropriate. One example of the appropriate application of sequential *SS* is when imbalances in cell sizes are the result of a difference in the proportions in the population sampled. Sequential *SS* can then be used to weight the analysis to obtain accurate population estimates of the population means (if that is desired).

Box 13.1 The cell means model

The cell means model is an alternative parameterization of the ANOVA model that can be more transparent than the sigma-restricted or overparameterized general linear models commonly implemented in software. One of its main advantages is that by parameterizing the model in terms of cell means, the individual parameters are easier to interpret. This is achieved by fitting a model with J rather than $J-1$ dummy coded predictors. Dropping the intercept ensures that the model is not overparameterized:

$$y_{ij} = \mu_j + \varepsilon_{ij} \qquad \text{Equation 13.21}$$

There is therefore a single parameter for each category and no need to designate a reference category. This makes it, like effect coding, a good choice for situations where there is no obvious baseline or comparison condition (but without the awkwardness of obtaining the level means).

The downside of the cell means model is that the parameterization leads to default inferences and summary statistics that can be confusing if you are more familiar with dummy or effect coded models (or their overparameterized cousins). In the cell means model the intercept is, in effect, zero and inferences are expressed relative to the hypothesis that H_0: $\mu = 0$. The R^2 value reported for the model therefore expresses the proportion of variance explained in terms of the total deviations of Y from zero (rather than from the grand mean). This has the appearance of inflating R^2 (when the grand mean is not zero) unless you understand how the model fit has been assessed. Inferences for individual predictors are also tests of H_0: $\mu_j = 0$. This is sometimes of interest (being a form of one sample t test for each category mean with a pooled error term). In addition, the corresponding CIs are constructed around individual means rather than differences between means. They therefore indicate the precision of measurement of each of the J means.

The cell means parameterization supports model comparison in the usual way (e.g., by looking at the change in R^2 between models or information criteria such as AIC). This is one method to obtain the standard omnibus F test for one-way ANOVA (by comparing the fit of the cell means model to that of an intercept-only model). Kirk (1995) discusses further advantages of the cell means model for a number of ANOVA designs.

13.4 Exploring differences between level means

While one-way ANOVA is widely used, it is rarely the end point of an analysis. An obvious exception is when $J = 2$ and the ANOVA main effect is equivalent to a t test with $t^2 = F$. With $J > 2$, most researchers are interested in more than merely rejecting the null hypothesis that all level means are unequal. There are several ways to explore differences between the level means. In many cases it is sufficient to plot the means and associated CIs. If the precision of measurement for each mean is suitably high, formal tests may not be required (as the pattern of differences in the means will be evident from the plot).

In this kind of plot it is customary to use a pooled estimate of error variance (MS_{error}) to calculate the CI, unless the homogeneity of variance assumption is thought to be untenable. If there are differences in the variances, plotting the CIs without pooling variance estimates has the added advantage of also revealing any patterns in the variances of the levels (assuming equal n). If interest is in the differences between pairs of level means then it may be better to plot error bars adjusted so that absence of overlap corresponds to a 95% CI for the difference in means. These can be plotted on their own or combined with CIs for the precision of individual means using two-tiered error bars (see Figure 3.8).

These solutions are satisfactory for informal inference or when displaying very clear patterns of effects, but are not appropriate for formal inference. If formal inference is required then there are two main strategies. One is to make *pairwise comparisons* between level means. The other is to explore patterns among the means using *contrasts*. The following sections provide a brief introduction to the most popular strategy – that of pairwise comparisons – before reviewing some of the limitations of the approach. Although, this strategy is strongly identified with frequentist inference, a potential alternative based on information criteria is also considered here. The second strategy – use of contrasts – is the focus of Chapter 15.

13.4.1 Pairwise comparisons and corrections for multiple testing

One-way ANOVA provides a natural way to formulate a test for the null hypothesis of no differences between level means for a factor. If the test of a factor leads to the rejection of H_0, a reasonable starting point for further exploration is to look at the pattern of observed means in a table or plot. Many researchers also follow-up the omnibus test with formal tests of the differences between pairs of level means.

These pairwise comparisons could take the form of multiple t tests (or CIs). Performing multiple t tests raises a number of awkward statistical issues. The most prominent is the problem of multiple testing (or, in this context, multiple comparisons). As more significance tests are conducted, the chance of Type I error for a set or 'family' of tests increases. Each individual t test or CI will have a long-run Type I error rate under H_0 equal to α. This can be labeled *per test* α (α_{PT}). However, the chance of a Type I error for a set of n tests will be much higher than α_{PT}.

This rate, known as *familywise* α (α_{FW}), is defined as the probability of at least one Type I error if the omnibus null hypothesis (H_0: $\mu_1 = \mu_2 = \ldots = \mu_j$) is true. Assuming the tests are independent, the familywise error rate is:

$$\alpha_{FW} = 1 - (1 - \alpha_{PT})^{n_{test}} \qquad \text{Equation 13.22}$$

For $n_{test} = 10$ there will be around a .40 (40%) chance of at least one Type I error. The consequences are serious, because the number of tests grows rapidly with the number of levels of a factor. With J levels, the number of possible pairwise comparisons is:

$$n_{test} = \frac{J(J-1)}{2} \qquad \text{Equation 13.23}$$

For instance, with $J = 5$ levels $n_{test} = 10$ and with $J = 6$ levels $n_{test} = 15$. Exactly the same problem applies in other multiple testing contexts. Thus a correlation matrix reporting tests among $J = 8$ variables involves 28 hypothesis tests. Analogous problems occur when comparing large numbers of regression models (e.g., using stepwise methods).

The following sections do not attempt a complete survey of the literature on multiple testing and pairwise comparisons. The principal focus is on procedures that provide strong control of the Type I error rate, and many of these procedures are sufficiently general that they can be applied to a wide range of statistical problems (not just pairwise testing) and can be implemented without specialist software. This generality tends to have a cost in terms of statistical power. A later section reviews options for increasing statistical power (though this may require specialist software or some loss of generality).

Statistical power can also be increased by opting for weak control of Type I error. This involves protecting familywise error only for the omnibus null hypothesis. In the event that the omnibus null hypothesis is false, familywise error is not necessarily protected (i.e., both the number of errors and probability of a Type I error could be very high). Consider a situation in which the true pattern of differences among J means is that L are equal and $J - L$ differ from all others. This pattern is at least as plausible as the omnibus null hypothesis (and probably more plausible). In this situation, the Type I error rate for some of the tests is uncontrolled if $L > 2$. Procedures with only weak control of Type I error are therefore usually undesirable.

13.4.2 *A priori* (planned) tests

The best solution is usually to restrict testing to a small set of plausible hypotheses. The tests should be motivated by theory or otherwise defined by the aims of the research. These tests are known as *a priori* or *planned* comparisons and should be planned before data are collected. Where possible they should also have some prior theoretical justification or other support. If the number of *a priori* tests is low it is considered reasonable to make no adjustment to α_{PT}. Otherwise the number of planned tests can be used to adjust α_{PT} (in order to control α_{FW}). This control usually involves keeping α_{FW} at some desired level (e.g., $\alpha_{FW} = .05$).

Dozens, perhaps hundreds, of procedures exist for making adjustments to α_{FW}. One of the simplest and most versatile adjustments is the *Bonferroni correction*. It is versatile because it is based on Boole's inequality (a very general law of probability). This states that for a finite set of events, the probability of at least one event occurring cannot exceed the sum of their individual probabilities. The probability that at least one of a set of tests is statistically significant by chance (if H_0 is true) cannot exceed the sum of their individual Type I error rates: n_{test} times α_{PT}. The Bonferroni correction adjusts α_{FW} for this worst-case scenario through division by the number of tests:

$$\alpha_{PT} = \frac{\alpha_{FW}}{n_{test}} \qquad \text{Equation 13.24}$$

This correction requires minimal calculation and few assumptions (e.g., it does not require that the tests are independent) and can be applied to any testing situation. A downside is that it is too strict (particularly when the number of tests is large) and can dramatically reduce statistical power (or precision if α_{PT} is used to correct the width of a CI).

A marginally more powerful alternative is the Šidák correction. This inverts the probability of at least one Type I error, under the assumption of independence of the individual tests (though this assumption can often be relaxed), to give:

$$\alpha_{PT} = 1 - (1 - \alpha_{FW})^{1/n_{test}}$$ Equation 13.25

It is slightly more powerful than the Bonferroni correction. This can be demonstrated by comparing α_{PT} for both corrections. If the number of tests to be controlled is 10 and α_{FW} = .05 then α_{PT} for the Bonferroni correction is $.05/10 = .005$. The corresponding value for the Šidák correction is $\alpha_{PT} = 1 - (.95)^{1/10} \approx .00512$. The difference tends to be modest when the desired familywise error rate is low (which it usually is).

More interesting and powerful modified Bonferroni procedures exist. Of these, one that stands out is a sequential procedure developed separately by Holm (1979) for ANOVA and Larzelere and Mulaik (1977) for correlation matrices. It is more powerful than the Bonferroni or Šidák corrections, only marginally harder to carry out and is very general (e.g., independent tests are not assumed). The *Larzelere-Mulaik-Holm* (LMH) procedure or Holm test works using the p values reported by each NHST. The first step is to rank in order the set of tests in terms of p value, from $i = 1$ lowest (most significant) to $i = n$ highest (least significant). The procedure is sequential because α_{PT} increases from $i = 1$ through to n according to the formula:

$$\alpha_i = \frac{\alpha_{FW}}{n_{test} + 1 - i}$$ Equation 13.26

Each successive test thus uses a Bonferroni correction, but with the effective number of tests decreasing by one each time (in what is termed a 'step-down' procedure). For $n = 4$ tests and $\alpha_{FW} = .05$ the first test would adopt the criterion $\alpha = .0125$, the second $\alpha = .0167$, the third $\alpha = .025$ and the fourth $\alpha = .05$. A crucial safeguard in the sequential procedure is that it stops at the first test that is non-significant. On reaching a non-significant test, all tests with larger p values are declared non-significant.

The way the LMH procedure controls the familywise error rate is rather clever. The first test uses the Bonferroni correction for all n tests, but if it is significant, the second test only needs to control for $n - 1$ tests. This is because the first test could not contribute to raising the Type I error rate over α_{FW} even if it were false (by Boole's inequality). The second test can therefore discount the first test for the purposes of calculating its correction and so on. Last of all, no individual test has $\alpha > \alpha_{FW}$. More powerful modified Bonferroni procedures exist, but they are either not as general or are considerably more difficult to implement (e.g., being tailored to a specific statistical model or a particular set of hypotheses).

Does it matter that the LMH procedure starts by applying the smallest α level to the most significant p value? Hochberg (1988) developed a variant of the LMH procedure that works in the opposite direction. It starts by applying unadjusted α to the largest uncorrected p value and ends applying the full α/n_{test} correction to the smallest p value. Once a test is found to be statistically significant with the Hochberg procedure all subsequent tests in the sequence (those with smaller p values) are also declared statistically significant. The Hochberg procedure can be substantially more powerful than LMH, but is more restrictive in its assumptions.

Like the Šidák procedure, one of the conditions under which the Hochberg procedure can be applied is if the distributions of tests statistics under H_0 are independent. Both Šidák and Hochberg also apply when the test statistics have a multivariate t distribution and are positively correlated. This situation includes pairwise comparisons on a factor in ANOVA (provided the test statistics have at least an approximate t distribution). Further examples of situations that relax the independence requirement of the Šidák and Hochberg procedures are detailed in the literature (e.g., Karlin and Rinott, 1981; Holland and Copenhaver, 1987; Sarkar, 2008).

Applying an adjustment directly to α makes it possible to employ these corrections without specialist software. Non-sequential corrections (e.g., Bonferroni or Šidák) can also be used to adjust the width of a set of CIs to account for multiple comparisons. If the assumptions of the t test are in doubt, general procedures such as LMH can be applied to robust alternatives such as the Welch-Satterthwaite or the Yuen-Hall bootstrap t test. All of the above approaches also provide strong control over the Type I error rate (controlling both α_{FW} and the α_{PT}).

Example 13.3 For the diagram data there are $J(J-1)/2 = 6$ possible pairwise comparisons. Of these up to five are relevant to the researcher's predictions. These are the comparison between full diagram and segmented diagrams, and the comparisons of each of the two separate diagram conditions versus the text condition and picture condition. The text and picture conditions act as control or baseline conditions to test the effectiveness of the diagrams. Although it might be sensible to employ a *post hoc* test to control for all six possible tests, I'll stick to five to demonstrate how the Bonferroni, Šidák, LMH and Hochberg procedures perform.

Start with five uncorrected pairwise t tests using a pooled error term. The Welch-Satterthwaite correction would be appropriate if either sample sizes or variances were dissimilar. MS_{error} for the one-way ANOVA was 67.8. This is a pooled variance estimate and so $\hat{\sigma}_{pooled} = \sqrt{67.8} \approx 8.23$ and the pooled SE for the difference in means is:

$$\hat{\sigma}_{\hat{\mu}_1 - \hat{\mu}_2} = \hat{\sigma}_{pooled}\sqrt{\frac{1}{n_1} + \frac{1}{n_2}} = 8.23\sqrt{\frac{1}{10} + \frac{1}{10}} \approx 3.68$$

The five t statistics are therefore computed from the relevant difference in means divided by 3.68. Using a pooled error term allows t to be evaluated against a distribution with 36 df (as all groups in the ANOVA contribute to estimation of error term). The equivalent 95% CI would have a margin of error (MOE) of roughly $\pm$ 7.47 (because $t_{36,.975} \approx 2.028$). If $\alpha_{FW} = .05$, the Bonferroni correction suggests $\alpha_{PT} = .05/5 = .01$. The uncorrected t tests can therefore be compared against the criterion $\alpha_{PT} = .01$ to determine statistical significance (and this guarantees $\alpha_{FW} \leq .05$). A 95% CI based on a Bonferroni correction has $MOE = t_{36,.995} \times \hat{\sigma}_{\mu_1 - \mu_2} = 2.72 \times 3.68 = 10.01$. The Šidák correction is barely different. For five tests $\alpha_{PT} \approx .01021$ and the $MOE = 9.98$.

The LMH procedure increments α_{PT} sequentially, starting with the smallest p value. It stops if any test is non-significant and any remaining tests in the sequence are declared non-significant. For $n = 5$ tests and $\alpha_{FW} = .05$ the first test will use $\alpha = .01$, the second .0125, the third 0.0167, the fourth .025 and the last .05. The Hochberg procedure uses a 'step-up' sequence that applies the same sequence of α levels, but starts with the largest p value. However, the Hochberg procedure terminates on a statistically significant test (with all subsequent tests in the sequence then declared statistically significant).

How do they compare in practice? Table 13.7 shows the t statistics and mean differences for each of the five *a priori* comparisons (ordered from most to least statistically significant). Below that, α_{PT}

for the Bonferroni, LMH and Hochberg procedures are reported. Last of all, uncorrected *p* values are reported for each test, followed by adjusted *p* values for Bonferroni, LMH and Hochberg.

Table 13.7 Performance of procedures for controlling familywise error for five *a priori* tests on the diagram data

	***A priori* tests**				
	1. Text vs segmented	**2. Picture vs segmented**	**3. Full vs segmented**	**4. Text vs full**	**5. Picture vs full**
$M_1 - M_2$	9.50	9.00	4.90	4.60	4.10
t	2.58	2.44	1.33	1.25	1.11
$\alpha_{Bonferroni}$	.010	.010	.010	.010	.010
α_{LMH}	.010	.013	.017	.025	.050
$\alpha_{Hochberg}$	.010	.013	.017	.025	.050
Uncorrected p	.014	.022	.192	.220	.273
$p_{Bonferroni}$	.071	.098	.958	1.098	1.365
p_{LMH}	.071	.078	.575	.575	.575
$p_{Hochberg}$	.071	.078	.273	.273	.273

The procedure for determining adjusted *p* values is explained by Wright (1992). An adjusted *p* value is the smallest *p* at which H_0 for a comparison would be rejected using a particular procedure. For the Bonferroni correction, adjusted *p* is the uncorrected *p* value multiplied by the number of tests to be conducted. This can result in adjusted *p* values larger than one (which, under the preceding definition, ought to be capped at $p = 1$).[11] Following Wright (*ibid.*), Table 13.7 departs from this strict definition. This helps illustrate the poor performance of the Bonferroni tests.

Calculating adjusted *p* values for the LMH and Hochberg procedures is more challenging, because sequential testing is terminated when non-significance (LMH) or significance (Hochberg) is found. α_{PT} for these procedures is identical, but the sequence of testing starts with text vs segmented diagram (for LMH) or picture vs full diagram (for Hochberg). Adjusted *p* is initially determined by multiplying uncorrected *p* by the number of tests to be corrected for. This would be five for the first test, four for the second test and so on. For LMH the testing stops at the first non-significant test. Wright suggested that the remaining tests should be assigned their initial adjusted *p* only if it is larger than the adjusted *p* value of the earlier tests. For the present analysis the fourth and fifth tests have initial adjusted *p* values of $2 \times .220 = .440$ and .273. It would illogical for a larger difference in means to produce a larger *p* value. For this reason the fourth and fifth tests are assigned the largest preceding adjusted *p* value (which is .575). This ensures that the order of the adjusted *p* values is not inconsistent with the order of the uncorrected ones. A similar principle applies to the Hochberg procedure. Here the uncorrected *p* value for the first test (text vs segmented diagram) is .273 and because this uses unadjusted α (i.e., corrects for only one test) *p* is also unadjusted. At the second step, correcting for two tests, initial *p* is around .44. This is inconsistent with the order of uncorrected *p* values and so it is replaced with the smallest earlier adjusted *p* value in the sequence (which is .273). Continuing from right to left, the third test also gets assigned .273 (for the same reason). The remaining initial adjusted *p* values are $.0196 \times 4 = .078$ and $.0141 \times 5 = .071$.

None of the adjusted *p* values is statistically significant with $\alpha_{FW} = .05$. Even so, the LMH procedure offers a substantial improvement over the Bonferroni correction. Hochberg is better still.

Nevertheless, the corrected *a priori* tests don't provide much support for the research hypotheses. This is a little misleading. It would be more common to apply *post hoc* methods when nearly all of the possible tests are of interest (and *a priori* tests would offer greater power if fewer tests had been selected). Most important of all, the strategy of treating a pattern of predictions involving four means as five separate tests is very inefficient. A more sensible strategy would be to test the pattern directly (e.g., via a contrast or by comparing models that match or don't match the hypothesized pattern).

13.4.3 *Post hoc* (unplanned) tests

Even in studies with *a priori* hypotheses and a strong theoretical motivation there will occasionally be tests that suggest themselves only after data is collected. Such *post hoc* or *unplanned tests* present a particular problem when there are many possible tests (e.g., when J is large). The fundamental problem for *post hoc* tests is that the Type I error rate is not determined by the number of tests conducted, but by the number of tests that might have been conducted. For pairwise comparisons with a pooled error term, performing a *post hoc* test on the largest difference between means has the same Type I error rate as conducting all possible pairwise comparisons. If the omnibus null hypothesis is true and only one test is statistically significant, it is, by definition, a Type I error. This Type I error must be for the effect with the smallest observed p value (and therefore the largest observed difference in means).

Provided it is possible to determine – or at least estimate – all the tests that might have been conducted, Bonferroni and modified Bonferroni procedures can also be applied as *post hoc* tests. This is accomplished by replacing the number of tests conducted with the total number of possible tests. For pairwise tests (e.g., in ANOVA or for simple correlations), the maximum number of tests is given by Equation 13.23. Unless J is small this produces adjustments that are very conservative for both the Bonferroni and Šidák correction. Sequential variants such as the LMH or Hochberg procedures are therefore preferable. In fact, LMH is always superior to the Bonferroni and Šidák corrections, and is no more restrictive in terms of assumptions. It is a safe choice for any situation.

There are many other options. Some will provide greater statistical power or offer more stringent protection of Type I error than the procedures discussed here. We will consider only a few of the most popular choices. The first of these is *Fisher's least significant difference* (Fisher's LSD). Fisher's LSD involves the application of uncorrected t tests following a significant omnibus test of an ANOVA main effect (i.e., a significant F ratio). These tests use a pooled error term if homogeneity of variances among groups is tenable. If not, more robust alternatives can be employed (e.g., Welch-Satterthwaite t tests). The LSD procedure protects against Type I errors only through the omnibus ANOVA test. It is unusual in this respect (because most popular procedures are not conditional on an earlier test). With large values of J it should be avoided, as it provides only weak control of Type I error. However, when $J = 3$ it is effective at controlling both the rate and number of Type I errors (and, because the individual tests are uncorrected, it maximizes statistical power for a given level of α).

Specialist *post hoc* procedures exist for a range of situations (see Kirk, 1995; Howell, 2002; Shaffer, 1995). Of these, Tukey's *honestly significant difference* (HSD) is among the most widely used for balanced designs, being popular for its strong control of Type I error. Procedures for unequal n designs have also been developed (see Kirk, 1995). The ideal test would have strong Type I error control, be robust to unequal cell sizes or violations of assumptions, and have high statistical power. Progress has been made in developing such procedures, but at some cost in terms of loss of generality or increase in complexity. At present there is no simple, general procedure for *post hoc* (or indeed *a priori*) comparisons that is easy to implement or widely available in software.

Example 13.4 If the priority is strict control of Type I error for all possible pairwise comparisons, many researchers will select Tukey's HSD procedure (though Fisher's LSD is a better choice when $J = 3$). This procedure will also produce interval estimates – a distinct advantage over some alternatives. Tukey's HSD is therefore a common choice for plotting CIs for differences (even if formal testing is not required).

One drawback of the conventional implementation of Tukey's HSD is that it assumes homogeneity of variances and equal cell sizes for the J independent means. SPSS implements a version using the

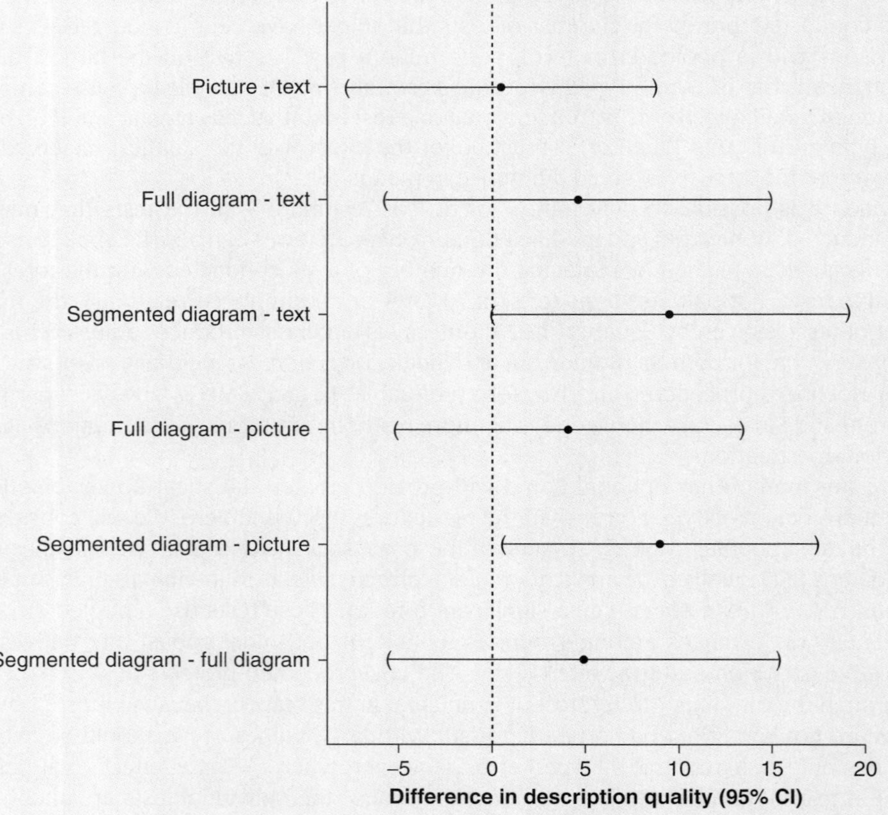

Figure 13.3 Tukey's HSD tests with robust standard errors, presented as 95% CIs of the differences between conditions for the diagram data

harmonic mean (but also warns that this does not necessarily control the Type I error rate). A more radical alternative is to implement the HSD procedure with robust standard errors. This procedure is available via the `R multcomp` package (Hothorn *et al.*, 2008). The robust standard errors incorporate a 'sandwich estimator' obtained from the `R sandwich` package (Zeileis, 2004, 2006). Figure 13.3 plots 95% confidence intervals for the Tukey HSD with robust standard errors for the diagram data comparisons.

The pattern of statistical significance differs slightly from that obtained from the earlier planned comparisons. With robust standard errors one of the comparisons is statistically significant at $\alpha_{FW} =$ .05 (the difference between the segmented diagram and the picture condition).

This comparison is marginally non-significant without robust standard errors, and suggests that the modest differences in the group variances (the smallest of which is for the picture condition) have some impact on the analysis. On average, the robust standard errors tend to be conservative – leading to larger standard errors and p values than the standard Tukey HSD procedure, but it can increase power for some tests (where the variance of the difference is smaller than the pooled average).

13.4.4 Using logical dependencies to increase statistical power

Despite the limitations of existing procedures, it is possible to increase the statistical power of pairwise comparisons (or other multiple testing procedures) by taking into account the specific structure of the testing situation. Shaffer (1986) explains how to modify the LMH procedure to take into account logical constraints between the hypotheses of individual tests. The rationale for the LMH procedure is that each statistically significant result reduces the number of Type I errors that are possible later in the sequence. This, in itself, can be considered a form of logical constraint on the error rate.

Shaffer demonstrated that some testing situations, including pairwise tests on a factor in ANOVA, allow further constraints to be added. Consider a one-way ANOVA with $J = 3$ levels (labeled A, B and C). For the first test all three null hypotheses (i.e., $\mu_A = \mu_B$, $\mu_A = \mu_C$ and $\mu_B = \mu_C$) could be true and therefore α_1 should be set at $\alpha/3$. If this test is non-significant, testing halts and no Type I errors are possible. If the first test has $p < \alpha_1$ then testing continues. Assume this test rejects the null hypothesis $\mu_A = \mu_B$. For the remaining null hypotheses, if both $\mu_A = \mu_C$ and $\mu_B = \mu_C$ were true then this would imply $\mu_A = \mu_B = \mu_C$ (a logical relationship termed 'transitivity'). This in turn implies with certainty that the decision on the first test was a Type I error. This creates a logical contradiction. It is not possible for $\mu_A = \mu_B$ to be false (with some non-zero probability) and to be true (with certainty). Accordingly, either $\mu_A = \mu_C$ or $\mu_B = \mu_C$, but not both, can be true. Thus the second test needs only to control for one true null hypothesis (rather than two under the LMH procedure).

The procedure can be formally defined as setting α_{PT} as

$$\alpha_i = \frac{\alpha_{FW}}{n_i} \qquad \text{Equation 13.27}$$

where n_i is the maximum number of null hypotheses that could be true given that $i - 1$ have been rejected. The Shaffer procedure is, at worst, as powerful as LMH (being equivalent when there are no logical constraints) and typically much more powerful. The difficulty is that, even in a simple example (e.g., all pairwise tests on a factor with $J = 3$ levels, where $n_1 = 3$, $n_2 = 1$, and $n_3 = 1$), n_i can be difficult to derive. Shaffer (1986) provides a method for deriving n_i in some common situations.

Holland and Copenhaver (1987) provide a table setting out the maximum number of null hypotheses that could be true for all pairwise tests on a factor for values of $J = 3$ to $J = 10$. A portion of this table (for $J = 3$ to $J = 6$) is reproduced in Table 13.8. When not all possible pairwise comparisons are conducted (e.g., in *a priori* testing), J is large, or some other testing situation pertains, deriving the maximum number of true null hypotheses is more challenging.

The Shaffer procedure can be further modified to increase statistical power. One modification is to base it on the Šidák procedure rather than Bonferroni, but at the cost of reduced generality (see *ibid.*). This typically provides only a small improvement in power (Shaffer, 1995). A more radical solution is to incorporate not just the logical structure of the testing situation, but also its correlation structure. Westfall (1997) describes a resampling-based approach to multiple comparisons that modifies the LMH procedure to take into account both logical constraints and the correlations between test statistics. The Westfall procedure typically has greater statistical power than the Shaffer procedure, but requires specialist software to implement (whereas the Shaffer procedure can be computed by hand once the logical constraints are known). Both the Shaffer and the Westfall procedure are modifications of the Bonferroni and LMH procedures and provide strong control of the Type I error rate. Their chief deficiency is that, like LMH (but unlike Bonferroni, Fisher's LSD or Tukey's HSD), they cannot be used to derive CIs for means or differences between means.

The generality and power of the Shaffer and Westfall procedures suggests that they should be preferred when it is feasible to compute them. Of the options discussed so far, only the Hochberg procedure is not guaranteed to have lower statistical power than Shaffer or Westfall. However,

Table 13.8 Maximum number of true null hypotheses if $i - 1$ have been rejected, for all $J(J - 1)/2$ pairwise comparisons of a factor with J levels

i	$J = 3$	$J = 4$	$J = 5$	$J = 6$
1	3	6	10	15
2	1	3	6	10
3	1	3	6	10
4		3	6	10
5		2	6	10
6		1	4	10
7			4	7
8			3	7
9			2	7
10			1	6
11				4
12				4
13				3
14				2
15				1

the Hochberg procedure is less general (e.g., it may not apply to pairwise comparisons if the test statistics do not have a t distribution under H_0).

The Westfall procedure has superior statistical power to the Shaffer procedure (Westfall, 1997), whereas the Hochberg procedure is sometimes superior to either Shaffer or Westfall and sometimes worse (*ibid.*). However, it seems likely that the Westfall is, on average, more powerful than the Hochberg procedure, though the difference may marginal for ANOVA designs (see Lix and Sajobi, 2010). As of writing, alternatives with equivalent or better power exist, but require the control of Type I error to be relaxed, are not widely available in software or are less general in their application (e.g., Fisher's LSD when $J = 3$).

Example 13.5 It is possible to illustrate the improved power of the Shaffer and Westfall procedures by revisiting the *a priori* tests conducted on the diagram data. As only five of the six possible pairwise tests are to be conducted it is not possible obtain n_i values from Table 13.8 to plug into Equation 13.27. It would be necessary to derive the logical constraints from first principles or use specialized software. The `R multcomp` package, used earlier to obtain Tukey's HSD with robust standard errors, also supports the LMH, Hochberg, Shaffer and Westfall procedures (among others). Table 13.9 compares adjusted p values for of each of these procedures for five *a priori* comparisons based on a one-way ANOVA of the diagram data with robust standard errors. Robust standard errors are used because Example 13.4 suggested that the differences in variances between groups were sufficient to have a modest impact on the outcome (though this does not change the pattern of results in Table 13.9).

Table 13.9 Adjusted p values for five *a priori* tests, derived from the LMH, Hochberg, Shaffer and Westfall procedures for a one-way ANOVA of the diagram data

	***A priori* tests**				
Adjusted *p*	**1. Text vs segmented**	**2. Picture vs segmented**	**3. Full vs segmented**	**4. Text vs full**	**5. Picture vs full**
p_{LMH}	.033	.044	.642	.642	.642
$p_{Hochberg}$	.033	.044	.242	.242	.242
$p_{Shaffer}$	.033	.033	.214	.474	.474
$p_{Westfall}$	.029	.027	.214	.366	.366

All tests now show the same pattern of statistical significance (though this is not guaranteed). An advantage for segmented diagram condition relative to both the text and picture control has been detected.

As anticipated, Hochberg, Shaffer and Westfall all return adjusted p values less than or equal to the LMH procedure, while Westfall returns p values less than or equal to the Shaffer procedure. The Hochberg procedure sometimes exhibits worse power and sometimes greater power than the Shaffer or Westfall procedure. The more general Westfall procedure should be preferred where available (and probably has slightly greater power on average). For hand calculation, either the Shaffer or Hochberg procedures should be considered.

13.4.5 Criticisms of corrections based on familywise error rates

Correcting for multiple comparisons by controlling familywise error rates is slightly controversial. One criticism is that researchers who use NHSTs and CIs are inconsistent in their application. The corrections are almost routinely applied for pairwise comparisons in ANOVA, but rarely applied under other circumstances (e.g., for main effects in ANOVA, for tests with different *DV*s in the same experiment, individual predictors in a regression model or multiple correlations). In part this is because it can be hard to define a family of tests in a rigorous way (and therefore know how many tests to correct for). A second criticism is that many of the popular methods tend to over-correct when the number of tests to be corrected for is large (e.g., in *post hoc* testing).[12] Research in many fields is probably already underpowered. The routine use of low-power correction procedures shifts the balance away from avoiding Type II errors toward avoiding Type I errors.

This state of affairs is made substantially worse when corrections are made conditional on an earlier significance test. This mistake is common in ANOVA. Few of the most popular *post hoc* correction procedures control the familywise error rate using the omnibus *F* test (a notable exception being Fisher's LSD). If a procedure that doesn't require omnibus *F* significance (e.g., Tukey's HSD or any of the modified Bonferroni procedures) implements it as a precondition, then it will inevitably fail to detect genuine differences on some occasions, thus increasing the Type II error rate (perhaps dramatically).

The role of the omnibus *F* test in ANOVA is widely misunderstood. Many researchers believe that a significant *F* ratio implies at least one of the pairwise comparisons is statistically significant with an uncorrected *t* test. This, accompanied by the mistaken belief that non-significance implies no pairwise tests can reach statistical significance, may explain the common mistake of applying a *post hoc* test conditional on rejecting the omnibus null hypothesis. A significant omnibus test guarantees only that some pattern of differences (one of the possible contrasts) among the means is statistically significant with an uncorrected test. Rejecting H_0: $\mu_1 = \mu_2 = \ldots = \mu_j$ does not guarantee that this contrast is a pairwise difference. An example might be the comparison of several treatments against a single control. None of the treatments might differ from each other, but their average effect might differ from the control.

While these criticisms are cogent, particularly those relating to a reduction in statistical power, they may be symptoms of a deeper problem. Pairwise comparisons, by definition, attempt to break down complex patterns in data into their component parts. Quite often – perhaps most of the time – the finding of genuine interest is the overall pattern rather than its components. Furthermore, even when the pattern can be represented faithfully in terms of its constituent elements, breaking it down in this way tends to decrease statistical power. Decreased power arises for several reasons (e.g., because effective *n* is reduced), but most often because some of the components of the pattern involve small effects and some large effects. Thus a very clear overall pattern may end up being rejected because its weakest component is tested in isolation.

Breaking down the overall pattern in this way can also lead to logical inconsistencies between findings. It is well known that pairwise tests frequently produce results that violate transitivity (Loftus, 2001; Dayton, 2003). For instance, a one-way ANOVA design with $J = 3$ might produce level means $\hat{\mu}_1 = 30$, $\hat{\mu}_2 = 28$ and $\hat{\mu}_3 = 12$. Pairwise tests might reveal the difference $\hat{\mu}_1 - \hat{\mu}_3$ to be statistically significant, but $\hat{\mu}_1 - \hat{\mu}_2$ and $\hat{\mu}_2 - \hat{\mu}_3$ to be non-significant. The overall pattern of statistical significance suggests $\mu_1 > \mu_3, \mu_1 = \mu_2$ and $\mu_2 = \mu_3$. This violates transitivity because $\mu_1 = \mu_2$ and $\mu_2 = \mu_3$ together imply $\mu_1 = \mu_3$. The pattern of differences in the true population differences will never violate transitivity (e.g., if $\mu_1 = \mu_2$ and $\mu_2 = \mu_3$ then $\mu_1 = \mu_3$ must also be true).

This kind of decomposition can be avoided by setting out to compare models that capture patterns of interest. The ideal approach is to focus on *a priori* hypotheses and to evaluate a model that captures a pattern of interest against plausible competing models. As this is not always possible – some research being exploratory and some interesting findings being unanticipated, there is a role for *post hoc* testing. One avenue for this is the likelihood approach. What matters, according to likelihood inference, is the evidence that the data provide. There is no need to correct for multiple testing (because the evidence does not change if more tests are performed). The burden then shifts to careful selection of the models to be compared (rather than merely maximizing a likelihood ratio). Similar arguments can be made for the Bayesian approach, although in Bayesian inference the issue of multiple testing should be addressed through selecting an appropriate prior (see Dienes, 2008).

Two further alternatives to conventional corrections for multiple testing are considered here. The first is a radical alternative to control familywise error. Benjamini and colleagues argued that focusing on the familywise error rate is the wrong strategy (Benjamini and Hochberg, 1995; Benjamini and Yekutieli, 2001). It reduces statistical power too far if there are many tests to control. A better approach for situations with many tests may be to accept that Type I errors will occur and control the proportion of these errors: the *false discovery rate* (FDR). The FDR approach is often adopted in fields such as neuroimaging, where very large numbers of tests are routine (and where the occasional false discovery among that large set is not regarded a serious problem).

An entirely different solution is to apply information criteria such as AIC and BIC to the multiple testing context. Dayton's (2003) paired-comparisons information-criterion (PCIC) procedure does exactly this. PCIC treats the problem of testing differences between means as a form of model comparison. A factor with $J = 4$ levels leads naturally to comparisons between models in which all means are equal, represented in Dayton's notation as {1234}, through to a model where all means differ: {1,2,3,4}. Testing only coherent patterns of means avoids violations of transitivity. The use of AIC or BIC also takes into account the complexity of the different models (in terms of the number of parameters being estimated). Dayton also extends PCIC to deal with heterogeneity of variance.

As well as directly addressing the question of the pattern of differences among the population means, the PCIC approach tends to have high statistical power relative to conventional pairwise comparison procedures. If AIC is used, it controls Type I error rates when all models are compared (provided the omnibus F test of the factor is statistically significant). BIC provides a more conservative test that avoids the need for a preliminary test of the main effect to control Type I error (Dayton, 2003). AIC_C corrects AIC for small sample size and is likely to be similarly conservative when n per group is small.

Example 13.6 FDR methods tend not to be used unless the number of tests to be controlled is very large. Switching to a different criterion (the rate at which false discoveries are made) increases sensitivity to detect real differences. The cost of this approach is weak control of the Type I error rate (and in large sets some Type I errors are more or less guaranteed). The increased sensitivity is illustrated by calculating an adjusted p value for the FDR test. This is the smallest p value that keeps the rate of false discoveries below α_{FW}. In comparison to the values reported in Table 13.7

the FDR adjusted p values are .049 for the first two tests and .273 for the remaining three tests. This is a marginal improvement over the LMH procedure (or indeed Tukey's HSD). Larger numbers of tests would provide a more substantial advantage. With respect to the pairwise comparisons in Table 13.9 (also incorporating robust standard errors) the FDR tests are comparable to the Westfall procedure with adjusted $p=.027$ for the first two tests and $p=.242$ for the remaining tests. The FDR is likely to be more powerful than the Shaffer or Westfall procedure for large numbers of tests (see Keselman *et al.*, 1999). However, the FDR procedure requires independence or positively correlated test statistics with particular distributions (e.g., multivariate t) and does not provide strong Type I error control. For this reason the Westfall procedure should be preferred outside situations that the FDR procedure was designed for (i.e., for very large numbers of tests in which some Type I errors may be tolerated).

All of the approaches considered so far are, to some extent, unsatisfactory. First, multiple pairwise tests are inefficient if more precise hypotheses can be set out. Second, the pattern of significance is sometimes intransitive (e.g., as with the Tukey HSD test in Example 13.4). Dayton's PCIC approach is one way to resolve this kind of intransitivity (and also has high 'all-pairs' statistical power and sensitivity to the set of all true differences). A full treatment of this approach is not possible in the limited space here, but it is possible to give a brief illustration using AIC_C (which, for this sample size, should be more conservative than AIC or BIC).

Table 13.10 Dayton's PCIC procedure using AIC_C applied to the diagram ANOVA data

Model	**AIC_c**	***df***	**ΔAIC_c**	**Akaike weight**
{12,34}	286.6	3	0.0	.2606
{123,4}	286.7	3	0.1	.2485
{12,3,4}	287.1	4	0.6	.1974
{1,23,4}	288.5	4	1.9	.1013
{1,2,34}	289.0	4	2.5	.0763
{1,2,3,4}	289.7	5	3.2	.0538
{1,234}	290.8	3	4.2	.0317
{1234}	290.9	2	4.3	.0304

The first step is to order the means from one (smallest) to four (largest). Assuming homogeneity of variance, all that is required is to fit a series of eight models that range from the grand mean (intercept-only) model {1234} to the usual ANOVA model with separate parameters for each of the four group means {1,2,3,4}. Table 13.10 summarizes AIC_C for the eight possible models. These are ordered from most to least probable (by Akaike weight) with the best-supported model as the reference model. The most probable and best-supported model is {12,34}. It suggests the two diagram conditions are different from the two non-diagram conditions. Close behind is model {123,4} in which only the segmented diagram condition is different from the other conditions. Also reasonably plausible is {12,3,4}, in which the two diagram conditions are different from the two non-diagram conditions, but the segmented diagram condition produces better results than the full diagram condition. This model is the precise pattern predicted by the researcher. Taken together these results provide fairly strong evidence that the diagrams aid learning from the text, but weaker evidence favoring the segmented diagram over the full diagram.

A major advantage of the PCIC approach is that there is an intuitive mapping between its results and patterns of means predicted by the researcher. It is also parsimonious, in that it favors the models with fewest parameters (all other things being equal). On the other hand, some properties of the procedure are not yet as well known as for competing methods (e.g., its robustness to violations of assumptions). An alternative to the PCIC approach is to compare patterns of means using contrasts.

13.5 Analysis of covariance

ANCOVA is a powerful extension of ANOVA models to include continuous as well as categorical predictors. Like ANOVA, it is a special case of multiple regression. ANCOVA has several applications, but the best known are: i) to increase statistical power in randomized controlled experiments and ii) to remove bias or confounding in observational or quasi-experimental studies.

13.5.1 One-way ANCOVA

The simplest ANCOVA model involves the addition of a single covariate to a two independent groups design (normally analyzed using a t test, but equivalent to one-way ANOVA with two levels). To make the interpretation of the model easier it is best to center the continuous covariate (see Box 13.2). The centered covariate $(C_i - \hat{\mu}_C)$ keeps the link between the grand or weighted grand mean and the intercept in a model with effect coding:

$$y_i = \hat{\mu}_{grand} + b_1 x_i + b_2 (C_i - \hat{\mu}_C) + e_i \qquad \text{Equation 13.28}$$

Here, X is a categorical predictor that can take the values -1 or $+1$ whereas C is a continuous predictor. This model therefore describes the following two regression lines:

$$\begin{aligned} &\hat{\mu}_{grand} - b_1 + b_2 (C_i - \hat{\mu}_C) + e_i \quad (X = -1) \\ &\hat{\mu}_{grand} + b_1 + b_2 (C_i - \hat{\mu}_C) + e_i \quad (X = 1) \end{aligned} \qquad \text{Equation 13.29}$$

Figure 13.4 shows an example of regression lines for a two group ANCOVA design (with one group represented by the shaded circles and the other by open circles).

With effect coding, the intercepts of the two regression lines are $\hat{\mu}_{grand} - b_1$ and $\hat{\mu}_{grand} + b_1$. The slope of the categorical predictor b_1 is therefore the deviation of the regression line for each group from the grand mean (and half the vertical distance between the lines).

If the covariate is not centered, the slope of the categorical predictor would be the deviation relative to an adjusted grand mean (the average expected value of Y when the covariate is zero). By changing the value of C in the prediction equation it is possible to adjust the expected mean value in each group. Adjusted means for the groups play the same role in interpreting ANCOVA as the level means do in ANOVA (see Box 13.2).

Exactly the same plot would be obtained if dummy coding had been used. Under dummy coding with two groups, the interpretation is perhaps even clearer. The regression intercept

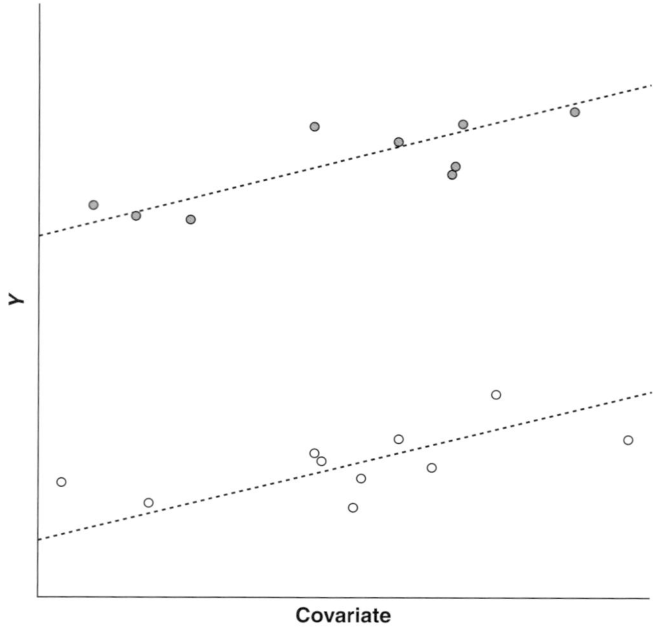

Figure 13.4 ANCOVA with two groups and one covariate

would represent the intercept for the group coded zero, whereas the slope of the categorical predictor would represent the difference in the intercepts and therefore the vertical distance between regression lines:

$$\begin{aligned} &\hat{\mu}_0 + b_2(C_i - \hat{\mu}_C) + e_i &\quad (X=0) \\ &\hat{\mu}_0 + b_1 + b_2(C_i - \hat{\mu}_C) + e_i &\quad (X=1) \end{aligned}$$

Equation 13.30

An important feature of this basic ANCOVA model is that the effects of the covariate for the groups are identical. The regression lines are therefore parallel. This will always happen whenever a covariate has a single slope parameter. This kind of ANCOVA model is suitable only when the effects of the covariate are the same (or at least similar) between groups. This is sometimes known as the assumption of *homogeneity of covariance* (or perhaps *homogeneity of regression* or *parallel slopes*). Using more sophisticated regression models it is possible to relax this constraint by adding slopes for different groups.

ANCOVA is not restricted to two groups. Covariates can be added to any one-way ANOVA model and fitted using any software that will run multiple regression or specific ANCOVA commands. For more complex models, effect coding is usually preferred. Setting out an ANCOVA with one factor in an ANOVA table is instructive. Table 13.11 shows how the total sample variance (in terms of sums of squares) is partitioned into variance associated with the covariate, the factor (adjusted for the presence of the covariate) and what remains (error).

If the covariate is uncorrelated with the factor levels (i.e., all predictors are orthogonal) SS_{factor} will be identical to that of a one-way ANOVA excluding the covariate. The effect of

Table 13.11 The structure of the ANOVA table for a one-way ANCOVA, with independent measures and a single covariate

Source	*df*	*SS*	*MS*	*F*
Covariate	1	$SS_{covariate}$	$\frac{SS_{covariate}}{df_{factor}}$	$\frac{MS_{covariate}}{MS_{error}}$
Factor (adjusted)	$J-1$	SS_{factor}	$\frac{SS_{factor}}{df_{factor}}$	$\frac{MS_{factor}}{MS_{error}}$
Error	$N-J-1$	$SS_{residual}$	$\frac{SS_{residual}}{df_{error}}$	
Total	$N-1$	SS_{total}		

adding a covariate is then almost solely to reduce error (its only other impact being to reduce df_{error} by one).

This is the classic application of ANCOVA. Provided the covariate has a non-negligible correlation with the outcome Y (but not with the factor) the reduction in error should more than compensate for the loss of 1 *df*. This application is particularly suitable when applied to a randomized design. In such a design the value of the covariate will typically be similar for both groups (though rarely identical). Adding a covariate should therefore adjust for any chance differences between the groups in terms of the covariate (e.g., arising through randomization). Given that differences are usually small, it is the reduction in error that is typically more useful. For instance, in a randomized experiment comparing a new and old asthma treatment, the participants will differ in the severity of their disease. Random allocation of sufficiently large samples will ensure that the new and old treatment groups are, on average, similar in severity, but much of the resulting variance in outcomes will still depend on the severity of the disease. Adding the covariate will decrease the size of the error term and therefore – if the treatments do differ in effectiveness – generate a larger F ratio for the test of the factor. Both F ratio for the factor and F or t ratio for the covariate can be tested in the usual way. The reduction in error will also influence CIs and other inferential procedures such as information criteria or Bayes factor (as these also depend on the error term).

A proportion of variance explained measures such as η^2 or R^2 no longer necessarily agree in ANCOVA. The overall R^2 measure is now the sum of covariate effects and the adjusted effect of the factors. In one-way ANCOVA with a single covariate R^2 is defined as $SS_{covariate} + SS_{factor}$ as a proportion of SS_{total}, while η^2 for the factor is SS_{factor} divided by SS_{total}. What may not be obvious is that η_p^2 will now tend to be larger than η^2 because it has the denominator $SS_{factor} + SS_{residual}$ rather than SS_{total}. Some software (e.g., SPSS) provides η_p^2 as the default effect size measure for ANOVA and ANCOVA designs. This will be misleading if researchers interpret it as a proportion of overall variance explained. In fact, it is the proportion of variance explained ignoring other (possibly highly relevant) effects. Ignoring the presence of a covariate may be dangerous if you want to interpret the practical or clinical effect of a factor. In many cases, the covariate is not merely a nuisance variable, but an important variable for understanding what is going on (e.g., disease severity in the asthma example).

Being able to detect the effect of a factor with increased sensitivity is very useful, but ANCOVA adds a layer of complexity to interpreting differences between the means of the factor levels. Unless the covariate has exactly zero correlation with the categorical predictors (i.e., the covariate has the same mean for all levels of the factor), the effect of the factor does not indicate differences in the level means. It now indicates differences in the *adjusted means* (the level means after adjustment for the influence of the covariate). It tests the null hypothesis that the level means are all equal for situations where the covariate is identical. The regression equation can also be used to obtain estimates of the differences when the covariate is held constant (and software packages often report these adjusted means in ANCOVA output). The adjusted means are usually reported as if the covariate were at its mean value (though other values can be selected). Adjusted means are a form of prediction and can be obtained using the prediction equation (with the appropriate covariate and predictor values as input).

The ability to adjust the means for the presence of a covariate has led to ANCOVA being widely adopted for observational as well as experimental designs. In these designs, ANCOVA is typically presented as a 'statistical control' of a confounding variable. This application is controversial. There are two main problems with it. One is statistical and the other philosophical. The statistical issue is that the covariate may not be successful at removing all the bias – and in some cases can lead to overestimates or underestimates of other effects (see Snedecor and Cochran, 1989). If the covariate is not perfectly reliable it will only partly remove bias owing to a confounding variable. If the covariate is uncorrelated with the factor (as is common in an experimental design) it will not bias the estimates of mean differences. This may not be true in an observational design. As a consequence, effects can be distorted by the presence of an unreliable covariate (Ree and Carretta, 2006). This does not necessarily invalidate the approach, as even with an unreliable covariate it may be the case that the adjusted effects are less biased than the unadjusted ones (but never assume that all bias has been removed).

The philosophical problem is more troubling. For the idea of a statistical control to be tenable, it must be plausible that X could be observed at the adjusted levels of the covariate. What if the covariate is inextricably linked to different levels of the factor? A study looking at levels of aggression might look at predictors such as the sex of participants, testosterone levels or alcohol consumption. One could argue that testosterone levels are intrinsically linked to the sex of participants and that treating them as a covariate is problematic, in a way that adjusting for differing levels of alcohol consumption might not be. The application of ANCOVA as a method of statistical control may therefore be difficult to defend, with some authors arguing that it is rarely, if ever, justified (Miller and Chapman, 2001). One indicator that it may be reasonable is the degree of overlap between groups with respect to the covariate. With at least partial overlap there is some indication that members of different groups can be equated with respect to the covariate in a meaningful way (see Gelman and Hill, 2007).[13]

Box 13.2 Adjusted means and their standard errors

In a one-way independent measures ANOVA the predictions are defined by the means of groups defined by the factor levels. In ANCOVA the expected mean value of the outcome Y is not a simple function of the categorical predictor (except in the rare case that all groups have the same mean covariate score). If the mean value of Y depends on the covariate, then it would be unfair to compare the group means if (as is likely) the groups differ on the covariate.

In a study of weight loss it might be that weight loss is predicted by weight at the start of the study (the baseline). It would be unfair to compare the unadjusted mean weight of the experimental and control group at the end of the study if they differed at baseline. A sensible analysis for the study might therefore incorporate baseline weight as a covariate. This allows you to compare the weight of participants adjusted for the differences in the covariate.

Adjusted group means can be calculated from the prediction equation. The prediction equation for one-way ANCOVA with a single covariate (for either dummy or effect coding) takes the form:

$$\hat{Y} = b_0 + b_1 X + b_2 C \qquad \text{Equation 13.31}$$

Centering the covariate makes a huge difference to the interpretation. To derive the adjusted means you first have to decide which value of the covariate to pick (as they will change with the covariate). Sometimes the right value to pick will be obvious, but often the choice is arbitrary. Picking zero as the default value for the covariate (by fitting an uncentered model) is generally a bad idea. For many covariates (e.g., age, weight, or IQ) zero is an unlikely or impossible value. Evaluating the adjusted means at zero produces hard-to-interpret and perhaps meaningless values when the covariate is uncentered (e.g., evaluating weight loss as if participants had started the study with a weight of zero).

Centering the covariate simplifies the arithmetic and aids interpretation. The prediction equation then becomes:

$$\hat{Y} = b_0 + b_1 X + b_2 \left(C - \hat{\mu}_C\right) \qquad \text{Equation 13.32}$$

The intercept b_0 is now meaningful because it represents the adjusted mean when $C - \hat{\mu}_C$ is zero and X is zero. For a dummy coded model b_0 will be the adjusted mean of the group coded zero. This property is sometimes used as a quick way to obtain adjusted or predicted means in regressions with categorical predictors. By selecting different reference categories you can get adjusted means for each group in turn. Rescaling the covariate gives you adjusted means evaluated at different points (e.g., for low, medium and high values of the covariate).

The presence of the covariate complicates the analysis of group means in another way. Even if the homogeneity of variance assumption is plausible, it is not appropriate to test for differences in the adjusted means with the pooled error term from the ANCOVA. The standard errors also require adjustment (unless the means of the covariate within each group are identical). Groups that are extreme on the covariate will have larger standard errors than groups that are average on the covariate. This happens for the same reason that $\hat{\sigma}_{prediction}$ depends on the predictor values in any regression; extreme values have high leverage and are estimated with less precision than central values.

The pooled error term for a single adjusted level (i.e., group) mean is:

$$\hat{\sigma}_{\hat{\mu}*} = \sqrt{MS_{error}\left(\frac{1}{n_j} + \frac{\left(\hat{\mu}_{C_j} - \hat{\mu}_C\right)^2}{SS_{residual(\mathrm{cov})}}\right)} \qquad \text{Equation 13.33}$$

MS_{error} here is the pooled error term from the ANCOVA. The other terms need further explanation: n_j is the sample size for group j and $\hat{\mu}_{C_j}$ is the mean value of the covariate in group j. $\hat{\mu}_C$ is therefore the grand mean value of the covariate calculated over all J groups. $SS_{residual(\mathrm{cov})}$ is the residual sum of squares from a one-way ANOVA with the covariate replacing Y as the outcome. The standard error for an unadjusted mean ($\hat{\sigma}_{\hat{\mu}}$) can be expressed as $\sqrt{MS_{error}\left(1/n_j\right)}$. Thus $\hat{\sigma}_{\hat{\mu}*}$ is equivalent only when $\hat{\mu}_{C_j} = \hat{\mu}_C$ (ignoring the fact that MS_{error} is often smaller for ANCOVA than for ANOVA).

This quantity is sufficient to construct a CI for a single adjusted mean. Inference about a difference between adjusted means depends on the separation of the covariate mean $(\hat{\mu}_{C_1} - \hat{\mu}_{C_1})$ for the groups in question:

$$\hat{\sigma}_{\hat{\mu}_1-\hat{\mu}_2*} = \sqrt{MS_{error}\left(\frac{1}{n_1} + \frac{1}{n_2} + \frac{(\hat{\mu}_{C_1} - \hat{\mu}_{C_2})^2}{SS_{residual(cov)}}\right)} \qquad \text{Equation 13.34}$$

The size of $\hat{\sigma}_{\hat{\mu}_1-\hat{\mu}_2*}$ thus depends on the similarity of the groups in terms of their covariate score.

Adjusted means and their standard errors can be obtained in several ways. Because the adjusted means are predictions, matrix algebra solutions for obtaining predictions also work for adjusted means. Coefficients from a fitted ANCOVA model, in addition, provide either adjusted means or differences between adjusted means (and report appropriate standard errors). For dummy coded predictors, the intercept is the adjusted mean of the reference category. The coefficients for the $J - 1$ dummy coded predictors represent differences in adjusted means relative to the mean of the reference category. This is one way to obtain adjusted means and standard errors (by refitting the model with different reference categories). Fitting a cell means model (see Box 13.1) provides an elegant way to obtain all J adjusted means and their standard errors in a single analysis.

One final point should be noted. Some of the potential efficiency advantage of ANCOVA (which typically has a smaller error term) will be lost if covariate values vary substantially between groups. In extreme cases, the efficiency gains may be wiped out completely (see Liu, 2011). This is most likely when n is small and the covariate is only weakly associated with the outcome Y.

Example 13.7 Earlier analyses of the diagram data focused only on the impact of the experimental group. The study also recorded the time participants took to read the descriptions. As participants were free to take as long as they wished to read the text, it seems likely that participants who took longer would have learned more. The mean reading times (in seconds) also vary somewhat between conditions: 639 for text, 646 for picture, 518.2 for full diagram and 448.1 for segmented diagram. The confounding variable of reading time may therefore be masking or exaggerating differences in description quality between the groups. ANCOVA provides a way to take account of these differences by including time as a covariate.

There are (at least) two different models that could be employed here. Either the reading time or the logarithm of the reading time could be added. The logarithm of reading time might be preferred *a priori* because reading times tends to be positively skewed. It is also plausible to view learning as proportionate to time spent on a task rather than as a simple additive function. Inspection of the normal probability plot (not reported here) for each model suggests little to choose between them (and both plots are similar to Figure 13.2). The AIC for the two models marginally favors the use of ln(*time*) as a covariate (ΔAIC = 1.013). This is equivalent to $LR_{AIC} = 1.66$ in favor of the model with the transformed covariate. This suggests that ln(*time*) should be entered as a covariate rather than *time*.

Table 13.12 shows the ANCOVA output for a model with experimental group as the factor, ln(*time*) as the covariate and description quality as the outcome. As the predictors in this model are not orthogonal it matters very much how the sums of squares are calculated, with non-sequential SS being appropriate (i.e., hierarchical or unique SS which are equivalent in balanced designs).

Table 13.12 The ANOVA table for a one-way ANCOVA of the diagram data

Source	*df*	*SS*	*MS*	*F*	*p*
ln(*time*)	1	339.66	339.66	5.66	.023
Group (adjusted)	3	879.26	293.09	4.88	.006
Error	35	2100.54	60.02		
Total	39	3023.90			

The overall model is statistically significant, $F_{4,35} = 3.85$, $p < .05$, $R^2 = .31$. As the only difference between this model and the one-way ANOVA is the inclusion of the covariate, the test of the covariate is also a test of the change in R^2 between the ANCOVA and ANOVA model. The test of the covariate is statistically significant, $F_{1,35} = 5.66$, $p < .05$, indicating that an effect of reading time on description quality has been detected. η^2 for the covariate ($339.66/3023.90 = .112$) is also ΔR^2 for the ANCOVA relative to the ANOVA. The effect of the experimental group is statistically significant and the observed *p* value somewhat smaller than in the one-way ANOVA.

Two things are at work here. One is the effect of a marginal decrease in error variance from 67.78 to 60.02. The other is the impact of covariate adjustments to the means (which has increased the spread of the scores). The covariate has behaved a little like a suppressor variable. Its simple correlation with description quality is $r = .12$. Its correlation with the residuals of the one-way ANOVA is $r = .34$. Its impact on the ANCOVA is large because it explains residual variance that the ANOVA doesn't (rather than because it is a good predictor of learning on the task). For it to be a suppressor under Darlington's definition, the simple correlation with the outcome would need to be zero or negative (rather than $r = .12$). There is nothing particularly mysterious about how suppressor variables work – they are only marginally more extreme than a typical confounding variable in their effects.

To interpret the effects of the covariate it is sensible to look at the coefficients for the model. For a dummy coded factor and a centered covariate they are:

Intercept	16.618
Picture	0.286
Full diagram	6.465
Segmented diagram	12.579
ln(*time*)	7.252

The coefficient for ln(*time*) is the increase in description quality associated with a one-unit increase in the natural logarithm of the reading time. This is positive, indicating that longer reading times are associated with better description quality. As the natural logarithm has been used, this implies that when reading time increases by a factor of $e^1 \approx 2.72$ then description quality goes up by an average of around 7.25 points. Scaling that down, a $1/7.25 = 0.14$ increase in ln(*time*) would give a one-unit increase in description quality. This would require an increase in reading time by factor $e^{0.14} \approx 1.15$. So spending 15% longer reading the text is associated with a one-unit increase in description quality.

Turning to the other coefficients, the intercept is the adjusted group mean for the *text* condition (evaluated, because of centering, at the mean of the covariate). The remaining coefficients are the differences in adjusted means of the groups relative to the text only reference group (e.g., the adjusted mean for the picture condition is $16.618 + 0.286 = 16.904$). Under effect coding the coefficients are:

Intercept	21.450
Text	−4.832
Picture	−4.547
Full diagram	1.632
ln(*time*)	7.252

The coefficient for the covariate is unchanged. The intercept is the grand mean. The coefficients for the other groups are now deviations from the grand mean (e.g., the adjusted mean for the picture condition is $21.45 + (-4.547) = 16.90$). To get the coefficient for the segmented diagram condition you can either change the reference category or use the knowledge that the group coefficients must sum to zero. The reported coefficients have the sum −7.747. The coefficient for the segmented diagram condition is therefore +7.747 (and its adjusted mean is $21.45 + 7.747 = 29.20$).

Another parameterization, perhaps the easiest to interpret (in terms of coefficients), is the cell means model:

Text	16.618
Picture	16.903
Full diagram	23.082
Segmented diagram	29.197
ln(*time*)	7.252

This provides all four adjusted means and the covariate effect. The only problem is that the default inferences for this model are now rather uninteresting (e.g., *t* tests of the null hypothesis that description quality is zero).

The adjusted means for the analysis can also be obtained as predictions for the group means at a particular value of the covariate. Evaluated at the mean value of the covariate, the adjusted means are as indicated for the cell means model. The range of the means and the separation between diagram and non-diagram conditions has increased. A plausible explanation is that the diagrams may make the text easier to read, so that participants both take less time to read and learn better.

There are several ways to compare the adjusted means. To construct a pairwise comparison or a CI for a difference involves obtaining the standard errors. I'll illustrate this for the comparison of full and segmented diagrams (groups three and four). The *SE* for this difference is:

$$\hat{\sigma}_{\hat{\mu}_3 - \hat{\mu}_4 *} = \sqrt{MS_{error}\left(\frac{1}{n_1} + \frac{1}{n_2} + \frac{(\hat{\mu}_{C_3} - \hat{\mu}_{C_4})^2}{SS_{residual(cov)}}\right)}$$

$$= \sqrt{60.02\left(\frac{1}{10} + \frac{1}{10} + \frac{[\ln(518.2) - \ln(448.1)]^2}{6.4576}\right)} \approx 3.49$$

The difference in the adjusted means is $29.20 - 23.08 = 6.12$, $t_{crit} = 2.03$ and the 95% CI is [−0.96, 13.20]. Alternatively, using the PCIC approach from Example 13.6, the most informative model, in terms of AIC_C, is now {12,3,4}. This is the model that supports the conclusion that the diagram conditions are better than the non-diagram conditions, and the segmented diagram superior to the full diagram. Although this is exactly the hypothesized pattern, models {12,34} and {123,4} are almost as probable. ANCOVA therefore provides moderate support for the hypothesis that the diagrams facilitate learning, and some evidence for the superiority of the segmented diagrams over the full diagrams. Stronger conclusions would require larger samples or less noisy data.

13.6 ANOVA, ANCOVA and multiple regression

Treating regression models with categorical predictors, continuous predictors or a mix of the two all as special cases of the same family of regression models has several advantages. One of these is that the regression approach is more flexible (e.g., making it easy to cope with unequal group sizes in ANOVA and ANCOVA). Another is that procedures for interpreting and checking a model (e.g., plotting residuals, influence and leverage diagnostics) are shared between models. Adjustment for covariates is also simplified when treating it as prediction from a regression model. Issues related to planning a study (e.g., statistical power and sample size estimation) are common to many of the models.

Where there are differences, they often arise because the structure of some models is simpler than others. In models with orthogonal predictors, such as balanced ANOVA models, collinearity never arises and this simplifies interpretation of the effects. For ANOVA with independent measures the homogeneity of variance assumption for regression reduces to the assumption of equal variances in the populations the groups are sampled from. The distribution of residuals in an ANOVA model is identical to the distribution of Y within groups for such a model. This happens because $y_{ij} = \mu + \tau_j + \varepsilon_{ij}$ implies $\varepsilon_{ij} = y_{ij} - \mu - \tau_j$ and because μ and τ_j are constants. This can sometimes lead to apparently conflicting expert advice (e.g., plotting the residuals of the model versus plotting the raw scores within groups to check distributional assumptions). On the whole, it is safer to get into the habit of checking model assumptions using tools and procedures designed for regression, as the diagnostic tools available for regression models (e.g., leverage and influence statistics) are often superior to those implemented for specialist ANOVA commands. One exception is that specialist ANOVA software often comes with customized procedures for displaying means or adjusted means in plots or tables.

13.7 R code for Chapter 13

13.7.1 One-way ANOVA models (Examples 13.1 and 13.2)

Many ANOVA models can be fitted using the `lm()` function. This can be accomplished directly or via the `aov()` or `anova()` functions (which are ways to get an ANOVA style of output from a linear model). To see the differences, first read the diagram data from SPSS as a data frame.

```
library(foreign)
diag.data <- read.spss('diagram.sav', to.data.frame=TRUE)
```

Compare output from the following commands:

```
summary(lm(descript ~ group, data = diag.data))
anova(lm(descript ~ group, data = diag.data))
summary(aov(descript ~ group, data = diag.data))
```

The `anova()` function applied to the linear model output produces identical results to that of the summary of the `aov()` function. This is a conventional ANOVA table for a one-way independent measures design. In contrast, the linear model function returns multiple regression output for the dummy coded predictors for the variable group (though all three functions use a parameterization of the general linear model with what amounts to dummy coding). R has also done something rather clever in this analysis. It recognized, without being instructed, that group is a categorical predictor (a 'factor') and treated it as such in the analysis. R usually codes any imported variable containing text (here the condition names) as a factor. For groups identified only by number, R will default to treating them as a continuous predictor. This may not matter if the factor has only two levels, but can sometimes cause problems. See what happens when the groups are coded as the numbers one to four:

```
new.group <- c(rep(1,10), rep(2,10), rep(3,10), rep(4,10))
summary(lm(descript ~ new.group, data=diag.data))
```

The group codes can be defined by exploiting each argument of the `rep()` function. Here the sequence 1:4 is repeated in multiples of ten:

```
new.group <- rep(1:4, each = 10)
```

The results have changed because new.group is treated (incorrectly) as a continuous predictor. There are ways to treat this object as a factor:

```
new.group <- factor(new.group)
summary(lm(descript ~ new.group, data=diag.data))

summary(lm(descript ~ factor(new.group), data = diag.data))
```

The `gl()` function can also generate levels for a factor. Here the command generates a new factor with four levels and $n = 10$ per level:

```
new.factor <- gl(4,10)
```

The `expand.grid()` function, often used with `predict()`, can help set up factor structures in a data frame, and works with multiple predictors:

```
expand.grid(parts=seq(1,10,1), factor1=gl(4,1))
```

Although R defaults to dummy coding in the treatment of factors, this can be altered. To check the default settings use:

```
options('contrasts')
```

This will usually return:

```
$contrasts
     unordered            ordered
'contr.treatment'      'contr.poly'
```

For unordered factors, the default is 'treatment contrasts' (dummy coding for each 'treatment' or category). The following commands set it to effect coding and then back to dummy coding for unordered factors:

```
options(contrasts=c('contr.sum', 'contr.poly'))
options(contrasts=c('contr.treatment', 'contr.poly'))
```

Effect coding is referred to as 'sum' contrasts because the codes all sum to zero. (Polynomial contrasts are dealt with in Chapter 15.) This isn't the only way to set up effect coding. You could code the indicator variables directly. This command produces the effect codes for the first condition versus the second (assuming the first condition is the reference category):

```
ec1 <- new.group <- c(rep(-1,10), rep(1,10), rep(0,20))
```

Coding things directly in this way is tedious (and mistakes are easy to make) and people rarely bother to unless there are only two levels. To the see the effect coded output for the diagram data ANOVA try:

```
options(contrasts=c('contr.sum', 'contr.poly'))
summary(lm(descript ~ group, data = diag.data))
```

R defaults to using the last category as the reference category.

The regression output doesn't make it easy to work out the expected values (i.e., means of each group). This can be done for a single factor using `tapply()`. This applies another function to a variable in a data frame or similar structure. Using `tapply()` with an `index` (here diag.data$group) applies that function to subsets of the data frame, though it is cleaner to use `with()`. Here it is used to obtain the mean and *SD* for each condition:

```
tapply(diag.data$descript, diag.data$group, mean)

with(diag.data, tapply(descript, group, mean))
with(diag.data, tapply(descript, group, sd))
```

A more versatile function is the `summaryBy()` function in the doBy package. It defaults to the mean, but can report several functions, taking arguments in a formula style:

```
install.packages('doBy')
library(doBy)
```

```
summaryBy(descript ~ group, data=diag.data)
summaryBy(descript ~ group, data=diag.data, FUN = mean)
summaryBy(descript ~ group, data=diag.data, FUN = sd)
summaryBy(descript ~ group, data=diag.data, FUN = c(mean, sd))
```

The `summaryBy()` function generalizes nicely to more complex designs, but for a data frame or a single vector the psych functions `describe()` and `describe.by()` can be preferable. These are simpler to use and report other statistics (including skewness and excess kurtosis):

```
library(psych)
describe(diag.data)
describe.by(diag.data, group=diag.data$group)
```

My preferred route to ANOVA output that provides the means directly is to fit a cell means model. This involves fitting a no-intercept model with a single factor. R fits a model with J indicator variables, one for each level of the factor. The parameter estimates for these predictors are the four cell means:

```
diag.cell.model <- lm(descript ~ 0 + group, data = diag.data)
diag.cell.model <- lm(descript ~ group - 1, data = diag.data)
summary(diag.cell.model)
```

The cell means model allows the parameters in the regression to be interpreted directly as level means, but has the drawback that statistics such R^2, F and t are relative to an expected outcome of zero. Each t test is now a test of whether the level mean is zero. R^2 is the proportion of variance explained relative to a model in which the grand mean is zero. For this reason the cell means model is more useful for model comparison than for testing individual parameters. A quick way to obtain the usual R^2 for an ANOVA model (equal to η^2 and η_p^2 in this case) is to center the outcome in the cell means model. The F ratio for the main effect can be obtained by comparison with an intercept-only model:

```
summary(lm(scale(descript, scale = F) ~ 0 + group, data =
  diag.data))$r.sq

anova(diag.cell.model, lm(descript ~ 1, diag.data))
```

The hand calculations in Example 13.2 can be checked in R (though bear in mind that these formulas assume balanced designs). The mean square for the group factor is the variance of the group means multiplied by the cell size:

```
n <- 10
J <- 4
group.means <- with(diag.data, tapply(descript, group, mean))
ms.group <- var(group.means) * n
```

MS_{error} is the average of the squared standard deviations of the groups:

```
group.sds <- with(diag.data, tapply(descript, group, sd))
ms.error <- mean((group.sds)^2)
```

SS_{total} is the variance of the outcome variable multiplied by the total *df*, and *F* is the ratio of the mean squares:

```
SS.tot <- var(diag.data$descript) * (n * J - 1)
ms.group / ms.error
```

Using regression or GLM commands to run ANOVA makes it possible to draw on a wide range of diagnostic and other tools. A normal probability plot for the standardized residuals, like the one in Figure 13.2, uses the `rstandard()` and `qqnorm()` functions:

```
qqnorm(rstandard (lm(descript ~ group, data=diag.data)) )
abline(0, 1, lty=3)
```

The maximum Cook's distance is given by:

```
cd.diag <- cooks.distance(lm(descript ~ group,
  data=diag.data))
max(cd.diag)
```

For statistical power the first step (for an ANOVA) is to calculate Cohen's *f*. Then use the ANOVA power function in the `pwr` package:

```
f <- (.193/(1 - .193))^0.5
library(pwr)
pwr.anova.test(k = 4, n = 20, f)
```

This matches the output from other software such as G*Power. Sensitivity to effect size can be explored by plotting the effect of changing *f* on required sample size:

```
f.seq <- seq(.2, .6, .01)
power <- pwr.anova.test(k = 4, n = 20, f.seq)$power
plot(f.seq, power, xlab=expression(italic(f.seq)),
  ylab='Power')
```

13.7.2 *A priori* comparisons (Example 13.3)

A *t* test or CI for a single *a priori* comparison between means usually uses the pooled error term from an ANOVA (for independent designs). This pooled error term is MS_{error} and its square root is $\hat{\sigma}_{pooled}$. Assuming equality of variance, this will be a more accurate measure of error than that from the individual levels. The following commands calculate $\hat{\sigma}_{pooled}$, $\hat{\sigma}_{\hat{\mu}_1-\hat{\mu}_2}$ and the margin of error for a 95% CI of the differences in level means:

```
sd.p <- 67.8^0.5
se.p <- sd.p * (1/10 + 1/10)^0.5
moe <- qt(.005, 36, lower.tail=FALSE) * se.p
```

The ratio of the differences between means to $\hat{\sigma}_{\hat{\mu}_1-\hat{\mu}_2}$ generates the t statistics for the pairwise tests. These are then used to derive p values:

```
m.diffs <- c(9.5, 9.0, 4.9, 4.6, 4.1)
t.obs <- m.diffs/se.p
p.obs <- pt(t.obs, df = 36, lower.tail=FALSE)*2
```

From a set of unadjusted p values, like those in `p.obs`, the `p.adjust()` function can be used to calculate LMH (Holm), Hochberg and other corrections:

```
p.adjust(p.obs, method = 'holm')
p.adjust(p.obs, method = 'hochberg')
p.adjust(p.obs, method = 'bonferroni')
```

As the `p.adjust()` function works with the observed p values it is not restricted to ANOVA.

13.7.3 *Post hoc* tests (Example 13.4)

R implements *post hoc* testing using any of the methods available for p value adjustment from the `p.adjust()` function. These also include false discovery rate (FDR) methods. Unlike *a priori* tests, the adjustment, using `pairwise.t.test()` is made for all possible pairwise tests. For uncorrected tests using a pooled error term and for the LMH (Holm) procedure:

```
pairwise.t.test(diag.data$descript, diag.data$group,
  p.adjust.method='none')

pairwise.t.test(diag.data$descript, diag.data$group,
  p.adjust.method='holm')
```

It is possible to specify a non-pooled error term (this being the default if paired t tests are specified). Some specialized *post hoc* tests, notably Tukey's HSD, are available and it is also easy to plot the differences as CIs:

```
TukeyHSD(aov(formula = descript ~ group, data=diag.data))

plot(TukeyHSD(aov(formula = descript ~ group,
  data=diag.data)))
```

More sophisticated *post hoc* testing requires something like the `multcomp` package (Hothorn *et al.*, 2008). A full exploration of the package is not possible here, but the `glht()` or general linear hypotheses function is very versatile (and not restricted to models fitted with the `lm()` function). It takes as basic input a fitted model and set of linear functions via the `linfct` argument. The linear functions can be set up in various ways, with some options (e.g., Tukey HSD) built in. The built in functions involve a call to `mcp()`. This sets up the linear functions for a named factor in the model automatically, and is designed to be applied within `glht()`. Thus the following code runs Tukey HSD pairwise tests for the diagram data:

```
install.packages('multcomp')
library(multcomp)
diag.anova <- aov(formula = descript ~ group, data=diag.data)
summary(glht(diag.anova, linfct = mcp(group='Tukey')))
```

The Dunnett test of all conditions versus a single control (assumed to be the first level of the factor) is also built in. Thus this command displays tests of the picture, full diagram and segmented diagram versus the text condition:

```
summary(glht(diag.anova, linfct = mcp(group='Dunnett')))
```

Hothorn *et al.* (2008) show how to use a sandwich estimator to deal with potential violations of the homogeneity of variance assumption. A sandwich estimator is a robust method of estimating variances and covariances for a regression model (Zeileis, 2004, 2006). This is useful because the Tukey test is not designed for unequal variances between groups.

```
install.packages('sandwich')
library(sandwich)
summary(glht(diag.anova, linfct = mcp(group = 'Tukey'),
  vcov=sandwich))
```

The `multcomp` package allows plotting of the Tukey HSD CIs.

```
par(mar=c(4,13,.5,.5))
plot(confint(glht(diag.anova, linfct = mcp(group = 'Tukey'),
  vcov=sandwich)), xlab='Difference in description quality
  (95% CI)', cex.axis = .85, main = NA, ylim=c(6,1))
segments(0,0, 0,7, lty=3, lwd = 0.5)
```

The `par()` function is used here to make the margins wider and `cex.axis` to make the axis text smaller. This allows the full label text to fit on the left-hand side of the plot. Specifying the limits of the y-axis backwards as `ylim=c(6,1)` rather than the default `ylim=c(1,6)` coerces it to plot the tests in reverse order (which seems more natural here). The `segments()` function adds a line for zero difference in means.

13.7.4 Incorporating logical constraints (Example 13.5)

Adding logical constraints to *a priori* or *post hoc* tests is possible using the `multcomp` package. The precise tests required need to be specified as user-defined linear functions, but the `glht()` function can determine the constraints automatically. The linear functions are specified as a matrix of linear contrasts (of which pairwise comparisons are a special case). The columns of the matrix are the fixed parameters of the model (including the intercept, if there is one), while the rows define the tests. I find it easier to fit a cell means model first. This creates a model with J cell means as parameters and therefore each column in the matrix represents a mean. Each row of the matrix represents a test. The two means to be compared are set to -1 and 1 respectively (and all other means to zero). In a cell means model each test can therefore be specified using a form of effect coding. The following matrix creates labels for the columns and rows and then codes for the five *a priori* tests conducted in Example 13.5.

```
cnames <- c('Text', 'Picture', 'Full', 'Segmented')
rnames <- c('S-F', 'S-P', 'S-T', 'F-P', 'F-T')
C.mat <- matrix(,5,4, dimnames=list(rnames, cnames))
C.mat[1,] <- c(0, 0, -1, 1)
C.mat[2,] <- c(0, -1, 0, 1)
C.mat[3,] <- c(-1, 0, 0, 1)
C.mat[4,] <- c(0, -1, 1, 0)
C.mat[5,] <- c(-1, 0, 1, 0)
C.mat
```

There is no need to fill the matrix row-by-row or add labels (but it can help to keep track of the hypotheses being tested). The remaining commands fit a cell means model to the diagram data and then run the pairwise tests with logical constraints according to the Shaffer procedure. As before, robust standard errors are requested (but need not be).

```
diag.cmm <- aov(formula = descript ~ 0 + group, data =
  diag.data)

summary(glht(diag.cmm, linfct=C.mat, vcov = sandwich),
  test=adjusted('Shaffer'))
```

The test argument can accept any of the standard `p.adjust()` methods such as `holm` or `fdr`. If it is set to `Westfall` the adjusted p values take into account correlations between test statistics. This is the recommended option unless CIs are required.

```
summary(glht(diag.cmm, linfct=C.mat, vcov = sandwich),
  test=adjusted('Westfall'))
```

13.7.5 Dayton's PCIC approach to *post hoc* testing (Example 13.6)

The group means are already ordered smallest to largest, so Dayton's method involves fitting all eight models and comparing AIC or BIC. Given the small sample size for the diagram data set it makes sense to use AIC_C in place of AIC. Again this involves the `bbmle` package. The commands below fit the eight different models and then use the `ICtab()` function to tabulate the results:

```
g1234 <- lm(descript ~ 1, data=diag.data)

group <- c(rep(0,10),rep(1,30))
g1v234 <- lm(diag.data$descript ~ group)

group <- c(rep(0,20),rep(1,20))
g12v34 <- lm(diag.data$descript ~ group)

group <- c(rep(0,30),rep(1,10))
g123v4 <- lm(diag.data$descript ~ group)
```

```
group <- as.factor(c(rep(0,10),rep(1,10), rep(2,20)))
g1v2v34 <- lm(diag.data$descript ~ group)

group <- as.factor(c(rep(0,10),rep(1,20), rep(2,10)))
g1v23v4 <- lm(diag.data$descript ~ group)

group <- as.factor(c(rep(0,20),rep(1,10), rep(2,10)))
g12v3v4 <- lm(diag.data$descript ~ group)

g1v2v3v4 <- lm(descript ~ group, data=diag.data)

library(bbmle)

ICtab(g1234, g1v234,g12v34, g123v4, g1v2v34, g1v23v4, g12v3v4,
  g1v2v3v4, weights=TRUE, base=TRUE, type='AICc', nobs=40)
```

The simplest model is the intercept-only (grand mean) model and the most complex is the usual ANOVA. The intermediate models set up dummy variables or factors to code differences between the groups.

13.7.6 One-way ANCOVA (Example 13.7)

The choice of covariate to add is between *time* and ln(*time*). Here it is convenient to use the `add1()` function. This confirms that there is little to choose between the two ANCOVA models, but the model using the logarithm of the reading time as a covariate is slightly more informative and probably more plausible.

```
add1(diag.anova, scope = ~ group + time + log(time), test='F')
```

The second argument `~ group + time + log(time)` is the `scope` of the model and must include all predictors in the original model as well as the ones to be added (one at a time).

The mean reading time for each description can be obtained in several ways:

```
with(diag.data, tapply(descript, group, mean))

library(psych)
describe.by(diag.data, diag.data$group)
```

As this is ANCOVA there are two sensible approaches to fitting the model. One is to fit the model with sequential *SS*, and ensure that the covariate is entered first. The other is to use non-sequential *SS* (e.g., hierarchical/Type II or unique/Type III *SS*) in which case the order will not matter. Sequential *SS* is the R default for linear models. One way to get hierarchical *SS* tests is to use the `drop1()` function (other methods will be considered later).

```
diag.ancov <- aov(descript ~ log(time) + group,
  data=diag.data)
summary (diag.ancov)

drop1(diag.ancov, test = 'F')
```

With this order of entry both the sequential and non-sequential methods give the group *SS* as 879.26. They differ in the *SS* attributed to the covariate. This is 44.09 for sequential *SS* and 339.66 for non-sequential *SS*. If there is no inherent interest in the covariate the distinction is immaterial (what matters is that the fit of the model improves). The non-sequential fit gives the *SS* after the other predictor is added to the model (or equivalently the reduction in *SS* when that term is dropped). This better reflects its impact on the model (although it can be confusing when the predictors are collinear because they will not sum to the model *SS*).

The coefficients can be obtained from the `lm()` function in the usual way using dummy coding, provided the covariate is centered:

```
cltime <- scale(log(diag.data$time), scale=FALSE)
options(contrasts=c('contr.treatment', 'contr.poly'))
lm(descript ~ group + cltime, data=diag.data)
```

The same commands work for effect coding if the defaults are changed:

```
options(contrasts=c('contr.sum', 'contr.poly'))
lm(descript ~ group + cltime, data=diag.data)
```

The cell means model provides a quick way to get the adjusted means and their standard errors:

```
lm(descript ~ 0 + group + cltime, data=diag.data)
summary(lm(descript ~ 0 + group + cltime, data=diag.data))
```

Centering the covariate is essential if the aim is to report adjusted means where the covariate is at its average. To get them for other values apply the prediction equation (or refit one of the above models with an appropriate constant added to the centered covariate).

As the adjusted means are really just predictions, the `predict()` function will also work (and is preferred for complex modes). The `epicalc` package provides a user-friendly function `adjust()` for returning the adjusted means and their *SE*s. It uses `glm()` which, for present purposes, is identical to the `lm()` function.

```
install.packages('epicalc')
library(epicalc)

diag.mod <- glm(descript ~ cltime + group, data=diag.data)
adjust(cltime, list(group), diag.mod)
```

To calculate the standard error for a difference in means in ANCOVA is harder. This is an instance where the default dummy coding of treatments in R is quite helpful. Using dummy coding the difference in adjusted means for three of the levels and the reference category are reported and the `summary()` function also reports standard errors, *t* and *p*.

```
options(contrasts=c('contr.treatment', 'contr.poly'))
summary(lm(descript ~ group + cltime, data=diag.data))
```

This gives the difference in adjusted means for the full diagram, segmented diagram and picture groups relative to the text group (and the appropriate *SE*s). The example in the text was calculated for the segmented versus the full diagram. To obtain this difference and its *SE* requires a change of reference category. The order of reference categories can be interrogated using `factor()` and the reference category changed using `relevel()`:

```
factor(diag.data$group)
new.group <- relevel(diag.data$group, 'Segmented Diagram')
factor(new.group)
summary(lm(descript ~ new.group + cltime, data=diag.data))
```

This gives the difference in adjusted means for the full and segmented diagram conditions as 6.114 and its *SE* as 3.502. This broadly matches with the results of the hand calculations in Example 13.7. The `confint()` function can also be used here to gain accurate CIs for the adjusted differences in means or adjusted means (depending on the model):

```
confint(lm(descript ~ new.group + cltime, data=diag.data))
```

An alternative to resetting the default contrasts for all analyses is to use the `contrasts()` function to set the preferred contrasts for a particular factor. Compare these results:

```
contrasts(new.group) <- 'contr.sum'
contrasts(new.group)
contrasts(new.group) <- 'contr.treatment'
contrasts(new.group)
```

The `multcomp` package happily performs pairwise comparisons of adjusted means using a range of methods:

```
summary(glht(diag.ancov, linfct = mcp(group = 'Tukey')))
summary(glht(diag.anova, linfct = mcp(group = 'Tukey'), vcov =
  sandwich))
confint(glht(diag.anova, linfct = mcp(group = 'Tukey'), vcov =
  sandwich))
```

This facility includes the Shaffer and Westfall procedures, but the contrast matrix has to take into account the extra parameter required for each covariate. The following matrix sets up and runs all pairwise tests between adjusted means for the diagram data ANCOVA (using a cell means model) with the Westfall procedure:

```
cnames <- c('Text', 'Picture', 'Full', 'Segmented', 'Time')
rnames <- c('S-F', 'S-P', 'S-T', 'F-P', 'F-T', 'P-T')

C.mat <- matrix(,6,5, dimnames=list(rnames, cnames))
C.mat[1,] <- c(0, 0, -1, 1, 0)
C.mat[2,] <- c(0, -1, 0, 1, 0)
C.mat[3,] <- c(-1, 0, 0, 1, 0)
C.mat[4,] <- c(0, -1, 1, 0, 0)
```

```
C.mat[5,] <- c(-1, 0, 1, 0, 0)
C.mat[6,] <- c(-1, 1, 0, 0, 0)
C.mat

diag.ancova <- aov(formula = descript ~ 0 + group + time, data
  = diag.data)
summary(glht(diag.ancova, linfct=C.mat, vcov = sandwich), test
  = adjusted('Westfall'))
```

13.7.7 R packages

Bolker, B. M., and R Development Core Team (2011) *bbmle*: Tools for General Maximum Likelihood Estimation. R package version 0.9.7.

Champely, S. (2009) *pwr*: Basic Functions for Power Analysis. R package version 1.1.1.

Chongsuvivatwong, V. (2011) *epicalc*: Epidemiological Calculator. R package version 2.12.2.3.

Højsgaard, S., Wright, K. and Leidi, A. A. (2010) *doBy*: Groupwise Computations of Summary Statistics, General Linear Contrasts and Other Utilities. R package version 4.0.6.

Hothorn, T., Bretz, F., and Westfall. P. (2008) Simultaneous Inference in General Parametric Models. *Biometrical Journal*, 50, 346–63.

Revelle, W. (2011) *psych*: Procedures for Psychological, Psychometric, and Personality Research. R package version 1.0–95.

Zeileis, A. (2004) Econometric Computing with HC and HAC Covariance Matrix Estimators. *Journal of Statistical Software*, 11, 1–17.

Zeileis, A. (2006) Object-oriented Computation of Sandwich Estimators. *Journal of Statistical Software*, 16, 1–16.

13.8 Notes on SPSS syntax for Chapter 13

13.8.1 Independent measures ANOVA

It is possible to run ANOVA and ANCOVA models in SPSS using regression commands by careful use of dummy or effect coding. This is sometimes a good way to approach an analysis, but for most independent measures designs it is probably better to use the dedicated ANOVA commands. For more complex analyses, the SPSS general linear model commands run ANOVA and ANCOVA as overparameterized models. The major advantage of this approach is that it deals elegantly with categorical predictors. However, there are situations where manual coding of categorical predictors and use of regression commands will be preferred (e.g., for the flexibility and range of subcommands it offers).

For one-way independent measures designs it makes sense to use the basic `ONEWAY` command. To run the ANOVA with group as the factor and description quality as the outcome:

SPSS data file: `diagram.sav`

```
ONEWAY descript BY group.
```

This can be accessed via <Analyze> <Compare means> <One-Way ANOVA ...>. In practice, you'd always want to request some additional statistics such as the means and *SD*s for each group.

```
ONEWAY descript BY group
  /STATISTICS DESCRIPTIVES BROWNFORSYTHE WELCH.
```

The HOMOGENEITY statement added to the /STATISTICS subcommand gives a version of Levene's test of equality of variances based on absolute deviations from the sample mean (see Example 9.3). The procedure is not recommended, but if you do want to test the equality of the variances a more robust version (using absolute deviations from the median) from the EXAMINE subcommand should be selected:

```
EXAMINE VARIABLES=descript BY group
 /PLOT=SPREADLEVEL.
```

If there are doubts about homogeneity of variance – or if the sample sizes in the groups are very unequal – there is good reason to consider a robust version of the ANOVA *F* test. SPSS offers the Brown-Forsyth and Satterthwaite-Welch corrections as options by adding BROWNFORSYTHE or WELCH to the /STATISTICS subcommand.

A means plot can be requested, but an error bar plot is recommended for both its visual appeal and the richer range of chart options for manual editing.

```
GRAPH
  /ERRORBAR(CI 95)=descript BY group
  /TITLE='Description quality by group for the diagram data'.
```

The ONEWAY command doesn't allow you to save residuals, influence or other useful quantities into the spreadsheet. As this is an independent measures design, the outcome can be plotted directly (as the residuals have the same distribution as the outcome). If the predictions, influence and so forth are important, switch to the general linear model commands described below.

To run the one-way independent measures ANOVA as a general linear model use the UNIANOVA command. (Note that the names of the commands in SPSS can be misleading. Not all analyses run via these commands are univariate ANOVAs and it is not helpful to describe an analysis using SPSS software command names.) For example, to run the same ANOVA and save predictions, Cook's distance and studentized residuals to the spreadsheet:

```
UNIANOVA descript BY group
  /METHOD=SSTYPE(3)
  /SAVE PRED SRESID COOK
  /PRINT ETASQ HOMOGENEITY DESCRIPTIVE GEF.
```

The /METHOD=SSTYPE(3) subcommand can be omitted as it specifies the SPSS default of 'Type III' unique sums of squares. Switching to Type I gives sequential and Type II hierarchical sums of squares (though for one-way independent measures ANOVA the choice is immaterial). The syntax here is a little like the one-way ANOVA and regression commands, but with some differences (e.g., options from the statistics subcommand now appear under /PRINT). The GEF statement prints the generalized estimating function – a table of the coding scheme used for the overparameterized ANOVA. ETASQ adds partial eta-squared to the ANOVA output. The ANOVA table here is more cluttered than it needs to be: overparameterized model information is reported as well as the corrected model that matches the ONEWAY output.

An annoying absence is the ability to add information criteria to the output of either ONEWAY or UNIANOVA. The obvious solution (within SPSS at least) is to run the model as a regression. The main obstacle is recoding the group variable (with values one to four) into four different dummy indicator variables. This can be done via the RECODE command, via.

<Transform> < Recode into different variables ...>. It is slightly easier and quicker to use SPSS syntax:

```
RECODE group (1=1) (ELSE=0) INTO dummy1.
RECODE group (2=1) (ELSE=0) INTO dummy2.
RECODE group (3=1) (ELSE=0) INTO dummy3.
RECODE group (4=1) (ELSE=0) INTO dummy4.
EXECUTE.
```

This creates four dummy variables (dummy, dummy2, etc.) in the spreadsheet. The syntax can be adapted to get effect coding. The indicator variables can now be selected as predictors. To get AIC and BIC run the ANOVA model using the regression syntax:

```
REGRESSION
  /DESCRIPTIVES MEAN STDDEV
  /STATISTICS ANOVA SELECTION
  /DEPENDENT descript
  /METHOD=ENTER dummy2 dummy3 dummy4.
```

The AIC and BIC output here should match that obtained from the simplified loglikelihood formulas (and the extractAIC() function in R). This assumes you want a dummy coded model. For a cell means model try:

```
REGRESSION
  /STATISTICS COEFF OUTS R ANOVA SELECTION
  /ORIGIN
  /DEPENDENT descript
  /METHOD=ENTER dummy1 dummy2 dummy3 dummy4.
```

13.8.2 Independent measures ANCOVA

For an ANCOVA analysis with independent measures the options are either to use the general linear model approach with UNIANOVA or the regression approach (e.g., with dummy coding). For the diagram data the examples use the natural logarithm of the reading time as the covariate, so some pre-processing is required to compute the covariate and assign it to a new variable:

```
COMPUTE ln_time=ln(time).
EXECUTE.
```

The basic ANCOVA syntax using the former method is:

```
UNIANOVA descript BY group WITH ln_time
  /METHOD SSTYPE(3)
  /EMMEANS TABLES(group) WITH(ln_time=MEAN)
  /PRINT PARAMETER.
```

The /PRINT subcommand with the PARAMETER statement is not necessary but is helpful to illustrate that this is really a linear regression model with indicator variables. In this model the choice of sums of squares matters – with non-sequential (Type II or Type III) commonly being preferred (and giving the same output here). For any ANCOVA the adjusted group means and a CI for the adjusted means are vital to be able to interpret the output sensibly (and DESCRIPTIVE added to the /PRINT subcommand gives the unadjusted group means for comparison). The adjusted means are obtained with the estimated marginal means subcommand. Šidàk or Bonferroni adjustments for the CI are also possible:

```
/EMMEANS TABLES(group) WITH(ln_time=MEAN) COMPARE ADJ(SIDAK)
```

The default behavior of SPSS is to adjust the means using the mean of the covariate (here the natural logarithm of the reading time). An advantage of using syntax is the ability to adjust at different values other than the mean – should that be required. For instance, to adjust for a reading time of five minutes the subcommand would be:

```
/EMMEANS TABLES(group) WITH(ln_time=5.703782)
```

The value 5.703782 is the natural logarithm of a 300 second reading time. The interval estimates are 95% CIs by default but this can be altered – here to a 99% CI – by adjusting alpha by inserting the following subcommand:

```
/CRITERIA=ALPHA(.01)
```

To obtain the AIC or BIC for the model, regression commands are necessary (though, in general, the GLM ANOVA approach is more convenient for getting adjusted means and so forth). Try the following syntax:

```
REGRESSION
  /STATISTICS ANOVA SELECTION
  /DEPENDENT descript
  /METHOD=ENTER dummy2 dummy3 dummy4 ln_time.
```

The AIC is reported as 168.443. This matches (to three decimal places) the output of the R extractAIC() function, which gives the AIC as 168.4429.

13.8.3 Multiple comparisons

For independent measures designs the ONEWAY and UNIANOVA commands offer a wide and potentially confusing choice of pairwise comparison procedures. In practice most users only ever consider a fraction of these. SPSS help gives brief information about each, but it is worth consulting a text such as Howell (2002) for a more detailed explanation if the choice of pairwise comparisons is very important. For a conservative test that also provides CIs, Tukey's HSD is likely to be a good choice. Fisher's LSD is unlikely to be a sensible option unless the $J = 3$, but is nonetheless useful if you want to obtain uncorrected pairwise t tests using a pooled error term. This output can be used to carry out the LMH, Hochberg or Shaffer procedures by hand. Howell (*ibid.*) recommends the Ryan procedure (implemented in two variants as REGWQ or REGWF in SPSS). This is a more liberal test than Tukey's HSD, but still controls the omnibus null hypothesis at α for any number of pairwise comparisons.

Syntax for the Tukey HSD, Fisher LSD and REGWQ is given below for both commands:

```
ONEWAY descript BY group
  /POSTHOC TUKEY LSD QREGW ALPHA(0.05).

UNIANOVA descript BY group
  /METHOD SSTYPE(3)
  /POSTHOC group(TUKEY LSD FREGW QREGW)
  /DESIGN group.
```

The `/POSTHOC` subcommand works slightly differently in each case, but provides tests and CIs for all pairwise comparisons for the first two procedures. The REGWQ output is more unusual, because exact p values are not provided. Instead it provides 'homogeneous subsets' output in which level means are grouped into subsets. All means within a subset are not significantly different from each other and all means in different subsets are statistically significant at $p < \alpha$. The subset output can be difficult to interpret – particularly where the pattern of significant differences violates transitivity.

All the above methods assume homogeneity of variance and use a pooled error term. Various options exist when this assumption is violated, including the Games-Howell procedure. This can be specified using the `GH` statement in the `/POSTHOC` subcommand. The Bonferroni and Šidàk corrections can be implemented as *post hoc* tests (i.e., controlling for all possible pairwise comparisons) by adding the `BONFERRONI` or `SIDAK` to the *post hoc* list. These can also be obtained as CIs using the `/EMMEANS` subcommand in `UNIANOVA`. For *a priori* testing the corrections need to be made by hand (in which case the LMH, Hochberg and Shaffer procedures are potential options). This can be very useful because the `/POSTHOC` subcommand will not run if there are covariates in the design (whereas `/EMMEANS` will).

13.9 Bibliography and further reading

Cohen, B. H. (2002) Calculating a Factorial ANOVA from Means and Standard Deviations. *Understanding Statistics*, 1, 191–203.

Kirk, R. E. (1995) *Experimental Design* (3rd edn) Belmont, CA: Brooks/Cole.

Snedecor, G. W., and Cochran, W. G. (1989) *Statistical Methods* (8th edn). Ames, IA: Iowa State University Press.

14
Interactions

Contents

14.1 Chapter overview

This chapter explores the role of interaction effects in modeling the non-additive effects of predictors in regression. The chapter starts by introducing the use of product terms to model bilinear interactions between continuous predictors (sometimes termed moderated multiple regression). Strategies for interpreting interactions between continuous predictors such as centering and analysis of simple slopes are explained, and the special case of polynomial regression is considered. This is followed by discussion of interactions between categorical predictors in factorial ANOVA and ANCOVA. Emphasis throughout is on interpretation of interaction effects (e.g., through graphical methods).

14.2 Modeling interaction effects

The aim of a statistical model is to build up a representation of data that allows us to explore, understand and predict outcomes of interest. The models looked at so far focused on either the aggregate behavior of predictors or on individual predictors within the model. While this is sometimes sufficient, there are also times when the patterns that matter are not captured by either aggregate or individual effects.

In the behavioral and human sciences, theories involve often relationships between several variables. Looking at the overall model may allow you to test whether these variables contribute to an outcome, but won't necessarily allow you to test the relative contribution of each predictor. There are, however, ways to refine a statistical model to test subtle or complex patterns in data. As well as providing tools to compare different theories and hypotheses, being aware of these tools can also have a beneficial effect on the construction of theories and generation of hypotheses. The kinds of patterns that can readily be modeled by a researcher also help him or her generate and communicate theoretical ideas. Statistical and mathematical tools provide a language to explore and express these ideas as hypotheses – hypotheses that might otherwise be hard to distinguish when expressed in words alone.

The focus of this chapter is on *interactions*. Interactions between variables are fundamental to understanding many complex systems. By studying the effects of a predictor on an outcome in isolation (e.g., between X and Y in simple linear regression) you ignore the potential effects of other predictors on the relationship. As soon as a third variable is added to a system, the effects can be surprising (relative to known relationships between pairs of variables). In a system with two predictors (X_1 and X_2) there are at least three potential effects to consider. These are the separate effects X_1 and X_2 on Y (main effects) plus the effect of the interaction between X_1 and X_2 on Y.

People deal with interaction effects every day without thinking too deeply about them. You might like the taste of salt on popcorn and you might like the taste of sugar on popcorn. But you are unlikely to believe that putting salt and sugar on popcorn together will be better than either on its own. People tend to understand that when you add two different flavors to the same food you have to consider not just their individual effects, but also the interaction of the two. In the case of popcorn, salt and sugar probably interact to make the taste worse (though I have not been brave enough to try this myself). Once you start thinking about it, it is easy to come up with examples from other domains (e.g., a medicine that interacts with alcohol to produce a side-effect not otherwise present). To build interesting, sensible and useful models about the world, it is important to consider patterns of effects relating to predictors and the interactions between them.

14.3 Interactions in regression: moderated multiple regression

A *moderator* is a variable that influences or moderates the effects of another predictor in a regression model. If a moderator relationship exists then two or more predictors in the model interact to produce an effect on the outcome that is different from that obtained by adding up the individual effects of the predictors. Despite the name, *moderated multiple regression* is really only a multiple regression that includes interaction effects. Not only that, but while it may often be reasonable to think of one predictor as the moderator variable and another as the moderated variable, there is no formal distinction between the two (and supposing that one predictor *causes* another predictor's effects to change has obvious risks).

14.3.1 Adding a product term to represent an interaction effect

Setting up a moderated multiple regression model is not at all difficult (though interpreting the model can be). A good starting point is to think about how a multiple regression model with $q=2$ predictors works. In this model the outcome is an additive function of the predictors:

$$y_i = b_0 + b_1 x_{1,i} + b_2 x_{2,i} + e_i \qquad \text{Equation 14.1}$$

In the language of ANOVA, the effects of individual predictors on Y are 'main effects'. With two predictors there are separate main effects of both X_1 and X_2. These effects are additive (that is to say that their joint effect on Y is obtained by adding the two effects together). This model assumes that the effects of X_1 and X_2 on Y do not interact. In mathematical terms, additive effects such as these imply independent effects of the two predictors on Y. The effect of X_1 on Y is not correlated with the effect of X_2 on Y.

It is essential to realize that it is the effects of the predictors on the outcome that are at issue here. It is quite possible for two predictors to be correlated in the population they are sampled from (and therefore not be independent of each other), but to be independent in their effects. Having high blood pressure and being old may be correlated in the population, but that does not imply that the effect of high blood pressure on risk of heart disease interacts with the effects of age on risk of heart disease. The effects of high blood pressure could, in principle, be identical for younger and older people (even though older people are more likely to have high blood pressure).[1]

Once you understand that a model with no interactions has additive effects of its predictors, it should be clear that modeling moderator or interaction effects involves constructing a model in which some effects are non-additive (and therefore non-independent). The trick to modeling interaction effects is to add a predictor to the linear model that can account for their non-additive contribution. This new effect is formed as the product of X_1 and X_2. For $q=2$ this gives the following regression model:

$$y_i = b_0 + b_1 x_{1,i} + b_2 x_{2,i} + b_3 x_{3,i} + e_i \qquad \text{Equation 14.2}$$

As $X_3 = X_1 \times X_2$ the model can also be written as:

$$y_i = b_0 + b_1x_{1,i} + b_2x_{2,i} + b_3(x_{1,i} \times x_{2,i}) + e_i \quad \text{Equation 14.3}$$

The beauty of this model is that it is still additive in its form (and hence acceptable as a linear regression model) and yet any non-additive effects of X_1 and X_2 are estimated by the multiplicative product term $X_1 \times X_2$. No special software is required to set up and fit the model.

Focusing on the equations sometimes obscures the simplicity of the process. If for observation y_1 the value of $x_{1,1} = 8$ and $x_{2,1} = -3$, then the value of $x_{3,1}$ will be $8 \times -3 = -24$. All $i = 1$ to N values of X_3 are computed in exactly the same way. The product term $(X_1 \times X_2)$ is then entered into the regression as a regular predictor, with only one restriction: an interaction term should not be entered without the constituent lower-order terms in the model (in this case the main effects X_1 and X_2). X_3 might, very rarely, be considered a legitimate predictor in its own right, but it is not necessarily an estimate of the interaction effect unless X_1 and X_2 are also in the model. Moreover, the predictors X_1, X_2 and X_3 will often be collinear. Predictions that do not jointly consider all three terms will not make much sense.

An interaction between two predictors is referred to as a *two-way interaction*. If both predictors are continuous it may also be termed a *bilinear interaction* (see Jaccard *et al.*, 1990). Interactions are not limited to two variables. The preceding approach can be extended to any number of predictors. For practical purposes it is rare to have models with higher-order terms more complex than a three-way or four-way interaction. This kind of model is usually only justified when the goal is purely to predict an outcome (and interpreting the effects is unimportant) or if an interaction is predicted in advance (e.g., from a theory that makes precise quantitative predictions about the form of the interaction). The practicalities of fitting models with higher-order interactions can be illustrated by just looking at the model for a three-way interaction effect. The main effects only model is:

$$y_i = b_0 + b_1x_{1,i} + b_2x_{2,i} + b_3x_{3,i} + e_i \quad \text{Equation 14.4}$$

To test the three-way interaction you need to add not only a three three-way interaction term (the product of X_1, X_2 and X_3), but also all $q(q-1)/2 = 3$ two-way terms. It helps to simplify the notation from this point on. An interaction term between X_1 and X_2 will be denoted as $X_{1\cdot2}$. Even with this simpler notation, a three-way interaction model is quite formidable:

$$y_i = b_0 + b_1x_{1,i} + b_2x_{2,i} + b_3x_{3,i} + b_4x_{1\cdot2,i} + b_5x_{1\cdot3,i} + b_6x_{2\cdot3,i} + b_7x_{1\cdot2\cdot3,i} + e_i \quad \text{Equation 14.5}$$

As with the two-way model, interaction terms must not be included without also including all constituent lower-order terms. So a four-way interaction effect requires that all three-way interactions, two-way interactions and main effects terms involving those four predictors are also included. A common short-hand for this kind of model is to use asterisks to represent the product terms and any constituent lower-order terms in the model. Thus a four-way model with all lower order terms could be summarized as $X_1 * X_2 * X_3 * X_4$. Fitting complex interaction terms is costly in terms of the number of parameters and difficulty of interpretation. It is often desirable, and sometimes necessary, to work with a simpler model. If so, moderated multiple regression is often approached using a hierarchical modeling strategy (see Box 14.1).

This principle of including lower-order terms also extends to prediction. In fact, considering the relationships between predictors in a moderated multiple regression model is fundamental. In a main effects regression model (with no interactions) predictors can sometimes be interpreted in isolation (e.g., when they are orthogonal or near-orthogonal). In a model with interactions, prediction involves summing across several terms in the model. If an interaction is present, the individual components should not normally be interpreted in isolation.

Interpretation of interactions with continuous predictors is known to be difficult. Start with the prediction equation itself:

$$\hat{Y} = b_0 + b_1X_1 + b_2X_2 + b_3X_{1 \cdot 2} \qquad \text{Equation 14.6}$$

By plugging in a range of low, medium and high values of each of the predictors you can record what happens to Y. Good options for low and high values include the sample or population minimum and maximum, and ± 1 or ± 2 *SD* around the mean. You may also want to plug in combinations of values for plausible scenarios (e.g., representative of a particular individual or class of individual). You can do this and note down the effects on Y by hand, or use spreadsheet software to keep track of the calculations and results. This can be followed up by plotting Y as a function of the predictors. A common display for a two-way bilinear interaction is to plot Y as a function of X_1 by including separate regression lines for low, medium and high values of X_2. Such plots can be misleading. Care must be taken to select a sensible range of values to be plotted. Preacher *et al.* (2006) describe tools for exploring two-way and three-way interactions in multiple regression (some of which are considered in more detail below).

Example 14.1 Jarvis (2003) looked at the endowment effect (placing a higher value on something you own than an equivalent item that you don't own). A sample of 184 students was asked how much money they required to part with a lottery ticket (purchase price £1). The research questions included whether performance depended on the present financial resources or anticipated future finances of participants. To assess their present finances they were asked to rate their wealth on a one to five scale (going from 1 substantial debt through to 5 substantial cash savings). To assess future financial resources, students were asked to estimate the annual income they expected after graduation (measured in thousand pounds per annum). Subsequent examples will refer to this data set as the lottery data.

Summary statistics for the outcome variable (*money*), and the predictors *present finances* and *future income* are:

	M	*SD*	*min*	*max*
Money	£654,731	£2,179,384	£0	£10,000,000
Present finances	2.73	1.53	1	5
Future income	£19,000	£5118	£5000	£50,000

For present finances most students are in the range 1 to 3 (indicating no savings or slight debt.) For future income there looks to be some skew (as you would expect for an estimate of income). The money variable is bounded at zero and, having enormous skew, is unsuitable as an outcome measure in a regression model. For theoretical reasons it would be sensible to use a logarithmic transformation, as people seem to represent gains in money on a multiplicative rather than additive scale. As zeroes are present, it is necessary to add a small constant (in this case 0.5) prior to transformation. This example uses the logarithm to base ten (as it makes interpretation slightly easier when many of the responses are multiples of ten such as £100). Figure 14.1 plots the kernel

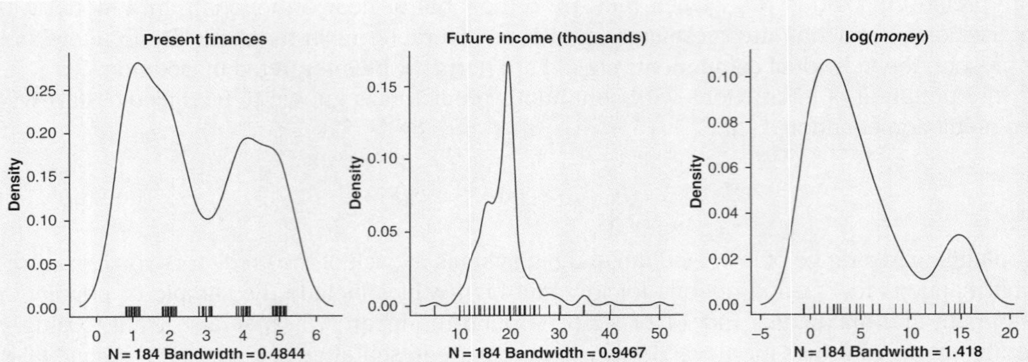

Figure 14.1 Density plots of predictors and outcome for lottery data analysis

density estimates (adding a rug to each plot) for the transformed outcome measure log(*money*) and the two predictors.

Both present finances and log(*money*) look to be bimodal, and all three variables show some degree of positive skew (notably for future income, though perhaps not sufficient to warrant a transformation). For this reason it will be important to check the residuals of the model. The bimodality may not be a big problem. It is quite possible that the sample is a mix of two somewhat distinct subgroups, one relatively financially secure or wealthy and the other in a more financially precarious position.

A multiple regression of log(*money*) with both predictors is statistically significant, $F_{2,181} = 4.22$, $p < .05$, $R^2 = .045$, and AIC (using full maximum likelihood) is 798.6. The prediction equation is:

$$\log(money) = 3.3660 - 0.2727\,present - 0.0294\,future$$

Remember that future income is scaled in thousands of pounds. Hence a value of ten for future income represents £10,000 (not £10). This choice is helpful for interpreting the regression equation because its coefficient is already very small (and would otherwise be −0.0000294). Of the individual predictors, only present finances is statistically significant, $t_{181} = 2.69$, $p < .05$. Both predictors are negatively related to the outcome. This suggests that, on average, the worse a student's perceived financial resources, the more money they require to part with the lottery ticket. So a student with high debt (*present* = 1) and low expected annual income on graduation (£5000) has an expected outcome of $3.3660 - 0.2727 \times 1 - 0.0294 \times 5$. This is about 2.9463 on a base 10 logarithmic scale or $10^{2.9463} - 0.5$ on the untransformed scale (about £880). The corresponding prediction for *present* = 5, and anticipated income of £50,000 is about £3. One interpretation of these results is in terms of anticipated regret. Students with worse financial positions might anticipate greater regret on discovering that they had sold a ticket that subsequently won than students with good finances.

While these results were broadly in line with what was expected, it was suspected that the two variables might interact. Perhaps having large debt now would have less influence on the endowment effect if a student anticipated a high-earning job in a couple of years' time? This can be tested by moderated multiple regression, adding the product of present finances and future income to the regression model as an interaction term. The resulting model is also statistically significant, $F_{3,180} = 4.22$, $p < .05$, and seems to have better explanatory power than the main effects model ($R^2 = .072$ and AIC = 795.3). Tests of moderator effects are notoriously difficult in terms of statistical power (though bimodality of some predictors may be helpful). Modest absolute differences in R^2 should not be of too much concern. In any case, the most important test in this context is the change in R^2. As the interaction term has 1 *df* this is equivalent to the test of the interaction effect in the moderated multiple regression. This test is statistically significant, $t_{180} = 2.29$, $p < .05$, and the difference in AIC of 3.27 is equivalent to a likelihood ratio of about 5.1 in favor of the model including the interaction.

The prediction equation for this model is:

$$\log(money) = 5.7935 - 1.2309\,present - 0.1586\,future + 0.0506\,present \times future$$

It is now possible to revise the earlier predictions. For a student with $present = 1$ and $future = £5000$ the predicted outcome is:

$$5.7935 - 1.2309 \times 1 - 0.1586 \times 5 + 0.0506 \times 1 \times 5 = 4.0226$$

On the untransformed scale this is about £10,500. For a student with $present = 5$ and $future = £50,000$ the figure is about £22,850. Something very different is happening in the interaction model relative to the main effects model.

As always, it is important to check the model. Analysis of the model residuals indicates that the bimodality is still present (as well as some skew), but there seem to be no extremely influential observations (all Cook's distances are < 0.20). Given the sample size, it is likely that the model is not too misleading. Running a robust linear regression (not reported here) leads to similar parameter estimates.

Box 14.1 Hierarchical regression strategies

Hierarchical regression is a modeling strategy in which all predictors are entered into a statistical model according to a predetermined order. It differs from automatic methods such as stepwise regression because the order of entry and choice of models is determined in advance by theoretical or pragmatic concerns.

A common application of hierarchical regression is to compare models with and without interaction effects. This approach is recommended when there is no strong theory predicting interactions between specific predictors. The popularity of hierarchical strategies when working with interactions is partly because interaction effects should not be included in a model that doesn't already include all lower-order effects. A second advantage is that with many predictors in the model there are many potential interaction effects. A hierarchical approach usually simplifies the process of exploring higher-order interaction effects (which are frequently hard to interpret and of limited theoretical interest) without completely excluding them.

For a model with q continuous predictors it is common to start with main effects and work 'up' the hierarchy. If q is small it may be convenient to fit all effects and work down the hierarchy. If $q = 7$, the first model might be a main effects only model. The second model would then add all $q(q-1)/2 = 21$ two-way interactions. Given the large number of parameters being estimated it is sensible to judge the fit of the two-way model using a method that favors parsimonious models (e.g., by examining adjusted R^2 or, better still, via AIC_C or BIC). The next step would be to add three-way interactions, followed by four-way interactions and so forth. Higher-order terms would not normally be added unless the terms added at the previous step suggested an improvement in fit. For small values of q, or if theoretical reasons suggest higher-order interactions are likely or important, working down the hierarchy is preferable (particularly in larger data sets where there are sufficient *df* to estimate many parameters accurately).

If $q = 3$ a hierarchical regression might start with the model A * B * C (the model with all main effects, all three two-way interactions and the three-way interaction). This model would then be compared to a model with only the two-way interactions and main effects: A * B + A * C + B * C. The last step compares this model with the main effects model: A + B + C.

Hierarchical modeling strategies can be applied in any situation where there is a theoretical reason to order the predictors in the model. The ordering could be at the level of individual variables (e.g., an *a priori* ranking of importance or causality) or sets of predictors. For instance, when working with data from human participants you might start with a model that includes demographic factors, then add another distinct set of effects (e.g., individual differences), before fitting a model with the effects of primary theoretical interest.

This approach to fitting models with interaction terms is not universal, but can be useful for preventing over-fitting when working with large number of predictors. There are alternative ways to fit models with interaction effects. For instance a Bayesian approach might be to fit all interaction effects and prevent over-fitting by selecting appropriate priors.

14.3.2 Centering, collinearity and moderated multiple regression

People often assume that if predictors are orthogonal then the product of those predictors will also be orthogonal. This is not so. Consider two predictors with values {−2, 0, 2} and {3, 5, 3} respectively. Their product is {−6, 0, 6} and is perfectly correlated with the first predictor. Adding a product term can introduce multicollinearity between predictors where none existed before. This is an extreme example, but the phenomenon is far from uncommon. Many predictors are measured on scales that give rise only to positive numbers. Multiplying two positive numbers generates a new positive number somewhat correlated to each of the others. When predictors are measured only on positive scales (or indeed only on negative scales) adding a product term will nearly always produce high levels of multicollinearity. This can make the interpretation of multiple regression with interaction terms more difficult.

Remember, however, that the overall regression model is unaffected by the collinearity of the predictors (except where predictors are perfectly collinear). Because the contribution of an interaction term should always be considered relative to a model containing all the relevant lower-order terms, this means that the test of an interaction effect depends on its unique contribution to the model. This test is therefore unaffected by multicollinearity with lower-order product terms. Adding a product term for a two-way interaction is therefore sufficient to assess the overall impact of the interaction on R^2 or to test the effect (e.g., using a *t* test or other methods such as change in AIC or BIC).

Even so, it can be confusing when multicollinearity arises. Notably, the parameter estimates and tests of main effects (or lower-order interaction terms) could be markedly different between models with and without the product term. At one level this should not matter (because the main effects should not be interpreted on their own), but getting rid of the multicollinearity caused by adding an interaction effect can improve the interpretability of a model.

A simple solution is to center continuous predictors by subtracting their mean prior to calculating the product term. For a two-way moderated multiple regression this produces the model:

$$y_i = b_0 + b_1 (x_{1,i} - \hat{\mu}_{X_1}) + b_2 (x_{2,i} - \hat{\mu}_{X_2}) + b_3 (x_{1,i} - \hat{\mu}_{X_1}) (x_{2,i} - \hat{\mu}_{X_2}) + e_i \qquad \text{Equation 14.7}$$

As the centered predictors $x_{1,i} - \hat{\mu}_{X_1}$ and $x_{2,i} - \hat{\mu}_{X_2}$ have a mean of zero, their product $(x_{1,i} - \hat{\mu}_{X_1})(x_{2,i} - \hat{\mu}_{X_2})$ does not need to be centered. Centering and computing product terms are routine operations. The order of the operations is, however, vital. Centering of X_1 and X_2 must precede the creation of the product term (Friedrich, 1982). An important warning is that standardizing variables (as conducted by default in many regression packages) is not equivalent to centering the predictors in the required way. Although standardizing predictors involves centering, most software implements centering after computing the product term is used to code the interaction. This means that the usual standardized regression coefficients are generally unsafe to interpret in a moderated multiple regression. Even if computed correctly, the standard errors for an interaction effect between standardized predictors will be incorrect. Standardization is best avoided completely in moderated regression models (Preacher, 2003).

If predictors are centered prior to computing the product term, the main effects will have similar parameter estimates and tests in the main effects model to those in the moderated regression model.[2] This has several advantages. First, it is not necessary to run separate regression models with and without interaction effects (though you may wish to for other reasons). Second, it can reduce confusion caused by lower-order terms that appear to have unstable parameter estimates. Third, if the predictors are on arbitrary scales (e.g., rating scales) it can make the interpretation of the model much easier. With centered predictors, the intercept is the expected value of Y when all predictors are at their mean value. If the outcome is also on an arbitrary scale there may be further benefits to centering Y (in which case the intercept will be zero).[3]

It may not always be best to center continuous predictors relative to the observed mean. Some predictors (e.g., rating scales) have a natural mid-point and it may be easier to interpret the model by 'centering' at this value. For instance, a scale coded from one (strongly disagree) through to four (neutral) and seven (strongly agree) might have an observed mean of 3.71, but may be easier to interpret if centered around four. Alternatively, you might want to center values around the population mean (if an accurate estimate exists). Perhaps most important of all, if the scale of the predictor is not arbitrary – if it is a ratio scale with true zero point – centering could make the model harder to interpret. Whether to rescale predictors depends on whether it helps you interpret or communicate your interpretation of a model. There is no correct solution for all models, but some form of centering or rescaling is generally a good idea if all predictors are continuous and on arbitrary scales (even if no interactions are being modeled).

Example 14.2 The analysis of the lottery data in Example 14.1 ignored the potential collinearity of the predictors. The predictors in the main effects model are only modestly correlated ($r = .045$), but as they are both positive they will be highly correlated with the product term. The correlation between *present* and the product term is .89, while between *future* and the product term it is .43. Collinearity is likely to be severe in the model with the uncentered predictors. To illustrate this, the variance inflation factor (VIF) for predictors in the main effects model is only 1.002 (as this is determined by their bivariate correlation it is identical for both predictors). In the interaction model the VIF values are 18.56 for present finances, 4.58 for future income and 22.84 for the interaction. Looking back at Example 14.1 it is also clear that the coefficients for the main effects are very different between the two models. Of more practical relevance is that the intercept in both models represents the expected outcome when a person scores zero on both predictors. As the lowest possible value for present finances is one and the lowest observed value for future income is five (i.e., £5000) neither intercept is directly interpretable.

Centering both predictors before calculating the product term is a good idea. The centered main effects model now has the prediction equation:

$$\log(money) = 2.0648 - 0.2727\, present - 0.0294\, future$$

Only the intercept has changed. All other parameter estimates and tests are unaffected. The intercept of 2.0648 can now be interpreted as the expected outcome for a student with average financial resources (with mean values on both predictors). This is equivalent to about £115. How does this compare with the interaction model? The prediction equation is now:

$$\log(money) = 2.0472 - 0.2689\, present - 0.0208\, future + 0.0506\, present \times future$$

The interaction effect (and its test) is identical to that in the uncentered model, but the other coefficients are all very different. Centering has two main advantages. As with the centered main effects model, the intercept is directly interpretable as the expected outcome for a student with average financial resources. The other is that the intercept and the main effects have coefficients and tests similar to those in the main effects model (e.g., the intercept is equivalent to about £110 on the untransformed scale).

This does not imply that it is a good idea to interpret the effects of the main effects in isolation from the interaction. The main effects in the centered interaction model represent the effects of one predictor evaluated at the mean of the other (and could be misleading). The effects might change markedly when evaluated at other values. For the present example this is probably not too dangerous (because the two predictors are uncorrelated), but the best way to understand what is going on is to investigate the two-way interaction in greater detail.

One remaining puzzle is worth resolving here. Why is the test of the interaction effect identical in both the centered and uncentered models? This must be so, because (as noted earlier) these tests are of the unique contribution of the product term as set out in Equation 12.25. Each new predictor's contribution depends on its correlation with the residuals of the model prior to its entry, and this is unchanged by centering. The puzzle is that the VIF for the product term is very different in the two models. This should inflate the standard errors and would seem to imply a reduction in the power to detect the effect. Shieh (2011) explains how these phenomena are reconciled. VIF differs between models, but there is a corresponding adjustment to the sums of squares in the interaction model to offset this difference.

14.3.3 Probing interactions: simple intercepts and simple slopes

The test of an interaction effect in moderated multiple regression can be interpreted in several ways. It can be considered a test of the unique contribution (semi-partial correlation or change in R^2) attributed to the interaction. It can also be interpreted as a test of whether the slope of X_1 depends on the slope of X_2. The presence of a two-way interaction indicates that the slope of X_1 changes as a continuous function of X_2 (or equivalently that the slope of X_2 varies as a function of X_1). In some cases these interpretations, combined with predictions from the model, are sufficient to address the questions of interest to a researcher. In other cases, especially where one variable is considered a moderator of another, it can be useful to explore the interaction further.

Many experienced researchers will explore a multiple regression model, including one with interaction effects, by plugging in plausible values of X into the prediction equation and seeing what happens to Y. This informal 'pick-a-point' method is widely used, but has drawbacks (Bauer and Curran, 2005). It relies heavily on being able to select sensible points, otherwise the selected values might lie outside the range of sampled values or those plausible in the population. A more formal approach can be taken (*ibid.*; Preacher *et al.*, 2006). This involves rearranging the prediction equation. For the simple two-way interaction case this involves designating one variable as the *focal predictor* (X_f) and the other as the *moderator* (X_m).[4] The focal predictor is usually the predictor of primary interest in the research. If the regression equation is

$$y_i = b_0 + b_1 x_{f,i} + b_2 x_{m,i} + b_3 x_{m \cdot f,i} + e_i \qquad \text{Equation 14.8}$$

the corresponding prediction equation is:

$$\hat{Y} = E\left(Y | X_f, X_m\right) = (b_0 + b_2 X_m) + (b_1 + b_3 X_m) X_f \qquad \text{Equation 14.9}$$

This may look odd, but all that has happened is that the regression between X_f and Y is expressed so that the intercept and slope are a function of X_m. The $b_0 + b_2 X_m$ term is the *simple intercept* (w_0) and $b_1 + b_3 X_m$ is the *simple slope* (w_1) of the moderated multiple regression.[5] This may be clearer if the relationship between Y and X_f is written in terms of the simple slope and intercept:

$$y_i = w_0 + w_1 x_{f,i} \qquad \text{Equation 14.10}$$

This is a formal way to extend the pick-a-point method to derive null hypothesis significance tests (NHSTs) and confidence intervals (CIs) for a fixed value of X_m. As the CI is more informative than the NHST I'll explain how to obtain the interval estimate. Where a conventional CI would describe a plausible range of Y for a given value of X, the CI based on the simple slope or intercept describes a plausible range for the selected value of X_f when X_m is also fixed. The first step in constructing the CI is to decide what values of X_f and X_m to use. As noted earlier, a common strategy is to pick low, middle and high values of both X_f and X_m and to compare the interval estimates across these values. For the moment, imagine that you only want to evaluate the effect of X_f at one value of X_m. The interval for the slope is constructed in the usual way:

$$w_1 \pm t_{N-q-1, 1-\alpha/2} \hat{\sigma}_{w_1} \qquad \text{Equation 14.11}$$

The standard error of the simple slope $\hat{\sigma}_{w_1}$ can be obtained by calculating the sampling variance of w_1. As the simple slope is the sum of b_1 and $b_3 X_m$ it is possible to use the variance sum law (see Key Concept 3.2) to combine these variances for a chosen value of X_m (Bauer and Curran, 2005; Preacher *et al.*, 2006):

$$\hat{\sigma}^2_{w_1} \Big| X_m = \hat{\sigma}^2_{b_1} + \hat{\sigma}^2_{b_3} X_m^2 + 2\hat{\sigma}_{b_1, b_3} X_m \qquad \text{Equation 14.12}$$

X_m enters this equation through the $b_3 X_m$ term (because b_3 is a function of X_m, its standard error is too). All the estimates of the sampling variances (i.e., squared standard errors) are available from $\hat{\mathbf{V}}$, the variance-covariance matrix of the regression coefficients (see Key Concept 12.2). The intercept equations are obtained in the same way (using b_0 and b_2), but there is no need to specify a value of X_f (because the intercept is constant for all X_f).

These CIs allow researchers to address more specific questions than the test of interaction effect. Because the effect of X_f varies with X_m you will sometimes want to know whether the CI excludes some value (e.g., zero) for a given value of X_f or X_m. Nevertheless, the approach is still cumbersome. Bauer and Curran (2005) show how to extend this approach to add confidence bands to a plot, and Preacher *et al.* (2006) describe an online tool to generate R code to plot these confidence bands. Using confidence bands makes it possible to simultaneously view the interval estimates of the simple slopes for a range of X_f values (without the need to pre-select a specific set of points). This is the best approach (unless formal hypothesis tests for particular points are required).

Example 14.3 For the lottery data present finances and future income appear to interact to influence the value participants place on a lottery ticket. A good start to exploring a bilinear interaction is to plot it in some way. One method is to plot separate regression lines for one predictor evaluated at low, high and medium values of the other predictor. Figure 14.2 shows the expected outcome as a function of *present finances* in the form of three different lines: one each for *future income* = £5000, *future income* = £19,000 and *future income* = £50,000. These values are the minimum, mean and maximum observed in the sample. While it is more realistic to plot ±1 or ±2 standard deviations, for exploratory purposes it is interesting to plot more extreme (but possible) patterns. Plotting for extreme values is revealing about the deficiencies of the model and can highlight unusual, interesting or implausible outcomes. The left-hand panel log(*money*) is plotted on the *y*-axis, while the right-hand pattern shows the same pattern for the untransformed data. After looking at Figure 14.2, the findings of the lottery analysis should be easier to interpret.

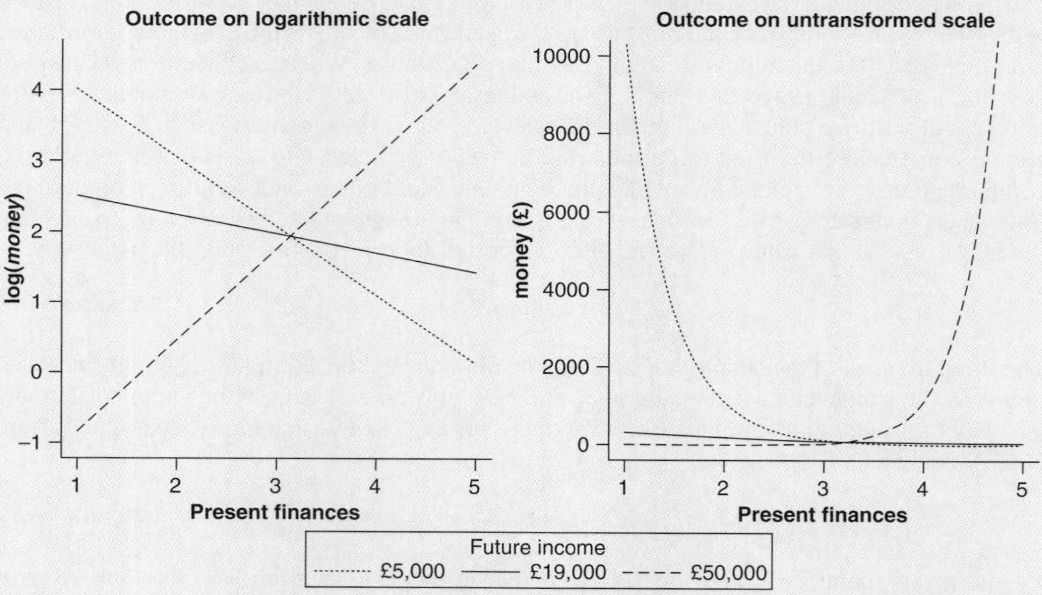

Figure 14.2 Plots of the bilinear interaction between perceived personal finances and future income on money required to part with a lottery ticket

Participants with low and average expected future incomes have downward-sloping lines for the outcome on the logarithmic scale. For these students, poor present finances are associated with a larger endowment effect (i.e., requiring more money to part with the lottery ticket). This effect is stronger for the poorest students. For students with very high expectations of future earnings the slope is reversed. The better off they are, the more money they require to part with the lottery ticket.

The effect is even more striking looking at the untransformed data. Here the outcome curves upwards very steeply for the poorest students if they expect low future income, or for the wealthiest students if they expect high future incomes. The curve for the students with average expected incomes appears fairly flat (on the untransformed scale), but still represents a decline from £325 to £25 pounds.

These plots are quite striking, but there are issues about how to interpret effects that may or may not be statistically significant. Performing dozens of tests for different values of slopes is a rather clumsy way to proceed (unless there are specific hypotheses to be tested). A more appealing strategy is to look at the confidence bands for the simple slopes of one or more predictors. This gives an idea of the uncertainty in the estimates without reducing an interesting pattern to a series of uninteresting tests. Figure 14.3 plots the simple slope of present finances as a function of future income with 90% confidence bands added. This level of confidence is chosen, in part, because tests of interaction effects tend to have low power. It also helps illustrate the features of the plot (by showing where both confidence bands cross zero). The plot indicates how the effect of personal finances switches from negative to positive as expected future income changes from low to high. The confidence bands exclude zero for future income up to about £20,000 (which is the majority of

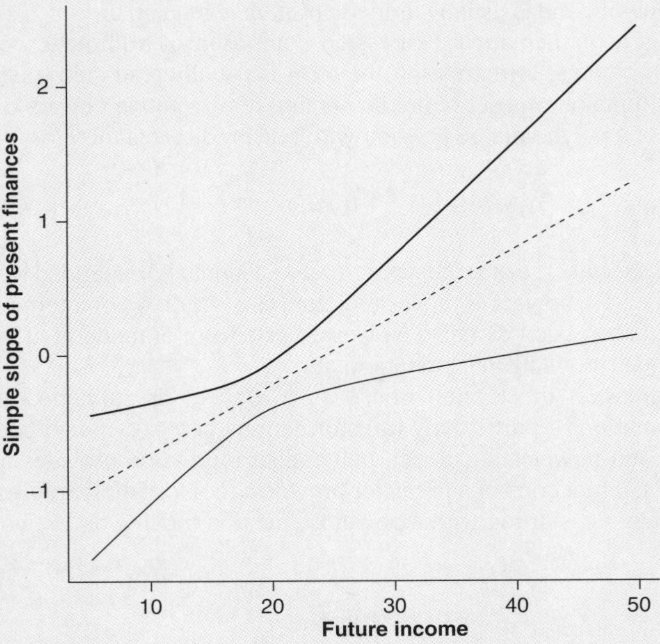

Figure 14.3 Simple slope of personal finances (with 90% confidence bands) as a function of future income

the sample) and so suggest that for these students worse personal finances may indeed be predictive of a greater endowment effect. Only for the very highest levels of future income (e.g., £40,000) does the plot suggest that better personal finances predict an increased endowment effect. The latter effect is somewhat tentative. For the range £21,000 to £39,000 the effect of personal finances cannot be distinguished from zero with any great confidence.

Although there is evidence of an interaction, the sample size is not sufficient to estimate the effect precisely. If neither confidence band excluded zero for the range of observed data, this would not indicate absence of an interaction, merely uncertainty over the magnitude of the effect within the plotted range. For theoretical research it may be sufficient to detect an effect. For applied research a typical aim is to estimate the magnitude of the effect to some degree of precision. This may require additional data.

14.4 Polynomial regression

Interaction terms in regression allow an additive model to be fitted even when the effects of the predictors are not strictly additive. This is possible because the effect of a predictor on Y depends upon another predictor in the model. This is not the only type of non-additivity that might occur.[6] Rather than varying as a function of another predictor, the effect of X on Y could vary as a function of X itself. This type of model can also be incorporated within the general linear model framework and is usually termed *polynomial regression*.

A polynomial is a mathematical expression composed of arithmetic operators and non-negative (i.e., ≥ 0) powers. In regression the term is usually restricted to situations in which Y is modeled as a function of a set of predictors and non-negative powers of those predictors. The general form of a polynomial regression with one predictor is therefore:

$$y_i = b_0 + b_1 x_{1,i} + b_2 x_{1,i}^2 + \ldots + b_q x_{1,i}^q + e_i \qquad \text{Equation 14.13}$$

This is yet another special case of multiple regression. It could be expanded to include additional predictors (e.g., X_2 or X_3), powers of those predictors (e.g., X_2^2 or X_3^2) or interactions between predictors. Polynomial regression can also be viewed as a form of moderated multiple regression (and similar issues surround its interpretation).

Polynomial regression most often arises as a way to fit curvilinear patterns in data. Although transformations – particularly transformations of Y – can also be used to fit curves (e.g., exponential and power law curves), polynomial regression provides a more systematic approach. Polynomial functions of a predictor provide a tool for fitting progressively more complex curves to a data set, starting with a power of one and moving on to two and three and so on in turn:

$$y_i = b_0 + b_1 x_{1,i} + e_i$$
$$y_i = b_0 + b_1 x_{1,i} + b_2 x_{1,i}^2 + e_i$$
$$y_i = b_0 + b_1 x_{1,i} + b_2 x_{1,i}^2 + b_3 x_{1,i}^3 + e_i$$
$$\ldots$$

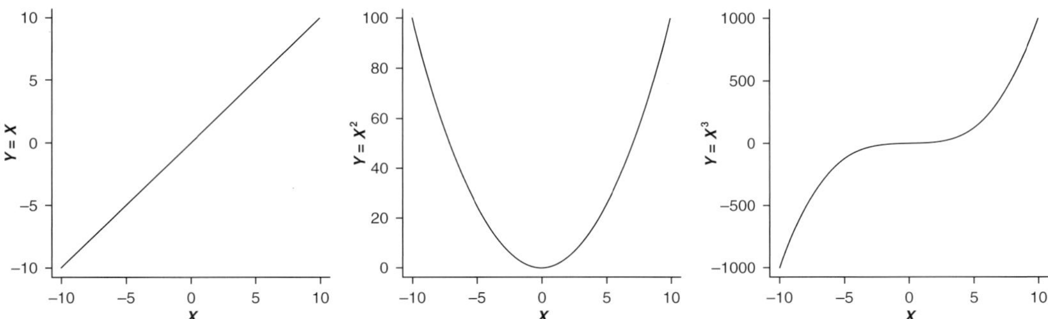

Figure 14.4 Examples of linear, quadratic and cubic functions of X

Each lower-order polynomial regression is nested within the next more complex model. The simplest polynomial function of X is a straight line, the next most complex adds a *quadratic* (X^2) term, followed by a *cubic* (X^3) term, a *quartic* (X^4) term and so on. Figure 14.4 shows examples of linear, quadratic and cubic functions of X.

Each additional polynomial term requires an additional parameter in the regression and allows the model to fit a slightly more complex curve (i.e., with one an additional 'bend'). A straight line has no bends at all. A quadratic function has a distinctive curved shape (a *parabola*) with a single bend, while a cubic function adds a second bend.

Each polynomial regression can also be viewed as a form of interaction model. The difference is that what is being added to the model is not the product of two different predictors (e.g., $X_1 \times X_2$) but the product of a single predictor with itself (e.g., $X \times X = X^2$). As with interaction models in general, it is natural to fit these models with a hierarchical strategy – comparing the fit of simpler polynomials with successively more or less complex ones. There are also other similarities. It makes no sense to fit the quadratic term X^2 without also including the linear X term in the model; all lower-order polynomial terms need to be retained in the model. Likewise, lower-order terms in a polynomial regression should not be interpreted in isolation, because they will typically be highly correlated with the higher-order terms. Centering X prior to calculating the higher-order terms can reduce this collinearity. Again, this is not a requirement of polynomial regression, merely a strategy to aid interpretation of the coefficients. Predictions from a polynomial regression will be unaffected by collinearity of the constituent terms. If a higher-order term is present it is probably unreasonable to try and interpret any of the polynomial terms in isolation.

There are some disadvantages of polynomial regression that need to be carefully considered. One is that complex polynomial models tend to over-fit data. This problem can be ameliorated by incorporating a penalty to the fit, perhaps using information criteria such as AIC_C or BIC (see Glover and Dixon, 2004). Polynomial fits also tend to be atheoretical (e.g., for cubic or more complex fits). This may not matter if the primary goal is prediction, but functions with a clear theoretical rationale have better properties in terms of robustness and out of sample generalization. A final problem is that polynomial functions provide non-local fits. The fit of the curve at any point depends on observations that are far from that point. For this reason 'local' fitting methods such as *loess* or *regression splines* are sometimes better solutions for complex curvilinear patterns or exploratory analyses (see Wright and London, 2009). On the other hand, simple polynomials such as quadratics may have a plausible theoretical interpretation, and be preferable on the grounds of parsimony (relative to complex polynomial functions or non-local curve fits that estimate dozens of parameters).

Example 14.4 This example uses the Anscombe data (designed to illustrate the importance of graphical exploration of data). One of the Anscombe data sets (that plotted in Figure 9.14a) shows a pronounced curvilinear pattern. Fitting a linear regression to the curve gives a superficially reasonable fit, $F_{1,9} = 17.97$, $p < .05$, $R^2 = .67$, AIC = 39.7, with the prediction equation $\hat{Y} = 3 + 0.5X$. Entering a quadratic term to the model provides a more or less perfect fit to the data, $F_{1,9} = 17.97$, $p < .05$, $R^2 \approx 1$, AIC = −104.9. The prediction equation for the quadratic model is $\hat{Y} = -6.00 + 2.78X - 0.127X^2$. Figure 14.5 displays both the linear and quadratic fits on the same graph. Given that the fit is near perfect, there is no point attempting a cubic or higher-order polynomial regression model.

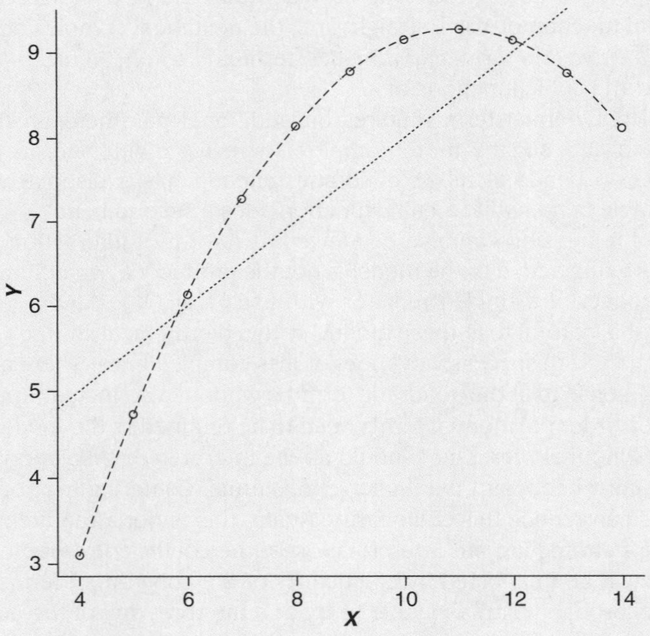

Figure 14.5 Linear and quadratic fits to the curvilinear Anscombe data

14.5 Factorial ANOVA

One of the main attractions of analysis of variance (ANOVA) is its application to experimental designs in which there are two factors (i.e., categorical predictors) each with two or more levels. This form of design is appealing to experimenters because it can be efficient (combining multiple independent variables in a single study), but mostly because it allows researchers to investigate interactions between factors.

A balanced ANOVA design has equal cell sizes and orthogonal predictors. In addition, if a balanced ANOVA has two or more *fully crossed* factors then the design is *fully factorial*.[7] Fully crossed factors are ones in which every level of each factor occurs in conjunction with each level of the other factors. The combinations of levels of different factors are the *cells* in the design (and correspond to groups in an independent measures design). If the factorial design has equal cell sizes the factors will be orthogonal (see Chapter 13). Thus the term factor in ANOVA is not a mere synonym for an independent variable or categorical predictor. It refers to a factorial design when several categorical predictors are fully crossed.

14.5.1 The 2 × 2 factorial design

There are many forms of ANOVA model (see Kirk, 1995), but the main features of factorial ANOVA can be introduced by focusing on independent measures designs with two or three factors: two-way and three-way independent measures (between-subjects) ANOVA designs. The simplest such design is a two-way ANOVA in which each factor has two levels: a 2 × 2 ANOVA. In factorial ANOVA it makes sense to assume effect coding and to adopt an ANOVA parameterization of the model. Remember that a one-way ANOVA with independent measures can be represented as $y_{ij} = \mu + \tau_j + \varepsilon_{ij}$ with the restriction that $\sum_{j=1}^{J} \tau_j = 0$ and with the usual $N(0, \sigma^2)$ distributional assumptions for ε_{ij} (the errors). Parameterized in this way, a two-way ANOVA with factors labeled A and B has the form:

$$y_{iab} = \mu + \alpha_a + \beta_b + \alpha\beta_{ab} + \varepsilon_{iab} \qquad \text{Equation 14.14}$$

Under this parameterization the restrictions $\sum_{a=1}^{a} \alpha_a = 0$, $\sum_{b=1}^{b} \beta_b = 0$ and $\sum_{a=1,b=1}^{a,b} \alpha\beta_{ab} = 0$ apply. The coefficients α_a and β_b are the respective deviations of the level means of factors A and B from the grand mean μ while $\alpha\beta$ denotes the interaction. If the number of levels on each factor (a and b) is two then the design could be set out in a table divided into 2 × 2 = 4 cells. This is a common way to set out data for analysis or to present summary statistics such as means for the design.

A crucial feature of the factorial ANOVA design is that the default model includes an interaction term. The $\alpha\beta$ interaction term need not be included in the model, but is only very rarely excluded (e.g., if there are insufficient df to estimate it). One reason is that the interaction term is often the *raison d'être* of factorial ANOVA and of focal interest in the analysis. A second is that if the factor effects are orthogonal (e.g., in a fully factorial design with effect coding) the interaction term will be estimated independently of other effects. Its interpretation tends to be straightforward (relative to bilinear interactions in multiple regression). The cost of estimating the interaction is to reduce df_{error} by one. Unless the sample size is small relative to the number of parameters (which depends on the number of levels on each factor), any loss in efficiency from including the interaction is likely to be minimal. Furthermore, unless the interaction is negligible, the smaller error term for the model compensates for the reduction in df_{error}.

Example 14.5 Imagine a 2 × 2 design in which factor *A* is the presence or absence of a drug and factor *B* is the sex of a patient. The outcome variable is a measure of general health. This study is not a true, randomized experiment because only the drug (and not sex of patient) can be randomly allocated. However, it is a fairly typical application of ANOVA. Table 14.1 sets out the raw data and cell means for such a study.

Table 14.1 Raw data and means for a 2 × 2 factorial ANOVA design

	Raw data		**Cell means**		
	B_1 male	**B_2 female**	**B_1 male**	**B_2 female**	
A_1 placebo	8 10 10 12	8 9 11 12	10.0	10.0	10.0
A_2 drug	12 13 17 18	16 19 21 24	15.0	20.0	17.5
			12.5	15.0	

Arranged in this way, standard ANOVA terminology such as cell means and *n* per cell should be clear. Here *n* per cell is four and the cell means are computed for each combination of levels; for the male participants in the placebo condition (10), the male participants in the drug condition (15) and so on. The level means of each factor A_1, A_2, B_1 and B_2 are therefore also marginal means.

In a factorial design, the main effect of each factor is the average effect of that factor ignoring the presence of other factors. The main effects are therefore comparisons of the marginal (i.e., level) means of each factor. The main effect of factor *A* (the drug) is therefore a test of the difference between the placebo condition ($\hat{\mu}_{A_1} = 10$) and drug condition ($\hat{\mu}_{A_2} = 17.5$). The main effect of factor *B* (sex) is the test of the difference between male ($\hat{\mu}_{B_1} = 12.5$) and female ($\hat{\mu}_{B_2} = 15$) participants. The null hypotheses for the main effects can be expressed as H_0: $\mu_{A_1} = \mu_{A_2}$ and H_0: $\mu_{B_1} = \mu_{B_2}$.

What about the interaction? The null hypothesis in this case is not immediately obvious. Let's think about what a 2 × 2 interaction involves. It implies that the effects of drug and sex of patient on health in Table 14.1 are not additive. This is mathematically equivalent to saying that the effects are not independent. If they were perfectly additive (independent) the effect of the drug on males and the effect of the drug on females would have to be identical. In other words, the effect of factor *A* at each level of *B* (called a *simple main effect*) would the same. So within each level of *B* (B_1 or B_2) the difference between levels of *A* ($A_1 - A_2$) would be the same. Expressed as an equation this becomes:

$$H_0 : (\mu_{B_1A_1} - \mu_{B_1A_2}) - (\mu_{B_2A_1} - \mu_{B_2A_2}) = 0$$

This suggests a definition of the interaction in 2 × 2 ANOVA as a *difference of differences*.* For the data in Table 14.1, the interaction represents the difference in the effect of the drug (i.e., drug minus placebo) between male and female participants.

A practical consequence of this interpretation is that if you plot the cell means of a two-way ANOVA and add lines (slopes) representing the simple main effects of *A* at each level *B*, the lines will be parallel if the interaction is exactly zero. Figure 14.6 shows an example of this kind of *profile* or *interaction plot* of the cell means for the data at hand.

The interaction, being the difference in the drug effect for males and females, is shown by the differences in slopes for males and females. These differences are +5 for males and +10 for females and the difference of the differences is $10 - 5 = 5$. It won't matter which way round the calculation is done, the interaction effect has the same absolute magnitude. In terms of the difference between males and females (zero for the placebo conditions and five for the drug condition) this is $5 - 0 = 5$.

Although the magnitude of the interaction effect is the same, the graph of the interaction will look different when the roles of *A* and *B* are reversed. Figure 14.7 shows Figure 14.6 replotted with

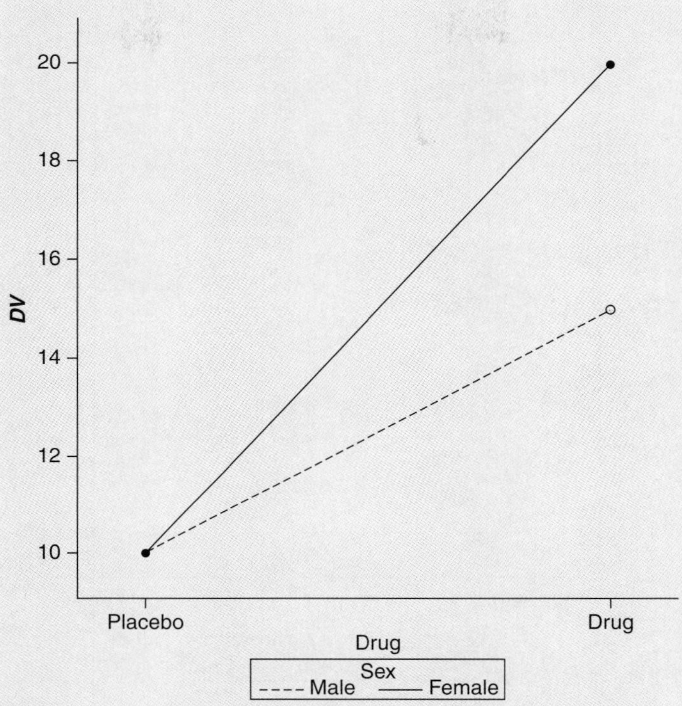

Figure 14.6 Interaction plot of cell means for the data in Table 14.1

sex on the x-axis and the levels of the drug factor as separate lines. The explanation for the different appearance of the two plots is that a conventional interaction or profile plot is not a pure depiction of the interaction effect. Each plot shows the interaction effect superimposed on a plot of the main effects. As a different main effect is plotted on the x-axis in each case, the striking difference between the graphs is due to differences in the main effects of A and B.

Fitting the regression (as a multiple linear regression model with effect coding of the factors) gives the prediction equation:

$$health = 13.75 + 3.75\,drug + 1.25\,sex + 1.25\,drug \times sex$$

In the ANOVA parameterization $y_{iab} = \mu + \alpha_a + \beta_b + \alpha\beta_{ab} + \varepsilon_{iab}$ this is equivalent to $\mu = 13.75$, $\alpha_a = \pm 3.75$, $\beta_b = \pm 1.25$ and $\alpha\beta_{ab} = \pm 1.25$. With equal n and only two levels, the constraint that deviations sum to zero ensures that all the deviations are equidistant from μ.

Had the regression been fitted using dummy coding, the parameter estimates would look like this (with the placebo condition and the male group used as the reference categories):

$$Y = 10 + 5\,drug + 0\,female + 5\,drug \times female$$

Although this appears different to the earlier equation, it is identical for the purposes of prediction. By expressing the effects relative to the male placebo mean (the intercept), individual predictors are interpreted differently. The effect of *drug* and *female* are now simple main effects rather than main effects. They express the effect of drug for the male group only (an increase of five) and the effect

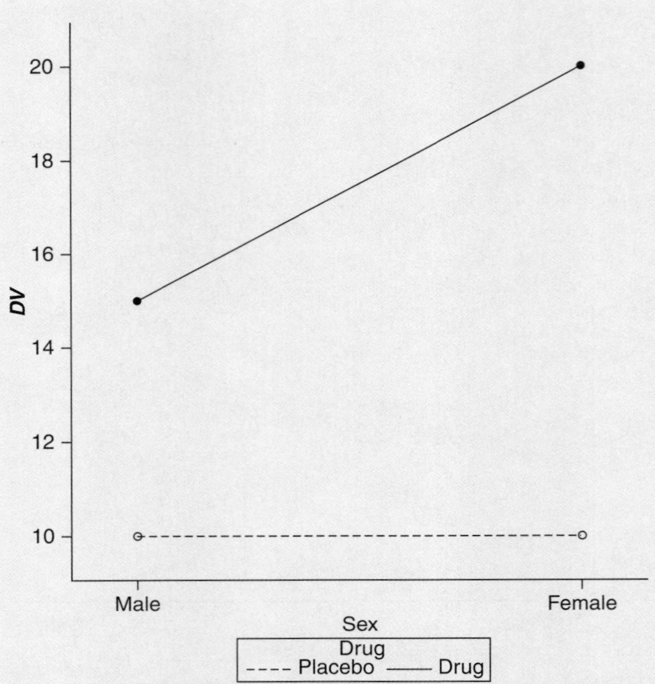

Figure 14.7 Alternative interaction plot of cell means for the data in Table 14.1

of female for the placebo group only (zero). The drug by female interaction is now the additional effect of drug for the female group (or the additional effect of being female for the drug condition). Simple main effects and simple interaction effects (effects restricted only to one level of another factor) can be confusing to interpret. Unless it is the simple main effects you are interested in, it is probably wise to use effect coding for factorial designs (or an appropriate ANOVA parameterization of the general linear model).

One of enduring puzzles of interpreting interaction effects is the question of whether the presence of an interaction changes the interpretation of the main effects. In this case (without formal tests) there appears to be some evidence of a main effect of drug. On average, health scores are 3.75 higher for the drug condition relative to the placebo condition. The evidence for a main effect of sex or of a sex by drug interaction is less convincing.** If the interaction can be dismissed as nonexistent, or at least negligible in its impact, then both main effects can be interpreted as if they had arisen in a separate one-way ANOVA (or a *t* test if they have two levels). If the impact of the interaction is not negligible, the relationship between main effects and interactions can cause confusion (see Box 14.2).

* Alternative expressions of the null hypothesis such as $\mu_{B_1A_1} - \mu_{B_1A_2} - \mu_{B_2A_1} + \mu_{B_2A_2} = 0$, $\mu_{B_1A_1} + \mu_{B_2A_2} - \mu_{B_1A_2} - \mu_{B_2A_1} = 0$ or $\mu_{B_1A_1} - \mu_{B_1A_2} = \mu_{B_2A_1} - \mu_{B_2A_2}$ do not necessarily emphasize the difference of differences interpretation.

** All three effects use the same estimate of error variance, so the simple differences in health scores are a crude measure of the strength of evidence against each null hypothesis.

Box 14.2 Does the presence of an interaction change ANOVA main effects?

A strict, technical answer to this question (for an orthogonal design) is 'no'. The main effects and interaction effects are independent of each other. If this is the case, why do people get confused? One cause for confusion relates to the hypothesis being tested by a main effect. There are two equally valid interpretations of what a main effect is. One is (for want of a better term) that it is a substantive hypothesis about some state of affairs in the world. The other is that it is the statistical hypothesis implied by the ANOVA model.

Take a study looking at disease symptoms in relation to the presence or absence of a drug in male and female participants. The substantive 'main effect' hypothesis might be 'men have more severe symptoms than women' or 'presence of the drug reduces symptoms'. These are general statements about the world and may be quite nuanced (e.g., there is a meaningful distinction between 'men have more severe symptoms than women' and 'men like those in the sample have more severe symptoms than women like those in the sample'). The corresponding statistical hypotheses are $\mu_{male} > \mu_{female}$ and $\mu_{placebo} > \mu_{drug}$. If there is no interaction (or one of negligible magnitude) in the population, then it isn't too difficult to align the statistical hypotheses with the substantive ones (and most experienced researchers are able to avoid the trap of thinking that statistical and substantive hypotheses are the same thing).

If an interaction is present and has a big enough effect then this changes. It becomes much harder to align the statistical and the substantive hypotheses. Why? The statistical hypothesis being tested now has a subtly different interpretation.* The statistical hypothesis is now that the marginal means for one factor (averaged over levels of the other factors) differ from each other.

Here is a concrete example. If the substantive hypothesis is that 'men have more severe symptoms than women' it is tempting to map this onto the statistical hypothesis $\mu_{male} > \mu_{female}$. This is reasonable if there is no interaction, but it could well be misleading if there is an interaction. This is because the statistical hypothesis is more accurately represented as:

$$(\mu_{male,placebo} + \mu_{male,drug})/2 > (\mu_{female,placebo} + \mu_{female,drug})/2$$

Only if the interaction is zero is this equivalent to $\mu_{male} > \mu_{female}$ (because $\mu_{male} = \mu_{male,placebo} = \mu_{male,drug}$ and $\mu_{female} = \mu_{female,placebo} = \mu_{female,drug}$). A conclusion such as 'men like those in the sample have more severe symptoms than women like those in the sample' is not necessarily supported by the presence of a main effect. To check the correct interpretation you need to look quite carefully at the interaction.

If there is a main effect of the drug, this implies that on average the drug line in Figure 14.7 is higher than the placebo line. To see if a general statement like 'presence of the drug improves health' is reasonable (as a substantive conclusion) look at the plot. The clear separation of the drug and placebo lines (for both men and women) suggests that this substantive interpretation is reasonable. This visual check could be replaced by formal hypothesis tests (e.g., a test of the simple main effects drug for males and females).

In Figure 14.6 the female line is also (on average) higher than the male line. However, a substantive conclusion such as 'men have worse health than women' would be misleading. There is no clear separation between the lines (and no formal hypothesis test is required). Furthermore, the context of the study is relevant here. The general statement 'men have worse health than women' can probably only be justified if it applies in the placebo conditions. Common sense demands that such a broad claim requires support among the conditions of the experiment that are typical of the population you want to generalize to. It is likely that only participants in the placebo condition can be considered typical of the population.

Although the technical answer to this question is 'no', a more refined answer is to say that an interaction can't change the ANOVA main effects (in an orthogonal design), but it can change the interpretation of the effects. The interpretation will also change according to the context of the study and the precise formulation of the substantive hypothesis you wish to test.

As a fallback, there is a 'safe' way to interpret any main effect in the presence of an interaction. First, report the main effects as average effects of a factor over all levels of the other factor. Second, place more emphasis on explaining the pattern of the interaction. If a main effect of gender in Figure 14.6 is detected, it indicates that on average (weighting drug and placebo conditions equally) men had worse health status than women. The interaction suggests that this is probably only true for the drug condition, because the drug has a larger effect for women than for men.

* The hypothesis has not really changed (in a statistical sense), but it needs to be interpreted differently because the state of affairs in the world being modeled is more complex than in the 'no interaction' case.

14.5.2 Types of 2 × 2 interactions

There is some debate in the literature about the wisdom of plotting interaction effects with main effects present (Rosnow and Rosenthal, 1995; Abelson, 1996; Petty *et al.*, 1996; Rosnow and Rosenthal, 1996a). Related to this debate, it is not uncommon to categorize interactions as 'ordinal' or 'disordinal' according to the pattern of cell means.

Figure 14.8 illustrates some of the possible patterns found in 2 × 2 ANOVA. In panel (a) the lines are perfectly parallel. There is no interaction, though one or both main effects may be present. The presence of a main effect for B is suggested by the higher line for B_1 than B_2, while the increase from A_1 to A_2 suggests a main effect of A. The remaining panels all suggest an interaction is present: none of the lines are parallel. Panel (b) is what some would call an ordinal interaction. In an ordinal interaction, the rank order of the means for one predictor doesn't change across levels of the other predictor (for the levels included in the study). As a consequence, the interaction has the appearance of enhancing a main effect. Panel (d) shows an interaction that is disordinal in the extreme (usually referred to as a *crossover interaction*). In a disordinal interaction the rank order of the means for the predictor is not the same across levels of another predictor. The main effects in (d) are exactly zero (it is a pure interaction effect) and so the effects of A are completely reversed between B_1 and B_2 (and vice versa).

Rosnow and Rosenthal (1995) suggest that to interpret an interaction it is important to strip out the main effects and look at the 'residual' effects of the interaction. This is equivalent to the $\alpha\beta_{ab}$ term in the ANOVA model, and expresses the interaction as deviations relative to the grand mean and ignoring main effects. Petty *et al.* (1996) and Abelson (1996) are much more cautious about the wisdom of interpreting interaction effects in isolation. Both positions have merit. Rosnow and Rosenthal's argument could be interpreted as pointing out that all interaction effects are disordinal by definition. Once you strip out any main effects, all 2 × 2 interactions look rather like panel (d) of Figure 14.8. An ordinal interaction requires that the slopes in an interaction plot do not cross within the range of levels sampled in the analysis. However, if an interaction exists, the slopes of the lines differ. This implies that at some point the lines

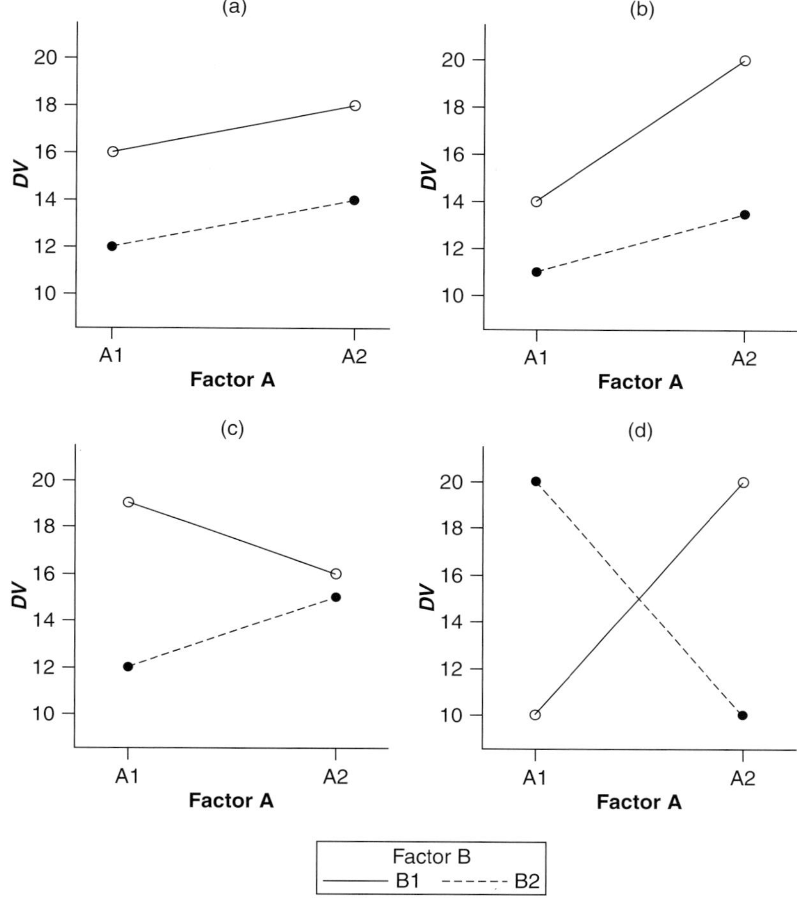

Figure 14.8 Examples of potential patterns of cell means in 2 × 2 ANOVA

must cross for any interaction effect, though the point at which the lines cross could be outside the sampled values of the predictors (i.e., off the edge of the graph). It is in this sense that all interactions are disordinal.

On the other hand, the fact that all non-parallel lines cross somewhere is irrelevant to some analyses. It will be irrelevant if the levels in the study are the only ones of interest or if they don't represent an ordinal or continuous quantity (e.g., a categorical distinction such as sex). However, if the levels are sampled from an ordered set of categories (e.g., year groups in a school) or from a continuum (e.g., dose of a drug) the fact that the lines cross somewhere may be hugely important. For these reasons, avoiding the terms ordinal and disordinal is recommended (though the term 'crossover' interaction applied to a pure interaction with no main effects is worth retaining). It is not the interaction *per se* that is ordinal or disordinal, but the combination of interaction and main effects.

14.5.3 Partitioning sums of squares when cell sizes are unequal

In a balanced ANOVA design, all factors are orthogonal and there is no difficulty unambiguously allocating sums of squares for the regression model to main effects and interaction effects. In an unbalanced design, the factors are no longer orthogonal and unambiguous allocation of sums of squares to effects is no longer possible.

There are, as noted in Section 13.3.3, three main solutions to the problem of partitioning sums of squares: sequential (Type I) *SS*, hierarchical (Type II) *SS* and unique (Type III) *SS*. Sequential *SS* offers the most flexible approach – allowing you to tailor the model to the hypotheses you are interested in. By varying the sequence of effects entered into the model, you can replicate the hierarchical and unique *SS* solutions. Non-sequential *SS* are preferred as a default solution for partitioning effects. For simple models, hierarchical and unique *SS* partition variance in the same way.

The crucial distinction between the solutions is that unique *SS* assesses the contribution of an effect added to a model containing all other effects, while hierarchical *SS* assesses its contribution to a model containing effects of equal or lower order. If a model contains only effects of equal order (e.g., main effects) then the two solutions are equivalent. The difference therefore only arises for unbalanced ANOVA or ANCOVA models with interaction or polynomial terms. The question of which solution is correct is a matter of historical and, to some extent, continuing interest (Herr, 1986; Venables, 1998).

Hierarchical (Type II) *SS* are an appropriate default for most situations (Langsrud, 2003; Venables, 1998). The arguments against unique *SS* (the default in SPSS and some other packages) are twofold. The first is pragmatic. By and large, hierarchical *SS* leads to tests with greater statistical power than unique *SS* (Langsrud, 2003). The second is conceptual. Partitioning effects via unique *SS* implicitly involves testing hypotheses that are uninteresting and perhaps meaningless. Partitioning sums of squares according to the additional contribution of an effect to a model containing other effects is a form of model comparison. If one of the two models is uninteresting or implausible, then the comparison won't make much sense.

In a two-way ANOVA with factors A and B, there are three effects of interest: the main effect of A, the main effect of B and the A × B interaction. The concerns with unique *SS* can be demonstrated when partitioning variance for a main effect such as A or B. To assess the main effect of A, the variance is partitioned by comparing a model with A, B and A × B (the full model) to a model with B and A × B. The reference model in this case is problematic because it includes an interaction term without both lower-order terms (i.e., A is not present in a model containing A × B). The A × B term in such a model is at best uninteresting and at worst meaningless (e.g., it is unlikely to be a pure estimate of the interaction effect). Hierarchical *SS* avoids this problem by implicitly setting up a hierarchical sequence of model comparisons. The *SS* for the interaction is the additional sample variance accounted for by the full interaction model (A, B and A × B) over and above the additive, main effects model (A and B). The *SS* for a main effect (e.g., A) is the increase in sample variance of the additive model (A and B) relative to a model without the main effect (e.g., B only). Thus hierarchical *SS* restricts the model comparisons to models with a clear interpretation and (by partialing out fewer effects) tends to provide more powerful tests.

While the conceptual distinction between hierarchical and unique *SS* is far from trivial, the practical consequences of the choice may not matter much for experimental research (where ANOVA and ANCOVA designs tend to be balanced). The problem of a default choice can also be avoided by taking a model comparison approach to ANOVA and ANCOVA models, in which the hypotheses to be tested are explicit in the choice of the models being compared.

14.5.4 Beyond 2 × 2 factorial ANOVA

A 2 × 2 factorial ANOVA can be extended in several ways: by including factors with more than two levels, adding factors to the design or by adding covariates. Adding levels to a two-way factorial design requires coding a and b levels of the predictors using $a-1$ and $b-1$ indicator variables. Both dummy and effect coding are frequently used for this, though effect coding is more popular. A cell means parameterization of the model is also possible (but uncommon for factorial designs).

Table 14.2a shows dummy coding applied to 2 × 3 ANOVA design. The factors are labeled A and B (with levels A_1 and B_1 designated as reference categories). Table 14.2b shows the same design with effect coding. Note that whenever the reference category (level 1 in this instance) appears, the code is -1.

Dummy or effect coding for the main effects is established in the same way it would be for a one-way ANOVA with more than two levels. The origin of the interaction terms A_2B_2 and A_2B_3 may not be immediately obvious. In the 2 × 2 case there is one interaction term, and it is the product of the two indicator variables. Exactly the same process applies here, but as there are $a-1$ and $b-1$ predictors coding the factors, it will take $(a-1) \times (b-1)$ indicator variables to code

Table 14.2a Dummy coding for 2 × 3 factorial ANOVA

Participant	Factor A	Factor B	A_2	B_2	B_3	A_2B_2	A_2B_3
1	Level 1	Level 1	0	0	0	0	0
2	Level 1	Level 1	0	0	0	0	0
3	Level 1	Level 2	0	1	0	0	0
4	Level 1	Level 2	0	1	0	0	0
5	Level 1	Level 3	0	0	1	0	0
6	Level 1	Level 3	0	0	1	0	0
7	Level 2	Level 1	1	0	0	0	0
8	Level 2	Level 1	1	0	0	0	0
9	Level 2	Level 2	1	1	0	1	0
...	...	...	...	...	...	...	...

Table 14.2b Effect coding for 2 × 3 factorial ANOVA

Participant	Factor A	Factor B	A_2	B_2	B_3	A_2B_2	A_2B_3
1	Level 1	Level 1	−1	−1	−1	1	1
2	Level 1	Level 1	−1	−1	−1	1	1
3	Level 1	Level 2	−1	1	0	−1	0
4	Level 1	Level 2	−1	1	0	−1	0
5	Level 1	Level 3	−1	0	1	0	−1
6	Level 1	Level 3	−1	0	1	0	−1
7	Level 2	Level 1	1	−1	−1	−1	−1
8	Level 2	Level 1	1	−1	−1	−1	−1
9	Level 2	Level 2	1	1	0	1	0
...	...	...	...	...	...	...	...

all of the possible product terms for a two-way factorial ANOVA. Indicator variables are created for the interaction by multiplying every possible pair of the original indicator variables. Dummy coding therefore produces product terms with many zeroes (because anything multiplied by zero is zero). Effect coding has product terms with zeroes when any of terms being multiplied is zero, and if both are 1 or -1 the product term will be one. Only if one indicator is positive and one negative will the product be -1.

The general form of the two-way ANOVA table with independent measures is set out in Table 14.3. For a balanced design the *MS* for each factor is *n* per level (n_A or n_B) times the variance of the level means (just as it is for a one-way ANOVA with independent measures). This approach expresses the *MS* for factor A as

$$MS_A = \frac{n_A \sum_{i=1}^{a} \left(\hat{\mu}_a - \hat{\mu}_{grand}\right)^2}{a-1} = n_A \hat{\sigma}^2_{means_A} \qquad \text{Equation 14.15}$$

and the *MS* for factor *B* as

$$MS_B = \frac{n_B \sum_{i=1}^{b} \left(\hat{\mu}_b - \hat{\mu}_{grand}\right)^2}{b-1} = n_B \hat{\sigma}^2_{means_B} \qquad \text{Equation 14.16}$$

MS_{error} is defined as the average of the variances of the separate cells in independent measures ANOVA (Cohen, 2002). By squaring the standard deviations of each cell you get the variance for each *ab* condition. Summing these and dividing by *ab* gives MS_{error}. Sums of squares can then be computed in the usual way. $SS_{A\times B}$ is most easily obtained by subtraction from SS_{total} (the sums of squares of the outcome *Y*). This allows $MS_{A\times B}$ to be computed as $SS_{A\times B}/df_{A\times B}$.

$MS_{A\times B}$ can't be computed directly from the cell means, because these also include the influence of the main effects, though their effects could be stripped out (see Key Concept 15.1). These equations illustrate the link between the variances of levels and combinations of levels and the *MS* and *SS* columns in an ANOVA. They are also useful for secondary analysis (e.g., reproducing an ANOVA analysis from summary statistics in published research where raw data is unavailable).

Table 14.3 The ANOVA table for a two-way independent measures design

Source	***df***	***SS***	***MS***	***F***
Factor *A*	$a-1$	SS_A	$\frac{SS_A}{df_A}$	$\frac{MS_A}{MS_{error}}$
Factor *B*	$b-1$	SS_B	$\frac{SS_B}{df_B}$	$\frac{MS_B}{MS_{error}}$
$A \times B$ interaction	$(a-1)(b-1)$	$SS_{A\times B}$	$\frac{SS_{A\times B}}{df_{A\times B}}$	$\frac{MS_{A\times B}}{MS_{error}}$
Error	$N-ab$	$SS_{residual}$	$\frac{SS_{residual}}{df_{error}}$	
Total	$N-1$	SS_{total}		

Table 14.4 The ANOVA table for a three-way independent measures design

Source	*df*	*SS*	*MS*	*F*
Factor *A*	$a-1$	SS_A	$\frac{SS_A}{df_A}$	$\frac{MS_A}{MS_{error}}$
Factor *B*	$b-1$	SS_B	$\frac{SS_B}{df_B}$	$\frac{MS_B}{MS_{error}}$
Factor *C*	$c-1$	SS_C	$\frac{SS_C}{df_C}$	$\frac{MS_C}{MS_{error}}$
$A \times B$ interaction	$(a-1)(b-1)$	$SS_{A\times B}$	$\frac{SS_{A\times B}}{df_{A\times B}}$	$\frac{MS_{A\times B}}{MS_{error}}$
$A \times C$ interaction	$(a-1)(c-1)$	$SS_{A\times C}$	$\frac{SS_{A\times C}}{df_{A\times C}}$	$\frac{MS_{A\times C}}{MS_{error}}$
$B \times C$ interaction	$(b-1)(c-1)$	$SS_{B\times C}$	$\frac{SS_{B\times C}}{df_{B\times C}}$	$\frac{MS_{B\times C}}{MS_{error}}$
$A \times B \times C$ interaction	$(a-1)(b-1)(c-1)$	$SS_{A\times B\times C}$	$\frac{SS_{A\times B\times C}}{df_{A\times B\times C}}$	$\frac{MS_{A\times B\times C}}{MS_{error}}$
Error	$N-abc$	$SS_{residual}$	$\frac{SS_{residual}}{df_{error}}$	
Total	$N-1$	SS_{total}		

Extending the calculations to more than two factors is not too challenging. A three-way ANOVA design is sufficient to demonstrate the process of setting out and interpreting such designs. Table 14.4 shows the table for three-way independent measures ANOVA. The usual relationships between *F*, *MS*, *SS* and *df* are maintained in these tables. *F* is the ratio of the estimated population variance of an effect to the estimate of error. Each *MS* is an estimate of population variance and computed from the average *SS* per *df* for each source of variance. The *df* for the effects are the number of indicator variables required to code the effect. These are the number of levels minus one for the main effects. Two-way interaction effects are obtained by pooling the effects of these indicator variables. Three-way interaction terms are coded using the products of the indicator variables of all three main effects. Thus, in a $2 \times 3 \times 4$ design, the $A \times B$ interaction would have only $1 \times 2 = 2$ *df*, but the $A \times B \times C$ interaction would have $1 \times 2 \times 3 = 6$ *df* (and involves estimating six parameters – one for each of the indicator variables required to code it).

The *df* for the error term may at first seem mysterious. This is simply the number of data points minus the number of parameters being estimated: $N - abc$. It could also be represented as the *df* per group $(n - 1)$ multiplied by the number of groups: $(n - 1) \times a \times b \times c$.

In a fully factorial design, $a \times b \times c$ parameters are estimated (including the intercept). Factorial ANOVA designs with large numbers of levels and large numbers of factors are therefore rare. Not only is the interpretation tricky, but unless *N* is large, statistical power to detect effects will suffer. As these analyses are usually applied to experimental data, experiments are often designed with only two or three factors to minimize these problems.

If the ANOVA is unbalanced, the factors won't be orthogonal and the hand calculations become increasingly cumbersome. For a small degree of imbalance, using the harmonic mean cell size in place of n provides an approximate solution to the unique *SS* method (Cohen, 2002). However, there is no agreed method for quantifying the degree of imbalance and this solution is no longer considered satisfactory (Herr, 1986). Regression solutions using general linear models are now almost invariably employed.

Example 14.6 Kvavilashvili *et al.* (2001, Experiment 3) looked at performance on a prospective memory task (in which participants have to remember an intention to do something in the future). Children aged four, five or seven ($n = 32$ per group) were asked to name pictures on stacks of cards, having earlier been instructed to hide any picture of an animal that they encountered. Each child received four stacks of cards and a single animal card was inserted either at the end of the stack (the *no interruption* condition) or the middle of the stack (the *interruption* condition). Thus half the children had to remember the prospective memory instruction (to hide the card) after the naming task was completed and half had to remember it during the task. The mean and *SD* of the frequency with which the instruction was successfully acted upon (ranging from zero to four) are set out in Table 14.5 below. Subsequent examples will refer to this data set as the prospective memory data.

Table 14.5 Summary data for the prospective memory study

Age	**Interruption**		**No interruption**		
	M	**SD**	**M**	**SD**	$\hat{\mu}$
4 years	0.94	1.69	2.50	2.00	1.720
5 years	2.06	1.91	2.68	1.89	2.370
7 years	2.25	1.84	3.50	1.36	2.875
$\hat{\mu}$	1.750		2.893		

These data are suitable for a balanced 3×2 independent measures analysis with age and condition as factors (and $n = 16$ per cell). The variance of the level means of the age groups and the grand mean of 2.32167 can be used to compute the mean square for the age factor (given that there are 32 children per level):

$$MS_{age} = n_{age}\hat{\sigma}^2_{means} = 32\left(\frac{1.72^2 + 2.37^2 + 2.875^2 - 3 \times 2.32167^2}{3-1}\right) \approx 10.728$$

The corresponding result for the condition factor, with 48 children per level, is:

$$MS_{cond} = n_{cond}\hat{\sigma}^2_{means} = 48\left(\frac{1.75^2 + 2.893^2 - 2 \times 2.32167^2}{2-1}\right) \approx 31.355$$

The error term is given by the average of the reported variances in each *ab* cell:

$$MS_{error} = \frac{\sum_{i=1}^{ab} \hat{\sigma}_i^2}{ab} = \frac{1.69^2 + 1.91^2 + 1.84^2 + 2^2 + 1.89^2 + 1.36^2}{6} \approx 3.219$$

Working out $MS_{interaction}$ is trickier and the easiest route is to calculate $SS_{interaction}$. Multiplying MS_{error} by the error df of $96-6=90$ gives $SS_{residual}=289.67$. With only two levels, $SS_{cond}=MS_{cond}=31.355$, but with $a=3$ levels $SS_{age}=MS_{age}\times(3-1)=21.456$. SS_{total} can't be calculated from Y because $\hat{\sigma}_Y$ is not reported. However, the total SS not explained by $SS_{residual}$ can be calculated from the sums of squares of the cell means. This makes it possible to calculate $SS_{interaction}$ by subtracting the sums of squares for the main effects from those of the cell means:

$$SS_{interaction} = SS_{cells} - \left(SS_{age} + SS_{cond}\right)$$

This gives the following results:

$$SS_{cells} = n\hat{\sigma}^2_{cells} = 16\left(0.94^2 + 2.06^2 + 2.25^2 + 2.5^2 + 2.68^2 + 3.5^2 - 6 \times 2.32167^2\right) = 56.501$$

$$SS_{age\times cond} = 56.501 - (21.456 + 31.355) = 3.690$$

$$MS_{age\times cond} = \frac{SS_{age\times cond}}{df_{age\times cond}} = \frac{3.690}{(3-1)(2-1)} \approx 1.845$$

$MS_{interaction}$ could also be obtained from the sums of squares of the double-centered cell means (see Key Concept 15.1).

Table 14.6 sets out the output from the ANOVA calculations including F ratios and p values. These results are very close to those of Kvavilashvili *et al.* (2001).

Table 14.6 ANOVA table for the proactive memory data

Source	***df***	***SS***	***MS***	***F***	***p***
Age	2	21.46	10.73	3.33	.040
Condition	1	31.35	31.35	9.74	.002
Age × condition	2	3.69	1.85	0.57	.566
Error	90	289.67	3.22		
Total	95	346.17			

Although there are more efficient formulas for working with raw data, these formulas are convenient for secondary analysis (and for illustrating how variance is partitioned in ANOVA).

14.5.5 Exploring and interpreting interaction effects

Graphical methods are the most widely used methods for exploring interaction effects. Plotting cell means for a two-way ANOVA, with or without CIs, is an important method for understanding the pattern of effects. Interaction plots for two-way ANOVA with more than two levels per factor are plotted in the same format as for a 2×2 design. The choice of factor to assign to the x-axis matters a little more for these plots. The mathematics of the interaction won't change, but the interpretation may be clearer plotting the interaction one way rather than another (because of the confounding influence of the main effects).

Two tricks can help to get the plot right. First, if the levels of a factor take the form of an ordered category (e.g., academic grades) or are discrete points along a continuum (e.g., 0, 10 or 20 *mg* doses of a drug) then that factor is a sensible candidate for plotting on the *x*-axis. People are used to plotting ordinal or continuous information on the *x*-axis of a plot and prefer plots designed this way. A second trick is to plot the factor with the most levels on the *x*-axis. The number of levels of the factor not on the *x*-axis determines the number of lines on the plot. Cluttered plots can be difficult to interpret (e.g., a plot with five points connected by two lines typically appears less cluttered than one with five lines connecting two points each). These tricks will often help produce a user-friendly plot.

Figure 14.9 illustrates this advice for a 5 × 3 ANOVA (with five levels on A and three levels on B). The top row shows an example in which an interaction and both main effects are present. In panel (a) the five levels of factor *A* are plotted on the *x*-axis. This produces a less cluttered plot than panel (b) where the same data are plotted with *B* on the *x*-axis. The bottom row shows similar plots for a 5 × 3 ANOVA with no interaction. Here, if anything, the advantage of plotting the factor with five levels on the *x*-axis is even greater. The plots in the left-hand side

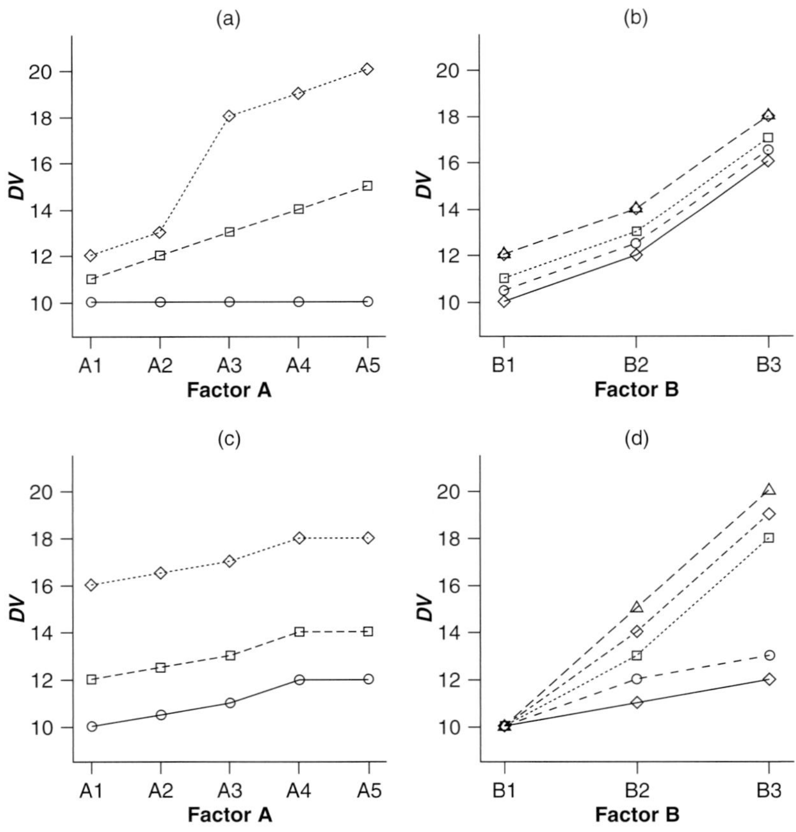

Figure 14.9 Alternative plots for a 5 × 3 ANOVA, with interaction in (a) and (b) or without interaction in (c) and (d)

panels (a) and (c) would be particularly appropriate if the levels of factor A were ordered (e.g., increasing dose of a drug).

Graphical methods are capable of revealing potential interactions regardless of the number of levels on each factor. If the effects of each factor are independent, the differences in levels of one factor will remain constant across all levels of the other factor. If so, the lines in the interaction plot will be parallel. This should be apparent in panels (c) and (d) of Figure 14.9. People encountering ANOVA for the first time occasionally find it hard to detect departures from parallel lines in an interaction plot. One culprit is that the lines can still be parallel even if they aren't straight. Parallel lines are defined by constant separation between lines, not by straightness. A second culprit is that a single point shifted up or down could cause the separation of the lines to be unequal. Even a tiny departure from parallelism could, in theory, indicate the presence of an interaction. Such subtle patterns can be difficult to spot.

With real data, small departures from independence and hence slightly non-parallel lines will often reflect statistical noise (error). Non-parallel lines alert you to the potential presence of an interaction and help you interpret one if it is present. However, they are not a substitute for formal tests of an interaction effect. Adding CIs to the plot will sometimes help, but, because the interaction depends on differences of differences, this approach can be equivocal and formal inference (but not necessarily a significance test) may be required.

There are a number of statistical procedures that can be applied to probe a two-way interaction in more detail. The most common of these approaches is to break the interaction down into the simple main effects of one factor at a given level of another factor. This approach lends itself to constructing an NHST for each simple main effect. To keep things simple, we'll assume that this is the preferred approach for the discussion that follows.[8] For independent measures ANOVA, the test of a simple main effect involves computing an F ratio of the form:

$$F_{df_{SME},df_{error}} = \frac{SS_{SME}/df_{SME}}{SS_{residual}/df_{error}} = \frac{MS_{SME}}{MS_{error}} \qquad \text{Equation 14.17}$$

The first step is to decide which simple main effect to calculate. A common approach is to calculate all simple main effects. For a 2×3 ANOVA these would be the effect of factor A at B_1, B_2, and B_3 plus the effects of factor B at A_1 and A_2. For an independent measures design MS_{error} is the pooled error term from the original ANOVA (already available from the full analysis). This error term is preferred because each participant contributes one independent observation and pooling the errors across as many observations as possible gives the most accurate estimate of the error in the population. This logic holds only if the assumptions of normality, independence and homogeneity of variance are met. If not, it may be more accurate to compute separate error terms for each effect.

If the effect of interest is the simple main effect of A at B_1, then MS_{SME} is a variance estimate for A within the first level of B. This can be computed from the variance of the cell means for that level of B multiplied by n per level of A at B_1 (which is n per cell for the full ANOVA). An important check on this calculation is that sums of squares for all simple main effects of factor A at levels of B will sum to SS_A plus $SS_{A \times B}$.

A standard method for calculating the MS for the simple main effect you are interested in is to rerun the ANOVA including only the data from B_1. If the full design has two factors, this analysis will be a one-way ANOVA with A as the factor and the outcome Y taken only from the appropriate level of B. This analysis will provide the correct SS, MS and numerator df $(a - 1)$ for the effect, but the denominator of the F ratio will be incorrect. The correct F ratio can be calculated using the pooled error term from the original analysis (from which df_{error} is inherited). This is the calculation set out in Equation 14.17, where the numerator MS_{SME} is calculated afresh for each simple main effect but the denominator is taken from the full ANOVA.

Although simple main effects seem like a logical way to decompose an interaction effect, they can lead you into difficulty. First, they are not pure tests of an interaction effect. They do not really decompose the interaction into its component parts. In the most basic 2×2 case the interaction has a coherent interpretation as a difference of differences. Because the effect has 1 *df*, there is, from the perspective of the ANOVA model, no logical way to it break down further. It is therefore unsurprising that trying to follow-up an interaction by reducing it to its simple effects can lead to confusion. For instance, it is possible that an interaction is statistically significant, but all simple effects are non-significant. In fact, this occurs frequently when *SS* accounted for by the main effects are small relative to the *SS* for the interaction. Simple main effects are most appropriate when they map directly onto a set of hypotheses that a researcher is interested in. If so, it may make sense to run the analysis so that only the simple main effects of interest are tested (thus limiting the overall number of tests performed).

If the interaction has multiple *df* there is a strong argument for breaking down the interaction and looking for patterns within it. However, the appropriate tool in this case is an interaction contrast (not a simple main effect).

Example 14.7 The proactive memory data in the previous example did not suggest the presence of an interaction between age and condition. An interaction plot of the cell means is given in Figure 14.10. This illustrates the pattern of effects quite clearly. Even without formal tests (e.g., pairwise comparisons) it seems reasonable to conclude that prospective memory performance increases with the age of the child (and almost certainly from four to seven). Interruption leads to worse performance on the task than if there is no interruption. This difference does not seem to vary much with the age of the child (consistent with a non-significant interaction effect).

It would be unusual in this situation to calculate simple main effects, but because a simple main effect decomposes the combined interaction and main effect variance, it is still possible to calculate and interpret one if an interaction effect is not present (or negligible).

For instance, if the prime theoretical issue was whether seven-year-olds showed an interruption effect (e.g., because previous studies had shown that they did not), the most direct test of this hypothesis is the simple main effect of condition at age seven. To calculate this effect requires df_{error} and MS_{error} from the original analysis. These are 90 and 3.22 respectively, while $df_{SME} = 1$ because only two means are being compared. The final input, MS_{SME}, is calculated from the cell means of experimental condition at age seven. These means are 2.25 and 3.50. Their average is 2.875, making the numerator for the *F* ratio:

$$MS_{SME} = n\hat{\sigma}^2_{means} = 16\left(2.25^2 + 3.5^2 - 2 \times 2.875^2\right) = 12.5$$

Combining this with the error term gives:

$$F_{1,90} = \frac{MS_{SME}}{MS_{error}} = \frac{12.5}{3.22} \approx 3.88$$

This could reported as: $F_{1,90} = 3.88$, $MSe = 3.22$, $p = .052$. Although the overall main effect is statistically significant and the test of the interaction effect does not indicate that the effect of condition differs across the age groups, the direct test of the effect of condition for seven-year-olds is not quite statistically significant.

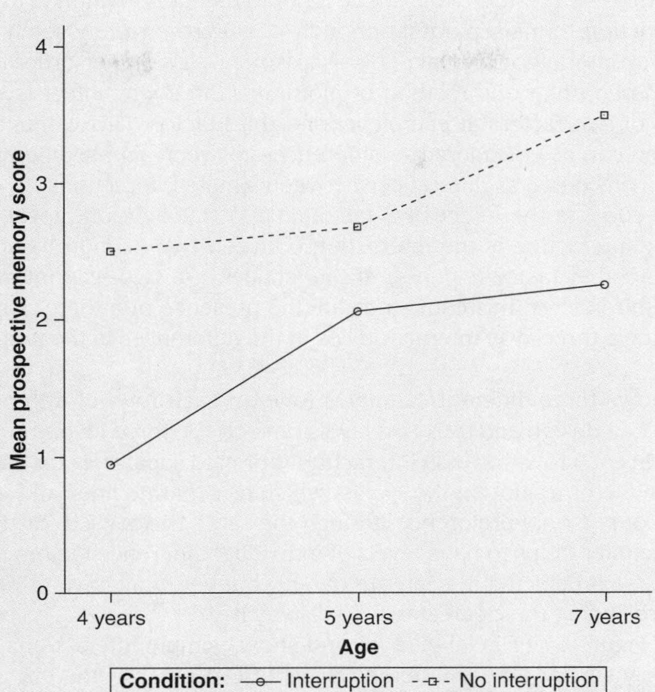

Figure 14.10 Interaction plot of the cell means by condition and age for the prospective memory data

The explanation for the discrepancy is prosaic: the individual test of the effect at age seven has less statistical power than the omnibus test of the main effect (because it is based on fewer observations and a smaller *SS* value). This problem would be less obvious if an interaction were present. This is one of the chief dangers of testing simple main effects. They tend to have less power than the omnibus tests they usually follow. For the prospective memory data the non-significant simple main effect is unimportant. The main effect is more relevant. The simple main effect is only appropriate if the hypothesis of an effect for one factor at a given level of another is critical.

This example also demonstrates the other main danger of simple main effects: interpreting them as if they are decomposed interaction effects. Here the interaction effect is negligible (having $F < 1$ and therefore smaller than that expected from sampling error), yet it is still quite possible to construct a test of the simple main effects (although they may not be that interesting). The sum of the main effect and interaction variance is being partitioned by this analysis. The sums of squares for the simple main effects of condition at age four, five and seven are 19.4688, 3.0752 and 12.5 respectively. These sum to 35.044 (which exactly equals the sum of the *SS* for the main effect of condition and the age by condition interaction).

14.5.6 Plotting a three-way interaction

Two-way interactions can be plotted by separating out one factor (e.g., using separate lines for each level). A three-way interaction is somewhat harder to squeeze into a 2D plot. If you are confident that the three-way interaction can be ignored then it is legitimate to plot and interpret the two-way interaction terms separately (though it is unwise to rely solely on a significance test of the three-way interaction to make this assessment). If a higher-order interaction cannot legitimately be ignored, then one method of plotting a three-way effect is to plot the simple interaction effects of two factors at each level of a third factor. This works because, just as a two-way interaction can be considered as differences between simple differences, a three-way interaction can be considered as differences between simple interactions.

A simple main effect is the effect of a factor (e.g., A) at only one level of another factor (e.g., B_1). A simple interaction is the interaction between two or more factors (e.g., $A \times B$) at only one level of another factor (e.g., C_1). If the 'shape' of a two-way interaction is different across levels of a third factor, this could indicate the presence of a three-way interaction. The secret of interpreting a three-way interaction lies in the differences in the patterns of the simple interactions.

Figure 14.11 shows three different examples (one on each row) of a three-way interaction plot. Each has $2 \times 3 \times 3$ design and thus two levels on factor A, three levels on factor B and three levels on factor C. In each row the $A \times B$ interaction is plotted separately for the levels C_1, C_2 and C_3. Deciding which factor to plot on the x-axis, which as separate lines and which on separate panels is a matter of personal preference (though the same tricks used for two-way plots also work here). It sometimes helps to have levels of individual difference factors representing types of participant (e.g., sex) depicted in separate panels, but you may have to plot the interaction several ways before finding the clearest way to display it.

The top row of Figure 14.11 is labeled (a) and shows simple interactions between A and B that are qualitatively similar across different levels of C. However, the size of the interaction effect clearly increases over levels of C. This suggests that a three-way interaction is present. The simple interactions show that the difference between A_1 and A_2 (the separation of the lines) increases over levels of B. This three-way interaction indicates that the increase in the differences between levels of A over levels of B also increases over levels of C. This is a fairly straightforward three-way interaction to interpret, but is complex enough for most people! One way to reduce the complexity is to strip out A altogether (by considering the difference between the lines). Across levels of B the differences are roughly +3 for C_1, +5 for C_2 and +9 for C_3. This is a common tactic in interpreting three-way interactions; to consider them as changes in the effect size of one factor over levels of the other factors (and this could also be plotted).

The second row of Figure 14.11, labeled (b), shows an example of a $2 \times 3 \times 3$ design when a three-way interaction is not likely to be present. Although each panel in row (b) is different, the shape of the simple interaction is the same in each case. This is a rather unusual example as all three plots show roughly parallel lines (indicating no simple interactions are likely to be present). None of the lines are perfectly parallel. In theory this means that a large enough sample size (or small enough error variance) might just about detect a three-way interaction effect. If all the panels in row (b) had shown a simple interaction effect, but the shape had been similar (e.g., they had all looked like a single panels from the row above) then this would still suggest no three-way interaction was present. A point of particular importance is that the absence of simple interactions in this kind of plot can conceal two-way interactions. The panels of row (b) conceal a potential $A \times C$ interaction. In practice this should not matter, as you should check all the two-way plots if the three-way interaction is negligible.

The third row of Figure 14.11, labeled (c), shows what is probably the simplest kind of three-way interaction to interpret. This is where there is no hint of a simple interaction in some panels and a very clear simple interaction in another. This form of 'all-or-none' interaction effect is a

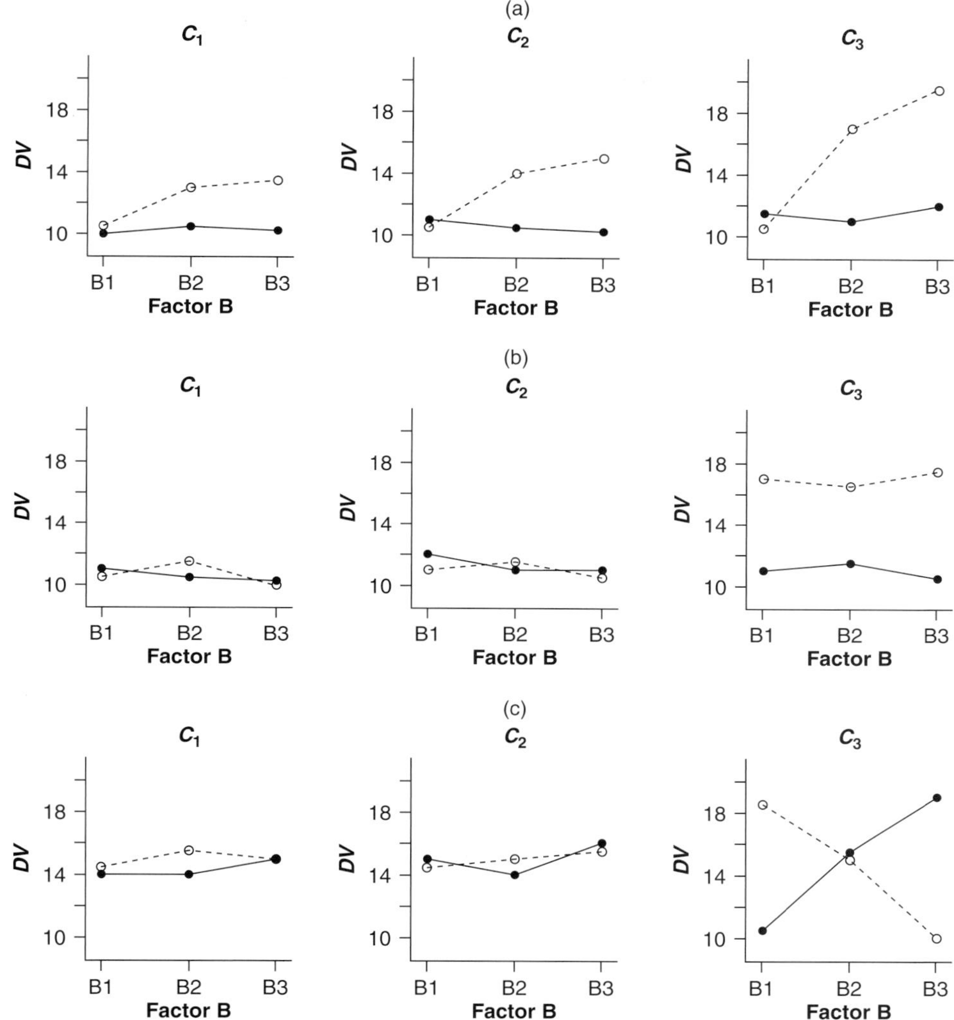

Figure 14.11 Three-way interaction plots for ANOVA with and without interaction

two-way interaction that only occurs for some levels of a third factor. These effects are easy to interpret, because you can compartmentalize what is happening (e.g., the interaction occurs for the experimental group, but not for the control group). They are more likely to occur in designed experiments (where a researcher can set up the experiment to maximize the potential for an interaction in one condition relative to the others). In this case the panels on the left, for C_1 and C_2, show little indication of a simple interaction while C_3 shows a very clear crossover interaction.

Just as tests of simple main effects can be used to follow-up or explore interaction effects, tests of simple interaction effects can also be constructed. This is a relatively trivial extension of the logic of simple main effects. For an independent measures design with three factors, these tests will use the pooled error term from the original ANOVA. The *SS* can be obtained by running a separate two-way ANOVA for each level of the third factor. The interaction term for the two-way ANOVA provides the required *SS* and *MS* for the simple main effect (e.g., the $A \times B$ interaction term for a two-way analysis of participants in the first level of C is used to give the *SS* and *MS* for the simple interaction of $A \times B$ at C_1). If the simple interaction has 1 *df* (i.e., it is a 2×2 interaction), then the dummy coded regression method could also be used.

Moving up to four or more factors makes plotting the patterns very difficult. Unless the pattern is extremely clear it will be hard to interpret. On the other hand, computing simple interaction effects for lower-order interactions across levels of another factor is relatively easy. Most researchers avoid testing higher-order interactions where possible, and if they do test them, hope that their impact is ignorable. If your primary goal is to test a higher-order interaction effect such a complex design may be worthwhile, but *a priori* interaction contrasts rather than the general factorial ANOVA approach should be considered (unless all factors have two levels).

For any graph, and for interaction plots in particular, it is vital that appropriate limits for the *y*-axis are selected. Selecting a very narrow range will exaggerate any effects and selecting an excessively wide range will make effects look smaller. The default axes used for plots in software tend to be good choices for two-way interactions. For three-way interaction plots it is particularly important that each panel be plotted using the same *y*-axis limits (e.g., as in Figure 14.11). In some software packages (e.g., SPSS) the default plot of a three-way interaction does not force the same *Y* limits for all panels. This can be very misleading (e.g., because simple interaction effects such as those in Figure 14.11a might look identical).

14.6 ANCOVA and homogeneity of covariance

A one-way ANCOVA model can be represented as a regression with dummy or effect coding of the factor. This model is readily extended to factorial designs with two or more factors. A two-way ANCOVA with a single covariate could be represented as:

$$y_{iab} = \mu + \alpha_a + \beta_b + \alpha\beta_{ab} + b(C_i - \mu_C) + \varepsilon_{iab} \qquad \text{Equation 14.18}$$

In this model C is the covariate, μ_C is its mean and b is its slope. This equation thus includes the covariate as a centered predictor. This is appropriate for the ANOVA parameterization because it preserves the grand mean as the intercept. As with the one-way ANCOVA model considered previously, the two-way model forces the covariate to have the same effect for all combinations of levels of the factors. In an independent measures design where each observation is sampled from a different person, the combinations of levels define groups of participants. This is therefore equivalent to assuming that the covariate has an identical slope for each group. In the context of one-way ANCOVA, this was identified as the homogeneity of covariance 'assumption' of ANCOVA. However, it is slightly different from other regression assumptions. It arises merely because the effects of the covariate are modeled using only a single slope parameter. By adding additional parameters it is possible to model separate slopes for each group (rather than a common slope).

Just as adding an interaction term for categorical predictors allows the effect of one predictor to vary across levels of another parameter, so adding an interaction term allows the slope of a covariate to vary across levels of a factor. Consider a simple ANCOVA model with one factor:

$$y_{ij} = \mu + \tau_j + b(C_i - \mu_C) + \varepsilon_{ij} \qquad \text{Equation 14.19}$$

Adding a covariate by factor interaction produces

$$y_{ij} = \mu + \tau_j + \bar{b}(C_i - \mu_C) + b_{\tau_j}(C_i - \mu_C) + \varepsilon_{ij} \qquad \text{Equation 14.20}$$

where $\bar{b}$ represents the average (or weighted average if the design is unbalanced) slope of the covariate and b_{τ_j} is the difference in the slope of the covariate for level j of the factor. The usual constraints apply (i.e., that τ_j and b_{τ_j} sum to zero). You could also represent this as separate regression equations for each of the J levels of the factor. Assuming $J = 2$ this gives the following equations for $j = 1$ and $j = 2$:

$$y_{i,1} = \mu + \tau_1 + \left(\bar{b} + b_{\tau_1}\right)(C_i - \mu_C) + \varepsilon_{i1}$$

$$y_{i,2} = \mu + \tau_2 + \left(\bar{b} + b_{\tau_2}\right)(C_i - \mu_C) + \varepsilon_{i2}$$

Arranging the equations this way should make it clear that a different slope is being fitted for the effect of the covariate in each group. This parameterization is equivalent to that of an effect coded factor and a centered covariate. Employing dummy coding with a centered covariate would produce an equivalent model in which the covariate main effect would not be the average slope, but the slope of the covariate at the reference category. The difference in the slope between the reference category and the other levels of the factor would be captured by a set of product terms between the covariate and the set of dummy coded indicator variables.

The upshot of this is that homogeneity of covariance is no more (and no less) an assumption of ANCOVA than the assumption of independence of linear effects in a multiple regression with two continuous predictors. Fitting models without interaction effects means that non-additivity of predictor effects cannot be captured. The solution is to add interaction terms between predictors. A main effects only model is generally implausible for ANCOVA, but it is not uncommon for models with many higher-order interactions to provide only marginal improvements in model fit. An advantage of the regression approach to ANCOVA is that it makes it easier to test models with interaction terms between combinations of categorical and continuous predictors (e.g., in a hierarchical regression).

The form of the ANOVA table for ANCOVA depends on the number of factors and covariates in the design as well as whether interaction effects are included. The F tests of factors and interactions between factors are tests of adjusted means in factorial ANCOVA. If covariate levels are unequal across levels of factors, the differences in adjusted means can be very different from the unadjusted differences in means. It is customary to report adjusted means with all covariates at their mean value (though other meaningful values of the covariate can be substituted). The adjusted means are simply predictions from the regression equation and can be obtained by plugging the appropriate covariate values into a prediction equation.

Homogeneity of covariance is particularly important in certain study designs. Yzerbyt *et al.* (2004) looked at designs involving an individual difference factor (termed a *measured factor*) A, a factor manipulated by the experimenter (termed a *manipulated factor*) B and a covariate C. In many such designs, the covariate is included because it correlates with a measured factor (e.g., gender). Yzerbyt *et al.* (*ibid.*) show that just including a covariate, without also including the covariate by measured factor interaction ($A \times C$), biases the estimates and tests of the $A \times B$ interaction. This kind of confounding is probably very common, but is easily avoided if there are sufficient data to estimate all covariates by measured factor interactions.

Example 14.8 Homogeneity of covariance is something that should be checked for any ANCOVA. In the analysis of the diagram data in Example 13.7, the covariate (reading time) was found to have a multiplicative effect on description quality. The model employed in that analysis assumed that the covariate had the same multiplicative effect for each of the four experimental conditions. Analysis of homogeneity of covariance involves testing the main effects model against a model with the group by covariate interaction terms. Prior to fitting this model it is wise to switch to effect coding and to center the covariate. If the covariate is transformed – as here – it is important to center after transformation. As the factor has more than two levels, the interaction model will fit $J - 1 = 3$ new slopes (requiring three more parameters).

The fit of the effects model from Example 13.7 can be summarized as $F_{4,35} = 3.85$, $R^2 = .31$, AIC = 284.0. In comparison, the fit of the covariate by factor interaction model (with the three extra parameters) is summarized as $F_{7,32} = 2.13$, $R^2 = .32$, AIC = 289.2. The difference in R^2 is very modest (.01) for the extra three parameters and ΔAIC = 5.2. This is equivalent to a likelihood ratio of about 14 in favor of the (less complex) main effects model. There is no reason to prefer the interaction model. Homogeneity of covariance seems plausible. This doesn't mean that the effects of the covariate are identical for the groups, but any differences are not large enough to be worth including in the model (or to be detected in such a small sample).

14.7 Effect size in factorial ANOVA, ANCOVA and multiple regression

Adding multiple predictors to a regression model, whether categorical or continuous, complicates the interpretation of effects. This applies also to the problem of estimating the magnitude of effects and selecting an appropriate effect size statistic. One approach, advocated earlier, is to emphasize effect size metrics such as simple differences in means and unstandardized slopes – particularly where the original units of measurement are not arbitrary (Baguley, 2004, 2009). Some of the advantages of simple effect size metrics are reduced in non-experimental designs if some of the predictors are unreliable (Ree and Carretta, 2006; Hunter and Schmidt, 2004). However, selecting an appropriate standardized effect size metric presents additional difficulties.

Several difficulties with R^2 type measures emerge from the large number of parameters in the model. First, proportion of variance explained needs to be corrected to account for over-fitting. The most common correction is adjusted R^2. This adjusts R^2 for the number of parameters in the model, but not from over-fitting arising from other sources (e.g., cherry-picking the best model from a large set of models). Second, when more than one predictor is included in the model, the choice of partial effect size statistic will matter (e.g., η_p^2 or η^2). Third, effect size statistics for multiple *df* effects don't distinguish the direction or pattern of the effect. This makes them dangerous when interpreted unthinkingly. Two effects of a similar size could represent completely different effects (e.g., in opposite directions).

These problems are particularly acute for ANOVA and ANCOVA designs. In multiple regression analyses it is more common to focus on individual predictors and there is more emphasis on the sign and magnitude of their slopes. Of particular importance in ANOVA and ANCOVA is whether to use a partial effect size statistic. These statistics are used to compare the contribution of categorical or continuous predictors within and between models. For these comparisons to be sensible it is important to consider the possible presence of factors such as range restriction or differences in reliability. Even if these factors do not distort the result, any comparison needs to consider the design of the study.

To understand the basic problem, consider two studies. One in which the factor *A* is investigated on its own (i.e., in a one-way ANOVA) and another in which both factor *A* and factor *B* are investigated (in a two-way factorial design). What effect size metric will make it possible to compare factor *A* across the two designs? The most common choice in this situation is η_p^2 (partial eta-squared). Using η_p^2, the argument goes, strips out the extra variance in the two-way design (associated with *B* and the $A \times B$ interaction). It does this by using $SS_A + SS_{error}$ in place of SS_{total} as the denominator for the proportion. A hidden assumption is that including factor *B* increases the total sums of squares in the study. This assumption is probably only reasonable if *B* is a manipulated factor – as found in a completely randomized experimental design (Gillett, 2003; Olejnik and Algina, 2003). A manipulated factor (if it has an effect) adds to the total variance in the sample by causing differences in the means that would not have otherwise have been present. In contrast, measured (individual difference) factors (Olejnik and Algina, 2003) are not expected to increase the total variance. If factor *B* were the sex of the participants, there would be no expectation that the total sums of squares would increase in the two-factor design relative to the one-factor design. This counter-argument assumes that the one-factor design sampled all levels of *B*. However, on the rare occasions that the one-factor design sampled only males or only females, *B* would behave like a manipulated factor rather than a measured one. Thus the crucial distinction is whether the second factor adds variation relative to the one-factor comparator design.

A partial statistic such as η_p^2 is appropriate if the extra predictors in a model add variance to the model and the objective is to compare effects common to each model. This most often (but not always) happens with manipulated factors. If the extra predictors don't add variance (as tends to be the case with measured factors) η^2 is more appropriate. This argument extends to ANCOVA. More often than not, covariates and continuous predictors will be measured rather than manipulated variables – particularly where a covariate is added to increase power in a randomized design or to control for a confound. While η_p^2 is a tempting choice for researchers, because it is always at least as large as η^2, it is nearly always a bad choice for ANCOVA designs. Even in ANOVA with apparently manipulated factors it can be misleading. Consider an experiment looking at memory for faces. One factor might be the symmetry of the face (symmetrical or asymmetrical). This is manipulated by the experimenter (using image processing software), but the choice of the effect size statistic is not trivial. Faces used as experimental stimuli and those encountered in everyday life vary in symmetry. To generalize to another study involves knowing whether the variability in the experiment is similar or dissimilar to that in the experimental materials used by others (which may be unknown). Generalizing to everyday life requires knowing the degree of symmetry typically encountered in the population. Baguley (2009) also points out that variance explained measures traditionally treat factors as fixed effects (see Key Concept OS1 and section 16.3). Where levels of a factor are samples from a larger population, and that population is the target of generalization, standard measures may greatly overestimate standardized effect size.

Where it is known that a predictor adds to the variability in one study (relative to another) it is possible to compute Olejnik and Algina's η_g^2 (generalized eta-squared). Olejnik and Algina

(2003) provide detailed examples, but the general principle is to compute proportion of variance explained including only factors and covariates that add to the total variance (that for convenience will be referred to as manipulated variables):

$$\eta_g^2 = \frac{SS_{effect}}{I \times SS_{effect} + \sum_{meas} SS_{meas} + \sum_{error} SS_{error}} \quad \text{Equation 14.21}$$

In this formula I is a dummy indicator variable that equals one if the effect is manipulated and zero otherwise. The $\sum_{meas} SS_{meas}$ term is the sum of SS for measured factors or covariates and $\sum_{error} SS_{error}$ is the sum of all sources of error variance (e.g., the pooled error term for a typical independent measures design). The $\sum_{meas} SS_{meas}$ term also includes any interactions terms between measured and manipulated factors.

As eta-squared statistics are based on sums of squares they are descriptive measures of sample variance and inevitably overestimate the proportion of population variance accounted for by a factor or covariate. One alternative is ω^2 (omega-squared). This is an estimate of the proportion of explained population variance in ANOVA. Olejnik and Algina (*ibid.*) describe how to calculate a generalized version of the statistic. For an independent measures design it can be represented as:

$$\omega_g^2 = \frac{SS_{effect} - df_{effect} \times MS_{error}}{I \times \left(SS_{effect} - df_{effect} \times MS_{error}\right) + \sum_{meas} (SS_{meas} - df_{meas} \times MS_{error}) + N \times MS_{error}} \quad \text{Equation 14.22}$$

The $\sum_{meas} (SS_{meas} - df_{meas} \times MS_{error})$ term sums over all measured variables whether factors or covariates (and including their interactions with manipulated variables). As before, manipulated and measured variables are short-hand for variables that do or don't add variance to what is being measured. Olejnik and Algina (*ibid.*) provide tables of formulas for specific designs with different combinations of manipulated and measured variables. These tables can simplify computation of ω_g^2 or η_g^2.

Of these statistics only η_p^2 is routinely reported by statistics packages. It has a direct connection to R^2, being the change in R^2 when a factor or covariate is added to a regression. It is therefore convenient for sample size estimation (at least if an identical or near-identical replication is assumed). It overestimates the proportion of variance explained, either because of its bias as a population estimate or because it excludes measured variables. It should not be relied on for comparing effects within or between studies. Its generalized counterpart η_g^2 should be preferred and is almost as easy to calculate (provided you can evaluate whether a factor or covariate adds variance to the analysis relative to some comparator study). A safer option may be to focus on simple, unstandardized effect size metrics. For generalizing to a population, ω_g^2 is preferable to η_g^2, but is hardly ever reported (which limits its usefulness for comparing between studies). Although both statistics are biased, the bias is smaller for omega-squared based measures (Howell, 2002; Olejnik and Algina, 2003).

A final concern is that any measure that decomposes the total sums of squares is only really meaningful in ANOVA or ANCOVA with orthogonal factors (or where imbalance is negligible). If the choice of method for partitioning SS changes the outcome of the calculation (as it does in unbalanced designs) then ω^2 and η^2 metrics may not be interpretable.

Example 14.9 Consider the diagram data from Example 13.7. The model for these data had a single factor and a single covariate. For any model, η^2 is the proportion of effect *SS* relative to total *SS*. SS_{total} is 3023.9 so the η^2 statistics are:

$$\eta^2_{(factor)} = \frac{879.26}{3023.90} = .291 \quad \eta^2_{(covariate)} = \frac{339.65}{3023.90} = .112$$

The η_p^2 statistic replaces the denominator with the sum of SS_{effect} and $SS_{residual}$. As $SS_{residual} =$ 2100.54, the η_p^2 statistics are:

$$\eta^2_{p(group)} = \frac{879.26}{583.70 + 2100.54} = .328 \quad \eta^2_{p(covariate)} = \frac{339.65}{339.65 + 2100.54} = .139$$

This statistic partials out the effect of any other predictors in the model.

Calculating generalized versions of the statistic involves determining whether factors and covariates are measured or manipulated. The factor would usually be considered a manipulated variable because it represents an experimental manipulation (the type of instructional text participants are exposed to). This manipulation adds to the variability of *Y* (the description quality). A covariate would normally be considered a measured variable that varies naturally and is not manipulated by the experimenter. This is probably true for the diagram study. If so, η_g^2 for the group effect is:

$$\eta_g^2 = \frac{SS_{factor}}{I \times SS_{factor} + \sum\limits_{meas} SS_{meas} + \sum\limits_{error} SS_{error}} = \frac{879.26}{1 \times 879.26 + 339.65 + 2100.54} = \eta^2 = .265$$

For the covariate it is:

$$\eta_g^2 = \frac{SS_{covariate}}{I \times SS_{covariate} + \sum\limits_{meas} SS_{meas} + \sum\limits_{error} SS_{error}} = \frac{339.65}{0 \times 339.65 + 339.65 + 2100.54} = \eta_p^2 = .139$$

The calculations clarify the role of the indicator *I*. If the indicator were not present, $SS_{covariate}$ would be counted twice. The indicator is there to stop an effect that is itself a measured variable contributing more than once.

What is the interpretation of the generalized statistic? For the factor, η_g^2 is the proportion of sample variance accounted for by the group. For the covariate it is the proportion of sample variance that would be accounted for by the covariate had there been no experimental manipulation. In principle, both statistics are now comparable to similar studies with different combinations of predictors. The logic is that the manipulated factor needs to account for the extra variation it introduces to the study, but the measured factor does not. The variation due to a measured factor should be present in the error term of other similar studies (regardless of whether it is included in the model).

There is one further thing to reflect on. Olejnik and Algina (2003) treat covariates as measured variables. This is reasonable most of the time, but sometimes not. Reading time presumably varies from text to text and person to person. Treating it as a measured variable makes sense if the goal is to determine the practical impact of the covariate on reading an instructional text. If so, ω_g^2 (which is a population estimate) would be better. But if the goal is to compare proportion of variance explained between experiments (a reasonable aim for η^2 measures) then perhaps reading time should be treated as a manipulated factor. Many similar experiments control exposure to the text by limiting reading time to a fixed period (e.g., 15 minutes). In such studies reading time is not free to vary. To compare between experiments it would be necessary to treat this particular covariate as a manipulated factor (i.e., additional variation attributable to the design). The decision regarding whether a variable is manipulated or measured therefore depends on the type of variable, the context of the study and the design of the study you wish to compare the statistic with.

14.8 Statistical power to detect interactions

The statistical power to detect an interaction effect is often very low. McClelland and Judd (1993) reviewed a number of factors thought to be responsible for this lack of power. The problem is most acute in observational as opposed to experimental research. There are several reasons for the difference, but the most important have to do with the increased power that comes from being able to manipulate variables or minimize error in an experiment. McClelland and Judd focused on multiple regression, but similar concerns apply to interactions in ANOVA and ANCOVA.

McClelland and Judd (*ibid.*) explain the lack of power by reviewing the distinction between interactions and main effects. The test of an interaction effect depends on the joint distribution of the interacting variables. In a model with predictors X_1 and X_2, statistical power to detect an effect of a predictor tends to be large when the range of that predictor is maximized. Statistical power to detect the interaction term, the product of X_1 and X_2 tends to be large when the range of the product is maximized.

McClelland and Judd (*ibid.*) provide a detailed mathematical account of the problem and show that the joint distribution of X_1 and X_2 will almost always produce dramatically less powerful tests. One way to explain this is in terms of range restriction. Restricting the range of X_1 or X_2 would decrease the statistical power of their tests (and depress standardized effect size). But even if X_1 and X_2 are not restricted, their product will suffer from an effect analogous to range restriction. This is because the product $X_1 \times X_2$ is extreme only if both X_1 and X_2 are extreme. An interaction effect tends to disproportionately sample from the middle of the distribution of the product rather than its extremes (relative to X_1 and X_2). Just as range restriction results in lower power, so will tests of interaction effects. Sampling observations with high leverage increases the power to test effects in a regression model. For the individual tests of X_1 and X_2 this just involves sampling extreme values relative to the mean. For the product term, observation extremes in both X_1 and X_2 are required for leverage to be high.

How big is the reduction in power for detecting interaction effects? There is no set answer because the precise power depends on the distribution of X_1 and X_2 (and by implication their product). Collinear predictors will typically reduce power further. Normally distributed predictors produce particularly low power because most values are close to the mean. Judd and McClelland (*ibid.*) give an example of approximately bivariate normal predictors, each on a five-point scale, and show that the efficiency of the interaction test relative to the main effects is about 6%. A uniform distribution would also give low power (though not as bad as the normal case).

This problem is more severe for observational research because of the ability to sample extremes in many experimental contexts. In a two-way factorial experiment factors are sampled at the same, often relatively extreme levels. Dummy or effect coding demonstrates this. This assigns 0 and 1 or −1 and 1 to the two extremes (with no values in-between). In an experiment, the values are typically selected to maximize the effect (within practical constraints such as time, cost or risk to participants). For example, a researcher looking at the effects of caffeine in a laboratory study could compare doses of exactly 0 and 30 *mg*. Experimental research is not entirely immune to the problem, though. Interactions with covariates can be very difficult to detect and not all experiments involve easy-to-manipulate variables.

The problem of low power to detect interactions necessarily also applies for polynomial terms. A quadratic term can be considered an interaction of a predictor with itself. The precise power to detect the quadratic term is complex and depends on the variability of X as well as its skew and kurtosis (*ibid*.). For this reason we'll just consider the case of a centered, symmetrical predictor (X). The X^2 term is necessarily extreme if X is extreme, but as both X and X^2 compete to explain Y, what matters is the relative predictive power of the two. Normally distributed predictors are not particularly high in kurtosis and therefore have relatively few observations at the extremes. This decreases power to detect quadratic effects because relative to X, the predictor X^2 will have even fewer extreme observations. Perhaps the observed *min* and *max* of X are -10 and 10, but most values are between -2 and $+2$. The range of X^2 will be zero to 100, with most values between zero and four. Additional weight in the tails of the distribution (and therefore increased kurtosis) would lead to greater power to detect quadratic effects. Increased variability also implies more extreme X^2 values and increased power. In contrast, skew decreases power to detect quadratic effects.

If the aim of research is to detect an interaction effect (or related effects such as polynomial terms) it is important to consider the optimal sampling strategy (McClelland, 1997). For interaction effects involving continuous predictors or covariates (including tests of homogeneity of covariance) serious thought should be given to over-sampling the extremes. This is the standard practice for experimental designs with two levels, but less common for designs with more than two levels or for observational designs. This kind of study is a form of extreme-groups analysis (see Preacher *et al.*, 2005). As it is not possible to design a study with optimal power to detect all potential effects of interest, the focus is usually to increase power to detect *a priori* effects. Factorial designs are optimized to detect main effects and interactions if all effects are of equal interest. In practice this is unlikely (except perhaps for a 2×2 design). An interesting alternative is to design studies with optimal power to detect a particular contrast (McClelland, 1997).

14.9 Problems with interactions in ANOVA and regression

Testing interaction effects can pose a range of problems, some unique to interaction effects and others also found in a main effects analysis. Several of these issues, such as collinearity and lack of power, have already been considered. Others such as multiple testing are a variation of the more general problem of adding predictors to a model. As predictors are added to a model the number of interaction effects that can be included increases rapidly (e.g., from one with two predictors to seven with three predictors). The principal solution is to try and minimize the number of models to be considered. One approach is a hierarchical modeling strategy (see Box 14.1) or to test only *a priori* hypotheses, but more radical options can also be considered. If there are sufficient *df*, modeling all interactions is sometimes sensible (e.g., for prediction).

This section will briefly consider additional problems that are particularly relevant to interactions. The first is that of ceiling and floor effects. When an outcome measure is bounded, this can make it hard to detect effect if any mean is close to either of the boundaries. For instance, memory is often measured in terms of percentage or number of items recalled from a list. If the lists have ten items then mean scores close to either zero or ten could produce *ceiling* or *floor* effects. Proximity to the boundary can have quite surprising effects. It can artificially reduce variability within levels of a factor (and hence error variance), as well as suppressing differences between means. More often than not, it makes simple differences harder to detect. In contrast, ceiling or floor effects will sometimes introduce spurious interaction effects, or prevent detection of genuine interactions.

This is illustrated in Figure 14.12. This depicts data from four hypothetical memory experiments with a two-way factorial design in which lists with either 15 or 20 items are presented. Panels (a) and (c) on the left-hand side depict scenarios for 20-item lists, while (b) and (d) on the right-hand side present corresponding results for a 15-item list.

Panel (a) shows a situation where no interaction is detected and the lines are near parallel. In panel (b), with only 15 words, the task is too easy and performance across of levels of B_1 is at ceiling. This introduces a spurious interaction effect that isn't present with the longer list in panel (a). The opposite occurs in the bottom row of Figure 14.12. The interaction is detected in panel (c) with the longer list, but not in panel (d) with the shorter list. Analogous problems arise with floor effects. To get around this problem it is best to design studies to avoid floor and

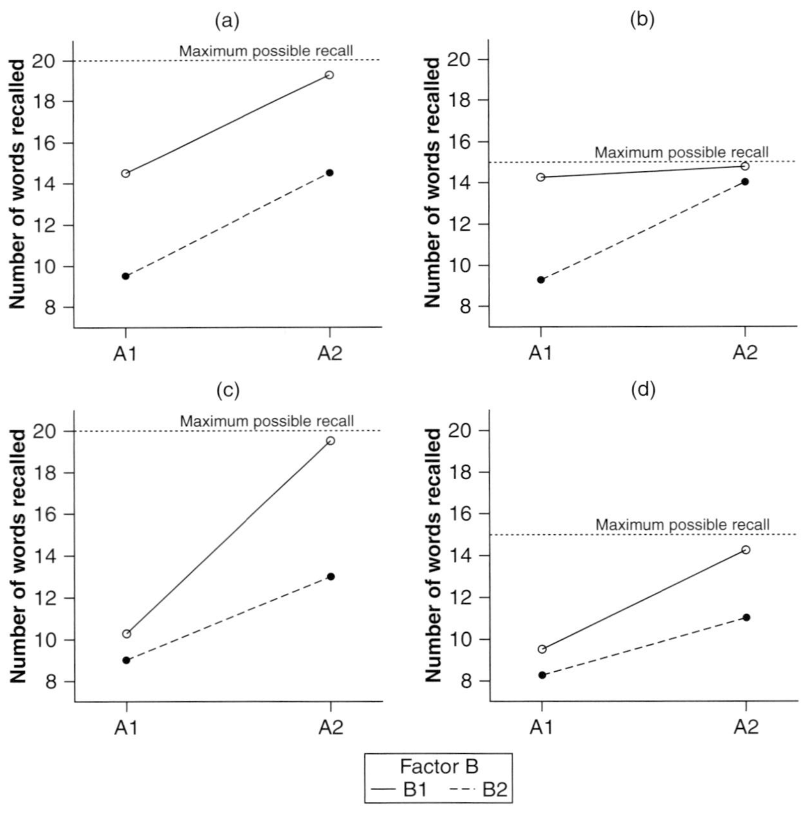

Figure 14.12 How a ceiling effect can influence detection of an interaction

ceiling effects. Where this is not possible, there are models that are less vulnerable to ceiling or floor effects. These include some models for dealing with bounded, discrete outcomes as well as models for truncated or censored distributions (the latter being beyond the scope of this book).

A theoretically sophisticated issue concerns the mathematical form of the relationship captured by an interaction. A product term captures non-additivity of the effects in a regression model, but the effects could be non-additive in many different ways. Often an appealing interpretation is that the effects are multiplicative rather than additive. In a multiplicative model the predictors have a proportionate effect on the outcome. That is, each unit increase in X is associated with a fixed proportion or percentage change in Y. This kind of model naturally leads to the use of a logarithmic transformation of Y to produce an additive linear model. What sometimes upsets researchers is that this logarithmic transformation may make an interesting interaction effect disappear from an analysis. This is exactly what you'd expect if the true effect were multiplicative rather than additive. Perfectly multiplicative effects of A and B will be perfectly additive after a logarithmic transformation of Y. In practice, a typical interaction design might not have the statistical power to distinguish additive from multiplicative effects with confidence unless sample sizes are high. Graphical methods can often help elucidate the relationship between the effects (see Loftus, 2001).

A corollary of this is that an interaction for a logarithmically transformed outcome might sometimes represent additivity of the untransformed effects. Where the transformation is applied atheoretically (e.g., purely to make residuals look more normal), additive untransformed effects could show up as sub-multiplicity in the transformed data. Whether an interaction effect is present cannot therefore be disentangled from the mathematical form of the relationship between predictors and outcome. If there is no theory to guide your interpretation of the findings (or the theory is too vague to discriminate between additive and multiplicative models) there won't be a clear answer to the question of whether an interaction exists.

Theories that make precise, quantitative predictions about the form of the relationship between variables are thus very valuable. It is easy to test the predictions of these models and to compare competing models – particularly with likelihood and Bayesian inference (Dienes, 2008). In addition, graphical methods such as *state-trace analysis* have been developed to explore the dimensionality of domain (Bamber, 1979; Loftus, 2001; Newell and Dunn, 2008). One advantage of state-trace analysis is that it does not require the mathematical form of the underlying function to be known.

14.10 R code for Chapter 14

14.10.1 Interactions in multiple regression (Example 14.1)

In any regression model it is a good idea to start by getting an idea of the range of values the predictor and outcome variables take. The `summary()` function provides this for variables in a data frame, but does not provide the *SD*, which can be obtained using `sd()`. The `describe()` function from the psych package is more informative:

```
lottery.data <- read.csv('lottery.csv')
summary(lottery.data)
sd(lottery.data)
```

```
library(psych)
describe(lottery.data)
```

As the *SD* of the `money` outcome variable is very large, R reports them in scientific notation.

```
present      future       money
1.527282e+00 5.111863e+00 2.179384e+06
```

The `e+` part of the notation is short-hand for 'multiply by the ten to the positive power of the number that follows'. (Whereas `e-` would stand for 'multiply by the ten to the negative power of the number that follows'). As 10^0 is one, the first two *SD*s are 1.527282 and 5.111863, but the third *SD* is 2.179384×10^6. This resolves as $2.179384 \times 1,000,000 = 2,179,384$. As base ten is used, the decimal point is shifted right or left along the number according to the sign and magnitude of the exponent.

The severe positive skew for the outcome variable suggests that a logarithmic transformation may be a good idea (and a multiplicative model is plausible for other reasons). To explore the distribution of the variables in more detail, Figure 14.1 shows kernel density plots of the data. The raw data are also added as a rug to each plot:

```
par(mar = c(4, 4, 2, 2), mfrow = c(1, 3), pty = 's', font.main
  = 1, cex.main = 1.5)
with(lottery.data, plot(density(present, main = 'Present
  finances')))
with(lottery.data, rug(jitter(present), ticksize=0.04))
with(lottery.data, plot(density(future), main = 'Future income
  (thousands)'))
with(lottery.data, rug(future, ticksize=0.04))
with(lottery.data, plot(density(log(money + 0.5)), main =
  expression(paste('log(', italic(money), ')'))))
with(lottery.data, rug(jitter(log(money + 0.5)),
  ticksize=0.04))
```

Running a multiple regression with main effects of present and future finances on the money outcome is problematic because there are some zero outcomes. For this reason the model includes a small constant. A detailed summary of the fit and the AIC is also given:

```
lot.main <- lm(log(money + 0.5, 10) ~ present + future,
  lottery.data)
summary(lot.main)
AIC(lot.main)
```

The interaction model adds an uncentered product term. The following commands illustrate how a comparison with the main effects model made using either `drop1()` or `anova()` is identical to the test of the interaction term. The formula term `present * future` fits a model with both main effects and the interaction:

```
lot.int <- lm(log(money+.5,10) ~ present * future,
  lottery.data)
summary(lot.int)
drop1(lot.int, test='F')
anova(lot.main, lot.int)
```

In this case, `drop1()` only drops the interaction term. Thus it mimics hierarchical (Type II) sums of squares by dropping all predictors of equal 'order' in turn. As the interaction is the highest order term in the model, it is dropped in preference to all other terms. The interaction model can also be 'built' in different ways. One is to explicitly fit each term of the additive model with the interaction indicated by `present:future`. Another is to use the formula expression `(present + future)^2`.

```
lm(log(money+0.5, 10) ~ present + future + present:future,
  lottery.data)

lm(log(money+0.5, 10) ~ (present + future)^2, lottery.data)

lm(log(money+0.5, 10) ~ present * future, lottery.data)
```

As it is possible to get confused between arithmetic and formula expressions, a special function called `AsIs()` or `I()` exists to incorporate ordinary arithmetic into formulas. Thus `I(present + future)` treats the enclosed terms as a single outcome or predictor variable that is the sum of `present` and `future`.

Model checks are also worth making (e.g., analysis of residuals, Cook's distance or perhaps a robust regression). The density plot of residuals reveals the bimodality (hard to spot in the normal probability plot). A robust regression has broadly similar parameter estimates and favors the interaction model.

```
qqnorm(rstandard(lot.int))
plot(density(rstandard(lot.int)))
max(cooks.distance(lot.int))

library(MASS)

lot.rob <- rlm(log(money+0.5, 10) ~ present*future, method =
  'M', lottery.data)
summary(lot.rob)
AIC(lot.rob)-AIC(rlm(log(money+0.5, 10) ~ present+future,
  method = 'M', lottery.data))
```

14.10.2 Centering in moderated multiple regression (Example 14.2)

A correlation matrix for the lottery data (including the product term) is given by:

```
cor.dat <- cbind(lottery.data, lottery.data$present *
  lottery.data$future)
names(cor.dat) <- c('present', 'future', 'money',
```

```
'interaction')
cor(cor.dat)
```

The `cbind()` function is useful for binding an extra column onto the `lottery.data` data frame. The second command above is not necessary, but makes the correlation matrix easier to read by shortening the name of the interaction term. The `car` package can be used to check the VIF of the predictors in the main effect model and the interaction model from Example 14.1.

```
library(car)
vif(lot.main)
vif(lot.int)
```

Centered versions of the predictors can be created by subtracting the mean or using the `scale()` function. The default of this function is to standardize rather than just center (hence the `scale=FALSE` argument). The centered versions of the main effects and interaction model are:

```
p.c <- scale(lottery.data$present, scale=FALSE)
.c <- scale(lottery.data$future, scale=FALSE)
lot.mc <- lm(log(money+0.5, 10) ~ p.c + f.c, lottery.data)
lot.ic <- lm(log(money+0.5, 10) ~ p.c * f.c, lottery.data)
summary(lot.mc)
summary(lot.ic)
```

The scale function can also be called within a formula. Thus the following command would also fit the main effects model:

```
lm(log(money+0.5, 10) ~ scale(present, scale=FALSE) +
  scale(future, scale=FALSE), lottery.data)
```

14.10.3 Plotting bilinear interactions (Example 14.3)

Interpreting interaction effects is greatly assisted by suitable plots. In Figure 14.2 the bilinear interaction of present and future finances was plotted as separate regression lines for present finances at low, medium and high values of future finances. For the left panel of Figure 14.2 regression lines for the fitted model with log(*money*) as outcome were plotted. The initial commands set the low, medium and high values of the future predictor. It would be easy to switch these with lower values such as ± 1 *SD* or ± 2 *SD* (and this would give a less dramatic plot). Each regression line uses the `curve()` function for the prediction equation. Some care needs to be taken to select appropriate axes for the first `curve()` command (with subsequent commands using `add=TRUE` to avoid calling a new plot).

```
h.f <- max(lottery.data$future)
m.f <- mean(lottery.data$future)
l.f <- min(lottery.data$future)
```

```
curve(5.79 - m.f * 0.15864 - 1.23094 * x + 0.05063 * m.f * x,
  xlim=c(1,5), ylim=c(-1,4.5), ylab=expression(paste('log(',
  italic(money), ')')), xlab = 'Present finances', main =
  'Outcome on logarithmic scale', cex.main= 0.85)
curve(5.79 - l.f * 0.15864 - 1.23094 * x + 0.05063 * l.f * x,
  xlim=c(1,5), add=TRUE, lty=3)
curve(5.79 - h.f * 0.15864 - 1.23094 * x + 0.05063 * h.f * x,
  xlim=c(1,5), add=TRUE, lty=2)
```

Interpretation on the untransformed scale is perhaps preferable and can be addressed by tweaking the commands to reverse the transformation via the function: 10^X. It helps to add a legend labeling the lines.

```
curve(10^(5.79 - m.f*.15864-1.23094*x + .05063*m.f*x)-
  .5,xlim=c(1,5), ylim=c(0,10000), ylab='money (£)', xlab =
  'Present finances', main = 'Outcome on untransformed scale',
  cex.main= 0.85)
curve(10^(5.79 - l.f*.15864-1.23094*x + .05063*l.f*x)-0.5,
  xlim=c(1,5), add=TRUE, lty=3)
curve(10^(5.79 - h.f*.15864-1.23094*x + .05063*h.f*x)-0.5,
  xlim=c(1,5), add=TRUE, lty=2)
legend(4.25, 2000, legend = c('£5,000', '£19,000', '£50,000'),
  lty=c(3,1,2), xpd=TRUE, cex=0.8, title='Future income',
  bty='n')
```

Another method of exploring the interaction is to plot the simple slope of one or both predictors. An interaction implies that the simple slope varies as a function of one (or more) other predictors. Here the simple slope of *present* varies as a function of *future* (or vice versa). The basic plotting of the simple effects is straightforward. Preacher *et al.* (2006) provide interactive calculation tools that are recommended. These require information from standard regression output (coefficients and error *df*). The asymptotic variances and covariances of the regression coefficients are also required. These are obtained from the covariance matrix of the fitted regression model using `vcov()`.

```
vcov(lot.int)
```

Figure 14.3 uses the uncentered model, and this seems to produce a more interpretable scale (but as long as you are consistent there is no statistical reason to prefer one over the other).

The Preacher *et al.* calculation tools provide *t* tests of simple effects at different values, but plotting the confidence bands is the recommended approach. Entering the information into the calculator as instructed provides the R code. The basic R code it supplies for the lottery data interaction model (for 90% confidence bands) is:

```
z1=-10 #supply lower bound for z
z2=10  #supply upper bound for z
z <- seq(z1,z2,length=1000)
fz <- c(z,z)
y1 <- (-1.23094+0.05063*z)+(1.6534*sqrt(0.185775465+(2*z*-
  0.0092859615)+((z^2)*0.0004906467)))
```

```
y2 <- (-1.23094+0.05063*z)-(1.6534*sqrt(0.185775465+(2*z*-
  0.0092859615)+((z^2)*0.0004906467)))
fy <- c(y1,y2)
fline <- (-1.23094+0.05063*z)
plot(fz,fy,type='p',pch='.',font=2,font.lab=2,col=2,xlab='Mode
  rator',ylab='Simple Slope',main='Confidence Bands')
lines(z,fline)
f0 <- array(0,c(1000))
lines(z,f0,col=8)
abline(v=20.7782,col=4,lty=2)
abline(v=39.6696,col=4,lty=2)
```

This needs to be edited by changing the range of the moderator (z) to be plotted from the default −10 to 10 to something more sensible (such as the observed range of five to 50). The labels and colors also have been edited. A further tweak is to switch from using dots as a plot character `pch='.'` to using smooth lines for the confidence bands. This is done by producing an empty plot (`pch=NA`) and adding two new calls to the `lines()` function.

```
z1= 5  #lower plot bound for moderator (future finances)
z2= 50 #upper plot bound for moderator (future finances)
z <- seq(z1,z2,length=1000)
fz <- c(z,z)
y1 <- (-1.23094+0.05063*z)+(1.6534*sqrt(0.185775465+(2*z*-
  0.0092859615)+((z^2)*0.0004906467)))
y2 <- (-1.23094+0.05063*z)-(1.6534*sqrt(0.185775465+(2*z*-
  0.0092859615)+((z 2)*0.0004906467)))
fy <- c(y1,y2)
fline <- (-1.23094+0.05063*z)
plot(fz,fy,type='p',pch=NA,font=2,font.lab=2,cex=0.5,
  xlab='Future Income', ylab='Simple slope of Present
  finances', main=NA)
lines(z,y1, lty=1)
lines(z,y2, lty=1)
lines(z,fline, lty= 2)
f0 <- array(0,c(1000))
lines(z,f0, lwd = .2)
abline(v=20.7782, lty=3, lwd= 0.5)
abline(v=39.6696, lty=3, lwd= 0.5)
```

14.10.4 Polynomial regression (Example 14.4 and Figure 14.5)

The linear fit of the curvilinear Anscombe data and its plot is given by:

```
data(anscombe)
lin.fit <- lm(lm(y2 ~ x2, data = anscombe))
with(anscombe, plot(x2,y2, xlab=expression(italic(X)),
```

```
ylab=expression(italic(Y))))
abline(lin.fit, lwd = 0.8, lty=3)
```

The quadratic fit can be obtained by adding in a second predictor equal to `x2` squared. This can be done by creating a new predictor or within the formula:

```
quad.fit <- lm(y2 ~ x2 + I(x2^2), data=anscombe)
```

The `poly()` function can be used to automate this process and is excellent for more complex polynomials. Its default is to create orthogonal polynomials (useful for contrasts, but not necessary or convenient here). Adding the argument `raw=TRUE` gives non-orthogonal polynomials:

```
quad.fit <- lm(y2 ~ poly(x2, order=2, raw=TRUE), anscombe)
```

The second argument `order` can be set to give linear polynomials with `order=1`, cubic with `order=3` and so forth.

```
cub.fit <- lm(y2 ~ poly(x2, 3, raw= TRUE), anscombe)
```

The usual functions can be used to compare fits using *F* tests or using AIC.

```
AIC(lin.fit)
AIC(quad.fit)
AIC(cub.fit)

library(bbmle)
ICtab(lin.fit, quad.fit, cub.fit, type = 'AICc', nobs=11)
```

Adding the quadratic fit to the earlier plot gives Figure 14.5:

```
curve(-5.9957 + 2.7808*x -0.1267*x^2, add=TRUE, lty=2)
```

14.10.5 Factorial ANOVA with independent measures (Example 14.5)

After reading the Table 14.1 data into R as a data frame, the 2 × 2 ANOVA can be run as a linear regression model with either dummy or effect coding.

```
tab14.1 <- read.csv('Tab.14_1.csv')
```

For the factors `drug` and `sex` a fully factorial model can be fitted in several ways. The formula can be specified by listing all the terms: `drug + sex + drug:sex` (where `drug:sex` denotes the interaction term). Alternatively, the short-hand syntax `drug * sex` can be specified in the call to `lm()` or `aov()`.

```
lm(health ~ drug + sex + drug:sex, data = tab14.1)
lm(health ~ drug * sex, data = tab14.1)
```

The ANOVA table can be obtained in the usual way:

```
summary(aov(health ~ drug * sex : sex, data = tab14.1))
anova(lm(health ~ drug * sex, data = tab14.1))
```

The cell means can be obtained in several ways. Functions for two-way tables include `ezStats()` in `ez` and `summaryBy()` in `doBy`. First consider `summaryBy()` for the data in Table 14.1:

```
library(doBy)
summaryBy(health ~ sex, data = tab14.1)
summaryBy(health ~ drug, data = tab14.1)
summaryBy(health ~ sex + drug, FUN=c(mean,sd), data=tab14.1)
```

The ANOVA can be fitted via dummy or effect coding by changing the default contrasts. Compare the following models:

```
options(contrasts=c('contr.treatment','contr.poly'))
anov.dc <- lm(health ~ drug * sex, tab14.1)

options(contrasts=c('contr.sum','contr.poly'))
anov.ec <- lm(health ~ drug * sex, tab14.1)

summary(anov.dc) ; summary(anov.ec)
```

The `ez` package provides a simple, general interface for ANOVA (drawing on several other packages including `car`). It requires a data frame with a column identifying the participants by number. These commands first create the new data frame with the participant numbers and then demonstrate descriptive statistics (including *SD*) and factorial ANOVA:

```
install.packages('ez')
library(ez)
parts <- 1:16
tab.data <- cbind(parts, tab14.1)

ezStats(tab.data, wid=.(parts), between=.(sex, drug),
  dv=.(health))
ezANOVA(tab.data, wid=.(parts), between=.(sex, drug),
  dv=.(health))
```

The `ezANOVA()` command also provides η_g^2 as part of the output. It defaults to treating fixed factors as manipulated factors unless an `observed` argument is added to indicate any measured factors (see `?ezANOVA`). You can check these by looking at the *SS*, which can be requested by detailed output:

```
ezANOVA(tab.data, wid=.(parts), between=.(sex, drug),
  dv=.(health), detailed=TRUE)
```

For pure independent measures designs there is also an option for robust errors via the Huber-White sandwich estimator, by adding the argument `white.adjust=TRUE` (similar to that obtained through `multcomp`).

14.10.6 ANOVA interaction plots (Example 14.5 and Figures 14.6 to 14.7)

An interaction can be plotted from raw data via `interaction.plot()`, though the output is not particularly pretty. The `ezPlot()` function from the `ez` package is a good alternative (and the output is a `ggplot2` object that can be edited via that package).

Creating your own plot is not too difficult. Here is a simple function that plots a 2×2 interaction from cell means (rather than raw data):

```
plot.2by2 <- function(A1B1, A1B2, A2B1, A2B2, group.names,
  legend = TRUE, leg.loc = NULL, factor.labels = c('Factor A',
  'Factor B'), swap = FALSE, ylab = NULL, main = NULL) {
    group.means <- c(A1B1, A2B1, A1B2, A2B2)
    if (missing(ylab))
        ylab <- expression(italic(DV))
    if (swap == TRUE) {
        group.names <- list(group.names[[2]],
  group.names[[1]])
        group.means <- c(A1B1, A1B2, A2B1, A2B2)
        factor.labels <- c(factor.labels[2], factor.labels[1])
    }
    plot(group.means, pch = NA, ylim = c(min(group.means) *
  0.95, max(group.means) * 1.025), xlim = c(0.8, 2.2), ylab =
  ylab, xaxt = 'n', xlab = factor.labels[1], main = main)
    points(group.means[1:2], pch = 21)
    points(group.means[3:4], pch = 19)
    axis(side = 1, at = c(1:2), labels = group.names[[1]])
    lines(group.means[1:2], lwd = 0.6, lty = 2)
    lines(group.means[3:4], lwd = 0.6)
    if (missing(leg.loc))
        leg.loc <- c(1, max(group.means))
    if (legend == TRUE)
        legend(leg.loc[1], leg.loc[2], legend =
  group.names[[2]], title = factor.labels[2], lty = c(3, 1))
}
```

The following command plots Figure 14.6:

```
group.names <- list(c('placebo','drug'), c('male', 'female'))

plot.2by2(10,10,15,20, group.names, factor.labels=c('Drug',
  'Sex'), swap = FALSE)
```

The function will pass on coordinates for the location of the legend (which can also be dropped by specifying `legend=FALSE`) and a main title or y-axis label can be added. It can also swap the factor placed on the x-axis:

```
plot.2by2(10,10,15,20, group.names, factor.labels=c('Drug',
  'Sex'), swap = TRUE)
```

For color plots from data try:

```
ezPlot(tab.data, wid=.(parts), between=.(drug, sex),
  dv=.(health), x =.(drug), split=.(sex))

ezPlot(tab.data, wid=.(parts), between=.(drug, sex),
  dv=.(health), x =.(sex), split=.(drug))
```

Note that it provides Fisher LSD CIs by default. For a pure independent measures design these should be equivalent to difference-adjusted 95% CIs with a pooled error term (though the `bar_size` argument allows the width of the CI to be altered).

14.10.7 Factorial ANOVA calculations (Example 14.6)

Provided sufficient information is reported in a study, it is possible to reproduce ANOVA calculations. The prospective memory data in Example 14.6 are taken from a published paper. For a factorial design it is convenient to enter the data in matrix form:

```
cell.means <- matrix(c(0.94, 2.06, 2.25, 2.5, 2.68, 3.5), 3, 2)
cell.sds <- matrix(c(1.69, 1.91, 1.84, 2, 1.89, 1.36), 3, 2)
n <- matrix(16, 3, 2)
```

The *MS* (variance estimates) for the age and condition factors are calculated from the cell size multiplied by the variance of the level means. Using the harmonic mean gives an approximation if the cell sizes are unequal (though exact n should be used if available). The cell sizes are equal here, but the harmonic mean approach is illustrated for completeness (and gives the exact n per cell or level in this case). The `harmonic.mean()` function is taken from the `psych` library:

```
library(psych)
ms.age <- harmonic.mean(apply(n,1,sum)) *
  var(apply(cell.means,1,mean))
ms.cond <- harmonic.mean(apply(n,2,sum)) *
  var(apply(cell.means,2,mean))
```

MS_{error} is calculated from the *SD*s of the groups and the *df* error used to calculate $SS_{residual}$. The F ratios for the main effects are calculated from the earlier variance estimates divided by the pooled error term.

```
N <- sum(n)
df.error <- N - length(cell.means)
ms.error <- mean(cell.sds 2)
ss.res <- df.error * ms.error

F.age <- ms.age/ms.error ; F.age

F.cond <- ms.cond/ms.error ; F.cond
```

Double-centering the cell means (see Key Concept 15.1) of the matrix gives the residualized cell means (i.e., removes the main effects). These can then be used to obtain $MS_{interaction}$ and the F ratio for the interaction.

```
dc.out <- sweep(cell.means,1,apply(cell.means,1,mean))
dc.out <- sweep(dc.out,2,apply(dc.out,2,mean))
dc.out

ss.int <- harmonic.mean(n)*sum(dc.out 2)
ms.int <- ss.int / prod(dim(cell.means)-1)
F.int <- ms.int/ms.error ; F.int
```

An alternative method, used in Example 14.6, involves subtracting the total sums of squares for the main effects from the overall *SS* for the cell means.

```
ss.cells <- (sum(cell.means 2)-
  mean(cell.means)^ 2*length(cell.means))*(harmonic.mean(n))

ss.int <- ss.cells - (ms.cond * (ncol(cell.means)-1) + ms.age
  * (nrow(cell.means)-1))
```

The p values are:

```
pf(F.age, 2, 90, lower.tail=FALSE)
pf(F.cond, 1, 90, lower.tail=FALSE)
pf(F.int, 2, 90, lower.tail=FALSE)
```

These are very close to the published values (though, for unequal sample sizes, the approximation using the harmonic mean cell size might not be as accurate).

14.10.8 Simple main effects (Example 14.7)

In Example 14.7 the proactive memory data are used to illustrate methods for exploring two-way interactions. Plotting the means could be done using `interaction.plot()` or via basic plot functions as done in Figure 14.10.

```
groups <- c('4 years','5 years','7 years')
levels <- c(1:3)
l1 <- c(0.94, 2.06, 2.25)
l2 <- c(2.5, 2.68, 3.5)
```

```
par(mar = c(3.5,3.5,.5,.5), pty='s', mgp = c(2.5, 1, 0), xpd
  = TRUE)
plot(l1, pch=NA, ylim=c(0.15,4), xlim= c(0.9,3.1), ylab='Mean
  prospective memory score', xaxt='n', xlab = 'Condition')
points(l1, pch = 21)
points(l2, pch = 22)
axis(side = 1, at = levels, labels = groups)
lines(l1, lwd = .6)
lines(l2, lwd = .6, lty = 2)
legend(2.5, 1, legend = c('Interruption', 'No interruption'),
  pch=c(21,22), lty=c(1,2), bty='n')
```

There are several ways to compute the simple main effects of a factor across levels of another. One way is to replicate the hand calculations by computing the *SS* for the simple main effect and combining it with the MS_{error} from the original analysis. Here the calculation is for the simple main effect of condition at age seven. The steps here are generic and should work for two-way designs with different levels per factor. The term `cell.means[3,]` extracts the appropriate means from row three of the matrix.

```
ss.sme <- harmonic.mean(n[3,]) * var(cell.means[3,])
df.sme <- length(cell.means[3,])-1
ms.sme <- ss.sme / df.sme
F.sme <- ms.sme / ms.error ; F.sme
pf(F.sme, df.sme, df.error, lower.tail=FALSE)
```

The resulting *F* ratio and *p* value match the hand calculation in Example 14.7.

There is a cleverer method using dummy coding, but this only works if you have raw data. Recall, that dummy coded predictor effects in a linear model are simple main effects. This next example uses the data from Table 14.1.

```
summary(anov.dc)
```

Because the intercept here is the mean of the female, drug condition this reports the simple main effect of drug at female as:

```
                    Estimate Std. Error t value  Pr(>|t|)
drugno drug          -10.000      1.803  -5.547  0.000126 ***
```

Likewise the simple main effect of sex at drug is:

```
                    Estimate Std. Error t value Pr(>|t|)
sexmale               -5.000      1.803  -2.774 0.016852 *
```

Squaring the *t* statistic would give the appropriate *F* ratio. However, this approach relies on the factor being tested having just two levels. If it has more than two levels the simple main effect depends on the pooled effect of all $J - 1$ dummy coded predictors for the effect of the factor at that level. If $J > 2$ a one-way ANOVA of the appropriate subset of the data will give the correct

SS (but the error term is usually taken from the original). For instance, the following code runs a one-way ANOVA of the drug factor on only the female participants.

```
fem.data <- subset(tab14.1, sex =='female')
aov(health ~ drug, fem.data)
```

The sums of squares for the factor can be read from the table (probably the easiest option), or (with a little effort) extracted from the summary object:

```
ss.sme <- summary(aov(health ~ drug, fem.data))[[1]]$Sum[1]
```

The *F* ratio and *p* value can then be found using the pooled error term from the full ANOVA. This can be done as follows (though you may prefer to read values from the appropriate tables and combine them by hand):

```
ms.error <- summary(aov(health ~ sex*drug,
  tab14.1))[[1]]$Mean[4]
df.sme <- summary(aov(health ~ drug, fem.data))[[1]]$Df[1]
df.error <- aov(health ~ sex*drug, tab14.1)$df.residual
ms.sme <- ss.sme / df.sme
F.sme <- ms.sme / ms.error ; F.sme
pf(F.sme, df.sme, df.error, lower.tail=FALSE)
```

The appropriate test statistic here is *F*, because the effect *df* may be greater than one (though note that the *F* ratio 30.76923 is the square of the –5.547 *t* statistic reported above).

14.10.9 Three-way interaction plots (Figure 14.11)

Figure 14.11 is a fairly complex plot. Rather than plot all nine panels, this section will explain how to build up the first row (Figure 14.11a) element-by-element. The `par()` function is used to create the nine panels, but for this row only three panels are needed:

```
par(mfrow=c(1,3), pty='s')
```

For all panels the plot needs the labels for factor B and the number of levels for B.

```
B.gps <- c('B1','B2','B3')
levels <- c(1:3)
```

This calls an 'empty' plot with suitable labels and suitably wide *x* and *y* limits.

```
plot(0, pch=NA, ylim=c(9,21), xlim= c(0.9,3.1),
  ylab=expression(italic(DV)), xaxt='n', xlab = 'Factor B')
```

As the left-hand panel is for the simple interaction of A × B at C1, a vector of means has been created for B at A1 and at A2. Plotting each vector as a set of points with different plot characters (`pch = 19` or `pch = 21`) gives the basic plot.

```
l1 <- c(10, 10.5, 10.25)
l2 <- c(10.5 ,13, 13.5)
points(l1, pch = 19)
points(l2, pch = 21)
```

Adding lines with different styles (the default solid line and the dashed `lty=2`) completes the panel (apart from the level labels for B and the text label in the margin above the panel).

```
lines(l1, lwd = 0.6)
lines(l2, lwd = 0.6, lty = 2)
axis(side = 1, at = levels, labels = B.gps)
mtext(expression(italic(C[1])), line = 0.25, at = 2, cex =
  0.8)
```

The remaining panels are created in the same way but with different means.

```
l1 <- c(11, 10.5, 10.25)
l2 <- c(10.5, 14, 15)
plot(l1, pch=NA, ylim=c(9,21), xlim= c(0.9,3.1),
  ylab=expression(italic(DV)), xaxt='n', xlab = 'Factor B',
  cex.main = 1.2)
points(l1, pch = 19)
points(l2, pch = 21)
axis(side = 1, at = levels, labels = B.gps)
lines(l1, lwd = 0.6)
lines(l2, lwd = 0.6, lty = 2)
mtext(expression(italic(C[2])), line = 0.25, at = 2, cex =
  0.8)

l1 <- c(11.5, 11, 12)
l2 <- c(10.5, 17, 19.5)
plot(l1, pch=NA, ylim=c(9,21), xlim= c(0.9,3.1),
  ylab=expression(italic(DV)), xaxt='n', xlab = 'Factor B')
points(l1, pch = 19)
points(l2, pch = 21)
axis(side = 1, at = levels, labels = B.gps)
lines(l1, lwd = 0.6)
lines(l2, lwd = 0.6, lty = 2)
mtext(expression(italic(C[3])), line = 0.25, at = 2, cex =
  0.8)
```

As this code repeats, it is easy to cut, paste and edit to refine the output. It would also be possible to automate it by writing a function. For plotting a three-way interaction from data, looking at the examples for the `ezPlot()` function is recommended:

```
library(ez)
example(ezPlot)
```

14.10.10 Homogeneity of covariance in ANCOVA (Example 14.8)

The important question when considering homogeneity of regression is whether it is reasonable to fit a single slope for all combinations of factor levels (groups in an independent measures design) or whether varying slopes are required. Although the constant slope assumption might not be plausible (except possibly for some randomized experiments), it may still be preferable to fit a model with a common slope to avoid over-fitting in noisy samples. In Example 14.8 the common slope ANCOVA model for the diagram data was compared to a model with separate slopes for each group. The common slope model is the ANCOVA model for the diagram data that has centered log(*time*) as a covariate.

```
library(foreign)
diag.data <- read.spss('diagram.sav', to.data.frame = TRUE)

ltime <- scale(log(diag.data$time), scale=FALSE)

options(contrasts=c('contr.sum', 'contr.poly'))
diag.ancov <- lm(descript ~ group + cltime, data=diag.data)
summary(diag.ancov)
```

In this case the choice of coding and centering isn't important, as the objective is to compare the two models rather than interpret the effects in detail. Fitting the interaction model is now trivial (as is comparing the two models using AIC or an F test of the change in R^2).

```
diag.int <- lm(descript ~ group * cltime, data=diag.data)
summary(diag.int)

anova(diag.int, diag.ancov)

delta.AIC <- AIC(diag.int) - AIC(diag.ancov)
LR.aic <- exp(delta.AIC/2)
LR.aic
```

Given the sample size it would be better to use AIC_C (which would give an even larger LR in favor of the main effects model of around 80:1).

```
library(bbmle)
AICc(diag.int) - AICc(diag.ancov)
LR.aicc <- exp((AICc(diag.int) - AICc(diag.ancov))/2)
LR.aicc
```

14.10.11 R packages

Bolker, B. M., and R Development Core Team (2011) *bbmle*: Tools for General Maximum Likelihood Estimation. R package version 0.9.7
Fox, J., and Weisberg, S. (2010) *An R Companion to Applied Regression* (2nd edn). Thousand Oaks CA: Sage.
Højsgaard, S., Wright, K. and Leidi, A. A. (2010) *doBy*: Groupwise Computations of Summary Statistics, General Linear Contrasts and Other Utilities. R package version 4.0.6.
Hothorn, T., Bretz, F., and Westfall. P. (2008) Simultaneous Inference in General Parametric Models. *Biometrical Journal*, 50, 346–63.
Lawrence, M. A. (2011) *ez*: Easy Analysis and Visualization of Factorial Experiments. R package version 3.0-0.
R-core members, DebRoy, S., Bivand, R., *et al.* (2011) *foreign*: Read Data Stored by Minitab, S, SAS, SPSS, Stata, Systat, dBase. R package version 0.8-42.
Revelle, W. (2011) *psych*: Procedures for Psychological, Psychometric, and Personality Research. R package version 1.0-95.
Venables, W. N., and Ripley, B. D. (2002) *MASS*: Modern Applied Statistics with S. (4th edn) Springer: New York.
Wickham, H. (2009) *ggplot2*: Elegant Graphics for Data Analysis. Springer: New York.

14.11 Notes on SPSS syntax for Chapter 14

14.11.1 Interactions in multiple regression (Examples 14.1 and 14.2)

Models with bilinear interaction terms can be fitted in SPSS in several ways. The preferred route is to create the product term using COMPUTE and add it to the model as you would any other predictor. The following commands therefore fit a moderated multiple regression model to the lottery data with the logarithm (to base 10) of the money variable as *Y* and *present* and *future* as predictors. CIs, descriptive and collinearity statistics are also requested:

SPSS data file: lottery.sav

```
COMPUTE log_money=LG10(money+ 0.5).
EXECUTE.

COMPUTE interaction=present*future.
EXECUTE.

REGRESSION
  /DESCRIPTIVES MEAN STDDEV CORR SIG N
  /STATISTICS COEFF OUTS CI(95) R ANOVA COLLIN TOL
  /NOORIGIN
  /DEPENDENT log_money
  /METHOD=ENTER present future interaction.
```

This output already includes a correlation matrix and it would be trivial to add plots. If centering is required, you can fit the model after computing centered main effects and taking their product (remembering to compute the product after centering and not centering the product term itself).

As the mean of present is 2.7228 and the mean of future is 19, this could be accomplished with the following syntax:

```
COMPUTE c_present = present - 2.722826086956522.
COMPUTE c_future = future - 19.
COMPUTE c_interaction = c_present * c_future.
EXECUTE.

REGRESSION
  /DESCRIPTIVES MEAN STDDEV CORR SIG N
  /STATISTICS COEFF OUTS CI(95) R ANOVA COLLIN TOL
  /NOORIGIN
  /DEPENDENT log_money
  /METHOD=ENTER c_present c_future c_interaction.
```

To compare the AIC and R^2 of the model with and without interaction:

```
REGRESSION
  /STATISTICS COEFF OUTS CI(95) CHANGE SELECTION
  /NOORIGIN
  /DEPENDENT log_money
  /METHOD=ENTER c_present c_future
  /METHOD=ENTER c_interaction.
```

14.11.2 Getting the asymptotic covariance matrix (Example 14.3)

SPSS provides the variance-covariance of the regression coefficients (the asymptotic covariance matrix), but does not give the sampling variance for the intercept. This can be used to provide input for the online tools for plotting bilinear interactions provided by Preacher *et al.* (2006). To get SPSS into providing it, fit a no-intercept regression, but add a column of constants (one) as a predictor. Here is possible syntax for the uncentered lottery data set:

```
COMPUTE constant=future*0+1.
EXECUTE.

REGRESSION
  /STATISTICS BCOV
  /ORIGIN
  /DEPENDENT log_money
  /METHOD=ENTER constant present future interaction.
```

14.11.3 Polynomial regression (Example 14.4 and Figure 14.5)

The linear fit and quadratic of the curvilinear Anscombe data and its plot are easily obtained with the CURVEFIT command.

SPSS data file: `anscombe.sav`

```
CURVEFIT
  /VARIABLES=y2 WITH x2
  /CONSTANT
  /MODEL=LINEAR QUADRATIC
  /PRINT ANOVA
  /PLOT FIT.
```

It would be easy to change the fitted model via menus or by adding (e.g., `CUBIC`) to the `MODEL` subcommand.

The model could also be fitted as a regression by using COMPUTE to calculate the square of *x*2 and add it to the model. The advantage of this route is that it allows you to get AIC or BIC if `SELECTION` is added to the `STATISTICS` subcommand.

14.11.4 ANOVA

The `UNIVARIATE` command will run independent measures ANOVA designs as an over-parameterized general linear model. Note that we have switched to Type II *SS* from the default Type III (though this is not really necessary in a balanced design).

SPSS data file: `tab14_1.sav`

```
UNIANOVA health BY drug sex
  /METHOD=SSTYPE(2)
  /INTERCEPT=INCLUDE
  /PLOT=PROFILE(drug*sex)
  /PRINT PARAMETER DESCRIPTIVE
  /DESIGN=drug sex drug*sex.
```

The `PLOT` subcommand will give a profile plot of the cell means and the factor on the *x*-axis can be swapped by changing the order to `sex*drug`. A three-way plot can be specified as `A*B*C` with the third factor spread across separate plots. One thing to watch is the scale of the *y*-axis as this will not necessarily be the same on all of the plots. You can manually rescale the axes in the output window by double-clicking on the plot and opening it in the chart editor.

To get AIC or BIC it is necessary to set up the model as a regression with dummy or effect coding for each factor and for the interaction. Residuals and other useful statistics (such as Cook's distance) can be obtained in the usual way for a `UNIVARIATE` or `REGRESSION` command.

14.11.5 Simple main effects

The table of parameter estimates automatically gives you the dummy coded parameter estimates and hence the simple main effects of drug at female and sex at drug. Other simple main effects can be obtained by rerunning the analysis with another reference category, though this route only works for testing effects of a factor with two levels. Running a one-way ANOVA for a subset of the data would allow you to extract the appropriate *SS* for the test and then compute the *F* ratio by hand. However, the UNIANOVA command can be modified with the estimated marginal means subcommand EMMEANS in order to produce the simple main effects. This syntax gives the simple main effects of drug at male and female by the statement COMPARE(drug) for the cell means defined by TABLES(sex*drug).

```
UNIANOVA health BY drug sex
  /METHOD=SSTYPE(2)
  /EMMEANS=TABLES(sex*drug) COMPARE(drug)
  /DESIGN=drug sex drug*sex.
```

To get the simple main effects of sex at no drug and for drug just change COMPARE(drug) to COMPARE(sex).

14.11.6 Homogeneity of covariance (Example 14.8)

There are a number of ways to test homogeneity of covariance in SPSS. You can use the regression commands or specify a custom model via UNIANOVA.

SPSS data file: diagram.sav

```
UNIANOVA descript BY group WITH ln_time
  /METHOD=SSTYPE(2)
  /DESIGN=group ln_time group*ln_time.
```

Effect or dummy coding would allow you to run the model as a regression and then obtain AIC for the mode with and without the interaction (though if $F < 1$ for the interaction, as here, this is not going to be worth the effort).

14.12 Bibliography and further reading

Cohen, J., Cohen, P., West, S. G., and Aiken, L. S. (2003) *Applied Multiple Regression/Correlation Analysis for the Behavioral Sciences*. Mahwah, NJ: Erlbaum.

Jaccard, J., Turrisi, R., and Wan, C. K. (1990) *Interaction Effects in Multiple Regression*. Thousand Oaks: Sage.

Preacher, K. J., Curran, P. J., and Bauer, D. J. (2006) Computational Tools for Probing Interaction Effects in Multiple Linear Regression, Multilevel Modeling, and Latent Curve Analysis. *Journal of Educational and Behavioral Statistics*, 31, 437–48. http://quantpsy.org/interact/index.html.

15
Contrasts

Contents

15.1 Chapter overview

This chapter focuses on contrasts: weighted linear functions of means or other statistics in ANOVA, ANCOVA and related models. The chapter begins by considering the central role of orthogonal contrasts in fitting models with categorical predictors, before introducing their role as a focused test of a substantive hypothesis. Effect size statistics, methods for deriving contrast weights and inference for factors or interactions in balanced and unbalanced designs are reviewed. The chapter ends with a discussion of the problem of *post hoc* contrasts and briefly considers examples of contrasts in relation to other statistical models.

15.2 Contrasts and the design matrix

The concept of a contrast, although strongly associated with ANOVA, is central to a number of statistical models. A contrast is a weighted linear function of means (or occasionally other statistics). The weights of the contrast must sum to zero and at least one weight must be different from zero. In this way, a contrast can express a hypothesized pattern of performance among a set of means as if were the effect of a single predictor in a regression model. Each contrast thus uses up only a single degree of freedom (*df*) in the model. Contrasts are central to ANOVA, and all ANOVA effects can be considered either as contrasts or as sets of contrasts. They also play a role in ANCOVA or any general linear regression model that has categorical predictors.

One way of representing contrasts is in terms of the ANOVA *design matrix*. This is the **X** matrix in a general linear model. Any ANOVA design can be defined in terms of this matrix of predictor effects. To show how this works, look at the design matrix for a 2×2 ANOVA with eight participants (assuming effect coding):

$$\mathbf{y} = \mathbf{X}\hat{\mathbf{b}} + \hat{\mathbf{e}}$$

$$\begin{bmatrix} y_1 \\ y_2 \\ y_3 \\ y_4 \\ y_5 \\ y_6 \\ y_7 \\ y_8 \end{bmatrix} = \begin{bmatrix} 1 & -1 & -1 & 1 \\ 1 & -1 & -1 & 1 \\ 1 & -1 & 1 & -1 \\ 1 & -1 & 1 & -1 \\ 1 & 1 & -1 & -1 \\ 1 & 1 & -1 & -1 \\ 1 & 1 & 1 & 1 \\ 1 & 1 & 1 & 1 \end{bmatrix} \begin{bmatrix} b_0 \\ b_1 \\ b_2 \\ b_3 \end{bmatrix} + \begin{bmatrix} e_1 \\ e_2 \\ e_3 \\ e_4 \\ e_5 \\ e_6 \\ e_7 \\ e_8 \end{bmatrix}$$

The first column in the **X** matrix is for the constant intercept term and the remaining columns are the predictors defined by effect coding. Each of the predictors in a 2×2 design is itself a contrast. For convenience the matrix of contrasts is often condensed into a simpler format, by presenting it in terms of level or group means (rather than raw scores):

$$\begin{bmatrix} 1 & -1 & -1 & 1 \\ 1 & -1 & 1 & -1 \\ 1 & 1 & -1 & -1 \\ 1 & 1 & 1 & 1 \end{bmatrix}$$

Even if you have trouble interpreting matrix algebra it is important to appreciate that contrasts are in many ways more fundamental to ANOVA than factors and interaction terms (which are either contrasts themselves or sets of contrasts that are pooled for the purposes of testing).

Contrasts are not just important because of their prominence in matrix algebra calculations. They provide an important alternative to the default omnibus testing approach in ANOVA and ANCOVA. This approach has been hotly debated in the literature (Rosnow and Rosenthal, 1995; Abelson, 1996; Petty *et al.*, 1996; Rosnow and Rosenthal, 1996a), but is generally reasonable for applications such as a 2×2 design. As soon as a factor has more than two levels the wisdom of the omnibus testing approach is questionable. The usual practice is to follow up the omnibus test with pairwise comparisons. Each pairwise comparison is itself a contrast (with all weights except those of the two means being compared set to zero). The problem with this approach is that testing only pairwise differences among the level means unnecessarily restricts the set of hypotheses that can be assessed. It can also decrease statistical power for the hypotheses of real interest.[1]

A superior approach is to specify *a priori* contrasts of means in place of omnibus tests. Because an *a priori* contrast has one a single degree of freedom it has greater focus. A contrast will map each hypothesis onto a unique pattern of differences between means (Abelson and Prentice, 1997; Rosenthal *et al.*, 2000; Furr and Rosenthal, 2003). Moreover, although contrasts are usually presented in terms of null hypothesis significance testing, there is absolutely no reason that they should be. The idea of a focused test of a hypothesis is central to testing scientific theories (Dienes, 2008). Contrasts can take the form of interval estimates or model comparisons, and inferences can be based on frequentist, likelihood or Bayesian methods.

It is important to realize that the increase in sensitivity or power of the approach arises from the precision of the hypothesis expressed by a contrast. Aside from the restriction that it has one *df*, increased precision is not an intrinsic property of a contrast. A hypothesis that is imprecise (in the sense of only loosely matching the pattern of means in the population) may have less sensitivity than a general test (Abelson and Prentice, 1997). This is analogous to the benefits and costs of having an informative or uninformative prior in a Bayesian analysis (Dienes, 2008).

15.2.1 Orthogonal versus non-orthogonal contrasts

One way to think of a contrast is as a method of decomposing an omnibus test of a factor or interaction in ANOVA or ANCOVA. This kind of decomposition is only possible if the original effect has more than 1 *df*. Omnibus effects are fundamentally just sets of contrasts bundled together, but in classical ANOVA or ANCOVA the contrasts are rarely unbundled.[2] Grouping the contrasts together in this way can make it hard to work out what is going on in the ANOVA, but the bundled contrasts have a very useful property: the sum of squares (*SS*) for the omnibus effect is the total *SS* accounted for by the differences among all means contributing to the effect. This happens because the bundled contrasts are orthogonal. An effect with ν degrees of freedom can be decomposed into up to ν orthogonal contrasts. For example, if it is a factor with J levels, ν will be $J - 1$.

If you want to decompose an effect with ν *df*, one option is therefore to construct your own set of ν orthogonal contrasts to explore what is going on. Using orthogonal contrasts has several advantages. First, each contrast will account for a separate portion of the overall *SS* for the effect. Because each effect will be independent of the others, it can be interpreted with greater clarity. Second, orthogonal contrasts place a sensible limit on the number of tests that can be performed. Pairwise comparisons, the most widely used type of contrast, are not necessarily orthogonal (e.g., if all $J(J-1)/2$ contrasts are conducted then they cannot all be orthogonal). Orthogonal contrasts do not eliminate problems arising from multiple testing, but any strategy that limits the number of tests will reduce the severity of the problem.

To check that a contrast is orthogonal you can just correlate the contrast weights. If W and Z are contrasts with weights $\sum_{j=1}^{J} w_j = 0$ and $\sum_{j=1}^{J} z_j = 0$, then the contrasts are uncorrelated if $\sum_{j=1}^{J} w_j z_j = 0$. If you prefer, you can calculate the correlation r_{WZ} between the two sets of contrast weights. A simple strategy for generating contrast weights that are orthogonal is to construct contrasts that split the means into subgroups such as $\{\hat{\mu}_1, \hat{\mu}_2, \hat{\mu}_3\}$ versus $\{\hat{\mu}_4, \hat{\mu}_5, \hat{\mu}_6\}$. Successive contrasts that only compare within these subgroups – such as $\{\hat{\mu}_1\}$ versus $\{\hat{\mu}_2\}$ – are guaranteed to be orthogonal to previous contrasts.

Decomposing a factor in this way does not necessarily require the omnibus test to reach statistical significance (assuming that classical frequentist inference is employed). Contrasts work best as *a priori* tests of a specific hypothesis or hypotheses. Omnibus tests are less useful because they lack focus. For this reason, they tend to be employed when the research questions are vague or hard to quantify. There is some debate surrounding the use of contrasts to test a theory (e.g., Rosnow and Rosenthal, 1995; Abelson, 1996). Abelson (1996) points out the dangers of being too flexible in fitting contrasts to data. It is easy to find a contrast that matches the pattern predicted by a theory quite well, but there are often other plausible contrasts that fit the means as well or better.

Selecting a contrast to match a specific hypothesis or set of hypotheses sometimes leads to non-orthogonal contrasts being tested. One example is the case of contrasts based on two established theories. Often both theories will account for well-known patterns in the data and the contrasts weights will be correlated.

For orthogonal contrasts it is rare to correct for multiple testing. Each contrast is usually treated as a separate 'family' for the purposes of the Type I error rates (Kirk, 1995). This matches practice in orthogonal ANOVA designs where main effects and interaction terms are not usually corrected for the number of tests performed. Should a correction be required (e.g., if several *a priori* contrasts are being conducted) modified Bonferroni corrections such as the Shaffer or Westfall procedures can be used to adjust α for the number of *a priori* contrasts.

A final observation is that if you run only one *a priori* contrast, the question of orthogonality is irrelevant. Such a contrast will always be 'orthogonal' (because there are no other contrasts for it to be correlated with).

15.2.2 Effect size statistics for linear contrasts

Comparing correlated or overlapping contrasts is trickier than working with orthogonal ones, but there are methods that make comparison easier. One method is to explore the leftover ('residual') *SS* for the omnibus effect after a contrast has been added. This is because decomposing an omnibus effect using orthogonal contrasts is analogous to partitioning the total *SS* in ANOVA. In this analogy SS_{effect} (the *SS* for the omnibus effect with $J-1$ *df*) is the total *SS* to be explained. $SS_{contrast}$ is the effect variance explained by the contrast. The unexplained or residual effect variance is $SS_{effect} - SS_{contrast}$ and has $J-2$ *df*. Thinking about things this way allows you to express the variance explained by the contrast as a proportion of the total variance of the effect:

$$\frac{SS_{contrast}}{SS_{effect}} \qquad \text{Equation 15.1}$$

When n is equal for each mean, this quantity is sometimes called $r^2_{alerting}$ and provides a metric to compare contrasts – especially non-orthogonal ones. The difference in the two $r^2_{alerting}$ values can also be tested as a difference in contrasts. One handy property of $r^2_{alerting}$ is that its square root ($r_{alerting}$) is the Pearson correlation between the contrast weights and the observed means.[3] This relationship makes it easy to compute $SS_{contrast}$ in a balanced ANOVA from the means and SS_{effect}:

$$SS_{contrast} = r^2_{alerting} \times SS_{effect} \qquad \text{Equation 15.2}$$

The $r^2_{alerting}$ statistic is a very important tool for comparing contrasts, but requires that contrasts are computed over the same set of sample means. Unlike R^2 in a regression model, it is quite plausible that a contrast could account for nearly all of the observed variance of an effect. If so, $r^2_{alerting}$ should be close to one. It is also possible for a contrast to be supported by the data (e.g., in terms of statistical significance), but only explain a modest proportion of the total effect. Abelson and Prentice (1997) suggest distinguishing these situations with the terms *canonical* and *ecumenical* outcome. For a canonical outcome the residual effect variance is negligible, whereas for an ecumenical outcome there is additional systematic variation unexplained by the contrast. It is possible to test the residual effect variance (using its SS to construct a t or F statistic), though the proportion of effect variance left unexplained is typically more informative than a formal test. This is for the usual reasons: in small samples the proportion of unexplained variance can be high and the residual test non-significant, while in large samples even negligible residual variance could be statistically significant.

The $r^2_{alerting}$ statistic is a powerful tool for comparing contrasts as explanations of the differences among a set of means in a particular data set. It is not useful as a general effect size metric. Any contrast can also be expressed as a difference in means on the original scale used in the analysis. This implies that it is always possible to express the size of a contrast effect as a simple, unstandardized difference in means (or more correctly as a difference in weighted means). This provides a useful point estimate and can be accompanied by a suitable interval estimate such as a confidence, likelihood or posterior probability interval. SS_{contrast} can also be used to calculate eta-squared statistics. A simple way to accomplish this is to use $r^2_{alerting}$ to rescale the corresponding omnibus statistic (e.g., $\eta^2_{g(contrast)} = r^2_{alerting} \times \eta^2_g$).

15.2.3 Decomposing main effects in ANOVA

The first step in constructing a contrast is to decide on the contrast weights. For a test involving J means there will be one weight for each of the J means:

$$\{w_1, w_2 \ldots w_j\}$$

In many cases the choice of weights will follow, in an obvious way, from the hypothesis being tested. For instance, a researcher may want to compare the mean of the first group against the average of the other three in a one-way ANOVA with four levels. The corresponding set of contrast weights is either $\{-1, 1/3, 1/3, 1/3\}$ or $\{1, -1/3, -1/3, -1/3\}$. Coming up with appropriate weights is sometimes difficult, but provided a researcher can generate a pattern of means consistent with his or her predictions there are tricks that can help (see Box 15.1).

Once selected, the weights are multiplied by the respective level means ($\hat{\mu}_1$ to $\hat{\mu}_j$) to generate a contrast score:

$$C = \sum_{j=1}^{J} w_j \hat{\mu}_j \qquad \text{Equation 15.3}$$

The integer weights $\{3, -1, -1, -1\}$ and level means $\{14, 11, 9, 12\}$ would then produce the contrast score:

$$C = \sum_{j=1}^{J} w_j \hat{\mu}_j = 3\hat{\mu}_1 - (\hat{\mu}_2 + \hat{\mu}_3 + \hat{\mu}_4) = 42 - (11 + 9 + 12) = 10$$

The sign of the weights is important (because they must sum to zero), and common practice is to assign them so that weights produce a positive contrast score (though the test of a negative score would be equivalent).

It is occasionally convenient to scale the weights so that they are all integers. This rescaling is accomplished by multiplying through by an appropriate constant. For instance, multiplying the weights $\{1, -1/3, -1/3, -1/3\}$ by three produces the contrast weights: $\{3, -1, -1, -1\}$. An alternative approach is to rescale the weights so that the sum of their absolute values is two (Kirk, 1995):

$$\sum_{j=1}^{J} \left| w_j \right| = 2 \qquad \text{Equation 15.4}$$

This may seem like a strange maneuver, but it scales each contrast to have the same sum as a contrast between two means; as if it were a pairwise comparison of the two weighted means. This places the contrast score on the same scale as the original means (e.g., a contrast score of $C = 25$, for observations measured in milliseconds would then be equivalent to a 25 *ms* difference between the weighted means). Rescaling the weights in this way turns the contrast score into a measure of simple effect size.

A contrast can be used to form a null hypothesis significance test (NHST) using either the *t* or *F* distribution. In an independent measures design the *F* test statistic takes the form:

$$F_{1,df_{error}} = \frac{MS_{contrast}}{MS_{error}} = \frac{SS_{contrast}}{MS_{error}} \qquad \text{Equation 15.5}$$

The identity between $MS_{contrast}$ and $SS_{contrast}$ only holds because $df_{contrast}$ is always one. The df_{error} and MS_{error} terms are those from the usual ANOVA model. The only new information required in an independent measures design is $SS_{contrast}$. This can be obtained from the correlation between the contrast weights and the means (as described earlier), but both SS_{effect} and

$SS_{contrast}$ can also be calculated directly. Assuming a balanced one-way ANOVA design, SS_{effect} is equal to SS_{factor}.

$$SS_{effect} = SS_{factor} = n \sum_{j=1}^{J} \left(\hat{\mu}_j - \hat{\mu}_{grand} \right)^2 \qquad \text{Equation 15.6}$$

The sum of squares for the contrast can be computed from:

$$SS_{contrast} = \frac{C^2}{\frac{1}{n}\left(\sum_{j=1}^{J} w_j^2 \right)} \qquad \text{Equation 15.7}$$

The $\sum_{j=1}^{J} w_j^2$ term is the sum of the squared contrasts weights and adjusts the result to account for the scaling of the weights (and the denominator in this equation is therefore the variance of the weights). Doubling the weights would double the contrast score, but this cancels out if Equation 15.7 is employed.

Because the F ratio for a 1 df contrast is equivalent to a t test (i.e., $t_{df_{error}} = \sqrt{F_{1,df_{error}}}$), it is possible to form a CI for the contrast as:

$$\frac{2C}{\sum_{j=1}^{J} \left| w_j \right|} \pm t_{df_{error},1-\alpha/2} \sqrt{MS_{error} \left(\frac{1}{n} \sum_{j=1}^{J} w_j^2 \right)} \qquad \text{Equation 15.8}$$

If the absolute values of contrast weights already sum to two this reduces to:

$$C \pm t_{df_{error},1-\alpha/2} \sqrt{MS_{error} \left(\frac{1}{n} \sum_{j=1}^{J} w_j^2 \right)} \qquad \text{Equation 15.9}$$

This is the regular CI for a difference except that a weighted linear combination rather than a simple difference of means is employed. For this reason, the weighted mean difference, *SE* and *df* could also be used to obtain a likelihood interval or Bayesian posterior probability interval. Information-theoretic model comparison methods such as AIC can also be employed.

In factorial designs with independent measures, contrasts for main effects can be constructed in the same way as for one-way designs. The only changes are to the error term and the error *df* (because there are additional predictors in the model). If the pattern of interest involves more than one factor other types of contrast can be constructed. If it involves decomposing multiple *df* interaction effects an *interaction contrast* can be formed. If the pattern involves more than one effect (e.g., a main effect and an interaction), it can be addressed by ignoring the factorial structure. The analysis then treats all means as obtained under a one-way design (see Rosenthal *et al.*, 2000). Equivalently, the contrast can be treated as a single predictor in a regression model, by computing a contrast weight for each of the n outcomes. The latter approach is very flexible – possibly too flexible – and care must be taken to match the contrast to the hypothesis of interest (and create interpretable parameter estimates), rather than simply trying to maximize the effect variance explained.

Example 15.1 Since Example 13.3, various tests for the predicted pattern of differences among a set of group means have been reported for the diagram data. Testing the hypotheses of interest via pairwise tests alone was considered unsatisfactory. The predicted pattern of means was: i) that the text only (T) condition ($M = 17.8$) and picture (P) condition ($M = 18.3$) would be worse than the diagram conditions and ii) that the full diagram (F) condition ($M = 22.4$) would be worse than the segmented diagram (S) condition ($M = 27.3$). Rather than explore these predictions using five separate pairwise tests, it is possible to test the predicted pattern with a single contrast.

The first challenge is to determine an appropriate set of weights. The pattern to be tested is $T = P < F < S$. The first two weights must therefore be equal. For the remaining weights F should be smaller than S. One option is that $F = 1$ and $S = 2$. This forces T and P to sum to -3 and thus resolves to $\{-1.5, -1.5, +1, +2\}$. Multiplying by two results in the weights $\{-3, -3, +2, +4\}$. These weights would work, but they are not the simplest set of integer weights for the pattern $T = P < F < S$. A simpler set is obtained by setting $T = P = -2$, and hence $F = 1$ and $S = 3$. Alternatively $T = P = -1$, and thus $F = 0$ and $S = 2$. This gives a choice of $\{-2, -2, +1, +3\}$ or $\{-1, -1, +0, +2\}$. In practice there is little to choose between them.

Although or $\{-1, -1, +0, +2\}$ is simpler, I'll select $\{-2, -2, +1, +3\}$ because it places more emphasis on the difference between diagram and non-diagram conditions (which seems to capture the spirit of the predictions slightly better). I'll also scale the absolute values of the weights to sum to two (thus turning the contrast score into a weighted mean on the original scale). Rescaling in this way, the weights are $\{-0.5, -0.5, +0.25, +0.75\}$. As n per condition is ten, the contrast score and sums of squares are:

$$C = \sum_{j=1}^{J} w_j \hat{\mu}_j = (-0.5 \times 17.8) + (-0.5 \times 18.3) + (0.25 \times 22.4) + (0.75 \times 27.3) = 8.025$$

$$SS_{contrast} = \frac{C^2}{\frac{1}{n}\left(\sum_{j=1}^{J} w_j^2\right)} = \frac{8.025^2}{(2 \times 0.5^2 + 0.25^2 + 0.75^2)/10} = 572.45$$

The original ANOVA output reports MS_{error} as 67.78. So the F ratio for the contrast is:

$$F_{1,36} = \frac{572.45}{67.78} = 8.45$$

The square root gives the equivalent t test of the contrast, $t_{36} = 2.91$, $p = .006$. This can also be presented as a 95% CI of the weighted contrast mean:

$$C \pm t_{df_{error},1-\alpha/2}\sqrt{MS_{error}\left(\frac{1}{n}\sum_{j=1}^{J} w_j^2\right)} = 8.025 \pm -2.028 \times 2.761 = 8.025 \pm 5.600$$

Thus $C = 5.6$, 95% CI is [2.42, 13.63]. A plausible range of values for the true difference in description quality for the contrast excludes zero and (given that observed range is seven to 38) includes differences of a substantial magnitude.

A good way to establish the explanatory power of the contrast is to calculate $r^2_{alerting}$; the proportion of the group factor main effect that it explains. This is the ratio of $SS_{contrast}$ to the SS_{factor} (the sums of squares of the main effect). From the original ANOVA, $SS_{factor} = 583.7$, so $r^2_{alerting} = 572.45/583.7 = .98$. This contrast therefore explains 98% of the variance of the main effect (i.e., 98% of the variation between the means of the experimental conditions). It only explains $\eta^2 = 572.45/3023.9 = .189$ or about 19% of the total sample variance. The two figures have different uses. $r^2_{alerting}$ indicates how good the contrast is as an explanation of the effect. You would expect a good explanation to account for a very high proportion of the variation among means (certainly 80% or 90% and perhaps close to 100%). The lower value of η^2 indicates that most of the variation in the sample is unexplained. This could be because there are other variables at work (or because of measurement error).

Had the weights {−1, −1, +0, +2} been used, the test statistic would have been $F = 8.42$ and the proportion of variance explained would have been virtually unchanged. Only rarely will switching between weights expressing a similar pattern have a material impact on the analysis.

Box 15.1 Generating contrast weights to test a hypothesis

One of the easiest methods to generate contrast weights is to start with a pattern of means consistent with the hypothesis. Previous research may suggest such a pattern or you may have a theory that makes precise quantitative predictions. Often it will be acceptable to generate plausible values for the means; values that seem about right. Consider a factor with $J = 5$ levels and a *DV* that usually ranges from zero to 25. If a theory predicts no difference for the first two conditions and progressively larger means for the last three conditions you might start with a set of means such as:

$$\{8, 8, 10, 14, 20\}$$

You can turn these into contrast weights by *centering* (subtracting the grand mean of the five levels). The grand mean of the levels is $(8 + 8 + 10 + 14 + 20)/5 = 60/5 = 12$. Subtracting 12 from each of the starting values gives:

$$\{-4, -4, -2, 2, 8\}$$

These weights will work just fine, but can be simplified through division by a common factor. For instance, dividing by two gives:

$$\{-2, -2, -1, 1, 4\}$$

If you end up with fractional weights (e.g., obtained when the original pattern or average contained fractions), these can be turned into integers through multiplication by a common factor. To get the absolute sum of the weights to equal two you could divide the original weights (with an absolute sum of 20) by ten to get:

$$\{-0.4, -0.4, -0.2, 0.2, 0.8\}$$

What if it is possible to come up with several plausible sets of weights? For example, the same general pattern is also captured by:

$$\{-3, -3, -2, 1, 7\}$$

In most cases it won't matter, but a good rule of thumb is to select the simplest set of integers that matches the desired pattern. This prevents people searching for combinations of weights that produce the 'best' results for a given data set.

Sometimes the levels themselves provide the information to construct the weights. For example, Lansdale *et al.* (2005, Experiment 2) looked at location memory as a function of stimulus duration. They used durations of 5, 10, 20 and 30 seconds. These durations could have been used to generate contrast coefficients in the same way as for a predicted pattern of means (assuming that longer duration is expected to improve recall in a linear fashion). The weights can be obtained from the values {5, 10, 20, 30} by subtracting the mean duration of 16.25 to give:

$$\{-11.25, -6.25, 3.75, 13.75\}$$

Multiplying through by four to get $\{-45, -25, 15, 55\}$ and dividing by the common factor of five gives:

$$\{-9, -5, 3, 11\}$$

These can be used as convenient contrast weights. A near-equivalent strategy is to treat the stimulus duration as a continuous predictor in a linear regression. The choice depends on what other predictors are included in the model and whether they are coded as categorical or continuous predictors. Lansdale *et al.* (2005) reported the simple linear regression (though the results are similar either way).

15.2.4 Contrasts in unbalanced designs

Unbalanced designs, with unequal n per mean, make the contrast formulas a little more complicated. They also pose the additional challenge of determining an appropriate effect size metric. Rosenthal *et al.* (2000) propose different solutions depending on the quantity calculated. In particular, they make the case that $r^2_{alerting}$ and $r_{alerting}$ should be calculated as if means are equal for unbalanced designs. The easiest way to do this is to calculate $r_{alerting}$ as the simple correlation of the level means and the contrast weights (but it could also be done by calculating SS_{effect} and $SS_{contrast}$ and substituting N/J, the arithmetic mean sample size per group, for n in the original formulas). The justification for this approach is that $r^2_{alerting}$ is an estimate of the variance accounted for by the contrast among the population means (rather than an estimate of what would happen in a similarly unbalanced study). In general, this argument is sensible. However, the argument doesn't work as well for eta-squared based statistics. These have a very specific definition and interpretation as descriptive (rather than inferential) sample statistics. These should be calculated based on unbalanced sample sizes. Rosenthal *et al.* (*ibid.*) take a slightly different view and advocate calculating variants of eta-square statistics in these cases.[4] Unless the sample sizes are very unequal, the differences between the approaches should not be too large. Furthermore, contrast effect sizes are not particularly useful for comparing between studies (because the choice of levels often varies between studies). It makes more sense to use simple effect sizes (e.g., the weighted difference in means).

Regardless, it is important to calculate tests, standard errors (*SE*s) and confidence intervals (*CI*s) differently in the unequal n case. An approximate, but unsatisfactory solution would be to use a weighted harmonic mean sample size. A superior solution involves a Welch-Satterthwaite correction (Kirk, 1995). This statistic uses separate variance estimates rather than the usual pooled estimate and is robust against both unequal sample sizes and unequal variances. Denoting the contrast weight and sample size for each of the J means as w_j and n_j, it takes the form:

$$\frac{C}{\hat{\sigma}_{\mu_C}} = \frac{C}{\sqrt{\sum_{j=1}^{J} \frac{w_j^2 \hat{\sigma}_j^2}{n_j}}} \quad : t'(\nu') \qquad \text{Equation 15.10}$$

Calculating the CI from the contrast score gives:

$$C \pm t_{\nu', 1-\alpha/2} \sqrt{\sum_{j=1}^{J} \frac{w_j^2 \hat{\sigma}_j^2}{n_j}} \qquad \text{Equation 15.11}$$

As before, it may be convenient to choose contrast weights with an absolute sum of two so that the CI is on the same scale as the original means.

The Welch-Satterthwaite solution to the Behrens-Fisher problem produces a contrast test statistic that does not follow a t distribution with the usual *df*. However, if evaluated against ν' degrees of freedom, the approximation is highly accurate, provided the normality assumption is satisfied:

$$\nu' = \frac{\left(\sum_{j=1}^{J} \frac{w_j^2 \hat{\sigma}_j^2}{n_j} \right)^2}{\sum_{j=1}^{J} \frac{w_j^4 \hat{\sigma}_j^4}{n_j^2 (n_j - 1)}} \qquad \text{Equation 15.12}$$

Bonett (2008, p. 107) suggests that Welch-Satterthwaite contrasts 'are robust to moderate amounts of nonnormality and become increasingly robust as the sample size increases'. Other solutions such as transformations or bootstrapping should be preferred if violations of normality are very severe (e.g., for extremely heavy-tailed, leptokurtotic distributions). Bonett and Price (2002) also describe methods for linear contrasts of medians.

15.2.5 Polynomial contrasts

A number of coding schemes exist that describe sets of orthogonal contrasts (e.g., Kirk, 1995). Polynomial contrasts are a good example of these, and are particularly useful when factor levels possess a meaningful order (e.g., school year groups). Polynomial contrasts are also often employed when the underlying dimension that factor levels are drawn from is quantitative (e.g., doses of a drug). One restriction is that they require that levels are equally spaced (or at least approximately so). For instance: 0, 10, 20, and 30 *mg* doses of a drug are equally spaced, whereas 0, 5, 10, and 20 *mg* are not. For unequal spacing, customized contrast coefficients can be created or levels can be treated as values of a continuous predictor in regression (see Box 15.1).

Polynomial contrasts can be considered a special case of polynomial regression. The logic of the approach is that with J levels it is possible to have $J - 1$ orthogonal contrasts and, if the levels are ordered, it seems sensible to use this information to structure a set of tests. It is essential that the order is either intrinsic to the levels of the factor (e.g., year groups or doses of a drug) or specified *a priori* by the researcher. Almost any set of means could be rearranged *post hoc* to produce evidence of a polynomial trend, and *post hoc* ordering of means is bad practice. As with regression, polynomial contrasts start with the most parsimonious explanation – a linear contrast – and increase complexity by considering quadratic, cubic, quartic or higher-order contrasts in turn. Linear, quadratic and cubic fits suffice to explain most patterns of means. There is little advantage in going beyond these contrasts to higher-order polynomial functions (unless there is a clear theoretical or practical interpretation of the polynomial).

Abelson and Prentice (1997) argue that if the 'residual' effect variance (the portion of SS_{effect} unexplained by polynomial or other contrasts) is substantial, it is sensible to explore whether further orthogonal contrasts may improve the fit. These additional contrasts don't have to be polynomial ones. For instance, for a linear contrast, there may be one mean that falls far from the straight line fit. An additional contrast of this mean versus the remaining means could test this departure from the pattern. However, such a contrast might not be particularly meaningful unless there were some *a priori* reason to suppose that the mean should be different from the others.

A linear contrast is one that predicts a fixed increase or decrease across a set of means. Weights for a linear contrast are evenly spaced (and therefore assume equal spacing between the levels being compared). Any set of evenly spaced weights that sum to zero will do. A general method for eliciting the weights is to adapt the approach described in Box 15.1. Start with the integers 1 to J (where J is the number of means in the contrast). Then subtract $(J+1)/2$, the arithmetic mean of the uncentered weights, to get the centered weights. If J is odd these weights will be integers. When $J=5$ the starting values are {1, 2, 3, 4, 5} and subtracting their mean of three produces:

$$\{-2, -1, 0, 1, 2\}$$

If J is even, the weights will be integers or multiples of 0.5. So for $J=6$ the weights start as {1, 2, 3, 4, 5, 6} and, after subtracting the mean of 3.5, become:

$$\{-2.5, -1.5, -0.5, 0.5, 1.5, 2.5\}$$

When integer weights are required these values can multiplied by two. For example, for $J=6$ you would get:

$$\{-5, -3, -1, 1, 3, 5\}$$

Because this procedure is so easy, people often jump directly from J to the weights. This works well when J is odd. When J is even, people tend to make errors. The errors are usually of the form $\{\ldots -2, -1, 1, 2 \ldots\}$. This pattern looks linear at first glance, but the central weights -1 and 1 are two units rather than one unit apart. Linear contrasts with integer weights thus take the general form:

$$J = odd \quad \left\{ \ldots \quad -2 \quad -1 \quad 0 \quad 1 \quad 2 \quad \ldots \right\}$$

$$J = even \quad \left\{ \ldots \quad -5 \quad -3 \quad -1 \quad 1 \quad 3 \quad 5 \quad \ldots \right\}$$

Table 15.1 Sets of linear, quadratic and (where possible) cubic integer contrast weights, for $J = 3$ to $J = 6$ means

J	Linear	Quadratic	Cubic
3	{−1, 0, 1}	{1, −2, 1}	–
4	{−3, −1, 1, 3}	{1, −1, −1, 1}	{−1, 3, −3, 1}
5	{−2, −1, 0, 1, 2}	{2, −1, −2, −1, 2}	{−1, 2, 0, −2, 1}
6	{−5, −3, −1, 1, 3, 5}	{5, −1, −4, −4, −1, 5}	{−5, 7, 4, −4, −7, 5}

Generating contrast weights for quadratic and higher-order polynomials is non-trivial. The difficulty is with maintaining a set of integer coefficients that are orthogonal (see Snedecor and Cochran, 1989). Your software may have built-in procedures for calculating coefficients for orthogonal polynomial contrasts and many texts include tables of such contrasts (e.g., Howell, 2002). Table 15.1 gives sets of linear, quadratic and cubic contrast coefficients for $J = 3$, 4, 5 and 6. If non-orthogonal sets of weights are employed, the contrasts would not decompose the total effect variance into independent components and the effects would no longer be uncorrelated.

With $J - 1$ orthogonal contrasts it is always possible to account for all the variance of the omnibus effect. For this reason care should be taken when fitting quadratic contrasts when $J = 3$ (or cubic contrasts when $J = 4$) because the total *SS* for these contrasts will necessarily exhaust SS_{effect}. The same applies for polynomials of order $J - 1$ in general. For a linear contrast, analysis of the 'residual' effect variance can be particularly revealing. One strategy is to form an *F* ratio to test the residual effect variance in what is known as a *test of non-linearity*:

$$F_{nonlinear} = \frac{SS_{effect} - SS_{linear}}{MS_{error}} \sim F(J-2, df_{error}) \quad \text{Equation 15.13}$$

The logic of the procedure is that if SS_{effect} is the total sample variance owing to the effect, and SS_{linear} is the contribution due to the linear increase among means, the remaining portion must be owing to non-linear effects. It is also possible to test the remaining higher-order terms after having fitted a quadratic or cubic contrast. For instance, if a cubic contrast had been fitted the test of higher-order terms would be:

$$F = \frac{SS_{effect} - \left(SS_{linear} + SS_{quadratic} + SS_{cubic}\right)}{MS_{error}} \sim F(J-4, df_{error}) \quad \text{Equation 15.14}$$

If your primary objective is to test for a linear, quadratic or other polynomial contrast, it is worth considering this at the design stage (see McClelland, 1997). For instance, power to detect a linear trend is maximized by two extreme groups. It is also possible to increase statistical power by adjusting the weights. Miller (1986) points out that weighting the extremes more heavily (e.g., with weights such as $\{-4, -1, 1, 4\}$ for $J = 4$) increases power to detect a linear trend (though the revised weights will now be optimized to detect a sigmoidal pattern).

Example 15.2 Gatz and Hurwitz (1990) investigated levels of depression across different age groups. They reported depression scores (using the CES-D scale) for groups aged 20–39 years (G1), 40–54 years (G2), 55–69 years (G3) and 70–98 years (G4). Subsequent examples will refer to this data set as the lifespan depression data. The age intervals are not quite evenly spaced. The authors argued that they are close enough that orthogonal polynomial contrasts can be applied without distorting the results. Their analysis controls for several covariates, though the data here are unadjusted. Means, *SD*s and *n* for the conditions are:

	n	*M*	*SD*
G1	548	10.85	9.03
G2	218	10.36	10.19
G3	352	8.63	8.31
G4	212	12.11	8.73

The coefficients for a linear contrast are $\{-3,-1,+1,+3\}$ and the linear contrast score is:

$$C_{linear} = \sum_{j=1}^{J} w_j \hat{\mu}_j = (-3 \times 10.85) + (-1 \times 10.36) + (1 \times 8.63) + (3 \times 12.11) = 2.05$$

This is an unbalanced design and, using a Welch-Satterthwaite correction, the *SE* is:

$$\hat{\sigma}_{\hat{\mu}_{linear}} = \sqrt{\sum_{j=1}^{J} \frac{w_j^2 \hat{\sigma}_j^2}{n_j}} = \sqrt{\frac{9 \times 9.03^2}{548} + \frac{1 \times 10.19^2}{218} + \frac{1 \times 8.31^2}{352} + \frac{9 \times 8.73^2}{212}} = \sqrt{5.247} \approx 2.29$$

Hence $t = 2.05/2.29 = 0.90$. The *df* are best calculated by computer, which gives $\nu' = 509.4$. The linear contrast is not statistically significant: $t_{509.4} < 1$, $p > .05$ and $r^2_{alerting} = .034$. It accounts for about only 3.4% of the main effect. Because the design is unbalanced, $r^2_{alerting}$ is calculated as the squared correlation between contrast weights and group means. The linear contrast is not a convincing explanation of the pattern of depression scores between the age groups.

The quadratic contrast is more promising. The coefficients for this contrast are $\{+1,-1,-1,+1\}$ and the contrast score is:

$$C_{quadratic} = (1 \times 10.85) + (-1 \times 10.36) + (-1 \times 8.63) + (1 \times 12.11) = 3.97$$

The error term for this contrast differs from that of the linear trend (because the contrast weights are scaled differently and have a smaller variance):

$$\hat{\sigma}_{\hat{\mu}_{quadratic}} = \sqrt{\frac{9.03^2}{548} + \frac{10.19^2}{218} + \frac{8.31^2}{352} + \frac{8.73^2}{212}} = \sqrt{1.181} \approx 1.09$$

The *t* statistic is therefore $3.97/1.09 = 3.65$. As $\nu' = 771.1$, $t_{771.1} = 3.65$, $p < .05$. The quadratic effect has greater explanatory power, with $r^2_{alerting} = .63$. The quadratic trend explains around 63% of the variation in the sample means. The pattern also seems plausible – depression is more marked for the youngest and oldest age groups and lowest for those in between (roughly following a U-shaped curve). It would be unreasonable to claim that this reflects a quadratic function of age. The value of $r^2_{alerting}$ is not close to one and without theoretical support for this specific function almost any roughly U-shaped curve would be just as plausible.

At this point it would be possible to fit a cubic contrast. This would be hard to interpret (because most patterns among four means can be fitted rather well by a cubic contrast). Around (100 − 63 − 3) = 34% of the variation between means is unaccounted for. A test is not necessary. Such an effect would undoubtedly be statistically significant. It is more useful to consider covariates such as physical health, which might explain some of the residual variation in depression or that may be confounded with age group (see Gatz and Hurwitz, 1990).

15.2.6 Contrasts and model comparison

A solitary contrast can suggest data are consistent with a hypothesis, but the true test of any hypothesis is to compare it with one or more plausible alternatives. Tools for these comparisons are possible within the contrast approach or within the broader model comparison framework. Within the contrast approach, two contrasts can themselves be compared using a *difference contrast* (Rosenthal *et al.*, 2000).

A difference contrast is a contrast using weights obtained from subtracting one pattern of contrasts from another. The starting point is simple subtraction of the two sets of weights, but this ignores the fact that the set of weights with the greater variance has a better chance of explaining the data. This can be seen by comparing two contrasts such as $\{-1, -1, 1, 1\}$ and $\{-7, -1, 4, 4\}$. The simple difference between the weights is $\{-6, 0, 3, 3\}$. This set of differences correlates about .82 with the first contrast and .99 with the second. The contrast with more variable weights will have greater explanatory power than the one with less variable weights. The solution is to standardize each set of weights prior to subtraction. To do this, calculate the standard deviation of the J weights for each contrast:

$$SD_W = \sqrt{\frac{\sum_{j=1}^{J} w_j^2}{J}} \qquad \text{Equation 15.15}$$

This formula provides the descriptive SD of the weights (and note that the mean, being zero, does not need to be subtracted from w before squaring). The difference contrast uses the simple difference between the standardized weights of two contrasts, but is otherwise calculated using standard formulas. The standardization process generally produces weights that are hard to turn into integers, so it is best to use a computer to handle the calculations (otherwise there may be substantial rounding error).

As a contrast is itself a form of regression model, it is also possible to compare contrasts using more general model comparison techniques. In one-way designs it may be interesting to compare a model with a single contrast to the full ANOVA model. This can be done by assessing change in R^2 for the model (e.g., using an F ratio). This is often best accomplished in regression software by creating a new predictor for the contrast (using contrast coding in place of effect coding of the factor). By fitting separate regression models it is also possible to obtain information criteria such as AIC or BIC. Glover and Dixon (2004) and Wagenmakers (2007) describe how to compare different polynomial contrasts using AIC or BIC (allowing for the extra parameter of a quadratic model over a linear model).

Example 15.3 Imagine that theory A predicts the following pattern of four means: {−3, −1, 1, 3}, while theory B predicts the pattern: {−4, −1, −1, 6}. As the contrasts are somewhat similar, if contrast A is statistically significant, it is likely that B will be too. More worrying is the fact that even if B is non-significant it doesn't necessarily mean that A is a much better fit to the data than B. To address this you need to construct a contrast of the difference between A and B. Start by calculating the *SD* of the contrast weights for each hypothesis. For contrast A this is

$$SD_W = \sqrt{\frac{(-3)^2+(-1)^2+1^2+3^2}{4}} = \sqrt{\frac{20}{4}} = \sqrt{5} \approx 2.236$$

while for contrast B it is

$$SD_W = \sqrt{\frac{(-4)^2+(-1)^2+(-1)^2+6^2}{4}} = \sqrt{\frac{54}{4}} = \sqrt{13.5} \approx 3.674$$

Dividing by the *SD* of each set of weights produces:

$$\begin{array}{ll} A & \{-1.342, -0.447, 0.447, 1.342\} \\ B & \{-1.089, -0.272, -0.272, 1.633\} \end{array}$$

Thus the weights for the difference contrast are:

$$A - B = \{-0.253, -0.175, 0.719, -0.291\}$$

Multiplying all weights through by 1000 would produce integer weights (even if the resulting weights are somewhat awkward).

This kind of model comparison can also be used to test the vulnerability of a contrast to competing explanations. For the diagram data the contrast {−2, −2, +1, +3} was found to explain the 98% of the variation in sample means in Example 15.1. An alternative explanation is that just having a diagram of any kind improves description quality (relative to the no diagram conditions). This contrast has the weights: {−1, −1, 1, 1}. These two contrasts are correlated, so a difference contrast could be used to compare the competing explanations. This produces the weights {0.0572, 0.0571, −0.5286, 0.4142}. The resulting *F* ratio is 0.76 and therefore statistically non-significant. Also of interest is the comparison between $r^2_{alerting}$ for the two contrasts. The original contrast explained 98% of variation in means whereas the {−1, −1, 1, 1} contrast explains 79% of the variation in means. Both are good explanations, but there are insufficient data to allow us to choose between them (even if the explanatory power of the original contrast is much higher).

15.3 Interaction contrasts

There are several ways to follow up the presence of an interaction effect in ANOVA using contrasts. One, already considered, is to look at simple effects (although simple main effects with

1 *df* are themselves a form of contrast). Another alternative is to treat a factorial design as if it were a one-way design; testing contrasts representing patterns of variation among the cell means. These approaches lump together interaction and main effect variance to be explained by a contrast. A more elegant approach, the interaction contrast, is available if the goal is to decompose an interaction effect with multiple degrees of freedom. Interaction effects with a single *df* cannot be decomposed in this way; they are differences of differences and cannot be simplified further (e.g., as in 2×2 ANOVA).[5]

Contrast weights in a one-way ANOVA are centered (i.e., sum to zero). Contrast weights in an interaction contrast must be double-centered. Double-centering ensures that the row and column marginals representing the main effects sum to zero. For this reason both the cell means and weights are often represented in matrix format, with J rows and K columns for the J and K levels of the two factors. Through double-centering, also known as 'sweeping out', it is possible to generate weights for an interaction contrast from a predicted pattern of cell means (see Key Concept 15.1). The purpose of double-centering is to strip out the influence of the main effects from the cell means, leaving a 'pure' interaction effect. The interaction contrast score C_I can be obtained directly from the interaction score (the 'residuals' of the cell means after double-centring) or from the raw cell means multiplied by the interaction contrast weights:

$$C_I = \sum_{j=1,k=1}^{J,K} w_{jk} I_{jk} = \sum_{j=1,k=1}^{J,K} w_{jk} \hat{\mu}_{jk} \qquad \text{Equation 15.16}$$

The contrast score is identical via either route because I_{jk} (the residualized cell means) and $\hat{\mu}_{jk}$ (the observed cell means) differ only in terms of the presence of main effects. Thus multiplying the observed cell means by the double-centered weights has the benefit of stripping out the influence of main effects (Abelson and Prentice, 1997).

The chief obstacle to constructing interaction contrasts, once you have mastered double-centering, is translating hypotheses into sensible patterns of weights. Interactions can be difficult to interpret and predicting appropriate patterns of means is also difficult. Abelson and Prentice (*ibid.*) provide worked examples for several plausible hypotheses that might be considered. These include *matching, opposed concavities, differential linear trends* and *differential curvilinear trends*.

The matching hypothesis is pertinent when levels of one factor are in some way paired with levels of another factor (and by implication $J = K$). This could occur in a memory experiment where characteristics of learning and test are paired (e.g., three different contexts are present at learning and reinstated at test). The expectation of a matching hypothesis is that the cell means of paired levels should be different from non-paired levels (e.g., testing in the same context as learning will lead to better memory). This matching hypothesis is tested by weights selected so that the main diagonal of the matrix is positive whereas weights on the off-diagonals are negative:

$$\begin{Bmatrix} 2 & -1 & -1 \\ -1 & 2 & -1 \\ -1 & -1 & 2 \end{Bmatrix}$$

A concavity hypothesis is one in which an ordered set of levels shows a quadratic-like, concave pattern among the means (see the central panel of Figure 14.4). This pattern is captured by the main effect of a factor. If it also varies between levels of a second factor, curving upwards for one or more levels and downwards for one or more others, this is an opposed concavities interaction. This pattern is appropriate if the mid-point of the ordered levels represents the predicted peak response for one group and the predicted trough for another (e.g., preferred group size for extroverts and introverts, if introverts prefer either to be in very small groups or very large groups). In its purest form, and assuming a 2×4 interaction, this would produce the following pattern of weights:

$$\begin{Bmatrix} -1 & 1 & 1 & -1 \\ 1 & -1 & -1 & 1 \end{Bmatrix}$$

Abelson and Prentice point out that a weaker hypothesis – in which a concave quadratic is contrasted with a flat set of weights – is also possible. The latter hypothesis is less focused and will tend to have less statistical power.

A contrast of differential linear trends is one in which a linear relationship for one group is predicted to be larger than that of another. Abelson and Prentice (*ibid.*) show that this is tested by weights that increase linearly for one factor at one or more levels of a second factor, but decrease linearly for the remaining levels of the second factor. For instance, in an experiment contrasting the effects of two different drugs on some outcome, the effects of the drugs might be linear across four doses. If one drug is expected to show a larger linear effect than another this could be tested by the weights:

$$\begin{Bmatrix} -3 & -1 & 1 & 3 \\ 3 & 1 & -1 & -3 \end{Bmatrix}$$

The selection of weights here may appear puzzling; it looks as though it predicts a linear contrast that increases for one group and decreases for another. This interpretation is incorrect as it assumes that the main effects are still present. If the original means in each group increased equally and linearly, the residualized means would show a flat profile after stripping out the main effects. But if there is an additional linear component for one condition relative to another it necessarily shows as depicted above (because the main effect overestimates one linear trend and underestimates the other). This is yet another variant of the earlier insight: all interactions are disordinal once the main effects are stripped out.

A differential curvilinear trend is a more complex variant of the differential linear trend. One simple kind – a quadratic – has already been considered (for hypotheses of opposed concavities). The difficulty for other curvilinear patterns is that there will be a large number of curves to choose from. Having excluded the quadratic (one of the simplest), it is difficult to select from among the remaining candidates on *a priori* grounds (unless a theory makes very precise quantitative predictions).

Abelson and Prentice (*ibid.*), based on earlier work by Tukey, suggest using the observed curvilinear trend among the level means of a factor to define the contrast pattern. Modeling the weights from the observed level means is not sensible for the main effects (as weights constructed from the observed level means always account for 100% of the main effect sums of squares). However, in an orthogonal ANOVA design, the main effect and interaction effects are unrelated (because the main effects have been stripped out from the interaction). In the absence of other information, the level means provide the best estimate of the curvilinear pattern revealed by the main effect. Thus, if the level means for a factor are {10, 11, 14, 22, 45} they suggest contrast weights of $\{-5.2, -4.7, -3.2, 0.8, 12.3\}$ after subtracting the mean and dividing by two. A test of differential curvilinear trends between two levels of a different factor could then use the weights:

$$\begin{Bmatrix} -5.2 & -4.7 & -3.2 & 0.8 & 12.3 \\ 5.2 & 4.7 & 3.2 & -0.8 & -12.3 \end{Bmatrix}$$

This follows the same reasoning that provided weights for the differential linear trend. In the absence of *a priori* information about the nature of the true curvilinear pattern they are sensible choices for the interaction contrast.

$SS_{contrast}$ can be used to compute effect size statistics such as $r^2_{alerting}$ (using $SS_{interaction}$ from the original ANOVA). These statistics have to be interpreted slightly differently because the main effects have been stripped out. Thus $r_{alerting}$ is the correlation between the contrast weights and the double-centered residuals of the cell means (not the raw means) and $r^2_{alerting}$ is its square. These are useful measures of the explanatory power of the interaction contrast. A worked example for the calculation of an interaction contrast is provided in Example 16.5.

KEY CONCEPT 15.1

Double-centering (sweeping out) main effects and interaction residuals

Double-centering is a technique for getting at the two-way interaction effect in a two-way contingency table of means. It works by stripping out the main effects to reveal the 'residual' effect of the interaction on the cell means. The double-centered, residualized cell means are described by the equation

$$I_{jk} = \hat{\mu}_{jk} - \hat{\mu}_j - \hat{\mu}_k + \hat{\mu}_{grand}$$

where I_{jk} is the residual interaction effect in each cell, $\hat{\mu}_{jk}$ are the observed cell means, $\hat{\mu}_j$ and $\hat{\mu}_k$ are the marginal means and $\hat{\mu}_{grand}$ is the grand mean. The subscripts *j* and *k* refer to each of the *J* levels on factor *A* and the *K* levels on factor *B* in the two-way design.

Abelson and Prentice (1997) use a sequential sweeping out procedure to illustrate the approach. Consider the means for the 2 × 2 ANOVA in Table 14.1 (with the marginals and grand means in italics):

	Male	*Female*	Σ
Placebo	10.00	10.00	*10.00*
Drug	15.00	20.00	*17.50*
Σ	*12.50*	*15.00*	*13.75*

The sweeping out procedure first removes the grand mean to give:

	Male	*Female*	Σ
Placebo	−3.75	−3.75	*−3.75*
Drug	1.25	6.25	*3.75*
Σ	*−1.25*	*1.25*	*0.00*

This table still includes the effects of gender and drug. The main effect of drug is stripped out by subtracting the row means of −3.75 and 3.75 from the placebo and drug conditions:

	Male	*Female*	Σ
Placebo	0.00	0.00	*0.00*
Drug	−2.50	2.50	*0.00*
Σ	*−1.25*	*1.25*	*0.00*

Repeating the procedure to subtract the male marginal of −1.25 and the female marginal of 1.25 from the columns gives the double-centered table:

	Male	*Female*	Σ
Placebo	1.25	−1.25	*0.00*
Drug	−1.25	1.25	*0.00*
Σ	*0.00*	*0.00*	*0.00*

The double-centered table has row and column marginals that are exactly zero. It is not influenced by either main effect. This reveals interaction effect in its purest form. These 'residuals' would also be given by the coefficient or coefficients of a regression model that used effect coding for both factors. This implies that the double-centered cell means could be used to compute sums of squares for a two-way interaction effect in ANOVA. The squared values of the double-centered cell means are all 1.5625. This multiplied by the number of cells (which is four) and n per cell (also four) gives $SS_{A\times B} = 4 \times 4 \times 1.5625 = 25$.

This again demonstrates that (once the main effects are stripped out) all interactions are 'disordinal' crossover interactions. Both the direct equation and sweeping out produce the same results. The direct equation works by subtracting the original row and column marginals simultaneously (rather than sequentially). It therefore has to add the grand mean back in (having effectively subtracted it twice). The same procedure can be applied to cell means for a $J \times K$ ANOVA where $J > 2$ or $K > 2$. It can also create double-centered contrast weights from a predicted or expected pattern of means.

15.4 Post hoc contrasts and correction for multiple testing

Contrasts work best when a small set of plausible *a priori* hypotheses are compared. Selecting orthogonal contrasts or comparing competing hypotheses (especially if Bayesian or likelihood methods are employed) can further reduce the impact of multiple comparisons. Nevertheless, there are situations in which researchers wish to test contrasts that are identified *post hoc*. In some cases a *post hoc* hypothesis can be considered without worrying about multiple testing. The most obvious example is where the contrast represents a plausible alternative explanation of a predicted effect (and it seems unfair to penalize a plausible competing hypothesis of this kind). In other contexts more caution is required.

When the set of contrasts to be corrected for is small – either because the set of *post hoc* hypotheses is well defined (e.g., all pairwise comparisons) or because the set is defined *a priori*, conventional methods for controlling familywise Type I error can be employed. The approach advocated here is to use powerful modified Bonferroni procedures such as Shaffer or Westfall's, as these take into account logical relations between hypotheses and, in the case of the Westfall procedure, correlations between test statistics (Westfall, 1997). Methods for dealing with pairwise tests can be readily extended to deal with a set of contrasts, by setting up an appropriate contrast matrix (Hothorn *et al.*, 2008). However, these methods are unsuitable if the set of contrasts is not well defined (which is typically the case for *post hoc* testing).

A cautious approach to null hypothesis significance testing of a *post hoc* contrast is to use the *Scheffé F test*. This test controls the familywise error rate for all possible contrasts based on linear functions of means (which is an infinitely large set when there are more than two means).[6] The test statistic for $F_{Scheffé}$ is the usual $F_{contrast}$ obtained for the test of the contrast. What differs is that this is evaluated with respect to a critical value for an F statistic equal to $(J-1)F_{\alpha}$ and with $J-1$ and df_{error} degrees of freedom (in place of the usual critical value F_{α} with 1 and df_{error} degrees of freedom). This procedure is highly conservative, because the majority of the infinite contrasts being controlled for are probably both uninteresting and implausible (and would not have been seriously considered). Scheffé suggested testing such contrasts at $\alpha = .10$ (Howell, 2002).

A seemingly sensible alternative is to correct for the set of contrasts that were or might have been considered. This set is usually unknown but can sometimes be determined with some precision (e.g., for all contrasts of a single mean against the average of all others). If so, multiple testing can readily be controlled by powerful modified procedures as described above. The set of contrasts that might have been considered is the implicit number of contrasts implicated by performing the test (Rosenthal *et al.*, 2000). Rather than correcting the contrast, Rosenthal *et al.* propose reporting T_{ic}, an estimate of the tolerance of the test to implicit contrasts:

$$T_{ic} = \frac{\alpha_{contrast}}{p_{contrast}} \qquad \text{Equation 15.17}$$

This equation estimates the number of implicit contrasts required to render a statistically significant test non-significant (i.e., where $p_{contrast} < \alpha$) at the chosen significance threshold ($\alpha_{contrast}$). The calculation assumes an unmodified Bonferroni correction and is therefore rather conservative. Even so, small T_{ic} values (e.g., in the single digits) are likely to be far from compelling, whereas large T_{ic} (e.g., in the hundreds) provide some comfort that the observed pattern is supported by the data. To be persuasive this argument needs to be coupled with a plausible explanation of the pattern. For a large set of means it is nearly always possible to search for a contrast with a moderate to high T_{ic}. A plausible explanation of the pattern gives some protection against this kind of cherry picking, but may still be unconvincing unless replicated.

Example 15.4 For the lifespan depression data in Example 15.2, the G3 mean (for the 55–69-year-olds) is the lowest. A *post hoc* contrast to test the hypothesis that this mean is lower than the average of the other groups has coefficients $\{1, 1, -3, 1\}$. This contrast is statistically significant, $t_{714.9} = 4.48$, and explains about 74% of the variation in mean depression scores. Is it reasonable to conclude that this age group is the least depressed?

Assuming no *a priori* (e.g., theoretical) justification for the test, its vulnerability to implicit contrasts is revealing. The p value in this case is approximately 4.34×10^{-6}. The T_{ic} is therefore

$$\frac{\alpha_{contrast}}{p_{contrast}} \approx \frac{.05}{0.00000434} \approx 11523$$

It is safe to say that this contrast would be statistically significant even if many hundreds of alternatives were corrected for.

15.5 Contrasts of adjusted means in ANCOVA

ANCOVA provides estimates of group means adjusted for a covariate. It is quite possible to test contrasts among these adjusted means. However, the standard errors for comparisons between adjusted means depend on the covariates (see Kirk, 1995). Equation 13.34 explained how ANCOVA standard errors are adjusted for a pairwise comparison. This formula for the *SE* of a difference between adjusted means in Equation 13.34 is a special case of that for a contrast of *J* adjusted means:

$$\hat{\sigma}_{\hat{\mu}*} = \sqrt{MS_{error}\left(\sum_{j=1}^{J}\frac{w_j^2}{n_j} + \frac{\left(\sum_{j=1}^{J} w_j\hat{\mu}_{C_j}\right)^2}{SS_{residual(\text{cov})}}\right)} \qquad \text{Equation 15.18}$$

The term n_j is the sample size per level, w_j is its contrast weight and $\hat{\mu}_{C_j}$ is the mean of the covariate within each level. $SS_{residual(\text{cov})}$ is the residual sum of squares from ANOVA with the covariate as outcome, MS_{error} is taken from the ANCOVA output, and the contrast score is calculated by replacing the cell means with the adjusted means. It is possible to adjust *SE*s for more complex models, including additional covariates or interactions, but this is best done via regression software.

Example 15.5 With Equation 15.18 it is possible to recalculate the diagram data contrast in Example 15.1 to adjust for the influence of reading times (in the ANCOVA model with the logarithm of the reading times added as a covariate). The adjusted means for this model, taken from Example 13.7 are: 16.62 (T), 16.90 (P), 23.08 (F) and 29.20 (S). The present example will use the integer weights $\{-2, -2, 1, 3\}$. The contrast score for the adjusted means is therefore:

$$C = \sum_{j=1}^{J} w_j\hat{\mu}_j = (-2 \times 16.62) + (-2 \times 16.90) + (1 \times 23.08) + (3 \times 29.20) = 43.64$$

MS_{error} from the ANCOVA is 60.02 and $SS_{residual(cov)} = 6.4576$ (from an ANOVA with the covariate as the outcome). The adjusted *SE* is:

$$\sqrt{60.02\left(\frac{18}{10} + \frac{(-2 \times 6.405512 - 2 \times 6.435045 + 1 \times 6.148393 + 3 \times 5.980962)^2}{6.4576}\right)} = 11.47$$

The *t* statistic for the contrast is therefore:

$$t_{35} = \frac{C}{\hat{\sigma}_{\hat{\mu}*}} = \frac{43.64}{11.47} = 3.81$$

This contrast of adjusted means is statistically significant, $t_{35} = 3.81$, $p < 001$ and $r^2_{alerting}$ has increased from .98 to .99. This may not seem much, but it is a 50% decrease in the proportion of error between the group means (from 2% to 1%). The analysis of adjusted means strengthens the conclusions of the original ANOVA contrast. Using a *t* statistic for the contrast also means that the NHST could be replaced by a 95% CI, likelihood ratio or Bayes factor.

15.6 The role of contrasts in other statistical models

Although the concept of a contrast is fundamental to ANOVA and ANCOVA it generalizes to a number of other situations. One example is in meta-analysis where contrasts can be used to test for moderator effects.[7] Another, in relation to contingency tables, is briefly considered here.

15.6.1 Contrasts for contingency tables

Rosnow and Rosenthal (1996b) also describe an approximate method for constructing contrasts for $2 \times J$ contingency tables where $J > 2$. For these tables the usual χ^2 test will have multiple *df* and can be difficult to interpret. They propose using a normal approximation to the binomial to construct a contrast test using a z statistic. The first step is to obtain $\hat{P}_j$, the sample estimate of the proportion of 'successes' falling into each of the J columns. The variance of each of the J proportions is then given by the binomial distribution with n_j defined as the number of independent observations in each column of the contingency table (i.e., in each of the J categories collapsing across both rows):

$$\hat{\sigma}^2_{\hat{P}_j} = \frac{\hat{P}_j\left(1-\hat{P}_j\right)}{n_j} \qquad \text{Equation 15.19}$$

From the proportions and their variances the contrast test statistic is:

$$z_{contrast} = \frac{\sum_{j=1}^{J} \hat{P}_j w_j}{\sqrt{\sum_{j=1}^{J} \hat{\sigma}^2_{\hat{P}_j} w_j}} \qquad \text{Equation 15.20}$$

The w_j contrast weights are determined for a hypothesis by the usual methods for contrasts among means (e.g., from theory or polynomial functions). Being based on the binomial distribution, this approximation should be reasonably accurate for independent counts if N is not too small and P not too extreme.

Rosnow and Rosenthal (1996b) propose calculating a standardized measure of effect size based on ϕ equal to $z/\sqrt{N}$. Because $z^2 = \chi^2_1$ this could also be used to express the 'variance' explained by the contrast as a proportion of the omnibus statistic χ^2_{J-1} via the ratio $z^2_{contrast}/\chi^2_{J-1}$.

These approximate methods can work quite well, but sometimes break down (notably for sparse tables and small N). Regression methods developed for discrete outcomes, which also support contrasts, provide a more principled approach.

15.7 R code for Chapter 15

15.7.1 ANOVA contrasts (Example 15.1)

To calculate the contrast in example 15.1, the means of the four conditions and MS_{error} for the original ANOVA are required:

```
diag.data <- read.spss('diagram.sav', to.data.frame=TRUE)
with(diag.data, tapply(descript, group, mean))

anova(lm(descript ~ group, data = diag.data))$M[2]
ms.error <- anova(lm(descript ~ group, data = diag.data))$M[2]
```

Here MS_{error} is 67.78. To run the contrast it helps to specify the contrast coefficients in matrix form. It helps to give the contrast an obvious label such as 'contrast'.

```
cont <- matrix(c(-2,-2,1,3), 1, 4, dimnames=list('contrast', NULL))
```

The default contrasts for the `group` factor can be reported by the `contrasts()` function. This will normally reveal dummy-coded contrasts for the `group` factor. The beauty of setting up the contrasts via a matrix is that you can now run the contrast as part of a linear model. One way to do this is to reset the default contrasts for the factor and then run a linear model in the usual way.[8]

```
contrasts(diag.data$group)
contrasts(diag.data$group) <- t(cont)
contrasts(diag.data$group)

diag.cont <- lm(descript ~ group, diag.data)
summary(diag.cont)
```

The linear model output now includes as its first row (under coefficients) the contrast output with $t = 2.906$ and $p = .00623$. For the overall regression model to match the one-way ANOVA output any $J - 1$ orthogonal contrasts can be used. The remaining coefficients are for orthogonal contrasts that have no sensible interpretation. Cohen (1968) terms these 'nonsense' contrasts. The remaining contrasts only matter if you have specific hypotheses to test (so the nonsense contrasts can be safely ignored).

A more flexible way to obtain the contrasts is to set them up as linear functions of means for the `glht()` function of the `multcomp` package (Hothorn *et al.*, 2008). Doing it this way, it is convenient to refit the cell means ANOVA model.

```
diag.cmm <- lm(descript ~ 0 + group, diag.data)

library(multcomp)
summary(glht(diag.cmm, linfct=cont), test=adjusted('none'))
```

This method allows you to just fit the contrast you want (with no nonsense contrasts) and to change run contrasts for other models (such as factorial ANOVA or ANCOVA). It even allows you to specify more than one contrast and incorporate a correction for multiple testing such as the Shaffer or Westfall procedure. The main practical limitation is being able to define the correct contrast weights in matrix form when a model has many parameters.

Calculation of the CI for the contrast in the linear model will be influenced by the nonsense contrasts. So if you are interested in a 95% CI on the same scale as the mean you can mimic the hand calculations in Example 15.1.

```
alpha <- .05
means <- c(17.8, 18.3, 22.4, 27.3)
new.cont <- cont/4
c.score <- sum(means * new.cont)
se.cont <- (ms.error * (sum(new.cont^2)/10))^0.5
moe <- qt(1-alpha/2, 36) * se.cont
c(c.score - moe, c.score + moe)
```

This gives the same 95% CI of [2.42, 13.63]. A neat trick is to rescale the integer weights for the contrast within `glht()`. Thus the same CI is obtained from:

```
confint(glht(diag.cmm, linfct=cont/4))
```

The `glht()` function also provides a way to test an interaction contrast. First, fit a one-way ANOVA with levels defined by the cell means of the factorial ANOVA in which the interaction is found. For instance, a 2×3 ANOVA would have $2 \times 3 = 6$ levels. The grouping factor can be set up manually or using `gl()` for a balanced design. For instance, imagine that the diagram data had an extra grouping factor with two levels (for a 2×4 ANOVA design). This could be fitted as:

```
g2 <- gl(2,5,40)
anova(lm(descript ~ group*g2, diag.data))
```

Note that the MS_{error} in this ANOVA is 62.35. Now fit a restructured one-way ANOVA with $2 \times 4 =$ 8 levels as a cell means model:

```
int.groups <- gl(8, 5)
diag.restruc <- lm(descript ~ 0 + int.groups, diag.data)
anova(diag.restruc)
```

This has the same MS_{error} because the same cell means are fitted in each case (and because the design has independent measures). Now `glht()` can fit an interaction contrast with the restructured model. Here the example is for differential linear trends (Abelson and Prentice, 1997), rescaled appropriately for the subsequent CI:

```
contr.int <- matrix(,1, 8)
contr.int[1,] <- c(-3, 3, -1, 1, 1, -1, 3, -3)/8

summary(glht(diag.restruc, linfct=contr.int),
  test=adjusted('none'))
confint(glht(diag.restruc, linfct=contr.int))
```

This method of restructuring is a bit clumsy (but worth illustrating because the solution is easy to adapt for any software that can run a contrast for a one-way ANOVA model). A more elegant approach involves fitting a cell means model for the two-way ANOVA. This can make the contrast easier to set up and avoids creating a new factor. The cell means model for a two-way design removes the intercept and has the appearance of fitting a model with the interaction effect on its own:

```
diag2.cmm <- lm(descript ~ 0 + group:g2, diag.data)
summary(diag2.cmm)
```

This fits the same model (e.g., the error term is identical) but tests of individual effects are different. The reason why it is OK to drop the main effects is that in the cell means model the main effects and interaction term are normally estimated as contrasts or sets of contrasts that decompose the overall model (and can be 'put back in' if required – perhaps through the `glht()` function). Here they are not required. The goal is simply to obtain the interaction contrast:

```
ic.wts <- c(-3, -1, 1, 3, 3, 1, -1, -3)
contr.int <- matrix(ic.wts, 1, 8)/8

summary(glht(diag2.cmm, linfct=contr.int),
  test=adjusted('none'))

confint(glht(diag2.cmm, linfct=contr.int))
```

The contrast weights are reordered here, because the cell means model orders the effects differently from the previous model. Regardless of what approach you take, making sure that the contrast weights fit your hypothesis is probably the most important step. You can check the names and order of coefficients by requesting their names:

```
names(coef(diag.restruc))
names(coef(diag2.cmm))
```

The `glht()` function is not the only one that could be used here. Its big advantage is being able to incorporate powerful multiple comparison procedures.

15.7.2 Polynomial contrasts (Example 15.2)

Polynomial contrasts are the default contrasts for ordered factors in R. With access to raw data, running the contrasts involves creating an ordered factor. A quick way is to use the generate factor levels function `gl()`. The default is an unordered factor, but is easily altered. The following code creates an ordered factor for the diagram data set (with four groups of $n = 10$) and then runs a linear model.

```
group.ord <- gl(4, 10, ordered=TRUE)
diag.lin <- lm(descript ~ group.ord, diag.data)
```

The ANOVA table for this model is identical to that for dummy coding or effect coded contrasts (though dummy codes are not true contrasts because they don't sum to zero). In this case the polynomial contrasts don't have a clear interpretation because the groups are only loosely ordered (though the linear contrast could be interpreted as an approximate test of the research predictions). Polynomial contrasts that are not meaningful are nonsense contrasts in the sense described by Cohen (1968). The summary of the individual effects reports tests of the linear, quadratic and cubic contrasts (there being only $J-1=3$ *df* for the main effect).

```
anova(diag.lin)
summary(diag.lin)
```

Even without raw data, it is possible to calculate the linear and quadratic contrasts with relative ease. The mean, *SD* and sample size of each group is required. Here the data are from the lifespan depression data in Example 15.2.

```
g.means <- c(10.85, 10.36, 8.63, 12.11)
g.n <- c(548, 218, 352, 212)
g.sd <- c(9.03, 10.19, 8.31, 8.73)
```

As the group sizes and variances are unequal, a Welch-Satterthwaite correction is adopted:

```
lin.cont <- c(-3,-1,1,3)
c.lin <- sum(lin.cont * g.means)
se.lin <- sum((lin.cont^2 * g.sd^2)/g.n)^0.5
t.lin <- c.lin/se.lin ; t.lin
```

The quadratic and cubic contrasts use the same method, though only the quadratic contrast is shown here:

```
quad.cont <- c(1,-1,-1,1)
c.quad <- sum(quad.cont * g.means)
se.quad <- sum((quad.cont^2 * g.sd^2)/g.n)^0.5
t.quad <- c.quad/se.quad ; t.quad
```

The hardest part is to obtain ν' (the corrected *df*). A relatively painless method is to write a function to do the calculations:

```
nu.prime <- function(means, sds, ns, weights = 1) {
    sum(weights^2 * sds^2/ns)^2/sum((weights^4 * sds^4)/(ns^2
         * (ns - 1)))
}
```

For a simple Welch-Satterthwaite t test and for some contrasts (e.g., the quadratic contrast when $J=4$) the squared weights all equal to one, and the function defaults to a constant weight equal to one. So ν' for the linear and quadratic contrast can respectively be calculated with the following commands:

```
nu.prime(g.means, g.sd, g.n, lin.cont)
nu.prime(g.means, g.sd, g.n)
```

The explanatory power of each contrast is assessed by $r^2_{alerting}$.

```
r2a.lin <- cor(lin.cont, g.means)^2
r2a.quad <- cor(quad.cont, g.means)^2
c(r2a.lin, r2a.quad)
```

Calculating contrasts from summary statistics like this is a good way to perform supplementary analyses for published data.

15.7.3 Difference contrasts (Example 15.3)

A difference contrast expresses the difference between two other contrasts. Difference contrasts are awkward to calculate because the variance of the contrast weights will influence a contrast's ability to explain patterns among means. Correcting for the difference in variance of the contrast weights often results in rounding errors. For this reason we would write a function to calculate the weights of the difference contrast:

```
wts.diff <- function(weights.A, weights.B, rescale = FALSE) {
    sd.A <- (sum(weights.A^2)/length(weights.A))^0.5
    sd.B <- (sum(wights.B^2)/length(weights.B))^0.5
    contrast.weights <- weights.A/sd.A - weights.B/sd.B
    if (rescale == TRUE)
          contrast.weights <- 2/sum(abs(contrast.weights)) *
               contrast.weights
    contrast.weights
}
```

Now enter the weights as vectors and call the function:

```
wts.A <- c(-3, -1, 1, 3)
wts.B <- c(-4, -1, -1, 6)
wts.diff(wts.A, wts.B)
```

The difference contrast for the diagram data can therefore be obtained from the following code:

```
wts.A <- c(-2, -2, 1, 3)
wts.B <- c(-1, -1, 1, 1)
wts.diff(wts.A,wts.B)

c.diag <- matrix(wts.diff(wts.A, wts.B), 1, 4,
  dimnames=list('d contrast', NULL))

library(multcomp)
summary(glht(diag.cmm, linfct=c.diag), test=adjusted('none'))
```

The first contrast is the difference contrast and has a t statistic of 0.87, equivalent to $F = 0.87^2 \approx 0.76$. The `wts.diff()` function also rescales the weights to have an absolute sum of two if you set the argument `rescale=TRUE`. This is useful for CIs on the original scale of the means:

```
c.diag <- matrix(wts.diff(wts.A, wts.B, rescale=TRUE), 1, 4,
  dimnames=list('d contrast', NULL))

confint(glht(diag.cmm, linfct=c.diag))
```

15.7.4 Tolerance to implicit contrasts (Example 15.4)

Returning to the lifespan depression data, it is possible to construct a *post hoc* contrast using the coefficients $\{1, 1, -3, 1\}$. This is not prompted by a specific theory, but by the observed pattern of means. The contrast itself is calculated using the Welch-Satterthwaite correction.

```
ph.cont <- c(1,1,-3,1)
c.ph <- sum(ph.cont * g.means)
se.ph <- sum((ph.cont^2 * g.sd^2)/g.n)^0.5
t.ph <- c.ph/se.ph ; t.ph
```

The explanatory power of the test is from the squared correlation between contrast weights and means:

```
cor(ph.cont, g.means)^2
```

To calculate the tolerance to implicit contrasts it is necessary to know the precise p value (and therefore ν').

```
df.ph <- nu.prime(g.means, g.sd, g.n, ph.cont)
df.ph
p.ph <- pt(t.ph, df.ph, lower.tail = FALSE)
p.ph
T.ic <- .05/p.ph
T.ic
```

Out of interest, the conservative $F_{\text{Scheffé}}$ test is also statistically significant. The F ratio of the contrast being larger than the critical value:

```
F.ph <- t.ph^2
F.ph

J <- 4
alpha <- .05
Fsheffe.crit <- (J-1)*qf(alpha,J-1,df.ph, lower.tail=FALSE)
Fsheffe.crit
```

The huge sample size compensates for the conservatism of $F_{\text{Scheffé}}$.

15.7.5 ANCOVA contrasts (Example 15.5)

It is possible to obtain a t and p value for a contrast of adjusted means in several ways. The most versatile (and one of the easiest) is to set up a cell means model for the ANCOVA with centered covariates and use `glht()` from `multcomp`. The covariates also need to be included in the contrast matrix (but should be set to zero).

```
C1 <- matrix(c(-2,-2,1,3,0), 1, 5, dimnames=list('C1', NULL))

diag.ancov.cmm <- lm(descript ~ 0 + group + scale(log(time),
  scale=F), diag.data)
summary(diag.ancov.cmm)
library(multcomp)
summary(glht(diag.ancov.cmm, linfct=C1),
  test=adjusted('none'))
```

To calculate a 95% CI of the weighted means you could use the more long-winded method in Example 15.5.

```
adj.means <- c(16.618, 16.903, 23.082, 29.197)
MS.e <- 60.02
n <- 10
ltime.means <- c(6.405512, 6.435045 ,6.148393, 5.980962)
SS <- 6.4576
cont <- c(-.5, -.5, .25, .75)
c.score <- sum(cont * adj.means)
contr.se <- (MS.e * (sum(cont^2)/10 + sum(ltime.means *
  cont)^2/SS))^0.5
moe <- qt(.025,35, lower.tail = FALSE) * contr.se
c(c.score-moe, c.score+moe)
```

A far simpler route uses the `glht()` function, rescaling the contrast weights first. Their absolute value sums to eight so dividing the contrast weights by four will work:

```
confint(glht(diag.ancov.cmm, linfct=C1/4))
```

15.7.6 R packages

Hothorn, T., Bretz, F., and Westfall. P. (2008) Simultaneous Inference in General Parametric Models. *Biometrical Journal, 50*, 346–63.

15.8 Notes on SPSS syntax for Chapter 15

15.8.1 Contrasts in SPSS (Examples 15.1 and 15.5)

SPSS can run many forms of contrasts, but a full range of contrasts is available only via syntax, and it can be difficult to set out the syntax correctly. Field (2009) includes supplementary material that describes how to set up SPSS contrasts via syntax in greater detail than the brief notes provided here. For contrasts in one-way ANOVA, the ONEWAY command can be accessed via menus or syntax.

SPSS data file: `diagram.sav`

```
ONEWAY descript BY group
  /CONTRAST= -2 -2 1 3.
```

The default output also includes a Welch-Satterthwaite corrected t statistic. Rescaling the contrast weights gives a contrast score on the original scale:

```
ONEWAY descript BY group
  /CONTRAST= -0.5 -0.5 0.25 0.75.
```

The same command also runs polynomial contrasts. Here the syntax specifies that the order is three and so linear, quadratic and cubic contrasts are fitted:

```
ONEWAY descript BY group
  /POLYNOMIAL=3.
```

The contrast can also be run via UNIANOVA, but only via syntax (not from menus). The main advantage of this approach is that it also gives the 95% CI (but not Welch-Satterthwaite correction). It can be extended to ANCOVA or factorial models without too much additional work. This is the syntax for a one-way ANOVA contrast:

```
UNIANOVA descript BY group
/METHOD=SSTYPE(2)
/CONTRAST (group)=SPECIAL(-0.5 -0.5 0.25 0.75).
```

A polynomial contrast would be:

```
UNIANOVA descript BY group
    /METHOD=SSTYPE(2)
    /CONTRAST(group)=Polynomial.
```

To run the ANCOVA contrast:

```
COMPUTE ln_time=ln(time).
EXECUTE.

UNIANOVA descript BY group WITH ln_time
/METHOD=SSTYPE(2)
/CONTRAST (group)=SPECIAL(-0.5 -0.5 0.25 0.75).
```

The /LMEANS subcommand also allows you to specify an interaction contrast. This can be difficult to set up, but the following syntax would run a contrast of differential linear trends in a 2×3 ANOVA (with three levels on factor *B*).

```
UNIANOVA DV BY A B
/METHOD=SSTYPE(2)
/LMATRIX A*B
-1 0 1
1 0 -1.
```

The contrast weights do not need to be spread over two lines (though it makes it easier to check the weights). The first line is for levels of B within A_1 and the second line for B within A_2. Had the order of the factors been switched, the subcommand would have to be restructured (e.g., with two levels of A over three lines).

```
/LMATRIX A*B
-1 1
0 0
1 -1.
```

It can be hard to work out the correct way to code a contrast in SPSS, but there is a way to simplify the process. This is to fit a cell means model for the interaction (i.e., an interaction-only model with no intercept). This forces SPSS to interpret the contrast coefficients in terms of the cell means, and allows you to set any combination of cell weights for the contrast, provided they sum to zero. For instance, the following contrast compares two cell means (but simple main effects or interaction contrasts could, in theory, be set up this way):

```
GLM DV BY A B
  /METHOD=SSTYPE(2)
  /INTERCEPT=EXCLUDE
  /LMATRIX A*B
    1 0
    0 0
    0 -1
/DESIGN=A*B.
```

15.9 Bibliography and further reading

Abelson, R. P., and Prentice, D. A. (1997) Contrast Tests of Interaction Hypotheses. *Psychological Methods*, 2, 315–28.

Kirk, R. E. (1995) *Experimental Design* (3rd edn) Belmont, CA: Brooks/Cole.

Rosenthal, R., Rosnow, R. L., and Rubin, D. B. (2000) *Contrasts and Correlations in Behavioral Research*. New York: Cambridge University Press.

16

Repeated measures ANOVA

Contents

16.1 Chapter overview

This chapter introduces repeated measures and mixed measures ANOVA as methods for dealing with correlated measures arising from paired, repeated or matched designs. Advantages and disadvantages of repeated measures models are considered, with focus on the increased statistical power arising when individual differences are prevalent, and on the assumptions of sphericity and multisample sphericity. Later sections provide a brief overview of several related models including MANOVA, repeated measures ANCOVA and analysis of gain scores.

16.2 Modeling correlated or repeated measures

A typical least squares regression model assumes measures are independent. For measures to be independent, each observation in the analysis should carry no information about the value of any other observation. Specifically, it will provide no additional information over and above that already accounted for by the structure of the model (e.g., factor or covariate values). If people are measured only once and randomly allocated to the conditions of an experiment this assumption is likely to be reasonable.[1] It is often plausible even if random assignment is not possible. On the other hand, if people are measured more than once, the responses for a given person are almost certainly correlated. This gives rise to what is termed a 'repeated measures' or 'within-subjects' design.

Correlated measures can also arise by design or because of the way the world is structured (e.g., if people are tested in pairs, or participants sampled from pre-existing groups). For field research with human participants, this kind of clustering is probably the norm rather than the exception. People have a tendency to create and associate within groups in many aspects of their lives: families, classrooms, schools or teams being good examples.

Correlated measures have historically been regarded as nuisance variables to be eliminated or controlled by careful experimental design (not least because independent measures are easier to work with). Correlated measures can also be viewed as an asset. A repeated measures or matched design might be selected because the resulting model has greater statistical power or precision. It is also increasingly common, as statistical models for correlated measures have become more sophisticated, that the clusters or correlated measures themselves are a focus of research. A researcher may be interested in the performance of individual children in a school, but they may also be interested in the performance of different schools. The main focus of this chapter is on ANOVA models with repeated measures on one or more factors. Multilevel regression models (that attempt to model the clustered structure of the data directly) are considered in a subsequent chapter.

16.3 ANOVA with repeated measures

Correlated measures present an obvious problem for a least squares regression model that assumes residuals are sampled from an independent, normal population of errors. In the simplest repeated measures models there are only two measurement points: the familiar paired design. By using the difference between pairs as the outcome Y it is possible to treat the differences as independent observations (e.g., in a one sample t test). This won't work if there more than two levels on a factor or for a factorial design, but a similarly creative solution is feasible.

In a one-way independent measures design, the ANOVA parameterization of the model (with the usual sum-to-zero constraint for τ_j) is:

$$y_{ij} = \mu + \tau_j + \varepsilon_{ij}$$

What if you represent the deviations of each participant from the grand mean in a similar way? This gives a repeated measures model of the form:

$$y_{ij} = \mu + \pi_i + \tau_j + \varepsilon_{ij} \qquad \text{Equation 16.1}$$

In this model both τ_j and π_i must each sum to zero. Figure 16.1 shows the deviations of participant and level means for a trivial repeated measures ANOVA model with three levels and only two participants. The π_i term represents the deviation of each person's own mean (over all J levels of the factor) from the grand mean (after stripping out the average effect of the factor τ).

At first glance this looks almost exactly like a two-way independent measures ANOVA model incorporating only main effects (and no interaction). An important difference is that whereas the treatment τ is a fixed factor, π is a random factor.[2,3] Participants are viewed as randomly sampled from an infinite population, whereas the levels of the treatment are considered completely representative of the population of interest. The variance accounted for by the π_i term is due to systematic differences between participants: individual differences in Y (often termed *within-subject variance*). The shared subscript i of the participant and error variance indicates what is happening. In one-way independent measures ANOVA the variance not captured by

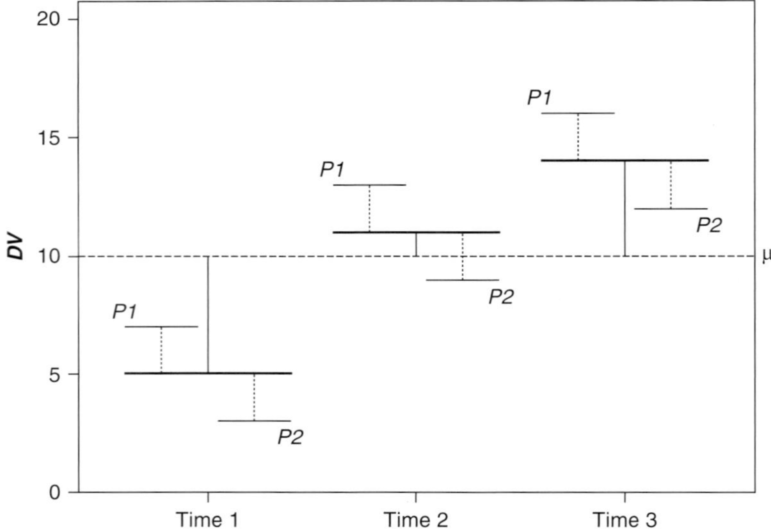

Figure 16.1 Deviations from the grand mean for a one-way repeated measures ANOVA, with three time points and two participants

the factor is subsumed within the ε_i term, whereas in the repeated measures design it is split between ε_i and π_i.

This model is implausible because it assumes that the effect of individual differences is exactly identical for all levels of the treatment. The model can be improved by permitting individual differences to vary across levels of τ. Allowing individual differences to vary in this way requires adding an interaction term:

$$y_{ij} = \mu + \pi_i + \tau_j + \tau\pi_{ij} + \varepsilon_{ij} \qquad \text{Equation 16.2}$$

This type of model is the one implemented in repeated measures ANOVA analysis, and if a subject-by-treatment interaction is present it will, in theory, produce more accurate tests of the factor (see Howell, 2002).[4]

Estimating this model in a repeated measures design is challenging because a typical application has exactly one measurement per participant in each combination of the levels of the fixed factor.[5] With only one observation per cell for the $\pi \times \tau$ interaction, the ε_i and $\tau\pi_{ij}$ terms cannot be estimated separately (and are said to be completely 'aliased'). This is not a problem for the test of the fixed factor (because its error term is formed from estimates of both ε_i and $\tau\pi_{ij}$ terms). Problems do arise for the test of the π_i subject term. Although a large *F* ratio provides evidence of systematic individual differences, a small *F* ratio is ambiguous (Kirk, 1995; Howell, 2002). It could occur because π_i is small relative to ε_i or because $\tau\pi_{ij}$ is large relative to π_i (e.g., if $\pi_i \approx \tau\pi_{ij}$).

It is possible to test whether the additive or non-additive interaction model is appropriate (see Kirk, 1995), but the choice of model ought to be decided *a priori* (Howell, 2002). The assumption of zero subject-by-treatment interaction is probably unjustified in research with human participants. To understand why, imagine a memory experiment comparing recall of own-race and other-race faces. If the subject by face interaction term were excluded from the model, this would be equivalent to assuming that individual differences in memory for faces are unaffected by the race of the face. This is highly implausible (e.g., it is contradicted by research that suggests lifetime exposure to other-race face influences ability to remember them). It is hard to come up with examples where one would be confident that individual differences are constant over all levels of a fixed factor unless individual differences or factor effects are themselves negligible. If $\tau\pi_{ij}$ is zero there will be no appreciable loss of power through adopting the non-additive model. What about the test of individual differences? The mere fact that you have decided to adopt a repeated measures model implies that you believe *a priori* that individual differences are present. A null hypothesis significance test (NHST) – particularly one with low statistical power – should not reverse that belief. Therefore a test of the π_i subject effect is only rarely of interest to researchers (and rarely reported or interpreted).

16.3.1 Advantages of repeated measures designs

A repeated measures design has one principal advantage over an independent measures design. In situations where both designs are feasible, it produces more accurate estimates of the fixed factor *F* ratio. This follows from the way in which the error term is constructed (and the logic of expected mean squares explained in Box 16.1). The error term in an independent measures design is influenced by at least two different sources of variation in the population.

These are experimental error and systematic between-subject variation (i.e., individual differences):

$$\sigma_E^2 = \sigma_{error}^2 + \sigma_{subjects}^2 \qquad \text{Equation 16.3}$$

In a repeated measures design, the individual differences can be separated out from the error term to get a purer estimate of error (i.e., $\hat{\sigma}_E^2 = \hat{\sigma}_{error}^2$). This is possible because multiple observations for each person allow $\sigma_{subjects}^2$ to be estimated from the variation between them. Having one observation per person per level of a factor (the state of affairs in an independent measures design) makes it impossible to untangle systematic individual differences from other sources of error. You can't tell if someone has scored high through chance or because their true score in the population is high.

There may be other advantages to repeated measures designs. One is practical: fewer participants need to be recruited to a study to obtain N data points. This is sometimes helpful if participants are scarce or difficult to recruit (because it allows a researcher to maximize the value of each participant's contribution). A further advantage of the repeated measures model is that the same equations also apply to matched or stratified designs. The calculations do not require that the same person be measured several times, just that observations are correlated with a particular structure. Equivalent correlations between measures arise for observations matched at the individual level (e.g., if each person is matched with a similar person in one or more comparisons on control conditions).

The main difference between matched and repeated measures designs is in their interpretation. A repeated measures design (assuming random or otherwise representative sampling) generalizes to all members of the population sampled, while a matched design generalizes only to the population of matched sets of individuals (Kirk, 1995). The matched design and repeated measures design thus reach similar conclusions only to the extent that matching is representative of the wider population. The difficulty of finding matches for some people might introduce bias into the sampling. Kirk also discusses the relative merits of matching (stratification) and ANCOVA for increasing statistical power. ANOVA with matched observations tends to be superior for low correlations between the confounding variable and the response, while ANCOVA is superior for high correlations. In practice, the difficulty of obtaining good matches makes ANCOVA more popular. In addition, ANCOVA usually assumes a linear effect of the covariate. Matching is a better strategy if the effect is curvilinear (Maris, 1998).

These characteristics imply certain disadvantages of repeated measures designs. The principal disadvantage is that, because measurements are typically spread over time, they may be influenced by the order in which they are obtained. If the order of measurement is controlled (e.g., by randomization or by counterbalancing) order effects can be reduced and perhaps eliminated, though this is only possible if the fixed factors can be manipulated by the experimenter. If order effects are controlled the study is a true experiment. Randomizing or counterbalancing the order of repeated measurements is essential if you want to infer that an experimental manipulation is causing differences in the outcome.

Order effects come in many different flavors (e.g., practice effects, fatigue effects or carry-over effects) and are a particularly dangerous source of confounding. If the experimenter is not able to control the order of measurement it may be possible to reduce the influence of order effects (e.g., building in breaks to reduce fatigue effects) but not eliminate them. These additional controls are also useful for counterbalanced or randomized orders of testing because they should reduce error variance. It is also useful to model order of testing as a factor or covariate. This strategy may increase statistical power in the same way that a covariate can in ANCOVA.

A final disadvantage of repeated measures designs is the increased complexity of the analysis and the assumptions of the model. Repeated measures ANOVA models can be inflexible. Analysis of an unbalanced design (in which some repeated measures are missing) is a good illustration. Multiple imputation provides a potential solution, if data are missing at random (MAR) or missing completely at random (MCAR).[6] A more flexible alternative for missing outcome data (one that overcomes these and other ANOVA limitations) is to use a multilevel model.

Box 16.1 Expected mean squares in one-way ANOVA

The smaller error term for a repeated measures design leads to tests with greater statistical power. Consider a pair of one-way designs with exactly the same sampling strategy and experimental manipulations: one with an independent measures design and one with a repeated measures design. All other things being equal, the test of the treatment (fixed factor) in each experiment would address the same null hypothesis: H_0: $\mu_1 = \mu_2 = \ldots = \mu_j$ (i.e., $\sigma^2_{factor} = 0$). The F ratio for the independent measures design is an estimate of the following ratio in the population:

$$F_{independent} = \frac{\sigma^2_{factor} + \sigma^2_{error} + \sigma^2_{subjects}}{\sigma^2_{error} + \sigma^2_{subjects}}$$

The true population variance associated with systematic differences between levels of the fixed factor σ^2_{factor}, systematic individual differences $\sigma^2_{subjects}$, and experimental error σ^2_{error} will be unknown, but imagine that they are 15, 10 and 5 respectively. The expected value of the F ratio for the values stated earlier will be:

$$E\left(F_{independent}\right) = \frac{15+10+5}{10+5} = \frac{30}{15} = 2$$

Doing the same arithmetic for the repeated measures design gives:

$$E\left(F_{repeated}\right) = \frac{\sigma^2_{factor} + \sigma^2_{error}}{\sigma^2_{error}} = \frac{15+5}{5} = \frac{20}{5} = 4$$

This illustrates why a repeated measures design has greater statistical power, and results in a more sensitive test of H_0.

A crucial feature of the expected F ratio is that, regardless of the design, $F = 1$ if the population effect of the fixed factor is zero. The numerator and denominator of the statistics are identical when $\sigma^2_{factor} = 0$. The increased power of the repeated measures therefore depends on the presence of systematic individual differences between the participants. The larger the population variance attributable to individual differences, the more sensitive the repeated measures design is (relative to an independent measures design). As the increased sensitivity to the effects of the factor is a consequence of the way that error variance is estimated, the statistical power advantage also applies to any inferential tool where the precision of estimation and hence estimation of error variance is fundamental (e.g., confidence intervals, as well as likelihood and Bayesian inference).

Up to this point, a number of technical points about expected F ratios have been glossed over (Howell, 2002; Kirk, 1995). A more detailed presentation of expected mean squares for one-way independent measures ANOVA takes the form:

$$E(MS_{factor}) = \sigma_\varepsilon^2 + n\sigma_\tau^2$$
$$E(MS_{error}) = \sigma_\varepsilon^2$$

Greek letter subscripts are used to differentiate these quantities from the 'rough and ready' versions used earlier. An expected mean square is a long-run average (as if calculated over many samples). The constant n is the sample size per group (assuming a balanced design) and reflects the increase in observed treatment variance expected when larger samples are taken. The expected value of the F ratio thus depends on σ_τ^2 (the treatment variance, accounted for by a factor in the population). This expectation is one if $\sigma_\tau^2 = 0$ and greater than one if $\sigma_\tau^2 > 0$.

The expected mean squares for one-way repeated measures ANOVA depend on the presence of subject-by-treatment interactions. As the complete absence of subject-by-treatment variance is somewhat implausible, it is usual to adopt a structural model with interactions included. The mean squares for this structural model are:

$$E(MS_{subjects}) = \sigma_\varepsilon^2 + k\sigma_\pi^2$$
$$E(MS_{factor}) = \sigma_\varepsilon^2 + n\sigma_\tau^2 + \sigma_{\tau\pi}^2$$
$$E(MS_{error}) = \sigma_\varepsilon^2 + \sigma_{\tau\pi}^2$$

This leads to an F ratio for the factor that uses MS_{error} as the denominator (so that, on average, the $\sigma_{\tau\pi}^2$ terms cancel out). The F ratio for the subjects in this structural model is:

$$E(F_{subjects}) = \frac{\sigma_\varepsilon^2 + k\sigma_\pi^2}{\sigma_\varepsilon^2 + \sigma_{\tau\pi}^2}$$

This quantity is biased and can't be relied on as a test of systematic individual differences (at least if $\sigma_{\tau\pi}^2$ is not zero). In factorial repeated measures ANOVA, assuming that subject-by-treatment interactions are present leads to the aliasing of the error term with subject-by-treatment interactions. For this reason it is not wise to pool the error terms in factorial repeated measures designs. However, by using the treatment-by-subject interaction terms as error terms for treatment effects it is possible to construct true F ratios with an expected value of one when H_0 is true (Howell, 2002; Kirk, 1995).

16.3.2 ANOVA with repeated measures on all factors

The calculations for repeated measures ANOVA can be conducted using a similar approach to that of independent measures ANOVA. Hand calculation typically involves setting out *SS*, *df*, *MS* and *F* in an ANOVA table, though most computer software employs a general linear model solution. The standard sigma-restricted ANOVA parameterization treats the participants like an effect coded categorical predictor (using $n - 1$ indicator variables to code the n participants). Rutherford (2001) illustrates this by demonstrating how to run repeated measures ANOVA as a multiple regression with effect coding.

Table 16.1 One-way ANOVA with repeated measures

Source	df	SS	MS	F
Subjects	$n-1$	$SS_{subjects}$		
Factor A	$a-1$	SS_A	$\frac{SS_A}{df_A}$	$\frac{MS_A}{MS_{A\times subjects}}$
Error (A × subjects)	$(n-1)(a-1)$	$SS_{A\times subjects}$	$\frac{SS_{A\times subjects}}{df_{A\times subjects}}$	
Total	$N-1$			

One-way repeated measures ANOVA can be set out in a single table as illustrated in Table 16.1. In some software packages, the between-subjects and within-subjects components are split across separate tables. The *MS* and *F* ratio for the subjects is not included in Table 16.1. These can be derived in the usual manner if required (though the *F* ratio is not a pure measure of the ratio of effect variance to error variance).

The one-way table may be extended to incorporate additional factors. The extension to a two-way table is shown in Table 16.2. Several properties need to be emphasized. While the one-way design has only a single error term, the two-way design (and more generally any *k*-way design) has one error term for each fixed effect being estimated (i.e., for all effects other than the subjects and by-subjects interactions).

The logic for this is identical to that for use of A × subjects as the error term in a one-way design. With only one observation per cell, the residual term and by-subjects interaction terms are aliased. In addition, there is no longer an obvious route for testing the effect of subjects

Table 16.2 Two-way ANOVA with repeated measures

Source	df	SS	MS	F
Subjects	$n-1$	$SS_{subjects}$		
Factor A	$a-1$	SS_A	$\frac{SS_A}{df_A}$	$\frac{MS_A}{MS_{A\times subjects}}$
Error (A × subjects)	$(n-1)(a-1)$	$SS_{A\times subjects}$	$\frac{SS_{A\times subjects}}{df_{A\times subjects}}$	
Factor B	$b-1$	SS_B	$\frac{SS_B}{df_B}$	$\frac{MS_B}{MS_{B\times subjects}}$
Error (B × subjects)	$(n-1)(b-1)$	$SS_{B\times subjects}$	$\frac{SS_{B\times subjects}}{df_{B\times subjects}}$	
A × B	$(a-1)(b-1)$	$SS_{A\times B}$	$\frac{SS_{A\times B}}{df_{A\times B}}$	$\frac{MS_{A\times B}}{MS_{A\times B\times subjects}}$
Error (A × B × subjects)	$(n-1)(a-1)(b-1)$	$SS_{A\times B\times subjects}$	$\frac{SS_{A\times B\times subjects}}{df_{A\times B\times subjects}}$	
Total	$N-1$			

(though you would not, in general, want to). In spite of these differences, the basic interpretation of the test of the main effects of A and B, or of the A × B interaction, are unchanged from a two-way independent measures design. The familiar tools of inspecting the level means and cell means or inspecting interaction plots can all be employed.

Formulas for *SS* and *MS* of both random and fixed effects factors are identical for the independent and repeated measures models. The main effects calculations use the level or participant means (as appropriate) after averaging over the other factors. Calculating the interaction *SS* or *MS* might seem difficult, but in a balanced design (which is common for repeated measures) this is simply done by calculating the cell means for a two-way table for A × B, A × subjects or B × subjects. Armed with the *SS* for A, B and subjects it is possible to calculate each interaction *SS* by subtraction from total *SS* for the two-way table (or from the residuals of the double-centered table just as for the interaction in a two-way independent measures design). The A × B × subjects interaction can in turn be calculated by subtraction from SS_{total} for the analysis.

16.3.3 Assumptions in repeated measures ANOVA

Repeated measures ANOVA is a form of general linear model and inherits those assumptions common to all least squares designs. However, having correlated measures violates one of the standard ANOVA assumptions (independence of observations). As repeated measures are correlated, it is necessary to fall back on the pure regression form of the assumption: that residuals are sampled from an independent, normal population of errors with constant variance.

A new complication is that the distribution of residuals – in particular its variance – depends both on the variances of the repeated measurements and the covariances between them. Stripping out the subjects and by-subjects variation does not necessarily guarantee independence and homogeneity of variance of the residuals (Kirk, 1995). Only under a restrictive condition known as *sphericity* will the patterns of variance and covariances between repeated measures meet the standard regression or general linear model assumptions.

For repeated measures, the specific distributional assumptions of the ANOVA model can therefore be set out as:

i) *correlated measures,*
ii) *normal distribution of errors* and
iii) *sphericity.*

The correlated measures assumption is justified *a priori* where matched or repeated measurements are employed. Unless there is a compelling argument that the correlation between these measures is exactly zero, a repeated measures model is required. Researchers are occasionally tempted to test the correlations for significance before using a repeated measures analysis for repeated or matched measurements. This is dangerous, and it is possible to show (e.g., via simulation) that correlations too small to be detected by a preliminary test can nevertheless have a material impact on the analysis.

The normal distribution of error assumption is identical to that for independent measures designs or for multiple regression. The residuals (of which there are several for each individual being measured) are assumed to have been sampled from a normal population of errors. While this assumption is identical to that for independent measures designs, it is important to note that plotting the outcome Y by condition will no longer be an adequate procedure for checking the assumption. In independent measures ANOVA the outcome is merely a constant (the cell mean) plus the residual; residuals and Y therefore always show the same pattern within each group. In a repeated measures model this is no longer the case. In a one-way design, the outcome Y is a function of π, τ and ε. The distribution of Y for a given value of τ_j could be completely different from the distribution of ε. Although τ_j is constant within a group, π_j will vary. The outcome Y is therefore a joint function of both π and ε (i.e., the distribution of outcome depends on both individual differences and error).

The third assumption listed, that of sphericity, is the hardest to explain. It is considered in more detail in the next section. It can be summarized as entailing that the variances of the differences between pairs of repeated measures are equal. As with other distributional assumptions, it applies to the populations being sampled. Owing to sampling error, the assumption will rarely be met perfectly in a sample, whether or not it is true in the population (except where there are only two samples – as in a paired or matched pairs design).

16.3.4 Sphericity

Paired data provide a simple case in which to introduce the concept of sphericity. For a one-way repeated measures ANOVA design with two levels – equivalent to a paired t test – the population covariance matrix (see Key Concept 12.2) of the repeated measurements has this structure:

$$\begin{bmatrix} \sigma_1^2 & \sigma_{1,2} \\ \sigma_{2,1} & \sigma_2^2 \end{bmatrix}$$

The main diagonal contains the population variances sampled by the first and second paired measurements. The covariance between the measurements is given by $\sigma_{1,2}$ or by $\sigma_{2,1}$. These quantities are necessarily identical, demonstrating the mirroring of covariances above and below the main diagonal of the matrix. For a two-group independent measures design the population covariance matrix is assumed to have the following structure:

$$\begin{bmatrix} \sigma_1^2 & 0 \\ 0 & \sigma_2^2 \end{bmatrix}$$

Even though the sample covariance matrix may not have zeroes in the off-diagonal cells, an independent measures ANOVA assumes that the true population covariance is zero. Viewed in this light, both designs make assumptions about the form of the population covariance matrix. The independent measures design assumes that covariances are precisely zero and that the variances σ_1^2 to σ_k^2 are equal in the population (respectively the assumptions of independent measures and homogeneity of variance). The repeated measures design assumes correlated measures (i.e., that the population covariances are non-zero) and that the covariance matrix is 'spherical'.

Sphericity was defined earlier as the assumption that the variances of differences between repeated measurements are equal in the population. The variance of a difference is obtained by subtracting one repeated sample from another to create a new variable (their difference). Its variance is the variance of a difference. Repeating this procedure produces variances of differences for every possible pair of the repeated measures samples. For paired data there are two repeated measurements and therefore only one difference variable. The variance of the difference is therefore always consistent with the sphericity assumption for paired data; a single variance can't differ from itself. Violations of sphericity are only possible when a repeated measures factor has more than two levels.

The same logic applies to interaction terms. Sphericity is only a problem for effects with multiple degrees of freedom (*df*), and therefore coded by more than one indicator variable or contrast in a regression model. A factor with two levels or an interaction involving factors with more than two levels requires more than one predictor or contrast to code (regardless of whether dummy or effect coding is used). Sphericity is always true for effects with only 1 *df*.

Sphericity is a serious problem for multiple *df* effects in repeated measures ANOVA designs. For instance, Keselman *et al.* (2001) point out that violations of sphericity are likely to be common in longitudinal designs. This is because a commonly observed pattern is that of decreasing correlations over time (a pattern not consistent with sphericity). If sphericity is violated, the *F* ratio for an effect will not follow an *F* distribution with *df* defined by the numerator and denominator of the ratio. As a consequence, the *p* values for the usual test will be inaccurate. Violations of sphericity always lead to tests that are more liberal than suggested by the observed test statistic. The degree of inaccuracy is often substantial (e.g., the observed *p* value could be much smaller than a *p* value based on the true distribution of the test statistic). The degree of bias for the test increases with the severity of the violation. This, in turn, tends to increase as the number of repeated measurements rises (in essence because there is more room for severe departures to occur). If there are many repeated measures, serious violations of sphericity are likely to be common, leading to liberal inferences (e.g., increased Type I error rates).

It is therefore essential to check the sphericity assumption for all repeated measures ANOVA analyses (except those with two levels on all factors). An obvious starting point is the population covariance matrix for a one-way repeated measures design:

$$\begin{bmatrix} \sigma_1^2 & \sigma_{1,2} & \sigma_{1,3} & \dots & \sigma_{1,k} \\ \sigma_{2,1} & \sigma_2^2 & \sigma_{2,3} & \dots & \sigma_{2,k} \\ \sigma_{3,1} & \sigma_{3,2} & \sigma_3^2 & \dots & \sigma_{3,k} \\ \dots & \dots & \dots & \dots & \dots \\ \sigma_{k,1} & \sigma_{k,2} & \sigma_{k,3} & \dots & \sigma_k^2 \end{bmatrix}$$

The pattern of covariances corresponding to sphericity is difficult to spot, because the variances of differences are not displayed directly. It is possible to calculate them using the variance-sum law (see Key Concept 3.2). For instance, the variance of the differences between the first two repeated measurements would be $\sigma_1^2 + \sigma_2^2 - 2\sigma_{1,2}$. This becomes tedious for large matrices. Many textbooks, particularly older ones, recommend looking for a related (but more restrictive) pattern known as *compound symmetry*. Compound symmetry entails both that the population variances are equal ($\sigma_1^2 = \sigma_2^2 = \ldots = \sigma_k^2$) and that the population covariances are equal ($\sigma_{1,2} = \sigma_{1,3} = \ldots = \sigma_{k-1,k}$). To detect this pattern in the sample covariance matrix, requires that the values on the main diagonal are similar to each other ($\hat{\sigma}_1^2 \approx \hat{\sigma}_2^2 \approx \ldots \approx \hat{\sigma}_k^2$) and that the off-diagonal cells are also similar in value ($\hat{\sigma}_{1,2} \approx \hat{\sigma}_{1,3} \ldots \approx \hat{\sigma}_{k-1,k}$). If compound symmetry holds, then sphericity is always true (e.g., it holds when homogeneity of variance and independence are both true). Additionally, if approximate compound symmetry is present, sphericity is unlikely to be severely violated (though this can be hard to judge).

The trouble is that, while compound symmetry always implies sphericity, sphericity could be true even if compound symmetry is not. This is obvious from the covariance matrix for a paired design, where the sphericity assumption is always met, but compound symmetry might not be true (if the variances are unequal).

A better approach to detecting violations of sphericity is to look at the epsilon estimate ($\hat{\varepsilon}$). Box (1954a, 1954b) showed that if the sphericity assumption is false the F statistic in one-way repeated measures ANOVA with $(J-1)$ and $(n-1)(J-1)$ df has an approximate F distribution with $\varepsilon(J-1)$ and $\varepsilon(n-1)(J-1)$ df. The ε parameter therefore indicates the degree to which the population departs from sphericity (with $\varepsilon = 1$ indicating that sphericity holds). As the departure becomes more extreme, ε approaches its lower bound. This lower bound depends on the design (starting at .5 if $J = 3$ and approaching zero as J becomes large). The sample estimate of ε is therefore an excellent descriptive statistic for assessing the degree to which sphericity is violated.

The lower bound of epsilon is

$$\hat{\varepsilon}_{lb} = \frac{1}{J-1}, \quad \text{Equation 16.4}$$

where J is the number of levels of a repeated measures factor (and more generally the effective number of means be compared). Box (1954a, 1954b) provided an estimate of epsilon that was later explored by Geisser and Greenhouse (Geisser and Greenhouse, 1958; Greenhouse and Geisser, 1959). This estimate is now widely known as Greenhouse-Geisser epsilon ($\hat{\varepsilon}_{gg}$).[7] Huynh and Feldt (1976) proposed an alternative estimate $\hat{\varepsilon}_{hf}$.

There are several simulation studies comparing the performance of $\hat{\varepsilon}_{gg}$ and $\hat{\varepsilon}_{hf}$ under a range of different conditions. It can be established that $\hat{\varepsilon}_{gg} \leq \hat{\varepsilon}_{hf}$ and that $\hat{\varepsilon}_{gg}$ tends to be conservative, under-estimating ε (notably when departures from sphericity are modest). In contrast, $\hat{\varepsilon}_{hf}$ is liberal (overestimating ε and occasionally exceeding one). These results are relevant to repeated measures ANOVA because the estimates can be used to correct the effect and error df of the F ratio. The $\hat{\varepsilon}_{lb}$ statistic is extremely conservative and no longer of interest as a correction factor. It had previously been used as a first step in significance testing, because statistically significance with $\hat{\varepsilon}_{lb}$ eliminates the need for the more cumbersome calculation of $\hat{\varepsilon}_{gg}$ or $\hat{\varepsilon}_{hf}$.

The main choice is therefore between the conservative Greenhouse-Geisser estimate and the liberal Huynh-Feldt estimate. Huynh and Feldt (*ibid.*) proposed that the greater statistical power of the correction using $\hat{\varepsilon}_{hf}$ warranted its use when $\varepsilon \geq .75$. They also argued that it keeps the Type I error rate closer to nominal α than $\hat{\varepsilon}_{gg}$ does. Subsequent authors have tended to stick to this view, advocating $\hat{\varepsilon}_{gg}$ when ε is thought to be close to its lower bound and $\hat{\varepsilon}_{hf}$ when ε is thought to be high (e.g., greater than .75 or .80).

An important issue is how to decide whether sphericity is violated in the first place. One option is to form a test of the null hypothesis that $\varepsilon = 1$. The best-known such test (implemented in a number of software packages) is *Mauchly's sphericity test*. This kind of test of assumptions addresses a largely irrelevant hypothesis. What matters is the degree of violation rather than its presence. Furthermore, the Mauchly test is neither robust to violations of normality nor high in statistical power. It is therefore wise to ignore the procedure entirely. Instead, focus on $\hat{\varepsilon}_{gg}$ and $\hat{\varepsilon}_{hf}$. The average of these conservative and liberal estimates provides a reasonable guide to the extent of any sphericity violation. If this average is close to its lower bound then the Greenhouse-Geisser correction is a safe choice. If the average is around .75 or better $\hat{\varepsilon}_{hf}$ should offer greater power (with only modest risk of Type I error inflation). If both estimates are close to 1 (e.g., .95 or above) the uncorrected F test is defensible (with at most modest Type I error inflation). These decisions should be tempered by the relative cost of Type I or Type II errors. If Type I errors are considered the more costly of the two then $\hat{\varepsilon}_{gg}$ is a good choice. If statistical power is the main concern then $\hat{\varepsilon}_{hf}$ should be preferred (unless the degree of sphericity violation is severe).

There is a surprising amount published on the relative merits of different sphericity corrections. Recent work has focused more on the relative power of different procedures (see Kirk, 1995). Two further strategies for dealing with sphericity ought to be considered. Probably the best strategy is to avoid tests of multiple *df* effects altogether. Repeated measures contrasts have 1 *df* and therefore make it possible to avoid sphericity concerns altogether. A second strategy is to use a type of *multivariate analysis of variance* (MANOVA) known as *profile analysis*.[8] This MANOVA approach will, under some conditions, provide more powerful tests than those of epsilon-corrected *F* ratios (Kirk, 1995). The precise conditions under which this occurs depend, in a somewhat unpredictable way, on the form of the population covariance matrix. A crude survey of the literature finds that MANOVA tends to provide greater power (relative to corrections using ε_{gg}) when *n* and the number of repeated measures is large or if ε is close to its lower bound. With small *n* and few repeated measures experience suggests that MANOVA only rarely reports statistical significance when the Greenhouse-Geisser test does not.[9]

Example 16.1 Uppal (2006) investigated young children's ability to recognize different emotions. Particular interest focused on the ability to recognize and discriminate pride from other emotions (e.g., happiness or surprise). She showed 90 children (aged between seven and nine years) several sets of pictures, each showing actors expressing either pride, happiness or surprise. For each set the children were asked to point to the picture that expressed one of the three emotions (as cued by the experimenter). Subsequent examples will refer to this data set as the pride data. Mean accuracy for the three picture types (averaging over other conditions of the experiment not considered here) was 68.1% for pride, 71.1% for happiness and 78.9% for surprise. Table 16.3 summarizes the output for one-way repeated measures ANOVA with emotion as the fixed factor. The main effect of emotion is not statistically significant, $F_{2,178} = 1.82$, $MS_e = 1,544$ $p = .165$. No differences are detected in average accuracy of recognizing the three emotions.

Table 16.3 Table for one-way ANOVA on the pride data

Source	***df***	***SS***	***MS***	***F***
Subjects	89	241,262	2,711	
Emotion	2	5,616	2,808	1.82
Error (emotion × subjects)	178	274,801	1,544	
Total	269			

In this case there is little reason to worry about sphericity. Even though there are more than two levels on the repeated measures factor, sphericity would only decrease statistical significance (i.e., make the non-significant *p* value less significant). For completeness, $\hat{\varepsilon}_{gg} = .9879$ and $\hat{\varepsilon}_{hf} = 1.0102$. Both suggest no violation of sphericity, and the upward bias of $\hat{\varepsilon}_{hf}$ is evident (as it exceeds the maximum value of the parameter it is estimating). The Greenhouse-Geisser correction (if implemented) would produce an almost identical main effect: $F_{1.98,175.84} = 1.82$, $p = .166$ (although no correction is warranted when both ε statistics are so close to the upper bound).

The main effect of emotion could also be tested via likelihood or Bayesian inference. AIC for the main effect model is 2808.2, while AIC for the intercept-only model (modeling accuracy of each emotion by the grand mean) is 2807.9. $\Delta AIC = 0.4$, equivalent to $LR_{AIC} = 1.2$ in favor of the grand mean model.

16.3.5 Confidence intervals for repeated measures ANOVA

Calculating confidence intervals (CIs) for a repeated measures ANOVA presents additional difficulties that do not arise in an independent measures design. The standard approach in an independent measures design is to plot error bars around each mean using a pooled standard error. This is useful for depicting the precision with which each mean is measured. These can be adjusted to support inference about differences between means (and for other factors such as multiple testing). The same approach is problematic for repeated measures designs because CIs based on individual means (with or without a pooled error term) may appear to be excessively wide, as they incorporate variance due to systematic individual differences. This variance is eliminated from tests of differences between means in repeated measures designs. Loftus and Masson (1994) argue that a better approach, for ANOVA, is to plot CIs that similarly exclude individual differences. These intervals tend to be much narrower (at least when individual differences are substantial) and therefore give a clearer indication of the presence of systematic differences between means.

Loftus and Masson (*ibid.*) proposed methods for calculating CIs for repeated measures designs using the error term from the corresponding ANOVA. Being based on the same error term, the width of a CI for an individual mean is related to the CI of a difference between means by the familiar factor of $\sqrt{2}$. Although these interval estimates are fairly widely employed, the Loftus-Masson approach has a number of drawbacks (Cousineau, 2005; Morey, 2008). One is that for effects with multiple *df* the pooled error term will be inappropriate if sphericity (equality of variances of differences between means) is not met. A further problem is that they can be awkward to calculate.

Cousineau (2005) proposed a simple alternative that is equivalent to the Loftus-Masson method when paired designs are employed. Morey (2008) showed that the intervals proposed by Cousineau tend to be too narrow (and explained how to correct for this problem). Like the Loftus-Masson approach, the Cousineau-Morey method attempts to strip out individual differences from the calculation of the interval estimate. Where the methods differ is that the Cousineau-Morey interval removes individual differences directly from the data prior to analysis. This is achieved by *participant mean centering* (subtracting the mean of each participant from their observed scores). While this strips out the individual differences, it also alters the mean score per condition. The remedy for this problem is to add the grand mean back on to each score. This process of participant mean centering followed by addition of the grand mean is termed *normalizing* (Loftus and Masson, 1994; Masson and Loftus, 2003).[10] Normalizing relocates all condition effects relative to the grand mean rather than participant means (and therefore relative to an average participant).

The discussion below assumes a one-way repeated measures ANOVA design with J levels (representing J different experimental conditions). If y_{ij} is the score of the ith participant in condition j, and $\hat{\mu}_i$ is the mean of participant i across all J levels, normalized scores can be expressed as:

$$y'_{ij} = y_{ij} - \hat{\mu}_i + \hat{\mu}_{grand} \qquad \text{Equation 16.5}$$

Why does computing a CI based on the normalized scores lead to intervals that are too narrow? It happens because adding the grand mean to all values induces a positive correlation between the levels that wasn't there before (Morey, 2008). The degree of positive correlation is related to the number of levels J (being largest when $J = 2$ and decreasing as J rises). As the normalized scores are positively correlated, the estimate of error variance computed from them is lower by a factor of $(J-1)/J$ than it would be for the original scores (and hence the CI is too narrow). This factor can be used to correct the CI computed from normalized scores. Thus Morey (2008) suggests computing a CI of the form

$$\hat{\mu}_j \pm t_{df_j,1-\alpha/2}\sqrt{\frac{J}{J-1}}\hat{\sigma}'_{\mu_j} \qquad \text{Equation 16.6}$$

where $\hat{\sigma}'_{\mu_j}$ is the standard error of the mean computed from the normalized scores of the jth level. For factorial designs, Morey indicates that J should be replaced by the total number of conditions across all repeated measures fixed factors (i.e., excluding the subject's random factor). If the design also incorporates independent measures, the intervals can be computed separately for each of the groups defined by the independent measures factors. The intervals themselves have the same expected width as the Loftus-Masson CIs, but do not assume sphericity. Except when $J=2$, their width varies as a function of the variances and covariances of the repeated measures samples.

One criticism of this general approach is that it treats participants as a fixed effect rather than a random effect (Blouin and Riopelle, 2005). This does not matter if the focus is comparison between means, but it does overestimate the precision with which sample means are measured (because it neglects sampling error between participants). Blouin and Riopelle's solution is to obtain CIs for sample means from a multilevel model. A more pragmatic approach is to select the interval estimate to match the purpose of the plot. Cousineau-Morey intervals will be appropriate if means are being plotted to emphasize systematic differences between conditions. However, as the width of a Cousineau-Morey or Loftus-Masson interval is larger than that for a difference in means (by a factor of $\sqrt{2}$), plots of these intervals are easy to misinterpret. Overlap of 95% CIs around individual means is often misinterpreted as indicating that a 95% CI for the difference in means would include zero.

The same problem arises in independent designs and the solution proposed in Chapter 3 was to adjust the width so that absence of overlap corresponds to the required CI for the difference. For large numbers of means (or other statistics) an approach based on multipliers for standard errors can be used (Goldstein and Healy, 1995; Afshartous and Preston, 2010). For the small numbers of means encountered in repeated measures ANOVA analyses, Baguley (2011) proposes the following adjustment to the Cousineau-Morey interval:

$$\hat{\mu}_j \pm \frac{\sqrt{2}}{2}\left(t_{n-1,1-\alpha/2}\sqrt{\frac{J}{J-1}}\hat{\sigma}'_{\hat{\mu}_j}\right) \qquad \text{Equation 16.7}$$

This ensures that the joint width of the difference-adjusted Cousineau-Morey CI is $\sqrt{2}/2$ plus $\sqrt{2}/2 = \sqrt{2}$ times larger than their individual width (matching that for a CI of their difference).

Plotting these adjusted Cousineau-Morey intervals solves the problem of creating interval estimates that are informative about the pattern of differences between means. It is also possible to adjust the interval estimates in other ways (e.g., by incorporating corrections for multiple testing). If both the differences in means and their precision are of interest Baguley (2011) proposes using two-tiered error bars similar to those in Figure 3.8. For instance, the inner tier error bars could be used to display difference-adjusted Cousineau-Morey CIs, while the outer tier could display a 95% CI from a multilevel model (Blouin and Riopelle, 2005; Baguley, 2011). In small samples, the variances and covariances of the repeated measures may be poorly estimated and it may be better to plot CIs (e.g., Loftus-Masson intervals) that rely on a pooled estimate of the covariances between the repeated measures (Baguley, 2011).

Example 16.2 Table 16.4 reports the width and limits of 95% confidence intervals computed using the Loftus-Masson and Cousineau-Morey methods for the one-way ANOVA on the pride data.

Table 16.4 Comparison of Loftus-Masson and Cousineau-Morey 95% CIs, for accuracy of identifying emotions (from the one-way ANOVA of the pride data)

	Emotion		
95% CI	**Happiness**	**Pride**	**Surprise**
Loftus-Masson			
Lower	62.9	59.9	70.7
Upper	79.3	76.2	87.1
(Width)	(16.3)	(16.3)	(16.3)
Cousineau-Morey			
Lower	63.0	59.4	71.0
Upper	79.2	76.7	86.8
(Width)	(16.3)	(17.3)	(15.8)

The width of the Loftus-Masson CIs is constant, whereas the Cousineau-Morey intervals vary. They do not use a pooled error term (and assume neither homogeneity of variance nor homogeneity of covariance). Their expected value is equal to that of the Loftus-Masson intervals and is identical when $J = 2$.

When plotting the intervals, the main aims are to reveal the pattern of differences between means or the precision with which means are measured. Two-tiered error bar plots make it possible to display both in the same plot (Baguley, 2011). Figure 16.2 plots difference-adjusted Cousineau-Morey intervals constructed from Equation 16.7 as inner tier error bars, and CIs from a multilevel model as the outer tier.

The multilevel model for the outer tier CIs is fitted with an unstructured covariance matrix and, like the Cousineau-Morey interval, does not assume sphericity. The substantial overlap of the inner tiers of the error bars provides little indication of differences between means (consistent with the non-significant main effect of emotion). It is plausible that average accuracy to detect the different

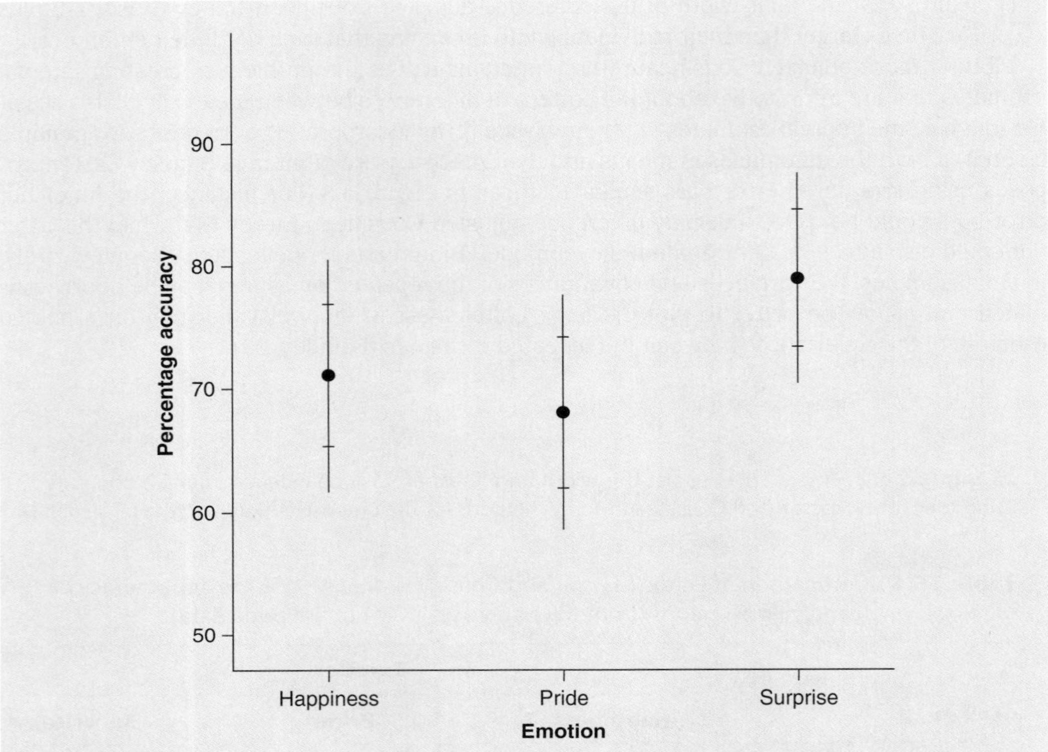

Figure 16.2 Two-tiered error bar plot for the one-way ANOVA of the pride data. The inner tier is a difference-adjusted 95% CI (so that overlapping CIs correspond to a 95% CI in the difference in means that includes zero). The outer tiers display 95% CIs for the individual means.

emotions is equal or similar in accuracy. The outer tier is also informative. Although the 95% CIs are rather wide, all comfortably exclude accuracy levels expected by random guessing (around 33%). There is evidence that children in this age range (seven to nine years) can recognize all three emotions.

16.4 Combining independent and repeated measures: mixed ANOVA designs

A design that includes both independent and repeated measures factors is termed a *mixed* or *mixed measures* design (though other labels such as *split-plot design* are also applied). A mixed ANOVA design allows a researcher to have some of the advantages of a repeated measures design (e.g., to account for individual differences) in the presence of one or more independent measures factors (e.g., individual difference factors). A common example is a pre-post design where different groups are compared at two or more time points (e.g., before and after an intervention).

Adopting a mixed design presents a number of challenges. These arise because individual differences can only be estimated between levels of repeated measures factors in a mixed design.[11] This carves up the design into repeated measures and independent measures components (and some software separates out these components into distinct ANOVA tables). The basic mixed design is a two-way design with a levels on the independent measures factor and b levels on the repeated measures factor. The ANOVA model for this design can be written as:

$$y_{iab} = \mu + \alpha_a + \pi_{i(a)} + \beta_b + \alpha\beta_{ab} + \beta\pi_{ib(a)} + \varepsilon_{iab} \qquad \text{Equation 16.8}$$

As with fully repeated measures designs, the error term is aliased with the $\beta\pi_{ib(a)}$ term (because there is only one observation per repeated measures condition).

Some explanation of the change in subscript notation is required: $\pi_{i(a)}$ represents the individual differences within the independent measures factor and is typically written as *subjects (A)* or *subjects within A* (which is also how it is spoken out loud). This acts as the error term for the independent measures (between subjects) factor. The $\beta\pi_{ib(a)}$ term is the interaction of the repeated measures factor B and subjects within A. This is used as the error term for both the effect of factor B and the A × B interaction. The ANOVA table for a two-way mixed design is shown in Table 16.5.

Mixed designs can be extended so that more than one repeated or independent measures factor is included (see Kirk, 1995; Howell, 2002). The general format remains the same. Independent measures effects are tested using a pooled error term (the subject variance within all independent measures factors) and repeated measures factors or interactions with independent measures factors are tested with the appropriate by-subjects error term.

A mixed design inherits characteristics from both repeated and independent measures designs. For a mixed design to be a true experiment, participants should be randomly assigned to independent measures conditions, and order effects should be controlled by randomization or counterbalancing for repeated measures conditions. It is also assumed that residuals are sampled from independent, normal populations with constant variance. As the residuals are represented by more than one error term, these assumptions should hold separately for both $\pi_{i(a)}$ and $\beta\pi_{ib(a)}$. For all repeated measures effects (e.g., B and A × B in the two-way mixed design) sphericity must be true for the residuals to be independent and have constant variance.

Table 16.5 Two-way ANOVA with mixed measures

Source	***df***	***SS***	***MS***	***F***
Factor A	$a-1$	SS_A	$\frac{SS_A}{df_A}$	$\frac{MS_A}{MS_{subjects(A)}}$
Subjects (A)	$a(n-1)$	$SS_{subjects(A)}$	$\frac{SS_{subjects(A)}}{df_{subjects(A)}}$	
Factor B	$b-1$	SS_B	$\frac{SS_B}{df_B}$	$\frac{MS_B}{MS_{B\times subjects(A)}}$
A × B	$(a-1)(b-1)$	$SS_{A\times B}$	$\frac{SS_{A\times B}}{df_{A\times B}}$	$\frac{MS_{A\times B}}{MS_{B\times subjects(A)}}$
B × subjects (A)	$a(n-1)(b-1)$	$SS_{B\times subjects(A)}$	$\frac{SS_{B\times subjects(A)}}{df_{B\times subjects(A)}}$	
Total	$N-1$			

This leads to one further difficulty. It is possible to represent each effect by a single population covariance matrix in a repeated measures design. Independent measures designs have a separate covariance matrix for each independent group in the population. It is necessary not only for sphericity to hold for the population each group is sampled from, but also for the covariance matrices of the groups to be equal in the population for the repeated measures test statistics to follow an F distribution. This assumption of mixed ANOVA designs is known as *multisample sphericity*. It is often difficult to satisfy in practice.

Keselman *et al.* (2001) review approaches to dealing with multisample sphericity. In balanced designs – those with equal cell sizes for the independent measures factors – the Greenhouse-Geisser and Huynh-Feldt adjusted tests are known to be robust. MANOVA approaches are also robust in balanced designs for main effects, but may not always be robust to sphericity for interaction tests, even in balanced designs (Keselman *et al.*, 2001). For this reason it is probably safest to employ mixed ANOVA designs with equal or near equal cell sizes wherever possible. It also makes sense to use epsilon-corrected tests in balanced mixed designs (which necessarily always include an interaction test).[12] Keselman *et al.* consider a number of alternative approaches for unbalanced ANOVA designs, but several are difficult to implement without specialist software. Among the approaches they propose are procedures equivalent to those in multilevel regression models. For this reason, switching from mixed ANOVA (or MANOVA) approaches to multilevel modeling is recommended if the design is unbalanced unless sphericity is not an issue.

However, if all repeated measures factors have only two levels (and each effect has 1 *df*) neither sphericity nor multisample sphericity can be violated. Moreover, with only a few repeated measures in each factor, departures from multisample sphericity may be minor (e.g., if all epsilon estimates are close to one). In these cases ANOVA will probably be preferable to either MANOVA or a multilevel model approach (though there are other reasons, such as missing outcome data, that favor multilevel regression models).

Example 16.3 In Example 16.1, accuracy differences in the pride data were analyzed, ignoring an independent measures factor. Uppal (2006) showed children pictures depicting emotion with face only, torso only, or both face and torso visible. Exactly 30 participants took part in each of the three experimental conditions and it is therefore a 3 × 3 mixed measures ANOVA design. Mean percentage accuracy for the nine conditions (all possible combinations of the levels of each factor) are set out in Table 16.6.

The cell means suggest a more subtle pattern than evident from the earlier one-way analysis. Table 16.7 shows the output of a 3 × 3 mixed ANOVA for these data. There is no indication that sphericity is violated. $\hat{\varepsilon}_{gg} = .9874$ and $\hat{\varepsilon}_{hf} = 1.0102$ for both the emotion and emotion × condition effect.

Table 16.6 Cell means by condition and emotion for the pride data

	Both	Face	Torso
Pride	74.2%	50.0%	80.0%
Happiness	90.0%	83.3%	40.0%
Surprise	93.3%	76.7%	66.7%

Table 16.7 Two-way ANOVA with mixed measures for the pride data

Source	***df***	***SS***	***MS***	***F***	***p***
Condition	2	26,060	13,030	5.27	.007
Subjects (condition)	87	215,201	2,474		
Emotion	2	5,616	2,808	2.12	.123
Condition × emotion	4	44,231	11,058	8.34	<.001
Emotion × subjects (condition)	174	230,569	1,325		
Total	269				

In this analysis, effects of both condition and condition × emotion have been detected. Participants appear to be more accurate on average when both face and torso are visible ($M = 85.8\%$) than for either face ($M = 70.0\%$) or torso ($M = 62.2\%$). The mean accuracy by emotion (ignoring condition) analyzed earlier conceals a more complex pattern. Recognition of emotion appears to be facilitated by different information depending on the type of emotion. Figure 16.3 shows an

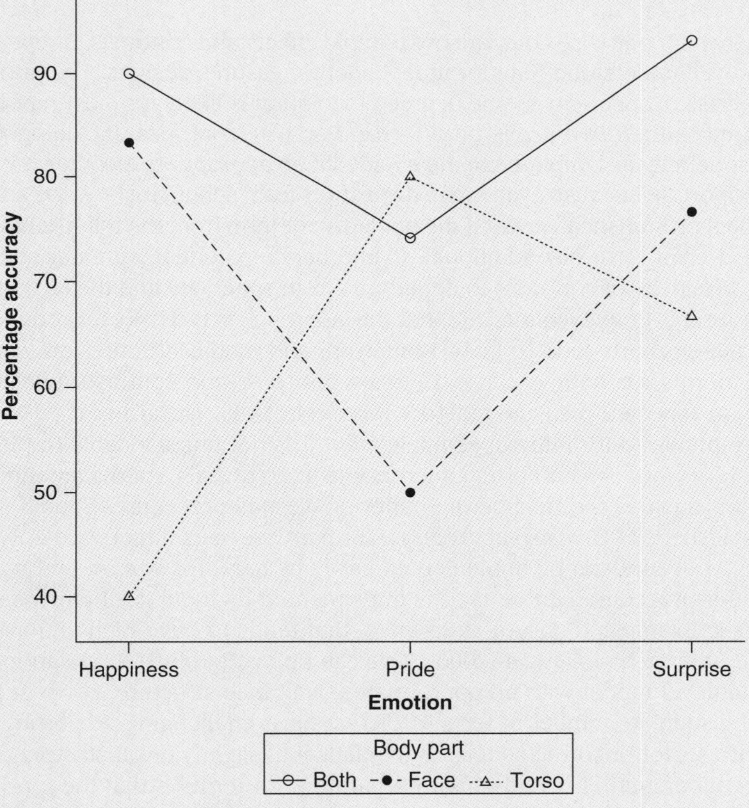

Figure 16.3 Cell means by condition and emotion for the pride data

interaction plot for the condition × emotion effect. The interaction plot suggests that having both face and torso visible produces consistently high performance (though there is a hint that pride is harder to identify than happiness).

Otherwise, it looks as though pride is very difficult to identify from facial expression alone, whereas as happiness is very hard to identify from body posture on its own. It seems likely that the interaction is largely down to this 'crossover' in performance between pride and happiness when only face or only torso is presented. Further exploration of the interaction is warranted to confirm this interpretation.

16.5 Comparisons, contrasts and simple effects with repeated measures

16.5.1 Comparisons, contrasts and simple effects with repeated measures on all factors

The best approach for pairwise comparisons, simple effects and contrasts in repeated measures ANOVA is less well understood than for independent measures designs. The principal problem is that of violations of sphericity. Some degree of violation is likely for most repeated measures analyses with more than two levels on a factor. For 1 *df* contrasts, including pairwise comparisons, the sphericity assumption can be avoided if an appropriate error term is selected. The error term is important because even small departures from sphericity (e.g., $.97 < \varepsilon < 1$) can have a material impact on statistical power if the pooled error term from the full ANOVA is used (Boik, 1981). A pooled error term has additional *df* and hence potentially greater statistical power. However, the sensitivity of contrasts to departures from sphericity and the lack of robustness if a pooled error term is employed indicate that this approach is too risky for routine application.

For this reason, experts tend to favor Bonferroni and modified Bonferroni corrections with separate error terms for both *a priori* contrasts and *post hoc* contrasts (including pairwise comparisons) on repeated measures factors (Maxwell, 1980; Jaccard *et al.*, 1984). Bonferroni corrections are preferred for interval estimates, but it is not unreasonable to plot uncorrected CIs for exploratory work or for informal inference (e.g., to reveal patterns among means). More powerful options such as the Hochberg, Shaffer or Westfall procedures should be adopted for formal testing. Fisher's LSD is also appropriate for pairwise tests if there are only three means. The Hochberg procedure can be implemented easily by hand for *a priori* and *post hoc* testing, while the Shaffer procedure can be readily implemented by hand if all pairwise comparisons are required (see Example 13.5). An alternative, that tends to have high all pairs power, is to adapt the PCIC approach of Dayton (2003). This can be made robust to violations of sphericity by fitting a multilevel model with an appropriate covariance structure. For *post hoc* contrasts, determining the suitable number of tests to correct for is challenging. Reporting the tolerance to implicit contrasts for uncorrected tests is a practical (if slightly unsatisfactory) solution.

One benefit of computing contrasts with separate error terms is that the procedure reduces to the calculation of a paired *t* test of weighted means. For pairwise comparisons this is merely the familiar paired *t* test of the differences between the level means you are interested in. For a contrast involving more than two means it may be necessary to calculate the contrast score in the usual manner. For this reason it will often be convenient to choose contrast weights with absolute values that sum to two. One method is to compute the weighted positive and negative scores for each participant and use a paired *t* test. Alternatively, you could calculate the contrast score *C* for each participant and compute a one sample *t* test of the null hypothesis that $C = 0$ in the population. Frequentist, likelihood or Bayesian inferences can be derived from the resulting *t* statistic.

Simple main effects follow the same pattern. Howell (2002) suggests calculating a one-way ANOVA for the effect of one repeated measures factor at each level of the second factor. The advantage of this procedure is it uses a separate error term for each simple effect. If the simple effect has only 1 *df* it is equivalent to the paired *t* test approach already described. Furthermore, the simple effect can adopt an epsilon correction for sphericity if more than two means are involved. The same rationale applies to simple interaction effects within pure repeated measures designs. A simple interaction effect for a three-way interaction can be tested via two-way repeated measures ANOVA at each level of the third factor. As with simple main effects and simple interactions in independent designs, care must be taken with these analyses. Simple effects are tests of aggregate effects (decomposing sums of squares from, for example, a main effect and a two-way interaction). The strategy can have very low power to detect patterns of interest. It is quite common that all simple effects are statistically non-significant, even if the overall ANOVA is not. Interaction contrasts provide a more principled (and potentially more powerful) route to follow up an omnibus interaction effect that has multiple *df*. Testing many simple effects in a complex factorial design will also lead to Type I error inflation – an almost paradoxical combination of low power for the effects you are most interested in and high Type I error rates for the overall analysis (Maxwell, 2004).

Example 16.4 In Example 16.1 the mean accuracy was 68.1% for pride, 71.1% for happiness and 78.9% for surprise. Previous research suggests that young children, and to some extent adults, have difficulty recognizing pride (e.g., it is not classed among basic emotions such as happiness, surprise, or disgust). This hypothesis could be tested by a contrast comparing accuracy for pride versus the average accuracy for surprise and happiness. This contrast could use integer weights $\{-2, +1, +1\}$ or $\{-1, +0.5, +0.5\}$ to keep the contrast score on the original percentage scale. The latter is suitable for a CI.

The first step is to create the weighted means. This can be done by computing a new variable (*non-pride*) as the arithmetic mean of happiness and surprise. A paired *t* test can then be run to compare *pride* and *non-pride* accuracy. The difference in weighted means is 6.94%, 95% CI of $[-3.65, 17.54]$, $t_{89} = 1.30$, $SE = 5.33$, $p = .196$. This CI is helpful because it tells us that the estimate of the difference between pride and the other emotions is not very precise (it could plausibly be zero, or approaching 20%). The study has insufficient power to measure this difference precisely.

The *t* statistic makes it possible to apply a Bayesian *t* test or calculate a likelihood interval. Using a JZS prior, the Bayes factor in favor of the null hypothesis that pride is not harder to recognize than the other emotions is 5.25, while the 1/8 likelihood interval is $[-3.99, 17.88]$.

16.5.2 Comparisons, contrasts and simple effects with mixed measures

Calculating contrasts and comparisons for mixed designs depends on the source of the effect being investigated. For a pure independent measures effect (a factor or interaction with no repeated measures), it is possible to treat the analysis exactly as for an independent measures design. For instance, with *a priori* contrasts and comparisons a powerful modified Bonferroni procedure such as the Westfall procedure could be employed. For repeated measures effects sphericity is a serious concern, and the approach set out for pure repeated measures designs is recommended.

The repeated measures approach of separate one-way ANOVAs (or factorial ANOVA for three-way and higher-order interactions) also works for repeated measures simple effects. For instance, if three types of problem (low, medium or high difficulty) were presented either to novice or expert problem solvers this could be analyzed with a 2 × 3 mixed design (with two levels on the independent factor and three levels on the repeated factor). The two simple main effects for the repeated measures factor test the effects of problem difficulty within the novice group and within the expert group. Each of these could be analyzed with a one-way ANOVA incorporating only one of the groups (and therefore not pooling error terms). Having three levels, there is a risk that sphericity is violated. This can be assessed by looking at the epsilon estimates and, if necessary, employing a correction.

Calculating a simple main effect for the independent factor in a mixed design is more treacherous. These effects are differences between groups (e.g., novices and experts) that are analyzed at just one measurement level of a repeated measures factor (e.g., only for low difficulty problems). The obstacle for the independent measures tests in this situation is that a simple main effect is not a method of decomposing an interaction. It decomposes *SS* attributable to both the main effect and the interaction. Hence the error variance for the independent factor simple main effect is distributed across the two error terms: subjects (A) and B × Subjects (A). The most accurate test will be obtained by pooling these two sources of error. The *SS* for the error term is the sum of the $SS_{\text{subjects}(A)}$ and $SS_{B\times\text{subjects}(A)}$, while the df is sum of $df_{\text{subjects}(A)}$ and $df_{B\times\text{subjects}(A)}$. The pooled error term is therefore:

$$MS_{error} = \frac{SS_{subjects(A)} + SS_{B\times subjects(A)}}{df_{subjects(A)} + df_{B\times subjects(A)}} \quad \text{Equation 16.9}$$

The trouble is that this pooled error term combines estimates of very unequal population variances and the resulting test statistic will not follow the usual *F* distribution. This is a variant of the Behrens-Fisher problem encountered in the context of the independent *t* test (see Howell, 2002). It can be dealt with by applying a similar correction to the *df*. Corrected df_{error} for the simple main effect are computed as:

$$\nu' = \frac{\left(SS_{subjects(A)} + SS_{B\times subjects(A)}\right)^2}{\frac{\left(SS_{subjects(A)}\right)^2}{df_{subjects(A)}} + \frac{\left(SS_{B\times subjects(A)}\right)^2}{df_{B\times subjects(A)}}} \quad \text{Equation 16.10}$$

For multiple *df* interactions, interaction contrasts can also be calculated. These can be generated along the same lines as those for an interaction contrast in an independent measures design. The contrast weights for the interaction effect define patterns of means that differ between groups (e.g., differential linear trends). The difficulty is deciding on what error term to use. If sphericity is not violated, the error term for the interaction in the mixed ANOVA should be employed. If sphericity is violated, but the design balanced, the error *df* could be adjusted using $\hat{\varepsilon}_{gg}$ or $\hat{\varepsilon}_{hf}$. If sphericity is violated and the design unbalanced, the contrast could be run via a multilevel model.

Example 16.5 Figure 16.3 shows a complex interaction among nine cell means. The interaction effect has 4 *df* and could be decomposed into one or more interaction contrasts. A hypothesis of particular interest in this case is how well the interaction is explained by a 2×2 interaction in which pride is better recognized from torso alone while happiness is better recognized by face alone. A reasonable choice of contrast weights for this hypothesis would be:

	Both	*Face*	*Torso*	Σ
Pride	0	−1	+1	*0*
Happiness	0	+1	−1	*0*
Surprise	0	0	0	*0*
Σ	*0*	*0*	*0*	*0*

Note that having absolute weights summing to two would have retained the original percentage scale.

The next step in the analysis would normally be to create a double-centered table of contrast weights (see Key Concept 15.1). By happenstance, the initial weights are already double-centered (with both row and column marginals summing to zero).

The contrast weights can then be multiplied by the cell means from Table 16.6 to give the contrast score:

	Both	*Face*	*Torso*	Σ
Pride	0	-1×50	$+1 \times 80$	*30*
Happiness	0	$+1 \times 83.3$	-1×40	*43.3*
Surprise	0	0	0	*0*
Σ	*0*	*33.3*	*40*	*73.3*

$SS_{contrast}$ is derived from the contrast score of 73.3, and is:

$$SS_{contrast} = \frac{C^2}{\frac{1}{n}\left(\sum_{j=1}^{J} w_j^2\right)} = \frac{73.3^2}{\frac{1}{30}(1+1+1+1)} = 40,296.7$$

The sphericity assumption was not violated in the earlier analysis. For this reason, it is reasonable to use the emotion $\times$ subjects (condition) MS_{error} term from the original ANOVA. This is 1,325, and so $F = 40,296.7/1,325$, and the contrast could be reported as: $F_{1,174} = 30.4$, $MS_e = 1,325$, $p < .01$.

As is often the case for a contrast, the explanatory power of the interaction contrast is of greater interest than the test. *SS* for the interaction is 44,231 and therefore the interaction contrast explains about 91% of the interaction effect ($r^2_{alerting} = .91$). This is equivalent to a correlation of .95 between contrast weights and the residualized cell means ($r_{alerting} = .95$). Although there is quite a bit going on in Figure 16.3, much of the variation is down to main effects. Of the variation that remains, the vast majority can be explained in terms of pride being harder to identify from facial expression than from body posture, and happiness being harder to identify from body posture than facial expression.

16.5.3 Effect size

Repeated measures and mixed designs are especially difficult to obtain appropriate standardized effect size metrics for. Many commonly calculated quantities (e.g., η_p^2 or g) are not comparable to similar metrics obtained from independent measures designs. It is a good idea to compare effects from different designs using unstandardized measures (e.g., simple mean differences) as a first – and possibly only – step. Standardized effect size metrics need to take into account factors that may distort the standardizer (the variance or standard deviation used to scale the effect). An important contributor to the standardizer in an independent measures design is individual differences (which in a repeated measures design are estimated separately from other sources of variance).

The generalized effect size measures of Olejnik and Algina (2003) provide a starting point for 'design neutral' standardized effect size metrics. Their approach is to calculate generalized statistics that treat repeated measures equivalently to independent measures designs. One proviso is that, for statistical power or sample size estimation, the appropriate metric is one that matches the design of the study being planned. In theory η_g^2 can be calculated with the formulas for other factorial designs by treating subjects as an additional measured factor. In practice, ANOVA software rarely provides the SS for such a calculation in a convenient format. Following Olejnik and Algina, calculating the required denominator for η_g^2 by subtraction is suggested. The goal is to exclude all manipulated factors or interactions with only manipulated factors (except the one under consideration). An indicator variable I is used to designate whether the effect under consideration is a manipulated factor ($I = 1$) or a measured factor ($I = 0$).

$$\eta_g^2 = \frac{SS_{effect}}{SS_{total} - \sum_{manip} SS_{manip} + I \times SS_{effect}} \qquad \text{Equation 16.11}$$

This formula excludes manipulated factors from the denominator (adding the focal effect back in only if the focal effect is a manipulated factor). Interactions with measured factors are considered measured factors. Repeated measures fixed factors tend to be manipulated factors, though it may be reasonable to treat them as measured factors in some situations.

Olejnik and Algina (2003) also extend ω_g^2 (generalized omega-squared) to designs with repeated measures factors. The correct formulas can become rather complex and the simplest solution is to refer to Tables 2, 3 and 4 of their paper.

Example 16.6 In the two-way mixed ANOVA for the pride data, the two factors are the emotion to be recognized and the experimental condition (whether the pictures showed face, torso or both face and torso). The experimental condition is a canonical example of a manipulated variable. Emotion is manipulated by the experimenter, and for comparisons with other experiments might be considered as such. For other purposes – for example to gauge impact on everyday performance – it may be considered a measured variable (because expressions of happiness, pride and surprise are a routine part of everyday experience).

Treating both variables as manipulated factors, η_g^2 for the interaction is:

$$\eta_g^2 = \frac{SS_{effect}}{SS_{total} + I \times SS_{effect} - \sum_{manip} SS_{manip}} = \frac{44231}{521678.2 + 1 \times 44231 - (44231 + 5616 + 26060)} = .090$$

The interaction would account for around 9% of the total sample variance in an equivalent independent measures design. Replacing SS_{effect} with $SS_{contrast}$ allows versions of η^2 to be calculated for a contrast. Thus η_g^2 for the interaction contrast is:

$$\eta_g^2 = \frac{SS_{effect}}{SS_{total} + I \times SS_{effect} - \sum_{manip} SS_{manip}}$$

$$= \frac{40296.7}{521678.2 + 1 \times 40296.7 - (40296.7 + 5616 + 26060)} = .083$$

In practice it is usually better to evaluate contrasts relative to the effect they are decomposed from, rather than in terms of total variance. The contrast explains about 91% of the interaction effect and about 8% of sample variance in an equivalent independent measures design.

16.6 MANOVA

Multivariate analysis of variance (MANOVA) is technique of potential interest whenever correlated measurements are obtained. MANOVA is designed for applications in which several correlated outcome variables or *DV*s (dependent variables) are measured.

An important application for repeated measures designs is a form of MANOVA called profile analysis. This does not assume sphericity and sometimes has greater statistical power than an epsilon-corrected ANOVA. In this application, already considered in passing, the repeated measures are treated as correlated outcome variables (which, in a sense, they are). Knowing in advance whether the MANOVA tests are more powerful than the corrected ANOVA analysis is far from simple. It would be possible to estimate the statistical power of each technique if the population covariance matrix Σ were known. Obtaining a good enough estimate of Σ (e.g., in a pilot study) to determine the relative power of the two approaches is likely to be difficult (but see Miles, 2003). Estimates of variances and covariances from small samples tend to be very imprecise. The MANOVA approach will tend to have greater power when many repeated measures are taken, when the degree of sphericity violation is large and when samples sizes are large (but there are departures from this general trend).

For designed experiments with small n and few repeated measurements, and certainly for designs with two levels on the repeated measures factors, ANOVA should probably be preferred. In unbalanced mixed designs MANOVA tests are not robust to violations of multisample sphericity. They may also be problematic for interaction tests in balanced designs (Keselman *et al.*, 2001; Olson, 1974). Keselman *et al.* (2001) also argue against combining MANOVA with epsilon corrections as this can produce unpredictable results. For mixed designs with imbalance, a multilevel model is recommended.

Two further applications of MANOVA, both controversial, need to be addressed. The first is the use of MANOVA to screen for effects prior to ANOVA. This is sometimes employed when a researcher has collected a number of different outcome measures. The second is to increase the statistical power to detect effects when correlated outcome measures are collected. Both practices should generally be avoided. Arguments against the MANOVA approach are part of a broader aversion both to screening tests and tests of multiple *df* effects.

Using MANOVA to screen for effects is analogous to using omnibus F tests prior to *post hoc* tests of all pairwise comparisons. If the omnibus H_0 is true (i.e., there are no differences between means for any of the outcome variables in the population) then the MANOVA test of an effect (e.g., a main effect of factor A) protects subsequent ANOVA tests on the separate outcome variables. This assumes that a researcher does not perform any further tests of differences, a rule that is not always adhered to (Huberty and Morris, 1989). Only very rarely should a researcher adopt this practice. Most research is conducted on the premise that some effects are likely to exist. Only rarely is the omnibus null hypothesis plausible.[13] It is more likely that a partial null hypothesis is true; that there are non-zero effects for some outcomes and zero or negligible effects for others (Huberty and Morris, 1989; Jaccard and Guillamo-Ramos, 2002).

Jaccard and Guillamo-Ramos (2002) provide a very clear illustration of the problem. Imagine a clinical study with one main outcome variable ($Y_1 =$ depression) and four secondary outcomes (Y_2 to Y_5 measuring anxiety, self-confidence and so forth). There may be a substantial effect for Y_1 but negligible or zero effects for Y_2 to Y_5. If the Y_1 effect is large enough, the overall MANOVA main effect might be statistically significant. Subsequent ANOVA tests on the secondary outcomes would then be unprotected with respect to familywise error (considering tests of the same treatment effect on different outcomes as the family). Jaccard and Guillamo-Ramos argue that modified Bonferroni corrections to separate univariate tests of secondary outcomes are a better solution (though the primary outcome should rarely if ever be corrected in this way). An alternative strategy is to report tests of all outcomes without correction. This may be sensible if the outcomes are correlated (though a powerful correction such as the Westfall procedure may be preferred). Reporting unmodified effects may be reasonable if the correlations between predictors are positive and substantial, provided care is taken not to conceal the true extent of testing when communicating the results.

Using MANOVA to screen for effects prior to ANOVA is generally a very bad idea. It will usually lead either to inadequate Type I error protection or to decreased statistical power. The latter occurs when the partial null is true, but the omnibus null is not rejected. This is a consequence of the screening test itself lacking statistical power (see Zimmerman, 2004). The power issue is subtle, and will be addressed shortly. The main issue is that the test of the omnibus null hypothesis lacks focus relative to the tests of individual outcomes such as Y_1 or Y_2.

It has already been hinted that the MANOVA omnibus tests will lack statistical power, but this isn't quite true. Think about the rationale for using MANOVA to provide more powerful tests. In Jaccard and Guillamo-Ramos's example there were five outcome measures all likely to be correlated with successful treatment for depression. In a small study, none of the individual outcomes might reach statistical significance, but all might show an effect in the right direction. Could you not use MANOVA to analyze the whole set of outcome variables for a more sensible test? This seems like a good idea, but MANOVA will not always provide a more powerful test. The power of the omnibus test in MANOVA depends on sample sizes, effect sizes and the pattern of correlations between the outcomes (Cole *et al.*, 1994). Interestingly, Cole *et al.* show that if the outcome variables have high positive correlations (a situation quite likely where the outcomes are repeated measures) MANOVA will not always have high power (depending on the mix of effect sizes). With the right mix of effect sizes and correlations, MANOVA can have greater power than univariate ANOVA. However, other approaches may also have good power. In fact, the most obvious choice of outcome in some studies is probably just to average the variables (e.g., taking their mean or the mean of their z scores depending on whether they have the same or different scales). This approach seems particularly attractive when there are positive correlations between outcome measures and fairly consistent effects across those measures.

Many misapplications of MANOVA stem from a lack of understanding of how MANOVA works. There are many good introductions to MANOVA (e.g., Field, 2009), but most focus on calculation and basic interpretation. It will help to explore the simple case of a two-group design with y outcome variables Y_1 to Y_y. A fundamental (and potentially surprising) characteristic of MANOVA is that it is not an analysis of the separate outcome variables at all. It is an analysis of a linear transformation or a combination of the outcomes that we will refer to as Y_C. Technical details of the mathematics of the combination are given by Grayson (2004), but the basic form of Y_C is similar to a contrast:

$$Y_C = c_1 Y_1 + \ldots + c_y Y_y \qquad \text{Equation 16.12}$$

The weights or coefficients (c_1 to c_y) for the combination are chosen to maximize the value of a one-way ANOVA F statistic for the differences between the means Y_1 to Y_y.[14] It is important to remember that this maximizes the F ratio of the combination for the effect being considered. Different effects in the same design nearly always end up with different weights. MANOVA therefore is really a 'disguised' ANOVA with a transformed Y variable. Grayson points out that Type I protection (for the omnibus H_0) is obtained because an ANOVA test of an individual outcome such as Y_1 is also a linear combination of the full set of Y variables (one in which the weights are one for Y_1 and zero for all other outcomes):

$$Y_1 = 1 \times Y_1 + 0 \times Y_2 \ldots + 0 \times Y_y$$

If the omnibus null were true and this 'combination' was statistically significant by chance alone (the definition of a Type I error), then the combination that maximizes the F statistic, Y_C, would also be statistically significant.

What gives cause for caution about MANOVA (at least as it is routinely applied) is that the linear combination that maximizes an F ratio is an inherently atheoretical approach. There is no guarantee that this linear combination (the *discriminant function*) is interpretable. Grayson (*ibid.*) provides several plausible examples of simple data sets that do not have an interpretable structure (or at least not one that makes any kind of theoretical sense).

If a researcher has a hypothesis about the differences in a particular outcome measure, it does not seem like a good idea to test the hypothesis using a different outcome measure (whether that outcome measure is theoretically interpretable or not). A number of experts advise against MANOVA if you are really are interested in the differences between the means of individual outcome measures (Huberty and Morris, 1989; Jaccard and Guillamo-Ramos, 2002; Grayson, 2004). If you have an *a priori* reason to think that some linear combination of several outcomes is meaningful, then a better approach might be to combine the outcomes yourself (e.g., using an average or weighted average).

Huberty and Morris (1989) discuss legitimate research questions for MANOVA. These rest on whether the inter-relationships between outcome measures themselves are of interest to a researcher. In particular, MANOVA will sometimes throw up theoretically meaningful linear combinations. Although this is true, other approaches to this problem should be considered. If the primary interest is in combinations of predictors that best discriminate different outcomes then *discriminant analysis* may be appropriate. Multilevel regression models can also be extended to deal with multiple outcome variables in what is termed a multivariate multilevel model (Hox, 2010). The multilevel approach is attractive because it may permit explicit modeling of the correlations between outcome variables and can handle missing outcomes.

MANOVA provides two additional causes for concern, one widely known and the other less so. The widely known issue is that MANOVA produces several different, rival test statistics. With only two outcome variables they all reduce to the same statistic, *Hotelling's* T^2.[15] With more than two outcomes *Wilk's* Λ (lambda),[16] *Pillai's trace*, *Hotelling's trace* and *Roy's largest root* are usually provided by MANOVA software. Olson (1976) recommends *Pillai's trace* as the most robust to violations of MANOVA assumptions, but *Wilk's* Λ is also popular (see Field, 2009). The final cause for concern is in relation to effect size. A number of MANOVA effect size metrics have been developed, but none seem particularly useful. For instance, eta-squared variants can be derived from *Wilk's* Λ (a measure of unexplained sample variance for Y_C), but have unattractive properties. Because Y_C is maximized separately for each test, the total proportion of variance explained by all effects can exceed one, and will not strictly be comparable even within an analysis. As different studies will capitalize on sampling variability to determine Y_C, MANOVA effect sizes are also not strictly comparable between studies (and this is true also for unstandardized differences in Y_C).

In summary, MANOVA has a potential application in pure repeated measures analyses (the focus here). It sometimes provides more powerful tests than epsilon-corrected tests when sphericity is violated. It is less useful for mixed designs, but may be appropriate for tests on main effects in balanced designs. However, the power advantage of MANOVA is not consistent; switching to a multilevel model is recommended. The multilevel model approach has the flexibility to mimic both ANOVA and MANOVA analyses and to relax constraints inherent in both models (e.g., sphericity and multisample sphericity). The common strategy of MANOVA followed by univariate ANOVA is inappropriate for testing multivariate hypotheses and should be replaced by genuinely multivariate approaches (Huberty and Morris, 1989; Enders, 2003).

16.7 ANCOVA with repeated measures

ANCOVA with repeated measures expands the familiar repeated measures designs to include a covariate. This approach is most appropriate for randomized experimental designs with continuous confounding variable, but can also be applied to non-experimental designs (provided the usual cautions about using the covariate as a 'statistical control' are borne in mind). Adding a covariate appears to be a relatively harmless process, but can end up being rather messy. A one-way design with single covariate would take the form:

$$y_{ij} = \mu + b\left(C_i - \mu_C\right) + \pi_i + \tau_j + \tau\pi_{ij} + \varepsilon_{ij} \qquad \text{Equation 16.13}$$

The covariate C in Equation 16.13 is centered (by subtracting its mean μ_C) and takes the same value for each of the $i = 1$ to n observations. Both these points turn out to be very important.

As it turns out, this form of pure repeated measures ANCOVA design may be uninteresting. In Equation 16.13, the covariate is measured between participants; there is one covariate score for each of the participants. Variation in the covariate equates to individual differences between participants. If the covariate was not present, this variation would get absorbed by the subjects term of the repeated measures analysis. If the covariate varied across repeated measures (often termed a *time-varying covariate*) then the model would also be inappropriate, because it would fail to capture important variation across observations indexed by i and j. Time-varying covariates can be dealt with in a number of ways, but multilevel regression models provide an elegant solution. The main motivation to add a time-stable covariate to a pure repeated measures model therefore differs from an independent measures design. The reason for including the covariate should be because its effect is of substantive interest, or because you are interested in testing covariate-by-treatment interactions.

Time-stable covariates are more interesting in mixed designs, because they potentially increase sensitivity to independent measures effects. Even so, there may still be advantages to separating out the independent measures analysis from the repeated measures analysis. In the basic one-way design ANCOVA above, it would perhaps be easier to run a one-way repeated measures ANOVA and a separate regression (or correlation) between outcome and covariate. One reason for this is that the way repeated measures ANCOVA is implemented in some software is problematic. A stronger reason to use a repeated measures ANCOVA model, in both mixed and pure repeated measures designs, is to include covariate-by-treatment interactions for the repeated measures factor. In some studies this will not be imperative, but in studies with measured factor by manipulated factor interactions it is strongly advisable (Yzerbyt *et al.*, 2004).

In the earlier presentation of factorial ANCOVA, centering of the covariate was a convenience. This is not so for tests of main effects of repeated measures factors in ANCOVA. For repeated measures analyses a number of packages use difference coding (as in MANOVA profile analyses). Difference coding strips out individual differences from the *SS* calculation on the repeated measures factor (because the means of differences between levels rather than the means of the levels are being compared). Delaney and Maxwell (1981) explain how adjusting the difference scores using a covariate messes up this calculation. One way to understand what happens is to realize that the difference scores have already eliminated the average effect of the covariate from the *SS*. A further adjustment for the covariate mean of each group confuses matters. It would, in effect, adjust the *SS* for the repeated measures main effect for the difference between the mean of the covariate and zero. This is not something you would usually want to do (*ibid.*).

Once a covariate is added, any tests of repeated measures main effects are no longer interpretable in isolation (though the overall model, including the prediction equation, is not compromised). This is a little like the problem with product terms between uncentered main effects in moderated multiple regression. The solution is the same: center the covariates prior to adding them to the ANOVA. For the same reasons that apply in moderated multiple regression, interactions between covariates and other predictors are unaffected. Adding any new predictor or set of predictors to a model allows you to test the effect of the predictor using standard model comparison approaches (e.g., F tests or ΔAIC).

As a general approach, repeated measures ANCOVA can be considered a mixed ANOVA in which the independent measures effect is a continuous covariate with a single *df*. This produces an ANOVA table resembling Table 16.5. Additional covariates and product terms to test covariate by factor interactions (moderator effects) can be added to the model. The product terms should be computed using the centered covariates and it is best to compute and add the centered covariate and product terms to the model yourself (unless you are certain that your software handles them correctly).

Two broad strategies for repeated measures ANCOVA are recommended. One is the full repeated measures ANCOVA with all repeated measures factors, all independent measures and all covariates of interest. If you adopt this strategy it is advisable that you use effect coding (or equivalent ANOVA parameterization) and center all covariates. If covariates are not centered, the repeated measures main effects may be uninterpretable. An alternative strategy is to conduct two separate analyses (see Rutherford, 2001). In the first analysis, no covariates are included but all factors of interest (independent or repeated measures) and their interactions are present. This first analysis is used only to assess interactions between and main effects of repeated measures factors. The second analysis adds all covariates of interest and any covariate by factor interactions. The second model can be used to assess the remaining effects (i.e., any that are not pure repeated measures effects).

The former 'global' strategy is probably the safest method, provided all covariates are centered. The alternative 'two phase' method is useful if you want to estimate effects at a value of a covariate other than its mean. This is useful, for example, in developmental trajectory analysis (Thomas *et al.*, 2009). It can also be also useful for obtaining contrasts and simple effects for repeated measures factors or interactions between repeated measures factors that do not need covariate adjustment.

16.7.1 ANCOVA, pre-post designs and gain scores

A *pre-post design* is a repeated measures design in which measurements of an outcome variable are taken before an intervention or experimental manipulation (the pre-test or baseline) and again afterwards (the post-test). When paired measures from a pre-post design are analyzed, a popular strategy is to simplify the analysis using *gain scores*. A gain score is the change in outcome between the pre-test and post-test (i.e., post-test score minus pre-test score). For a repeated measures design with more than two time points it is possible to generalize gain scores as *change relative to baseline*. Here the baseline score is subtracted from all repeated measures prior to ANOVA analysis (and is equivalent to calculating separate gain scores for each post-test measurement).

Analysis of gain scores isn't the only option. Think about a two independent group design in which the aim of the study is to determine whether the change between pre-test and post-test scores differs between the groups. Two other alternatives could be selected, one more interesting than the other. First, one could use mixed measures ANOVA with pre-test and post-test scores as levels of the repeated measures factor. This is a fairly uninteresting alternative, because the F ratio from the ANOVA interaction is equivalent to the independent t test of the difference in gain scores between groups ($t^2 = F$). Analysis of gain scores (or analysis of change relative to baseline) and ANOVA of the raw scores are equivalent with respect to the test of the differential change in outcome.

The second alternative is to use the pre-test or baseline score as a covariate in the analysis. This models the change between the pre-test and post-test outcome in a very different way. To illustrate what is going on, we'll adapt the approach of Wright (2006) and present the equations for ANOVA and ANCOVA as regression models where group is a dummy coded predictor (X). In the gain score model (equivalent to ANOVA) the regression model is:

$$gain_i = post_i - pre_i = b_0 + b_1 x_i + e_i \qquad \text{Equation 16.14}$$

The corresponding ANCOVA model is:

$$post_i = b_0 + b_2 pre_i + b_1 x_i + e_i \qquad \text{Equation 16.15}$$

Comparing the two will be easier if the gain score model is rearranged in terms of the post-test scores (by adding the pre-test scores to both sides). This produces:

$$post_i = b_0 + pre_i + b_1 x_i + e_i \qquad \text{Equation 16.16}$$

The crucial difference between Equation 16.15 and Equation 16.16 is that the ANCOVA model estimates an additional parameter: the slope of the pre-test scores b_2. In the gain score model, the pre-test scores are a constant and therefore the value of b_2 is implicitly assumed to be one.

Having presented the models in this way, it should be clear that the two models can lead to different conclusions, because the tests of the differences between groups (the test b_1) are not identical. The most famous demonstration of this is *Lord's paradox* (Lord, 1967). Lord showed that two groups could show no difference when compared using gain scores, but a large difference when comparing the means adjusted for their pre-test score. Lord used an artificial example, but the 'paradox' can also be found in real data sets (Wainer and Brown, 2004; Wright and London, 2009). In the Wright and London example (using data from London *et al.*, 2009), children's recall for an event (a magic show) was measured two weeks after the event and again ten months later. The age of the children at the start of the study varied from about five to nine years. Aside from the predictor X being a continuous covariate (the age in months of a child at the start of the study), this is identical to the earlier example. One of the research questions was whether the change in recall differed for younger and older children. The analysis of gain scores leads to the following prediction equation:

$$post = 3.061 + pre - 0.085\,age$$

The ANCOVA analysis gives a very different outcome:

$$post = -1.729 + 0.105\,pre + 0.044\,age$$

The effects are not only different, but they lie in opposite directions. Which model is correct? The literature on Lord's paradox is substantial and not easy to summarize. It turns out that there is no definitive answer. Because the models differ, each of them addresses a different hypothesis. The correct answer depends on the context of the study and its objective. That stated, there are ways to approach an answer. A number of commentators have pointed out that if you don't care what causes the difference in post-test scores (as may occur in some applied work) it may be reasonable just to focus on the observed differences using gain scores (Wright, 2006). More likely, a researcher will care about the relationships between predictors and the outcome measure. Wainer's (1991) position is that the choice of model depends on untestable assumptions about the relationship between pre-test and post-test scores (the parameter estimated by b_2). If $b_2 = 1$ in the population, the gain score approach will be correct, but if $b_2 \neq 1$ then ANCOVA is appropriate. If $b_1 = 1$ then you are assuming that, on average, the mean of the post-test and pre-test scores would be the same in the population if the effects of the other predictors were not present. It is the counterfactual nature of the assumption that makes it untestable; it depends on information not present in the sample. As Wainer (*ibid.*, p. 149) puts it: 'The very nature of untestable assumptions means that there is no statistical procedure that can be counted on to settle this issue. The answer to this question must come from other sources.'

Returning to Wright and London's example, would you expect the post-test recall to be on average the same (all other things equal) as pre-test recall? The simple answer is no. After ten months you'd expect all the children to have forgotten some of the information. This suggests the ANCOVA model is preferable. It is the more plausible of the two models, as it predicts older children remember more than younger children at the post-test (conditional on the initial level of recall). However, this is not necessarily the 'correct' answer. Even in this apparently clear-cut example Wright and London (2009) contrive a scenario in which the gain score model may be appropriate. What if an investigator has to select either an older or younger child to interview immediately after a crime (with the other child being interviewed much later)? The gain score model is useful here because it suggests that the older child should be interviewed first, because a delay would result in a larger absolute reduction in recall relative to the younger child.[17] Although the scenario is contrived it illustrates how great care should be taken in selecting the correct model. In addition, the usual ANCOVA concerns about the linearity of covariate effects and the absence of interactions apply (*ibid*.). In this case the linearity assumption is implausible and it might be sensible to assume an approximate power law relationship, though the precise nature of the forgetting curve is a matter of considerable debate (e.g., see Lansdale and Baguley, 2008).

Even though specifying the correct model can be hard, some guidelines are available. If the predictor of interest (e.g., group) is manipulated by the experimenter and therefore can be assigned at random, then all approaches produce unbiased tests, though ANCOVA tends to have greater statistical power (Wright, 2006). If pre-test score is confounded with the predictor of interest then ANCOVA can produce unbiased estimates of the de-confounded effects (though this is not necessarily the question of interest). ANCOVA is usually preferred in simple experimental and quasi-experimental studies looking to understand the effects of individual predictors. Maris (1998) also argues that ANCOVA is preferable if the pre-test is used to determine the assignment to the groups being compared. If the mechanism of assignment to groups is often unknown (e.g., because pre-existing 'groups' are measured) this presents a problem. These are the cases where it is necessary not only to know the precise hypothesis you wish to test, but also to try and work out which of the untestable assumptions about the model is most plausible. This issue is important because selecting the wrong model for the research question may introduce bias.

Some broad conclusions are possible. For randomized designs and situations where the pre-test determines assignment to groups ANCOVA has greater statistical power and is unbiased (Maris, 1998; Jamieson, 2004; Van Breukelen, 2006). For non-randomized studies where assignment to groups is not based on pre-test scores, it is argued that ANCOVA may have greater bias (Jamieson, 2004; Van Breukelen, 2006). However, recent work comparing randomized and non-randomized studies suggests that this is not inevitable (Cook *et al.*, 2008; Shadish *et al.*, 2008).

It appears that the key factor is being able to include predictors likely to have caused differential baseline performance, rather than just the usual range predictors used for matching or statistical control (e.g., easy to measure demographic factors such as age or sex). The argument here is closely related to that for dealing with missing data (e.g., drop out) by including predictors of missingness. This recent work is consistent with that of Senn (2006) who demonstrated that in situations where ANCOVA is biased it is difficult to design studies to detect a causal effect of a treatment in which change scores would not also be biased. It is sensible to take steps to remove as many sources of bias as possible (e.g., at the design stage or by inclusion of covariates). The question of which statistical model is best has no simple answer and will depend on the design and context of the study, with work on how best to select an analysis still ongoing (e.g., Dinh and Yang, 2011; Cousens *et al.*, 2011).

Box 16.2 Structuring repeated measures data: long form versus broad form

To run any repeated measures ANOVA it is necessary to structure the data in a way that preserves the relationship between repeated observations and the units being observed. To keep the explanation that follows manageable, assume that the repeated measures are on human participants and that the outcome is measured at two time points (*Time 1* and *Time 2*). Repeated measures analyses are tricky to deal with because different software requires data structured in different ways.

Independent measures data for regression and related analyses are usually represented in a data file or spreadsheet as follows:

Participant	*Predictor*	*Outcome*
P1	8.3	29
P2	6.1	12
P3	8.5	23
...	...	...

Each variable (a covariate or grouping variable) is a distinct column and each participant a separate row. These rows are often termed 'cases'.

The default repeated measures data structure in many packages is to represent data in what is sometimes called *broad form*:

Participant	*Predictor*	*Time 1*	*Time 2*
P1	8.3	29	33
P2	6.1	12	19
P3	8.5	23	20
...	...	...	...

This arrangement preserves the one case (row) per participant property of the independent measures data structure. It differs in the important respect that each repeated measures outcome is defined as a separate variable. Software that uses the broad form therefore has to have a method of linking the outcome variables in some way (e.g., requiring the user to define the appropriate columns as a repeated measures or within subjects factor).

An obvious alternative structure is to represent the data in *long form*:

Participant	*Predictor*	*Time*	*Outcome*
P1	8.3	1	29
P1	8.3	2	33
P2	6.1	1	12
P2	6.1	2	19
P3	8.5	1	23
P3	8.5	2	20
...	...	...	...

The long form violates the property that the data from a single participant is restricted on a single case, but retains the property of the standard independent measures structure that the outcome is described by observations in a single column. The broad form is popular because it provides a more efficient summary of the data (i.e., one with less repetition). However, for some regression models – especially multilevel models – it is easier to work with data in long form.

For multilevel data structures, the long form extends very easily to represent three, four or more levels. An important advantage is that it allows you to represent both cross-classified and nested data structures. In a nested design, observations are clustered uniquely within other measurement units. Here participants are nested within groups (with no participant in more than one group):

Group	*Participant*	*Outcome*
G1	P1	17
G1	P1	9
G1	P2	8
G1	P2	5
G2	P3	11
G2	P3	12
...	...	...

In a cross-classified design, lower-level observations are not clustered uniquely within high-level units. A fully crossed repeated measures structure is an extreme version where both measurement units are clustered within each other. Here the same four items in the experiment (I1 to I4) are clustered with every participant, though it would be just as valid to state that all *n* participants are clustered within every item:

Participant	*Item*	*Outcome*
P1	I1	10
P1	I2	11
P1	I3	7
P1	I4	9
P2	I1	15
P2	I2	8
...	...	...

Switching between the two formats can be time-consuming and is prone to error. Both SPSS and R have commands or functions for switching between the two data structures. For small data sets you may prefer to rearrange data in a spreadsheet such as Excel (because it is easy to check the results visually). In larger data sets it is better to use software to rearrange the data, but it is vital to check descriptive and other statistics to make sure the data are structured correctly.

16.8 R code for Chapter 16

16.8.1 One-way ANOVA with repeated measures (Example 16.1)

There are a number of different approaches to running repeated measures ANOVA models in R. There are pros and cons to each approach. Repeated measures ANOVA models with balanced data is one area in which the power and flexibility of R can be annoying; there are several very different methods to fit the same model (each with its own quirks).

For a basic model it is possible to use `aov()` by using the `Error()` function to specify the correct error terms to use in the analysis. It is also necessary to code a participant or subject variable as a factor for use within the `Error()` function. This approach uses the long form of the data rather than the broad form (used in most other software). The long form of the pride data from Example 16.1 is in a file named `pride_longS.csv` while the broad form is in `prideS.csv`. To run a one-way repeated measures ANOVA using `aov()` try the following code:

```
pride.long <- read.csv('pride_longS.csv')
pride.long$participant <- as.factor(pride.long$participant)

pride.anov <- aov(accuracy ~ emotion +
  Error(participant/emotion), pride.long)
summary(pride.anov)
```

The participant identifier can also be defined as a factor within the command:

```
pride.anov <- aov(accuracy ~ emotion +
  Error(factor(participant)/emotion), pride.long)
summary(pride.anov)
```

The `Error()` function is required to get R to recognize the repeated measures structure and select the correct error terms. The `participant/emotion` argument indicates that the `emotion` factor is fully nested within participants.

Had the original data used number and letter combinations (e.g., P1, P2 etc.), R would have converted `participant` to a factor by default. There are several ways to convert between the long and broad form (see Box 16.1). The following code uses the `stack()` and `unstack()` functions, which work well for simple cases. More complex data sets should use `reshape()`. The next example turns the long form into the broad form and then turns the broad form back. The default column names for `stack()` output are 'values' and 'ind', so the last command just updates these. Note that the column orders in the `pride.long2` are different from `pride.long`. The broad form is handy for getting the means or *SD*s of the repeated measures conditions.

```
pride.broad <- unstack(pride.long, accuracy ~ emotion)
mean(pride.broad)
sd(pride.broad)

pride.long2 <- stack(pride.broad)
names(pride.long2) <- c('accuracy', 'emotion')
```

The `car` package provides a range of powerful functions for running repeated measures ANOVAs and related analyses (and includes Greenhouse-Geisser and Huynh-Feldt corrections). The `ez` package provides a more user-friendly ('SPSS-like') way to access some `car` functions. `ez` will automatically load `car` and several other packages that it needs. Here is how to run a one-way repeated measures ANOVA using the `ezANOVA()` function:

```
library(ez)

ezANOVA(data=pride.long, dv=.(accuracy), wid =.(participant),
  within =.(emotion))
```

`ezANOVA()` has several useful features. As well as providing sphericity corrections it converts the subject term defined by `wid` to a factor automatically. In addition, `car` and therefore `ez` defaults to using hierarchical (Type II) sums of squares, whereas aov() defaults to sequential (Type I) sums of squares. ez also attempts to calculate η_g^2 (ges in the output) by treating subjects *SS* as a measured factor (other measured factors can be named using the observed argument). For one-way repeated measures designs this produces sensible output (equivalent to η^2).

Two additional methods could be mentioned at this point. One is to fit a MANOVA model using the car package, though this offers no advantage over the ez approach at this stage. The final method is to use a multilevel model (sometimes called a linear mixed model). This approach is more versatile than repeated measures ANOVA, but will produce equivalent results for a balanced design if the model is set up in the appropriate way. The example here uses the lme() function in the nlme package (part of the base distribution for R), although lmer() from lme4 could also be used (but it has slightly different syntax).

```
library(nlme)

lme.fit <- lme(accuracy ~ emotion, random = ~1|participant,
  pride.long)
anova(lme.fit)
```

Further explanation of this and related functions will be provided in Chapter 18. One advantage of this approach is that if they are fitted by maximum likelihood, R will calculate AIC and related statistics for repeated measures models using lme() or lmer(). These are unavailable from aov() objects fitted including Error(). The default fitting method for lme() is *restricted maximum likelihood* (RML). This produces inferences that are identical to repeated measures ANOVA in a completely balanced design with a fully nested data structure. To compare AIC (or AIC_C or BIC) for fixed effects it is necessary to switch to maximum likelihood methods (so that the log-likelihood is estimated correctly). The following commands compare the one-way model with emotion as a factor against the intercept-only model (in which all emotions have the same mean level of accuracy):

```
io.ml <- lme(accuracy ~ 1, random = ~1|participant,
  pride.long, method='ML')

ow.ml <- lme(accuracy ~ emotion, random = ~1|participant,
  pride.long, method='ML')

AIC(io.ml, ow.ml)
delta.aic <- AIC(ow.ml) - AIC(io.ml)
exp(delta.aic/2)
```

16.8.2 Plotting repeated measures CIs (Example 16.2)

The Loftus-Masson CIs in Table 16.4 can be obtained using functions provided by Baguley (2011). Similar code is available from Wright (2007), who also provides a bootstrap version. The functions in Baguley (2011) support plotting of difference-adjusted Cousineau-Morey CIs and CIs from multilevel models with different covariance structures (for both one-way repeated measures and two-way mixed designs). Afshartous and Preston (2010) provide R code for extending Goldstein-Healy intervals (Goldstein and Healy, 1995) to dependent designs.

The examples here use the Baguley (2011) functions. The functions for one-way repeated measures analyses take data in broad form (e.g., `pride.broad` from the preceding section). The first function `lm.ci()` gives an unadjusted Loftus-Masson function:

```
lm.ci(pride.broad)
```

The second function `cm.ci()` gives a Cousineau-Morey interval. Its default is a difference-adjusted CI (in which overlapping CIs correspond to a CI for a difference in means that includes zero), using the formula in Equation 16.7. To get an unadjusted CI use the call:

```
cm.ci(pride.broad, difference = FALSE)
```

The plot in Figure 16.2 uses the `two.tiered.ci()` function. The default is to plot the inner tier as a difference-adjusted Cousineau-Morey CI and the outer tier as 95% CIs for individual means with a covariance matrix estimate that does not assume sphericity:

```
two.tiered.ci(pride.broad, ylab = 'Percentage accuracy', xlab
  = 'Emotion', grid=TRUE)
```

16.8.3 ANOVA with mixed measures (Example 16.3)

In Example 16.1, an independent measures factor with three levels was ignored for the pride data. This manipulated whether children saw pictures of expression with face, torso or both face and torso visible. Including the additional grouping factor presents no difficulty once the full data set is loaded.

```
pride.long <- read.csv('pride_long.csv')

pride.mixed <- aov(accuracy ~ emotion*condition +
  Error(factor(participant)/emotion), pride.long)
summary(pride.mixed)
```

To obtain the cell means and other summary statistics for data in long form the `ezStats()` function from the `ez` package can be used. This takes more or less the same format as `ezANOVA()`.

```
ezStats(data=pride.long, dv=.(accuracy), wid =.(participant),
  within =.(emotion), between =.(condition))
```

The output includes *n*, mean and *SD* per cell as well as Fisher's least significant difference (though this is not suitable for designs with repeated measures factors). To obtain sphericity corrections you can again use `ezANOVA()`.

```
ezANOVA(data=pride.long, dv=.(accuracy), wid =.(participant),
  within =.(emotion), between =.(condition))
```

The `lme()` function also works, though the `car` package output reported via `ez` is more informative.

```
lme.fit <- lme(accuracy ~ emotion*condition, random =
  ~1|participant, pride.long)
anova(lme.fit)
```

To plot something similar to Figure 16.3, `interaction.plot()` could be used:

```
interaction.plot(pride.long$emotion, pride.long$condition,
  pride.long$accuracy, xlab='Emotion', ylab= 'Percentage
  accuracy', legend = FALSE)
```

A prettier, color plot could be specified using the `ez` package `ezPlot()` function. This function returns an object that can be edited further using the `ggplot2` package.

```
ezPlot(data=pride.long, wid = .(participant), dv=.(accuracy),
  within = .(emotion), between = .(condition), x = .(emotion),
  split = .(condition), do_bars=FALSE)
```

The *x* argument defines which of the repeated (within) or independent (between) factors is on the *x*-axis and `split` determines whether to split by levels of another factor (as separate lines). Setting `do_bars=TRUE` adds error bars based on Fisher's LSD (not desirable in this case). Baguley (2011) includes a two-tiered error bar function for mixed designs based on `two.tiered.ci()`. Below, `reshape()` is used to get the full pride data set into broad form and the participant ID stripped out so that the grouping variable is the first column in the new data frame `pride.mixed`. Shown here is a basic plot that can be edited or relabeled:

```
pride.broad2 <- reshape(pride.long, idvar = 'participant',
  direction = 'wide', timevar = 'emotion', v.names =
  'accuracy')[2:5]

two.tiered.mixed(pride.broad2, group.var='first', lines=TRUE)
```

16.8.4 Contrasts on a repeated measures factor (Example 16.4)

A contrast is a form of weighted comparison of means. With pure repeated measures designs, contrasts can be run as paired *t* tests between weighted means. To illustrate this Example 16.4 runs a contrast for the pride data set. Working with the broad form of the data set, first extract two vectors, one for the accuracy of the pride emotion and one for the mean happiness and surprise. The *t* test can then be run comparing the means of these vectors.

```
pride.mean <- pride.broad$pride
nonpride.mean <- (pride.broad$happiness +
  pride.broad$surprise)/2

t.test(nonpride.mean, pride.mean, paired=TRUE)
```

As an alternative to the t test or 95% CI the t statistic or mean and SE can be used calculate Bayes factors or likelihood intervals if desired (using functions from Chapter 11).

```
JZS.prior.Bf.1s(1.30, 90)
t.lik.int(6.94444, 5.33, 90)
```

There is nothing special about repeated measures contrasts – any ANOVA contrast that outputs a t statistic can be used to calculate a Bayes factor or a likelihood interval.

16.8.5 Interaction contrasts with repeated measures (Example 16.5)

Interaction contrasts for pure repeated measures effects can be calculated using the t test approach described earlier. This avoids sphericity problems (possibly with some loss of power), but does not extend to mixed measures interaction terms. One way to deal with mixed effects is to adopt the approach described in Example 16.5. To calculate an interaction contrast it is necessary to decide on the interaction weights and it is usually best to work with them in matrix form. For instance, the matrix for the contrast in Example 16.5 would be:

```
cont <- matrix(c(0,0,0,1,-1,0,-1,1,0), 3, 3)
```

The interaction residuals (the cell means after sweeping out the main effects) could be obtained in several ways. However, R can provide them directly using the `model.tables()` function. Using the interaction model from the `aov()` command fitted earlier (`pride.mixed`) the residuals are given in the table for the `emotion:condition` interaction.

```
model.tables(pride.mixed)
int.resids <-
  model.tables(pride.mixed)$tables$'emotion:condition'
```

The contrast score is the summed product of the interaction residuals multiplied by the contrast weights, while $SS_{contrast}$ is obtained from contrast score and n per cell.

```
c.score <- sum(cont*int.resids)
c.score

n <- 30
ss.contrast <- c.score^2/(sum(cont^2)/30)
ss.contrast
```

$SS_{contrast} = 40333.33$ and is slightly larger than in the worked example (because of rounding error). F, p, $r_{alerting}$ and $r^2_{alerting}$ are:

```
r.alerting <- cor(as.vector(resids),as.vector(cont))
r2.alerting <- r.alerting^2
c(r.alerting, r2.alerting)

ms.error <- 1325
F <- ss.contrast/ms.error
F ; pf(F, 1, 174, lower.tail = FALSE)
```

As the F ratio is very large the p value is tiny, though it is more interesting to focus on $r^2_{alerting}$. This suggests that the interaction contrast accounts for most of the variance of the interaction effect.

It is also possible to adapt the cell means approach described in Chapter 15 to mixed and repeated measures models. These analyses are run as multilevel models. First, the cell means interaction model needs to be fitted using `lme()`.

```
library(nlme)
pride.cmm <- lme(accuracy ~ 0 + emotion:condition, random =
  ~1|participant, pride.long)
pride.cmm
```

The `glht()` function isn't the most flexible option for running the contrast. Instead, we'll use `estimable()` from the package `gmodels`. This is used for calculating 'estimable functions' (linear functions of model parameters) which contrasts are a special case of. The function is more flexible than `glht()`, but doesn't directly support corrections for multiple testing. The key advantage of `estimable()` is that it takes input from a wide range of model objects plus a contrast matrix. To reduce confusion, the contrast matrix works with named parameters (with unnamed parameters set to zero). The following example grabs the names required for the contrast from the model object and adds them to the contrast matrix. Because a cell means model has been fitted, the names are those of the nine cell means (e.g., `emotionhappiness : conditionboth` is the cell mean for the happiness emotion with both torso and face presented).

```
library(gmodels)

labels <- names(coef(pride.cmm))[1:9]

contr <- matrix(c(0,0,0,1,-1,0,-1,1,0),1,9,
  dimnames=list('contrast',labels))

estimable(pride.cmm, contr)
```

The reported t statistic is 5.517036. Its squared value is 30.43769, identical, allowing for rounding error, to the 30.44025 obtained for F by the other method. The function provides a 95% CI if a `conf.int=.95` argument is added, but these are on the incorrect scale. The following code will rescale the contrast score, *SE* and CI without also (incorrectly) rescaling the df:

```
estimable(pride.cmm, contr, conf.int=.95)[1:2]/2
estimable(pride.cmm, contr, conf.int=.95)[6:7]/2
```

The multilevel approach has several advantages. It can be extended to deal with violations of sphericity and multisample sphericity or to more complex models (e.g., with unbalanced designs or time-varying covariates). The resulting models will not always produce statistics with an exact t or F distribution (though in this case, the statistics are known to be exact if the assumptions are met).

16.8.6 Generalized η^2 measures for repeated measures (Example 16.6)

Calculators for generalized η^2 are not easy to automate, because the decision over whether to consider variables as manipulated or measured is slightly subjective (and may vary with context). Using R can make the calculations easier – particularly for the total *SS*.

```
N <- 30*3*3
ss.tot <- var(pride.long$accuracy)*(N-1)
```

To get the generalized measures then involves manually adjusting the denominator using information from the ANOVA output:

```
ss.effect <- 44231
ges <- ss.effect / (ss.tot + ss.effect - sum(ss.effect + 5616
  + 26060))
ges.contrast <- ss.contrast / (ss.tot + ss.contrast -
  sum(ss.effect + 5616 + 26060))
c(ges, ges.contrast)
```

Note that `ezANOVA()` also provides η_g^2 output for the interaction. Its output of 0.09026790 matches that calculated in Example 16.6 – indicating that it is treating the repeated measures factor and the independent measures factor as manipulated factors. This is debatable. Emotions vary naturally in our environment so the repeated measures factor could be considered measured. The emotion factor should therefore be considered measured. If so, η_g^2 for the interaction should be:

```
ges <- ss.effect/(ss.tot - 26060)
ges
```

This can be checked with `ezANOVA()` where the observed argument allows you to override the defaults and treat a fixed factor as measured rather than manipulated.

```
ezANOVA(data=pride.long, dv=.(accuracy), wid =.(participant),
  within =.(emotion), between = .(condition), observed=
  .(emotion), detailed=TRUE)
```

16.8.7 R packages

Bates, D. M., Maechler, M., and Bolker, B. M. (2011) *lme4*: Linear mixed-effects models using S4 classes. R package version 0.999375-39.

Fox, J., and Weisberg, S. (2010) *An R Companion to Applied Regression*, (2nd edn). Thousand Oaks CA: Sage.

Lawrence, M. A. (2011) *ez*: Easy analysis and visualization of factorial experiments. R package version 3.0-0.

Pinheiro, J., Bates, D. M., DebRoy, S., Sarkar, D, and the R Core team (2011) *nlme*: Linear and Nonlinear Mixed Effects Models. R package version 3.1–98.

Warnes, G. R., *et al.* (2011) *gmodels*: Various R programming tools for model fitting. R package version 2.15.1.

16.9 Notes on SPSS syntax for Chapter 16

16.9.1 ANOVA with repeated measures (Examples 16.1 and 16.3)

Repeated measures ANOVA analyses in SPSS use the general linear model `GLM` command (which can also run `UNIANOVA` commands using the same syntax).

SPSS data file: `pride_rm.sav`

```
GLM pride happiness surprise
  /WSFACTOR=emotion 3
  /METHOD=SSTYPE(2)
  /PRINT=DESCRIPTIVE
  /WSDESIGN=emotion.
```

The statement `pride happiness surprise` defines the variables making up the within subjects (repeated measures factors) and `/WSFACTOR=emotion 3` tells SPSS that there is one repeated measures factor with three levels. The `/PRINT` subcommand requests descriptive statistics. Fitting a mixed ANOVA is straightforward with the same command:

```
GLM pride happiness surprise BY condition
  /WSFACTOR=emotion 3
  /METHOD=SSTYPE(2)
  /PRINT=DESCRIPTIVE
  /WSDESIGN=emotion.
```

A covariate could be added with a `WITH` statement. Additional repeated measures or independent measures can be added. For instance, a four-way mixed ANOVA with two repeated measures factors and two independent measures factors (`A` and `B`) could be run as:

```
GLM C1D1 C1D2 C2D1 C2D2 BY A B
  /WSFACTOR=factor1 2 Polynomial factor2 2 Polynomial
  /METHOD=SSTYPE(2)
  /WSDESIGN=factor1 factor2 factor1*factor2
  /DESIGN=A B A*B.
```

The repeated measures factors each have two levels and are defined across the variables `C1D1 C1D2 C2D1 C2D2`. The independent measures factors are defined using `BY A B` and the model is specified in the `/WSDESIGN` and `/DESIGN` subcommands. The `Polynomial` statement in the `/WSFACTOR` definition tells SPSS to run polynomial contrasts on the repeated measures factors and their interactions.

These models can also be fitted using the SPSS multilevel modeling `MIXED` command. As well as being able to relax the sphericity assumption for these models, it is also possible to obtain AIC, AIC_C and BIC.

16.9.2 Repeated measures CIs (Example 16.2)

Wright (2007) provides SPSS syntax for running Loftus-Masson CIs, while Cousineau provides SPSS syntax for the uncorrected CI using normalized data. To obtain the corrected Cousineau-Morey intervals for the pride data you can also adjust nominal confidence (in this case to 98.2%) to obtain the correct width for a 95% CI when $n = 30$ and $J = 3$ (see Baguley, 2011). The following syntax obtains the normalized data from the participant means and the grand mean (72.6851851851852). The latter is calculated from the participant means using `DESCRIPTIVES`.

SPSS data file: `pride_rm.sav`

```
COMPUTE pmeans=(pride+happiness+surprise)/3.
DESCRIPTIVES VARIABLES=pmeans
  /STATISTICS=MEAN.

COMPUTE n_pride = pride - pmeans + 72.6851851851852.
COMPUTE n_happiness = happiness - pmeans + 72.6851851851852.
COMPUTE n_surprise = pride - pmeans +72.6851851851852.
EXECUTE.

GRAPH
  /ERRORBAR(CI 98.2) = n_pride n_happiness n_surprise.
```

16.9.3 Contrasts for repeated measures designs (Examples 16.4 and 16.5)

Many repeated measures contrasts can be run using the paired t test commands. The following commands compute a weighted contrast for the pride versus other emotion contrast in Example 16.4.

SPSS data file: `pride_rm.sav`

```
COMPUTE pride_v_other=pride-(happiness+surprise)/2.
EXECUTE.

T-TEST
  /TESTVAL=0
  /VARIABLES=pride_v_other
  /CRITERIA=CI(.95).
```

This is a very versatile method for running contrasts on repeated measures. It avoids a pooled error term, but may sacrifice power if sphericity is true. The contrast can also be run using GLM, by changing the default within-subject contrasts:

```
GLM pride happiness surprise
/WSFACT = emotion(3)
special
(1 1 1
-1 .5 .5
0 -1 1).
```

This gives an *F* test of the contrast by default. With three levels there are two orthogonal contrasts by default (usually linear and quadratic polynomials specified by `Polynomial`). The contrasts are set out as a 'matrix' over several lines to reveal the structure (though it is not strictly necessary). The first row `1 1 1` defines the intercept, the second the contrast of interest and the third is an arbitrary contrast orthogonal to the first (which happens to compare the happiness and surprise means).

The default repeated and mixed measures ANOVA output (see the mixed ANOVA syntax above) includes polynomial contrasts for the repeated measures factors and interaction contrasts for effects involving repeated measures factors. Unfortunately, these are only really interpretable if the repeated measures factor is ordered (e.g., time points), which it is not for the pride data. In principle, it is possible to get SPSS to run custom interaction contrasts for mixed designs, but the difficulty of setting up the contrast coefficients often makes it easier to carry out the analysis by another route (e.g., by hand).

16.10 Bibliography and further reading

Keselman, H. J., Algina, J., and Kowalchuk, R. K. (2001) The Analysis of Repeated Measures Designs: A Review. *British Journal of Mathematical and Statistical Psychology*, 54, 1–20.

Kirk, R. E. (1995) *Experimental Design* (3rd edn) Belmont, CA: Brooks/Cole.

17
Modeling discrete outcomes

Contents

17.1 Chapter overview

The generalized linear model is an extension to the general linear model that will deal with discrete outcomes. This chapter provides a brief overview of the generalized linear model with particular focus on logistic regression for categorical outcomes and Poisson regression for count data. The links between logistic regression, Poisson regression and alternative models for categorical outcomes (multinomial, ordered logistic regression) and count data (negative binomial and zero-inflated models) are also reviewed. The chapter ends by considering the difficulty of modeling repeated measures data with discrete outcomes.

17.2 Modeling discrete outcomes in the general linear model

The general linear model is developed on the assumption that the outcome Y is continuous and unbounded. This limitation does not extend to the predictors in these models, which may be categorical or continuous. The solution to incorporating categorical predictors into regression models is to select an appropriate coding scheme (e.g., dummy or effect coding). Extending this approach to deal with a discrete outcome variable is less effective.

First, consider the case of a dichotomous variable. This could be coded as a continuous outcome taking either the value zero or the value one. The problem here is threefold: i) the usual linear regression model assumes Y is unbounded, ii) the predicted outcome is continuous and therefore can take values between zero and one and iii) distributional assumptions about the errors of the model will be violated. The first two problems are most relevant to prediction – as models that predict impossible values can be hard to interpret or lead to problems in application. On the other hand, if the focus is on predicting average rather than individual outcomes, the performance of the model could be satisfactory. Much will depend on the quality of the model (e.g., in terms of fit) and the precision you require. Recall also that, as a rule, it is the degree of distributional violations, not merely their presence, that matters. As each dichotomous observation is a Bernoulli trial, the outcome Y can be considered to have a binomial distribution (if independence of trials is plausible). Under circumstances where the normal approximation to the binomial is good, general linear models (e.g., t tests, regression and ANOVA) will tend to perform well. In practice, this is when the distribution is approximately symmetrical and sample sizes are moderate to large. Prediction using a general linear model will be poorest when the average value of Y approaches zero or one and best when it is close to .5.

An alternative way of conceptualizing the problem of dealing with discrete outcomes is to consider it an issue of linearity. A linear regression model predicts the same change in Y for a given change in X. If Y is bounded, then a linear model tends to run into problems. As Y approaches an upper or lower bound, a change in X that works well for mid-range values of Y may exceed the minimum or maximum possible value of Y.[1] Having a bounded range for the outcome variable is therefore a fundamental obstacle for a linear regression model. To correctly model a discrete outcome it is necessary to find a way to allow the effect of X to vary across the legitimate range of Y. In other words, having an upper or lower bound implies that the effect of X on Y is non-linear. Although a linear approximation will sometimes work well, the challenge is to find ways to capture the non-linear effect of X on Y explicitly. This does not necessarily require a non-linear regression model (e.g., transformations of X or Y may get around this restriction).

For count data, regression models pose similar challenges: i) counts are bounded at zero, ii) treating counts as continuous can lead to fractional rather than integer predictions and iii) the distributional assumptions of the model will be violated. Again, these problems are more pronounced for prediction than hypothesis testing. If the focus is hypothesis testing, a linear regression that assumes continuous responses will often suffice. This is particularly true for large samples where count data, often presumed to be Poisson distributed, are often well approximated by a normal distribution. Even in small samples the approximation may be reasonable and can be assisted by an appropriate transformation (e.g., a square root or Freeman-Tukey transformation).

The usual regression diagnostics for checking normality and homogeneity of variance help to determine the quality of the model. Even when the normal approximation is good, it will be wise to compare results with a model assuming a discrete outcome. Modeling a discrete outcome as continuous may make the results less persuasive (particularly as an appropriate discrete model is usually not difficult to fit). Furthermore, treating the outcome as discrete should lead to more precise estimates and accurate predictions (though these gains will sometimes be marginal). A corollary of this is that a regression model for discrete outcomes may also have greater statistical power. One strategy is to fit both kinds of models. If there are major discrepancies between the results, this is usually an indication that it is necessary to treat the outcome as discrete.[2]

17.3 Generalized linear models

17.3.1 A brief introduction to the generalized linear model

In a general linear model the mean of continuous outcome is modeled as an additive function of one or more predictors plus a random error component (assumed to have normal distribution). This approach to regression places restrictions on what can be modeled. In particular, the linearity of the model – the requirement to model the mean as an additive function of predictors – makes it difficult to cope with discrete, bounded outcomes. One solution is to apply a transformation (e.g., the square root for Poisson counts). This will sometimes work, but represents a somewhat *ad hoc* fix rather than a principled solution to the problem. A principled solution is to generalize the linear model to address both the problem that the mean is not a linear (i.e., additive) function of predictors and that the random component might not be a normal distribution. A *generalized linear model* does exactly this (Agresti, 1996).[3]

Agresti (*ibid.*) describes a generalized linear model in terms of three components. One component is the additive or linear combination of predictors (sometimes called the *systematic component*):

$$b_0 + b_1X_1 + \ldots + b_qX_q$$

The systematic component corresponds to the right-hand side of the of a standard regression equation. The other two components are the *random component* and the *link*. The random component specifies the outcome variable Y and a probability distribution for it. It is analogous to the left-hand side of a standard regression equation. The binomial distribution is a typical choice of random component for a dichotomous outcome, while for count data the Poisson distribution is a common default. Any distribution from the exponential family (a set of related distributions that includes the normal) can be selected as a random component.[4] The link is the component that determines the relationship between the systematic and random component. It works by specifying a function, the *link function* $g(.)$, which connects the random and systematic components. The link makes it possible to model any monotonic function of the mean of the original outcome. The expected value of the outcome $E(Y)$ is therefore related to the linear function of predictors via this link:

$$E(Y) = g(\mu) = b_0 + b_1X_1 + \ldots + b_qX_q \qquad \text{Equation 17.1}$$

This differs from a simple transformation of Y or X because the random component need not assume a normal distribution. This flexibility means that a transformation that produces an additive model doesn't also have to produce normality (provided its probability distribution can be captured by the chosen random component). Thus the link component separates the selection of a transformation from the choice of probability distribution.

The general linear model has a random component that is normal with a continuous, untransformed outcome. The generalized linear model therefore includes the general linear model as a special case. The link function for the general linear model is termed the *identity function*:

$$g(\mu) = \mu \qquad \text{Equation 17.2}$$

This is an example of a *canonical link function*. The definition of a canonical link function is somewhat technical, but it represents a natural or default choice associated with a particular random component. For a normal random component the identity function is a natural choice because it maps the range of the predictions of the regression onto the permitted range of Y. For a Poisson random component the canonical link function is the logarithm, while for the binomial distribution it is the logistic function. Although, the generalized linear model allows other random components (and permits non-canonical link functions), the following discussion is restricted to canonical link functions for the binomial, Poisson and a few closely related statistical models.

17.3.2 Estimation and inference

In the special case of a normal random component with an identity link function, the model can be fitted using least squares estimation. Otherwise generalized linear models require iterative methods to be fitted. Most software uses an iterative maximum likelihood (ML) estimation method (see Agresti, 1996), although Bayesian methods (e.g., MCMC estimation) are sometimes adopted (particularly where there are convergence problems). The algorithms for fitting these models are very similar to those used in obtaining parameter estimates for multilevel models (see Chapter 18).

Although the details of estimation for a generalized linear model are quite technical, the principle behind it is extremely simple. The model is first fitted with some vaguely plausible starting estimates for the parameters. The likelihood of the model with these parameter estimates is then calculated (i.e., a quantity proportional to the probability of these parameter estimates given the data at hand). The estimates are then altered and the likelihood recalculated. The process continues until changing the parameter estimates has no discernable impact on the likelihood (e.g., to a predetermined number of decimal places). Fitting a model this way requires greater computing power than for least squares estimation and models sometimes fail to converge on an adequate solution. For this reason, non-iterative solutions are preferred if available. This applies for models with a normal random component and identity link (standard least squares parameter estimates are therefore also maximum likelihood estimates).

A by-product of ML estimation is the maximized loglikelihood of the model (i.e., the value of the loglikelihood at convergence). This can be used to derive a *deviance* statistic equal to −2 times the loglikelihood of the model: $-2\ln(\ell)$. This statistic has an approximate χ^2 distribution. The quality of the approximation varies according to the type of generalized linear model (*ibid.*). Deviance statistics make it possible to test nested models by referring the difference between models to a χ^2 distribution with degrees of freedom *(df)* equal to the change in the number of parameters. This test is often termed a *likelihood ratio test* (LRT), though it is a conventional null hypothesis significance test (NHST). For comparisons of models differing by only a small number of parameters these χ^2 tests are generally very accurate (though the overall test of deviance of an individual model may not be). It is also straightforward to use likelihood or information-theoretic approaches to compare nested and non-nested methods (e.g., using AIC).

Individual parameters can be tested this way, but it is also common to use a normal approximation in the form of a Wald test. This Wald test involves deriving a χ^2 test statistic from the ratio of a squared model coefficient to its squared standard error (*SE*):

$$\frac{b^2}{\hat{\sigma}_b^2} \approx \chi_1^2 \qquad \text{Equation 17.3}$$

The Wald test can be extended to test several parameters simultaneously (e.g., a set of dummy variables coding a categorical predictor), by summing the test statistics and comparing them to a χ^2 distribution. Thus for J predictors this test would take the form:

$$\sum_{j=1}^{J} \frac{b_j^2}{\hat{\sigma}_{b_j}^2} \approx \chi_J^2 \qquad \text{Equation 17.4}$$

In addition, for a single parameter only, a test equivalent to that described by Equation 17.3 can be obtained using the standard normal distribution:

$$\frac{b}{\hat{\sigma}_b} \approx z \sim N(0,1) \qquad \text{Equation 17.5}$$

These are examples of a class of procedure that are often labeled Wald statistics.[5] The z version of the Wald test is commonly employed to obtain a quick, approximate test or confidence interval (CI) for a regression coefficient, though more accurate deviance tests should be preferred for formal inference in generalized linear models. The deviance of the model can also be used to provide CIs that are superior to the Wald CI, through what is called *profiling*. This involves finding confidence limits by adjusting a single parameter estimate until the deviance of the model differs by the required appropriate critical value above and below its maximum (e.g., 1.92 or approximately half of $\chi^2_{1,.95}$). This is a profile likelihood approach because all other parameters (including nuisance parameters) are fixed at their maximum likelihood estimate (*MLE*).

Taking a regression approach to modeling discrete outcomes has further advantages. Familiar concepts such as prediction equations, model checking, coding of categorical predictors and introducing product terms for moderator or interaction analyses remain useful. However, there is a cost. The additional complexity of the approach presents particular problems that would be relatively easy to resolve in least squares models.

Effect size statistics based on standardized metrics are particularly problematic when computed for generalized linear models. Unstandardized effect size metrics are more widely employed for these models than for least squares models (even among researchers who routinely report standardized metrics for least squares models). The use of a link function adds a layer of difficulty to the choice of unstandardized effect size metric, but transforming the model estimates and reporting effects in terms of the discrete outcome (e.g., counts or probability of a success) can be very effective. Statistical power for generalized models can also be tricky. A very basic first approximation is often to calculate power for a similar least squares model (perhaps incorporating a transformation). This will be sufficient for some applications. Software such as G*Power also has options for logistic and Poisson regression power calculations (Faul *et al.*, 2007). For complex generalized linear models it may be necessary to use Monte Carlo methods for sample size or statistical power estimates.

17.4 Logistic regression

In some fields, notably in clinical or health research, many of the outcome measures are dichotomous (e.g., correct or incorrect; dead or alive). Logistic regression is often the analysis of choice for such data. A logistic regression is a generalized linear model with a binomial distribution as its random component and the logistic transformation as its link function. The logistic transformation may already be familiar from its application in forming a CI for an odds ratio. Thus logistic regression uses a logit link of form:

$$g(\mu) = \ln\left(\frac{\mu}{1-\mu}\right) \qquad \text{Equation 17.6}$$

The logistic transformation has several important properties. Put simply, it copes with a discrete, dichotomous outcome by modeling the probability of obtaining successes from a binomial distribution (sticking to the convention of labeling the outcome coded one as success and the outcome coded zero as failure). Logits (or log odds) are required to model these probabilities using an additive model of predictors (see Key Concept 17.1). The logistic regression equation relates the probability of success P for the ith observation to a linear combination of predictors:

$$\ln\left(\frac{P_i}{1-P_i}\right) = b_0 + b_1 x_{1i} + \ldots + b_q x_{q,i} \qquad \text{Equation 17.7}$$

If the change in notation from μ to P is confusing, bear in mind that the expected value of the outcome Y is estimated by its mean (equivalent to the probability of success $\hat{P}$ for a binomial distribution).

Equation 17.7 expresses the relationship between the predictors and the outcome being modeled (the log odds of success), but for interpreting the parameter estimates it is typically much easier to work with the equation in its odds or probability form. The same equation can be represented in odds form by taking the exponent of each side:

$$o_i = \frac{P_i}{1 - P_i} = e^{b_0 + b_1 x_{1i} + \ldots + b_q x_{q,i}} \qquad \text{Equation 17.8}$$

Going one step further, it is possible to represent the equation in terms of the probability of success:

$$P_i = \frac{o_i}{1 + o_i} = \frac{e^{b_0 + b_1 x_{1i} + \ldots + b_q x_{q,i}}}{1 + e^{b_0 + b_1 x_{1i} + \ldots + b_q x_{q,i}}} \qquad \text{Equation 17.9}$$

You may also encounter the equation in the following form (obtained by algebraic rearrangement):

$$P_i = \frac{1}{1 + e^{-\left(b_0 + b_1 x_{1i} + \ldots + b_q x_{q,i}\right)}} \qquad \text{Equation 17.10}$$

Although Equation 17.10 is arguably somewhat simpler, the earlier format will be used here because it provides a more direct connection to the odds and log odds (logit) versions of the equations. Using these formulas it is possible to produce prediction equations from a fitted model either in log odds, odds or probability form.

Logistic regression relaxes some assumptions of least squares regression. There is no requirement that the residuals are sampled from a normal distribution and no requirement for homogeneity of variances. It does, however, assume both independence and additivity of effects on the logit scale. Violations of independence, in particular, can cause major problems for logistic regression models.

KEY CONCEPT 17.1

The logistic transformation

The logistic transformation takes P, the probability of event with only two possible outcomes, and turns in into a logit (natural logarithm of the odds of the event or log odds). Switching from a dichotomous outcome to the probability of that outcome is a clever way to turn a discrete variable into a continuous one. At the same time, it retains a relatively clear interpretation in terms of the original context. The downside is that a probability is still bounded at both zero and at one. The inherent problem of modeling a bounded outcome with a linear function has not been addressed. What is required is a function that maps the effect of one or more predictors onto a bounded probability in a systematic but non-linear way.

Transforming a probability to odds offers a partial solution:

$$o = \frac{P}{1 - P}$$

Odds (the ratio of the probability of occurrence to non-occurrence or of success to failures) are continuous and scaled from zero to infinity. Switching to odds removes a boundary at one end of the number line, but not boundary at zero. This problem is resolved by using the logarithm of the odds (with the logarithm to base e, the natural logarithm, being the default choice):

$$\text{logit} = \ln\left(\frac{P}{1 - P}\right)$$

Because the odds are always greater than zero, the logarithm of the odds ranges from $-\infty$ to ∞. At one level the transformation is merely a mathematical trick that turns a discrete binary outcome into a continuous, unbounded outcome. Yet the choice is not completely arbitrary. Both odds and probabilities are themselves directly interpretable. While in some situations it is preferable to work with probabilities, odds and odds ratios are preferable in others (depending on your goal and on factors such as whether you wish to incorporate or strip out the influence of the base rates). Furthermore, using log odds in a linear regression model implies that, while the predictors have an additive relationship with respect to the log odds, their influence on the odds is multiplicative.

A final insight is that the logistic transformation maps differences in the predictors onto a non-linear function with a particular form. To see this relationship between probability and predictors, the inverse of the logistic function (i.e., its cumulative distribution function or *cdf*) needs to be plotted:

$$P = \frac{e^x}{1 + e^x}$$

The inverse of the logistic function has a sigmoidal (S-shaped) curve.

Figure 17.1 depicts the inverse of a logistic function relating the aggregated effect of one or more predictors on the *x*-axis to the predicted probability on the *y*-axis. The curve has an almost linear section in the middle where a normal linear regression model would provide a good fit (e.g., within the range $.2 < P < .8$). It curves sharply at the extremes and converges either on zero or on one. This behavior neatly captures the required non-linearity of effects at the boundary. The function itself can be shifted up or

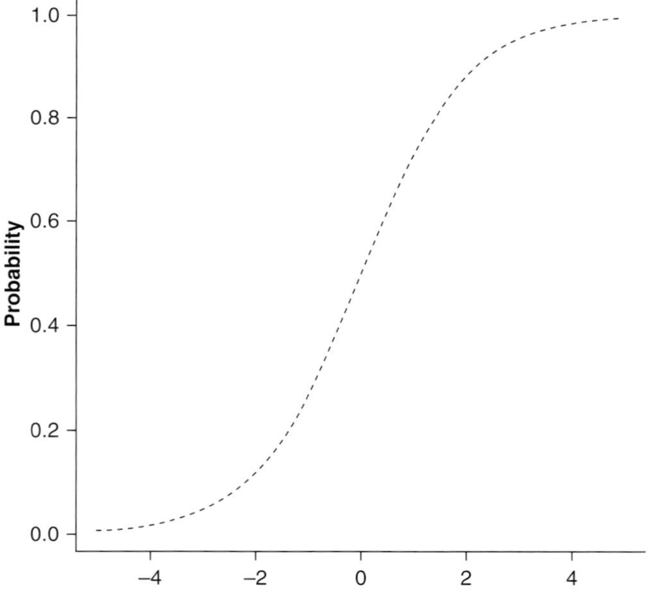

Figure 17.1 A sigmoidal curve produced by the inverse of the logistic function (the *cdf* of the logistic distribution)

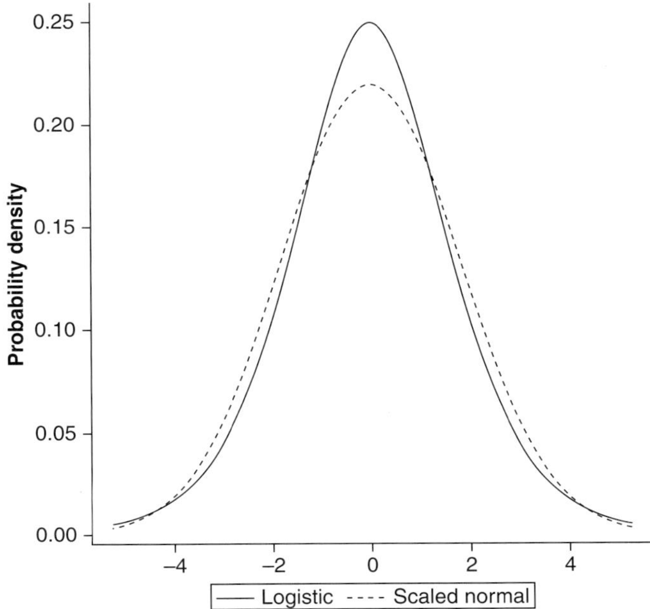

Figure 17.2 Probability distribution functions comparing the logistic distribution with a scaled normal distribution

down the *x*-axis by adding a constant to the equation (e.g., the intercept in systematic component) and the curve can become steeper or shallower by multiplying the log odds by a constant (e.g., changing the slope in a regression model). Changing the sign of the slope will change the direction of the slope so that the sigmoidal curve slopes down as it travels from left to right (required if the probability of success decreases as *X* increases).

The logistic function is not the only plausible sigmoidal function that might be adopted, but it is sufficiently flexible to work for many applications. The probability distribution for the log odds is symmetrical and approximately normal (see Section 7.5.6). This is very convenient for constructing CIs and tests. Figure 17.2 shows the *pdf* for the logistic distribution alongside a scaled normal distribution (scaled with parameters $\mu = 0$ and $\sigma = \pi/\sqrt{3}$ to match the standard logistic distribution). The rescaling is necessary because the standard logistic distribution has a variance of $\pi^2/3$, whereas the standard normal distribution has a variance of one).*

Of the other potential link functions for dichotomous data, the best known is the *probit*. The probit function maps a dichotomous outcome onto a standard normal (z) distribution (see Agresti, 1996). It does this by using the Φ function encountered in earlier chapters (or more formally, the *cdf* for the standard normal distribution). The sigmoidal form of the normal *cdf* is evident from Figure 2.8b. Logistic and probit regression produce very similar outputs for most applications (though probit regression should be superior if the dichotomous variable is derived from applying a cut-off to a continuous normal outcome).

* The logistic distribution can be altered in terms of 'spread' using a scale parameter. For many statistical applications – and all those considered here – this scale parameter is fixed at one and the variance is $\pi^2/3$.

Example 17.1 Subbotsky (2009, Experiment 3) reports an experiment looking at the impact of a suggested magical intervention on the content of dreams. Participants chose a target dream to focus on for three successive nights (e.g., involving them in some attractive role or activity). Some participants were offered a magical suggestion (a 'magic spell' to help them achieve their target dream) and some were not. One outcome of interest was the content of non-target dreams in the subsequent period. In the magical suggestion condition seven out of 21 non-target dreams were classified as 'scary', while in the no magical suggestion condition one out of 26 non-target dreams were classified as 'scary'. The total sample size (*N*) is therefore 47. Subsequent examples refer to this data set as the dream data.

It is possible to analyze these data via logistic regression. As the experimental condition is a categorical predictor it can be dummy coded (with magical suggestion coded one and no suggestion coded zero). Dream content is the outcome (with a scary dream coded as one and an ordinary dream as zero). The prediction equation is:

$$\ln\left(\frac{\hat{P}}{1-\hat{P}}\right) = -3.22 + 2.53 \times group$$

The deviance for this model is 35.211 and AIC is 39.211 (35.211 plus two times the total number of parameters $k=2$). The model has residual *df* equal to $N-q-1=45$. The term q is the number of predictors in the model (exactly as it would be in multiple regression).

The goodness-of-fit of the model could be assessed against a χ^2 distribution with 45 *df*. The NHST of goodness-of-fit is non-significant (as $df > \chi^2$). A non-significant goodness-of-fit test supposedly indicates a good fit (i.e., one not significantly different from a perfect fit), but the usual problems apply. In large samples the test will reject H_0 when there are only small departures from a model, while small samples will often fail to reject H_0 when the fit is relatively poor. Add to this the fact that the distribution of the deviance may only be poorly approximated by χ^2. The overall test of the deviance of the model is generally regarded as an unsatisfactory approach. A model comparison approach is preferred for inference.

For an individual predictor (such as the effect of group here) it is common to calculate a Wald test or CI. The *SE* for the intercept is 1.02 and the group slope is 1.12. A significance test of the intercept is uninteresting, but an interval estimate might be useful. With the dummy codes defined as above, the intercept is the estimate of the logits of a scary dream for the no magical suggestion condition. A 95% Wald CI for the intercept is:

$$b_0 \pm z_{.975} \times \hat{\sigma}_{b_0} \approx -3.2 \pm 1.96 \times 1.02 = -3.2 \pm 1.99$$

The Wald CI is not very accurate (tending to be too narrow). A more accurate approach is to use the profile likelihood: 95% CI [−6.10, −1.67]. There are several ways to get the CI for the other condition, but an easy way is to reverse the group coding (so that the magical suggestion condition is coded zero). Profile likelihood then gives a 95% CI of [−1.66, 0.18] for the magical suggestion condition. The interpretation of these point and interval estimates is quite tricky because they are on a logit scale. The issue of interpretation is explored in a later section (see Example 17.2). For the moment I'll just point out that when the odds are one the probability is .5 and the log odds are zero. As neither of the intervals include zero this suggests that the probability of a scary dream in either group is lower than .5 (as you would expect from the data).

The group effect (regardless of coding) is the difference in the logits for the two conditions. The Wald z test statistic is 2.53/1.12, and therefore $z = 2.26$, $p < .05$. Alternatively χ^2 $(1, N = 47) = 2.26^2 \approx 5.1$, $p < .05$. (The value of $p = .024$ is identical because these tests are equivalent).

An alternative test is obtained by comparing deviances for a model with and without the group predictor. The test of the difference in deviance is known as *likelihood ratio test* (sometimes labeled G^2 to distinguish it from the usual Pearson χ^2 test). The difference between the Pearson and likelihood statistics is discussed in Box 17.1. The model without the group predictor (an intercept-only model) has a deviance of 42.885. Subtracting 32.211 from 42.885 gives 7.674. The likelihood ratio test is therefore G^2 $(1, N=47)=7.67$, $p=.006$. Using profile likelihood, the corresponding 95% CI is [0.67, 5.51]. As this interval excludes zero it suggests that the odds of a scary dream are greater than one for the magical suggestion group. Out of interest, the Pearson chi-square test gives: χ^2 $(1, N=47)=7.15$, $p=.007$.

The likelihood ratio, Wald and Pearson χ^2 tests are asymptotically equivalent and should produce very similar results in large samples. In generalized linear models with small samples, the likelihood ratio test is typically more accurate than the Wald test (and should be preferred to it). In situations where both the Pearson χ^2 test of independence and the likelihood ratio test can be computed, the former is superior when some cells have small expected values and the latter when no cells have small expected values (see Box 17.1). Although the Pearson χ^2 test could have been applied here for identical or near-identical results, the logistic regression model is more flexible. It would be easy to add other categorical or continuous predictors or interactions to the model.

Box 17.1 Pearson versus likelihood χ^2 test statistics

The Pearson χ^2 statistic is best known for its application in the χ^2 test of independence, but has applications in other situations (e.g., goodness-of-fit tests). It is calculated by: i) obtaining the residual deviations of the observed cell counts from the expected cell counts for a statistical model and ii) summing the ratio of the squared deviations to the expected counts for all cells. A generic form (e.g., ignoring the subscripts) is:

$$\chi^2 = \sum \frac{(O-E)^2}{E}$$

The corresponding generic formula for the likelihood ratio chi-square is:

$$G^2 = 2\sum O \ln\left(\frac{O}{E}\right)$$

They are goodness-of-fit statistics because they increase as the difference between observed and expected values increases. Small test statistics therefore suggest a good fit to the assumed model (e.g., the model defined by a null hypothesis). Both have an asymptotic χ^2 distribution under H_0, but the Pearson chi-square converges on the χ^2 distribution more rapidly than G^2. Agresti (1996) suggests that the approximation for G^2 is poor when the ratio of total observations to cells is less than five. It tends to produce conservative inferences when data are very sparse (e.g., expected counts are less than .5) and liberal inferences when expected counts are between .5 and five. In contrast, the Pearson chi-square statistic is slightly more robust to small expected values (provided overall N is not too small and no expected counts fall below one).

The Pearson chi-square statistic is therefore typically preferred for tests in small samples. The likelihood ratio test also has properties that make it attractive – especially in fields where larger samples are more common. First, the likelihood χ^2 is the deviance (strictly the residual deviance) of the statistical model. It is therefore often employed because of its conceptual link to generalized linear models. A second useful property is that, because deviance is equal to $-2\ln(\ell)$, G^2 has a direct connection to likelihood inference (e.g., the calculation of information criteria such as AIC, AIC_C or BIC).

17.4.1 Interpreting parameter estimates in logistic regression

Interpretation of parameters in logistic regression can become convoluted. It helps to start by considering a model with only two predictors:

$$\ln\left(\frac{\hat{P}_i}{1-\hat{P}_i}\right) = b_0 + b_1 X_{1i} + b_2 X_{2i} \qquad \text{Equation 17.11}$$

The coefficient b_0 is the intercept of the generalized linear regression equation and determines the logits (log odds) when all predictors are zero. The coefficient b_1 is the slope, expressed in logits, of X_1 when X_2 is held constant. This is directly comparable to the interpretation of a coefficient in multiple regression. A one-unit increase in X_1 is associated with a b_1 increase in the log odds of success (assuming that X_2 is unchanged). If the predictors are orthogonal (or correlations between predictors are very low) the coefficients can reasonably be interpreted in isolation. Otherwise collinearity and multicollinearity present the usual difficulties for teasing apart effects of individual predictors (though, as usual, the overall fit and model predictions are unaffected as long as parameters can be estimated).

A logistic regression in logit form can be difficult to interpret (though it gets easier with experience). The slope of the inverse logistic curve (e.g., see Figure 17.1) for a given probability P and predictor is:

$$b_q P(1-P) \qquad \text{Equation 17.12}$$

For values close to $P = .5$ the slope of the predictor expressed on a probability scale is around 0.25 times the coefficient on the logit scale. This leads to an approximation using a 'divide by four rule' (Gelman and Hill, 2007). Using the rule, you can interpret the maximum effect of a predictor on the probability of an outcome by dividing its slope by four. This will be accurate for probabilities near .5, but will overestimate the impact of the predictor for probabilities approaching zero or one.

It is typically easier to interpret the regression coefficients in terms of their impact on the odds or probabilities of success. The odds of the logistic regression model with two predictors are obtained by applying the function e^x to each side of the logistic regression to give:

$$\hat{o}_i = \frac{\hat{P}_i}{1-\hat{P}_i} = e^{b_0 + b_1 X_{1i} + b_2 X_{2i}} \qquad \text{Equation 17.13}$$

This is a prediction equation for the odds of success. A useful feature is that each of the coefficients (including the intercept) has a direct interpretation in terms of odds. The intercept e^{b_0} is the odds of success when all the other predictors are coded zero. The slope e^{b_1} is the factor by which the odds of success are expected to increase for each unit increase in X_1 (with

X_2 held constant). Likewise, e^{b_2} is the multiplier for the odds of success associated with a one-unit increase in X_2. Thus the slopes in the odds form of the regression equation are a form of odds ratio (*OR*). The *OR* is therefore a useful effect size estimate in logistic regression (e.g., for situations where results from other studies with dichotomous outcomes are compared with results from logistic regression). The *OR* is particularly easy to interpret for categorical predictors with dummy coding. Under this parameterization, e^{b_q} would represent the *OR* for the category coded one relative to the category coded zero. The odds for the category coded zero would be represented by the intercept (assuming no other predictors in the model). The interpretation of predictors under effect coding is less transparent. The *OR* for an effect coded categorical predictor represents the square root of the change in odds of success.[6]

Comparing the *OR* for continuous predictors with categorical ones (on either coding scheme) should be done with caution. The *OR* for a continuous predictor will often be small in magnitude relative to those of categorical predictors. But, as in multiple regression, a one-unit change in *X* might be only a fraction of the possible change (in terms of the range in the sample or in the population). If you need to compare the two, make the comparison for a substantial change in the continuous predictor (e.g., two *SD* or the maximum possible change) or rescale the continuous predictor to facilitate the comparison you wish to make. Coefficients smaller than 0.1 or 0.01 tend to be awkward to work with (e.g., because software reports results to only two or three decimal places). Rescaling predictors can remove this sort of problem and make parameter estimates easier to interpret (without changing the fundamental model). CIs for the odds ratios are obtained by separately transforming the lower and upper bounds of the CI in log odds form, moving from a symmetrical interval estimate to an asymmetrical one.

A final option is to present the equation in probability form. Many people will find predicted probabilities intuitively more appealing than odds (and certainly than log odds). On the other hand, the mathematical properties of odds are sometimes very convenient for researchers. Effects on the odds scale are insensitive to the base rates of the outcome (i.e., to the proportion of successes). This makes them better for comparing effects that may have different base rates. The probability scale is better if you want to factor in the base rate (e.g., to show the impact of an effect for a specific individual or group). For this reason it is sensible to become familiar with both forms of the equation. The predicted probabilities for a model with two predictors are:

$$\hat{P}_i = \frac{e^{b_0+b_1x_{1i}+b_2x_{2i}}}{1+e^{b_0+b_1x_{1i}+b_2x_{2i}}} \qquad \text{Equation 17.14}$$

It is possible to interpret either effect on the probability scale by 'plugging' in particular values of other predictors. The obvious choices are the mean for continuous predictors and zero for dummy coded categorical predictors. However, it is important to realize that these choices can have a substantial impact on the predictions – because, in effect, they involve a shift in the base rates. For instance, a continuous predictor will produce a smaller absolute increase in the predicted probability of success for a group with a high average probability of success (e.g., .80) than for one with a low average probability of success (e.g., 0.20).

One solution to presenting such predictions is to plot the predicted probability as a function of one or more effects of interest. The prediction equation can be used to plot a sigmoidal logistic function relating the effects of a predictor (or combination of predictors) to the probability of success or failure. The observed or predicted values can also be added to the plot. Plotting the data on log odds scales (e.g., with confidence bands) helps to assess the linear fit of the

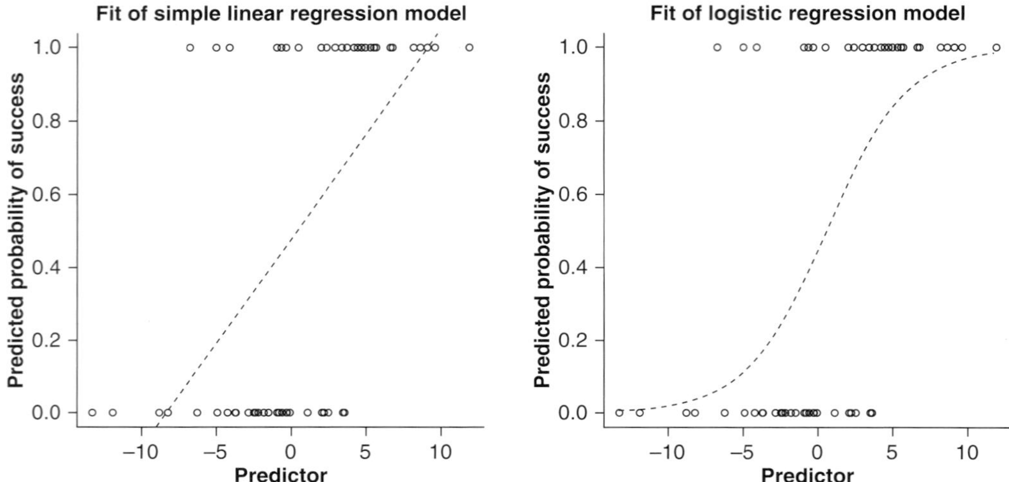

Figure 17.3 Comparing linear and logistic regression fits for a simulated data set with a single continuous predictor

systematic component (very much as you would in linear regression). Gelman and Hill (2007) provide examples of other ways to plot data from a logistic regression.

Figure 17.3 plots the predicted probabilities for a logistic regression involving a single continuous predictor (using simulated data). The panel on the left shows the line of best fit for a simple linear regression to the same data, while the panel on the right gives the fitted curve from a logistic regression. The observations are also plotted. These points fall either on one or zero (with darker circles indicating where more points have landed). The fit of the linear regression is poor at the extremes, but corresponds rather closely to the logistic fit for predicted probabilities in the middle of the distribution. This illustrates how a linear regression can produce satisfactory results when the average probability is close to .5.

Figure 17.3 also underlines an important property of the predictions. They are not predictions of the individual outcomes (successes or fails). They are predictive probabilities: predictions of the probability of an outcome (in this case the probability of a success). This is a subtle distinction, but one that is very important. Had the predicted probabilities been plotted, the points would all have fallen exactly on the regression line. Thus plotting the predictions can be a useful way to illustrate the fit of the model with continuous predictors.

Some authors (e.g., Gelman and Hill, 2007) advocate standardizing continuous predictors in logistic regression to aid interpretation. This can be done in the usual fashion (subtracting the mean and dividing by the *SD* prior to entering them in the regression). My own preference is to avoid standardization in most situations. For logistic regression this rescaling won't change the tests, but will change the coefficients (because a one-unit change will represent a one *SD* change in the predictor).

In a logistic regression with standardized dichotomous predictors, it may make sense to use effect coding for categorical predictors. Doing this ensures that, provided −1 and 1 codes are equally (or near equally) prevalent, the *SD* of the dichotomous predictor will be close to one. An equivalent option advocated by Gelman (2008c) involves dummy coding categorical predictors, and then rescaling continuous predictors by centering and dividing by twice the *SD*. This works because dummy coded predictors have an *SD* of .5 when there are equal numbers of zero and one codes. Because only the predictor has been standardized, this form of standardization does not produce standardized regression coefficients (beta weights) like those in multiple linear regression. For a review of standardized coefficients analogous to those in least squares models consult Menard (2004).

If you decide not to standardize continuous predictors, it frequently aids interpretation to center those that are not on ratio scales. Rescaling continuous predictors (e.g., multiplying or dividing by a constant) is also sensible if it produces coefficients that are easier to work with. Rescaling effect coded predictors by dividing by two, or (in equal *n* situations) centering dummy coded predictors produces the codes −.5 and .5. This has some of the desirable properties of dummy coding (e.g., the slope of the effect represents the difference in groups) and some of those of effect coding. Last of all, although the systematic component of a generalized linear model is additive, the usual options for dealing with non-additivity of predictor effects exist. The predictors can be transformed (e.g., taking logarithms if their effects are multiplicative) and interactions between predictors or polynomial terms can be included. As with linear regression, extra care must be taken if standardization is applied in moderated logistic or polynomial logistic regression models.

Example 17.2 In Example 17.1 logistic regression was applied to the dream data where both predictor and outcome were discrete. A big advantage of logistic regression is that the predictors can also be continuous. To illustrate this, consider a data set collated by blogger Mark Thompson.* During the recent UK parliamentary expenses scandal the *Daily Telegraph* published a series of articles (starting 8 July 2008) reporting alleged abuses of the parliamentary expenses system by individual members of parliament (MPs). Thompson looked to see if MPs reported as having a problem with their expenses (coded *problem* in the data set) were likely to come from safe seats. He used the parliamentary majority at the last general election (the number of votes exceeding that of his or her nearest rival) as a measure of 'safeness' and found a correlation between the two (using Pearson's *r*). Subsequent examples will refer to this data set as the expenses data.

The parliamentary majority is a count variable, but because of its range (from 37 to 19,519) can be considered continuous for many purposes. Even so, there may be advantages to analyzing the data as a logistic regression. We'll first fit a model with a single predictor: *majority* (scaled in units of 10,000 votes to make the coefficients easier to work with). The outcome is *problem* (zero for no reported expenses problem and one for reports of an expenses problem). The fitted regression equation for this model is:

$$\ln\left(\frac{\hat{P}_i}{1-\hat{P}_i}\right) = -1.039 + 0.6878 \times majority_i$$

Expressed in odds form it is:

$$\hat{o}_i = \frac{\hat{P}_i}{1-\hat{P}_i} = e^{-1.039+0.6878\times majority}$$

The *OR* for majority is therefore $e^{0.6878} = 1.99$. An approximate 95% CI using the Wald method is [1.38, 2.87]. The more accurate profile likelihood CI is [1.38, 2.88]. The close agreement is not surprising with such a large sample size, but for smaller samples the choice of CI could be important. As the majority is scaled in units of 10,000 votes, every 10,000 increase in parliamentary majority is associated with a near doubling of the odds of an expenses problem. Going from the smallest to largest majority is roughly an increase of 20,000 votes, so the *OR* for the most marginal to most safe seat is around $2 \times 2 = 4$. Putting it on a probability scale:

$$\hat{P}(problem) = \frac{e^{-1.039+0.6878 \times majority}}{1 + e^{-1.039+0.6878 \times majority}}$$

The probability of an expenses problem for a person in a seat with zero majority (which can arise if the election is a dead heat and decided by coin toss) would be:

$$\hat{P}(problem \mid majority = 0) = \frac{e^{-1.039}}{1 + e^{-1.039}} = \frac{0.3538}{1 + 0.3538} = .261$$

A similar calculation for $\hat{P}(problem \mid majority = 10{,}000) = .413$ and for $\hat{P}(problem \mid majority = 20{,}000) = .583$.

Figure 17.4 plots predictive probability of an expenses problem for this model against parliamentary majority (with approximate 95% confidence bands) and reveals a very clear pattern. The likelihood ratio test of the model (and therefore of the effect of majority) is statistically significant, $G^2 = 13.9$, $p = .002$, and $\Delta AIC = 11.9$ ($LR_{AIC} = 384$) favors the model containing the majority predictor. At this stage it is worth considering other possible predictors. Adding political party to the model doesn't improve the model fit once the 17 extra parameters are accounted for ($\Delta\chi^2_{17} = -29.0$, $\Delta AIC = 5.0$).

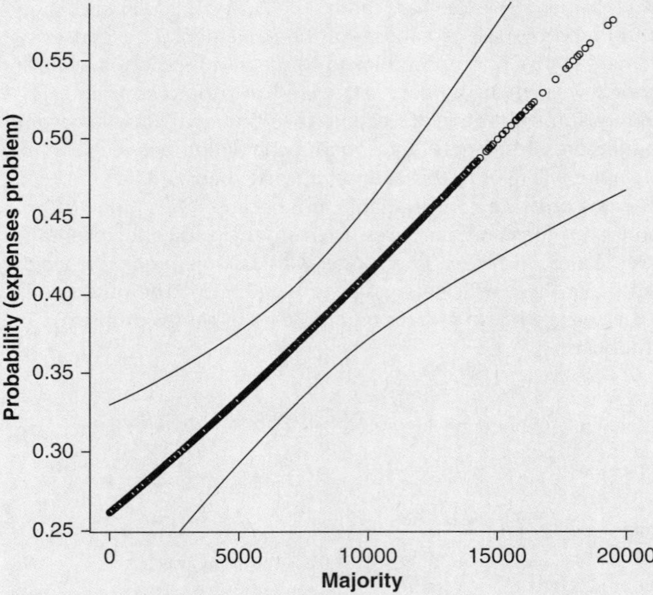

Figure 17.4 Predicted probability of expenses problem by parliamentary majority (with approximate 95% confidence bands) for the expenses data

A similar model (grouping minor parties together as 'Other') adds only four extra parameters, but barely improves the fit and is not more informative ($\Delta\chi^2_4 = -4.2$, ΔAIC = 3.8). Further predictors, such as number of years sitting as an MP could be added to test additional hypotheses or refine the model (but are not considered here).

One of the striking features of Figure 17.4 is just how straight the sigmoidal curve is for these data. This suggests that the methods such as linear regression or correlation would give similar results (at least for inference). Although the simple linear regression and logistic regression lead to similar inferences, the logistic regression is the more correct model and should be first choice when working with continuous predictors and independent, dichotomous outcomes. Even when the overall findings are similar (as for the expenses data) the predictions and the interval estimates from the logistic model will be superior.

* http://markreckons.blogspot.com/

17.4.2 Deviance and model fit

An obvious route to assessing model fit in logistic regression (given that the models are fitted using ML methods) is to determine the deviance of the model. If Y_i represents the ith observed values (zero or one) for each of the N outcomes and $\hat{P}_i$ is its predicted probability, the deviance is:

$$Deviance = -2\ln(\ell) = \sum_{i=1}^{N} -2\left[Y_i \ln\left(\hat{P}_i\right) + (1 - Y_i)\ln\left(1 - \hat{P}_i\right)\right] \quad \text{Equation 17.15}$$

The expression within the square brackets is the loglikelihood of the model (and is closely related to the binomial distribution and its likelihood function). The deviance therefore depends on the difference between the observed values and predicted probabilities, being small when the predicted probability is close to the observed outcome (e.g., if $Y = 1$ and $\hat{P} = .9$ the contribution from that observation to the deviance is $-2\ln\left(\hat{P}\right) = -0.211$). When the predicted probability is far from the observed outcome the deviance will be large (e.g., if $Y = 0$ and $\hat{P} = .95$ the contribution from that observation to the deviance is $-2\ln\left(1 - \hat{P}\right) = 5.99$). The deviance of the model – more properly the residual deviance of the model – therefore plays a role analogous to the residual sums of squares in a multiple linear regression. Larger deviance implies a worse fit. The deviance has an approximate χ^2 distribution with $N - q - 1$ df (where N is the total number of observations and q is the number of predictors). The approximation is not necessarily good when continuous predictors are in the model (Agresti, 1996). A significance test of the overall model should be avoided in any case. It is better to compare the change in deviance between models (see Example 17.1).

Another way to compare the fit of the model is relative to the deviance of the null model. The null deviance is obtained from an intercept-only model with no predictors. In a balanced design with categorical predictors, the null deviance can also be calculated by using the grand mean of P via Equation 17.15. As the null model has no predictors, its deviance can be used as a baseline for comparison (not unlike the SS_{total} in multiple regression). The deviance of the *saturated model* could also be used as a comparator. The saturated model is one with a predictor for each observation, thus resulting in perfect prediction. The deviance of a saturated model is therefore always exactly zero, and there is no need to fit the saturated model directly. Attempting to fit a saturated model will also produce errors in some software. Because its deviance is zero, this implies that the deviance of any other model is expressed relative to the saturated model (e.g., if D_S is the deviance of the saturated model and D_0 is the deviance of the null model, $D_0 = D_0 - D_S$).

The link between the residual deviance of a generalized linear model and $SS_{residual}$ makes it tempting to characterize the fit of the model in terms of the proportion of deviance or variance it explains. Several different forms of R^2 analog have been proposed for generalized linear models. These are known collectively as pseudo-R^2 measures (because none perfectly mimic the properties of R^2). All pseudo-R^2 measures have major limitations (in addition to the problems inherent in the use of standardized effect sizes – see Chapter 7). A major difficulty is that the total variance to be explained in a generalized linear model tends to vary as a function of the mean – and thus the proportion of variance explained is an ill-defined quantity (except in very restricted circumstances). Ultimately, using a predictive power measure – based on the correlation between observed and predictive values on the untransformed scale – is suggested (Zheng and Agresti, 2000). This measure has similar limitations to those of common pseudo-R^2 measures, can be applied to other generalized linear models, and has a clear interpretation in terms of the predictions of a model. For logistic regression it may sometimes also be useful to look at the percentage of outcomes (successes and fails) classified correctly by the model, though this approach has its drawbacks as well.[7]

17.4.3 Model checking and logistic regression diagnostics

It is one thing to assess the fit of a model, but another to detect or deal with any problems. In this section we'll briefly address residuals (and related leverage and influence statistics), collinearity diagnostics, sparse data and the phenomenon of *complete separation*. One further issue – *overdispersion* – will also be mentioned, but will be explored in more detail in relation to Poisson regression models.

A number of different regression diagnostics can be computed for generalized linear models. The two main types are *deviance residuals* and *Pearson residuals* (related to the fit of the likelihood and Pearson χ^2 statistics respectively). The raw residuals on the logit scale are usually avoided because they do not have particularly good distributional properties (but can be used to assess linearity of the systematic component). Pearson residuals are calculated from the difference between observed and predicted probabilities. This is scaled by the estimate of the standard deviation of the binomial distribution for each value. As the variance of a single Bernoulli trial from a binomial distribution is $P(1 - P)$, this produces the equation:

$$e_{P_i} = \frac{Y_i - \hat{P}_i}{\sqrt{\hat{P}\left(1 - \hat{P}\right)}} \qquad \text{Equation 17.16}$$

The formula for deviance residuals is:

$$e_{D_i} = \left(\frac{Y_i - \hat{P}_i}{\left|Y_i - \hat{P}\right|}\right)\sqrt{-2\left[Y_i \ln\left(\hat{P}_i\right) + (1 - Y_i)\ln\left(1 - \hat{P}_i\right)\right]} \qquad \text{Equation 17.17}$$

The right-hand term represents the square root of each observation's contribution to the overall deviance statistic. The sign of the residual depends on the direction of the discrepancy between Y_i and P_i and this is captured by the left-hand term (which evaluates as -1 if $Y_i=0$ and 1 for if $Y_i=1$).

Both types of residuals can be adjusted for leverage. The resulting quantities are termed either adjusted residuals or standardized residuals (and have an approximate *SD* of one). Standardizing involves dividing e_{Di} or e_{Pi} by $\sqrt{1-h_i}$ (where, as in linear regression, h_i is the leverage of the observation). It is also possible to calculate studentized residuals using estimates from a regression in which the ith point has been deleted (again matching the practice in linear regression).

The preference in the literature is for deviance residuals over Pearson residuals. The deviance residuals have an asymptotic normal distribution and tend to be more stable than Pearson residuals. The variance of both Pearson and deviance residuals tends to be lower than for a normal distribution, but large residuals can be used to identify extreme observations, with studentized deviance residuals being most useful for this. On the other hand, a normal probability plot of residuals is unlikely to be very useful for assessing the distributional assumptions of the model in small samples, though it may help reveal extreme or particularly influential observations. Using leverage and either Pearson or deviance residuals it is also possible to calculate a generalized version of Cook's distance. Influence measures such as this can help you to avoid drawing strong conclusions from a model where parameter estimates and inference depends strongly on one or two highly influential observations.

Collinearity or multicollinearity of predictors is problematic for any regression model that aims to investigate the individual effects of predictors. If the focus is on overall prediction or model fit then correlations between predictors may not matter (though perfect collinearity will prevent the model from being fitted). As collinearity and multicollinearity are defined in terms of the predictors, the nature of the response is not so important and familiar diagnostics from multiple linear regression such as tolerance and VIF can be computed. The range of solutions for dealing with correlated predictors is also unchanged. The best solutions are either to design a study to avoid collinearity, or to increase sample size to compensate for decreased precision. Where collinearity is a consequence of the structure of the model, arising from fitting polynomial or interaction terms, centering or other forms of rescaling may aid interpretation of the model. Combining, transforming or dropping predictors may also be sensible, depending on context.

Logistic regression can perform badly if data are sparse. Sparseness is a loosely defined term, but applies when there is a very high proportion of either failures or successes. When discrete data are sparse then statistical power and precision of parameter estimation tends to be poor. This should not be surprising, as in such a model there is very little information to use for estimation. Dichotomous data contain less information per observation than continuous outcomes (that can assume a range of intermediate outcomes). Estimation is difficult when modeling sparse data and ML estimates may not converge. Simulation and exact methods are popular alternatives for sparse data (e.g., methods such as MCMC estimation), though they may be very demanding in terms of computing power. The most obvious solution for sparse data is to increase the sample size, but it may also be possible to design the study to avoid or decrease sparseness.

Complete separation is a technical term applied to some logistic regression models. The problem is not unique to logistic regression. It arises when a predictor or combination of predictors perfectly predicts the observed outcomes. The name arises because the predictors can be used to completely separate the predicted outcomes into groups associated with distinct predictor values. While this seems like a good thing, it is not. Perfect prediction means that the model cannot be fitted and no parameter estimates can be obtained. This can happen for any regression model, but is unlikely for a truly continuous response (and rare for counts). In contrast, complete separation can easily happen when sampling dichotomous outcomes in a small sample or if too many predictors are added to a model and it becomes saturated. The same solutions that can work for sparse data (altering the study design or collecting additional observations) may also prevent complete separation. If complete separation arises due to over-fitting then it will make sense to reduce the number of predictors, though collecting more data may be the only viable option in small samples. *Quasi-complete separation* is also possible. This happens if subsets of values for one predictor are tied on the outcome variable (e.g., all values coded one for a predictor are associated with zero on the outcome variable). Quasi-complete separation is harder to detect and leads to large and unstable *SE*s (similar to the effects of collinearity). It is worth checking whenever the *SE*s are unreasonably large (and collecting more data is again often the best solution). Adding information to the model in the form of a Bayesian prior may also resolve separation problems, for the same reason that adding new data may provide a fix (Gelman and Hill, 2007).

Overdispersion is a potential problem if the probability distribution of the generalized linear model random component has a variance that is a function of the mean. Logistic and Poisson regression are good examples. For the binomial distribution used in logistic regression, the mean is $\hat{P}$ and the variance is $\hat{P}\left(1-\hat{P}\right)$. As a consequence, the expected residual deviance of the model D_M is equal to $\nu = N - q - 1$ (the residual *df* of the model). This implies the ratio $D_M/\nu = 1$ (though some variability is to be expected due to sampling error). Either the Pearson χ^2 or model deviance can be used to detect overdispersion using the estimate D_M/ν. This quantity is an estimate of the overdispersion parameter φ.[8] Overdispersion causes the *SE*s to be too small (and hence interval estimates will be too narrow and tests too liberal). It is also possible, if somewhat unusual, to get underdispersion (and hence *SE*s that are too large). Overdispersion parameters can be used to correct inferences (see Box 17.2) though this may not be the best way of dealing with the problem.

If overdispersion is suspected, try first to gauge the extent of the problem. If the estimate of φ is much greater than one then it is likely that the problem is serious enough to distort the analysis. A number of things can cause overdispersion in a logistic regression model. These include a poorly fitting model (e.g., missing one or more important predictors), not including interactions between predictors, and lack of independence between observations. Finding a better-fitting model by adding predictors, removing predictors or including interaction terms may help resolve the problem. If lack of independence is suspected (e.g., in repeated measures or clustered data), then it may be possible to model the extra random variation between observations (e.g., switching to a different random component or to a multilevel logistic regression model).

Example 17.3 Many of the methods for interrogating residuals in linear regression are available for logistic regression, but may be hard to interpret. Plots of residuals or influence (e.g., Cook's distance) are always worth checking. For the expenses data the residuals are not particularly extreme (studentized residuals range from −1.29 to 1.64). The influence statistics also suggest no reason for concern (all Cook's distances are lower than 0.01). Assessing overdispersion requires calculating an overdispersion parameter. This both provides an estimate of the dispersion parameter and provides a correction to *SE*s and tests. Doing so for the expenses data estimates the overdispersion parameter at 1.002876 (close to the desired value of one). The standard errors and tests are virtually unchanged. This should not be surprising, because the correction factor for the *SE*s is $\sqrt{1.002876} = 1.001437$ (see Box 17.2). Thus each *SE* is only 0.14% larger after the correction.

17.4.4 Multinomial logistic regression

An attractive feature of logistic regression is that is can be extended to deal with discrete data with more than two possible outcomes. This can be handled in two different ways. The simplest method is applicable only when the J outcomes are structured as a nested hierarchy of dichotomous outcomes or *nested dichotomies*. An example arises if several participants in an attention experiment were asked to respond if they had detected a target or not ('yes', 'no'). If they reported detecting a target they could then be asked if it was 'red' or 'blue'. This produces three possible outcomes 'yes-blue', 'yes-red' and 'no'. The effects of one or more predictor could be used to predict the probability of these outcomes by running two logistic regression models.[9] The first model would predict the probability of a 'yes' response among all N participants, while the second model (restricted only to the n 'yes' responses) would predict the probability of 'red' or 'blue'. In addition to separate tests provided within each of the nested logistic regressions it is possible to combine the deviance and *df* of each model. This gives an overall test of model fit. This is legitimate because each nested dichotomy is orthogonal to dichotomies nested elsewhere in the hierarchy and therefore deviances and *df* can be summed across submodels (which are independent). This kind of model can be useful where responses are naturally nested, and is flexible enough that multiple branches can be fitted (e.g., 'no' responses could be also be split by a further dichotomous outcome). The obvious drawback of this type of design is that, as outcomes split, n for each model decreases. The precision of estimates depends on n within each sub-model (requiring N to be very large to maintain statistical power for all effects).

If the outcomes cannot be represented as nested dichotomies, a *multinomial logistic regression* (or *polychotomous logistic regression*) model can be employed. In this model outcomes are assumed to have a multinomial distribution in which each independent trial has a fixed probability P_j of falling into one of J unordered outcome categories. As the probabilities P_1 to P_J exhaust all possible outcomes under consideration, their sum must equal one:

$$\sum_{j=1}^{J} P_j = 1$$

The multinomial distribution reduces to the binomial when $J = 2$ and the model becomes a regular logistic regression (though when $J = 2$ the outcomes can be ordered or unordered).

Fitting a multinomial logistic regression is a bit like fitting $J - 1$ separate logistic regression models (Agresti, 1996). The principle here is similar to that of using indicator variables to code categorical predictors in a statistical model: it takes $J - 1$ variables to represent J categories. Unlike the nested dichotomies approach it is necessary to fit the $J - 1$ sets of parameter estimates simultaneously (maximizing the likelihood of the joint equations). This is more efficient and produces more accurate parameter estimates than fitting the models separately. One outcome category (often the last outcome J) is chosen as a reference category and one or more slopes are estimated for the remaining $J-1$ outcomes. This produces $J-1$ equations of the form:

$$\ln\left(\frac{\hat{P}_{j,i}}{\hat{P}_{J,i}}\right) = b_0 + b_1 x_{1,i} + \ldots + b_q x_{q,i} \qquad \text{Equation 17.18}$$

This models each of the $J-1$ outcomes in terms of its log odds relative to an intercept. The subscript i is the index for all $i=1$ to N observations (but to simplify presentation of the equations the i subscript will be dropped for the rest of this discussion). No equation is required for outcome J because its predicted probability is a function of the probabilities of the other outcomes:

$$\hat{P}_J = 1 - \sum_{1}^{J-1} \hat{P}_j$$

This is identical to logistic regression when $J=2$ and where $\hat{P}_J = 1 - \hat{P}_1$ (the predicted probability of a failure, if $\hat{P}_1$ is a success).

For a model with two predictors and three outcome categories (labeled a, b and c) the $J-1=2$ regression equations are:

$$\ln\left(\frac{\hat{P}_a}{\hat{P}_c}\right) = b_{0_a} + b_{1_a} x_1 + b_{2_a} x_2$$

$$\ln\left(\frac{\hat{P}_b}{\hat{P}_c}\right) = b_{0_b} + b_{1_b} x_1 + b_{2_b} x_2 \qquad \text{Equation 17.19}$$

This defines the log odds of outcomes a and b relative to the reference outcome category c. What if you are interested in the log odds of a relative to b? Agresti (*ibid.*) explains how the log odds of any two categories can be determined from the differences in their coefficients. By this method, the log odds of a relative to b are:

$$\ln\left(\frac{\hat{P}_a}{\hat{P}_b}\right) = \ln\left(\frac{\hat{P}_a}{\hat{P}_c}\right) - \ln\left(\frac{\hat{P}_b}{\hat{P}_c}\right) = (b_{0_a} - b_{0_b}) + (b_{1_a} - b_{1_b})x_1 + (b_{2_a} - b_{2_b})x_2$$

Equation 17.20

This follows because odds are ratios of probabilities. Both the odds $\hat{P}_a/\hat{P}_c$ and $\hat{P}_b/\hat{P}_c$ have a common numerator (and division on the untransformed scale is equivalent to subtraction on the log scale). It is entirely legitimate to use a formula such as that in Equation 17.20 to extract individual coefficients. It is also possible to switch to another reference category (and this approach is superior if you want the *SE*s of the coefficients). This merely produces a change in sign of the log odds. The log odds of b relative to a for predictor X_2 are therefore equal to $b_{2b} - b_{2a}$. This is a property of all multinomial logistic regression models. In a model with six outcomes (labeled a to f) the intercept for outcome d relative to outcome a would be $b_{0d} - b_{0a}$.

The log odds forms of the equations are interpreted largely as they would be for logistic regression. The odds form of the equation can be obtained by applying the exponent function to both sides of the equation for each of the $J-1$ outcomes:

$$\left(\frac{\hat{P}_j}{\hat{P}_J}\right) = e^{b_0 + b_1 x_1 + \ldots + b_q x_q} \qquad \text{Equation 17.21}$$

These $J-1$ equations provide the *OR* for a unit increase in each predictor and the *OR* for the intercept. This has the usual interpretation, except that each outcome is represented relative to the reference outcome category (rather than to the probability of its own non-occurrence $1-\hat{P}_j$). The predictive probabilities can also be obtained. For an arbitrary outcome category a, the predictive probability is:

$$\hat{P}_a = \frac{e^{b_{0_a}+b_{1_a}x_1+\ldots+b_{q_a}x_q}}{1+\sum_{1=j}^{J-1} e^{b_{0_j}+b_{1_j}x_1+\ldots+b_{q_j}x_q}} \quad \text{Equation 17.22}$$

The term $\sum_{1=j}^{J-1} e^{b_{0_j}+b_{1_j}x_1+\ldots+b_{q_j}x_q}$ is the sum of $e^{b_{0_j}+b_{1_j}x_1+\ldots+b_{q_j}x_q}$ for all of the outcome categories excluding the reference category J. This reduces to Equation 17.9 when $J=2$.

Returning to a study with $J=3$ outcomes and two predictors, the respective probabilities for outcome a would be

$$\hat{P}_a = \frac{e^{b_{0_a}+b_{1_a}x_1+b_{2_a}x_2}}{1+e^{b_{0_a}+b_{1_a}x_1+b_{2_a}x_2}+e^{b_{0_b}+b_{1_b}x_1+b_{2_b}x_2}}, \quad \text{Equation 17.23}$$

while for outcome b they would be

$$\hat{P}_b = \frac{e^{b_{0_b}+b_{1_b}x_1+b_{2_b}x_2}}{1+e^{b_{0_a}+b_{1_a}x_1+b_{2_a}x_2}+e^{b_{0_b}+b_{1_b}x_1+b_{2_b}x_2}}, \quad \text{Equation 17.24}$$

and for the reference category c they would be

$$\hat{P}_c = \frac{1}{1+e^{b_{0_a}+b_{1_a}x_1+b_{2_a}x_2}+e^{b_{0_b}+b_{1_b}x_1+b_{2_b}x_2}} \quad \text{Equation 17.25}$$

The numerator for Equation 17.25 is 1 because it represents the odds of the reference category relative to itself.

Multinomial logistic regression, like its simpler namesake, can incorporate both categorical and continuous predictors. Categorical predictors are coded in the usual way. This typically involves dummy coding, but ANOVA- and ANCOVA-style models (e.g., using effect coding or a cell means model) are also possible. If all predictors in the model are categorical, the multinomial logistic regression (and indeed logistic regression) turn out to be a special case of a generalized linear model known as a loglinear regression model. It will often be a good idea to consider both logistic and loglinear regression models as candidates when all predictors are categorical.[10]

Multinomial logistic regression has three main restrictions. First, it assumes that the categories are unordered (and ignores order if it exists). Second, it is limited to situations where predictors take the same value for each outcome. This may be unduly restrictive. In a domain such as consumer choice, a researcher will be very interested in the factors that determine which product is chosen, but the potential outcomes (e.g., brand a, brand b and brand c) will have different values on some or all of the key predictors (e.g., price). These can be considered outcome-varying covariates (analogous to time-varying covariates in repeated measures).

Third, the model treats observations as independent. Models such as ordered logistic regression and generalized multilevel models relax these assumptions. The latter potentially allows all three limitations of a standard multinomial logistic regression model to be addressed (though other approaches are possible).

17.4.5 Ordered logistic regression

If categorical outcomes are ordered, fitting a multinomial logistic regression model for unordered outcomes ignores potentially crucial information about the data. Agresti (1996) discusses several approaches to the analysis of ordered categorical data. Of these, the *proportional odds model* is the most widely adopted model for bounded ordinal data.[11] The proportional odds model assumes that N independent observations fall into a set of J ordered categories. These are usually coded as a set of sequential integers (e.g., one to J). The coding of order should preserve the natural or logical order of the outcomes, but there is no requirement for the intervals to be equally spaced. Typical examples include grading of academic performance (e.g., where it is not reasonable to assume that the difference between a grade 'A' and a grade 'B' is the same as between 'E' and 'F') or Likert-style rating scales. Although ordinal outcomes lend themselves to ordered logistic regression, a least squares regression model with a good fit may well produce similar results (especially if the goal is hypothesis testing rather than prediction).

For discrete, ordinal outcomes the aim is to find a way of representing this order within the logistic regression framework. Logistic regression is ideally suited to dealing with dichotomous outcomes, and multinomial logistic regression extends this to polychotomous outcomes, by breaking down the model into pairs of dichotomous outcomes. The same solution can be adapted to deal with ordered categories. The key distinction is that ordered outcomes have greater constraints on them than unordered outcomes. These constraints are met by modeling the cumulative probability of each outcome rather than the probability of each separate outcome.

To see why using cumulative probability preserves the ordinal information in the data it helps to look at a simple case. For a rating scale with $J = 3$ possible responses, the outcomes could be 'disagree', 'neutral' and 'agree'. The cumulative probability of the first response is simply the probability that someone disagrees $\hat{P}_{disagree}$. The cumulative probability of the second response is $\hat{P}_{disagree}$ plus $\hat{P}_{neutral}$ and the cumulative probability of the third response is $\hat{P}_{disagree} + \hat{P}_{neutral} + \hat{P}_{agree} = 1$.[12] The constraint here is that the cumulative probability increases across the ordered outcomes; changes in a predictor either increase or decrease the probability of greater agreement (they cannot do both). For instance, a change in X could not increase $\hat{P}_{disagree}$ and $\hat{P}_{agree}$ at the expense of $\hat{P}_{neutral}$. Such a pattern could easily be modeled in an unordered multinomial regression (that treats agreement and disagreement as separate categories rather than two ends of a continuum).

The proportional odds model therefore treats ordered categories as if they were a series of logistic regression models for the $J - 1$ cumulative probabilities. As with unordered multinomial logistic regression, these logistic regression models are estimated simultaneously (with the constraint that the cumulative probability for the last category P_J equals one). In terms of equations, the J cumulative probabilities can be represented as:

$$\hat{P}(Y \leq j) = \hat{P}_1 + \ldots \hat{P}_j \qquad \text{Equation 17.26}$$

These probabilities will not sum to one, but the cumulative probability of the preceding outcome is constrained to be equal or lower than its successor:

$$\hat{P}_1 = \hat{P}(Y=1) \leq \ldots \leq \hat{P}(Y \leq j) \leq \hat{P}_J = 1 \qquad \text{Equation 17.27}$$

The cumulative logits (cumulative log odds) of the model are:

$$\ln\left(\frac{\hat{P}_1 + \cdots + \hat{P}_j}{\hat{P}_{j+1} + \cdots + \hat{P}_J}\right) = \ln\left(\frac{\hat{P}(Y \leq j)}{1 - \hat{P}(Y \leq j)}\right) \quad j = 1, \ldots, J-1 \qquad \text{Equation 17.28}$$

An important feature of this notation is the distinction between the predictive probability of an outcome $\hat{P}_j$ and its cumulative predictive probability $\hat{P}(Y \leq j)$. These are only identical for the first outcome $\hat{P}_1$ (assuming that the probabilities are cumulated from lowest to highest). At the level of the cumulative logits, the model is just a series of logistic regressions with dichotomous outcomes (just as if outcomes one to j had been coded as failure and outcomes $j+1$ to J had been coded as success).

The proportional odds model has several interesting features. The regression equation (excluding the subscript indexing the N independent observations) is:

$$\ln\left(\frac{\hat{P}(Y \leq j)}{1 - \hat{P}(Y \leq j)}\right) = b_{0_j} + b_1 x_1 + \ldots + b_q x_q \qquad j = 1, \ldots, J-1 \qquad \text{Equation 17.29}$$

The first feature to note is that there are multiple intercepts represented by the b_{0_j} term. Each of the $J-1$ cut-points for the regression has its own intercept. If $J=3$ the two intercepts would represent the cut-points for a logistic regression equation comparing $j=1$ against $j>1$ and the cut-point for comparing $j<3$ with $j=3$. In an intercept-only model (or a model with centered predictors) these intercepts can be interpreted directly as average values for the sample. The second feature is that the coefficients for the q predictors X_1 to X_q are identical for all the cut-points. The log odds are therefore constant for all cut-points. This in turn implies that the effect of a predictor on the odds is to multiply them by a constant proportion, leading to the designation of the model as a proportional odds model. Each unit increase in a predictor X is associated with an increase of odds of the next highest outcome by a factor of e^{b_k}.

The cumulative odds and cumulative probabilities can be obtained by applying the familiar transformations to the cumulative logit form of the ordered logistic regression in Equation 17.29. The cumulative odds are given by

$$\frac{\hat{P}(Y \leq j)}{1 - \hat{P}(Y \leq j)} = e^{b_{0_j} + b_1 x_1 + \ldots + b_q x_q} \quad j = 1, \ldots, J-1 \qquad \text{Equation 17.30}$$

while the cumulative predictive probabilities are:

$$\hat{P}(Y \leq j) = \frac{e^{b_{0_j} + b_1 x_1 + \ldots + b_q x_q}}{1 + e^{b_{0_j} + b_1 x_1 + \ldots + b_q x_q}} \quad j = 1, \ldots, J-1 \qquad \text{Equation 17.31}$$

The log odds and odds ratios for the predictors can be interpreted without too much difficulty. They refer to the log odds and odds of shifting from a lower to higher outcome category based on a one-unit increase in X. The cumulative probabilities are harder to interpret (e.g., the cumulative probability for outcome J, the last outcome is one). Instead, the predictive probabilities of the separate outcomes can be derived with a little arithmetic. The predictive probability of outcome j can be defined as:

$$P(Y=j)=P(Y \leq j)-P(Y \leq j-1) \quad \text{Equation 17.32}$$

The predictive probability for an outcome is therefore the cumulative probability for outcome j minus the cumulative probability for the preceding outcome (if there is one). If $J=3$ (with $j=$coded 1, 2 or 3) and the predicted cumulative probabilities are .36 and .82, the predictive probability of j_1 is .36. It follows that the probability of $j_2=.80-.36=.44$ and the probability of $j_3=1-.80=.20$.

The most obvious limitation of this form of ordered logistic regression model is the proportional odds restriction itself. Sometimes the effect of a predictor will vary between cut-points and a more flexible model is required. Often, even though the proportional odds assumption is unlikely to be met exactly, the odds will be sufficiently similar for each outcome that the proportional odds model provides a pretty good fit. Some software (e.g., SPSS) will provide a null hypothesis test of the proportional odds assumption, but often with large samples these tests tend to reject the assumption even when it holds up quite well (Harrell, 2001). A better check is to compare the coefficients between separate logistic regression models with identical predictors for each cut-point. The proportional odds assumption implies that effects of a predictor on the logit scale should be similar for each of these models. Modeling the effects of predictors at different cut-points substantially increases the number of parameters to be fitted when J is large (up to an additional $J-2$ effects per predictor). The assumption of proportional odds is rather like fitting a straight line to a messy X-Y relationship. Looking for a curve that fits better than the straight line might lead to over-fitting (unless there are ways to narrow down the scope of possible models).

The independence assumption can also be a major limitation (e.g., for rating data with repeated measures models). Some specialist software (e.g., MLwiN) permits multilevel proportional odds models to be fitted for repeated measures data and also allows separate slopes to be fitted for each intercept. Other approaches can also be used to relax the proportional odds assumption (see Agresti, 1996; Yee, 2010).

Example 17.4 Underwood *et al.* (2007) investigated perceptions of road safety in 119 children from two UK schools in years three, five and seven (roughly seven, nine and eleven years old). They looked at a number of measures, including a free sort task involving 20 pictures of road scenes. Responses on the free sort task were coded and analyzed in several different ways. One analysis used multiple regression to predict the use of a 'safe to cross' code based on gender, year group and two other codes: 'visibility' (*vis*) and 'other road users' (*oru*). This analysis suggested that the safe to cross codes were predicted by other road users for girls, but not boys. However, the safe to cross code occurred infrequently (either zero, one, two or three times). Because zero was the most common response the data are sparse (and less than ideal for multiple regression). One possible alternative is ordered logistic regression.

A first step is to fit a main effects only proportional odds logistic regression model with safe to cross (*stc*) as the outcome and year group (three, five or seven), female, *vis* and *oru* as predictors. The improvement in deviance of this model over the null model is statistically significant, $G^2 = 13.7$, $p = .018$ (ΔAIC = 3.7). However, the *SE* for the predictor *vis* is very high, suggesting quasi-complete separation. Only two of the children have visibility codes that are non-zero. Without additional data, the best option may be to drop *vis* from the model. The resulting model is also statistically significant, $G^2 = 11.6$, $p = .020$ (ΔAIC = 3.6 versus the null model). Particular interest rests on differences between girls and boys (because proportionately more boys than girls are killed or injured in road traffic accidents). Underwood *et al.* (2007) fitted separate regressions for boys and girls and found *oru* predicted *stc* for girls, but not boys. A better model fits a *female* by *oru* interaction. The interaction model provides a marked improvement in fit relative to the main effects model: $G^2 = 17.0$, $p = .00046$ (ΔAIC = 7.0). The coefficients *SE*s on the logit scale, Wald statistics as well as the OR and its 95% CI, are reported in Table 17.1.

Table 17.1 Regression coefficients, standard errors, Wald statistics and odds ratios for ordered logistic regression of the traffic data (including 95% CI for the *OR*)

					95% CI (Wald)	
	b	***SE***	**Wald *z***	***OR***	**Lower**	**Upper**
$stc > 0$	−1.026	0.530	−1.94	0.358	0.127	1.128
$stc > 1$	−2.240	0.613	−3.66	0.106	0.032	0.354
$stc > 2$	−4.769	1.330	−3.58	0.008	0.001	0.115
year 5	−2.873	1.124	−0.75	0.057	0.006	0.512
year 7	−0.263	0.572	−2.55	0.769	0.251	2.358
female	−0.472	0.631	−0.46	0.624	0.181	2.146
oru	−0.091	0.353	−0.26	0.913	0.457	1.825
female × *oru*	1.403	0.607	2.31	4.066	2.146	13.348

Note: The coefficients and inferences arise from a model including year group, gender, other road users and a gender by other road user interaction.

The intercepts are the thresholds for the cumulative log odds of the model when all predictors are zero (i.e., for a year three male child with $oru = 0$). Here the first outcome ($stc = 0$) is the reference category and so the first threshold defines the log odds of $stc > 0$ versus 0. The middle threshold defines log odds for $stc = 2$ or 3 versus 0 or 1 and the last threshold splits $stc = 3$ from $stc < 3$. As the coefficients are cumulative log odds, the cumulative odds for each threshold are $e^{-1.026}$, $e^{-2.240}$ and $e^{-4.769}$ or 0.358, 0.106 and 0.00849. The respective cumulative probabilities defined by $\hat{P} = \hat{o}/(1 + \hat{o})$ are:

$$
\begin{array}{ll}
stc > 0 & .26377 \\
stc > 1 & .09619 \\
stc > 2 & .00842
\end{array}
$$

The conditional probability that $stc = 0$ is 1 minus the sum of these probabilities. By subtraction, the probabilities of each outcome (conditional on the other predictors being zero) are therefore:

$$
\begin{array}{ll}
stc = 0 & .73624 \\
stc = 1 & .16757 \\
stc = 2 & .08777 \\
stc = 3 & .00842
\end{array}
$$

Cumulative probabilities incorporating predictor effects can be obtained from the regression equation in probability form:

$$P(Y \leq stc) = \frac{e^{b_{0_{stc}} - 2.873 year5 - 0.263 year7 - 0.472\ female - 0.091\, oru + 1.403\ female \times oru}}{1 + e^{b_{0_{stc}} - 2.873 year5 - 0.263 year7 - 0.472\ female - 0.091\, oru + 1.403\ female \times oru}}$$

The effect of particular interest here is the *female* × *oru* interaction. This indicates that the *oru* effect is negligible for males ($OR = e^{-0.907} = 0.91$) but positive for females ($OR = e^{1.403} = 4.07$). So the odds of a moving up a threshold (to the next highest *stc* value) increase by roughly four for a one-unit increase in *oru*, but only for girls. Thus the 'other road user' codes in the free sort predict safe to cross responses in girls, but not boys. Figure 17.5 shows the predicted probability of zero, one, two or three safe to cross codes as a function of the sex of a child and the number of *oru* codes for year three children. The other year groups show a similar pattern.

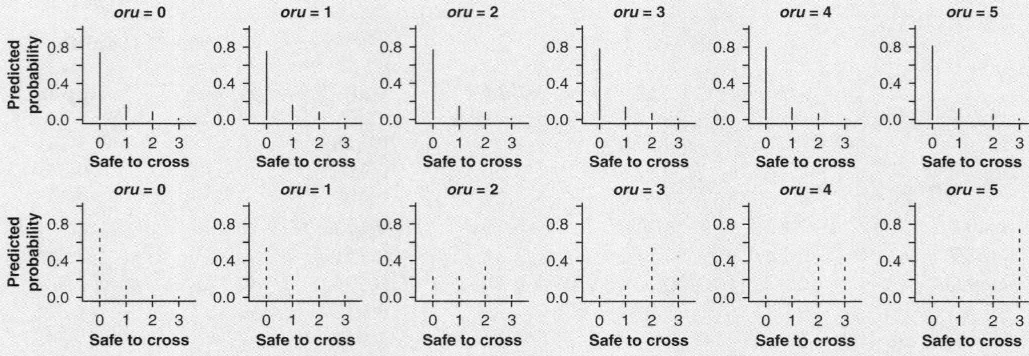

Figure 17.5 The predicted probability of zero, one, two or three safe to cross codes as a function of other road user (*oru*) codes by sex of child

Note: The upper panels show the predicted probabilities for boys (solid lines). The lower panels show the predicted probabilities for girls (dashed lines).

This illustrates the potential impact of the interaction effect. For boys (upper panel, solid lines) the presence of an *oru* code has little impact on a safe to cross response, whereas the probability of such a code increases markedly for girls (lower panel, dashed lines) as the number of *oru* codes increases.

Although this model produces broadly similar results to the multiple regression it would probably not be a good idea to rely on either analysis too heavily. The findings suggest an interesting and potentially important difference in how the boys and girls assess road conditions, but the data are too sparse to warrant high confidence in these conclusions. The proportional odds assumption could be checked for fitting separate logistic regression models for each cut-point (see Harrell, 2001).

17.5 Modeling count data

There are several potentially reasonable approaches when an outcome variable consists of independent counts. The starting point for modeling count data is very often the choice between a least squares linear regression model and Poisson regression. The residuals of least squares regression with count data are often well approximated by a normal distribution in large samples, and a transformation will often produce an adequate model for moderate sample sizes. Poisson regression (a generalized linear model with a Poisson random component) is a logical alternative when the normal approximation is poor and may well produce a better predictive model. Models specialized for count data may also have superior statistical power and precision relative to least squares alternatives (see Atkins and Gallup 2007; Hilbe, 2007).

Because Poisson regression is somewhat restrictive, alternative models such as quasipoisson and negative binomial regression may be employed. Together these options provide great flexibility with pure count data. Sometimes, however, count data may arise from what can be considered a mixture of different processes. One process is dichotomous and determines whether an event occurs, while a second process determines the frequency of the event. Count data from this kind of mixture of processes may have an excess of zeroes relative to a Poisson or negative binomial model. Models for this kind of data are termed *zero-inflated* regression models and present additional difficulties to modelers. A related approach, that does not assume a mixture of processes, is the *hurdle* model in which all zeroes (excess or otherwise) are modeled in one component of the model and non-zero counts in another component. Count data with excess zeroes will rarely be adequately modeled using normal linear regression models (with or without a transformation) and present a particularly difficult challenge for researchers.

Box 17.2 Overdispersion parameters and corrected standard errors

The overdispersion parameter φ represents the degree to which data are overdispersed in the population being modeled (relative to variance implied by the choice of random component in a generalized linear model). This parameter is the ratio of the modeled variance to the expected population variance. It is therefore an indication of the degree to which the model underestimates the true variance. Overdispersion is meaningful only for statistical models in which the variance is a function of the mean. It is not relevant if the mean and variance are modeled by separate free parameters (e.g., in a model with normal distributed errors). A sample estimate of ϕ can be calculated from either the Pearson χ^2 or the residual deviance of the model (dividing them by the residual degrees of freedom ν). The estimate using deviance is therefore

$$\hat{\varphi} = \frac{D_M}{\nu},$$

and the estimate using the Pearson χ^2 is:

$$\hat{\varphi} = \frac{\chi^2_\nu}{\nu}$$

Both estimates should be similar in magnitude.

The expected value of $\hat{\varphi}$ in a model that is neither overdispersed nor underdispersed is one. Owing to sampling error, it will hardly ever be exactly one for real data. Values greater than one suggest overdispersion, while values less than one suggest underdispersion (rare for logistic regression, but a plausible, if infrequent, outcome in Poisson regression). Some authors (e.g., Field, 2009) recommend the cautious approach of picking the more extreme statistic to assess overdispersion. More commonly, people report the Pearson χ^2 estimate of φ (and the choice of statistic is rarely critical). It is even possible to construct a NHST for the overdispersion parameter, though this is generally undesirable; what matters is the degree of overdispersion (or underdispersion) and not whether it is present.

The effects of overdispersion are to underestimate the variance and therefore the *SEs*, while underdispersion overestimates them. This is one reason why more emphasis is placed on the former rather than the latter. The overdispersion parameter, being an estimate of the ratio of the true variance to the model estimate can be used to correct the inferences. This is usually accomplished by adjusting the *SEs*. The corrected *SE* is $\sqrt{\hat{\varphi}}$ larger than that in the overdispersed or underdispersed model, because the sampling variance of the statistic is proportional to the variance of the model. If the uncorrected *SE* for a parameter estimate is $\hat{\sigma}_{\hat{\theta}}$, the corrected *SE* is therefore:

$$\hat{\sigma}_{\hat{\theta}}\sqrt{\hat{\varphi}}$$

This should explain why $\hat{\varphi} \geq 2$ is considered a serious problem. If $\hat{\varphi} = 2$ then the $\sigma_{\hat{\theta}}$ will be too small by a factor of $1/\sqrt{2} \approx .71$. This is nearly 30% smaller than it should be. Even if φ is as low as 1.2 the uncorrected *SEs* will be almost 10% smaller than required. Many researchers are cautious about overdispersion and take steps to deal with it. Correcting the *SEs* manually is one method, but can be cumbersome for complex models. You could also incorporate the overdispersion parameter (or an equivalent parameter) within your statistical model (e.g., using a quasipoisson or negative binomial random component in place of the Poisson distribution).

Overdispersion or underdispersion is a difficulty for all forms of inference (not merely NHSTs), and the overdispersion parameter can be used to correct interval estimates (e.g., by adjusting the *SE* for a Wald CI). A correction to AIC *quasi-AIC* (qAIC or qAIC_C) has also been proposed (Lebreton *et al.*, 1992; Bolker *et al.*, 2009). This uses φ to rescale the deviance. Thus qAIC would be computed as:

$$qAIC = \frac{-2\ln(\ell)}{\hat{\varphi}_C} + 2k \qquad \text{Equation 17.33}$$

The extension to qAIC_C (for small samples) is straightforward:

$$qAIC_C = \frac{-2\ln(\ell)}{\hat{\varphi}_C} + 2k + \frac{2k(k+1)}{N-k-1} \qquad \text{Equation 17.34}$$

Here $\hat{\varphi}_C$ is the best available estimate of the dispersion parameter – usually the estimate from the most complex model under consideration other than the saturated model (Richards, 2008).

17.5.1 Poisson regression

Outcomes in Poisson regression are assumed to be independent counts with a Poisson distribution. This distribution has a single rate parameter λ (lambda) that is both its mean and its variance. In a Poisson regression model, the goal is to model λ as a linear function of the predictors. The main complication is that count data are bounded at zero (they can not be negative) and, particularly when counts are small, a linear (additive) function for predicting λ is problematic.

Poisson regression is a form of generalized linear model in which a logarithmic link function is employed (Agresti, 1996). The random component consists of the *Y* counts assumed to have a Poisson distribution. The canonical link function is:

$$g(\lambda) = \ln(Y) \qquad \text{Equation 17.35}$$

Given that the rate parameter is the mean of a Poisson distribution it could also be expressed as $g(\mu) = \ln(Y)$. Putting this together with the systematic component gives a generalized linear regression equation:

$$\ln(y_i) = b_0 + b_1 x_{1,i} + \ldots + b_q x_{q,i} \qquad \text{Equation 17.36}$$

As with logistic regression, this equation in the generalized linear equation can be rearranged to place the original untransformed outcome (the y_i counts) on the left-hand side. Applying the exponential function to both sides gives:

$$y_i = e^{b_0 + b_1 x_{1,i} + \ldots + b_q x_{q,i}} \qquad \text{Equation 17.37}$$

Although Equation 17.37 expresses the formula in terms of the population, it is trivial to express this in terms of the expected or predicted counts:

$$\hat{Y} = e^{b_0 + b_1 X_1 + \ldots + b_q X_q} \qquad \text{Equation 17.38}$$

This is a multiplicative model in the sense that a one-unit increase in X is associated with a fixed proportion change in Y. When a coefficient is zero the proportionate change is one and the expected count is unchanged; the predictor has no effect. The multiplicative relationship between predictor effects can be reflected directly in the regression or prediction equation. For instance, Equation 17.37 could be expressed as:

$$y_i = e^{b_0} \times e^{b_1 x_{1,i}} \times \ldots \times e^{b_q x_{q,i}} \qquad \text{Equation 17.39}$$

The interpretation of Poisson coefficients is less complex than for logistic regression. The multiplicative effect of a coefficient b_q on the counts is given by e^{b_q}. If you prefer, this can be converted into a percentage or proportion increase. For example the percentage increase or decrease would be:

$$\Delta\hat{Y} = 100\left(e^{b_q} - 1\right)\% \qquad \text{Equation 17.40}$$

For very small values of b_q it turns out that the value of the coefficient is approximately equal to the proportion of change (Gelman and Hill, 2007). A coefficient of $b_q = 0.08$ would be roughly equal to a 0.08 or 8% increase in Y for each unit increase in X. Thus if X increased by two you would expect the observed count to increase by about 16%. So a coefficient of -0.04 equates to roughly a 4% decrease in Y for a one-unit increase in X. This holds only for coefficients close to zero. As the coefficient departs from zero (e.g., above ±0.2) the underestimate of the change is progressively large (being substantial at ±0.5 and grossly inaccurate above this). If the time period or area of which counts are observed is fixed and known, each of the multiplicative coefficients e^{b_q} also can be interpreted as a risk or rate ratio (*RR*). If the time period or area varies between observations, the *RR* interpretation can sometimes be restored by including an *offset* (see Section 17.5.2).

A Poisson regression, like other generalized linear models, is fitted by ML estimation and supports model comparisons using deviance statistics or information criteria. CIs and large sample tests can be obtained from the asymptotic Wald statistics (though profiling gives more accurate CIs in small samples). The deviance of a Poisson model is:

$$Deviance = -2\ln(\ell) = 2\sum_{i=1}^{N}\left(y_i \ln\left(\frac{y_i}{\hat{y}_i}\right) - (y_i - \hat{y}_i)\right) \qquad \text{Equation 17.41}$$

This calculation requires only y_i (the observed counts) and $\hat{y}_i$ (the predicted counts from the model). The difficulty therefore stems from estimating parameters that maximize the likelihood (as opposed to the formulas themselves). This expression implies that the deviance residuals, the square root of the contribution of each observation to the total deviance, take the form:

$$e_{D_i} = \left(\frac{y_i - \hat{y}_i}{|y_i - \hat{y}_i|}\right)\sqrt{2\left(y_i \ln\left(\frac{y_i}{\hat{y}_i}\right) - (y_i - \hat{y}_i)\right)} \qquad \text{Equation 17.42}$$

The Pearson residuals are the difference between the observed and predicted counts divided by their estimated *SD*. This *SD* is estimated from the square root of the estimated mean (which is also the variance of the Poisson distribution):

$$e_{P_i} = \frac{y_i - \hat{y}_i}{\sqrt{\hat{y}_i}} \qquad \text{Equation 17.43}$$

To obtain approximately constant variance for the residuals it is usual to get the adjusted or standardized residuals. Again this involves dividing by $\sqrt{1-h_i}$. The standardized residuals are preferred for assessing the distributional assumptions of Poisson regression, though studentized residuals (calculated in the usual way) are superior for detecting extreme observations. Corresponding influence measures such as Cook's distance can also be derived.

For model checking, deviance residuals tend to have better distributional properties than Pearson residuals. In large samples the approximate χ^2 distribution of the deviance and can be used to assess the goodness-of-fit of the model (though as always, comparisons between models are preferred). Plots of residuals can highlight extreme observations and sometimes reveal lack of independence (e.g., by plotting standardized residuals versus a potential source of dependency such as order of data collection or time of day), or departures from linearity (e.g., plotted against predictor or fitted values), but are less useful than for least squares models.

A serious concern for any Poisson regression model is overdispersion (see Box 17.2). Overdispersion (and sometimes underdispersion) occurs because a Poisson distribution has a single rate parameter that is both its mean and its variance. As in logistic regression, its variance is therefore a function of the mean. Poisson regression models can underestimate or overestimate the true variance if the population of counts being modeled is more or less variable than expected by its mean. For data where each observation is a count accumulated over the same units (e.g., a count of six represents six arguments for the same couple) overdispersion or underdispersion tends to be very common. Lindsey (1999) argues that correctly dispersed Poisson models are plausible only if the observations are accumulations of independent frequencies rather than counts *per se*. While overdispersion is common, it is still important to explore a number of models before concluding that overdispersion is both present and sufficient to distort the results. A poorly fitting model will make it difficult to gauge the degree of overdispersion or underdispersion correctly. For repeated measures data, multilevel Poisson or multilevel logistic regression should also be investigated.

If overdispersion is found to be a serious problem, then one option is to correct the standard errors using $\sqrt{\hat{\varphi}}$ (see Box 17.2). In recent years this approach has fallen slightly out of favor. Fitting an alternative model that allows both the variance and mean to vary is the preferred approach. In a multilevel model this can be accomplished indirectly (by modeling variation between higher-level units separately). In single-level models the preferred options are quasipoisson regression and negative binomial regression.

Example 17.5 This example again uses the surgical checklist data introduced in Example 7.7. These data came from eight hospitals in eight different countries. Factors other than the presence of the checklist might predict mortality. These include the quality of the healthcare in the hospital. This is hard to measure, but one possible proxy is the per capita GDP of the country the hospital is in. Haynes *et al.* (2009) coded this as a dichotomous predictor: *income* (low or high). Using Poisson regression it is possible to model the mortality count before and after introduction of the checklist as a function of *time* (pre or post), *op.k* (total number of operations in thousands) and *income*.

A main effects model with all three predictors has the prediction equation:

$$\ln(mortality) = -1.113 + 0.752 \times pre + 0.786 \times low + 3.904 \times op.k$$

Note that *time* and *income* are dummy coded with $pre = 1$ and $low = 1$ (hence the labeling of coefficients in the model). Scaling operations in thousands makes the operations coefficient easier to work with (e.g., 3.904 instead of 0.003904). There are 16 observations (two per hospital), so a main effects model with $16 - 3 - 1 = 12$ *df* can be compared with the (intercept-only) null model with $16 - 1 = 15$ *df*.

	df	*Deviance*	*AIC*
Null model	15	57.5	108.3
Main effects model	12	32.1	89.0

The change in deviance is $57.5 - 32.1 = 25.4$. The likelihood ratio test is statistically significant, $G^2 = 25.4$, $df = 3$, $p < .0001$, and the change in AIC substantial. A model with all two-way interactions requires three extra parameters, hardly improves model fit and slightly increases AIC ($\Delta df = 3$, $\Delta G^2 = -3.6$, $\Delta \text{AIC} = +2.4$).

The interpretation of coefficients is also clear. The predictors *pre* and *low* have positive coefficients. This indicates that mortality was higher before the checklist was introduced and is higher for low-income countries. The number of operations also increases mortality rates for trivial reasons; the fewer procedures, the fewer opportunities for patients to experience adverse health problems. The coefficients are on a log scale, so it is very helpful to reverse the transformation for interpretation. For *pre*, $e^{0.7524} = 2.1$, and it suggests the mortality rate was 2.1 times higher in hospitals before the checklist was introduced. Hospitals in low-income countries have mortality counts that are roughly 2.2 times higher than for hospitals in high-income countries, and every additional 1000 operations increases the mortality rate in a hospital by a factor of about 50. To gauge the impact of each predictor it is better to look at interval estimates rather than significance tests. Using profile likelihood, the 95% CIs (on the count scale) are:

pre	[1.34, 3.42]
op.k	[2.53, 1293.01]
low	[1.41, 3.49]

None of the intervals includes zero (though the effect of operations seems to be measured rather imprecisely).

There are several things worth checking at this stage. Several of the hospitals have quite influential points (e.g., Cook's distance of .53 and .64), but this is hardly surprising in a model with low residual *df*. What about overdispersion? The residual deviance is 32.8 with 12 *df*. This suggests $\hat{\varphi} = 32.1/12 = 2.68$. For Pearson χ^2, $\hat{\varphi} = 28.2/12 = 2.35$. Both statistics indicate substantial overdispersion (not too surprising given the paired mortality counts from within the same hospitals).

17.5.2 Offsets and rates

The Poisson distribution is often used to compare rates of occurrence of discrete events spread over time or over an area. Unlike a simple Poisson model, Poisson regression treats the rate as an additive function of a set of predictors. Modeling rates in this way is straightforward when the exposure to events is equivalent for all observations. Under such circumstances the model for the rates and the counts is equivalent. If a mean of ten counts were observed in a period of ten seconds, this is a rate of ten per ten seconds or (less clumsily) one event per second. In these situations it is possible to determine the expected rate from the predicted mean count after fitting the model. The rate can also be obtained directly from the model by adding an *offset*. If the opportunity to observe events is not equivalent for all observations, then adding an offset is a requirement.[13] From this perspective, an offset is merely an adjustment to a Poisson regression model that permits the predicted outcome to be interpreted as a rate rather than a count when exposure varies between units.[14]

To understand how an offset works, envisage a data set that consists of counts sampled over a period of ten days. These might represent the number of arguments for a married couple or accidents reported in a workplace. The data can therefore be represented as number of events (arguments, accidents) over a given time period (ten days). The number of events is the observed count Y and the time period is the *exposure* E. The rate is therefore defined as Y/E. Even in a laboratory experiment it may not be possible to fully control the exposure period. The exposure may vary naturally, by design or by misfortune (e.g., some workplaces or couples may contribute data for only seven or eight days rather than the full ten). To model the rate now requires a regression equation of the form:

$$\ln\left(\frac{y_i}{E_i}\right) = b_0 + b_1x_{1,i} + \ldots + b_qx_{q,i} \qquad \text{Equation 17.44}$$

As the logarithm of a ratio is the difference between the logarithm of the numerator and denominator, this model can also be expressed as,

$$\ln(y_i) - \ln(E_i) = b_0 + b_1x_{1,i} + \ldots + b_qx_{q,i} \qquad \text{Equation 17.45}$$

where the $-\ln(E_i)$ term is the offset. Most software for generalized linear models has options to include an offset. If the software doesn't, it can still incorporate an offset (provided it is possible to place constraints on the parameter estimate). This is because Equation 17.45 can be rearranged (by subtracting the offset from both sides) to take the form:

$$\ln(y_i) = \ln(E_i) + b_0 + b_1 x_{1,i} + \ldots + b_q x_{q,i} \qquad \text{Equation 17.46}$$

This is a Poisson regression model in which the natural logarithm of the exposure has been added as a predictor, and where the slope of the predictor $\ln(E_i)$ has been forced to equal one. So an alternative (and more general) way of thinking about an offset is that it involves adding a predictor with a slope of exactly one into the model. In a sense, the exposure is a predictor with privileged status in the model – its effect is assumed to take precedence in adjusting the model (it doesn't compete with other predictors to explain variance and its coefficient is taken as given rather than estimated). This is a logical model to fit if the goal is to de-confound the effects of differential exposure from the outcome. There may be other occasions where it makes more sense to treat exposure as a regular predictor (e.g., if there is good reason to think that its effects vary from occasion to occasion) or if determining its influence on the outcome is part of the research. There may also be other situations in which it makes sense to treat a variable as an offset, rather than estimate its effects as an ordinary predictor.

Example 17.6 In Example 17.5 the outcome variable in the Poisson regression was the mortality count in eight hospitals before and after an intervention. In that model the number of operations in each hospital was used as a predictor in the regression. An alternative model, probably a better one, is to compare the mortality rates between hospitals. As the number of operations in each hospital varies considerably, the predicted outcomes cannot be converted to a rate per 1000 operations by dividing it by a common denominator. To model this mortality rate involves adding the logarithm of the number of operations (in 1000s) as an offset to the model. The model with no offset was:

$$\ln(\mathit{mortality}) = b_0 + b_1\,\mathit{pre} + b_2\,\mathit{low} + b_3\,\mathit{op.k}$$

The model with the offset becomes:

$$\ln(\mathit{mortality}) = b_0 + b_1\,\mathit{pre} + b_2\,\mathit{low} + \ln(\mathit{op.k})$$

Fitting this model gives the prediction equation:

$$\ln(\mathit{mortality}) = 1.604 + 0.655\,\mathit{pre} + 0.768\,\mathit{low} + \ln(\mathit{op.k})$$

Expressing this as a rate gives:

$$\frac{\mathit{mortality}}{\mathit{op.k}} = e^{1.604+0.655\,\mathit{pre}+0.768\,\mathit{low}}$$

This model has deviance of 32.7 with 13 *df* and AIC = 87.5. Relative to the null model ($G^2 = 53.5$, $df = 15$, AIC = 104.3) the main effects model with the offset provides a superior fit ($\Delta df = 2$, $\Delta G^2 = -20.8$, $\Delta\text{AIC} = -16.8$). The profile likelihood CIs for the rate ratios are:

pre 95% CI [1.25, 3.02]
low 95% CI [1.39, 3.43]

Although the coefficients have changed slightly, the biggest shift has been in the intercept.

The predicted mortality rate per 1000 operations for a hospital in a low-income country after the surgical checklist has been introduced is:

$$\frac{mortality}{op.k} = e^{1.604+0.655\times 0+0.768\times 1} = e^{1.604+0.768} = e^{2.372} = 10.7$$

For a similar hospital without the checklist, the rate would be 20.6. The overall ratio (risk ratio) for mortality post-checklist is .52, 95% CI [0.33, 0.80], indicating a substantial decrease in risk.

The overdispersion parameter (calculated from the Pearson χ^2) has also decreased slightly from 2.35 to 2.14. This is still a clear signal of overdispersion.

17.5.3 Negative binomial and quasipoisson regression

Adjusting standard errors for a fitted Poisson model using an overdispersion parameter can be time-consuming and rather inflexible. A more satisfactory approach is to model the dispersion of the data separately from the mean – using a quasipoisson or a negative binomial model.[15] Quasipoisson regression does this by fitting a model with a random component in which the variance is a linear function of the mean determined by an additional parameter:

$$\sigma^2_{Y_i} = \varphi \mu_i \qquad \text{Equation 17.47}$$

This parameter has been labeled φ because it is functionally equivalent to an overdispersion parameter (the difference being that it is incorporated directly into the model rather than being applied as a correction *post hoc*). A disadvantage is that software that fits a quasipoisson model can't readily assess its relative fit to the Poisson model. It provides the same parameter estimates, but with revised standard errors.

Quasipoisson isn't the only option. The negative binomial can be adopted as an alternative to the Poisson distribution. The negative binomial distribution is usually first encountered as a distribution for modeling n, the number of Bernoulli trials to observe r failures for a fixed probability P.[16] For this reason it is convenient to treat the parameters of the negative binomial in a generalized linear model as μ and σ^2 (which can be expressed as functions of P and r) and which are both constrained to be greater than zero. Cook (2009) shows how the mean of a negative binomial distribution can be written as:

$$\mu = r\frac{(1-P)}{P} \qquad \text{Equation 17.48}$$

For modeling the dispersion of count data, the crucial property of the negative binomial is that the variance can be expressed as:

$$\sigma^2 = r\frac{(1-P)}{P^2} = \mu + \frac{1}{r}\mu^2 \qquad \text{Equation 17.49}$$

Thus, at one level, the negative binomial distribution is just a convenient probability function with an extra parameter. What makes it particularly attractive is that when r is large, $1/r$ shrinks

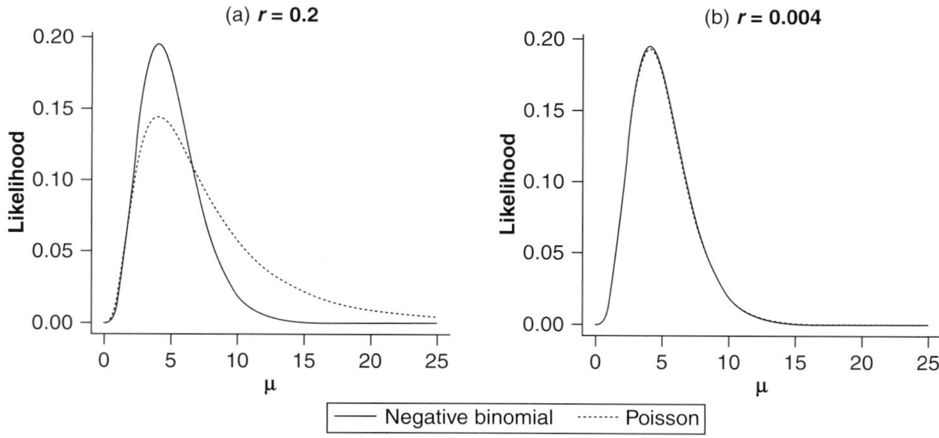

Figure 17.6 Likelihood functions for negative binomial and Poisson distributions, when $\hat{\lambda} = 4$ and (a) $r = 0.2$, or (b) $r = 0.004$

toward zero and the variance converges on μ (and therefore the probability mass function (*pmf*) of the negative binomial converges on the Poisson). Cook (*ibid.*) calls $1/r$ a 'clumping factor' that behaves like an inverted dispersion parameter. For large r, the counts clump together, but for small values they spread apart and hence overdispersion is observed. Figure 17.6 shows the relationship between the Poisson and negative binomial distributions. For convenience, the likelihood functions for the parameter μ of the Poisson and negative binomial distribution have been plotted for an observed count of $\hat{\lambda} = 4$.[17] Panel (a) indicates that even for moderately large values of r the probability distributions diverge and the Poisson is noticeably overdispersed relative to the negative binomial. In panel (b), when r is very small the probability distributions are not detectably different. This pattern is comforting because it indicates that the negative binomial will mimic the fit of the Poisson model if overdispersion is not present.

When should negative binomial regression be preferred over quasipoisson? Negative binomial regression has some practical advantages. The deviance of the model can readily be compared to that of a Poisson regression and it is in some senses a more natural model (Atkins and Gallup, 2007). Ver Hoef and Boveng (2007) point out that a fundamental difference is that the quasipoisson assumes a linear relationship between mean and variance, while the negative binomial distribution assumes a quadratic relationship. They suggest a diagnostic plot of the squared residuals of the model versus the mean (this is best done by grouping or binning data). Alternatively, if there are theoretical reasons to believe that a linear or quadratic function is more plausible this could also motivate selection of the appropriate model.

Example 17.7 The Poisson regressions of the surgical checklist data in Example 17.5 and Example 17.6 indicated that the counts were overdispersed. One option for dealing with this is to manually correct the *SE*s of the coefficients using the square root of the dispersion parameter. For example, the *SE* for the *pre* effect is 0.224. The Pearson overdispersion parameter is 2.14 and so, correcting for overdispersion, the *SE* should be $\sqrt{2.14} \times 0.224 = 0.327$. This procedure is useful if your software does not offer quasipoisson or negative binomial regression as an option. qAIC or $qAIC_C$ can also be obtained manually if required. For instance, qAIC for the main effects model with offset is 41.33, while qAIC for the two-way interaction model with offset is 43.33. This suggests that the simpler model is slightly more informative ($\Delta qAIC = 2.0$).

Running the quasipoisson regression in R produces the corrected *SE* for each coefficient automatically. Even better, it also provides profile likelihood CIs for the quasipoisson model. Fitting this model with the offset ln(*op.k*) will necessarily produce identical coefficients to those from the Poisson regression. The 95% profile likelihood CIs for mortality rate ratios from the quasipoisson model (corrected for overdispersion and including the offset) are:

pre [1.03, 3.75]
low [1.14, 4.30]

Both CIs are wider than before. In addition, the interval estimate for the pre-post difference in mortality now only barely excludes one. The *p* value from the Wald test is .067 and from the more accurate likelihood ratio test it is .041.

Fitting a negative binomial model is also an option here. The negative binomial regression is more than a linear adjustment to the variance – it fits a different distribution – and so may produce different parameter estimates. In a negative binomial model with the same predictors and an offset the prediction equation is:

$$\ln(mortality) = 1.613 + 0.653\,pre + 0.736\,low + \ln(op.k)$$

This model has deviance 20.6 with 13 *df* and AIC = 84.6. The coefficients are indeed slightly different (e.g., the difference between *pre* and *post* checklist mortality is a little larger). The profile likelihood CIs for the mortality rate ratios are:

pre [1.06, 3.52]
low [1.15, 3.85]

Both 95% CIs now exclude one and the likelihood ratio *p* value for the test of time is .031.

The choice between negative binomial and quasipoisson is not necessarily an easy one (though they often produce similar models). Given that the negative binomial is perhaps a more principled approach to overdispersion it would be my default choice. Here both models point to very similar models of the data (and it would be unwise to focus too much on the difference in *p* values). Diagnostics such as Cook's distance also hint at a marginal preference for the negative binomial model, which has slightly lower influence statistics (all now < .30).

17.5.4 Dealing with zero-inflated count data

A feature of count data is that zeroes are not infrequent, even if the rate at which events occur exceeds zero. Poisson and negative binomial models both assume a rate of occurrence greater than zero, so (in these models) the absence of events is either bad luck or indicates an exposure too narrow to observe them. This handles the presence of zero counts for some phenomena, but is unreasonable for others. What if some of the zero counts represent a true absence of the event; measurements on a unit that simply doesn't generate them? A well-known illustration is for criminal behavior. A study might look at a large sample of teenagers to determine what factors influence violent criminal behavior. Some of the teenagers will commit one or more violent crimes, but the majority (if the sample is representative) won't. One way to consider this is to suppose that there are two subpopulations of teenagers – one with a zero rate of violent crime and one with a non-zero rate.[18] A potential solution is to fit separate statistical models: one to predict whether a teenager has a zero or non-zero rate of violent crime and one to predict the number of crimes for the latter. This strategy leads to a class of models termed 'mixture models' (Atkins and Gallup, 2007). For the first model a way of predicting the occurrence of an event is required. Coding occurrence as one and non-occurrence as zero leads to the problem of predicting a dichotomous outcome from a set of predictors, and thus a logistic regression model can be employed. To predict the non-zero crime counts several models could be considered, but Poisson and negative binomial regression are the obvious choices (depending on the dispersion of the counts).

A *zero-inflated Poisson regression* is therefore a mixture model with a Poisson regression nested within a logistic regression:

$$Y \sim f(y_i)\begin{cases} 0 & \textit{with} \quad P(Y=0)=1-P_i \\ \sim \textit{Poisson}\left(e^{b_0+b_1x_{1,i}+\ldots+b_qx_{q,i}}\right) & \textit{with} \quad P(Y>0)=P_i \end{cases} \qquad \text{Equation 17.50}$$

A zero-inflated negative binomial regression is a mixture model of the form:

$$Y \sim f(y_i)\begin{cases} 0 & \textit{with} \quad P(Y=0)=1-P_i \\ \sim NB\left(e^{b_0+b_1x_{1,i}+\ldots+b_qx_{q,i}}, \sigma^2\right) & \textit{with} \quad P(Y>0)=P_i \end{cases} \qquad \text{Equation 17.51}$$

In both equations $f(y_i)$ designates a function of two other probability distributions – one producing zeroes (with a fixed probability $1 - P_i$) and one producing Y counts of the modeled outcome according to a Poisson or negative binomial distribution with fixed probability P_i.

Figure 17.7 shows the differences between Poisson, zero-inflated Poisson and zero-inflated negative binomial distributions for the same population mean. Each plot shows histogram of a simulated random sample of 10,000 observations for an expected mean count of seven. Panel (a) shows the Poisson distribution, (b) the zero-inflated Poisson when the probability of a zero (ignoring the Poisson counts) is $P=.2$ and (c) shows the negative binomial distribution for $P=.2$ and $r=0.2$. The zero-inflated Poisson is very similar to the Poisson distribution, with about 20% of the observations 'shaved off' the distribution and allocated to zero. The zero-inflated negative binomial in panel (c) has greater dispersion and a more pronounced spike at zero (comprising nearly 25% of the observations). Because the population parameters are known for these simulated data, this is in excess of the 20% 'structural' zeroes expected when $P=.2$. For a real data set the probability would have to be estimated from what is likely to be a very noisy sample.

Mixture models are particularly difficult to fit (Atkins and Gallup, 2007). It isn't good enough to fit separate models to the zeroes and non-zeroes in the sample. The difficulty is that a zero could arise either from the logistic regression with probability $1 - P_i$, or it could arise from the Poisson or negative binomial count distribution. It may help to refer back to Figure 2.4a. This shows the *pmf* for a Poisson distribution with $\lambda=2$. Zero counts are fairly common when λ, the population rate parameter, is small. Fitting zero-inflated count data therefore involves optimizing both fits simultaneously to provide the best overall explanation of the observed data. In addition, predictors may have different effects for the probability and count parts of the model.

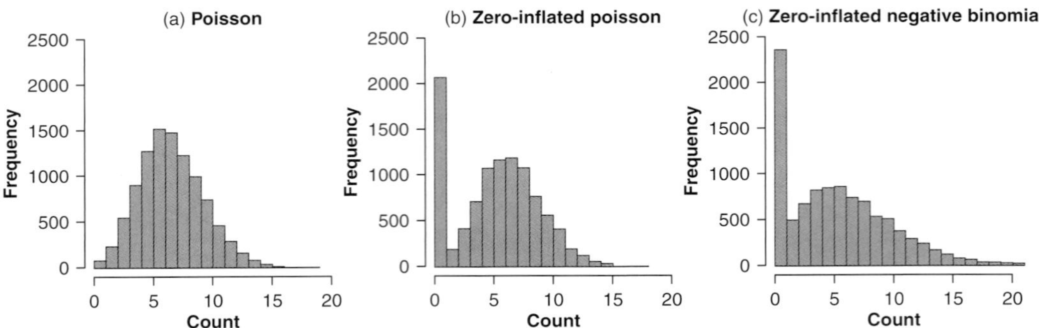

Figure 17.7 Counts sampled from simulated data, with $\mu = 7$ and either (a) a Poisson distribution, (b) a zero-inflated Poisson distribution with $P = .2$, or (c) a zero-inflated negative binomial distribution with $P = .2$ and $r = 0.2$

Modeling the data as a mixture in this way can lead to difficulties of interpretation. Perhaps the most important point is that it will always be safer to interpret the overall fit and predictions of the model rather than interpret the components separately. Zeroes in the model arise from both components, so interpreting the components in isolation could lead to misleading conclusions. An analogy here can be made with interpreting interaction terms in a regression model; interpretation of the product term in isolation will be misleading relative to plotting the predictions of the model. One situation in which the separate interpretation of the components can be defended is if there is strong theoretical justification for the view that a mixture of two populations is being modeled. If this mixed population interpretation is appropriate then inferences based on separate components can be restricted to the population of interest. If this interpretation is not justified there may be advantages to switching to a different approach such as a hurdle model. A hurdle model also separates performance into two components, but one component (typically a logistic regression) models all the zeroes, while the other component (a truncated Poisson or negative binomial) models the non-zero counts (see Zeileis *et al.*, 2008). Hurdle models and zero-inflated models tend to produce very similar overall fits, so the choice between them relates to the interpretation of the separate components. In a hurdle model it is easier to separate out the effects of predictors on zero responses and non-zero responses.

17.6 Modeling discrete outcomes with correlated measures

The generalized linear models considered so far have all assumed independent observations. The random component of the models has distribution such as the normal, binomial, Poisson or negative binomial that requires independence. In the case of a normal generalized linear model it is possible to develop models that explicitly account for the correlation and assume independence of residuals. In addition, for both logistic regression and Poisson regression, correlated observations can be a cause of overdispersion (or even underdispersion). Modeling the dispersion (e.g., using negative binomial regression) may also provide a partial solution to problems with correlated or repeated outcomes. A more principled approach is possible by setting up a *generalized estimating equation* (GEE) or a multilevel generalized linear model (see Chapter 18).

More restrictive, but simpler approaches also exist for some situations (see Agresti, 1996). One well-known approach, for working with paired dichotomies, is illustrated here.

17.6.1 Logistic regression with paired observations

A relatively simple approach to dealing with repeated or correlated measures where outcomes are dichotomous is possible for paired data (e.g., from matched pairs or repeated measures designs). The approach is known as *conditional maximum likelihood* or *conditional logistic regression*. Agresti (*ibid.*) shows how this is related to simpler procedures such as McNemar's test of change in 2 × 2 tables (and can be extended to more complex study designs).

For paired data, the model of interest is probably of the form:

$$\ln\left(\frac{\hat{P}_{ij}}{1-\hat{P}_{ij}}\right)=b_{0,j}+b_1 x_{1i,j}+\ldots+b_q x_{q,ij} \qquad \text{Equation 17.52}$$

This looks to be a regular logistic regression except that the intercept b_{0j} is a random variable equivalent to a subject term in a one-way repeated measures ANOVA. Unfortunately, fitting multiple intercepts causes estimation difficulties if there are large numbers of participants (*ibid.*). Conditional logistic regression works by eliminating the subject effect from the likelihood estimate entirely. The conditional maximum likelihood is therefore estimated for the parameters (in the sense that the estimates are all conditional on the subject term).

This can be done using specialized software, but it is also possible to arrive at the conditional estimates using standard logistic regression software. This is done by fitting a no-intercept model with a constant as the outcome (i.e., $Y = 1$ for all cases) and with the difference between the paired cases (a series of values equal to −1, 0 or 1) as the predictor. Applied to a 2 × 2 table, the difference between the deviance of the null and residual model would be roughly equivalent to the more familiar McNemar test. However, unlike the McNemar test, other predictors can be added to the model. These are included as additional predictors (along with the differences) in the usual way. If the cases differ in terms of some predictor value it is also possible to use the between-pair difference in predictor as an explanatory variable.

Although conditional logistic regression is useful, it can be awkward to implement (even using the shortcuts described here), and is inflexible. On the other hand, it can cope with paired repeated measures, with 1:1 matching or 1:x matching between cases and controls (where there are several controls for each case). Other forms of repeated or correlated measures designs require different solutions. A final issue is that the random effect is treated as a nuisance variable rather than being explicitly modeled (as it would be in a multilevel model).

Example 17.8 To illustrate how conditional logistic regression can be fitted, I'll use an imaginary case-control study (in which 30 cases are matched with 30 controls). The question of interest is whether a potential risk factor (*prf*) is associated with increased odds of being a case versus a control. The contingency table looks like this:

		Controls		
		no prf	*prf*	
Cases	*no prf*	8	4	*12*
	prf	17	1	*18*
		25	*5*	*30*

To run a conditional logistic regression using standard logistic regression software requires data arranged as two columns: one for cases and one for controls. As there are 30 case-control pairs, there will be 30 rows. Of these, one row will contain one for both cases and controls (indicating both have the potential risk factor). Seventeen rows will have one entered for cases and zero for controls. Four rows will have zero for case and one for controls. The remaining eight cases will have zero for both cases and controls. For the analysis you will also need a column of constants (with 30 rows containing one in each cell). Last, you will need a column of differences (created by subtracting the control column from the case column).

After setting the data up as described, the next step is to run a logistic regression with no intercept and with the column of constants the outcome. The model has one predictor: the difference scores (though it would be possible to add others). The cases and controls are not entered into the analysis directly – they are just used to create the difference scores. The log odds estimated from this model (for the difference predictor) are the log odds of cases having the risk factor relative to controls. These log odds are 1.45. The corresponding odds ratio is therefore $e^{1.45} = 4.25$, or .81 expressed as a probability. This odds ratio is identical to that obtained from the McNemar test ($17/4 = 4.25$). Using profile likelihood, the 95% CI for the odds ratio is [1.57, 14.77]. The likelihood ratio or deviance test is: $G^2\ (1, N = 30) = 8.66$, $p = .0032$.

This procedure ought to work with most logistic regression software (but may not in practice). It is also possible to 'trick' other procedures to run the analysis – including survival analysis in SPSS or R (though this requires data arranged in a slightly different form).

17.7 R code for Chapter 17

17.7.1 The logistic function

The logistic function can be plotted via several routes. Figure 17.1 used the `curve()` function and specified the equation directly:

```
curve(exp(x)/(1+exp(x)), ylab = 'Probability', xlab = NA,
  xlim=c(-5,5), lwd=2, lty=3)
```

This shows how the predictive probability depends on the predictors (in this case *x*). It is also instructive to see the probability density plotted against that of the normal distribution (as in Figure 17.2). The normal distribution needs to be scaled to have the same standard deviation (defined by the first command below). The remaining functions plot the density of a standard logistic distribution and add the scaled normal on top (with an appropriate legend).

```
logis.sd <- pi/3^0.5
curve(dlogis(x), xlim=c(-5,5), ylab = 'Probability density',
  lwd=1)
curve(dnorm(x,0,logis.sd), lty= 3, add = TRUE, lw=1.5)
legend(1.6, 0.23, legend = c('Logistic', 'Scaled normal'), lty
  =c(1,3), cex = 1, lwd=c(1.5,1))
```

Note that a similar figure to that in Figure 17.1 could have been obtained directly using the *cdf* or inverse *quantile* function for the logistic distribution. This is simpler, but hides the form of the equation (which is worth becoming familiar with):

```
curve(plogis(x), xlim =c(-5,5))
```

17.7.2 Logistic regression and χ^2 (Example 17.1)

For the dream data set it is quite easy to set up the data by creating a numeric vector with either zero or one for group membership or the 'scary dream' response. Using the `rep()` reduces the need to type in lots of numbers (e.g., `rep(0,26)` repeats the value zero 26 times). The first vector specifies the group (zero for no suggestion and one for suggestion). The second specifies the response (zero for no scary dream and one for scary dream).

```
group <- c(rep(0,26), rep(1,21))
scary <- c(1, rep(0,25), rep(1,7), rep(0,14))
```

The logistic regression is run using the `glm()` function. This specifies a general linear model using a formula similar to that of the `lm()` function. One difference is that a family is now specified for the random component of the generalized linear model. This defaults to `family=normal`. The `family()` function used as an argument to `glm()` also determines the link function (which defaults to the canonical link function and can therefore often be ignored). Thus the following are identical in output:

```
glm(scary ~ group, family=binomial(link = logit))
glm(scary ~ group, family=binomial)
```

If the family is not specified, `glm()` is equivalent to `lm()` for most purposes. For this reason `glm()` is often used as a convenient generic function for regression modeling. However, because the output from the functions is delivered slightly differently, there can be differences in how other functions act on objects (models) created by the two functions.

Wald tests are given by the `summary()` function for the model:

```
subbot.mod <- glm(scary ~ group, family=binomial)
summary(subbot.mod)
```

The change in deviance for the group effect can be obtained by the `anova()` function. The `drop1()` function also gives the change in deviance, AIC and, if requested, the likelihood ratio test of the change in deviance:

```
anova(subbot.mod)
drop1(subbot.mod, test = 'Chisq')
```

The `confint()` command gives the profile likelihood CIs for generalized linear models.

```
confint(subbot.mod)
```

As dummy coding is being used for the grouping variable it is also very simple to reverse the coding. The main reason to do this is simply to change the intercept to obtain the CI for the other group:

```
summary(glm(scary ~ I(1 - group), family=binomial))
confint(glm(scary ~ I(1 - group), family=binomial))
```

The usual Pearson χ^2 test of independence can be obtained by creating a contingency table and using `chisq.test()`:

```
ctable <- matrix(nrow=2, ncol=2)
ctable[1:4] <- c(1, 7, 25, 14)
ctable
chisq.test(ctable, correct=FALSE)
```

17.7.3 Interpreting logistic regression coefficients (Example 17.2)

Example 17.2 modeled the effect of a continuous predictor – the electoral majority of a UK member of parliament – on a discrete outcome (whether there was a reported allegation of expenses abuse). As the majority data range from 37 to nearly 20,000 it is convenient to rescale the majorities by expressing them in units of 10,000:

```
expenses <- read.csv('expenses.csv')
majority.10k <- expenses$majority/10000
```

The model with majority as predictor and problem as outcome can then be fitted using `glm()`.

```
model.10k <- glm(problem ~ majority.10k, family=binomial,
  data = expenses)
summary(model.10k)
```

Wald CIs on the logit scale are computed by adding or subtracting the appropriate margin of error (e.g., ±1.96 SE for a 95% CI). However, the profile indicates the likelihood CIs that should be more accurate:

```
confint(model.10k)
```

In most cases the odds ratios are easier to interpret than the logit scale coefficients. The CIs on the odds scale can be obtained by exponentiation:

```
exp(model.10k$coefficients)
exp(confint(model.10k))
```

The predictions for each MP on the logit scale are easily obtained using the `predict()` function. To change the scale to the predicted probabilities (by using the inverse of the link function), `type='response'` can be specified. Alternatively the fitted values of the model can be used (as these are calculated on the untransformed response scale). Compare the following outputs:

```
predict(model.10k)
predict(model.10k, type='response')
model.10k$fitted.values
```

Plotting predicted values on the probability scale versus a predictor such as majority is now easy:

```
plot(expenses$majority,model.10k$fitted.values,
  ylab='Probability(Expenses problem)', xlab='Majority')
```

This is similar to the plots in Figures 17.3 and 17.4. Figure 17.4 also adds approximate Wald confidence bands. This is done by using the predict function to obtain standard errors for 20,000 or so predicted new values (with a range of zero to two for the majority variable scaled in units of 10,000) and using these to calculate a margin of error at each point. Adding or subtracting these to the fitted values gives upper or lower bounds for the log odds.

```
maj <- data.frame(majority.10k = seq(0, 2, 1/10000))
moe <- predict(model.10k, newdata=maj, se.fit=TRUE)[[2]] *
  qnorm(.975)
ub <- predict(model.10k, newdata=maj, se.fit=FALSE) + moe
lb <- predict(model.10k, newdata=maj, se.fit=FALSE) - moe
```

Adding these to a plot `lines()` joins the points and gives the appearance of a smooth function:

```
lines(c(0:20000),exp(lb)/(1+exp(lb)), col='dark gray')
lines(c(0:20000),exp(ub)/(1+exp(ub)), col='dark gray')
```

The rest of the example considers the deviance and AIC for the model:

```
anova(model.10k, test = 'Chisq')
drop1(model.10k, test = 'Chisq')

model.null <- glm(problem ~ 1, family=binomial, data =
  expenses)

AIC(model.10k) - AIC(model.null)

LR.aic <- 1/exp((AIC(model.10k) - AIC(model.null))/2)
LR.aic
```

The model isn't improved by adding party affiliation (given that this requires an extra 17 *df*) or the extra four parameters when minor parties are categorized as 'other'.

```
all.parties <- glm(problem ~ majority.10k + factor(Party),
  family=binomial, data = expenses)
drop1(all.parties)
main.parties <- glm(problem ~ majority.10k + Lab + Con +
  LibDem + SNP + Other, family=binomial, data = expenses)
drop1(main.parties)
```

Note that if the conventional significance test is applied for the `all.parties` model the more complex model is a statistically significantly better fit:

```
drop1(all.parties, test = 'Chisq')
```

This is a good example where throwing predictors at a model will often produce a substantial shift in fit. This is a doubly bad model; because it ignores the problem of over-fitting and because some of the smaller 'party' labels are for MPs who had been ejected from a main party because of expenses allegations.

17.7.4 Model checking in logistic regression (Example 17.3)

Quantities such as the standardized and unstandardized residuals, Cook's distance and leverage can be obtained from a `glm()` model in the same way as for a linear regression model.

```
cooks.distance(model.10k)
resid(model.10k)
```

By default the residuals are the working residuals of the model (on the transformed scale – not in terms of the untransformed response). The standardized and studentized residuals may also be useful and can be obtained with familiar commands:

```
rstandard(model.10k)
rstudent(model.10k)
```

The summary command also provides the dispersion parameter used for the model. This should be one for a logistic regression, and refitting the model as a quasipoisson model gives a simple method to extract the dispersion parameter:

```
summary(model.10k)$dispersion
model.10k.q <- glm(problem ~ majority.10k,
  family=quasibinomial, data = expenses)
summary(model.10k.q)$dispersion
```

17.7.5 Ordered logistic regression (Example 17.4)

The traffic data used in this example can be read into R from an SPSS file.

```
library(foreign)
traffic <- read.spss('traffic.sav', to.data.frame=TRUE)
```

To run an ordered logistic regression there are several options including `lrm()` in the `rms` package and `polr()` in `MASS`. The data here are very sparse and difficult to fit. The `lrm()` function seems to cope best. The following model fits indicate the problem with the visibility predictor `vis`.

```
install.packages('rms')
library(rms)

traf.me <- lrm(stc ~ female + year + oru + vis, data=traffic)
traf.me
traf.null <- lrm(stc ~ 1, data=traffic)
traf.null
```

A better model drops `vis` and there is also some indication that the fit is improved by adding the `female:oru` interaction:

```
traf.me2 <- lrm(stc ~ female + year + oru, data=traffic)
traf.int <- lrm(stc ~ female + year + oru + female:oru,
  data=traffic)
traf.me2
traf.int
```

The formula for the `traf.int` model could be represented more succinctly as stc ~ year + female*oru.

17.7.6 Poisson regression (Example 17.5)

Example 17.5 returns to the surgical checklist data. It models the mortality rates across the eight different hospitals, using data in the 'checklist.csv' data file. Again, it helps to rescale some of the predictors. In this case the number of operations is scaled in terms of units of 1000. A main effects model adds predictors for the number of operations and dummy indicators for time (pre or post checklist) and income (low or high income per capita countries).

```
checklist <- read.csv('checklist.csv')
op.k <- checklist$operations/1000

mort.me <- glm(mortality ~ time + op.k + income,
  data=checklist, family=poisson)

summary(mort.me)
```

For the difference in deviance and likelihood ratio test versus the null model use the `anova()` function:

```
anova(mort.me, update(mort.me, ~ 1), test = 'Chisq')
```

The model with all two-way interactions can be tested in same way:

```
mort.int <- glm(mortality ~ (time + operations + income)^2,
  data=checklist, family= poisson)
```

```
anova(mort.me, mort.int, test = 'Chisq')
AIC(mort.int) - AIC(mort.me)
```

The CIs (using profile methods) for the log scale and the count scale are given by:

```
confint(mort.me)
exp(confint(mort.me))
```

Residuals and Cook's distance can be obtained with the usual commands:

```
residuals(mort.me)
cooks.distance(mort.me)
```

The residual deviance obtained directly from the model object could also be calculated from the residuals directly:

```
mort.me$deviance
sum(residuals(mort.me)^2)
```

The Pearson χ^2 statistic of 28.2 is also easy to calculate from residuals, but it is necessary to use the Pearson residuals:

```
sum(residuals(mort.me, type='pearson')^2)
```

Either quantity can be used to estimate the dispersion parameter by dividing by the residual *df*, though the Pearson χ^2 produces larger estimates and tends to be preferred.

```
sum(residuals(mort.me)^2)/12
sum(residuals(mort.me, type='pearson')^2)/12
```

The latter is the parameter reported by R for a fitted quasipoisson model:

```
summary(update(mort.me, family = quasipoisson))$dispersion
```

17.7.7 Offsets and rates (Example 17.6)

Treating the number of operations in the previous example as a predictor is probably not the best approach. A better approach, that allows the Poisson model to treat the mortality as a rate per operation (strictly per 1000 operations) is to enter the number of operations as an offset.

```
mort.off <- glm(mortality ~ time + income, data=checklist,
  offset=log(op.k), family=poisson)
```

An equivalent way to express the model with the offset explicit in the formula is also sometimes useful:

```
glm(mortality ~ time + income + offset(log(op.k)),
  data=checklist, family=poisson)
```

The CIs for the main predictors are broadly similar in this instance, but the overdispersion is slightly less severe:

```
exp(confint(mort.off))
sum(resid(mort.off, type = 'pearson')^2)/13
```

The `drop1()` function is also useful for investigating the effects of individual predictors with AIC or with an NHST of the change in deviance:

```
drop1(mort.off, test = 'Chisq')
```

17.7.8 Negative binomial and quasipoisson regression (Example 17.7)

Figure 17.6 shows how the negative binomial distribution and the Poisson are almost indistinguishable when the 'clumping factor' r is very small (and overdispersion negligible). A continuous likelihood function (rather than discrete *pmf*) is used to make the plots clearer (and easier to produce). The likelihoods are generated using the `dpois()` and `dnbinom()` functions. The `dnbinom()` function uses a slightly different parameterization than that in Equation 17.48, using a 'size' parameter equal to $1/r$. The following plot matches panel (b) of Figure 17.6 and shows the similarity of the two distributions when 'clumpiness' is low.

```
siz <- 250
curve(dpois(4, x), xlim=c(0,25), xlab=expression(mu),
  main=expression(paste('(b) ',italic(r),'= 0.004')),
  cex.main =0.95, ylab = 'Likelihood')

curve(dnbinom(4, size=siz, mu=x), add = TRUE, lty = 3)

legend(12.5, 0.175, legend = c('negative binomial','Poisson'),
  lty=c(1,3), cex = 0.8)
```

To show the potential difference in the distribution as 'clumpiness' increases, compare it with panel (a):

```
siz <- 5

curve(dpois(4, x), xlim=c(0,25), lty = 1, xlab=expression(mu),
  main=expression(paste('(a)', italic(r),'= 0.2')), cex.main
  =0.95, ylab = 'Likelihood')
curve(dnbinom(4, size=siz, mu=x), add = TRUE, lty = 3)
legend(12.5,.175, legend = c('negative binomial','Poisson'),
  lty=c(1,3), cex = 0.8)
```

To deal with the overdispersion in the checklist data, one option is to adjust the *SE*s using the overdispersion parameter. R makes this option simpler by fitting a quasipoisson model that also supports profile likelihood CIs. The `drop1()` function also provides accurate NHSTs (but not AIC).

```
mort.oq <- glm(mortality~time+income, data=checklist,
  offset=log(op.k), family=quasipoisson)
summary(mort.oq)

exp(confint(mort.oq))
drop1(mort.oq, test = 'Chisq')
```

The `bbmle` package provides functions to compute qAIC and $qAIC_C$. These require the estimated dispersion parameter as input. Here the dispersion parameter is extracted from a quasipoisson model and qAIC computed for the two-way interaction model (the most complex under consideration):

```
library(bbmle)
disp <- summary(glm(mortality ~ time * income, data=checklist,
  offset=log(op.k), family=quasipoisson))$dispersion

mort.off.int <- glm(mortality ~ time * income, data=checklist,
  offset=log(op.k), family=poisson)

qAIC(mort.off, dispersion = disp)
qAIC(mort.off.int, dispersion = disp)
qAIC(mort.off, dispersion = disp) - qAIC(mort.off.int,
  dispersion = disp)
```

As qAIC is rather simple to compute, it may be easier to do it directly from the dispersion and loglikelihood. This calculation should match for the `mort.off.int` model above:

```
(logLik(mort.off.int)[1]*-2)/disp + 4 * 2
```

The negative binomial model is less limited than the quasipoisson, but requires a package such as MASS to fit it. MASS provides the `glm.nb()` function to fit negative binomial generalized linear models. This has a default 'log' link function and works slightly differently from `glm()` (e.g., in requiring an offset to be part of the formula). Refitting the checklist main effect model with an offset is done as follows:

```
library(MASS)
mort.nb <- glm.nb(mortality ~ time + income +
  offset(log(op.k)), data=checklist)
summary(mort.nb)
```

Again the profile likelihood CI and tests of the predictors are obtained using familiar functions:

```
mort.nb <- glm.nb(mortality ~ time + income +
  offset(log(op.k)), data=checklist)
summary(mort.nb)
```

```
exp(confint(mort.nb))
drop1(mort.nb, test = 'Chisq')
```

Residuals, Cook's distance and so forth are also provided:

```
resid(mort.nb, type ='pearson')
predict(mort.nb, type = 'response')
cooks.distance(mort.nb)
```

17.7.9 Modeling zero-inflated count data

Zero-inflated Poisson, negative binomial models and other mixture models are not yet routinely available in statistical software. Functions for working with these models are found in a number of R packages. The plots in Figure 17.7 use the `rzipois()` function from the `VGAM` package and the `rzinbinom()` function from the `emdbook` package.[19] Using these functions, Figure 17.7 is:

```
install.packages('emdbook')
install.packages('VGAM')

library(emdbook)
library(VGAM)

count <- 7
prob <- .2
n <- 10000
size <- 5

par(mfrow=c(1,3), mar=c(4,4,2,1)+.1, pty='s', cex=1)
hist(rpois(n, count), xlim=c(0,20), ylim=c(0,2500), main='(a)
  Poisson', cex.main=1.1, xlab = 'Count', col='light gray')

hist(rzipois(n, count, prob), xlim=c(0,20), ylim=c(0,2500),
  main =' (b) Zero-inflated Poisson', cex.main=1.1, xlab =
  'Count', col='light gray')

hist(rzinbinom(n, count, size, prob), xlim=c(0,20),
  ylim=c(0,2500), breaks = 25, main='(c) Zero-inflated
  negative binomial', cex.main = 1.1, xlab='Count', col='light
  gray')
```

`VGAM` can be used to fit zero-inflated count models with the `vglm()` function. Although `vglm()` is very powerful, a more user-friendly option for extending Poisson and negative binomial regression models is the `zeroinfl()` function from the `pscl` package. For instance, to fit an intercept only zero-inflated Poisson or negative binomial model for the checklist data you'd specify the formula like this:

```
install.packages('pscl')
library(pscl)
```

```
zeroinfl(mortality ~ 1, dist='poisson', link = 'logit',
  data=checklist)

zeroinfl(mortality ~ 1, dist='negbin', link = 'logit',
  data=checklist)
```

The `dist` argument indicates the family used for the count part of the mixture model (the link function here is always the log and need not be specified). The `link` argument specifies the link function for the zero-inflation part of the mixture model. The defaults are `dist='poisson'` and `link = 'logit'`. The following model adds `income` as a predictor to both parts of the model:

```
zeroinfl(mortality ~ income, data=checklist)
```

Sometimes it makes sense to add predictors only to the count part of the model (or possibly only the zero-inflation part). Here, although a zero-inflation model doesn't look that plausible, it is more plausible (and fits better) if the predictors (including offset) are added to the count part of the model only. This is achieved by separating the predictors in each component using `|` (not to be confused with its role in other functions such as multilevel models).

```
zeroinfl(mortality ~ time + income + offset(log(op.k))|1,
  data=checklist)
```

You may prefer to fit a hurdle model in place of the zero-inflated model. This is also possible within the `pscl` package by using the `hurdle()` function with the same formula structure:

```
hurdle(mortality ~ time + income + offset(log(op.k))|1,
  data=checklist)
```

In general the models will have very similar overall fits and predictions (but slightly different parameter estimates because of the way excess zeroes are modeled). Thus the choice between them rests on the appeal of the mixed population interpretation versus a single population interpretation.

17.7.10 Logistic regression with paired data (Example 17.8)

Analyzing paired outcomes when data are dichotomous can be accomplished via several routes. One of the simplest is conditional logistic regression. A very basic illustration uses case-control data where two groups of participants (cases and controls) are compared on some risk factor (coded zero for risk factor not present and one for risk factor present). What distinguishes this from an independent groups analysis is that the cases and controls are matched in pairs (e.g., for age, gender and so forth).

The first step is to load in the case-control pairs into a data frame with two columns (one for cases and one for controls).

```
cc.dat <- read.csv('case_control.csv')
```

There also needs to be a vector of 30 constants and a separate vector of 30 risk factor differences (one difference for each pair):

```
const <- rep(1,30)
diff <- cc.dat$case - cc.dat$control
```

To fit the conditional logistic regression, just run a logistic regression with no intercept with the constant as outcome and the differences as a predictor:

```
cc.fit <- glm(const ~ 0 + diff, family=binomial)
```

The log odds, odds ratio and probability of having the risk factor for the cases relative to the controls are:

```
cc.fit$coefficients
exp(cc.fit$coefficients)
exp(cc.fit$coefficients)/(1 + exp(cc.fit$coefficients))
```

The CI for the odds ratio is:

```
exp(confint(cc.fit))
```

To fit the same model using conditional logistic regression commands requires a different data structure, with separate variables for an identifier (the case number for case-control pairs or the participant number for repeated measures), case and predictor such as the risk factor in the example above. This format differs because it uses the repeated measures long form rather than the broad form. The file `cond_lg.csv` has data structured in this way.

```
clg.dat <- read.csv('cond_lg.csv')
```

To run the conditional logistic regression, use case as outcome, the identifier to define the repeated measures 'strata' and add the predictor in the usual way. The `clogit()` function in the `survival` package will fit this model:

```
library(survival)
clg.fit <- clogit(case ~ prf + strata(id), data = clg.dat)
```

However, this method doesn't provide profile likelihood CIs (and the Wald CI it does report is quite a bit wider here).

```
summary(clg.fit)
```

17.7.11 R packages

Bolker, B. M. (2009) *emdbook*: Ecological Models and Data (Book Support). R package version 1.2.

Bolker, B. M., and R Development Core Team (2011) *bbmle*: Tools for General Maximum Likelihood Estimation. R package version 0.9.7

Harrell, F. E. Jr. (2011) *rms*: Regression Modeling Strategies. R package version 3.3–1.

R-core members, DebRoy, S., Bivand, R., *et al.* (2011) *foreign*: Read Data Stored by Minitab, S, SAS, SPSS, Stata, Systat, dBase. R package version 0.8–42.
Therneau T., and Lumley, T. (2009) *survival*: Survival Analysis, including Penalised Likelihood. R package version 2.35–7.
Venables, W. N., and Ripley, B. D. (2002) *MASS*: Modern Applied Statistics with S. (4th edn) Springer: New York.
Yee, T. W. (2009) *VGAM*: Vector Generalized Linear and Additive Models. R package version 0.7–9.
Zeileis, A., Kleiber, C., and Jackman, S. (2008) Regression Models for Count Data in R. *Journal of Statistical Software*, 27(8).

17.8 Notes on SPSS syntax for Chapter 17

17.8.1 Generalized linear models

SPSS has both specialized commands (e.g., for binary logistic regression, ordinal logistic regression and loglinear models) and a very powerful generalized linear model command. For a basic logistic regression the `LOGISTIC REGRESSION` command can be used. This example uses the dream data, but input requires a dichotomous outcome for each participant (rather than as a contingency table):

SPSS data file: `dream.sav`

```
LOGISTIC REGRESSION VARIABLES scary
  /METHOD=ENTER group
  /SAVE=PRED
  /PRINT=CI(95).
```

The odds ratios are reported as `EXP(B)` where `B` is the coefficient on the log odds (logit) scale. Here the `/PRINT` subcommand requests a CI for the odds ratio and `/SAVE` requests predicted probabilities saved to the spreadsheet. Additional predictors can be entered by listing them after `group`.

As a rule these SPSS commands are quite easy to run via menus, but less flexible. In contrast, the generalized linear model command `GENLIN` is incredibly powerful, but can be rather fiddly to run using menus. For most models you can reply on the SPSS defaults to set up the model correctly with some basic syntax. Here is the same logistic regression via `GENLIN`.

```
GENLIN scary BY group
  /MODEL group DISTRIBUTION=BINOMIAL LINK=LOGIT.
```

The point of using `GENLIN` is that it can do a lot more than the simpler command and (even for a basic model such as this) automatically provides AIC, BIC and, most useful of all, AIC_C (as well as other information criteria and fit indices). It also provides profile likelihood CIs if requested:

```
GENLIN scary BY group
  /MODEL group DISTRIBUTION=BINOMIAL LINK=LOGIT
/CRITERIA CILEVEL=95 CITYPE=PROFILE(.0001).
```

The `PROFILE(.0001)` argument sets the required accuracy of the CI (which is obtained by iterative fitting). It is also trivial to change the reference category for the outcome:

```
GENLIN scary (REFERENCE=LAST) BY group
  /MODEL group DISTRIBUTION=BINOMIAL LINK=LOGIT
/CRITERIA CILEVEL=95 CITYPE=PROFILE(.0001).
```

The syntax is similar for all `GENLIN` models. Thus, for a Poisson regression the syntax takes the form:

```
GENLIN
outcome BY factor1 WITH covariate1
/MODEL factor1 covariate1 INTERCEPT=YES
DISTRIBUTION=POISSON LINK=LOG.
```

Diagnostics, predictions and so forth can be obtained from `/SAVE` and profile intervals from a `/CRITERIA` subcommand as above. SPSS command syntax reference (from the <Help> menu) will list all the options for different subcommands. The following example fits a main effects Poisson regression model for the surgical checklist data for counts arranged in a contingency table. The default is to include intercept and use a canonical link function so this syntax should work fine. The number of operations is first rescaled (as in Example 17.4) using the `COMPUTE` command:

SPSS data file: `mortality.sav`

```
COMPUTE op_k=operations/1000.
EXECUTE.

GENLIN mortality BY income time WITH op_k
  /MODEL income time op_k DISTRIBUTION=POISSON
  /CRITERIA CILEVEL=95 CITYPE=PROFILE(.0001).
```

In practice the number of operations should be an offset, in which case the following syntax can be used:

```
COMPUTE log_op_k = LN(op_k).
EXECUTE.

GENLIN mortality BY income time
  /MODEL income time DISTRIBUTION=POISSON OFFSET=log_op_k
  /CRITERIA CILEVEL=95 CITYPE=PROFILE(.0001).
```

It is also possible to change the distribution to negative binomial by altering the `DISTRIBUTION` statement. However, the dispersion is fixed equal to one by default. To fit estimate the dispersion add `DISTRIBUTION=NEGBIN(MLE)` to the `MODEL` subcommand:

```
GENLIN mortality BY income time
  /MODEL income time DISTRIBUTION=NEGBIN(MLE) OFFSET=log_op_k
  /CRITERIA CILEVEL=95 CITYPE=PROFILE(.0001).
```

This produces output similar to (but not quite the same as) that from `glm.nb()` in R.

Ordered logistic regression uses similar syntax within the `PLUM` command:

```
PLUM outcome BY factor1 WITH covariate1
  /CRITERIA=CIN(95)
  /LINK=LOGIT
  /PRINT TPARALLEL.
```

The `TPARALLEL` statement requests a test of parallel lines (in effect a significance test of the proportional odds assumption – though as already noted this NHST tends to reject the assumption too often in larger samples). The GENLIN command does a similar analysis but supports profile likelihood CIs:

```
GENLIN outcome (ORDER=ASCENDING) BY factor1 WITH covariate1
  /MODEL factor1 covariate1
DISTRIBUTION=MULTINOMIAL LINK=CUMLOGIT
  /CRITERIA CILEVEL=95 CITYPE=PROFILE(.0001).
```

17.8.2 Conditional logistic regression

SPSS won't accept a constant as an outcome for logistic regression, so regular logistic regression commands won't work for the case-control data in Example 17.8. However, the survival model approach will work. As with the example using R, the data needs to be in long form (as in the file `cond_lg.sav`). First, use `COMPUTE` to get a *time* variable that codes time as one when case = 1 and two when case = 0 (i.e., for controls), then run the survival using the following syntax:

SPSS data file: `cond_lg.sav`

```
COMPUTE time=1+(case=0).
EXECUTE.

COXREG time WITH prf
  /STATUS=case(1)
  /STRATA=id
  /PRINT=CI(95).
```

Other predictors can be added as covariates or factors in the normal way using `WITH` or `BY`. Note that the measures don't really need to be separated in time (the correlation between case and control or other matched observations just needs to be treated as if it is a repeated measure).

17.9 Bibliography and further reading

Agresti, A. (1996) *An Introduction to Categorical Data Analysis*. New York: Wiley.

Atkins, D. C., and Gallop, R. J. (2007) Rethinking How Family Researchers Model Infrequent Outcomes: A Tutorial on Count Regression and Zero-inflated Models. *Journal of Family Psychology*, 21, 726–35.

Hilbe, J. M. (2007) *Negative Binomial Regression*. Cambridge: Cambridge University Press.

17.10 Online supplement 4: Pseudo-R^2 and related measures

For pseudo-R^2 statistics as well as alternatives such as predictive power (Zheng & Agresti, 2000) and percentage correct classification, go to online supplement 4 at www.palgrave.com/psychology/baguley.

17.11 Online supplement 5: Loglinear models

For a detailed introduction to loglinear models go to online supplement 5 at www.palgrave.com/psychology/baguley. These models are closely related to both logistic regression and Poisson regression and are widely employed for analysis of contingency table data. Examples of how to fit loglinear models in R and SPSS are provided.

18
Multilevel models

Contents

18.1 Chapter overview

Multilevel models provide a powerful and flexible extension to repeated measures ANOVA and regression models. This chapter starts by considering the challenge of modeling hierarchical data structures and the limitations of standard repeated measures analyses, followed by a brief introduction to multilevel regression. This is supported by examples of how to build up a random intercept model, a random slope model and how to model different covariance structures. These examples are followed by an introduction to models for cross-classified data, with particular emphasis on fully crossed data structures. The chapter ends with a brief overview of multilevel generalized linear models.

18.2 From repeated measures ANOVA to multilevel models

18.2.1 Modeling hierarchical data structures

The first obstacle in understanding multilevel regression models is to get to grips with the range of different terminology used to describe them. You may encounter similar or identical models under names such as *linear mixed models*, *hierarchical linear models* or *random coefficient models* (and this list is not exhaustive). The term *multilevel model* best captures the defining feature of this technique: the ability to model variation at different levels of a data set. A standard multilevel model assumes that data have a hierarchical structure, with effects of predictors modeled at multiple levels of the hierarchy.[1] Hierarchical structure can be imposed by the design of a study, the sampling strategy adopted by a researcher, or arise from the natural clustering of the units being measured. No matter how these structures occur, they are more likely than not to be associated with dependencies between measurements within a 'node' of the hierarchy. Multilevel models are a relatively recent development in statistics, devised to overcome the limitations of existing methods for dealing with hierarchical data structures. It is not possible to do justice to the full range of possibilities opened up by multilevel modeling here, but looking at the first and subsequent editions of the book by Goldstein (1987, 1995, 2003) will give a flavor of the history and scope of the approach.

Much of the early work on multilevel models (including Goldstein's) is concerned with modeling educational data. Data in educational contexts are inherently clustered, with individuals (children) usually being nested within classes, which are, in turn, nested within schools. Additional levels of clustering can also occur (with measurements nested within individuals or schools nested in education authorities, states or nations). Similar natural clusters occur in occupational and health settings where researchers only very rarely have the luxury of randomly assigning individuals to experimental groups. Multilevel modeling is especially important in these contexts because it also allows researchers to tease apart effects at different levels of the hierarchy. In education research, people are interested in the factors that impact on academic attainment both at the individual level and also at the level of a school or classroom. Figure 18.1 shows the structure of a typical two-level multilevel model (with individuals at the lower level and schools at the higher level). The most common convention, and the one adopted here, numbers the levels from the bottom so that level one (here pupils) is always the lowest, more detailed level.

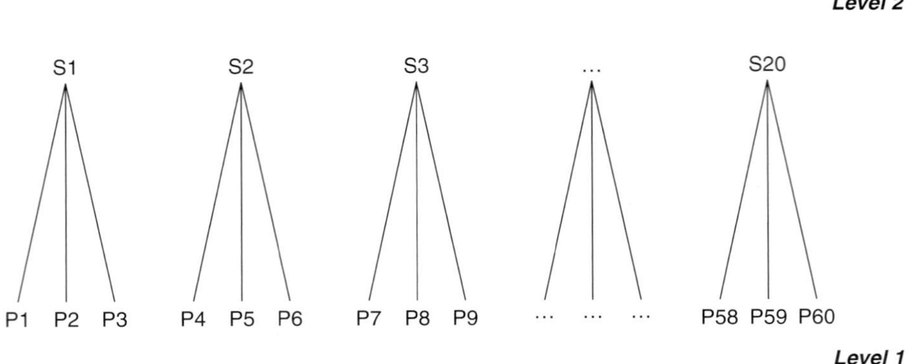

Figure 18.1 Multilevel structure for a two-level model, with pupils ($N = 60$) nested in schools ($n = 20$)

Although much of the interest in multilevel models relates to natural clustering, as found in educational or clinical settings, the focus of this chapter is on multilevel models as extensions of familiar repeated measures designs (including those with mixed measures). Repeated measures ANOVA designs provide a natural bridge between standard least squares regression models and multilevel models. Some repeated measures models, particularly those from designed experiments, can be analyzed adequately with standard ANOVA models. But sometimes the usual repeated measures models may be unwieldy or be too restrictive to fully capture the structure of the data (even with designed experiments). Multilevel models are more flexible – and not necessarily much more complex – than repeated measures ANOVA (e.g., when unbalanced designs and violations of sphericity or multisample sphericity are a concern).

The strength of multilevel modeling – its flexibility – is also one of its drawbacks. The other main drawback is the additional complexity of the approach (though this is becoming less problematic as the availability of suitable software increases). The flexibility of the approach allows a wide range of models and a rich set of hypotheses to be explored. In principle, this is an advantage (because hypotheses that cannot easily be modeled by traditional approaches can be explored). Yet it is possible to become overwhelmed by these possibilities or to intentionally or unintentionally abuse the flexibility by selecting models that fit your prejudices. For this reason, beginning with the following principles is recommended:

- build models that are guided by strong theory, using them to test *a priori* hypotheses;
- build models that are strongly constrained by the structure of the data.

The former is a restatement of the view that theory-driven *a priori* hypotheses should guide research (e.g., a preference for 1 *df* contrasts over omnibus tests). The latter is implicit in all statistical modeling, which can be characterized as a search for a model that matches the structure of the data. Experimental and quasi-experimental studies with repeated measures data often provide precisely the strong structural constraints that make constructing a multilevel model relatively easy.

18.2.2 Limitations of repeated measures analyses

Multilevel regression is an attractive alternative to the rather restricted model imposed by repeated measures ANOVA. The most obvious limitation of the ANOVA model is that it incorporates only categorical predictors. ANCOVA or regression with repeated measures is awkward to implement and rather restrictive (Misangyi *et al.*, 2006). This section will review the limitations of repeated and mixed measures ANOVA, before briefly assessing those of repeated measures regression models.

A classical ANOVA model has only categorical predictors and a balanced design (with equal *n* per cell). In a pure repeated measures design this usually entails having no missing measurements for any cells, though sometimes repeated measures are unbalanced for other reasons. For instance, Wright (1998) looked at autobiographical memories – memories of personally meaningful events. These may not fall neatly into cells of an analysis in a balanced way (e.g., the frequency of events such as getting married or having a job interview varies between people). Lack of balance is relevant to the analysis for several reasons. It complicates the analysis because predictors in an unbalanced design will not be orthogonal. Even worse, it can introduce bias to the estimates if the imbalance arises from missing data or bias in sampling. Moreover, imbalance in a mixed design arising from unequal group sizes renders epsilon-corrected tests in ANOVA highly vulnerable to violations of multisample sphericity. MANOVA (i.e., profile analysis) shares these limitations. Repeated measures ANOVA should generally be restricted to balanced designs where sphericity is not violated (McCulloch, 2005; Misangyi *et al.*, 2006).

Repeated measures ANOVA has a further limitation. While it assumes that the *subject* 'factor' is a random effect, it assumes that any other factors are fixed effects. What if one or more other factors is also a random effect? For instance, an experiment looking at memory for English nouns will sample only a tiny proportion of the total population of English nouns. It can't legitimately be considered a fixed effect. Although ANOVA models exist that can incorporate random factors (see Hays, 1973), it is not easy to estimate more than one random effect in a repeated measures model (where only one measurement per subject is taken for each combination of levels of the other factors). Many researchers either ignore or remain unaware of the problem, which has come to be known as the *language-as-fixed-effect fallacy* after the title of a paper by Clark (1973; see Box 18.1). This paper had a big impact on the field of psycholinguistics (though researchers did not necessarily understand the problem or follow Clark's advice), but – perhaps owing to the title – it has largely been ignored or gone unnoticed in other fields. Clark suggested a number of possible solutions to the problem (see Box 18.1). These solutions are either difficult to implement or suboptimal (e.g., in terms of statistical power).

If a researcher is also interested in the effects continuous predictors, then repeated measures ANCOVA is a possibility. Estimating such a model with covariates that do not vary across the repeated measures is relatively easy, but if the covariates vary between measurements (i.e., *time-varying covariates*) this can be a major headache. If the measurements are thought to vary only due to measurement error (not systematically in relation to the outcome over time) then including them as separate predictors or including their average value is reasonable. Otherwise a regression solution is required. A repeated measures regression analysis is sometimes adopted in these situations (Misangyi *et al.*, 2006; Lorch and Myers, 1990). This approach also allows a researcher to incorporate non-orthogonal categorical predictors (and can therefore be used for unbalanced designs). One difficulty is that it assumes missing data are MCAR.[2] Restoring balance through multiple imputation is required if the data are thought to be MAR (in which case the simpler ANOVA or ANCOVA model might be preferable). In this kind of repeated measures regression, participants are treated as categorical predictors and coded with indicator variables (e.g., using dummy or effect coding).

Misangyi *et al.* (2006) review this dummy variable regression approach and compare it with both ANOVA and multilevel models. They conclude that there is little or no benefit to using the repeated measures regression approach.[3] ANOVA is sufficient for simple designs (and sometimes superior to the regression approach), while for more complex designs it can be difficult to obtain the correct regression solution and multilevel models are preferable (Misangyi *et al.*, 2006). The dummy variable regression approach does not solve the problems with sphericity, multisample sphericity or multiple random effects. Furthermore, as each indicator variable uses up a degree of freedom, the approach is very data hungry (Wright, 1998; Gelman and Hill, 2007). Indeed, there may be insufficient degrees of freedom (*df*) to estimate the model.

A developing consensus (McCulloch, 2005; Misangyi *et al.*, 2006; Gellman and Hill, 2007) is that repeated measures ANOVA has a role for simple balanced models, but that for anything much more sophisticated a different approach is required. Multilevel modeling provides a framework for incorporating a range of alternative models (as well as applying more generally to models with clustered or correlated measurements). These models are more complex than single-level regression models and the jump from traditional ANOVA models to multilevel approaches is sometimes seen as quite abrupt. Being familiar with the regression approach to ANOVA will help with transition. In addition, many of the tricks used to fit general or generalized linear models (e.g., coding schemes, transformations, product and polynomial terms) are also useful in multilevel modeling.

Box 18.1 The language-as-fixed-effect fallacy

Coleman (1964) was one of the first to point out the problems in generalizing linguistic stimuli in a sample to a language population. Clark (1973) addressed the potential solutions in greater detail and popularized the *language-as-fixed-effect* fallacy. At the time, a number of respondents to Clark's paper were critical of his arguments. A particular concern was that stimuli in language experiments were not sampled at random – as implied by treating them as a random effect (Wike and Church, 1976; Cohen, 1976; Keppel, 1976). Subsequent authors have tended to side with Clark (see Raaijmakers *et al.*, 1999). To understand why, it is helpful to review the basis for the problem.

To illustrate that the problem is not confined to linguistic stimuli, consider a different a hypothetical experiment looking at memory for facial expressions, in which participants are presented with five faces displaying either happy or sad expressions. They are later tested to see if they can recognize the same faces with neutral expressions. A researcher interested in whether happy faces are easier to recognize than sad faces might run a *t* test or ANOVA comparing mean response times (e.g., in milliseconds). The mean times would be computed by averaging performance over all five faces in each condition for each participant. This is known as a *by-subjects* analysis because subjects are treated as a random factor. Any variability between the faces is completely ignored. This can be seen by looking at hypothetical data from two participants: S_1 and S_2. The first five response times are for the happy faces and the next five for sad faces.

	Happy faces					*Sad faces*				
	I_1	I_2	I_3	I_4	I_5	I_1	I_2	I_3	I_4	I_5
S_1	510	<u>485</u>	490	500	515	<u>605</u>	610	590	600	595
S_2	<u>350</u>	650	600	500	400	550	700	650	<u>750</u>	<u>350</u>

The minimum and maximum values for each participant are underlined. Although these numbers are somewhat contrived it should be fairly obvious that the times for S_2 are rather more variable than for S_1.

In a by-subjects analysis, the differences in variability between items is ignored. The mean times for all happy faces ($M = 500$) and sad faces ($M = 600$), which happen to be the same for both participants, would enter the analysis. If the differences between faces were purely measurement error, this might be a good thing. However, the differences are not pure measurement error. The faces vary, in part, because there are individual differences in facial appearance, expressiveness and so forth between people. The by-subjects analysis ignores this source of variability entirely.

Does the fact that the by-subjects analysis ignores variability among faces matter? Perhaps not. If you want only to demonstrate an effect for the ten faces used in the experiment, it is an irrelevance (e.g., under the slightly implausible scenario of wanting to know whether five particular criminals will be easier to recognize if shown with happy or sad faces). However, in most domains you'd probably want to know whether your results generalized beyond the particular stimuli used in the experiment.

One test of this is a *by-items* analysis. Here the faces take the place of the random factor and response times are collapsed over participants:

	Happy faces		*Sad faces*	
	S_1	S_2	S_1	S_2
I_1	510	350	605	550
I_2	485	650	610	700
I_3	490	600	590	650
I_4	500	500	600	750
I_5	515	400	595	350

A by-items analysis compares the mean of the two participants for happy faces with the mean of the two participants for sad faces. The first face is I_1. Its mean response time with a happy expression is $(510 + 350)/2 = 430\,ms$, and its mean response time with a sad expression is $(605 + 550)/2 = 577.5\,ms$. Although the overall means for each condition (happy or sad) are unchanged, the raw outcome measures and sample sizes are not the same as for the by-subjects analysis. The resulting test of the overall difference between happy and sad times (using t or F) would generalize to the population of faces from which these five faces were sampled. The problem is that the analysis entirely ignores variability between participants, and does not therefore assess whether the effect generalizes to new participants.*

Although Clark advocated several superior solutions, researchers since Clark have often reported separate by-subjects analysis and by-items ANOVA tests (with F statistics typically labeled to F_1 and F_2 respectively). The separate test statistics approach appears sensible, but each test underestimates the error variance in the raw data. It therefore fails to control Type I error for null hypothesis significance tests (NHSTs). This is true even if the overall test of the effect requires both F_1 and F_2 to be statistically significant (Clark, 1973; Raaijmakers *et al.*, 1999). Even in this situation it is possible that a test with the correct error term would be non-significant. Clark's preference is to calculate a statistic that captures the variability of both random factors. One such statistic is a *quasi-F* ratio (F'), but this is not easy to estimate. Instead, Clark proposed that its lower bound (*min* F') be reported. Switching to *min* F' leads to some loss of statistical power, but simulation studies reviewed by Raaijmakers *et al.* (1999) suggest that it is generally robust and not excessively conservative (becoming less conservative as sample sizes increase). Furthermore, *min* F' is trivial to calculate if F_1 and F_2 are already available:

$$minF' = \frac{F_1 \times F_2}{F_1 + F_2} \qquad \text{Equation 18.1}$$

This F ratio can be tested against $J-1$ and $df_{minF'}$ degrees of freedom where J is the number of levels on the factor (e.g., $J=2$ for the above example where the facial emotion factor has two levels: happy and sad). If df_1 and df_2 are the respective df_{error} for by-subjects and by-items analyses then:

$$df_{minF'} = \frac{(F_1 + F_2)^2}{\frac{F_1^2}{df_2} + \frac{F_2^2}{df_1}} \qquad \text{Equation 18.2}$$

A common error in calculating Equation 18.2 is not to notice that, in the denominator, each squared F ratio is divided by df_{error} from the other analysis.

The *min F′* statistic can never exceed one unless both $F_1 > 1$ and $F_2 > 1$. In fact, *min F′* will never reach statistical significance unless both F_1 and F_2 are statistically significant. The opposite is not true: *min F′* is not always significant when both F_1 and F_2 are statistically significant. There is some loss of statistical power using this method, though avoiding small samples for both participants and stimuli ameliorates this. The ability to generalize to both populations is compromised if either sample size is small.

Clark offered other ingenious solutions to the problem of generalizing to stimulus populations as well as participant populations. One of the most interesting is to use different random samples of stimuli for each participant. For instance in an experiment presenting 20 items to 30 participants, the by-subjects analyses will correctly account for variability in sampling items if each participant receives a different set of 20 randomly sampled items. Raaijmakers *et al.* (1999) discuss using matching and counterbalancing to provide similarly accurate test statistics, though matching and counterbalancing may compromise the generality of the findings (although the tests will be accurate). Kirk (1995) discusses this in the context of matched or stratified designs – generalization is necessarily restricted to the population of potential matches. The same is logically true of counterbalancing. Counterbalancing using several sets of materials will produce tests that reflect the variability within those sets (and is therefore better than using a single set). This leads to an inevitable trade-off in experimental design. If you restrict the variability of materials (e.g., by matching) to obtain more powerful tests and better experimental control over confounding variables, the population of stimuli being sampled (and therefore generalizability) is restricted.

What about the chief historic criticism of Clark's paper: how important is random sampling of stimuli? Random sampling is a good idea, but tricky to implement. Absence of random sampling does not eliminate the main problem. Whether randomly sampled or not, the presence of a second random factor implies that there is extra variability that the by-subjects analysis ignores. So the safe approach is to use *min F′* or adopt an analysis (such as a multilevel model) that can cope with more than one random factor.

Baguley (2009) also notes that standardized effect sizes are likely to be problematic when a fixed effect analysis is used and a second random factor is present. A standardized effect size statistic computed from a by-subjects analysis (e.g., r, d or η^2) could be huge even if the variability accounted for in the population of items is negligible. Baguley (*ibid.*) suggests that *min F′* could be used to derive an η^2 or ω^2 style statistic (though there is little or no published literature evaluating this form of effect size metric). The simple, unstandardized difference between level means is, as noted earlier, stable across by-subjects and by-item analyses.

* In this scenario both the by-items and by-subjects analyses are repeated measures analyses, but this will not always be the case. If the happy and sad faces had been presented using ten different faces (five for each expression) the by-items analysis would have been an independent measures analysis (though the by-subjects analysis would still be repeated measures).

18.3 Multilevel regression models

18.3.1 A brief introduction to multilevel regression

The fundamental objective of a multilevel regression model is to build a mathematical representation that captures the structure of the data. The basic structure assumed by a typical multilevel model is hierarchical. This introduction focuses on repeated measures models where the hierarchy represents individual observations nested within participants. A basic scenario involves n participants, each with m measurements (for a total of $nm = N$ observations). A good starting point is to consider how to reflect this structure in terms of a regression model.[4]

A very basic model involves fitting a simple linear regression for each participant of the form:

$$y_i = b_0 + b_1 x_{1,i} + e_i \quad e_i \sim N\left(0, \sigma^2_{error}\right)$$

The n separate equations for each of the $j = 1$ to n participants could be summarized as:

$$y_i = \beta_{0,j} + \beta_{1,j} X + \varepsilon_{ij} \quad \varepsilon_{ij} \sim N\left(0, \sigma^2_{error}\right) \qquad \text{Equation 18.3}$$

The parameters $\beta_{0,j}$ and $\beta_{1,j}$ represent the separate population intercepts and slopes for the jth participant in the analysis. Such a model can be fitted by regressing X on Y for each of the n participants. The resulting parameter estimates would take the form:

$$y_i = b_{0,j} + b_{1,j} X + e_{ij} \qquad \text{Equation 18.4}$$

For inference the averages of the n intercepts and n slopes are sometimes tested against a t distribution with $n - 1$ df in a form of one sample t test or CI (Lorch and Myers, 1990; Hoffman and Rovine, 2007). A model like this treats the intercepts and slopes as fixed parameters and would therefore be somewhat inefficient. In addition, and like a dummy variable repeated measures regression, the approach could also introduce bias (Hoffman and Rovine, 2007). The bias arises because each slope and intercept in this form of analysis has equal weighting, even though some parameters are estimated with more error than others (Kreft and de Leeuw, 1998).[5] The single-level approach illustrated by Equation 18.4 is not, as a rule, a sensible one.

The multilevel solution is rather ingenious. Replace the $j = 1$ to n intercepts or slopes of the participants with a single parameter. If this were a single, fixed parameter for the intercept or slope it would just be a regression model with a common intercept or slope for all participants. Such a simplistic model would be both uninteresting and implausible; what is required is a model that captures the variation in b_0 or b_1 with a random parameter for each coefficient. If you think about it, this is exactly how the variability in a single-level least squares regression is modeled: with the nuisance parameter σ^2_{error}. The e_i residuals are regarded as if sampled from an independent, normal population of ε_i errors with mean zero and unknown variance. The same ploy can be recruited to construct a multilevel model. This involves estimating the $b_{0,j}$ intercept term as

$$b_{0,j} = b_0 + u_{0,j} \quad u_{0,j} \sim N\left(0, \sigma^2_{u_0}\right) \qquad \text{Equation 18.5}$$

and the slope as

$$b_{1,j} = b_0 + u_{1,j} \quad u_{1,j} \sim N\left(0, \sigma^2_{u_1}\right) \qquad \text{Equation 18.6}$$

These estimates can be incorporated into a single regression equation for the model:

$$y_{ij} = b_0 + b_1 x_{1,ij} + u_{0,j} + u_{1,j} x_{1,ij} + e_{ij} \quad \begin{array}{l} u_{1,j} \sim N\left(0, \sigma^2_{u_1}\right) \\ u_{0,j} \sim N\left(0, \sigma^2_{u_0}\right) \\ e_{0,ij} \sim N\left(0, \sigma^2_{e}\right) \end{array} \qquad \text{Equation 18.7}$$

These equations are often split into separate parts for the fixed effect estimates $b_0 + b_1 x_{1,ij}$ and the variances $u_{0,j} + u_{1,j} x_{1,ij} + e_{ij}$ (the latter are usually called random effects).[6] Although this separation is a convenient way to simplify the presentation of the model, it can conceal the fundamental insight that there is only one regression equation for the model.

A key change is that, unlike a general linear model, there is no longer just one variance parameter to estimate.[7] Equation 18.7 requires not only the variances $\sigma^2_{u_0}$, $\sigma^2_{u_1}$ and σ^2_e, but also $\sigma_{u_{01}}$ (the covariance between $u_{0,j}$ and $u_{1,j}$) to be estimated. The random effects are assumed to have a normal distribution with mean zero, but only the error variance σ^2_e is assumed to be independent of the others. The covariance $\sigma_{u_{12}}$ thus allows the correlation between the intercept and slope to be non-zero. This necessarily complicates the model. It is as if three separate 'error' terms are being modeled: one each for the variance of the level 2 slope ($\sigma^2_{u_1}$), the level 2 intercept ($\sigma^2_{u_0}$) and the residuals between predicted and observed (σ^2_e) at level 1.

Another way of looking at it is that the covariance matrix of effects at each level is being explicitly modeled. The random effects in this kind of model will sometimes be nuisance parameters, but don't have to be looked at in that way. There are several benefits to modeling variances and covariances explicitly:

(1) Individual differences in an intercept (e.g., $u_{0,j}$) or slope $u_{1,j}$ (e.g., $u_{1,j}$) are treated as random effects: random samples from an infinite population. A multilevel model therefore avoids the language-as-fixed-effect fallacy.[8]

(2) By modeling the variances and covariances explicitly, there is no need to assume sphericity. Multilevel models therefore offer the choice of modeling an *unstructured covariance matrix* at each level of the model or placing constraints on the structure. A good starting point is to model the variances and covariances without too many constraints. This tends to work well for relatively simple models because the cost is low (see also Gelman and Hill, 2007). If there is good reason to believe that the variances follow a particular pattern, then constraining the covariance matrices will probably produce a more precise model (but there are dangers in assuming patterns such as sphericity or compound symmetry by default). If there are practical difficulties in estimating the model when sample sizes are small or when the number of random effects being modeled is very large, constraining the number of variance parameters is more attractive. However, there is no need to limit the choice of covariance structures to sphericity or compound symmetry.

(3) Effects can be tested at different levels of the hierarchy. A fundamental insight is that effects can differ in magnitude (and occasionally direction) at different levels of the hierarchy. Enders and Tofighi (2007) give the example of a repeated measures study looking at the

effect of anxiety on pain over a fixed number of occasions (e.g., trials in an experiment). The overall effect of anxiety might reflect contributions of a particular trial (state anxiety) and the general level of anxiety of that person (trait anxiety). The effects of state anxiety are at level 1 of the multilevel model, whereas trait anxiety is at level 2. Multilevel models provide a potential way to tease apart these different effects.

(4) When variances and covariances are free parameters in a model, then it is possible to use the free parameters for inference. With a multilevel model it is possible to test hypotheses about variability of effects and the relationship between them. In a repeated measures model, for instance, it is possible to test hypotheses about the variability of effects between individuals. A fixed effect model only allows inference about the presence or magnitude of an effect. Variability in the magnitude of the effect is subsumed under the error term. It is therefore extremely difficult to disentangle systematic individual differences from error in conventional repeated measures designs.[9] Individual differences in a multilevel repeated measures model are represented by parameters estimated at level 2 or higher in the model.

The final two advantages, taken together, can be considered the 'unique selling points' of the multilevel and related approaches. They expand the range of hypotheses that a researcher can test and, to some extent, broaden the class of theories that a researcher can both conceive of and model. Multilevel models are not, however, the only option for clustered data. The increased complexity of the models provides more scope for getting things wrong. This applies both to the process of selecting an appropriate model and to the statistical assumptions that are made when estimating models with complex random effects. Although these problems are reduced by building models that are constrained by the structure of the data, it isn't always necessary to fit such models.

Sometimes the goal of research is merely to explore or test fixed effects. Multilevel models can be applied to account for what are considered nuisance parameters (e.g., variability in stimuli or variability in participants) in a rigorous manner. Alternatively, it is possible to use one of several methods for adjusting standard errors (*SE*s) of inferences to account for the variance-covariance structure of repeated measures and other clustered data. Hedges (2009) and Hedges and Rhoads (2011) describe how to make these adjustments for some common designs. Several alternative methods for dealing with nuisance parameters exist. A particularly important class is what are sometimes called generalized estimating equations or GEEs (Hanley *et al.*, 2003; Ballinger, 2004; Hox, 2010). This class of model is closely related to the robust *SE*s obtained with the sandwich estimator (Hardin, 2003; Wooldridge, 2003; Zeileis, 2004, 2006). These models make weaker assumptions about the true pattern of variances and covariances and therefore tend to be more robust than multilevel models, though they have other limitations (e.g., for unbalanced designs or where there is missing data).

18.3.2 Aggregation, statistical power and the design effect

What happens if the structure of a hierarchical data set is ignored? There are two main ways to approach such an analysis. An aggregated data analysis is one where the lower level of the hierarchical structure is ignored and only data at some higher level are analyzed. Usually, but not always, this involves calculating the mean of the m lower-level observations for each of n higher-level units. A good example is a by-subjects analysis, which involves the analysis of item means aggregated at the subject level (see Box 18.1). A disaggregated analysis is the opposite: analysis of individual observations at the lowest level that ignores the hierarchical structure entirely. For a repeated measures analysis with m observations per n participants this would involve treating all $mn = N$ observations as if they were independent. Aggregation and disaggregation are troublesome because they impact on the nature of the hypotheses being tested and the statistical power of the analysis (Snijders and Bosker, 1999).

It has been known at least as far back as Robinson (1950) that aggregation can produce misleading effects. Robinson showed that for grouped data the correlation between mean of X and mean of Y will only rarely be the same as the correlation between X and Y when pooling observations across groups. One of his original examples is the correlation between illiteracy and being of foreign birth (using 1930 US Census data). The correlation computed from individual level data is $\phi = .118$. Computed from average illiteracy in each US state, the correlation is $r = -.516$ (*ibid.*). Not only are the correlations very different in magnitude, but they have different signs.

Robinson (*ibid.*) termed the correlation of data aggregated by groups an *ecological correlation*. Consequently, the belief that analysis of aggregated data can support inferences about data at the individual level is known as the *ecological fallacy*. It should be emphasized that there is nothing inherently wrong with an aggregate analysis, provided that you are really interested in inference at the level of the aggregated data (though the aggregate analysis may introduce other difficulties depending on how it is handled). Ecological correlations, however, are particularly tricky. The size of a correlation coefficient depends on both the magnitude of an effect and its variability. Ecological correlations tend to be much higher than individual-level correlations because they ignore variability at the individual level. This makes the usual interpretation of r^2 as proportion of variance explained even more problematic than usual; by excluding unexplained variance at the individual level, the unexplained variance at the aggregate level is probably artificially low.

Ecological fallacies come in different forms, and a pertinent one for multilevel modeling is the *atomistic fallacy* or *individualistic fallacy* (Alker, 1969). This is a corollary of the ecological fallacy. The atomistic fallacy is the belief that an inference at the individual level is revealing with respect to a higher level. Robinson argued that looking at ecological correlations was misleading because the usual focus of interest is the individual effects, but this is not necessarily the case. A researcher interested in whether immigrants tended to settle in states with high literacy levels would be misled by looking at the individual-level correlation. Modeling both effects simultaneously (e.g., in a multilevel model) can avoid these and other traps.

Disaggregation has additional problems as an analytic strategy in relation to statistical power. An analysis of m level 1 observations clustered within n level 2 observations will have $mn = N$ observations in total. In a balanced design (where m is constant for all n level 2 units) it is reasonable to estimate the mean effect of a predictor at level 1 from the N disaggregated observations. In an unbalanced design the mean weighted by m for each of the n level 2 units could be used. The point estimate of the fixed effect of the predictor should be unbiased. What about the standard error (*SE*) of the effect? The standard error is the standard deviation (*SD*) of the sampling distribution (i.e., the square root of the variance of the parameter estimate). Estimation of an *SE* involves the square root of the sample size, but the *SE* will almost always be too small if N is employed. This happens because the N observations will hardly ever be independent. The effective sample size of the analysis N_{eff} is therefore much smaller.

This reduction in effect sample size (and consequent impact on the *SE*) is a special case of a more general phenomenon: the *design effect of two-stage sampling*. A design effect is an adjustment to N that accounts for the reduction in effective sample size for a study with a particular sampling strategy (Kish, 1965; Snijders and Bosker, 1999). Effective sample size in the simple case considered here is given by the relationship

$$N_{eff} = \frac{N}{D_{eff}} \qquad \text{Equation 18.8}$$

where D_{eff} is the design effect. It follows that the *SE*s of the usual analysis in a balanced, single predictor model (e.g., a t test or simple linear regression) are too small by a factor of $\sqrt{D_{eff}}$, where:

$$D_{eff} = 1 + (m - 1)\,\rho_I \qquad \text{Equation 18.9}$$

and m is the number of observations per level 2 unit (e.g., the number of repeated measures per participant). The quantity ρ_I is the *intraclass correlation coefficient* or *ICC* (see Box 18.2). For $m = 1$ the design effect is one. As m and ρ_I increase, so does the design effect, resulting in spurious statistical power if the disaggregated data are treated as independent. Equation 18.9 presents a way to correct the *SE* for a single mean when there are no other complicating factors present. Different design effects arise for slopes and intercepts in more complex models (Skinner, 1989; Hedges, 2009).

Although the design effect can be used to adjust the *SE*s of an analysis, this approach is no longer widely used in the survey literature – being recognized as rather inaccurate (e.g., Hedges, 2009). It is still, however, widely used in some fields (see Musca *et al.*, 2011) and examples of both disaggregation and aggregation are still found in published work. The main purpose of reviewing the design effect here is to illustrate the potential dangers of ignoring the hierarchical structure of a data set.

In addition to its role in the design effect, the *ICC* is an important parameter in statistical power or sample size estimation for a multilevel model, and it is useful as a descriptive statistic indicating the degree of clustering between observations (and its potential impact on the power of a study). For statistical power to detect an effect in repeated measures ANOVA it is possible to use conventional power estimates (e.g., using G*Power). For general guidance in planning a multilevel study, exploring the effects of the *ICC* and sample size at each level of the model can be instructive (Maas and Hox, 2005). Estimates of intra-class correlation coefficients can be obtained from similar studies or from surveys of *ICC* values reported within a field (e.g., Hedges and Hedberg, 2007; Murray and Blitstein, 2003). Except for very simple designs, this approach is likely to be inadequate for a full power analysis.

For some repeated measures designs (e.g., with time-varying covariates or imbalance) and for many multilevel models, estimating statistical power or precision is difficult using standard methods. Monte Carlo simulation is the recommended method for complex designs. Gelman and Hill (2007) give an introduction to simulation methods for statistical power analyses. Cools *et al.* (2008) describe a user-friendly tool that uses R to set up simulations via the specialist multilevel modeling package MLwiN (Rasbash *et al.*, 2009). MLPowSim provides a more extensive approach to simulation models for power analysis via MLwiN and R (Browne *et al.*, 2009).

Box 18.2 Intraclass correlation coefficients

The *ICC* (ρ_I) plays a central role in what may appear to be two distinct areas of statistics (though the areas are closely related). One is in statistical models for clustered data and the other is reliability. An *ICC* is a form of correlation related to Pearson's *r*. It can be computed when measurements within a unit (e.g., person or group) are unordered or unstructured;* for instance, units that are pairs of individuals (or *dyads*). Sometimes it is obvious what structure exists within the dyad (e.g., male and female members of heterosexual couples; doctors and patients). In other dyads there is no general structure or order that holds for all units (e.g., homosexual couples; twins). The key property here is exchangeability. Only if the units are exchangeable for the purposes of the analysis is the *ICC* appropriate. Otherwise it would make sense to compute a standard correlation coefficient such as Pearson's *r*.

The *ICC* can be defined in at least two ways, but for relatively simple models (e.g., single-level regressions or two-level multilevel models) the definitions converge on the same quantity:

$$\rho_I = \frac{\tau^2}{\tau^2 + \sigma^2} \qquad \text{Equation 18.10}$$

τ^2 is the variance between level 2 units and σ^2 the variance within level 2 units. Thus one definition of the *ICC* is the proportion of total ($\tau^2 + \sigma^2$) variance accounted for by variation between level 2 units. In a repeated measures design the level 2 units are typically participants (but are usually groups in other nested designs). A second definition is that the *ICC* is the average correlation between all the possible pairs of observations within level 2 units. Thus it is the expected value of the standardized difference from the level 2 mean for a random pair of level 1 observations within a randomly selected level 2 unit. The *ICC* therefore represents the degree to which measurements within the same level 2 unit resemble each other.

According to the definitions above, the *ICC* is always ≤ 1, and its upper bound of one is only reached if the variance within classes (σ^2) is zero. If the variance within classes is zero, the level 2 units all resemble each other perfectly. The *ICC* is related to reliability for measurements of the level 2 units (Snijders and Bosker, 1999). This is because level 1 observations can be considered repeated measurements of the level 2 unit, differing in terms of random error. For instance, in a repeated measures model it reflects the consistency of responses within an individual. The reliability ρ_{YY} of an aggregated measurement is:

$$\rho_{YY} = \frac{\tau^2}{\tau^2 + \sigma^2/m} = \frac{m\rho_I}{1 + (m-1)\,\rho_I} \qquad \text{Equation 18.11}$$

The link to reliability is that with $m = 1$ (i.e., one measurement per level 2 unit) the reliability of ρ_{YY} is equal to ρ_I. As the number of level 1 measurements becomes large, the reliability of the measurement *Y* for the level 2 units approaches one.

Intra-class correlation coefficients are important measures for calculating reliability in other situations also. McGraw and Wong (1996) review how to calculate *ICC*s for a range of different designs. *ICC*s are also used as proportion of variance explained effect size metrics, as well as for reliability. Like omega-squared statistics (to which they are related), an *ICC* is an inferential measure (because estimates of the population variances are used to calculate them). Confidence intervals (CIs) for *ICC*s can be constructed (*ibid.*), but – as with other standardized measures – they tend to be very wide.

* Kish regarded an *ICC* as sufficiently distinct from *r* to refer to it as 'roh' (short for rate of homogeneity) rather than 'rho'.

18.3.3 Estimation, inference and model comparison

A characteristic that increases the difficulty of working with a multilevel model is that it is only rarely possible to fit them using conventional least squares methods. They are similar to generalized linear models in this respect, and both generalized linear models and multilevel models are usually fitted using iterative solutions. These generally look for parameter estimates that maximize the likelihood of the model given the data. A variety of iterative methods are used in multilevel modeling to obtain maximum likelihood (ML) estimates of the regression parameters (see Box 18.3). Of these, FML and RML methods are the most widely implemented, but *Markov chain Monte Carlo* (MCMC) methods are increasingly popular (see Box 18.3).

Both RML and FML methods seek out sets of parameter estimates that maximize the overall likelihood of the regression model. To make estimation more efficient, the logarithm of the likelihood (loglikelihood) is usually the quantity that is maximized. This necessarily converges on the same solution. Working with more tractable numbers can make the process faster and reduce rounding error. Estimation proceeds until the parameter estimates and the likelihood of the model is unchanged (to the desired degree of precision) for two successive iterations. In addition to the parameter estimates and the variances of the parameter estimates (used to derive their *SE*s), the likelihood or loglikelihood of the model is also part of the output. This provides a natural way to compare two models fitted for the same data. One approach to such model comparisons involves using the deviance of the model. This is the same quantity – a generalization of variance – used to compare fit in generalized linear models and has the same formal definition: $D = -2\ln(\ell)$. Having obtained the deviance of a model it can be compared to the deviance of another model using NHSTs, CIs or information criteria (among other approaches).

NHSTs based on the change in deviance between two models are likelihood ratio tests and can be distinguished from tests based on the *SE*s of the model. The former compare the change in deviance (ΔD) from adding parameters against a χ^2 statistic with *df* equal to Δk (the change in number of parameters). The latter involve constructing a test statistic to be compared against a χ^2, z, t or F distribution. These are often termed 'Wald tests' (though the term applies most strictly to those using the χ^2 distribution). The tests based on χ^2 or z are large sample approximations. The Wald test statistic for a single parameter has 1 *df* and is formed from the ratio $b^2/\hat{\sigma}_b$ where b is the parameter estimate of interest and $\hat{\sigma}_b$ its *SE* under maximum likelihood estimation. If several parameters are tested simultaneously, the individual test statistics can be summed (as indicated in Equation 17.4). In the single parameter case, the Wald test is equivalent to an asymptotic normal approximation: a z test where $z = b/\hat{\sigma}_b$. The z test is simple to compute, preserves the sign of b and can be used to form CI for the parameter estimate as $b \pm z_{1-\alpha/2}\hat{\sigma}_b$.

As the Wald test is a large sample approximation, it is somewhat liberal in small samples (having Type I error rates in excess of nominal α). In principle, it is possible to construct more accurate tests using the F distribution (or with t in place of z). This is uncontroversial for balanced ANOVA designs with repeated measures, where the estimates are equivalent to the usual repeated measures tests (Searle *et al.*, 1992; Hox 2010), but causes complications in other situations.

For tests of fixed effects, the Wald test (and Wald-style tests using F or t) are preferred to likelihood ratio tests. Although asymptotically identical, the likelihood ratio test is not considered robust for multilevel models unless sample sizes are very large (Bolker *et al.*, 2009; Hox, 2010). For random effects, a likelihood ratio test with RML estimation to obtain the difference in deviance generally performs better than Wald-style tests (Bolker *et al.*, 2009; Hox, 2010). In general, inference with multilevel models is more complex than for general linear or generalized linear models. Two challenges need to be overcome: the problem of boundary effects and the difficulty of determining residual *df* for inferences using F or t.

The general procedure for determining a p value from a test statistic assumes that the value of the parameter under H_0 is not at (or close to) the boundary of the possible values it can take (Berkhof and Snijders, 2001; Bolker *et al.*, 2009; Hox, 2010).[10] This is generally true for tests of fixed effects and covariances, but not for tests of variances (which are bounded at zero). Owing to the bounded parameter space, the test statistic of likelihood ratio and Wald tests will no longer have the anticipated χ^2 distribution with ν *df*. The true distribution of the test statistic under the null hypothesis will be a mixture of different distributions. For instance, the correct distribution for the test of whether a single variance parameter is zero is an equal-weighted mixture of a χ_0^2 and a χ_1^2 distribution (Stoel *et al.*, 2006).[11] As $\chi_0^2 = 0$ this resolves to a p value that is half the usual right-tail probability for the χ_1^2 distribution (in essence because negative parameter values are impossible and these contribute half of the unbounded parameter space). Calculating an accurate p value is a major challenge for models differing by more than a single variance parameter. Stoel *et al.* (*ibid.*) describe how to calculate accurate likelihood ratio tests for different mixtures of χ^2 distributions.

Boundary effects are awkward because it is not always possible to avoid them when comparing models that differ in their random effects. It is not always possible or desirable to add a variance estimate without also adding one or more covariance estimates. Some software will allow you to constrain one or more covariances to equal zero when estimating an additional variance. This will permit sensible tests of that variance parameter, but the same procedure will not work for covariances. The problem in this case is that the covariance is not defined under the null hypothesis, and a different solution is required (Davies, 1987; Andrews and Ploberger, 1994). Unless the distribution of the test statistic is accounted for in some way, boundary effects will bias inference involving variances. The p values from the resulting tests will be too large and statistical power will suffer.

A Wald χ^2 or z test is not appropriate for inference in small samples. Switching to the F or t distribution is attractive, but raises the challenge of determining the residual *df*. Except in the case of balanced ANOVA designs, there is no agreed solution. The problem is that the *df* required to estimate each random effect lies somewhere between one and $n-1$, where n is number of units the random effect is estimated over (Bolker *et al.*, 2009). Different software packages implement different solutions to the problem (*ibid.*). For instance, one relatively conservative estimate is to use $n-q-1$ (where n is the sample size at the highest level of the model and q is the total number of predictors in the model; see Hox, 2010). These problems should diminish for designs that are close in structure to a balanced repeated measures ANOVA model and when sample sizes at both level 1 and level 2 are large.

Several alternatives to NHSTs are widely used for inference with multilevel models. The two most common are CIs and information criteria. CIs can be constructed for parameter estimates using the z or t distribution (in which case the problem of determining the residual *df* also arises). Where a likelihood ratio test is preferred (e.g., for inference about a variance) a CI can be formed through profiling. Information criteria have a close connection to the deviance of a statistical model. AIC (calculated using FML) is simply the deviance of a model plus two times the number of parameters k:

$$AIC = -2\ln(\ell) + 2k = D_M + 2k$$

Information criteria are particularly attractive because (as long as the data being modeled are identical) it is possible to compare non-nested models using AIC, whereas a significance test of the deviance requires nested models. Recall that two models are non-nested if one model can't be expressed in terms of the other model just by dropping one or more parameter. Such models arise when comparing theories that include different predictors (e.g., model *A* includes gender but not age, while model *B* includes age but not gender). Hox (2010) proposes using FML estimates of loglikelihood to calculate information criteria for models differing in terms of fixed effects and RML estimates for models differing only in terms of random effects. It is also very easy to transform the AIC for two models into a difference in AIC (ΔAIC), a likelihood ratio (LR_{AIC}) or Akaike weights to aid interpretation.

It is considered good practice to report AIC or similar statistics for a set of plausible models. BIC is less likely to be reported than AIC, mainly because there is some debate as to the correct source of n to adopt in the $k\ln(n)$ 'penalty' term for BIC. Wagenmakers (2007) recommends using n at the higher (participant) level for repeated measures, while some software defaults to using N at the lowest level (i.e., the total number of observations). This is arguably a variant of the residual *df* problem for NHSTs (Bolker *et al.*, 2009). The question of determining the appropriate sample size for BIC, or indeed AIC_C, has led to many researchers adopting AIC by default. A further argument in favor of AIC is it has a strong link to the predictive performance of a model. The emphasis on prediction to check models leads some Bayesian multilevel models to prefer AIC to BIC (Gelman and Hill, 2007). An additional concern is that information criteria are also subject to boundary effects when the models being compared differ in terms of variance parameters.

It is not possible to obtain a direct equivalent of AIC for models fitted using MCMC estimation. More generally, AIC is argued to be problematic in multilevel models because determining the *df* required to model each random effect may not be straightforward. This is another variant of the residual *df* problem (though, in the case of a Bayesian model, information in the prior also influences the effective number of parameters in the model). One way to view this is as a problem of determining the complexity of the model – the effective number of parameters being estimated (Spiegelhalter *et al.*, 2002; Bolker *et al.*, 2009). In a least squares regression model it is possible to identify the number of parameters being estimated as the trace (the sum of the main diagonal elements) of the hat matrix. Spiegelhalter *et al.* (2002) extend this idea to multilevel and related models and describe a measure known as *deviance information criterion* (DIC) that exploits it. DIC is closely related to AIC, but explicitly developed from a Bayesian perspective (and designed for working with MCMC estimation). This measure is defined as

$$DIC = \hat{D} + 2\hat{p}_D, \qquad \text{Equation 18.12}$$

where $\hat{p}_D$ is the estimate of the effective number of parameters in the model (derived from the hat matrix) and $\hat{D}$ is the posterior deviance of the model estimated from the raw MCMC output. DIC is frequently reported by specialist multilevel software that uses MCMC estimation (see Browne, 2009; Gelman and Hill, 2007). DIC is not without critics and makes some assumptions that may not hold in practice. For instance, it is a large sample approximation that assumes that the posterior distribution is multivariate normal.

It is also possible to obtain interval estimates from the MCMC output. Among the most popular are highest posterior density (HPD) intervals. The MCMC output includes samples from the posterior distribution of the parameters. A 95% HPD interval would find the shortest interval that included 95% of the posterior density of these samples (Baayen *et al.*, 2008; Kruschke, 2010).[12]

It therefore needn't be continuous or symmetrical. Importantly, the simulation methods used to derive HPD intervals avoid boundary effects and the difficulty of determining the residual *df*. Some forms of bootstrapping may also avoid these problems.

Your choice of inferential tools will be constrained by the software you are using and the complexity of the model being fitted. It is important to look at the documentation carefully and review the latest recommendations in the literature before deciding what tools to adopt. The papers by Baayen *et al.* (2008) and Bolker *et al.* (2009) provide a good overview of some of the pitfalls and solutions.

Box 18.3 Maximum likelihood estimation of multilevel models

Early multilevel models used fairly straightforward iterative solutions that maximize the likelihood of the model. A drawback of these methods is that they assume that the variances are known. Moreover, the variances and covariances tend to underestimate the true population values. This is a form of small sample bias (and is negligible in sufficiently large samples). However, multilevel models with modest sample sizes at the highest levels are extremely common (e.g., a study with 30 countries or 30 schools). The importance of accurate variance estimates for inference (and their prominent role in multilevel modeling) led to development of several other approaches.

A popular alternative estimation method is *restricted maximum likelihood* (RML or REML). RML reduces, but doesn't eliminate, the bias in estimating variance parameters.* Maximum likelihood methods are often termed *full information maximum likelihood* (FML or FIML) methods to make the distinction between the methods clearer.

RML will tend to agree with FML estimates in large samples, but be more accurate (in terms of variances and covariances) in small samples, though FML has a couple of useful properties that ensure that it is still widely employed. Iterative estimation methods can run into convergence problems (getting stuck or running out of computing power, or both). FML tends to have less difficulty converging than RML. This is useful because it may give a solution when other methods fail, and because the FML solution can be used to provide starting values for other methods. The starting values shouldn't influence the final solution, but can reduce the time or computing power required to find the solution or help avoid nasty regions of the search space. This is a common estimation strategy in multilevel models; using an inferior method to get starting values for a better, but more computationally demanding method. The second useful feature is that FML tends to give more accurate tests of fixed effects. It is therefore often used in place of RML when comparing models differing only in terms of one or more fixed parameters, whereas RML tends to be adopted for comparing models differing only in terms of random effects.

Because random effects under both FML and RML are underestimated, this tends to produce *SE*s for the fixed effects that are too large. The degree of underestimate is sensitive to the sample size at each level of the model. Maas and Hox (2005) explored the impact of sample size on parameter estimates and *SE*s for a two-level model. They concluded that the impact on the fixed effects and their *SE*s is generally negligible at level 1 of the model when n at the highest level was 30 (the lowest level they considered). However, *SE*s for level 2 fixed effects were about 15% too small on average for $n = 30$ (and around 7% too small when $n = 50$). Their simulation included level 1 sample sizes of $m = 5$, $m = 30$ or $m = 50$ per level 2 unit. Even when $m = 5$ there was little impact on either parameter estimates or *SE*s. These results suggest that samples sizes of 30 may be adequate for inference on level 1 effects, but sample sizes of at least 50 are desirable for inference about level 2 effects.** These simulations assume a normal distribution of errors at each level – though other work suggests that inferences for fixed effects are robust to non-normal residuals at level 2 of the model (Maas and Hox, 2004).

These are the basic approaches to estimation used in multilevel models. Hox (2010) reviews a range of alternative approaches including bootstrapping and Monte Carlo methods. Bayesian approaches to multilevel modeling often use simulation in the form of MCMC methods. MCMC estimation is favored because there are often no analytic solutions for the integrals needed to implement complex Bayesian models. One caveat, common to all simulation methods (and quite likely to arise in practice), is that MCMC methods can require very large numbers of iterations to converge. For this reason it is not uncommon to use other methods for exploratory analysis, and MCMC methods with a large number of iterations to fit a smaller subset of theoretically interesting or important models. For an introduction to MCMC methods in multilevel modeling see Gill (2007) or Browne (2009).

* In a sense they are generalizations of linear regression approaches for unknown variances using *t* and *F*. In balanced designs multilevel models fitted via RML reduce to conventional repeated measures ANOVA models (see Searle *et al.*, 1992; Hox, 2010).
** These are very rough guidelines. In some cases you might get sensible results with $n=14$ and in others you might need $n=50$ or $n=100$.

18.4 Building up a multilevel model

18.4.1 Random intercept models

When explaining how multilevel modeling works it often helps to go through the process of constructing a complex model step-by-step. This is the recommended method for fitting a multilevel model for beginners: building up from a basic model to a more sophisticated one. A good starting point is the *empty model* (also called the null model). This model is really just a one-way ANOVA with a single random factor. The link may be clearer if presented in the following form:

$$y_{ij} = \mu + \pi_j + \varepsilon_{ij} \qquad \text{Equation 18.13}$$

Equation 18.13 uses π_j in place of u_j to illustrate that this is just a repeated measures ANOVA without a fixed factor. An identical model using multilevel notation[13] is:

$$y_{ij} = b_0 + u_j + e_{ij} \qquad \text{Equation 18.14}$$

This model has no predictors. It contains only the intercept b_0, a random effect for the level 2 units u_j, and a random error term e_{ij} (representing variation within level 1 units). The separation of the model into a fixed component $y_{ij} = b_{0,j}$ and a random component $b_{0,j} = b_0 + u_j + e_{ij}$ is trivial in this case. The empty model can be used to estimate the *ICC* of *Y* for the data set. Calculating the *ICC* with predictors in the model will change the results, making the *ICC* estimate conditional on those predictors – an estimate of the *ICC* of *Y* after controlling for covariates (Snijders and Bosker, 1999; Hedges and Hedberg, 2007). For this reason, standard practice is to estimate the *ICC* and proportion of variance explained at different levels of a multilevel model only for the empty model.[14] This produces estimates broadly consistent with ANOVA.

Deriving standardized effect size analogues for multilevel models is rarely wise and interpretation usually emphasizes the unstandardized parameter estimates. There are well-known anomalies in the use of variance explained statistics when predictors are added to a model.

The *ICC* for an empty model has a clear, but limited, interpretation in several contexts (see Box 18.2). When predictors are added, the change in variance explained can be informative, but needs careful interpretation (see Snijders and Bosker, 1999; Hox, 2010). Unlike conventional linear regression models, the total variance often changes when predictors are added: multilevel models do not decompose sample variance unambiguously in the sense that single-level models do. Thus, it is quite possible for the proportion of variance explained in the sample to decrease when predictors are added to the model (an impossibility in a single-level model). There are no variance explained measures that faithfully mimic the properties of R^2 and related ANOVA or multiple regression effect size metrics (see Hox, 2010).

Standardized regression slopes (β weights) are not routinely used in the multilevel context. One reason is that standardization is an obstacle to correct estimation of variance parameters and *SE*s (as it is in linear regression with interactions). Should you still wish to compare standardized effects (bearing in mind the usual caveats as well as the additional difficulties for a multilevel model), the appropriate procedure is to standardize the regression weights after fitting the model with unstandardized predictor and outcome variables. This is readily accomplished by adapting Equation 6.8 to convert from an unstandardized to a standardized metric. If b is the unstandardized estimate for a parameter, and $\hat{\sigma}_X$ and $\hat{\sigma}_Y$ are the *SD*s of the predictor and outcome in the sample, the standardized effect of the predictor is:

$$\beta = b\frac{\hat{\sigma}_X}{\hat{\sigma}_Y} \qquad \text{Equation 18.15}$$

It is less common to express effects in terms of d family metrics. Versions of d, g, Δ and $\hat{\delta}$ can be computed much as they would be for a repeated measures design. For instance, a version of g could be computed by dividing a difference between groups (the unstandardized slope for a dummy coded categorical predictor) by the *SD* of the outcome pooled across those groups.

The next step is usually to add predictors to the empty model as fixed effects. This form of model is termed a *random intercept model*, because the random effects are random variables used to model differences between the intercepts of higher-level units. Thus systematic variation between higher-level units is modeled solely in terms of differences in their means. A general form of the random intercept model with q fixed (predictors) effects is:

$$y_{ij} = b_0 + b_1x_{1,ij} + \ldots + b_qx_{q,ij} + u_j + e_{ij} \qquad \text{Equation 18.16}$$

Random intercept models are modest extensions of standard ANOVA and ANCOVA models that have fewer restrictions (e.g., dealing with unequal cell sizes and non-orthogonal predictors). An important property of the model is its ability to cope with missing observations for the outcome variable. As the model is fitted via maximum likelihood, estimates of the parameters are conditional on predictors present in the model. The resulting estimates should therefore be equivalent to those from multiple imputation with missing outcome data (because they both assume outcomes are MAR).

Figure 18.2 depicts a basic random intercept model with a single predictor and five level 2 units, each with ten observations. This model could be written as:

$$y_{ij} = b_0 + b_1x_{ij} + u_j + e_{ij} \quad u_j \sim N\left(0, \sigma_u^2\right) \quad e_{ij} \sim N\left(0, \sigma_e^2\right) \qquad \text{Equation 18.17}$$

A key feature of the model – evident in Figure 18.2 – is that the estimate of the slope of X is common to all level 2 units. In a repeated measures model this would model the effect of the

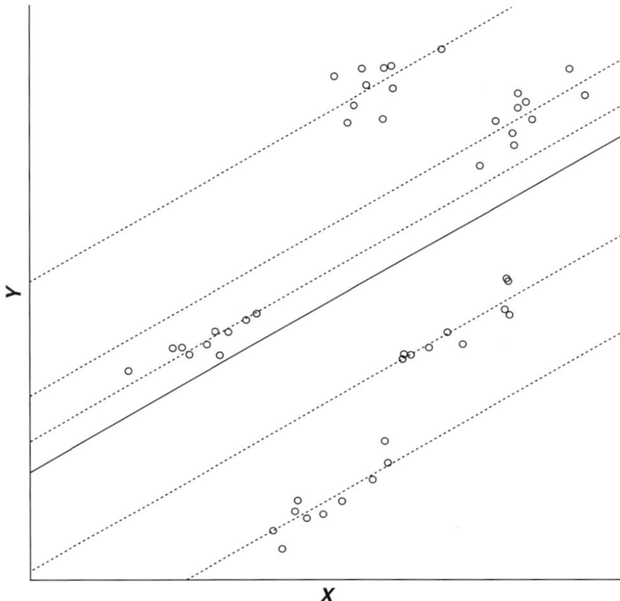

Figure 18.2 A random intercept model, with the overall average regression line (the solid line) and individual regression lines (the dashed lines) displayed for each level 2 unit

predictor as constant for all individuals – any individual differences in the observed effect of *X* are being attributed to error. Although the slope doesn't change, the intercept does vary between level 2 units. In a repeated measures model this indicates that individuals have different mean values of the outcome *Y*.

This is clear from Figure 18.2, where the regression lines fitted within each group (estimated from a multilevel model) are shifted up and down the *y*-axis. This sort of model is plausible if the effect of *X* is pretty much the same for all participants, but participants themselves vary quite a bit in terms of the outcome.

A basic random intercept model is somewhat restrictive for repeated measures data because it assumes homogeneity of variances and covariances between conditions. These restrictions can be relaxed by modeling alternative patterns of variances and covariances. A further limitation is that the variance at each level is usually assumed to follow a normal distribution. It is possible to check these distributions by plotting the residuals separately at each level of the model. If appropriate, transformations can be applied to reduce departures from normality. Fortunately, estimation of fixed effects in a two-level model is reasonably robust to violations of normality for residuals at level 2. However, very skewed residual distributions at level 2 make estimation of variance parameters and their *SE*s inaccurate unless the number of level 2 units is large (Maas and Hox, 2004). If the distributional assumptions are too restrictive, it is possible to relax these also. The main alternatives are to use robust *SE*s (e.g., GEEs), a multilevel generalized linear model, or a fully Bayesian approach (see Wooldridge, 2003; Gelman and Hill, 2007; Hox, 2010).

Up to this point only models with two levels have been discussed. Random intercept models can also be defined with additional levels. Three-level models are common and, in principle, three, four, five or more levels can be fitted (depending on software). What matters most is the structure of the modeled situation and the availability of suitable data. A three-level model is sensible if you have collected data from pupils nested in classrooms within different schools, but you won't be able to set up the model unless you know both the classroom and the school each child is in. The extension to three levels is sufficient to illustrate the process of modeling data from complex nested structures.

A three-level random intercept model with q fixed effects takes the form:

$$y_{ijk} = b_0 + b_1 x_{1,ijk} + \ldots + b_q x_{q,ijk} + v_k + u_{jk} + e_{ijk} \qquad \text{Equation 18.18}$$

The corresponding empty (null) model would be:

$$y_{ijk} = b_0 + v_k + u_{jk} + e_{ijk} \qquad \text{Equation 18.19}$$

Having three or more levels complicates the calculation of the *ICC* of Y. One complication is that a different *ICC* can be calculated for the level 2 and level 3 units. A second complication is that the proportion of variance explained and the average correlation interpretations of the *ICC* no longer agree for the third level of the model (see Box 18.4).

Predictors need not vary at all levels of the model. Indeed, if your primary interest is explanation at a particular level (e.g., level 2) you might well include predictors that vary only at that level. Yet, because of the hierarchical structure of the model, predictors varying at a lower level most likely also vary at the upper levels of the model. For example, in a repeated measures study looking the reading times for different texts, each participant might read several different texts and each text might contain several different sentences. The sentences are the level 1 units, the texts the level 2 units and participants the level 3 units. The length of the sentence (e.g., measured in number of syllables) would be an obvious predictor to include in the model. Sentence length probably varies at level 1, but this variability necessarily also impacts on texts (which contain multiple sentences) and participants (who read several texts, each containing multiple sentences). Some predictors, such as type of text, will vary only at the text level. Other predictors will vary only across participants – these will include individual difference variables such as the age or sex of the participant (and may also include treatment variables such as those designating experimental conditions). It is sometimes useful to vary the subscript of a predictor to indicate the levels at which it varies. Thus, in the earlier example predicting reading time by sentence, the following model might be fitted:

$$y_{ijk} = b_0 + b_1 x_{1,ijk} + b_2 x_{2,jk} + b_3 x_{3,k} + v_k + u_{jk} + e_{ijk} \qquad \text{Equation 18.20}$$

In this model X_1 could be sentence length, X_2 could represent text type and X_3 the age of the participant. The subscripts are not strictly necessary; what matters to the model is how the predictor varies. Some multilevel software does separate the predictors into separate data files at each level. This is highly efficient when working with large data sets, and more economical for data entry (see Gelman and Hill, 2007). This less efficient, but simpler method of entering all predictors at level 1 is preferable.[15] Having predictors that vary at different levels of the model also complicates the model in other ways (see Box 18.5).

Box 18.4 Intraclass correlation coefficients in three-level models

Several different *ICCs* can be calculated for a three-level model (Snijders and Bosker, 1999; Hox, 2010). The correct calculations depend on: i) whether one is interested in the proportion of variance explained or in the expected correlation between two units and ii) the level of the unit you are interested in.

The expected correlation between two level 1 units chosen at random depends on whether they are sampled from the same level 2 unit or not. If they are sampled from the same level 2 unit, the expected correlation is:

$$\rho_{I_2} = \frac{\sigma^2_{u0} + \sigma^2_{v0}}{\sigma^2_{u0} + \sigma^2_{v0} + \sigma^2_e}$$

If they share the same level 3 unit (but are from different level 2 units) the expected correlation is:

$$\rho_{I_3} = \frac{\sigma^2_{v0}}{\sigma^2_{u0} + \sigma^2_{v0} + \sigma^2_e}$$

These definitions assume a fully nested model in which sharing a level 2 unit also implies sharing a level 3 unit (but not vice versa). For instance, two children in the same class share the same school, but two children in the same school are not necessarily in the same class.

The *ICC* corresponding to the proportion of total variance explained at level 2 is:

$$\rho_{I_2} = \frac{\sigma^2_{u0}}{\sigma^2_{u0} + \sigma^2_{v0} + \sigma^2_e}$$

The proportion of total variance explained at level 3 is:

$$\rho_{I_3} = \frac{\sigma^2_{v0}}{\sigma^2_{u0} + \sigma^2_{v0} + \sigma^2_e}$$

These formulas indicate the estimated variance at each level as a proportion of the total (using estimates from the empty model, as usual). It is quite possible to express this proportion relative to a different denominator (Snijders and Bosker, 1999). For instance, if you were interested in the proportion of variance accounted for by level 2 effects out of the total level 2 and level 3 variation you would calculate:

$$\rho_{I_{2'}} = \frac{\sigma^2_{u0}}{\sigma^2_{u0} + \sigma^2_{v0}}$$

If level 3 was school, level 2 was classroom and level 1 was child, this would be the proportion of variance explained by classroom-level effects alone (excluding individual differences between children and schools).

Example 18.1 This example involves a re-analysis of data taken from a series of experiments in which reading times for sentences from spatial descriptions were measured (Baguley and Payne, 2000b). Subsequent examples will refer to this data set as the determinacy data. Each participant read eight different descriptions, each made up of four sentences describing the spatial locations of several objects (e.g., 'The city is below the lake' or 'The mountain is to the right of the city'). Every sentence was constructed in a similar way, but each participant received a slightly different set of sentences and descriptions. This analysis can be set up as a two-level repeated measures model with sentences nested within participants. Because reading times are positively skewed, the natural logarithm of the reading times (in seconds) plus a small constant $\ln(time + 0.5)$ is used as the outcome (Y). The null model with no predictors is:

$$y_{ij} = b_0 + u_j + e_{ij}$$

Remember that j subscripts refer to level 2 units (participants) and i subscripts refer to level 1 units (sentences). There are 88 participants and 2164 sentences. Reading times for some descriptions were excluded (based on performance on a comprehension task). Using a multilevel model makes it possible to estimate the reading times for the remaining data without bias if data are MAR (which is plausible because the outcome and many of the predictors are correlated with comprehension difficulty). A random intercept model with FML estimation and no predictors can be summarized as:

$$\begin{aligned} y_{ij} &= 2.002\,(0.045) + u_j + e_{ij} \\ var\left[u_j\right] &= [0.165] \\ var\left[e_{ij}\right] &= [0.250] \\ -2\ln(\ell) &= 3387.6 \end{aligned}$$

The fixed effect here is the intercept 2.002 and its *SE* follows it (in parenthesis). The covariance matrix at each level is in square brackets (though in a random intercept model each matrix has only one variance estimate). The *ICC* is estimated as $0.165/(0.165 + 0.250) = 0.398$. Thus the average correlation between any two reading times within a participant is about .40. The $-2\ln(\ell)$ (deviance) of the model is also reported, but is not very useful without having another model for comparison.

Adding many predictors as fixed effects is easy, but it is worth starting with a very simple model. For this reason I'll just add dummy coded predictors for the sentences (though we could use effect coding or fit a cell means model). As there are $J = 4$ sentences, three dummy indicators are required. In this case we will use the second, third and fourth sentences (LINE2, LINE3 and LINE4) from each description. It seems likely that the reading times for sentences within a description will be correlated (as, unlike the descriptions they come from, the order of presentation can't be randomized). The sentences also vary from participant to participant. Thus sentence length (the number of syllables in the sentence) also varies. This is an example of a time-varying covariate. Including sentence length as a predictor produces a multilevel model that, although quite simple in many respects, is already beyond the scope of most single-level regression models. This model, again fitted using FML, is:

$$\begin{aligned} y_{ij} = b_{0,ij} &- 0.114\,(0.028)\,LINE2_{ij} - 0.195\,(0.029)\,LINE3_{ij} \\ &- 0.472\,(0.029)\,LINE4_{ij} + 0.031\,(0.014)\,LENGTH_{ij} \\ b_{0,ij} &= 1.874\,(0.153) + u_j + e_{ij} \\ var\left[u_j\right] &= [0.167] \\ var\left[e_{ij}\right] &= [0.217] \\ -2\ln(\ell) &= 3091.0 \end{aligned}$$

The random intercept is separated out from the fixed effects and is given by $b_{0,ij} = 1.874 + u_j + e_{ij}$. This is a common strategy for presenting the equation, and the combined equation would be:

$$y_{ij} = 1.874\,(0.153) - 0.114\,(0.028)\,LINE2_{ij} - 0.195\,(0.029)\,LINE3_{ij}$$
$$-0.472\,(0.029)\,LINE4_{ij} + 0.031\,(0.014)\,LENGTH_{ij} + u_{0,j} + e_{ij}$$

As the categorical predictors are dummy coded, the intercept is the mean reading time (on the log scale) of the first sentence (LINE1) adjusted for the covariate (sentence length). The coefficients for the other sentences are differences (contrasts) relative to the reading time for the first sentence. These reading times show a gradual decline in reading time from first to third sentence, culminating in a sharp drop at the end. This is an uncentered model, so the intercept is the reading time of the first sentence on the assumption that it has zero syllables. Length appears to have only a small effect (though this is deceptive because the sentences are from nine to 11 syllables long). Even so, it might be easier to interpret the model if LENGTH is centered. Except for the intercept, the resulting model is unchanged. In the model with the LENGTH centered the intercept is:

$$b_{0,ij} = 2.197\,(0.048) + u_j + e_{ij}$$

This is now evaluated as the mean of syllable length and represents the adjusted grand mean of the reading times for a first sentence with an average number of syllables. On an untransformed scale this is $e^{2.197} - 0.5 = 9.0 - 0.5 = 8.5$ seconds.

One useful check on the model is to look at the residuals of the model. Figure 18.3 plots the standardized (Pearson) residuals of the model at level 1 and level 2 (the latter representing estimates of individual differences in the average reading times of the participants).

The residuals at level 1 look reasonably straight in the middle of the distribution with some curvature at the extremes – suggesting leptokurtosis and perhaps some skew. This is consistent with

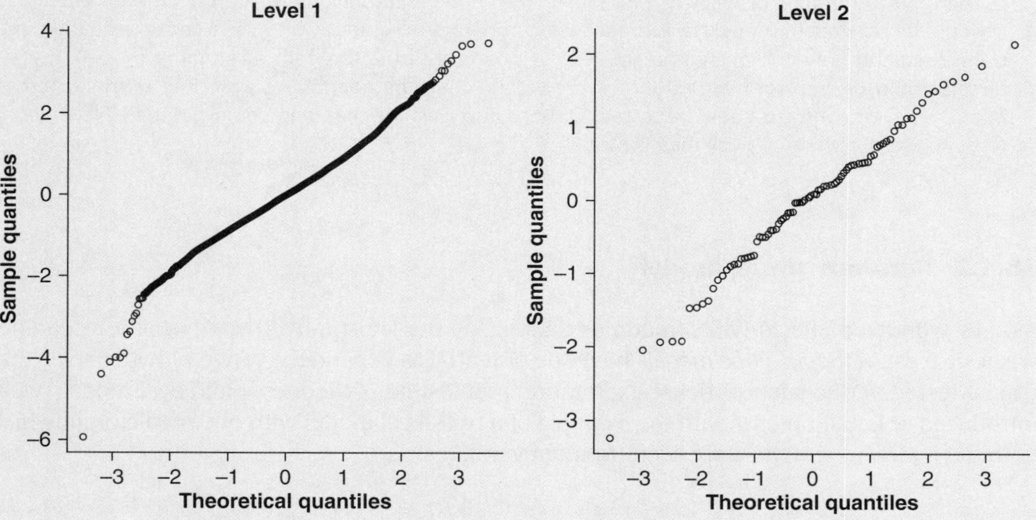

Figure 18.3 Normal probability plots of standardized residuals at level 1 and level 2 for a random intercept model of the determinacy data

the handful of very fast responses in the lower tail. This pattern may improve if additional predictors are added. Another option would be to exclude participants with responses with very fast reading times (though avoiding this is preferable, if possible). Doing so wouldn't alter the fixed estimates too much (though the level 2 variance would decrease and the intercept increase slightly). In contrast, the level 2 residuals look remarkably well behaved and there is only one extreme residual ($z = 3.25$).

The difference in deviance between model with sentence number and length and the null model is very large ($\Delta\chi^2 = 3091.0 - 3387.6 = -296.6$). This could be compared to a χ^2 distribution with 4 *df* (for the four additional parameters), but with such a large difference in deviance almost any type of inference would favor the more complex model. Given that four parameters were added, the reduction in AIC would be $-296.6 + 8 = -292.8$. When exploring a model it is reasonable to rely on rough rules of thumb such as ± 2 standard errors indicating statistical significance for individual predictors. For instance, the length effect is $0.031/0.014 = 2.14$ standard errors greater than zero. An approximate 95% Wald CI would be 0.031 [0.003, 0.059]. All the *SE*s are relatively small and the effects of the predictors are sensible (e.g., syllable length increases reading times), so there would be little reason to exclude any of them at this stage.

These estimates and inferences all depend on fitting the model using FML. Switching to RML has only one discernible effect on the estimates (the estimate of level 2 variance increases from 0.167 to 0.169). A final check is to consider a three-level model. Adding an intermediate level for the descriptions does not have any impact on the model. The variance of the description level is estimated to be close to zero. The parameter estimates are unchanged and deviance is also unchanged. Zero variance at a level is not uncommon in small samples, but for an intermediate level with 541 observations (descriptions) to be zero it suggests negligible variation between descriptions. This is not too surprising. The order of presenting the descriptions was randomized and each description, while based on one of eight common templates, varied in a number of ways (including the wording and length of sentences). Nearly all the variation is at the sentence or participant level because the templates themselves don't (and were not expected to) have much impact on the task.

There are a number of ways to tinker with the model without going beyond random effects. It would be possible to model the sentence effect more parsimoniously (e.g., as a linear or quadratic trend requiring only one or two parameters, as opposed to the three for a saturated model). Predictors could be transformed, additional predictors, could be added (e.g., product terms to test interactions) or contrasts could be tested. Options also exist for changing coding of the LINE effect (e.g., to effect coding or a cell means model).

18.4.2 Random slope models

Models with fixed effects will sometimes address all the substantive hypotheses a researcher wishes to test. *Random slope models* have the potential to expand the range of hypotheses that can be tested and to support richer exploration and testing of theories. Multilevel models were introduced in Equation 18.7 with the example of a two-level model with one predictor, in which both the intercept and the slope were random variables:

$$y_{ij} = b_0 + b_1 x_{1,ij} + u_{0,j} + u_{1,j} x_{1,ij} + e_{ij}$$

This is a simple random slopes model. A model of this form is shown in Figure 18.4.

The effects of X_1 vary across the level 2 units (indexed by the subscript j). This can be seen in Figure 18.4, where the slopes of the regression lines within each level 2 unit differ from the

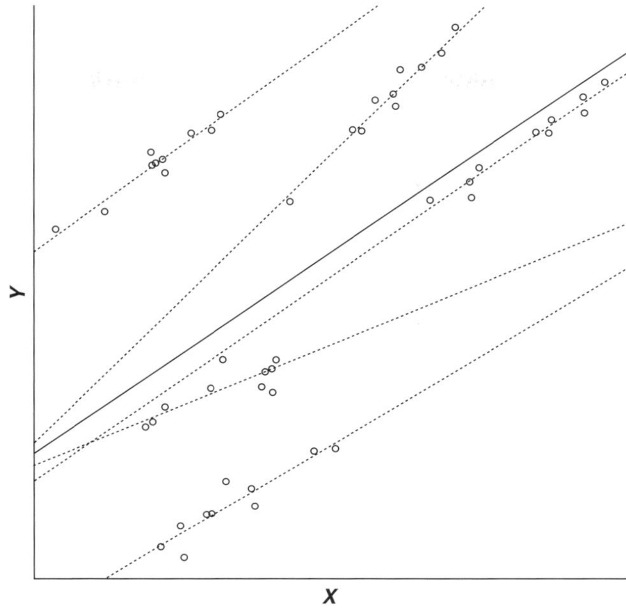

Figure 18.4 A random slope model, with the overall average regression line (the solid line) and individual regression lines (the dashed lines) displayed for each level 2 unit

overall average from the model. This contrasts with the random intercept model in Figure 18.3, where only the intercepts vary between level 2 units. In a repeated measures model the variance $u_{0,j}$ represents individual differences in the intercept (and therefore the average of the outcome Y) of the participants and $u_{1,j}$ represents the individual differences in the slopes (and therefore the magnitude of the effect of X_1). Both variance components are assumed to have a normal distribution:

$$u_{0,j} \sim N\left(0, \sigma^2_{u_0}\right) \quad u_{1,j} \sim N\left(0, \sigma^2_{u_1}\right)$$

The intercept for a given individual is therefore given by b_0 plus the jth residual for u_0. The slope for the same individual is given by b_1 plus the jth residual for u_1.

Unlike residuals in more familiar linear regression models, the residuals of higher-level units are interpretable as estimates of the effect of predictors for that unit. The distribution of the effects can, provided the assumption of normality is not unreasonable, also be used to make predictions about the range of effects likely to be obtained in the population sampled. Assuming approximate normality for an intercept with variance $\sigma^2_{u_0}$, around 95% of values would be expected to lie $\pm 1.96\sqrt{\sigma^2_{u_0}}$ or $\pm 1.96\sigma_{u_0}$ from b_0. Similarly, for a slope with variance $\sigma^2_{u_1}$, around 95% of values would be expected to fall in the range $b_1 \pm 1.96\sigma_{u_1}$.

The level 2 residuals in a multilevel model differ from those in a single-level regression. They are *empirical Bayes estimates* (or *shrinkage estimates*) of the intercepts and slopes of those units. So far we have presented multilevel models as if they are a clever extension of familiar regression methods (usually introduced as frequentist methods). However, switching to a multilevel model involves modeling data in a way that is Bayesian in flavor. The idea of representing variation in slopes or intercepts as random variables with a particular (e.g., normal) distribution is central to Bayesian statistics. Empirical Bayes estimation involves estimating these random values from the data (e.g., the variance of the level 2 units) rather than the traditional priors of a fully Bayesian analysis, but there are strong parallels between multilevel modeling and fully Bayesian methods (see Snijders and Bosker, 1999; Gelman and Hill, 2007).

Obtaining the residuals in this way has a very important consequence for the model. If the residuals had been obtained by conventional parameter estimation (i.e., requiring a dummy predictor for each intercept and slope) they would have been estimates and not predictions.[16] Obtaining them as empirical Bayes estimates ensures that the uncertainty in estimating the variance of the distribution is taken into account. Accordingly, the estimated values of the effects are closer to the population mean than the observed values are. This is easiest to demonstrate for the case of a two-level empty model in which only the means of the level 2 units are estimated. The estimates in a single-level model would be obtained from $\hat{\mu}_j$ (the means of the j 'groups' defined by level 2 units). The same estimate could be used in a two-level model. Alternatively, you might treat the random variation at level 2 as a nuisance variable. This leaves the grand mean $\hat{\mu}$ (b_0 in the empty model) as the estimate of any unit 2 mean. Neither estimate is totally satisfactory. The empirical Bayes estimate is:

$$\hat{b}_{1j} = \hat{\rho}_{YY}\hat{\mu}_j + (1 - \hat{\rho}_{YY})\,\hat{\mu} \qquad \text{Equation 18.21}$$

This is an average of the estimated population and group mean, weighted by the reliability ($\hat{\rho}_{YY}$) of the level 2 measurements (see Box 18.2). This weighting of unreliable estimates toward the population mean is known as *shrinkage* to the mean. The empirical Bayes residuals are sometimes termed *shrunken residuals* for this reason. Shrunken residuals are sometimes viewed as a drawback of multilevel models, but proponents of multilevel models point to their advantages. The squared error of these residuals is smaller than for residuals without shrinkage, because shrunken estimates of extreme level 2 units are closer to the population value than their observed value (though only if the level 2 measurements are unreliable). Shrunken residuals thus attempt to correct for unreliability in the measurement of effects in the multilevel model. If the true values are estimated with error (and hence unreliable) then this is probably a good thing.[17] The estimates are also optimal in the sense of minimizing the mean squared error of prediction. This increased precision of estimation comes at a cost: the estimates are biased. This is a classic instance of the trade-off between efficiency and bias. This bias is greatest for level 2 units that are far from the mean and where the level 1 sample size within that unit is small. Whether this bias is acceptable will depend on what your goal is. For instance, a common application of shrinkage estimates is in education (e.g., to estimate school or teacher impacts on children's learning). Tate (2004) argues that the bias in the empirical Bayes estimates of teacher or school effectiveness makes them problematic when used to assess individual teachers or schools.

A random slope model is not limited to a single predictor or to two levels. Additional predictors can be added, with or without random slopes, at any level of the model. The main limitation is that adding random slopes greatly increases the difficulty of interpreting the model. A practical consideration is that modeling a large number of variances and covariances may also lead to estimation problems (even if the model makes sense).

Adopting an appropriate centering strategy is potentially crucial for a multilevel model (see Box 18.5). Separating the effects of predictors at different levels of a multilevel model is difficult. The specific problem is that the effect of a predictor at one level can, in principle, be confounded with its effects at other levels (Enders and Tofighi, 2007). This problem is confined to the effect of a predictor at lower levels of the model. A predictor that varies only at the highest level of the model is constant at lower levels and cannot influence effects elsewhere (e.g., it is not a problem for a variable such as sex in a repeated measures design).

The effects of centering in random slope models are complex (see Box 18.5). CWC (*centering within cluster* or *centering within context*) is advocated by some experts. In a two-level model this involves subtracting the level 2 mean of a predictor from each level 1 predictor value (and is equivalent to participant-mean centering in a repeated measures model with two levels). Under CWC, the effect being modeled at level 1 is the impact on *Y* of the deviation of participants from their own mean for that predictor. The attraction of this approach is that it will strip out the influence of the predictor at level 2 (which may be desirable if the level 2 influence is considered a nuisance or confounding variable). Nevertheless, it will not always be appropriate, and Hox (2010) advises a more cautious approach. The CWC model strips out information from the analysis and might have unforeseen impacts on the model. By removing information from the analysis, it represents a shift away from the raw predictor to a transformed predictor (and the two analyses may produce very different results). Furthermore, the impact of CWC and of adding back level 2 (cluster) averages to the model is not fully understood – there may be situations where it is undesirable.

Box 18.5 Centering in multilevel models

In a single-level regression model, centering is used to aid the interpretation of a statistical model (e.g., one with interactions or polynomial terms). In a random slopes model, centering within clusters (CWC) may be desirable if the goal is to tease apart the effects of predictors at one level from their effects at a higher level. Without appropriate centering the effect of lower level predictors will be a potentially uninterpretable mixture of the different effects (Enders and Tofighi, 2007). Unlike the more familiar grand mean centering (CGM) approach, CWC is not a simple reparameterization of the model – it represents a fundamental change to what is being modeled.

Because it can be defined in different ways, centering in the multilevel context is more awkward than in single-level regression. CGM has a similar function to the centering in a single-level model, replacing an arbitrary zero point with a more meaningful one that should be easier to interpret. In contrast, the function of CWC is to strip out the effect of differences in the predictor between level 2 units. The level 2 units in repeated measures models are usually people and therefore CWC is a form of participant-mean centering (not dissimilar to normalized scores). CWC can, in principle, be extended to more than two levels of a hierarchy (in which case it helps to use specific terms such as group-mean centering or participant-mean centering to distinguish between levels).

Enders and Tofighi (*ibid.*) provide a detailed explanation of the effects of CGM and CWC on the estimates of different effects in a two-level model. However, before discussing their recommendations, you should realize that for level 2 predictors (and, in general, for the highest level of a model) only CGM is a possibility. As level 2 predictors have the same value at level 1, CWC would replace all the predictor values with zeroes! Centering predictors at the highest level of a model with respect to their grand mean is uncontroversial. It may help you interpret the effects (e.g., if there are interactions present or if the predictor is on an arbitrary scale), but is optional.

Enders and Tofighi show that under CGM, a two-level repeated measures model with a single predictor at level 1 ($X_{1,j}$) can be expressed as:

$$b_{0,j} = \hat{\mu}_{Yj} - b_{1,j}\left(\hat{\mu}_{X_1,j} - \hat{\mu}_{X_1}\right) \qquad \text{Equation 18.22}$$

This can be interpreted as $\hat{\mu}_{Y,j}$ (the mean of the outcome *Y* for person *j*) after adjusting by $\hat{\mu}_{X_1,j} - \hat{\mu}_{X_1}$ (how different X_1 for person *j* is from the mean of X_1 for all participants). This works like adjustment of means in ANCOVA; the intercept is the expected outcome of each person if they were exactly average in terms of X_1. Arguably, the slope may not have a clear interpretation (being a mixture of level 1 and level 2 effects).

Enders and Tofighi argue that if primary interest is in the effect of $X_{2,j}$, a second predictor that only varies at level 2, CGM of $X_{1,ij}$ could be useful. In this case the level 1 predictor is effectively a nuisance variable and CGM removes its influence on the intercept term. This allows the effect of $X_{2,j}$ to be assessed after adjustment (ANCOVA-style) for the nuisance variable $X_{1,ij}$. This might happen with repeated measures designs if the research question focused on individual differences (and any level 2 predictors were confounding variables).

CGM removes the influence of all variability in a predictor from the intercept. CWC, in contrast, only removes some of the variability: that associated with level 2 units. In repeated measures designs this involves stripping out individual differences. CWC thus strips out the level 2 effect from the estimate of the level 1 slope. The level 1 equation for a CWC centered predictor $X_{1,ij}$ can be expressed as:

$$y_{ij} = b_{0,j} + b_{1,j}\left(x_{1,ij} - \hat{\mu}_{X_{1,j}}\right) + e_{ij} \qquad \text{Equation 18.23}$$

This indicates, in a repeated measures model, that the outcome is a function of the intercept for person j plus the effect of the predictor adjusted for individual differences between participants (i.e., the level 2 mean) on the predictor X_1. Level 2 mean centering produces a 'pure' estimate of the effect of a predictor at level 1 (having stripped out the influence of differences at level 2). The variance estimates in this case (assuming all predictors are centered in this way) should be close to those in the empty model. This implies that (unless any other random effects are estimated) a CWC model will give similar estimates of the *ICC* to that of the empty model. CWC therefore seems to be the correct choice if a researcher is interested in getting uncontaminated estimates of the effects of a level 1 predictor.

What if you want 'pure' estimates of both level 1 and level 2 effects of a level 1 predictor? Enders and Tofighi propose adding an additional predictor to the model. This predictor is the mean of the level 1 predictor for each level 2 unit. In a repeated measures model this would be the mean of each person for that predictor. This 'restores' the variability stripped out by centering the predictor (by subtracting those same level 2 means). This approach involves estimating an additional parameter, though this is likely to have a negligible impact for data sets with few parameters relative to n at each level. Nevertheless, a model with the level 2 (cluster averages) added back into the model represents a further complication and its full impact for different situations (e.g., its effect on the covariances) have not been explored (Hox, 2010).

A final concern, addressed in much more detail by Enders and Tofighi (2007) is that of estimating interactions. For interactions between level 2 predictors, the usual interpretational concerns apply (in relation to collinearity) and CGM is preferred. For interactions involving level 1 predictors only (or for cross-level interactions), CWC may be a better option. The reasons are as outlined above: the interaction may not have a clear interpretation unless the level 1 effects have had level 2 variability stripped out.

The logic of Enders and Tofighi's recommendations applies equally to categorical predictors. Dummy or effect coded predictors should therefore also be centered by subtracting level 2 means. For a fully balanced design (e.g., equal m measures for each n level 2 units) effect coded predictors are already centered (they have a mean of zero). Dummy coded predictors in a fully balanced design have a mean of $(0+1)/2 = .5$ and so take the values $-.5$ and $.5$. The choice here is really between differently scaled predictors with effect coding (with slopes equal to half the difference in means for effect coding and the difference in means for centered dummy coding). For unbalanced designs centering should be implemented as it is for continuous predictors (though if the imbalance is not large the impact on the model will rarely be substantial).

Example 18.2 The random intercept model for the determinacy data in Example 18.1 is adequate for testing fixed effects, but doesn't allow individual differences for any effects to be explored. None of the fixed effects in the earlier model provides a strong theoretical rationale for modeling random slopes. However, about half of the descriptions describe spatial configurations that are indeterminate. For instance, participants may read 'The A is to the right of the B' and 'The A is to the right of the C'. The relative location of B and C are then unknown. If people try to work out the spatial locations of the objects then one would expect sentences that introduce a determinacy to be more difficult to understand than sentences in which the potential locations of the objects don't clash. These 'clash' sentences can introduce indeterminacy into the description either in the second, third or fourth sentence (but not the first). People should find the critical clash sentences harder to read and therefore take longer on them. People may also have different strategies for coping with the indeterminate descriptions. Some participants may give up at that point and switch to a more superficial strategy (e.g., remembering the sentences or guessing on the comprehension task). Others may respond by increasing mental effort (e.g., trying to keep track of all possible arrangements of the objects). This should manifest as individual differences in the size of the clash effect.

Starting with the two-level random intercept model with the same predictors as before, we added a predictor, CLASH, indicating the introduction of indeterminacy to a sentence. After fitting the model with FML estimation, the effect of clash was $+0.078\,(0.034)\,CLASH_{ij}$. FML estimation is appropriate here because the models differ only in their fixed effects. The deviance of the model decreased from 3091.0 to 3085.6 and $\Delta\text{AIC} = -5.4 + 2 = 3.4$ (equivalent to an LR in favor of the more complex model of around 5.5). The likelihood ratio test is also statistically significant, $G^2_1 = 5.4$, $p = .02$. The Wald-style t test is considered more appropriate for fixed tests, but produces similar results here: $b = 0.078$, 95% CI [0.012, 0.14], $t_{2071} = 2.33$, $p = .02$.

There is evidence of an increase in reading times (approaching ten per sentence) for the clash sentences. Adding a random effect for clash at level 2 (and thus estimating the variance of the clash effect and its covariance with the intercept) gives the following model (fitted with RML estimation):

$$
\begin{aligned}
y_{ij} &= b_{0,ij} - 0.114\,(0.028)\,LINE2_{ij} - 0.214\,(0.029)\,LINE3_{ij} - 0.490\,(0.029)\,LINE4_{ij} \\
&\quad + 0.032\,(0.014)\left(LENGTH - \hat{\mu}_{LENGTH}\right)_{ij} + b_{5,j}CLASH_{ij} \\
&\quad b_{0,ij} = 2.199\,(0.047) + u_{0,j} + e_{ij} \\
&\quad b_{5,j}CLASH_{ij} = 0.065\,(0.038) + u_{5,j} \\
&\quad var\begin{bmatrix} u_{0,j} \\ u_{5,j} \end{bmatrix} = \begin{bmatrix} 0.156 & \\ 0.050 & 0.027 \end{bmatrix} \\
&\quad var\left[e_{ij}\right] = [0.214] \\
&\quad RML - 2\ln(\ell) = 3101.6
\end{aligned}
$$

This model now includes the random slope $b_{5j}CLASH_{ij} = 0.065\,(0.038) + u_{5j}$ as well as a random intercept. The covariance matrix at level 2 has the form:

$$
\begin{bmatrix} \hat{\sigma}^2_{u0} & \\ \hat{\sigma}_{u05} & \hat{\sigma}^2_{u5} \end{bmatrix} = \begin{bmatrix} 0.156 & \\ 0.050 & 0.027 \end{bmatrix}
$$

Note that none of the variances or covariances comes with a standard error. These models were fitted in R using the `nlme` package, which does not provide them. This is by design. The authors believe that conventional p values and CIs are not appropriate ways to test random effects – because the distributions of variances are rarely even approximately normal. Some software does report standard errors, but this should not necessarily be taken to indicate that p values and CIs computed using them are accurate.

Although the fixed effect of CLASH has marginally decreased, there also seems to be evidence of individual differences in the size of the effect. In the random intercept model, the RML deviance was 3118.1. Estimating two extra parameters ($\hat{\sigma}_{u05}$ and $\hat{\sigma}^2_{u5}$) alters the RML deviance by (3101.6 − 3118.1) = −16.5. This decrease in deviance is statistically significant, $G^2_2 = 16.5$, $p = .0003$, and $\Delta AIC = -16.5 + 4 = -12.5$ (equivalent to an LR of 500 or so in favor of the random slope model). Moreover, owing to boundary effects, these tests are slightly conservative.

The variance for the CLASH predictor suggests that there is some variability in the size of effect between participants. Figure 18.5 shows separate regression lines for the CLASH effect for each of the first 20 participants. This gives a flavor of the variability present in the sample. From the

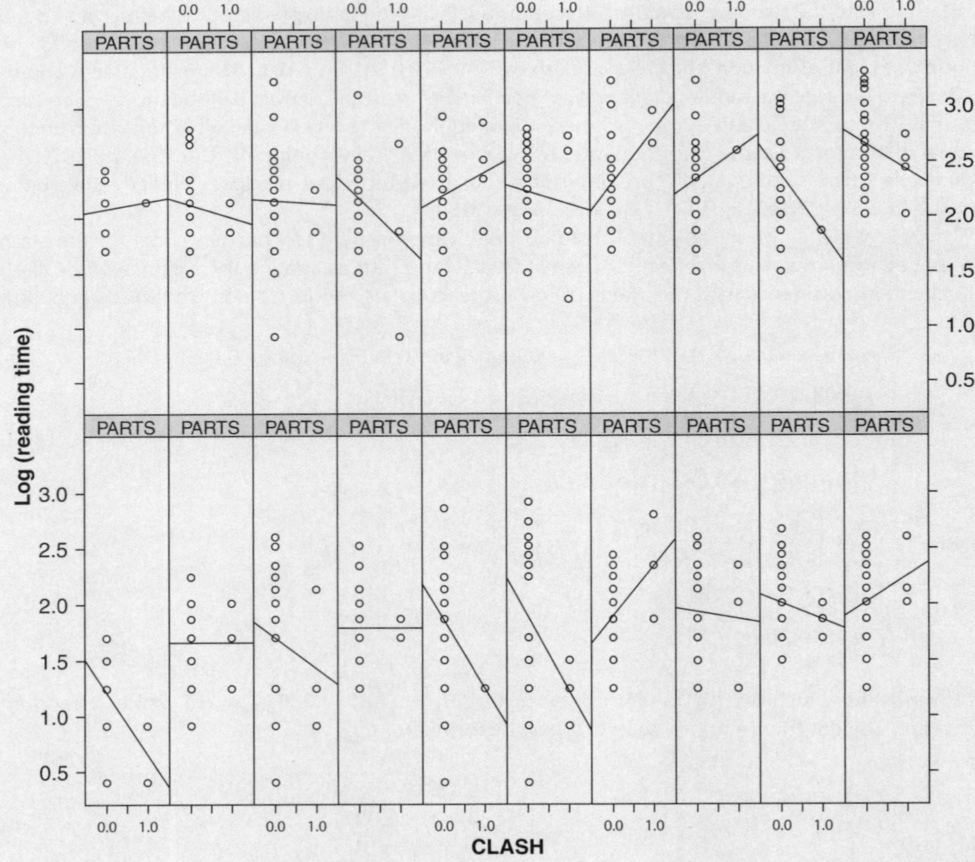

Figure 18.5 Separate regression lines for the CLASH effect, fitted to each of the first 20 participants in the determinacy data

plot it is very clear that the direction and size of the effect varies markedly from person to person. An important question is whether this variability is systematic or represents noise in the data.

One test of the variability of the slopes is to constrain the covariance to be zero and see how the deviance differs from the random intercept model. Doing so produces RML deviance of 3113.2. This suggests that the model with σ^2_{u5} (but not $\hat{\sigma}_{u05}$) offers a modest improvement over the random intercept model ($\Delta G^2 = -5.0$, $\Delta AIC = -3.0$). However, a boundary effect is present (because the variance is constrained to be ≥ 0). For this comparison, the likelihood ratio statistic under H_0 is an equally weighted mixture of χ^2_0 and χ^2_1 distributions, and the usual *p* value can be halved. Using this approach, the test of the CLASH variance would be, $G^2_1 = 5.0$, $p = .013$. This test uses RML, which is appropriate for comparing models varying only in their random component.

There is no real point in testing the covariance term (given the large change in deviance associated with it). What about its interpretation? The positive covariance indicates a positive relationship between the slope of the CLASH effect and the random intercept. People with longer average reading times take longer when encountering an indeterminacy (even greater than expected from the multiplicative model assumed by the ln(*time*) outcome variable). The absolute value of the covariance is misleading because the intercept variance is so large. It helps to standardize using the *SD*s of the intercept and CLASH effect. This just involves using the familiar equation for a standardized covariance (or correlation). As the *SD*s are the square roots of the variances 0.156 and 0.027, the calculation is:

$$r_{XY} = \frac{\hat{\sigma}_{XY}}{\hat{\sigma}_X \hat{\sigma}_Y} = \frac{.050}{\sqrt{0.156} \times \sqrt{0.027}} = .77$$

The correlation of the CLASH effect with average reading times for participants is .77 and it accounts for $.77^2 = .59$ of variation in the size of the CLASH effect. The usual caveats about interpreting correlations apply (e.g., range restriction). Even so, the small covariance is consistent with a fairly substantial relationship between average reading times and the size of the clash effect.

It would be quite reasonable to work with and report the correlation matrix for the random effects rather than the covariance matrix. Some software (e.g., MLwiN) reports the covariance matrix, while other software (e.g., `nlme` and `lme4` in R) reports the correlation between random effects rather than the covariance. The advantage of presenting the covariance matrix is that the variances are on the main diagonal of the matrix. Presenting the correlation matrix results in values on the main diagonal being one. `nlme` compromises by reporting *SD*s and the correlations (rather than variances and covariances).

It is possible to gauge the range of CLASH effects predicted by the model under the (strong) assumption of a normal distribution for the variance. About 95% of CLASH effects should be within ±1.96 standard deviations of the mean effect. This is a 'quick and dirty', but convenient, way to estimate the range of effects and gives:

$$0.065 \pm 1.96\sqrt{0.027} = 0.065 \pm 0.322$$

Although there are better approaches (such as simulating random slopes for the effect) the crude 95% posterior probability interval [−.257, .387] can help you interpret the impact of the effect. This is equivalent to a 25% decrease in reading times for the CLASH sentence participants at one end of the range (on the untransformed scale in seconds) or a 50% increase at the other. This is consistent with participants adopting very different strategies for dealing with indeterminacy. In addition, the participants who have longer reading times tend to be at the upper end of the range.

An important reservation is that the CLASH predictor varies at level 1 and at level 2. The level 1 effect of CLASH may therefore be confounded with the level 2 effect. CWC (centering around participant means) strips out the potential confounding influence of the level 2 effect. The level 1 effect is of particular theoretical interest (because it represents the effect of determinacy at the sentence level). The level 2 effect is the effect of the average number of CLASH sentences read by a participant. This is uninteresting (partly because it does not vary much and partly because it would be an identical except for the exclusion of some descriptions from the analysis).* For completeness, the model with the participant-mean centered CLASH effect added is summarized below:

$$y_{ij} = b_{0,ij} - 0.114\,(0.028)\,LINE2_{ij} - 0.214\,(0.029)\,LINE3_{ij} - 0.490\,(0.029)\,LINE4_{ij}$$
$$+ 0.035\,(0.014)\,(LENGTH - \hat{\mu}_{LENGTH})_{ij} + b_{5,j}\left(CLASH - \hat{\mu}_{CLASH_j}\right)_{ij}$$
$$b_{0,ij} = 2.206\,(0.048) + u_{0,j} + e_{ij}$$
$$b_{5,j}CLASH_{ij} = 0.066\,(0.048) + u_{5,j}$$
$$var\begin{bmatrix} u_{0,j} \\ u_{5,j} \end{bmatrix} = \begin{bmatrix} 0.162 & \\ 0.050 & 0.024 \end{bmatrix}$$
$$var\left[e_{0,ij}\right] = [0.213]$$
$$RML - 2\ln(\ell) = 3102.0$$

CWC has hardly any influence on the CLASH effect at level 1. There remains some evidence of individual differences in the size of the CLASH effect even after any level 2 effect is stripped out.

* The model does not change much if these descriptions are included, but in this area of research it is common to exclude time data from trials where subsequent performance was inaccurate. The rationale is that a researcher is usually not interested in performance on trials where the participant may have misread or misremembered the description.

18.4.3 Modeling variances and covariances

Estimating random effects in a multilevel model is one approach to modeling the variances and covariances of the effects at each level. The population covariance matrix being estimated in a random intercept model has a very basic form. For a two-level model it would be:

$$\left[\sigma^2_{u0}\right]$$
$$\left[\sigma^2_{e}\right]$$

As soon as random slopes are added, the covariance structure is more complex. For a predictor with random slopes at level 1 it would be:

$$\left[\sigma^2_{u0}\right]$$
$$\begin{bmatrix} \sigma^2_{e0} & \\ \sigma_{e01} & \sigma^2_{e1} \end{bmatrix}$$

It is possible, in principle, to estimate a large number of variances and covariances at each level. But, as more variances are estimated, the number of additional parameters required grows rapidly. If two random slopes were included in the model (e.g., at level 2), five additional parameters would be estimated (relative to a random intercept model):

$$\begin{bmatrix} \sigma^2_{u_0} & & \\ \sigma_{u_{01}} & \sigma^2_{u_1} & \\ \sigma_{u_{02}} & \sigma_{u_{12}} & \sigma^2_{u_2} \end{bmatrix}$$

$$\begin{bmatrix} \sigma^2_e \end{bmatrix}$$

The parsimony of a multilevel model rapidly diminishes if large numbers of random slopes are estimated in this way. Furthermore, the interpretability of the model may be prejudiced if random effects are added in an *ad hoc* way, rather than being driven by theoretical considerations or structural constraints imposed by the study.

Hox (2010) considers approaches to modeling variances and covariances (particularly in relation to repeated measures or longitudinal designs) in detail. Among the driving considerations are the assumptions that you wish to make about the data. The usual covariance matrices estimated for level 1 units implicitly assume that observations are unordered and therefore that the *ICC* is homogeneous within level 2 (or higher) units. This is a form of homogeneity of covariance. This is reasonable for many clustered designs, because there is no particular reason to assume that any two units are more similar than any two others. A form of homogeneity of variance is also assumed: a single variance is used to model all observations at a given level for a given slope or intercept.

Goldstein (2003) shows how to extend the model to cope with more complex variance structures. For instance if there are subgroups with different variances, this can be explicitly captured in the covariance matrix being estimated. A good illustration is for a two-level model of children in schools. For some measures, such as reading ability, boys and girls quite possibly differ, not only in their mean ability but also in the variability. Adding a dummy variable for gender to the model will capture the difference in the mean (through its fixed effect). Including the slope of this effect as a random effect will model separate variances for boys and girls. An important step here is to treat the variances as independent. This is achieved by constraining the covariance to be zero (which also reduces the required number of parameters by one). If boys are coded as 1 and girls as 0, the intercept would estimate the variance of the latter, and the covariance matrix being estimated at level 1 would be:

$$\begin{bmatrix} \sigma^2_{girls} & \\ 0 & \sigma^2_{boys} \end{bmatrix}$$

In some models – notably repeated measures models (but also multivariate response models) – the assumption of homogeneity of covariance will be problematic. The combination of homogeneity of variance and homogeneity of covariance assumptions is better known in this context as compound symmetry (see Snijders and Bosker, 1999; Hox, 2010). Compound symmetry is a slightly more restrictive assumption than that of sphericity (assumed in repeated measures ANOVA). If compound symmetry is met, then the estimates of the variances will be unbiased. If not, then estimates of the variances and covariances are biased. This has a knock-on effect on the *SE*s of all effects (including the fixed effects). Estimation of the fixed effects is usually robust to violations of compound symmetry but, as with repeated measures ANOVA, biased *SE*s lead to inaccurate tests and interval estimates.

A number of factors will influence the seriousness of any violation. The number of measures at level 1 of the model is particularly important. If $m = 2$, then compound symmetry reduces to homogeneity of variance (because there is only one covariance). By including a dummy variable for the second measurement occasion at level 2 it would be possible to deal with differences in variance (as described above for level 1 effects). As m increases, the potential for serious violations of compound symmetry also rises. Including random slopes will sometimes deal with these violations, because the departures from compound symmetry may reflect individual differences in the effects of predictors. This is more likely for experimental designs in which the order effects are controlled by counterbalancing or by randomization. There is no guarantee that controlling for order effects will produce homogeneity of covariance, but it should make the assumption of equal covariances more plausible. Adding the order of measurement as a categorical predictor (e.g., using dummy or effect coding) with a random slope is also possible in these designs (*ibid*.).

If there are many measurement occasions (and order effects are uncontrolled) serious violations of compound symmetry are more likely. This is particularly true if the outcome being measured is one that is slow to change. One option is to model the correlations between measurement occasions using an *unstructured covariance matrix*. This is, in essence, the solution employed in MANOVA. It therefore involves estimating a form of multivariate multilevel model (see Hox, 2010). The multilevel approach to multivariate regression is of interest in its own right, being generally superior to MANOVA (e.g., being able to cope with missing outcome data). However, the present discussion focuses on the repeated measures case. In this kind of model the level 1 residual variance is not estimated at all.[18] Instead, dummy variables for each of the m measurement occasions are added at level 2 (assuming a two-level model). The variances and covariances between each dummy variable are thus added as random effects. The drawback of this approach is that m variances and $m(m-1)/2$ covariances are estimated. For four measurement occasions this would require ten parameters to be estimated (rather than the two estimated in the basic random intercept model). The model would normally also have four fixed effects: one for each time point.

These covariance structures, compound symmetry at one end and the unstructured covariance matrix at the other, mark the two most extreme patterns you would probably want to consider for a repeated measures model. If there are plenty of degrees of freedom in the model, the unstructured solution is usually a safe bet (though modeling so many random effects can lead to problems fitting the model). If emphasis is primarily on the fixed effects and compound symmetry is plausible (or if $m = 2$) then the basic covariance structure may suffice. Otherwise variance structures of intermediate complexity are worth exploring. Several approaches are discussed by Hox (2010). For instance, changes in variance over time can be captured by linear or polynomial trends.

One pattern of covariation is particularly important for repeated measures. If each measurement is influenced by values in the preceding measurement then *autocorrelation* is said to be present. Autocorrelation is very common when an outcome measure is relatively slow to change (e.g., many measures of health or growth). An unstructured covariance matrix can be constrained to model autocorrelation in several ways. In first order autocorrelation it is assumed that each measurement only influences outcomes at one lag (i.e., the measurement immediately after it). First order autocorrelation is very efficient because it requires only a couple of extra parameters. This is sometimes sufficient, and can be extended to second or third order autocorrelation if necessary. Fitting autocorrelated models is complicated by the possibility of having autocorrelated observations, autocorrelated residuals or both. Hox (2010) also describes the *Toeplitz* model in which each lag is modeled with a separate parameter. This is also quite efficient and can be further simplified by pooling autocorrelation parameters for longer lags (which tend to be very small). Although fitting these covariance structures is fiddly, several software packages have built-in options for some of the more common structures (e.g., SPSS and R). An alternative strategy, exemplified by MLwiN, is to support very flexible modeling by explicitly fitting or constraining parameters (lending itself to more customized approaches). If in doubt, the unstructured covariance matrix is a safe option. Its main drawback is that it restricts options for modeling additional random effects (but if the focus is on the fixed effects that should not matter).

Example 18.3 The models of the determinacy data in Example 18.2 assume a restrictive form of compound symmetry in which the variances of the repeated measures at level 2 (the four sentences) are equal and the covariances are zero:

$$\begin{bmatrix} \sigma_u^2 & & & \\ 0 & \sigma_u^2 & & \\ 0 & 0 & \sigma_u^2 & \\ 0 & 0 & 0 & \sigma_u^2 \end{bmatrix} = \begin{bmatrix} \sigma_u^2 \end{bmatrix}$$

This covariance matrix is parsimonious (but extremely implausible). A more plausible covariance structure is an unstructured covariance matrix. This requires ten free parameters:

$$\begin{bmatrix} \sigma_{u_1}^2 & & & \\ \sigma_{u_{12}} & \sigma_{u_2}^2 & & \\ \sigma_{u_{13}} & \sigma_{u_{23}} & \sigma_{u_3}^2 & \\ \sigma_{u_{14}} & \sigma_{u_{24}} & \sigma_{u_{34}} & \sigma_{u_4}^2 \end{bmatrix}$$

The first stage in fitting this model for the determinacy data is to fit the structure to a model with no predictors. This is accomplished by adding four dummy predictors (one for each of the four repeated measurements at level 1) at level 2. The only fixed effect is the constant. In a random intercept model the constant would be allowed to vary at both level 1 and level 2. In this (multivariate) repeated measures model the usual set-up is for the intercept not to vary at either level 1 or level 2. This is because all the variance should already be captured by the measurement occasion dummy predictors (the four sentences). If the set-up of the model seems peculiar, bear in mind that it is just a variant of the cell means model in ANOVA. The difference is that four dummy variables are used to estimate four variances at level 2 (rather than four means in the fixed part of the model).

Fitting such a model to the determinacy data produces an error message in some software (e.g., MLwiN: 'numerical error calculating likelihood'). The reason for the error is that (unusually) the two-level model set-up doesn't capture all the level 1 residual variance for these data. Although there are only four measurement occasions within descriptions, there are up to eight descriptions per participant (because the third level defined by description was not included in the model). Thus modeling the variances for each sentence does not exhaust the residual variation. Adding back the intermediate level is a possibility, but would be an unnecessary complication (because the estimated variance at that level is so close to zero). Adding a residual term at level 1 is sufficient to soak up the extra variation for the multiple descriptions.

Fitting an unstructured covariance matrix at level 2 and with the level 1 error term retained (and no predictors) produces the following estimates:

$$y_{ij} = b_{0,i} + u_{1,j}LINE1_{ij} + u_{2,j}LINE2_{ij} + u_{3,j}LINE3_{ij} + u_{4,j}LINE4_{ij}$$

$$b_{0,i} = 2.162\,(0.041) + e_{ij}$$

$$var\begin{bmatrix} u_{1,j} \\ u_{2,j} \\ u_{3,j} \\ u_{4,j} \end{bmatrix} = \begin{bmatrix} 0.150 & & & \\ 0.118 & 0.154 & & \\ 0.124 & 0.164 & 0.215 & \\ 0.124 & 0.194 & 0.306 & 0.570 \end{bmatrix}$$

$$var\left[e_{ij}\right] = [0.178]$$

$$RML - 2\ln(\ell) = 2952.2$$

The unconstrained covariance matrix at level 2 is not consistent with compound symmetry (let alone the more restrictive form of compound symmetry implied by the random intercept model in which all the covariances are zero). One indication of this is that variances and covariances increase from the first to last sentence. Another is the deviance of the model. Even without predictors, the deviance is far lower than the deviance of the models considered earlier (the best of which had RML deviance of over 3000). Formal tests are unnecessary for changes in deviance this substantial.

The present model has no predictors, so it would be reasonable at this stage to model the fixed effects of sentence and syllable length that previously had an impact on the reading times. To aid interpretation we will add fixed effects for each of the four lines and remove the intercept. This is a fairly standard ANOVA-style cell means model. The advantage of this – in a regression context – is that the intercept is zero and the parameters for lines one to four are the adjusted means (adjusting for any covariates in the model). The new model is:

$$Y_{ij} = b_{0,i} + b_{1,j}LINE1_{ij} + b_{2,j}LINE2_{ij} + b_{3,j}LINE3_{ij} + b_{4,j}LINE4_{ij} + 0.036\,(0.013)\left(LENGTH - \hat{\mu}_{LENGTH}\right)_{ij} + e_{ij}$$

$$b_{1,j} = 2.208\,(0.045) + u_{1,j}$$

$$b_{2,j} = 2.091\,(0.045) + u_{2,j}$$

$$b_{3,j} = 1.997\,(0.050) + u_{3,j}$$

$$b_{4,j} = 1.708\,(0.067) + u_{4,j}$$

$$var\begin{bmatrix} u_{1,j} \\ u_{2,j} \\ u_{3,j} \\ u_{4,j} \end{bmatrix} = \begin{bmatrix} 0.146 & & & \\ 0.119 & 0.150 & & \\ 0.129 & 0.150 & 0.192 & \\ 0.143 & 0.160 & 0.235 & 0.362 \end{bmatrix}$$

$$var\left[e_{ij}\right] = [0.177]$$

$$RML - 2\ln(\ell) = 2904.2$$

Adding just four parameters (one for each predictor minus one for the intercept that was removed) produces a substantial improvement in fit. As the models differ only in their fixed effects, a proper comparison requires FML estimation (which would confirm the large reduction in deviance observed here). Several of the variance and covariance terms have also changed substantially; missing out important predictors can give the appearance of extra variation elsewhere in the model.

Before adding additional predictors to the model it is worth simplifying the covariance structure. In a standard two-level repeated measures model this would be essential to test hypotheses about individual differences of the predictors (other than measurement occasion). Here there is a little more freedom because of the extra observations having multiple descriptions; the model has not exhausted the *df* available within participants. Although adding predictors has reduced variability at level 2, it still looks as though there is some kind of autocorrelation (as covariances and variances increase for later sentences). One reason for this may also be that indeterminacy (CLASH sentences) can only arise in lines two to four.

There are several covariance structures that could be explored. Some plausible options are considered here. One option fits separate variances for each repeated measure, but sets all covariances to zero. This is effectively an independent measures model that does not assume homogeneity of variance. It is sometimes termed a diagonal covariance structure because it takes the form of a diagonal matrix (see Key Concept 12.1). The other is a less restricted form of compound symmetry in which covariances are equal (but not necessarily zero) and where variances are also equal. These are parsimonious models that make strong assumptions (in contrast to the unstructured model already fitted).

The diagonal structure produces a covariance matrix at level 2 that looks like this:

$$\begin{bmatrix} 0.142 & & & \\ 0.000 & 0.144 & & \\ 0.000 & 0.000 & 0.192 & \\ 0.000 & 0.000 & 0.000 & 0.358 \end{bmatrix}$$

This structure is a much worse fit than the unconstrained matrix (RML deviance is 3128.0), but has only ten parameters relative to the 16 required by the unconstrained model ($\Delta G^2 = +211.8$, $\Delta\text{AIC} = +199.8$). The terrible fit of this model is unsurprising. Independence of measures is extremely unlikely in most repeated measures models. The compound symmetry model produces:

$$\begin{bmatrix} 0.211 & & & \\ 0.158 & 0.211 & & \\ 0.158 & 0.158 & 0.211 & \\ 0.158 & 0.158 & 0.158 & 0.211 \end{bmatrix}$$

This is a much better fit, but with RML deviance of 2969.7 and eight parameters it is still worse than the unconstrained matrix with its 16 parameters ($\Delta G^2 = +65.5$, $\Delta\text{AIC} = +49.5$). Of the three models considered so far, the unconstrained (unstructured) covariance matrix is preferred. Further structures could be explored if necessary (e.g., the Toeplitz structure or an autogressive model).

For this example, an alternative approach seems reasonable. In the unstructured covariance matrix model the variances and covariances tend to increase with measurement occasion. Treating them as a polynomial function of the sentence number may produce a more parsimonious model. These models fail to converge using the `nlme` package in R, but can be fitted by switching to the `lmer()` function from the `lme4` package.

The number of parameters, RML deviance and AIC (computed as RML deviance plus 2 × *df*) for the unstructured covariance matrix model, the linear random effect of sentence number and the quadratic random effect of sentence number are set out below. In addition, DIC is obtained for each model (using the `arm` package).

	df	*RML deviance*	*AIC*	*DIC*
Linear	9	2949.2	2967.2	2895.6
Quadratic	12	2909.0	<u>2933.0</u>	2856.7
Unstructured	16	<u>2904.2</u>	2936.2	<u>2852.4</u>

In short, fitting a covariance matrix that is a quadratic function of the sentence number provides a model that fits almost as well as the unstructured matrix (and has four fewer parameters). The model is more parsimonious than the unstructured covariance matrix model according to AIC and slightly worse by DIC. This model would be a good starting point to explore models with additional random effects. It is also plausible that the variances of the reading times should be greater for the first and last sentences (a pattern captured by both the unstructured and quadratic models).

18.5 Crossed versus nested random factors

A typical multilevel model assumes a nested data structure. A nested structure assumes that each observation (e.g., a child) is located within only one higher-level unit (e.g., a classroom), which may itself be nested within single unit at an even higher level (e.g., each classroom is located within just one school). The key characteristic of this kind of nesting is the one-to-one relationship between low- and high-level units (see Figure 18.1). A nested structure is not inevitable. Consider a model with school years nested within pupils, and with pupils nested within both primary schools and secondary schools. For this context, a nested structure arises only in the unlikely scenario that all primary schools feed into the same secondary school (see Goldstein, 1994; Rasbash and Goldstein, 1994; Hox, 2010). This form of *cross-classified* structure is more difficult to model than the conventional nested structure. If cross-classification is rare (perhaps only 1% or 2% of units at a given level) it may not be too dangerous to ignore the cross-classification. In some contexts the cross-classification is more extreme. Figure 18.6 illustrates a *fully crossed* repeated measures structure in which the same three items (I1 to I3) are presented to 20 participants (P1 to P20).

Using notation adapted from Rasbash and Goldstein (1994), a basic intercept-only cross-classified model can be represented, as:

$$y_{i(j_1 j_2)} = b_0 + u_{1,j_1} + u_{2,j_2} + e_{i(j_1 j_2)} \qquad \text{Equation 18.24}$$

At first glance this may look like a three-level model, but the subscripts j_1 and j_2 refer to cross-classified units at level 2 of a two-level model. The parameters u_{1,j_1} and u_{2,j_2} are deviations from b_0 for each type of classification and have an assumed normal distribution with mean

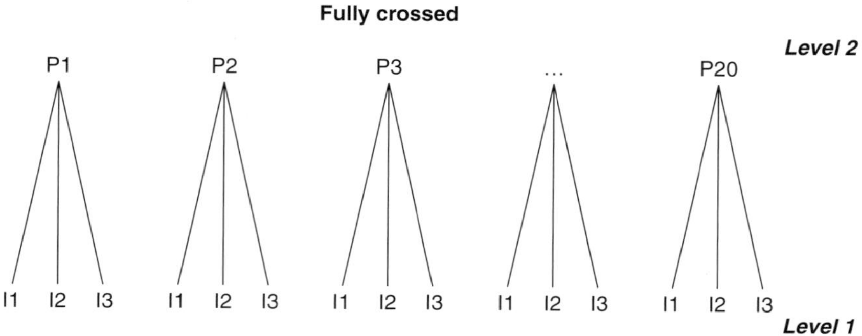

Figure 18.6 Multilevel structure for a fully crossed repeated measures design, with items ($n = 3$) crossed with participants ($n = 20$)

zero and variances $\sigma^2_{u_1}$ and $\sigma^2_{u_2}$. The total variance at level 2 is therefore $\sigma^2_{u_1} + \sigma^2_{u_2}$. To keep the level 2 variance estimates independent of each other, the covariance $\sigma_{u_1 u_2}$ is constrained to equal zero.

This model can be estimated via multilevel software by setting up a two-level model with level 1 units nested within one of the level 2 classifications (e.g., subscripted as j_1). A superordinate level is then added to the model with just one unit (for a constant). This level is not a true level of the model (and merely used to persuade the software to estimate $\sigma^2_{u_2}$). Accordingly, it is sometimes termed a 'dummy' level. n dummy variables are then added at level 1, one for each unit of the second classification (subscripted as j_2). These dummies would be set to one for each level 1 unit that belongs to that level 2 unit (e.g., each child attending a particular secondary school). No fixed effects are estimated for these n dummy variables. Instead random slopes are fitted to each of these dummy predictors at the dummy third level. The variances of these slopes are constrained to be equal and all covariances at the dummy level are constrained to be zero. In this manner, a single pooled variance is estimated across all the dummy variables representing the second level 2 classification (e.g., secondary school). The choice of which classification to act as a dummy level is arbitrary (though it is sensible to pick the classification with smaller n, thus limiting the number of dummies to be added). Estimation of cross-classified models is not possible in all software, but software such as MLwiN (that can constrain variances) and the R package *lme4* (Bates *et al.*, 2011) is capable of fitting them. The former use the step-by-step approach described above, while the latter allows the formula for a cross-classified model to be specified directly.

Data with a cross-classified structure are challenging to model, but there is an even more challenging case: that of designs with *fully crossed random factors*. These designs are ones where every unit is cross-classified among all higher-level units. This might seem an unusual situation, but is surprisingly common in experimental designs. Consider the examples mentioned in relation to the language-as-fixed-effect fallacy (see Box 18.1). In such designs it is common to use the same set of stimuli for all participants, and hence they are fully crossed rather than nested.

A good test of a fully crossed design is whether the stimulus and participant levels are interchangeable. If we collected one observation for each of 30 faces presented to 30 participants, we could model this as 30 observations (one for each face) at level 1, nested within 30 different people. On the other hand, we could also model it as 30 observations (one for each participant) at level 1, nested within 30 different faces at level 2. Which is the correct model? Neither. A model with fully crossed random factors is required (Baayen *et al.*, 2008; Baayen, 2008). In theory, this could be fitted using standard cross-classification methods (e.g., in MLwiN), but these are cumbersome to set up and run, and it is usually better to use specialized software such as the *lme4* package in R (Baayen *et al.*, 2008).

Baayen (2008) argues that using cross-classified multilevel models increases statistical power and should produce more accurate estimates of variance components than a nested design. In the simulations he reports, a conventional model (with stimuli nested within participants) slightly underestimates the participant variance and overestimates the level 1 residual variance. Earlier advocates of multilevel models for repeated measures data (e.g., Quené and van den Bergh, 2004) fitted models with nested structures for designs with fully crossed factors. Baayen (2008) suggests this is hardly ever appropriate. A nested structure with n participants at the highest level and m stimuli at a lower level implies that there are, in effect, $nm = N$ unique stimuli being modeled. This would be reasonable, according to Baayen, if each participant's experience of a stimulus (e.g., the word book) is as different from other participants' experiences of that stimulus as for two unrelated stimuli (e.g., book and waterfall). For linguistic stimuli this seems unreasonable.

Even so, the nested model may not be quite as restrictive as Baayen suggests.[19] Think about an autobiographical memory study of the kind reported by Wright (1998). Imagine that a researcher presented 30 adults with the same set of 30 cues: common nouns such as birthday, seaside, garden, breakfast and so on. The task is to recall a personal memory cued by that word and make some judgment based on it. The superficial structure here is identical to that of using 30 words in a psycholinguistic study, but it could be argued that two memories triggered by the same cue (e.g., birthday) in different people might be as different as two memories triggered by different cues (e.g., birthday and garden). If there is a golden rule in statistical modeling, it is that the correct model depends on subtle details of the research context (including the precise hypotheses you wish to investigate).

Example 18.4 Dunn *et al.* (2011) investigated the effects of female facial attractiveness on male voice pitch. Thirty male participants were presented with 32 female faces in a fully crossed design (the same 30 faces were used for each participant). The pitch (fundamental frequency in *Hz*) of spoken attractiveness ratings (on a one to nine scale) was measured for each response in one of two contexts (attractiveness as a short-term or long-term partner). In addition, baseline voice pitch was measured for each of the numbers (one to nine) spoken in a neutral context. The main research question is whether males change their voice pitch for attractive faces. Low male voice pitch is associated with testosterone levels, so male participants will perhaps decrease voice pitch to signal higher testosterone levels.

For the present example we'll focus on a random intercept model with attractiveness rating, baseline pitch and context as predictors. We'll contrast two different ways of modeling the data. The first is a three-level model with 32 faces nested within 30 participants. The second is a fully crossed model with 30 participants and 32 faces modeled at level 2. Alternative models are possible, but the focus here is on comparing the nested and fully crossed models. The nested model is:

$$pitch_{ij} = b_{0,ij} + 0.209\,(0.044)\, baseline_{ij} + 0.462\,(0.105)\, attractiveness_{ij} + 0.259\,(0.421)\, context_{ij}$$

$$b_{0,ij} = 89.185\,(5.574) + u_j + e_{ij}$$

$$var\left[u_j\right] = [170.15]$$

$$var\left[e_{ij}\right] = [84.94]$$

$$RML \quad -2\ln(\ell) = 14123$$

This model has considerable variation for both level 1 (faces) and level 2 (participants). The fixed effects of baseline pitch and attractiveness both have small standard errors in relation to their effects, but context looks to have little impact on the model (its standard error being larger than the estimate). The equivalent model fitted as a fully crossed structure is:

$$pitch_{ij} = b_{0,ij} + 0.206\,(0.044)\, baseline_{ij} + 0.455\,(0.112)\, attractiveness_{ij} + 0.260\,(0.420)\, context_{ij}$$

$$b_{0,ij} = 89.63\,(5.578) + u_{1,j} + u_{2,j} + e_{ij}$$

$$var\left[u_{1,j}\,(face)\right] = [0.45]$$

$$var\left[u_{2,j}\,(participant)\right] = [171.64]$$

$$\left[e_{ij}\right] = [84.50]$$

$$RML \quad -2\ln(\ell) = 14121$$

The deviance of the model (fitted with the default `lme()` estimation method) is now slightly lower ($\Delta G^2 = -2.0$) indicating a marginally improved fit. The parameter estimates are also very similar, but not identical. The AIC (provided by R) is 14135 for the crossed model and 14137 for the nested model. This marginally favors the crossed model (as does DIC, not reported here). This is interesting because, in theory, the fully crossed model is the correct model specification and the nested structure is inappropriate. Why are they so similar?

The chief distinction between the models (at least in terms of the R output) is the additional variance parameter estimated at level 2. In the crossed model both face and participant variances are at level 2 and the level 1 term is a residual term. The participant variance estimate is 171.64, slightly larger than the estimate of 170.15 for the nested model. Both are large relative to the level 1 residual (about 85 in both models). The face variance at level is, in relative terms, tiny. The intercept-only fully crossed model estimates are:

$$
\begin{aligned}
&pitch_{ij} = b_{0,ij} \\
&\quad b_{0,ij} = 114.95\,(2.97) + u_{1,j} + u_{2,j} + e_{ij} \\
&\quad var\left[u_{1,j}\,(face)\right] = [1.18] \\
&\quad var\left[u_{2,j}\,(participant)\right] = [261.55] \\
&\quad var\left[e_{ij}\right] = [85.02] \\
&RML \quad -2\ln(\ell) = 14151
\end{aligned}
$$

This suggests that about $1.18/(1.18 + 261.55 + 85.02) = .0034$ (0.34%) of the total proportion of variance is between faces and $261.55/(1.18 + 261.55 + 85.02) = .75$ (75%) between participants. The rest is residual (within face or within participant variation). This explains why the nested and crossed structures are so similar in their parameter estimates and fits. There is very little systematic variation between faces. Had there been substantial variation between faces this would almost certainly have had a bigger impact on the random effects and *SE*s for the fixed effects. Another reason to prefer the crossed model is that estimates and inferences from the nested model change dramatically if face is modeled as level 3 and participants at level 2 (and there is no *a priori* reason to prefer the nested structure with participants at level 3).

The `lmer()` function in R is powerful and flexible, but has a slightly different philosophy from other multilevel modeling packages (see Baayen *et al.*, 2008). The function does not report *p* values for tests of the fixed effects – just Wald-style *t* statistics. It and `lme()` also report *SE*s only for fixed effects, not for random effects. Attaching a *p* value to the *t* statistics, it could be argued, would encourage users to believe that the statistic really has a *t* distribution (or a *z* distribution in large samples). Unless the distribution of the statistic is fairly symmetrical it can take very large samples for the *t* approximation to become remotely accurate. Rather than provide *p* values with a 'health warning', the authors of the `lmer()` packages prefer not to report them at all. The variance components in particular are expected to have a highly skewed distribution and Wald-style tests will nearly always be pretty inaccurate – hence users are not provided with *SE*s to compute their own. On the other hand, `lme()` and `lmer()` do provide FML and RML deviance statistics as well as AIC and BIC statistics (defaulting to using *n* from the lowest level). Because of difficulty defining sample size in multilevel models, AIC tends to be preferred over BIC. AIC_C is also infrequently used (partly because multilevel sample sizes tend to be quite large). A version of DIC is available for `lmer()` via the `arm` package.

If it is necessary to obtain *p* values or (more reasonably) CIs for fixed effects it is possible to do so using MCMC sampling or via a parametric bootstrap. Plotting the density of the MCMC samples makes it possible to test the symmetry of the distribution – and get an idea of the adequacy of the method in each case. We will focus on interval estimates rather than *p* values (which are less useful). The most common approach in this case is to obtain Bayesian HPD intervals (estimates of the posterior probability of a parameter from the density of MCMC samples). Using 20,000 MCMC iterations, the HPD interval for the attractiveness effect in the fully crossed is [0.26, 0.66].

The other main alternative in `lmer()` is parametric bootstrapping. This first simulates data sets from a fitted model (conditional on both random and fixed effects). Statistics computed from the simulated samples can then be used to construct significance tests or CIs. A parametric bootstrap (with 1000 simulated samples) gives a 95% CI for the attractiveness effect of [0.25, 0.67]. A Wald CI from the fully crossed model is similar in magnitude: [0.23, 0.68]. This should not be too surprising. The fully crossed model is not too different from the nested model with participants at level 3 (by virtue of the small face variance). The nested model is for a balanced design with a fairly large sample size at level 1 – and is therefore close to a classical ANOVA design. Under these circumstances Wald-style tests should have acceptable performance.

18.6 Multilevel generalized linear models

Multilevel generalized linear models provide a versatile framework for repeated or correlated measures regression with discrete outcomes. This section provides a brief introduction to multilevel models for both dichotomous outcomes and for counts. A fuller treatment with examples using R can be found in Gelman and Hill (2007) and in the MLwiN manuals (Rasbash *et al.*, 2009; Browne, 2009). The focus here is on two-level repeated measures models (with repeated observations nested within higher-level units such as participants), though the logic of the approach encompasses other hierarchical data structures. Depending on available software, it is possible to extend the model to additional levels and to crossed factors.[20]

A single-level logistic regression assumes independence of observations. If observations are instead nested within units at a higher level of analysis, such as within participants in a repeated measures design, this assumption is violated. A multilevel model models accounts for the correlations between observations by explicitly modeling the variances and covariances. The starting point is a random intercept model such as that in Equation 18.16. This model is similar to the model of interest (but not fitted) in a conditional logistic regression, and reproduced here from Equation 17.52:

$$\ln\left(\frac{\hat{P}_{ij}}{1-\hat{P}_{ij}}\right) = b_{0,j} + b_1 x_{1,ij} + \ldots + b_q x_{q,ij}$$

The $b_{0,j}$ term is a random intercept. A crude approach in this situation is to model $b_{0,j}$ (the individual differences between participant mean outcomes) with a separate parameter for each participant. This is expensive in terms of parameters as well as being difficult when the data set is large (Agresti, 1996). The multilevel model solution is to treat the random effect as a probability distribution. In a repeated measures model with two levels, dichotomous observations at level 1 are modeled as a logistic regression in which the intercept is a normal, random variable at level 2:

$$b_{0,j} = b_0 + u_j \quad u_j \sim N\left(0, \sigma_u^2\right) \qquad \text{Equation 18.25}$$

Putting the two equations together gives:

$$\ln\left(\frac{\hat{P}_{ij}}{1-\hat{P}_{ij}}\right) = b_0 + b_1 x_{1,ij} + \ldots + b_q x_{q,ij} + u_j \quad u_j \sim N\left(0, \sigma_u^2\right) \qquad \text{Equation 18.26}$$

This differs from a multilevel normal model in that there is no e_{ij} error term at level 1. The only random variation being modeled is at level 2. The level 1 model is for a dichotomous outcome assumed to have a binomial distribution. The binomial distribution is modeled with a single free parameter (its mean $\hat{P}$). There is no level 1 variance to model (because all level 1 variance is a function of the mean).

In keeping with practice in single-level logistic regression models, the numeric value of the level 1 variance is fixed at $\pi^2/3$ (see Key Concept 17.1). This value is not interpretable on its own, but does act as a reference point for the level 2 variance. The estimated level 2 variance from the intercept-only model (one with a random intercept but no predictors) is $\hat{\sigma}_u^2$, and can be used to estimate an *ICC* for the logistic regression:

$$\hat{\rho}_I = \frac{\hat{\sigma}_u^2}{\hat{\sigma}_u^2 + \pi^2/3} \qquad \text{Equation 18.27}$$

This is not the only way to define the *ICC* (Snijders and Bosker, 1999), but is perhaps the most convenient (because it is a direct analogue of the method used for a two level normal model).[21] Keep in mind the usual concerns about interpreting proportion of variance explained measures in both multilevel and generalized linear models. Fixing the level 1 variance in this way also makes it difficult to compare coefficients between models with different random effects. Best practice is to focus on more meaningful quantities such as predictions on the odds or probability scale (Mroz and Zayats, 2008).

Adding predictors to the model at level 1 or level 2 allows a range of hypotheses to be tested. Level 1 predictors vary within level 2 units and therefore within participants in a repeated measures model. Level 2 predictors thus represent individual differences between participants. Individual differences need not be modeled only as fixed effects in a random-intercept model; random-slope models are also possible. The level 2 intercepts and slopes are typically assumed to have a normal distribution. Their interpretation is identical to that of random effects in a normal model, except that the random variation is on the logit scale. Obtaining the odds or predictive probabilities of the model is done in the same way as for a single-level logistic regression (i.e., by reversing the logistic transformation). For suggestions on exploring and plotting these models it is worth looking at a text such as Gelman and Hill (2007). Random slope models also typically model the covariances as well as variances of the random effects, and, in principle, it is possible to model complex variation at level 2 of the model.

The same strategy – modeling random intercepts or slopes as a normal probability distribution – can be applied to other generalized linear models including multinomial and ordered logistic regression, Poisson regression and negative binomial regression. Software varies greatly in the range of models that can be fitted and the estimation methods that are used. MLwiN can fit all of the models mentioned earlier, but is not able to estimate deviance for the models. This can make model comparison tricky and switching to MCMC estimation is often recommended (see Browne, 2009). The `lme4` package (Bates *et al.*, 2011) will fit multilevel generalized linear models with normal, binomial or log link functions (and hence multilevel logistic and Poisson regression). An R package specialized for generalized linear multilevel models, `MCMCglmm`, has also recently been developed and can fit a wider range of models – including multilevel ordered logistic regression and zero-inflated Poisson models (Hadfield, 2010). In theory, overdispersion due to correlations between observations should be resolved in multilevel generalized logistic and Poisson regression (see Skrondal and Rabe-Hesketh, 2007). However, overdispersion also arises from other factors, and there are reasons to model this overdispersion in some situations (Gelman and Hill, 2007).

Example 18.5 The surgical checklist data explored in Chapter 7 and Chapter 17 (e.g., Example 17.6) exhibited overdispersion. One possible cause is the repeated measures (pre and post checklist) for each hospital. A generalized multilevel model would allow us to model the dependency between cell counts in the same hospital. It also offers the potential to treat the eight hospitals as samples from a random population of hospitals. Such a model would be slightly controversial. It would treat the hospitals as level 2 observations and the counts within hospitals (alive and dead; before and after introducing the checklist) as observations at level 1. Many experts recommend against multilevel modeling when the number of level 2 units is this low. With only eight units, the variance at level 2 will probably be underestimated substantially and there may also be insufficient *df* to model random variation between units. Gelman and Hill (2007) take a slightly different line. Adopting a single-level model implicitly involves assuming that the random variation between hospitals is exactly zero.

This example re-analyzes the checklist data as a multilevel Poisson model. With so few units at level 2 it is important to proceed with caution (and it would be unwise to estimate random slopes). Estimates of fixed effects from the model should be fairly accurate, but variances, covariances and *SE*s will probably be underestimated.

Having decided to proceed with a multilevel model for the checklist data, there are two main options: multilevel logistic regression and multilevel Poisson regression. Of these, the Poisson model is easier to set up (as a data set) and is the model reported here. The model has two levels. Level 1 is composed of the cell counts defined by survival and time. These four counts are nested within the eight hospitals at level 2. This is a form of multilevel loglinear model, so a natural approach is to fit the 'saturated model' of time*survival as fixed effects.* Because hospital is modeled as a random variable this is not, in fact, a saturated model. The hospital random effect requires just one parameter to estimate, while time*survival requires three parameters. As there are 32 observations, the *df* of the model are not exhausted. The multilevel model therefore has additional freedom relative to the loglinear model. This makes it possible to model the income effect that was ignored in the earlier (single-level) loglinear analysis (because income was aliased with the hospital dummy variables in that model). The initial model has income*time*survival as fixed effects and hospital as the random effect at level 2.

The `glmer()` function in the `lme4` package can be used to fit the model. The model has deviance of 92.0 (AIC = 109.9, DIC = 91.9). Dropping the three-way interaction and running the model with all two-way interactions and main effects produces deviance of 92.0 (AIC = 108, DIC = 92). There is negligible improvement in fit with the three-way interaction in the model, so the simpler two-way model is preferred. A main effects only model is not a reasonable option. Although it has three fewer parameters, its deviance is 113.5 (AIC = 123.5, DIC = 113.5).

A slightly simpler model that also fits well can be obtained by dropping the income by pre interaction (but is not worth reporting separately). The model with all two-way interactions and all main effects is:

$$\ln(count_{ij}) = b_{0,ij} + 0.008\,(0.127)\,income_{ij} - 0.084\,(0.033)\,time_{ij} - 4.524\,(0.195)\,survival_{ij}$$

$$+ 0.037\,(0.046)\,income \times time_{ij} - 0.777\,(0.231)\,income \times survival_{ij} + 0.663\,(0.225)\,time \times survival_{ij}$$

$$b_{0,ij} = 6.178\,(0.090) + u_{0,j}$$

$$\left[u_{0,j}\,(hospital)\right] = [0.030]$$

$$-2\ln(\ell) = 92.0$$

Virtually identical parameter estimates are obtained with the same model in MLwiN (but deviance and AIC are not provided). MLwiN can also fit a negative binomial multilevel model, but not (as of writing) via MCMC estimation. For these data the negative binomial model has similar parameter estimates with only marginally larger standard errors.

As the main focus is still on the *time* × *survival* effect, it is worth obtaining a CI for this term. The model fit decreases if it is dropped (Wald $z = 2.95$ and $\Delta AIC = 7.0$). The Wald CI is easy to calculate and gives a 95% CI of the *time* × *survival* interaction (on the log scale) as $0.663 \pm 1.96 \times 0.225$ or [0.221, 1.104]. A more accurate estimate is possible from HPD intervals or a parametric bootstrap. For instance, the latter gives [0.248, 1.145]. The corresponding 95% CI for the rate ratio of the difference in pre-checklist and post-checklist survival (obtained using the function e^x) is [1.28, 3.14]. This suggests that the rate of survival after surgery is between 1.3 and 3.3 times higher after the checklist was introduced. This estimate should be treated with caution, but it is reassuring that the various different models produce similar estimates (and are not too different from the estimates in previous examples).

* See *Online Supplement 5: Loglinear models.*

18.7 R code for Chapter 18

18.7.1 Random intercept multilevel models (Example 18.1)

The random intercept models fitted in Example 18.1 can be replicated using either the `lme()` or the `lmer()` functions. The analysis begins by reading in the determinacy data, creating the transformed reading time outcome (by adding a constant and using a logarithmic transformation) and using `lme()` to fit the null model. Summary statistics for the predictors are also obtained at this stage. The data set is already structured in long form required by most multilevel software.

```
determ <- read.csv('determ.csv')
summary(determ)

LTIME <- log(determ$TIME + 0.5)

library(nlme)
det.null <- lme(LTIME ~ 1, random = ~1|PARTS, data=determ,
  method = 'ML')
summary(det.null)
```

The `lme()` function uses formulas in roughly the same way as the familiar `lm()` function, except that there is a separate formula for the fixed and random part of the model. For the random part, the intercept is nested within the participants and this is specified with the vertical bar |. This is, therefore, a two-level random intercept model with no predictors. The variances at level 1 and level 2 are not reported directly, though the *SD*s are reported as 0.4062447and 0.4999353. Squaring these gives the variances 0.1650348 and 0.2499353. Calculating the *ICC* from the *SD*s at level 1 and level 2 is (trivially):

```
0.4062447^2/(0.4062447^2 + 0.4999353^2)
```

You can also get the variances from the `VarCorr()` covariance matrix function:

```
VarCorr(det.null)
```

The default fitting method is RML, and it was necessary to specify `method = 'ML'` in the command (to match Example 18.1). The loglikelihood is −1693.8. Multiplied by −2, this is equivalent to the deviance of 3387.6 reported in the example. As fitting is iterative, different software sometimes produces slightly different results, but you should not expect large discrepancies between software.

Adding predictors to the fixed part is no different to other linear models in R. The first model adds the dummy predictors for the last three lines of the description and syllable length. The second model uses the centered syllable length.

```
det.ri1 <- lme(LTIME ~ LINE2 + LINE3 + LINE4 + LENGTH, random
  = ~1|PARTS, data=determ, method = 'ML')

det.ri2 <- lme(LTIME ~ LINE2 + LINE3 + LINE4 + scale(LENGTH,
  scale=FALSE), random = ~1|PARTS, data=determ, method = 'ML')
```

The model could also be fitted by designating the categorical predictor (LINE) as a factor (with the default contrasts being dummy coded):

```
lme(LTIME ~ factor(LINE) + LENGTH, random = ~1| PARTS,
  data=determ, method = 'ML')
```

This method has the advantage that `anova()` can be used to produce ANOVA-style output rather than regression output. It is possible to obtain the variances from the call:

```
VarCorr(det.ri2)
```

Plotting residuals at level 1 is straightforward, as this is the default for the `qqnorm()` method with `lme()` objects and also for `residuals()`. The following calls produce the level 1 residuals for the response (outcome) and standardized residuals (by dividing them by the residual *SD*).

```
residuals(det.ri2, type='response', level = 1)
residuals(det.ri2, type='pearson', level = 1)
```

The raw response at level 1 is the default, but standardized residuals may be more useful for a normal probability plot:

```
qqnorm(residuals(det.ri2, type='pearson', level = 1))
```

The level 2 residuals can be obtained in several ways. Empirical Bayes residuals are obtained from the random effects via the `ranef()` function:

```
ranef(det.ri2)
```

These are on the scale of the outcome variable. To standardize them it is necessary to divide by the estimated *SD* of the level 2 intercept. It is then trivial to get the normal probability plot:

```
l2.resids <- ranef(det.ri2)
l2.sd <- as.numeric(VarCorr(det.ri2)[3])
l2.resids.std <- l2.resids[[1]] / l2.sd
qqnorm(l2.resids.std)
```

Use `anova()` to compare the models:

```
anova(det.null, det.ri2)
```

Here BIC for the multilevel model is calculated using the total number of observations (2164) rather than the number of participants (88). You can check this by using the `AIC()` function to get BIC:

```
AIC(ri.fit2, k=log(2164))
AIC(ri.fit2, k=log(88))
```

In addition, both `AIC()` and `extractAIC()` use the same method for these models. These outputs would change if the model was fitted using RML (the default) rather than FML.

```
lme(LTIME ~ factor(LINE) + scale(LENGTH, scale=FALSE), random
  = ~1|PARTS, data=determ, method = 'REML')

det.ri.rml <- lme(LTIME ~ factor(LINE) + scale(LENGTH,
  scale=FALSE), random = ~1|PARTS, data=determ)
summary(det.ri.rml)
```

As with linear models, factors and ordered factors in multilevel models have default contrasts (dummy coded for unordered factors and polynomial for ordered factors). A model can be fitted using effect coding or polynomial contrasts if desired:

```
options(contrasts=c('contr.sum','contr.poly'))

lme(LTIME ~ factor(LINE) + scale(LENGTH, scale=FALSE), random
  = ~ 1|PARTS, data=determ, method = 'ML')

lme(LTIME ~ ordered(LINE) + scale(LENGTH, scale=FALSE), random
  = ~ 1|PARTS, data=determ, method = 'ML')
```

Fitting a three-level model is possible by adjusting the specification of the random part of the model. The null model with a third level is:

```
ri3.fit <- lme(LTIME ~ 1, random = ~ 1|PARTS/DESC,
  data=determ, method = 'ML')

summary (ri3.fit)
```

The term $\sim$ `1|PARTS/DESC` tells R to fit a random intercept for descriptions nested within participants. This formula style generalizes to additional levels.

For models fitted by `lme()` it is not possible to constrain variances, but contrasts are available via `fit.contrast()` or `estimable()` from the `gmodels` package. These functions also work for models fitted with `lm()`, `glm()` or `lmer()`. Note that the p values and CIs for the fixed effects in a multilevel model are not always exact. Balanced repeated measures ANOVA models fitted this way will, however, produce exact tests. Balanced ANOVA designs with appropriate covariance structures and large samples should produce at least adequate tests of fixed effects. An example was given of how to use `estimable()` in Chapter 16. A contrast of a single factor can be run via `fit.contrast()`, though it is necessary to ensure that the factor can be referred to directly by name (done here by directly coding the LINE variable as a factor in the `determ` data frame). This example compares the average reading times of the last three sentences with the first sentence.

```
determ$LINE <- factor(determ$LINE)

det.ri.fact <- lme(LTIME ~ LINE + scale(LENGTH, scale=FALSE),
  random = ~1|PARTS, data=determ)

library(gmodels)
fit.contrast(det.ri.fact, 'LINE', c(-1,1/3,1/3,1/3),
  conf.int=0.95)
```

This produces a t statistic, p value and 95% CI that are of debatable accuracy. Rerunning the model with a MANOVA-style unstructured covariance matrix prior to fitting the contrast should produce fairly accurate tests that don't assume sphericity. A more cautious approach would involve a parametric bootstrap or HPD intervals. Here the t statistic is sufficiently large that more accurate approaches are probably unnecessary.

These models can also be fitted in `lme4`. The formula for the random effects now follows a slightly different format. This simple example fits a two-level null model. In addition, if you are switching between `lme()` and `lmer()` it makes sense to detach the package you are not using.[22]

```
detach(package:nlme)

install.packages('lme4')
library(lme4)

lmer(LTIME ~ 1 + (1|PARTS), data=determ, REML=FALSE)
detach(package:lme4)
```

To fit a two-level random intercept model with the same predictors as before, the fixed effects need to be changed. One important difference is that `lmer()` does not assume that random factors are nested. It may therefore fit a non-nested model in some situations (depending on how the raw data are coded).

18.7.2 Random slope models (Example 18.2)

Example 18.2 starts by adding an additional predictor indicating a 'clash' sentence. The impact of this can be tested by using `drop1()`, provided that FML estimation (and not RML) is specified.

This function works in the usual way, but only drops the highest-order fixed effects one at a time.

```
library(nlme)

drop1(lme(LTIME ~ factor(LINE) + scale(LENGTH, scale=FALSE) +
  CLASH, random = ~1|PARTS, data=determ, method = 'ML'), test
  = 'Chisq')
```

This gives the likelihood ratio test as well as the AIC of the models created by dropping each of the fixed effects in turn.

The rest of the example uses RML estimation. Fitting the same model with this estimation method gives slightly different results.

```
clash.ri <- lme(LTIME ~ LINE2 + LINE3 + LINE4 + scale(LENGTH,
  scale=FALSE) + CLASH, random = ~1|PARTS, data=determ)

summary(clash.ri)
```

Fitting a random slope model, with the effect of clash sentences allowed to vary between participants, is now possible.

```
clash.rs <- lme(LTIME ~ LINE2 + LINE3 + LINE4 + scale(LENGTH,
  scale=FALSE) + CLASH, random = ~ CLASH|PARTS, data=determ)

summary(clash.rs)

VarCorr(clash.rs)
```

The formula here adds random effects to the left of |PARTS indicating that both the implied intercept and the clash effect are free to vary between participants in the model. The covariance is not reported directly. The correlation between intercept and clash variances of .775 is reported instead. This is equivalent to the covariance of 0.05 reported in Example 18.2. As a correlation is a standardized covariance, this can be checked by reversing the standardization (multiplying the correlation by the product of the *SD* estimate for the intercept and CLASH):

```
.775 * (0.3954614 * 0.1628789)
```

To compare the two multilevel models (both fitted using the same estimation method – in this case RML) use `anova()`.

```
anova(clash.ri, clash.rs)
```

Owing to boundary effects, this test is slightly conservative (though this does not matter here). An interesting thing to do at this point is to plot the random slopes. This could be done in several ways (including plotting simulated output from the model). A simpler approach is to plot separate regression lines for each participant. This kind of plot can be more persuasive than more sophisticated approaches (e.g., because it is easier to explain to non-experts). Figure 18.5 uses the `lattice` package to plot separate regression lines for each participant. This package should already be loaded (as it is usually installed with R and loaded as a dependency of `nlme`). The plot itself uses the `xyplot()` function, though a data frame with the first 20 participants is extracted first:

```
det20 <- subset(determ, PARTS<21)

xyplot(log(TIME+0.5) ~ CLASH | PARTS, det20, type =
  c('g','p','r'), index = function(x,y) coef(lm(y ~ x))[1],
  ylab = 'Log(reading time)', xlab = 'CLASH', aspect = 'xy',
  xlim=c(-.54,1.54))
```

The `lattice` plot functions are complex and cannot be covered in detail here (but see `?xyplot`). The key component is the formula `log(TIME+0.5) ~ CLASH | PARTS` indicating the outcome variable and the effect of interest. The vertical bar specifies the units of analysis for which the effect is plotted (here participants). The `index` argument is not required but allows you to order the plots in different ways. Here the order is determined by the intercept of the regression line. It therefore gives a rough idea of whether the slope co-varies with the intercept (e.g., if an increasing or decreasing trend is present). Testing the variance of the CLASH effect (without the covariance) is trickier because `lme()` doesn't support variance constraints. One solution is to fit a diagonal covariance matrix at level 2 (so the covariance is zero). This approach is described in the next section.

CWC centering involves calculating the means of the level 2 units (the participants) for the predictor being centered (CLASH). This can be done using the `aggregate()` function:

```
aggregate(determ$CLASH, by = list(parts = determ$PARTS), FUN =
  mean)
```

The above command takes a vector and applies a function to it according to values specified in a list. Here the vector is the clash predictor, the function is the mean and the list has one element containing the participant identifiers. To create a CWC predictor also requires the `merge()` function (though first the names need to be changed from the defaults).

```
clash.part.means <- aggregate(determ$CLASH, by = list(PARTS =
  determ$PARTS), FUN = mean)

names(clash.part.means) <- c('PARTS', 'clash.mean')

determ <- merge(determ, clash.part.means, by = 'PARTS')
```

The `merge()` function takes a vector of 88 average values (one for each participant) and merges it into the `determ` data frame (which has 2164 values). It therefore needs to assign each participant average to each participant multiple times. The final step is to add in a vector of CWC clash values to the data frame:

```
determ$clash.cwc <- determ$CLASH - determ$clash.mean
```

Fitting the CWC version of the model for the clash effect is now possible:

```
clash.rs.cwc <- lme(LTIME ~ LINE2 + LINE3 + LINE4 +
  scale(LENGTH, scale=FALSE) + clash.cwc, random= ~
  clash.cwc|PARTS, data=determ)

summary(clash.rs.cwc)
```

18.7.3 Modeling covariance structures (Example 18.3)

Fitting an unstructured covariance structure for the four repeated measures (sentences) of the determinacy data set is relatively simple in *nlme.* The dummy variables for the four sentences can be specified in the random part of the formula as a factor with no intercept:

```
null.unstruc <- lme(LTIME ~ 1, random = ~ 0 +
  factor(LINE)|PARTS, data=determ)

summary(null.unstruc)
```

Alternatively, they can be specified directly. In each case the model is similar to an ANOVA cell means model (if a cell means model was fitted only in the random part):

```
lme(LTIME ~ 1, random = ~ 0 + LINE1 + LINE2 + LINE3 + LINE4 |
  PARTS, data=determ)
```

To fit the model with additional predictors (in this case a cell means model for the fixed effect of sentence and the centered length predictor):

```
det.unstruc <- lme(LTIME ~ 0 + factor(LINE) + scale(LENGTH,
  scale = FALSE), random = ~ 0 + factor(LINE)|PARTS,
  data=determ)

summary(det.unstruc)
```

The above command involves describing the covariance structure directly. It is also possible to use the built-in capabilities of the `nlme` package to fit a wider variety of structures. To do this requires using what, in `nlme`, are called `pdClasses` (difference classes of a positive definite covariance matrix). The unstructured (unconstrained) covariance structure corresponds to the `pdSymm` class and is fitted with the following command:

```
lme(LTIME ~ 0 + factor(LINE) + scale(LENGTH, scale = FALSE),
  random=list(PARTS=pdSymm(form= ~ 0 + factor(LINE))),
  data=determ)
```

This mimics the cell means style of random effects fitted earlier, but the same overall model (with a regression parameterization of the random effects) is fitted by:

```
lme(LTIME ~ 0 + factor(LINE) + scale(LENGTH, scale = FALSE),
  random=list(PARTS=pdSymm(form= ~ factor(LINE))),
  data=determ)
```

The advantage of the cell means-style model is that the variance estimates are easier to interpret. It is possible to define new classes or fit from the existing set that can be reviewed with `?pdClasses` to fit other structures. For instance, the diagonal and compound symmetry covariance structures are fitted in the following way:

```
det.diag <- lme(LTIME ~ 0 + factor(LINE) + scale(LENGTH, scale
  = FALSE), random=list(PARTS=pdDiag(form= ~ 0 +
  factor(LINE))), data=determ)

det.cs <- lme(LTIME ~ 0 + factor(LINE) + scale(LENGTH, scale =
  FALSE), random=list(PARTS=pdCompSymm(form= ~ 0 +
  factor(LINE))), data=determ)

anova(det.unstruc, det.diag, det.cs)
```

It is also possible to fit an autoregressive correlation structure using the `correlation` argument (in addition to or instead of a covariance structure from `pdClasses`). A full discussion of autocorrelation in `nmle` is not possible in the space available here. For the determinacy data, models with autocorrelation don't really improve on the unstructured model fitted earlier. As these models take some time to fit it may be worth using the `update()` function to modify an existing model rather than start from scratch. Either of the following commands can be used to fit an AR(1) model with autocorrelated measures at lag 1:

```
summary(update(det.cs, correlation=corAR1()))

summary(update(det.cs, correlation=corARMA(p = 1, q = 0)))
```

A model with autocorrelated residuals at lag 1 is fitted as:

```
summary(update(det.cs, correlation=corARMA(p = 0, q = 1)))
```

The parameters `p` and `q` are the lags for observations and residuals respectively.

The option to specify the random part as a list in `nlme` is ideal for some complex models. A basic demonstration is for fitting a two-way mixed ANOVA model (i.e., a model with one independent measures factor and one repeated measures factor). The standard ANOVA approach assumes multisample sphericity (and the usual corrections are problematic for unbalanced designs). A neat solution is to run the ANOVA with a diagonal covariance matrix for the independent measures factor and an unstructured covariance matrix for the repeated measures factor. This example uses the pride data from Example 16.3.

```
pride.long <- read.csv('pride_long.csv')

pride.new <- lme(accuracy ~ emotion*condition, random =
  list(participant = pdDiag(form = ~ 0 + factor(condition)),
  participant = ~ 0 + factor(emotion)), data=pride.long)

anova(pride.new)
VarCorr(pride.new)
```

The test statistics are similar to those obtained with the standard ANOVA approach. This is not unexpected, as sphericity appeared to hold for those data, although the homogeneity of variance assumption may be untenable (explaining the slightly different results obtained here).

Some of the more complex models have difficulty converging if fitted with `lme()`. Fitting a linear or quadratic random effect of sentence number is possible in `nlme`, but faster and easier with `lme4`. The following commands refit the baseline unstructured covariance matrix model fitted earlier, and compare it to the models with linear or quadratic random effects of sentence number (LINE). This requires that LINE is recoded as numeric (given that a previous example coded it as a factor). The model reports both FML and RML deviance, but computes AIC and BIC based on the estimation method used to fit the model – in this case RML (appropriate because the models only differ in terms of random effects).

```
detach(package:nlme)
library(lme4)

determ$LINE <- as.vector(determ$LINE, mode='numeric')

det.base <- lmer(LTIME ~ 0 + factor(LINE) + scale(LENGTH,
  scale = FALSE) + (0 + factor(LINE)|PARTS), determ)
det.base

det.lin <- lmer(LTIME ~ 0 + factor(LINE) + scale(LENGTH, scale
  = FALSE) + (poly(LINE, degree = 1, raw = TRUE)|PARTS),
  determ)
det.lin

det.quad <- lmer(LTIME ~ 0 + factor(LINE) + scale(LENGTH,
  scale = FALSE) + (poly(LINE, degree = 2, raw= TRUE)|PARTS),
  determ)
det.quad
```

There is a trade-off here between the large range of structures that can be fitted using `lme()` and the speed and superior convergence of `lmer()`.

For models fitted in `lme4` it is possible to obtain DIC via the `arm` package. This can be done using `extractDIC()` or `display()`. The latter is an alternative to summary 'clean printout' of `lm()`, `glm()` and `lmer()` models. In addition to including DIC for multilevel models, it gives simple, uncluttered output (e.g., rounding to one or two decimal places).

```
install.packages('arm')
library(arm)

display(det.base) ; display(det.lin) ; display(det.quad)

detach(package:arm) ; detach(package:lme4)
```

18.7.4 Fully crossed versus nested models (Example 18.4)

Use `lme()` to fit a nested model to the voice pitch data in Example 18.4. The `lmer()` function would fit a fully crossed model because of the way that the participant, face and context identifier

(ID) variables are coded. To understand why, read the data into R and take a look at the coding scheme:

```
vp.data <- csv('pitch.csv')
vp.data
```

Each face is given a unique number from one to 32 and the same ID numbers reoccur for each participant (one to 30). To get `lmer()` to treat this as a nested structure, different face ID numbers would be required for each participant. On the other hand, `lme()` would treat either coding scheme as if it was from a nested design:

```
library(nlme)

pitch.lme <- lme(pitch ~ attract + base + Context, random = ~
  1|Participant, data=vp.data)

summary(pitch.lme)
```

For the rest of the example it will help to detach the `nlme` package before refitting a fully crossed model with `lmer()`.

```
detach(package:nlme)
library(lme4)
library(arm)

pitch.cross <- lmer(pitch ~ (1| Face) + (1|Participant) +
  attract + base + Context, data = vp.data)

summary(pitch.cross)
```

To show that the difference in models is due to the way the data are coded, recode the face ID variable so that each participant has unique numbers. A crude 'trick' for this is to use the participant ID to generate a new face ID and refit the model using this variable:

```
face.nested <- vp.data$Participant * 100 + vp.data$Face

pitch.nest <- lmer(pitch ~ (1| face.nested) + (1|Participant)
  + attract + base + Context, data = vp.data)

display(pitch.nest)
```

The parameter estimates of the two 'nested' models are almost identical. It is now possible to directly compare the crossed and nested models (which requires that both are fitted with the same function).

```
anova(pitch.nest, pitch.cross)
```

To calculate the proportion of variance explained by face and participant variance requires fitting an intercept-only fully crossed model. This model and the percentage of variance accounted for by each classification are reported by these calls:

```
cross.null <- lmer(pitch ~ (1| Face) + (1|Participant),
  data=vp.data)

display(cross.null)
VarCorr(cross.null)

1.18 /(1.18 + 261.5483 + 85.0212) * 100
261.5483/(1.18 + 261.5483 + 85.0212) * 100
```

To calculate HPD intervals, the first step is to obtain the MCMC samples for the model with the predictors of interest. A density plot gives an indication of the approximate symmetry (or lack thereof) for the parameters. In this instance, the symmetry of the fixed effects in the density plot is good (and they look reasonably close to normal).

```
cross.mcmc <- mcmcsamp(pitch.cross, n=10000)
densityplot(cross.mcmc, plot.points=FALSE)
```

Depending on the complexity of the model and the version of `lme4` that you are using, it may not be possible to get HPD intervals from models fitted via `lme()`. A safer alternative (within R) is to fit the model using the `MCMCglmm` package (Hadfeld, 2010). The formulas have a slightly different syntax from those of earlier regression functions (but one that is relatively intuitive for simple models such as these). The MCMC samples may take some time to collect, and the MCMC estimates will be influenced by Monte Carlo sampling error. A crude check is obtained by rerunning everything to see if the HPD intervals change substantially (and if so the number of iterations may need to be increased from the default of `nitt=13000`). The `pitch.cross` model from above is refitted below using `MCMCglmm()`.

```
install.packages('MCMCglmm')
library(MCMCglmm)

n.sims <- 20000
mcmc.mod <- MCMCglmm(fixed= pitch ~ Context + attract + base,
  random= ~ Participant + Face, data=vp.data, nitt=n.sims)
```

This package also provides MCMC diagnostics. These include density plots of the MCMC samples and an MCMC trace plot. The latter shows how the MCMC estimates for an effect changes over iterations (e.g., see Browne, 2009). A healthy plot should be have a thick black central band and have no discernable pattern (suggesting estimates that have converged and no autocorrelation in the MCMC simulations).

```
plot(mcmc.mod$Sol)
plot(mcmc.mod$VCV)
```

With 20,000 iterations the fixed effect solutions in `mcmc.mod$Sol` have fairly healthy trace plots and fairly symmetrical density estimates. The variances and covariances in `mcmc.mod$VCV` show a more mixed pattern, with the residual variance looking okay, the participant variance density estimates slightly skewed and the face variance showing a clear boundary effect (and being poorly estimated). With further iterations the MCMC estimates of the participant variance could be improved, but the present model is adequate to support inferences about the fixed effects.

These can be obtained from the `summary()` function. This will return HPD intervals, DIC and MCMC estimates of p values.

```
summary(mcmc.mod)
```

In general, the parameter estimates from `lmer()` and `MCMCglmm()` should be similar. Some statistics (e.g., DIC) may differ because of the estimation methods used by the approaches or because of Monte Carlo sampling error.

At present, the best available alternative with `lme()` is probably parametric bootstrapping. This makes use of the `lme4` version of the `simulate()` function. This is a general R function (implemented for many types of model object). It generates simulated data sets from a fitted model. Because the `mer` method conditions on both random and fixed parts of the fitted model, it should take into account concerns about boundary effects or the appropriate residual *df*. On the other hand, the approach is fairly novel and may be problematic in some cases. Here it produces similar results to the HPD intervals. The procedure works by first defining a function to simulate a sample from a fitted model and extract the statistics of interest. The `replicate()` function can then be used to obtain as many simulations as are required. The `quantile()` function is then used to obtain interval estimates from the bootstrap samples.

```
pb.sim <- function(model) {
  sim <- simulate(model)
  fixef(refit(model, sim))
}

n.sims <- 1000
sims.out <- replicate(n.sims, pb.sim(pitch.cross))

quantile(sims.out[2,], c(0.025, 0.975))
```

The quantiles are computed for `sims.out[2,]` because this is the first predictor defined in the model (so `sims.out[1,]` would be the intercept). As with any simulation method, the number of simulations can be increased to give more precise results. All the methods reviewed here (HPD intervals, parametric bootstrap or Wald CIs) give similar results for the attractiveness effect. The healthy MCMC diagnostics suggest that this will be true of most of the other effects (but not the face variance and perhaps not the participant variance).

18.7.5 Fitting multilevel generalized linear models (Example 18.5)

It is only possible provide a brief sketch of R functions for multilevel generalized linear models. This example focuses mainly on `glmer()` from `lme4`. The `MCMCglmm` package has a wider range of capabilities (that include multilevel zero-inflated Poisson and multilevel ordered regression models).

The following R code fits a Poisson model for the surgical checklist data, with a random intercept that varies between hospitals, and income, time (pre or post checklist) and survival as predictors. A three-way model is estimated first and then and compared to a model with only two-way or lower effects and to a main effects only model:

```
checklist.tab <- read.csv('checklist_tab.csv')
library(lme4) ; library(arm)
```

```
mlm.3way <- glmer(count ~ income*post*survival + (1|hospital),
  data=checklist.tab, family = poisson)

mlm.2way <- glmer(count ~ (income + post + survival)^2 +
  (1|hospital), data=checklist.tab, family = poisson)

mlm.me <- glmer(count ~ income + post + survival +
  (1|hospital), data=checklist.tab, family = poisson)
```

The model with all two-way and main effects seems to fit best:

```
anova(mlm.3way, mlm.2way, mlm.me)

display(mlm.3way)
display(mlm.2way)
display(mlm.me)
```

Note that the level 1 *SD* (and variance) is fixed at one for each of these models. The choice of constant influences the scale of the coefficients in the model – so care must be taken when comparing models estimated in different ways or with different random effects.

The coefficient for the time × survival interaction can be used to construct a Wald CI on the count scale:

```
lb <- fixef(mlm.2way)[7] - 1.96 * 0.225211
ub <- fixef(mlm.2way)[7] + 1.96 * 0.225211

c(exp(lb), exp(ub))
```

A sensible check is to obtain a CI from a parametric bootstrap or HPD interval. A bootstrap CI will take some time to run, but can be obtained from:

```
n.sims <- 1000
sim.pb <- replicate(n.sims, pb.sim(mlm.2way))

exp(quantile(sim.pb[7,], c(.025, .975)))
```

For additional options it is worth exploring the `MCMCglmm` package (Hadfield, 2010). For instance, the following R code will (almost) replicate the two-way Poisson model from above:

```
library(MCMCglmm)
n.sims <- 75000

checklist.mcmc <- MCMCglmm(count ~ (income+post+survival)^2,
  random= ~ hospital, data=checklist.tab, family = 'poisson',
  nitt=n.sims)

summary(checklist.mcmc)
```

Fitting a model by MCMC estimation may take some time (though the 75,000 iterations for this model can be fitted quite quickly). `MCMCglmm()` generates regular updates on its progress and reports the acceptance ratio in each update. The MCMC algorithm that it uses (Metropolis-Hastings) proposes new estimates from some distribution at random and then checks them to see if they are plausible. The proportion of plausible estimates is the acceptance ratio. This should be neither too high nor too low. Too high and it will be searching the parameter space too erratically to produce good estimates. Too low and it may not be exploring very much of the parameter space. Values in the range of 0.2 or 0.3 are probably close to ideal (with values close to zero or one problematic).

The key difference between this model and that estimated by `lmer()` is that an additional variance – a sort of overdispersion parameter – is fitted at level 1 (the patient level). In contrast, the level 1 variance for the `mlm.2way` model is a constant. This parameter is barely different from zero and thus the two models are very similar in their estimates of the fixed effects (and inferences on them). It would be possible to add a similar parameter to the `glmer()` model, though it is not necessary here.

18.7.6 R packages

Bates, D. M., Maechler, M., and Bolker, B. M. (2011). *lme4*: Linear Mixed-effects Models using S4 Classes. R package version 0.999375–39.

Gelman, A., Su, Y.-S., Yajima, M., Hill, J., Grazia Pittau, M., Kerman, J., and Zheng, T. (2011) *arm*: Data Analysis using Regression and Multilevel/Hierarchical Models. R package version 1.4–07.

Hadfield, J. (2010) MCMC Methods for Multi-Response Generalized Linear Mixed Models: The MCMCglmm R Package. *Journal of Statistical Software*, 33, 1–22.

Pinheiro, J., Bates, D. M., DebRoy, S., Sarkar, D., and the R Core team (2009) *nlme*: Linear and Nonlinear Mixed Effects Models. R package version 3.1–96.

Sarkar, D. (2008) *Lattice*: Multivariate Data Visualization with R. New York: Springer.

Warnes, G. R., *et al.* (2009) *gmodels*: Various R Programming Tools for Model Fitting. R package version 2.15.0.

18.8 Notes on SPSS syntax for Chapter 18

18.8.1 Multilevel models

The `MIXED` command in SPSS implements linear mixed models for normal responses and is set up to model several types of covariance structure. A fuller introduction can be found in Field (2009), and only a quick sketch is provided here. A major limitation is the type of response distribution modeled (continuous normal only). The range of models fitted is comparable to the `lme()` function in R.

The following example uses the pride data from Example 16.3. To do the analysis via `MIXED` it is necessary to convert the broad form data file to long form. This is possible using <Restructure . . . > from the <Data> menu. This invokes the `VARSTOCASES` command (shown here). The `MIXED` command is used to analyze the data.

SPSS data file: `pride_rm.sav`

```
VARSTOCASES
  /ID=id
  /MAKE accuracy FROM pride happiness surprise
  /INDEX=Index1(3)
  /KEEP=condition
  /NULL=KEEP.
```

```
MIXED accuracy BY condition Index1
  /FIXED=condition Index1 condition*Index1 | SSTYPE(3)
  /METHOD=REML
  /REPEATED=Index1 | SUBJECT(id) COVTYPE(CS).
```

The variable `Index1` created by `VARSTOCASES` needs some explaining (whereas the participant identifier `id` is fairly obvious). `Index1` identifies levels of the emotion factor, coding pride = 1, happiness = 2 and surprise = 3. Thus the `/FIXED` subcommand is just fitting a factorial ANOVA-style model in the fixed part. The `/REPEATED` subcommand fits the repeated measures emotion factor nested within subjects: `Index1 | SUBJECT(id)`. The `COVTYPE(CS)` fits a compound symmetry covariance structure and (in this case) the effects are equivalent to a standard repeated measures ANOVA model that assumes sphericity. Altering the covariance structure from `CS` to `UN` (unstructured) is a sensible check on the model when sphericity is in doubt (which it is not here). Alternative covariance structures include `TP` (Toeplitz), `TPH` (Toeplitz with heterogeneous variances) and `AR1` (first-order autoregressive). SPSS also provides AIC, AIC_C and BIC in the output, making it possible to compare repeated measures ANOVA models using AIC. Although AIC is calculated differently from R (e.g., here being based on two parameters, presumably the variance parameters) this will not matter if you compare change in AIC between models fitted in SPSS. For AIC_C and BIC you may wish to recalculate the values by hand to be sure what value for N and what number of parameters have been used. SPSS seems to use N at the lower level (as the reported BIC value is consistent with $k = 2$ parameters and $N \approx 270$). To compare models differing in their fixed part, AIC should be recalculated using `METHOD=ML` rather than `METHOD=REML`.

18.8.2 Generalized estimating equations

If you are interested in the fixed effects, a GEE provides an excellent alternative to a multilevel general or generalized linear model. These are run via the generalized linear model `GENLIN` command. The following illustrates a repeated measures logistic regression model with a single predictor and an unstructured covariance matrix:

SPSS data file: `gee_rm.sav`

```
GENLIN outcome (REFERENCE=LAST) WITH predictor
 /MODEL predictor INTERCEPT=YES
 DISTRIBUTION=BINOMIAL LINK=LOGIT
 /REPEATED SUBJECT=id WITHINSUBJECT=predictor SORT=YES
CORRTYPE=UNSTRUCTURED ADJUSTCORR=YES
  COVB=ROBUST
  /PRINT CPS DESCRIPTIVES MODELINFO FIT SUMMARY SOLUTION.
```

It is possible to fit repeated measures normal, Poisson, negative binomial and ordered logistic regression models with robust standard errors in this way. As a rule, the unstructured covariance matrix is a safe option, but specific alternatives such as `AR(1)` may appropriate in some situations. SPSS also reports information criteria, and these can be used to compare models.

18.9 Bibliography and further reading

Baayen, R. H., Davidson, D. J., and Bates, D. M. (2008) Mixed-effects Modeling with Crossed Random Effects for Subjects and Items. *Journal of Memory and Language*, 59, 390–412.

Bolker, B. M., Brooks, M. E., Clark, C. J., Geange, S. W., Poulsen, J. R., Stevens, M. H. H., and White, J. S. (2009) Generalized Linear Mixed Models: A Practical Guide for Ecology and Evolution. *Trends in Ecology and Evolution*, 24, 127–35.

Hox, J. J. (2010) *Multilevel Analysis: Techniques and Applications* (2nd edn). New York/Hove: Routledge.

Notes

1 Data, samples and statistics

1. Not all data are numbers, but this book focuses on the analysis of data that are collected in numeric form or that can be readily represented as numbers.
2. The symbol *N* is often used to denote the total number of observations in a data set. Here we've used *N* to represent population size.
3. This bar plot could also be considered a simple form of histogram (a bar plot of the frequency or density of observations of a sample).
4. This is the convention adopted here (except for some complex equations where is convenient to alter the notation).
5. In mathematics, the term 'product' refers to the number obtained by multiplying two or more other numbers together (e.g., the product of three and four is 12).
6. The numerator is the top element of a ratio (the bit above the line if it is represented as a fraction) and the denominator is the bottom element. In the ratio 1/2, one is the numerator and two is the denominator. If you ever get stuck trying to remember which is which, try to recall the well-known phrase 'lowest common denominator' (as the denominator is the lower half of the ratio).
7. It is important to be careful about the degree of trimming reported. Some authors refer to the total proportion or percentage of the sample trimmed, while others refer to the proportion or percentage trimmed in each tail. R uses the proportion of trimming in each tail (the convention adopted in this book).
8. The qualifier 'roughly' is used because this interpretation is more accurately applied to the *MAD*. It will also depend on the distribution of the data, working best for symmetrical, unimodal distributions (see Chapter 2).
9. It helps to give the objects you use names that are somewhat meaningful. It also helps to keep them short, and most object names are compromises between these competing tensions.
10. After working with R for a while you will develop your own strategies. R has a pretty good text editor built in which you can access by opening up a 'New Document' from the file menu.
11. Many R users will write examples of useful R code using a text editor and paste the code into the R console window to run it. This can make it easy to edit and re-run code. If you do this make sure to use a plain text editor (or use an editor that allows you to turn off 'smart quotes' as R will generate an error on encountering them.

2 Probability distributions

1. A possible objection in this case is that, under some definitions of male and female there may be other outcomes (albeit ones with a very low probability). Alternatively, the probability may fluctuate under certain conditions. If it does, the situation is only approximated by a Bernoulli trial (though the approximation will most likely be a good one).

2. If it strikes you as odd that a unimodal distribution can (sometimes) have two modes, it is important to realize that this can occur only for adjacent values of a discrete distribution. It is therefore unimodal in the sense of having a single peak, even though the peak spans two values.
3. A theorem is a mathematical statement that is accepted as true. Each theorem is derived from other proven results or fundamental propositions ('axioms') considered self-evident.
4. The Φ function is implemented in a number of software packages (e.g., `NORMSDIST()` in Excel or `pnorm()` in R). The inverse function Φ^{-1} is also widely available (e.g., `NORMSINV()` in Excel or `qnorm()` in R) and gives the *quantile function* for the standard normal, returning quantiles of z when a probability entered.
5. The terms chi-square and chi-squared are used interchangeably, though the former is more common. The name is derived from χ (the Greek lower-case letter 'chi').
6. The probability density functions of χ^2 and the closely related t and F distributions are rather more difficult to describe than for the distributions considered so far and will not be considered here (e.g., see Hays, 1973).
7. Ratios of distributions can be tricky to work with and often have awkward properties (e.g., undefined mean or variance).
8. Be aware that R treats a sequence such as `1:3` as a self-contained object – almost as if it is in brackets. Thus `1:3 + 1` evaluates as `[1] 2 3 4`, not `[1] 1 2 3 4` (which is produced by `1:(3+1)`.

3 Confidence intervals

1. The Greek letter theta is often employed denote a parameter and theta-hat its estimator.
2. Recall that a percentage is equivalent to a proportion of the total probability: C% corresponds to a proportion or probability of $C/100$ (e.g., 95% is equivalent to .95).
3. If n were known, it would be possible to construct a CI for a binomial proportion and use the relationship $\lambda = nP$ to obtain upper and lower limits for this rate.
4. Best practice would be to plot the data (e.g., using a histogram) before considering how to construct a CI for the difference.
5. This assumes the data values (e.g., percentage accuracy) are plotted on the y-axis and group or sample information on the x-axis. For some plots it may be preferable to plot data values on the x-axis.
6. The 1.39 multiplier is obtained by combining the appropriate quantile of the z distribution (1.96) with the $\sqrt{2}/2$ adjustment from Equation 3.31.

4 Significance tests

1. Although most significance tests are NHSTs, significance testing is a more general term (i.e., some significance tests do not involve rejecting or failing to reject a null hypothesis).
2. For experimental research it may also be termed the *experimental hypothesis*.
3. Although the Neyman-Pearson approach dominates the way NHST usually operates, the preference of 'failure to reject the null hypothesis' over 'accept the null hypothesis' reflects the influence of Fisher (Dienes, 2008). According to the Neyman-Pearson philosophy, accepting H_0 is a description of an outcome of a decision procedure rather than a statement of a belief about the population parameter. However, for a decision to accept H_0 to be reasonable, requires that Neyman-Pearson approach is implemented in its strict form (rather than the conventional hybrid approach outlined here).

4. Abelson (1995) points out that α need not be split evenly between each tail. In his one-and-a-half-sided test with $\alpha = .05$ statistical significance is declared if one-sided $p < .01$ in the non-predicted direction or one-sided $p < .04$ in the predicted direction.
5. These tests are often referred to as Student's t (after Student, 1908).
6. An alternative approximation preferred for some applications is the likelihood χ^2 (see Chapter 17).
7. A large reduced χ^2 statistic indicates a poor fit, but does not necessarily indicate a large departure from the ideal fit – as the statistic is sensitive to sample size (and may become very large when n is large).
8. As a square root has two solutions – one positive and one negative – it makes sense to assign the standardized residual the same sign as the raw residual. Some software does this automatically.
9. If $r = 1$ or $c = 1$ the test of independence is identical to the goodness-of-fit test with a null hypothesis of equiprobability.

5 Regression

1. The symbols used to represent the two variables (X and Y) and the two coefficients (b_0 and b_1) are arbitrary. The sequence of the b_0 and b_1X terms may also vary. If you have studied this topic before you may have been taught a different version of the equation (e.g., $Y = mX + c$ or $Y = a + bX$). What defines a straight line is the functional form of the equation.
2. This definition applies to both b_0 and b_1, though its application to b_0 may not be obvious at this point.
3. Although this convention is common in mathematics, software often plots the axes at other locations to make it easier to view the data being plotted.
4. Here the upper case Greek letter Δ (delta) is a standard symbol for a change in quantity such as X or Y.
5. The reasons for denoting this as R^2 will become apparent when more complex regression models are considered. A common alternative label for R^2 is the *coefficient of determination*.
6. For instance, a CI for the population mean of Y given a known value of X (the value used to predict it) could be formed from $\hat{Y} \pm t_{N-2,1-\alpha/2} \times \hat{\sigma}_E$. This quantity has the limitation that it does not generalize beyond the known, sampled values of X.
7. In very small samples all points tend to be quite influential.
8. See D'Agostino (1971).

6 Correlation and covariance

1. Percentages and proportions are other examples of dimensionless scales.
2. Provided there is sufficient variation in X and Y for both correlation and slope to be estimated.
3. N here refers to the total number of $X - Y$ pairs, whereas n in Equation 1.12 refers to the number of observations in the sample. These usually match, but this will not always be the case (e.g., if some of the outcomes are missing).
4. This is a further reminder, if one is needed, that a straight line relationship between two variables should never be assumed; a simple scatter plot of X and Y will often reveal whether a curvilinear relationship is likely.
5. Cohen (1988) proposed these labels "for use only when no better basis" for estimating the strength of effect was available.
6. This step is unnecessary when standardizing residuals because, by definition, they have a mean of zero.

7. SD_Y should not be confused with SD_{pooled}. SD_Y is calculated from deviations from the grand mean of Y (not deviations from the group means). It is therefore larger than SD_{pooled} when the group means are unequal.

7 Effect size

1. An introduction to meta-analysis is provided in *Online supplement 1: Meta-analysis*.
2. One caveat should be noted here. This does not necessarily mean that a large effect size statistic indicates a more important effect than a small effect size statistic. As these are estimates of population effect size they are subject to sampling error. Estimates from small samples are also more likely to be biased.
3. For a true categorical variable, dummy coding is reasonable. Assigning the values zero to one category and one to another ensures that a unit change in X (i.e., shifting from one category to the other) is associated with the difference in their outcomes.
4. The error in estimating σ is distinct from the error in estimating μ (or sample statistic). In a large sample μ is often estimated very precisely, whereas σ tends to be estimated with considerable uncertainty even in a large sample.
5. The parameter δ_{IG} is the population standardized difference δ for an equivalent independent groups design, if there is one. This differs from the parameter δ_{RM} for a repeated measures design that accounts for the correlation between paired or correlated measures. Cohen (1988) labels the latter parameter d_z to distinguish it from d.
6. Although r computed from r^2 it is assigned a positive sign by default, the correct sign can usually be recovered.
7. Intuitively, when the difference in means is also zero it feels as though δ and ρ should also be zero. In a technical sense the result is undefined and a more sensible conclusion is that there is insufficient information to estimate δ or ρ.
8. Other terms include the *risk difference* (*RD*) or *success rate difference* (*SRD*).
9. Notation varies. Here I have adapted the notation used by Fleiss (1994) and added the subscript Π (the Greek capital 'pi') to reduce confusion with Glass' Δ.
10. The base rates are determined by the row and column marginals of the contingency table. In a strict sense, the population proportions of each variable are the base rates and the sample proportions should therefore be referred to as marginals. The terminology here follows that of McGrath and Meyer (2006).
11. If the effects are harmful, *NNT* is the number needed to harm (*NNH*). Thus it is the number needed to achieve one success (failure) at the observed base rates.
12. The biserial or tetrachoric correlation coefficients are appropriate if one or both variables are dichotomized continuous variables.
13. Alternative labels for both *RR* and *RRR* exist. An important one, for future reference, is that relative risk is also known as a rate ratio or risk ratio (also abbreviated to *RR*).
14. In scientific work odds are almost invariably represented in decimal form as illustrated here. This has the advantage of being compact to report and easy to manipulate using a computer or calculator. Historically, a fractional odds format is used in betting (e.g., decimal odds of 1.5 can be represented as '3 to 2') and you may be familiar with that format.

8 Statistical power

1. Not to be confused with use of β to denote the population parameter for a regression coefficient (e.g., β_1) or an estimate of a standardized regression coefficient (e.g., $\hat{\beta}_1$).

2. Thus Sackett (2001) presents the 'only formula' of physiological statistics as

$$confidence = \frac{signal}{noise} \times \sqrt{samplesize}.$$

3. Methods exist to correct α for these problems, but methods are not always applied or applied correctly.
4. An objection to this view asserts that H_0 is never true (i.e., that there is always some effect, although it may be vanishingly small). We will ignore this argument for the moment, but the case for statistical power is not greatly diminished when considering the ability to distinguish large, interesting effects from tiny, uninteresting (but non-zero) effects.
5. For a probability density function (*pdf*), probability is represented by an area under the curve. Although Figure 8.1 makes a number of simplifications, the principles illustrated generalize to other situations (e.g., two-sided tests or test statistics with a t distribution).
6. The noncentrality parameter for t is sometimes labeled δ. The label ncp_t is adopted here to reduce confusion with other applications of these symbols.
7. Iterative solutions are sequential methods that work by gradually moving closer to a satisfactory solution. Many iterative methods eventually converge on an exact solution. If convergence is rapid it won't take too many steps to get to very close to the exact solution (within some acceptable margin of error). Sometimes iterative methods require extensive computing resources to obtain acceptable solutions in real time. For the procedures discussed here, convergence to an acceptable solution is very quick.
8. Because of inconsistency in labeling, it is particularly important to check standardized mean differences (see McGrath and Meyer, 2006). The values d, g or $\hat{\delta}$ are usually similar in large samples, but for repeated measures designs it is vital to know, for instance, whether d_{IG} or d_{RM} was reported.
9. The term γ ('gamma') is effectively a kind of Type I error rate for the expected width. 1 - γ is the long-run probability of obtaining an interval that is as narrow, or narrower, than W. The term 'degree of certainty' or 'assurance' is used to minimize confusion with confidence.
10. This value was determined by simulation.

9 Exploring messy data

1. You can check this by randomly generating 100 observations from a binomial distribution with $P = .5$ and calculating the mean (a first attempt produced $\hat{\mu} = .49$). With only ten participants an uneven split is much more likely (a first attempt produced $\hat{\mu} = .3$).
2. The population, having a lower bound, cannot have an exact normal distribution.
3. In a strict sense the extreme values also suggest skew – because the sample skewness will reflect their presence. For practical reasons it is helpful to distinguish these two patterns. One suggests a feature of the entire sample, while the other might merely reflect one or two aberrant observations. The two patterns are also not mutually exclusive; skewed populations increase the risk of extreme observations in the sample.
4. A histogram can also be considered a form of density estimator.
5. Robustness in this context simply means that, if the assumptions are violated, the performance of the test degrades gracefully (rather than being wildly inaccurate).
6. This is occurs for models as simple linear regression or an independent t test, where the outcome y_i is fitted by b_1x_i plus e_i (the residuals). As b_1x_i is constant for a particular value of X, the distribution of Y depends solely on the distribution of the residuals.

7. Methods for checking assumptions in meta-analysis are considered in *Online supplement 1: Meta-analysis*.
8. Wright and London (2009, p.165) refer to the Anscombe samples as the 'best made-up data set ever'.

10 Dealing with messy data

1. Researchers are, quite rightly, reluctant to adopt practices that involve editing or changing data. Altering data is not something that should be done lightly. However, there are legitimate ways to go about correcting data prior to analysis. The golden rule is always to report precisely what corrections were made and why. If you cannot report clearly and concisely what you did to the data, and why you did it, you probably shouldn't have done it.
2. Methods also exist for model averaging (combining or integrating results from a range of plausible models) which can be contrasted with the more common practice of model selection.
3. For some time it was believed that inference using t or F had good statistical power. Wilcox and Keselman (2003) state that this belief arose because older studies looked at power to detect a population standardized mean difference (δ). Heavy tailed or other distributions with extreme values increase σ and thus decrease δ. This obscured the loss of power to detect a simple mean difference of a particular magnitude by disguising the impact of extreme scores within the calculated value of δ.
4. One culprit here is the central limit theorem (CLT). If the sample sizes are large enough (and the CLT applies) then there may be little advantage to using robust methods.
5. One very common transformation, not discussed here, is standardization (having already been considered at length in relation to z scores, correlation and standardized effect size).
6. For the Haldane estimator of the odds ratio $c = 0.5$.
7. Zimmerman and Zumbo (1993b) note that the Welch-Satterthwaite t test applied to ranked data resolves problems with unequal variances, but does not address any distributional problems.
8. These can be loaded within R using the `source()` function (but check first to see whether a version more recent than 16 exists):

```
source('http://www-rcf.usc.edu/~rwilcox/Rallfun-v15')
```

11 Alternatives to classical statistical inference

1. This issue is so fundamental to hypothesis testing and experimental research that it will be considered in detail later in the chapter.
2. Lindley's paradox is not a true paradox – having the appearance of one only if you (incorrectly) believe that a small p value implies that the H_0 has a small probability of being true.
3. Often this point is zero, identified in the quote by Cohen as the 'nil hypothesis'.
4. Note that this is not the same as optional stopping. The argument here is that a sufficiently large sample will reject H_0 because H_0 is always false.
5. This target can be traced to examples in Cohen (1969; 1988). It needs to be viewed in the context of evidence suggesting that the median power of a study is somewhere between .50 and .60. Cohen was, in effect, proposing a decrease in typical Type II error rates from 50% to 20%.

6. Although potentially misleading, a p value may still be informative for secondary analysis (e.g., helping you to derive an effect size or some other statistic).
7. The p_{rep} statistic is discussed in more detail in *Online Supplement 3: Replication probabilities and* p_{rep}.
8. This result relies on the sampling distribution of t being similar to z when N is large.
9. The capture rate is bounded at 100% and so can fall far lower than the mean of 83% for a 95% CI, but cannot go much higher. These constraints produce the skewed distribution.
10. It has been argued that likelihood methods are frequentist (in essence because they are not Bayesian). In keeping with Dienes (2008) and others, this author classifies the likelihood approach as a distinct school of inference.
11. The calculation of a p value violates the likelihood principle. A p value is not the conditional probability of obtaining a particular value of a statistic in the observed data (e.g., $z = 1.96$), but of obtaining a statistic as extreme or more extreme than the observed data (e.g., $z > 1.96$). Therefore p values depend on unobserved data (in which z is more extreme than that observed). Those who adhere to the likelihood principle (which includes likelihood theorists and most Bayesians) tend to regard frequentist methods as inherently flawed.
12. Edwards (1972) quantifies support for one hypothesis over another by the natural logarithm of this ratio. Royall (1997) and others prefer the untransformed *LR*. The distinction is largely pragmatic. Logarithms are easier to work with when likelihoods are small or the ratios large.
13. Once you have observed the data, x and n are no longer free to vary. Hence a likelihood theorist focuses on the uncertainty of the parameter.
14. The concept of an *MLE* is central in frequentist statistics (e.g., many common descriptive statistics are also the *MLE* for a population parameter). Thus the arithmetic mean $\hat{\mu}$ is the *MLE* for the population mean μ of a sample from a normal distribution.
15. Blume (2002, p. 2589) states that this is 'so that, for small sample sizes, the probability of observing misleading evidence remains below the maximum of the bump function'.
16. It is common to use $p(\theta)$ rather than $P(\theta)$ or $Pr(\theta)$ to differentiate a probability distribution from a probability.
17. Turing's work, as part of the Bletchley Park code-breaking team during 1940 and 1941, was unpublished.

12 Multiple regression and the general linear model

1. The term orthogonal tends to be reserved for the predictors in a regression model. Terms like uncorrelated or independent are used in other contexts. It derives from geometry and means 'at right angles to'. Independent predictors have effects that are orthogonal when the equations are represented geometrically.
2. The technical term is a 'semi-partial slope'. As this is a bit of a mouthful, the 'semi-partial' bit is often dropped.
3. It may still be convenient to include composite predictors in a regression model. The maximum number of predictors in a multiple regression is $N - q - 2$ (because there must be at least 1 *df* left to estimate the error term). Composites reduce the number of predictors. Provided the composites are not obtained by optimizing the fit of individual parameters for the data in question, this can be useful. Optimizing the fit for a particular data set is dangerous. It disguises the number of parameters being estimated (and overstates the quality of the fit).
4. You can check that this is indeed a way to compute the intercept if your software has the option to fit a regression model without an intercept. If a new predictor with a constant value equal to one is added to the model, this will produce identical results to regression

with an intercept. This should explain why b_0 is a true regression coefficient (a constant, multiplicative term).

5. This matrix algebra solution is the clearest to explain, but is not computationally very efficient. Most software will implement more efficient (but mathematically equivalent) solutions.
6. This format (attributed to Fisher) is used more widely than in regression and is strongly associated with the family of regression models also known as ANOVA.
7. In addition, if you can design an experiment so that predictors are orthogonal and manipulated by the experimenter it becomes reasonable to attribute a causal relationship to the effect of the predictor on the outcome. Much effort in the design of a study is often expended on eliminating these correlations or determining which correlations are causal in their effects (see Gelman and Hill, 2007).
8. Grayson (2004) argues that Venn diagrams such as this one are therefore misleading as teaching aids for multiple regression. While there is some merit in this view, they can help convey some of the main ideas.
9. Even if the observed correlations between predictors are small you cannot unambiguously make attributions about individual contributions unless you are confident you have measured the predictor correlations accurately.
10. The equation $t = b/\hat{\sigma}_b$ implies that $\hat{\sigma}_b = b/t$.
11. The same is not true for general-purpose software (e.g., spreadsheet packages). The main problem is that high predictor correlations can produce very small numbers at intermediate stages. If software (or hand calculation) routinely rounds intermediate results to an inadequate number of decimal places calculations can go awry.
12. This assumes it is reasonable even to make the attempt. Take the example of two different measures of the same psychological construct (e.g., trait anxiety). It will only rarely be sensible to try and disentangle their effects (generally only if there is some theoretical rationale for thinking that the construct has different components).
13. This is how it behaves for a basic multiple regression model. For more sophisticated modes it behaves slightly differently.

13 ANOVA and ANCOVA with independent measures

1. Parameterization refers to the method of representing parameters in the model. Any statistical model of non-trivial complexity can be represented by a number of different, but equivalent equations, varying in terms of parameters and the relationships between them. The parameterization of a model does not, as a rule, change the overall model, but can (depending on what you want to do) make it easier or harder to interpret.
2. Switching from dummy to effect coding therefore has the same impact as multiplying X by two.
3. Often the categories represent group membership or identity, but they can represent other types of categorical distinction (e.g., time points in a repeated measures model).
4. This isn't true for all coding schemes, as it is possible to parameterize the model in a different way (without an intercept) that would make this possible (see Box 13.1).
5. The main difference is that we start by calculating the mean squares rather than sums of squares. Doing this makes it natural to employ the inferential formula for the *SD*. Cohen uses the descriptive formula (which facilitates calculation using electronic calculators or generic spreadsheet software – but is not the goal here).
6. See *Online supplement 2: Dealing with missing data*.
7. Were this model appropriate, a better solution would be to impute the 'missing' data.

8. There are other types, but the choice between sequential, hierarchical and unique sums of squares is more than sufficient for present purposes.
9. This question is revisited when ANOVA and ANCOVA with multiple factors are discussed in Chapter 14.
10. Other patterns are possible because the impact of a new predictor depends on its correlation with the residuals of the model containing earlier predictors. Adding a covariate might account for a small proportion of the overall *SS* but increase the impact of a factor added later (see Example 13.7).
11. This implies that adjusted *p* values are not true probabilities. Rather, they are convenient ways to present the outcome of a decision procedure that keeps α_{FW} below the desired level.
12. This can be alleviated with more powerful methods such as the Hochberg, Shaffer or Westfall procedures.
13. ANCOVA is an important topic and is returned to in relation to designs with multiple factors (in Chapter 14), contrasts (in Chapter 15) and repeated measures designs (in Chapter 16).

14 Interactions

1. Risk factors such as high blood pressure and age may well interact in their effects – but this is an empirical question (it not a logical consequence of their correlation in the population).
2. This principle also applies to lower-order terms in a moderated multiple regression with three-way and higher-order interaction effects, provided all the relevant continuous predictors are centered prior to computing product terms.
3. It is assumed here that all predictors are centered (not just those used to compute product terms). Centering continuous predictors is often helpful, but is not mandatory. For other predictors (e.g., categorical predictors) centering is not routinely practiced (though you might consider effect coding a form of centering).
4. If the choice is not obvious it can be instructive to repeat the procedure reversing the roles of the predictors.
5. The author has sympathy for anyone who thinks that neither is entitled to the label 'simple'. The origin of the label is that each term is itself a simple linear regression equation.
6. It is possible for *Y* to be a non-additive function of a predictor that cannot be modeled by conventional linear regression models. Such non-linear models are beyond the scope of this presentation. Fortunately, linear models are satisfactory (though perhaps not optimal) for many research questions.
7. Variants such as 'completely crossed', 'full factorial' or 'fully crossed' design are also common, but 'fully factorial' sounds better.
8. For a factor with two levels each simple main effect reduces to a *t* test. Any inferential tool designed to test differences in means is therefore available to test the effect (e.g., a *CI*, *LR* or Bayes factor).

15 Contrasts

1. To detect a pattern of differences among several means usually requires several pairwise tests to be statistically significant. This arguably reduces power to the level of the weakest test. Statistical power will suffer further, in comparison with a single *a priori* contrast, if corrections for multiple testing are applied.

2. Depending on how the model is run, the contrasts may be explicit or implicit in the analysis, though the contrasts are hidden away in most software.
3. The label $r_{alerting}$ is taken from Rosenthal *et al.* (2000).
4. They also use the labels $r_{effect\ size}$ and $r_{contrast}$ for η^2 and η_p^2 respectively.
5. This applies also to higher-order interaction terms. A $2 \times 2 \times 2$ interaction is a difference between 2×2 simple interactions and therefore a difference between differences of differences.
6. These contrasts need not be orthogonal (and indeed many are highly correlated).
7. See *Online Supplement 1: Meta-analysis.*
8. A more versatile method using `glht()` is described below. That approach sets up contrasts as separate rows of the matrix (rather than the columns required here) and this explains why the contrast matrix is transposed for use here.

16 Repeated measures ANOVA

1. The discussion that follows assumes that the fundamental unit of analysis is a person (but the same points apply for other units such as teams or families).
2. See Key Concept OS1.1 in *Online Supplement 1: Meta-analysis*. This issue is also considered further in Chapter 18.
3. A further difference is in the subscripts; each observation can be defined by its residual relative to the mean for participant *i* and mean level under level *j* of the factor (whereas in two-way independent measures ANOVA an additional subscript is required to distinguish different participants who experience the same level of factor A and factor B).
4. The convention is to refer to people who participate in a study voluntarily and with informed consent as participants, but to use 'subject' to describe a design or source of variance.
5. A repeated measures design is a special case of the more general *randomized blocks design* (see Kirk, 1995).
6. See *Online Supplement 2: Multiple imputation*.
7. Early authors refer to it as Box's $\hat{\varepsilon}$. This appears to be a case of Stigler' law, prolific in statistics, that no discovery is named after its original discoverer.
8. Although this kind of repeated measures MANOVA is slightly different from a standard MANOVA, most software and many texts refer to it as MANOVA rather than profile analysis. The more general term MANOVA is used here.
9. MANOVA reports a number of alternative test statistics. This comment is in relation to the two that are most widely reported: Wilk's lambda and the Pillai-Bartlett trace.
10. The terminology here has the potential to confuse, as other authors may use normalizing to describe a number of different statistical operations (e.g., transforming variables to have an approximate normal distribution).
11. Kirk (1995) characterizes this as *group-treatment confounding*. The effects of the independent measures factors are confounded with the group of participants sampled. This is not as serious as it seems because it occurs also for independent measures designs. The confounding is controlled, under ideal circumstances, by random assignment of participants to experimental conditions. However, it implies that independent measures effects are estimated with less precision than the repeated measures effects.
12. Under some circumstances MANOVA tests will provide more powerful tests of main effects than corrected *F* tests. However, it can be confusing to report completely different analyses for main effect and interaction tests. Where MANOVA is likely to be more powerful than ANOVA, it is probably sensible to switch to multilevel model analyses for all tests.

13. There is debate about whether the point null hypothesis can be true for a single outcome variable. It becomes less plausible as the number of outcome variables increases.
14. The difference between a profile analysis and regular MANOVA is that for profile analysis the linear combination is constructed from differences between pairs of repeated measures rather than the repeated measures directly (see Howell, 2002).
15. In profile analysis, two outcome variables produce just one difference, so all the statistics reduce to t^2 or F with 1 *df* for the effect.
16. Λ is the capital Greek letter λ (lambda).
17. Another way to look at this is in terms of a floor effect (Wright and London, 2009). The older children forget more, in part, because they have better pre-test recall (and thus recall has further to fall).

17 Modeling discrete outcomes

1. This problem can be seen for the Wald CI for a binomial proportion in Example 3.4. This uses a normal approximation that has the same properties as a linear regression model.
2. This will not always be the case. If modeling the outcome as discrete introduces additional assumptions – not present in the continuous regression model – then these considerations may weigh in favor of the simpler model. A good example is that of a repeated measures model with a continuous outcome. This might well be preferable to a model that assumes independence, but treats the outcome as discrete.
3. The generalized linear model is often abbreviated to GLM. This is avoided here because GLM is also used to abbreviate the general linear model (which can be confusing). If the abbreviation is adopted then it makes sense to use LM for the general linear model and GLM for the generalized linear model (noting that any LM is also a special case of the GLM).
4. Although the focus of this chapter is on generalized linear models for discrete outcomes, the random component is not restricted to discrete probability distributions (e.g., including continuous ones such as the normal distribution).
5. Agresti (1996) reserves the label Wald test for the χ^2 version of the test, but used loosely it can refer to almost any procedure that employs a test statistic from parameter estimates and standard errors derived from maximum likelihood estimation.
6. A unit increase under effect coding is half the full category change in the logit form of the model. The effect on the logit scale needs to be doubled to correspond to that for a full category change. As addition is equivalent to multiplication in the exponentiated equation, the full category effect under effect coding needs to be squared to match the *OR* for the dummy coded model. It follows that, under effect coding, the coefficient on the odds scale is the square root of the odds for the dummy coded coefficient.
7. Pseudo-R^2 measures predictive power and percentage of outcomes correctly classified are reviewed briefly in *Online Supplement 4: Pseudo-R^2 and related measures*.
8. This is represented by the lower case Greek letter phi. φ, an alternate form of phi, is used here (to reduce confusion with the correlation coefficient ϕ).
9. This is a slightly contrived example, because multiple trials per participant would probably be required in a real experiment of this type.
10. A detailed introduction to loglinear models is provided in *Online Supplement 5: Loglinear models*.
11. Rank-based methods are excluded here because they are not a method of modeling ordinal data, but of taking continuous measures and turning them into ordinal ones. Most rank-based methods are equivalent or approximately equivalent to least squares linear

regression models with ordinal measures. These models do not deal with the non-linearity implied by bounded outcomes and implicitly assume that all intervals between ranks are equal.

12. A common convention, adopted here, is to use the last category as the reference category, but it is also possible to use the first.
13. In any case, when the exposure is fixed (either because it is identical for all observations or through fitting an offset) the parameters of the model have a direct interpretation as logarithms of risk ratios or rate ratios.
14. The precise definition of an offset is more general than this, and is not restricted to Poisson models or models of count data.
15. Some authors class neither the quasipoisson nor the negative binomial as generalized linear models – though for different reasons. The quasipoisson model does not produce a true likelihood, while the form of negative binomial model discussed here is not a generalized linear model unless the overdispersion parameter is known (rather than estimated). Hilbe (2007) provides a more complete discussion of negative binomial and related count models.
16. It can also be expressed in terms of trials to achieve r successes.
17. The likelihood function is continuous regardless of whether a discrete or continuous probability distribution is plotted. The *pmf* of each distribution could be plotted instead, but a continuous function shows the differences more clearly.
18. Even if you doubt that an event can have a zero probability or rate, the probability that the rate is negligible for one subpopulation may be plausible.
19. The parameterization of this function is slightly easier to work with for producing plots such as these.

18 Multilevel models

1. For some situations – such as cross-classified data – the data do not fall neatly into a hierarchical structure, but can still be considered to have multiple levels.
2. For the distinction between MCAR (missing completely at random) and MAR (missing at random) and an explanation of multiple imputation see *Online Supplement 2: Dealing with missing* data.
3. This conclusion will not apply to all regression methods for dealing with repeated measures data. GEEs and models for panel data in economics are designed to overcome some of the limitations discussed here (see Wooldridge, 2003).
4. For a more general introduction see Goldstein (2003) or Hox (2010).
5. If the aggregate analysis uses weighted means, it becomes a form of fixed effect meta-analysis. This fixed effect model is widely regarded as problematic and the usual alternative, the random effects model, is a simple multilevel model (see Key Concept OS1 in *Online Supplement 1: Meta-analysis*).
6. In keeping with most publications, the terms 'fixed' and 'random' are employed here to differentiate these effects. Gelman and Hill (2007) consider the terms confusing and try and avoid them. For instance, you might conceptualize all effects as random, with some having variances that are zero or close to zero (equivalent to fixed effects). I have some sympathy with this position, but have stuck with the more common terminology for this brief introduction. As indicated in Box 18.1, the crucial consideration is whether there is additional systematic variability that can be incorporated into a model (rather than being ignored or lumped in with error). If so, the modeling strategy should be slanted toward exploring whether it can be included in the model as a random effect. This looks like a reversal of the usual assumption of parsimony, but it is warranted here. There are three main reasons for this: i) small samples often underestimate variance parameters, so it is difficult to reject

the assumption of no random variation, ii) ignoring covariances, in particular, seems to bias estimates of fixed effects and iii) in many domains there are *a priori* reasons to expect some, probably substantial, inter-unit and intra-unit variation at each level of a hierarchical data structure.

7. It is not strictly necessary to estimate them. They can be treated as 'nuisance' parameters and the model adjusted to cope with their presence. This is what happens with a GEE or with a sandwich estimator (Hanley *et al.*, 2003; Ballinger, 2004; Zeileis, 2004, 2006).
8. Although additional variability in sampling from a population of stimuli (or additional random effects) is modeled, it cannot alter the populations being sampled. If the samples are restricted in some way (e.g., by matching), the variability being modeled is also restricted.
9. Remember that the tests of subject effects in repeated measures ANOVA and regression models are either biased or aliased with an error term.
10. Analogous boundary effects arise in other contexts, such as inference with Pearson's r (which is bounded at -1 and 1). The solution in that case was to use the Fisher z transformation (which produces an unbounded test statistic for r but not r^2).
11. This assumes that, as is common in multilevel modeling, variances are constrained to be non-negative (Savalei and Kolenikov, 2008).
12. An alternative approach is to obtain a central interval (with equal tails). The two approaches are equivalent for equal symmetrical, unimodal densities.
13. Different authors use slightly different notation. Here notation is based on that of Goldstein (1987, 1995, 2003), though Greek letters (e.g., β) for coefficients are avoided. This is to emphasize the link with multiple linear regression. Hox (2010) discusses some of more common variations in notation.
14. Estimating the ICC with predictors in the model tends to reduce $\hat{\rho}_I$. This is important when using previous studies to estimate the *ICC* (e.g., when planning sample size for a new study). It is generally safer to ignore predictors when computing *ICC* unless you are confident that the new study has predictors that impact on *ICC* in the same way. In part this is because the ICC will almost always be estimated very imprecisely, and small changes in ρ_I can have a big impact on statistical power.
15. This involves duplicating values of higher-level predictors for lower-level units. This duplication is what makes the process less efficient.
16. This isn't entirely true, as means estimated for different values of predictors, such as adjusted means, are also predictions.
17. In an unreliable measurement, extreme observations are, on average, extreme partly because of measurement error. This can be demonstrated by measuring them again. Typically the second measurement will be less extreme. This phenomenon is known as *regression to the mean*. Shrinkage can be seen as a method for reducing the impact of regression to the mean on estimates from a multilevel model.
18. This is true for the simple example discussed here, but not always true in practice. In some situations it may be necessary to model residual variation at level 1 (see Example 18.3).
19. This is not a criticism of Baayen. He focuses on data in psycholinguistics, where his arguments are persuasive.
20. Discrete models can be difficult to fit. Having access to more than one multilevel package will widen the range of models that you can analyze.
21. Similar issues arise for other multilevel generalized linear models. For instance, the level 1 variance in a Poisson model is usually fixed at one.
22. When a library is loaded it reports whether the new package has functions that mask those in an already loaded package. This masking redirects 'old' functions to ones loaded with the new package (or one of its dependencies). This is necessary to make the new package operate smoothly, but can be problematic when switching between two different types of model (as in Example 18.5).

References

Aaron, B., Kromrey, J. D., and Ferron, J. M. (1998) Equating *r*-based and *d*-based Effect-size Indices: Problems with a Commonly Recommended Formula. Paper presented at the annual meeting of the Florida Educational Research Association, Orlando, FL, November.

Abelson, R. P. (1985) A Variance Explanation Paradox: When a Little is a Lot. *Psychological Bulletin*, 97, 128–32.

Abelson, R. P. (1995) *Statistics as Principled Argument*. Hillsdale, NJ: Erlbaum.

Abelson, R. P. (1996) Vulnerability of Contrasts to Simpler Interpretations: An Addendum to Rosnow and Rosenthal. *Psychological Science*, 7, 242–6.

Abelson, R. P. (1997) A Retrospective on the Significance Test Ban of 1999 (If there were no significance tests, they would have to be invented). In L.L. Harlow, S.A. Mulaik, and J.H. Steiger (eds), *What If There Were No Significance Tests?* Mahwah, NJ: Erlbaum, pp. 117–41.

Abelson, R. P., and Prentice, D. A. (1997) Contrast Tests of Interaction Hypotheses. *Psychological Methods*, 2, 315–28.

Afshartous D., and Preston R. A. (2010) Confidence Intervals for Dependent Data: Equating Nonoverlap with Statistical Significance. *Computational Statistics and Data Analysis*, 54, 2296–305.

Agresti, A. (1996) *An Introduction to Categorical Data Analysis*. New York: Wiley.

Agresti, A., and Coull, B. A. (1998) Approximate is Better Than 'Exact' for Interval Estimation of Binomial Proportions. *The American Statistician*, 52, 119–26.

Akaike, H. (1974) A New Look at the Statistical Model Identification. *IEEE Transactions on Automatic Control*, 19, 716–23.

Alker, H. (1969) A Typology of Ecological Fallacies. In M. Dogan and S. Rokkan (eds). *Quantitative Ecological Analysis in the Social Sciences*. Cambridge, MA: MIT Press.

Alter, A. L., and Oppenheimer, D. M. (2008) Effects of Fluency on Psychological Distance and Mental Construal (or why New York is a large city, but *New York* is a civilized jungle). *Psychological Science*, 19, 161–7.

Altman, D. G. (1998) Confidence Intervals for the Number Needed to Treat. *British Medical Journal*, 317, 1309–12.

Anderson, C., and Schumacker, R. E. (2003) A Comparison of Five Robust Regression Methods with Ordinary Least Squares Regression: Relative Efficiency, Bias, and Test of the Null Hypothesis. *Understanding Statistics*, 2, 79–103.

Andrews, D. W. K., and Ploberger, W. (1994) Optimal Tests when a Nuisance Parameter is Present only under the Alternative. *Econometrica*, 62, 1383–414.

Anscombe, F. J. (1973) Graphs in Statistical Analysis. *American Statistician, 27,* 17–21.

APA (2010) *Publication Manual of the American Psychological Association* (6th edn). Washington, D.C.: APA.

Armitage, P., Berry, G., and Matthews J. N. S. (2002) *Statistical Methods in Medical Research* (4th edn). Oxford: Blackwell.

Atkins, D. C., and Gallop, R. J. (2007) Rethinking How Family Researchers Model Infrequent Outcomes: A Tutorial on Count Regression and Zero-inflated Models. *Journal of Family Psychology*, 21, 726–35.

Atkinson, A. C. (1978) Posterior Probabilities for Choosing a Regression Model. *Biometrika*, 65, 39–48.

Baayen, R. H. (2008) *Analyzing Linguistic Data: A Practical Introduction to Statistics using R*. Cambridge: Cambridge University Press.

Baayen, R. H., Davidson, D. J., and Bates, D. M. (2008) Mixed-effects Modeling with Crossed Random Effects for Subjects and Items. *Journal of Memory and Language*, 59, 390–412.

Baguley, T. (2004) Understanding Statistical Power in the Context of Applied Research. *Applied Ergonomics*, 35, 73–80.

Baguley, T. (2009) Standardized or Simple Effect Size: What should be Reported? *British Journal of Psychology*, 100, 603–17.

Baguley, T. (2011) Calculating and Graphing Within-subject Confidence Intervals for ANOVA. *Behavior Research Methods*. doi: 10.3758/s13428-011-0123-7.

Baguley, T., and Kaye, W. S. (2010) Review of Understanding Psychology as a Science: An Introduction to Scientific and Statistical Inference. *British Journal of Mathematical and Statistical Psychology*, 63, 695–8.

Baguley, T., and Payne, S. J. (2000a) Long-term Memory for Spatial and Temporal Mental Models includes Construction Processes and Model Structure. *Quarterly Journal of Experimental Psychology*, 53A, 479–512.

Baguley, T., and Payne, S. J. (2000b) Given-new versus New-given? An Analysis of Reading Times for Spatial Descriptions. In S. ÓNualláin (ed.), *Spatial Cognition: Foundations and Applications*. Amsterdam: John Benjamins, pp. 317–28.

Baguley, T., Lansdale, M. W., Lines, L. K., and Parkin, J. (2006) Two Spatial Memories are not Better than One: Evidence of Exclusivity in Memory for Object Location. *Cognitive Psychology*, 52, 243–89.

Ballinger, G. A. (2004) Using Generalized Estimating Equations for Longitudinal Data Analysis. *Organizational Research Methods*, 7, 127–50.

Bamber, D. (1979) State-trace Analysis: A Method of Testing Simple Theories of Causation. *Journal of Mathematical Psychology*, 19, 137–81.

Bates, D. M., Maechler, M., and Bolker, B. M. (2011) *lme4*: Linear mixed-effects models using S4 classes. R package version 0.999375-39.

Bauer, D. J., and Curran, P. J. (2005) Probing Interactions in Fixed and Multilevel Regression: Inferential and Graphical Techniques. *Multivariate Behavioral Research*, 40, 373–400.

Beck, A. X., Ward, C. H., Mendelson, M., Mock, J., and Erbaugh, J. (1961) An Inventory for Measuring Depression. *Archives of General Psychiatry*, 4, 561–71.

Benjamini, Y., and Hochberg, Y. (1995) Controlling the False Discovery Rate: A Practical and Powerful Approach to Multiple Testing. *Journal of the Royal Statistical Society Series B, 57,* 289–30.

Benjamini, Y., and Yekutieli, D. (2001) The Control of the False Discovery Rate in Multiple Testing under Dependency. *Annals of Statistics*, 29, 1165–88.

Berkhof, J., and Snijders, T. A. B. (2001) Variance Component Testing in Multilevel Models. *Journal of Educational and Behavioral Statistics*, 26, 133–52.

Berry, D. (1995) *Basic Statistics: A Bayesian Perspective*. Belmont, CA: Wadsworth.

Bertenthal, B. I., and Fischer, K. W. (1978) The Development of Self-recognition in Infancy. *Developmental Psychology*, 14, 44–50.

Birnbaum, A. (1962) On the Foundations of Statistical Inference. *Journal of the American Statistical Association*, 57, 269–326.

Blaker, H. (2000) Confidence Curves and Improved Exact Confidence Intervals for Discrete Distributions. *Canadian Journal of Statistics*, 28, 783–98.

Bland J. M., and Altman, D. G. (1996) The Use of Transformations when Comparing Two Means. *British Medical Journal*, 312, 1153.

Blouin, D. C., and Riopelle, A. J. (2005) On Confidence Intervals for Within-subject Designs. *Psychological Methods*, 10, 397–412.

Blume, J. D. (2002) Likelihood Methods for Measuring Statistical Evidence. *Statistics in Medicine*, 21, 2563–99.

Boag J. W. (1949) Maximum Likelihood Estimates of the Proportion of Patients Cured by Cancer Therapy. *Journal of the Royal Statistical Society B*, 11, 15–53.

Bobko, P., Roth, P. L., and Bobko, C. (2001) Correcting the Effect Size of *d* for Range Restriction and Unreliability. *Organizational Research Methods*, 4, 46–61.

Boik, R. J. (1981) A priori Tests in Repeated Measures Designs: Effects of Nonsphericity, *Psychometrika*, 46, 241–55.

Bolker, B. M., Brooks, M. E., Clark, C. J., Geange, S. W., Poulsen, J. R., Stevens, M. H. H., and White, J. S. (2009) Generalized Linear Mixed Models: A Practical Guide for Ecology and Evolution. *Trends in Ecology and Evolution*, 24, 127–35.

Bond, C.F., Jr., and Richardson, K. (2004) Seeing the Fisher *z*-transformation. *Psychometrika*, 69, 291–303.

Bonett, D. G. (2008) Meta-analytic Interval Estimation for Bivariate Correlations. *Psychological Methods*,13, 173–89.

Bonett, D. G., and Price, R. M. (2002) Statistical Inference for Linear Function of Medians: Confidence Intervals, Hypothesis Testing, and Sample Size Requirements. *Psychological Methods*, 7, 380–3.

Boring, E. G. (1919) Mathematical versus Scientific Significance. *Psychological Bulletin*, 16, 335–8.

Botella, J., Ximénez, C., Revuelta, J., and Suero, M. (2006) Optmization of Sample Size in Controlled Experiments: The CLAST Rule. *Behavior Research Methods, Instruments, and Computers*, 38, 65–76.

Box, G. E. P. (1953) Non-normality and Tests on Variances. *Biometrika*, 40,318–35.

Box, G. E. P. (1954a) Some Theorems on Quadratic Forms Applied in the Study of Analysis of Variance Problems, I. Effects of Inequality of Variance in the One-way Classification. *Annals of Mathematical Statistics*, 25, 290–302.

Box, G. E. P. (1954b) Some Theorems on Quadratic Forms Applied in the Study of Analysis of Variance Problems, II. Effects of Inequality of Variance and of Correlation between Errors in the Two-way Classification. *Annals of Mathematical Statistics*, 25, 484–98.

Brennen, T., Baguley, T., Bright, J. E. and Bruce, V. B. (1990) Resolving Semantically Induced Tip-of-the-tongue States for Proper Nouns. *Memory and Cognition*, 18, 339–47.

Bring, J. (1994) How to Standardize Regression Coefficients. *American Statistician*, 48, 209–13.

Browne, R. H. (1995) On the Use of a Pilot Sample for Sample Size Determination. *Statistics in Medicine*, 14, 1933–40.

Browne, W. J. (2009) *MCMC estimation in MLwiN, v2.13*. Bristol: Centre for Multilevel Modelling, University of Bristol.

Browne, W. J., Golalizadeh Lahi, M., and Parker, R. M.A. (2009) *A Guide to Sample Size Calculations for Random Effect Models via Simulation and the MLPowSim Software Package.* Bristol: Centre for Multilevel Modelling, University of Bristol.

Buchner, A., and Mayr, S. (2004) Auditory Negative Priming in Younger and Older Adults. *Quarterly Journal of Experimental Psychology: Human Experimental Psychology*, 57A, 769–87.

Burnham, K. P. and Anderson, D. R. (2004) MultimodelInference: Understanding AIC and BIC in Model Selection. *Sociological Methods and Research*, 33, 261–304.

Carroll, J. B. (1961) The Nature of Data, or How to Choose a Correlation Coefficient. *Psychometrika*, 26, 347–72.

Clark, H. H. (1973) The Language-as-a-fixed-effect Fallacy: A Critique of Language Statistics in Psychological Research. *Journal of Verbal Learning and Verbal Behavior*, 12, 335–59.

Cleveland. W. S. (1985) *The Elements Of Graphing Data*. New York, NY: Chapman and Hall.

Cohen, B. H. (2002) Calculating a Factorial ANOVA from Means and Standard Deviations. *Understanding Statistics*, 1, 191–203.

Cohen, B. H. (2007) *Explaining Psychological Statistics* (3rd edn). New York: Wiley.

Cohen, J. (1968) Multiple Regression as a General Data-analytic System. *Psychological Bulletin*, 70, 426–43.

Cohen, J. (1969) *Statistical Power Analysis for the Behavioral Sciences*. Hillsdale, NJ: Erlbaum.

Cohen, J. (1976) Random Means Random. *Journal of Verbal Learning and Verbal Behavior*, 15, 261–2.

Cohen, J. (1988) *Statistical Power Analysis for the Behavioral Sciences*(2nd edn). Hillsdale, NJ: Erlbaum.

Cohen, J. (1992) A Power Primer. *Psychological Bulletin*, 112, 155–9.

Cohen, J. (1994) The Earth is Round ($p < .05$). *American Psychologist*, 49, 997–1003.

Cohen, P., Cohen, J., Aiken, L. S., and West, S. G. (1999) The Problem of Units and the Circumstance for POMP. *Multivariate Behavioral Research*, 34, 315–46.

Cohen, J., Cohen, P., West, S. G., and Aiken, L. S. (2003) *Applied Multiple Regression/Correlation Analysis for the Behavioral Sciences*. Mahwah, NJ: Erlbaum.

Cole, D. A., Maxwell, S. E., Arvey, R. D., and Salas, E. (1994) How the Power of MANOVA can both Increase and Decrease as a Function of the Intercorrelations among the Dependent Variables. *Psychological Bulletin*, 115, 465–74.

Coleman, E. B. (1964) Generalizing to a Language Population. *Psychological Reports*, 14, 219–26.

Conover, W. J. (1980) *Practical Nonparametric Statistics* (2nd edn). New York: Wiley.

Conover, W. J., and Iman, R. L. (1981) Rank Transformations as a Bridge between Parametric and Nonparametric Statistics. *American Statistician*, 35, 124–9.

Cook, J. D. (2009) Notes on the Negative Binomial Distribution. Accessed 14 November 2009, at http://www.johndcook.com/negative_binomial.pdf.

Cook, R. D. (1977) Detection of Influential Observations in Linear Regression. *Technometrics*, 19, 15–18.

Cook, R. J., and Sackett, D. L. (1995) The Number Needed to treat: A Clinically Useful Measure of Treatment Effect. *British Medical Journal*, 310, 452–4.

Cook, T. D., Shadish, W. R. and Wong, V. C. (2008) Three Conditions under which Observational Studies Produce the Same Results as Experiments. *Journal of Policy Analysis and Management*, 274, 724–50.

Cools, W., Van den Noortgate, W., and Onghena, P. (2008) ML-DEs: A Program for Designing Efficient Multilevel Studies, *Behavior Research Methods*, 40, 236–49.

Cornfield J. (1966) Sequential Trials, Sequential Analysis and the Likelihood Principle. *American Statistician*, 20, 18–23.

Cortina, J. M. (1993) What is Coefficient Alpha? An Examination of Theory and Applications. *Journal of Applied Psychology*, 78, 98–104.

Cousens, S., Hargreaves, J., Bonelli, C., Armstrong, B. Thomas, J., Kirkwood, B. R., and Hayes, R. (2011) Alternatives to Randomisation in the Evaluation of Public-health Interventions: Statistical Analysis and Causal Inference, *Journal of Epidemiology and Community Health*, 65, 582–7.

Cousineau, D. (2005) Confidence Intervals in Within-subject Designs: A Simpler Solution to Loftus and Masson's Method. *Tutorials in Quantitative Methods for Psychology*, 1, 42–5.

Cronbach, L. J. (1947) Test 'Reliability': Its Meaning and Determination. *Psychometrika*, 12,1–16.

Culpepper, S. A., and Aguinis, H. (2011) Using Analysis of Covariance (ANCOVA) with Fallible Covariates. *Psychological Methods*, 16, 166–78.

Cumming, G., and Fidler, F. (2009) Confidence Intervals Better Answers to Better Questions.*Zeitschrift für Psychologie*, 217, 15–26.

Cumming, G., and Finch, S.J. (2001) A Primer on the Understanding, Use and Calculation of Central and Noncentral Confidence Intervals. *Educational and Psychological Measurement*, 61, 530–72.

Cumming, G., and Finch, S. (2005) Inference by Eye: Confidence Intervals, and How to Read Pictures of Data. *American Psychologist*, 60, 170–80.

Cumming, G., and Maillardet, R. (2006) Confidence Intervals and Replication: Where Will the Next Mean Fall? *Psychological Methods*, 11, 217–27.

Cumming, G., Williams, J., and Fidler, F. (2004) Replication, and Researchers' Understanding of Confidence Intervals and Standard Error Bars. *Understanding Statistics*, 3, 299–311.

D'Agostino, R. B. (1971) A Second Look At Analysis Of Variance On Dichotomous data. *Journal of Educational Measurement*, 8, 327–33.

Darlington, R. B. (1968) Multiple Regression in Psychological Research and Practice. *Psychological Bulletin*, 69, 161–82.

Davies, R. B. (1987) Hypothesis Testing when a Nuisance Parameter is Present Only Under the Alternatives. *Biometrika*, 74, 33–43.

Dawes, R. M. (1979) The Robust Beauty of Improper Linear Models in Decision Making. *American Psychologist*, 34, 571–82.

Dayton, C. M. (2003) Information Criteria for Pairwise Comparisons. *Psychological Methods*, 8, 61–71.

DeCarlo, L. T. (1997) On the Meaning and Use of Kurtosis. *Psychological Methods*, 2, 292–307.

Dedousis-Wallace, A. and Shute, R. H. (2009) Indirect Bullying: Predictors of Teacher Intervention, and Outcome of a Pilot Educational Presentation about Impact on Adolescent Mental Health. *Australian Journal of Educational and Developmental Psychology*, 9, 2–17.

Deegan, J., Jr (1978) On the Occurrence of Standardized Regression Coefficients Greater than One. *Educational and Psychological Measurement*, 38, 873–88.

Delaney, H. D., and Maxwell, S. E. (1981) On Using Analysis of Covariance in Repeated Measures Designs. *Multivariate Behavioral Research*, 16, 105–23.

Delucchi, K. L. (1993) The Use and Misuse of Chi-Square. In G. Keren and C. Lewis (eds), *Methodological and Quantitative Issues in the Analysis of Psychological Data*. Hillsdale, NJ: Erlbaum.

DeShon, R. P. (2003) A Generalizability Perspective on Measurement Error Corrections in Validity Generalization. In K. R. Murphy (ed.), *Validity Generalization: A Critical Review*. Mahwah, NJ: Erlbaum, pp. 365–402.

DiCiccio, T. J, and Efron, B. (1996) Bootstrap Confidence Intervals. *Statistical Science*, 11, 189–228.

Dienes, Z. (2008) *Understanding Psychology as a Science: An Introduction to Scientific and Statistical Inference*. Basingstoke: Palgrave Macmillan.

Dinh, P., and Yang, P. (2011) Handling Baselines in Repeated Measures Analyses with Missing Data at Random. *Journal of Biopharmaceutical Statistics*, 21, 326–41.

Dixon, P. M. (1998) Assessing Effect and No Effect with Equivalence Tests. In M. C. Newman and C. L. Strojan (eds), *Risk Assessment: Logic and Measurement*. Chelsea, MI: Ann Arbor Press, pp. 275–301.

Dunlap, W. P., Cortina, J. M., Vaslow, J. B., and Burke, M. J. (1996) Meta-analysis of Experiments with Matched Groups or Repeated Measured Designs. *Psychological Methods*, 1, 170–7.

Dunn, A. D., Wells, T., and Baguley, T. (2011) Male Voice Pitch Modulation in Response to Attractive Female Faces. Unpublished manuscript.

Edlin, A., Gelman, A., and Kaplan, N. (2007) Voting as a Rational Choice: Why and how People Vote to Improve the Well-being of Others. *Rationality and Society*, 19, 293–314.

Edwards, A. L. (1948) Note on the 'Correction for Continuity' in Testing the Significance of the Difference between Correlated Proportions. *Psychometrika*, 13, 185–7.

Edwards, A. W. F. (1972) *Likelihood* (1st edn). Cambridge: Cambridge University Press.

Edwards, A. W. F. (1974) The History of Likelihood. *International Statistical Review*, 42, 9–15.

Edwards, W., Lindman, H., and Savage, L. J. (1963) Bayesian Statistical Inference for Psychological Research. *Psychological Review*, 70, 193–242.

Ellison, A. M. (1996) An Introduction to Bayesian Inference for Ecological Research and Environmental Decision-making. *Ecological Applications*, 6, 1036–46.

Enders, C. K. (2003) Performing Multivariate Group Comparisons following a Statistically Significant MANOVA. *Measurement and Evaluation in Counseling and Development*, 36, 40–56.

Enders, C. K., and Tofighi, D. (2007) Centering Predictor Variables in Cross-sectional Multilevel Models: A New Look at an Old Issue. *Psychological Methods*, 12, 121–13.

Ezekiel, M. (1929) The Application of the Theory of Error to Multiple and Curvilinear Correlation. *Journal of the American Statistical Association*, 24, 99–104.

Faul, F., Erdfelder, E., Lang, A.-G., and Buchner, A. (2007) G*Power 3: A Flexible Statistical Power Analysis for the Social, Behavioral, and Biomedical Sciences. *Behavior Research Methods*, 39, 175–91.

Faul, F., Erdfelder, E., Buchner, A., and Lang, A.-G. (2009) Statistical Power Analyses using G*Power 3.1: Tests for Correlation and Regression Analyses. *Behavior Research Methods*, 41, 1149–60.

Fay, M. P. (2009) Confidence Intervals that Match Fisher's Exact or Blaker's Exact Tests. *Biostatistics*, 11, 373–4.

Fay, M. P. (2010) Two-sided Exact Tests and Matching Confidence Intervals for Discrete Data. *The R Journal*, 2, 53–8.

Fidler, F., and Thompson, B. (2001) Computing Correct Confidence Intervals for ANOVA Fixed- and Random-effects Effect Sizes. *Educational and Psychological Measurement*, 61, 575–604.

Field, A. (2009) *Discovering Statistics Using SPSS (and sex and drugs and rock 'n' roll)* (3rd edn). London: Sage.

Fisher, R. A. (1915) Frequency Distribution of the Values of the Correlation Coefficient in Samples of an Indefinitely Large Population. *Biometrika*, 10, 507–21.

Fisher, R. A. (1925) *Statistical Methods for Research Workers*. London: Oliver and Boyd.

Fleiss, J. L. (1973) *Statistical Methods for Rates and Proportions*. New York: Wiley.

Fleiss, J. L. (1994) Measures of Effect Size for Categorical Data. In H. Cooper and L. V. Hedges (eds),*The Handbook of Research Synthesis*. New York: Sage, pp. 245–60.

Fox, J. (2002a) *An R and S-Plus Companion to Applied Regression*. Thousand Oaks, CA: Sage.

Fox, J. (2002b) Bootstrapping Regression Models: Appendix to an R and S-PLUS Companion to Applied Regression. Accessed 31 August 2010, at http://cran.r-project.org/doc/contrib/Fox-Companion/appendix-bootstrapping.pdf.

Freeman, M. F., and Tukey, J. W. (1950) Transformations Related to the Angular and the Square Root, *Annals of Mathematical Statistics*, 21, 607–11.

Frick, R. W. (1995) Accepting the Null Hypothesis. *Memory and Cognition*, 23, 132–8.

Frick, R. W. (1996) The Appropriate Use of Null Hypothesis Testing. *Psychological Methods*, 1, 379–90.

Frick, R. W. (1998) A Better Stopping Rule for Conventional Statistical Tests. *Behavior Research Methods, Instruments, and Computers*, 30, 690–7.

Frick, R. W. (1999) Defending the Statistical Status Quo. *Theory and Psychology*, 9, 183–9.

Friedrich, R. (1982) In Defense of Multiplicative Terms in Multiple Regression Equations. *American Journal of Political Science*, 26, 797–833.

Furr, R. M., and Rosenthal, R., (2003) Evaluating Theories Efficiently: The Nuts and Bolts of Contrast Analysis. *Understanding Statistics*, 2, 33–67.

Gardner, M. J., and Altman, D. G. (1986) Confidence Intervals Rather than *P* Values: Estimation Rather than Hypothesis Testing. *British Medical Journal*, 292, 746–50.

Gatz, M., and Hurwitz, M. (1990) Are Old People More Depressed? Cross-sectional Data on Center for Epidemiological Studies Depression Scale Factors. *Psychology and Aging*, 5, 284–90.

Gebauer, J. E., Riketta, M., Broemer, P., and Maio, G. R. (2008) Pleasure and Pressure Based Prosocial Motivation: Divergent Relations to Subjective Well-being. *Journal of Research in Personality*, 42,399–420.

Geisser, S., and Greenhouse, S W. (1958) An Extension of Box's Results on the Use of the *F* Distribution in Multivariate Analysis. *Annals of Mathematical Statistics*, 29, 885–91.

Gelman, A. (2008a) Objections to Bayesian Statistics. *Bayesian Analysis*, 3, 445–50.

Gelman, A. (2008b) Rejoinder. *Bayesian Analysis*, 3, 467–78.

Gelman, A. (2008c) Scaling Regression Inputs by Dividing by Two Standard Deviations. *Statistics in Medicine*, 27, 2865–73.

Gelman, A., and Hill, J. (2007) *Data Analysis using Regression and Multilevel/Hierarchical Models.* Cambridge: Cambridge University Press.

Gill, J. (2007) *Bayesian Methods: A Social and Behavioral Sciences Approach* (2nd edn). New York: Chapman and Hall.

Gillett, R. (2003) The Metric Comparability of Meta-analytic Effect-size Estimators from Factorial Designs. *Psychological Methods*, 8, 419–33.

Glass, G. (1976) Primary, Secondary, and Meta-analysis of Research. *Educational Researcher*, 5, 3–8.

Glover, S., and Dixon, P. (2004) Likelihood Ratios: A Simple and Flexible Statistic for Empirical Psychologists. *Psychonomic Bulletin and Review*, 11, 791–806.

Goertzen, J. R., and Cribbie, R. A. (2010) Detecting a Lack of Association: An Equivalence Testing Approach. *British Journal of Mathematical and Statistical Psychology*, 63, 527–37.

Goldstein, H. (1987) *Multilevel Statistical Models* (1st edn). London: Edward Arnold.

Goldstein H. (1994) Multilevel Crossclassified Models. *Sociological Methods and Research*, 22, 364–75.

Goldstein, H. (1995) *Multilevel Statistical Models* (2nd edn). London: Edward Arnold.

Goldstein, H. (2003) *Multilevel Statistical Models* (3rd edn). London: Edward Arnold.

Goldstein, H. and Healy, M. J. R. (1995) *Journal of the Royal Statistical Society. Series A (Statistics in Society)*, 158, 1, 175–7.

Gönen, M., Johnson, W. O., Lu, Y., and Westfall, P. H. (2005) The Bayesian Two-sample *t* Test. *American Statistician*, 59, 252–7.

Good, I. J. (1979) Studies in the History of Probability and Statistics. XXXVII A. M. Turing's Statistical Work in World War II. *Biometrika*, 66, 393–6.

Goodman, S. N. (1993) *p*-values, Hypothesis Tests, and Likelihood: Implications for Epidemiology of a Historical Debate. *American Journal of Epidemiology*,137, 485–95.

Goodman, S. N. (1999) Toward evidence-based medical statistics. 2: The Bayes factor. *Annals of Internal Medicine*, 130, 1005–13.

Gould, S. J. (1985) The Median isn't the Message. *Discover*, 6, 40–2.

Graham, J. W. (2009) Missing Data Analysis: Making it Work in the Real World. *Annual Review of Psychology*, 60, 549–76.

Graham, M. H. (2003) Confronting Multicollinearity in Ecological Multiple Regression. *Ecology*, 84, 2809–15.

Grayson, D. (2004) Some Myths and Legends in Quantitative Psychology. *Understanding Statistics*, 3, 101–34.

Green, S. B., Marquis, J. G., Hershberger, S. L., Thompson, M. S., and McCollam, K. M. (1999) The Overparameterized Analysis of Variance Model. *Psychological Methods*, 4, 214–33.

Greenhouse, S. W., and Geisser, S. (1959) On Methods in the Analysis of Profile Data. *Psychometrika*, 24, 95–112.

Greenland, S. (2006) Bayesian perspectives for epidemiologic research. I. Foundations and basic methods. *International Journal of Epidemiology*, 35, 765–78.

Grissom, R. J., and Kim, J. J. (2001) Review of Assumptions and Problems in the Appropriate Conceptualization of Effect Size. *Psychological Methods*, 6, 135–46.

Hacking, I. (1965) *Logic of Statistical Inference*. Cambridge: Cambridge University Press.

Haddock, C. K., Rindskopf, D., and Shadish, W. R. (1998) Using Odds Ratios as Effect Sizes for Meta-analysis of Dichotomous Data: A Primer on Methods and Issues. *Psychological Methods*, 3, 339–53.

Hadfield, J. (2010) MCMC Methods for Multi-Response Generalized Linear Mixed Models: The MCMCglmm R Package. *Journal of Statistical Software*, 33, 1–22.

Hall, P. (1986) On the Number of Bootstrap Simulations Required to Construct a Confidence Interval, *Annals of Statistics*, 14, 1453–62.

Hall, P. (1992) On the Removal of Skewness by Transformation. *Journal of the Royal Statistical Society, Series B*, 54, 221–28.

Hancock, K. J., and Rhodes, G. I. (2008) Contact, Configural Coding and the Other-race Effect in Face Recognition, *British Journal of Psychology*, 99, 45–56.

Hanley, J. A., Negassa, A., Edwardes, M. D., and Forrester, J. E. (2003) Statistical Analysis of Correlated Data Using Generalized Estimating Equations: An Orientation. *American Journal of Epidemiology*, 157, 364–75.

Hardin, J. W. (2003) The Sandwich Estimator of Variance. In T. B. Fomby, and C. R. Hill (eds), *Maximum Likelihood Estimation of Misspecified Models: Twenty Years Later*. New York: Elsevier.

Harlow, L. L., Mulaik, S. A., and Steiger, J. H. (eds) (1997) *What If There Were No Significance Tests?* Hillsdale, NJ: Erlbaum.

Harrell, F. E. Jr. (2001) *Regression Modeling Strategies: With Applications to Linear Models, Logistic Regression and Survival Analysis*. New York: Springer.

Hastie, T., Tibshirani, R., and Friedman, J. (2001) *The Elements of Statistical Learning; Data Mining, Inference and Prediction*. New York: Springer.

Haviland, M. G. (1990) Yates's Correction for Continuity and the Analysis of 2 x 2 Contingency Tables, *Statistics in Medicine*, 9, 363–83.

Hayden, R. W. (2005) A Dataset that is 44% Outliers. *Journal of Statistics Education*, 13, 1.

Hayes, A. F., and Cai, L. (2007) Further Evaluating the Validity of the Conditional Decision Rule for Comparing Two Independent Means. *British Journal of Mathematical and Statistical Psychology*, 60, 217–44.

Haynes A. B., Weiser, T. G., Berry, W. R., *et al.* (2009) A Surgical Safety Checklist to Reduce Morbidity and Mortality in a Global Population. *New England Journal of Medicine*, 360, 491–9.

Hays, W. (1973) *Statistics for the Social Sciences* (2nd edn). New York: Holt.

Healy, F. (2009) (Unpublished BSc. Psychology research project). Nottingham Trent University, Nottingham, UK.

Hedges, L. V. (1981) Distribution Theory for Glass's Estimator of Effect Size and Related Estimators. *Journal of Educational Statistics*, 6, 107–28.

Hedges, L. V. (2009) Adjusting a Significance Test for Clustering in Designs with Two Levels of Nesting. *Journal of Educational and Behavioral Statistics*,34, 464–90.

Hedges, L. V., and Hedberg, E. C. (2007) Intraclass Correlations for Planning Group-randomized Experiments in Education. *Educational Evaluation and Policy Analysis*, 29, 60–87.

Hedges, L. V., and Rhoads, C. H. (2011) Correcting an Analysis of Variance for Clustering. *British Journal of Mathematical and Statistical Psychology*, 64, 20–37.

Herr, D. G. (1986) On the History of ANOVA in Unbalanced, Factorial Designs: The First 30 Years. *The American Statistician*, 40, 265–70.

Hilbe, J. M. (2007) *Negative Binomial Regression.* Cambridge: Cambridge University Press.

Hill, R. (2004) Multiple Sudden Infant Deaths: Coincidence or Beyond Coincidence? *Paediatric and Perinatal Epidemiology*, 18, 320–6.

Hintze, J. L., and Nelson, R. D. (1998) Violin Plots: A Box Plot-Density Trace Synergism. *The American Statistician*, 52, 181–4.

Hochberg, Y. (1988) A Sharper Bonferroni Procedure for Multiple Tests of Significance. *Biometrika*, 75, 800–03.

Hoenig, J. M., and Heisey, D. M. (2001) The Abuse of Power: The Pervasive Fallacy of Power Calculations for Data Analysis. *American Statistician*, 55, 19–23.

Hoffmann, L., and Rovine, M. J. (2007) Multilevel Models for the Experimental Psychologist: Foundations and Illustrative Examples. *Behavior Research Methods*, 39, 101–17.

Holland, B. S., and Copenhaver, M. D. (1987) An Improved Sequentially Rejective Bonferroni Test Procedure. *Biometrics*, 43, 417–23.

Holm, S. (1979) A Simple Sequentially Rejective Multiple Test Procedure. *Scandinavian Journal of Statistics*, 6, 65–70.

Hothorn, T., Bretz, F., and Westfall. P. (2008) Simultaneous Inference in General Parametric Models. *Biometrical Journal*, 50, 346–63.

Howard, G., Maxwell, S. E., and Fleming, K. (2000) The Proof of the Pudding: An Illustration of the Relative Strengths of Null Hypothesis, Meta-analysis, and Bayesian Analysis. *Psychological Methods*, 5, 315–32.

Howell, D. C. (2002) *Statistical Methods for Psychology* (5th edn). Pacific Grove, CA: Duxberry.

Hox, J. J. (2010) *Multilevel Analysis: Techniques and Applications* (2nd edn). New York/Hove: Routledge.

Hubbard, R. (2004) Blurring the Distinctions Between P's and Alpha's in Psychological Research. *Theory and Psychology*,14, 295–327.

Huberty, C. J., and Morris, J. D. (1989) Multivariate Analysis versus Multiple Univariate Analyses. *Psychological Bulletin*, 105, 302–8.

Hunter, J. E., and Schmidt, F. L. (2004) *Methods of Meta-analysis: Correcting Error and Bias in Research Findings* (2nd edn). Thousand Oaks, CA: Sage.

Hunter, J. E., Schmidt, F. L., and Le, H. (2006) Implications for Direct and Indirect Range Restriction for Meta-analysis Methods and Findings. *Journal of Applied Psychology*, 91, 594–612.

Hurvich, C. M., and Tsai, C. L. (1989) Regression and Time Series Model Selection in Small Samples. *Biometrika*, 76, 297–307.

Huynh, H., and Feldt, L. S. (1976) Estimation of the Box Correction for Degrees of Freedom from Sample Data in Randomized Block and Splitplot Designs. *Journal of Educational Statistics*, 1, 69–82.

Hyndman, R. J., and Fan, Y. (1996) Sample Quantiles in Statistical Packages. *American Statistician*, 50, 361–5.

Ioannidis, J. P. A. (2005a) Contradicted and Initially Stronger Effects in Highly Cited Clinical Research, *Journal of American Medical Association*, 294, 218–28.

Ioannidis, J. P. A. (2005b) Why Most Published Research Findings are False. *PLoS Medicine*, 2, e124. doi:10.1371/journal.pmed.0020124.

Iverson, G. J., Lee, M. D., Zhang, S., and Wagenmakers, E.-J. (2009) p_{rep}: An Agony in Five Fits. *Journal of Mathematical Psychology*, 53, 195–202.

Jaccard, J., Becker, M. A, and Wood, G. (1984) Pairwise Multiple Comparison Procedures: A Review. *Psychological Bulletin*, 96, 589–96.

Jaccard, J. and Guilamo-Ramos, V. (2002) Analysis of Variance Frameworks in Clinical Child and Adolescent Psychology: Issues and Recommendations. *Journal of Clinical Child and Adolescent Psychology*, 31, 130–46.

Jaccard, J., Turrisi, R., and Wan, C. K. (1990) *Interaction Effects in Multiple Regression*.Thousand Oaks: Sage.

Jamieson, J., (2004) Analysis of Covariance (ANCOVA) with Difference Scores. *International Journal of Psychophysiology*, 52, 277–83.

Jarvis, H. (2003) (Unpublished BSc. Psychology research project). Loughborough University, Loughborough, UK.

Joliffe, I. T. (1995) Sample Sizes and the Central Limit Theorem: The Poisson Distribution as an Illustration. *The American Statistician*, 49, 269.

Kaas, R., and Buhrman, J. M. (2008) Mean, Median and Mode in Binomial Distributions. *Statistica Neerlandica*, 34, 13–18.

Kalbfleisch, J. D., and Sprott, D. A. (1970) Application of Likelihood Methods to Models Involving Large Numbers of Parameters, *Journal of the Royal Statistical Society Series B*, 32, 175–208.

Kampstra, K. (2008) *Beanplot*: A Boxplot Alternative for Visual Comparison of Distributions. *Journal of Statistical Software*, Code Snippets, 28.

Karlin, S., and Rinott, Y. (1981) Total Positivity Properties of Absolute Value Multinormal Variables with Applications to Confidence Interval Estimates and Related Probabilistic Inequalities. *The Annals of Statistics*, 9, 1035–49.

Kass, R. E., and Raftery, A. E. (1995) Bayes Factors. *Journal of the American Statistical Association*, 90, 773–95.

Kaye, W. S., and Baguley, T. (in prep.) *Bayesian t Tests.* Manuscript in preparation.

Kelley, K. (2005) The Effects of Nonnormal Distributions on Confidence Intervals around the Standardized Mean Difference: Bootstrap and Parametric Confidence Intervals. *Educational and Psychological Measurement*, 65, 51–69.

Kelley, K. (2007a) Constructing Confidence Intervals for Standardized Effect Sizes: Theory, Application, and Implementation. *Journal of Statistical Software*, 20(8).

Kelley, K. (2007b) Methods for the Behavioral, Educational, and Social Science: An R Package. *Behavior Research Methods*, 39, 979–84.

Kelley, K., Maxwell, S.E., and Rausch, J.R. (2003) Obtaining Power or Obtaining Precision: Delineating Methods of Sample-size Planning. *Evaluation and the Health Professions*, 26, 258–87.

Kelley K., and Rausch, J. R. (2006) Sample Size Planning for the Standardized Mean Difference: Accuracy in Parameter Estimation via Narrow Confidence Intervals. *Psychological Methods*, 11, 363–85.

Keppel, G. (1976) Words as Random Variables. *Journal of Verbal Learning and Verbal Behavior*,15, 263–5.

Keselman, H. J., Cribbie, R., and Holland B. (1999) The Pairwise Multiple Comparison Multiplicity Problem: an Alternative Approach to Familywise and Comparisonwise Type I Error Control. *Psychological Methods*, 4, 58–69.

Keselman, H. J., Algina, J., and Kowalchuk, R. K. (2001) The Analysis of Repeated Measures Designs: A Review. *British Journal of Mathematical and Statistical Psychology*, 54, 1–20.

Keselman, H. J., Othman, A. R., Wilcox, R. R., and Fradette, K. (2004) The New and Improved Two-sample *t* Test. *Psychological Science*, 15, 47–51.

Killeen, P. R. (2005) An Alternative to Null Hypothesis Statistical Tests. *Psychological Science*, 16, 345–53.

Kim, J.-Q, and Feree, G. D. (1981) Standardization in Causal Analysis. *Sociological Methods and Research*, 10,187–210.

Kirk, R. E. (1995) *Experimental Design* (3rd edn) Belmont, CA: Brooks/Cole.

Kirk, R. E. (1996) Practical Significance: A Concept whose Time has Come. *Educational and Psychological Measurement*, 56, 746–59.

Kirk, R. E. (2007) Effect Magnitude: A Different Focus. *Journal of Statistical Planning and Inference*, 137, 1634–46.

Kish, L. (1965) *Survey Sampling*. New York: Wiley.

Kline, R. B. (2010) *Principles and practice of structural equation modeling* (3rd edn). New York: Guilford Press.

Kraemer, H. C. and Kupfer, D. J. (2006) Size of Treatment Effects and their Importance to Clinical Research and Practice. *Biological Psychiatry*, 59, 990–6.

Kreft, I. G., and de Leeuw, J. (1998) *Introducing Multilevel Modeling*. London: Sage.

Krus, D. J., and Wilkinson, S. M. (1986) Demonstration of Properties of a Suppressor Variable. *Behavior Research Methods, Instruments, and Computers*, 18, 21–4.

Kruschke, J. K. (2010) *Doing Bayesian Data Analysis: A Tutorial with R and BUGS*. London: Academic Press/Elsevier.

Kvavilashvili, L., Messer, D. J., and Ebdon, P. (2001) Prospective Memory in Children: The effects of Age and Task Interruption. *Developmental Psychology*, 37, 418–30.

Langsrud, Ø. (2003) ANOVA for Unbalanced Data: Use Type II Instead of Type III Sums of Squares. *Statistics and Computing*, 13, 163–7.

Lansdale, M. W., Oliff, L., and Baguley, T., (2005). Quantifying Precision and Availability of Location Memory in Everyday Pictures and its Implications for Picture Database Design. *Journal of Experimental Psychology: Applied*, 11, 67–83.

Lansdale, M. W., and Baguley, T. (2008) Dilution as a Model of Long-term Forgetting. *Psychological Review*, 115, 864–92.

Larzerlere, R. E., and Mulaik, S. A. (1977) Single-sample Tests for Many Correlations. *Psychological Bulletin*, 84, 557–69.

Lebreton, J. D., Burnham, K. P., Clobert, J., and Anderson, D. R. (1992) Modeling Survival and Testing Biological Hypotheses using Marked Animals: A Unified Approach with Case-studies. *Ecological Monographs*, 62, 67–118.

Lecoutre M.-P., Poitevineau J., and Lecoutre B. (2003) Even Statisticians are not Immune to Misinterpretations of Null Hypothesis Significance Tests. *International Journal of Psychology*, 38, 37–45.

Lenth, R. V. (2001) Some Practical Guidelines for Effective Sample Size Determination. *The American Statistician*, 55, 187–93.

Lenth, R. V. (2009) *Java Applets for Power and Sample Size* [Computer software]. Accessed 8 March 2011,at http://www.stat.uiowa.edu/~rlenth/Power.

Liang, F., Paulo, R., Molina, G., Clyde, M. A., and Berger, J. O. (2008) Mixtures of *g* Priors for Bayesian Variable Selection. *Journal of the American Statistical Association*, 103, 410–23.

Limpert, E., Stahel, W. A. and Abbt, M. (2001) Log-normal Distributions Across the Sciences: Keys and Clues. *Biosciences*, 51, 341–52.

Lindley, D. V. (1957) A Statistical Paradox, *Biometrika*, 44, 187–92.

Lindsey, J. K. (1999) On the Use of Corrections for Overdispersion. *Applied Statistics*, 48, 553–61.

Liu, X. S. (2011) The Effect of Covariate Mean Differences on the Standard Error and Confidence Interval for the Comparison of Treatment Means. *British Journal of Mathematical and Statistical Psychology*, 64, 310–19.

Lix, L. M., and Sajobi, T. T. (2010) Testing Multiple Outcomes in Repeated Measures Designs. *Psychological Methods*, 15, 268–80.

Loftus, G. R. (2001) Analysis, Interpretation, and Visual Presentation of Experimental Data. In J. Wixted and H. Pashler (eds), *Stevens' Handbook of Experimental Psychology* (3rd edn), Vol. 4: Methodology in Experimental Psychology (pp. 339–90). New York: Wiley.

Loftus, G. R., and Masson, M. E. J. (1994) Using Confidence Intervals in Within-subject Designs. *Psychonomic Bulletin and Review*, 1, 476–90.

London, K., Bruck, M., and Melnyk, L. (2009) Post-event Information Affects Children's Autobiographical Memory After One Year. *Law and Human Behavior*, 33, 344–55.

Lorch, R. F. and Myers, J. L. (1990) Regression Analyses Of Repeated Measures Data in Cognitive Research. *Journal of Experimental Psychology: Learning, Memory, and Cognition*, 16, 149–57.

Lord, F. M. (1953) On the Statistical Treatment of Football Numbers. Reprinted in *Readings in Statistics*, A. Haber, R.P. Runyon, and P. Badia, P. (eds). Reading, MA: Addison-Wesley, 1970.

Lord, F M. (1967) A Paradox in the Interpretation of Group Comparisons. *Psychological Bulletin*, 68, 304–5.

Lord, F. M., and Novick, M. R. (1968) *Statistical Theories of Mental Test Scores*. Reading, MA: Addison-Welsley.

Maas, C. J. M., and Hox, J. J. (2004) Robustness Issues in Multilevel Regression Analysis. *Statistica Neerlandica*, 58, 127–37.

Maas, C. J. M., and Hox, J. J. (2005) Sufficient Sample Sizes for Multilevel Modeling. *Methodology*, 1, 86–92.

MacCallum, R. C., Zhang, S., Preacher, K. J., and Rucker, D. D. (2002) On the Practice of Dichotomization of Quantitative Variables. *Psychological Methods*, 7, 19–40.

Macdonald, R. R. (2002) The Incompleteness of Probability Models and the Resultant Implications for Theories of Statistical Inference. *Understanding Statistics*, 1, 167–89.

Macdonald, R. R. (2005) Why Replication Probabilities Depend on Prior Probability Distributions. *Psychological Science*, 16, 1007–8.

Maris, E. (1998) Covariance Adjustment versus Gain Scores: Revisited. *Psychological Methods*, 3, 309–27.

Marschner, I. C., Emberson, J., Irwig, L., and Walter, S. D. (2004) The Number Needed to Treat (NNT) can be Adjusted for Bias when the Outcome is Measured with Error, *Journal of Clinical Epidemiology*, 57, 1244–52.

Masson, M. E. J., and Loftus, G. R. (2003) Using Confidence Intervals for Graphically Based Data Interpretation. *Canadian Journal of Experimental Psychology*, 57, 203–20.

Maxwell, S. E. (1980) Pairwise Multiple Comparisons in Repeated Measures Designs. *Journal of Educational Statistics*, 5, 269–87.

Maxwell, S. E. (2004) The Persistence of Underpowered Studies in Psychological Research: Causes, Consequences, and Remedies. *Psychological Methods*, 9, 147–63.

Maxwell, S. E., Kelley, K., and Rausch, J. R. (2008) Sample Size Planning for Statistical Power and Accuracy in Parameter Estimation. *Annual Review of Psychology*, 59, 537–63.

McClelland, G. H. (1997) Optimal Design in Psychological Research. *Psychological Methods*, 2, 3–19.

McClelland, G. H., and Judd, C. M. (1993) Statistical Difficulties of Detecting Interactions and Moderator Effects. *Psychological Bulletin*, 114, 376–90.

McCulloch. C. E. (2005) Repeated Measures ANOVA, RIP? *Chance*, 18, 29–33.

McGrath, R. E. and Meyer, G. J. (2006) When Effect Sizes Disagree: The Case of r and d. *Psychological Methods*, 11, 386–401.

McGraw, K. O., and Wong, S. P. (1996) Forming Inferences about some Intraclass Correlation Coefficients. *Psychological Methods*, 1, 30–46.

Mellanby, J., Martin, M., and O'Doherty, J. (2000) The 'Gender Gap' In Final Examination Results at Oxford University. *British Journal of Psychology*, 91, 377–90.

Menard, S. (2004) Six Approaches to Calculating Standardized Logistic Regression Coefficients. *The American Statistician*, 58, 218–23.

Miles, J. N. V. (2003) A Framework for Power Analysis using a Structural Equation Modelling Procedure. *BMC Medical Research Methodology*, 1, 27.

Miller, G. M., and Chapman, J. P. (2001) Misunderstanding Analysis of Covariance. *Journal of Abnormal Psychology*, 110, 40–8.

Miller, R. G., Jr (1986) *Beyond ANOVA: Basics of Applied Statistics.* New York: Wiley.

Misangyi, V. F., LePine, J., Algina, J., and Goeddeke, F. (2006) The Adequacy of Repeated-measures Regression for Multilevel Research. *Organizational Research Methods*, 9, 5–28.

Morey, R. D. (2008) Confidence Intervals from Normalized Data: A Correction to Cousineau. *Tutorials in Quantitative Methods for Psychology*, 4, 61–4.

Morris, S. B., and DeShon, R. P. (2002) Combining Effect Size Estimates in Meta-analysis with Repeated Measures and Independent-groups Designs. *Psychological Methods*, 7, 105–25.

Mroz, T. A., and Zayats, Y. V. (2008) Arbitrarily Normalized Coefficients, Information Sets, and False Reports of 'Biases' in Binary Outcome Models. *The Review of Economics and Statistics*, 90, 406–13.

Murray, D. M., and Blitstein, J. L. (2003) Methods to Reduce the Impact of Intraclass Correlation in Group-randomized Trials, *Evaluation Review*, 27, 79–103.

Musca, S., Kamiejski, R., Nugier, A., Méot, A., Er-Rafiy, A., and Brauer, M. (2011) Data with Hierarchical Structure: Impact of Intraclass Correlation and Sample Size on Type-I error. *Frontiers in Psychology: Quantitative Psychology and Measurement*, 2, 74.

Newcombe, R. G. (1998a) Two-Sided Confidence Intervals for the Single Proportion: Comparison of Seven Methods. *Statistics in Medicine*,17, 857–72.

Newcombe, R. G. (1998b) Interval Estimation for the Difference Between Independent Proportions: Comparison of Eleven Methods. *Statistics in Medicine*,17, 873–90.

Newell, B. R., and Dunn, J. C. (2008) Dimensions in Data: Testing Psychological Models using State-trace Analysis. *Trends in Cognitive Sciences*, 12, 285–90.

Nickerson, R. S. (2000) Null Hypothesis Significance Testing: A Review of an Old and Continuing Controversy. *Psychological Methods*, 5, 241–301.

Nix, T. W., and Barnette, J. J. (1998) The Data Analysis Dilemma: Ban or Abandon. A Review of Null Hypothesis Significance Testing. *Research in the Schools*, 5, 3–14.

Nordstokke, D. W., and Zumbo B. D. (2007) A Cautionary Tale about Levene's: Tests for Equal Variances. *Journal of Educational Research and Policy Studies*, 7, 1–14.

O'Grady, K. E. (1982) Measures of Explained Variance: Cautions and Limitations. *Psychological Bulletin*, 92, 766–77.

O'Brien, R. M. (2007) A Caution Regarding Rule of Thumb for Variance Inflation Factors. *Quality and Quantity*, 41, 673–90.

Olejnik, S., and Algina, J. (2000) Measures of Effect Size for Comparative Studies: Applications, Interpretations, and Limitations. *Contemporary Educational Psychology*, 25, 241–86.

Olejnik, S., and Algina, J. (2003) Generalized Eta and Omega Squared Statistics: Measures of Effect Size for Some Common Research Designs. *Psychological Methods*, 8, 434–47.

Olson, C. L. (1974) Comparative Robustness of Six Tests in Multivariate Analysis of Variance. *Journal of the American Statistical Association*, 69, 894–908.

Olson, C. L. (1976) On Choosing a Test Statistic in Multivariate Analysis of Variance. *Psychological Bulletin*, 83, 579–86.

Pearson, K. (1903) Mathematical Contributions to the Theory of Evolution XI: On the Influence of Natural Selection on the Variability and Correlations of Organs. *Philosophical Transactions of the Royal Society, London, Series A*, 200,1–66.

Petty, R. E., Fabrigar, L. R.,Wegener, D. T., and Priester, J. R. (1996) Understanding Data when Interactions are Present or Hypothesized. *Psychological Science,* 7, 247–52.

Preacher, K. (2003) *A Primer on Interaction Effects in Multiple Linear Regression.* Accessed 11 November 2010, at http://quantpsy.org/interact/interactions.htm.

Preacher, K. J., Curran, P. J., and Bauer, D. J. (2006) Computational Tools for Probing Interaction Effects in Multiple Linear Regression, Multilevel Modeling, and Latent Curve Analysis. *Journal of Educational and Behavioral Statistics*, 31, 437–48. http://quantpsy.org/interact/index.html.

Preacher, K. J., and Hayes, A. F. (2008) Contemporary Approaches to Assessing Mediation in Communication Research. In A. F. Hayes, M. D. Slater, and L. B. Snyder (eds), *The Sage Sourcebook of Advanced Data Analysis Methods for Communication Research*. Thousand Oaks, CA: Sage, pp. 13–54.

Preacher, K. J., and Kelley, K. (2011) Effect Size Measures for Mediation Models: Quantitative Strategies for Communicating Indirect Effects. *Psychological Methods*, 16, 93–115.

Preacher, K. J., Rucker, D. D., MacCallum, R. C., and Nicewander, W. A. (2005) Use of the Extreme Groups Approach: A Critical Reexamination and New Recommendations. *Psychological Methods*, 10, 178–92.

Prentice, D. A., and Miller, D. T. (1992) When Small Effects are Impressive. *Psychological Bulletin*, 112, 160–4.

Quené, H., and van den Bergh, H. (2004). On Multi-level Modeling of Data from Repeated Measures Designs: A Tutorial. *Speech Communication*, 43, 103–21.

R Development Core Team (2011). *R: A language and environment for statistical computing.* Vienna, Austria: R Foundation for Statistical Computing.

Raaijmakers, J. G. W., Schrijnemakers, J. M. C., and Gremmen, F. (1999) How to Deal with 'The Language-as-fixed-effect Fallacy': Common Misconceptions and Alternative Solutions. *Journal of Memory and Language*, 41, 416–26.

Raftery, A. E. (1995) Bayesian Model Selection in Social Research. *Sociological Methodology*, 25, 111–96.

Rasbash, J. R., Charlton, C., Browne, W. J., Healy, M., and Cameron, B. (2009) *MLwiN Version 2.1*. Bristol: Centre for Multilevel Modelling, University of Bristol.

Rasbash, J. R., and Goldstein, H. (1994) Efficient Analysis of Mixed Hierarchical and Cross-classified Random Structures using a Multilevel Model, *Journal of Educational and Behavioral Statistics*, 19, 337–50.

Ree, M. J., and Carretta, T. R. (2006) The Role of Measurement Error in Familiar Statistics. *Organizational Research Methods*, 9, 99–112.

Richards, S. A. (2008) Dealing with Overdispersed Count Data in Applied Ecology. *Journal of Applied Ecology*, 45, 218–27.

Robinson, D. H., Whittaker, T., Williams, N., and Beretvas, S. N. (2003) It's Not Effect Sizes so much as Comments about their Magnitude that Mislead Readers. *Journal of Experimental Education*, 72, 51–64.

Robinson, W. S. (1950) Ecological Correlations and the Behavior of Individuals. *American Sociological Review*, 15, 351–7.

Robbins, H. (1970) Statistical Methods Related to the Law of the Iterated Logarithm. *Annals of Mathematical Statistics*, 41, 1397–409.

Rochon. J., and Kieser, M. (2011) A Closer Look at the Effect of Preliminary Goodness-of-fit Testing for Normality for the One-sample *t*-test. *British Journal of Mathematical and Statistical Psychology*, 64, 410–26.

Rogers, J. L., Howard, K. I., and Vessey, J. T. (1993) Using Significance Tests to Evaluate Equivalence between Two Experimental Groups. *Psychological Bulletin*, 113, 553–65.

Rodgers, J. L. (1999) The Bootstrap, the Jackknife, and the Randomization Test: A Sampling Taxonomy. *Multivariate Behavioral Research*, 34, 441–56.

Rodgers, J. L., and Nicewander, W. A. (1988) Thirteen Ways to Look at the Correlation Coefficient. *The American Statistician*, 42, 59–66.

Rosenberg, M. S. (2010) A Generalized Formula for Converting Chi-square Tests to Effect Sizes for Meta-analysis. *PLoS ONE 5(4)*, doi: 10.1371/journal.pone.0010059.

Rosenthal, R. (1994) Parametric Measures of Effect Size. In H. Cooper and L. V. Hedges (eds), *The Handbook of Research Synthesis*. New York: Sage, pp. 231–44.

Rosenthal, R., and Rubin, D. B., (1979) A Note on Percent Variance Explained as a Measure of the Importance of Effects. *Journal of Applied Social Psychology*, 9, 395–6.

Rosenthal, R., Rosnow, R. L., and Rubin, D. B. (2000) *Contrasts and Correlations in Behavioral Research*. New York: Cambridge University Press.

Rosnow, R. L., and Rosenthal, R. (1995) 'Some Things You Learn Aren't So': Cohen's Paradox, Asch's Paradigm, and the Interpretation of Interaction. *Psychological Science*, 6, 3–9.

Rosnow, R. L., and Rosenthal, R. (1996a) Contrasts and Interactions Redux: Five Easy Pieces. *Psychological Science*, 7, 253–7.

Rosnow, R. L., and Rosenthal, R. (1996b) Computing Contrasts, Effect Sizes, and Counternulls on Other People's Published Data: General Procedures for Research Consumers. *Psychological Methods*, 1, 331–40.

Rosnow, R. L., and Rosenthal, R. (2003) Effect Sizes for Experimenting Psychologists. *Canadian Journal of Experimental Psychology*, 57, 221–3.

Rouder, J. N., Speckman, P. L., Sun, D., Morey, R. D., and Iverson, G. (2009) Bayesian *t* Tests for Accepting and Rejecting the Null Hypothesis. *Psychonomic Bulletin and Review*, 16, 225–37.

Royall, R. M. (1986) The Effect of Sample Size on the Meaning of Significance Tests. *American Statistician*, 40, 313–15.

Royall, R. M. (1997) *Statistical Evidence: A Likelihood Paradigm*. New York: Chapman and Hall.

Royall, R. M. (2000) On the Probability of Observing Misleading Statistical Evidence (with Discussion). *Journal of the American Statistical Association*, 95, 760–7.

Royall, R. (2004) The Likelihood Paradigm for Statistical Evidence. In M. L. Taper and S. R. Lele (eds), *The Nature of Scientific Evidence: Statistical, Philosophical, and Empirical Considerations*. Chicago: University of Chicago Press, pp. 119–52.

Royall, R. M., and Tsou, T.-S. (2003) Interpreting Statistical Evidence using Imperfect Models: Robust Adjusted Likelihood Functions. *Journal of the Royal Statistical Society Series B*, 65, 391–404.

Rozeboom, W. W. (1960) The Fallacy of the Null-hypothesis Significance Test. *Psychological Bulletin*, 57, 416–28.

Rozencwajg P., and Bertoux, M. L. (2008) *Current Psychology Letters*, 24, 2.

Rutherford, A. (2001) *Introducing ANOVA and ANCOVA: A GLM Approach*. London: Sage.

Sackett, D. L. (2001) Why Randomized Controlled Trials Fail but Needn't: 2. Failure to Employ Physiological Statistics, or the Only Formula a Clinician-trialist is Ever Likely to Need (or Understand!). *Canadian Medical Association Journal*, 165, 1226–37.

Sackett, D. L., Deeks, J. J., and Altman, D. G. (1996) Down with Odds Ratios! *Evidence-Based Medicine*, 1, 164–6.

Sackett, P. R., and Yang, H. (2000) Correction for Range Restriction: An Expanded Typology. *Journal of Applied Psychology*, 85,112–18.

Sakia, R. M. (1992) The Box-Cox Transformation Technique: A Review. *The Statistician*, 41, 168–79.

Sánchez-Meca, J., Marín-Martínez, F., and Chacón-Moscoso, S. (2003) Effect-size Indices for Dichotomized Outcomes in Meta-analysis. *Psychological Methods*, 8, 448–4.

Sarkar, S. K. (2008) Generalizing Simes' Test and Hochberg's Stepup Procedure. *Annals of Statistics*, 36, 337–63.

Savalei, V., and Kolenikov, S. (2008) Constrained versus Unconstrained Estimation in Structural Equation Modeling. *Psychological Methods*, 13, 150–70.

Schafer, J. L., and Graham, J. W. (2002) Missing Data: Our View of the State of the Art. *Psychological Methods*, 7, 147–77.

Schenker, N., and Gentleman, J. F. (2001) On Judging the Significance of Differences by Examining the Overlap between Confidence Intervals. *The American Statistician*, 55, 182–6.

Schiffler, R. E. (1988) Maximum Z Scores and Outliers. *The American Statistician,* 42, 79–80.

Schmidt, F. L. (1992) What Do Data Really Mean? *American Psychologist*, 47, 1173–81.

Schmidt, F. L. (1996) Statistical Significance Testing and Cumulative Knowledge in Psychology: Implications for Training of Researchers. *Psychological Methods*, 1, 115–29.

Schmidt, F. L., and Hunter, J. E. (1999) Theory Testing and Measurement Error. *Intelligence*, 27, 183–98.

Schucany, W. R., and Ng, H. K. T. (2006) Preliminary Goodness-of-fit Tests for Normality do not Validate the One-sample Student *t*. *Communications in Statistics: Theory and Methods*, 35, 2275–86.

Schuirmann, D. L. (1981) On Hypothesis Testing to Determine if the Mean of a Normal Distribution is Contained in a Known Interval. *Biometrics*, 37, 617.

Schwarz, G. (1978) Estimating the dimension of a model. *Annals of Statistics*, 6, 461–4.

Searle, S. R., Casella, G., and McCulloch, C. E. (1992) *Variance Components*. New York: Wiley.

Sedlmeier, P. (2009) Beyond the Significance Test Ritual: What is There? *Zeitschrift für Psychologie*, 217, 1–5.

Seggar, L. B., Lambert, M. J., and Hansen, N. B. (2002) Assessing Clinical Significance: Application to the Beck Depression Inventory. *Behavior Therapy*, 33, 253–69.

Senn, S. J. (2006) Change from Baseline and Analysis of Covariance Revisited. *Statistics in Medicine*, 25, 4334–434.

Shadish, W. R., Clark, M. H., and Steiner, P. M. (2008) Can Nonrandomized Experiments Yield Accurate Answers? A Randomized Experiment Comparing Random to Nonrandom Assignment. *Journal of the American Statistical Association*, 103, 1334–43.

Shaffer, J. P. (1986) Modified Sequentially Rejective Multiple Test Procedures. *Journal of the American Statistical Association*, 81, 826–31.
Shaffer, J. P. (1995) Multiple Hypothesis Testing. *Annual Review of Psychology*, 46, 561–76.
Shieh, G. (2011) Clarifying the Role of Mean Centringin Multicollinearity of Interaction Effects. *British Journal of Mathematical and Statistical Psychology*, 64, 462–77.
Shrout, P. E. (1997) Should Significance Tests be Banned? Introduction to a Special Section Exploring the Pros and Cons. *Psychological Science*, 8, 1–2.
Siegel, S., and Castellan, N. J. Jr. (1988) *Nonparametric Statistics for the Behavioral Sciences* (2nd edn). New York, NY: McGraw-Hill.
Skinner, C. J. (1989) Domain Means, Regression and Multivariate Analysis. In C. J. Skinner, D. Holt and T. M. F. Smith (eds), *Analysis of Complex Surveys*. Chichester: Wiley, pp. 59–87.
Skrondal, A., and Rabe-Hesketh, S. (2007) Redundant Overdispersion Parameters in multilevel Models for Categorical Responses. *Journal of Educational and Behavioral Statistics*, 32, 419–30.
Slater, H., Davies, N., and Burgess, S. (2009). Do Teachers Matter? Measuring the Variation in Teacher Effectiveness in England. Working Paper No. 09/212, University of Bristol: Centre for Market and Public Organisation.
Smith, A. F. M. and Spiegelhalter, D. J. (1980) Bayes Factors and Choice Criteria for Linear Models. *Journal of the Royal Statistical Society*, 42, 213–20.
Smithson, M. (2001) Correct Confidence Intervals for Various Regression Effect Sizes and Parameters: The Importance of Noncentral Distributions in Computing Intervals. *Educational and Psychological Measurement*, 61, 605–32.
Snedecor, G. W., and Cochran, W. G. (1989) *Statistical Methods* (8th edn). Ames, IA: Iowa State University Press.
Snijders, T. A. B., and Bosker, R. J., (1999) *Multilevel Analysis: An Introduction to Basic and Advanced Multilevel Modeling*. London: Sage.
Spearman, C. (1904) The Proof and Measurement of Association Between Two Things. *American Journal of Psychology*, 15, 72–101.
Spiegelhalter, D. J., and Rice, K. (2009) Bayesian Statistics. *Scholarpedia*, 4(8), 5230.
Spiegelhalter, D. J., Best, N. G., Carlin, B. P., and van der Linde, A. (2002) Bayesian Measures of Model Complexity and Fit. *Journal of the Royal Statistical Society Series B*, 64, 583–639.
Steinberg, L., and Thissen, D. (2006) Using Effect Size for Research Reporting: Examples using Item Response Theory to Analyze Differential Item Functioning, *Psychological Methods*, 11, 402–15.
Stevens, S. S. (1946) On the Theory of Scales of Measurement. *Science*, 103, 677–80.
Stevens, S. S. (1951) Mathematics, Measurement and Psychophysics. In S. S. Stevens (ed.), *Handbook of Experimental Psychology*. New York: Wiley, pp. 1–49.
Stoel, R. D., Galindo-Garre, F., Dolan, C., and Van den Wittenboer, G. (2006). On the Likelihood Ratio Test in Structural Equation Modeling when Parameters are Subject to Boundary Constraints. *Psychological Methods*, 4, 439–55.
Student [Gosset, W. S.](1908) The Probable Error of a Mean. *Biometrika*, 6, 1–25.
Subbotsky, E. (2009) Can Magical Intervention Affect Subjective Experiences? Adults' Reactions to Magical Suggestion. *British Journal of Psychology*, 100, 517–37.
Sugiura, N. (1978) Further Analysis of the Data by Akaike'sInformation Criterion and the Finite Corrections. *Communications in Statistics*, A7, 13–26.
Tate, R. L. (2004) A Cautionary Note on Shrinkage Estimates of School and Teacher Effects. *Florida Journal of Educational Research*, 42, 1–21.
Thomas, M. S. C., Annaz, D., Ansari, D., Serif, G., Jarrold, C., and Karmiloff-Smith, A. (2009) The Use of Developmental Trajectories in Studying Developmental Disorders. *Journal of Speech, Language and Hearing Research*, 52, 336–58.

Thompson, B. (1999) If Statistical Significance Tests are Broken/Misused, What Practices Should Supplement or Replace Them? *Theory and Psychology*, 9, 165–81.

Thorburn, W. M. (1918) The Myth of Occam's Razor. *Mind*, 27, 345–53.

Tukey, J. W. (1954) Causation, Regression and Path Analysis. In O. Kempthorne, T. A. Bancroft, J. W. Gowen and J. L. Lush (eds), *Statistics and Mathematics in Biology*. Ames, IA: Iowa State College Press,pp. 35–66.

Tukey, J. W. (1957) On the Comparative Anatomy of Transformations. *Annals of Mathematical Statistics*, 28, 602–32.

Tukey, J. W. (1962) The Future of Data Analysis. *Annals of Mathematical Statistics*, 33, 1–67.

Tukey, J. W. (1969) AnalyzingData: Sanctification or Detective Work? *American Psychologist*, 24, 83–91.

Tukey, J. W. (1977) *Exploratory Data Analysis*. Reading, MA: Addison-Wesley.

Ulm, K. (1990) A Simple Method to Calculate the Confidence Interval of a Standardized Mortality Ratio. *American Journal of Epidemiology*, 131, 373–5.

Underwood, J. D. M., Dillon, G., Farnsworth, B., and Twiner, A. (2007) Reading the Road: The Influence of Age and Sex on Child Pedestrians' Perceptions of Road Risk. *British Journal of Psychology*, 98, 93–110.

Uppal, A. (2006) (Unpublished BSc psychology research project). Nottingham Trent University, Nottingham, UK.

Van Breukelen, G. J. P. (2006) ANCOVA versus Change from Baseline had more Power in Randomized Studies and More Bias in Nonrandomized Studies. *Journal of Clinical Epidemiology*, 59, 920–5.

Van der Tweel, I. (2005) Repeated Looks at Accumulating Data: To correct or Not to Correct? *European Journal of Epidemiology*, 20, 205–11.

Vasquez, G., Duval, S., Jacobs, D. R. Jr., and Silventoinen, K. (2007) Comparison of Body Mass Index, Waist Circumference, and Waist/Hip Ratio in Predicting Incident Diabetes: A Meta-Analysis. *Epidemiological Reviews*, 29, 115–28.

Velleman, P. F. and Wilkinson, L. (1993) Nominal, Ordinal, Interval, and Ratio Typologies are Misleading. *The American Statistician*, 47, 65–72.

Venables, W. N. (1998) *Exegeses on Linear Models*. Accessed 4 December 2009, at www.stats.ox.ac.uk/pub/MASS3/Exegeses.pdf.

Ver Hoef, J. M., and Boveng, P. L. (2007) Quasi-poisson vs Negative Binomial Regression: How Should We Model Overdispersed Count Data? *Ecology*, 88, 2766–72.

Vickers, A. J. (2003) Underpowering in Randomized Trials Reporting a Sample Size Calculation. *Journal of Clinical Epidemiology*, 56, 717–20.

von Hippel, P. T. (2005). Mean, Median, and Skew: Correcting a Textbook Rule. *Journal of Statistics Education*,13, 2.

Wagenmakers, E.-J. (2007) A Practical Solution to the Pervasive Problems of *p* Values. *Psychonomic Bulletin and Review*, 14, 779–804.

Wagenmakers, E.-J., and Farrell, S. (2004) AIC model selection using Akaike weights. *Psychonomic Bulletin & Review*, 11, 192–6.

Wagenmakers, E.-J., Lee, M. D., Lodewyckx, T., and Iverson, G. (2008) Bayesian versus Frequentist Inference. In H. Hoijtink, I. Klugkist, and P. A. Boelen (eds), *Bayesian Evaluation of Informative Hypotheses*. Springer: New York, pp. 181–207.

Wainer, H. (1991) Adjusting for Differential Base-rates: Lord's Paradox Again. *Psychological Bulletin*, 109, 147–51.

Wainer, H., and Brown, L. M. (2004) Two Statistical Paradoxes in the Interpretation of Group Differences: Illustrated with Medical School Admission and Licensing Data. *American Statistician*, 58, 117–23.

Walter, S. D. (1985) Small Sample Estimation of Log Odds Ratios From Logistic Regression and Fourfold Tables. *Statistics in Medicine*, 4, 437–44.

Walter, S. D. (2000) Choice of Effect Measure for Epidemiological Data. *Journal of Clinical Epidemiology*, 53, 931–9.

Walter, S. D. (2001) Number Needed to Treat (NNT): Estimation of a Measure of Clinical Benefit. *Statistics in Medicine*, 20, 3947–62.

Wang, Z., and Thompson, B. (2007) Is the Pearson r^2 Biased, and if so, What is the Best Correction Formula? *Journal of Experimental Education, 75*, 109–125.

Warren, R. D., White, J. K., and Fuller, W. A. (1974) An Errors-in-variables Analysis of Managerial Role Performance. *Journal of the American Statistical Association*, 69, 886–93.

Weakliem, D. L. (2004) Introduction to the Special Issue on Model Selection. *Sociological Methods and Research*, 33, 167–87.

Wenzel, J. (2004) (Unpublished BSc psychology research project). Loughbrough University, Loughbrough, UK.

Westfall, P. H. (1997) Multiple Testing of General Contrasts using Logical Constraints and Correlations. *Journal of the American Statistical Association*, 92, 299–306.

Westlake, W. J. (1981) Response to T. B. L. Kirkwood: Bioequivalence Testing: A Need to Rethink. *Biometrics*, 37, 589–94.

Wetzels, R., Lee, M. D., and Wagenmakers, E.-J. (2010) Bayesian Inference using WBDev: A Tutorial for Social Scientists. *Behavior Research Methods*, 42, 884–97.

Wetzels, R., Raaijmakers, J. G. W., Jakab, E., and Wagenmakers, E.-J. (2009) How to Quantify Support for and against the Null Hypothesis: A Flexible WinBUGS Implementation of a Default Bayesian *t* Test. *Psychonomic Bulletin and Review*, 16, 752–60.

Whittingham, M. J., Stephens, P., Bradbury, R. B. and Freckleton, R. P. (2006) Why Do We Still Use Stepwise Modelling in Ecology and Behaviour? *Journal of Animal Ecology, 75*, 1182–9.

Wike, E. L., and Church, J. D. (1976) Comments on Clark's 'The Language-as-fixed-effect Fallacy'. *Journal of Verbal Learning and Verbal Behavior*,15, 249–55.

Wilcox, R. R. (2004) Kernel Density Estimators: An Approach to Understanding How Groups Differ. *Understanding Statistics*, 3, 333–48.

Wilcox, R. R. (2005a) *Introduction to Robust Estimation and Hypothesis Testing* (2nd edn). San Diego, CA: Academic Press.

Wilcox, R. R. (2005b) New Methods for Comparing Groups: Strategies for Increasing the Probability of Detecting True Differences. *Current Directions in Psychological Science*, 14, 272–5.

Wilcox, R. R. (2005c) Comparing Medians: An Overview Plus New Results on Dealing with Heavy-tailed Distributions. *Journal of Experimental Education*. 73, 249–63.

Wilcox. R. R. (2009) *Update Info*. Accessed 17 July 2009, at http://www-rcf.usc.edu/~rwilcox/.

Wilcox, R. R., and Keselman, H. J. (2003) Modern Robust Data Analysis Methods: Measures of Central Tendency. *Psychological Methods*, 8, 254–74.

Wilcox, R. R.,and Keselman, H. J. (2004) Robust Regression Methods: Achieving Small Standard Errors when there is Heteroscedasticity. *Understanding Statistics*, 3, 349–64.

Wilkinson, L., and APA Task Force on Statistical Inference (1999) Statistical Methods in Psychology Journals: Guidelines and Explanations. *American Psychologist*, 54, 594–604.

Wiseman, R., and Greening, E. (2002) The Mind Machine: A Mass Participation Experiment into the Possible Existence of Extrasensory Perception. *British Journal of Psychology*, 93, 487–99.

Wooldridge, J. M. (2003) Cluster-Sample Methods in Applied Econometrics. *The American Economic Review*, 93,133–8.

Wright, D. B. (1998) Modeling Clustered Data in Autobiographical Memory Research: The Multilevel Approach. *Applied Cognitive Psychology*, 12, 339–57.

Wright, D. B. (2003) Making Friends with your Data: Improving how Statistics are Conducted and Reported. *British Journal of Educational Psychology*, 73, 123–36.

Wright, D. B. (2006) Comparing Groups in a Before-After Design: When *t*-test and ANCOVA Produce Different Results. *British Journal of Educational Psychology*, 76, 663–75.

Wright, D. B. (2007) Graphing within Subject Confidence Intervals(WSCI) using SPSS and S-Plus. *Behavior Research Methods*, 39, 82–5.

Wright, D. B., and Field, A. P. (2009) Giving your Data the Bootstrap. *The Psychologist, 22,* 413.

Wright, D. B. and London, K. (2009) *Modern Regression Techniques using R*. London: Sage.

Wright, S. P. (1992) Adjusted P-values for Simultaneous Inference. *Biometrics*, 48, 1005–13.

Ximénez, C., and Revuelta, J. (2007) Extending the CLAST Sequential Rule to One-way ANOVA under Group Sampling. *Behavior Research Methods*, 39, 86–100.

Yates, F. (1934) Contingency Table involving Small Numbers and the χ^2 Test. *Supplement to the Journal of the Royal Statistical Society*, 1, 217–35.

Yates, F., and Mather. K. (1963) Ronald Aylmer Fisher. *Biographical Memoirs of Fellows of the Royal Society of London*, 9, 91–120.

Yee, T. W. (2010) The VGAM Package for Categorical Data Analysis. *Journal of Statistical Software*, 32, 1–34.

Yohai, V. J. (1987) High Breakdown Point and High Efficiency Robust Estimates for Regression. *Annals of Statistics*, 15, 642–56.

Yuen, K. K. (1974) The Two-sample Trimmed *t* for Unequal Population Variances. *Biometrika*, 61, 165–70.

Yzerbyt, V. C., Muller, D., and Judd, C. M. (2004) Adjusting Researchers' Approach to Adjustment: On the use of Covariates when Testing Interactions. *Journal of Experimental Social Psychology*, 40, 424–31.

Zeileis, A. (2004) Econometric Computing with HC and HAC Covariance Matrix Estimators. *Journal of Statistical Software*, 11, 1–17.

Zeileis, A. (2006) Object-oriented Computation of Sandwich Estimators. *Journal of Statistical Software*, 16, 1–16.

Zeileis, A., Kleiber, C., and Jackman, S. (2008) Regression Models for Count Data in R. *Journal of Statistical Software*, 27(8).

Zheng, B., and Agresti, A. (2000) Summarizing the Predictive Power of a Generalized Linear Model. *Statistics in Medicine*, 19, 1771–81.

Ziliak, S. T., and McCloskey, D. N. (2004) Size Matters: The Standard Error of Regressions in the American Economic Review, *Journal of Socio-Economics*, 33, 527–46.

Zimmerman, D. W. (2004) A Note on Preliminary Test of Equality of Variances. *British Journal of Mathematical and Statistical Psychology*, 57, 173–81.

Zimmerman, D. W. (2007) Correction for Attenuation with Biased Reliability Estimates and Correlated Errors in Populations and Samples. *Educational and Psychological Measurement*, 67, 920–39.

Zimmerman, D. W. (2011) A Simple and Effective Decision Rule for Choosing a Significance Test to Protect Against Non-normality. *British Journal of Mathematical and Statistical Psychology*, 64, 388–409.

Zimmerman, D. W., and Zumbo, B. D. (1993a) Relative Power of the Wilcoxon Test, the Friedman Test, and the Repeated-measures ANOVA on Ranks. *Journal of Experimental Education*, 62, 75–86.

Zimmerman, D. W., and Zumbo, B. D. (1993b) Rank Transformations and the Power of the Student *t* Test and Welch *t′* Test for Non-normal Populations with Unequal Variances. *Canadian Journal of Experimental Psychology*, 47, 523–39.

Zimmerman, D. W., and Zumbo, B. D. (2009) Hazards in Choosing Between Pooled and Separate-variances *t*Tests. *Psicológica*, 30, 371–90.

Zou, G. Y. (2007) Toward using Confidence Intervals to Compare Correlations. *Psychological Methods*, 12, 399–413.

Zumbo, B. D., and Hubley, A. M. (1998) A Note on Misconceptions Concerning Prospective and Retrospective Power. *The Statistician*, 47, 385–3.

Author index

Subject index

N

T